Making America

A History of the United States

Making America
A History of the United States
Volume II: Since 1865

Carol Berkin
Baruch College, City University of New York

Christopher L. Miller
The University of Texas, Pan American

Robert W. Cherny
San Francisco State University

James L. Gormly
Washington and Jefferson College

HOUGHTON MIFFLIN COMPANY
Boston Toronto
Geneva, Illinois Palo Alto
Princeton, New Jersey

Sponsoring Editor: Sean W. Wakely
Senior Associate Editor: Jeffrey Greene
Senior Project Editor: Carol Newman
Senior Production/Design Coordinator: Jill Haber
Senior Manufacturing Coordinator: Marie Barnes
Marketing Manager: Pamela Shaffer

Cover design: Harold Burch, Harold Burch Design, NYC.
Cover image: Thomas Hart Benton "Instruments of Power" from *America Today*, 1930. Tempera with oil glaze on linen, 92" x 100". Copyright © The Equitable Life Assurance Society of the United States.
Text photo research: Pembroke Herbert/Picture Research Consultants.

Printed in the U.S.A.

Library of Congress Catalog Card Number: 94-76487

ISBN: 0-395-50253-5 (Student Edition)
      0-395-71712-4 (IAE)

3 4 5 6 7 8 9-VH-99 98 97 96 95

Brief Contents

Contents

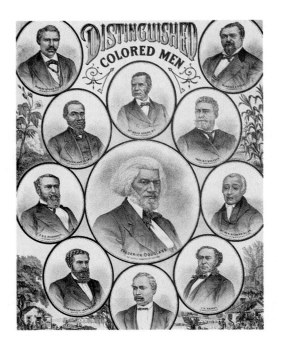

■ ■ ■

A FAIR FIELD AND NO FAVOR!
UNCLE SAM: "I'M OUT FOR COMMERCE, NOT CONQUEST."

Maps

Note: Maps listed in boldface type indicate chapter-opening maps.

Features

Tables

Preface

On a warm spring day in 1990, the authors of this textbook sat under a shade tree on a campus in southern Texas and argued the merits of the textbooks they used in their classes. Each of the books did something very well, but none of the books seemed to meet the real needs of our students. As professors at public universities, we knew that many students' formal skills lag behind their often keen interest and strong commitment to learning. And because we teach in universities located on three of the nation's borders—the Pacific Ocean, the Atlantic and the Rio Grande—we also knew that many of today's students are culturally diverse and a significant number of them have been educated outside of the United States. The textbook we dreamed of would help us teach the American past to every student—both native-born and those new to this country. We imagined a survey textbook that did not demand much prior knowledge about American history to understand and enjoy it, and one that progressed sequentially to avoid confusing students with topical digressions. It would provide integrated and supportive learning aids to help those students who were unfamiliar with the demands of college-level study to comprehend and retain what they have read.

As we talked, our "dream" textbook slowly took shape. It was a narrative account of the American past, firmly anchored by a political chronology that framed the many centuries under discussion. It was well written, with vivid descriptions of people and places. It featured maps, paintings, photos, and other visual aids that were not simply decorative, but further developed the themes of the narrative. Our dream book made every effort to communicate with students, defining words that were part of the formal language of scholarship and clarifying unfamiliar terms. Finally, the textbook presented history as a dynamic process rather than an endless, inevitable procession of people, places, dates, and events. This focus on history as a process promised to encourage students to think historically and to produce citizens who valued history.

Conversations like this one happen often when college instructors get together. They usually end with a wistful pledge: "Someday, we'll sit down and write that book ourselves!" What makes our conversation unusual is that we were given the oppor-

tunity to keep that promise. *Making America* is the result.

Approach

Making America follows the course of American history from the earliest human settlements to the present day. This is a remarkable story to tell—and a complex one. A look at the table of contents will show the reader that we have set this story within an explicit political chronology. This structure has the advantage of being basic and familiar to most readers, and it is broad enough to accommodate generous attention to social, economic, and diplomatic history. As scholars whose own work focuses on the experience of women, American Indians, political behavior, labor, and international policymakers, we wanted our book to integrate the best new scholarship in these and other important fields. We are confident that the political framework we have chosen, like the loom on which a weaver works, allows us to bring all these strands of the American story together over thirty-two chapters.

In *Making America*, we have made a conscious commitment to demonstrate the significance of race, gender, social class, region, ethnic background, age, and religion in shaping the historical experience of Americans. *Making America* does not adopt the perspective of any single group within American society as it narrates our national history. It does not tell the story from the perspective of a single region either. It does not assume that there is one group that makes history and others that simply survive it. *Making America* is built on the premise that all Americans are historically active figures, playing significant roles in creating the history the authors narrate.

This view of history as the product of the ideas and actions of *all* men and women, coupled with our desire to show history as a dynamic process, led to the creation of the ECCO model. ECCO is an acronym for four fundamental aspects of the historical process: Expectations, Constraints, Choices, and Outcomes. As we wrote, it helped the authors to organize the flow of the narrative. In execution, it also functions as an integrated learning aid for the student. In every chapter, *Making America* examines the variety of *expectations* people held about their futures; the *constraints* of time, place, and multiple social and economic factors that these historical figures faced; the *choices* they made, given the circumstances of their lives; and finally, the expected and unexpected *outcomes* produced by their decisions. The ECCO model does not force any historical interpretations upon the student. Instead, it offers a method by which students are able to understand the past as a rich human experience.

Too often, students come away from a textbook with the impression that people in the past behaved very differently from people in the present. Unlike themselves, their friends, their parents, or their nation's leaders, the historical women and men they encounter seem never to be confused by the decisions they face or uncertain about the consequences of their actions. Indeed, a mood of inevitability hangs over the lives of these past generations, as they live out their roles as actors in a drama written for them by destiny. Students find it difficult to relate to these earlier Americans who seem to inhabit a world with too many simple answers and too many clear solutions. Presenting the past in this manner may make it more manageable, but it does not make it good history. *Making America* offers students a way of thinking about history that scholars themselves employ as they research and reconstruct the past. ECCO is a device that will reinforce the reality of history as a dynamic, uncertain process, increase students' empathy for the men and women of the past, and help them to analyze critically and retain what they have read.

Themes

In keeping with our goal to create a clear and straightforward narrative chronology, a central theme in this text is the political development of the nation. The creation and revision of its federal and local governments, the contests over domestic and diplomatic policies, and the internal and external crises faced by the United States and its political institutions all play a major role in the book's organization. The reader will find this theme of political development throughout the book, for example, in the discussion of events leading to the American Revolution, in the detailed accounts of the constitutional debates of the 1770s and the 1780s, in the analysis of the political tensions and conflicts lead-

ing to the Civil War, in the close attention to federal Indian policy in the nineteenth century, in the examination of the American role in modern world wars, in the contest over the role of the federal government in the Great Depression, and in the economic crises of recent eras.

Political development serves as a broad umbrella for discussion of other significant themes as well. Among these is the understanding of American history as a story of immigrant societies. To do justice to this second theme, *Making America* explores not only English and European immigration, but immigrant communities from Paleolithic times to the present, including Indian societies before European colonization, the creation of African-American culture within slavery, and the great migration from the Pacific rim in recent time.

Making America's third theme recognizes the changing nature of relations between groups—racial, ethnic, class, and gender relations. Thus, *Making America* examines the changing nature of gender roles over several centuries, the way that relations between whites and African-Americans have changed, the development of Anglo-Latino relations (especially in the Southwest), and alterations in the relations between employers and employees. This book focuses on creating understanding about groups, their relation to each other, and the way that some groups have used politics to achieve their goals and define their relations with other groups.

Our fourth theme focuses on the significance of regional economies and cultures. This regional theme is developed, for example, in the discussion of the seventeenth and eighteenth century colonies, and in the examination of the striking social and cultural divergences that have existed between the American southwest and the Atlantic coastal region.

A fifth theme is the rise and impact of large social movements, prompted by changing material conditions or by new ideas that challenge the status quo. *Making America* explores movements such as the Great Awakening of the 1740s, the reform efforts of the early nineteenth century, including abolitionism, temperance, and women's rights, the Progressive Era, the emergence of organized labor, third-party organizations, and the rise of a youth culture in the post-World War II era.

The sixth, and final, theme is the relationship of the United States to other nations, which also fits well within the political framework of the text. *Making America* explores in depth the causes and consequences of this nation's role in world conflict and diplomacy, whether in the eighteenth and early nineteenth century struggles for dominance in Europe, the removal of Indian nations from their tribal lands, the impact of American policies of isolationism and interventionism, or the modern role of the United States as a dominant player in world affairs. These are not the only themes students will see threading through the text, but they are themes we believe are useful to identify from the beginning.

Learning Features

Each chapter in *Making America* follows the same format. Before the students are asked to immerse themselves in the past, we provide them with some essential study aids for the task ahead. As they read the narrative, we provide them with a second set of aids, designed both to ensure the best communication between the authors and their readers and to help bridge the gap between women and men of the past and those who are trying to understand them in the present. When the student has finished the chapter, we provide a final set of aids to reinforce what they have learned and to guide them if they want to pursue a topic in greater depth.

Chapter-Opening Features

Each chapter of *Making America* begins by placing historical events in space and in time. First, each chapter begins with a map to set the scene for the most significant events in the narrative to follow. Second, a timeline locates the major political events in the period under discussion within a larger time frame. Third, students are given an outline of new material they will encounter in the chapter. Fourth, several critical thinking questions help students focus on the larger, overarching themes of the material. Following the two pages of chapter-opening material, a chapter introduction demonstrates the dynamic process of history by applying the ECCO model to the subject matter the students will explore.

In-Text Features

As students read they will find a number of features in each chapter designed to make the text more accessible and the people and events it portrays more familiar. First, there are glossaries on each page that define terms and explain their historically specific usage in the narrative. These glossaries are precise and informative. They help students build their vocabularies and review for tests, and they reflect the authors' concern to communicate fully with their student readers. Second, the introductory critical thinking questions reappear at the beginning of each major chapter section. Third, the chapter's illustrations provide an exciting visual connection to the past. The caption for each illustration does more than identify the artist, the scene, or the physical location of an event; it also analyzes the subject of the painting, photograph, or artifact and comments on its significance. Finally, every chapter has an "Individual Choices" feature that helps students understand an important point raised in that chapter. "Individual Choices" provides an intimate portrait of individuals and how they arrived at a decision that shaped their lives. These features dramatically reinforce the essential point that historical events are not inevitable occurrences, but are the result of choices made by real people.

In addition, students are presented with a chance to read the words of Americans of the past as they debate over events or ideas that were critical in their era. This "Voices" feature contains a document relating to a controversial issue and quotations from supporting and opposing voices on that issue. This feature grew out of *Making America*'s conviction that students can learn much from the archival material through which the past speaks for itself.

End-of-Chapter Features

One of the most important obligations of a textbook is to help students reflect on the new information they have encountered and to suggest additional sources for further study. Thus, each chapter contains a summary of the chapter's main topics made dynamic by structuring it according to the ECCO model. The text also provides suggestions for further reading on events and personalities introduced in the chapter. After the last chapter, there is a selected bibliography citing the best scholarship in the field, both old and new, which is provided to assist professors and students who might want to explore the historiographical debates on a topic.

At the heart of *Making America* is the fascinating story of this nation's past. It is told by scholars and instructors who have a genuine enthusiasm for retelling that story to others. Our abiding interest in the experiences of earlier generations of Americans is not lost in an overly abstract style or buried by a narrative designed to impress students rather than inform them. We tell America's story clearly, and people it with women and men who are depicted as individuals rather than representative figures and as complex historical actors rather than simple heroes or villains. *Making America* provides more than a textbook that integrates new scholarship, raises questions about causes and consequences of historical events, and provides analyses of historical developments. The authors know that, above all, a text is a teaching tool, and we have designed *Making America* to be useful in the classrooms of our colleges and universities. Its structure, the themes it emphasizes, and the features it incorporates were chosen to assist our colleagues in their efforts to communicate effectively with students and impart to them a solid knowledge of the American past.

Study and Teaching Aids

A number of useful learning and teaching aids accompany *Making America*. They are designed to help the student get the most from the course and to provide the instructor with some useful teaching tools. The two-volume *Study Guide,* written by Eli Faber of John Jay College of Criminal Justice, City University of New York, provides students with many review exercises and tips on how to study and take tests effectively. Each chapter includes learning objectives, an annotated outline of the chapter, and approximately twenty-five key terms, concepts, and people. The fifteen multiple-choice questions per chapter include a text-page reference and a rejoinder for the correct answer. Also included in each chapter are three to five essay questions with answer guidelines, one analytical question based on an analysis of a primary source, and one map exercise.

A *Computerized Study Guide* is also available for students. It functions as a tutorial providing rejoinders to all multiple-choice questions that explain why the student's response is or is not correct.

The *Instructor's Resource Manual,* prepared by Kelly Woestman of Pittsburg State University, begins with a section on how to organize lectures effectively, how to handle large lecture classes efficiently, and provides tips on how to run discussion and activity groups. For every chapter, it includes instructional objectives that are drawn from the textbook's critical thinking questions, a chapter summary and annotated outline, and three lecture topics that include resource material and references to the text. Each chapter also includes discussion

questions, answers to the critical thinking questions that follow each main heading in the text, cooperative and individual learning activities, map activities (including activities for the Rand McNally *Atlas of American History*), ideas for paper topics, and a list of audio-visual resources including CD-ROM and videodisc products with addresses of suppliers.

A *Test Items* file, prepared by Orson Cooke of St. John's School and the University of Houston, provides twenty key terms and definitions, forty-five multiple-choice questions, seven to ten essay questions with answer guidelines, an analytical exercise to test critical thinking skills, and one map exercise per chapter. It also includes a section on creating a good testing environment, what constitutes a good test item, and how to construct test questions, as well as a sample midterm and final exam.

A *Computerized Test Item File* is available for IBM® PC or compatible and Macintosh computers.* This computerized version of the printed *Test Items* file allows professors to create customized tests by editing and adding questions.

There is also a set of over one hundred full-color *Map Transparencies* available on adoption.

A variety of *videos,* documentaries and docudramas by major film producers, is available for use with *Making America.*

Please contact your local Houghton Mifflin representative for more information about the ancillary program or to obtain desk copies.

Acknowledgments

The authors have benefited from the critical reading of the manuscript by our generous colleagues. We thank the following instructors:

Jack Bricker, Finger Lakes Community College

Sherri Broder, Boston College

Keith Bryant, University of Akron

Ken Chiano, Pima Community College

David Danbom, North Dakota State University

V. Baillie Dunlap, Rose State College

Lacy Ford, University of South Carolina

Larry Godel, Northeast Nebraska Community College

*IBM is the registered trademark of International Business Machines Corporation.

Wendell Griffith, Okaloosa Walton Community College

Paul Harvey, Hill College

Wallace Hutcheon, Northern Virginia Community College

Donald Jacobs, Northeastern University

Perry Kaufman, Burlington County College

Andrea Kluge, Simon Fraser University

Salvatore LaGumina, Nassau Community College

Peter Mancall, University of Kansas

Joe Mays, Jackson State Community College

Richard Means, Mountain View College

Steve Michot, Mississippi County Community College

Alexandra Nickliss, City College of San Francisco

Emmett Panzella, Point Park College

Howard Rabinowitz, University of New Mexico

David Rubiales, Yuba College

Lonnie Sinclair, San Jacinto College North

James Sweeney, Old Dominion University

Michael Tate, University of Nebraska at Omaha

Ken Weatherbie, Delmar College

Stephen Weisner, Springfield Technical Community College

Carol Berkin, who is responsible for Chapters 2 through 6, also wishes to acknowledge the help of her colleagues Eli Faber and Norman Fainstein of the City University of New York; graduate students Kerry Candaele and Michael Sappol of Columbia University, and Janis Ruden and Simon Middleton of the CUNY Graduate Center. And finally, her two works-in-progress, Hannah Berkin-Harper and Matthew Berkin-Harper, provided invaluable support.

Christopher L. Miller, who is responsible for Chapters 1 and 7 through 14, is indebted to many students—uncounted numbers at the University of Texas, Pan American, and several with whom he has discussed this project over the Internet. Of special note were those who volunteered to read, criticize, and discuss various parts of this book including Cristi DeJuana, Bobby Lovett, Lynn Lavigne, Allan Vassberg, Hays Traylor, Stacy Granger, Hai Pham, and Mattias Ohden. Colleagues at the University of

Texas, Pan American, were very forthcoming with sound advice and helpful criticism, especially David Vassberg, Sarah Neitzel, Chad Richardson, Bobby Wrinkle, Jerry Polinard, and Rudolfo Rocha. A number of colleagues around the country also helped in innumerable ways including Barbara DeWolfe, Drew McCoy, Patricia Nelson Limerick, Calvin Martin, Allen Howard, Peter Inveson, Albert Hurtado, Elliot Brownlee, and James Henretta. He especially wants to thank Terry Cargill for his contributions to Chapters 13 and 14 and to acknowledge his greatest scholarly debt to Wilbur R. Jacobs, a patient and caring mentor. His greatest personal debt is to Samantha Colt Miller, Parrish Kelley, and Ian Kelley, who always rallied when the demands seemed overwhelming.

Robert W. Cherny, who is responsible for Chapters 15 through 23, wishes to thank the students who have worked as research assistants over the three years that this book was in various stages and drafts: Marie Bolton, Sarah Cherny, Katherine Davis, Beth Haigen, Cynthia Taylor, and David Winn. Nancy Helfter provided valuable advice on art history. Among his colleagues at San Francisco State, Jerald Combs, William Issel, and Jules Tygiel stand out for their helpfulness and support in ways too complex to describe here. Rebecca Marshall Cherny has been not just understanding about the considerable demands made by this project, but has provided encouragement and support in other ways as well.

Jim Gormly, who is responsible for Chapters 24 through 32, would like to acknowledge the role that Bill Fleming played in moving the idea of this textbook along during its initial stages. He also thanks his colleagues at the University of Texas, Pan American, and Washington and Jefferson College, and provides a special thanks for the understanding, ideas, advice, and critical eye that his wife, Sharon, has provided. Without her support, his part in this project would not have been possible.

The editorial staff at Houghton Mifflin have all been superb, especially Jean Woy and Sean Wakely, without whom the project would never have made it out from under that shade tree in south Texas. Jan Fitter's questions, comments, and suggestions have helped to sharpen and focus every page and every paragraph. Jeff Greene, Carol Newman, and Charlotte Miller also deserve special thanks for their handling of the final production process and for putting up with a lot from us.

C. B.
C. L. M.
R. W. C.
J. L. G.

About the Authors

■ ■ ■

Carol Berkin

Born in Mobile, Alabama, Carol Berkin received her A.B. from Barnard College and her Ph.D. from Columbia University. Her dissertation won the Bancroft Award. She is now professor of history at Baruch College and the Graduate Center of City University of New York. She has written *Jonathan Sewall: Odyssey of an American Loyalist* (1974) and is currently completing *The American Eve: Women in Colonial American Society*. She has edited *Women of America: A History* (with Mary Beth Norton, 1979) and *Women, War, and Revolution* (with Clara M. Lovett, 1980). Her articles have appeared in such collections as *The American Revolution: Changing Perspectives, Around the Square: Greenwich Village, 1830–1890, Portraits of American Women,* and *The Underside of American History*. She was contributing editor on southern women for *The Encyclopedia of Southern Culture*.

Professor Berkin has chaired the Dunning-Beveridge Prize Committee for the American Historical Association and the Columbia University Seminar in Early American History and served on the program committees for both the Society for the History of the Early American Republic and the Organization of American Historians. In addition, she has been a historical consultant for the National Parks Commission and served on the Planning Committee for the Department of Education's National Assessment of Educational Progress.

Christopher L. Miller

Born and raised in Portland, Oregon, Christopher L. Miller received his undergraduate degree from Lewis and Clark College and his Ph.D. from the University of California, Santa Barbara. Before accepting his current position on the faculty of the University of Texas, Pan American, he served as an educational consultant for the Oregon Museum of Science and Industry, was a visiting assistant professor at Rutgers University, and a fellow at the Charles Warren Center for Studies in American History, Harvard University. He is the author of *Prophetic Worlds: Indians and Whites on the Columbian Plateau* (1985), and his articles and reviews have appeared in numerous scholarly journals. In addition to his scholarship in the areas of American West and American Indian history, Professor Miller has been active in projects designed to improve history teaching. He is a charter member of the American Textbook Council and has directed teaching improvement programs funded by the Meadows Foundation, the U.S. Department of Education, and other agencies.

Robert W. Cherny

Born in Marysville, Kansas, and raised in Beatrice, Nebraska, Robert W. Cherny received his B.A. from the University of Nebraska and his M.A. and Ph.D. from Columbia University. He is now professor of history at San Francisco University.

His books include *Populism, Progressivism, and the Transformation of Nebraska Politics, 1885–1915* (1981), *A Righteous Cause: The Life of William Jennings Bryan* (1985, 1994), and *San Francisco, 1865–1932* (with William Issel, 1986). His articles and reviews have appeared in *American Historical Review, Great Plains Quarterly, Journal of American History, Pacific Historical Review, Western Historical Quarterly,* and other journals and anthologies. He has contributed to *The American National Biography, The Reader's Companion to American History, The Dictionary of American Biography,* and other historical encyclopedias. He has served as a consultant for several documentary films.

He is president of the Society for Historians of the Gilded Age and Progressive Era, and has served on the council of the American Historical Association, Pacific Coast Branch, as president of the Southwest Labor Studies Association, on other professional committees, and on editorial boards.

James L. Gormly

Born in Riverside, California, James L. Gormly received a B.A. from the University of Arizona and his M.A. and Ph.D. from the University of Connecticut. He is now professor of history and chair of the history department at Washington and Jefferson College. He has written *The Collapse of the Grand Alliance* (1970) and *From Potsdam to the Cold War* (1979). His articles and reviews have appeared in *Diplomatic History, The Journal of American History, The American Historical Review, The Historian, The History Teacher,* and *The Journal of Interdisciplinary History*.

xxiii

Making America

A History of the United States

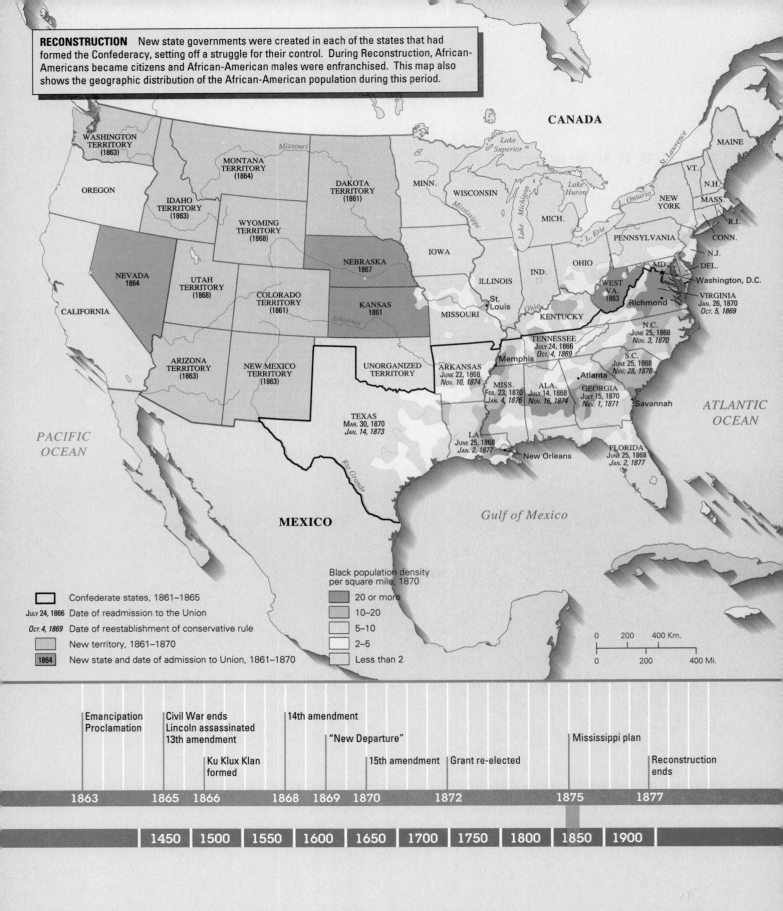

RECONSTRUCTION New state governments were created in each of the states that had formed the Confederacy, setting off a struggle for their control. During Reconstruction, African-Americans became citizens and African-American males were enfranchised. This map also shows the geographic distribution of the African-American population during this period.

CANADA

WASHINGTON TERRITORY (1863)

OREGON

IDAHO TERRITORY (1863)

MONTANA TERRITORY (1864)

DAKOTA TERRITORY (1861)

MINN.

WISCONSIN

MICH.

MAINE

VT.

N.H.

NEW YORK

MASS.

R.I.

CONN.

NEVADA 1864

UTAH TERRITORY (1868)

WYOMING TERRITORY (1868)

NEBRASKA 1867

IOWA

ILLINOIS

IND.

OHIO

PENNSYLVANIA

N.J.

DEL.

MD.

Washington, D.C.

CALIFORNIA

COLORADO TERRITORY (1861)

KANSAS 1861

MISSOURI

St. Louis

KENTUCKY

WEST VA. 1863

Richmond

VIRGINIA
JAN. 26, 1870
OCT. 5, 1869

ARIZONA TERRITORY (1863)

NEW MEXICO TERRITORY (1863)

UNORGANIZED TERRITORY

ARKANSAS
JUNE 22, 1868
NOV. 10, 1874

TENNESSEE
JULY 24, 1866
OCT. 4, 1869

Memphis

N.C.
JUNE 25, 1868
NOV. 3, 1870

S.C.
JUNE 25, 1868
NOV. 28, 1876

MISS.
FEB. 23, 1870
JAN. 4, 1876

ALA.
JULY 14, 1868
NOV. 16, 1874

GEORGIA
JULY 15, 1870
NOV. 1, 1871

Atlanta

Savannah

ATLANTIC OCEAN

TEXAS
MAR. 30, 1870
JAN. 14, 1873

LA.
JUNE 25, 1868
JAN. 2, 1877

New Orleans

FLORIDA
JUNE 25, 1868
JAN. 2, 1877

PACIFIC OCEAN

MEXICO

Rio Grande

Gulf of Mexico

Black population density per square mile, 1870

	20 or more
	10–20
	5–10
	2–5
	Less than 2

Confederate states, 1861–1865

JULY 24, 1866 Date of readmission to the Union

OCT. 4, 1869 Date of reestablishment of conservative rule

New territory, 1861–1870

1864 New state and date of admission to Union, 1861–1870

0   200   400 Km.

0   200   400 Mi.

Emancipation Proclamation

Civil War ends
Lincoln assassinated
13th amendment

Ku Klux Klan formed

14th amendment

"New Departure"

15th amendment

Grant re-elected

Mississippi plan

Reconstruction ends

1863   1865   1866   1868   1869   1870   1872   1875   1877

1450   1500   1550   1600   1650   1700   1750   1800   1850   1900

Reconstruction: High Hopes and Broken Dreams, 1865–1877

Presidential Reconstruction

- What did President Lincoln and President Johnson expect to accomplish through their Reconstruction plans?
- Why did each choose a lenient approach?

Freedom and the Legacy of Slavery

- What were freed people's expectations for freedom?
- What constraints on their freedom did African-Americans experience in the South during the first years of Reconstruction?

Congressional Reconstruction

- Why did Republicans in Congress choose to take control of Reconstruction?
- What did they expect to accomplish?

Black Reconstruction

- Who made up the Republican party in the South during Reconstruction?
- What important choices did Republican state administrations make during Reconstruction?
- Which choices brought the most lasting outcomes?

The End of Reconstruction

- What was the Mississippi Plan, and how was it related to the end of Reconstruction?
- What were the final outcomes of Reconstruction?

INTRODUCTION

E xpectations
C onstraints
C hoices
O utcomes

Recall that the preface identifies four components in the process of making history—*expectations, constraints, choices,* and *outcomes* (which we call ECCO). These components do not always operate in order, but they work together as a web of causes, influences, and effects. Each ECCO component can have an impact on any other one. For example, a certain *expectation* might point to what appears to be a natural *choice*. Yet, constraints may alter an *expectation* or limit the available choices to such a degree that new *expectations* or *choices* arise. A given *choice* can influence new *expectations*, change existing *constraints*, or limit or increase the variety of other *choices* available. All come together in *outcomes* that can, in turn, redefine other *expectations, constraints,* and *choices*. Each time any of the people connected with America's past went through the process we call ECCO, they created their own part in America's story. It was this process that is instrumental in describing how America was made, and it is this process that we will use to describe Reconstruction and much of the history of the United States in the nineteenth and twentieth centuries.

When the last Confederate military resistance collapsed in 1865, ending the bloody Civil War, some 2.6 million men had served in the Union or Confederate army since 1861, equal to almost 40 percent of all the men aged 15 to 40 in the United States in 1860. More than a half-million died—more deaths than in any other American war. Many women made important contributions to the war effort as civilians and more than a hundred—perhaps several hundred—women disguised themselves and fought as soldiers, mostly for the Union. By 1865, the war had touched the lives of nearly every person living in the nation.

Except for Gettysburg, the major battles in the Civil War occurred in the South or the border states. Toward the end of the war, Union armies swept across the South, leaving devastation behind them: burned and shelled buildings, ravaged fields, twisted railroad tracks. This destruction, and the collapse of the region's financial system, posed significant *constraints* on economic revival in the South.

More devastating for many white southerners than the property damage and destruction was the emancipation of 4 million slaves. In 1861, fearful *expectations* about the future of slavery under Republicans had caused the South to *choose* secession. With the *outcome* of the war, fears became reality. The end of slavery forced southerners—of both races—to reconsider most of their *expectations* and to make a series of *choices* that created new patterns of social, economic, and political relations between the races.

The years between 1865 and 1877 marked Reconstruction. Although the period was a time of physical rebuilding throughout the South, the term *Reconstruction* refers primarily to the rebuilding of the federal Union and to the political, economic, and social changes that came to the South as a result of defeat in war and the end of slavery. Reconstruction involved *choices* in response to some of the most momentous questions in American history. How was the defeated South to be treated? What was to be the future of the 4 million former slaves? Were key decisions to be made in Washington, by the federal government, or in state capitols and county courthouses throughout the South? Within the federal government, which branch of government—Congress or the president—was to establish policies?

As the dominant Republicans turned their attention from waging war to reconstructing the Union, they wrote into law and the Constitution new definitions of the very nature of the Union itself. They also made *choices* about the terms on which the South might rejoin the Union and about the rights of the former slaves. They also permanently changed the definition of American citizenship.

These changes conflicted with the *expectations* of most white southerners, some of whom *chose* to resist. Choices over the future of the South and the status of the former slaves also produced conflict between the president and Congress. A temporary *outcome* of this conflict was an increase in the power of Congress and a reduction in that of the president. A lasting *outcome* of these *choices* was a significant increase in the power of the federal government and new *constraints* on local and state governments.

The *outcome* of these government actions was some social change. In the end, however, the *outcome* of Reconstruction failed to fulfill most African-Americans' *expectations* for freedom and equality.

CHRONOLOGY

Reconstruction

1863	Emancipation Proclamation The Ten-Percent Plan
1864	Abraham Lincoln re-elected
1865	Freedmen's Bureau created Civil War ends Lincoln assassinated Johnson becomes president Thirteenth Amendment (abolishing slavery) ratified

1866	Ku Klux Klan formed
	Congress begins to assert control over
	    Reconstruction
	Civil Rights Act of 1866
	Riots by whites in Memphis and New
	    Orleans

1867	Military Reconstruction Act Command of the Army Act Tenure of Office Act
1868	Impeachment of President Johnson Fourteenth Amendment (defining citizen- ship) ratified Ulysses S. Grant elected president

1869–1870	Victories of "New Departure" Dem- ocrats in some southern states
1870	Fifteenth Amendment (guaranteeing voting rights) ratified
1870–1871	Ku Klux Klan Acts
1872	Grant re-elected
1875	Civil Rights Act of 1875 Mississippi Plan ends Reconstruction in Mississippi
1876	Disputed presidential election: Hayes vs. Tilden
1877:	Compromise of 1877 Hayes becomes president End of Reconstruction

Presidential Reconstruction

● What did President Lincoln and President Johnson expect to accomplish through their Reconstruction plans?

● Why did each choose a lenient approach?

On New Year's Day 1863, President Abraham Lincoln signed the *Emancipation Proclamation*. More than four years earlier, he had insisted that "this government cannot endure permanently half slave and half free. . . . It will become all one thing, or all the other." With the Emancipation Proclamation, Lincoln began the process by which the nation became all free. At the time, however, the Proclamation did not affect any slave, because it abolished slavery only in territory under Confederate control, where there was no way to enforce it. But every advance of a Union army after January 1, 1863, brought the reality of **emancipation** to the Confederacy.

Republican War Aims

The Emancipation Proclamation made clear that, for Lincoln and the Republican party, destroying slavery was a war aim second in importance only to preserving the Union. Freedom for the slaves became a central concern in part because **abolitionists** were an influential element within the Republican party.

Some Republican leaders in Congress—notably Senator Charles Sumner of Massachusetts and Congressman Thaddeus Stevens of Pennsylvania—not only favored abolition but argued that emancipation would be meaningless unless the government

---

emancipation   Release from bondage; freedom.

abolitionist   Someone who condemned slavery as morally wrong and believed that it should be abolished.

◆ This engraving celebrating the Emancipation Proclamation first appeared in 1863. While it places a white Union soldier in the center, it also portrays the important role of African-American troops and emphasizes the importance of education and literacy. *The Library Company of Philadelphia.*

guaranteed the civil and political rights of the freedmen. They were joined by abolitionists throughout the North—notably Frederick Douglass, an escaped slave who had become one of the most important leaders of the abolition movement. This powerful **faction** within the Republican party developed a third objective: citizenship for the former slaves and the equality of all citizens before the law. At the time, these were extreme views on abolition and equal rights, and the people who held them were called Radical Republicans or simply **Radicals.**

Thaddeus Stevens, the Radical leader in the House of Representatives, was born in Vermont and made a successful career as a Pennsylvania iron manufacturer before he won election to the House in 1858. Born with a clubfoot, he always seemed to identify with those outside the social mainstream. He had argued as early as 1838 that voting rights should be extended to the free African-Americans of his own state. A compelling spokesman for abolition, he became an uncompromising advocate of equal rights for African-Americans. Masterful at parliamentary maneuver, he was known for his honesty and his sarcasm.

Charles Sumner of Massachusetts, leading Radical in the Senate, had argued for **racial integration** of Massachusetts schools in 1849 and won election to the U.S. Senate in 1851. Immediately establishing himself as the Senate's foremost champion of abolition, he became a martyr to the cause after a severe beating he suffered in 1856 because of an antislavery speech. After emancipation, Sumner, like Stevens, fought for full political and civil rights for the freed people.

Most Radicals demanded a drastic restructuring not only of the South's political system but also of its economy. They had opposed slavery on moral grounds because they believed free labor was more productive and inventive. Whether on the farm, in small artisans' shops, or in the North's developing factories, free labor—according to the Radicals—had contributed centrally to the dynamism of the North's economy. Free labor, they argued, was crucial to democracy itself. "The middling classes who own the soil, and work it with their own hands," Stevens once proclaimed, "are the main support of every free government." Thus, the Radicals concluded, for the South to be fully democratic, it had to elevate free labor to a position of honor.

Not all Republicans accepted the proposals of the Radicals. All Republicans had objected to slavery, but not all Republicans had been abolitionists (some wanted only to ban slavery from the western territories), and not all Republicans wanted to extend full citizenship rights to the former slaves. Some were undecided about the proper course to take. Others favored rapid restoration of the South so that the federal government could concentrate on stimulating economic growth and developing the West. Republicans who did not immediately endorse severe punishment for the South or citizenship for the freed people are usually referred to as **moderates.**

---

faction   A group of people with shared opinions and goals who split off from a larger group.

Radicals   A faction of the Republican party that advocated citizenship for former slaves; Radical Republicans believed the South should be forced to meet congressional goals for reform.

racial integration   The bringing together of people of different racial groups into unrestricted and equal association in a society or organization.

moderates   Those whose views are midway between two more extreme positions; in this case, Republicans who favored some reforms but not all the Radicals' proposals.

Lincoln's Approach to Reconstruction: "With Malice Toward None"

President Lincoln and the congressional Radicals agreed that emancipation had to be a condition for the return of the South to the Union. However, major differences soon appeared over other terms for reunion and the roles of the president and Congress in establishing those terms. In his second inaugural address, a month before his death, Lincoln defined the task facing the nation:

> With malice toward none; with charity for all; with firmness in the right, as God gives us to see the right, let us strive on to finish the work we are in: to bind up the nation's wounds; to care for him who shall have borne the battle, and for his widow and orphan, to do all which may achieve and cherish a just and lasting peace among ourselves, and with all nations.

Lincoln had already laid out a policy for rebuilding the Union based on these principles.

When Union armies occupied portions of southern states, Lincoln appointed temporary **military governors** for those regions and tried to restore civil government as quickly as possible. Drawing on the president's constitutional power to issue pardons (Article II, Section 2), Lincoln issued a Proclamation of **Amnesty** and Reconstruction (also known as the "Ten-Percent Plan") in December 1863. Taking a lenient approach, he offered a full pardon and restoration of all rights to those who swore their loyalty to the Union and accepted the abolition of slavery. Only high-ranking Confederate leaders were not eligible. When those who took the oath in a state amounted to 10 percent of the number of votes cast by that state in the 1860 presidential election, the pardoned voters were to write a new state constitution that abolished slavery and then elect state officials to take over from the military governor. Lincoln hoped such leniency would encourage prominent southerners to abandon the Confederacy and accept emancipation.

Many congressional Republicans thought that Congress should be more involved in restoring the southern states to the Union. Two leading Radicals, Benjamin F. Wade and Henry W. Davis, introduced a bill to require 50 percent of all white males in a state to swear loyalty to the Union before the formation of a new civil government. The bill also guaranteed some black rights. Most Republicans voted in favor when Congress passed the Wade-Davis bill in July 1864. Lincoln, however, killed it with a **pocket veto,** fearing it would seriously slow the restoration of civil government. Wade and Davis, in a response known as the **Wade-Davis Manifesto,** denounced Lincoln for ignoring Congress.

Lincoln continued to hope that his Ten-Percent Plan might hasten the end of the war by creating new state governments with a broad base of support. New state governments were established in Arkansas, Louisiana, and Tennessee during 1864 and early 1865. In Louisiana, the new government denied voting rights to men who were one-quarter or more black, and it maintained restrictions on plantation laborers. Radicals complained loudly, but Lincoln urged patience, suggesting the reconstructed government in Louisiana was "as the egg to the fowl, and we shall sooner have the fowl by hatching the egg than by smashing it." Events in Louisiana and elsewhere, however, convinced Radicals that freed people were unlikely to receive equitable treatment from state governments formed under the Ten-Percent Plan. Such experiences pushed moderate Republicans toward accepting the Radicals' position that only **suffrage** could protect the freedmen in their rights and that only federal action could secure suffrage for blacks.

Abolishing Slavery Forever: The Thirteenth Amendment

Amid such questions about the rights of freed people, congressional Republicans prepared the final destruction of slavery. The Emancipation Proclamation had been a wartime measure, justified in part

---

military governor   Officer appointed to govern a region occupied by an army, as a substitute for civilian rule.

amnesty   A general pardon granted by a government, especially for political offenses.

pocket veto   The veto that occurs when Congress adjourns before the end of the ten-day period that the Constitution gives the president for considering whether to sign a bill and the president's decision is to "pocket"—that is, to not sign and let the bill expire.

Wade-Davis Manifesto   A statement, issued by leading Radicals, that denounced President Lincoln for rejecting the congressional plan for Reconstruction in favor of his own, more lenient policies.

suffrage   The right to vote.

by military necessity. Slavery was still legal in Delaware and Kentucky, which had been exempted from the Emancipation Proclamation and refused to change their laws. State laws—which might or might not be considered valid—permitted slavery in the Confederate states not yet reconstructed under Lincoln or his successor, Andrew Johnson. Opponents of slavery feared that if the legality of slavery were to be determined state by state, its ultimate status might remain uncertain. To destroy slavery forever, Congress in early 1865 approved the **Thirteenth Amendment,** which read simply: "Neither slavery nor involuntary servitude, except as a punishment for crime whereof the party shall have been duly convicted, shall exist within the United States, or any place subject to their jurisdition."

The Constitution requires any amendment to be ratified by three-fourths of the states—then 27 of 36. Eleven states—more than one-fourth—had seceded to form the Confederacy and seemed unlikely to vote to abolish slavery. The border states of Delaware and Kentucky had not seceded, but they rejected the amendment. By December 1865, only 19 of the 25 Union states had ratified the amendment; however, eight of the reconstructed southern states had ratified it, bringing the total to 27. In the end, therefore, the abolition of slavery hinged on action by reconstructed state governments in the South.

Andrew Johnson and Reconstruction

After the assassination of Lincoln in mid-April 1865, Vice President Andrew Johnson became president. He had little formal education and in his early life struggled continually against poverty. As a young man in Tennessee, he worked as a tailor, then turned to politics. A Democrat, he relied on his oratorical skills to win several terms in the Tennessee legislature. He was elected to Congress, then served two terms as governor before winning election to the U.S. Senate in 1857. His political support came especially from small-scale farmers and working people. The state's elite of plantation owners had usually opposed him, and the feeling was mutual. Johnson resented their wealth and power, and he blamed them for secession and the Civil War.

When **secession** came, Johnson was the only southern senator who rejected the Confederacy. Early in the war, Union forces captured Nashville, capital of Tennessee, and Lincoln appointed Johnson as military governor. Johnson dealt harshly

◆ Radical Republicans initially hoped that Andrew Johnson would be their ally. Instead he proved to be unsympathetic to most Radical goals. His self-righteous and uncompromising personality led to conflict that eventually produced an unsuccessful effort to remove him from office in 1868. *Library of Congress.*

with Tennessee secessionists, especially the wealthy planters. Radical Republicans thought that Johnson's severe treatment of former Confederates was what the South needed. He was elected vice president in 1864, receiving the nomination for vice president in part because Lincoln wanted to appeal to Democrats and to Unionists in border states.

When Johnson succeeded to the presidency, Radicals hoped he would join in their plans for transforming the South. Johnson, however, soon made clear that he held a strong commitment to **states' rights** and opposed the Radicals' concept of a powerful federal government able to impose policies on

---

Thirteenth Amendment   Constitutional amendment, ratified in 1865, that abolished slavery in the United States and its territories.

secession   The withdrawal of eleven southern states from the United States in 1860–1861, giving rise to the Civil War.

states' rights   A political position favoring the limitation of the federal Government's power and the greatest possible self-government by the individual states.

the states. "White men alone must manage the South," Johnson told one visitor, although he recommended that southerners give limited political roles to a few freedmen as a way of mollifying the Radicals. Johnson's support for emancipation seemed to derive largely from his desire to punish the wealthy planters who, he believed, were responsible for the war. Self-righteous and uncompromising, Johnson saw the major task of Reconstruction as empowering the region's white middle class and keeping the planters from regaining power.

In practice, Johnson's approach to Reconstruction differed little from Lincoln's. Like Lincoln, he relied on the president's constitutional power to grant pardons. Despite his bitterness toward the southern elite and his hatred of secession, he granted amnesty to most former Confederates who pledged loyalty to the Union and support for emancipation. In one of his last actions as president, he granted full pardon and amnesty to all southern rebels, although, by then (in 1868) the **Fourteenth Amendment** prevented him from restoring the right to hold office.

Johnson appointed provisional governors for the southern states that had not already been reconstructed. He instructed them to call constitutional conventions of delegates elected by pardoned voters. Some provisional governors, however, appointed former Confederates to state and local offices, outraging those who expected Reconstruction to bring to power loyal Unionists committed to a new southern society.

The Southern Response: Minimal Compliance

Johnson expected the state constitutional conventions to abolish slavery within each state, ratify the Thirteenth Amendment, renounce secession, and deny responsibility for the state's war debts. The states were then to hold elections and resume their place in the Union. State conventions during the summer of 1865 usually complied with these provisions. Nearly all of them ratified the Thirteenth Amendment. They renounced secession, though some did so grudgingly. However, they all rejected black suffrage.

By April 1866, all the southern states had fulfilled Johnson's requirements for rejoining the Union and had elected legislators, governors, and members of Congress. Unionists scored a few victories, but former Confederates won many positions. Johnson's policies had failed to create new political leaders in the South in the way he had hoped. The South's

support for the planters and for former Confederate officials troubled him, for he saw in it "something of a defiance, which is all out of place at this time."

Most white southerners, however, viewed Johnson as their protector, standing between them and the Radicals. His support for states' rights and his opposition to federal determination of voting rights led white southerners to expect that they would shape the transition from slavery to freedom—that they, and not Congress, would define the status of the former slaves.

Freedom and the Legacy of Slavery

- What were freed people's expectations for freedom?
- What constraints on their freedom did African-Americans experience in the South during the first years of Reconstruction?

As state conventions wrote new constitutions and as politicians argued in Washington, African-Americans throughout the South set about creating new, free lives for themselves. Before the Civil War, all slaves and most free blacks in the South had led lives tightly constrained by law and custom. They were permitted few social organizations of their own, separate from those of the white South. The freed people faced enormous changes in almost every aspect of their lives. They experimented with their new freedom and quickly developed expectations for a future free from the old constraints. From this ferment of freedom came new, black social institutions that provided the basis for southern African-American communities.

Eric Foner, in his comprehensive study *Reconstruction* (1988), described the central theme of the black response to emancipation as "a desire for independence from white control, for **autonomy** both as individuals and as members of a community." This desire for autonomy affected every aspect of life—family, churches, schools, newspapers, and a

---

Fourteenth Amendment Constitutional amendment, ratified in 1868, that extended citizenship to everyone born or naturalized in the United States, barred former rebels from holding state or federal office, and renounced responsibility for Confederate debts.

autonomy Self-government or the right of self-determination.

host of other social institutions. At the same time, the economic life of the South was shattered by the war and transformed by emancipation, and white southerners also faced drastic economic and social change.

Defining the Meaning of Freedom

At the most basic level, freedom was not something that Lincoln or the Union armies gave to enslaved blacks. It came, instead, when individual slaves stopped working for a master and claimed the right to be free. Freedom did not come to all slaves at the same time or in the same way. For some, freedom had come before the Emancipation Proclamation, when they had walked away from their owners, crossed into Union-held territory, and asserted their freedom. Toward the end of the war, as civil authority broke down throughout much of the South, many slaves simply declared their freedom and left their former masters. Owners were surprised and distressed as even their most favored slaves left them for the Yankee armies and freedom. For the slaves in Kentucky, however, freedom did not come until ratification of the Thirteenth Amendment.

Across the South, the approach of Yankee troops set off a joyous celebration—called a Jubilee—among those who knew that their enslavement was ending. One Virginia woman remembered that "when they knew that they were free they, oh! baby! began to sing. . . . Such rejoicing and shouting you never heard in your life." A man recalled that, with the appearance of the Union soldiers, "We was all walking on golden clouds. Hallelujah!" **W. E. B. Du Bois,** an African-American and one of the pioneers in the study of black history, described it this way in his classic work *Black Reconstruction in America* (1935): "A great human sob shrieked in the wind, and tossed its tears on the sea,—free, free, free." For generations afterward, freed people from Texas and their descendants across the nation celebrated "Juneteenth Day"—June 19, the day in 1863 when Texas's African-Americans learned of their freedom. Once the celebrating was over, however, the freed people faced difficult choices: what to do now; how best to use one's freedom.

The freed people expressed their new freedom in many ways. Some chose new names to symbolize their new identity and new beginnings. Many changed their style of dress, discarding the cheap clothing provided to slaves. Some acquired guns. A significant benefit of freedom was the ability to travel without a pass and without being checked by the patrols that had enforced the **pass system.** Many freed people took advantage of this new opportunity. Most who chose to move, however, traveled only short distances and usually for well-defined reasons: to find work or land to farm, to seek family members separated from them by slavery, or to return to homes that war had forced them to leave.

Many African-Americans felt they had to leave the site of their enslavement to experience full freedom. One woman explained that she chose to leave the plantation where she had been a slave because "if I stay here I'll never know I'm free." Dr. Daniel Norton, an African-American who testified before the congressional Joint Committee on Reconstruction in 1866, pointed out that many freed people did not return to their former homes because of the poor treatment they had received there.

The towns and cities of the South attracted many freed people. The presence of Union troops and officials seemed to offer protection from the random violence against freed people that occurred in many rural areas. The cities and towns also offered black churches, schools, and other social institutions begun by free blacks before the war. Many African-Americans came to the towns and cities looking for work, for urban wages were usually better than those on the plantations. Cities and towns had little housing for the influx of former slaves, however, and most crowded into black neighborhoods of hastily built shanties. Sanitation was poor and disease a common scourge. In just two weeks in September 1866, for example, more than a hundred died of cholera in Vicksburg, Mississippi. Such conditions improved only very slowly.

Creating Communities

During Reconstruction, African-Americans created their own communities with their own social institutions. Freed people hoped to strengthen family ties. Some families were reunited after years of separation caused by the sale of children away from parents or husband away from wife. Some people spent years searching for lost family members.

W. E. B. Du Bois American historian and civil rights activist who helped found the National Association for the Advancement of Colored People and wrote several influential studies of black life in America.

pass system Laws that forbade slaves from traveling without written authorization from their owners.

The new freedom to conduct religious services without white supervision—prohibited under slavery—was centrally important. Churches quickly became the most prominent social organization in African-American communities. W. E. B. Du Bois later pointed to these churches as "the first social institution[s] fully controlled by black men in America." He might have mentioned black women too, for they also took leading roles in the new churches. Black ministers advised and helped to educate congregation members as they adjusted to the changes brought by freedom. Ministers emerged as important leaders within developing African-American communities, and many of them provided political leadership. One explained that a person "cannot do his whole duty as a minister except he looks out for the political interests of his people."

Freed people understood the importance of education. Setting up a school, said one, was "the first proof" of independence. Throughout the cities of the South, blacks—especially ministers and church members—worked to establish schools. Many of the new schools were not just for children but also for adults who had been barred from learning by state laws that had prohibited education for slaves. The desire to learn was widespread and intense. One freedman in Georgia wrote to a friend about learning to read and write: "The Lord has sent books and teachers. We must not hesitate a moment, but go on and learn all we can."

There had not been a public school system in much of the South before the war. In many places, freed people created the first public schools. The region faced a severe shortage of teachers, books, and schoolrooms—everything but students. As abolitionists and northern reformers tried to assist the transition from slavery to freedom, many of them focused especially on education.

In March 1865, Congress created the **Freedmen's Bureau,** an agency run by the War Department to assist the freed people in their transition to freedom. It helped freed people find employment or become farmers, but its most lasting contribution was helping to establish a black educational system by coordinating aid from the North—especially from the Freedmen's Aid Societies, which sprang up in most northern cities. Northern churches often took an active role too, especially through the American Missionary Association. Northern aid and missionary societies, together with the Freedmen's Bureau, also established schools to train black teachers. Some of those schools evolved into black colleges. At first, many teachers—mostly women, many from New

◆ Churches were among the first social institutions created and controlled by African-Americans after Emancipation. Such churches became important elements in the development of African-American communities, and church leaders, such as this female minister, were usually influential community leaders. *Collection of William Gladstone.*

England, many acting on religious impulses—came from the North. By 1870, the Bureau supervised more than 4,000 schools, with more than 9,000 teachers and 247,000 students. Still, in 1870, the schools had room for only one black child in ten of school age.

In addition to churches and schools, other African-American social institutions included **fraternal orders** and **benevolent societies.** *L'Union,* the first black newspaper in the South, appeared in 1862 in New Orleans, which was then occupied by Union troops. By 1866, the South had ten black newspapers led by the New Orleans *Tribune,* and black newspapers came to play important roles in emerging African-American communities.

Freedmen's Bureau   Agency established in 1865 to aid former slaves in their transition to freedom, especially by administering relief and sponsoring education.

fraternal order   Group of people, usually men, associated for a common purpose; often formed with the idea that social connections may lead to mutual economic or political advancement.

benevolent society   Group of people associated for some charitable purpose.

◆ Republicans enfranchised the black male population of Washington, D.C., early in Reconstruction. This drawing of the second city election in which black voters took part shows a black voter placing his ballot in the ballot box under the watchful eyes of election officials, one of whom is black. *Northwind.*

African-Americans also developed political organizations. In politics, their first objective was recognition of their equal rights as citizens. Frederick Douglass insisted that "Slavery is not abolished until the black man has the ballot." Political conventions of African-Americans in 1865 attracted hundreds of delegates, including many ministers, artisans, and former soldiers. In calling for equality and voting rights, these conventions pointed to black contributions in the American Revolution and the Civil War as evidence of patriotism and devotion. They also appealed to the nation's republican traditions, especially the Declaration of Independence and its dictum that "all men are created equal."

Land and Labor

Former slaveowners reacted to emancipation in a variety of ways. Some tried to keep their slaves from learning of their freedom. A very few, like Mary Chesnut (a member of the plantation aristocracy from South Carolina), actually welcomed an end to slavery. Few provided any compensation (whether money, supplies, or land) to assist their former slaves in the transition to freedom. One freedman

later stated, "I do know some of dem old slave owners to be nice enough to start der slaves off in freedom wid somethin' to live on . . . but dey wasn't in droves, I tell you."

Many freed people began their new lives with virtually nothing, and many looked to the Union troops for assistance. When General Sherman led his army through Georgia in the closing months of the war, thousands of African-American men, women, and children chose to leave their plantations, claim their freedom, and follow the Yankee troops. Their leaders told Sherman that what they wanted more than anything else was to "reap the fruit of our own labor." In January 1865, Sherman responded, by issuing Special Field Order No. 15, setting aside the Sea Islands and land along the South Carolina coast for freed families. Each family, he specified, was to receive 40 acres and the loan of an army mule. By June, the area had filled with some forty thousand freed people settled on 400,000 acres of "Sherman land."

Sherman's action encouraged many African-Americans to expect that the federal government would order a similar redistribution of land throughout the South. "Forty acres and a mule" became a rallying cry. Land, Thaddeus Stevens proclaimed, was the only thing that would give the freed people control of their own labor. "If we do not furnish them with homesteads," Stevens once said, "we had better left them in bondage."

The Freedmen's Bureau took the lead in the efforts to assist the freed people toward landownership and free labor. At the end of the war, the Bureau controlled more than 850,000 acres of land abandoned by former owners or confiscated from leading Confederates. In July 1865, General Oliver O. Howard, head of the Bureau, directed Bureau agents to divide this land into 40-acre plots to be given to freed people.

The widespread expectation of "forty acres and a mule" came to an end when President Johnson issued pardons to the former owners of the confiscated land and ordered Howard to halt **land redistribution** and to reclaim land already given to freed people and return it to its former owners. Johnson's order displaced tens of thousands of African-Americans who had already taken their 40 acres. They and

---

land redistribution The division of land held by large landowners into small plots that are turned over to people without property.

♦ Sharecropping gave African-Americans more control over their labor than did labor contracts. But sharecropping also contributed to the South's dependence on one-crop agriculture and helped to perpetuate widespread rural poverty. Notice that the child standing on the right is holding her kitten, probably to be certain it is included in this family photograph. *Library of Congress.*

others who had hoped for land now felt disappointed and betrayed. One recalled years later that they had expected "a heap from freedom dey didn't git."

Sharecropping slowly emerged across much of the South as an alternative both to land redistribution and to wage labor on the plantations. Sharecropping derived directly from the central realities of the southern agricultural economy. A great deal of land was in large holdings, but the landowners had no one to work the land. A large number of families, both black and white, wanted to raise their own crops with their own labor but had no land, no supplies, and no money to buy them. The entire region was short of **capital.** Under sharecropping, an individual—usually a family head—signed a contract with a landowner to rent land as a home and farm. The tenant—the sharecropper—was typically to pay, as rent, a share of the harvest. The share might be half or even two-thirds of the year's crop if the landlord provided not only the land but also mules, tools, seed, and fertilizer. If the landlord provided only the land, the share was usually a quarter or a third. Many landowners preferred sharecrop-

ping because it encouraged tenants to be productive, to get as much value as possible from their shares of the crop. Some tenants preferred sharecropping to wage labor because sharecroppers had more control over their day-to-day work than did laborers.

Southern farmers—whether black or white, sharecroppers or owners of small plots—often found themselves in debt to a local merchant who had advanced supplies on credit until the harvest came. Many landlords ran stores for their tenants and required the tenants to patronize those stores. All too often, the share paid as rent and the debt owed the store exceeded the value of the entire harvest. Many contracts included provisions that automatically renewed them if all debts were not paid off at the end of a year.

By becoming tenants and taking responsibility for a plot of land, sharecropping families hoped to achieve greater control over their lives and labor than was possible for wage-earning contract laborers. In the end, however, many southerners, black and white alike, felt trapped by sharecropping and debts.

In a time before the **secret ballot,** the power of the landlord and merchant often extended to the ballot box. When a landlord or merchant advocated a particular candidate, the unspoken message was often an implicit threat to cut off credit at the store or to evict a farmer from his plot if he did not vote as directed. Such forms of economic coercion had the potential to undercut the significance of voting rights.

The White South: Confronting Change

The slow spread of sharecropping through much of the South, among white tenant farmers as well as black, was just one of many ways that the end of slavery transformed the lives of white southerners. For some white southerners, the changes were nearly as profound as for the freed people. With

---

sharecropping   Agricultural system in which tenant farmers give landlords a share of the crops as rent, rather than cash.

capital   Money needed to start a commercial enterprise.

secret ballot   System of voting in which ballots are cast anonymously and voters thus do not have to fear reprisals if they vote against a powerful candidate.

Confederate money worthless, savings vanished. Some found their homes and other buildings destroyed. Thousands sold their landholdings and left the South.

Before the war, few white southerners had owned slaves, and even fewer had owned large numbers. Distrust or even hostility had always existed between the few privileged planter families and whites who farmed small plots and had either a few slaves or none. Some regions populated by small-scale farmers had resisted secession, and some of them welcomed the Union victory and supported the Republicans during Reconstruction. A few white southerners welcomed the prospect of the economic transformation that northern capital might bring.

Most white southerners, however, shared what one North Carolinian in 1866 described as "the bitterest hatred toward the North." United in detesting Yankees and in affection for the "lost cause" of the Confederacy, southern whites were largely unprepared for the extent of change facing them. The historian E. Merton Coulter suggested that they expected their society "to be mended as of old—that Humpty Dumpty might after all be put back on the wall." The early response of white southerners to emancipation reflects such an expectation that things might "be mended as of old."

As civil governments created under presidential Reconstruction began to function in late 1865 and 1866, state legislatures passed **black codes** defining the new legal status of African-Americans. Black codes varied from state to state, but every state placed significant restraints on the freedom of black people. Various black codes required all African-Americans to have an annual employment contract, limited them to agricultural work except with court permission, restricted them from moving about the countryside without permission, forbade them from owning guns or carrying weapons, restricted ownership of land, and provided for forced labor by those found guilty of **vagrancy**—which usually meant anyone without a job. Some codes originated in prewar restrictions placed on both slaves and free blacks. Some reflected efforts to ensure that farm workers would be on hand at crucial times in the annual cycle of planting, cultivating, and harvesting. Taken together, however, the black codes clearly represented an effort by white southerners to define a legally subordinate place for African-Americans.

While white southern lawmakers were creating the black codes, some white southerners were using violence to coerce freed people into accepting a subordinate status within the new southern society. Clara Barton, who had organized women to serve as nurses for the Union Army, visited the South from 1866 to 1870 and observed "a condition of lawlessness toward the blacks" and "a disposition . . . to injure or kill them on slight or no provocation." Most southern whites seem to have tolerated this kind of treatment.

Violence and terror became closely associated with the **Ku Klux Klan,** a secret organization formed in 1866 and led by a former Confederate general, Nathan Bedford Forrest. Most Klan members were small-scale farmers and workers, but the leaders were often prominent citizens—planters, merchants, lawyers, and ministers. As one Freedmen's Bureau agent said, "the most respectable citizens are engaged in it." Klan groups existed throughout the South, but there was little central control. Their major goal, however, was everywhere the same: to restore **white supremacy** and to destroy the Republican party. Other, similar organizations also formed and adopted terrorist tactics.

In the Klan's bizarre ritual, members were called ghouls. Officers included cyclops, night-hawks, and grand dragons, and the national leader was called the grand wizard. Klan members covered their faces with hoods, wore white robes, and rode horses draped in white. So attired, they set out to intimidate Republicans, typically targeting leading black Republicans and their Radical white allies. Klan members also attacked less politically prominent people, often whipping African-Americans accused of not showing deference to whites. Night-riders burned black churches and schools. Using violence and threats, the Klan devastated Republican organizations in many communities.

In 1866, two events dramatized for the nation the violence that some white southerners routinely in-

---

black codes   Laws passed by the southern states after the Civil War to limit the freedoms of African-Americans and force them to return to agricultural labor.

vagrancy   Not having a permanent home or means of support and thus being a public nuisance; a charge of vagrancy was often used to deprive blacks of freedom in the years after the Civil War.

Ku Klux Klan   A secret society organized in tne South after the Civil War to resurrect white supremacy by means of violence and intimidation.

white supremacy   The racist belief that whites are inherently superior to all other races and are therefore entitled to rule over them.

♦ In this picture, the artist has portrayed a group of bizarrely dressed Klansmen contemplating the murder of a white Republican. *Library of Congress.*

flicted on African-Americans. In early May, in Memphis, Tennessee, a three-day riot by whites, including police, left forty-five blacks and three whites dead. In late July, in New Orleans, some forty people died, most of them African-Americans, in an altercation between police and a largely black prosuffrage group. "It was not a riot," insisted General Philip Sheridan, the military commander of the district. "It was an absolute massacre by the police." Memphis and New Orleans were unusual only in the number involved and the number killed. Local authorities seemed uninterested in stopping such violence, and federal troops were often not available where they were needed.

Congressional Reconstruction

● Why did Republicans in Congress choose to take control of Reconstruction?

● What did they expect to accomplish?

Carl Schurz, a prominent Republican, traveled through the South in 1865. "One reason why the Southern people are so slow in accommodating

themselves to the new order of things," he concluded, was "that they confidently expect soon to be permitted to regulate matters according to their own notions." By early 1866, most congressional Republicans—Radicals and moderates alike—had concluded that Johnson's Reconstruction policies had encouraged the white South in that expectation. The black codes, violence against freed people, and the failure of southern authorities to stem the violence turned opinion in Washington, and in the North more generally, against the president's approach to Reconstruction. Increasing numbers of moderate Republicans now joined the Radicals in concluding that southern whites must be constrained. As President Johnson proved unable to attract a popular following in the North, choices about the future of the South became intertwined with efforts to establish congressional control over Reconstruction.

Challenging Presidential Reconstruction

In December 1865, the thirty-ninth Congress (elected in 1864) met for the first time. In both houses of Congress, Republicans outnumbered Democrats by more than three to one. The president's annual message proclaimed Reconstruction complete and the Union restored, but few Republicans agreed. Radical Republicans, especially, had been angered by Johnson's lack of support for black suffrage. To accomplish black suffrage, they needed both to assert congressional power over Reconstruction and to move decisions on suffrage from the state to the federal level. Most Republicans agreed with the Radicals' commitment to creating a southern economy based on free labor and to defining and protecting basic rights for the freed people. Most also agreed that Congress had the right to withhold representation from the South until state governments there met these conditions.

On the first day of the thirty-ninth Congress, the newly elected congressmen from the South—including many former Confederates—were excluded. Republicans set up a Joint Committee on Reconstruction to evaluate the qualifications of the excluded southerners under Article II, Section 5, of the Constitution and to determine whether the southern states were entitled to representation. Thaddeus Stevens, head of the committee, announced his intent to make an extensive investigation of the whole question of Reconstruction and the president's policy. While the committee worked, the former Confederate states were to have no representation in Congress.

At the same time, Republicans in Congress moved to assist the freed people by extending the life of the Freedmen's Bureau. Lyman Trumbull of Illinois, chairman of the Senate Judiciary Committee, wielded great influence among moderates. He proposed a bill to extend the life of the Freedmen's Bureau and give it greater authority to act against racial discrimination. Trumbull also sponsored a civil rights bill, a far-reaching measure to extend citizenship to African-Americans and define some of the rights of all citizens. Johnson vetoed both of Trumbull's bills, but Congress passed them over his veto. With creation of the Joint Committee on Reconstruction and passage of the Civil Rights and Freedmen's Bureau acts, Congress asserted its control over Reconstruction.

The Civil Rights Act of 1866

The Civil Rights Act of 1866, prompted by the black codes, defined all persons born in the United States (except Indians not taxed) as citizens. It also listed certain rights of all citizens, including the right to testify in court, own property, make contracts, bring lawsuits, and enjoy "full and equal benefit of all laws and proceedings for the security of person and property." It authorized federal officials to bring suit against violations of civil rights, and it specified that federal courts—not state courts—were to decide such suits.

The Civil Rights Act of 1866 was the first effort to define in law some of the rights of American citizenship. It placed significant restrictions on state actions on the ground that the rights of *national* citizenship took precedence over the powers of *state* governments. By expanding the power of the federal government in unprecedented ways, the law not only challenged traditional concepts of states' rights but did so on behalf of African-Americans.

Much of the debate in Congress focused on the immediate situation of the freed people. Moderates intended the measure as a way to secure the freed people's basic rights rather than as something that redefined federal-state relations. Some moderates feared that failure to extend rights to freed people in the South might cause them to move to the North. They saw Trumbull's proposal as a way to encourage freed people to stay in the South. For Radical Republicans, however, the bill carried broader implications, because it empowered the federal gov-

ernment to force states to abide by the principle of equality before the law. Senator Lot Morrill of Maine described it as "absolutely revolutionary" but added, "Are we not in the midst of a revolution?"

When President Johnson vetoed the civil rights bill, he argued that it violated states' rights. By defending states' rights and taking aim at the Radicals, Johnson may have hoped to generate enough political support to elect a more cooperative Congress in 1866 and to elect him to the presidency in his own right in 1868. He probably expected the veto to appeal to antiblack sentiments among voters in both North and South and to turn them against the Radicals. Instead, the veto led most moderate Republicans in Congress to give up all hope of cooperation with him. In April 1866, when Congress passed the Civil Rights Act over Johnson's veto, it was the first time that Congress had overridden a veto of major legislation.

Defining Citizenship: The Fourteenth Amendment

Leading Republicans worried that the Civil Rights Act could be amended or repealed by a later Congress or declared unconstitutional by the Supreme Court. They concluded that only another constitutional amendment could permanently safeguard the freed people's rights as citizens.

The Fourteenth Amendment began as a proposal made by the Radicals within the Joint Committee on Reconstruction who wanted a constitutional guarantee of equality before the law. But the final wording—the longest of any amendment—resulted from many compromises within the Republican party. Section 1 of the amendment defined American citizenship in much the same way as the Civil Rights Act of 1866, then specified that

> No State shall make or enforce any law which shall abridge the privileges or immunities of citizens of the United States; nor shall any State deprive any person of life, liberty, or property, without due process of law; nor deny to any person within its jurisdiction the equal protection of the laws.

The Constitution and Bill of Rights prohibited *federal* interference with basic civil rights. The Fourteenth Amendment extended this protection against action by *state* governments. The amendment was vague on some points, however. For example, it penalized states that did not **enfranchise** African-Americans—by reducing their congressional and electoral representation proportionate to the number of adult males disfranchised—but it did not specifically guarantee to African-Americans the right to vote.

Some provisions of the amendment stemmed from Republicans' fears that a restored South, in alliance with northern Democrats, might try to undo the outcome of the war. One section barred from public office anyone who had sworn to uphold the federal Constitution and then "engaged in insurrection or rebellion against the same." Only a two-thirds vote of both houses of Congress could counteract this provision. (In 1872, Congress passed a blanket measure pardoning nearly all former Confederates.) The amendment also pledged to honor the federal debt, including that part incurred in "suppressing insurrection or rebellion," and it prohibited either federal or state governments from assuming any of the Confederate debt or from paying any claim arising from emancipation.

Not everyone approved of the compromise. Sumner condemned the provision that permitted a state to deny suffrage to male citizens if it accepted a penalty in congressional representation. Stevens wanted not just to bar former Confederates from holding office but to disfranchise them as well. Woman-suffrage advocates, led by **Susan B. Anthony** and Elizabeth Cady Stanton, protested that the amendment, for the first time, introduced the word *male* into the Constitution in connection with voting rights.

Despite such concerns, Congress approved the Fourteenth Amendment by a straight party vote in June 1866 and sent it to the states for ratification. Johnson opposed that action, arguing that Congress should not propose constitutional amendments until the representatives of all the southern states had taken their seats. (Tennessee ratified the amendment promptly, became the first reconstructed state government to be recognized by Congress, and was therefore exempted from most later Reconstruction legislation.)

Although Congress adjourned in the summer of 1866, the nation's attention remained fixed on the issues of Reconstruction. In May and July, the bloody riots in Memphis and New Orleans turned more northerners and moderates against Johnson's Reconstruction policies. Some interpreted the congressional elections that fall as a **referendum** on Reconstruction and specifically on the Fourteenth

Amendment, pitting Johnson against the Radicals. Johnson undertook a speaking tour—dubbed a "Swing Around the Circle"—to promote his views, but his reckless tirades alienated many who heard him. Republicans swept the 1866 elections, outnumbering Democrats 143 to 49 in the new House of Representatives, and 42 to 11 in the Senate. Lyman Trumbull voiced the view of most congressional Republicans: Congress should now "hurl from power the disloyal element which controls and governs" in the South.

Radicals in Control: Impeachment of the President

As Congress—and the Radicals—took charge of Reconstruction, it became clear that the Fourteenth Amendment was falling short of ratification. Rejection by ten states could prevent ratification. By March 1867, the amendment had been rejected by twelve states—Delaware, Kentucky, and all the Confederate states except Tennessee. Moderates who had expected the Fourteenth Amendment to be the final federal Reconstruction measure became more receptive to other proposals put forth by the Radicals.

The Military Reconstruction Act of 1867, passed on March 2 over Johnson's veto, divided the Confederate states (except Tennessee) into five military districts. Each district was governed by a military commander authorized by Congress to use military force to protect life and property (see Map 15.1). The ten states were to hold constitutional conventions, and all adult male citizens were to vote, except former Confederates barred from office under the proposed Fourteenth Amendment. The constitutional conventions were to create new state governments that permitted black suffrage, and the new governments were to ratify the Fourteenth Amendment. Then, perhaps, Congress might recognize those

---

enfranchise To grant the right to vote to a person or group of people.

Susan B. Anthony Feminist and reformer who worked to secure the vote for women and to protect the economic rights of married women.

referendum The submission to the public for its approval or disapproval of a law passed or proposed by the legislature.

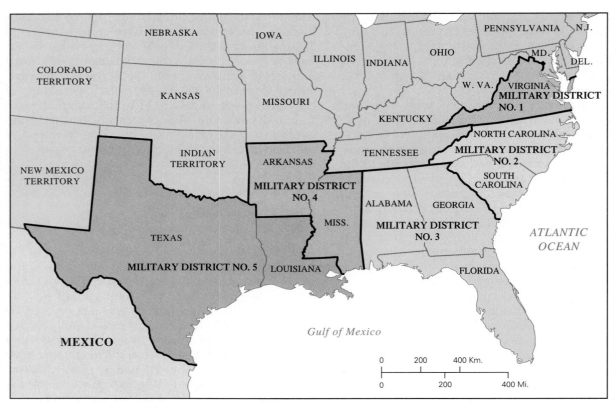

◆   **MAP 15.1 Reconstruction Military Districts**   This map displays the five military districts created when Congress approved the *Reconstruction Act* of 1867. Tennessee was exempted from military rule because it had been so quick to ratify the Fourteenth Amendment.

state governments as valid. While awaiting congressional recognition, they were to be considered provisional.

On the same day, March 2, Congress limited some of Johnson's constitutional powers. The Command of the Army Act specified that the president could issue military orders only through the general of the army (Ulysses S. Grant, who was thought to be sympathetic to Congress). It also specified that he could not be removed or sent outside Washington without Senate permission. Congress thereby blocked Johnson from direct communication with military commanders in the South. The Tenure of Office Act specified that officials appointed with the Senate's consent were to remain in office until the Senate approved a successor. This measure was intended to prevent Johnson from replacing federal officials who opposed his policies.

Early in 1867, some Radicals had begun to consider impeaching President Johnson. (The Constitu-

tion, in Article I, Sections 2 and 3, gives the House of Representatives exclusive power to **impeach** the president—that is, to bring charges of misconduct. The Senate has exclusive power to hold trial on those charges, with the chief justice of the Supreme Court presiding. If found guilty by a two-thirds vote of the Senate, the president is removed from office.) In January 1867, the House Judiciary Committee began to investigate charges against Johnson but failed to find convincing evidence of misconduct. Johnson, however, confronted Congress over the Tenure of Office Act by removing Edwin Stanton, a Lincoln appointee and a Radical, from his cabinet post as secretary of war. This action provided the Radicals

> **impeach**   To formally charge a public official with improper conduct in office and bring the official to trial for that offense.

with something resembling a violation of law by the president.

Led by Thaddeus Stevens, the Joint Committee on Reconstruction recommended impeachment. On February 24, 1868, the House approved the recommendation and adopted eleven articles, or charges, nearly all dealing with the Stanton affair. The actual reasons the Radicals wanted Johnson removed were clear to all: they disagreed with his actions and disliked him personally.

To convict Johnson and remove him from the presidency required a two-thirds vote of the Senate. Johnson's defense attorneys argued that Johnson had dismissed Stanton only to test the constitutionality of the Tenure in Office Act and that he had done nothing to warrant impeachment. The Radicals' case was weak, but they urged senators to base their vote on whether they wished Johnson to remain as president. Some moderate Republicans, however, questioned the wisdom of removing Johnson, because they feared the **precedent** it might set. The vote, on May 16 and 26, 1868, was 35 in favor of conviction and 19 against, one vote short of the required two-thirds. By this narrow margin, the nation maintained the principle that Congress should not remove the president from office simply because they disagreed with or disliked each other (see Individual Choices: Lyman Trumbull).

Political Terrorism and the Election of 1868

The Radicals' failure to unseat Johnson left him with less than a year remaining in office, and the furor over impeachment quickly passed. The Republicans nominated Ulysses S. Grant for president. A war hero, popular throughout the North, Grant seemed the right person to end the conflict between the White House and Congress. During the war, he had fully supported Lincoln and Congress in implementing emancipation. By 1868, he had committed himself to the congressional view of Reconstruction. The Democrats nominated Horatio Seymour, a former governor of New York, and focused most of their campaign against Reconstruction.

In the South, the campaign stirred up fierce activity by the Ku Klux Klan and similar groups. **Terrorists** assassinated an Arkansas congressman, three members of the South Carolina legislature, and several delegates to state constitutional conventions. Throughout the South, mobs attacked Republican newspaper offices and campaign meetings, and sometimes they attacked any black person they

◆ Tickets such as these were in high demand, for they permitted the holder to watch the historic proceedings as the Radical leaders presented their evidence to justify removing Andrew Johnson from the presidency. *Collection of David J. and Janice L. Frent.*

could find. Such coercion had its intended effect. For example, during the campaign, as many as two hundred blacks were killed in St. Landry Parish, Louisiana, where the Republicans had more than a thousand-vote majority among registered voters. On election day, not a single Republican vote was recorded from the parish.

Despite such violence, by election day many Americans probably expected a calmer political future. In June 1868, Congress had readmitted seven southern states that met the requirements of congressional Reconstruction. In July, the secretary of state had declared the Fourteenth Amendment ratified. In August, Thaddeus Stevens had died. In November, Grant won the presidency, taking twenty-six of the thirty-four states and 53 percent of the vote.

Voting Rights and Civil Rights

Grant's election confirmed that Reconstruction was not likely to be overturned. Radical Republicans now addressed voting rights for all African-Ameri-

---

precedent   An event or decision that may be used as an example in similar cases later on.

terrorists   Those who use threats and violence, often against innocent parties, to achieve ideological or political goals.

Choosing Principle Over Party

Lyman Trumbull

Lyman Trumbull, a former judge and chairman of the Senate Judiciary Committee, faced a choice between his party and his commitment to judicial principles when he had to vote on removing Andrew Johnson from presidency. Chicago Historical Society.

The sun was shining in Washington, D.C., on May 16, 1868, as a crowd swarmed around the entrance to the visitors' gallery of the Senate. Seats were in great demand, for at noon the Senate was to vote on the impeachment of President Andrew Johnson. Promptly at noon, Salmon P. Chase, Chief Justice of the Supreme Court, arrived to carry out his constitutionally mandated role of presiding over the proceedings. The roll call was delayed to permit the last of the 54 senators—weakened by a recent stroke—to take his seat.

Chase began to call the roll on the eleventh charge, the one considered most likely to be approved, asking each senator, "Is the respondent, Andrew Johnson, President of the United States, guilty or not guilty of a high misdemeanor, as charged in this article?" All Democrats voted not guilty. Nearly all Republicans voted guilty. Seven Republicans, however, made the difficult choice to break with their party, producing a final outcome of 35 for conviction and 19 opposed—one vote short of the two-thirds majority needed to convict Johnson and remove him from office.

cans, whether in the North or the South. In 1867, Republicans in Congress had removed racial barriers to voting in the District of Columbia and in the territories, but elsewhere voting rights were still defined by the states. Congress had required southern states to enfranchise black males as the price of readmission to the Union, but only seven northern states had taken that step by 1869. States that had enfranchised African-Americans could change their suffrage laws at any time and, once again, disfranchise black voters. To extend to African-Americans in the North the same suffrage rights that African-Ameri-

cans exercised in the South, and to guarantee their voting rights everywhere, Congress approved the **Fifteenth Amendment** in February 1869. Widely considered to be the final step in Reconstruction, the amendment prohibited states from denying the

> **Fifteenth Amendment** Constitutional amendment, ratified in 1870, that prohibited states from denying the right to vote because of a person's race or because a person used to be a slave.

Lyman Trumbull, chairman of the Senate Judiciary Committee and one of the leading Republicans in the Senate, had listened carefully to all the testimony on the case, sometimes bringing his young son Henry to observe the historic proceedings. Trumbull, who had represented Illinois in the Senate for thirteen years, was one of the seven Republicans choosing to vote not guilty, despite the overwhelming majority of Republican leaders in his state who favored conviction. By his choice, he set himself not only against most of the leaders of his party and many of his friends, but even against his wife Julia, described by a Chicago newspaper only nine days before the vote as "a warm impeacher."

Trumbull's choice reflected, in part, his expectations as a lawyer. As early as December 1866, he had called on Republicans to deal with the possibility of impeachment "coolly and deliberately" and not to be misled by "excited demagogues." As a former judge, Trumbull expected more proof of guilt than the leaders of the impeachment effort provided.

One of the important leaders of Congressional Reconstruction, Trumbull had little regard for Johnson, but had great respect for the constitutional separation of powers. Removing Johnson on flimsy evidence, he argued, would pose "far greater danger to the future of the country than can arise from leaving Mr. Johnson in office." Trumbull feared, too, that removal of Johnson would place a major constraint on all future presidents. "Once set an example of impeaching a President for what,

when the excitement of the hour has subsided, will be regarded as insufficient causes," Trumbull warned the Senate, "and no future President will be safe who happens to differ with the majority of the House and two-thirds of the Senate."

Trumbull must have expected that his choice would bring harsh reprimands from Republicans in his home state. One Chicago newspaper even suggested that Trumbull was too unclean even to be touched by decent people. Longtime friendships were shattered by his action. One major Chicago newspaper defended his action, however, and he regained his high standing among the Republican leaders of the Senate.

For Trumbull, however, one outcome of the impeachment trial was that he began to rethink the constitutional issues involved in Reconstruction at the same time that he became more concerned about corruption. He grew more and more critical of the Radicals, the Black Reconstruction governments in southern states, and the Grant administration. In 1872, he joined the Liberal Republicans hoping to defeat Grant. Afterward he became a Democrat. He lost his bid for reelection to the Senate in 1873 and returned to the practice of law. His last major political appearance came in 1894 at the age of 81, when he condemned both the Republican and Democratic parties for failing to protect working people against the mighty industrial corporations and announced that he had become a Populist (see page 590).

right to vote because of a person's race:

The right of citizens of the United States to vote shall not be denied or abridged by the United States or by any State on account of race, color, or previous condition of servitude.

Like the Fourteenth Amendment, the Fifteenth marked a compromise between moderate and Radical Republicans. Some African-American leaders had argued for language guaranteeing voting rights to all male citizens, because language that prohibited some grounds for limitation might imply the

legitimacy of other grounds. Similarly, some Radicals tried, unsuccessfully, to add "nativity [place of birth], property, education, or religious beliefs" to the prohibited grounds. Democrats in both North and South condemned the Fifteenth Amendment, even in its restricted form, as a "revolutionary" change in the rights of states.

Susan B. Anthony and the newly formed National Woman Suffrage Association opposed the amendment for a different reason: it ignored restrictions based on sex. Before emancipation, supporters of woman suffrage had been among the staunchest

◆ This lithograph celebrates approval of the Fifteenth Amendment in 1870. That amendment eliminated race, color, or previous condition of servitude as barriers to voting. Frederick Douglass, the most prominent black abolitionist, is depicted at top center. *Library of Congress.*

opponents of slavery. Now, nearly all male abolitionist leaders agreed that this was, as one said, "the Negro's hour" and that women's issues had to take second place to black suffrage. Many woman-suffrage advocates, however, urged that the vote be extended to women and black men at the same time. Anthony vowed that she "would sooner cut off my right hand than ask the ballot for the black man and not for women." The break between the women's movement and the black movement was patched over somewhat once black suffrage was accomplished, but the wounds never completely healed. (For additional information on the woman-suffrage movement at this time, see pages 565–567 and pages 581–582.)

Despite such opposition, within thirteen months the proposed amendment received the approval of enough states to take effect. Success came in part because Republicans who might otherwise have been reluctant to impose black suffrage in the North recognized that the future success of their party required black suffrage in the South.

The Fifteenth Amendment did nothing to reduce the violence—especially at election time—that had become almost routine in the South after 1865. When Klan activity escalated in the elections of 1870, southern Republicans began to look to Washington for support. In 1870 and 1871, Congress enacted a series of force bills—often called the Ku Klux Klan Acts—to enforce the rights specified in the Fourteenth and Fifteenth Amendments. These laws

for the first time made certain crimes committed against individuals punishable under *federal* law.

Despite a limited budget and many obstacles, the prosecution of Klansmen began in 1871. Hundreds were indicted in North Carolina, and many were convicted. In Mississippi, federal officials indicted nearly seven hundred. In South Carolina, President Grant declared martial law and sent federal troops to occupy the region. Hundreds of arrests followed, and as many as two thousand Klansmen fled the state. By 1872, federal intervention had broken the strength of the Klan.

Congress passed one final Reconstruction measure, largely because of the persistence of Charles Sumner, who introduced a bill prohibiting **discrimination** in 1870 and in each subsequent session of Congress until his death in 1874. Passed after Sumner's death, the Civil Rights Act of 1875 prohibited racial discrimination in the selection of juries and in public transportation and **public accommodations.** Provisions prohibiting **segregated** schools, churches, and cemeteries were deleted as too controversial—in both North and South.

Black Reconstruction

● Who made up the Republican party in the South during Reconstruction?

● What important choices did Republican state administrations make during Reconstruction?

● Which choices brought the most lasting outcomes?

Congressional Reconstruction set the stage for new developments at state and local levels throughout the South, as newly enfranchised black men organized for political action. African-Americans never completely controlled any state government, but they did form a large and important element in the governments of several states. The period when African-Americans participated prominently in state and local politics, and sometimes took the

---

discrimination   Treatment based on class or racial category rather than on merit; prejudice.

public accommodations   Places such as hotels, bars and restaurants, and theaters set up to do business with anyone who can pay the price of admission.

segregated   Characterized by the separation of a race or class from the rest of society, such as the separation of blacks from whites in most southern school systems.

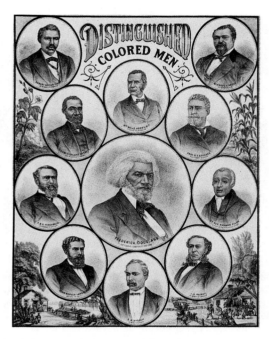

♦ This lithograph from 1883 depicts prominent African-American men, several of whom had leading roles in Black Reconstruction. *Library of Congress.*

lead in pushing through new laws, is usually called **Black Reconstruction.** It began with the efforts of African-Americans to take part in politics as early as 1865 and lasted for more than a decade. Some African-Americans continued to hold elective office in the South long after 1877, but they could do little to bring about significant political change.

The Republican Party in the South

Not surprisingly, nearly all blacks who took an active part in politics did so as Republicans. Throughout Reconstruction, African-Americans formed a large majority of those who supported the Republican party in the South. Nearly all black Republicans were new to politics, and they often braved considerable personal danger by participating in a political party that many white southerners saw as a tool of the conquering Yankees. In the South, the Republican party also included transplanted northerners—both black and white—and some whites born in the South.

Suffrage made politics a centrally important activity for African-American communities. The state constitutional conventions that met in 1868 included 265 black delegates. In Louisiana and South Car-

olina, half or more of the delegates were black, and blacks made up 40 percent in Florida and 20 percent in Arkansas, North Carolina, and Texas. With suffrage established, southern Republicans (black and white) began to elect African-Americans to public office. Between 1869 and 1877, fourteen black men served in the national House of Representatives, six of them from South Carolina, three from Alabama, and one each from Florida, Georgia, Louisiana, Mississippi, and North Carolina. Mississippi sent two African-Americans to the U.S. Senate: Hiram R. Revels and Blanche K. Bruce.

Across the South, the state-level offices that black men were most likely to hold were lieutenant governor and secretary of state—typically the least consequential offices in state government. Six blacks served as lieutenant governors, and one of them, P. B. S. Pinchback, succeeded to the governorship of Louisiana for forty-three days. More than six hundred black men served in southern state legislatures during Reconstruction, three-quarters of them in just four states: South Carolina, Mississippi, Louisiana, and Alabama. Only in South Carolina did blacks ever have a majority in the state legislature. Elsewhere they formed part of a Republican majority and rarely held key legislative positions. Only in South Carolina and Mississippi did legislatures elect black Speakers.

Although politically inexperienced, most of the African-Americans who held office during Reconstruction had some education. Many had been free before the war—of eighteen who served in statewide offices, all but three are known to have been born free. Blanche K. Bruce was born a slave but was educated by a private tutor and, after the Civil War, attended Oberlin College in Ohio. He moved to Bolivar County, Mississippi, in 1868 and served as U.S. senator from Mississippi from 1875 to 1881. P. B. S. Pinchback was educated in Ohio and served in the army as a captain before entering politics in Louisiana. Most black politicians first achieved prominence through army service or work in the Freedmen's Bureau, the new schools, or the religious and civic organizations of black communities.

Even in states with large black populations, southern Republicans achieved power only by securing at least some support from whites. Two

---

Black Reconstruction The period of Reconstruction when African-Americans took an active role in state and local government.

groups of white Republicans are usually remembered by the names fastened on them by their political opponents: "carpetbaggers" and "scalawags." Both groups included idealists who hoped to create a new southern society, but both also included some opportunists who hoped only to fatten their own purses by exploiting the unstable politics of the day.

Southern Democrats used the term **carpetbagger** to suggest that northerners who came to the South after the war were a pack of second-rate opportunists, with their belongings packed in a cheap bag made of carpet material. In fact, most northerners who came south were well-educated men and women from middle-class backgrounds. Most of the men had served in the Union Army and moved South soon afterward, before blacks could vote. Some were lawyers, businessmen, or newspaper editors, and some left behind prominent roles in northern communities. As investors in agricultural land, teachers in the new schools, or agents of the Freedmen's Bureau, most of these northerners hoped to transform the South by creating new institutions based on northern models, especially free labor and free, public schools. Carpetbaggers made up a sixth of the delegates to the state constitutional conventions. In the conventions and in state legislatures, they often took leading roles and chaired key committees. Everywhere, transplanted northerners emerged as advocates of economic modernization.

Southern Democrats reserved their greatest contempt for those they called **scalawags,** slang for someone completely unscrupulous and worthless. Scalawags were white southerners who aligned themselves with the Republican party. They made up the largest single category of delegates to the state constitutional conventions, indicating the extent to which southern whites themselves were divided over Reconstruction. Scalawags included many southern Unionists, who had opposed secession in 1860–1861, and others who thought alliance with the Republicans of the North offered the best hope for economic recovery. Scalawags included small-town merchants, artisans, and professionals who favored a modernized South. Others were small-scale farmers from the backcountry, who had traditionally opposed the political leadership of the plantation owners. For them, Reconstruction promised an end to political domination by the plantation counties. Still others, including some aristocratic plantation owners, had been Whigs before the Civil War.

Despite differences, freedmen, carpetbaggers, and scalawags used the Republican party to inject

◆ Bags made of carpeting, like this one, were inexpensive sacks used to pack things for traveling. Southern opponents of Reconstruction fastened the label "carpetbaggers" on northerners who came south to participate in Reconstruction, suggesting that they were cheap opportunists. *Collection of Antique Textile Resource, Nancy Gerwin.*

new ideas into the South. Throughout the South, Republican governments extended the role of state and local government and expanded public institutions, seeking to make southern states more like states in the North. They established or expanded schools, hospitals, orphanages, and penitentiaries.

Creating an Educational System and Fighting Discrimination

Free public education was perhaps the most permanent legacy of Black Reconstruction. Reconstruction constitutions throughout the South required tax-supported public schools. Implementation, however, was expensive and proceeded slowly. By the mid-1870s, only half of southern children attended public schools.

In creating public school systems, the Reconstruction state governments faced a central question: would white and black children attend the

---

carpetbagger Derogatory southern term for the northerners who came to the South after the Civil War to take part in Reconstruction.

scalawag Derogatory southern term for white southerners who aligned themselves with the Republican party.

same schools? Most blacks probably favored **integrated** schools. As W. E. B. Du Bois later wrote, "They wanted the advantages of contact with white children, and they wanted to have this evidence of their equality." Southern white leaders, however, including many southern white Republicans, warned that integration would destroy the fledgling public school system by driving whites away. Only Louisiana and South Carolina mandated that schools not be segregated. Florida took this step in 1873, but it was not enforced. Nor did South Carolina and Louisiana enforce their laws, although a third of the New Orleans public schools were racially mixed for several years. Similarly, most southern states set up separate black public colleges and universities, although South Carolina experimented, briefly, with integrating its university.

On balance, most blacks probably agreed with Frederick Douglass's newspaper that separate schools were "infinitely superior" to no public education. Some found other reasons to accept segregated schools: separate black schools gave a larger role to black parents, and they hired black teachers, who were beginning to graduate from the new black colleges.

Funding for the new schools was rarely adequate. In some rural areas in the North, public schools had been supported by land set aside for that purpose by the Northwest Ordinance of 1787, but elsewhere school funds came from **property taxes.** In the South, the new schools had to be funded largely through property taxes, and property-tax revenues declined during the 1870s as property values fell. Creating and operating two educational systems, one white and one black, was expensive. The division of limited funds posed an additional problem, and black schools almost always received less support than white schools. Despite their accomplishments, the segregated schools institutionalized discrimination.

Reconstruction state governments moved toward protection of equal rights in areas other than education. The federal occupation forces had canceled the black codes, and Congress had followed up with the Civil Rights acts of 1866 and 1875. As Republicans gained control in the South, they often wrote into the new state constitutions prohibitions against discrimination and protections for civil rights. Some Reconstruction state governments enacted laws guaranteeing **equal access** to public transportation and public accommodations, but elsewhere efforts to pass equal access laws foundered on the opposition of southern white Republicans (scalawags).

◆ Howard University, Washington, D.C., was chartered by Congress in 1867 and quickly became the leading African-American university. Its first president and namesake was General Oliver O. Howard, former head of the Freedmen's Bureau. Over the years, the university has produced many of the nation's black leaders. *Collection of William Gladstone.*

Like southern Democrats, scalawags often favored separate facilities for blacks. Such conflicts pointed up the internal divisions within the southern Republican party. Even when equal access laws were passed, they were often not enforced.

Railroad Development and Corruption

Republicans everywhere, not just in the South, sought to use the power of government to encourage economic growth and development. Efforts to promote economic development, in both North and South alike, often focused on encouraging railroad

---

integrated   Open to people of all races and ethnic groups without restriction.

property taxes   Taxes paid by property owners according to the value of their property; often used in the United States to provide funding for local schools.

equal access   The right of any group to use a public facility such as streetcars as freely as all other groups in the society.

construction. In the South, Reconstruction governments sometimes granted state lands to railroads, or lent them money, or committed the state's credit to **underwrite** bonds for construction. Sometimes they promoted railroads without adequate planning and without finding out whether companies were financially sound. Such efforts to promote railroad construction sometimes failed, as companies squandered their funds without building rail lines. During the 1870s, only 7,000 miles of new track were laid in the South, compared to 45,000 miles in the North.

Railroad companies sometimes tried to secure favorable treatment by bribing public officials, and all too many officeholders—in the North, South, and West—accepted their offers. Indeed, during the post–Civil War period, the ethics of public officials reached one of the lowest points in the nation's history. From New York City to Mississippi to California, revelations and allegations of corruption became staples in political campaigning.

Conditions in the South were especially ripe for political corruption, as government responsibilities expanded rapidly and created opportunities for the ambitious and unscrupulous. Reconstruction governments included many men—white and black—who had only modest holdings of their own and aspired to better things. One South Carolina legislator bluntly described his attitude toward electing a U.S. senator: "I was pretty hard up, and I did not care who the candidate was if I got two hundred dollars." Corruption was usually nonpartisan—it seemed especially prominent among Republicans only because they held the most important offices. Henry C. Warmoth, the Republican governor of Louisiana, claimed that, in his state, "Corruption is the fashion." Still, in the midst of one of the most corrupt periods in the nation's history, some Reconstruction Republicans maintained reputations for scrupulous honesty.

The End of Reconstruction

• What was the Mississippi Plan, and how was it related to the end of Reconstruction?

• What were the final outcomes of Reconstruction?

Most white southerners resisted the new social order imposed on them by the conquering Yankees. They created the black codes to maintain white supremacy and restore elements of a bound labor system. They used terrorism against the advocates of black rights. Instead of producing the results they hoped, such resistance led Congress to pass still more severe terms for Reconstruction. This backlash drove some southern opponents of Reconstruction to rethink their strategy.

The "New Departure"

By 1869, some leading southern Democrats had abandoned their last-ditch resistance to change and had chosen instead to accept key Reconstruction measures and African-American suffrage. At the same time, they also tried to secure restoration of political rights for former Confederates. Behind this **New Departure** for southern Democrats lay the belief that continued resistance would cause more regional turmoil and would prolong federal intervention in state politics.

Sometimes southern Democrats supported conservative Republicans for state and local offices instead of members of their own party. The outcome of this strategy was to defuse concern in Washington and dilute Radical influence in state government. This strategy was tried first in Virginia, where William Mahone, a railroad promoter and leading Democrat, forged a broad political **coalition** that accepted black suffrage. Mahone's organization managed to elect a candidate for governor, a northern-born Republican banker. In this way, Mahone got state support for his railroad plans, and Virginia became the only Confederate state to avoid Radical Republican rule.

Similar coalitions of Democrats and moderate Republicans won in Tennessee in 1869 and in Missouri in 1870. Elsewhere leading Democrats also endorsed the New Departure, accepted black suffrage, and attacked Republicans more for raising taxes and increasing state spending than for their racial policies. Whenever possible they added charges of corruption. Such campaigns brought a positive response from many taxpayers, because southern tax rates

---

underwrite To assume financial responsibility for; in this case, to guarantee the purchase of bonds so that a project can go forward.

New Departure A policy of cooperation with key Reconstruction measures that leading southern Democrats adopted in the hope of winning compromises favorable to their party.

coalition An alliance, especially a temporary one of different people or groups.

had risen dramatically to support the new educational systems, subsidies for railroads, and other new programs. In 1870, Democrats won the governorship in Alabama and Georgia. For Georgia, that meant the effective end of Reconstruction.

The victories of so-called **Redeemers** and New Departure Democrats in 1869–1870 coincided with terrorist activity aimed at Republicans. The worst single incident occurred in 1872. A group of armed freedmen fortified the town of Colfax, Louisiana, to hold off Democrats suspected of planning to seize the county government. After a three-week siege, well-armed whites overcame the black defenders and killed 280 African-Americans—"the bloodiest single instance of racial carnage in the Reconstruction era," according to Foner's *Reconstruction.* Leading Democrats rarely endorsed such bloodshed, but they reaped political advantages from it.

A few southern Republicans who favored countering force with force proposed creating black militias. Most Republican governors, however, feared that use of armed black militia units might provoke a race war. The Arkansas militia and the Texas state police, both of which included whites and blacks, played important roles in the struggle against the Klan in those states. In most of the South, however, the suppression of Klan terrorism came only with federal action.

The 1872 Election

The New Departure movement, at its peak in 1872, coincided with a division within the Republican party in the North. The Liberal Republican movement began in Missouri in 1870 as a revolt by some Republicans against corruption in the Grant administration. It soon spread nationwide, opposing both corruption and the Radicals. Liberal Republicans found allies among Democrats when they argued against further Reconstruction measures.

Horace Greeley, editor of the New York *Tribune,* won the Liberal nomination for president. Greeley had been an ardent opponent of slavery before the Civil War and had given strong support to the Fourteenth and Fifteenth Amendments. But he had sometimes taken puzzling positions, including a willingness to let the South secede in 1860–1861. His unkempt appearance and whining voice conveyed little of a presidential image. One political observer described him as "honest, but . . . so conceited, fussy, and foolish that he damages every cause he wants to support."

Greeley had long ripped the Democrats in his newspaper columns. Even so, the Democrats made him their nominee in an effort to unite the forces opposing the re-election of Grant. Many voters saw the Democrats' action as pure opportunism.

The Liberal Republicans and Democrats were united almost solely by their opposition to Grant and the Radicals. Few Republicans found Greeley an attractive alternative to Grant, and Greeley alienated many northern Democrats by his preference for prohibiting the sale of alcohol. Grant easily overcame the stigma of corruption and won convincingly, carrying 56 percent of the vote and winning every northern state and ten of the sixteen southern and border states (see Map 15.2).

Redemption by Terror: The "Mississippi Plan"

After 1872, southern whites began to abandon the Republicans, but African-Americans maintained their Republican loyalties. The region polarized largely along racial lines, and the elections of 1874 proved disastrous for Republicans. Democrats won over two-thirds of the South's seats in the House of Representatives and "redeemed" Alabama, Arkansas, and Texas.

Republican candidates in 1874 lost all across the North because of the economic **depression** that began in 1873 and the continuing scandals of the Grant administration. Before the 1874 elections, the House of Representatives included 194 Republicans and 92 Democrats. After the 1874 elections, Democrats outnumbered Republicans in the House by 169 to 109. Southern Republicans could no longer look to Congress for assistance, for the Democratic majority in the House of Representatives could now block legislation even though Republicans still controlled the Senate.

As had been the case before, terrorism against black Republicans and their remaining white allies played a role in the victory of the Redeemers in 1874. The Klan had worn disguises and ridden at night, but Democrats now openly formed rifle com-

---

Redeemers Southern Democrats who hoped to bring the Democratic party back into power and to suppress Black Reconstruction.

depression A period of drastic decline in a national or international economy, characterized by decreasing business activity, falling prices, and unemployment.

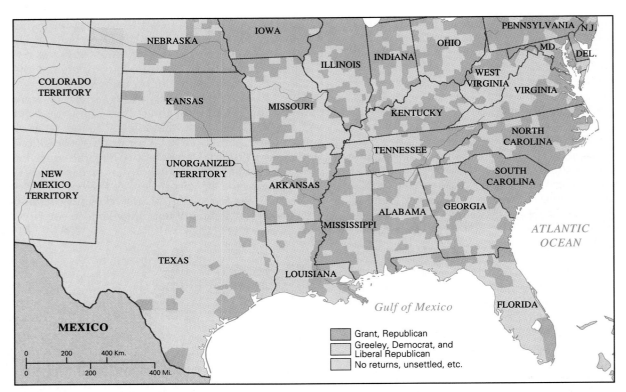

♦ **MAP 15.2 Popular Vote for President in the South, 1872** This map shows which candidate carried each county in the southeastern United States in 1872. Looking at both this map and the chapter-opening map, you can see the relation between Republican voting and African-American population in some areas, as well as where the southern Republican party drew strong support from white voters.

panies, put on red-flannel shirts (the most common article of clothing among southern males), and marched and drilled in public, armed with weapons sometimes sent by fellow Democrats from the North. In some areas, armed whites prevented African-Americans from voting.

During 1875 in Mississippi, political violence reached such an extreme that the use of terror against African-Americans to overthrow Reconstruction became known as the **Mississippi Plan.** Democratic rifle clubs operated freely, breaking up Republican meetings and attacking Republican leaders in broad daylight. One black Mississippian described the election campaign of 1875 as "the most violent time we have ever seen." When Mississippi's carpetbagger governor, Adelbert Ames, requested federal help, President Grant hesitated, fearful that intervention might damage Republican candidates in the Midwest. In one particularly blatant act of political terrorism, armed whites in Ya-

zoo County drove out the carpetbagger sheriff and murdered several prominent African-Americans, including a member of the state legislature. On election day, only seven Republican votes were cast in Yazoo County.

The Democrats swept the Mississippi elections, winning four-fifths of the state legislature. When the legislature convened, it impeached and removed from office Alexander Davis, the black Republican lieutenant governor, on grounds no more serious than those brought against Andrew Johnson. The legislature then brought similar impeachment charges against Governor Ames, who resigned

Mississippi Plan The use of threats, violence, and lynching by Mississippi Democrats in 1875 to drive out Republicans and bring the Democratic party to power.

♦ *Harper's Weekly,* a leading northern periodical, used this cartoon in 1875 to argue that the presence of federal troops and federal law enforcement officials was necessary if African-Americans were to exercise equal rights in the South. *Library of Congress.*

and left the state. Ames had foreseen the result during the campaign when he wrote, "a *revolution* has taken place—by force of arms."

The Compromise of 1877

In 1876, on the centennial of American independence, the nation stumbled through a deeply troubled—and potentially dangerous presidential election. As revelations of corruption grew in both the North and the South, the issue of reform took center stage. The Democratic party nominated Samuel J. Tilden, governor of New York, as its presidential candidate. A wealthy lawyer and businessman, Tilden had earned a reputation for reform by opposing the Tweed Ring, the corrupt Democratic political machine that had dominated New York City government (see pages 550–551). The Republicans also selected a reform candidate, **Rutherford B.**

Hayes, a Civil War general and governor of Ohio. Hayes's unblemished reputation proved to be his greatest asset. Not well known outside Ohio, he was a candidate nobody could object to.

First election reports indicated a victory for Tilden (see Map 15.3). Most politicians assumed that Tilden would carry the border states and the South. He also secured majorities in crucial northern states, including New York, New Jersey, and Indiana. Tilden received 51 percent of the popular vote to 48 percent for Hayes. But in South Carolina, Florida, and Louisiana, the Republican party still controlled the counting and reporting of ballots. Charging **voting fraud** by Democrats in those states, Republican election boards rejected enough ballots so that the official count gave Hayes majorities in those three states and thus a one-vote margin of victory in the Electoral College.

Democrats cried fraud, and Democratic officials in all three states submitted their own versions of the vote count. In addition, the Democratic governor of Oregon (where Hayes won an unquestioned majority) certified a Democratic elector in place of a Republican who, the governor claimed, was ineligible—thereby creating the possibility of switching the one-vote margin to Tilden's favor. Some Democrats vowed to see Tilden inaugurated by force if necessary, and some Democratic newspapers ran headlines that read "Tilden or War."

For the first time, Congress had to face the problem of disputed electoral votes that could decide the outcome of an election. To count the electoral votes and, more important, resolve the challenges, Congress created a fifteen-member commission: five senators, five representatives, and five Supreme Court justices. By party, the commission consisted of eight Republicans and seven Democrats. Initially, the balance was seven to seven with one independent from the Supreme Court, but he withdrew and a Republican replaced him.

Democrats and Republicans braced themselves for a potentially violent confrontation. However, as commission hearings droned on through January

---

Rutherford B. Hayes   Ohio governor and former Union general who won the Republican nomination in 1876 and became president of the United States in 1877.

voting fraud   Altering election results by stuffing ballot boxes or through other illegal measures, in order to bring about the victory of a particular candidate.

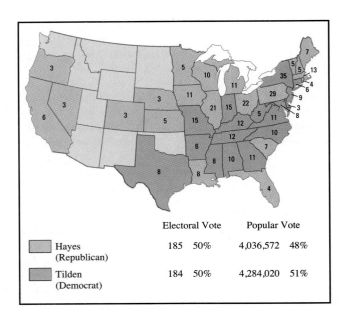

		Electoral Vote		Popular Vote	
Hayes (Republican)		185	50%	4,036,572	48%
Tilden (Democrat)		184	50%	4,284,020	51%

◆ **MAP 15.3 Election of 1876** The end of Black Reconstruction in most of the South combined with Democratic gains in the North to give a popular majority to Samuel Tilden, the Democratic candidate. The electoral vote was disputed, however, and was ultimately resolved in favor of Rutherford B. Hayes, the Republican.

and into February 1877, a series of informal discussions took place across Washington among leading Republicans and Democrats. The result was the **Compromise of 1877.** Southern Democrats demanded **home rule,** by which they meant an end to federal intervention in southern politics. They also called for federal subsidies for railroad construction and waterways in the South. And they wanted one of their own as postmaster general, because that office held the key to most federal patronage. In return, southern Democrats were willing to abandon Tilden's claim to the White House if the commission ruled for Hayes.

Although the Compromise of 1877 was never set down in one place or agreed to by all parties, most of its conditions were met. By a straight party vote, the commission confirmed the election of Hayes. Soon after his peaceful inauguration, he ordered the last of the federal troops withdrawn from occupation duties in the South. The Radical era of a powerful federal government pledged to protect "equality before the law" for all citizens was over. Without federal protection, the last three Republican state

governments fell in 1877, completing the "Redemption" of the South. The Democrats, the self-described party of white supremacy, held sway in every southern state capital. One Radical journal bitterly concluded that African-Americans had been forced "to relinquish the artificial right to vote for the natural right to live." In parts of the South thereafter, election fraud and violence became routine. One Mississippi judge in 1890 acknowledged that "since 1875 . . . we have been preserving the ascendancy of the white people by . . . stuffing ballot boxes, committing perjury and here and there in the state carrying the elections by fraud and violence."

The Compromise of 1877 marked the end of Reconstruction. The war was more than ten years in the past, and the passions it had stirred had slowly cooled. Many who had yearned to punish the South for its treason turned to other matters. Some reformers concentrated on civil service or currency issues. A major depression in the mid-1870s, unemployment and labor disputes, the growth of industry, the emergence of big business, and the economic development of the West (see Chapters 16 and 17) focused public attention on economic issues. In 1875, when Grant refused to use federal troops to protect black rights, he declared that "the whole public are tired out with these . . . outbreaks in the South." He was quoted widely and with approval throughout the North.

By then, southern Democrats had mounted a campaign to persuade northerners—on paltry evidence—that carpetbaggers and scalawags were corrupt and self-serving, manipulating black voters to keep themselves in power; that all African-American officeholders were ignorant and illiterate and could not participate in politics without guidance by whites; and that southern Democrats wanted only to establish honest self-government. The truth of the situation seemed to make little difference. Northern Democrats had always opposed Reconstruction and readily adopted the southern Democrats' version of reality.

Such racist portrayals found growing acceptance among other northerners too, for many people in

Compromise of 1877 Compromise in which southern Democrats agreed to allow the Republican candidate the victory in the disputed presidential election in return for the removal of federal troops from the South.

home rule Self-government; in this case, an end to federal intervention in the South.

the North had shown their own racial bias when they resisted black suffrage and kept their public schools segregated. Some Republicans, to be certain, kept the faith of their abolitionist and Radical forebears and hoped the federal government might again protect black rights (for example, see pages 589–590). The majority of the Republican party, however, condemned violations of black rights but showed little interest in taking action to prevent such outrages.

After Reconstruction

Southern Democrats read the events of 1877 as their permit to establish new systems of politics and race relations. Most Redeemers set out to reduce taxes, to dismantle Reconstruction legislation and agencies, to take political influence away from black citizens, and eventually to reshape the South's legal system to establish African-Americans as subordinate and to restrict the rights of laborers. They also began the process of turning the South into a one-party region, a situation that reached its fullest development around 1900 and persisted until the 1950s and in some areas later.

Although voting and officeholding by African-Americans did not cease with Redemption, the political context changed profoundly once they lost federal enforcement of their rights. The threat of violence from night-riders and the potential for economic retaliation by landlords and merchants sharply reduced independent action by African-Americans. Black political leaders increasingly recognized that efforts to mobilize black voters posed dangers to both candidates and voters, and they concluded that their political survival depended on favors from influential white Republicans or even from Democratic leaders. The public schools remained, segregated and underfunded, but important both as a symbol and as a real opportunity to learn. Many Reconstruction-era laws remained on the books, and blacks in many places continued to be admitted to theaters, bars and restaurants, and hotels and to receive equal seating on streetcars and railroads.

Not until the 1890s did black disfranchisement and thoroughgoing racial segregation become widely embedded in southern law (see pages 562–565). For a time, from the mid-1870s to the late 1890s, the South lived an uneasy compromise: African-Americans had certain constitutional rights, but white supremacy had been established by force of arms, and blacks exercised their rights at the sufferance of the dominant whites. Such a compromise bore the seeds of future conflict.

For generations after 1877, Reconstruction was held up as a failure. Although far from accurate, the southern version of Reconstruction—that conniving carpetbaggers and scalawags had manipulated ignorant freedmen—appealed to the racial bias of many white Americans in the North and South alike, and it gained widespread acceptance among popular novelists, journalists, and historians. William A. Dunning, for example, fully endorsed that interpretation in his history of Reconstruction, published in 1907. Thomas Dixon's popular novel *The Clansman* (1905) inspired the highly influential film *The Birth of a Nation* (1915). Historically inaccurate and luridly racist, the book and the movie portrayed Ku Klux Klan members as heroes who rescued the white South, and especially white southern women, from domination and debauchery at the hands of depraved freedmen and carpetbaggers.

Against this pattern stood some of the first black historians, notably George Washington Williams, a Union army veteran whose two-volume history of African-Americans appeared in 1882. W. E. B. Du Bois's study *Black Reconstruction in America* appeared in 1935. Both presented fully the role that African-Americans played in the biracial southern Republican party of the Reconstruction era. Both pointed to the accomplishments of the Reconstruction state governments and tried to rescue the reputations of black leaders from the abuse that had been heaped on them. Not until the civil rights movement of the 1950s and 1960s, however, did large numbers of American historians begin to reconsider their interpretation of Reconstruction.

Historians today recognize that Reconstruction was not the failure that had earlier been claimed. The creation of public schools was but the most important of the changes in southern life produced by the Reconstruction state governments. At a federal level, the Fourteenth and Fifteenth Amendments eventually provided the constitutional leverage used to restore the principle of equality before the law that so concerned the Radicals. Historians also recognize that Reconstruction collapsed without gaining all its objectives not so much because of internal flaws as because of the political terrorism unleashed in the South and the refusal of the North to commit the force required to protect the constitutional rights of African-Americans.

SUMMARY

E xpectations

C onstraints

C hoices

O utcomes

At the end of the Civil War, the nation held conflicting *expectations* and faced difficult *choices* regarding the future of the defeated South and the future of the freed people. Committed to an end to slavery, President Lincoln nevertheless *chose* a lenient approach to restoring states to the Union, partly to persuade southerners to accept emancipation and abandon the Confederacy. When Johnson became president, he continued Lincoln's approach.

The end of slavery brought new *expectations* for all African-Americans, whether they had been slaves or not. Taking advantage of the new *choices* that freedom opened, they tried to create independent lives for themselves, and they developed social institutions that helped to define black communities. Few were able to acquire land of their own—a significant *constraint* on their economic choices—and most became either wage laborers or sharecroppers. White southerners *expected* to keep African-Americans in a subordinate role through black codes and violence.

In reaction against the black codes and violence, Congress *chose* to wrest control over Reconstruction from President Johnson and passed the Civil Rights Act of 1866, the Fourteenth Amendment, and the Reconstruction acts of 1867. An attempt to remove Johnson from the presidency was unsuccessful. Additional federal Reconstruction measures included the Fifteenth Amendment, laws directed against the Ku Klux Klan, and the Civil Rights Act of 1875. One outcome of these measures was to strengthen the federal government at the expense of the states.

Enfranchised freedmen, white and black northerners who now moved to the South, and some southern whites created a southern Republican party that governed most southern states for a time. The most lasting contribution of these state governments was the creation of public school systems. Like government officials elsewhere in the nation, however, some southerners fell prey to corruption.

In the late 1860s, many southern Democrats *chose* a "New Departure": they grudgingly accepted some features of Reconstruction and sought to recapture control of state governments. The 1876 presidential election was very close and hotly disputed, but key Republicans and Democrats in both North and South *chose* to compromise. The Compromise of 1877 permitted Hayes to take office and brought Reconstruction to an end. Without further federal protection for their civil rights and political activities, African-Americans faced severe *constraints* in exercising those rights fully. Sharecropping consigned most African-Americans to a subordinate economic status. Terrorism, violence, and even death became the lot of African-Americans who *chose* to challenge their subordinate social role. Thus the *outcome* of Reconstruction in the South was white supremacy in politics and government, the economy, and social relations.

SUGGESTED READINGS

Donald, David. *Charles Sumner and the Rights of Man* (1970).

A good account not just of this important Radical leader but of important Reconstruction issues.

Du Bois, W. E. B. *Black Reconstruction in America: An Essay Toward a History of the Part Which Black Folk Played in the Attempt to Reconstruct Democracy in America, 1860–1880* (1935; reprint, 1969).

Written more than a half-century ago, Du Bois's book is still useful for both information and insights.

Foner, Eric. *Reconstruction: America's Unfinished Revolution, 1863–1877* (1988).

The most thorough of recent treatments, incorporating insights from many historians who have written on the subject during the past forty years. Also available in a condensed version.

Litwack, Leon F. *Been in the Storm So Long: The Aftermath of Slavery* (1979).

Focuses especially on the experience of the freed people.

Woodward, C. Vann. *Reunion and Reaction: The Compromise of 1877 and the End of Reconstruction,* rev. ed. (1956).

The classic account of the Compromise of 1877.

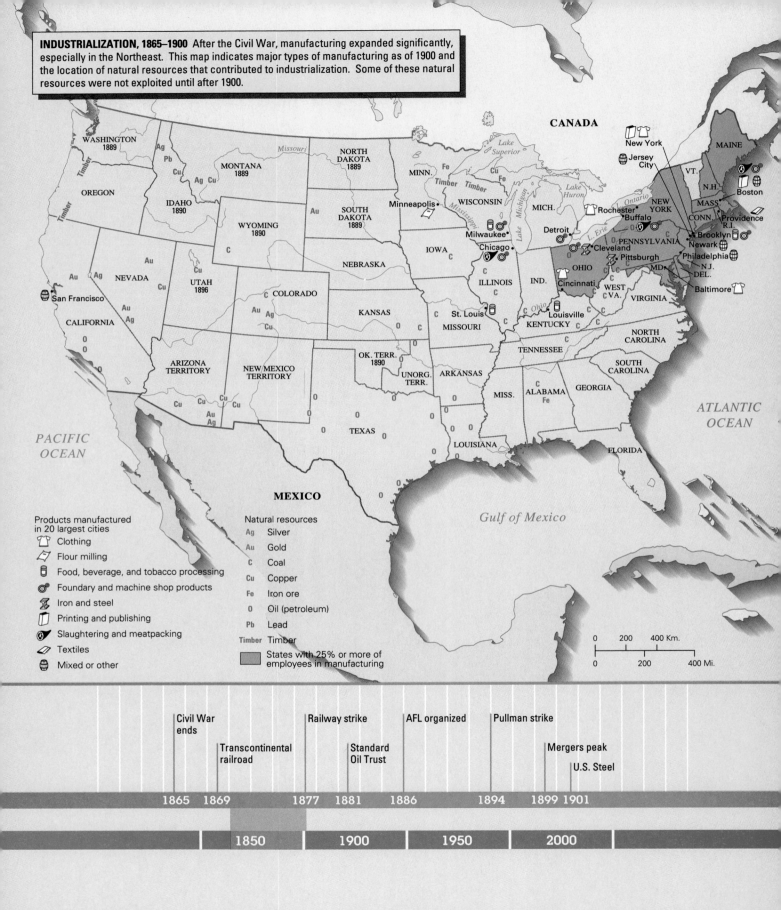

INDUSTRIALIZATION, 1865–1900 After the Civil War, manufacturing expanded significantly, especially in the Northeast. This map indicates major types of manufacturing as of 1900 and the location of natural resources that contributed to industrialization. Some of these natural resources were not exploited until after 1900.

CANADA

WASHINGTON 1889

OREGON

MONTANA 1889

NORTH DAKOTA 1889

MINN.

IDAHO 1890

WYOMING 1890

SOUTH DAKOTA 1889

WISCONSIN

Minneapolis

MICH.

Milwaukee

Chicago

Detroit

NEVADA

UTAH 1896

NEBRASKA

IOWA

ILLINOIS

IND.

OHIO

Cleveland

Pittsburgh

Cincinnati

WEST VA.

PENNSYLVANIA

NEW YORK

Rochester

Buffalo

MAINE

VT.

N.H.

MASS.

Boston

CONN.

R.I.

Providence

Brooklyn

Newark

N.J.

Philadelphia

DEL.

Baltimore

MD.

New York

Jersey City

San Francisco

CALIFORNIA

COLORADO

KANSAS

MISSOURI

St. Louis

KENTUCKY

Louisville

VIRGINIA

NORTH CAROLINA

ARIZONA TERRITORY

NEW MEXICO TERRITORY

OK. TERR. 1890

UNORG. TERR.

ARKANSAS

TENNESSEE

SOUTH CAROLINA

MISS.

ALABAMA

GEORGIA

TEXAS

LOUISIANA

FLORIDA

PACIFIC OCEAN

MEXICO

Gulf of Mexico

ATLANTIC OCEAN

Lake Superior

Lake Michigan

Lake Huron

Lake Erie

Ontario

Missouri

Mississippi

Ohio

Products manufactured in 20 largest cities

Clothing
Flour milling
Food, beverage, and tobacco processing
Foundary and machine shop products
Iron and steel
Printing and publishing
Slaughtering and meatpacking
Textiles
Mixed or other

Natural resources

Ag Silver
Au Gold
C   Coal
Cu Copper
Fe Iron ore
O   Oil (petroleum)
Pb Lead
Timber Timber

States with 25% or more of employees in manufacturing

0   200   400 Km.
0   200   400 Mi.

Civil War ends

Transcontinental railroad

Railway strike

Standard Oil Trust

AFL organized

Pullman strike

Mergers peak

U.S. Steel

1865   1869   1877 1881   1886   1894   1899 1901

1850   1900   1950   2000

CHAPTER 16

Survival of the Fittest: Entrepreneurs and Workers in Industrial America, 1865–1900

Foundation for Industrialization

- What expectations and policy choices encouraged economic growth in the late nineteenth century?

Railroads and Economic Growth

- In the post–Civil War era, what constraints did railroad entrepreneurs and investment bankers face, what choices did they make, and what was the outcome of those decisions?

Entrepreneurs and Industrial Transformation

- How did entrepreneurs like Carnegie and Rockefeller choose to deal with competition and other constraints?
- What outcome did they expect from their choices?

Workers in Industrial America

- What were Americans' expectations regarding economic mobility in the late nineteenth century?
- What constraints did workers face in seeking mobility, and what choices were they able to make?

The Varieties of Labor Organization and Action, 1865–1900

- Compare the expectations of American workers who joined craft unions with those who chose organizations like the Knights of Labor.
- What were some outcomes of labor unrest in the late nineteenth century?

The Nation Transformed

- How did Americans respond to the transformation of the economy?

INTRODUCTION

E xpectations
C onstraints
C hoices
O utcomes

In January 1901, 65-year-old Andrew Carnegie used a blunt pencil to write several lines on a sheet of paper. He handed the paper to his business associate, Charles Schwab, who delivered it to J. P. Morgan. Morgan glanced at it and murmured, "I accept this price." Thereby did Carnegie sell his steel company—the nation's largest—for $480 million. Thereby did Morgan—the nation's most prominent banker—acquire the central element for his plan to create the United States Steel Corporation, the first corporation in the world to be capitalized at more than a billion dollars.

Carnegie had come a long way since his poverty-stricken parents had brought him to America as immigrants from Scotland. Morgan had started with much more, but he too had moved far in his lifetime. Both men, nevertheless, carried out one of the most extraordinary sales in American history in a manner that simple country shopkeepers would have recognized. Such behavior was increasingly rare in the complex and fast-changing business world.

By the time Morgan accepted Carnegie's scribbled offer, the economy of the United States was dramatically and profoundly transformed from what it had been during the Civil War, when both men had entered business. Back then, more than half of all American workers toiled in agriculture. And anyone contemplating the prospects for manufacturing would have noted many potential *constraints:* a poorly developed transportation system, limited amounts of capital, an unsophisticated system for mobilizing capital, and a potential shortage of workers. Some, however, would have pointed to the great potential evident in America's vast natural resources and skilled workers.

A generation later, much of that potential had been realized, and the United States stood as a major industrial power. The changes in the nation's economy far exceeded the wildest *expectations* of Americans living in 1865. Many expected continued economic growth, but few could have imagined that steel production could increase a thousand times by 1900, or that railroads could operate nearly six times as many miles of tracks, or that farms could triple their harvests. Few too could have expected the torrent of inventions that transformed many people's lives—adding machines, telephones, electric lights,

electric streetcars, electric sewing machines, automobiles, motion pictures. By the 1890s, rapid and far-reaching change had become an ingrained part of Americans' *expectations.*

These economic changes were the result of *choices* made by many individuals—where to seek work, where to invest, whether to expand production, how to react to a business competitor, whom to trust. Among the many economic choices Americans made, however, two general areas of decision making stand out: competition and cooperation.

As the industrial economy took off, many entrepreneurs found themselves in a love-hate relationship with competition. Carnegie loved it, expressing the *expectation* that it "insures the survival of the fittest" and "insures the future progress of the race" by producing the highest quality, the largest quantity, and lowest prices. Morgan, in contrast, saw competition as the single most unpredictable factor in the economy and as a serious *constraint* on economic progress. Carnegie's zeal for competition was, in fact, unusual. Although many entrepreneurs paid lip service to the idea of the "survival of the fittest," most resembled Morgan more than Carnegie: they loved competition in the abstract but preferred to find alternatives to it in the reality of their own business *choices.*

Other Americans found themselves making *choices* regarding cooperation. Individualism was deeply entrenched in the American psyche, yet the increasing complexity of the economy presented repeated opportunities for cooperation. Entrepreneurs sometimes chose to cooperate by dividing a market rather than competing in it. Wage earners sometimes chose to join with other workers in standing up to their employer and demanding better wages or working conditions. In the process, some workers found themselves not just cooperating in a union but even questioning capitalism, the economic system that paid their wages. The *outcome* of these many *choices* was the industrialization of the nation and the transformation of the economy.

CHRONOLOGY

The Growth of Industry

1850s	Development of Bessemer and Kelly steel-making processes
1861	Protective tariff
1862	Homestead Act Land-Grant College Act Pacific Railroad Act
1865	Civil War ends
1866	National Labor Union organized
1869	First transcontinental railroad completed Knights of Labor founded
1870	Standard Oil incorporated Patent Office registers the first trademark
1872	Montgomery Ward opens its mail-order business
1873–1878	Depression
1875	Andrew Carnegie opens Edgar Thomson Works
1876	Invention of the telephone
1877	Great Strike Reconstruction ends
1879	Invention of the light bulb Henry George's *Progress and Poverty*

1880s	Railroad expansion and consolidation
1881	Standard Oil Trust organized United Brotherhood of Carpenters and Joiners organized
1882–1885	Recession
1886	Last major railroad converts to the standard gauge First Sears and Roebuck catalogue Peak membership in Knights of Labor Haymarket Square bombing American Federation of Labor founded
1887	American Sugar Refining Company formed
1890–1891	Recession
1892	Homestead strike
1893–1897	Depression
1893	World's Columbian Exposition opens
1894	Pullman strike
1901	United States Steel organized
1902	International Harvester organized

Foundation for Industrialization

● What expectations and policy choices encouraged economic growth in the late nineteenth century?

By 1865, conditions in the United States were ripe for rapid industrialization. A wealth of natural resources, a capable work force, an agricultural base that produced enough food for a large urban population, and favorable government policies laid the foundation.

Resources, Skills, and Capital

At the end of the Civil War, entrepreneurs could draw on vast and virtually untapped natural resources. Americans had long since plowed the fertile farmlands of the Midwest (where corn and wheat dominated) and the South (where cotton was king). At the end of the war, they had just begun to farm the rich black soils of Minnesota, Nebraska, Kansas, Iowa, and the Dakotas, as well as the productive valleys of California. Through the central part of the nation stretched vast grasslands that re-

◆ Many white Americans and Europeans saw much of the American West as a vast reservoir of resources, largely devoid of human inhabitants. Trees such as these redwoods, painted by Albert Bierstadt, were logged to provide lumber for construction in booming western cities. American Indians, however, considered the western regions to be their ancestral homeland. *Courtesy of The Berkshire Museum, Pittsfield, MA.*

ceived too little rain for farming but were well suited for grazing. The Pacific Northwest, the western Great Lakes region, and the South all held extensive forests untouched by the lumberman's saw.

The nation was also rich in mineral resources. Before the Civil War, the iron industry had become centered in Pennsylvania as a result of easy access to iron ore and coal. Pennsylvania was also the site of early efforts to tap underground pools of crude oil. The California Gold Rush, beginning in 1848, had drawn many people west, and some of them had found great riches. Reserves of other minerals lay unused and, in most cases, undiscovered at the end of the war, including iron ore in Michigan, Minnesota, and Alabama; coal throughout the Ohio Valley and in Wyoming and Colorado; oil in the Midwest, Oklahoma, Texas, Louisiana, southern California, and Alaska; gold or silver in Nevada,

Colorado, and Alaska; and copper in Michigan, Montana, Utah, and Arizona. Many of these natural resources were far from population centers, and their use awaited adequate transportation facilities. Exploitation of some of these resources also required new technologies.

Like natural resources, the work force and the skills and experience of workers were important for economic growth. In the 1790s and early nineteenth century, New Englanders had developed manufacturing systems based on **interchangeable parts** (first used for manufacturing guns and clocks) and factories for producing cotton cloth. These accomplishments gave them a reputation for "Yankee ingenuity"—a talent for devising new tools and inventive methods. Such skills and problem-solving abilities, however, were not limited to New England. They were, in fact, essential to the emergence of large-scale manufacturing nearly everywhere, because most early factories relied on skilled artisans to direct less-skilled workers in assembling products.

Another crucial element for industrialization was capital and institutions that could mobilize capital. These too had developed before the Civil War. During the years before the war, capital became centered in the seaport cities of the Northeast—Boston, New York, and Philadelphia, especially—where merchants had prospered from shipping and invested their profits in both banks and factories. Banks were an important tool for mobilizing capital. Before the Civil War, some bankers had specialized in arranging financing for large-scale enterprises, and some of them had opened permanent branch offices in Britain to tap sources of capital there. **Stock exchanges** had also developed long before the Civil War as important institutions for raising capital for new ventures.

The Transformation of Agriculture

The expanding economy of the nineteenth century rested on a productive agricultural base. Improved transportation—canals early in the nineteenth cen-

---

interchangeable parts   Parts that are identical and can be substituted for each other.

stock exchange   A place where people meet to buy and sell stocks and bonds.

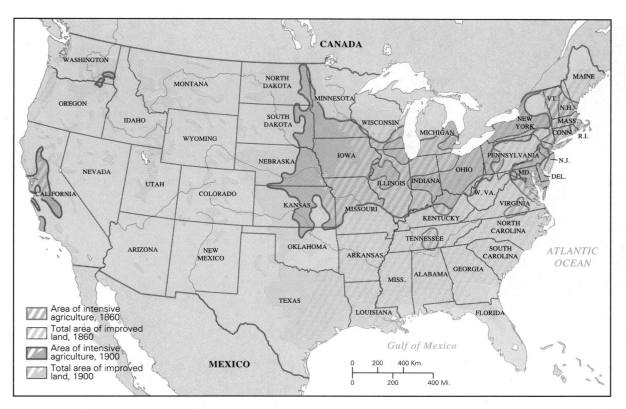

♦ **MAP 16.1 Expansion of Agriculture, 1860–1900**   The amount of improved farmland more than doubled during these forty years. This map shows how agricultural expansion came in two ways—first, western lands were brought under cultivation; second, in other areas, especially the Midwest, land was cultivated much more intensely than before.

tury and railroads later—speeded the expansion of agriculture by making it possible to move large amounts of agricultural produce over long distances. Up to 1865, farmers had developed 407 million acres. During the next thirty-five years, this acreage more than doubled, to 841 million acres. Map 16.1 indicates where this expansion occurred.

The federal government contributed to the rapid settlement of Kansas, Nebraska, the Dakotas, and Minnesota through the **Homestead Act of 1862,** a leading example of the Republicans' commitment to using federal landholdings to speed economic development. Under this act, any person could receive free as much as 160 acres (a quarter of a square mile) of government land by building a house, living on the land for five years, and farming it. Between 1862 and 1890, 48 million acres passed from government ownership to private hands in this way. Other federally owned land could be purchased for as little as

$1.25 per acre, and much more was purchased than was acquired free under the Homestead Act.

Production of leading commercial crops increased more rapidly than the overall expansion of farming. The total number of acres in farmland doubled from 1866 to 1900, but the number of acres planted in corn, wheat, and cotton more than tripled. New farming methods pushed up the harvests even more—corn by 264 percent, wheat by 252 percent, and cotton by 383 percent. Through these years, farm output increased more than twice as much as the population.

Homestead Act of 1862   Law passed by Congress in 1862 promising ownership of 160 acres of public land to any citizen who lived on and cultivated the land for five years.

♦ Mechanization greatly increased the amount of land that an individual could farm. This 1878 lithograph depicts a California crew setting a world's record for the amount of wheat harvested in a single day. *Department of Special Collections, F. Hal Higgins Library of Agricultural Technology, University of California, Davis.*

As production of major crops rose, prices for them fell. Corn sold for 66 cents per bushel in 1866, but fell steadily to its lowest point, 21 cents, in 1896. Wheat prices fell too, from $2.06 per bushel in 1866 to a low of 49 cents in 1894. Cotton prices followed the same trend, from 9.7 cents per pound in 1876, to 8.39 cents in 1885, to 4.6 cents in 1894.

Several factors contributed to the decline in farm prices, but the most obvious was that supply rose faster than demand. Production increased more rapidly than both the population (which largely determined the demand within the nation) and the demand from other countries. According to economic theory, oversupply causes prices to fall, and falling prices lead producers to reduce their output. American farmers, however, made different choices. When they received less for their crops, they raised *more* in the expectation that they might maintain the same level of income. To increase their yield, they bought fertilizers and new, elaborate machinery. Between 1870 and 1890, the amount of fertilizer consumed in the nation more than quadrupled.

New machinery especially affected the production of grain crops. More efficient equipment was available to prepare the soil (steel-bladed sulky plows and **harrows**), plant seeds (grain **drills**), cut stalks (reapers), and remove the grain from the stalks (threshing machines). Such equipment greatly increased the amount of land one person could farm. Wheat provides an extreme example. A single farmer with a hand-held scythe and cradle could harvest 2 acres of wheat in a day. Using the McCormick reaper (first produced in 1849), a single farmer and a team of horses could harvest 2 acres in an hour. For other crops too, a person with modern machinery could farm two or three times as much land as a farmer fifty years before.

The growth of agriculture affected other parts of the economy. The expansion of farming stimulated the farm equipment industry and, in turn, the iron and steel industry. Throughout the nineteenth century, agricultural products (cotton, tobacco, wheat, and meat) formed the bulk of American exports, ranging from two-thirds to seven-eighths of the total. Hefty exports spurred oceanic shipping and shipbuilding, and increased shipbuilding also increased demand for iron and steel. Railroads played a crucial role in the expansion and commercialization of agriculture by carrying farm products to distant markets and transporting fertilizer and machinery from factories (usually in distant cities) to farming regions.

harrow A farm machine consisting of a heavy frame with sharp teeth, used to break up and smooth plowed ground.

drill A machine for planting seeds in holes or furrows.

The Impact of War and New Government Policies

At the end of the Civil War, nearly three times as many Americans worked in agriculture as in manufacturing. Most manufacturing was small in scale and served people nearby—a shop with a few workers who made barrels or a shop with a half-dozen employees who built farm wagons. The war encouraged some entrepreneurs to deliver military supplies to distant parts of the nation, and they thereby developed new expectations for peacetime business. At the end of the war too, some people found themselves looking for places to invest their wartime profits. But, in the short run, by diverting labor and capital into war production, the Civil War probably slowed an expansion of manufacturing already under way. Although the war did not directly cause an expansion of manufacturing, it brought important changes in the experience and expectations of some entrepreneurs. And it was accompanied by new government policies that quickened the rate of growth after the war.

When Republicans took command of the federal government in 1861, the South seceded in reaction to the new administration's opposition to slavery, and secession in turn produced the four-year-long war. But the Republicans were never a single-interest party. While they made war against the Confederacy, abolished slavery, and undertook Reconstruction, they also made policy choices intended to stimulate economic growth. First came a new **protective tariff**, passed in 1861. The tariff was intended to protect products made in America from competition with foreign-made products, by increasing the price of imports to exceed the price of American-made goods. Republicans expected the tariff to stimulate investment in manufacturing.

At the beginning of the Civil War, the federal government claimed more than a billion acres of land as federal property—the **public domain**—more than half of the land area of the nation. The Republicans chose to use this land to encourage economic development in a variety of ways, including free land for farmers, beginning with the Homestead Act (1862). Recognizing the key role of higher education in economic growth, the **Land-Grant College Act** (1862) gave land to states to fund public universities that were required, among other things, to provide education in engineering and agriculture. Also in 1862, by approving a land grant for the first transcontinental railroad, Congress began a series of subsidies to railroads.

Railroads and Economic Growth

● In the post–Civil War era, what constraints did railroad entrepreneurs and investment bankers face, what choices did they make, and what was the outcome of those decisions?

To many Americans of the late nineteenth century, nothing symbolized change so effectively as a locomotive—a huge, powerful, noisy, rapidly moving machine. Railroads set much of the pace for economic expansion after the Civil War. Growth of the rail network stimulated industries that supplied materials for railroad construction and operation—especially steel and coal—and industries that needed railroads to connect them to the emerging national economy. Railroad companies also came to symbolize "big business"—huge corporations with a life and personality of their own—and some Americans began to fear their power.

Railroad Expansion

At the end of the Civil War, the lack of a national rail network posed a significant constraint on economic development. Railroad companies operated on tracks of varying **gauges.** Thus it was impossible to transfer railcars from one line to another, and freight had to be carried, sometimes over a considerable distance, from the railcars of one line to the railcars of another. Few bridges crossed major rivers. Until 1869, no railroad connected the eastern half of the country to the booming Pacific coast region. Every route between the Atlantic and Pacific coasts required more than a month and posed serious discomfort and often outright danger—a sea voyage around the storm-tossed tip of South America; or a boat trip to Central America, transit over

---

protective tariff   Tax on imported goods intended to make them more expensive than similar domestic goods, thus protecting the market for goods produced at home.

public domain   Land owned and controlled by the federal government.

Land-Grant College Act   Law, passed by Congress in 1862, that gave public land to each state; income from the land by the states was to provide funding for engineering and agricultural colleges.

gauge   The distance between the iron rails in a railroad track.

◆ In his novel *The Octopus* (1901), Frank Norris described not just the physical power of the railroad, but also its economic and political prowess: "the galloping terror of steam and steel, with its single eye, cyclopean, red, shooting from horizon to horizon, symbol of a vast power, huge and terrible; the leviathan with tentacles of steel, to oppose which meant to be ground to instant destruction beneath the clashing wheels." *Picture Research Consultants, Inc.*

mountains and through malaria-infested jungles to the Pacific, and another boat trip up the Pacific Coast; or a seemingly endless overland journey by train, riverboat, and stagecoach.

By the 1880s, the final elements had fallen into place to create a national rail network. The first transcontinental rail line was completed in 1869, connecting Sacramento, California, to Omaha, Nebraska, and ultimately to eastern cities. Within the next fifteen years, three more rail lines linked the Pacific coast to the eastern half of the nation, and a fourth was completed in 1893. Between 1865 and 1890, railroads grew from 35,000 miles of track to 167,000 miles (see Map 16.2). By the mid-1880s, most major rivers had been bridged. Companies had replaced many iron rails with steel ones, making it possible to haul heavier loads. New inventions increased the speed, carrying capacity, and efficiency of trains. In 1886, the last major lines converted to a standard gauge, making it possible to transfer railcars from one line to another simply by throwing a switch. This rail network enabled entrepreneurs to make choices in terms of a national economic sys-

tem in which raw materials and finished products might move fairly easily from one region to another.

Railroads, especially in the West, expanded with generous assistance from government. The first transcontinental rail line had benefited from the **Pacific Railroad Act** of 1862. Congress had provided the Union Pacific and Central Pacific companies not only with sizable loans but also with 10 square miles of the public domain for every mile of track laid—an amount that was doubled in a subsequent act in 1864. By 1871, Congress had authorized some seventy railroad land grants, involving 128 million acres—more than one-tenth of the entire public domain, an area approximately equal to Colorado and Wyoming together. Most railroads sold their land to raise capital for railroad operations, and most preferred to sell it to farmers, companies, or organizations that wanted to develop it economically. That way, the railroads would have guaranteed business hauling supplies to the new settlers along their tracks and, soon, carrying their products (wheat, cattle, lumber, ore) to market.

Railroads: Defining Big Business

Railroad companies differed in kind from earlier business organizations. Because of the size of their operations they encountered problems of scale that other industrial entrepreneurs had to face later, and later businesses often adopted solutions that railroads first developed.

Railroad companies required a much higher degree of coordination and long-range planning than most businesses up to that time. Earlier companies typically operated at a single location, but railroads functioned over long distances. They had to keep up numerous maintenance and repair facilities and maintain many stations to receive and discharge both freight and passengers. Financial transactions carried on over hundreds of miles by scores of employees required a centralized accounting office. One result was development of a company bureaucracy of clerks, accountants, managers, and agents. Railroads became training grounds for administrators, some of whom later entered other industries.

Pacific Railroad Act   Law, passed by Congress in 1862, that encouraged the construction of a transcontinental railroad by providing loans and public lands to the Union Pacific and Central Pacific companies.

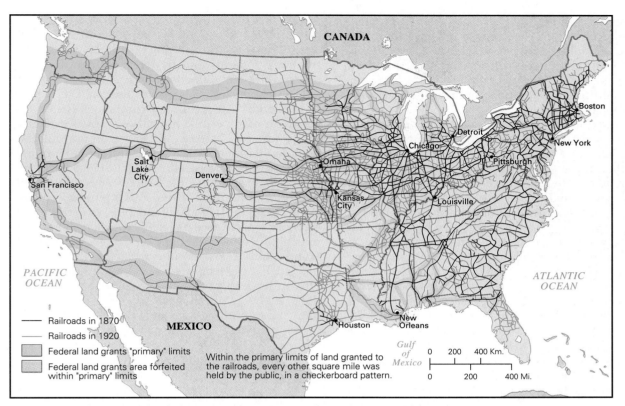

◆ **MAP 16.2 Railroad Expansion and Railroad Land Grants**   Post-Civil War railroad expansion produced the transportation base for an industrial economy. In the West, federal land grants encouraged railroad construction. Within a grant, railroads received every other square mile. Land could be forfeited if construction did not meet the terms of the grant legislation.

Indeed, the experience of the railroads helped to define the meaning of business administration when it began to be taught in colleges in the early twentieth century.

Railroads required far more capital than most manufacturing concerns. In 1875, the largest steel furnaces in the world cost $741,000; at the same time, the Pennsylvania Railroad was capitalized at $400 million. Even railroads that received government subsidies required a large amount of private capital—and Congress gave out the last federal land grant in 1871. Private capital and support from state and local governments underwrote the enormous railroad expansion of the 1880s. The railroads' huge appetite for capital made them the first American businesses to seek investors on a nationwide and international scale. Those who invested their money could choose to buy either stocks or **bonds.** Before the Civil War, the New York Stock Exchange had emerged as the leading place where brokers sold railroad stocks, and those sales provided the major activity for the New York exchange through the second half of the nineteenth century.

Railroads faced higher **fixed costs** than most previous companies. These costs included commitments to bondholders and the cost of maintaining and protecting far-flung equipment and property. To pay their fixed costs and keep profits high, railroad companies chose to operate at full capacity

> **bond**   A certificate of debt issued by a government or corporation guaranteeing payment of the original investment plus interest by a specified future date.
>
> **fixed costs**   Costs that a company must pay even if it closes down all its operations—for example, interest on loans, dividends on bonds, and property taxes.

whenever possible. Doing so, however, sometimes proved difficult. Where two or more lines competed for the same traffic, one might choose to cut rates in an effort to lure business from the other. But if the other company responded with cuts in its rates, neither stood to gain significantly more business, and both took in less income.

Competition between railroad companies sometimes became so intense that no line could show a profit. Charles Francis Adams, a railroad executive, described the results in a book published in 1879: "Railroads sprang up as if by magic, and after they were constructed, as it was impossible to move them from places where they were not wanted to places where they were wanted, they lived upon the land where they could, and, when the business of the land would not support them, they fought and ruined each other." A railroad that failed to generate enough income to cover its fixed costs faced bankruptcy.

Some railroad operators chose to defuse such intense competition by forming a **pool.** The most famous was the Iowa Pool, made up of the railroads operating between Chicago and Omaha, across Iowa. Formed in 1870, the Iowa Pool operated until 1874. Some pooling continued until the mid-1880s, but few pools lasted that long. Often one or more pool members tired of a restricted market share and broke the pool arrangement in an effort to expand, thereby starting a new price war. When a pooling arrangement became known, it brought loud complaints from customers, who concluded that they paid higher rates because of the pool.

To compete more effectively, railroads adjusted their rates to attract companies that did a great deal of shipping. Favored customers sometimes received a **rebate.** Large shipments sent over long distances cost the railroad companies less per mile than small shipments sent over short distances, so companies developed different rate structures for long hauls and short hauls. Thus the largest shippers, with the power to secure rebates and low rates, put small businesses and farmers at a comparative disadvantage. Railroad companies explained the differences in rates in terms of differences in costs, but small shippers who paid full price saw themselves as victims of rate discrimination. Some rate differentials were so great that they seemed to confirm complaints of rate discrimination.

Railroads saw state and federal governments as sources of valuable subsidies. At the same time, they constantly guarded against efforts by their customers to use government to restrict or regulate

their enterprises—by outlawing rate discrimination, for example. Companies sometimes campaigned openly to secure the election of friendly representatives and senators and to defeat unfriendly candidates. They maintained well-organized operations to **lobby** public officials in Washington, D.C., and in state capitals. Most railroad companies issued free passes to many public officials—a practice reformers attacked as a form of bribery. Some railroads won reputations as the most influential political power in entire states—the Southern Pacific in California, for example, or the Santa Fe in Kansas.

Stories of railroad officials bribing politicians became commonplace after the Civil War. The Crédit Mobilier scandal (see page 585) touched some of the most influential members of Congress. Collis P. Huntington of the Southern Pacific candidly explained his expectations regarding public officials: "If you have to pay money to have the right thing done, it is only just and fair to do it." For Huntington, "the right thing" meant favorable treatment for his company.

Investment Bankers and "Morganization"

The railroad expansion of the 1880s involved the laying of 75,000 miles of new track, but some of the new lines earned little profit. Some ran through sparsely populated areas of the West. Others were in eastern areas already served by railways. In the 1880s, however, a few ambitious, talented, and occasionally unscrupulous railway executives made choices that produced great regional railway systems. The Santa Fe and the Southern Pacific, for example, came to dominate the Southwest, and the Great Northern and the Northern Pacific held sway in the Northwest. The Pennsylvania and the New York Central controlled much of the shipping in the Northeast. By consolidating major lines within a region under a single management, railway execu-

---

pool An agreement among businesses in the same industry to divide up the market and charge equal prices instead of competing.

rebate The refund of part of the amount given in payment for something.

lobby To try to influence the thinking of public officials for or against a specific cause.

tives expected to create more efficient systems with less duplication, fewer price wars, and more dependable profits.

In this consolidation process, system builders sometimes paid inflated prices for their acquisitions. To raise the funds, some companies issued **watered stock.** Sometimes the new company proved to be so profitable that investors received good returns and the watered stock caused no problem. In other cases, however, it drove down the value of the stock or even forced the company into bankruptcy. Sometimes entrepreneurs were ruined along with their companies. In other watered-stock deals, unscrupulous promoters managed to pocket a sizable fortune at the expense of stockholders and bondholders.

To raise the enormous amounts of capital necessary for construction and consolidation, railroad executives turned increasingly to investment bankers. Among investment bankers, **John Pierpont Morgan** emerged as the most prominent by the late 1880s. Born in Connecticut in 1837, Morgan was the son of Junius Morgan, a successful merchant who turned to investment banking and relocated the family to London when Morgan was 17. After schooling in Switzerland and Germany, young Morgan began working in his father's London bank. In 1857, he moved to New York, where his father had arranged a banking position for him. There he gradually emerged as a major banking figure.

Morgan's background and his growing stature in banking gave him access to capital within the United States and in London and Paris. His investors wanted to put their money where it would be safe and would give them a reliable **return.** Morgan therefore tried to bring the unstable aspects of railroads under control, especially the cut-throat rate competition that often resulted when several companies served one market. Financially ailing railroad companies that turned to Morgan for help in raising capital found that he insisted on reorganization to simplify corporate structures and to combine small lines into larger, centrally controlled systems. He often insisted that he or one of his partners be seated on the board of directors, to guard against risky decisions in the future. After a time, some began to refer to this process as "Morganization." "Morganized" lines included some of the largest in the country: the Reading, the Baltimore & Ohio, and the Chesapeake & Ohio in the 1880s; the Santa Fe, the Erie, the Northern Pacific, and the Southern in the 1890s. A few other investment bankers followed similar patterns.

By the early 1900s, the outcome of the efforts of railroad entrepreneurs and investment bankers was that twelve large railroad systems controlled more than half of the nation's track mileage. Twenty others operated most of the rest. The largest systems, in turn, were interlocked with each other into a half-dozen massive networks, each affiliated with one of the leading New York banking houses.

Chicago: Railroad Metropolis

The financing of railroads was centered in New York, but no city challenged Chicago as the nation's leading rail center (see Map 16.3). Between 1850 and 1900, railroads transformed Chicago from a town of 30,000 residents to the nation's second largest city, with 1.7 million people. Thanks in part to the tireless efforts of local promoters and in part to its geographic location, Chicago emerged as the rail center not just of the Midwest but of much of the nation. By 1880, more than twenty railroad lines connected Chicago with all parts of the United States and much of Canada, and the boom in railroad construction during the 1880s reinforced the city's prominence. Many eastern railroad companies located their western **terminus** in Chicago, and some western railroad companies situated their eastern terminus there. A major north-south line linked Chicago and New Orleans.

Visitors to Chicago in the late nineteenth century marveled at its vitality. Louis Sullivan, later a leading architect, remembered his first impressions of the city in 1873: "An intoxicating rawness; a sense of big things to be done. . . . 'Biggest in the world' was the braggart phrase on every tongue." A French visitor called Chicago "the most active, the boldest, the most American, of the cities of the Union."

A central location and unrivaled rail connections made Chicago the logical center for the new business of mail-order sales, and the two pioneers in

---

watered stock Shares of stock whose combined value exceeds the value of the physical assets of the company.

John Pierpont Morgan American banker and industrialist who used investments in railroads and steel to turn his family fortune into a colossal financial empire.

return The yield on money that has been invested in an enterprise or product.

terminus The end point of a transportation line.

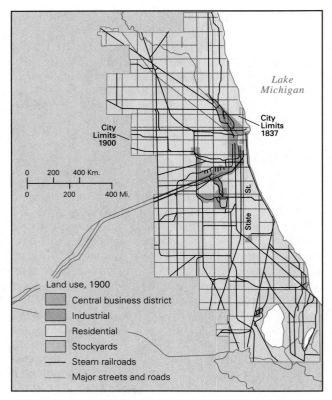

◆ **MAP 16.3 Chicago, 1900** Railroads transformed Chicago into a major city. This map shows the city's boundaries in 1837 and in 1900, when more than twenty railroad lines entered the city from every direction. This map also indicates how industry, including the stockyards, developed along major rail lines.

that field— Montgomery Ward and Sears and Roebuck—began business there. Central location and rail connections also made it a manufacturing center. By the 1880s, Chicago's factories produced more farm equipment than the factories of any other city, and its iron and steel production rivaled that of Pittsburgh. Other leading Chicago industries produced railway cars and equipment, metal products and **machine tools,** and clothing. In the 1880s, the city claimed title as the world's largest grain market.

Location and rail lines made Chicago the largest center for meatpacking. Livestock from across the Midwest and from as far away as south Texas was unloaded in Chicago's Union Stockyards—over 400 acres of railroad sidings, chutes, and pens filled with cattle, hogs, and sheep. Huge slaughterhouses flanking the stockyards received a steady stream of live animals and disgorged an equally steady

stream of canned and fresh meat. The development in the 1870s of refrigeration for railroad cars and ships permitted fresh meat to be sent throughout the nation and to Europe.

The poet Carl Sandburg celebrated Chicago in his poem by that name in 1914:

> *Hog Butcher for the World,*
> *Tool Maker, Stacker of Wheat,*
> *Player with Railroads and the Nation's Freight*
>   *Handler;*
> *Stormy, husky, brawling,*
> *City of the Big Shoulders:*
>
> *They tell me you are wicked and I believe them, for I*
>   *have seen your painted women under the gas*
>   *lamps luring the farm boys.*
> *And they tell me you are crooked and I answer: Yes,*
>   *it is true I have seen the gunman kill and go free*
>   *to kill again.*
> *And they tell me you are brutal and my reply is: On*
>   *the faces of women and children I have seen the*
>   *marks of wanton hunger.*
> *And having answered so I turn once more to those*
>   *who sneer at this my city, and I give them back*
>   *the sneer and say to them:*
> *Come and show me another city with lifted head*
>   *singing so proud to be alive and coarse and*
>   *strong and cunning. . . .*

Entrepreneurs and Industrial Transformation

● How did entrepreneurs like Carnegie and Rockefeller choose to deal with competition and other constraints?

● What outcome did they expect from their choices?

In 1889, economist David A. Wells published *Recent Economic Changes*, a survey of developments in the American economy. In it, he remarked on the "wholly unprecedented" size of recent new businesses, the "rapidity" with which they emerged, and their tendency to be "far more complex than what has been familiar." Such giant enterprises, he noted, "are regarded to some extent as evils." But, he added, "they are necessary, as there is apparently no other way in which the work of production and

---

machine tool A power-driven tool used to cut and shape metal and other substances.

BIRD'S-EYE VIEW OF THE BUSINESS DISTRICT OF CHICAGO

◆ In this lithograph, the railroad metropolis is depicted from a spot high over Lake Michigan, looking south toward the financial and commercial center of the city. The many railroad tracks and plumes of smoke were important symbols of progress and prosperity. *Chicago Historical Society.*

distribution . . . can be prosecuted." During the ten years before the publication of Wells's book, and during the fifteen years that followed it, American business changed profoundly—in size, function, and structure. By 1905, major American business enterprises resembled those of today more than those of 1865.

In 1865 and before, most American businesses were relatively small. As late as 1899, nearly 60 percent of all manufacturing establishments were so small that they averaged only two production workers. Such businesses typically operated in a single shop, were run by the owner, and produced one particular item or service for local sale. For example, a wheelwright turned out wheels one at a time, or a dressmaker made dresses to order. As early as the 1820s and 1830s, a few factories employed a hundred workers or more—New England textile mills are the leading example—but these companies often made only one product in only one location with the owner as boss. Entrepreneurs in the late nineteenth century challenged all these patterns.

Andrew Carnegie and the Age of Steel

The new industrial economy rode on a network of steel rails, propelled by locomotives made of steel. Steel plows broke the tough sod of the western prairies. Skyscrapers with steel frames boldly shaped urban skylines. Steel, a relative latecomer to

the industrial revolution, defined the age. Made by combining carbon and molten iron and then burning out impurities, steel has greater strength, resilience, and durability than iron. This superior metal was difficult and expensive to make until the 1850s, when Henry Bessemer in England and William Kelly in Kentucky independently discovered ways to make steel in large quantities at a reasonable cost. Even so, the first Bessemer or Kelly process plants did not begin production in the United States until 1864. In that year, the entire nation produced only 10,000 tons of steel.

In 1875, just south of Pittsburgh, Pennsylvania, **Andrew Carnegie** opened his giant new Edgar Thomson Works—the nation's largest steel plant, named for Carnegie's former boss, the president of the Pennsylvania Railroad. From then until 1901, Carnegie held central place in the steel industry. Born in Scotland in 1835, Carnegie and his penniless parents came to the United States in 1848. Young Andrew worked first in a textile mill. He soon became a messenger in a telegraph office and then a telegraph operator. Because of his great skill at the telegraph key, Carnegie became the personal telegrapher for a high official of the Pennsylvania Railroad. Carnegie rose rapidly and became a superin-

> **Andrew Carnegie** Scottish-born industrialist who made a fortune in steel and believed the rich had a duty to act for the public benefit.

◆ When this photograph of Andrew Carnegie was taken in 1911, inside his golfing cottage near his favorite American golf course, he had been retired from the steel industry for ten years. A fierce competitor during his career, Carnegie devoted most of his retirement to philanthropy. *Library of Congress.*

tendent (a high management position) at the age of 25. At the end of the Civil War, he chose to leave railroading and to devote full attention to the iron and steel industry, in which he had already invested money. He quickly began to apply to his iron companies the management lessons he had learned with the railroad.

Carnegie's basic rule was "Cut the prices; scoop the market; run the mills full." An aggressive competitor, he took every opportunity to cut costs so that he might show a profit while charging less than his rivals. He occasionally participated in pools with other steel-making companies, but he usually chose to undersell competitors rather than cooperate with them. In 1864, steel rails sold for $126 per ton; by 1875, Carnegie was selling them for $69 per ton. Driven by improved technology and Carnegie's competitiveness, steel prices continued to fall, reaching $29 in 1885 and less than $20 in the late 1890s. By then, the nation produced nearly 10 million tons of steel each year.

Carnegie's company was larger and more complex than any manufacturing enterprise in pre–Civil War America. In its own day, however, it was by no means unique. Other companies operated plants that were as complex, and several challenged it in

size. By 1900, three steel plants each employed between 8,000 and 10,000 workers, and seventy factories employed more than 2,000 wage earners, producing everything from watches to locomotives, from cotton cloth to processed meat. Some companies operated more than one giant factory. Carnegie Steel ran two of the seventy largest factories, as did General Electric and Western Electric.

During the late nineteenth century, drawing in part on railroads' innovations in managing large-scale operations, entrepreneurs transformed the organizational structure of manufacturing. The result was **vertical integration**, as entrepreneurs chose to take over and own the suppliers of their raw materials and the distributors of their finished products. Companies usually resorted to vertical integration to eliminate constraints and to gain a competitive advantage. Control over the sources and transportation of raw materials, for example, guaranteed a reliable flow of crucial supplies at predictable prices. Such control may also have denied materials to a competitor.

Steel plants stood at one end of a long chain of operations that Carnegie owned or controlled: iron ore mines in Michigan and Wisconsin, a fleet of ships that transported iron ore across the Great Lakes, hundreds of miles of railway lines, tens of thousands of acres of coal lands, ovens to produce **coke** (coal treated to burn at high temperatures), and plants for turning iron ore into bars of crude iron. Carnegie Steel was vertically integrated from the point where the raw materials came out of the ground through the production of steel rails and beams.

Standard Oil: Model for Monopoly

As Carnegie provided a model for other steel companies and for heavy industry in general, **John D. Rockefeller** revolutionized the petroleum industry.

---

vertical integration   The bringing together of a wide range of business activities—such as acquiring raw materials, manufacturing, and marketing and selling finished products—into a single organization.

coke   Coal from which most of the gases have been removed by heating; it burns with intense heat and is used in making steel.

John D. Rockefeller   American industrialist who amassed great wealth through the Standard Oil Company and donated much of his fortune to promote learning and research.

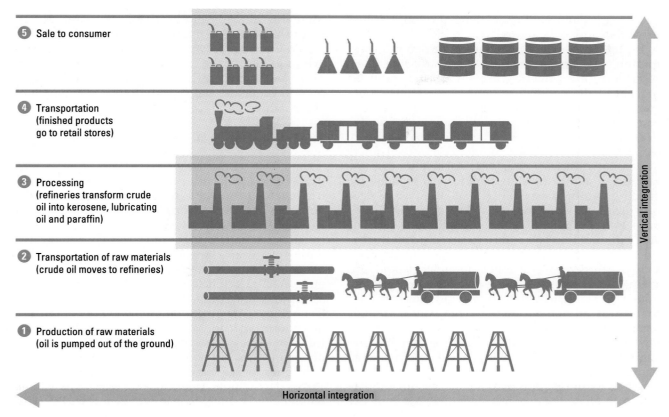

① Sale to consumer

② Transportation
(finished products
go to retail stores)

③ Processing
(refineries transform crude
oil into kerosene, lubricating
oil and paraffin)

④ Transportation of raw materials
(crude oil moves to refineries)

⑤ Production of raw materials
(oil is pumped out of the ground)

Vertical integration

Horizontal integration

● Steps in petroleum production/distribution

◆ **FIGURE 16.1 Vertical and Horizontal Integration of the Petroleum Industry**   This diagram represents the petroleum industry before Standard Oil achieved its dominance. The symbols represent different specialized companies, each engaged in a different step in the production of kerosene. Rockefeller entered the industry by investing in a refinery, and first expanded *horizontally* by absorbing several other refineries (indicated by the blue band). His Standard Oil company then practiced *vertical integration* by acquiring oil leases, oil wells, pipelines, advantageous contracts with railroads, and eventually even retail stores (an example of vertical integration is indicated by the green band). For a time, Standard Oil controlled nearly 90 percent of the industry.

Rockefeller was born in upper New York state in 1839 and educated in Cleveland, Ohio. After working as a bookkeeper and clerk, he became a partner in a grain and livestock business in 1859 and earned large profits during the Civil War.

At that time, Cleveland was a major center for refining oil from northwestern Pennsylvania, then the nation's main source for crude oil. The major product of oil refining was kerosene, used primarily for home lighting. Rockefeller, in 1863, chose to invest his wartime profits in a refinery (see Figure 16.1). After the war, he bought control of more refineries and incorporated them as Standard Oil in 1870.

The refining business was relatively easy to enter and highly competitive. Aggressive competi-

tion became a distinctive Standard Oil characteristic. Recognizing that state-of-the-art technology could bring a competitive advantage, Rockefeller recruited technical experts to make Standard the most efficient refiner. He secured reduced rates or rebates from the railroads by offering a heavy volume of traffic on a predictable basis. He usually sought to persuade his competitors to join the **cartel**

cartel   A group of independent business organizations that cooperate to control the production, pricing, and marketing of goods by group members; another term for *pool*.

he was creating. Failing in that, he would try to drive them out of business.

By 1881, following a strategy of **horizontal integration,** Rockefeller and his associates controlled some forty oil refineries, accounting for about 90 percent of the nation's refining capacity. The outcome of Rockefeller's strategy of taking over the companies of his competitors was a **monopoly:** Rockefeller's company, Standard Oil, had nearly exclusive control over the refining of oil in the United States. Between 1879 and 1881, Rockefeller centralized decision making among all forty companies by creating the Standard Oil trust. The **trust** was a new organizational form designed to get around state laws that prohibited one company from owning stock in another. To create the Standard Oil trust, Rockefeller and others who held shares in the individual companies exchanged their stock and the voting rights that went with it for trust certificates issued by Standard Oil. Standard Oil thus was able to control all the individual companies, though technically it did not own them. Eventually, new laws in New Jersey made it legal for corporations chartered in New Jersey to own stock in other companies. So Rockefeller set up Standard Oil of New Jersey as a **holding company,** which assumed ownership of all of the companies in the Standard Oil trust.

Standard Oil chose to consolidate operations by closing more than half of its refineries and building several larger plants that incorporated the newest technology. One outcome was greater efficiency—the cost of producing petroleum products fell by more than two-thirds. Another outcome was a decline in the price of fuel and lighting products by more than half from 1866 to 1890. In the 1880s, Standard moved to vertical integration by gaining control of existing oil fields, building its own transportation facilities (including pipelines and ocean-going tanker ships), and creating its own marketing operations. Standard also took a leading role in the world market, producing nearly all American petroleum products sold in Asia, Africa, and Latin America during the 1880s. By the early 1890s, Standard Oil had achieved virtually complete vertical and horizontal integration of the American petroleum industry—a near-monopoly over an entire industry.

Rockefeller retired from active participation in business in the mid-1890s. The "Rockefeller interests" (companies dominated by Rockefeller or his managers), however, became even more powerful. They included the National City Bank of New York (an **investment bank** second only to the House of

Morgan), railroads, mining, real estate, steel plants, steamship lines, and other industries. Standard's petroleum monopoly proved to be short-lived, however, because of the discovery of new oil fields in Texas and elsewhere. New companies emerged, tapping those fields, and quickly followed the path of vertical integration.

Technology and Economic Change

By the late nineteenth century, most American entrepreneurs had joined Rockefeller in viewing technology as an important competitive device. Railroads wanted more powerful locomotives, larger freight cars, and stronger rails, so they could carry more freight at a lower cost. Steel companies demanded larger and more efficient furnaces to make more steel more cheaply. Ordinary citizens as well as famous entrepreneurs seemed infatuated with technology. One invention followed after another: a machine that made ice in 1865, the air brake for trains in 1868, the vacuum cleaner in 1869, the telephone in 1876, the phonograph in 1878, the electric light bulb in 1879, an electric welding machine in 1886, and the first American-made gasoline-engine automobile in 1895, to name only a few. By 1900, many Americans had almost come to expect a steady flow of new and astounding creations.

Many new inventions relied on electricity, and in the field of electricity one person stood out: **Thomas A. Edison.** Born in 1847, Edison left school early because his teachers considered him a slow learner. Like Carnegie, he became a telegraph operator as a

---

horizontal integration The bringing together of a series of related business activities performing similar functions—such as oil refining—into a single organization.

monopoly Exclusive control by one group of the means of producing or selling a product.

trust A combination of firms or corporations for the purpose of reducing competition and controlling prices throughout an industry.

holding company A company that exists to own other companies, usually through holding a controlling interest in their stocks or bonds.

investment bank A bank that provides capital to new or expanding companies by buying their securities and reselling them to investors.

Thomas A. Edison American inventor, especially of electrical devices, among them the microphone (1877), the phonograph (1878), and the light bulb (1879).

♦ This photograph from 1893 shows Thomas A. Edison in his laboratory, the world's leading research facility when it opened in 1876. By creating research teams, the Edison laboratories could pursue several projects at once. They developed a dazzling stream of new products, most based on electrical power. *Library of Congress.*

teenager. He began to experiment with electrical devices and in 1869 secured the first of the thousand-plus **patents** that he would obtain.

In 1876, in Menlo Park, New Jersey, Edison set up the first modern research laboratory, where he and his staff could work at improving technology, especially involving electricity. In 1887, in West Orange, New Jersey, he opened a new laboratory, which became the leading research and development facility in the world. Edison promised "a minor invention every ten days and a big thing every six months," and he backed up his words with results. Sometimes building on the work of others, Edison's laboratories invented or significantly improved electrical lighting, electrical motors, the storage battery, the electric locomotive, the phonograph, the mimeograph, and many other products. Such research and development by Edison's laboratories and by others soon translated into production and sales. Nationwide, sales of electrical equipment were insignificant in 1870 but reached nearly $2 million ten years later and nearly $22 million in 1890.

The sale of light bulbs and other new electrical devices depended on the availability of electric-ity. Generating and distribution systems had to be constructed, and wires for carrying electrical current had to be installed along city streets and in homes. Early developers of electrical devices realized quickly that they needed major financial assistance, and investment bankers played an important role in the development of the new companies that manufactured electrical equipment and sold electricity to consumers. General Electric, for example, came about through a series of **mergers** arranged by the banking firm of J. P. Morgan.

Selling to the Nation

Large, vertically integrated manufacturers of consumer goods often produced goods that differed little from each other and that cost virtually the same to produce. Such companies sometimes chose not to compete on the basis of price but instead to use advertising to differentiate their products. By 1900, many of the new consumer-goods manufacturers began to make extensive use of advertising.

Most advertising in the mid-nineteenth century promoted **patent medicines** and books. By 1890, however, large-scale advertising also featured packaged foods, clothing, soap, and petroleum products. Advertisements in newspapers and magazines became larger and more complex. In some cases—notably cigarettes—advertising actually created demand and expanded the market for the product. After the federal Patent Office registered the first **trademark** in 1870, companies rushed to develop logos that, they expected, would distinguish their product from its nearly identical rivals.

Advertising popularized new ways of selling goods to customers. Up until this time, most people expected to purchase the goods they needed (for example, hardware or **dry goods**) in small specialty stores, or directly from artisans who made goods

---

patent A government grant that gives the creator of an invention the sole right to produce, use, or sell that invention for a set period of time.

merger The union of two or more organizations.

patent medicine A medical preparation that is advertised by brand name and can be bought without a physician's prescription.

trademark A name or symbol that identifies a product and is officially registered and legally restricted for use by the owner or manufacturer.

dry goods Textiles, clothing, and thread.

on order (shoes, clothes, furniture), or in **general stores,** or from door-to-door peddlers. In urban areas after the Civil War, department stores appeared and flourished, offering a wide range of choices in ready-made products—clothing, household furnishings, shoes, and much more. They relied heavily on newspaper advertising to attract customers, especially women, from throughout the city and its suburbs. The variety presented by department stores paled, however, when compared to the vast array of goods available through the new mail-order catalogues. Led by Montgomery Ward (which issued its first catalogue in 1872) and Sears and Roebuck (1886)—both based in Chicago—mail-order houses aimed at rural America. They offered a wider range of choices than most rural-dwellers had ever before seen—everything from clothing to farm equipment—most illustrated with attractive line drawings. Department stores and mail-order houses were possible because manufacturers now produced all sorts of ready-made goods. Mail-order houses depended on railroads to deliver their catalogues and products across great distances.

◆ Mail-order companies, led by Montgomery Ward and Sears and Roebuck, both based in Chicago, issued advertising catalogs that brought the most remote farm family into contact with the latest fashions in clothing and the most recent developments in equipment. These pages are from the spring catalog for 1896. *Sears Roebuck and Co.*

Economic Concentration and the Merger Movement

Carnegie, Rockefeller, and a few others helped to redefine the expectations of other entrepreneurs and provided models for the choices that they made in their own businesses. One outcome was that large, complex companies—vertically integrated, sometimes horizontally integrated, often employing extensive advertising—appeared relatively suddenly in the 1880s. At first they were concentrated in consumer-goods industries.

James B. Duke, for example, used efficient machinery, extensive advertising, and vertical integration to become the largest manufacturer of cigarettes. In 1890, he merged with his four largest competitors to create the American Tobacco Company, which dominated the cigarette industry. Gustavus Swift in the early 1880s began to ship fresh meat from his slaughterhouse in Chicago to markets in the East using his own refrigerated railcars. He eventually added refrigerated storage plants in each city, along with a sales and delivery staff. Other meatpacking companies followed Swift's lead. By 1890, a half-dozen firms, all vertically integrated, dominated meatpacking.

The American Sugar Refining Company, a horizontally integrated trust modeled after Standard

Oil, was created in 1887. It controlled three-quarters of the nation's sugar-refining capacity in the early 1890s but did not become vertically integrated until after 1907, by which time it had lost ground to competitors. Monopolies like Standard Oil and American Sugar were fairly rare. More typical was the situation in meatpacking, where a small number of firms dominated an industry; such a market is called an **oligopoly.**

Many new manufacturing companies in the 1870s and early 1880s did not sell stock or use investment bankers to raise capital. Standard Oil and Carnegie Steel, two of the largest of the new companies, never "went public"—that is, they never sold stocks on a stock exchange as a means of raising capital. Rockefeller chose to expand either through mergers or by

---

general store   A store, common in rural areas, that sells a lot of different goods but is not divided into departments.

oligopoly   A market or industry dominated by a few firms.

making purchases paid for from the profits of the business itself. Similarly, Carnegie chose to expand by adding partners or by investing profits.

Rockefeller and Carnegie concentrated ownership and control in their own hands. The same held true for many others among the new industrial companies until late in the nineteenth century. In 1896, for example, the New York Stock Exchange sold stock in only twenty manufacturing concerns. At the turn of the century, however, a second phase of vertical and horizontal integration created the need for more capital, and investment bankers began to turn their attention from railroads to the reorganization of heavy industry.

In the late 1890s, J. P. Morgan began combining separate steel-related companies to create a vertically integrated operation that might challenge Carnegie's dominance. Carnegie had never carried vertical integration to the point of making final steel products such as wire, barrels, or tubes. By vertically integrating to include companies making such finished products, Morgan threatened to close off a significant part of Carnegie's market. Faced with the prospect of building his own plants for finished products, Carnegie seemed at first to relish the prospect of no-holds-barred competition with what he called "the Trust." When Morgan offered to buy him out, however, he agreed, allowing Morgan in 1901 to create United States Steel, the nation's first corporation capitalized at over a billion dollars.

In 1902, competition between the two largest companies making harvesting machines became so intense that each considered vertical integration by creating its own steel plant. Realizing that the outcome of that strategy was likely to be a loss of business for United States Steel, Morgan intervened. Using his access to capital as a lever and promising that profits would be higher and more predictable through consolidation, Morgan merged the two largest and three smaller harvester firms into International Harvester in 1902, creating a company that dominated 85 percent of the market for harvesting machines.

United States Steel and International Harvester were just two of the many new combinations in manufacturing and mining created in a relatively short time at the turn of the century. Between 1898 and 1902, the nation witnessed an astonishing number of mergers. The high point came in 1899, with 1,208 mergers involving $2.3 billion in capital. This merger movement resulted partly from economic weaknesses revealed by a depression that had begun in 1893 and lasted for four years. Railroads were hit especially hard. Several large lines declared bankruptcy and had to be reorganized. At the end of the depression, the threat of vicious competition among manufacturing companies prompted reorganization there too.

As had been true with railroad reorganization, an investment banker usually sought two primary objectives in reorganizing an industry: to make the industry stable, so that investments would yield predictable **dividends;** and to make the industry efficient and productive, so that dividends would be high. Toward that end, investment bankers not only created new combinations but also placed their representatives on the boards of directors of the new companies, to guarantee that the companies would continue to meet those objectives. By 1912, the three leading New York banking firms together occupied 341 directorships in 112 major companies. Investment bankers argued that benefits from their activities extended far beyond the dividends received by shareholders. One of Morgan's associates claimed in 1901 that, as a result of Morganization, "production would become more regular, labor would be more steadily employed at better wages, and panics caused by over-production would become a thing of the past."

In fact, the new industrial combinations failed to have much impact on economic cycles. Throughout the late nineteenth and early twentieth centuries, the economy alternated between periods of boom and bust—periods of growth and prosperity and those of decline and unemployment. Severe depressions occurred from 1873 to 1878 and from 1893 to 1897, and less severe downturns came from 1882 to 1885 and in 1890–1891. After the mergers of 1899–1902, financial panics struck in 1903 and 1907–1908 and recessions in 1910–1911 and 1913–1914.

Thus, by 1900 or so, many of the characteristics of modern business had emerged. Many industries were oligopolistic, dominated by a few vertically integrated companies. **Product differentiation** through advertising had begun. The stock market had moved beyond the sale of railroad securities to play an important role in raising capital for industry.

Gradually, too, with the passing of the first generation of industrial empire builders, ownership

---

dividend   A share of profits received by a stockholder.
product differentiation   The use of advertising to distinguish one product from similar products.

◆ In the crowded and noisy factories of industrial America, workers toiled under the foreman's watchful eye. In the McCormick plant in Chicago (left), these machines were driven from a central source through a system of belts and shafts. This permitted the foreman to control the speed of the work. In this cigar factory in Richmond, Virginia (right), women rolled cigars. *McCormack factory: State Historical Society of Wisconsin; Cigar factory: Valentine Museum.*

grew apart from management. Many new business executives were simply hired managers. Ownership rested with hundreds or thousands of stockholders, all of whom wanted a reliable return on their investment though the vast majority of them remained uninvolved with business operations. The huge size of the new companies also meant that most managers rarely saw or talked with most of their employees, especially those not involved in management or accounting. Careful **cost analysis,** the desire for efficiency, and the need to pay regular dividends led many companies to treat most of their employees as expenses to be increased or cut as necessary, with little regard to the impact on people.

Workers in Industrial America

• What were Americans' expectations regarding economic mobility in the late nineteenth century?

• What constraints did workers face in seeking mobility, and what choices were they able to make?

The rapid expansion of railroads, mining, and manufacturing created a demand for labor to lay the rails, dig out the ore, tend the furnaces, operate the refineries, and carry out a thousand other tasks. America's new workers—men, women, and children from many ethnic groups—came from across the nation and around the world. For many of them, the nature of work itself changed during these years. Despite the lure of a rags-to-riches triumph like that of Andrew Carnegie, very few rose from the shop floor to the manager's office.

Labor and Mobility

Horatio Alger emerged as one of the most prominent popular novelists in the nation after the success of his first novel, *Ragged Dick* (1868). He eventually produced 108 more books with total sales of nearly a hundred million copies. Aimed at young people,

---

cost analysis   Detailed study of the cost of operations, intended to make them more efficient through careful planning.

Horatio Alger   American writer of rags-to-riches stories about impoverished boys who become wealthy through hard work, virtue, and luck.

his books repeated one refrain: a poor but hard-working youth, through some unusual opportunity to do good—saving a child from danger, for example—attracts the attention of a wealthy and powerful person and thereby achieves success, wealth, and happiness. Alger's stories often emphasized the element of luck, but his name became a symbol of the expectation that in America anyone who worked hard and saved carefully could succeed.

The reality of life in industrial America bore little resemblance to Alger's tales. In the new industrial economy, nearly all successful business leaders came from middle-class or upper-class families. Few workers could expect to move more than a step or so up the economic scale. An unskilled laborer might become a semiskilled worker, or a skilled worker might become a foreman, but few wage earners moved into the middle class. If they did, it was usually as the owner of small business.

In industrial America, the treatment that labor received differed little from the treatment of the raw materials that went into the production of a finished product. During efforts to cut manufacturing costs, workers' wages were always a tempting target for savings. During boom periods, companies advertised for labor and ran their operations at full capacity. When the demand for manufactured goods fell, companies reduced production or even closed down entirely. At such times, they expected to lay off workers, cut wages, or reduce hours. Unemployed workers had little to fall back on but their savings or the earnings of other family members. Some churches and private charity organizations gave out food, but state and federal governments provided no unemployment benefits. Families that failed to find work—for any member of the family, including the children—might become homeless and go hungry. In a depression, jobs of any sort were scarce, and competition for them was intense.

Workers for Industry

After the Civil War, the labor force more than doubled. The largest increases occurred in industries undergoing the greatest changes (see Figure 16.2). Agriculture continued to employ the largest share of the labor force, ranging downward from more than half in 1870 to two-fifths in 1900, but the proportional growth of workers engaged in agriculture was the smallest of all major categories of workers.

Workers for the rapidly expanding economy came from within the nation and from abroad. Throughout rural parts of New England and the

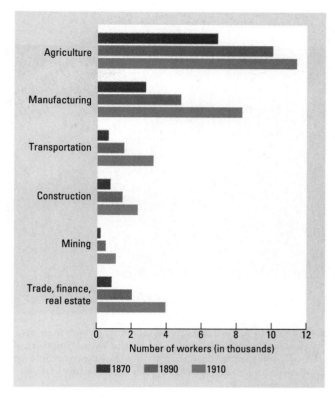

♦ **FIGURE 16.2 Industrial Distribution of the Work Force, 1870, 1890, 1910**

Middle Atlantic states especially, large numbers of people moved to urban or industrial areas. In New England, some farms—usually small and unproductive—were abandoned when their owners chose to take a job in a nearby factory town or to move west. Country towns that served the surrounding countryside also lost population in such areas.

The expanding economy, however, needed more workers than the nation could supply. As a result, the period from the Civil War to World War I (1865–1914) witnessed the largest influx of immigrants in American history: more than 26 million people, equivalent to three-quarters of the nation's entire population in 1865. By 1910, immigrants and their children made up more than 35 percent of the total population.

Large-scale immigration contributed many adult males to the work force—especially in mining, manufacturing, and transportation. But the expanding economy also pulled many women and children into the ranks of industrial wage earners. The 1910 census revealed that nearly 2 million children worked for wages, many in mining, manufacturing,

♦ The coal mines of Pennsylvania employed more than ten thousand boys under the age of 16. Known as "breaker boys," they sorted coal. Such work was dangerous and sometimes fatal, as attested by this 1911 headline. *Library of Congress.*

and agriculture. Others worked as newsboys, bootblacks, or domestic servants. More children were employed in the textile industry, especially in the South, than in any other kind of manufacturing. Mostly girls, they worked 70-hour weeks for between 10 and 20 cents per day.

Children worked in tobacco and cotton fields in the South, operated sewing machines in New York, assisted glass blowers in West Virginia factories, and sorted vegetables in Delaware canneries. Other children worked at home, alongside their parents who brought home **piecework.** Most working children turned over all their wages to their parents.

Women as well as children found employment outside the home in the new industrial economy. Between 1890 and 1910, nearly half of all single women worked for wages, along with a third of widowed or divorced women. Among married women, only 5 or 10 percent did so. Black women were employed at much higher rates in all categories. Young women who lived at home and earned wages usually gave most of their pay to their parents.

A report of the Illinois Bureau of Labor Statistics for 1884 explained that some children and mothers worked for wages because of the "meager earnings of many heads of families." A study in 1875 showed that the average male factory worker in Lawrence, Massachusetts, earned $500 per year. The study also showed that the average family in Lawrence required a minimum annual income of $600 to provide sufficient food, clothing, and shelter. In such circumstances, a family could not make ends meet without two or more incomes.

By 1900, some occupations were filled mainly by women. Females—adults and children—made up more than 70 percent of the workers in clothing factories, knitting mills, and other textile factories. Women also dominated certain types of office work. By 1900, women made up more than 70 percent of the nation's secretaries and typists and 80 percent of telephone operators. Office work usually paid even less than factory work but was considered safer and of higher status. Women and children workers almost always earned much less than their male counterparts. In most industries, work was separated by age and gender, and the jobs requiring the most skill and commanding the best pay were reserved for adult males. Even when men and women did the same work, there was usually a pay differential (see Figure 16.3), which was sometimes explained by the argument that a man had to support a family but a woman worked to supplement the income of her husband or father.

Not all women worked as wage earners. Some took in laundry in their own homes, did sewing for neighbors, or rented a room to a boarder. In one eastern factory town in 1912, 90 percent of the families where the husband was the only wage earner took in one or more boarders.

The Transformation of Work

Most adult industrial workers had been born into a rural society, either in the United States or in another part of the world. They found industrial work quite different from whatever work they had done in the past. Farm families might expect to work from sunrise to sunset, but they worked at their own speed and could take a break whenever they felt like it. Self-employed blacksmiths, carpenters, dressmakers, and other skilled workers also controlled

---

piecework   Work paid for according to the number of items turned out, rather than by the hour.

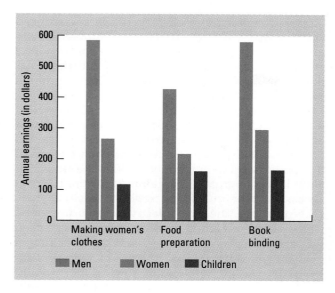

♦ **FIGURE 16.3 Average Annual Earnings for Men, Women, and Children, in Selected Industries, 1890**

the speed and intensity of their work. Like the farmer, they might work from sunrise to sunset, but they could pace themselves to avoid exhaustion.

In early factories, before the Civil War, work hours were often those of the farm: from daybreak to dark. But eventually the workday in most industries settled down to ten or twelve hours, six days a week. People from rural settings expected to work long hours, but they found that industrial work controlled them, rather than the other way around. The speed of the machines set the pace of the work, and machine speeds were centrally controlled. If managers ordered a speedup, workers worked faster. When a Massachusetts law limited daily work to ten hours, a textile-mill worker grumbled that "the manufacturers have counteracted [it] by an increase of speed, and the work is much more tiresome."

Ten or twelve hour days at a constant, rapid pace drained the workers. A woman textile worker in 1882 said, "I get so exhausted that I can scarcely drag myself home when night comes." Steel mills operated twenty-four hours a day. Beginning in the 1890s, most converted their shifts from eight hours to twelve. During times of high demand for steel, most companies required seven-day workweeks. A 27-year-old steelworker in 1910 was blunt: "It's simply a killing pace in the steel works." The pace sometimes proved, literally, to be killing, as exhausted workers were injured or killed in industrial accidents.

Some factory managers saw their dependence on skilled workers as a constraint on their control of production, for skilled workers often understood a plant's operations better than any manager did. They set the pace of work around them, earned more than other workers, and were difficult to replace. Industrial engineer Frederick W. Taylor built a national reputation on his ability to take a complex operation, requiring a high level of skill, and break it down into its component parts. Taylor designed each task so that it could be done by relatively unskilled workers, who earned low wages, required little training, and were easily replaced. Once tasks were simplified in this way, **efficiency experts** conducted time-and-motion studies to determine the ideal speed at which each one should be performed. Such "de-skilling" was intended to increase manager's control over the process of work.

The Varieties of Labor Organization and Action, 1865–1900

● Compare the expectations of American workers who joined craft unions with those who chose organizations like the Knights of Labor.

● What were some outcomes of labor unrest in the late nineteenth century?

As the industrial economy grew, some workers reacted to the far-reaching changes in the nature of work by choosing to join with other workers in efforts to maintain or regain control over their working conditions. They experimented with a variety of organizations. **Craft unions** drew their strength from skilled workers. Some craft unionists joined in reform or **radical** causes; others held themselves apart. Some organizations sought reform, hoping

---

efficiency expert Consultant who studies industrial workplaces to determine how to minimize wasted motion and perform tasks in the shortest amount of time.

craft union Labor union that organizes skilled workers engaged in a specific craft or trade; also called a trade union.

radical Advocating fundamental or revolutionary changes in current practices or institutions.

to use the power of government to assist workers. Others proposed alternatives to capitalism itself. European immigrants sometimes contributed to the diversity of organizations by bringing union experience or a commitment to socialism.

Strikes erupted on an unprecedented scale. Faced with striking workers, entrepreneurs began to call on government, both state and federal, to protect property and maintain order—and to assist in suppressing the strikes.

Craft Unionism—and Its Limits

Skilled workers in many fields outside manufacturing often remained indispensable. In construction, only an experienced carpenter could build stairs or hang doors properly. In railroading, only a highly trained engineer could operate a locomotive. In publishing, only a skilled typesetter could transform handwritten copy into lines of lead type. Such workers took pride in the quality of their work and knew that their skill was crucial to their employer's success. William D. ("Big Bill") Haywood, a leader of the **Industrial Workers of the World** was referring to such workers when he said that "the manager's brains are under the workman's cap."

Skilled workers formed the first unions, called craft unions or trade unions because membership was limited to skilled workers in a particular craft or trade. Before the Civil War, workers in most American cities created local trade unions in attempts to regulate the quality of work, wages, hours, and working conditions for their craft. Local unions eventually formed national trade organizations—twenty-six of them by 1873, thirty-nine by 1880. They sometimes called themselves brotherhoods—for example, the United Brotherhood of Carpenters and Joiners, formed in 1881—and they drew on their craft traditions to forge bonds of unity.

The skills that defined craft unions' membership also provided the basis for their success. Skills made craftworkers valuable to their employers. Some skills took years to develop, and there was no substitute for them. If most craftworkers within a city belonged to the local union, a strike could badly disrupt or shut down the affected businesses. The strike, therefore, was a powerful weapon in the effort of skilled workers to define working conditions.

Strikes most often succeeded in times of prosperity, when the employer wanted to continue operating and was best able financially to make concessions to workers. When the economy experienced a serious downturn and employers sharply reduced work hours or laid off workers, craft unions usually disintegrated because they could not use the strike effectively. Only after the 1880s did local and national unions develop strategies that permitted them to survive depressions.

The craft union tradition served some skilled workers well but by the late nineteenth century was of little help to most industrial workers. Unskilled or semiskilled workers—the majority of employees in many emerging industries—lacked the skills that gave the craft unions bargaining power. Without such skills, they could be replaced easily if they chose to strike. The most effective unions, therefore, were groups of skilled workers—sometimes called the "aristocracy of labor." Such unions often limited their membership not just to workers with particular skills but to white males with those skills. Unions controlled access to apprenticeship programs through which workers acquired the skills of the craft, so restrictions based on gender or ethnicity were major obstacles to the economic advancement of women and people of color.

Shortly after the Civil War, in 1866, craft unionists and reformers formed the **National Labor Union (NLU).** The founders represented craft union locals, national craft unions, citywide federations of local unions, and reform organizations, especially those committed to establishing eight hours as the proper workday. The NLU admitted representatives of women's organizations and, after vigorous, even bitter, debate, also decided to encourage the organization of black workers. The most important of the NLU objectives was the eight-hour day, which NLU leaders hoped to secure through political action. In 1870, the NLU divided itself into a labor organization and a political party. In 1872, the political party, the National Labor Reform party, nominated candidates for president and vice president, but the campaign was so unsuccessful and divisive that neither the NLU nor the party met again.

Industrial Workers of the World   Revolutionary labor organization launched in Chicago in 1905; it demanded the eventual overthrow of capitalism through political and economic action, including strikes, boycotts, and sabotage.

National Labor Union   Federation organized at Baltimore in 1866; it lasted only six years but helped push through a law limiting government employees to an eight-hour workday.

The Great Strike of 1877

In 1877, for the first time, the nation witnessed the implications of labor strife on a wide scale. When a depression began in 1873, railroad companies reduced operating costs by repeatedly cutting wages. Railroad workers' pay fell by more than a third between 1873 and early 1877. Union leaders talked of organizing a strike but failed to bring one off.

Without union leadership, railway workers chose to take matters into their own hands when companies announced additional pay cuts of 10 percent. On July 16, 1877, a group of firemen and brakemen on the Baltimore & Ohio Railroad stopped work in Maryland. The next day, nearby in West Virginia, a group of railway workers refused to work until the company restored their wages. Some members of the local community supported the strikers. The governor of West Virginia sent in the state militia, but the strikers still prevented the trains from running. The governor then requested federal troops, and President Rutherford B. Hayes sent them.

Federal troops restored service on the Baltimore & Ohio, but the strike spread to other lines. Strikers shut down the trains in Pittsburgh. When the local militia refused to act against the strikers, the governor of Pennsylvania ordered in militia units from Philadelphia. The troops killed twenty-six people. Strikers and their sympathizers then attacked the militia, forced the troops to retreat, and burned and looted railroad property throughout Pittsburgh.

Strikes and demonstrations of support for strikers erupted across Pennsylvania and New York and throughout the Midwest. Everywhere, the strikers drew support from other members of their local communities. In various places, coal miners, factory workers, owners of small businesses, farmers, black workers, and women demonstrated their support. In St. Louis, local unions declared a **general strike** to secure the eight-hour day and to end child labor. State militia, federal troops, and local police eventually broke up the strikes, but not before hundreds had lost their lives. By the strikes' end, railroad companies had suffered property damage worth $10 million, half of it in Pittsburgh.

The **Great Strike of 1877** revealed widespread dislike for the new railroad companies and significant community support for strikers. However, the strike deeply worried many Americans who did not identify with the strikers' cause. Some considered the use of troops only a temporary expedient and, like President Hayes, hoped for "education of the strikers," "judicious control of the capitalists," and some way to "remove the distress which afflicts laborers." Others saw in the strike a forecast of future labor unrest and even revolution, and they called for better means to enforce law and order by training and equipping state militia units to suppress such domestic disorders.

The Knights of Labor

The Great Strike suggested that working people could unite across lines of occupation, race, and gender. No organization drew on that potential, however, until the early 1880s, when the **Knights of Labor** emerged as an alternative to craft unions.

The Noble and Holy Order of the Knights of Labor grew out of an organization of Philadelphia garment workers. Founded in 1869, the Knights proclaimed that labor was "the only creator of values or capital" and opened their ranks to all members of "the producing class"—those who, by their labor, produced value. All Knights were required to have worked for wages sometime, but the organization specifically excluded only professional gamblers, stockbrokers, lawyers, bankers, and liquor dealers.

The Knights accepted African-Americans as members, and some sixty thousand joined by 1886. After one organizer formed an all-woman local organization in 1881, the Knights officially opened their ranks to women and enrolled about fifty thousand by 1886. A few women and African-Americans held leadership positions at local and regional levels, and the Knights briefly appointed a woman, Leonora M. Barry, as a national organizer. The Knights helped to provide both women and African-Americans with experience in labor organizing—including the first endeavors of the legendary **Mary Harris ("Mother") Jones** (see Individual Choices: Mother Jones). The organization adopted the racism

---

general strike   A strike by all union members in a particular region.

Great Strike of 1877   A series of strikes in American cities triggered by railroad wage cuts; the strikes showed widespread support for the demands of workers but were put down by government troops.

Knights of Labor   Labor organization founded in 1869; membership, open to all workers, peaked in 1886.

Mary Harris ("Mother") Jones   A labor organizer in the 1890s who traveled from region to region organizing strikes and protests among coal miners.

Choosing to Serve Labor

Mother Jones

Mary Harris Jones, known as Mother Jones, faced many difficult choices in her long career as a union organizer, sometimes involving threats to her personal safety. This picture is from a protest march in 1910, when she was nearly 70 years old. Archives of Labor & Union Affairs, Wayne State University.

In 1891, a white-haired woman more than 60 years old stepped down from a train in an Appalachian mining town. A man anxiously asked her name, and she told him. Thirty years later, she still recalled his response: "The superintendent [manager for the coal-mining company] told me that if you came down here he would blow out your brains. He said he didn't want to see you 'round these parts." The threat had no effect, for she had long since chosen her life's direction. "You tell the superintendent that I am not coming to see him anyway. I am coming to see the miners." For almost fifty years, Mary Harris Jones chose "to see the miners" and to bring them the message of unionism in the face of hostility and threats from mining companies and the local officials who did the companies' bidding.

According to her own account, Mary Harris was born in Ireland in 1830 and came to the United States as a child, with her father. As a young woman, she taught school and worked as a dressmaker or seamstress, then married George Jones, an iron molder and union activist. Her expectations as a wife and mother were shattered, however, when she lost her entire family—her husband and their four children—in a yellow-fever epidemic in 1867.

of unionists on the Pacific coast, however, when it refused to accept Chinese immigrants as members.

Terence V. Powderly, a machinist, led the Knights from 1879 to 1893. Under his leadership, they chose organization, education, and cooperation as their chief objectives. Powderly generally opposed strikes. A lost strike, he argued, often destroyed the local organization and thereby delayed the more important tasks of education and cooperation. The Knights favored political action to accomplish a range of labor reforms, including health and safety laws for workers, the eight-hour workday, prohibition of child labor, equal pay for equal work regardless of gender, and the graduated income tax.

Terence V. Powderly   Leader of the Knights of Labor who called for cooperative production instead of a wage system.

On her own, she opened a dressmaking shop in Chicago. Her clients included those she called "the aristocrats of Chicago," and she witnessed "the luxury and extravagance of their lives." The contrast between the opulent expectations of her wealthy clients and tightly constrained lives of the poor left her deeply disturbed.

"Often while sewing for the lords and barons who lived in magnificent houses on the Lake Shore Drive," she recalled in her autobiography, "I would look out of the plate glass windows and see the poor, shivering wretches, jobless and hungry, walking along the frozen lake front. The contrast of their condition with that of the tropical comfort of the people for whom I sewed was painful to me."

In 1871, her shop burned in the great fire that swept much of the city. Thereafter, she chose to give much of her time to helping workers, first through the Knights of Labor. In 1882, she first took part in a strike by coal miners.

As the Knights of Labor began to disintegrate after 1886, some of its trade assemblies (organizations limited to workers in one trade) chose to affiliate with the American Federation of Labor. In 1890, one received an AFL charter as the United Mine Workers of America (UMW), but it remained an industrial union that admitted both white and black members. Until her death, in 1930, Mother Jones fought for the UMW. She became a familiar figure throughout the sooty valleys of Appalachia, where miners' families lived in wretched, company-owned shacks, their lives closely constrained by the power of the mining companies, the often brutal company guards, and compliant local officials.

Jones's white hair, grandmotherly appearance, and deep loyalty to those she called "her boys" earned her the nickname "Mother." Others called her the "miners' angel." One county attorney, however, labeled her "the most dangerous woman in the country" in recognition of her ability to inspire men and women to oppose the mining companies. Her admirers recounted stories of her bravery in the face of danger. One insisted that "she wasn't afraid of the devil."

Mother Jones's talents lay in public speaking and in organizing demonstrations to capture public attention and sympathy. In one strike in 1900, she organized miners' wives to protest against strikebreakers by pounding on pots and pans and frightening the mules that pulled the mine carts. In 1903, she took up the cause of the children who worked in textile mills. By organizing a march of mill children to the home of President Theodore Roosevelt, she captured headlines with her living, walking display of the children's deformities and injuries caused by mill work.

Mother Jones made an unusual choice in her decision to spend the last half of her life as a labor organizer and agitator. But she apparently held traditional expectations about the role of women in society, arguing that their place was in the home. She seems to have seen her own work as an extension of her role as mother. Deprived of her own family, she sought to nurture and protect a much larger family of workers.

They later endorsed government ownership of the telephone, telegraph, and railroad systems. In 1878, 1880, and 1882, Powderly won election as mayor of Scranton, Pennsylvania, as the candidate of a labor party.

The Knights' endorsement of cooperation was related to the labor theory of value. A major objective of the Knights was "to secure to the workers the full enjoyment of the wealth they create." Toward that end, they committed themselves in their first national meeting in 1878 to create a system of producers' and consumers' **cooperatives,** which they hoped would "tend to supersede the wage-system." The Knights saw cooperatives as an alternative to a

> **cooperative** A business enterprise in which workers and consumers share in ownership and take part in management.

capitalistic system based on the payment of wages. They established some 135 cooperatives by the mid-1880s, but few lasted very long. Some folded because of lack of capital, some because of opposition from businesses with which they competed, some because of poor organization.

By the 1880s, the Knights of Labor was the most prominent labor organization in the country. Members numbered 9,000 in 1879 and 703,000—peak membership—in 1886. Although the Knights opposed striking, a large part of the increase in membership in 1885–1886 came because local Knights' organizers played major roles in helping to organize and win strikes against prominent railroads in 1884 and 1885—strikes that had started when workers refused to accept changes in their wages and in working conditions.

The willingness of local Knights' organizations to strike despite the national organization's disapproval of striking points to an internal conflict. Many members seem to have joined in order to unite against their employer, but the national leadership played down such conflicts in the interests of long-term economic and political change. Nevertheless, the Knights' meteoric growth in membership suggested that many working people would choose to respond to efforts to unite in opposition to the emerging corporate behemoths.

1886: Turning Point for Labor?

The Great Strike of 1877 and the rise of the Knights of Labor were signs of a sense of common purpose among large numbers of working people. After 1886, however, labor organizations often found themselves on the defensive and were divided between those trying to adjust to the new realities of industrial capitalism and those seeking to change it.

On May 1, 1886, some eighty thousand Chicagoans marched through the streets in support of an eight-hour workday, a cause that united a wide variety of unions and radical groups. Three days later, Chicago police killed several strikers at the McCormick Harvester Works. Hoping to build on the unity demonstrated by the May Day parade, a group of Chicago **anarchists** called a protest meeting for the next day at Haymarket Square. When police tried to break up the rally, someone threw a bomb into the police ranks. The police opened fire on the crowd, and some of the protesters fired back. Eight policemen eventually died, along with an unknown number of demonstrators. About a hundred people, including sixty policemen, suffered injuries.

The Haymarket bombing sparked public anxiety and antiunion feelings. Employers who had opposed unions before now tried to discredit them by playing on fears of radical-inspired terrorism. Some people who supported what they saw as legitimate union goals now shrank back in horror. In Chicago, amid public furor over the violence, eight leading anarchists stood trial for inciting the bombing and, on flimsy evidence, were convicted. Four were hanged, one committed suicide, and three remained in jail until they were released in 1893 by a sympathetic governor, John Peter Altgeld.

Preserving the Craft Union Tradition: The American Federation of Labor

Two weeks after the Haymarket bombing, trade union leaders met in Philadelphia to discuss the inroads that the Knights of Labor had made among their members. They proposed an agreement between the trade unions and the Knights: trade unions would recruit skilled workers, and the Knights would limit themselves to unskilled workers. When the Knights refused to go along with this plan, the trade unions formed the **American Federation of Labor (AFL)** to coordinate their struggles with the Knights for the loyalty of skilled workers. The AFL was to be limited to national trade unions. The combined membership of the thirteen founding unions amounted only to 140,000.

Samuel Gompers became the first president of the new organization. Born in London in 1850 to Dutch Jewish parents, he learned the cigarmaker's trade before coming to the United States in 1863. He joined the Cigarmakers' Union in 1864 and became its president in 1877. Except for one year in the 1890s, Gompers continued as president of the AFL from 1886 until his death in 1924. A socialist in his youth, Gompers moved to a more conservative stance as AFL president, opposing labor involve-

---

anarchist A person who believes that all forms of government are oppressive and should be abolished.

American Federation of Labor National organization of trade unions founded in 1886; it used strikes and boycotts to improve the lot of workers.

Samuel Gompers First president of the American Federation of Labor; he eventually argued to divorce labor organizing from political theory and stressed practical demands involving wages and hours.

ment with radicalism or politics. Instead, he came to favor what he called "pure and simple" unionism, focusing on higher wages, shorter hours, and improved working conditions for members of craft unions.

Such attitudes indicated acceptance of industrial capitalism and willingness to work toward accommodation with employers. Even so, AFL unions used the strike to achieve their goals, and they sometimes engaged in long and bitter struggles with their employers. Most AFL leaders, however, chose to define their task as the limited one of winning immediate struggles over wages and hours rather than the radical one of changing capitalism. The Knights of Labor tried to improve the lives of workers as a class and opposed strikes. In contrast, many trade union leaders argued that unions should focus solely on improving the specific working conditions of their own members.

After the 1880s, in any case, the AFL suffered little competition from the Knights of Labor. The decline of the Knights came swiftly: 703,000 members in 1886, 260,000 in 1888, 100,000 in 1890. This collapse stemmed only in part from the opposition of the trade unions. The failure of several strikes involving the Knights in the late 1880s cost them many supporters. Then, too, the organization's highly centralized and cumbersome decision-making structure sometimes interfered with effective communication between the national leadership and local members.

Labor on the Defensive: Homestead and Pullman

In the late 1880s and 1890s, even highly skilled workers often found that their craft unions could not withstand the power of the new industrial companies. A major demonstration of this came in 1892 in Pennsylvania, at Carnegie's **Homestead steel plant,** a stronghold of the Amalgamated Association of Iron, Steel, and Tin Workers, the largest AFL union. One of Carnegie's partners, Henry Clay Frick, managed the Homestead plant. The Amalgamated Association had a contract with Carnegie Steel covering the plant. As the contract's expiration date approached, Frick proposed major cuts in workers' wages. When the union refused, Frick locked union members out of the plant and prepared to bring in replacements.

Frick's first step was to bring in, as guards, three hundred agents of the Pinkerton detective agency.

They came by riverboat, but ten thousand strikers and community supporters resisted when they tried to land. Shots rang out. In the ensuing gun battle, seven Pinkertons and nine strikers were killed and sixty people injured. The Pinkertons surrendered, leaving the strikers in control of the town and the plant. Soon after, the governor of Pennsylvania sent in the state militia to wrest control from the strikers and protect the strikebreakers. The militia did its job. The Amalgamated Association never recovered. This crushing defeat of the largest craft union in the nation seemed a vivid lesson that no union could stand up to the new industrial companies, especially when those companies could call on the government for assistance.

A similar fate befell the most ambitious organizing drive of the 1890s. In 1893, under the leadership of **Eugene V. Debs,** railway workers launched the American Railway Union (ARU). Born in Indiana in 1855, Debs had served for many years as an officer of the locomotive firemen's union. Railway workers had organized separate craft unions for engineers, firemen, switchmen, and conductors. Debs hoped to bring them all together into one union. Instead of using skill as the qualification for membership, he proposed employment in an industry as the basis for membership, thereby creating an **industrial union.** Success came quickly. Within a year, the ARU claimed 150,000 members and was the largest single union in the nation. The ARU did not affiliate with the AFL.

To counter the growing strength of organized labor, the twenty-four railway companies that entered Chicago had formed the General Managers Association (GMA). Railway company managers viewed with alarm the rise of the ARU and decided to challenge the union at the earliest opportunity. In 1894, workers at the Pullman Palace Car Company (a manufacturer of luxury railway cars) asked the ARU to support a strike of Pullman workers by boycotting

---

Homestead steel plant   Carnegie steel plant in Pennsylvania where state troops in 1892 put down a strike after a violent clash between striking workers and Pinkerton detectives.

Eugene V. Debs   American Railway Union leader who was jailed after the Pullman strike; he converted to socialism and later ran for president.

industrial union   Labor union that organizes all workers in an industry, skilled or unskilled, without categorizing them by occupation.

◆ In 1894, a boycott of Pullman cars by the new American Railway Union quickly escalated into a nationwide railroad strike. President Grover Cleveland used federal troops and marshals to protect trains operated by strike-breakers. *Library of Congress.*

Pullman cars—disconnecting them from every train and proceeding without them. When the ARU agreed, it found itself on a collision course with the GMA, which insisted that only railway managers had the authority to determine which cars would make up a train. The managers promised to fire any worker who observed the boycott, but their real purpose—as expressed by the GMA chairman—was to eliminate the ARU and "to wipe him [Debs] out."

As soon as an ARU member was fired for refusing to handle a Pullman car, the other ARU members in that area immediately went out on strike. Within a short time, all 150,000 ARU members were on strike. Rail traffic in and out of Chicago came to a halt, affecting railways from the Pacific coast to New York State. The General Managers Association, however, found an ally in U.S. Attorney General Richard Olney, a former railroad lawyer. Olney obtained an **injunction** against the strikers by arguing that the strike prevented delivery of the mail. He also argued that it violated the Sherman Anti-Trust Act (see pages 589–590). Olney convinced President **Grover Cleveland** to use thousands of **U.S. marshals** and federal troops to protect trains operated by strikebreakers. Mobs lashed out at railroad property, especially in Chicago, burning trains and buildings. ARU leaders condemned the violence, but a dozen people died before it ended. Union leaders, including Debs, were jailed, and the union was destroyed.

The depression that began in 1893 further weakened the unions. Many union members were unemployed. In 1894, Gompers acknowledged that nearly all AFL affiliates "had their resources greatly diminished and their efforts largely crippled" through a combination of lost strikes and unemployment. Nevertheless, the AFL hung on. By 1897, the organization claimed fifty-eight national unions as affiliates and a combined membership of nearly 270,000. By then, working people had repeatedly made choices that demonstrated their discontent with the constraints they faced in the new economic order and their expectation that united, cooperative action might improve matters.

The Nation Transformed

● How did Americans respond to the transformation of the economy?

By 1901, Americans could be excused if they seemed anxious about the economic changes of the previous thirty years or if they appeared uncertain about the outcome of their many individual choices. While some Americans wandered through great **expositions** that celebrated the outcomes of the economic transformation, others argued whether competition and cooperation were the best choices for achieving and maintaining progress.

Celebrating the New Age

In 1893, when the World's Columbian Exposition opened in Chicago, Hamlin Garland, a writer living there, wrote to his parents in South Dakota, "Sell the cook stove if necessary and come. . . . You *must* see this fair." Between 1876 and 1915, Americans re-

---

Pullman car   A railroad car with private compartments or seats that can be made up into berths for sleeping.

injunction   A court order requiring a person or group to do or refrain from doing something; courts often used injunctions to force strikers to return to work.

Grover Cleveland   New York politician and advocate of clean government who was president of the United States from 1885 through 1889 and again from 1893 through 1897.

U.S. marshal   A federal officer who carries out court orders and discharges duties similar to those of a sheriff.

exposition   A public exhibition, often of cultural and industrial developments.

In this painting, Childe Hassam depicts the Electricity Building at Chicago's Columbian Exposition, designed in classical style but lit and filled with modern technology. Because its buildings were white, the Chicago exposition was called the "White City." This architectural style profoundly affected city planning and the design of public buildings. *"The Electricity Building" by Childe Hassam, Chicago Historical Society.*

peatedly held great expositions, beginning with one in Philadelphia in 1876 that commemorated the centennial of independence and concluding with one in San Francisco in 1915 that celebrated the opening of the Panama Canal. Others, on various pretexts, took place in Atlanta, Buffalo, Omaha, Portland (Oregon), San Diego, and St. Louis. The most impressive and influential was the Columbian Exposition in Chicago, marking the 400th anniversary of Columbus's voyage to the New World.

These expositions typically featured vast exhibition halls where companies displayed their latest technological marvels, artists exhibited their creations, and farmers presented their most impressive produce. In other halls, states and foreign nations showed their accomplishments. People of color rarely played important roles in such expositions except, perhaps, as part of an insulting display of exotic "happy primitives." Women sometimes had a building to display women's contributions to culture. Most exhibits, however, implied that women took no part in the worlds of work or business. Somewhere on the edge of the exposition grounds an amusement area provided a Ferris wheel, other rides, and exhibits of a more titillating nature than those in the formal exhibit halls—like the belly dancer "Little Egypt," who scandalized Chicago by violating prevailing notions of proper behavior for women.

In 1982, Alan Trachtenberg, a cultural historian, called these expositions "ritual celebrations of machinery and fervently optimistic prophecies of abundance." All of the exhibits expressed the expectation that technology and industry would inevitably break through all constraints and improve the lives of all. Behind the gleaming machines in the imitation marble palaces, however, lurked troubling questions that never appeared in the exhibits glorifying "Progress." Were democratic institutions compatible with tendencies toward the ever-increasing concentration of power and control in industry and finance? What were the working conditions of those whose labor created such technological marvels?

Survival of the Fittest?

The concentration of power and wealth during the late nineteenth century generated comment and concern at the time. The most prominent statement on the subject was known as **Social Darwinism,** reflecting its roots in Charles Darwin's work on evolution. Darwin had concluded that only the toughest, strongest, or cleverest creatures survive in competition against other creatures and an often inhospitable environment, and that this competition leads to evolution of different species, each adapted to a particular ecological niche.

Herbert Spencer in England and William Graham Sumner in the United States, both philosophers, adapted Darwin's reasoning to the human situation, producing Social Darwinism. Social Darwinists contended that competition among people produced "progress" through "survival of the fittest," that competition provided the best possible route for improving humankind and advancing civilization. Further, they argued that efforts to ease the harsh impact of competition only protected the unfit and thereby worked to the long-term disadvantage of

Social Darwinism   The application of Darwinism to the study of human society; a theory that people who succeed in competition do so because of genetic and biological superiority.

all. Some concluded that powerful entrepreneurs constituted "the fittest" and benefited all humankind by their accomplishments.

Andrew Carnegie enthusiastically embraced Spencer's arguments and endorsed **individualism** as the cornerstone of progress. "Civilization took its start from that day that the capable, industrious workman said to his incompetent and lazy fellow, 'If thou dost not sow, thou shalt not reap,'" Carnegie wrote. Carnegie also preached what he called the **Gospel of Wealth:** the idea that the wealthy should return their riches to the community from which they came by creating "the ladders upon which the aspiring can rise"—parks, art museums, educational institutions. The person who dies rich, Carnegie proclaimed, "dies disgraced."

Carnegie did not die disgraced. He spent his final eighteen years giving away his fortune: 3,000 public library buildings and 4,100 church organs all across the nation, gifts to universities, Carnegie Hall in New York, the Peace Palace in the Netherlands, and several foundations. After John D. Rockefeller largely retired from business in the mid-1890s, he too gave much of his attention to disbursing his fortune—to the University of Chicago and other universities, the Baptist church, and the Rockefeller Foundation.

Carnegie and Rockefeller were unusual because of the amount of their wealth and the emphasis they placed on the obligation of the wealthy toward the community, but they were not the only nineteenth-century industrialists and financiers who gave generously. Duke University, Stanford University, Vanderbilt University, the Morgan Library in New York City, and the Huntington Library in southern California all carry the names of men who amassed fortunes in the new, industrial economy and used their fortunes to promote learning and research.

Although many Americans subscribed to the vision of Social Darwinism propounded by Spencer, Sumner, and Carnegie, many others did not. One humorist poked fun at Carnegie's libraries by suggesting that they would serve the community better if they contained a kitchen and beds so that the poor might eat and sleep in them. Entrepreneurs themselves welcomed some forms of government intervention in the economy—from railroad land grants to the protective tariff to suppression of strikes—although most agreed with Carnegie that government should not assist the poor and destitute. Henry George, a San Francisco journalist, pointed out in *Progress and Poverty* (1879) that "amid the greatest accumulations of wealth, men die of starvation,"

and he concluded that "material progress does not merely fail to relieve poverty—it actually produces it." Lester Frank Ward, a sociologist, posed a carefully reasoned refutation of the basic tenets of Social Darwinism, suggesting that biological competition produced bare survival, not civilization. Civilization, he argued, derived not from competition but from rationality and cooperation. Civilization, he concluded, represented "a triumph of mind" over "ceaseless and aimless competition."

Robber Barons?

Americans disagreed over the deeds of the powerful industrialists and financiers. Some accepted them as benefactors of the nation. Others agreed with E. L. Godkin, a journalist who in 1869 compared one railroad magnate, Cornelius Vanderbilt, to a medieval robber baron—a feudal lord who robbed travelers passing through his domain. Those who have called the wealthy industrialists and bankers **robber barons** point out that they were unscrupulous, greedy, exploitative, and antisocial. Looking only at the deeds or misdeeds of individual entrepreneurs, however, hides more about the economy than it reveals. Understanding these men and the larger economic changes of the era requires more than an examination of individual behavior, whether despicable or praiseworthy.

Thomas C. Cochran, a historian, looked at the broad cultural context that affected not just prominent entrepreneurs but also most Americans. He identified three broadly shared "cultural themes" as central for understanding the period: (1) a belief that the economy operated according to self-correcting principles, especially the law of supply and demand; (2) the ideas of Social Darwinism; and (3) an assumption that people were motivated primarily by a desire for material gain. These themes shed light not only on the actions of the entrepreneurs of the late nineteenth century but also on the reception they received from other Americans.

---

individualism   Belief in the primary importance of the individual and the virtues of self-reliance.

Gospel of Wealth   Andrew Carnegie's idea that all possessors of great wealth have an obligation to spend their money on good works, to help people who are inclined to help themselves.

robber baron   Disapproving term applied to the financial giants of the late nineteenth century, especially those who flaunted their wealth.

SUMMARY

E **xpectations**
C **onstraints**
C **hoices**
O **utcomes**

After 1865, large-scale manufacturing developed quite quickly in the United States, built on a foundation of abundant natural resources, a pool of skilled workers, expanding harvests, and favorable government policies. The *outcome* was the transformation of the U.S. economy.

Entrepreneurs made *choices* that improved and extended railway lines, eliminating *constraints* of distance and natural barriers and creating a national transportation network. Manufacturers and merchants developed new *expectations* based on a national market for raw materials and finished goods. Railroads were first to grapple with many problems related to size, and they made *choices* that other businesses imitated. Investment bankers, notably J. P. Morgan, led in combining separate rail companies into larger and more profitable systems.

Andrew Carnegie and John D. Rockefeller were the best known of many entrepreneurs whose *choices* produced manufacturing operations of unprecedented size and complexity. By 1900, choices spurred by competition had produced oligopoly and vertical integration in many industries. Technology and advertising emerged as important competitive devices. At the turn of the century, investment bankers led a wave of mergers in a number of industries.

Workers *chose* to migrate to expanding industrial centers from rural areas either in the United States or in another country. The new work force included not only adult males but also women and children. Industrial workers had little control over the pace or hours of their work and often faced unpleasant or dangerous working conditions.

Expecting that cooperation might improve their lot, some workers *chose* to form labor organizations to fight the *constraints* of low wages, long hours, and poor conditions. Espousing cooperatives and reform, the Knights of Labor *chose* to open their membership to the unskilled, to African-Americans, and to women—groups usually not admitted to craft unions. The Knights died out after 1890. The American Federation of Labor was formed by craft unions. The AFL *chose* to reject radicalism and instead to work within capitalism to improve wages, hours, and conditions for its members. Major strikes between 1877 and 1894 revealed both the depth of workers' discontent and the strength of their organizations. By the mid-1890s, however, labor organizations were on the defensive.

Great expositions celebrated manufacturing and new technologies. Social Darwinists acclaimed unrestricted competition for producing progress and survival of the fittest. Others criticized the negative aspects of the era's economy. Some simply condemned the great entrepreneurs as robber barons, but more complex treatments analyze such figures within the cultural context of their own time.

SUGGESTED READINGS

Brody, David. *Steelworkers in America: The Nonunion Era* (1960).

　　The lives of steelworkers and the nature of their work.

Dubofsky, Melvyn. *Industrialism and the American Worker, 1865–1920,* 2d ed. (1985).

　　A brief introduction to the topic, organized chronologically.

Jones, Mary Harris "Mother." *The Autobiography of Mother Jones,* ed. by Mary Field Parton (1925, 1980).

　　A self-portrait by the feisty union activist; not always precise regarding facts and dates, but fascinating for its account of one woman's activism.

Lamoreaux, Naomi. *The Great Merger Movement in American Business, 1895–1904* (1985).

　　An impressive study of the merger movement using detailed case histories of particular industries.

Montgomery, David. *The Fall of the House of Labor: The Workplace, the State, and American Labor Activism, 1865–1925* (1987).

　　Looks at the workplace and develops workers' responses to their situation from that perspective.

Porter, Glenn. *The Rise of Big Business, 1860–1910,* 2d ed. (1992).

　　A brief introduction to the topic, including the role of the railroads, vertical and horizontal integration, and the merger movement.

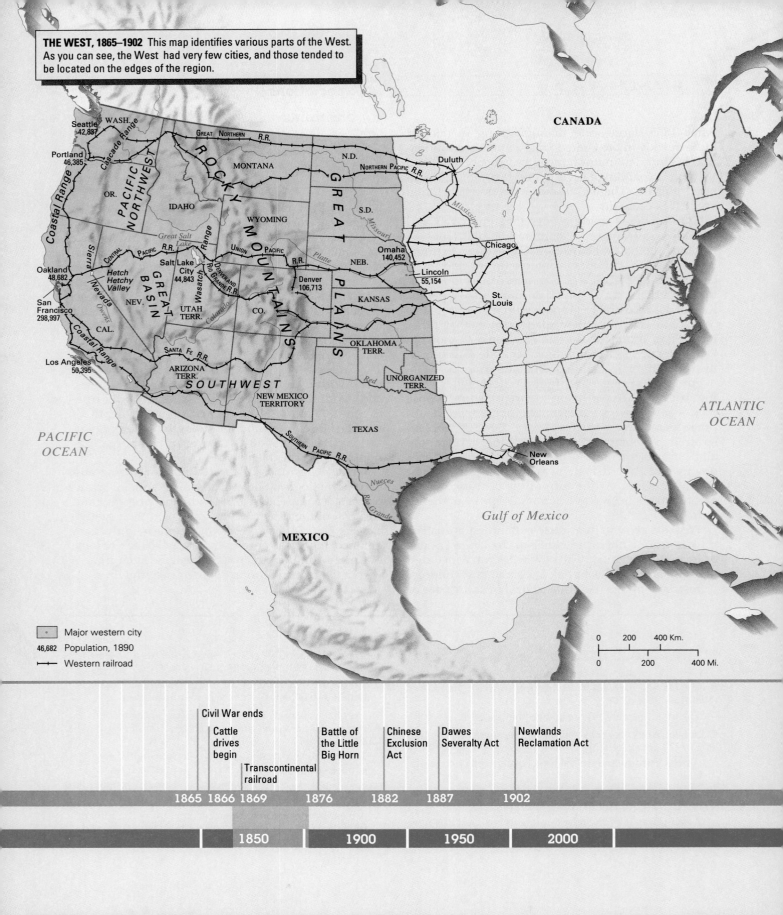

THE WEST, 1865–1902 This map identifies various parts of the West. As you can see, the West had very few cities, and those tended to be located on the edges of the region.

CANADA

ATLANTIC OCEAN

PACIFIC OCEAN

Gulf of Mexico

MEXICO

Seattle 42,837
Portland 46,385
WASH.
OR.
IDAHO
MONTANA
N.D.
S.D.
GREAT NORTHERN R.R.
NORTHERN PACIFIC R.R.
Duluth
ROCKY MOUNTAINS
Cascade Range
PACIFIC NORTHWEST
Coastal Range
Great Salt Lake
WYOMING
GREAT PLAINS
Sierra Nevada
CENTRAL PACIFIC R.R.
UNION PACIFIC
R.R.
Platte
Omaha 140,452
Chicago
Oakland 48,682
San Francisco 298,997
Hetch Hetchy Valley
GREAT BASIN
Salt Lake City 44,843
DENVER AND RIO GRANDE R.R.
Wasatch Range
NEV.
UTAH TERR.
CO.
Denver 106,713
NEB.
Lincoln 55,154
KANSAS
St. Louis
Owens
CAL.
Coastal Range
Los Angeles 50,395
SANTA FE R.R.
ARIZONA TERR.
SOUTHWEST
NEW MEXICO TERRITORY
Colorado
OKLAHOMA TERR.
Red
UNORGANIZED TERR.
TEXAS
SOUTHERN PACIFIC R.R.
New Orleans
Nueces
Rio Grande
Mississippi
Missouri

- ▪ Major western city
- 46,682 Population, 1890
- —⊢—⊢— Western railroad

| 0 | 200 | 400 Km. |
| 0 | 200 | 400 Mi. |

Civil War ends
Cattle drives begin
Transcontinental railroad
Battle of the Little Big Horn
Chinese Exclusion Act
Dawes Severalty Act
Newlands Reclamation Act

1865 1866 1869   1876   1882   1887   1902

1850   1900   1950   2000

Conflict and Change in the West, 1865–1902

War for the West

- What expectations led to federal policymakers' choices regarding American Indians after the Civil War?
- In what ways did western Indians choose to respond?
- What expectations probably lay behind their responses?

Mormons, Cowboys, Sodbusters, and Loggers: The Transformation of the West, Part I

- How did Mormons, the range cattle industry, and farmers respond to the constraints they faced in the West?
- What were the outcomes of their choices for western development?

Railroads, Mining, and Agribusiness: The Transformation of the West, Part II

- How did choices regarding railroads, mining, agribusiness, finance capitalism, and water promote the development of the West?

Ethnicity and Race in the West

- Compare the constraints faced by Indians, Latinos, and Chinese immigrants between the mid-nineteenth century and 1900, and the choices that each made.

The West in American Thought

- How does the myth of the West compare with the reality?

INTRODUCTION

E xpectations
C onstraints
C hoices
O utcomes

While Andrew Carnegie and John D. Rockefeller were building industrial empires in the East, the U.S. Army was eliminating the last armed Indian resistance in the West, where entrepreneurs had already begun their own empire building. Americans have shown a long-lasting interest in the West of the late nineteenth century. Popular fiction and drama have glorified the West as a land where **rugged individualism** held sway and pioneers overcame great odds, but the reality of western life was somewhat different.

At the close of the Civil War, many Americans looked to the West with high *expectations.* For years before the war, the issue of slavery had *constrained* federal action to develop the West. The secession of the southern states removed that *constraint*, and the Republicans who took charge in Washington in 1861 moved quickly to use federal power to open the West to economic development and white settlement, through measures such as the Pacific Railroad Act and the Homestead Act, both passed in 1862.

As Americans faced west, they held some contradictory *expectations.* On the one hand, prior experience suggested the steady westward extension of family farms. It had taken American farmers more than a half-century to fill the area between the Appalachian Mountains and the Mississippi River and might take as long to extend cultivation to the Rocky Mountains. In 1827, in fact, a cabinet officer had predicted that the nation would take five hundred years to fill up the West. On the other hand, travelers to the West had described it as an area of vast deserts, forbidding mountains, and well-armed, mounted Indian warriors. Potential *constraints*, such as these, suggested that parts of the West might never be developed like the eastern half of the nation.

In most of the West, rainfall was markedly less than in the eastern United States, where sufficient water was simply taken for granted. In the West, the scarcity of water *constrained* development and presented a new set of *choices.* What sort of development was appropriate in a region with little rain? How could western water be harnessed to support development? Who would control the water, and who would benefit from it?

Similarly, the ethnic and racial composition of the West differed significantly from patterns in the East and South. At the end of the Civil War, the northeastern and north-central United States was almost entirely of European descent. The South was a biracial society—white and black. Some Indians lived east of the Mississippi, but larger numbers of Indians had been pushed beyond the river and shared parts of the West with tribal groups that claimed it as their ancestral homeland. The Southwest was home to significant numbers of people who spoke Spanish, who were often of mixed white and Indian ancestry, and whose families had lived in the region long before the arrival of the first Yankees. By the time of the Civil War, the Pacific coast had attracted immigrants from Asia, especially China, who had *chosen* to cross the Pacific going east in the *expectation* of making their fortune in America, much as European immigrants crossed the Atlantic going west. In the late nineteenth century, these concentrations of ethnic groups marked the West as a distinctive place.

As individual Americans made *choices* that shaped the development of the West—from seeking free land under the Homestead Act to speculating in mining stock to deciding how to deal with environmental *constraints*—federal officials also faced important *choices.* The basic choice to use the public domain to speed economic development had already been made by 1862. But a related *choice* remained—what to do about the Indians who occupied much of the land. Given the *choices* and *constraints* facing Americans in the West, the *outcome* of efforts to develop the land was sometimes quite different from previous experience and from the *expectations* of those involved. Overall, though, the *outcome* was that during this period the western half of the United States underwent immense change.

Conflict and Change in the West

1700s	Horse culture spreads throughout the Great Plains
1847	First Mormon settlements near Great Salt Lake
1848	Treaty of Guadalupe Hidalgo California Gold rush begins
1851	Fort Laramie Treaty
1862	Homestead Act Pacific Railroad Act Land-Grant College Act
1865	Civil War ends
1866–1880	Cattle drives north from Texas
1867–1868	Treaties establish major western reservations
1868–1869	Army's winter campaign against southern Plains Indians
1869	First transcontinental railroad completed
Early 1870s	Cattle raising begins on northern Plains
1870s	Destruction of buffalo herds Silver mining boom in Nevada
1870s–1880s	Extension of farming to the Great Plains
1871–1885	Anti-Chinese riots across the West
1874	Indian resistance ends on southern Plains Patent issued for barbed wire
1876	Spring and summer campaign on northern Plains Indian victory in Battle of Little Big Horn
1877	Army subdues last major Indian resistance on northern Plains Surrender and death of Crazy Horse Chief Joseph and the Nez Perce flee Workingmen's party of California attacks Chinese Reconstruction ends

1881	Surrender of Sitting Bull
1882	Chinese Exclusion Act
1883	Northern Pacific Railroad completed to Portland
1884	Federal court prohibits hydraulic mining
1886	Surrender of Geronimo *Yick Wo v. Hopkins*
1886–1887	Severe winter damages northern cattle business
1887	Dawes Severalty Act
Late 1880s	Reduced rainfall
1890	Conflict at Wounded Knee Creek
1892	Sierra Club formed
1893	Great Northern Railway completed Frederick Jackson Turner presents his frontier thesis
1899	National Irrigation Association formed
1902	Reclamation Act
1907	Japanese immigration ends
1913	Congress approves Hetch Hetchy dam
1920s	Western movies help make cowboy a mythical figure

War for the West

- What expectations led to federal policymakers' choices regarding American Indians after the Civil War?
- In what ways did western Indians choose to respond?
- What expectations probably lay behind their responses?

When Congress chose to use the public domain—western land—to encourage economic development, most white Americans considered the West to be largely vacant. In fact, however, American Indians lived throughout most of the West, and their understanding of their relationship to the land differed greatly from that of most white Americans. The most tragic outcome of the development of the West was certainly the experience of the Indians.

The Plains Indians

By the time white Americans began to move west, the acquisition of horses and, to a lesser extent, guns had already transformed the lives of many American Indians. This transformation occurred most dramatically among the tribes living on or near the **Great Plains**—the vast, relatively flat and treeless region that stretches from north to south across the center of the nation and was home to huge herds of buffalo. The introduction of the horse to the Great Plains took place slowly, primarily from Spanish settlements in what is now New Mexico. In 1680, the **Pueblo Indians** of that region revolted against the Spanish, briefly drove them out, and took their herds of horses. The Pueblos traded horses to surrounding tribes, thus introducing substantial numbers of them to the Plains for the first time. Even so, horses did not reach the northern Plains in large numbers until the eighteenth century. At the same time, the expanding white settlements along the Atlantic coast pushed all tribes westward, toward the Great Plains. By the mid-eighteenth century, French and English traders to the northeast of the Plains had begun to provide guns to the Indians in return for furs. Thus guns entered the Plains from the East and Northeast, and horses entered from the Southwest. Together they transformed the culture of many of the Plains tribes.

Two different ways of life were evident among the Indians of the Plains: sedentary farming and nomadic buffalo hunting. Living a settled life in river valleys in large, permanent villages with dome-shaped houses made of logs were the Pawnees, Arikaras, and Wichitas (who spoke languages of the Caddoan family) and the Hidatsas, Mandans, Omahas, Otos, Osages, and others (who spoke Siouan languages). On the northern Plains, their houses were covered with dirt. In southern areas, their houses were covered with grass. These Indians farmed the fertile river valleys, harvesting corn, squash, pumpkins, beans, sunflowers, and tobacco. They gathered wild fruit and vegetables and hunted and fished near their villages. Men were responsible for hunting, fishing, and cultivating tobacco. Women were responsible for the other farming and for food preparation. Before the arrival of horses, twice a year entire villages went—on foot—on extended hunting trips for buffalo, once in the early summer after the crops were planted, then again in the fall after the harvest. During these hunts, the people lived in **tipis,** cone-shaped tents of buffalo hide that could be easily moved. The acquisition of horses changed the culture of these Indians only slightly.

In contrast, the horse revolutionized the way of life of another group of Plains Indians. Indians on horseback would kill twice as many buffalo as Indians on foot. By increasing the killing capacity of the hunters, the horse substantially increased the number of people the Plains could support. At the same time, the horse increased mobility, permitting a band to follow the buffalo herds as they moved across the Plains. The buffalo provided most essentials: food (meat), clothing and shelter (made from hides), implements (made from bones and horns), and even fuel for fires (dried dung). Some groups completely abandoned farming and became nomadic, living in tipis year round and following the buffalo herds. The Cheyenne, for example, made this transition within one generation after 1770, when a neighboring tribe destroyed their permanent village. By the early nineteenth century, the horse culture existed throughout the Plains. The largest groups practicing it included—from North

---

Great Plains High grassland of western North America, stretching from the Mississippi Valley to the Rocky Mountains; it is generally level, treeless, and semiarid.

Pueblo Indians Hopis, Zunis, and other village Indians of the Southwest who lived in multilevel stone or adobe apartment houses; they were primarily farmers.

tipi Tent made from buffalo hide and used as a portable dwelling by Indians on the Great Plains.

◆ In the 1830s, George Catlin painted this buffalo hunt in what is now Montana. The aquisition of horses greatly increased the Indians' ability to kill buffalo. The Cheyenne, for extreme example, abandoned farming and staked their livelihood entirely on hunting. *"Buffalo Chase, Mouth of the Yellowstone" by George Catlin. National Museum of American Art, Washington, DC/Art Resource, NY.*

to South—the Blackfeet, Crows, **Dakotas** (largest of all the groups), **Cheyennes** and Arapahos, Kiowas, and Comanches.

Whether nomadic buffalo hunters or sedentary farming people, Indians living on the Plains and in other areas of North America had a view of the land that was very different from the view that white settlers brought with them from Europe. Europeans believed in individual ownership of land. According to Indian tradition, land was to be used but not owned. Horses, weapons, tipis, and clothing were all individually owned, but the land was not. Among farming peoples, a tribal leader divided farmland among the female heads of each family on the basis of family size.

Before the arrival of horses, status among young men derived from a raid on a neighboring tribe to seize agricultural produce, capture a member of that tribe as a slave, or seek revenge for a similar raid. With the development of the horse culture, wealth was measured in horses. After the arrival of horses, raids were staged primarily to steal horses, seek revenge, or accomplish both. A young man acquired status through demonstrations of daring and bravery in raids. Signs of success were the number of horses captured, the number of opponents defeated in battle, and returning home uninjured. An individual won special glory by counting coup—that is, by touching an enemy, either with one's hand or with a stick. (*Coup* is a French word meaning "stroke" or "blow.") Raiding occurred frequently among the Plains Indians, but its purpose was rarely to seize territory.

A nomadic family needed at least fifteen horses. Wealthy families had several times that number. For the most part, however, the individual ownership of property was not a pressing goal. A person achieved high social standing not by accumulating possessions but by sharing. Francis La Flesche, son of an Omaha leader, learned from his father that "the persecution of the poor, the sneer at their poverty is a wrong for which no punishment is too severe." His mother reinforced the lesson: "When you see a boy barefooted and lame, take off your moccasins and give them to him. When you see a boy hungry, bring him to your home and give him food."

The Plains Wars

In 1851, Congress approved a new Indian policy intended to provide each tribe with a definite territory "of limited extent and well-defined boundaries," within which the tribe was to live. The government was to supply those needs the tribes could not meet themselves from the lands they were assigned. Federal officials initially planned large reservations taking up much of the Great Plains. At a great conference held at Fort Laramie, they signed treaties that guaranteed extensive territory to the northern Plains tribes.

At the end of the Civil War, federal policymakers chose to create three great reservations in the West. One was for northern Plains tribes, north of the new state of Nebraska. Another was for southern Plains tribes, south of Kansas. The third was for the tribes of the mountains and the Southwest and was to be located somewhere in the Southwest. The remainder of the West was to be cleared of all but a few small reservations, thereby opening it for development—railroad building, mining, and farming. Indians on the reservations were to receive food and shelter and were to be taught how to farm and raise cattle.

> **Dakotas** Indian people who lived on the northern Great Plains; hostile tribes called them *Sioux*, which means "enemy."
>
> **Cheyennes** Indian people who became nomadic buffalo hunters after migrating to the Great Plains in the eighteenth century.

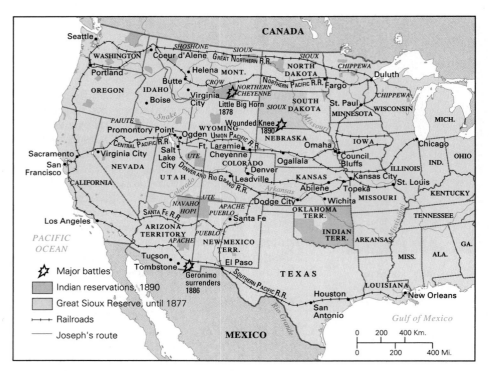

♦ **MAP 17.1 Indian Reservations** This map indicates the location of most western Indian reservations in 1890, as well as the Great Sioux Reservation before it was broken up and severely reduced in size. Note how the development of a large reservation on the northern Plains and another on the southern Plains opened the central Plains for railroad construction and agricultural development.

At the same time, federal officials permitted and even encouraged growing numbers of white buffalo hunters to kill the buffalo—for sport, for meat to feed railroad construction workers, for the profit to be made from the hides. Given the importance of the buffalo in the lives of the Plains Indians, their way of life was doomed once the slaughter began.

Slaughter of the buffalo proceeded rapidly. Uncounted millions of the creatures lived on the Plains, as their ancestors had done since ancient times. Railroad construction split them into southern and northern herds. Their demise came quickly once **tanneries** in the East began to buy buffalo hides. In the mid-1870s, more than 10 million buffalo were killed and stripped of their hides, which sold for a dollar or more. The carcasses were left to rot. The southern herd was wiped out by 1878, the northern herd by 1883. Only 200 animals survived the butchery. Hunters almost eliminated an entire species whose numbers had once seemed as vast as the stars.

After the army mounted a major show of force on the southern Plains, a conference at Medicine Lodge Creek in 1867 led to treaties by which the major southern tribes accepted reservations in Indian Territory—now western Oklahoma (see Map 17.1). In April 1868, many of the northern Plains tribes met at Fort Laramie and agreed to a Great Sioux Reservation in what is now the western half of South Dakota. They believed that they would retain "unceded lands" for hunting in the Powder River country—present-day northeastern Wyoming and southeastern Montana. By the end of summer, the army abandoned its posts along the **Bozeman Trail** in eastern Wyoming, a victory for the Dakotas and northern Cheyennes who, led by **Red Cloud**, had

> **tannery** An establishment where skins and hides are made into leather.
>
> **Bozeman Trail** Trail that ran from Fort Laramie, Wyoming, to the gold fields of Montana.
>
> **Red Cloud** Dakota chief who led a successful fight to prevent the United States from building forts along the Bozeman Trail.

fought a two-year battle over construction of the posts. In May 1868, the Crows agreed to a reservation in Montana. In June 1868, the Navahos accepted a large reservation in the area of the Southwest where Arizona, New Mexico, Colorado, and Utah now meet. By mid-1868, federal officials thought their new reservation policy had made a promising start.

Some members of the southern Plains tribes, however, refused to accept the terms of the Medicine Lodge Creek treaties. They continued to live in their traditional territory, resisted efforts to move them onto the reservations, and occasionally attacked stagecoach stations, ranches, travelers crossing the Plains, and even military units. General William Tecumseh Sherman, who during the Civil War had devastated a wide swath of Georgia and South Carolina, served as commander of the army on the Plains. After a group of southern Cheyennes inflicted heavy losses on an army unit, Sherman remarked that all Indians not on reservations "are hostile and will remain so till killed off."

Sherman's comment was the usual reaction of a conventional military force to guerrilla warfare: concentrate the friendly population in defined areas (reservations in this case), and then open fire on anyone outside those areas. In 1868–1869, the army launched a winter campaign on the southern Plains. The troops were under the command of General Philip Sheridan, another Union Army veteran. Sheridan directed his men to "destroy their villages and ponies, to kill and hang all warriors, and bring back all women and children." The brutal campaign that followed convinced most southern Plains tribes that further resistance was pointless.

In the early 1870s, sizable buffalo herds still remained west and south of Indian Territory, in the Red River region of Texas. The Medicine Lodge Creek treaties permitted hunting in the region as long as buffalo were there. When white buffalo hunters began operations in that area in 1874, young men from the Kiowa, Comanche, and southern Cheyenne tribes sought to stop them and extended their attacks. Sheridan launched another war of **attrition,** destroying tipis, food, and animals. When winter came, the cold and hungry Indians had to surrender in order to avoid starvation. At the end of the Red River war, tribal war leaders were imprisoned in Florida, far from their families. Given free rein, buffalo hunters quickly exterminated all remaining buffalo from the southern Plains.

Hunting grounds outside the Great Sioux Reservation were a cause of conflict on the northern Plains. Many Dakotas and some northern Chey-

♦ This painting by Yellow Nose, a Ute, was done in 1891. It depicts the Ghost Dance, a religion that promised to restore the buffalo and banish the whites. The dancers' shirts were thought to make them immune to harm. The cult began in Nevada in the 1880s and gained support throughout the West until the Wounded Knee massacre. *Smithsonian Institution.*

enne lived on unceded lands in the Powder River region, led by **Crazy Horse** and **Sitting Bull.** As the Northern Pacific Railroad prepared to lay track in southern Montana, uncertainty over the boundaries of the unceded lands raised the prospect of strife. So the government took steps to force all Indians out of the Powder River region and onto the reservation, producing a conflict sometimes called the **Great Sioux War.**

Military operations in the Powder River region began in the spring of 1876. Sheridan directed troops to enter the area from three directions and then to converge on the Indians. One part of the operation went dreadfully wrong when Lieutenant Colonel George A. Custer, without waiting for the other units, sent his Seventh Cavalry against an Indian

---

attrition A gradual decrease in number or strength caused by constant stress.

Crazy Horse Dakota leader who resisted white encroachment in the Black Hills and fought at the Little Big Horn River in 1876; he was killed by U.S. soldiers in 1877.

Sitting Bull Dakota leader who fought at the Little Big Horn River in 1876 and fled with his people to Canada before surrendering in 1881.

Great Sioux War War between the tribes that took part in the Battle of Little Big Horn and the U.S. Army; it ended in 1881 with the surrender of Sitting Bull.

Choosing Peace

Chief Joseph

*Joseph and the Nez Perce faced the diffi-
cult choice of being expelled from their
ancestral homeland and turning over
several young men to federal authorities
for trial, or leaving their ancestral homeland forever and fleeing to Canada.*
Library of Congress.

Hinmatonyalatkit, known to whites as Joseph
(often called Young Joseph to distinguish him
from his father, also named Joseph), led the
Chopunnish, or Nez Perce tribe, whose traditional homeland was in what is now western
Idaho. When the U.S. government pressured
the Nez Perce to leave their ancestral homeland, one part of the tribe agreed to sell tribal
lands to the government. But others, including
Joseph, refused to sell and refused to recognize
the validity of the government's claim to their
lands. Joseph later explained his people's understanding of the sale: "In the treaty councils
the commissioners have claimed that our country had been sold to the Government. Suppose
a white man should come to me and say,
'Joseph, I like your horses, and I want to buy
them.' I say to him, 'No, my horses suit me, I
will not sell them.' Then he goes to my neighbor, and says to him: 'Joseph has some good
horses. I want to buy them, but he refuses to
sell.' My neighbor answers, 'Pay me the money,
and I will sell you Joseph's horses.' The white
man returns to me and says, 'Joseph, I have
bought your horses, and you must let me have
them.' If we sold our lands to the Government,
this is the way they were bought."

camp that his scouts had located. The encampment,
on the **Little Big Horn River,** proved to be one of the
largest ever on the northern Plains, combining several bands of Dakota and Cheyenne led by Crazy
Horse and Sitting Bull. Custer unwisely divided his
force and lost nearly three hundred men, including
himself. The Indians then scattered, knowing that
their victory would bring massive retaliation.

In the winter of 1876–1877, Sheridan launched
another campaign of attrition. Troops defeated
some Indian bands. Hunger and cold drove most
others to surrender. Crazy Horse and his band held
out until spring and surrendered only when the

government promised that they could live in the
Powder River region. Several months later, Crazy
Horse was brought to Fort Robinson, the major
army post for the reservation. There he was killed
when he resisted being put into the jail. Sitting Bull
and his band escaped to Canada and remained there

Little Big Horn River   River in Montana where in
1876 Lieutenant Colonel George Custer discovered a
large Indian encampment and ordered an attack in
which he and many of his men were killed.

Nevertheless, in 1877, army forces, commanded by General Oliver O. Howard (former head of the Freedmen's Bureau), tried to force the Nez Perce to leave their traditional homeland and move to a newly designated reservation. Conflict erupted between young men of the tribe and nearby white settlers, and the army came to punish the Nez Perce. Joseph was dismayed at the conflict but felt he had only two choices: to fight the army or to flee.

Joseph was not a war chief, but he knew that if the Indians fought, they could not expect to win. He explained his expectations this way: "I have carried a heavy load on my back ever since I was a boy. I learned then that we were but a few, while the white men were many, and that we could not hold our own with them. We were like deer. They were like grizzly bears. We had a small country. Their country was large. We were contented to let things remain as the Great Spirit Chief had made them. They were not; and would change the rivers and mountains if they did not suit them." So Joseph determined to flee—to lead his people, some 650 in number, to Canada, where he thought they would be safe.

They traveled for two months and some 1,300 miles, skirmishing with and eluding the troops that followed them. They were within a day's journey of their goal when the troops caught them. Joseph surrendered. About 50 Nez Perce managed to make their way into Canada. There had been 250 deaths along the way.

In 1879, Joseph asked the government to reconsider the choices it had made in its treatment of his people: "If the white man wants to live in peace with the Indian he can live in peace. There need be no trouble. Treat all men alike. Give them all the same law. Give them all an even chance to live and grow. . . . Let me be a free man—free to travel, free to shop, free to work, free to trade, where I choose, free to choose my own teachers, free to follow the religion of my fathers, free to think and talk and act for myself—and I will obey every law, or submit to the penalty. Whenever the white man treats the Indian as they treat each other, then we shall have no more wars. We shall be all alike—brothers of one father and one mother, with one sky above us and one country around us, and one government for all. . . . For this time the Indian race are waiting and praying. I hope that no more groans of wounded men and women will ever go to the ear of the Great Spirit Chief above, and that all the people may be one people."

The outcome, however, was that the Nez Perce were not allowed to return to their home in Idaho but were sent instead to Indian Territory (Oklahoma), where many died of malaria. Eventually the survivors were permitted to return to Idaho. Joseph, however, was considered too dangerous for that. He was sent instead to a reservation in Washington, where he died in 1904.

until 1881, when he finally surrendered. The Great Sioux War ended. At its close, the government cut up the Great Sioux Reservation into several smaller units and took away the Powder River region, the Black Hills (which the Dakotas considered sacred), and other lands.

The Last Indian Wars

After the Great Sioux War, no Indian group had the capacity for sustained resistance. Small groups occasionally left their reservations but were promptly tracked down by troops. One notable instance was the effort by the Nez Perce, led by **Chief Joseph,** who attempted to flee to Canada in 1877 when the army tried to force them to leave their reservation in western Idaho (see Individual Choices: Chief Joseph). Between July and early October they managed to elude the army as they traveled east and

Chief Joseph   Nez Perce chief who led his people in an attempt to escape to Canada in 1877; after a grueling journey they were forced to surrender and were exiled to Indian Territory.

north through Montana toward Canada. More than two hundred died along the way. Joseph surrendered on the specific condition that the Nez Perce be permitted to return to their previous home. His surrender speech is often quoted to illustrate the hopelessness of further resistance:

> *I am tired of fighting. Our chiefs are killed. . . . The old men are dead. . . . It is cold and we have no blankets. The little children are freezing to death. . . . Hear me my chiefs, I am tired; my heart is sick and sad. From where the sun now stands, I will fight no more forever!*

Federal officials sent the Nez Perce to Indian Territory where, in an unfamiliar climate, many soon died of disease.

The last sizable group to refuse to live on a reservation was Geronimo's band of Chiricahua Apaches, who long managed to elude the army in the mountains of the Southwest. They finally gave up in 1886, and the men were sent to prison in Florida.

The last major armed confrontation between the army and the Indians came late in 1890, on the Pine Ridge Reservation in South Dakota. There, some Dakotas had taken up a new religion, the **Ghost Dance,** that promised to return the land to the Indians, restore the buffalo, and sweep away the whites. Fearing an uprising, federal authorities ordered the Dakotas to stop their dance ritual. Most did so, although there was some resistance. Concerned that Sitting Bull might use the occasion to encourage further defiance, federal authorities ordered his arrest. Some Ghost Dancers tried to prevent it, and Sitting Bull was killed in the ensuing scuffle. A small band of Dakotas, led by Big Foot, tried to flee but was captured by the Seventh Cavalry and taken to a site near **Wounded Knee Creek.** When an Indian refused to surrender a gun, a brief battle took place. Some 250 Indians died, as did 25 soldiers.

The events at Wounded Knee marked the symbolic end of armed conflict on the Plains. In fact, the end of the horse culture was written long before, even before the Battle of Little Big Horn. Once the federal government chose to encourage rapid economic development in the West, rather than reserving it for the Indians, much of the outcome was inevitable. From the beginning, the struggle was a mismatch, for the Indians faced overwhelming odds. The desperate nature of their resistance suggests that they understood that they were facing the loss not only of hunting grounds but also of their very culture.

Mormons, Cowboys, Sodbusters, and Loggers: The Transformation of the West, Part I

● How did Mormons, the range cattle industry, and farmers respond to the constraints they faced in the West?

● What were the outcomes of their choices for western development?

Long before the last battles between the army and the Indians, various economic activities aimed at transforming the West were under way. At the end of the Civil War, the West constituted more than half of the land area of the nation. Its subsequent development was the outcome of many choices reflecting environmental and other constraints and the cultural expectations of men and women seeking to live in that region. Thus choices made by the Mormons who established themselves in the Great Basin differed significantly from choices made by the ranchers and farmers of the Great Plains and also from choices made by those developing the lumber industry of the Pacific Northwest.

Zion in the Great Basin

By the end of the Civil War, development of the Great Basin region (between the Rocky Mountains and the Sierra Nevada) was already well advanced as a result of the efforts of the **Mormons.** The Mormons were controversial because of their religious beliefs, which included **polygamy.** Led by Brigham Young, Mormons in 1847 had chosen to settle near the Great Salt Lake, in what was then northern Mexico. They expected to establish a settlement so remote that no one would interfere with them. Young planned to build a great Mormon state outside the

---

Ghost Dance   Indian religion centered on a ritual dance; it promised the coming of an Indian messiah who would banish the whites and restore the land to the Indians.

Wounded Knee Creek   Site of a conflict in 1890 between Dakota Indians and U.S. troops attempting to suppress the Ghost Dance religion; it was the last major encounter between Indians and the army.

Mormons   Members of the Church of Jesus Christ of Latter-Day Saints, founded in New York in 1830.

polygamy   The practice of having more than one wife at a time.

United States. The Great Basin region, however, was incorporated into the United States by the Treaty of Guadalupe Hidalgo (1848), which ended the Mexican War, and it became Utah Territory in 1850.

Nevertheless, in the remoteness of the Great Basin—isolated by mountains and deserts from the rest of the nation—the Mormons created their Zion. The Mormon community was a **theocracy,** a society in which church officials governed every aspect of life. Church authority extended to politics—a church-sponsored political party dominated elections for local and territorial officials. Although streams flowed from the nearby Wasatch mountain range, meager rainfall and poor soil constrained farming. Young decreed communal ownership of both land and streams, and church officials made choices about the use of water. Ignoring legal definitions of the rights of property owners toward streams on their property, Young chose a system for creating farms and irrigation projects based on the right to divert water for irrigation. Congress recognized this new definition in 1866, and it became the basis for laws on water rights in all western states. The communal ownership of land ended after 1869, when the Homestead Act was extended to the territory.

With all aspects of development directed by the church, the settlement thrived and established satellite communities. By the time of the Civil War, more than twenty thousand Mormons were living in Utah Territory. As the region became more populated, the church established a consumers' cooperative known as the Zion's Cooperative Mercantile Institute, or ZCMI. The cooperative manufactured some products, sold through ZCMI, and engaged in the production of sugar from sugar beets. Such cooperative enterprises mirrored practices within the 20 to 40 percent of families that practiced polygamy. The division of household tasks among several wives gave each woman time to pursue other activities, and church officials urged them to take up home industries (such as silk production) or outside professional employment (such as teaching).

With the end of the Civil War and with greater federal assistance for the economic development of the West, Mormons came under more pressure to renounce polygamy. Efforts to make Utah a state were blocked again and again because of that issue. The Republican party, in its 1888 national **platform,** called polygamy "wickedness." Behind concern over the morality of polygamy was concern over the potential political power of the Mormon church, which the Republicans considered "dangerous" and

♦ At some time in the 1870s, these cowboys put on good clothes and sat for a photographer's portrait before a painted background. They probably worked together and were friends. Most cowboys were young African-Americans, Mexican-Americans, or poor southern whites. *Collection of William Gladstone.*

"a menace to free institutions." In 1890, to clear the way for statehood, the leadership of the church dissolved the church-sponsored political party, encouraged Mormons to divide themselves among the national political parties, and disavowed polygamy. Utah became a state in 1896.

Cattle Kingdom on the Plains

As the Mormons were building their centralized and cooperative society in the Great Basin, a more individualistic enterprise was emerging on the western Great Plains. There, cattle came to dominate the economy.

The expanding cities of the eastern United States were hungry for meat. At the same time, many cattle were wandering the ranges of south Texas. Cattle had first been brought into south Texas—then part of New Spain (Mexico)—in the eighteenth century.

> **theocracy**   A state governed by religious authority.
> **platform**   A formal statement of the principles, policies, and promises on which a political party bases its appeal to the public.

Climate encouraged the growth of the herds, and Mexican ranchers developed an open-range system of cattle raising. The cattle grazed on the unfenced plains, and vaqueros (cowboys) herded the half-wild longhorns from horseback. Many of the patterns that developed in south Texas were subsequently transferred to the range-cattle industry, including **branding** and **roundups.**

Between 1836, when Texas separated from Mexico, and the Civil War, few changes occurred in south Texas. Texans occasionally drove their cattle to distant markets, but cattle drives ended during the Civil War, when Union forces effectively cut Texas off from the rest of the Confederacy. At the end of the war, 5 million cattle ranged across Texas, many unbranded and thus free for the taking. Others could be purchased for a few dollars each. At the slaughterhouses of Chicago, cattle brought ten times or more their price in Texas, but no railroad ran from Texas to Chicago.

To get cattle from south Texas to markets in the Midwest, Texans revived the cattle drive. They herded cattle north through Texas and Indian Territory (now Oklahoma) to the railroads then being built westward. A half-dozen cowboys, a cook, and a foreman (the trail boss) could drive one or two thousand cattle. Not all the animals survived the drive, but enough did to yield a good profit. Between 1866 and 1880, some 4 million cattle walked north from Texas.

The first cattle drives, in 1866, went to Sedalia, Missouri. As railroad construction pushed westward, it created a series of Kansas cattle towns—notably Abilene, Ellsworth, Newton, and Dodge City (see Map 17.2). Later drives followed more westerly routes to Ogallala, Nebraska, to Denver, Colorado, or to Cheyenne, Wyoming. In cattle towns, the trail boss sold his herd and paid off his cowboys, and many cowboys spent their earnings in saloons, brothels, and gambling houses. There too eastern journalists and dime-novel authors discovered and embroidered the exploits of town marshals like **James B. ("Wild Bill") Hickok** (who started his career as a cold-blooded killer) and **Wyatt Earp,** giving them national reputations. The popular press credited such "town-tamers" with heroic exploits, although the most important changes in the cattle towns really came when a town's middle class—especially the women in the town—organized churches and schools and determined to create law-abiding communities.

Although most Texas cattle were loaded on trains to go east for slaughtering, some continued north, to northern ranges where cattlemen had virtually free access to vast lands still in the public domain. One result of these "long drives," as they were called, was an extension of open-range cattle raising from Texas into the northern Great Plains (the western parts of Kansas, Nebraska, and the Dakotas, and eastern Colorado, Wyoming, and Montana). Beginning in the early 1870s, cattle raising on the northern Plains, almost entirely in the public domain, attracted attention in the East, partly because popular fiction was glamorizing the "Wild West." The more important reason, however, was newspaper and business journal reports about profits as high as 50 percent that investors could make from cattle raising. From the East, England, continental Europe, and elsewhere came investors eager to make a fortune. Some brought in new breeds of cattle, which they bred with the longhorn stock from Texas. The result was hardy range cattle that yielded more meat.

In the early 1880s so many cattle ranches began operation that beef prices began to fall. The severe winter of 1886–1887 broke the boom. Uncounted thousands of cattle froze or starved to death on the northern Plains. Many investors went bankrupt. Cattle raising then became more of a business and less of a romantic adventure. Surviving ranchers fenced their ranges and made certain that they could feed their cattle during the winter.

Texas became known for its huge ranches—the King Ranch eventually reached a million acres, larger than the state of Rhode Island. But on the northern Plains and much of the southern Plains as well holdings tended to be smaller. By 1900, the average ranch in Wyoming occupied about 2 square miles.

Another important change, both on the northern Plains and in the Southwest, was the rise of sheep

---

branding   Using a hot iron to burn a unique design on the hide of cattle and other animals; the design, or brand, is used to establish ownership.

roundup   A spring event in which cowboys gathered together the cattle, branded newborn calves, and castrated most male calves.

James B. Hickok   Western gambler and gunman; in 1876, he was shot in the back and killed while playing poker in Deadwood, Dakota Territory.

Wyatt Earp   American frontier law officer and gunfighter involved in 1881 in a controversial shootout at the O.K. Corral in Tombstone, Arizona, in which several men were killed.

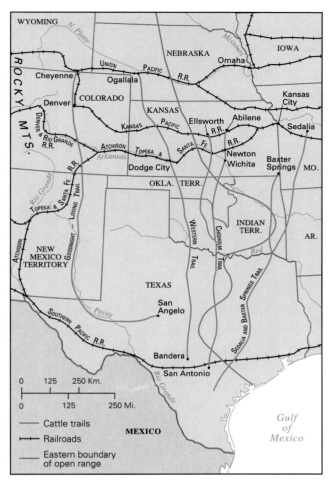

♦ **MAP 17.2 Western Cattle Trails and Railroads, 1865–1890**   The demand for beef in northeastern cities encouraged Texans to drive cattle north to the railroads, which carried the cattle to eastern slaughterhouses. As railroad construction moved west, cattle trails did, too, creating a series of "cattle towns" where the trails met the tracks.

raising. By 1900, Montana had more sheep than any other state, and the western states accounted for more than half of the sheep raised in the nation.

As the cattle industry expanded, so did the romanticizing of the cowboy. Popular fiction beginning in the 1870s and then motion pictures in the 1920s created the image of the cowboy as a brave, clean-cut hero, white and often blond, who spent most of his time defeating villains and rescuing fair-haired white women from danger. Most real cowboys were young and unschooled. Many were African-American or of Mexican descent, and others were former Confederate soldiers. On a cattle drive,

they worked as much as twenty hours a day, faced serious danger if a herd stampeded, slept on the ground, and lived on biscuits and beans. Between drives, when working on a cattle ranch, most found conditions little better, for they earned about a dollar a day and spent much of their working time in the saddle with no human companionship. Some joined unions, notably the Knights of Labor.

Plowing the Plains

Removal of the Indians and buffalo from most of the Plains facilitated the construction of railroads and the extension of the cattle industry into areas once home to the great buffalo herds and to the Indians who had depended on them for their livelihood. Farmers entering this region, however, encountered unfamiliar environmental constraints. Unlike the Indians, whose way of life was in harmony with the Plains environment, the new residents chose to alter the environment to bring it into line with their expectations. Some succeeded, but others failed and left.

After the Civil War, the land most easily available for establishing new farms stretched from what is now the northern boundary of North Dakota and Minnesota southward through the current state of Oklahoma. Mapmakers in the early nineteenth century had labeled this region the Great American Desert. It was not a desert, however, and some parts of it were very fertile. But west of the so-called line of **aridity**—roughly the 98th or 100th **meridian**—sparse rainfall was a serious constraint on farming (see Map 17.3). Farmers there who expected to follow their usual farming practices ran the risk not only of failing but also of severely damaging an **ecosystem** that was unexpectedly fragile.

When the vast region was opened for development, after the **Kansas-Nebraska Act** (1854), the first settlers stuck to eastern areas, where the terrain

---

aridity   Dryness; the lack of sufficient rainfall to support trees or woody plants.

meridian   Any of the imaginary lines representing degrees of longitude that pass through the North and South Poles and encircle the earth.

ecosystem   A community of animals, plants, and bacteria, considered together with the environment in which they are found.

Kansas-Nebraska Act   Law, passed by Congress in 1854, that created Kansas and Nebraska Territories.

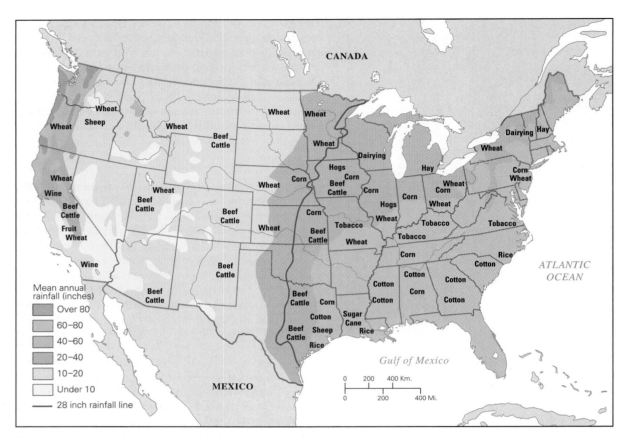

♦ **MAP 17.3 Rainfall and Agriculture, c. 1890**   The agricultural produce of any given area depended upon the type of soil, the terrain, and the rainfall. Most of the western half of the nation received relatively little rainfall compared to the eastern half, and crops such as corn and cotton could not be raised in the West without irrigation.

and climate were similar to those they knew. After the Civil War, farmers pressed steadily westward, spurred by the promise of free land under the Homestead Act or lured by railroad advertising that promised fertile and productive land at little cost.

Those who expected to take advantage of the opportunities for land were as diverse as the nation itself. Thousands of African-Americans left the "redeemed" South, seeking farms of their own. Immigrants from Europe—especially Scandinavia, Germany, **Bohemia,** and Russia—flooded in, attracted by railroad advertising in their lands. Most homesteaders, however, were families who moved from areas a short distance to the east, where farmland had become too expensive for them to buy.

Single women, some of whom came west as schoolteachers, could and did claim 160 acres of their own land. Sometimes the wife of a male homesteader did the same, claiming 160 acres in her own name next to the claim of her husband. According to one estimate, by 1886, one-third of all homestead claims in Dakota Territory were held by women. Single women seem more likely than families to have seen homesteading as a speculative venture. Many single women never intended to do more than meet the minimum requirements for acquiring title and then sell the land to acquire money for other purposes, such as starting a business, paying college tuition, or creating a nest egg for marriage.

Although the Homestead Act, as well as the lure of cheap railroad land, brought many people west, the Homestead Act had clear limits. The 160 acres that it provided were sufficient for a farm only in ar-

---

Bohemia   A region of central Europe now part of the Czech Republic.

eas lying east of the line of aridity. West of that line, most of the land required irrigation or was suitable only for cattle raising (an activity requiring much more than 160 acres).

Federal officials were often lax in enforcing the Homestead Act's requirements for establishing ownership. The law required a homesteader to build a house on the land. A husband and wife who filed separate claims, each for 160 acres, could build a house on the boundary between their claims, thereby doubling their land and using the same house to "prove up" on both claims. Lax enforcement seemed to invite fraud. Cattle ranchers sometimes manipulated the law by having all their cowboys file claims and then transfer the land to the rancher after they received title to it. Thus much land was acquired by individuals who did little to earn it and who obtained it for purposes other than those intended by the law.

Pioneers who had opened eastern areas for farming usually had to clear away trees before planting and usually had an abundance of wood for fuel, shelter, and fencing. On the Plains, however, there were few trees. They grew only alongside streams, and streams were often many miles apart. People who wished to live in this region had to find substitutes for the things that their eastern counterparts obtained from trees.

At first, many families carved homes out of the land itself. Some tunneled into the side of a low hill or embankment to make a cavelike dugout. Others cut the tough prairie **sod** into blocks from which they fashioned a one- or two-room house. Many combined dugout and sod construction. "Soddies" became common throughout the Plains but seldom made satisfactory dwellings. The roof usually leaked during rain. Forty years later, women still told their grandchildren of their horror when snakes dropped from the ceiling or slithered out of the walls. For fuel to use in cooking or heating, women sometimes burned dry cow dung or dry sunflower stalks. Sod houses were usually so dark inside that sewing, washing clothes, and many other household tasks were done outside whenever the weather permitted. Grim as such dwellings may have been, photographs of them speak eloquently of the expectations that the men and women had for them and of their efforts to make them homelike—with curtains and potted flowers at the windows and spindly trees planted outside.

Plains families looked to technology to meet many of their needs. Barbed wire, first patented in 1874, provided a cheap and easy alternative to wooden fences. The barbs effectively kept ranchers' cattle off farmland. Ranchers eventually used it too, to keep their herds from straying. Much of the Plains had abundant **ground water,** but at depths greater than in the East. Windmills, powered by the wind, pumped water from great depths. Because the sod was so tough, special plows were developed to make the initial cut through it. These plows were so expensive that most farmers hired a specialist (a "sodbuster") to break their sod.

The most serious problem for pioneers on the Plains was a much-reduced level of rainfall compared to precipitation in eastern farming areas. During the late 1870s and well into the 1880s, when the central Plains were farmed for the first time, the area received unusually heavy rainfall, and one university professor naively suggested that "Rainfall follows the plow." He thought that farming changed the environment sufficiently to increase rainfall. The error of that theory became clear after the late 1880s, when rainfall fell below normal and crop failures drove many homesteaders off the Plains. By one estimate, half of the population of western Kansas left between 1888 and 1892. One covered wagon heading east bore the legend "In God we trusted, in Kansas we busted." Only after farmers learned better techniques of **dry farming,** secured improved strains of wheat (some brought by **Russian-German** immigrants), and began to practice irrigation did agriculture become viable. Even so, farming practices in some western areas failed to protect soil that had formerly been covered by natural vegetation. This exposed soil became subject to severe wind erosion in years of low rainfall.

Logging in the Pacific Northwest

The coastal areas of the Pacific Northwest—Washington, Oregon, and northern California—are very different from the remainder of the West. Rainfall is

---

sod   A section of grass-covered surface soil held together by the matted roots of grass.

ground water   Water beneath the earth's surface, often between soil and rock, that supplies wells and springs.

dry farming   Farming that makes maximum use of available moisture by using techniques such as planting drought-resistant crops and harrowing after a rainfall.

Russian-Germans   Immigrants from Russia of German descent, often from farmig colonies in the Ukraine in the eighteenth century.

so heavy that the region supports one of the few rain forests outside the tropics. Heavy winter rains and cool, damp, summer fogs nurture thick stands of evergreens, especially tall Douglas firs and giant redwoods.

After the coastal redwoods of California were cut for use in San Francisco and other nearby cities, attention shifted north to Oregon and Washington. Seattle developed as a lumber town, as companies in San Francisco helped to finance an industry geared to providing lumber for San Francisco and other California cities. Some companies quickly became vertically integrated, owning lumber mills in the Northwest, a fleet of schooners that hauled logs up and down the coast, and lumber yards in the San Francisco Bay area. In 1883, the Northern Pacific Railroad reached Portland, Oregon, and was extended to the Puget Sound area a few years later. The Great Northern completed its line to Seattle in 1893. Both railroads actively promoted the development of the lumber industry by offering cheap rates for logs to be shipped east. Lumber production in Oregon and Washington boomed, leaving behind treeless hillsides subject to severe soil erosion during heavy winter rains.

Railroads, Mining, and Agribusiness: The Transformation of the West, Part II

● How did choices regarding railroads, mining, agribusiness, finance capitalism, and water promote the development of the West?

At the end of the Civil War, most of the West was sparsely populated. (Many parts of it remain so at the end of the twentieth century.) From 1865 onward, the West of the lone cowboy and solitary prospector was also a region in which most people lived in cities. In a region of great distances, relatively few people, and widely scattered population centers, effective transportation was a necessity for economic development. Just as western cattle raisers required rail connections to send their cattle east to market, so too did western miners and farmers need railroads to carry the products of their labor to markets in the East or in San Francisco, the burgeoning metropolis of western America. Given the scarcity of water in much of the West, by 1900 many westerners had concluded that an adequate supply

of water was as important for economic development as was their network of steel rails.

Western Railroads

In the eastern United States railroad construction usually involved laying track to connect already established population centers. In the sparsely populated West, population centers were few and far between. For eastern railroads moving through areas with developed economies and connecting major cities, there was no shortage of freight to be hauled to and from the many towns along the line. At the end of the Civil War, however, such a situation existed almost nowhere in the West.

Most western railroads were built first to connect the Pacific coast to the eastern half of the country. Only slowly did they begin to find business along their routes. Railroad promoters understood that building a transcontinental line was very expensive and that such a line stood little immediate chance of carrying sufficient freight to justify the cost of construction. Thus they turned to the federal government for assistance in the cost of construction. The Pacific Railroad Act of 1862 (see page 482) provided loans and also 10 square miles (later increased to 20) of the public domain for every mile of track laid. This generosity was intended to promote railroad construction for at least two major purposes: to tie the Pacific coast, with its rich deposits of gold and silver to the Union; and to stimulate the economic development of the intervening region.

The recipients of federal support for the first transcontinental railroad were two companies: the Union Pacific, which began laying tracks westward from Omaha, Nebraska, and the Central Pacific, which began building eastward from Sacramento, California. Construction began slowly, partly because crucial supplies—especially rails and locomotives—had to be brought to each starting point by boat. For the Central Pacific, most supplies came from the eastern United States by ship, around South America. The cost of shipping a locomotive to Sacramento could equal four-fifths of the cost of the locomotive itself. For the Union Pacific, supplies at first came by riverboat up the Missouri River. Both lines experienced labor shortages. The Union Pacific solved its labor shortages only after the end of the Civil War, when former soldiers and construction workers flooded west. Many were Irish immigrants. The Central Pacific found the solution to its labor shortage earlier, by recruiting Chinese immigrant laborers.

The Central Pacific laid only 18 miles of track during 1863, and the Union Pacific laid no track at all until mid-1864. Construction of the Central Pacific was slowed to a crawl by the sheer cliffs and rocky ravines of the Sierra Nevada range. Chinese laborers sometimes dangled from ropes to create a roadbed by chiseling away the solid rock face of a mountain. Because the companies earned their subsidies by laying track, however, construction became a race in which each company tried to build faster than the other. By 1868, Central Pacific construction crews totaled 6,000 workers, Union Pacific crews 5,000. In 1869, as the project neared completion and with the Sierra far behind, the Central Pacific boasted of laying 10 miles of track in a single day.

The tracks of the two companies finally met at **Promontory Summit,** north of the Great Salt Lake (see Map 16.2 on page 483), on May 10, 1869, joined by a series of spikes made of precious metals from the regions served by rails, including two solid gold spikes from California. Other lines followed during the next twenty years, bringing most of the West into the national market system and speeding the development of western mining, lumbering, and agriculture.

Westerners greeted the arrival of the railroads in their communities with joyful celebrations, but some soon wondered if they had traded isolation for dependence on a greedy monopoly. The Southern Pacific, successor to the Central Pacific, became known as the "Octopus" because of its efforts to establish a monopoly over rail and water transportation throughout California. It had a reputation for charging whatever seemed to be the most that a customer could afford. Not all western railroads acquired such bad reputations. James J. Hill of the Great Northern, for example, was called the "Empire Builder" for his efforts to build up the economy and prosperity of the region alongside his rails. He introduced improved varieties of crops and livestock, helped to build churches, and provided assistance to victims of fire and other disasters. Whether "Octopus" or "Empire Builder," railroads provided the crucial transportation network for the economic development of the West. The outcome was the rapid expansion of agriculture and mining.

Western Mining

Between 1859 and 1885, prospectors discovered gold or silver in Colorado, Nevada, Arizona, Idaho, Montana, Wyoming, and South Dakota. Such dis-coveries brought a rush of fortune seekers to the area. **Boom towns** seemed to spring up overnight to meet the needs of the miners. Stores that sold picks and shovels, clothing, and groceries quickly appeared, along with boarding houses, saloons, gambling halls, and brothels. Once the valuable ore gave out, such towns were likely to be abandoned and to become ghost towns. Discoveries of precious metals and other valuable minerals in the mountainous regions of the West inevitably prompted the construction of rail lines to the sites of discovery, and the rail lines in turn permitted rapid exploitation of the mineral resources by bringing in supplies and heavy equipment.

Many of the first miners collected gold by **placer mining.** The only equipment they needed was a pan—even a frying pan would do. Miners "panning" for gold simply washed gravel that they hoped contained gold. If present, the gold sank to the bottom of the pan as the gravel was washed away by the water.

After the early gold seekers had taken the most easily accessible ore, elaborate mining equipment became necessary. Gold-mining companies especially in California developed **hydraulic** systems that used great amounts of water under high pressure to demolish entire mountainsides. In the process, they wreaked havoc on the environment downstream. By 1880, such companies had constructed 6,000 miles of ditches to divert water to their operations. This practice ended only when a federal court ruled in 1884 that it inevitably damaged the property of others.

In most parts of the West, the exhaustion of surface deposits led to the construction of shafts and tunnels deep underground, as miners followed veins of ore. In Butte, Montana, for example, a gold discovery in 1864 led to additional discoveries of copper, silver, and zinc in what has been called the richest hill on earth. Mine shafts there eventually

---

Promontory Summit   Site in northwest Utah where in 1869 the Central Pacific and Union Pacific railroads were linked, thus completing the first transcontinental railroad in the United States.

boom town   A town experiencing a sudden increase in prosperity and population.

placer mining   Washing minerals from placers—deposits of sand or gravel that contain eroded particles of gold and other valuable minerals.

hydraulic   Making use of water under pressure.

♦ William Hahn, a German-born artist, painted *Harvest Time* in 1875. The horses on the left provide power to the threshing machine, separating grain from stalks. Bags of grain are piled near the thresher. Within a few years, steam-powered combines had been developed that could cut and thresh the grain in one operation. *"Harvest Time" by William Hahn 1875 oil on canvas 36" x 70". The Fine Arts Museums of San Francisco. Gift of Mrs. Harold R. McKinnon and Mrs. Harry L. Brown.*

reached depths of a mile and required 3,000 miles of underground rail lines.

Such operations required machinery to move men and equipment thousands of feet into the earth and to keep the tunnels cool and dry. By the mid-1870s, the Comstock silver mines in Nevada boasted the most advanced and efficient mining equipment in the world. There, temperatures soared to 120 degrees in shafts more than 2,200 feet deep. Mighty air pumps circulated air from the surface to the depths, and ice was used to reduce temperatures. Massive water pumps kept the shafts dry. Everywhere, powerful drills speeded the job of removing the ore, and enormous ore-crushing machines operated day and night on the surface.

The mining industry changed rapidly. Solitary prospectors panning for gold in mountain streams gave way to large mining companies whose operations were financed by banks in San Francisco and eastern cities. Mining companies became vertically integrated, operating not only mines but also ore-crushing mills, railroads, and even the companies that supplied fuel and water for the heavy mining equipment. Western miners organized too, forming strong unions. Beginning in Butte and spreading throughout the major mining regions of the West, miners' unions helped to secure wages five to ten times higher than wages paid to miners in Britain or Germany.

The Birth of Western Agribusiness

Throughout the northeastern part of the nation, the family farm was the typical agricultural unit. In the South, after the Civil War, family-operated farms, whether run by owners or by sharecroppers, also became typical. There were always some very large

farming operations in the East and South, but they tended to be the exception. In California and other parts of the West, agriculture developed on a different scale, involving huge areas, the intensive use of heavy equipment, and wage labor. Today agriculture on such a large scale is known as **agribusiness.**

Wheat growing lent itself to large-scale farming both because of the nature of the crop—it was the first major crop for which farming could be entirely mechanized—and because of the heavy demand for wheat in both the United States and Britain. In 1880, in the Red River Valley of what is now North Dakota and in the San Joaquin Valley in central California, wheat farms were as large as 100 square miles. Such farming businesses required major capital investments in land, equipment, and livestock. One Dakota farm required 150 workers during spring planting and 250 or more at harvest time. In California especially, wheat raising became highly mechanized, utilizing steam-powered tractors and steam-powered **combines** in the late 1880s, well before similar machinery was widely used east of the Rockies.

The huge wheat farms of Dakota proved to be only temporary. Most of them were broken into smaller units by the 1890s. In California, however, agriculture continued to flourish on a scale largely unknown in other parts of the country. One Califor-

---

agribusiness   Farming that is a large-scale business operation using heavy farm machinery and involving processing and distribution as well as the growing of crops.

combine   A power-operated harvesting machine that combines the cutting and threshing of grain.

nia company, Miller and Lux, held more than a million acres, an area as large as the King Ranch in Texas but scattered through three states. In California, wheat raising had declined in significance by 1900, but large-scale agriculture employing many seasonal laborers had become established for a variety of crops, producing the earliest examples of what Carey McWilliams, a journalist, later called "factories in the field." At first the growers relied on Chinese immigrants for their field labor. But after the Exclusion Act of 1882 (see page 532) the number of Chinese began to fall, and growers turned to other immigrant groups—Japanese and eventually Mexicans. California farmers were quick to take advantage of the refrigerator car and refrigerator ship. Fresh fruit from California was being sold in London by 1892.

Western Metropolis: San Francisco

The Miller and Lux land company, several major mining companies, and the Southern Pacific Railroad all located their headquarters in San Francisco. Between the end of the Civil War and 1900, that city emerged as the metropolis of the West and was long unchallenged as the commercial, financial, and manufacturing center for the entire region west of the Rockies.

From 1864 to 1875, the Bank of California, led by William Ralston, determined the course of development in San Francisco and the West. Like many western entrepreneurs, Ralston saw himself as a bringer of civilization to the wilderness, and he expected to profit from his efforts. He once argued that "what is for the good of the *masses* will in the *end* be of *equal* benefit to the bankers"—although, in choosing his investments, Ralston himself decided what was for the good of the masses. Seeking to build a diversified economy, he channeled profits from Nevada's silver mines into a variety of enterprises: factories, ranging from furniture making to sugar refining to making woolen goods; transportation facilities; and the Palace Hotel, one of the most luxurious hotels in the world.

Although the rails and locomotives for the Central Pacific had to be shipped to California by sea, by 1880 San Francisco was home to foundries that produced not only rails but also locomotives, the world's most advanced mining equipment, agricultural implements for large-scale farming, and ships. By the late 1880s, James Bryce, an English visitor,

could write that "California, more than any other part of the Union, is a country by itself, and San Francisco a capital." The city, he explained, "dwarfs the other cities" and "is ... more powerful over them than is any Eastern city over its neighbourhood."

William Ralston died in 1875, but his bank and a few other banks in San Francisco continued to play roles in the western economy comparable to those played by eastern investment bankers. By the early twentieth century, for example, William H. Crocker, son of one of the founders of the Central Pacific Railroad, was president of Crocker Bank and controlled investments in electrical power companies, western mining enterprises, the southern California oil industry, and extensive agricultural property. By 1900, San Francisco was home not just to the banks and companies that dominated the western economy but also to a strong and growing union movement. By 1900, other western cities—Denver, Salt Lake City, Seattle, Portland, and especially Los Angeles—had begun to challenge the economic dominance of San Francisco.

Water Wars

From the first efforts at western economic development, water was a central concern. Prospectors in the California Gold Rush needed water to separate worthless gravel from gold. Californians worked out a system of **water rights** that closely paralleled the Mormons' system. On the Great Plains, a cattle rancher staked out grazing land by establishing control over a stream. Throughout much of the West, would-be farmers learned that irrigation was vital to their success. As early as 1899, irrigated land in the eleven westernmost states produced $84 million in crops. Only in California, however, was irrigation used extensively to raise fruits and vegetables. Western cities saw lack of water as a major constraint on their ability to grow.

Competition for scarce supplies of water sometimes led to conflict. Such disputes occasionally turned violent, but courtroom battles were more typical. Henry Miller, of Miller and Lux, once grumbled that he had spent $25 million in legal fees, mostly to protect his water rights. One of the most

> **water rights** The right to draw water from a particular source, such as a lake, an irrigation canal, or a river.

◆ The upper picture, a painting by Albert Bierstadt done in the 1870s, depicts the Hetch Hetchy valley as an idyllic wilderness. After 1913, the valley was dammed to create a reservoir. The lower picture shows the valley filling with water. *Top: "Hetch Hetchy Valley, California" by Albert Bierstadt, Wadsworth Atheneum, Hartford. Bequest of Mrs. Theodore Lyman in Memory of Her Husband. Bottom: UPI/Bettman Archives.*

Cities also battled for access to water. Beginning in 1901, San Francisco sought federal permission to put a dam across the Hetch Hetchy Valley, on federal land adjacent to Yosemite National Park in the Sierra Nevada, in order to create a reservoir (see Voices: Hetch Hetchy Valley). Opposition came primarily from the **Sierra Club,** formed in 1892 in an effort to preserve Sierra Nevada wilderness in its natural state. Congressional approval did not come until 1913, and the enormous construction project took another twenty-one years to complete. Los Angeles resolved its water problems in a similar way, by diverting the water of the Owens River to its use—even though Owens Valley residents tried to dynamite the **aqueduct** in resistance.

Although individual entrepreneurs and companies undertook significant irrigation projects in the late nineteenth century, the magnitude of the efforts needed to provide enough water led many westerners to look increasingly for federal assistance, just as they had sought federal assistance to encourage railroad development. "When Uncle Sam puts his hand to a task, we know it will be done," wrote one irrigation proponent. "When he waves his hand toward the desert and says, '*Let there be water!*' we know that the stream will obey his commands."

The National Irrigation Association, created in 1899, organized lobbying efforts, and Francis Newlands, member of Congress from Nevada, introduced legislation. The **Reclamation Act** of 1902 promised federal construction of irrigation facilities. In an effort to promote family farms rather than agribusiness interests, the law specified that only farms of 160 acres or less could have access to the facilities. The Reclamation Service, established by the law, eventually became a major power in the West as it sought to move the region's water to areas where it could be used for irrigation. Agribusiness often managed to avoid the acreage limitation, however, and reclamation projects sometimes drew criticism for benefiting large landowners.

important legal decisions, *Lux v. Haggin* (1886), involved two of the largest landowners in the West: Charles Lux, of Miller and Lux, and James Ben Ali Haggin, head of the Kern County [California] Land and Water Company and owner of even more land than Miller and Lux. When Haggin built a dam that prevented water from reaching land owned by Miller and Lux, Lux went to court. The final decision of the court was that the rights of those who diverted water for irrigation were second to the rights of those downstream who had been using the water.

Sierra Club Environmental organization dedicated to preserving and expanding the world's parks, wildlife, and wilderness areas.

aqueduct A pipe or channel designed to transport water from a remote source, usually by gravity.

Reclamation Act Law, passed by Congress in 1902, that provided for publicly funded irrigation of western lands and created the Reclamation Service to oversee the process.

Ethnicity and Race in the West

• Compare the constraints faced by Indians, Latinos, and Chinese immigrants between the mid-nineteenth century and 1900, and the choices that each made.

In ethnic and racial composition, the West has always differed significantly from the rest of the nation. In 1900, the western half of the nation included 15 percent of all white Americans, 10 percent of all African-Americans, 81 percent of Americans of Chinese or Japanese ancestry, 82 percent of all American Indians, and 98 percent of immigrants born in Mexico (see Figure 17.1).

Immigrants to the Golden Mountain

Between 1854 and 1882, some three hundred thousand Chinese immigrants entered the United States. Most came from southern China, which in the 1840s and 1850s suffered from political instability and economic distress so acute as to produce famine. The California Gold Rush attracted large numbers of Chinese, just as it attracted prospectors from many other parts of the world. Among the early Chinese immigrants, California became known as "Land of the Golden Mountain."

Many Chinese worked in mining in the mid-nineteenth century, accounting for a third of all miners in California in 1860 and more than half in 1870. They also formed a major part of construction labor in the West, especially for railroad building, not just for the Central Pacific but for other lines as well. Many hundreds, perhaps a thousand, of them perished in the construction of the Central Pacific. Chinese immigrants also worked as agricultural laborers and farmers, especially in California, throughout the late nineteenth century. Some of them made important contributions to crop development, especially fruit growing.

In San Francisco and elsewhere in the West on a smaller scale, they established **Chinatowns**—relatively autonomous and largely self-contained Chinese communities. In San Francisco's Chinatown, immigrants formed kinship organizations and district associations (whose members had come from the same part of China) in order to assist and protect each other. A confederation of such associations, the Chinese Consolidated Benevolent Association (called the "Six Companies"), eventually exercised

♦ This public letter writer in San Francisco represents an institution that Chinese immigrants brought with them to America. By the 1880s, the Chinatowns of large western cities had become places of refuge that provided immigrants with some degree of safety from anti-Chinese agitation. *California Historical Society, San Francisco E.N. Sewell FN-01003.*

great power over the social and economic life of Chinatown and of Chinese communities in other parts of the West. Such communities were largely male, for immigration officials prevented most Chinese women from entering the country, apparently to prevent an American-born generation. As was true in many largely male communities, gambling and prostitution flourished, giving Chinatowns reputations as centers for vice.

Almost from the beginning, Chinese immigrants encountered discrimination and violence. In 1854, the California Supreme Court prohibited Chinese (as well as Indians and African-Americans) from testifying in court against a white person. After early Gold Rush prosperity had passed, and especially when the depression of the 1870s set in, white workers in the West began to blame the Chinese for driving down wages and causing unemployment. Despite the fact that wage levels and employment

---

Chinatown A section of a city that is inhabited chiefly by Chinese people.

Hetch Hetchy Valley

Preservation vs. Development

The City of San Francisco requested permission from Congress to construct a dam, 300 feet in height, across the end of the Hetch Hetchy Valley, a part of Yosemite National Park. The dam created a large lake in the Hetch Hetchy Valley, which serves as a reservoir for San Francisco and nearby areas. It holds water produced by snow melting from the mountains surrounding the valley and releases it throughout the dry summer and autumn months. The dam also generates electrical power. Until the dam was built, the city and its residents depended on privately owned companies for their water and electricity. The proposal was widely discussed throughout the country.

HETCH HETCHY DAM SITE

HEARING

BEFORE THE

COMMITTEE ON THE PUBLIC LANDS

HOUSE OF REPRESENTATIVES
SIXTY-THIRD CONGRESS
FIRST SESSION

ON

H. R. 6281

A BILL GRANTING TO THE CITY AND COUNTY OF SAN FRANCISCO
CERTAIN RIGHTS OF WAY IN, OVER, AND THROUGH CERTAIN
PUBLIC LANDS, THE YOSEMITE NATIONAL PARK, AND
STANISLAUS NATIONAL FOREST, AND CERTAIN LANDS
IN THE YOSEMITE NATIONAL PARK, THE STANIS-
LAUS NATIONAL FOREST, AND THE PUBLIC
LANDS IN THE STATE OF CALIFORNIA,
AND FOR OTHER PURPOSES

WASHINGTON
GOVERNMENT PRINTING OFFICE
1913

Supporters Had This to Say

■ A city surrounded by a region that is semi-arid or has an uncertain amount of annual rainfall, like San Francisco or Los Angeles, presents far more serious problems in providing for the future than any found in the Eastern or Central cities of the United States. . . . [There is not] known to exist within reach on any of the other California rivers a damsite which gives so large a volume of storage for an equal quantity of masonry, as the Hetch Hetchy. . . . Very few campers go there for pleasure [17 from outside California in 1909, 16 in 1910, 37 in 1911, and 2 in 1912 up to August 15]. . . . [Denying San Francisco permission to build the dam] would injure some hundreds of thousands of good citizens of the United States, by increasing their water rates and taxes for the benefit of a dozen or so solitude lovers [that is, the campers and their defenders, the Sierra Club]. *John R. Freeman, a civil engineer working for the City of San Francisco.*

■ Secretary of Interior Lane and [conservation leader] Gifford Pinchot suggest openly and unequivocally that the hydro-electric power companies are the most interested opponents of the bill. . . . [San Francisco] procured lawfully and by purchase the ownership of the water. Ever since this project was started the city has been frustrated by the water monopoly and the hydroelectric interests. *Washington Times.*

Opponents Had This to Say

■ [The question is] whether, for the benefit of a single city of less than half a million, a public park set aside for the public . . . shall be diverted from its present use to save San Francisco money. A single city is asked the whole nation to sacrifice a cherished possession and delight in order to help out with its financing, and the House of Representatives has not been able to see that this is graft. *Milwaukee Journal.*

■ The city . . . is after [electrical] power rights, which Government engineers say are worth $45,000,000. The city wants to supply its public utilities with electric light and power current at the nation's expense. *Literary Digest.*

■ Imagine yourself in Hetch Hetchy on a sunny day in June, standing waist-deep in grass and flowers (as I have often stood), while the great pines sway dreamily with scarcely perceptible motion. Looking northward across the Valley you see a plain, gray granite cliff rising abruptly out of the gardens and groves to a height of 1800 feet, and in front of it Tueeulala's silvery scarf [a waterfall] burning with irised sun-fire. . . . [Hetch Hetchy] is a grand landscape garden, one of Nature's rarest and most precious mountain temples. . . . These temple destroyers, devotees of ravaging commercialism, seem to have a perfect contempt for Nature, and instead of lifting their eyes to the God of the mountains, lift them to the Almighty Dollar. Dam Hetch Hetchy! As well dam for water-tanks the people's cathedrals and churches, for no holier temple has ever been consecrated by the heart of man. *John Muir, a leader of the Sierra Club.* **531**

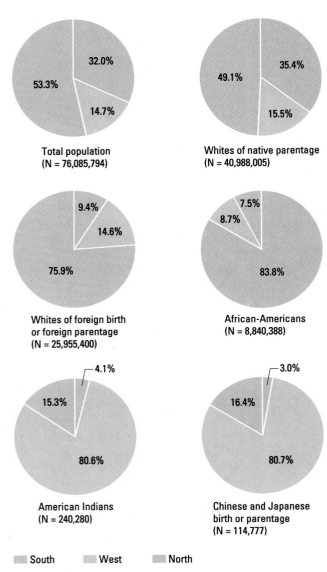

32.0%

53.3%

14.7%

Total population
(N = 76,085,794)

35.4%

49.1%

15.5%

Whites of native parentage
(N = 40,988,005)

9.4%

14.6%

75.9%

Whites of foreign birth
or foreign parentage
(N = 25,955,400)

7.5%

8.7%

83.8%

African-Americans
(N = 8,840,388)

4.1%

15.3%

80.6%

American Indians
(N = 240,280)

3.0%

16.4%

80.7%

Chinese and Japanese
birth or parentage
(N = 114,777)

▇ South   ▇ West   ▇ North

◆ **FIGURE 17.1 Regional Distribution of Population, by Race, 1900** These pie charts indicate the distinctiveness of the West with respect to race and ethnicity. Note that the West held about 15 percent of the nation's total population and about the same proportion of the nation's white population (including whites who were foreign-born or of foreign-parentage), but included more than four-fifths of American Indians and those of Chinese and Japanese birth or parentage. *Source:* Data from *Twelfth Census of the United States: 1900* (Washington, 1901), Population Reports, vol. 1, p. 483, Table 9.

were depressed by different economic factors, anti-Chinese riots occurred across the West: in Los Angeles in 1871, in San Francisco in 1877 and after, and in

small cities throughout the West in 1885. A mob of white miners in 1885 burned the Chinatown in Rock Springs, Wyoming, and killed twenty-eight Chinese, mostly mineworkers.

In these riots, the message was usually the same: "The Chinese Must Go." This slogan first gained popularity in San Francisco in 1877 as part of the appeal of the Workingmen's party of California, a political organization that blamed unemployment and low wages on the Chinese and on the capitalists who hired them to build the railroads and work in the mines. Cities passed ordinances to harass the Chinese. Congress passed a law prohibiting Asians from becoming naturalized citizens. In 1882, Congress responded to repeated pressures from unions, especially Pacific coast unions, by passing the **Chinese Exclusion Act,** prohibiting entry to all Chinese people except teachers, students, merchants, tourists, and officials.

In the West, the Chinese were subjected to varieties of segregation similar to those imposed on blacks in the South. Chinese students were barred from the San Francisco public schools from 1871 until 1885, when the parents of **Mamie Tape** convinced the courts to order the city to provide education for their daughter. The city then chose to open a segregated Chinese school. Segregated schools for Chinese-American children were also set up in Sacramento and a few other towns.

Local custom, enforced occasionally by mob violence, promoted residential segregation. Chinese lived outside Chinatown only as servants or in laundries. Occupational segregation was similarly enforced. Gim Chang, who lived in San Francisco in the early years of the twentieth century, recalled that Chinese who ventured outside Chinatown "were often attacked by thugs. . . . All of us had to have a police whistle with us all the time [to call for help]. But once we were inside Chinatown, the thugs didn't bother us."

Anti-Chinese violence in small towns in the West in the mid-1880s prompted many Chinese to retreat to the large Chinatowns, especially the one in San

---

Chinese Exclusion Act Law, passed by Congress in 1882, that prohibited Chinese laborers from entering the United States; it was extended in 1892 and again in 1902.

Mamie Tape Chinese girl in San Francisco whose parents sued the city in 1885 to end the exclusion of Chinese students from the public schools.

Francisco. Chinese merchants took the lead in establishing a strong economic base. Organizations based on kinship, region, or occupation sometimes took the lead in opposing discrimination and segregation. They were sometimes successful in fighting restrictions through the courts. When San Francisco passed a city law requiring laundry licenses, the organization of Chinese laundry owners brought a court challenge. In the case of *Yick Wo v. Hopkins* (1886), the U.S. Supreme Court for the first time declared a licensing law unconstitutional because local authorities had used it to discriminate on the basis of race. School segregation began to break down shortly before World War I.

When other immigrants began to arrive from Asia, they too concentrated in the West. Most Japanese immigrants at first went to Hawaii, an independent nation until 1898. Significant numbers of Japanese began coming to the United States after 1890. From 1891 through 1907, nearly 150,000 arrived. After 1907, immigration of Japanese laborers stopped because of an agreement between the United States and Japan. Whites in the West, especially organized labor, had come to view Japanese immigrants in much the same way as they had earlier viewed immigrants from China.

Forced Assimilation

After the end of Reconstruction in 1877, the federal government largely abandoned any defense of the rights of black people and chose to look away as state governments imposed disfranchisement and segregation laws based on assumptions of white superiority. Federal laws denied citizenship to Asian immigrants and excluded Chinese from entering after 1882. Federal policy toward American Indians, however, proceeded from the expectation that Indians could and should be rapidly **assimilated** into white society. The final outcome, however, was that federal policies tried to eradicate the Indians' cultures but failed to integrate the Indians into the mainstream economy and society.

After 1871, federal policy shifted from treating Indian tribes as sovereign nations, with which federal officials negotiated treaties, to viewing them as wards of the federal government. Few federal policymakers understood that the Indians had complex cultures that were significantly different from—but *not* inferior to—the culture of Americans of European descent. Instead, leading scholars of the day, notably Lewis Henry Morgan of the Smithsonian Institution, viewed the acquisition of culture as an evo-

lutionary process. Rather than seeing each culture as unique, they considered all peoples to be at different stages of cultural development, ranging from savagery to civilization. All peoples, they thought, were evolving toward "higher" cultural types. Most white Americans thought that western Europeans and their descendants in the United States and other parts of the world had reached the highest level of culture and were the most civilized people of all. Acting on this view of culture and civilization, federal policymakers sought to speed up the evolutionary process for the Indians, so that they would be more like their white contemporaries.

Education was an important element in the "civilizing" of the Indians. Federal officials worked with churches and philanthropic organizations to establish schools at some distance from the reservations, and many Indian children were sent to them to live and study. Teachers at these schools prohibited Indian boys and girls from speaking their own language, practicing their religion, or otherwise displaying their own culture. The teachers' goal was to educate the children so that they would be able to live in white society and to separate them from Indian culture.

Other educational programs aimed to train adult Indian men to be farmers or mechanics. The effort to teach Indian men farming, however, was at odds with traditional gender roles in Indian society: typically women raised crops, and men hunted and fought. Many Indian men viewed farming in the same way as their white male contemporaries viewed housework: as women's work.

Federal Indian Affairs officials also tried to prohibit some religious observances, notably the **Sun Dance** of the Plains tribes and the Snake Dance and kachina ceremony of the Hopis in the Southwest.

The **Dawes Severalty Act** (1887) was an important tool of rapid assimilation. Its objective was to make the Indians into self-sufficient, property-conscious, profit-oriented, individual farmers—model citizens of nineteenth-century white America. The

---

assimilate   To absorb immigrants or members of a culturally distinct group into the prevailing culture.

Sun Dance   A ritual in honor of the sun.

Dawes Severalty Act   Law, passed by Congress in 1887, that broke up reservations into 160-acre family plots and sought to assimilate Indians into white culture by making them farmers.

law committed the government to a policy of **severalty**—that is, individual ownership of land. It divided the reservations into individual family farms of 160 acres each. Once the reservation lands were divided up and each family had received its allotment, any surplus was to be sold by the government. This policy therefore found support among those who coveted Indian lands.

Individual landownership and acquisitiveness, however, were also at odds with traditional beliefs and practices. Indians maintained that the land was for the use of all and that sharing was a major obligation. Some Indian leaders urged Congress not to pass the Dawes Act. D. W. Bushyhead, principal chief of the Cherokee Nation, joined with delegates from the Cherokee, Creek, and Choctaw nations in a petition to Congress. "Our people have not asked for or authorized this," they stressed in the petition, and they explained that "Our own laws regulate a system of land tenure suited to our condition."

Despite such protests, Congress approved the Dawes Act. The result bore out the warning of Senator Henry Teller of Colorado, who had called the proposed legislation "a bill to despoil the Indians of their land and to make them vagabonds on the face of the earth." Time after time, Indians were given plots of land before they were prepared to take them or even when they didn't want them. Many were cheated out of their holdings. Once all the allotments had been made, about 70 percent of the land area of the reservations remained, and much of it was sold outright. In the end, the Dawes Act did not end the reservation system, nor did it reduce the Indians' dependence on the federal government. It did separate the Indians from some of their land, often the areas that were most valuable.

Indians responded to their situation in various ways. After 1877, armed resistance virtually disappeared. From the 1880s into the early twentieth century, a few Indians performed in Wild West shows. The best known was led by **William F. Cody,** known as "Buffalo Bill," who became famous when a popular writer glorified his exploits as a buffalo hunter and Indian fighter. These traveling troupes featured demonstrations of riding and shooting and mock battles between cowboys and Indians. Those who took part—including Sitting Bull—earned some money and were able, at least briefly, to take pride in their horsemanship and marksmanship.

Response to the assimilation programs varied widely. Some Indians tried to cooperate and to become a part of white society. Susan La Flesche, for example, daughter of an Omaha leader, graduated

◆ Susan La Flesche was the first Indian woman to graduate from medical college. Her sister, Susette, was a prominent crusader for Indian rights and her brother, Francis, was a leading ethnologist. Well-educated, they chose to live in and mediate between two societies—the Omaha and the dominant whites.   *Nebraska State Historical Society.*

from medical college in 1889 at the head of her class. But she disappointed some of her teachers when she set up her medical practice near the Omaha reservation, treated both white and Omaha patients, took part in tribal affairs, and managed her land allotment and that of her sister and father. However, Dr. La Flesche also participated in the local white community by taking an active part in the **temperance movement** and sometimes preaching in the local Presbyterian church.

By contrast, some Indians tried to cling to the old ways, hiding their children to keep them out of school and secretly practicing traditional religious ceremonies. In the late nineteenth century, the peyote cult, based on the hallucinogenic properties of the **peyote cactus,** emerged as an alternative relig-

---

severalty   The holding of property by individuals.

William F. Cody   Frontier army scout and buffalo hunter who became the hero of a series of dime novels and toured the United States with his Wild West show.

temperance movement   A movement advocating the avoidance of alcoholic drinks.

peyote cactus   A cactus, native to Mexico and the southwestern United States, able to produce a hallucinogenic effect.

ion. It evolved into the Native American Church by combining elements of traditional Indian culture, elements of Christianity, and peyote use. Some Indians also took solace in alcohol.

Mexican-Americans in the Southwest

The United States annexed Texas in 1845 and three years later acquired vast territories from Mexico at the end of the Mexican War. Living in those territories were many people who spoke Spanish, most of them **mestizos**—people of mixed Spanish and Indian ancestry. The treaties by which the United States acquired those territories specified that Mexicans living there automatically became American citizens.

Throughout the Southwest during the late nineteenth century, many Mexican-Americans had similar experiences as the region began to attract large numbers of **Anglos**—English-speaking whites. Mexican-Americans' landholdings were guaranteed by the Treaty of Guadalupe Hidalgo, which ended the war with Mexico, but the vagueness of Spanish and Mexican land grants often opened the door to legal challenges. In some instances, Mexican-Americans were cheated of their land through outright fraud. In California and Texas and to some extent elsewhere, some Mexican-American families with large landholdings kept their land if a daughter married a prominent Anglo—especially a lawyer—who could help them. Except in New Mexico, however, most found themselves landless laborers in areas that their forebears had once dominated.

In California, some **Californios**—Spanish-speaking people born in California—had welcomed the break with Mexico. A number were elected to office during the early years of California statehood. Romualdo Pacheco, for example, won election as state treasurer and lieutenant governor and succeeded to the governorship for the last year of his term. Two other Californios also held the office of state treasurer, and at least a few Californios served in most sessions of the state legislature until the 1880s. On occasion a Californio represented California in Congress, and many Californios won local offices, especially in southern California.

The California Gold Rush, beginning in 1848, attracted fortune seekers from around the world, including Mexico and other parts of Latin America, especially Chile. Most, however, came from the eastern United States and Europe. In northern Cali-

◆ Cinco de Mayo (the 5th of May) celebrates an 1862 victory of Mexicans over the French occupation army. It became an important festival in Mexican communities throughout the United States, but it is celebrated in Mexico only at the site of the actual battle. *Library of Congress.*

fornia, the few thousand Mexican-Americans were inundated by a hundred thousand gold seekers. By the 1880s, the English-speaking majority had pushed them aside. Latinos (people from anywhere in Latin America) who came to California as gold seekers were often driven from the mines by racist harassment and a special tax on foreign miners. They sometimes settled into the pueblos (towns) created during Mexican or Spanish rule, joining the Mexican-Americans who lived there.

By the 1870s, many of these pueblos had become **barrios** centered around a Catholic church. In some ways, the barrios resembled the neighborhoods of European immigrants in the eastern United States at the same time. Both had mutual benefit societies, political associations, and newspapers published in the language of the community, and both often centered on a church. There was an important difference, however. Neighborhoods of European immi-

---

mestizo   A person of mixed Spanish and Indian ancestry.

Anglo   A term applied in the Southwest to English-speaking whites.

Californios   Spanish-speaking people born in California.

barrio   A Spanish-speaking community, especially of poor laborers.

grants consisted of people who had come to a new land where they anticipated making some changes in their own lives in order to adjust. The residents of the barrios, in contrast, lived in regions that had been home to Mexicans for generations, but they now found themselves surrounded by English-speaking Americans who hired them for cheap wages, sometimes sneered at their culture, and urged them to assimilate.

A different pattern developed in Texas. As was true in California, some of the Tejanos (Spanish-speaking people born in Texas) welcomed the break with Mexico. Lorenzo de Zavala served briefly as the first vice president of the Texas Republic. Like the Californios, many Tejanos lost their lands through fraud or coercion. Juan Seguin, a Tejano who helped to lead the revolt against Mexico, described them as victims of "dark intrigues against the native families, whose only crime was, that they owned large tracts of land and desirable property." By 1900 much of the land in south Texas had passed out of the hands of Tejano families—sometimes legally, sometimes fraudulently—but the new, Anglo ranchowners usually maintained the social patterns characteristic of Tejano ranchers. In the early 1880s, railroad construction and the introduction of cotton growing in some coastal regions brought more Anglos, and new types of jobs, into south Texas.

A large section of Texas—between the Nueces River and Rio Grande and west to El Paso—remained culturally Mexican, home both to Tejanos and to two-thirds of all Mexican immigrants who came to the United States before 1900. Most people living there spoke Spanish. In the 1890s, one journalist described the area as "an overlapping of Mexico into the United States." Three times—in 1859–1860, 1873–1875, and 1877—south Texas witnessed armed conflict, as Mexican-Americans challenged the political and economic power of Anglo newcomers. In social relations and in politics, all but a few wealthy Tejanos came to be subordinate to the Anglos who dominated the economy at the region and the professions.

New Mexico presented a third pattern in the late nineteenth century. In California, the Latino population quickly became a minority, mostly scattered in barrios and not composing a majority in any city or county. In Texas, the population of Mexican descent composed a majority within one part of the state but was unable to hold onto political power. In New Mexico Territory, by contrast, Hispanos (Spanish-speaking New Mexicans) were clearly the majority of the population and the voters. They consistently composed a majority in the territorial legislature and were frequently elected as territorial delegate to Congress (the only position elected by the entire territory). Republicans usually prevailed in territorial politics, their party led by wealthy Hispanos and Anglos who began to arrive in significant numbers after the entrance of the first railroad in 1879. Although Hispanos were the unquestioned majority and could dominate elections, many who had small landholdings lost their land in ways similar to patterns in California and Texas—except that some who enriched themselves in New Mexico were wealthy Hispanos.

From 1856 to 1910 throughout the Southwest, the Latino population grew more slowly than the Anglo population. After 1910, however, that situation reversed itself, as political and social upheavals in Mexico prompted massive migration to the United States. Probably a million people—equivalent to one-tenth of the entire population of Mexico—arrived over the next twenty years. More than half stayed in Texas, but significant numbers settled in southern California and throughout other parts of the Southwest where Latino communities already existed. Inevitably, this new stream of emigrants changed some of the patterns of ethnic relations that had characterized the region since the mid-nineteenth century.

The West in American Thought

• How does the myth of the West compare with the reality?

The West has long fascinated Americans, and the "winning of the West" has become something of a national myth—a myth that has obscured or distorted the actual facts. Since at least the 1890s, many Americans have thought of the West in terms of the frontier, an imaginary line that marked the westward advance of mining, cattle raising, farming, commerce, and the social patterns associated with them. According to this way of thinking, to the east of the frontier line lay established society, and to the west of it lay the wild, untamed West. Often this view was closely related to evolutionary notions of civilization like those put forth by Lewis Henry Morgan and the Social Darwinists. For those who thought about the West in this way, the frontier represented the dividing point between savagery and civilization.

The West as Utopia and Myth

During the nineteenth and much of the twentieth century, the West seemed a potential **utopia** to those who thought of the frontier as a line dividing emptiness from civilization. Many Americans could dream of a better life there, even if they never ventured forth. What was the origin of this utopian view of the West? In the popular mind of the late nineteenth century, the West was vacant, waiting to be formed. There, nothing was predetermined. A person could make a fresh start. The Mormons had done so, moving west, creating a theocratic state, and for a long time living in isolation from the rest of American society. And other people who dreamed of creating communities based on new social values also looked to the West, especially to California.

The West appealed as well to Americans who sought to fulfill the American dream of improving their social and economic standing. The presence of free or cheap land, the ability to start over, the idea of creating a place of one's own, all were part of the West's attraction—even for those who never acted on their dream. Some of those who tried to fulfill their dream did not succeed, but enough did to provide some justification for the utopian image of the West as a land of promise.

The West achieved mythical status as popular novels, movies, and eventually television used it as the setting for stories that spoke to Americans' anxieties as well as their hopes. The development of the West gave rise to the myth of the winning of the West. As depicted in popular novels, art, and movies, the myth begins with the grandeur of wide grassy plains, towering craggy mountains, and vast silent deserts. In most versions, the western Indians face a tragic destiny. They are usually portrayed as a proud, noble people whose demise clears the way for the transformation of the vacated land by bold men and women of European descent. The starring roles in this drama are played by white pioneers—miners, ranchers, cowboys, farmers, railroad builders—who struggle to overcome both natural and human obstacles. These pioneers personify rugged individualism—the virtues of self-reliance and independence—as they triumph through hard work and personal integrity. Many of the human obstacles are villainous characters: greedy speculators, vicious cattle rustlers, unscrupulous moneylenders, selfish railroad barons. Some are only doubters, too skeptical of the promise of the West to be willing to risk all in the struggle to succeed.

◆ Popular fiction and Hollywood movies have contributed much to the creation of the "winning of the West" myth, which depicted much of the West as empty wilderness waiting for the transforming hand of bold white settlers. This myth either ignored or minimized previous inhabitants of the West. *The Michael Barson Collection/Past Perfect.*

Novelist **Willa Cather** presents a sophisticated—and woman-centered—version of many elements in this myth in *O Pioneers!* (1913) and *My Ántonia* (1918). The major character in *O Pioneers!* is Alexandra Bergson, daughter of Swedish immigrant homesteaders on the Great Plains. When her father dies, Alexandra struggles with the land, the climate, and the skepticism of her brothers to create a lush and productive farm.

My Ántonia presents Ántonia Shimerda, daughter of Czech immigrants, who survives run-ins with a land speculator, grain buyer, and moneylender, only to become pregnant outside marriage by a railroad conductor. Dishonored, Ántonia regains the respect of the community through her hard work. She builds a thriving farm, marries, raises a large family, and becomes "a rich mine of life, like the founders of early races." *My Ántonia* explicitly presents another aspect of the myth. Jim Burden, the

---

utopia   An ideally perfect place.
Willa Cather   Writer of the early twentieth century whose novels chronicle the lives of immigrants and others on the American frontier.

narrator of the story, grows up on the frontier with Ántonia but becomes a prosperous New York lawyer whose own marriage is childless. Ántonia, symbolizing western fecundity, is thus contrasted with eastern sterility.

The Frontier and the West

Starting in the 1870s, accounts of the winning of the West suggested to many Americans the existence of an America more attractive than the steel mills and urban slums of their own day, a place where people were more virtuous than the barons of industry and corrupt city politicians and individual success was possible without labor strife or racial and ethnic discord. The myth has evolved and continues to exert a hold on Americans' imagination. From at least the 1920s onward, the cowboy has been the most prominent embodiment of the myth. The mythical cowboy is a brave and resourceful loner, riding across the West and dispelling trouble from his path and from the lives of others. A modern version of the medieval knight in shining armor, he rarely does the actual work of a cowboy.

In the 1920s, this image seemed to have special appeal to Americans dissatisfied with the routine of their lives and work. In the 1950s, some found the cowboy symbolic of the American role in the Cold War, as the nation strode across the globe, rescuing grateful nations from the threat of Communist domination. In a more recent incarnation, the "urban cowboy," wearing cowboy boots and mastering mechanical bucking broncos, kicks aside the restraints of society.

Like all myths, the myth of the winning of the West contains elements of truth but also ignores some truths. The myth usually treats Indians as victims of progress. It rarely considers their fate after they meet defeat at the hands of the cavalry. Instead, they obligingly disappear from the scene. The myth rarely tempers its celebration of rugged individualism by acknowledging the fundamental role of government at every stage in the transformation of the West: dispossessing the Indians, subsidizing railroad construction, using the public domain to underwrite economic development, suppressing unions among miners, and rerouting rivers to bring their precious water to both farmland and cities. The myth often overlooks the role of ethnic and racial minorities—from African-American and Tejano cowboys to Chinese railroad construction crews—and it especially overlooks the extent to which these people were exploited as sources of cheap labor.

Women typically appear only in the role of helpless victim or noble helpmate. Finally, the myth generally ignores the extent to which the economic development of the West in fact replicated economic conditions in the East, including monopolistic, vertically integrated corporations and labor unions. If such influences appear in the myth, they are usually as constraints that the hardy pioneers overcame.

In 1893, **Frederick Jackson Turner,** a young historian, presented an essay called "The Significance of the Frontier in American History." In that essay, he challenged the prevailing idea among American historians that answers to questions about the nature of American institutions and values were to be found by studying the European societies to which white Americans traced their ancestry. Turner focused instead on the frontier as a uniquely defining factor, long absent from the European experience but characteristic of North America from the time of Jamestown to his own day, when the development of the West had finally progressed to the point where there was no longer a frontier line. Turner argued that "American social development has been continually beginning over again on the frontier" and that these experiences constituted "the forces dominating American character." The western frontier, he claimed, was the region of maximum opportunity and widest equality, where individualism and democracy most flourished.

Turner's view of the West and the importance of the frontier dominated the thinking of historians for many years. Today, however, historians focus on many elements missing from Turner's analysis: the importance of cultural conflicts among different groups of people; the experiences of American Indians, the original inhabitants of the West, and of the Spanish-speaking mestizo peoples of the Southwest, and of Asian Americans; gender issues and the experiences of women; the natural environment and ecological issues, especially those involving water; the growth and development of western cities; and the ways that the western economy resembles and differs from the economy of the East. If frontier individualism and mobility have been important elements in the American experience, as Turner suggested, so too have been these other elements in western history.

> **Frederick Jackson Turner**   American historian who argued that the receding frontier and cheap land were dominant factors in creating American democracy and shaping national character.

SUMMARY

Expectations

Constraints

Choices

Outcomes

The West changed greatly during the thirty or forty years following the Civil War. Federal policy toward that region derived from the *expectation* of rapid development, and policymakers usually *chose* to use the public domain to accomplish that purpose. American Indians, especially those of the Great Plains, posed *constraints* on development, but most were defeated by the army by 1877.

Patterns of development varied in different parts of the West. In the Great Basin, Mormons created a theocracy and *chose* new approaches to irrigation to meet *constraints* posed by scarce water. A cattle kingdom emerged on the western Great Plains, as railroad construction made it possible to carry cattle east for slaughter and processing. As farming moved west, lack of rainfall *constrained* farmers' *expectations*, leading to the *choice* of crops and farming methods. The coniferous forests of the Pacific Northwest attracted lumbering companies.

Throughout the West, change was driven by *choices* made in the face of *constraints*. Railroad construction overcame *constraints* posed by vast distances, making possible most other forms of economic development. As western mining became highly mechanized, control shifted to large mining companies able to secure the necessary capital. In California, especially, landowners made *choices* that led to the development of western agriculture into a large-scale commercial undertaking. By the 1870s, many entrepreneurs had made *choices* that, taken together, made San Francisco the center of much of the western economy. Water posed a significant *constraint* on economic development in many parts of the West, prompting *choices* to reroute water sources.

Immigrants from Asia, American Indians, and Latino peoples all formed substantial parts of the western population but had significantly different *expectations* and experiences. White westerners *chose* to use politics and, sometimes, terrorism to exclude and segregate Asian immigrants. Federal policy toward American Indians proceeded from the *expectation* that they could and should be rapidly assimilated and lose their separate cultural identity, but such policies largely failed. Latinos—descendants of those living in the Southwest before it became part of the United States and those who came later from Mexico or elsewhere in Latin America—had their lives and culture *constrained* by Anglo newcomers.

The *outcome* of the many *choices* made in the late nineteenth century was explosive economic development and population change. Americans have viewed the West both as a utopia and as the source of a national myth. But, those views overlook important realities in the nature of western development and in the people who accomplished it.

SUGGESTED READINGS

Billington, Ray Allen, and Ridge, Martin. *Westward Expansion: A History of the American Frontier*, 5th ed. (1982).

   Presents the most detailed treatment of the West and the frontier, largely from a Turnerian perspective.

Brown, Dee. *Bury My Heart at Wounded Knee: An Indian History of the American West* (1971).

   One of the first efforts to write western history from the Indians' perspective, drawing on oral histories.

Chan, Sucheng. *Asian Americans: An Interpretive History* (1990).

   A good introduction to the history of Asian-Americans.

Hundley, Norris, Jr. *The Great Thirst: Californians and Water, 1770s–1990s* (1992).

   The most recent of a number of studies surveying the role of water in the West.

Limerick, Patricia Nelson. *The Legacy of Conquest: The Unbroken Past of the American West* (1987).

   The major recent criticism of the Turner thesis, posing an alternative framework for viewing western history.

Montejano, David. *Anglos and Mexicans in the Making of Texas, 1836–1986* (1987).

   An award-winning study of south Texas.

Weeks, Philip. *Farewell, My Nation: The American Indian and the United States, 1820–1890* (1990).

   A good, short synthesis.

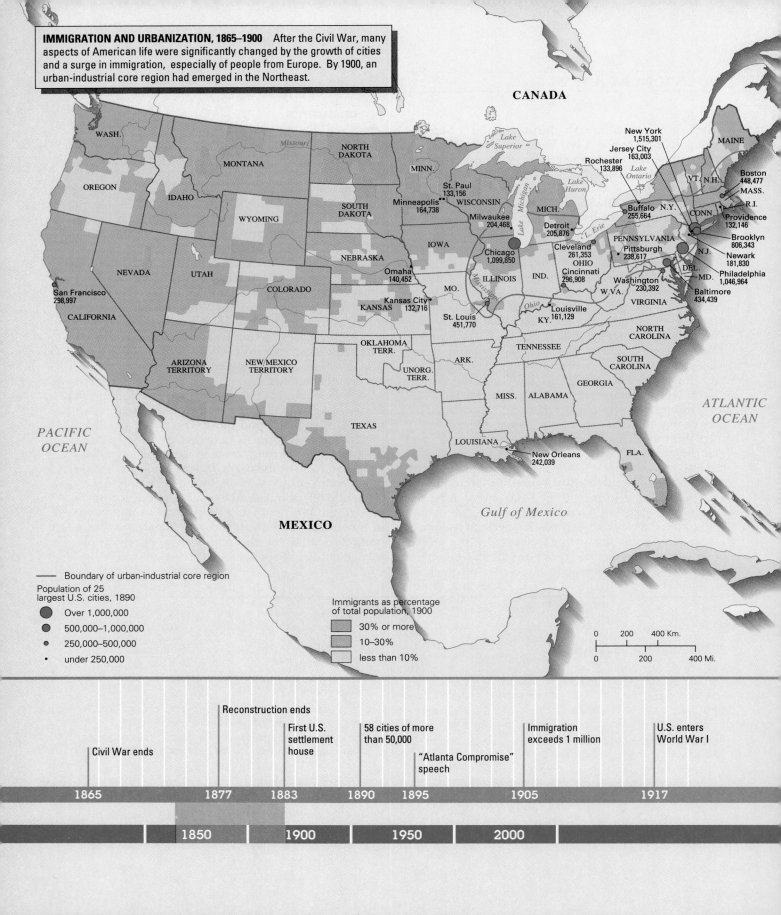

IMMIGRATION AND URBANIZATION, 1865–1900 After the Civil War, many aspects of American life were significantly changed by the growth of cities and a surge in immigration, especially of people from Europe. By 1900, an urban-industrial core region had emerged in the Northeast.

CANADA

WASH.
MONTANA
NORTH DAKOTA
MINN.
OREGON
IDAHO
WYOMING
SOUTH DAKOTA
WISCONSIN
St. Paul 133,156
Minneapolis 164,738
Milwaukee 204,468
MICH.
Detroit 205,876
IOWA
NEBRASKA
Chicago 1,099,850
ILLINOIS
IND.
Omaha 140,452
NEVADA
UTAH
COLORADO
San Francisco 298,997
Kansas City 132,716
KANSAS
MO.
St. Louis 451,770
CALIFORNIA
ARIZONA TERRITORY
NEW MEXICO TERRITORY
OKLAHOMA TERR.
UNORG. TERR.
ARK.
TENNESSEE
TEXAS
MISS.
ALABAMA
GEORGIA

CANADA
MAINE
Lake Superior
Lake Huron
Lake Ontario
VT. N.H.
Boston 448,477
MASS.
R.I.
Buffalo 255,664
N.Y.
CONN.
Providence 132,146
Rochester 133,896
New York 1,515,301
Jersey City 163,003
Brooklyn 806,343
Newark 181,830
PENNSYLVANIA
Pittsburgh 238,617
L. Erie
Cleveland 261,353
OHIO
Cincinnati 296,908
N.J.
DEL.
Philadelphia 1,046,964
MD.
Washington 230,392
W.VA.
Baltimore 434,439
VIRGINIA
Louisville 161,129
KY.
NORTH CAROLINA
SOUTH CAROLINA

Missouri
Mississippi
Ohio

PACIFIC OCEAN

ATLANTIC OCEAN

LOUISIANA
New Orleans 242,039
FLA.

MEXICO

Gulf of Mexico

— Boundary of urban-industrial core region

Population of 25 largest U.S. cities, 1890

● Over 1,000,000
● 500,000–1,000,000
● 250,000–500,000
• under 250,000

Immigrants as percentage of total population, 1900
30% or more
10–30%
less than 10%

0   200   400 Km.
0   200   400 Mi.

Reconstruction ends

First U.S. settlement house

58 cities of more than 50,000

Immigration exceeds 1 million

U.S. enters World War I

Civil War ends

"Atlanta Compromise" speech

1865   1877   1883   1890   1895   1905   1917

1850   1900   1950   2000

18

The New Social Patterns of Urban and Industrial America, 1865–1917

The New Urban Environment

- How did choices by Americans transform cities during late nineteenth and early twentieth centuries?
- What constraints did urban Americans have to overcome?

Poverty and the City

- What were the expectations of newcomers to the growing American cities?
- How did different groups analyze the constraints of urban poverty?
- What were the outcomes of efforts to help the poor?

New Americans from Europe

- Compare immigrants' expectations and choices regarding assimilation with those of nativists.
- What were the outcomes of immigrants' choices?

New South, Old Issues

- What were the expectations and choices of white and black southerners regarding race relations?
- What was the outcome?

New Patterns of American Social and Cultural Life

- How did Americans' expectations and choices contribute to important social and cultural trends during the late nineteenth and early twentieth centuries?

INTRODUCTION

In 1872, two neighboring families in Hartford, Connecticut, shared dinner. As they argued over popular fiction, the two men concluded they could write a better novel than the ones then in vogue. They did, the first time either had written a novel. Charles Dudley Warner and Samuel L. Clemens titled their book *The Gilded Age: A Tale of Today*. In it, they satirized the business and politics of their day. The novel gave its name to the years from the 1860s through the 1890s: the *Gilded Age,* suggesting both the golden gleam of a gilded surface and the cheap nature of the base metal underneath. Clemens went on to fame, under the pen name Mark Twain, as author of *Huckleberry Finn* and other classics.

Chapters 16 and 17 portrayed some aspects of late nineteenth-century life that might justify terming it "gilded." The dramatic expansion of business, the technology that typified "progress" for many people, the glittering wealth and great power of the new industrial entrepreneurs, and the rapid economic development of the West all provided the gleaming surface. The grim realities of life for most industrial workers and the plight of racial and ethnic minorities, however, lay uncomfortably just below that golden surface and made it possible. This chapter continues to examine the expectations, constraints, choices, and outcomes of the period by looking at social and cultural changes in the late nineteenth and early twentieth centuries. New patterns of life rocked the burgeoning cities; ethnic and racial groups related to each other in new ways; new developments revolutionized education, gender roles, creative expression, and cultural participation.

Most of these *choices* and *outcomes* were related to the great transforming experiences of the late 1800s—industrialization, urbanization, immigration, and development of the West. Together they changed many aspects of American life, breaking down old *constraints* and creating new ones. As changes occurred, they fostered new *expectations* among many Americans about how people should live and how social groups should relate to each other. Americans' expectations sometimes expanded individual choices and opportunities and, other times, led some groups to try to impose their values and behaviors on others.

E xpectations
C onstraints
C hoices
O utcomes

As Americans revised old expectations for social relations and forged new ones, the very pace of growth created *constraints* that sometimes forced troubling *choices*. Cities expanded so rapidly that municipal governments, sometimes unable to meet all the demands placed on them, faced difficult choices. For example, should they pave streets or build sewers? At the same time, however, the expansion of the educational system removed *constraints* on Americans' opportunities to learn and presented many Americans with new *choices*—whether to go to college, which college to choose, what courses to take. Educational opportunities for women helped to expand career choices, including such previously all-male professions as medicine or law, or the new profession created largely by women, social work. In the South, where industrialization and urbanization lagged, some made *choices* intended to develop new social and economic patterns.

The expanding industrial economy and rapidly growing cities convinced people throughout Europe to come to America. Such *choices* were often made with the *expectation* of acquiring free land or earning high wages. Some succeeded, and turned their dreams to reality. Other times, such hopes foundered on *constraints* posed by the difficulty of getting to areas of available land, or the unemployment and wage cuts that came when the economy turned down.

Chapter 16 depicted how the outcome of choices by many entrepreneurs and workers was the transformation of the economy during the years between the Civil War and the early twentieth century. Chapter 17 indicated how the outcome of choices by government and individuals was the transformation of life in the West during the same time period. So, too, the *outcome* of the many *choices* by individuals and groups about where they lived, how they lived, and how they related to other groups was the transformation of many aspects of American society and culture during those years.

CHRONOLOGY

Social and Cultural Change

1865	Civil War ends 248,120 immigrants enter the U.S.	**1892**	Walt Whitman's *Leaves of Grass,* final edition Stephen Crane's *Maggie: A Girl of the Streets*
1868	First medical school for women		
1870	25 cities exceed 50,000 people	**1894**	Pullman strike
1871	Great Chicago fire Boss Tweed indicted	**1895**	Booker T. Washington delivers Atlanta Compromise
1872	Clemens and Warner name the Gilded Age	**1896**	South Carolina adopts white primary *Plessy v. Ferguson* McKinley elected
1873	Steel industry launched		
1874	Women's Christian Temperance Union founded	**1897**	President Cleveland vetoes immigration restriction First southern steel mill
1876	National League (professional baseball) formed "Compromise of 1877" ends Reconstruction	**1899**	Scott Joplin's *Maple Leaf Rag*
		1901	Frank Norris's *The Octopus* Anarchists barred from U.S. Oil discovered in Texas, Oklahoma, Louisiana U.S. Steel organized
1877	Nicodemus, Kansas, all-black community Widespread railroad strikes		
1879	Henry George's *Progress and Poverty* Standard Oil trust formed	**1902**	Columbia University offers program in social work
1882	788,992 immigrants enter the U.S.	**1903**	First World Series
1883	Civil Rights cases	**1903–06**	Pogroms against Russian Jews
1885	William LeBaron Jenney designs first U.S. skyscraper Mark Twain's *Huckleberry Finn*	**1907**	1,285,349 immigrants enter the U.S.
		1913	President Taft vetoes immigration restriction Armory Show
1886	First U.S. settlement house		
1887	American Protective Association founded Florida segregates railroads	**1916**	Madison Grant's *The Passing of the Great Race*
1888	First electric streetcar system AFL formed	**1917**	Congress requires literacy test to limit immigration, overriding President Wilson's veto U.S. enters World War I
1889	Hull House opens		
1890	58 cities exceed 50,000 people Louis Sullivan designs Wainwright building Jacob Riis's *How the Other Half Lives* Second Mississippi Plan		

The New Urban Environment

- How did choices by Americans transform cities during late nineteenth and early twentieth centuries?
- What constraints did urban Americans have to overcome?

"The city is the nerve center of our civilization. It is also the storm center." So said Josiah Strong, a leading Protestant minister, pointing up the ambivalence with which many Americans viewed their rapidly growing cities. For recent immigrants and those whose families had lived in the United States for generations, for men and women, for industrial workers and farmers, the ever-expanding cities seemed to pose the greatest challenge to their expectations and to give them the widest range of choices.

Surging Urban Growth

What Americans saw in their cities often fascinated them. Cities boasted the technological innovations that many equated with progress. When William Allen White, a journalist, moved to Kansas City in 1891, the city's streetcars were "marvels" to him and its telephones "a miracle." But the lure of the city stemmed from far more than telephones, streetcars, and technological gadgetry. Reverend Samuel Lane Loomis in 1887 listed the many choices to be found in cities: "The churches and the schools, the theatres and concerts, the lectures, fairs, exhibitions, and galleries . . . and the mighty streams of human beings that forever flow up and down the thoroughfares."

Not every urban vista was so appealing, however. Other visitors were shocked and repulsed by what they saw in American cities. A British traveler in 1898 described Pittsburgh as "a most chaotic city": "A cloud of smoke hangs over it by day. The glow of scores of furnaces light the river banks by night. . . . All nations are jumbled up here, the poor living in tenement dens or wooden shanties thrown up or dumped down with very little reference to roads." Guillermo Prieto, visiting San Francisco in 1877, was struck by the contrast of luxurious wealth and desperate poverty: "Behind the palaces run filthy alleys, or rather nasty dungheaps without sidewalks or illumination, whose loiterers smell of the gallows."

The odd mixture of fascination and repulsion Americans felt toward cities stemmed in part from the rapidity of urban growth. Cities with more than 50,000 people grew almost twice as fast as rural areas (see Figure 18.1). The nation had twenty-five

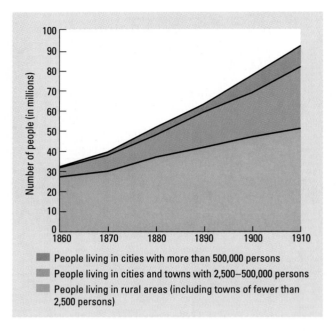

◆ **FIGURE 18.1 Urban and Rural Population of the United States, 1860–1910** Although much of the population increase between 1860 and 1910 came in urban areas, the number of people living in rural areas increased as well. Notice, too, that the largest increase was in towns and cities that had between 2,500 and 500,000 people. *Source:* U.S. Bureau of the Census, Department of Commerce, *Historical Statistics of the United States*, 2 vols. (Washington, D.C.: U.S. Government Printing Office, 1975), Series A-58, A-59, A-69, A-119.

cities of that size in 1870, with a total population of 5 million. By 1890, fifty-eight cities had reached that size and held nearly 12 million people. Most of these cities were in the Northeast and near the Great Lakes.

Where did all these city-dwellers come from so suddenly? Urban growth came largely through migration from rural areas in the United States and Europe, as millions of families and individuals made choices about their futures. The mechanization of farm work (see pages 478–480) meant that agriculture required fewer workers per acre than ever before. Rural birth rates remained high, however, and rural death rates were lower than in the cities. America's farmlands, then, contributed significantly to the growth of the cities, but even more of the new urban residents came from Europe.

Growth of manufacturing went hand in hand with urban expansion. By the late nineteenth cen-

◆ A major center for manufacturing, transportation, commerce, and finance, turn-of-the-century Chicago contained all the jarring contrasts of the new, urban, industrial America—bold skyscrapers and shabby slums, poor immigrants and affluent entrepreneurs, corrupt politicians and altruistic settlement-house workers, and more—including traffic jams. *Chicago Historical Society.*

tury, the nation had developed a **manufacturing belt.** This region, which included nearly all the largest cities as well as the bulk of the nation's manufacturing and finance, may be thought of as constituting the nation's industrial "core." (See the chapter-opening map.) Some of the port cities in this region had long been among the busiest in the nation. Boston, New York, Baltimore, Buffalo, and St. Louis, for example, all were born as ports, with their early economies centered on the goods that flowed across their docks. In some port cities, manufacturing flourished and came to be nearly as important as trade. In other cases, cities developed as industrial centers from their beginnings. Some cities became known for a particular product: iron and steel in Pittsburgh, clothing in New York City, textiles in Massachusetts, meat packing in Chicago, flour milling in Minneapolis. A few cities, especially New York, also stood out as major centers for finance.

New Cities of Skyscrapers and Streetcars

As the urban population swelled and the urban economy grew more complex, technological ad-

vances permitted cities to expand upward and outward. In the early 1800s, most cities measured only a few miles across, and most residents chose to get around by foot. Buildings were low (three stories was unusual) and often not designed for a specific economic function. Small factories existed here and there among warehouses and commercial offices near the docks. In the late nineteenth century, however, new technologies for building and transportation removed many previous limits on growth, spelling the end of the "walking city."

Until the 1880s, construction techniques constrained building height because the lower walls carried the structure's full weight. The higher a building, the thicker its lower walls had to be. New York architects experimented with tall buildings in the 1870s, but William LeBaron Jenney usually receives credit for designing the first skyscraper—ten stories high—built in Chicago in 1885. Chicago architects also took the lead in designing even taller buildings. Such ventures were possible through new construction technology, in which a metal frame carried the weight of the walls. Although Jenney's first skyscraper used an iron frame, architects quickly turned to steel instead, both for its greater strength and because (under Carnegie's constant pressure) steel prices kept falling. Economical and efficient, tall buildings created unique city skylines.

Among the Chicago architects who developed the skyscraper, **Louis Sullivan** stands out. He recognized it as the architectural form of the future and he introduced a new way of thinking about height. In the nine-story Wainwright building (St. Louis, 1890), Sullivan chose to emphasize its height while trying to diminish its bulk, to create in his own words a "proud and soaring thing." He also designed an exterior that largely reflected the interior function, thus keeping to his rule that "form follows function." Frank Lloyd Wright, perhaps the greatest American architect of the twentieth century, described the Wainwright building as signifying the birth of "the 'skyscraper' as a new thing under the sun."

manufacturing belt   A region of the country in which an urban population, transportation systems, and other infrastructure support heavy industry.

Louis Sullivan   American architect of the late nineteenth century whose designs reflected his theory that the outward form of a building should express its function.

◆ Louis Sullivan designed the Wainwright Building (1890) with the intention of creating a new way of thinking about height and about the relationship between form and function. The building was widely acclaimed and often imitated. *Missouri Historical Society/Emil Boehl.*

Just as steel-frame buildings allowed cities to grow upward, so new forms of transportation allowed cities to expand outward. In the 1850s, horses pulled the first streetcars over iron rails laid in city streets. By the 1870s and 1880s, some cities boasted streetcar lines powered by an underground moving cable. It was electricity, however, that transformed urban transit. Frank Sprague, a protege of Thomas Edison, designed a streetcar driven by an electric motor that drew its power from an overhead wire. Sprague's system was first installed in Richmond, Virginia, in 1888. Electric streetcars quickly replaced horse-cars and cable-cars in most cities. By 1902, 97 percent of the nation's streetcar tracks operated on electricity.

In the early 1900s, some large cities, choked with traffic congestion, moved their streetcars either above or below street level, thereby creating **elevated trains** and subways. New construction technologies also launched bridges spanning rivers and bays that had once posed serious constraints on urban growth. And where bridges went, streetcars followed.

By the early 1900s, elaborate networks of streetcar lines criss-crossed most large cities, connecting neighborhoods to downtown. Some carried middle-class women wearing white gloves and stylish hats to downtown department stores. Skilled workers rode others to and from their factory jobs. Still other lines carried typists and corporate executives to and from banks and offices.

As streetcar lines pushed outward from the city's center, the old "walking city" expanded by annexing suburban areas that grew up along the spreading transportation lines. In 1860, Chicago occupied 17 square miles. By 1890 it took in 178 square miles. During the same years, Boston grew from 5 square miles to 39, and St. Louis, from 14 square miles to 61.

As horse-drawn streetcars had first expanded the city beyond distances that residents could easily walk, new railroad lines began to bring outlying villages within commuting distance of urban centers. Wealthier urban residents who could afford the passenger fare now could choose to escape the disorder of the city at the end of the workday. As early as 1873, nearly a hundred suburban communities sent 5,000 to 6,000 commuters into Chicago each day, and by 1890 70,000 suburbanites poured in daily. At about the same time, commuter lines brought more than 100,000 workers daily into New York City just from its northern suburbs.

The New Urban Geography

More than just the skyline and the streetmap of cities was in flux. New technologies in construction and transportation interacted with the growth of manufacturing, commerce, and finance to change the geography of American cities. As the largest cities grew, areas within them became increasingly specialized by economic function.

Early manufacturing in port cities was often scattered among warehouses near the waterfront. Clothing factories, for example, sometimes began in buildings formerly used by sailmakers or as warehouses. All that was necessary was open floor space to set up cutting tables and sewing and pressing machines. Other types of manufacturing required more space and specially designed buildings. Iron and steel making, meat packing, shipbuilding, and oil refining, for several examples, had to be established

---

elevated train A train running on a steel framework above a street leaving the street itself free for other traffic.

on the outskirts of a city. There, open land was plentiful and relatively cheap, and the city center suffered less from the noise, smoke, and odor of heavy industry.

Most manufacturing workers, however, were constrained by cost from riding the new streetcars, so they often had no choice but to live within walking distance of their work. Construction of industrial plants outside cities, therefore, usually meant working-class residential neighborhoods nearby. Some companies established planned communities that centered on a manufacturing plant surrounded by multifamily houses, stores, and even parks and schools. Such *company towns* were sometimes well intended, but few earned good reputations among their residents. Workers whose employer was also their landlord and storekeeper usually resented the ever-present authority of the company—and the lack of alternatives to the rents and prices it charged.

At the same time that heavy manufacturing moved to the outskirts of the cities, areas in the city centers tended to become more specialized. By 1900 or so, the center of a large city usually had developed distinct districts. A district of light manufacturing might include clothing and printing. Next to, or overlapping with, light manufacturing was often a **wholesale** trade district with warehouses and offices of wholesalers. **Retail** shopping districts, anchored by "modern" department stores, emerged in a central location, where streetcar and railroad lines could bring shoppers from outlying areas. In the largest cities, banks, insurance companies, and headquarters of large corporations clustered near one another to form a financial district. A hotel and entertainment district often lay close to both the financial and retail blocks. These areas together made up a *central business district.*

Just as specialized downtown areas emerged according to economic function, so too did residential areas develop according to economic status. New suburbs ranged outward from the city center in order of wealth. Those who could afford to travel the farthest could also afford the most expensive homes. Those too poor to ride the new transportation lines lived in apartments or small houses in the center of the city or clustered around its industrial plants, within walking distance of their work.

Building an Urban Infrastructure

During the rapid urban growth after the Civil War, local governments did little to regulate expansion or construction practices in the public interest. Cities grew with only the most basic planning. Most choices about land use and construction were made by individual land owners, developers, and builders—typically focusing on a few projects at a time. Everywhere, builders and owners hoped to achieve a high return on their investment by producing the most living space for the least cost. Such profit calculations rarely left room for such amenities as varied designs or open space.

Given the rapid and largely unplanned nature of most urban growth, utilities and services provided by city government—fire and police protection, schools, sewage disposal, street maintenance, water supply—rarely kept pace with growth of new neighborhoods. As a result, city residents sometimes faced contaminated drinking water, inadequate disposal for sewage and garbage, and—as the consequence—epidemic disease. Throughout the Gilded Age, most cities played "catch up" when it came to their **infrastructure,** but significant progress appeared by 1900.

Certain city utilities and services—gas, electricity, telephone service, public transit, and sometimes water—were supplied by private companies, operating under **franchises** from the city. Companies eagerly competed with each other for such franchises, sometimes bribing city officials to secure one. As a result, cities usually found themselves well supplied with franchised utilities. New residential areas sometimes had gas and electric lines before any houses were framed, and had streetcars long before streets were paved.

The quality and quantity of the water supply varied greatly from city to city. To enlarge its water supply, New York City spent seven years and $24 million constructing what was then the largest aqueduct in the world, carrying 300 million gallons of water a day. Baltimore and Boston also built huge

---

wholesale   Engaged in the sale of goods in large quantities, usually for resale by a retailer.

retail   Engaged in the sale of goods in small quantities directly to consumers.

infrastructure   The basic facilities that a society needs to function, such as transportation systems, water and power lines, and public institutions such as schools, post offices, and prisons.

franchise   Government authorization allowing a private company to provide a public service in a certain area.

water projects. Water quality, though, remained a problem. As more and more city officials understood that germs caused many diseases, cities introduced filtration and **chlorination** of their water to eliminate disease-carrying organisms. Even so, by the early twentieth century, only 6 percent of urban residents received filtered water.

Cities faced similar constraints in disposing of sewage, cleaning streets (especially given the ever-present horse), and removing garbage. Even when cities built sewer lines, they usually emptied the untreated sewage into some nearby body of water. One sanitary expert in 1877 called Boston Harbor "one vast cesspool, a threat to all the towns it washed." The mayor of Cleveland in 1881 considered the Cuyahoga River "an open sewer through the center of the city." In most cities, few streets were paved. The rest became mudholes in the rain, threw up clouds of dust in dry weather, and froze into deep ruts in the winter. Chicago in 1890 counted 2,048 miles of streets, but only 629 miles were paved, often with wooden blocks. Of Cleveland's 462 miles of streets, only 69 miles were paved. In the late nineteenth century, however, most eastern cities began using asphalt paving, following the lead of Washington, D.C. Sometimes cities found it easier to pave streets than to maintain them: after clearing garbage from a street in the 1890s, one Chicagoan discovered pavement buried under 18 inches of trash.

Everywhere, urban growth seemed at first to outstrip cities' abilities to provide for it. After New York City created the first uniformed police force in 1845, seven other cities followed by the mid-1860s, and more did so afterward. Nonetheless, urban crime mushroomed faster than the number of police. Fire protection also became professionalized. Earlier, most cities relied on volunteer fire companies. By 1871, however, all major cities had switched to paid, professional firefighters. The **great Chicago fire** of 1871 dramatically demonstrated that the new system was inadequate. The fire devastated three square miles, including much of the downtown, killed more than 250 people, and left 18,000 homeless. The Chicago fire and other serious fires elsewhere spurred further efforts to improve fire protection. Such efforts attacked two separate problems: first, create a well-trained and well-equipped staff of firefighters and, second, regulate construction practices that encouraged fires to spread. By 1900, progress toward the first goal was impressive in most American cities, especially compared to other parts of the world. Chicago had more fire-fighters and fire engines than London, England, a city three times its size.

Although change came slowly, most city utilities and services improved significantly between 1870 and 1900. By the early twentieth century, large American cities had more extensive sewer systems than cities of similar size in Germany, and provided more water to each resident than comparable cities in Britain or Germany. Nevertheless, if city residents had enough water, many of them still had no hot water or bathtubs. And no city larger than 150,000 people had a sewage treatment plant as late as 1900.

Poverty and the City

- What were the expectations of newcomers to the growing American cities?
- How did different groups analyze the constraints of urban poverty?
- What were the outcomes of efforts to help the poor?

In 1879, in *Progress and Poverty*, Henry George pointed out that the "enormous increase in productive power" had failed to eliminate poverty or to improve the lives of working people. He concluded that experience demonstrated that progress and poverty went hand in hand: "The 'tramp' comes with the locomotive, and almshouses and prisons are as surely the marks of 'material progress' as are costly dwellings, rich warehouses, and magnificent churches." George was one of many at that time who focused public attention on the growing numbers of the urban poor and on the massive and expanding slums of the cities.

"How the Other Half Lives"

In 1890, **Jacob Riis** shocked many Americans with the revelations in his book, *How the Other Half Lives: Studies Among the Tenements of New York*, which de-

---

chlorination The treatment of water with the chemical chlorine in order to purify and disinfect it.

great Chicago fire The 1871 Chicago disaster that destroyed much of the city and spurred national efforts to improve fire protection.

Jacob Riis New York journalist whose exposure of slum conditions in American cities appalled middle-class Americans and led to calls for slum clearance and new building codes.

In poor urban neighborhoods, children often had no other place to play than the streets, which were usually dirty and sometimes dangerous. When a horse died in the street, as has occurred here, it was sometimes just cut loose from its harness and left for sanitation or rendering crews to pick up. *Library of Congress.*

scribed the lives of the poorest New Yorkers. In a city of a million and a half inhabitants, Riis claimed, half a million (136,000 families) had begged for food at some time over the preceding eight years. Of them, more than half were unemployed but only 6 percent were physically unable to work. Most of Riis's book described the appalling conditions of tenement housing—home, he claimed, to three-quarters of the city's population.

Strictly speaking, a **tenement** is an apartment house occupied by three or more families, but the term came also to imply housing so overcrowded and badly maintained that it was hazardous to the health and safety of its residents. Riis described the typical, cramped New York tenement of his day as

a brick building from four to six stories high on the street, frequently with a store on the first floor. . . . Four families occupy each floor, and a set of rooms consists of one or two dark closets, used as bedrooms, with a living room twelve feet by ten. The staircase is too often a dark well in the center of the house, and no direct through ventilation is possible, each family being separated from the other by partitions.

Such buildings, Riis insisted, "make for evil; because they are the hotbeds of the epidemics that carry death to rich and poor alike; the nurseries of pauperism and crime that fill our jails and police courts; . . . above all, they touch the family life with deadly moral contagion." He especially deplored the impact of poverty and miserable housing conditions on children and families.

Crowded conditions in the working-class sections of large cities developed in part because so many of the poor were constrained by the need to live within walking distance of their work. By choosing to divide buildings into small rental units, landlords packed in more tenants and collected more rent. Rents were high compared to wages, so tenants often chose to take in boarders. The outcome of such choices was alarmingly high population densities in the lower income neighborhoods of the great cities.

No other city was as densely populated as New York, but nearly all urban, working-class neighborhoods were crowded. Most Chicago stockyard workers, for example, lived in small rowhouses near the slaughterhouses. Unlike New Yorkers, many owned their own homes. In 1911, however, three-quarters of the houses were subdivided into two or more living units, and a small shanty often sat in the backyard. Nearly all the homeowners were, therefore, also landlords. Half of all the living units (including both entire houses and apartments) had four rooms, a few had five, and none had more. More than half of all families—owners and tenants alike—took in **lodgers.** Lodgers who worked different shifts at the stockyards sometimes took turns sleeping in the same bed.

Despite widespread urban poverty, few agreed on the causes or cures. Riis divided the blame among greedy landlords, corrupt officials, and the poor themselves. Henry George, in *Progress and Poverty,* pointed to private ownership of property as the culprit. The Charity Organization Society (COS), by contrast, argued for individual responsibility. With chapters in one hundred cities by 1895, COS claimed that, in most cases, individual character defects produced poverty and that assistance for such

---

tenement An unsafe and often unsanitary apartment building often occupied by poor families.

lodger A person who rents a room or a bed in a family's home.

♦ Doing laundry was typically a woman's task, whether rural or urban. When many women were hanging out their laundry at the same time in a neigborhood like this one (New York, about 1900), the domestic chore acquired a social dimension, as neighbors exchanged greetings and discussed neighborhood matters. *Library of Congress.*

people only rewarded immorality or laziness. Assistance, COS insisted, should be given only after careful investigation and should be temporary, only until the man or woman could secure work. Recipients of COS aid were expected to be moral, thrifty, and hard-working. Under COS influence, some cities chose to reduce their public relief efforts.

The Mixed Blessings of Machine Politics

Not everyone blamed the urban poor for their own distress and extracted promises of moral uprightness in return for help. In most cities, in the late nineteenth century, there emerged political organizations that extracted promises of another kind. Politicians built loyal followings among the residents of poor neighborhoods by addressing their most desperate needs in a direct and personal way. Instead of repentance they wanted gratitude from the poor.

Born in a poor Irish neighborhood of New York City, George W. Plunkitt left school at the age of 11. He chose a career in politics, eventually becoming a district leader of **Tammany Hall,** which dominated the city's Democratic party. In 1905, newspaper reporter William Riordon published a series of conversations with Plunkitt. In one, Plunkitt described how he kept the loyalty of the voters in his neighborhood.

Go right down among the poor families and help them in the different ways they need help. . . . It's philanthropy, but it's politics, too—mighty good politics. . . . The poor are the most grateful people in the world, and, let me tell you, they have more friends in their neighborhoods than the rich have in theirs. If there's a family in my district in want I know it before the charitable societies, and me and my men are first on the ground. . . . The consequence is that the poor look up to George W. Plunkitt as a father, come to him in trouble—and don't forget him on election day.

Plunkitt typified many big-city politicians across the country. Neighborhood **saloons** often served as social gathering places, especially for working-class men. Not surprisingly, would-be politicians chose to frequent neighborhood saloons—in fact, they often owned them—and tried to build a personal rapport with the voters they met there. They responded to the needs of the urban poor by providing a bucket of coal on a cold winter day, or a basket of food at Thanksgiving, or a job on a city crew. In return, they expected the people they assisted to follow their lead in politics. Political organizations based among working-class and poor voters, usually led by men of poor, immigrant parentage, emerged in nearly all large cities and experienced varying degrees of political success. Where they amassed great power, their opponents denounced the leader as a **boss** and the organization itself as a machine.

One of the earliest city bosses was **William Marcy Tweed,** whose name became synonymous with urban political corruption. Tweed entered New York City politics in the 1850s and became head of the Tammany Hall organization in 1863. By

Tammany Hall A New York political organization whose "machines" dominated city and sometimes state politics.

saloon A place common to middle-class and working-class neighborhoods where patrons could buy and drink alcoholic beverages.

boss Name applied to the head of urban political organizations that based their success on lower-income voters.

William Marcy Tweed New York City political boss who used the Tammany machine to maintain control over city and state government from 1860s until his downfall in 1871.

1868, this organization had nearly complete control of city and state government. Bribes to state legislators bought laws enlarging the power of the city to tax, borrow, and spend. Tweed and his associates built public support by spending tax funds on various charities, and they gave to the poor from their own pockets—pockets often lined with public funds or bribes. Under Tweed's direction, city government launched such major construction projects as buildings and improvements in streets, parks, sewers, and docks. Much of the construction was riddled with corruption. During the years between 1868 and 1871, the so-called **Tweed Ring** may have systematically plundered $200 million from the city, mostly by giving bloated construction contracts to businesses that gave a **kickback** to the Ring. In 1871, evidence of corruption led to Tweed's indictment and ultimately his conviction and imprisonment.

The machine's opponents in every city charged corruption, although most bosses were more cautious than Tweed. Plunkitt, who began his political career in the late 1870s, maintained that Tammany leaders in his day "didn't steal a dollar from the city treasury." Some urban political leaders nonetheless managed to accumulate sizable fortunes, sometimes through gifts or **retainers** from companies seeking franchises or city contracts, and sometimes through advance knowledge of city planning.

Perhaps the most important single function the bosses served was to centralize political decision-making. According to Martin Lomasney of Boston, "There's got to be in every ward somebody that any bloke can come to—no matter what he's done—to get help." An organization that could elect city officials and, through them, appoint most other city decision makers could help many voters to deal with the intricacies of city government. If a pushcart vender needed a permit to sell tinware, or a railroad president needed permission to build a bridge, or a saloon-keeper wanted to stay open on Sunday in violation of the law, the machine could help them all—if they showed the proper gratitude in return. Always, the machine cultivated its base of support among poor and working-class voters.

Combating Urban Poverty: The Settlement Houses

By the 1890s, in several cities, young, college-educated men and women chose to confront urban poverty differently from either the Charity Organization Societies or the political machines. These humanitarians took an environmental approach, seeking to assist the poor in dealing with the constraints of inadequate housing, diet, and sanitation. The settlement house idea, first practiced in London's Toynbee Hall in 1884, involved opening a house in the slums where idealistic university graduates lived among the poor and tried to help them. The concept spread to the United States with the establishment of a **settlement house** in New York in 1886.

Men staffed this first settlement house. In 1889, however, several women who had graduated from Smith College opened a New York settlement house. The same year, **Jane Addams** and Ellen

♦ This visiting nurse from the Henry Street settlement house is taking a shortcut between two New York tenement buildings in 1908. She has apparently gone up the stairs in one tenement, seeing families along the way, and is now crossing to the next building where she will work her way down the stairs. *Photograph by Jessie Tarbox Beals/Museum of the City of New York.*

Tweed Ring The political organization of William M. Tweed, accused of using bribery, kickbacks, and padded accounts to steal money from New York City.

kickback A sum of money illegally deduced from the payment made to a contractor and given "under the table" to the official who awarded the contract.

retainer A fee paid for advice or service from a professional.

settlement house Community centers operated by resident social reformers in slum areas in order to help poor people in their own neighborhoods.

Jane Addams Illinois social worker who sponsored child labor laws and was a leader in the settlement house movement. She won the Nobel Peace Prize in 1931.

Choosing to Help the Poor

Jane Addams

Jane Addams, born to a prosperous family, lived a life of leisure as a young woman, until she made the choice to devote her life to serving those less privileged than herself. This portrait was done in 1896 by Alice Kellogg Tyler, an artist at Hull House, the settlement house Addams established to serve the poor. Chicago Historical Society.

In her autobiography, *Twenty Years at Hull House,* Jane Addams devoted a full chapter to one difficult choice she faced as a young woman. Born in 1860 in a small town in Illinois, the youngest daughter of a bank president, Addams lived a childhood filled with higher expectations and more choices than were possible for most young women of her day. Her father believed women as well as men should go to college, and his wealth freed his daughters from the economic constraints that restricted most young women even if they wanted to attend college. In 1877, Addams entered Rockford Seminary, then transforming itself into a full-fledged women's college. There she met Ellen Gates Starr, who became a close friend and later an associate at Hull House.

Like many among the first generation of college women, Addams became a feminist at Rockford. In one of her college speeches, she defined her feminism in terms of expectations and choices: "She [the feminist of her day] wishes not to be a man, nor like a man, but she claims the same right to independent thought and action." After completing her studies at the seminary, she entered the Woman's Medical

Gates Starr opened **Hull House,** the first settlement house in Chicago. For many Americans, Jane Addams became synonymous with the settlement house movement (See Individual Choices: Jane Addams). Settlement house workers provided a wide range of assistance to slum families: cooking and sewing classes, public baths, childcare facilities, instruction in English, housing for unmarried working women. Some houses were sponsored by churches, others were secular. Church-sponsored houses blended the movement's environmental approach to alleviating poverty with a moral emphasis. Nearly all of them chose to minimize class con-

> **Hull House** Settlement house founded by Jane Addams and Ellen Gates Starr in Chicago in 1889 in order to improve community and civic life in the slums.

College in Philadelphia in 1881, but soon her own health problems caused her to drop out.

A college graduate, of independent financial means, Addams spent many of the next several years traveling in Europe. But in her visits to art galleries, museums, and concerts she found little purpose or satisfaction, and she began to consider ways to spend her life more productively. A Spanish bullfight pushed her to make the pivotal choice.

> We had been to see a bullfight rendered in the most magnificent Spanish style, where greatly to my surprise and horror, I found that I had seen, with comparative indifference, five bulls and many more horses killed. . . . I had not thought much about the bloodshed; but in the evening the natural and inevitable reaction came, and in deep chagrin I felt myself tried and condemned, not only by this disgusting experience, but by the entire moral situation which it revealed. It was suddenly made quite clear to me that I was lulling my conscience. . . . I had fallen into the meanest type of self-deception in making myself believe that all this was in preparation for great things to come.

She immediately determined that the very next day she would speak to her friend and traveling companion, Ellen Gates Starr, about this compelling new desire to seek a more productive life of service. Addams not only shared the decision but also invited Starr to join her—and she did. Before returning to the United States, Addams visited Toynbee Hall in London, to learn about its revolutionary approach to helping the urban poor.

Inspired by what she saw in England, Addams made the choice to commit her life to such endeavors. Upon her return to the United States, she and Starr set up Hull House in a working-class, immigrant neighborhood in Chicago. By then, Addams seems to have chosen not to marry, a choice made by about half of the first generation of college-educated women in the United States, who seem to have considered the combination of career and family impossible.

Addams lived at Hull House for the rest of her life, attracting a circle of impressive associates and making Hull House the best-known example of settlement work. Hull House offered a variety of services to the families of its neighborhood: a nursery, a kindergarten (childcare for preschool children), classes in child rearing, a playground and gymnasium. Unlike some settlement house workers, Addams chose to confront directly some of the political factors that constrained her neighborhood's efforts at self-improvement. She and other Hull House activists challenged the power of city bosses and lobbied state legislators, seeking cleaner streets, the abolition of child labor, health and safety regulations for factories, compulsory school attendance, and more. Her efforts brought her national recognition. A delegate to the convention that nominated Theodore Roosevelt for president as a Progressive in 1912, she seconded his nomination. Her opposition to war brought her the Nobel Peace Prize in 1931, four years before her death.

flict and to accomplish the realization that, as Jane Addams said, "the dependence of classes on each other is reciprocal." Some settlement house workers, including Addams, became forces for urban reform, promoting better education, improved public health and sanitation, and honest government.

Settlement houses spread rapidly, with some four hundred operating by 1910, staffed largely by middle-class, college-educated women. In fact, three-quarters of settlement workers were women, and the settlement houses became the first institutions to be created and staffed primarily by college-educated women. When universities began to offer courses of study in social work (first at Columbia, in 1902), women tended to dominate that field too. Women college graduates thus created a new, and uniquely urban, profession at a time when many other careers still remained closed to them.

Church-affiliated settlement houses often reflected the **Social Gospel,** a movement popularized by urban Protestant ministers who were concerned about the social and economic problems of the cities. One of the best known, Washington Gladden, of Columbus, Ohio, called for an "Applied Christianity," by which he meant the application to business relations of Christ's injunctions to love one another and to treat others as you would have them treat you. Another minister, C. S. Sheldon, wrote *In His Steps* (1896), the story of a fictional church congregation whose members chose to live for one year in full compliance with the teachings of Jesus. The book suggested that if all Americans did the same, both unemployment and the saloon would soon disappear. A similar, socially oriented approach appeared among some Catholics, especially those inspired by *Rerum Novarum,* a message from Pope Leo XIII urging support for labor.

New Americans from Europe

● Compare immigrants' expectations and choices regarding assimilation with those of nativists.

● What were the outcomes of immigrants' choices?

The United States has attracted large numbers of immigrants throughout its history. But the flood of immigrants that fed the burgeoning cities and industrial labor force during the period from the Civil War to World War I represents the highest level of immigration the nation ever experienced. Most immigrants at this time came from Europe, and many settled in cities. By 1910, in eighteen of the twenty-five largest cities, immigrants and their children made up more than half the total population. In New York and Chicago, the nation's two largest cities, more than three-fourths of the people were first- or second-generation immigrants.

A Flood of Immigrants

Though the numbers of immigrants varied from year to year, higher in prosperous years, lower in depression years, the trend was constantly upward. A quarter of a million foreigners arrived in 1865, two-thirds of a million in 1881, a million in 1905. In the 1870s and 1880s, most immigrants came from Great Britain, Ireland, Germany, and **Scandinavia.** After the depression of the mid-1890s, immigration rose far above any previous levels. After 1900, most

immigrants came from southern and eastern Europe, especially Austria-Hungary, Italy, and Russia. Austria-Hungary and Russia both contained peoples with many languages and cultures. The 3.4 million immigrants from those two empires who lived in America in 1910 included nearly a million Jews, 750,000 Poles, 353,000 Germans, 228,000 Hungarians, 222,000 Czechs, and smaller numbers of Slovaks, Slovenes, Croats, Serbs, Lithuanians, Latvians, and others (see Figure 18.2).

Immigrants left their former homes for a variety of reasons, but most chose to come to the United States because of its reputation as the "land of opportunity," where farm land was cheap or free, labor was in demand, and wages were high. They came, as one bluntly said, for "jobs," and as another declared, "for money." Some were also attracted by the reputation of the United States for toleration of religious difference and commitment to democracy. Some, too, were recruited by agents sent to Europe by the governments of sparsely populated western states or by railroad companies seeking buyers for their land grants. In fact, the reasons for coming to America varied from country to country, year to year, and person to person. Groups also exhibited distinctive patterns of settlement in the United States. A few examples will illustrate some of the forces that uprooted different groups of Europeans, and the settlement patterns they established in the United States.

In Ireland, a four-fold population increase between 1750 and 1850 combined with changes in agriculture to constrain possibilities for farming. Repeated failure of potato crops after 1845 produced widespread famine and starvation. For some, English oppression contributed to the choice to leave, and America's reputation for political and religious freedom attracted them. Irish immigrants, many desperately poor, arrived in their greatest numbers between 1847 and 1854, but Irish immigration continued at high levels until the 1890s. Ninety percent were Catholic. They settled initially in the cities of the Northeast, composing a quarter of the popula-

---

Social Gospel A moral reform movement of the late nineteenth century led by Protestant clergymen, who drew attention to urban problems and advocated social justice for the poor.

Scandinavia The region of northern Europe consisting of Norway, Sweden, and Denmark.

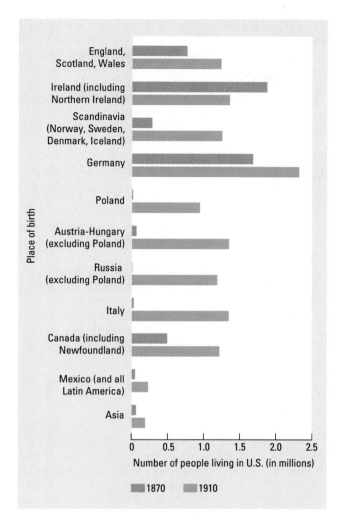

◆ **FIGURE 18.2 Place of Birth of the Foreign-Born Population, 1870 and 1910**   This figure compares the number of people born in other countries who were living in the United States in 1870 and 1910. Notice the large increases from eastern and southern Europe, but also notice that in 1910 the total number of immigrants from those regions was still smaller than the total from northwestern Europe and Great Britain. *Source:* U.S. Bureau of the Census, Department of Commerce, *Historical Statistics of the United States,* 2 vols. (Washington, D.C.: U.S. Government Printing Office, 1975), Series A-58, A-59, A-69, A-119.

tion in New York City and Boston as early as 1860. Although many Irish immigrants worked in the West, the Irish as a group remained very urban.

Throughout the late nineteenth and early twentieth centuries, Germans outnumbered all other immigrant groups in the United States, but most arrived before 1900. Rural overpopulation, changes in agriculture, and crop failures in the 1840s and 1850s all contributed to the desire to move. Religious and political persecutions affected some as well. Many German peasants chose to sell their holdings and, thus, arrived in the United States with some capital. Many expected to acquire farm land, and some succeeded, especially in the north central states. Most German immigrants, however, settled in towns and cities, especially in the Middle West. Germans were of diverse religious backgrounds, including Catholics (about a third of the total), Lutherans, Calvinists, Jews, and other groups.

In many ways, Scandinavian immigration followed the German patterns. The high point of Scandinavian immigration came in the 1880s and 1890s, when they accounted for 12 percent of the immigrants to the United States—and for about a quarter of the entire population of Sweden and Norway. Scandinavian farmers were pushed from the land by overpopulation and changes in agriculture as well as the by the hardships of farming the stony Nordic soil. Religious groups who challenged the state Lutheran church met persecution. Many Scandinavians settled in Minnesota, the Dakotas, Montana, and Nebraska, where many became farmers, and others landed in Washington state. Many Scandinavian Mormons went to Utah.

Italian immigrants illustrate a different situation. Residents of southern Italy and Sicily, especially landless farm laborers (the *contadini*), began to leave in significant numbers in the 1880s. Their numbers increased slowly through the 1890s until, between 1900 and 1915, Italians outnumbered any other single group of immigrants to the United States. Four out of five came from the overpopulated and depressed regions of southern Italy and Sicily. At first, many young men worked in construction or agriculture during summers and returned to Italy during winters. Eventually some chose to stay and sent for their families to join them. Large numbers of Italians made the cities of the Northeast their home and worked in construction and in textile and clothing factories. In California, Italians became prominent in farming, especially in growing grapes for wine making.

The migration of eastern European Jews reveals still a different pattern. In the late nineteenth and early twentieth centuries, one-third of the Jews living in eastern Europe left there, and 90 percent of those came to the United States. The largest number of eastern European Jews came from Russia, comprising nearly one-eighth of all immigrants

♦ This family from eastern Europe arrived in the United States in 1905. After 1890, immigrants came ashore at Ellis Island and were processed by the Immigration Service. For millions of immigrants, Ellis Island was their portal to America. *Courtesy George Eastman House.*

after 1900. **Overpopulation,** industrialization that reduced the demand for skilled craftsmen, and legal constraints on Jews all contributed to the choice to leave. Religious persecution, however, was undoubtedly the most important single reason for their migration. **Pogroms** occurred sporadically throughout these decades, notably in Russia in the early 1880s and from 1903 to 1906. This religious dimension marked Jewish immigration as different: whole communities chose to emigrate, including businessmen, professionals, and intellectuals as well as workers and farmers. They became the most urban of immigrant groups, settling initially in the cities of the Northeast, especially New York, where half of all eastern European Jews in the United States resided in 1914.

Although Czechs arrived in significant numbers in the 1870s, large numbers of other Slavic-speaking immigrant groups came only in the 1890s and after, accounting for more than a third of all European immigrants between 1900 and 1914. They emigrated primarily for economic opportunity. Poles, the largest single group, included some fleeing efforts by the German and Russian governments to suppress

Polish nationalism. Like the Irish, Poles were nearly all Catholic. Poles settled in New York and in the cities of the Midwest. By 1910, Chicago had the largest number of Polish immigrants, with significant concentrations in Milwaukee, Detroit, and Buffalo as well. Most Slavic-speaking groups tended to locate in urban and industrial areas.

An Ethnic Patchwork

Jacob Riis, himself a Danish immigrant, provided this striking description of Manhattan in 1890:

> A map of the city, colored to designate nationalities, would show more stripes than on the skin of a zebra, and more colors than any rainbow. The city on such a map would fall into two great halves, green for the Irish prevailing in the West Side tenement districts, and blue for the Germans on the East Side. But intermingled with these ground colors would be an odd variety of tints that would give the whole the appearance of an extraordinary crazy quilt.

Riis then pieced in some smaller parts of the ethnic patchwork by describing neighborhoods of Italians, African Americans, Jews, Chinese, Czechs, Arabs, Finns, Greeks, and Swiss.

Ethnic patchworks composed of distinctive immigrant communities were not limited to cities. The numbers of immigrants in the north central region points to some immigrants' success in becoming farmers, for there farmland was relatively cheap, either acquired through the Homestead Law or purchased from a railroad. Scandinavians, Dutch, Swiss, Czechs, and Germans were most likely to be farmers, but there were rural farming settlements of many groups. One woman recalled that, in the 1880s, when growing up on a farm in Nebraska, her family could attend Sunday church services in Norwegian, Danish, Swedish, French, Czech, or German. "There were, of course, American congregations also," she added. The chapter-opening map reveals concentrations of immigrants in the urban-industrial core region, or manufacturing belt, especially in urban areas.

---

overpopulation The growth of a population beyond the point where it can be supported by its environment.

pogrom Violent mob attacks on Jewish communities, often resulting in massacres.

These patterns of immigrant settlement obviously reflect the expectations, opportunities, constraints, and choices that various groups faced when they arrived in America. The British, Germans, Scandinavians, Czechs, and a few others came in the 1870s and 1880s, when good farmland could still be acquired relatively cheaply in the north central states. Many of them expected to become farmers and came with enough capital to get a start in agriculture. By contrast, fewer Irish had the necessary capital and so fewer came with the expectation of becoming farmers. Some of the post-1900 immigrants, especially among Italians and Poles, came with no expectation even of staying in America permanently. They wanted, instead, to work for a time and then return home with pockets full of their earnings. After 1890, farmland was more difficult to obtain—a significant constraint, whatever the immigrants' expectations. Newcomers at that point were more likely to find work in the rapidly expanding industrial sectors of the economy: mining, transportation, and manufacturing. Of course, there were many individual variations on these patterns. Some immigrants coming after 1890 certainly intended to become farmers and they succeeded. Many who came before 1890 intended to become farmers but ended up as industrial workers.

Hyphenated America

In the nineteenth century, most **old-stock Americans** assumed that immigrants should quickly learn English, become citizens, and restructure their lives and values to resemble those of old-stock Americans. Immigrants from Britain were often rapid assimilators, for they already spoke English and their religious values were similar to those of major old-stock Protestant denominations. Most immigrants, however, resisted rapid assimilation.

For most immigrants, assimilation took place over a lifetime or over generations. Most held fast to elements in their own culture at the same time that they took up a new life in America. Their sense of identity drew on two elements: where they came from and where they were now. Being conscious of their new identity as a German in America, or an Italian in America, they often came to think of themselves as **hyphenated Americans:** German-American, Italian-American, Polish-American.

On arriving in America, with its strange language and unfamiliar customs, many immigrants reacted by seeking people who shared their cultural values, practiced their religion, and, especially, spoke their language. Ethnic communities emerged throughout regions with large numbers of immigrants. These communities played significant roles in newcomers' transition from the old country to America. They gave immigrants a chance to learn about their new home with the assistance of those who had come before. At the same time, they could retain the values and behavior from their old country that they found most important without awkwardness.

Hyphenated America developed a unique blend of ethnic institutions, often unlike anything in the old country but also unlike those of old-stock America. Fraternal lodges based on ethnicity sprang up, and often provided not only social ties but also benefits in case of illness or death. Among these lodges were the Ancient Order of Hibernians (Irish), the Sons of Hermann (German), and the Sons of Italy. Social groups often included singing societies devoted to the music of the old country. Foreign-language newspapers were vital in developing a sense of identity that connected the old country to the new, for they provided news from the old country as well as from other similar communities in the United States.

For nearly every group, the church provided the single most important building block of ethnic group identity. In most of Europe, a state church was officially sanctioned to perform certain functions. In many countries, citizens were expected to belong to the state church. Though church membership was voluntary in America, religious ties often became stronger here, partly because churches provided such an important link to people with a similar language and cultural values. Protestant immigrant groups created new church organizations based on both theology and language. By 1900, for example, there were separate Lutheran churches speaking German, Norwegian, Swedish, Danish, Finnish, and Icelandic, and distinct Calvinist churches conducted in German, Dutch, and Welsh. Catholic parishes in immigrant neighborhoods often took on the ethnic characteristics of the community, with

---

old-stock Americans Term used by the Census Bureau to describe people who were born in the United States and whose parents were born in the United States.

hyphenated Americans Americans with a strong ethnic identity based on their ancestry who feel that they have been shaped by two cultures—Irish-American, for example.

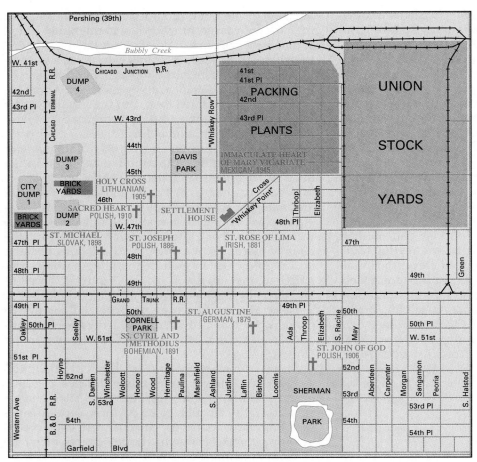

◆ **MAP 18.1 "Back of the Yards" Neighborhood** Many of the workers in Chicago's stockyards and packing plants lived in this area called "Back of the Yards." The founding dates for the neighborhood's Catholic parish churches point to the successive waves of immigrants who lived and worked there. The neighborhood also had several ethnically identifiable Protestant churches.

services conducted in that language and special observances transplanted from the old country. (Map 18.1 shows the ethnic Catholic parishes in the Chicago neighborhood where stockyard workers lived.)

Nativism

Many old-stock Americans (sometimes only a generation removed from immigrant forebears themselves) expected that immigrants would lay aside their previous identities, embrace the behavior and beliefs of old-stock Americans, and blend neatly into old-stock American culture. These expectations

came to be identified with the image of the **melting pot,** after the appearance of a play by that name in 1908. But the melting-pot metaphor rarely described the reality of immigrants' lives. Most immigrants *had* to change in some ways upon coming to a new land. But most did so slowly, over lifetimes, gradually adopting new patterns of thinking and behavior or modifying previous beliefs and practices.

> **melting pot** A phrase describing the vision of American society as a place where immigrants set aside their distinctive cultural identities and were absorbed into a homogeneous culture.

Few old-stock Americans appreciated or even understood the long-term nature of immigrants' adjustment to their new home. Instead of seeing the ways immigrants changed, many old-stock Americans saw only immigrants' efforts to retain their own culture. They fretted over the multiplication of foreign-language newspapers and feared to go into communities where they rarely heard an English sentence. Such fears and misgivings fostered the growth of *nativism:* the view that old-stock values and social patterns were preferable to those of immigrants. Nativists argued that only their values and institutions were genuinely American, and they feared that immigrants posed a potential constraint on those comfortable traditions.

American nativism was often linked to anti-Catholicism. Many immigrant groups included large numbers of Catholics, and inevitably many old-stock Americans came to identify the Catholic church as an immigrant church. The American Protective Association (APA), founded in 1887, noisily proclaimed itself the voice of anti-Catholicism. Its members pledged not to hire Catholics, not to vote for them, and not to strike with them. They recruited Protestant immigrants and Protestant African-Americans as well as old-stock white Protestants, claiming a half million members by 1894. They dominated the Republican party in parts of the Middle West, and, in a few instances, fomented mob violence against Catholics. Their rampages led to deaths in Butte, Montana, and Kansas City, Missouri.

Jews, too, faced religious antagonism. Beginning in the 1870s, increasing numbers of organizations and businesses began to discriminate against Jews, refusing to admit them. By the early twentieth century, such discrimination intensified. Some employers refused to hire Jews, many college fraternities and sororities refused to admit them, and **restrictive covenants** constrained them from buying homes in certain areas.

Labor organizations sometimes looked at unlimited immigration as a threat to jobs and wage levels—especially when economic depression brought widespread unemployment and wage reductions. Anti-Chinese sentiment among Pacific Coast unions contributed to passage of the Chinese Exclusion Act in 1882 (see page 532). The depression of the 1890s seemed to convince the American Federation of Labor to seek ways to cut the number of laborers entering the nation. In 1897, the AFL called for a literacy test as a way to reduce the influx of immigrants.

The rise of labor organizations and, especially, radical political organizations also contributed to anti-immigrant sentiment. By 1900 or so, a few employers had begun to argue that unions violated American traditions of individualism and represented foreign, un-American interests. Far more serious was the association of immigrants with radicalism, especially anarchism. Newspapers claimed that "there is no such thing as an American anarchist." In 1901, Leon Czolgosz, an American-born anarchist with a foreign-sounding name, assassinated President William McKinley. Congress promptly passed a bill barring anarchists from immigrating. After 1900, Socialist party candidates received strong support from voters in some areas heavily populated with immigrants, confirming to many a link between immigrants and radicalism.

The shift in the sources of immigration from northwestern Europe to southern and eastern Europe—bringing large numbers of Italians, Poles, and eastern European Jews—also contributed to the rise of nativism in the 1890s through the turn of the century. Anti-Catholicism and anti-Semitism combined with cruel stereotypes of Catholics and Jews to create a sense that these **new immigrants** were less-desirable than **old immigrants** from northwestern Europe. More of old immigrants were Protestant, and by 1900 many had managed to establish themselves as farmers, artisans, or merchants. By contrast, many of the new immigrants worked in factories or mines, or as unskilled laborers.

The arrival of significant numbers of new immigrants in the late nineteenth century coincided with a wave of sentiment that glorified Anglo-Saxons (Germanic ancestors of the English) and accomplishments of the English and English-Americans. Relying on Social Darwinism and its argument for the survival of the fittest (see pages 505–506), proponents of Anglo-Saxonism took alarm from statistics that showed old-stock Americans having fewer children than the new immigrants. Some voiced fears of

---

restrictive covenant   Provision in a property title designed to restrict subsequent sale or use of the property, often specifying sale only to a white Christian.

new immigrants   Newcomers to America from eastern and southern Europe, who began to arrive in large numbers in the 1880s.

old immigrants   Newcomers to America from Britain, Germany, Ireland, and Scandinavia, who came in waves that peaked during the years 1840–1880.

a "race suicide" in which Anglo-Saxons allowed themselves to be bred out of existence.

These concepts eventually came together in the thinking of Madison Grant, a wealthy New Yorker who read widely in physical anthropology and genetics. In 1916, he published *The Passing of the Great Race*, in which he claimed that all civilization had been created by Nordics—tall, blond, blue-eyed northern Europeans. Other Europeans, he argued, had proven themselves unable to create or protect civilization, and he feared their descendants might overwhelm American culture. Though based on selective research and faulty reasoning, his conclusions fed the anxieties of many old-stock Americans by seeming to confirm their prejudices. With Grant, nativism became blatant racism.

By the 1890s, these religious, economic, political, and racist strains began to result in demands that the government restrict immigration from Europe. Advocates of restriction focused initially on requiring immigrants to pass a literacy test before being admitted. Opposition came from immigrants' organizations and, usually, from employers seeking a larger supply of labor. Congress passed literacy measures in 1897 and again in 1913, but both met presidential vetoes. A third effort, in 1917, was vetoed by **President Woodrow Wilson,** but Congress overrode the veto and enacted the measure into law. It had little impact. Most immigrants, by then, were literate in their own language, and the law did not specify English. A more sweeping restriction came in the early 1920s (see page 721).

New South, Old Issues

- What were the expectations and choices of white and black southerners regarding race relations?
- What was the outcome?

The term **New South** is sometimes used to refer to the South after Reconstruction. More specifically, however, it refers to efforts by some southerners, notably Henry Grady, editor of the Atlanta *Constitution,* to promote a more diverse economic base, with more manufacturing and less reliance on a few staple agricultural crops. As some southerners developed expectations and made choices based on promoting economic change, their neighbors—white and black alike—grappled with the legacy of slavery, Civil War, and Reconstruction. One outcome to these efforts was a modest diversification in the southern economy. Another outcome was that, after

1890, white southerners created a social structure, centered on racial segregation, that persisted with little change for more than a half-century.

The New South

Following the Civil War, the state of southern transportation, especially railroads, posed a critical constraint on the region's economic growth. During the 1880s, however, southern railroads more than doubled their miles of track. In the 1890s, J. P. Morgan led in reorganizing southern railroads into three large and presumably efficient systems, dominated by the Southern Railway.

There had been efforts to establish cotton textile manufacturing in the South before the Civil War, but the 1880s stand out as the industry's boom era. The South counted 161 textile mills in 1880, and 400 in 1900. The new mills had more modern equipment and were larger and more productive than the mills of New England. By the 1890s, New England firms often chose to move their operations southward rather than compete with the products of southern mills. Southern textile mills had cheaper labor costs than those in New England, partly because they relied extensively on child labor. One official of the American Cotton Manufacturers' Association estimated that 70 percent of southern cotton-mill workers were under 21 years of age. Another estimated that 75 percent of the cotton spinners in North Carolina were under 14. A few other industries also developed in the South, including tobacco and cotton-seed oil processing. For the most part, however, these enterprises did little to transform the regional economy. Nearly all the new plants paid low wages and some had located in the South specifically to take advantage of its large pool of cheap, unskilled, nonunionized labor.

Of greater potential to transform part of the South was the iron and steel industry that emerged in northern Alabama. Dominated by the Tennessee Coal, Iron, and Railroad Company, the industry drew on coal from Tennessee and Alabama mines

---

President Woodrow Wilson Scholar and politician who established a reputation for reform and a strong progressive record as governor of New Jersey and who was elected president in 1812.

New South Term first used by southern journalist Henry Grady to promote the image of an industrialized South as the region recovered from the devastation of the Civil War.

◆ Much of the new southern textile industry was based on child labor. These children were photographed by Lewis Hines in 1908. *National Archives/Lewis Hines.*

and iron ore from northern Alabama. By the late 1890s, Birmingham, Alabama, had become one of the world's largest producers of pig iron. In 1897, the first southern steel mill opened in Ensley, Alabama, and soon established itself as a serious rival to those of Pittsburgh. In 1907, J. P. Morgan arranged the merger of the Tennessee Company into his United States Steel Corporation.

The turn of the century also saw the beginning of a southern oil industry near Beaumont, Texas, with the tapping of the Spindletop Pool—so productive the press labeled it "the world's greatest oil well." The center of petroleum production now shifted from the Midwest to Texas, Oklahoma, and Louisiana, where important discoveries also came in 1901. In addition to attracting attention from Standard Oil, the new discoveries prompted the growth or creation of new companies, notably Gulf and Texaco.

As the South sought to become industrialized, some southerners also tried to diversify the region's agriculture. In doing so, however, they ran up against the cotton textile and cigarette industries, both of which had located to the South in part to be near their raw materials. In the end, southern agriculture changed little: owners and sharecroppers farmed small plots, obligated by their rental contracts or **crop liens** to raise cotton or tobacco. In some parts of the South, farmers became even more dependent on cotton than before the Civil War. The Georgia upcountry, for example, produced almost

200 percent more bales of cotton in 1880 than in 1860. Fencing laws brought some long-term improvement of livestock. States adopted such laws to end the practice of allowing cattle and hogs to run free in unfenced, wooded areas. Fencing permitted more prosperous farmers to introduce new breeds, control breeding, and thereby improve the stock. But the law disadvantaged many small-scale farmers who now had to fence their grazing areas but could not afford to buy the new breeds.

Despite repeated backing for the idea of a New South by some southern leaders, and despite growth of some industry in the South, the late nineteenth century was also the time when the myth of the Old South and the so-called Lost Cause reached into nearly every aspect of southern life. Popular fiction and song, North and South, romanticized the pre–Civil War Old South as a place of gentility and gallantry, where "kindly" plantation owners cared for "loyal" slaves. The Lost Cause myth portrayed the Confederacy as a heroic, even noble, effort to retain the life and values of the Old South. Leading southerners—especially Democratic party leaders—promoted the Lost Cause myth. Hundreds of statues of Confederate soldiers appeared on courthouse lawns and gala commemorative events and organizations reflected devotion to the myth among many white southerners.

The Second Mississippi Plan and the Atlanta Compromise

Dreams of the **Old South** and the **Lost Cause** helped to fuel the politics of white supremacy that dominated the South after Reconstruction. So long as the Civil Rights Act of 1875 remained in place, African-Americans were, at least in theory, protected against discrimination in public places (see page 462). In the South, from the mid-1870s to the early 1890s, states prohibited racial intermarriage. Most communities required separate school systems, cemeteries, and hospitals, and nearly all churches

---

crop lien A claim against a growing crop, typically held by a store keeper as the price for extending credit.

Old South Term used to describe the antebellum, or pre–Civil War, South, especially by those who characterized the period as a time of gentility and gallantry.

Lost Cause Term used to describe the Confederate struggle in the Civil War, especially by white southerners who characterized it as a noble but doomed effort to preserve a way of life.

and other voluntary organizations were segregated. African-Americans, though they shared steamboat and railroad facilities with whites, were expected to ride only in second-class accommodations. Even so, in 1885, African-American lawyer T. McCants Stewart traveled in integrated first-class railroad cars and ate in integrated restaurants all through Virginia and the Carolinas. Segregation existed in many places, to be certain, but largely without force of law, enforced by local custom and the ever-present threat of violence. Restrictions on black political voting and office holding were also extra-legal, through coercion or intimidation.

Then, in the **Civil Rights cases** (1883), the United States Supreme Court ruled unconstitutional the Civil Rights Act of 1875. The court's decision specified that the "equal protection" of the Fourteenth Amendment applied only to state governments, not to individuals and companies. This meant that state governments were obligated to treat all citizens as equal before the law, but that private businesses need not offer equal access to their facilities. Given this court interpretation, southern lawmakers slowly began to require businesses to practice segregation. In 1887, the Florida legislature required separate accommodations on railroad trains. Mississippi passed a similar law the next year, and added separate waiting rooms. Louisiana required segregated railroad facilities in 1890, and four more states did the same in 1891. During those years, both social custom and local laws also began to specify greater racial separation in other ways too, but patterns remained inconsistent.

Mississippi whites took a bolder step in 1890, holding a state constitutional convention to eliminate political participation by African-Americans. Shrewdly, the new provisions did not mention the word *race*. Instead they specified payment of a **poll tax,** passing a literacy test, and other requirements for voting. Everyone involved understood that these measures were intended to disfranchise black voters. Those who failed the literacy test could still vote if they could understand a section of the state constitution or law after a local official read it to them. This "understanding" clause was widely accepted as granting local (white) officials discretion in deciding who passed the test. The outcome often was that the only illiterates who could vote were white. Most of the South followed this so-called Second Mississippi Plan (see pages 467–469 for the first Mississippi Plan) with great interest. Except for the poll tax, however, no other state moved immediately to imitate its provisions.

Then, in 1895, a black educator signaled his apparent willingness to accept disfranchisement and segregation for the moment. Born in 1856, **Booker T. Washington** had worked as a janitor while studying at Hampton Institute, a school that combined preparation for elementary school teaching with vocational education in agriculture and industrial work. Before long, Washington returned to Hampton as a teacher. In 1881, the Alabama legislature authorized establishment of a black normal school at Tuskegee. Washington became its principal and made Tuskegee Normal and Industrial Institute into a leading black educational institution.

In 1895, Atlanta played host to the Cotton States and International Exposition, one of the many spin-offs from the Chicago Columbian Exposition. Given the state of southern race relations, the exposition directors took an unusual step: they invited an African-American, Booker T. Washington, to speak at the opening ceremonies. They felt he could speak successfully to the mixed crowd of southern whites, southern blacks, and northern whites who would be present.

Washington did not disappoint the directors. In his speech, he seemed to accept an inferior status for blacks, at least for the present: "No race can prosper till it learns that there is as much dignity in tilling a field as in writing a poem. It is at the bottom of life we must begin, and not at the top." He also seemed to condone segregation: "In all things that are purely social, we can be as separate as the fingers, yet one as the hand in all things essential to mutual progress. . . . The wisest among my race understand that the agitation of questions of social equality is the extremest folly." He agreed that equal rights had to be earned, rather than belonging to all citizens: "It is important and right that all privileges of the law be ours, but it is vastly more important that we be prepared for the exercise of these privileges."

Civil Rights cases   A series of cases that came before the Supreme Court in 1883, in which the Court ruled that private companies could legally discriminate against blacks.

poll tax   A tax that many Southern states used as a prerequisite to voting in order to discourage blacks from taking part in the electoral process.

Booker T. Washington   A former slave, this educator founded and built the Tuskegee Institute into a leading black educational institution and urged blacks to accept segregation for the time being.

Booker T. Washington's message of racial self-help and accommodation to discrimination brought him national attention and made him the most powerful African-American of his day, with access to funds of northern philanthropists and influence over Republican political patronage. *Brown Brothers.*

The speech—soon dubbed the **Atlanta Compromise**—earned great acclaim for Washington, especially among whites, at Atlanta and across the nation. His message was one that southern whites wanted to hear: a black educator urged his race to accept segregation and disfranchisement in return for interracial peace and economic opportunity. Northern whites, too, were receptive to the notion that the South would work out its race relations by itself. Until his death in 1915, Washington held sway as the most prominent black leader in the nation, at least among white Americans. His message found a mixed reception among African-Americans, however. Some not only accepted, but even anticipated, his approach as the best that might be secured at the time. Others criticized his willingness to sacrifice black rights. Henry M. Turner, a bishop of the African Methodist Episcopal church in Atlanta, declared that Washington "will have to live a long time to undo the harm he has done our race." Some black newspapers criticized Washington's "sycophantic attitude." Privately, Washington never accepted disfranchisement and segregation as permanent fixtures in southern life, and he quietly financed some court challenges to segregation.

Separate But Not Equal

During the years following Washington's Atlanta speech, southern lawmakers continued to redefine the legal status of African Americans. State after state followed the lead of Mississippi and disfranchised black voters. Louisiana, in 1898, added the infamous **grandfather clause,** which specified that men prevented from voting by the various changes would temporarily be permitted to enroll to vote if their fathers or grandfathers had been eligible to vote in 1867 (before the Fourteenth Amendment extended the suffrage to African-Americans). The ruling reinstated whites into the electorate but kept blacks out. Although each state worked out its own variation on the pattern, the general model was the same everywhere: the state set up substantial barriers to voting and then carved holes through which only whites could squeeze.

A number of southern states added an additional barrier in the form of the white primary, which specified that political parties had the right to limit participation in the process by which they chose their candidates. Southern Democrats, who had long proclaimed themselves to be the "white man's party" or the party of white supremacy, quickly restricted their primaries and conventions to whites only. South Carolina took this step first, in 1896, and other states soon followed.

Southern lawmakers also began to extend segregation by law. The advocates of legally mandated segregation were given a major assist by the decision of the United States Supreme Court in *Plessy v. Ferguson* (1896), a case that involved a Louisiana law requiring segregated railroad cars. The Court ruled that "separate but equal" facilities did not violate the equal protection clause of the 14th Amendment. Southern legislators soon applied that reasoning to other areas of life, requiring segregation of

---

Atlanta Compromise Landmark speech given by Booker T. Washington in 1895, in which he encouraged blacks to accommodate to segregation and work for economic advancement in the available paths.

grandfather clause Provision in various southern state constitutions restricting suffrage to those whose fathers or grandfathers could vote in 1867, thus depriving blacks of the vote.

Plessy v. Ferguson Case in 1896 in which the Supreme Court upheld a Louisiana law requiring segregated railroad facilities on the grounds that "separate but equal" accommodations were constitutional.

everything from prisons to telephone booths—and especially places open to the public like parks and restaurants. Baltimore, in 1910, first established legally segregated residential neighborhoods and other southern cities soon followed.

Violence directed against blacks accompanied the new laws, providing an ever-present lesson in the consequences of resistance. From 1885 to 1900, when the South was redefining relations between the races, the region witnessed more than 2,500 deaths by lynching—almost one every two days. The victims were almost all African-Americans, with the largest numbers in the states with the most black residents: Mississippi, Alabama, Georgia, and Louisiana. Once the new order was in place, lynching deaths declined slightly, to about 1,100 during the years 1900 to 1915.

African-Americans fought against lynching in various ways, but especially by publicizing the record of brutality. One of the most prominent opponents of the horror was **Ida B. Wells.** Born in Mississippi in 1862, she attended a school set up by the Freedman's Bureau and worked as a rural teacher from 1884 to 1891. In 1891 in Memphis, Tennessee, she helped to found, and began to write for, the black newspaper *Free Speech.* She began to attack lynching, arguing that several local victims had been targeted as a means of eliminating successful black businessmen. In response, a mob destroyed her newspaper office. She moved north and, throughout the 1890s, spent most of her time crusading against lynching, speaking in the North and in England, and writing a pamphlet, *A Red Record* (1895).

African Americans also sought ways to resist disfranchisement and segregation. With the violent end of Reconstruction, some began to promote an exodus from the South. Many focused their attention on **Liberia,** the nation created in western Africa before the Civil War as a home for free blacks. Interest in Liberia swept the South, but few could afford to establish themselves in a new country. One shipload that left from South Carolina in 1878 met such financial difficulties as to discourage others. Senator Blanche K. Bruce of Mississippi argued against moving to Liberia both for African Americans' own good and for the good of Liberia, which, he felt, needed financial help to assist its modernization more than it needed "dependent, uneducated emigrants."

Other African Americans proposed leaving the South and taking advantage of homestead and railroad land in Kansas. Kansas Fever swept through

♦ During the 1890s, Ida B. Wells emerged as the leading opponent of lynching, refusing to be silenced even when threatened herself. She appealed to women especially, through the various women's organizations that developed in the late nineteenth century. *Schomburg Center for Research in Black Culture/New York Public Library/photo by Oscar B. Willis.*

the South in the late 1870s and early 1880s. A group of Kentuckians established Nicodemus, Kansas, as a black community in 1877. Well over 6,000 blacks from Louisiana, Mississippi, and Texas moved north in just a few months in mid-1879, and the total may have been as high as 20,000. Not all who left joined the "Kansas Exodus," but Kansas probably received the largest number. The 1890s saw another swell of interest in migration.

In the 1880s, interest began to grow in the creation of all-black communities as places where African-Americans could exercise their full political rights and enjoy full economic opportunities. Several communities were organized, most of them in

---

Ida B. Wells Reformer and journalist who crusaded against lynching and advocated racial justice and woman's suffrage. Upon marrying in 1895 she changed her name to Wells-Barnett.

Liberia A nation on the west coast of Africa founded through the efforts of the American Colonization Society and settled mainly by freed slaves between 1822 and the Civil War.

the South but others scattered from Whitesboro, New Jersey, to Allensworth, California. Between 1892 and 1910, African-Americans created some twenty-five all-black towns in Oklahoma. A few black leaders even hoped that Oklahoma might become an all-black state, but those hopes were dashed by adoption of the white Democratic primary in 1907 and other disfranchisement provisions in 1910.

New Patterns of American Social and Cultural Life

● How did Americans' expectations and choices contribute to important social and cultural trends during the late nineteenth and early twentieth centuries?

Many aspects of American society and culture underwent significant change in the late nineteenth and early twentieth centuries. The educational system, gender roles, sexual relationships, artistic expression, and popular participation in cultural and leisure activities all took on new features during the period.

Ferment in Education

The Gilded Age witnessed important changes in education, from kindergarten through the university. The number of kindergartens—first created outside the public schools to provide childcare for working mothers—grew from two hundred in 1880 to three thousand in 1900. In some areas, kindergartens began to be included in the public school system. Between 1870 and 1900, most northern and western states and territories established school attendance laws, requiring children between certain ages (usually eight to fourteen) to attend school for a minimum number of weeks each year, typically twelve to sixteen. In the 1880s, the New York City schools began to provide textbooks to students free of charge, and the practice expanded slowly, despite those who criticized it as "communism." By 1898, ten states required that textbooks be provided without charge.

Between 1870 and 1910, school enrollment among those aged 5 to 19 increased from 48 percent to 59 percent, with the largest increase at the secondary level. By 1890, high schools had extended to a fourth year (grades 9 through 12) everywhere but in the South. The high school curriculum changed significantly, adding courses on the sciences, civics, business, home economics, and skills needed by industry, such as drafting, woodworking, and the mechanical trades. The entire nation counted fewer than 800 high schools in 1878, but 5,500 by 1898, and the proportion of high school graduates tripled. From 1870 onward, women outnumbered men among high school graduates.

College enrollments also grew, with the largest gains in the new state universities created under the Land-Grant College Act of 1862. Even so, college students still came disproportionately from middle-class and upper-class families and rarely from farms. The college curriculum changed greatly, from a set of courses required of all students (mostly Latin, Greek, mathematics, rhetoric, and religion), to the elective system in which students focused on a major and chose courses from a long list of alternatives. New subjects included economics, political science, modern languages, and laboratory sciences. Many universities also began to offer courses on engineering, business administration, and teaching for elementary and secondary schools. In 1870, the curricula in most college still resembled those of a century before. By 1900, curricula looked more like those of today than like those of 1870.

Despite the growing female majority through the high school level, far fewer women than men marched in college graduation processions. Only one college graduate in seven was a woman in 1870, and this improved only to one in four by 1900 (see Figure 18.3). In 1879, fewer than half the nation's colleges even admitted women, although most state universities did so. In just twenty years, four-fifths of all colleges, universities, and professional schools enrolled women.

Regardless of such gains for coeducation, some colleges remained all-male enclaves, especially such prestigious private institutions as Harvard, Princeton, and Yale. Colleges exclusively for women began to appear after the Civil War, partly because so many colleges still refused to admit women and partly in keeping with the notion that men and women should occupy "separate spheres." The first, founded in 1861, was **Vassar College,** whose faculty of eight men and twenty-two women included Maria Mitchell, a leading astronomer and the first woman member of the American Academy of Arts and Sciences.

Vassar College   The first collegiate institution for women, founded in Poughkeepsie, New York, in 1861.

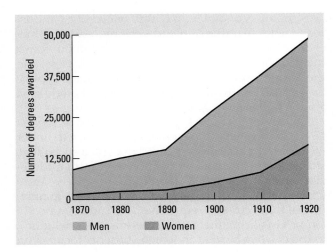

◆ **FIGURE 18.3 Number of First Degrees Awarded by Colleges and Universities, 1870–1920** This figure shows the change in the number of people receiving B.A., B.S., or other first college degrees, at ten-year intervals from 1870 to 1920. Notice that after 1890, the number of women increased more rapidly than the number of men. *Source:* U.S. Bureau of the Census, Department of Commerce, *Historical Statistics of the United States,* 2 vols. (Washington, D.C.: U.S. Government Printing Office, 1975), Series A-58, A-59, A-69, A-119.

Redefining Women's Gender Roles

Greater educational opportunities for women marked part of a change in social definitions of gender roles. Throughout the nineteenth century, most Americans defined women's social role in terms of the **cult of domesticity,** the notion that the proper place for a woman was in the home as wife and mother, and that in her wife-mother role she was guardian of the family, responsible for its moral, spiritual, and physical well-being. Advocates of domesticity conceded that women might also have important roles outside the home, but only in the church and the classroom. Beyond this, they contended that women ought not experience much of the world, claiming that business or politics, with their sometimes lax moral standards, might corrupt women. The best choice, they argued, was for women to occupy a **separate sphere,** immune from such dangers. The Illinois state supreme court even ruled, in 1870, that "God designed the sexes to occupy different spheres of action." Widely advocated in the pulpits and journals of the day, the concepts of domesticity and separate spheres proved most typical of white middle-class and upper-class

women in towns and cities. Farm women and working-class women (including most women of color) worked too hard and witnessed too much of the world to fit easily into the patterns of innocence and daintiness prescribed by advocates of domesticity.

The late nineteenth century saw an increasing number of challenges to domesticity. One challenge came through education, especially at colleges. As more and more women finished college, some chose to enter the professions. Important early successes came in medicine. In 1849, Elizabeth Blackwell became the first woman to complete medical school, and she helped to open a medical school for women in 1868. By the 1880s, some 2,500 women held medical degrees. About 3 percent of all physicians were women, more proportionately than in most of the twentieth century. After 1900, however, medical schools began to impose enrollment restrictions on women. Access to the legal profession proved surprisingly difficult. Arabella Mansfield was the first woman to be admitted to the bar, in 1869, but the entire nation counted only sixty practicing women attorneys ten years later. Most law schools refused to admit women until the 1890s. Other professions yielded very slowly to women seeking admission.

Professional careers attracted relatively few women, but many more middle-class and upper-class women, especially in towns and cities, became involved outside their homes through women's clubs or in reform activities. Women's clubs became popular among middle- and upper-class women in the late nineteenth century, claiming 100,000 members nationwide in the 1890s, and 800,000 by 1910. Crusader Ida Wells-Barnett actively promoted the development of black women's clubs. Such clubs often began within the separate women's sphere, as forums to discuss literature or art. But they sometimes led women out of their separate sphere and to involvement with reform, however. (Of course, women had publicly participated in reform before, especially the movement to abolish slavery.) In 1904, Sarah Platt Decker, president of the General Federation of Women's Clubs, bluntly proclaimed,

---

cult of domesticity The Gilded Age notion that women's activities were ideally rooted in domestic labor and the nurture of children.

separate sphere The notion that women were meant to pursue occupations having to do with family, church, or school and not those in such traditionally male fields as business or politics, which were considered too competitive and corrupt for women.

"**Dante** is dead. He has been dead for several centuries, and I think it is time that we dropped the study of his Inferno and turned our attention to our own." Female participation swelled the ranks and produced leaders for a variety of reform organizations, especially those with some link to domesticity—temperance, opposition to prostitution, and abolition of child labor. The **Women's Christian Temperance Union,** one of the most prominent, was formed in 1874.

Women's church organizations, clubs, and reform societies all provided experience in working together under the leadership of women, sometimes seeking changes in public policy. Through them, women developed networks of working relationships. These experiences and contacts contributed to the growing effectiveness of women's efforts to establish their right to vote, a movement that came to fruition in the early twentieth century (see page 581).

Emergence of a Gay and Lesbian Subculture

Challenges to domesticity and separate spheres mostly involved women seeking to redefine the society's gender roles. A quite different redefinition occurred at the same time, as burgeoning cities permitted development of gay and lesbian subcultures.

Homosexual behavior was illegal in all states and territories throughout the nineteenth and into the early twentieth centuries. At the same time, however, there was a wider variety of socially acceptable same-sex relationships than later. The concept of separate spheres and the related tendency for schools and workplaces to be segregated by sex meant that many men and women spent much of their time with others of their own sex. In many occupations, a worker worked closely with a partner, sometimes over long periods of time. Such partners—both male or both female—could speak of each other with deep affection without violating prevailing social norms. Many women expressed deep affection for other women. Such same-sex relationships may or may not have involved physical contact, although kisses and hugs— and sleeping in the same bed—were common expressions of affection, especially among women. Participants in such same-sex relationships did not consider themselves to be committing what the laws called "an unnatural act," and most of them also married partners of the opposite sex.

Same-sex relationships that involved genital contact, however, violated both the laws and the expectations of society. In rural communities, where most people knew each other, people physically attracted to those of their own sex seem to have suppressed such tendencies or to have exercised them very discreetly. The record of convictions for **sodomy** indicates, however, that some failed to conceal their activities. A few men and somewhat more women changed their dress and behavior, passed for a member of the other sex, and married someone of their own sex.

In the late nineteenth century, in the United States and in Europe, homosexuals and lesbians recognized that the burgeoning cities permitted an anonymity not possible in rural societies. They gravitated toward the largest cities and began to create distinctive **subcultures.** By the 1890s, one researcher reported that "perverts of both sexes maintained a sort of social set-up in New York City, had their places of meeting, and [the] advantage of police protection." Reports of regular meeting places for homosexuals—clubs, restaurants, steambaths, parks, streets—also came from Boston, Chicago, New Orleans, St. Louis, and San Francisco. Though most participants in these subcultures were secretive, some flouted their sexuality. In a few places, "drag balls" featured cross-dressing, especially by men.

In the 1880s, physicians began to study members of these emerging subcultures, and created medical names for them, including "homosexual," "lesbian," "invert," and "pervert." Earlier, law and religion had defined particular *actions* as illegal or immoral. The new, medical definitions emphasized not the actions but instead the *persons* taking the action. Some theorists in the late 1800s proposed that such behavior resulted from a mental disease but others concluded that homosexuals and lesbians were born that way.

The definition of *homosexual* was accompanied by definition of its opposite, *heterosexual.* As medical and legal definitions shifted from actions to persons, the larger society also witnessed a change in

---

Dante   Italian poet (1265–1321), best known for his *Inferno,* about a descent into hell.
Women's Christian Temperance Union   Women's organization founded in 1874, which opposed the evils of drink and supported reforms such as women's suffrage.
sodomy   Varieties of sexual intercourse prohibited by law.
subculture   A cultural subgroup unified by status, interests, or practices, which differentiates its members from the dominant culture on the basis of shared values or loyalties.

the nature of same-sex relationships. Once-acceptable behavior, including expressions of deep affection between heterosexuals of the same sex, became less common as individuals tried to avoid any suggestion that they were anything but heterosexual.

New Patterns in Cultural Expression: From Realism to Ragtime

Shortly after 1900, the director of the nation's most prominent art museum, the Metropolitan Museum of New York, observed "a state of unrest all over the world" in art, literature, music, painting, and sculpture. "And," he added, "I dislike unrest." Unrest, like it or not, meant change and Americans at that time witnessed dramatic changes in art, literature, and music—many of them directly influenced by the new urban, industrial, multi-ethnic society.

Walt Whitman's *Leaves of Grass,* first published in 1855 and reissued in revised and enlarged editions until his death in 1892, stands as a major work in world literature. His poetry gloried in democracy, in the scenes and rhythms of New York City, and in the faces and forms of working people. He dealt, too, with topics often considered inappropriate for public print, including intimate same-sex relationships and the human body:

> *Have you ever loved the body of a woman?*
> *Have you ever loved the body of a man?*
>
> *Do you not see that they are exactly the same to all*
> *in all nations and times all over the earth?*
>
> *If anything is sacred the human body is sacred,*
> *And the glory and sweet of a man is the token of*
> *manhood untainted,*
> *And in man or woman a clean, strong, firm-fibred*
> *body,*
> *is more beautiful than the most beautiful face.*

Emily Dickinson, whose poetry was first published in 1890, after her death, rejected the formal structures of most previous verse, and probed depths of anxiety and emotion.

> *I can wade Grief—*
> *Whole Pools of it—*
> *I'm used to that—*
> *But the least push of Joy*
> *Breaks up my feet*
> *And I tip—drunken—*

American novelists increasingly turned to a realistic—and sometimes quite critical—portrayal of life, rejecting the romantic idealism characteristic of the pre–Civil War period. The towering figure of the era was **Mark Twain** (Samuel Langhorne Clemens), whose *Huckleberry Finn* (1885) may be read at many levels, from a nostalgic account of boyhood adventures to profound social satire. In this masterpiece, Twain humorously reproduced the everyday speech of unschooled whites and blacks, poked fun at social pretensions of the day, scorned the Old South myth, and challenged prevailing, racially biased attitudes toward African-Americans. The novels of William Dean Howells and Henry James, by contrast, presented restrained, realistic portrayals of upper-class men and women. After 1890, Stephen Crane, Theodore Dreiser, and Frank Norris sharpened the critical edge of fiction. Crane's *Maggie: A Girl of the Streets* (1893) depicted how urban squalor could turn a young woman to prostitution. Norris's *The Octopus* (1901) portrayed the abusive power that a railroad could wield over people. Kate Chopin sounded feminist themes in *The Awakening* (1899), dealing with repression of a woman's desires.

As American literature moved toward realism during these years, most American painting was moving in the opposite direction. An important exception was Thomas Eakins, the most impressive painter working in the United States in the 1870s and 1880s. Although he received little recognition at the time, his work is now considered a major contribution to realism. American painting changed late in the century, but largely in response to French **impressionism,** which emphasized less an exact reproduction of the world and more the artist's impression of it. James Whistler, for example, studied and

---

Walt Whitman American poet whose free-verse poems were collected in *Leaves of Grass,* which celebrates the self, universal brotherhood, and the greatness of democracy.

Emily Dickinson American poet who lived her entire life as a recluse in her family home in Amherst, Massachusetts. Her intense and lyrical poems were not published until after her death.

Mark Twain Pen name of Samuel Clemens, an American author who drew on his childhood along the Mississippi River to create novels such as *The Adventures of Huckleberry Finn.*

impressionism A style of painting that developed in France in the 1870s, which emphasized the play of light on surfaces and attempted to convey the impression of observing nature directly.

♦ In this painting of 6th Avenue at 30th Street, done in 1906, John Sloan seems to glory in the diversity and excitement of life in New York City. He was a member of the Ash Can School of painters, who often focused on ordinary life in the cities, sometimes including unpleasant subjects. *"6th Avenue at 30th St., 1907" by John Sloan/Vivian and Meyer P. Potamkin Collection.*

worked in France, and his work showed impressionist influences. Mary Cassatt was the only American—and the only woman—to rank among the leaders of impressionism, but she lived and painted mostly in France. Among artists in the United States who adopted an impressionist style, one of the most prominent was Childe Hassam, who often presented urban landscapes. Attention to the city was also characteristic of work by Robert Henri and his associates in the early 1900s. Labeled the **Ash Can School** because of their preoccupation with urban poverty and ordinary people, they produced the artistic counterpart to critical realism in literature.

The Ash Can adherents faced a challenge, however, from artists influenced by the abstract approach then becoming prominent in France. In 1913, the most widely publicized art exhibit of the era permitted a half-million Americans in New York, Chicago, and Boston to view examples of this shocking new style. Known as the Armory Show, for its opening in New York's National Guard Armory, it presented art from the previous century. The works that drew the most attention, however, were pieces by the radical European innovators: Pablo Picasso, Henri Matisse, Marcel Duchamp, Wassily Kandinsky, and others. Critics and newspapers alike dismissed these modernists as either insane or anarchists. One reviewer scornfully suggested that Duchamp's *Nude Descending a Staircase* be retitled

"explosion in a shingle factory." The abstract, modernist style, however outrageous to some, was firmly established.

Just as with painting, many aspects of American music derived from European models. However, the most influential musician at the turn of the century was African-American composer Scott Joplin, who contributed significantly to **ragtime.** Born in Texarkana, Texas, in 1869, Joplin studied piano with a German-born music teacher and then traveled through African-American communities from New Orleans to Chicago. As he traveled, he encountered ragtime music and soon began to write his own. In 1899, he published *The Maple Leaf Rag* and soared to fame as the best-known ragtime composer in the country. Though condemned by some at the time as vulgar, ragtime formed a major element in the development of jazz (see below and pages 715–716). Joplin's African-American opera *Treemonisha* was first performed in Harlem in 1915.

The Origins of Mass Entertainment

Changes in transportation (the railroads) and communication (telegraph and telephone) combined with new forms of corporate organization and increased leisure time (especially among the middle class and skilled workers) to foster new forms of entertainment. Companies now organized entertainers into traveling groups and sent them from city to city, and even to small towns, to perform. Thus mass entertainment had its birth.

The American public had long enjoyed traveling dramatic and musical troupes, but in the Gilded Age booking agencies managed to schedule such arts and amusements into every corner of the country. Traveling groups of actors, singers, and other performers provided the entertainment mainstay in many areas throughout the late nineteenth and early twentieth century, performing everything from Shakespeare to **slapstick,** and from opera to

---

Ash Can School New York artists of varying styles who shared a dislike of academicism.

ragtime Music blending African rhythms and European form to create a unique style, popularized by Scott Joplin and others in the late nineteenth century.

slapstick A boisterous form of comedy marked by chases, collisions, and crude practical jokes.

♦ Professional baseball developed a strong popular appeal in the years after the Civil War, as most major cities acquired one or more teams. Thomas Eakins, who depicted these ballplayers at work in 1875, was the most impressive realist painter in the country at the time. *"Baseball Players Practicing" by Thomas Eakins 1875/Museum of Art, Rhode Island School of Design, Jesse Metcalf and Walter H. Kimball Funds. Photo by Cathy Carver.*

a few companies which scheduled bookings far in advance and arranged for performers and crews to ride from one location to the next by train.

Immediately after the Civil War, a quite different form of mass entertainment appeared: professional baseball. Teams traveled by train from city to city, and urban rivalries built loyalty among hometown fans. The formation of the National League in 1876 established a cartel, through which team owners (often drawn initially from the ranks of players) in the larger cities tried to monopolize the industry by excluding rival clubs and leagues from their territories and controlling the movement of players from team to team. Because African-Americans were barred from the National League and, after the 1880s, from all minor leagues as well, separate black clubs and Negro Leagues emerged. In the 1880s and 1890s, the National League successfully warded off challenges from rival leagues and also defeated a players' union. Not until 1901 did another league—the American League—successfully organize. In 1903, the two leagues merged into a new, stronger cartel, and staged the first World Series. (The Boston Red Socks beat the Pittsburgh Pirates.) As other professional spectator sports developed, they often adopted the patterns of organization, labor relations, and racial discrimination first established in baseball.

melodrama. In the late nineteenth century, these booking agencies helped develop the star system, in which each traveling company had one or two popular performers who attracted the audience and helped to make up for the inadequacies of the bit-players. Other traveling spectacles also took advantage of improved transportation and communication to establish regular circuits, including circuses and Wild West shows.

One of the most unusual traveling shows was the **Chautauqua,** a blend of inspirational oratory, education, and entertainment. By 1900, some seventy towns offered such programs, often a week or two in length, attracting hundreds, even thousands, of people from the surrounding countryside. At their high point, thousands of towns held annual Chautauqua assemblies and millions of people came to see and hear political figures, comedians, inspirational orators, opera, glee clubs, lectures on ancient history, string quartets, or magic-lantern shows on foreign countries. Large tents accommodated enthusiastic crowds, and electric lights permitted regular evening offerings. The programs were organized by

melodrama   A sensational or romantic stage play with exaggerated conflicts and stereotyped characters.

Chautauqua   Traveling shows offering educational, religious, and recreational activities, part of a nationwide movement of adult education that began in the town of Chautauqua, New York.

SUMMARY

E xpectations
C onstraints
C hoices
O utcomes

In the Gilded Age, as industrialization transformed the economy, urbanization and immigration challenged many established social patterns. In the midst of economic and social change, Americans developed new *expectations* and faced new *choices* about their relations with each other. The *outcomes* of their many individual *choices* marked a major re-definition of American social and cultural life.

As rural Americans and European immigrants sought better lives in the cities, urban America changed dramatically. New technologies in transportation and communication broke down old *constraints* on individual *choices* about where to live and work. The *outcome* was a new urban geography with separate retail, wholesale, finance, and manufacturing areas and residential neighborhoods defined by economic status.

Many urban Americans struggled under the *constraints* of poverty. To gain support from the poor, urban political machines, like Tammany Hall in New York City, helped them in various ways. Social reformers established settlement houses as a different way of addressing the problems of the urban poor.

Many Europeans emigrated because of economic and political *constraints* in their homelands and their *expectations* of better opportunities in America. Immigrants often formed separate communities, usually centered around a church. The flood of immigrants, particularly from eastern and southern Europe, spawned nativist reactions among some old-stock Americans, who sought to limit immigration.

Some southerners proclaimed the creation of a New South and promoted industrialization and a more diversified agricultural base. The *outcome* was mixed—the South did acquire significant industry, but the region's poverty was little reduced. After 1890, white southerners disfranchised African-Americans and extended racial segregation. Booker T. Washington emerged as the best-known African-American in the nation, and he accepted such *constraints*, at least for the moment.

Education underwent far-reaching changes, from kindergartens through universities. Challenged in part by the *expectations* of a generation of college-educated women, socially defined gender roles began to change as some women chose professional careers. Some also chose active roles in reform. Urbanization offered new *choices* to gay men and lesbians by permitting the development of urban subcultures. In response, medical specialists tried to define homosexuality and lesbianism. The new *expectations* and choices generated by an urban, industrial, multiethnic society contributed to critical realism in literature, new patterns in painting, and ragtime music. Urbanization and changes in transportation and communication also fostered the emergence of an entertainment industry.

SUGGESTED READINGS

Addams, Jane. *Twenty Years at Hull House* (1910, rpt. 1960).

Nothing can convey the complex world of Hull House and the striking personality of Addams as well as her own account.

McDonald, Terrence J., ed. *Plunkitt of Tammany Hall,* by William L. Riordon (1993).

McDonald has provided excellent context and editing for this classic account of Tammany's relationships to voters.

Mohl, Raymond A. *The New City: Urban American in the Industrial Age, 1860–1920* (1985).

An informative but concise introduction to nearly all aspects of the growth of the cities.

Clinton, Catherine. *The Other Civil War: American Women in the Nineteenth Century* (1984).

The section on the post-Civil War period surveys the subject, although so many recent works have appeared that no synthesis could cover them all.

Kraut, Alan M. *The Huddled Masses: The Immigrant in American Society, 1880–1921* (1982).

A helpful introduction to immigration, especially the so-called "new" immigration.

Higham, John. *Strangers in the Land: Patterns of American Nativism, 1860–1925* (1965).

This classic of American history played a major role in defining the contours of American nativism and still provides an excellent introduction to the subject.

Ayers, Edward L. *The Promise of the New South: Life After Reconstruction* (1992).

A recent and comprehensive survey of developments in the South during this period.

REGIONAL BASES OF POLITICAL PARTIES IN THE GILDED AGE After Reconstruction ended, competition between Republicans and Democrats settled into distinct regional patterns, as revealed by this map showing the party that carried presidential elections in each state.

CANADA

WASH. TERRITORY

OREGON

IDAHO TERRITORY

MONTANA TERRITORY

DAKOTA TERRITORY

MINNESOTA

WISCONSIN

MICHIGAN

ME.

VT.

N.H.

NEW YORK

MASS.

R.I.

CONN.

WYOMING TERRITORY

IOWA

PENNSYLVANIA

N.J

NEVADA

UTAH TERRITORY

NEBRASKA

ILLINOIS

IND.

OHIO

MD.

DEL.

CALIFORNIA

COLORADO

KANSAS

CHEROKEE OUTLET

MISSOURI

KENTUCKY

W.VA.

VIRGINIA

NORTH CAROLINA

ARIZONA TERRITORY

NEW MEXICO TERRITORY

OK. TERR.

INDIAN TERR.

ARKANSAS

TENNESSEE

SOUTH CAROLINA

MISS.

ALABAMA

GEORGIA

TEXAS

LOUISIANA

FLORIDA

PACIFIC OCEAN

MEXICO

Gulf of Mexico

ATLANTIC OCEAN

States consistently voting Republican, 1876–1888
States voting Republican 3 times out of 4
States voting Republican 2 times , Democratic 2 times
States voting Democratic 3 times out of 4
States consistently voting Democratic
Territories, 1876–1888

0   200   400 Km.
0   200   400 Mi.

Civil War ends

Grange formed

Reconstruction ends

Pendleton Act

1890 Populist movement begins

McKinley elected

Gold Standard Act

1865 1867   1877   1883   1890   1896 1900

1850   1900   1950   2000

Political Stalemate and Political Upheaval, 1868–1900

Parties, Voters, and Reformers

- What were people's expectations about the role of parties in the politics of the Gilded Age?
- What choices did the political parties offer voters?

Political Stalemate

- How did the stalemate that deadlocked politics from 1874 into the 1890s constrain both parties?

Agricultural Distress and Political Upheaval

- Why did farmers choose to take political action outside the major parties?
- What did they expect to accomplish?
- What was the immediate outcome?

Economic Collapse and Political Upheaval

- What choices did voters face in the 1896 presidential election?
- What were the long-term outcomes of that election?

INTRODUCTION

E xpectations
C onstraints
C hoices
O utcomes

In July 1892, a new political party, the People's party, met in Omaha to choose its candidates for president and vice president. Born in protest against the economic and political events of the previous quarter-century, the new party—soon called the Populists—drafted a platform that presented their understanding of the *outcome* of industrialization: material and moral ruin, political corruption, and exploited labor. The Populists also proclaimed their *choices* for dealing with the outcome of industrialization. They urged immediate federal action to rescue debtors, break up monopolies, and bring railroads under government ownership. They proposed reforms to increase the power of voters to control the government. And they made clear the expected *outcome* of these changes: that "oppression, injustice, and poverty shall eventually cease in the land."

Most Americans, however, held different *expectations* than did the Populists. Consequently, most were unwilling to create a vastly more powerful federal government, or to place severe *constraints* on the rights of property owners, or to entrust the federal government to self-proclaimed representatives of impoverished farmers and angry workers. In the end, those who gathered at Omaha failed to establish their new party as a major factor in American politics. The *outcome* of their efforts, however, was significant change in the nature of politics in the 1890s—and in the twentieth century as well.

Although most Americans rejected the Populists' remedies, few doubted that the *outcome* of industrialization, the economic development of the West, urbanization, and immigration had been a profound transformation of the nation's social and economic life during the years following the Civil War. During the same years, Congress and the president had grappled with complex choices affecting the South and Reconstruction, the future of American Indians, and the role of the federal government in developing the West. They also faced difficult *choices* regarding the nature of the federal civil service, a persistent federal budget surplus, federal tariff and monetary policies, and the relation between the federal government and the recently developed industrial corporations. However, a protracted stalemate gripped national politics from 1875 to 1896, *con-*

straining those who advocated political changes. Even so, during the same years, the economy was transformed through the activities of John D. Rockefeller, Andrew Carnegie, J. P. Morgan, and the corporate giants that they helped to create.

Throughout those years, men were *expected* to hold intense party loyalties—to the point that such loyalties were even seen as part of a man's gender role. (Nearly all women were *constrained* from voting throughout this period.) Despite such expectations, a few people *chose* to break with the major parties to call for changes in policies or in the nature of politics. Prominent among those demanding change were advocates of woman suffrage. But those who attracted the most attention at that time were a succession of organizations and parties that spoke out for impoverished farmers and that tried, largely unsuccessfully, to forge an alliance among all the disadvantaged—rural and urban, black and white.

The Populist party was the *outcome* of a quarter-century of agrarian radicalism that began shortly after the Civil War and was fueled by the economic misfortunes of farmers. Eventually the Populists *chose* to merge with the Democrats in support of the presidential candidacy of William Jennings Bryan in 1896. In the process, the Democratic party shed its deep commitment to minimal government and embraced a more activist role for the government in the economy as a way to protect and assist farmers, workers, and small businesspeople. In 1896, however, voters *chose* not Bryan but William McKinley, the Republican candidate for president, thereby endorsing a more conservative approach to the role of government in the economy. The long-term *outcome*, however, was the transformation of the very nature of American politics.

CHRONOLOGY

Politics

1865	End of the Civil War
1867	First Grange
1868	Grant elected president
1869	National Woman Suffrage Association and American Woman Suffrage Association formed Wyoming Territory adopts woman suffrage
1870	Utah Territory adopts woman suffrage Standard Oil of Ohio organized
1872	Crédit Mobilier scandal Grant reelected
1873	"Salary Grab" Act
1872–1874	Granger laws
1874	Whiskey Ring scandal
mid-1870s	Grange membership peaks
1876	Secretary of War Belknap impeached Custer dies in battle Disputed presidential election "Compromise of 1877" ends Reconstruction
1877	*Munn v. Illinois* Widespread railroad strikes
1878	Greenback party peaks Bland-Allison Act
1879	Standard Oil trust formed
1880	Garfield elected president
1881	Garfield assassinated Arthur becomes president
1883	Pendleton Act
1884	Cleveland elected president
1885	Mark Twain's *Huckleberry Finn* published
1886	*Wabash Railway v. Illinois* Knights of Labor peaks
1887	Congress disfranchises women in Utah Territory Interstate Commerce Act
late 1880s	Farmers' Alliances spread
1888	Harrison elected president
1888–1892	Australian ballot adopted
1889	North Dakota, South Dakota, Montana, and Washington become states Hull House opened
1890	National American Woman Suffrage Association Wyoming becomes a state, with woman suffrage Idaho becomes a state McKinley Tariff, Sherman Anti-Trust Act, and Sherman Silver Purchase Act "Force Bill" defeated Populist movement begins
1892	Homestead strike Cleveland elected president again
1893	Colorado adopts woman suffrage Nationwide depression Sherman Silver Purchase Act repealed
1894	Coxey's Army Wilson-Gorman Tariff Pullman strike
1895	Morgan stabilizes gold reserve
1896	Utah becomes a state, with woman suffrage Bryan's "Cross of Gold" speech McKinley elected president Idaho adopts woman suffrage
1897	Dingley Tariff
1900	Gold Standard Act

Parties, Voters, and Reformers

• What were people's expectations about the role of parties in the politics of the Gilded Age?

• What choices did the political parties offer voters?

Political parties dominated nearly every aspect of the political process from the 1830s until the early 1900s, more so than before or since. During those years, Americans expected that *politics* meant *party politics*, and that all meaningful political choices came through the structure of parties. An understanding of politics, therefore, must begin with an analysis of political parties: what they were, what they did, what they stood for, and what choices they offered to voters.

Parties and Patronage

The two major parties—Democrats and Republicans—had similar organizations and purposes. Both nominated candidates, tried to elect them to office, and attempted to write their objectives into law.

Throughout the years after the 1830s, nominations for office came from **party conventions,** which were gatherings of delegates chosen at earlier meetings. At the most basic level, neighborhood voters gathered in party caucuses to choose one or more delegates to represent them at party conventions. Conventions took place at local, county, state, and national levels, and at the level of congressional districts and various state districts too. Conventions featured many of the same procedures. The delegates listened to speech after speech glorifying their party and denouncing the opposition. They chose candidates for elective offices or chose delegates to yet another convention. And they adopted a platform, a written explanation of their position on important issues and their promises for policy change. Party leaders often worked out the intricate compromises that satisfied various sections of their party in informal settings—hotel rooms thick with cigar smoke and cluttered with whiskey bottles. Such behind-the-scenes negotiations reinforced the notion of political parties as all-male institutions into which no self-respecting women would venture.

After choosing their candidates, the parties conducted their campaign. Party organizers tried to identify all their supporters and worked to get them to vote on election day. Such party organizing was often done in places like saloons, where males congregated and women were barred. No wonder participation in party politics was regarded as gender-based. Candidates campaigned as party candidates, and campaigns were almost entirely party-oriented. Nearly every newspaper identified itself with a political party. A party expected to subsidize the newspapers that gave it support and, in return, expected both sympathetic treatment of its candidates and officeholders and slashing criticism of the other party. During the month or so before an election, local party organizations sponsored many activities: parades of marching clubs, free barbecues with speeches for dessert, and rallies capped by speeches that lasted for two hours or more. Such activities were intended to confirm the loyalty of the party's supporters, whip up enthusiasm for the candidates, and perhaps even attract new or undecided voters.

Once the votes were counted, the winners immediately turned their attention to appointing people to government jobs. In the nineteenth century, government positions not filled by elections were filled through patronage. That is, newly elected presidents or governors or mayors appointed their loyal supporters to the many government jobs at their disposal. Appointment to a government job was considered the appropriate reward for working hard during a campaign and getting party candidates elected. Everyone also understood that those appointed to such jobs were expected to return part of their salaries gratefully to the party. The use of patronage for party purposes was often called the spoils system after the statement by Senator William Marcy in 1831, "to the victor belongs the spoils." Its defenders were labeled **spoilsmen.**

Party loyalists inevitably seemed to outnumber patronage jobs, so competition for appointments was always fierce. In 1869, when Ulysses S. Grant took office as president, Congressman James A. Garfield grumbled that all "the adult population of the United States" seemed involved in "the rush for office," a spectacle he found "absolutely appalling." When Garfield himself became president in 1881, he was so overwhelmed with demands for jobs that he

---

party convention Party meeting to nominate candidates for elective offices and to adopt a political platform.

spoilsmen Defenders of the spoils system, under which the successful party in an election distributes government jobs to its supporters.

A NICE FAMILY PARTY.

◆ This cartoon depicts government patronage as "cake" and all party leaders as greedily clamoring for a piece, despite the president's efforts to maintain peace in his party. Such frantic scrambles eventually brought reform and the introduction of the merit system for appointing people to governmental positions. *Library of Congress.*

exclaimed in disgust, "My God! What is there in this place that a man should ever want to get into it?" Even after some reforms—precipitated in part by the assassination of Garfield—Secretary of the Interior L. Q. C. Lamar complained in the late 1880s that "I eat my breakfast and dinner and supper always in the company of some two or three eager and hungry applicants for office."

All government jobs were eagerly sought, but those most in demand involved purchasing supplies or otherwise handling government contracts. Purchasing and contracts themselves became another form of spoils, awarded to entrepreneurs who supported the party. This system invited corruption and the invitation was all too often accepted. In the 1890s, for example, a Post Office Department official pressured **postmasters** across the country to buy clocks from a political associate of his. Business owners competing to receive government contracts sometimes paid bribes to the officials who made the decisions. Opportunities were limited only by the imagination of the spoilsmen. In 1880, government funds were diverted from the Treasury Department to redecorate the home of the secretary of the treasury.

Some critics found a more fundamental defect in the system, beyond its capacity for corruption. By concentrating on patronage so much, politics ignored principles and issues and revolved instead around greed for government employment. George F. Hoar, a Republican congressman from Massachu-

setts, condemned this aspect of the spoils system when he complained in 1876 that some of his colleagues believed that the only way to win power was "to bribe the people with the offices," and that they used power primarily for "promotion of selfish ambition and the gratification of personal revenge." The spoils system had its defenders, however. George Plunkitt explained, "You can't keep an organization together without patronage. Men ain't in politics for nothin'. They want to get somethin' out of it." Plunkitt was describing the reality that all local party activists faced: given the enormous numbers of party workers needed to identify supporters, to mobilize voters, and to distribute ballots, politics required some sort of reward system.

The most persistent critics of the spoils systems were a group called "genteel reformers" by some historians but known as **Mugwumps** to their contemporaries. Centered in Boston and New York, these reformers were largely Republicans who enjoyed high social status. They traced many of the

---

postmaster   An official appointed to oversee the operations of a local post office.

Mugwumps   A group of Republicans who opposed political corruption and campaigned for reform in the 1880s and 1890s, sometimes crossing party boundaries to achieve their goals.

evils they saw in politics to the spoils system, and they argued that eliminating patronage would drive out the machines and opportunists. Only then, they insisted, would political purity and decency be restored. Instead of basing appointments on political loyalty, the Mugwumps advocated a **merit system** based on a job-seeker's ability to pass a comprehensive examination. Educated, dedicated civil servants, they believed, would stand above party politics and provide capable and honest administration.

Because the Mugwumps sometimes broke with their party, they drew the contempt of most party politicians. James G. Blaine, a leading Republican, called them "conceited, foolish . . . pretentious but not powerful." Other party politicians questioned the Mugwumps' manhood, reflecting the extent to which being a loyal party member was closely tied to men's gender role in the minds of many.

Republicans and Democrats

Beyond the hoopla, fireworks, and interminable speeches, important differences characterized the two parties in their campaign arguments, their actions at state and local levels, and the voters who chose between them. Some of those differences appear in the ways the two parties described themselves in their platforms, newspapers, speeches, and other campaign appeals.

Republicans asserted a virtual monopoly on patriotism by pointing to their defense of the Union during the Civil War and claiming that Democrats—especially southern Democrats—had proven themselves disloyal during the conflict. Trumpeting this accusation was often called "waving the bloody shirt," in reference to the action of a Republican congressman who displayed the bloodstained shirt of a northerner beaten by white supremacists. "Every man that shot a Union soldier," Robert Ingersoll, a Republican orator, repeatedly proclaimed, "was a Democrat." Republicans exploited the Civil War legacy in other ways too. Republicans in Congress voted to provide generous federal pensions to disabled Union Army veterans and to the widows and orphans of those who died. Republican party leaders carefully cultivated the Grand Army of the Republic (GAR), the organization of Union veterans, attending their meetings and urging them to "vote as you shot." Republican presidential candidates were almost all Union veterans, as were many state and local officials throughout the north.

Prosperity formed another persistent Republican campaign theme. Republicans pointed to the economic growth of the post-war era and boasted that it stemmed largely from their wise policies. They especially accused the Democrats of endangering prosperity by pledging to reduce the protective tariff. Many Republicans also claimed to be the party of decency and morality. Senator George Hoar of Massachusetts claimed in 1889 that all upright and virtuous citizens "commonly, and as a rule, by the natural law of their being, find their place in the Republican party." Republicans may never have committed themselves in favor of **prohibition,** but they were proud to be the party of sobriety and moderation. The 1888 national convention pronounced itself in favor of "all wise and well-directed efforts for the promotion of temperance and morality." Republican campaigners delighted in portraying as typical Democrats "the old slave-owner and slave-driver, the saloon-keeper, the ballot-box-stuffer, the Kuklux [Klan], the criminal class of the great cities, the men who cannot read or write," and they usually threw in Boss Tweed for good measure.

Where Republicans defined themselves in terms of what their party did and who they were, Democrats typically explained what they opposed. Most leading Democrats stood firm against what one called "governmental interference" in the economy, especially tariffs and land grants. The protective tariff, they claimed, protected manufacturers from international competition at the expense of consumers who paid higher prices. And land grants for railroads, they maintained, should provide farms for citizens, not subsidies for corporations. All in all, Democrats favored a strictly limited role for the government in the economy, a position much closer to **laissez faire** than that of the Republicans. Such a commitment to minimal government harked back to the days of Andrew Jackson, who equated governmental activism with privileges for a favored few.

---

merit system   Practice of hiring government workers based on their abilities and their scores on competency tests instead of through patronage.

prohibition   A legal ban on the manufacture, sale, and use of alcoholic beverages.

laissez faire   An economic doctrine under which the free-enterprise system operates with little government interference.

◆ Using an elephant to symbolize the Republicans and a donkey for the Democrats dates to the 1870s and the work of Thomas Nast, the most talented cartoonist of his age. At the time, Republicans often preferred an eagle or star and Democrats usually chose a rooster. *Library of Congress.*

Just as the Democrats opposed governmental interference in the economy, so too did they oppose governmental interference in social relations and behavior. In the North, especially in Irish and German communities, they condemned prohibition, which they called a violation of personal liberty. And they defended Catholics against the political attacks of groups like the American Protective Association (APA). In the South, Democrats rejected federal enforcement of equal rights for African-Americans, which they called a violation of states' rights. There, Democrats called for white supremacy and appealed to the memory of the Lost Cause.

On election day, each party tried to mobilize all its supporters and make certain that they voted. This form of political campaigning produced all-time records for voter participation. In 1876, more than 80 percent of the eligible voters cast their ballots. Turnout sometimes rose even higher (see Figure 19.1), although exact percentages were affected by poor record keeping or fraud. At the polling places, party workers distributed lists or "tickets" of their party's candidates, which voters then used as ballots. Voting was not secret until the 1890s. Before then, everyone could see which party's ballot a

voter deposited in the ballot box. Such a system discouraged voters from crossing party lines when they voted.

Most voters developed strong loyalties to one party or the other, often on the basis of **ethnicity,** or race, or religion. Nearly all Catholics and many Irish, German, and other immigrants supported the Democrats as the party that defended them against the APA, nativism, and prohibition. Poor voters in the disproportionately Catholic big cities usually supported the local machine, whether Democratic or Republican—but far more were Democrats. Most southern whites supported the Democrats as the party that opposed federal enforcement of black rights. After 1876, the Democrats dominated the South and usually the Border States and also found pockets of ethnic supporters throughout the North. The Democrats' opposition to the protective tariff attracted a few businessmen and professionals who

---

ethnicity   Ethnicity, or ethnic background, can include a shared racial, religious, linguistic, cultural, or national heritage.

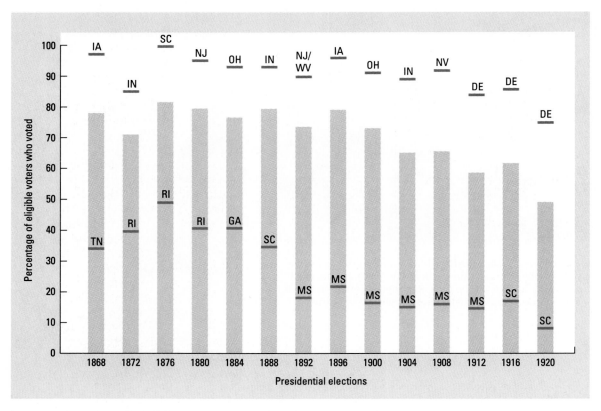

◆ **FIGURE 19.1 Voter Participation Rates for Presidential Elections, 1868–1920** This
figure indicates the proportion of eligible voters who actually cast ballots. The bar represents the national average, and the two states indicate the highest and lowest rates
of turnout. The average and the highs and lows all move downward after 1896. Notice
the impact of the "Mississippi Plan" of 1890. *Source:* U.S. Department of Commerce,
Bureau of the Census, *Historical Statistics of the United States,* 2 vols. (Washington, D.C.:
U.S. Government Printing Office, 1975), pp. 1071–1072.

favored more competition. The Democrats, all in all,
composed a very diverse coalition, one that held together primarily because its various components
could unite against government action on social or
economic matters.

Outside the South, most old-stock Protestants
voted Republican, as did most Scandinavian and
English immigrants. Most African-Americans supported the Republicans too, as the party of emancipation, as did most veterans of the abolition movement. So many Union veterans supported the
Republicans that someone suggested the initials
GAR stood for "generally all Republicans," not
"Grand Army of the Republic." Republicans al-

ways did well among the voters of New England,
Pennsylvania, and much of the Midwest. In the
Southwest, many Hispanics voted Republican. For
the most part, the Republicans composed a more coherent political organization than the Democrats,
united around a set of policies that involved federal
government action to encourage economic growth
and to protect black rights.

Grand Army of the Republic (GAR)   Organization
of Union Army veterans.

Challenging the Male Bastion: Woman Suffrage

In the masculine political world of the Gilded Age, men expected one another to display strong loyalty to a political party, but they considered women—who could not vote—to stand outside the party system. The concepts of domesticity and separate spheres dictated that women avoid politics, especially party politics. In fact, women did involve themselves in political struggles by taking part in a variety of reform efforts, even though they could not cast a ballot on election day. In the late nineteenth century, some bold women accelerated the efforts to secure full political participation through the right to vote.

The struggle for woman suffrage was of long standing. In 1848, Elizabeth Cady Stanton and four other women had organized the world's first Women's Rights Convention, held at Seneca Falls, New York. The participants drafted a Declaration of Principles that announced, in part, "It is the duty of the women of this country to secure to themselves their sacred right to the elective franchise." Stanton became the most prominent leader in the struggle for women's rights, especially voting rights, from 1848 to her death in 1902. After 1851, Susan B. Anthony became her constant partner in these efforts. They achieved important successes in convincing lawmakers to modify laws that discriminated against women, but all their labor could not change the laws that limited voting to men. During those years, women increasingly participated in public affairs: movements to abolish slavery, mobilize support for the Union, improve educational opportunities, and more.

In 1866, Stanton and Anthony unsuccessfully opposed inclusion of the word *male* in the Fourteenth Amendment. Later, in 1869, they formed the **National Woman Suffrage Association (NWSA),** its membership open only to women. The NWSA sought an amendment to the Constitution as the only sure route to woman suffrage. They built alliances with other reform and radical organizations and worked to improve women's status. For example, members pressed for easier divorce laws and birth control (which Stanton called "self-sovereignty") and promoted women's unions. The **American Woman Suffrage Association (AWSA),** organized by other suffrage advocates in 1869, kept a narrower focus, concentrating on winning the right to vote on a state-by-state basis and avoiding all is-sues that distracted from that goal. For twenty years, these two organizations led the suffrage cause, disagreeing not on the final goal but on the way to achieve it. They merged in 1890, under Stanton's leadership, to become the National American Woman Suffrage Association.

The first victories for suffrage came in the West. In 1869, in Wyoming Territory, the territorial legislature extended the **franchise** to women and the Republican governor approved. At the time, about 7,000 men but only 2,000 women lived in the territory, and the men may have hoped to attract more women by enfranchising them. Women exercised the suffrage without controversy in Wyoming, voting for local and territorial officials (residents of a territory could not vote for president) and also serving on juries and as public officials. In 1889, when Wyoming asked for statehood, many congressmen balked at admitting a state that permitted women to vote. When the Wyoming legislators learned that they might have to give up women suffrage to become a state, they replied, "We will remain out of the Union a hundred years rather than come in without the women." Congress finally voted to approve Wyoming statehood in 1890. In 1893, Colorado voters (all male) approved woman suffrage, making it the first state to adopt woman suffrage through a popular vote.

Utah Territory, where men and women had nearly equal numbers, adopted woman suffrage in 1870. Mormons formed the majority in Utah Territory, but there were many Mormon women and relatively few non-Mormon women. By enfranchising women, Mormons strengthened their voting majority and may have hoped, at the same time, to silence the critics who claimed that polygamy degraded women. However, in an act aimed primarily at the

National Woman Suffrage Association   New York–based women's suffrage organization led by Elizabeth Cady Stanton and Susan B. Anthony; it accepted only women and worked for such related issues as unionizing female workers.

American Woman Suffrage Association   Boston-based women's suffrage organization led by Lucy Stone, Julia Ward Howe, and others; it welcomed men and worked solely to win the vote for women.

franchise   The right to vote; another word for *suffrage*.

♦ This sketch of women voting in Cheyenne, Wyoming Territory appeared in 1888. In 1869, Wyoming became the first state or territory to extend the suffrage to women. This drawing appeared shortly before Wyoming requested statehood, a request made controversial by the issue of woman suffrage. *Library of Congress.*

Mormons, Congress outlawed polygamy in 1887 and disfranchised the women in Utah Territory at the same time. Not until Utah became a state, in 1896, did Utah women regain the vote. In neighboring Idaho, where Mormon influence was also strong, male voters approved woman suffrage in 1896.

Several states began to permit women limited voting rights, especially on matters outside party politics, such as school board elections and school bond issues. These concessions perhaps reflected the widespread assumption that women's gender roles included child rearing. By 1890, women could vote in school elections in nineteen states, and on bond and tax issues in three. Despite valiant efforts

by suffrage advocates, however, not one state passed a suffrage proposal between 1896 and 1910.

Structural Change and Policy Change

The genteel reformers and the advocates of woman suffrage both challenged basic features of the political system of the Gilded Age. These were only two of many different, although occasionally overlapping, groups organized to seek measures rarely addressed by the major parties: abolition of the spoils system, woman suffrage, prohibition, the **secret ballot,** regulation of business, an end to child labor, a monetary policy that did not disadvantage debtors, and more. Most groups pushing for political change called themselves reformers, meaning that they wanted to change the form of politics. Most reforms fall into one of two categories—structural change and policy change. *Structural change,* or *structural reform,* refers to efforts to change the structure of political decision making. Structural issues include the way in which public officials are chosen. For example, the convention system, voting, the selection of government employees are all matters of structure. Those seeking to eliminate the spoils system and substitute the merit system, therefore, addressed one element in the structure of politics. The eligibility to vote was another. Woman suffrage was therefore a structural change, and so was disfranchisement of African-American voters in the South. Structural issues can even involve basic constitutional matters: the Electoral College as the means for choosing the president, the method of electing members of the Senate, the nature of the president's veto power.

Policy issues, by contrast, have to do with the way that the government uses its power. The debate over federal economic policy in the Gilded Age provides an array of contrasting positions. Many Democrats favored laissez faire, believing that the outcome of federal interference in the economy was to create a privileged class. Most Republicans, by contrast, followed a policy of *distribution,* meaning that

---

secret ballot Voting method in which individual votes are marked in private, so no one knows how an individual is voting.

they wanted to distribute benefits to companies and individuals (land, tariff protection) in order to encourage economic growth. The Grangers (discussed later) favored *regulation:* they wanted the government to enforce basic rules governing economic activity, in this case, by prohibiting pools and rebates and setting maximum rates. The Greenbackers (also discussed later) wanted to use **monetary policy** to benefit debtors—or, as they would have put it, to create a monetary policy that would not benefit lenders.

Groups seeking change may find little in common with each other, or they may overlook differences to form alliances with other groups. The genteel reformers, for example, generally opposed regulation and woman suffrage. One key distinction between the National Woman Suffrage Association and the American Woman Suffrage Association was that Stanton and Anthony's NWSA often welcomed political alliances with groups like the Greenbackers who endorsed woman suffrage. The AWSA, fearing that such alliances would lose more support for suffrage than they gained, preferred to keep a narrow focus on the suffrage issue.

Some groups combined structural and policy proposals. The tiny Prohibition party, for example, wanted government to eliminate alcohol but they also favored woman suffrage because they assumed that most women voters would oppose alcohol. In this instance, they promoted a structural reform, woman suffrage, not just for its own sake but also in order to accomplish a policy reform, prohibition of alcohol.

One important structural change received widespread support from many political groups, and many states chose to adopt it soon after its first appearance. The **Australian ballot**—printed and distributed by the government not by political parties, listing all candidates of all parties, and marked in a private voting booth—was adopted by the first states in the late 1880s but spread rapidly and was in use in most states by 1892. This reform carried important implications for political parties. No longer would it be difficult for voters to cross party lines and vote a **split ticket.** No longer would party activists see which party's ballot a voter dropped into the ballot box. No longer was it necessary for a party to have an army of campaign workers to distribute ballots. The switch to the Australian ballot and the subsequent adoption of the merit system for the civil service marked the first significant efforts to limit parties' power and influence.

Political Stalemate

● How did the stalemate that deadlocked politics from 1874 into the 1890s constrain both parties?

During the Civil War and early years of Reconstruction, the dominant Republicans had created far-reaching changes in the very nature of the federal government. Specifically, they adopted major alterations in the nature of citizenship, relations between the federal government and the states, and the relation between the federal government and the economy. Most of the economic policies established in the 1860s persisted with little change for more than a generation. Notably, the protective tariff and the policy of using the public domain to encourage rapid economic development both involved an active federal role to stimulate economic development and diversification. Thus, federal economic policy during these years should not be described as pure laissez faire, even though there was little regulation, restriction, or taxation of economic activity.

A political **stalemate** made it difficult for either party to put through major changes in federal policy between 1875 and 1896. Instead, politics often revolved around scandal and spoils rather than issues of policy. The few significant new laws tended to be relatively uncontroversial, to draw support from both parties, and to have little immediate effect on the economy or society. When Republicans briefly broke the stalemate, in 1889 and 1890, by passing nearly their full party agenda, they found themselves rejected by the voters.

Formula for Stalemate

Competition between Republicans and Democrats at a national level was very close during the years 1874 to 1896. Table 19.1 presents the popular vote

---

monetary policy A government course of action that seeks to influence the economy through methods such as controlling interest rates or printing money.

Australian ballot A printed ballot prepared by government officials and bearing the names of all qualified candidates of all parties, which is distributed to voters at the polls and marked in privacy.

split ticket A ballot cast by an individual who has voted for candidates of more than one political party.

stalemate A deadlock, in which neither side can advance.

TABLE 19.1 POPULAR AND ELECTORAL VOTE FOR PRESIDENT, 1872–1896

	Popular Vote (totals)		Popular Vote (percentage)		Electoral Vote	
	Demo-cratic	Repub-lican	Demo-cratic	Repub-lican	Demo-cratic	Repub-lican
1872	2,843,446	3,596,745	44.0%	55.6%	66[a]	286
1876	4,284,020	4,036,572	51.0	48.0	184	185
1880	4,414,082	4,453,295	48.0	48.5	155	214
1884	4,879,507	4,850,293	48.5	48.2	219	182
1888	5,537,857	5,447,129	48.7	47.9	168	233
1892[b]	5,555,426	5,182,690	46.1	43.0	277	145
1896	6,492,559	7,102,246	46.7	51.1	176	271

[a]In 1872, the Democratic presidential candidate, Horace Greeley, died between election day and the day when electoral votes were counted. Sixty-six electoral votes were cast for various Democrats, including three for Greeley, which were not officially tabulated. Seventeen electoral votes were not cast.
[b]In 1892, the Populist party received 1,029,846 popular votes, equal to 8.5 percent, and 22 electoral votes.

Source: Series Y 79–83, U.S. Department of Commerce, Bureau of the Census, *Historical Statistics of the United States,* 2 vols. (Washington: U.S. Government Printing Office, 1975), p. 1073.

and electoral vote for president during these years. Although the parties' popular vote was usually virtually identical, the electoral vote appears more decisive. But those figures are deceiving. In the elections of 1880, 1884, and 1888, New York state cast its electoral votes for the winning candidate. Had that one state voted for the other candidate, he would have won. In each of those elections, a different choice by one or two voters out of every hundred in New York would have changed the result there and for the nation.

Although most presidential elections during these decades were very close, the Republicans usually won. Democrats carried only two of the eleven presidential elections between 1860 and 1900. However, from the end of Reconstruction in 1877 until 1895, the two parties had nearly equal numbers in the Senate and House of Representatives. The Democrats held a slim majority in the House in most years, and the Republicans usually held sway by a similar margin in the Senate. What was the outcome of this situation? The Republican majority in the Senate could block any proposal by a Democratic president, and the Democratic majority in the House of Representatives could block any proposal by a Republican president.

Other factors also made significant changes in policy unlikely. The struggle between Andrew Johnson and the congressional radicals had tipped the balance of power from the presidency to the Congress, and after Johnson came a succession of presidents who did little to challenge that dominance. In fact, both parties held attitudes toward the presidency that made it improbable that a president would seek a leadership role in policy. John Sherman, a highly influential Republican who spent nearly fifty years in government—in the House, the Senate, and the cabinet—stated a view that most Republicans probably shared: the executive "should be subordinate to the legislative department." Outside of his responsibilities for war and diplomacy, the president was expected only to administer the laws and to point out to Congress, usually in an annual report delivered by a messenger, any problems requiring legislation. In the late nineteenth century, virtually no one expected the president to be a major policy initiator. And no president was.

The Grant Administration: Spoils and Scandals

The dogged determination that made Ulysses S. Grant a winning general failed to make him a great, or even a satisfactory, president. Grant seems never to have grasped the potential for leadership in the office of president. Congress had taken control of domestic policymaking during Andrew Johnson's troubled presidency, and Grant accepted that situation.

When making appointments, all too often Grant named his friends or acquaintances to federal posts for which they possessed no particular qualifications. He proved unable to form a competent cabinet and faced constant turnover among his executive advisers. Although many of his appointees seemed to view their positions as little more than the spoils of party victory, Grant himself was untouched by scandal. He did choose a highly capable secretary of state, Hamilton Fish, and he eventually found in Benjamin Bristow a secretary of the treasury who vigorously combated corruption.

Congress also supplied its full share of scandal. Visiting Washington in 1869, young Henry Adams was surprised to hear a member of the cabinet bellow, "You can't use tact with a Congressman! A Congressman is a hog! You must take a stick and hit him on the snout!" All too many members of Congress behaved in a way that confirmed such a cynical view. In 1868, before Grant became president, several prominent congressional leaders had become stockholders in the **Crédit Mobilier,** a construction company created by the chief shareholders in the Union Pacific Railroad. The Union Pacific officers awarded to Crédit Mobilier a very generous contract to build the railroad. Thus the company's chief shareholders paid themselves handsomely for constructing their own railroad. To protect this arrangement from congressional scrutiny, the company sold shares cheaply to key members of Congress. Purchasers included many leading Republicans, two of whom later became vice president. Revelation of these arrangements in 1872 and 1873 scandalized the nation. No sooner did that furor pass than Congress voted itself a 50 percent pay raise and made the increase two years retroactive. Only after widespread public protest did Congress repeal its "salary grab."

In 1875, Treasury Secretary Bristow took the lead in fighting widespread corruption in the collection of whiskey taxes. A **Whiskey Ring** of federal officials and distillers, centered in St. Louis, had conspired to evade payment of taxes. The 230 men indicted included several of Grant's appointees and even his private secretary. Despite the evidence, Grant could not believe his close associates were guilty. He helped his secretary avoid conviction and forced Bristow to resign. The next year, William

Belknap, Grant's secretary of war, resigned shortly before he was impeached for accepting bribes in connection with an appointment to a potentially lucrative position in Indian Territory.

Hayes, Garfield, and Arthur: The Politics of Faction

Repeated exposures of corruption led the embarrassed Republicans, in 1876, to nominate **Rutherford B. Hayes,** whose reputation was unblemished. All in all, Hayes helped to restore the reputation of the Republican party after the scandals of the Grant administration. In Congress, however, Hayes found few allies when he tried to modify the patronage system. In the House of Representatives, the Democrats had a majority and were interested in rolling back parts of Reconstruction but not in reforming the civil service. In the Senate, Republicans held the majority but key positions were occupied by committed spoilsmen. Hayes undercut his own arguments when he gave jobs to his own supporters, thereby alienating both the spoilsmen and those who favored civil service reforms. He did not seek reelection in 1880.

The Republicans were badly divided in 1880. James G. Blaine of Maine, a powerful leader in Congress and spokesman of a faction called the Half-Breeds, sought the presidential nomination. Roscoe Conkling of New York, who led the other major Republican faction, the **Stalwarts,** promoted the candidacy of former president Grant. Both factions grew largely out of personal connections rather than issues of policy—although Conkling's faction was more deeply committed to the spoils system and

---

Crédit Mobilier   Company created to build the Union Pacific Railroad. It sold shares cheaply to congressmen who approved federal subsidies for railroad construction. The scandalous deal was uncovered in 1872–1873.

Whiskey Ring   Distillers and revenue officials in St. Louis who were revealed in 1875 to have defrauded the government of millions of dollars in whiskey taxes, with the collusion of federal officials.

Rutherford B. Hayes   Reform governor of Ohio elected president in 1876 on the Republican ticket.

Stalwart   Faction of the Republican party led by Roscoe Conkling, which was committed wholeheartedly as their name implies to the spoils system.

Blaine's faction included many of the more respected Republican leaders. The convention deadlocked for 36 ballots before compromising on **James A. Garfield,** an able congressman from Ohio (with its crucial electoral votes). Born in a log cabin, Garfield grew up in poverty, became a minister, college president, and lawyer before the Civil War, then became the Union's youngest major general. The Democrats nominated Winfield Scott Hancock, a distinguished Civil War general with little political experience. The campaign dealt less with policy issues than with Garfield's minor role in the Crédit Mobilier scandal and with the religion of Hancock's wife. Elizabeth Hoxworth Hancock, a Catholic, drew attacks from nativists who charged that, if Hancock became president, she would turn the White House over to priests. Garfield won by a tiny margin—48.5 percent to 48.0 percent.

Long known as a compromiser, Garfield hoped to work with both Half-Breeds and Stalwarts. He respected Blaine and chose him for secretary of state. Conkling then jealously tried to maintain his standing by demanding the right to name appointees to many positions. Garfield refused to accept all of Conkling's proposals, especially for the most crucial offices. At first Conkling prepared to do battle with the president, but the discovery that Stalwart spoilsmen had committed widespread fraud in the Post Office Department instead pushed Conkling into resigning his Senate seat. Garfield's firm stand marked an important victory for presidential control over appointments rather than control by powerful senators.

On July 2, 1881, four months after taking office, Garfield was shot while walking through a Washington railroad station. His assassin, Charles Guiteau, was a mentally unstable religious fanatic who called himself "a Stalwart of the Stalwarts" and claimed he had acted to save the Republican party. Garfield clung to life for several months but died in September.

The vice president who stepped into the presidency was **Chester A. Arthur.** A close ally of Conkling, Arthur was known as a dapper dresser and capable administrator. Defying his previous reputation as a loyal Stalwart, Arthur proved that the presidential office can improve the stature of its occupant. He favored Stalwarts in his handling of patronage, but he also maintained Garfield's appointments that had so antagonized Conkling. He prosecuted the Stalwarts involved in post office corruption and even suggested that Congress should reform the spoils system. After the 1882 elections,

however, Arthur faced a Democratic majority in the House, with little interest in promoting the program of a Republican president. Also in 1882, he learned that he had Bright's disease, a fatal kidney condition that produced fatigue and depression. He told only his closest family and friends of his illness.

In 1883, Congress passed and Arthur signed the **Pendleton Act,** named for its sponsor, George Pendleton of Ohio. This measure finally established the merit system for government employment. In their successful efforts to secure passage of the Pendleton Act, civil service reformers took advantage of the widespread—but incorrect—belief that Garfield's assassin had acted out of disappointment at being denied a patronage position. Passed with bipartisan support, the act provided for competitive examinations as the basis for appointment to **classified positions,** which were removed from the patronage system. Initially only 15 percent of federal positions were classified, but the law authorized the president to add positions to the list. The person who held an office when it was first classified was protected from removal on political grounds, so presidents used the law to protect their own patronage appointees. Once those people retired, however, their replacements came through the merit system. In this way, positions were gradually withdrawn from the patronage system. By 1901, the law applied to 44 percent of federal employees. The Pendleton Act laid the basis for the current civil service system, and most state and local governments slowly came to adopt merit systems too.

Cleveland and the Democrats

In the end, Arthur proved more capable than anyone might have predicted. Given his failing health, however, he exerted little effort to win his party's

---

James A. Garfield   Ohio congressman who was chosen as a compromise candidate at the 1880 Republican convention, elected twentieth president of the United States and shot to death only four months after taking office.

Chester A. Arthur   Stalwart Republican elected vice president in 1880, who took over the presidency on Garfield's death.

Pendleton Act   1883 law that created the Civil Service Commission and the merit system for government hiring and jobs.

classified position   Government job filled through the merit system instead of by patronage.

nomination in 1884. Blaine—charming and quick-witted—had been rejected by his party in 1876 and 1880, but he now won the Republican nomination. The Democrats nominated Grover Cleveland of New York state, who had gone quickly from election as mayor of Buffalo in 1881 to election as governor in 1882. As governor he earned a reputation for integrity and political courage, particularly by attacking Tammany Hall. Many Irish voters, who made up a large component in Tammany, liked Blaine even though they were Democrats.

The campaign quickly turned nasty. Many Mugwumps disliked Blaine and embarrassed him by revealing an old letter of his regarding allegations that he had profited from pro-railroad legislation. Blaine supporters gleefully trumpeted the fact that Cleveland had avoided military service during the Civil War and had once fathered a child outside marriage. Democrats chanted, "Blaine, Blaine, James G. Blaine! The continental liar from the state of Maine." Republicans shouted back, "Ma! Ma! Where's my pa?" The election hinged on New York state, where Blaine expected to cut deeply into the usually Democratic Irish vote. A few days before the election, however, Blaine heard a preacher in New York City call the Democrats the party of "rum, Romanism [Catholicism], and rebellion." Blaine ignored this insult to his Irish Catholic supporters until newspapers blasted it the next day. By then the damage was done. Cleveland won New York state by a tiny margin, and New York's electoral votes gave him victory.

Cleveland won with support from many who opposed the spoils system. He chose not to dismantle it, but he did insist on demonstrated ability in those he appointed to office. Deeply committed to minimal government and to restraining spending, Cleveland vetoed 414 bills—most of them granting pensions to individual Union veterans—between 1885 and 1889. This amounted to twice as many vetoes as all previous presidents put together. Cleveland provided little leadership regarding legislation but did approve several important measures produced by the Democratic House and Republican Senate, including the Dawes Severalty Act (see page 533) and the Interstate Commerce Act.

The Interstate Commerce Act grew out of political pressure from farmers and small businesses that led several states to regulate railroads. Illinois acted first, in 1871, creating a railroad and warehouse commission to set maximum rates companies could charge. Iowa and Wisconsin passed laws regulating railroad freight rates in 1874 (called Granger laws,

see page 592). In 1877, in *Munn v. Illinois,* the Supreme Court held that businesses with "a public interest," including warehouses and railroads, "must submit to be controlled by the public for the common good." In *Wabash Railway v. Illinois* (1886), however, the Supreme Court put severe limits on the states' power to regulate railroad rates involving interstate commerce.

In response to the *Wabash* decision as well as to continuing protests over railroad rate discrimination, Congress passed the Interstate Commerce Act in 1887, creating the **Interstate Commerce Commission (ICC),** the first federal regulatory commission. The law prohibited pools, rebates, and different rates for short and long hauls, and required that rates be "reasonable and just." The prohibitions in the act proved to be largely unenforceable, however, partly because of vague provisions in the law itself and partly because the ICC had little real power. As a result, the impact of the ICC was negligible until the Hepburn Act of 1906 strengthened its muscle.

Cleveland considered the nation's greatest problem to be the persistent federal budget surplus. After the Civil War, the tariff usually generated more income than the country needed to pay federal expenses (see Figure 19.2). Throughout the 1880s, the surplus was often more than $100 million per year. Worried that the surplus encouraged wasteful spending, Cleveland demanded in 1887 that Congress cut tariff rates on raw materials and necessities. He hoped not only to reduce federal income but also, by lowering prices on raw materials, to encourage companies to compete with recently developed monopolies.

Cleveland's action provoked a serious division within his own party. So long as Democrats did not have responsibility for the tariff, they freely criticized Republican policies. Now, urged to act by their own party chief, they failed. Cleveland himself exerted little leadership, leaving the initiative to congressional leaders. House Democrats treated it as an exercise in party politics, creating a bill with little resemblance to Cleveland's proposal but with ample benefits for the South. Republicans in the Senate responded with amendments aimed at southern economic interests. But when Congress adjourned without voting on the bill, Cleveland's call for tariff reform came to nothing.

Interstate Commerce Commission (ICC)   Federal commission established in 1877 to oversee railroads.

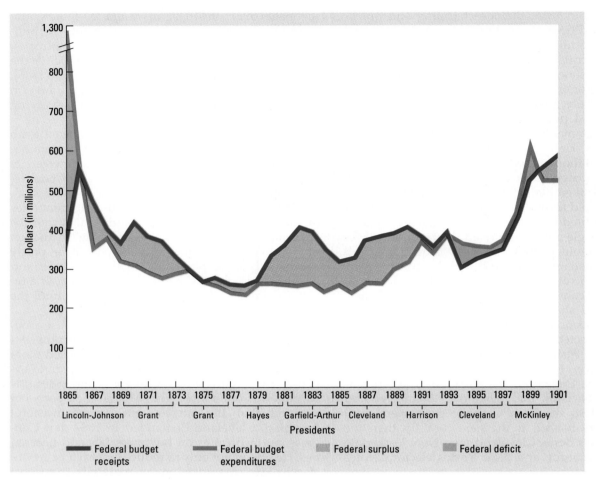

◆ **FIGURE 19.2 Federal Receipts and Expenditures, 1865–1901** The surplus usually shrank during economic downturns (the mid–1870s and mid–1890s) and grew in more prosperous periods (1880s). During the Harrison administration, however, the surplus virtually disappeared although the economy remained generally prosperous, reflecting efforts to reduce income and increase expenditures. *Source:* U.S. Department of Commerce, *Historical Statistics of the United States* (Washington, D.C.: U.S. Government Printing Office, 1975), p. 1104.

In the 1888 presidential election, the Democrats renominated Cleveland, but he backed off from the tariff issue and refused to campaign actively. The Republicans nominated **Benjamin Harrison,** senator from Indiana and yet another former Civil War general. Known as thoughtful, responsible, and cautious, Harrison nonetheless impressed many visitors as cool and distant. The Republicans launched a vigorous campaign, focused on the virtues of the protective tariff. They raised unprecedented amounts of campaign money by systematically approaching business leaders on the tariff issue, and they used the money to print more campaign materials than ever before. Republicans also attacked Cleveland's vetoes of pensions for Union veterans, especially when speaking to audiences of Union veterans.

> **Benjamin Harrison** Indiana Republican senator who was elected president in 1888 on a platform of high protective tariffs and a strengthened navy.

The effects of a Tariff exclusively for Revenue as laid down in the Democratic Plat-form and which the Democratic Congressmen tried to enact last winter at Washington.

The effects of Protection to American Industries as Guaranteed by the Republican Party and Platform.

Democratic Free-Trade Means low wages, children in rags and ignorance
If you are satisfied with this picture vote for Cleveland and Hendricks.
And G. M. WOODWARD, the Free Trader.

Republican Protection Means good wages, happy homes and education for your children.
If you prefer this picture vote for Blaine and Logan.
And O. B. THOMAS.

◆ Republicans circulated this cartoon in 1884, claiming that the Democrats' proposed tariff reform would threaten wage levels and endanger little children, but Republicans' commitment to the protective tariff would protect wage levels and make families more secure. *Museum of American Political Life/photo by Steve Laschever.*

Harrison won in the electoral voting but received fewer popular votes than Cleveland: 47.9 percent to Cleveland's 48.7 percent. As important for the Republicans as their narrow presidential victory, however, were the majorities they secured in both the House and Senate. In 1889, Republicans stood poised to create new public policies.

Harrison: Ending the Stalemate?

With Harrison in the White House and Republican majorities in both houses of Congress, the Republicans set out to do a lot, and to do it quickly. When the fifty-first session of Congress opened in 1889, Harrison worked more closely with Republican congressional leaders than any president in anyone's memory. Democrats in the House of Representatives tried to delay action, but Speaker Thomas B. Reed—an enormous but quick-witted man—announced new rules, designed to speed up House business.

The Republicans' first major task was tariff revision. They wanted to cut the troublesome federal surplus without reducing protection. Led by William McKinley of Ohio, the House Ways and Means Committee drafted a tariff that moved some items to the free list (notably sugar, a major source of tariff revenue) but raised tariff rates on other items, sometimes so high as to be prohibitive. The House passed the **McKinley Tariff** in late May and sent it on to the Senate.

On July 2, the House approved the Federal Elections Bill, nicknamed the "Force Bill" by its Democratic opponents. Proposed by Representative Henry Cabot Lodge, the bill would have permitted federal supervision over congressional election procedures to prevent disfranchisement, fraud, or violence. The bill did not single out the South, but everyone knew that the South was its target. The measure passed the House and went to the Senate, where approval by the Republican majority seemed likely.

The Senate, in the meantime, was laboring over two measures named for their sponsor Senator John Sherman of Ohio: the **Sherman Anti-Trust Act** and the Sherman Silver Purchase Act. The Anti-Trust Act, actually the work of several Republican senators close to Harrison, was potentially the most significant measure passed that year. Congress approved it with only a single dissenting vote, and Harrison signed it on July 2. Created in response to growing public concern about the trusts and mo-

---

McKinley Tariff Tariff passed by Congress in 1890 that sought not only to protect established industries but by prohibitory duties to create new industries; it soon became extremely unpopular.

Sherman Anti-Trust Act 1890 law authorizing the federal government to prosecute any "combination" "in restraint of trade"; because of adverse court rulings, it initially proved ineffective as a weapon against monopolies.

◆ This trinket from the 1888 presidential campaign is a balance scale with Benjamin Harrison on the left and Grover Cleveland on the right. This scale permitted the voter to demonstrate which candidate was the light-weight and which was the more substantial (heavy). *Collection of David J. and Janice L. Frent.*

nopolies that had developed during the 1880s, the law declared that "every contract, combination in the form of trust or otherwise, or conspiracy, in restraint of trade or commerce among the several states, or with foreign nations, is hereby declared to be illegal." Republicans thereby demonstrated their responsiveness to public concern about monopoly power, and the United States became the first industrial nation to attempt to regulate business combinations. In fact, however, the law proved difficult to interpret or enforce, and antitrust legislation had little immediate adverse impact on any companies.

The tariff and election bills still awaited Senate approval. Harrison wanted them passed as a party package. Some Senate Republicans, however, feared that a Democratic filibuster against the election bill would prevent passage of either measure. Finally a compromise emerged: if Republicans put off the elections bill until later, the Democrats would not delay the tariff bill. The deal was made. Over the strong protests of a few New England Republicans, the rest of their party sacrificed African-Americans' voting rights to gain the revised tariff. (Some seventy more years were to pass before Congress finally acted to protect black voting rights in the South.) Harrison signed the McKinley Tariff on Oc-

tober 1, and the revised tariff soon produced the intended result: it reduced the surplus by cutting tariff income.

The McKinley Tariff and Sherman Anti-Trust Act were only the tip of the iceberg. In ten months the Republicans had passed what one Democrat called "a raging sea of ravenous legislation." Among the record number of new laws were a major increase in pension eligibility for disabled Union Army veterans and their dependents, admission to statehood of Idaho and Wyoming, creation of territorial government in Oklahoma, and appropriations that laid the basis for a modern navy. After the long federal stalemate, Republicans hoped that they had broken the political logjam.

Agricultural Distress and Political Upheaval

● Why did farmers choose to take political action outside the major parties?

● What did they expect to accomplish?

● What was the immediate outcome?

Curiously enough, the first strong winds of political change blew not in the industrial cities, but in the farm communities of the Great Plains and the South and in the mining camps of the Rocky Mountain region. In the early 1890s, those regions witnessed the birth of a new political party, the People's party or **Populists.**

The Farmers' Complaints

During the Gilded Age, farmers became more and more dependent on the national railroad network, on fertilizer and labor-saving equipment, on grain and cotton brokers, and on sources of credit in distant cities. At the same time, some of them began to feel more and more helpless in the face of the great concentrations of economic power that seemed to be taking over their lives.

Perhaps most troubling to farmers were the prices they received for their crops. Those prices fell steadily during the years after the Civil War, follow-

Populists Members of the People's party, who held their first presidential nominating convention in 1892 and called for reforms such as the eight-hour workday, direct election of senators, and the secret ballot.

ing the fluctuations of supply and demand in this country and around the world. Some farmers, however, denied that prices were falling solely because of overproduction. They looked at the poor residents of the great cities and concluded that overproduction could hardly exist so long as multitudes went hungry and dressed in rags. Farmers also condemned the monopolistic practices of grain and cotton buyers. **Commodity markets** in distant cities determined the prices farmers received for crops. Most agricultural regions were served by only one buyer, who paid the prices set by those markets, especially in Chicago and New York. When farmers came to sell their crops, they had no choice but to accept the price that was offered. They needed cash to pay their debts, few of them had the resources to store their crops for sale later, and no other buyer would offer a better deal. Farmers knew, too, that the bushel of corn they sold for ten cents in Kansas in October brought three or four times that amount in New York in December, and they blamed commodity brokers for their misery.

Farmers had accomplished much of the post–Civil War agricultural expansion on borrowed money, and the impact of falling prices was magnified by debt. For example, suppose a farmer borrowed $1,000 for five years in 1881, when corn sold for 63 cents per bushel at best. The borrowed $1,000 would, therefore, have been equivalent to 1,587 bushels of corn. In 1886, when the loan came due, corn sold for 36 cents per bushel, requiring 2,777 bushels to repay the $1,000. And this increase of nearly 50 percent was over and above the annual interest on the loan. Further, prices of most farm supplies and consumer goods did not fall as rapidly as crop prices. As a result, farmers raised more and more each year just to pay their mortgage and buy necessities. Given the relation between supply and demand, the more they raised, the lower prices fell. The historian Carl N. Degler compared the farmers' plight to that of Alice in Wonderland: they had to run faster and faster just to stay in the same place.

The railroads also angered farmers, who relied on trains to carry their crops to market and to bring supplies in return. The railroads, farmers claimed, were greedy monopolies that charged as much as possible because small rural shippers had no choice but to pay. It sometimes cost four times as much to ship freight in the West as to ship the same amount over the same distance in the East. Farmers also protested the railroads' involvement in politics. Railroads dominated state nominating conventions and state legislatures and distributed free passes to politicians and influential members of local communities in return for favorable treatment. One North Carolina farm editor, in 1888, bemoaned the railroads' power in his state: "Do they not own the newspapers? Are not all the politicians their dependents? Has not every Judge in the State a free pass in his pocket? Do they not control all the best legal talent in the State?"

Crop prices and railroad practices were only two of the farmers' complaints. They protested, too, that local bankers charged 8, 9, or 10 percent interest—or even more—in western and southern states, compared to 6 percent or less in the Northeast. They argued that federal monetary policies contributed to falling prices and thereby compounded their debts. Southern farmers, especially, condemned the tariff for protecting manufacturers against competition from foreign imports, creating artificially high prices on manufactured goods the farmers had to buy. The tariff, however, did nothing for farmers who had to sell their crops abroad and remained, therefore, at the mercy of international cotton and grain markets. Farmers complained that the giant corporations that made farm equipment and fertilizer overcharged them. Even local merchants drew farmers' reproach for charging too much. In the South, where all these problems combined with the sharecrop and crop-lien systems, many farmers were so deeply in debt they saw little prospect of ever getting out.

Grangers, Greenbackers, and Silverites

Following the Civil War, farmers joined organizations that they hoped would provide them some relief. Oliver H. Kelley formed the first, a lodge for farm families, in 1867. Kelley called it the Patrons of Husbandry and gave it a secret ritual modeled on the Masons. Usually known as the **Grange,** the new organization extended full participation to women

---

commodity market   Financial market in which brokers buy and sell agricultural products in large quantities, thus determining the prices paid to farmers for their harvests.

Grange   The Grange (or Patrons of Husbandry) combined social activities with education on new methods of farming and cooperative economic efforts.

◆ This poster appeared in 1869, two years after the founding of the Grange. It depicts the farmer as a member of the producing class, laboring in the soil to produce value. It shows a military officer, railroad magnate, physician, politician, lawyer, merchant, and preacher as living off the farmer's labor. *Library of Congress.*

as well as men. Kelley hoped that the Grange would not only provide a social outlet for farm families but would also educate them to new methods of agriculture. It far exceeded his expectations.

The Grange grew rapidly, especially in the Midwest and the central South. In the 1870s, it became a leading proponent of cooperative buying and selling. Many local Grange organizations set up cooperative stores, and some even tried to sell their crops cooperatively. Two state Granges began manufacturing farm machinery, and Grangers laid ambitious plans for cooperative factories producing everything from wagons to sewing machines. Some Grangers formed mutual insurance companies and a few experimented with cooperative banks.

The Grange defined itself as nonpartisan. As Grange membership rapidly expanded in the 1870s, however, its midwestern and western members soon talked of political action. New political parties emerged in eleven states, usually called "Granger

parties." Their most prominent demand was state legislation to prohibit railroad rate discrimination. So crucial was their role in agitating for regulation that the resulting state laws were called **Granger laws.**

The Grange reached its zenith in the mid-1870s. Hastily organized cooperatives then began to suffer financial problems. In the late 1870s, the nationwide depression compounded difficulties for Grange cooperatives, and the collapse of cooperatives often pulled down Grange organizations. Political activity brought some successes but also generated bitter disputes within the Granges. These setbacks contributed to a decline in the Grange after the late 1870s, after which the surviving Granges usually avoided both cooperatives and politics.

With the decline of the Grange and its cooperatives, some farmers looked to monetary policy for relief. Following the Civil War, *most* prices fell (a situation called **deflation**) for several reasons: increased production, more efficient techniques in agriculture and manufacturing, the federal surplus taking money out of circulation, and the failure of the money supply to grow as rapidly as the economy. The Greenback party argued that prices could be stabilized through printing more **greenbacks,** the paper money issued during the Civil War. The Greenbackers were arguing for the quantity theory of money. According to this view, if the currency (money in circulation, whether of paper or precious metal) grew more rapidly than the economy, the result was inflation (rising prices), but if the currency failed to grow as rapidly as the economy, the outcome was deflation (falling prices).

Greenbackers calling for the federal government to issue more greenbacks found their most receptive audience among farmers who were in debt. In the congressional elections of 1878, the Greenback party received nearly a million votes and elected fourteen congressmen. However, they proved unsuccessful in attracting votes nationwide. In the 1880 presidential election, the Greenback party endorsed not only inflation but also the eight-hour workday, legisla-

---

Granger laws   Laws establishing standard freight and passenger rates on railroads, passed in various states in response to the lobbying of the Grange.

deflation   Falling prices, a situation in which the purchasing power of the dollar increases.

greenbacks   Paper money, not backed up by gold, that the federal government issued during the Civil War.

♦ The Grange tries to awaken the public to the approaching locomotive (a symbol of monopoly power) that is bringing consolidation (mergers), extortion (high prices), bribery, and other evils. *Culver Pictures.*

tion to protect workers, the abolition of child labor, regulation of transportation and communication, a **graduated income tax,** and woman suffrage. For president, they nominated James B. Weaver of Iowa, a Greenback congressman and former Union Army general. Weaver got only 3.3 percent of the vote. In 1884, with a similar platform and the erratic Benjamin Butler as their presidential nominee, the Greenbackers did even worse.

A similar monetary analysis motivated those who wanted the government to resume issuing silver dollars. Until 1873, federal mints had accepted gold and silver in unlimited quantities and made them into coins at virtually no charge, as the easiest way to get money into circulation. Throughout most of the nineteenth century, however, owners of silver made more money selling it commercially than taking it to the mint. Hence, no silver dollars existed for many years. In 1873, Congress dropped the silver dollar from the list of approved coins, following the lead of Britain and Germany who had specified that only gold was to serve as money. Some Americans believed that adhering to this **gold standard** was essential if American businesses were to compete ef-

fectively in international markets for capital and for the sale of goods.

Soon after 1873, silver discoveries in Nevada and elsewhere in the West drove down the commercial price of silver. The rallying cry was "**Free silver** at 16 to 1," which meant unlimited coinage of gold and silver, with the weight of the silver in a silver dollar sixteen times the weight of the gold in a gold dollar. The proposal quickly found support not just among farmers who wanted inflation but also among silver-mining interests. Members of this farming-mining coalition were soon called "silverites." In 1878, Congress passed the **Bland-Allison Act,** authorizing a limited amount of silver dollars. It was not enough to counteract deflation, however, and satisfied neither the proponents of the gold standard nor the silverites. The Sherman Silver Purchase Act of 1890 was a Republican attempt to satisfy silverites without alienating eastern Republicans who supported the gold standard. It increased the amount of silver to be coined but did not require free coinage of silver. Again, both silverites and advocates of the gold standard were unhappy.

Birth of the People's Party

The Grange had demonstrated the importance of group action, but its decline after the late 1870s left a vacuum among farmers, and the Greenback party had not taken its place. In the 1880s, three organizations emerged to fill the vacuum, all called **Farmers' Alliances.** One was centered in the north central states. Another, usually called the Southern Alliance, began in Texas and spread eastward across the South, absorbing similar local groups along its way.

---

graduated income tax Percentage tax levied on income that varies with income. People who earn more money pay a higher rate of taxes.

gold standard A monetary system in which the basic unit is defined by a fixed quantity of gold.

free silver The proposal to allow the coinage of all available silver to supplement gold as currency, which was repeatedly suggested as a solution to the nation's economic troubles.

Bland-Allison Act 1878 law providing for federal purchase of silver to be coined into silver dollars.

Farmers' Alliances Agricultural organizations of the 1880s and 1890s that carried forward the agrarian cause after the decline of the Grange.

Because its membership was limited to white farmers, a third, the Colored Farmers' Alliance, was formed as an offshoot of the Southern Alliance, for black farmers. Like the Grange and Knights of Labor, the Alliances defined themselves as part of the "producing classes" and looked to cooperatives as a partial solution to their problems. Alliance stores were most common, but the Texas Alliance experimented with cooperative cotton selling and some midwestern local Alliances built cooperative **grain elevators.** In cooperative selling, farmers tried to hold their crops back from market and to negotiate over prices rather than simply accepting the prices they were offered.

Local Alliance meetings featured social and educational activities. The educational program might present information on new agricultural techniques and sometimes focused on political topics, discussing a wide range of concerns and remedies. By the late 1880s, a host of weekly newspapers across the South and West presented Alliance views. One Kansas woman described the outcome: "People commenced to think who had never thought before, and people talked who had seldom spoken. . . . Everyone was talking and everyone was thinking. . . . Thoughts and theories sprouted like weeds after a May shower."

The Alliances defined themselves as nonpartisan and expected their members to work for Alliance aims within the framework of the major parties. This was especially important in the South, where any white person who challenged the dominant Democratic party ran the risk of being viewed as a traitor to both race and region. Many midwestern Alliance leaders, however, continued the Granger party tradition and some took part in the Greenback efforts of the 1880s. Not until the winter of 1889–1890 did widespread farmer support materialize for independent political action in the Midwest. Corn prices had fallen so low that some farmers found it cheaper to burn their corn than to sell it and buy fuel. During that winter, local Alliance meetings hummed with talk of political action.

As the fifty-first Congress argued over the McKinley Tariff and the Sherman Silver Purchase Act through the hot summer of 1890, members of the Farmers' Alliance in Kansas, Nebraska, the Dakotas, Minnesota, and surrounding states formed new political parties to contest state and local elections. One leader explained that the political battle they waged was "between the insatiable greed of organized wealth and the rights of the great plain people." Organization of the new party launched a decade of political change, a time when politics seized the nation's attention and when both politics and policies changed in dramatic ways.

Soon dubbed the People's party, or Populists, the grassroots party was launched by parades of farm wagons passing down the hot, dusty main streets of scores of country towns. The festivities ended with a picnic and rally, where speakers decried the plight of the farmer and proclaimed the sacred cause of the new party. Women took a prominent part in Populist campaigning, especially in Kansas and Nebraska. Mary Elizabeth Lease—a tall, red-haired woman from Kansas who had studied law while doing housework—was widely quoted in newspapers as urging farmers, "Raise less corn and more hell!" Alliance newspapers throughout the region published new words to familiar songs.

I was once a tool of oppression,
And as green as a sucker could be,
And monopolies banded together
To beat a poor hayseed like me.

The railroads and old party bosses
Together did sweetly agree;
And they thought there would be little trouble
In working a hayseed like me. . . .

But now I've roused up a little
And their greed and corruption I see . . .
And the ticket we vote next November
Will be made up of hayseeds like me.

(Sung to the tune of "Save a Poor Sinner Like Me")

The Populists emphasized three elements in their platforms, speeches, and other campaign materials: antimonopolism, government action on behalf of farmers and workers, and increased popular control of government. Their antimonopolism drew on their own unhappy experiences with railroads, grain buyers, and the companies that manufactured farm equipment and supplies. But it derived as well from a long American tradition of opposition to concentrated economic power. Populists liked to quote Thomas Jefferson on the need for equal rights for all, and often compared themselves to Andrew Jackson in his fight against the Bank of the United States.

---

grain elevator Storehouses equipped with mechanical lifting devices and usually located near railroad tracks, where farmers stored grain prior to shipping.
Sherman Silver Purchase Act 1890 law requiring the federal government to increase its purchases of silver.

The Populists' solution to the dangers of monopoly was government action on behalf of farmers and workers, including federal ownership of the railroads and the telegraph and telephone systems, and government alternatives to private banks. They endorsed a scheme of the Southern Alliance called the Sub-Treasury Plan, under which crops stored in government warehouses might be collateral for low-interest loans to farmers. "We believe the time has come," Populists proclaimed in 1892, "when the railroad companies will either own the people or the people must own the railroads." They also demanded inflation (through either greenbacks or silver or both) and a graduated income tax to replace the tariff. They had some following within what remained of the Knights of Labor, and hoped to gain broad support among urban and industrial workers. Their platform called for the eight-hour day for workers and the prohibition of private armies like the **Pinkertons** used against the Homestead strikers (see page 503).

Finally, the People's party favored a series of structural changes to make government more responsive to the people, including expansion of the merit system for government employees, election of United States senators by direct ballot instead of by state legislatures, a one-term limit for the president, the secret ballot, and the **initiative** and **referendum**. Many of them also favored woman suffrage. In the South, they not only opposed disfranchisement of black voters, but also posed a serious challenge to the prevailing patterns of politics by seeking to forge a political alliance of the disadvantaged of both races.

Thus, the Populists wanted to use government to control, even to own, the corporate behemoths that had evolved in their lifetimes, and they wanted to increase the influence of the individual voter in political decision making, an antiparty attitude rooted in their distrust of the old parties.

◆ When the Populists launched their new party, one cartoonist depicted them as a hot-air balloon of political malcontents. This cartoon may have inspired Frank Baum, author of *The Wizard of Oz*, whose wizard arrived in Oz in a hot-air balloon launched from Omaha, the site of the Populists' 1892 nominating convention. *Library of Congress.*

Democratic party to secure candidates committed to the farmers' cause. In the Northeast, Democrats attacked the McKinley Tariff for producing higher prices for consumers. In the Rocky Mountain region, nearly all candidates pledged their support for

The Elections of 1890 and 1892

The issues in the 1890 elections for members of the House of Representatives and for state and local offices varied by region. In the West, the Populists stood at the center of the campaign, lambasting both major parties for ignoring the needs of the people. In the South, Democrats held up Lodge's "Force Bill" as a symbol of the dangers posed by any who bolted the party of white supremacy. There, members of the Farmers' Alliance worked within the

Pinkertons Detectives of the Pinkerton agency, the first private detective agency in America, who were often employed as strikebreakers and industrial police against labor movements.

initiative Procedure allowing any group of people to propose a law by gathering signatures on a petition; the proposed law is then voted on by the electorate.

referendum Procedure whereby a bill or constitutional amendment is submitted to the voters for their approval after having been passed by a legislative body.

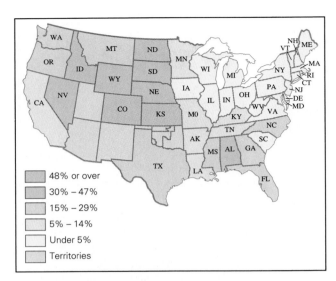

48% or over

30% – 47%

15% – 29%

5% – 14%

Under 5%

Territories

◆ **MAP 19.1 Popular Vote for Weaver, 1892** The Populist party's presidential candidate, James B. Weaver, made a strong showing in 1892. This map indicates that his support was concentrated regionally in the West and South, and that he had relatively little support in the northeastern states.

unlimited silver coinage. In various states and localities, Democrats scourged Republicans for their support of prohibition.

Perhaps the most surprising results were victories by Populists, the most successful new party since the appearance of the Republicans themselves in the 1850s. Kansas Republican senator John J. Ingalls had dismissed them as "a sort of turnip crusade," but so many Populists won election to the Kansas legislature that they were able to elect a Populist to replace Ingalls in the Senate. Populists in other states also elected state legislators, representatives in the House, and one other United States senator. All across the South, the Alliance claimed that successful Democratic candidates owed their victories to Alliance voters.

Everywhere Republicans suffered defeat. In the House of Representatives, the Republicans went from 166 seats in 1889 to only 88 in 1891. Many Republican candidates for state and local offices also lost. Republican disappointment in the results of the 1890 elections bred dissension within the party, and Harrison failed to maintain even a semblance of party unity.

The Republicans renominated Harrison, despite a lack of enthusiasm among many party leaders. The Democrats chose Grover Cleveland as their candidate again. Farmers' Alliance activists from the

South joined western Populists to form a national People's party, and to nominate James Weaver, who had run for president as a Greenbacker twelve years earlier. Democrats and Populists again earned the most impressive victories. Cleveland secured 46.1 percent of the popular vote, becoming the only president in American history to win two nonconsecutive terms. Harrison got 43.0 percent, and Weaver captured 8.5 percent (see Map 19.1). The Democrats kept control of the House of Representatives and, for the first time in twelve years, also won the Senate. Despite their weak showing nationally, Populist candidates displayed strength in the West and South. The Democrats now found themselves where the Republicans stood four years before: in control of the presidency and the Congress and fully able to translate their campaign promises into law.

Economic Collapse and Political Upheaval

● What choices did voters face in the 1896 presidential election?

● What were the long-term outcomes of that election?

After the Democrats swept to power in the 1892 elections, they suddenly faced difficult choices. Could they fulfill their campaign promises for tariff reform? Could they also halt the collapse of the national economy into a serious depression? The Democrats' failure to stabilize the economy opened the door to Republican victories in 1894 and 1896. When the Democrats in 1896 adopted some of the Populists' more moderate issues and nominated a candidate sympathetic to many Populist goals, they forced the new party to make a critical choice. Should they support the Democrats and risk losing their own identity as a party, or should they run their own candidate and guarantee a Republican victory?

Economic Collapse and Depression

Ten days before Cleveland took office, the Reading Railroad declared bankruptcy. A financial panic soon set in as other companies followed it into bankruptcy. One business journal reported in August that "never before has there been such a sudden and striking cessation of industrial activity.... Mills, factories, furnaces, mines nearly everywhere shut down in large numbers." More than 15,000 businesses failed in 1893, more than ever before in a single year, and more proportionately than in any year since the depression of the 1870s.

At the time, no one really understood why the economy collapsed so suddenly and so completely. In retrospect, it seems to have resulted from both immediate precipitating events and underlying structural weaknesses. The collapse of a major English bank led some British investors to call back some of their investments in the United States. This setback, combined with the reduction in revenues caused by the McKinley Tariff, resulted in a sharp decline in federal **gold reserves.** And this calamity, in turn, combined with the bankruptcy of a few large companies. As a result, the stock market crashed in May and June 1893, and the crash precipitated the depression.

The major underlying factors included the end of agricultural expansion and railroad construction. The difficulties that the agricultural economy encountered before 1893 produced a decline in sales of farm machinery and, hence, steel. More important were the railroads. Railroad building drove the industrial economy in the 1880s. In the 1890s, however, some companies found they did not have sufficient traffic on their new tracks to pay their fixed costs. Several large lines declared bankruptcy, including the Erie, Northern Pacific, Santa Fe, and Union Pacific. By 1894, almost one-fifth of the nation's railroad mileage had fallen into bankruptcy, and railroad construction fell by half between 1893 and 1895.

The sharp decline in railroad construction produced a domino effect, toppling industries that supplied the railroads, especially steel. Production of steel rails fell by more than a third between 1892 and 1894, and thirty-two steel companies joined the early business failures. Banks that had invested in railroads and steel companies collapsed along with those companies. Nearly five hundred banks failed just in 1893, and more than five hundred more closed down by the end of 1897, equivalent to one bank out of every ten.

No agency kept careful records on unemployment, but a third or even more of the wage earners in manufacturing may have been out of work. During the winter of 1893–1894, Chicago counted 100,000 unemployed—roughly two workers out of five. Crowds would swarm at factory gates in response to a rumor the plant was hiring. Throngs clustered around newspaper offices, hoping to be the first to see ads for work. Many who kept their

jobs received smaller paychecks, as employers cut wages and hours. In 1892, the average nonfarm wage earner received $482 per year. By 1894, this fell to $420.

The depression produced widespread suffering. Many of those who lost their jobs had little to fall back on except the soup dispensed by charities—if soup kitchens could be found. Newspapers told of people who chose suicide when faced with starving to death or stealing food. Susan Orcutt, a Kansas farm wife nearly nine months pregnant, saw the worst of both farm poverty and depression unemployment:

> I take my Pen In hand to let you know that we are Starving to death It is Pretty hard to do without any thing to Eat hear in this God for saken country we would have had Plenty to Eat if the hail hadent cut our rye down and ruined our corn and Potatoes . . . My Husband went a way to find work and came home last night and told me that we would have to Starve he has bin in ten countys and did not Get no work

Like Orcutt's husband, many men and some women left home desperate to find work, hoping to send money to their families as soon as they could. Some walked the roads, but most hopped on freight trains, riding in **boxcars** or—if the boxcars were packed with other itinerants—clinging outside them. A few found work, but most failed. Some families were never reunited. Those who kept their jobs and homes could not escape the pitiful sight of jobless, homeless men and women walking the streets.

A dramatic demonstration against unemployment began in late January 1894, when Ohio Populist Jacob S. Coxey proposed that the government hire the unemployed to build roads and repair public works and pay them with greenbacks, thereby inflating the currency. When he called on the unemployed to join him in a march on Washington to push this program, the response electrified the nation. All across the country, but especially in the West, hundreds of men and a few women tried to join the march. Given the vast distances, some western groups hijacked trains (fifty in all) and headed east pulling boxcars loaded with unemployed men.

---

gold reserves   The stockpile of gold with which the federal government backs up the currency.

boxcar   An enclosed railroad car with sliding side doors, used to transport freight.

♦ In 1894, Jacob Coxey, an Ohio Populist, led his "petition in boots" on a march from Ohio to Washington, D.C., demanding that Congress provide public-works jobs to the unemployed. *Library of Congress.*

(None of the pirated trains traveled far before authorities stopped them and arrested the leaders.) Several thousand people took part in Coxey's march in some way, but most never reached Washington, or reached it too late.

When Coxey and his group of several hundred did arrive in Washington, they learned that he would not be permitted to speak at the Capitol building. When he tried to do so anyway, on May 1, police arrested him and others for trespassing on the grounds of the Capitol. Mounted police with clubs dispersed the crowd. Even so, the trek of **Coxey's Army** marked the first time that so many protesters had gone to Washington, and the first time that so many had urged federal officials to create jobs for the unemployed.

The Divided Democrats

When Congress met in 1893, the majority Democrats faced several demanding issues. Their platform committed them to cut the tariff, but the party disagreed over how to do that. The other thorn in their side was the Sherman Silver Purchase Act. Many business leaders opposed the Sherman legislation as the cause of the gold drain that set off the depres-

sion, but many western and southern Democrats supported it as better than no silver coinage at all. On top of these issues, the depression and unemployment demanded attention. President Cleveland held to his staunch beliefs in minimal government and laissez faire. To him, it was inappropriate for the government to alleviate the suffering of the unemployed. Further, in the midst of the nation's financial crisis, Cleveland suffered a personal crisis. Doctors detected cancer in the roof of his mouth. Fearing that news of his condition might contribute to further financial panic, the president chose to keep his surgery and recuperation secret.

Convinced that silver coinage had contributed to the economic collapse, Cleveland asked Congress to repeal the Sherman Act (see Individual Choices: Grover Cleveland). In the House of Representatives, most Republicans voted for repeal, but more than a third of the Democrats voted against their own exec-

---

Coxey's Army   Unemployed workers led by Jacob S. Coxey who marched to Washington to demand relief measures from Congress following the Panic of 1893.

utive. In the Senate, Republicans supported Cleveland by 2 to 1, but Democrats divided almost evenly. Cleveland won, but at a disastrous political cost: he divided his party, pitting the Northeast against the West and much of the South. On other occasions when Cleveland encountered opportunities to restore party unity, he consistently took positions that conservatives applauded as "principled" and "courageous" but that failed to unite the increasingly divided Democrats.

The Democrats still faced the major challenge of the tariff. After their outspoken condemnation of the McKinley Tariff, they now had to demonstrate that they kept their word. The tariff bill produced by the House Ways and Means Committee in late 1893 reduced duties, tried to balance sectional interests, and created an income tax as a means of recovering lost federal revenue. The House passed it in February 1894. In the Senate, however, Democrats held a thin majority. There some Democrats, trying to protect their state's industries, produced so many amendments and compromises that Cleveland characterized the resulting Wilson-Gorman Tariff as "party dishonor." He refused to sign it, and it became law without his signature. (The Supreme Court soon declared the income tax unconstitutional.)

The 1894 elections gave voters a chance to register their response to the disorganized Democrats. The response was unmistakable. Democrats lost everywhere but the deep South, giving up 113 seats. Republicans, on the other hand, scored their biggest gain in Congress ever, adding 117. Populists had expected to capitalize on voter dissatisfaction with the old parties. In only a few places, however, did the voters turn to the Populists, and the party lost support in some of their previous strongholds. Most voters turned decisively to the Republicans, who began to look forward eagerly to the approaching 1896 presidential election.

Repeal of the Sherman Act badly damaged the Democratic party but failed to stop the flow of gold from the treasury as investors responded to economic uncertainties by converting their securities to gold. The gold reserve fell dangerously low, causing some to fear that the government might be unable to meet its obligations. In desperation, Cleveland turned to J. P. Morgan for assistance in floating a bond issue to restore the gold reserve. Morgan, the nation's leading investment banker and symbol of the power of Wall Street, extracted a high price for his services, but he did stabilize the gold reserve. Cleveland came under heavy criticism, both for the price paid to Morgan and for going to Morgan—symbol of Wall Street and the trusts—in the first place.

The 1896 Election: Bryan versus McKinley, Silver versus Protection

When Republicans met in St. Louis to nominate a candidate for president, **William McKinley** was the leading prospect. A Union veteran who had risen to the rank of major, he won election to the House of Representatives in 1876 and built a solid reputation there, specializing in the tariff. He lost his congressional seat in 1890 but won the Ohio governorship the next year and was reelected by a large margin in 1893. Known as a calm and competent leader, able to manage people and affairs without making enemies, McKinley billed himself as the "Advance Agent of Prosperity." He and his campaign manager, Marcus A. Hanna, planned their preconvention strategy so well that McKinley won on the first ballot, by a 3 to 1 margin over four rivals. Hanna, a retired Ohio industrialist known as both amiable and blunt, cared for organizational details, but the direction of the campaign rested with McKinley. The Republican platform pronounced in favor of the gold standard and against silver, but McKinley preferred to focus on the tariff. When the convention voted against silver, several western Republicans walked out of the convention and out of the party.

When the Democratic convention met, silverites held the majority but were not united behind any one candidate. The platform committee chose **William Jennings Bryan** of Nebraska to close a convention debate on silver. Blessed with a commanding voice, Bryan had won election to the House of Representatives in 1890 and 1892 and had achieved national attention for his eloquent defense of silver during debate on repeal of the Sherman Act.

Bryan's speech at the convention was masterful. Defining the issue as a conflict between "the producing masses" and "the idle holders of idle capi-

---

William McKinley   Republican who defeated Bryan in presidential elections in 1896 and 1900; he led the country into the Spanish-American War and was shot by an anarchist in 1901.

William Jennings Bryan   Nebraska congressman who advocated free coinage of silver, opposed imperialism, and ran for president unsuccessfully three times on the Democratic ticket.

Choosing Principle over Party

Grover Cleveland

President Grover Cleveland, confronted with a shattered economy, had to choose between his conservative principles and maintaining the unity of his party. Portrait Grover Cleveland by Anders Zorn. National Portrait Gallery, Smithsonian Institution/ Art Resource, NY.

Grover Cleveland took the presidential oath of office for the second time on March 4, 1893. Soon after, he faced a series of choices so difficult that he had every reason to expect intense criticism no matter what choice he made or what outcome resulted. He could not escape from making the choices, either, for he was afraid that the economic collapse that began shortly before he took office might threaten even the federal government itself.

Like many in his day, Cleveland held a traditional expectation about money. Because money must have intrinsic value, he contended, only precious metals could serve as money. In 1885, during his first term as president, he urged Congress to repeal the silver coinage act passed in 1878, on the grounds that the United States could not, by itself, maintain both gold and silver as money. To attempt to do so, Cleveland feared, would inevitably mean that gold would leave the country. Congress, however, refused to follow his advice in 1885.

When Cleveland's first presidency ended in 1889, the government's gold reserves stood at

tal," he argued that the first priority of federal policy should be "to make the masses prosperous," rather than to benefit the rich and hope that "their prosperity will leak through on those below." His closing rang defiant: "We will answer their demand for a gold standard by saying to them: You shall not press down upon the brow of labor this crown of thorns. You shall not crucify mankind upon a cross of gold." The speech stunned the convention and provoked an enthusiastic half-hour demonstration in support of silver and, even more so, of Bryan. Only 36 years old and not a declared candidate be-

fore his speech, Bryan nonetheless won the nomination on the fifth ballot.

Populists and another splinter party, the Silver Republicans, held nominating conventions next, amid frustration that the Democrats had stolen their thunder. Given Bryan's commitment to silver, to the income tax, and to a broad range of reforms that they also favored—and given the close working relationship he had developed with Populists in his home state—Populists felt compelled to give him their nomination too. Silver Republicans did the same. Subsequently, a group of Cleveland support-

$197 million. When he took office again in 1893, it seemed that his earlier fears were coming true, for the gold reserves had fallen to $103.5 million. This was dangerously close to the $100 million mark that Congress had earlier fixed as the point below which the nation might not be able to maintain the gold standard. The decline in gold reserves was in part the result of cuts in tariff revenues and greatly increased federal expenditures approved by the Republican Congress of 1889–1890. Another factor was widespread anxiety about the economy. Uncertain about the future, many investors chose to liquidate their holdings in return for gold. The shrinking gold reserves alarmed Cleveland.

Because so many business and financial leaders shared the expectation that money must have intrinsic value, they argued that silver coinage (authorized under the Sherman Silver Purchase Act) was dishonest, because it required that silver worth only 53 cents on the open market be made into a dollar coin. The president was pressured from one side by bankers and manufacturers eager to end silver coinage and to restore the gold reserve, and from the other side by members of his own party hostile to banking interests and favorable to silver coinage. Cleveland thus faced a difficult choice. Should he do what he believed to be necessary to maintain the nation's financial integrity? Or should he compromise and thereby preserve the unity of the Democratic party and his own political popularity?

In the midst of these pressures and counter-pressures, Cleveland demonstrated his courage when he underwent surgery to remove a cancer from the roof of his mouth and kept his illness secret. Seriously weakened by the surgery and uncertain that he was out of danger, Cleveland labored over a message to a special session of Congress. In his message, he made his choice clear: he asked Congress to repeal the Sherman Silver Purchase Act, knowing his action would badly divide his own party and bring upon him an avalanche of criticism.

The battle in Congress over repeal of the Sherman Silver Purchase Act was hard fought. Cleveland at times felt depressed about the prospects for success, once writing that "if I did not believe in God I should be sick at heart." But he stubbornly refused all efforts at compromise, and took comfort in the knowledge that he was following his sense of integrity and duty. "I think so often of Martin Luther's 'Here I stand—God help me,' " he told a friend.

The immediate outcome was that Cleveland won in Congress, with the assistance of most Republicans and some Democrats, including some who had previously opposed him. Another outcome was that Cleveland confirmed his personal reputation for integrity, courage, and stubbornness. But the most far-reaching outcome was that the president had splintered the Democratic party and doomed any hopes he may have had for leading it.

ers held a convention and nominated a Gold Democratic candidate.

Bryan and McKinley both fought an all-out campaign, but they used sharply contrasting tactics. Bryan, vigorous and young, knew that his speaking voice was his greatest campaign tool. He took his case directly to the voters in four grueling train journeys through 26 states and more than 250 cites. Delivering as many as 600 speeches—up to 30 a day—and speaking to a total of perhaps 5 million people, he stressed over and over that the most important issue was silver and that other reforms would fol-low once it was settled. He found large crowds of excited and enthusiastic supporters nearly everywhere he went.

McKinley stayed at home in Canton, Ohio, and campaigned from his front porch, but the Republican party carried the campaign to the voters for him, flooding the country with speakers, pamphlets, and campaign paraphernalia. They also chartered trains and brought thousands of supporters to hear McKinley. Canton became accustomed to daily parades marching from the train station to McKinley's house. Many business leaders feared that Bryan and

♦ In 1896, William Jennings Bryan (left), candidate of the Democratic, Populist, and Silver Republican parties, traveled some eighteen thousand miles in three months, speaking to about five million people. William McKinley (right), the Republican, stayed home in Canton, Ohio, greeting thousands of well-wishers. *Bryan: Nebraska State Historical Society; McKinley: Ohio Historical Society.*

silver coinage would bring complete financial collapse, and they opposed his other proposals such as the income tax and lower tariff rates. Hanna played on such fears to secure a campaign fund of $10 to $16 million. Far more than ever before, the sum was twenty or forty times as much as the Democrats raised.

McKinley won, taking 51.1 percent of the popular vote and 23 states with 271 electoral votes. Bryan received 46.7 percent of the vote, and won 22 states and 176 electoral votes. In both the popular vote and the electoral vote, McKinley scored the largest margin of victory since 1872. As Map 19.2 indicates, Bryan carried the South and nearly all of the West. McKinley's victory came in the urban, industrial Northeast (compare Map 19.2 to the opening map in Chapter 18). Of the twenty largest cities in the nation, only New Orleans went for Bryan.

Bryan's defeat spelled the end of the Populist party as a significant political organization. Some Populists moved into the Democratic party, and some returned to the Republicans. A few joined the Socialist party and a few simply ignored politics. The Populists' influence lived on, however, especially in Bryan's wing of the Democratic party.

After 1896: The New Republican Majority

The presidential election of 1896 stands as one of the most important in American history. The campaigns of 1896 focused on economic issues, sharpened by the depression. Bryan's silver crusade appealed most to debt-ridden farmers and western miners. McKinley forged a broader appeal by emphasizing

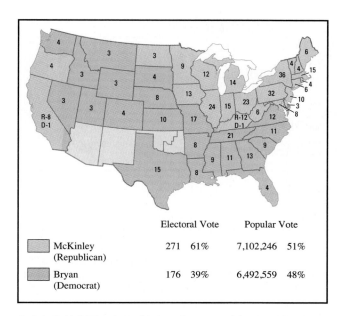

		Electoral Vote	Popular Vote	
▢	McKinley (Republican)	271 61%	7,102,246 51%	
▢	Bryan (Democrat)	176 39%	6,492,559 48%	

◆ **MAP 19.2 Election of 1896** Bryan could not win with just the votes of the South and West, for they had few electoral votes. Even if he won all the West, South, and border states, he still needed one or more northeastern states. McKinley won in the urban, industrial core region and the more prosperous farming areas of the Midwest.

the gold standard and protective tariff as keys to economic recovery. For many urban residents— workers and the middle class alike—silver seemed to promise inflation and higher prices, but the protective tariff meant manufacturing jobs. McKinley also won, at least in part, because he put a damper on his party's usual sympathy for moral reforms such as prohibition. Playing down ethnic divisions and condemning the anti-Catholic **American Protective Association** (see page 559) made it easier for McKinley to win support among immigrants, especially Germans, who approved of his stand on gold and the tariff.

McKinley's victory ushered in a generation of Republican dominance of national politics. The depression and the political campaigns of the 1890s caused some voters to reevaluate their partisan commitments, and to change parties. After 1896, no one could doubt that the Republicans were the national majority. Republicans ruled in the House of Representatives for twenty-eight of the thirty-six years after 1894, and in the Senate for thirty of those

thirty-six years. Republicans won seven of the nine presidential elections between 1896 and 1932. Similar patterns of Republican dominance appeared in state and local government, especially in the manufacturing belt.

The events of the 1890s also worked significant changes in the Democratic party. As Bryan solidified his hold on the leadership of the Democratic party over the next sixteen years, he and his allies moved the party away from its commitment to minimal government and laissez faire. While retaining the Jacksonians' distrust of monopoly and their opposition to governmental favoritism toward business, Bryan and other new Democratic leaders now agreed with the Populists that the solution to the problems of economic concentration lay in an active government that could limit monopoly power. "A private monopoly," Bryan never tired of repeating, "is indefensible and intolerable." In other ways, the Democrats changed little. They remained committed to states' rights that permitted the southern wing of the party to perpetuate white supremacist regimes. Most northern Democrats continued to oppose nativism and moral reform.

McKinley provided strong executive leadership and worked closely with leaders of his party in Congress to develop and implement new policies. In 1897, a revised protective tariff, the **Dingley Tariff,** fulfilled Republican campaign promises. It reduced the list of imports that could enter the nation without paying the tariff and drove tariff rates even higher than had the 1890 McKinley Tariff. The surplus disappeared as an issue after 1892, primarily as a result of significantly larger military and naval expenditures. In 1900, the **Gold Standard Act** wrote that Republican commitment into law. Fabulous gold discoveries in the **Klondike** and Alaska increased the

---

American Protective Association An anti-Catholic organization founded in Iowa in 1887 and active during the next decade.

Dingley Tariff 1897 bill enacting a high protective tariff, averaging 57 percent.

Gold Standard Act 1900 law that declared all forms of money redeemable in gold and made gold the monetary standard for all currency issued.

Klondike A region of Canada's Yukon Territory where gold was discovered in 1896, triggering a gold rush that attracted more than 25,000 people to the frozen north.

nation's currency supply without abandoning the gold standard.

Although the majority of American voters considered themselves Republican, many of them held their new party commitments less intensely than before. Before 1890, for most voters, ethnicity and choice of party went hand in hand. Now voters sometimes felt pulled toward one party by their economic situation, and toward the other party by their ethnicity. Such voters sometimes voted a split ticket, supporting Republicans for some offices and Democrats for others. This was now much easier because of the Australian ballot. Sometimes voters resolved their conflicts by not voting. As more and more government positions became subject to the merit system, there were fewer and fewer rewards for the party workers who once labored so strenuously to mobilize voters on election day. Voter participation began to decline, dropping from 79 percent in 1896 to 65 percent in 1908 to 59 percent in 1912.

The political role of newspapers also changed. In the 1890s, technological advances in paper manufacturing and printing, together with increasing numbers of literate adults, made possible the emergence of mass circulation newspapers. Enterprising publishers, notably William Randolph Hearst and Joseph Pulitzer, transformed large urban newspapers through **yellow journalism,** competing for the largest circulation through eye-catching headlines and questionable stories. As they focused on increasing their circulation and advertising, they also played down their tie to a political party. Some journalists began to develop the idea of providing balanced coverage to both parties.

American politics in 1888 looked much like American politics in 1876 or even 1844. But in 1896 American politics turned a corner and never looked back. In the early 1900s, the continued decline of political parties and partisan loyalties among voters combined with the emergence of organized interest groups to create even more change, producing the major structural features of American politics in the twentieth century.

---

yellow journalism Journalism that exploits or exaggerates the news in order to attract readers.

SUMMARY

E xpectations
C onstraints
C hoices
O utcomes

Americans in the late nineteen century *expected* political parties to dominate politics. All elected public officials were nominated by party conventions and elected through efforts of party campaigners. Most civil service employees were appointed in return for party loyalty. Republicans *chose* to use government to promote rapid economic development, but Democrats argued that government is best when it governs least. Voters tended to choose between the major parties along the lines of ethnicity, race, and religion.

Some people rejected the *constraints* of party government and sought reform. Mugwumps argued for the merit system in the civil service, accomplished through the Pendleton Act of 1883. By the late nineteenth century, a well-organized woman suffrage movement had also emerged. Gilded Age reformers sought both structural changes and policy changes.

The closely balanced strengths of the two parties contributed to a long-term political stalemate. The presidency of Ulysses S. Grant was plagued by scandals. Presidents Rutherford B. Hayes, James A. Garfield, and Chester A. Arthur faced stormy conflict between Republican factions. As president, Grover Cleveland approved the Interstate Commerce Act. Republicans broke the *constraints* of stalemate in 1889, passing the McKinley Tariff, Sherman Anti-Trust Act, Sherman Silver Purchase Act, and other measures. But voters turned against the Republicans in 1890.

The 1890s saw important and long-lasting changes in political patterns and people's *expectations* for politics. The political upheaval began when western and southern farmers turned to political action. In the 1870s, the Grange organized cooperatives and promoted regulatory laws to resolve farmers' economic problems. In the 1880s, several groups proposed currency inflation through paper or silver money. In 1890, members of the Farmers' Alliances *chose* to launch a new political party, usually called Populists. In 1892, voters rejected the Republicans in many areas, *choosing* either the new Populist party or the Democrats.

President Grover Cleveland proved unable to meet the political challenges of a major depression that began in 1893. In 1896, the Democrats nominated for president William Jennings Bryan, a critic of Cleveland and supporter of silver coinage. The Republicans chose William McKinley, who favored the protective tariff as most likely to end the depression. McKinley won, and important long-term *outcomes* were felt well into the twentieth century. First was the beginning of Republican dominance in national politics that lasted until 1930. And second, under Bryan's leadership, the Democratic party discarded its commitment to minimal government and instead adopted a willingness to use government against monopolies and other powerful economic interests.

SUGGESTED READINGS

Bryce, James. *The American Commonwealth*. 2 vols. (1889).
  Fascinating first-hand account of the politics of this period.

Cherny, Robert W. *A Righteous Cause: The Life of William Jennings Bryan*. (1986, rpt. 1994).
  Introduces Gilded Age politics through the busy life of a leading political figure.

Lebsock, Suzanne. "Women and American Politics, 1880–1920," in Louise A. Tilly and Patricia Gurin, eds., *Women, Politics, and Change* (1990).
  An overview of women and politics, incorporating summaries of much of the most interesting recent research.

Littlefield, Henry M. "The Wizard of Oz: Parable on Populism." *American Quarterly* 16 (1964): 47–58.
  Interesting account of populism's influence on a children's classic.

McMath, Robert C., Jr. *American Populism: A Social History, 1877–1898*. (1993).
  A recent, concise introduction to the populist movement.

Williams, R. Hal. *Years of Decision: American Politics in the 1890s*. (1978).
  A concise survey of national politics; strongest on congressional decision making.

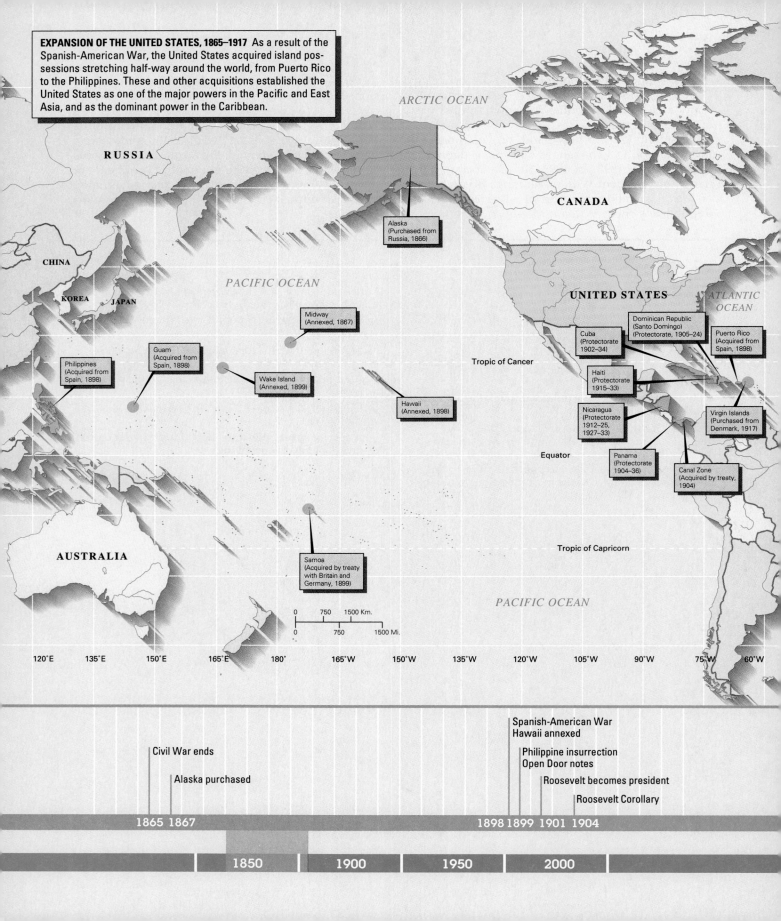

EXPANSION OF THE UNITED STATES, 1865–1917 As a result of the Spanish-American War, the United States acquired island possessions stretching half-way around the world, from Puerto Rico to the Philippines. These and other acquisitions established the United States as one of the major powers in the Pacific and East Asia, and as the dominant power in the Caribbean.

ARCTIC OCEAN

RUSSIA

CANADA

CHINA

KOREA   JAPAN

PACIFIC OCEAN

UNITED STATES

ATLANTIC OCEAN

Alaska
(Purchased from
Russia, 1866)

Midway
(Annexed, 1867)

Tropic of Cancer

Dominican Republic
(Santo Domingo)
(Protectorate, 1905–24)

Cuba
(Protectorate
1902–34)

Puerto Rico
(Acquired from
Spain, 1898)

Philippines
(Acquired from
Spain, 1898)

Guam
(Acquired from
Spain, 1898)

Wake Island
(Annexed, 1899)

Hawaii
(Annexed, 1898)

Haiti
(Protectorate
1915–33)

Nicaragua
(Protectorate
1912–25,
1927–33)

Virgin Islands
(Purchased from
Denmark, 1917)

Equator

Panama
(Protectorate
1904–36)

Canal Zone
(Acquired by treaty,
1904)

AUSTRALIA

Tropic of Capricorn

Samoa
(Acquired by treaty
with Britain and
Germany, 1899)

PACIFIC OCEAN

0   750   1500 Km.

0   750   1500 Mi.

120°E   135°E   150°E   165°E   180°   165°W   150°W   135°W   120°W   105°W   90°W   75°W   60°W

Spanish-American War
Hawaii annexed

Civil War ends

Philippine insurrection
Open Door notes

Alaska purchased

Roosevelt becomes president

Roosevelt Corollary

1865 1867   1898 1899 1901 1904

1850   1900   1950   2000

Becoming a World Power: America and World Affairs, 1865–1913

The United States and World Affairs, 1865–1889

- How did American choices with regard to Alaska, Mexico, and eastern Asia reflect traditional American expectations regarding world affairs?

Stepping Cautiously in World Affairs, 1889–1897

- How did some Americans' expectations about the U.S. role in world affairs begin to change between 1889 and 1897?

- Why?

Striding Boldly: War and Imperialism, 1897–1901

- What were the outcomes of the war with Spain?

- How did the acquisition of new possessions reflect the new expectations about America's role in world affairs?

"Carry a Big Stick": The United States and World Affairs, 1901–1913

- What were Theodore Roosevelt's expectations about the role of the United States in world affairs?

- What choices did he make to bring about the outcomes he desired?

INTRODUCTION

E xpectations

C onstraints

C hoices

O utcomes

In 1898, the United States went to war with Spain and quickly inflicted a stinging defeat. The *choice* to go to war climaxed a turnabout in American *expectations* regarding foreign affairs. During much of the nineteenth century, a time of far-reaching economic, social, and political change, the nation's role in world affairs was slight at best, and most Americans expected that their nation would stay out of foreign conflicts. George Washington had recommended that the nation "steer clear of permanent alliances with any portion of the foreign world." In 1823, President James Monroe warned the nations of Europe to stay out of the affairs of the independent nations of North and South America.

Through much of the nineteenth century, Americans had few worries about being pulled into European wars, for Europe remained relatively peaceful. The insulation imposed by the Atlantic and Pacific reinforced Americans' feeling of security, and the powerful British navy provided a protective umbrella for American commercial shipping. Thus, Washington's advice against foreign alliances became the cornerstone of American foreign relations at a time when the world little threatened American territory or commerce.

At the same time, as the *outcome* of treaties with European nations and war against Mexico, the nation expanded across the North American continent. Manifest destiny—the belief that God or Nature had destined the United States to spread its republican institutions throughout North America—fueled widespread *expectations* of continued expansion.

In the late nineteenth century, however, the United States took a place among the leading industrial nations of the world and had the potential to play a powerful role in world affairs if it chose. The simultaneous emergence of two other industrial and, soon, naval giants—Germany and Japan—contributed to a growing instability in world affairs, as the British navy faced serious challenges to its domination of the seas. Japan joined the European powers in a race for empire in which much of the world seemed fair game for colonial capture. In Africa, major European nations scrambled to claim territory. In eastern Asia, they were joined by Russia and Japan. Britain and Germany sometimes seemed to look toward Latin America as another field for ex-

pansion. In eastern Asia, the Pacific, and Latin America, the United States also had long-standing interests, often derived from commerce.

Toward the end of the nineteenth century, some Americans began urging that the nation's policymakers should boldly *choose* not just an increased role in world affairs, but a prominent one. Most presidents after the Civil War, however, were highly cautious about such a commitment. At times they seemed to take a step back for every step toward greater involvement. During the same years, a revolution in transportation and communication wiped out many *constraints* on foreign relations. American diplomatic representatives abroad had once been connected to Washington only by an occasional memorandum carried by an American ship. Now they could communicate daily by telegraph. Sailing ships had once taken weeks to traverse the Atlantic and Pacific. Now steam-powered, steel-hulled vessels crossed in days and carried many times as much cargo—whether passengers and freight or troops and military equipment. Previous American representatives abroad had usually been chosen through the patronage system, with little or no regard for their diplomatic abilities, but the rise of the merit system in the civil service had its parallel in the diplomatic service, producing more capable representation.

Challenges to traditional *expectations* of U.S. isolationism and the dissolving of long-standing *constraints* on action presented American policymakers of the late nineteenth century with more *choices* in foreign relations than had faced their predecessors. One *outcome* of their choices was a foreign policy usually described as *imperialism*. Its foundation was the acquisition of possessions scattered half-way around the world (see chapter-opening map). But the emerging U.S. foreign policy resulted in more than just colonies and the navy necessary to maintain and protect them. The larger *outcome* was a redefinition of nearly every aspect of American relations with the rest of the world.

CHRONOLOGY

The United States and World Affairs

1823	Monroe Doctrine
1865	Civil War ends
1867	French troops leave Mexico Danish West Indies purchase rejected by Senate Alaska purchased from Russia
1870	Santo Domingo annexation rejected by Senate
1872	Arbitration of *Alabama* claims
1877	Morgan's *Ancient Society* Reconstruction ends
1882	U.S. Navy opens Korean trade Congress authorizes modern navy
1885	Strong's *Our Country*
1887	Constitution forced on Hawaiian monarchy Pearl Harbor granted to U.S. Navy
1889	First Samoa treaty
1890	Mahan's *Influence of Sea Power upon History* McKinley Tariff
1891	Liliuokalani becomes Hawaiian queen Harrison threatens war with Chile
1893	Queen Liliuokalani overthrown
1894	Wilson-Gorman Tariff
1895–1896	Venezuelan boundary crisis
1896	Reconcentration policy in Cuba Insurrection in the Philippines McKinley elected
1898	De Lôme letter U.S. warship *Maine* explodes Spanish-American War Hawaii annexed by joint resolution Treaty of Paris signed
1899	Senate debates imperialism Treaty of Paris ratified Treaty of Berlin divides Samoa Open Door notes Permanent Court of Arbitration created
1899–1902	Philippine insurrection suppressed
1900	Foraker Act McKinley reelected Boxer Rebellion
1901	McKinley assassinated Roosevelt becomes president Insular cases Hay-Pauncefote Treaty
1902	Civil government in the Philippines Cuba becomes a protectorate
1903	Arbitration of Alaska-Canada boundary dispute
1904	Hay–Bunau-Varilla Treaty Panama becomes a protectorate Roosevelt Corollary
1904–1914	Panama Canal constructed
1905	Dominican Republic becomes a protectorate Roosevelt mediates Russo-Japanese War
1906	U.S. participates in Algeciras Conference
1907	Roosevelt's "Great White Fleet"
1912	Nicaragua becomes a protectorate
1914	Panama Canal completed

The United States and World Affairs, 1865–1889

● How did American choices with regard to Alaska, Mexico, and eastern Asia reflect traditional American expectations regarding world affairs?

Americans took their first steps toward a new foreign policy in the years following the Civil War, but those steps occurred largely in isolation from each other. Until the 1890s, the various components did not add up to a coherent policy. Instead, particular events were treated individually and separately from other events. Some were motivated by the lingering, pre–Civil War notion of manifest destiny. Others forecast concerns that emerged clearly only in the 1890s.

Alaska, Canada, and the *Alabama* Claims

In 1866, the Russian minister to the United States hinted to Secretary of State **William H. Seward** that Czar Alexander II might dispose of Russian holdings in North America if the price were right. Seward, one of the most capable secretaries of state in the nineteenth century, had often proclaimed his belief in America's destiny to expand across the North American continent. He made an offer and in 1867 the two diplomats agreed on a price slightly over $7 million. The deal was done, and the land that was to become the state of Alaska was in U.S. hands. The treaty differed from earlier territory agreements in one significant way. Previous treaties had all specified that the inhabitants of the territories (except Indians) would immediately become American citizens and that the territories themselves would eventually become states. The Alaska treaty extended full citizenship but carried no promise of eventual statehood. It therefore moved a half-step away from earlier patterns of territorial expansion and toward later patterns of colonial acquisition.

Some journalists derided the new purchase as a frozen, worthless wasteland and labeled the bargain "Seward's Folly." The Senate, however, greeted it with little opposition and considerable enthusiasm. Charles Sumner, the chairman of the **Senate Foreign Relations Committee,** and others looked on the purchase of Alaska as the first step to the ultimate possession of Canada. Sumner's hope that owning Alaska would lead to obtaining Canada was widely shared. The always extravagant Ben Butler,

for example, once exhorted expansion so far north that people "will mistake the flashings of the midnight sun reflected from our glorious flag for the scintillations of an aurora borealis."

Expansion by acquiring Canada was certainly on Sumner's mind as he considered a set of claims against Great Britain arising out of the Civil War. Several Confederate naval vessels, notably the *Alabama* and its sister ship the *Florida*, had badly disrupted northern shipping. English shipyards had built the *Alabama* and the *Florida* for the Confederacy. And English ports had offered refuge, repairs, and supplies to Confederate ships. The Union claimed that Britain had violated its neutrality by allowing these activities, but Britain proved unresponsive to American demands for compensation for the depredations by the Confederate cruisers. In 1869, however, as relations between Britain and Russia grew tense, the British began to fret that American shipyards might provide similar services for the Russians.

The major obstacle to settling the dispute was Sumner's argument that the damages caused by the Confederate navy included not just direct claims for shipping losses but many indirect claims as well. In fact, Sumner insisted that these related expenses should include the entire cost of the last two years of the war. The total, by Sumner's calculations, was more than $2 billion—so much, he suggested, that Britain could best meet its obligation by ceding its North American possessions, including Canada, to the United States. Grant's secretary of state, Hamilton Fish, found Sumner's claims unrealistic and convinced Grant not to support them. Instead, in the Treaty of Washington (1871), the two countries agreed to **arbitration.** The 1872 arbitration decision held Britain responsible for the direct claims and set $15.5 million as damages to be paid to the United States.

William H. Seward U.S. Secretary of State under Lincoln and Johnson, a former abolitionist who had expansionist views and who arranged the purchase of Alaska from Russia.

Senate Foreign Relations Committee One of the standing, or permanent, committees of the Senate; it deals with foreign affairs, and its chairman wields considerable power.

arbitration Process by which parties to a dispute submit their case to the judgment of an impartial person or group and agree to abide by the decision of the arbiter.

Testing the Monroe Doctrine: The United States and Latin America

After the Civil War, American diplomats turned their attention to Latin America, partly in reaction to the influence European powers had recently extended in that direction and partly because some Americans wanted the United States to exercise power in that region.

In late 1861, as the United States lurched into civil war, France, Spain, and Britain sent a joint force to Mexico to collect debts that Mexico could not pay. Spain and Britain soon withdrew their contingents but France remained. Despite resistance led by Benito Juarez, president of Mexico, French troops occupied key areas. Some of Juarez's conservative political opponents cooperated with the French emperor, Napoleon III, to name **Archduke Maximilian** of Austria as emperor of Mexico. Maximilian, an idealistic young man, apparently believed that the Mexican people genuinely wanted him as their leader, and he hoped to serve them well. He quickly antagonized some of his conservative supporters with talk of reform, but he failed to win support from any other quarter. Resistance became war, and Maximilian held power only because of the French army.

During these events, the United States was involved in its own civil war. The Union continued to recognize Juarez as president of Mexico but could do little else. As soon as the Civil War ended, however, Secretary of State Seward demanded that Napoleon withdraw his troops. At that point, the United States possessed the most experienced, and perhaps the largest, army in the world. Seward underscored his demand when 50,000 battle-hardened troops moved to the Mexican border. Thus confronted, Napoleon III agreed to withdraw his army. The last French soldiers sailed home in early 1867, but Maximilian unwisely remained behind, where he was defeated in battle by Juarez and then executed.

In his communications with France, Seward did not refer to the Monroe Doctrine by name. It had been, until then, a statement with no standing in international affairs unless backed by sufficient military or naval force. However, the withdrawal of the French troops, in the face of substantial American military force, helped to create new respect in Europe for the role of the United States in Latin America.

Some Americans had long regarded the Caribbean and Central America as potential areas for expansion. One driving vision was a canal to shorten the coast-to-coast shipping route. Central America was the logical location for a canal that would eliminate the need for ships from the eastern United States to travel around South America to reach the west coast or Asia. After the Civil War, both the Caribbean and the Pacific attracted attention as sites where the navy might need bases. In 1867, seeking naval bases, Secretary of State Seward negotiated a treaty with Denmark to buy part of the **Danish West Indies,** but the Senate withheld its approval partly out of concern over the price (more than for Alaska) and partly because of hurricanes and earthquakes in the area. Seward also tried to secure control of a base site in **Santo Domingo,** but that attempt too failed to win the approval of Congress.

In 1870, with Grant in the White House and Hamilton Fish as secretary of state, the dictator of Santo Domingo offered either to annex his entire country to the United States or to lease a major bay for a naval base. Grant found annexation attractive but Fish did not. Urged on by Americans eager to invest in the area, Grant asked the Senate to ratify a treaty of annexation. Sumner led the opposition, arguing that annexation might endanger the independence of Haiti, among other problems. The only black republic in the Western Hemisphere, Haiti shared the same island with Santo Domingo and periodically faced its neighbor on the battlefield. Sumner—erstwhile abolitionist, leader of the Senate Radical Republicans—found himself in unusual company, with support from southern Democrats and members of the emerging Liberal Republican movement. Some treaty opponents attacked it in bigoted terms for bringing Spanish-speaking Catholics into the nation. Approval required support of two-thirds of the Senate, and the treaty failed by a vote of 28 to 28. Grant nonetheless proclaimed an extension, or **corollary,** of the Monroe Doctrine,

---

Archduke Maximilian   Austrian archduke appointed by France to be emperor of Mexico in 1864; he lacked popular support and was executed by Mexican republicans when the French withdrew from the country.

Danish West Indies   Island group in the West Indies, including St. Croix and St. Thomas, which the United States finally purchased from Denmark in 1917; now known as the U.S. Virgin Islands.

Santo Domingo   Nation in the Caribbean, now known as the Dominican Republic, which shared an island with Haiti; it became independent from Spain in 1865.

corollary   A proposition that follows logically and naturally from an already proven point.

specifying that no territory in the Western Hemisphere could ever be transferred to a European power.

Rather than annexation of territory, Secretary of State Fish pressed for expansion of trade with Latin America. Trade with Latin America was also central to the thinking of James G. Blaine, secretary of state under Garfield (in 1881) and Harrison (from 1889 to 1892). Blaine promoted closer relations with Latin America in part to create additional markets for American products. He believed, too, that the United States should take a more active role among Latin American nations in resolving problems that might lead to war or European intervention.

Eastern Asia and the Pacific

Americans had long taken a strong commercial interest in eastern Asia. The China trade dated to 1784, and goods from Asia and the Pacific accounted for about 8 percent of all U.S. imports following the Civil War. Exports to that area made up less than 2 percent of all exports, however, and some Americans dreamed of profits from selling to China's hundreds of millions of potential consumers. American missionaries began to penetrate China in 1830. Although they counted few converts, the lectures they gave when back in the United States stimulated public interest in the Asian nation.

From 1839 to 1842, the British navy humiliated Chinese naval forces in a war conducted largely in Chinese waters. Although the war began over Chinese efforts to prevent British merchants from importing and selling **opium** in China, the British defined the issue as one of free trade. Previously the Chinese government had placed severe restrictions on foreign trade. In defeat, China granted privileges to Britain and subsequently to other nations who wished to sell goods there. The first treaty between China and the United States, in 1844, included a provision granting **"most favored nation" status** to the United States, laying the basis for the American **Open Door policy.**

Japan and Korea had insulated themselves from European imperial expansion by refusing to engage in trade, thereby keeping out western influences. In 1854, American naval forces, commanded by **Commodore Matthew C. Perry** and under orders from President Millard Fillmore, convinced the Japanese government to open its ports to foreign trade. A similar navy action opened Korea in 1882.

Growing trade prospects between eastern Asia and the United States fueled American interest in

the ocean that separated the two, the Pacific. Whether in sailing ships or steamships, the American merchant marine needed ports in the Pacific for supplies and repairs. Interest focused especially on two groups of islands with excellent harbors, Hawaii and Samoa. Hawaii had attracted Christian missionaries from New England as early as 1819, shortly after King Kamehameha the Great united the islands into one nation. Initially concerned with preaching the gospel and convincing the unabashed Hawaiians to wear clothes, the missionaries eventually came to exercise great influence over several Hawaiian monarchs in the early nineteenth century.

The Hawaiian Islands' location near the center of the Pacific made them an ideal supply depot for ships crossing the Pacific and for whaling vessels. After 1848, ships traveling from New York around South America to San Francisco also routinely stopped in Hawaii for supplies. As early as 1842, President John Tyler stated that the United States would not allow the islands to pass under the control of another power, but Britain and France continued to take a close interest in the islands.

In 1874 and 1875, King Kalakaua of Hawaii became the first monarch ever to visit the United States. Soon after, yielding to pressures from **haole** sugar growers, the Senate approved a treaty that exempted Hawaiian imports from the tariff. The outcome was a rapid expansion of the Hawaiian sugar industry as children of New England missionaries joined representatives of American sugar refiners in developing huge sugar plantations. Sugar soon tied the Hawaiian economy closely to the United States. In 1887, a group of haole business leaders and plantation owners pressured King Kalakaua into accepting a constitution that limited the monarch's powers

---

opium An addictive drug made from poppies.

"most favored nation" status In a treaty between two nations, a "most favored nation" clause means that commercial privileges extended by nation A to other nations automatically become available to nation B.

Open Door policy Advocated by the United States in 1899 under which all nations would have equal access to trading and development rights in China.

Commodore Matthew C. Perry American naval commander who sailed an armed squadron into Tokyo Bay and, using diplomacy and the threat of force, persuaded the Japanese to open their ports to American trade in 1854.

haole Hawaiian word used to describe persons not of indigenous Hawaiian ancestry, especially whites.

and permitted haoles to dominate the government. Among the royal family, resentment grew over the new constitution and haole control of the government. Nonetheless, they reluctantly granted Pearl Harbor to the American navy the same year in order to secure the renewal of the treaty that exempted Hawaiian sugar from tariff duties.

Samoa, in the South Pacific, drew attention not just from the United States but also from Britain and Germany. When German meddling in the islands suggested an attempt at annexation, President Cleveland vowed to maintain Samoan independence. All three nations dispatched warships to the vicinity in 1889, and conflict seemed likely until a typhoon scattered and damaged the ships. A conference in Berlin then produced a treaty that provided for Samoan independence under the protection of all three western nations.

Stepping Cautiously in World Affairs, 1889–1897

- How did some Americans' expectations about the U.S. role in world affairs begin to change between 1889 and 1897?
- Why?

During the administration of Benjamin Harrison (1889–1893), the United States began to take its first, cautious steps toward redefining its role in the world affairs. One step involved a new role for the U.S. Navy, and the commissioning of modern ships able to carry it out. Another involved the emergence of a more coherent and consistent set of foreign objectives and commitments.

Building a Navy

At the end of the Civil War, the navy, like the army, was rapidly **demobilized.** Unlike the army, which was needed to fight Indians in the West, the Navy was largely ignored. No political decision makers thought that establishing command of the high seas was an appropriate role for the U.S. Navy, and only a few Americans appreciated the significance of the Civil War experiments with heavily armored, steam-powered ships. As late as 1870, in fact, the U.S. Navy prohibited the use of steam power except when unavoidable. These attitudes fostered disastrous neglect. The navy's wooden sailing vessels deteriorated to the point that some people ridiculed them as fit only for firewood. When a coal barge accidentally ran down a navy ship, one congressman joked that the worn-out navy was too slow even to get out of the way.

Things began to change somewhat in 1882, when Congress authorized construction of two steam-powered cruisers—the first new ships since the Civil War. However, work at the shipyards soon became bogged down in political infighting and accusations of corruption and incompetence. Although Congress appropriated funds for four more new ships in 1883, Secretary of the Navy William C. Whitney announced in 1885 that "we have nothing which deserves to be called a navy." During Cleveland's first administration (1885–1889), Whitney prodded Congress into approving construction of several more cruisers and the first two modern battleships.

Alfred Thayer Mahan played a key role in the emergence of the modern navy. As president of the Naval War College, Captain Mahan exerted a powerful influence, especially during the Harrison administration. In lectures in several books—especially *The Influence of Sea Power upon History, 1660–1783* (1890)—and in articles in popular magazines, Mahan argued that sea power had been the determining factor in the great European power struggles from the mid-seventeenth to the early nineteenth centuries. From his study of history, he identified three elements as central to greatness on the seas: (1) production of goods for foreign trade, (2) shipping to carry on this commerce, and (3) colonies to provide both markets (usually for manufactured goods) and products (usually raw materials) to be used in the home country.

Mahan also explored the significance of geography, population, and government as they related to establishing sea power. From these studies, he drew lessons for government policy in his own day. First, Mahan urged support for a strong **merchant marine.** Second, he advocated a large, modern navy centered around huge, powerful battleships. And

---

Samoa A group of volcanic and mountainous islands in the South Pacific; the independence of the islands under three-power supervision lasted only until 1899.

demobilize To discharge from military service.

Alfred Thayer Mahan Lecturer and writer on naval history who stressed the importance of sea power in determining political history and who justified imperialism on the basis of national self-interest.

merchant marine Ships engaged in commerce.

◆ Located on the Hawaiian island of Oahu, Pearl Harbor is one of the finest harbors in the Pacific. This painting was done in 1889, two years after the Hawaiian king granted use of the harbor to the United States. In return, the United States granted preferred status to Hawaiian sugar in the American market. *"Pearl Harbor from the Ocean" by Joseph Strong, 1889. Bishop Museum, Honolulu, Hawaii.*

third, he stressed a vision for empire. Extend American power beyond the national boundaries, he exhorted, in order to establish and control a canal through Central America, command the Caribbean, dominate Hawaii and other strategic locations in the Pacific, and create naval bases at key points in the Atlantic and Pacific. His arguments were influential not just in the United States but also in Great Britain and Germany, which began large naval construction programs at about the same time as the United States.

In 1889, with Harrison in the White House and Republican majorities in both houses of Congress, Secretary of the Navy Benjamin F. Tracy urged Congress to modernize the navy and to expand it significantly: eighteen more battleships (up from two), nearly fifty more cruisers, and more smaller vessels. Tracy's ambitious proposal might have eliminated the federal budget surplus all by itself (see page 589). Congress did not give him all that he asked but did begin to create a modern, two-ocean navy centered on battleships. When construction was underway on three new battleships equal to the best in the world, Tracy happily announced that "we shall rule [the sea] as certainly as the sun doth rise!"

A New American Mission?

Mahan's strategic arguments and Tracy's battleship launchings came as some Americans began, in Mahan's phrase, to "look outward." The appeals for change came from many sources: Protestant ministers, historians, business figures, politicians. Together they redefined the way American policymakers viewed the world and the role of the nation in world affairs. Josiah Strong, for example, offered the perspective of a Protestant minister and missionary. His book *Our Country* (1885) argued that expansion of American Protestant ideals to the world constituted a Christian duty and was practically inevitable. "The world is to be Christianized and civilized," he predicted, and added that "commerce follows the missionary."

Such beliefs were widespread in the late nineteenth century. According to Lewis Henry Morgan, whose book *Ancient Society* (1877) was long considered the authoritative work on its subject, the peoples of the world ranged themselves on a ladder of civilization in three major categories: savagery, barbarism, and civilization. The nations of western Europe and the United States represented the highest steps of "civilization." All people, he argued, were moving in the same direction, up the ladder of evolution toward the ideal represented by the United States and Europe. Some policymakers—including future president Theodore Roosevelt—implicitly accepted Morgan's analysis and used his categories in arguing that conflict was inevitable when "civilized" and "barbarian" peoples came into contact because barbarians were inherently warlike. In such a situation, Roosevelt argued in 1899, expansion by "a great civilized power" not only extended peace, but also meant "a victory for law, order, and righteousness."

"Progress" and Social Darwinism merged with a belief in the superiority of the Anglo-Saxons—the people of England and their descendants. In the 1880s, popular books claimed that Anglo-Saxons had demonstrated a unique capacity for civilization and that they had a duty toward other peoples. Albert Beveridge, a Republican Senator from Indiana, was to combine some of these ideas with American nationalism during the debate over acquisition of the Philippines in 1899 and 1900. "[God] has made us the master organizers of the world to establish system where chaos reigns," Beveridge proclaimed. "He has marked the American people as His chosen Nation to finally lead in the regeneration of the world." Rudyard Kipling, an English poet, expressed this feeling in 1899 when he urged the United States to "take up the white man's burden," a phrase that came to describe a self-imposed obligation to go into distant lands, bring the supposed blessings of Anglo-Saxon civilization to their peoples, Christianize them, and sell them western products.

Today historians understand Anglo-Saxonism and the "white-man's-burden" argument to represent a perspective deeply tinged with racism. Such views assumed that some people, by virtue of race, possessed superior capability for self-government and cultural accomplishment than others. Further, this thinking elevated only one cultural pattern as real civilization, dismissing other cultural patterns as inferior and ignoring their accomplishments.

Revolution in Hawaii

In 1890, the McKinley Tariff put sugar on the free list (see page 589), meaning that *all* imported sugar entered without paying tariff duties. Hawaiian sugar now faced stiff competition in the American market, notably from Cuban sugar. To protect domestic sugar producers, sugar grown within the United States received a subsidy of two cents per pound. Facing economic disaster, many Hawaiian planters craved the two-cent subsidy and began to talk of annexation to the United States. In 1891, King Kalakaua died and was succeeded by his more assertive sister, **Liliuokalani.** She hoped to restore Hawaii to the **indigenous** Hawaiians and planned a new constitution returning political power to the monarchy. Fearing that they might lose not only their political clout but also their economic holdings, haole entrepreneurs set out to overthrow the monarchy. On January 17, 1893, the plotters an-

♦ As late as 1880, the U.S. Navy specified that ship captains should only use steam power when "absolutely necessary" and otherwise should rely on sail. Alfred Thayer Mahan, pictured here, took the lead in revolutionizing American thinking about sea power. *U.S. Naval Historical Center.*

nounced a provisional republican government that would seek annexation by the United States. John L. Stevens, the U.S. minister to Hawaii, provided crucial assistance for the rebellion by ordering the landing of 150 marines. Liliuokalani surrendered, as she put it, "to the superior force of the United States." Stevens immediately recognized the new republic, declared it a **protectorate** of the United States, and raised the American flag.

The Harrison administration, then in its closing days, **repudiated** Steven's overzealous action insist-

---

Liliuokalani Last reigning queen of Hawaii, whose desire to restore land to the Hawaiian people and perpetuate the monarchy prompted haole planters to depose her in 1893.

indigenous Original to or belonging in an area or environment.

protectorate A country partially controlled by a stronger power and dependent on that power for protection from foreign threats.

repudiate To reject the validity or authority of.

♦ Queen Liliuokalani came to the Hawaiian throne in 1891 and hoped to regain royal power that had been lost by her predecessor, King Kalakaua. Instead, in 1893, *haole* planters and businessmen overthrew the monarchy, aided by 150 U.S. marines ordered ashore by the American minister to Hawaii. *The Liliuokalani Trust.*

ing he had neither authorization nor authority to establish a protectorate. At the same time, however, the administration opened negotiations with representatives of the republic. Within thirty days after Stevens brought the marines into Honolulu, Harrison sent the Senate a treaty of annexation. There it rested when Grover Cleveland became president soon after.

Cleveland was willing to consider annexing Hawaii if the Hawaiian people requested it, but he withdrew the annexation treaty in order to study it further. Having earlier blocked German moves to subvert the government of Samoa, the president was upset to learn that his own nation was guilty of similar manipulation in Hawaii. When he discovered that the revolution could not have succeeded without the marines' involvement, he asked the new officials to restore the queen. They refused, and Hawaii became a republic, dominated by its haole business and planter community.

Crises in Latin America

Although Harrison and Cleveland acted at cross purposes regarding Hawaii, they moved in similar directions with regard to Latin America. Both presidents extended American involvement, and both threatened the use of force.

A rebellion in Chile in 1891 ended with victory for the rebels. Because the American minister to Chile had seemed to side against the rebels, providing protection to several high-ranking officials of the deposed government, anti-American feelings ran high. In October 1891, in Valparaiso, Chile, a mob set upon a group of American sailors on shore leave, beat them, injured several, and killed two. The Chilean government gave no sign of apologizing, so Harrison threatened "such action as may be necessary." Using language Americans considered insulting, the Chilean government insinuated that Harrison was wrong. When Harrison responded with plans for a naval war and threats to cut off diplomatic relations, Chile gave in, apologized, and promised to pay damages and to meet any other terms.

In 1895 and 1896, Grover Cleveland also took the nation to the edge of war. At issue was a long-standing boundary dispute between Venezuela and **British Guiana.** Venezuela repeatedly proposed arbitration, which Cleveland also favored, but Britain refused. Discovery of gold in the contested region intensified claims by both sides. In July 1895, Secretary of State Richard Olney demanded that Britain submit the boundary issue to arbitration. Resting his argument on the Monroe Doctrine, he bombastically proclaimed the United States to be preeminent throughout the Western Hemisphere. The British waited until December to respond, then rejected the notion that the Monroe Doctrine held any standing in international law and refused arbitration. Cleveland in turn asked Congress for authority to determine the boundary and enforce it. Britain faced the possibility of conflict with the United States at a time when it was becoming increasingly concerned about the colonial schemes of Germany and when tensions were mounting between the English colony

---

British Guiana   British colony in northeast South America on the Atlantic coast; its boundary with Venezuela was the source of a long-standing dispute with Great Britain.

in South Africa and neighboring independent **Boer republics.** Britain agreed to arbitration.

In both instances, American presidents behaved more forcefully toward other nations than had happened in twenty years. Both times, the firm American response had surprised its adversary. Harrison's action toward Chile involved a heavy-handed assertion of American power unlikely to encourage the closer relations with Latin America envisioned by Harrison's secretary of state, James Blaine. His role in the episode was limited largely to urging moderation from his sickbed. Cleveland and Olney did not even consult with the Venezuelan government at any time during the Venezuelan boundary crisis, and Venezuela was clearly secondary to a showdown between Cleveland and Britain. While Cleveland certainly may have hoped that standing up to Britain would help the Democrats in upcoming elections, his major objective was to serve notice to *all* European imperial powers that the Western Hemisphere was strictly off-limits in the ongoing contest for colonies.

At the same time, Cleveland faced a very different situation in Cuba, and there he took a more restrained position. Cuba and Puerto Rico were all that remained of the once mighty Spanish empire in the Americas, and Cuba had rebelled against the mother country repeatedly. In the early 1890s, the sugar provisions of the McKinley Tariff produced in Cuba the opposite of their effect in Hawaii. Hawaii lost its special access to the American market, and Cuban sugar now entered the United States tariff-free. The Cuban sugar industry boomed in response, just as the Hawaiian sugar industry crashed. By 1894, the United States received nearly 90 percent of Cuba's exports, primarily sugar. That year, however, the Wilson-Gorman Tariff restored a high duty on Cuban sugar, removed it on Hawaiian sugar, and caused a depression in Cuba.

Fueled by economic distress, a new insurrection erupted against Spanish rule, and the advocates of *Cuba libre* ("a free Cuba") received support from sympathizers in the United States. In 1896, in an effort to combat guerrilla warfare waged by the **insurgents,** General Valeriano Weyler, the Spanish commander in Cuba, established a **reconcentration** policy, by which the civilian population was ordered into fortified towns or camps. Everyone who choose to remain outside these fortified areas was assumed to be an insurgent, subject to military action. The insurgents responded by ravaging sugar and tobacco plantations, including those owned by

Americans. Before the conflict, the bulk of Cuban trade was with the United States. The **guerrillas** managed to reduce that commerce to a mere trickle.

The United States government vehemently protested reconcentration, particularly after disease and starvation swept through the camps. Within two years, by one estimate, these conditions killed one of every eight Cubans. American newspapers—especially **Joseph Pulitzer's** New York *World* and **William Randolph Hearst's** New York *Journal*—vied with each other in portraying Spanish atrocities. Papers sent their best reporters to Cuba and exaggerated the reports to attract readers, a practice called yellow journalism. Sickened from the steady diet of yellow press stories, many Americans began clamoring for action to rescue the Cubans from Spanish oppression.

Cleveland reacted cautiously, intent on avoiding American involvement. He proclaimed American neutrality and warned Americans not to support the insurrection. When members of Congress began to push Cleveland to take action to secure Cuban independence, he ignored the pressures. He urged Spain to grant concessions to the insurgents to allay their complaints, but he considered the insurgents incapable of replacing Spanish rule. Just as he had opposed annexation of Hawaii, so now Cleveland resisted the notion of intervening in Cuba, for the

---

Boer republics   Self-governing nations established by white South Africans of Dutch descent; they were formed in an effort to escape British rule but were eventually annexed by Britain into its South African colony.

insurgents   Rebels or revolutionaries.

reconcentration   Spanish policy in Cuba in 1896 under which the civilian population was ordered into fortified camps as part of a plan to isolate and annihilate Cuban revolutionaries.

guerrillas   Guerrillas fight in small groups, usually hiding in the countryside and among the noncombatant population, rather than directly confronting an opposing army.

Joseph Pulitzer   Hungarian-born newspaper publisher whose New York *World* printed sensational stories about Cuba that helped precipitate the Spanish-American War.

William Randolph Hearst   Publisher and rival to Pulitzer, whose newspaper the New York *Journal* thrived on exaggeration and distortion of facts and who actively promoted the war with Spain.

same reason. He feared that intervention might lead to annexation regardless of the will of the Cuban people. Nonetheless, by the time he left the presidency in early 1897, he had begun to warn Spain of possible American intervention.

Striding Boldly: War and Imperialism, 1897–1901

● What were the outcomes of the war with Spain?

● How did the acquisition of new possessions reflect the new expectations about America's role in world affairs?

In 1898, the United States went to war with Spain over Cuba. John Hay, the American ambassador to Great Britain and far from combat, celebrated it as "a splendid little war," and the description stuck. Some who promoted American intervention on behalf of the suffering Cubans envisioned a quick war to establish a Cuban republic. Others saw war with Spain as an opportunity to seize territory and acquire a colonial empire for the United States.

McKinley and War

William McKinley took the presidency in early 1897, amid increasing demands for action regarding Cuba. Unlike Cleveland, he was not willing to let Spain end the conflict by crushing the insurgents. McKinley moved cautiously, however, gradually stepping up diplomatic efforts to resolve the crisis. Late that year Spain responded by recalling General Weyler, softening the reconcentration policy, and offering the Cubans limited self-government but not independence. In February 1898, however, two events scuttled progress toward a negotiated solution.

First, Cuban insurgents stole a letter written by **Enrique Dupuy de Lôme,** the Spanish minister to the United States, and released it to the New York *Journal*. In it, de Lôme criticized President McKinley as "weak and a bidder for the admiration of the crowd." The letter also implied that the Spanish government's commitment to reform in Cuba was not serious. De Lôme's immediate resignation could not undo the damage. The letter aroused intense anti-Spanish feeling among Americans.

On February 15, a few days after publication of the de Lôme letter, an explosion ripped open the American warship *Maine,* anchored in Havana harbor. The *Maine* sank, with the loss of more than 260

American officers and sailors. The yellow press accused Spain of sabotage but produced no evidence. An official inquiry the next month blamed a submarine mine but could not determine whose. Regardless of how the explosion occurred, those advocating intervention now had a rallying cry: "Remember the *Maine!*"

McKinley now extended his demands on Spain: an immediate end to the fighting, an end to reconcentration and measures to relieve the suffering, and **mediation** by McKinley. As mediator between Spain and the insurgents, he would seek to resolve their differences but would also be able to specify Cuban independence. In reply, the Spanish government promised reforms, agreed to end reconcentration, and consented to end the fighting if the insurgents asked for an **armistice.** Spain was silent, though, on mediation by McKinley and independence for Cuba. McKinley responded on April 11 by telling Congress that "the war in Cuba must stop" and asking for authority to act. Congress acted on April 19, passing four resolutions that (1) declared that Cuba was and should be independent, (2) demanded that Spain withdraw "at once," (3) authorized the president to use force to accomplish Spanish withdrawal, and (4) disavowed any intention to annex the island. The first three resolutions were equivalent to a declaration of war. The fourth was usually called the **Teller Amendment** for its sponsor, Senator Henry M. Teller, a Silver Republican from Colorado. In response, Spain declared war.

Nearly all Americans reacted enthusiastically to what they understood to be a war undertaken for the humanitarian purpose of bringing independence to the long-suffering Cubans. From the beginning, however, some voiced distrust of the

---

Enrique Dupuy de Lôme Spanish minister to the United States whose private letter criticizing President McKinley was stolen and printed in the New York *Journal*, increasing anti-Spanish sentiment.

Maine American warship that exploded in Havana harbor in 1898; the incident supplied the motto that spurred the Spanish-American War.

mediation An attempt to bring about the peaceful settlement of a dispute through the intervention of a neutral party.

armistice An agreement to halt fighting at least temporarily.

Teller Amendment Resolution approved by U.S. Senate in 1898, by which the United States promised not to annex Cuba.

♦ On February 15, 1898, an explosion destroyed the American warship *Maine* as it lay at anchor in the harbor at Havana, Cuba. Some two hundred sixty Americans lost their lives. Many Americans blamed the Spanish government of Cuba, although there was no evidence to suggest who was responsible. *Library of Congress.*

McKinley administration's motives in battling an enfeebled colonial power. In Congress, Democrats, Silver Republicans, and Populists had urged the formal recognition of the insurgents as the legitimate government of Cuba, but the McKinley administration and Republican Congressional leaders defeated their efforts. The Teller Amendment also reflected a fear among legislators that McKinley might try to make Cuba an American possession rather than granting it independence.

The "Splendid Little War"

From 1895 onward, American attention had been riveted on Cuba. Thus many Americans were taken by surprise when the first engagement in the war occurred not in Cuba but in the **Philippine Islands,** on the other side of the world. A Spanish colony for more than three hundred years, the Philippines had rebelled repeatedly against Spanish rule. One such revolt had begun in 1896, shortly after the insurrection in Cuba.

Assistant Secretary of the Navy **Theodore Roosevelt** was among those Americans who well understood the islands' strategic location with regard to eastern Asia. In late February 1898, more than six weeks before McKinley's war message to Congress, Roosevelt cabled the American naval commander in the Pacific, George Dewey, and instructed him to lay in a supply of coal. In the event of war, Dewey was to immediately crush the Spanish fleet at Manila Bay.

At sunrise on Sunday, May 1, Dewey carried out those orders. His squadron of four cruisers and three smaller vessels steamed into Manila Bay and quickly destroyed or captured ten Spanish cruisers and gunboats. The Spanish commander knew he stood no chance against superior American firepower. His only response to Dewey's presence was to move his ships away from Manila so that stray shells would not endanger civilian lives. The Spanish lost 381 men. The Americans lost one, a victim of heat prostration. An English writer described it as "a military execution rather than a real contest." Nonetheless, Dewey instantly became a national hero.

Dewey's victory at Manila focused public attention on the Pacific and immediately raised, for some, the prospect of establishing a permanent

Philippine Islands   A group of islands in the Pacific Ocean southeast of China that came under U.S. control in 1898 after the Spanish-American War.

Theodore Roosevelt   American politician and writer who advocated war against Spain in 1898; McKinley's vice president in 1900, he became president in 1901 upon McKinley's assassination.

American presence in that area. This, in turn, revived interest in annexing the Hawaiian Islands as a base for supplying and protecting any future American role in eastern Asia. The McKinley administration had negotiated a treaty of annexation with the Hawaiian government in 1897, shortly after Cleveland left the White House, but anti-imperialist sentiment in the Senate had made approval unlikely. Now, with Dewey's victory and the prospect of a permanent American base in the Philippines, McKinley revived the joint-resolution precedent by which the annexation of Texas came about. Only a majority vote in both houses of Congress was required to adopt a joint resolution, rather than a two-thirds vote of the Senate to approve a treaty. Annexation of Hawaii was accomplished on July 7, more than five years after the planters had **deposed** Queen Liliuokalani.

Dewey's victory demonstrated that the American navy was clearly superior to that of Spain. In contrast, the Spanish army in Cuba outnumbered the entire American army by more than 5 to 1. The Spanish troops, too, had years of experience fighting in Cuba. When war was declared, the American army numbered only 28,000 soldiers, but a call for volunteers brought nearly a million—five times as many as the army wanted or could take. The volunteers represented a broad cross-section of American males. Many African-Americans, who were mustered into segregated units, joined up even though some black leaders voiced concern that the army might become the instrument for transplanting American patterns of racial segregation to Cuba.

The army needed many weeks to train and supply those who rallied to the call. Congress declared war in late April, but not until June did the first troop transports leave for Cuba. Sent to training camps in the South, the new soldiers found chaos and confusion. Food, uniforms, and equipment arrived at one location while the men for whom they were intended stood hungry and idle at another. Uniforms were often of heavy wool, totally unsuited for the climate and season. Disease raged through some camps, killing many men. Others died from tainted food, called "embalmed beef" by the troops. Some African-American soldiers refused to comply with racial segregation, and many white southerners objected to the presence in their communities of so many uniformed and armed black men.

At the outbreak of war, Theodore Roosevelt resigned as assistant secretary of the navy and ordered Brooks Brothers to make him an "ordinary cavalry lieutenant colonel's uniform." Then he and his friend Leonard Wood, a physician and career army officer, took command of the First Volunteer Cavalry, soon to be known as "Roosevelt's Rough Riders"—even though Wood was commander and Roosevelt the second-in-command. Roosevelt quickly recruited an impressive mounted regiment. Some were western cowboys and rangers who fit his qualifications exactly, being "young, good shots, and good riders." Others were upper-class easterners like himself, whose riding experience came more from polo and **steeplechase** competition.

Once in Cuba, American forces concentrated on the port city of Santiago, where the Spanish Atlantic fleet had taken refuge. Inexperienced, poorly equipped, and unfamiliar with the terrain, the Americans doggedly assaulted the fortified hills surrounding the city. Roosevelt—now in command of the **Rough Riders** after Wood was promoted— was the only one on horseback because the regiment's horses had not reached Cuba in time. At Kettle Hill, he led a successful but costly charge of Rough Riders and regular army units, including parts of the Ninth and Tenth Cavalry, made up of African-Americans. Driving the Spanish from the crest of Kettle Hill cleared a serious impediment to the assault on nearby, and strategically more important, San Juan Heights and San Juan Hill. Roosevelt then led his units to take a minor part in the attack on those heights. With little regard for accuracy but a good sense of politics, newspapers declared Roosevelt the hero of the Battle of San Juan Hill. Roosevelt himself thought he deserved the Congressional Medal of Honor. Americans suffered heavy casualties during the first few days of the attack on Santiago, with nearly 10 percent of the troops killed or wounded. Worsening the situation, the surgeon in charge of medical facilities refused assistance from trained Red Cross nurses because he thought field hospitals were not appropriate places for women. He was later overruled. Red Cross nurses, led by Clara Barton, also helped to care for injured Cuban insurgents and civilians.

Once the Americans secured control of the high ground around Santiago Harbor, the Spanish fleet of

---

depose   To dethrone or remove from power.
steeplechase   A horserace across open country or over an obstacle course.
Rough Riders   Cavalry volunteers in the Spanish-American War recruited by their lieutenant colonel Theodore Roosevelt.

◆ Theodore Roosevelt's Rough Riders joined parts of the Ninth and Tenth Cavalry (in the foreground) in a successful assault on Kettle Hill. This engagement became famous as the Battle of San Juan Hill. *Chicago Historical Society.*

four cruisers and two destroyers tried to escape from the harbor. A larger American fleet under Admiral William Sampson and Commodore Winfield Schley met them and repeated Dewey's rout at Manila. Every Spanish ship was sunk or run aground. The Spanish suffered 323 deaths, the Americans one.

Their fleet destroyed and the surrounding hills in American hands, the Spanish in Santiago still waited two weeks before surrendering. A week later American forces took over Puerto Rico. Early in the war, on June 21, an American cruiser had secured the surrender of Spanish forces on Guam without a contest. Spanish land forces in the Philippines surrendered when the first American troops arrived in mid-August. (For all locations, see Map 20.1) The "splendid little war" lasted only sixteen weeks. More than 306,000 men served in the American forces—385 of them died in battle and more than 2,000 died of disease and other causes.

The Treaty of Paris

On August 12, the United States and Spain agreed to stop fighting. The truce specified that Spain was to give up Cuba and transfer to the United States both Puerto Rico and one of the **Ladrone Islands.** Until a peace conference determined the final fate of the Philippines, the United States was to occupy Manila.

The only real question centered on the Philippines. Finley Peter Dunne, a popular humorist, par-odied the national debate on the acquisition of the Philippines in a discussion between his fictional characters, Chicago saloonkeeper Mr. Dooley and a customer named Hennessy.

"I know what I'd do if I was McKinley," said Mr. Hennessy. *"I'd hoist a flag over the Philippines, and I'd take in the whole lot of them."*

"And yet," said Mr. Dooley, *"it's not more than two months since you learned whether they were islands or canned goods. . . . If your son Packy was to ask you where the Philippines are, could you give him any idea whether they are in Russia or just west of the tracks?"*

"Maybe I couldn't," said Mr. Hennessy, haughtily, *"but I'm for taking them in, anyhow."*

"So might I be," said Mr. Dooley, *"if I could only get my mind on it. . . . I can't annex them because I don't know where they are. I can't let go of them because someone else will take them if I do. . . . It would break my heart to think of giving people I've never seen or heard of back to other people I don't know. . . . I don't know what to do about the Philippines. And I'm all alone in the world. Everybody else has made up his mind."*

Ladrone Islands   Islands in the western Pacific now known as the Marianas; they include the island of Guam, which the United States acquired from Spain under the 1898 Treaty of Paris.

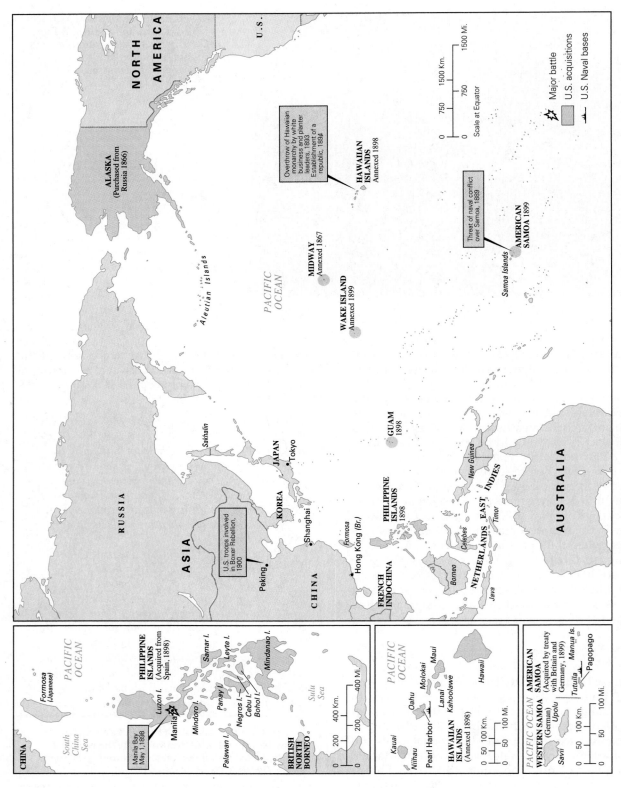

MAP 20.1 The United States and the Pacific, 1866–1900 In the 1890s, the United States became a major power in the Pacific and in eastern Asia. This map indicates major acquisitions and activities up to 1900.

McKinley apparently made up his mind early in favor of annexation, but in public he voiced as many doubts as Mr. Dooley. At first, he seemed inclined to request only a naval base and to leave Spain the remainder of the islands. Spanish authority collapsed everywhere on the islands by mid-August, however, as Filipino insurgents took charge. Britain, Japan, and Germany carefully watched these events and one or another seemed likely to step in if the United States withdrew. McKinley and his advisers had apparently decided by then that defending a naval base on Manila Bay would require control of the entire island group. No one seems to have seriously considered Filipino desires for independence.

McKinley was well aware of the political and strategic importance of the Philippines for establishing an American presence in eastern Asia. He invoked other reasons, however, when he explained his decision to a group of visiting Methodists. He repeatedly prayed for guidance on the Philippine question, he told them. Late one night, perhaps in answer to his prayers, he realized that "there was nothing left for us to do but to take them all, and to educate the Filipinos, and uplift and civilize and Christianize them and by God's grace do the very best we could by them, as our fellow men, for whom Christ also died." In fact, most Filipinos had been Catholics for centuries, but no one ever expressed more clearly the concept of the "white-man's burden."

All through the peace conference in Paris, Spain resisted giving up the Philippines, but McKinley's representatives remained adamant. The **Treaty of Paris,** signed in December 1898, required Spain to surrender all claim to Cuba, cede Puerto Rico and the island of Guam to the United States, and sell the Philippines for $20 million. For the first time in American history, a treaty acquiring new territory failed to confer U.S. citizenship on the residents. Nor did the treaty even mention future statehood. Thus these acquisitions represented a step beyond the Alaska treaty toward a new kind of expansion. The United States now owned territories with no prospect for statehood and whose residents lacked the rights of American citizens. America had become a colonial power.

The terms of the Treaty of Paris dismayed Democrats, Populists, and some conservative Republicans. They immediately launched a public debate over acquisition of the Philippines in particular and imperialism in general. An active anti-imperialist movement quickly formed, including Bryan, Grover Cleveland, Andrew Carnegie, Mark Twain, Jane Addams, and others. The treaty provisions, they argued, amounted to a denial of self-government for the newly acquired territories and therefore violated the Declaration of Independence. For the United States to hold colonies, they claimed, threatened the very concept of democracy. "If you teach suppressed people at all," Carnegie wrote, "you make them rebels." And he warned, "The Declaration of Independence will make every Filipino a thoroughly dissatisfied subject." Others worried over the perversion of American values. "God Almighty help the party that seeks to give civilization and Christianity hypodermically with 13-inch guns," prayed Senator William Morris of Illinois. Some anti-imperialists argued from a racist perspective that Filipinos were incapable of taking part in a western-style democracy, and that the United States would be corrupted by ruling over a people unable to govern themselves. Union leaders, fearing Filipino migration to the United States, repeated arguments once used to demand Chinese exclusion.

Those who defended the acquisition of the Philippines echoed McKinley's lofty pronouncements about America's solemn duty along with more mundane claims about economic benefits. Albert Beveridge, senator from Indiana after 1899, persuasively put forth the commercial benefits of expansion: "Today, we are raising more than we can consume, making more than we can use. Therefore we must find new markets for our produce." Such "new markets" were not limited to the Philippines or other new possessions. Having a major naval and military presence in the Philippines, proponents suggested, would make the United States a leading power in eastern Asia. American business could therefore anticipate access to the China market, then being divided among European imperialist nations and Japan. In contrast to the heated debates over the Philippines, virtually no one challenged the appropriateness of acquiring Puerto Rico.

William Jennings Bryan, the Democratic presidential candidate in 1896, had volunteered and been appointed a colonel (see Individual Choices: William Jennings Bryan). He now resigned his commission, returned to politics, and urged his followers in the Senate to approve the treaty. That way, he

---

Treaty of Paris Treaty ending the Spanish-American War, under which Spain granted independence to Cuba, ceded Puerto Rico and Guam, and sold the Philippines to the United States for $20 million.

The Choice for War

William Jennings Bryan

In 1898, William Jennings Bryan had to choose between joining the American effort to liberate Cuba or staying safely at home with his family and leaving the fighting to others. This photo shows Bryan in uniform, waiting for orders to go to Cuba—orders that never came. Nebraska State Historical Society.

When President McKinley asked Congress, in April 1898, to pass the resolutions that led to war with Spain, he presented a tough choice to William Jennings Bryan, his opponent in the 1896 election. Bryan had urged that the United States help the Cuban people to secure their independence—by war if necessary. Other leaders of Bryan's political coalition of Silver Democrats, Populists, and Silver Republicans (see pages 599–602) had voiced similar demands.

Once war was declared, Bryan had to choose whether he should volunteer to serve. There were important constraints against doing so: he was 39 years old and father of three young children. Most Americans reasonably expected him to do little more than use his oratorical gifts in speeches cheering departing troops. But Bryan had grown to political maturity at a time when leaders of his party, the Democrats, had come under severe and repeated political attack for failing to join the Union Army during the Civil War. When Bryan was 12 years old his own father had been so maligned when he ran for the House of Representatives. The issue had plagued Grover Cleveland in each of his campaigns for president. Bryan had every reason to expect that those who failed to serve would face similar unpleasant treatment in the future.

reasoned, the United States alone could determine the future of the Philippines. Once the treaty was approved, he argued, the United States should immediately grant them independence. By a narrow margin, the Senate approved the treaty on February 6, 1899, but soon after, Senators rejected a proposal for Philippine independence.

Republic or Empire? The Election of 1900

Bryan hoped to make independence for the Philippines the central issue in the 1900 presidential election. He easily won the Democrats' nomination for a second time, and the Democratic platform condemned the McKinley administration for its "imperialism." Bryan found, however, that many conservative anti-imperialists would not support his candidacy because he insisted on silver coinage and attacked big business.

The Republicans renominated McKinley. For vice president, they chose Theodore Roosevelt, "hero of San Juan Hill." Elected governor of New York in 1898, Roosevelt's popularity and independence frightened New York's established Republican leaders, who expected him to challenge their control of state politics. In fact, they pushed Roosevelt for the vice presidency as a means of getting him out of the

Thus, on April 25, when Congress declared war on Spain, Bryan wrote to McKinley: "I hereby place my services at your command during the war with Spain." Other young and aspiring politicians did the same, notably Theodore Roosevelt, two years older than Bryan and with similar family duties. The offer of Roosevelt, a rising Republican, was accepted quickly and with great publicity. Bryan's offer, however, brought no response. Volunteers began to depart for training, and Dewey smashed the Spanish fleet in Manila, but still Bryan waited at home in Nebraska. Finally, on May 7, McKinley responded cautiously but without accepting Bryan's offer to serve.

Meanwhile, Bryan's political allies were begging him to reconsider his choice. Most echoed the argument one friend sent to Bryan's wife Mary, trying to convince her to persuade him to stay in politics at home because "he [can not] be spared from the mighty contest now waging in favor of the rights of the people." With Dewey's action in Manila, especially, many began to fear that a war undertaken to free the Cubans was being transformed into a war for empire. William V. Allen, a Populist elected to the U.S. Senate with Bryan's support, complained that Bryan's enlistment "would dignify the war beyond its merit."

Bryan, however, decided to carry out his choice to serve and joined the Nebraska National Guard. Silas Holcomb, governor of Nebraska (another Populist elected with Bryan's support), promptly named him colonel of a new regiment, the Third Nebraska Volunteers.

Bryan's doubts about accepting such a command were resolved when a Nebraska Democrat with professional military education and Civil War experience chose to serve as his lieutenant colonel.

The army sent Bryan's regiment to Florida in mid-July. There they waited out the war, suffering from typhus and other diseases, while Roosevelt's Rough Riders captured newspaper headlines as well as Cuban hills. Rumors flourished that the McKinley administration intended to keep Bryan in uniform but far from action, thereby denying him any possibility of military glory and, at the same time, eliminating him from the fall political campaigns.

In September 22, with the fighting over for two months—and Roosevelt out of uniform and running for governor of New York—Bryan went to see McKinley and requested that his unit be sent home. "They did not volunteer," he lectured the president, "to subjugate other peoples." But McKinley still refused to release them. Bryan feared that if he chose to resign his commission, Republicans might accuse him of running out on his responsibilities. Finally, in December, when the peace treaty was signed, Bryan resigned his commission and front pages blared his return to politics. Thus, the outcome of Bryan's adventure as a political colonel was very different from that of Roosevelt. Bryan left uniform a committed anti-imperialist, and his reflections on world affairs eventually led him to a stand very close to pacifism.

statehouse. For most of its occupants in the previous century, the vice presidency had been a one-way ticket to political oblivion. Roosevelt, however, eyed the presidency itself, an ambition obvious to McKinley's political adviser Mark Hanna, who warned, "There's only one life between this madman and the White House."

The McKinley reelection campaign seemed unstoppable. Republican campaigners pointed proudly to a short and highly successful war, legislation that had fulfilled party campaign promises on the tariff and the gold standard, and the return of prosperity. Where Bryan repeatedly attacked imperialism, McKinley and Roosevelt never used the term *imperi-* *alism* at all and instead took pride in *expansion*. Republican campaigners questioned the patriotism of anyone who proposed to pull down the flag where it had once been raised. McKinley easily won a second term with 51.7 percent of the vote, carrying not only the states that had given him his victory in 1896 but also most of the western states where Populism had once flourished.

Organizing an Insular Empire

The Teller Amendment specified that the United States would not annex Cuba (see Map 20.2 for all Carribbean locations). The McKinley administra-

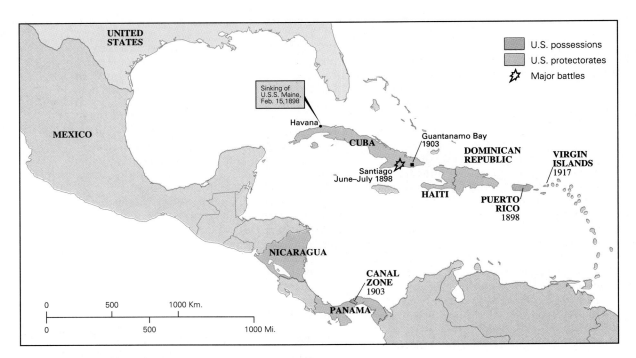

◆ **MAP 20.2 The United States and the Caribbean, 1898–1917** Between 1898 and 1917, the United States expanded into the Caribbean by acquiring possessions and establishing protectorates. As a result, the United States was the dominant power in the region throughout this time period.

tion, though, consistently refused to recognize the insurgents as a legitimate government, so the United States Army took over the job of running the island when the Spanish left. Among other tasks, the army undertook public improvements, including sanitation projects intended to reduce disease, especially yellow fever. After two years of army rule, the McKinley administration permitted Cuban voters to hold a constitutional convention.

The convention met late in 1900 and drafted a constitution modeled on that of the United States. It did not define relations between Cuba and the United States, however. General Leonard Wood, now military governor of Cuba, made clear that the army would not leave the island until the Cuban constitution established what McKinley had earlier called "ties of singular intimacy and strength" between the two nations.

In March 1901, the McKinley administration specified, and Congress adopted, detailed provisions for Cuba to adopt before the army would withdraw, including these stipulations: (1) Cuba was not to make any agreement with a foreign power that impaired the island's independence, (2)

the United States could intervene in Cuba to preserve Cuban independence and maintain law and order, and (3) Cuba was to lease facilities to the United States for naval and coaling stations. Cubans reluctantly accepted the conditions, amended them to their constitution, and agreed to a treaty with the United States stating the same conditions. Cuba thereby became a protectorate of the United States.

The Teller Amendment did not apply to Puerto Rico. On that island, too, the army provided a military government until 1900, when Congress approved the **Foraker Act.** That act made Puerto Ricans citizens of Puerto Rico but not citizens of the United States. It specified that Puerto Rican voters were to elect a legislature but that final authority was to rest with a governor and council appointed by the President of the United States. In 1901, in the

---

Foraker Act Law passed by Congress in 1900 that established civilian government in Puerto Rico; it provided for an elected legislature and a governor appointed by the U.S. president.

◆ The Spanish banished Emilio Aguinaldo y Famy (on horseback) from the Philippines because of his efforts to end Spanish rule. American naval officials returned him to the islands. There he helped to establish an independent Filipino government and later led armed resistance to American authority, until he was captured in 1901. *UPI/Bettmann Archives.*

Insular cases, the United States Supreme Court issued a complex decision that, in effect, confirmed the colonial status of Puerto Rico and, by implication, the other new possessions. The Court ruled that they were not equivalent to earlier territorial acquisitions, and that their people did not possess the constitutional rights of citizens.

Establishment of a civil government in the Philippines took longer. Between Dewey's victory and arrival of the first American soldiers three months later, a Philippine independence movement, led by **Emilio Aguinaldo,** had established a provisional government. Its forces controlled all the islands except Manila, which remained in Spanish hands until American troops arrived. Aguinaldo and his government had no interest in simply exchanging colonial masters—they wanted independence. When the United States decided to keep the islands, the Filipinos resisted and eventually turned to guerrilla warfare. In an ironic turn of events, the United States now found itself in the role that Spain had previously played, seeking to impose its rule on a people fighting for independence.

Quelling what American authorities called the "Philippine insurrection" required three years, took the lives of more than 4,200 American soldiers (more losses than in the Spanish-American War) and perhaps 20,000 guerrillas, and cost $400 million (twenty times the price of the islands). In crushing the resistance, U.S. troops resorted to the same practice of reconcentration that the American public and Congress had so widely condemned when Spain

used it in Cuba. Both sides committed atrocities during the conflict, and those by American troops confirmed for anti-imperialists their fears that a colonial policy would corrupt American values. Resistance continued into mid-1902 although American troops captured Aguinaldo in 1901.

Aguinaldo's defeat and McKinley's reelection ended any prospect for immediate Philippine independence. In 1902 Congress set up a government for the Philippines similar to that of Puerto Rico. Filipinos became citizens of the Philippine Islands, not citizens of the United States. The president of the United States appointed the governor. Filipino voters elected one house in the two-house legislature, and the governor appointed the other. Both the governor and the United States Congress could veto laws passed by the legislature. **William Howard Taft,** governor of the islands from 1901 to 1904, tried to build local support for American control, brought

---

Insular cases   1901 Supreme Court cases concerning Puerto Rico, in which the Court ruled that people in new island territories did not automatically receive the constitutional rights of U.S. citizens.

Emilio Aguinaldo   Leader of struggles for Philippine independence, first against Spain and then against the United States.

William Howard Taft   Appointed governor of the Philippines from 1901 to 1904; he was elected president of the United States in 1908 and became chief justice of the Supreme Court in 1921.

about some reform in land ownership, and initiated projects to build public schools and hospitals and to bring modern sanitation to the islands. However, when the first Philippine legislature met, in 1907, over half of its members favored independence from the United States.

The Open Door and the Boxer Rebellion in China

Late in 1899, Britain, Germany, and the United States signed a treaty that divided Samoa between Germany and the United States. The new Pacific acquisitions of the United States—Samoa, Hawaii, the Philippines, and Guam—were all endowed with excellent harbors and sites for naval bases. Combined with the modernized navy, these acquisitions greatly strengthened American ability to protect access both to its new possessions and to commercial markets in eastern Asia, especially China. They also laid a more general basis for assertion of American power in eastern Asia and the Pacific. The McKinley administration now began to act like a major east Asian power.

Weakened by war with Japan in 1894–1895, the Chinese government could not resist attempts by European nations to gain control over parts of its territory. By 1899, Britain, Germany, Russia, and France had all carved out **spheres of influence,** areas where they claimed special rights, usually a monopoly over trade. In keeping with the open door approach first adopted in the treaty of 1844, the United States claimed no such privileges in China. Now, however, American diplomats began to fear the break-up of China into separate European colonies and the consequent exclusion of American commerce.

In 1899, Secretary of State John Hay circulated a letter to Germany, Russia, Britain, France, Italy, and Japan, asking them to permit Chinese authorities to continue to collect tariff duties within their spheres of influence. Hay hoped that this measure would preserve some semblance of Chinese sovereignty. He also urged them not to discriminate against citizens of other nations engaged in commerce within their spheres. Thus, Hay sought to prevent other nations from carving up China and, at the same time, to make American trade possible throughout China. Although some replies proved less than fully supportive, he announced that the Open Door policy was in effect.

DEAN C. WORCESTER ON THE PHILIPPINES

A FAIR FIELD AND NO FAVOR!
UNCLE SAM: "I'M OUT FOR COMMERCE, NOT CONQUEST"

◆ In this 1899 cartoon celebrating the Open Door policy, Uncle Sam insists that the nations of Europe must compete fairly for China's commerce and must not seize Chinese territory. In the background, John Bull (Britain) lifts his hat in approval. *Library of Congress.*

The next year, in 1900, a Chinese secret society took up arms to expel foreigners and foreign influence from China. Because the rebels used a clenched fist as their symbol, westerners called them Boxers. After attacking missionaries, the Boxers laid siege to the section of Peking, the Chinese capital, that housed foreign **legations.** Hay foresaw that the major powers, in rescuing their citizens, might use the

> **sphere of influence** A territorial area where a foreign nation is given significant authority.
> **legation** A diplomatic mission in a foreign country.

Boxer Rebellion as a pretext to take full control and divide China among themselves, slamming shut the Open Door. To block such a move, the United States took full part in a joint international military expedition—with Japan and Russia supplying the largest numbers—to rescue the Peking hostages and to crush the Boxer Rebellion. Hay insisted, however, that American action was not against the Chinese government but the rebels.

Although China did not lose territory after the Boxer Rebellion, the intervening nations required it to pay an **indemnity.** After compensating United States citizens for actual losses suffered during the rebellion, the United States government returned the remainder of its indemnity to China. To show its appreciation for the return of the funds, the Chinese government used the money to send Chinese students to the United States to develop good will between the two countries.

"Carry a Big Stick": The United States and World Affairs, 1901–1913

- What were Theodore Roosevelt's expectations about the role of the United States in world affairs?

- What choices did he make to bring about the outcomes he desired?

In 1901, an assassin's bullet cut down President McKinley and put Theodore Roosevelt in the White House. Roosevelt remolded the presidency, established new federal powers in the economy, and expanded America's role in world affairs. Few presidents have had so great an impact. He once expressed his fondness for what he described as a West African proverb, "Speak softly and carry a big stick; you will go far." As president, however, Roosevelt seldom spoke softly. Everything he did, it seemed, he did strenuously. Well read in history and current events, Roosevelt entered the presidency with definite ideas on the proper role for the United States in the world. He envisioned a future in which major powers would exercise international police powers. As he advised Congress in 1902, "The increasing interdependence and complexity of international political and economic relations render it incumbent on all civilized and orderly powers

to insist on the proper policing of the world." The United States, Roosevelt made clear, stood ready to do its share of "proper policing."

Taking Panama

While McKinley was still president, following the American victory over Spain, American diplomats pursued efforts to build, control, and protect a canal through Central America. Many people, and not just in the United States, had long dreamed of such a passage between the Atlantic and Pacific oceans. In 1897, for example, Roosevelt wrote to Mahan, agreeing that the United States should give highest priority to building an isthmian canal and to dominating the Caribbean to protect it. Construction had actually gotten underway in the late 1870s, by a French company. But the task proved too great for its resources, and the builders abandoned the project.

During the Spanish-American War, the battleship *Oregon* took well over two months to steam from Portland, Oregon, around South America, to the southern coast of Cuba. A canal would have permitted the *Oregon* to reach Cuba in three weeks or less. McKinley soon pronounced an American-controlled canal "indispensable." In the **Clayton-Bulwer Treaty** of 1850, however, Britain and the United States had agreed that neither would exercise exclusive control over a canal. Between 1900 and 1901, Secretary of State Hay negotiated a new agreement with Britain, the **Hay-Pauncefote Treaty,** which yielded the canal project to the United States alone.

Experts identified two possible locations for a canal, Nicaragua and Panama (then part of Colombia). In its favor, the Panama route was shorter, and the French canal company had completed some

---

Boxer Rebellion   Uprising in China in 1900 directed against foreign powers; it was suppressed by an international army that included American participation.

indemnity   Payment for damage, loss, or injury.

Clayton-Bulwer Treaty   Treaty signed in 1850 under which the United States and Britain agreed to guarantee jointly the neutrality of a canal through Central America.

Hay-Pauncefote Treaty   Two separate treaties (1900 and 1901) signed by the United States and Britain, which gave the United States the exclusive right to build, control, and fortify a canal through Central America.

♦ Theodore Roosevelt, in his 1904 Corollary to the Monroe Doctrine, asserted that the United States was dominant in the Caribbean. Here a cartoonist capitalized on Roosevelt's boyish nature, depicting the Caribbean as Roosevelt's pond. *Culver Pictures, Inc.*

work. **Philippe Bunau-Varilla**—formerly the chief project engineer, now a major stockholder and an indefatigable lobbyist—did his utmost to sell that company's interests to the United States. Building through Panama, however, meant overcoming both formidable mountains and fever-ridden swamps. Previous studies had preferred Nicaragua. Its geography posed fewer natural obstacles and much of the route lay through Lake Nicaragua.

In 1902, shortly before Congress was to vote between the two routes, a volcano erupted in Nicaragua. Bunau-Varilla underscored its relation to the canal by distributing to senators a Nicaraguan postage stamp showing a smoldering volcano looming over a lake. Bunau-Varilla's lobbying—and his stamps—reinforced efforts by such prominent Republican senators as Mark Hanna. The Senate approved the route through Panama, provided that Colombia agreed to give up land for a canal, and designated Nicaragua as the alternative location should Colombia hold back.

Negotiations with Colombia bogged down over treaty language that significantly limited its sovereignty. When the United States put on pressure, the Colombian government offered to accept the limitations on its sovereignty in return for more money. Roosevelt, outraged, called it "pure bandit morality." To break the impasse, Bunau-Varilla and his associates encouraged and financed a revolution in Panama. Anticipating such a possibility, Roosevelt

had ordered U.S. warships in the area to prevent Colombian troops from crushing the uprising. The revolution quickly succeeded and Panama declared its independence. The United States immediately extended diplomatic recognition. Bunau-Varilla, named Panama's minister to the United States, promptly signed a treaty that gave the United States much the same arrangement earlier rejected by Colombia.

The **Hay–Bunau-Varilla Treaty** (1904) granted the United States perpetual control over a strip of Panamanian territory ten miles wide, for a price of $10 million and annual rent of $250,000, and made Panama the second American protectorate (see Map 20.3). The United States also purchased the assets of the French company and in 1904 began construction of the canal. Roosevelt considered the Panama Canal his crowning deed in foreign affairs. "When

---

Philippe Bunau-Varilla   Chief engineer of the French company contracted to build the Panama Canal and later minister to the United States from the new Republic of Panama.

Hay–Bunau-Varilla Treaty   Treaty with Panama that granted the United States sovereignty over the Canal Zone in return for a $10 million payment plus an annual rent.

nobody else could or would exercise efficient authority, I exercised it," he wrote in his *Autobiography* (1911). He always denied, however, that he took part in planning the revolution. "I did not lift my finger to incite the revolutionists," he wrote. "I simply ceased to stamp out the different revolutionary fuses that were already burning." On another occasion, however, he bluntly claimed, "I took the canal zone."

Building the canal, though, proved difficult. Just over 40 miles long, the canal took ten years to build and cost nearly $400 million. Completed in 1914, just as World War I began, the canal was considered one of the world's great engineering feats.

Making the Caribbean an American Lake

Well before the canal was finished, American policymakers debated how best to protect it. Roosevelt determined to establish American dominance in the Caribbean and Central America, where the many islands and harbors might permit a naval build-up for a strike against the canal or even the Gulf Coast of the United States. Acquisition of Puerto Rico, protectorates over Cuba and Panama, and naval facilities in all three locations as well as on the Gulf Coast made the United States a powerful presence in the region.

The Caribbean and the area around it contained twelve independent nations. Britain, France, Denmark, and the Netherlands held nearly all the smaller islands as well as a coastal colony. Several Caribbean nations had borrowed large amounts of money from European bankers, raising the prospect of European intervention to secure loan payments. In 1902, for example, Britain and Germany declared a blockade of Venezuela over debts owed their citizens. In 1904, when several European nations hinted that they might similarly intervene in the Dominican Republic, Roosevelt waved his "big stick." He presented to Congress what became known as the **Roosevelt Corollary** to the Monroe Doctrine.

Chronic wrongdoing, or an impotence which results in a general loosening of the ties of civilized society, may in America, as elsewhere, ultimately require intervention by some civilized nation, and in the Western Hemisphere the adherence of the United States to the Monroe Doctrine may force the United States, however reluctantly, in flagrant cases of such wrongdoing or impotence, to the exercise of an international police power.

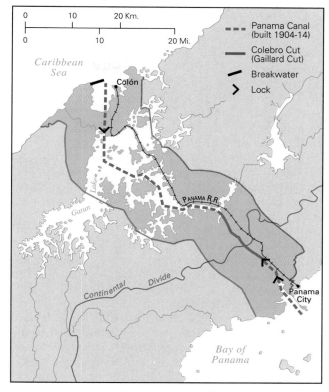

◆ **MAP 20.3 The Panama Canal**   The Panama Canal could take advantage of some natural waterways. The most difficult part of the construction, however, was devising some way to move ships over the mountains near the Pacific end of the canal. This was done through a combination of cutting a route through the mountains and constructing massive locks.

Roosevelt thus warned European nations against any intervention whatsoever in the Western Hemisphere, even if provoked by loan default or other action. If outside authority became necessary in the Caribbean and Central America, Roosevelt insisted that the United States would handle it, acting as an international police officer. Roosevelt exempted Argentina, Brazil, and Chile from application of the Roosevelt Corollary. He considered them "civilized" powers in their own right, and he hoped they might wield a similar police power in Latin America south of the Caribbean region.

Roosevelt Corollary   Extension of the Monroe Doctrine voiced by Theodore Roosevelt in 1904, in which he proclaimed the right of the United States to police Caribbean areas.

Roosevelt acted forcefully to establish his new policy. In 1905, the Dominican Republic agreed to permit the United States to collect customs and supervise government expenditures, including payment of debts. Thus the island nation became a third U.S. protectorate. The Senate initially rejected this arrangement but approved an amended version in 1907. In the meantime, Roosevelt ordered the navy to collect Dominican customs, claiming that he could do so under his presidential powers.

Roosevelt's successors, William Howard Taft and Woodrow Wilson, continued and expanded his policy of American domination in the Caribbean region. Under Taft, the United States encouraged Americans to invest in the region. Taft hoped that diplomacy could open doors for American investments, and American investments in turn could advance foreign policy objectives by blocking investment by other nations and by stabilizing and developing the Caribbean economies. Taft supported such **dollar diplomacy** throughout the region, especially in Nicaragua. In 1912, Taft sent marines there to suppress a rebellion against President Adolfo Días. They remained after the turmoil settled, ostensibly to guard the American legation but actually to prop up the Días government—making Nicaragua a fourth protectorate. A treaty was drafted giving the United States responsibility for collecting customs, but the Senate rejected it. At that point, the State Department, several American banks, and Nicaragua agreed to set up a customs **receivership** through the banks.

Roosevelt and Eastern Asia

In developing American policy in eastern Asia, Roosevelt built on the Open Door notes and American participation in the international force that had suppressed the Boxer Rebellion. He found cause for both concern and optimism in the rise of Japan as a major industrial and imperial power. His friend and naval strategist, Alfred Thayer Mahan, had warned of the potential danger to the United States, a rising power on one rim of the Pacific, posed by Japan, a rising power on the opposite rim. But Roosevelt was also hopeful. He admired Japanese accomplishments and looked forward to Japan exercising the same degree of international police power in its vicinity that the United States wielded under the Roosevelt Corollary.

In 1904, Russia and Japan went to war over **Manchuria,** the northern part of China. Russia had

never withdrawn the many troops moved into the area during the Boxer Rebellion. Backed by that military presence, Russia pressured China repeatedly to grant concessions by which Manchuria slowly seemed to be turning into a Russian colony. Russia seemed also to have designs on Korea, a nominally independent kingdom. Japan saw the steady expansion of Russia as a threat to its own predominance in Korea and the region, and responded with force. The Japanese scored smashing naval and military victories over the Russians but had too few resources to sustain a long-term war.

Roosevelt concluded that American interests were best served by reducing Russian influence in the region so as to maintain a balance of power. Such a balance, he thought, would be most likely to preserve at least the fiction of Chinese sovereignty in Manchuria. Early in the war, he indicated some support for Japan, and—as its resources ran low—Japan asked Roosevelt to act as mediator. The president agreed, concerned by then that the Japanese victories might pose as great a danger as Russian expansion. The peace conference took place in Portsmouth, New Hampshire. The **Treaty of Portsmouth** (1905) recognized Japan's dominance in Korea and gave Japan both the southern half of Sakhalin Island and Russian concessions in southern Manchuria. Russia kept its railroad in northern Manchuria. China was to have responsibility for civil authority in Manchuria. For his mediation, Roosevelt received the 1906 Nobel Peace Prize.

That same year, Roosevelt mediated another significant dispute. An order by the San Francisco school board stipulated that children of Japanese parentage were to attend the city's segregated Chinese school. The Japanese government protested what they considered a serious insult, and Japanese newspaper headlines even hinted of war. Roosevelt

---

dollar diplomacy   Policy during the Taft administration of supporting U.S. commercial interests abroad for strategic purposes, especially in Latin America.

receivership   An office appointed to receive and account for money due.

Manchuria   A region of northeast China that the Russians and Japanese fought to control in the late nineteenth and early twentieth centuries.

Treaty of Portsmouth   Treaty in 1905 ending the Russo-Japanese War, which was negotiated at a conference in Portsmouth, New Hampshire, through Theodore Roosevelt's mediation.

brought the city's school officials to Washington and convinced them to withdraw the segregation order in return for his efforts to cut off Japanese immigration. He soon carried out his part of the bargain through a so-called **gentlemen's agreement,** by which Japan agreed informally to limit the departure of laborers to the United States. In 1908, the American and Japanese governments further agreed to respect each other's territorial possessions (the Philippines and Hawaii for the United States, Korea, Formosa, and southern Manchuria for Japan) and to honor as well "the independence and integrity of China" and the Open Door.

During the presidential administration of William Howard Taft, Roosevelt's successor, the United States extended the concept of dollar diplomacy to China. Proponents sought Chinese permission for American citizens not just to trade with China, but also to invest there, especially in railroad construction. Taft and his secretary of state, Philander C. Knox, hoped that such investments could head off further Japanese expansion. The effort received Chinese governmental sanction, but little ever came of it, apart from alienating Japan somewhat.

The United States and the World: 1901–1913

Before the 1890s, the United States had no clear or consistent set of foreign policy commitments or objectives. After then, its commitments were obvious to all. Acquisition of the Philippines, Guam, Hawaii, Puerto Rico, eastern Samoa, and the **Canal Zone** represented highly visible components in a new concept of America's role in world affairs.

Central to that concept was a large, modern, two-ocean navy, without which other commitments lacked anything more than moral force. Roosevelt was so proud of the navy that, in 1907, he dispatched sixteen battleships—painted white to indicate their peaceful intent—on a fourteen-month around-the-world tour, as a demonstration of American naval might. Although it is clear that his action came initially in response to saber-rattling by the Japanese press, Roosevelt later claimed that his primary purpose in sending the Great White Fleet "was to impress the American people." But he was clearly interested in impressing other nations too, and, even more, in demonstrating that the American navy was a two-ocean navy, fully capable of moving quickly from Atlantic to Pacific ports. When one senator argued that insufficient funds had been ap-

propriated for such a showy undertaking, Roosevelt retorted that he had enough money to get the fleet to the middle of the Pacific, and that he expected Congress to pay to bring it back.

Another aspect of America's new role in the world revolved around the principle that the United States should control an **isthmian** canal, a principle that derived from considerations of both commercial enterprise and naval strategy. Protecting that canal led the United States to establish **hegemony** in the Caribbean and Central America as a means of preventing any other major power from gaining a foothold that might threaten the canal. The new American role also focused on the Pacific. Captain Mahan and other naval strategists pointed out that the Atlantic Ocean had been the theater of conflict among European nations in the eighteenth century, a conflict whose outcome was unrivalled British naval supremacy in the nineteenth century. They looked to the Pacific Ocean as the likely theater of twentieth-century conflict. Again, considerations of commercial enterprise, such as the China trade, and naval strategy coincided in leading the United States to acquire naval bases at strategic points in the central Pacific (Hawaii), south Pacific (eastern Samoa), and off eastern Asia (the Philippines).

America's new vision of the world divided nations into two broad categories. On the one hand were all the "civilized" nations. On the other were those nations that Theodore Roosevelt described, at various times, as "barbarous," "impotent," or simply unable to meet their obligations. American policy toward "civilized" countries—the European powers, Japan, and the large, stable nations of Latin America—focused on efforts to find peaceful ways to realize mutual objectives, especially through arbitration. In eastern Asia, McKinley, Roosevelt, and Taft all looked to a balance of power among the contending "civilized" powers as most likely to realize the American objective of maintaining commercial

---

gentlemen's agreement　An agreement bound only by the word of the parties; in this case, Japan agreed in 1907 to limit Japanese emigration to the United States.

Canal Zone　Territory under U.S. control including the Panama Canal and land extending five miles on either side of it.

isthmian　Of an isthmus, which is a narrow strip of land connecting two larger land masses; in this case, the isthmus was Panama.

hegemony　The dominance of one over other.

◆ The artist Henry Reuterdahl has captured the White Fleet, entering San Francisco Bay through the Golden Gate, shortly before its round-the-world voyage in 1907–1908. Roosevelt sent the fleet around the world to demonstrate American naval power, but had it painted white as sign of its peaceful intent. *The Beverly R. Robinson Collection, U.S. Naval Academy Museum.*

access to the China market. In Europe, Roosevelt proved far more willing than any of his successors to take part in maintaining the balance of power, as he proved in 1906 by sending representatives to a conference at Algeciras, Spain, to resolve disputes over the role of the European powers in Morocco.

The conviction that arbitration was the appropriate means to settle disputes among "civilized" countries was widespread. An international conference in 1899 created a Permanent Court of Arbitration in the Netherlands. Housed in a marble "peace palace" built through a donation from Andrew Carnegie, the **Hague Court** functioned as a source of neutral arbitrators for international disputes. Both Roosevelt and Taft tried to negotiate arbitration treaties with major powers, only to find that the Senate was not willing to ratify them. Senators feared that such treaties might diminish its future role in approving agreements with other countries.

The United States and Britain repeatedly used arbitration to settle disputes between themselves. In addition to the *Alabama* claims, they used arbitration in 1903 to settle questions over the boundary between Alaska and Canada and in 1909 to end a dispute over the rights of American fishermen operating off the coast of Canada. In each instance, however, Canadians complained that Britain sacrificed Canadian interests to maintain good relations with the United States.

Throughout the late nineteenth and early twentieth centuries, American relations improved steadily with Great Britain, primarily as a consequence of British policy choices. From at least the time of the Venezuelan boundary dispute (1895–1896), Britain proceeded cautiously in its relations with the United States. As Germany expanded its army and navy and increasingly challenged Britain, British policymakers sought to improve ties with the United States, the only nation besides Great Britain with a navy comparable to Germany's. During the Spanish-American war, Britain alone among the major European powers sided with the United States and encouraged its acquisition of the Philippines. In signing the Hay-Pauncefote Treaty and reducing its naval forces in the Caribbean, Britain delivered a clear signal: it not only accepted American dominance there but even depended on the good will of the United States to protect its own holdings in the region.

> **Hague Court**   Body of delegates from about fifty member nations, created in the Netherlands in 1899 for the purpose of peacefully resolving international conflicts; also known as the Permanent Court of Arbitration.

SUMMARY

E xpectations
C onstraints
C hoices
O utcomes

From 1865 to 1889, few Americans *expected* their nation to take a major part in world affairs, at least outside North America. The United States did make *choices* to acquire Alaska and to expel the French from Mexico, and some Americans even hoped that Canada might become U.S. territory. Other American *choices* brought some involvement in the Caribbean and Central America, and in eastern Asia and the Pacific.

The 1890s witnessed the development of enlarged *expectations* and daring *choices* in foreign affairs. During the administration of Benjamin Harrison, Congress approved creation of a modern navy. Although a revolution presented the United States with an opportunity to annex Hawaii, President Grover Cleveland *chose* to reject that course. However, Cleveland boldly threatened war with Great Britain over a disputed boundary between Venezuela and British Guiana, and Britain *chose* to back down.

A revolution in Cuba led the United States into a one-sided war with Spain in 1898. The immediate *outcome* of winning the war was acquisition of an American colonial empire that included not only Cuba, but also the Philippines, Guam, and Puerto Rico. Congress annexed Hawaii in the midst of the war and the United States acquired Samoa by treaty in 1899. Filipinos *chose* to resist the imposition of American authority, leading to a three-year war that cost more lives than the Spanish-American War. With the Philippines in hand and an improved navy on the seas, the United States was free of old *con-*straints on its influence in east Asia. It now *chose* to assert the principle of the Open Door in China, where American troops took part in suppressing the Boxer Rebellion.

President Theodore Roosevelt's *choices* played an important role in defining America's status as a world power. He secured rights to build a U.S.-controlled canal through Panama and established Panama as an American protectorate. The Roosevelt Corollary declared outright that the United States was the dominant power in the Caribbean and Central America. In eastern Asia, by contrast, Roosevelt chose to bolster the Open Door policy by maintaining a balance of power.

Roosevelt, and many others, *expected* that "civilized" nations had no need to go to war. Thus he *chose* to seek arbitration treaties with leading nations, efforts that failed because of Senate opposition. Faced with the rise of German military and naval power, Great Britain *chose* to improve its relations with the United States.

One *outcome* of America's *choices* in foreign affairs was the acquisition of colonies in a foreign policy usually described as imperialism. A larger *outcome* was that the United States took on the role of a world power, thereby redefining its relations with the rest of the world.

SUGGESTED READINGS

Beisner, Robert L. *From the Old Diplomacy to the New, 1865–1900.* 2nd ed. (1986).
    A concise introduction to American foreign relations for this period.

Gould, Lewis L. *The Spanish-American War and President McKinley* (1980).
    The political decisions involved in war, peacemaking, and the acquisition of Spanish possessions.

LaFeber, Walter. *The New Empire: An Interpretation of American Expansion, 1860–1898* (1963).
    A leading treatment, the first to emphasize the notion of a commercial empire.

Langley, Lester D. *The Banana Wars: United States' Intervention in the Caribbean, 1898–1934* (1983, rpt. 1988).
    Sprightly and succinct account of the role of the United States in the Caribbean and Central America.

McCullough, David G. *The Path Between the Seas: The Creation of the Panama Canal, 1870–1914* (1977).
    Perhaps the most lively engrossing coverage of its subject.

Miller, Stuart Creighton. *"Benevolent Assimilation": The American Conquest of the Philippines, 1899–1903* (1982).
    A thorough account of its subject.

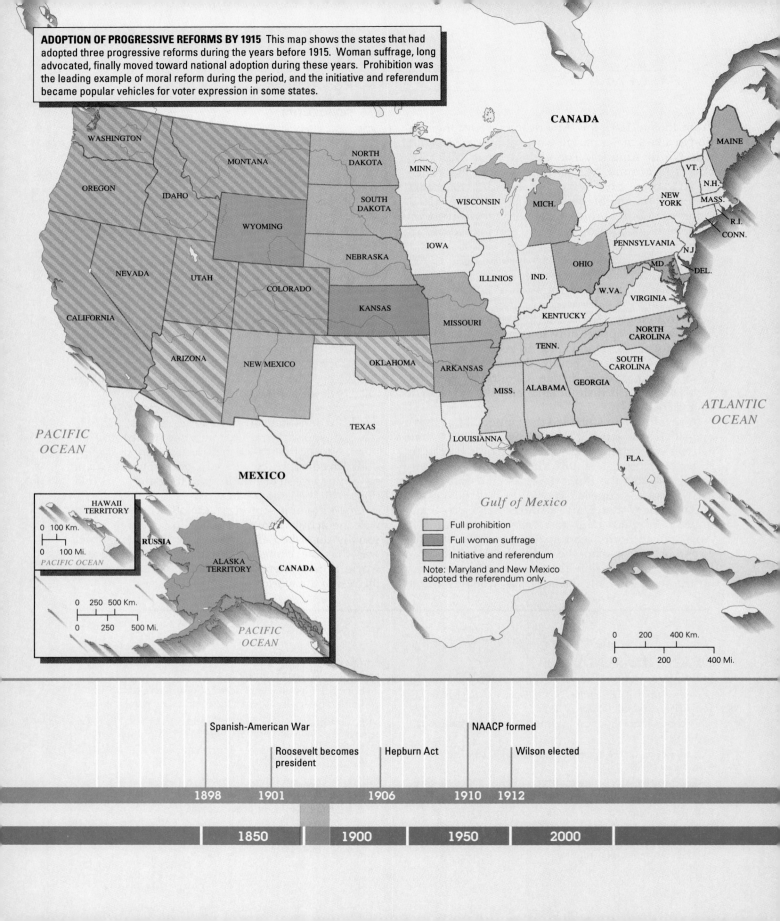

ADOPTION OF PROGRESSIVE REFORMS BY 1915 This map shows the states that had adopted three progressive reforms during the years before 1915. Woman suffrage, long advocated, finally moved toward national adoption during these years. Prohibition was the leading example of moral reform during the period, and the initiative and referendum became popular vehicles for voter expression in some states.

CANADA

WASHINGTON

MONTANA

NORTH DAKOTA

MINN.

WISCONSIN

MICH.

MAINE

VT.

N.H.

NEW YORK

MASS.

R.I.

CONN.

OREGON

IDAHO

SOUTH DAKOTA

WYOMING

IOWA

PENNSYLVANIA

NJ

NEVADA

UTAH

NEBRASKA

ILLINIOS

IND.

OHIO

MD.

DEL.

W.VA.

CALIFORNIA

COLORADO

KANSAS

MISSOURI

KENTUCKY

VIRGINIA

NORTH CAROLINA

ARIZONA

NEW MEXICO

OKLAHOMA

ARKANSAS

TENN.

SOUTH CAROLINA

MISS.

ALABAMA

GEORGIA

ATLANTIC OCEAN

TEXAS

LOUISIANNA

FLA.

PACIFIC OCEAN

MEXICO

Gulf of Mexico

HAWAII TERRITORY

0 100 Km.

0 100 Mi.

PACIFIC OCEAN

RUSSIA

ALASKA TERRITORY

CANADA

0 250 500 Km.

0 250 500 Mi.

PACIFIC OCEAN

Full prohibition

Full woman suffrage

Initiative and referendum

Note: Maryland and New Mexico adopted the referendum only.

0 200 400 Km.

0 200 400 Mi.

Spanish-American War

NAACP formed

Roosevelt becomes president

Hepburn Act

Wilson elected

1898 1901 1906 1910 1912

1850 1900 1950 2000

CHAPTER 21

The Progressive Era, 1900–1917

Progressivism: Organizing for Change

- How did progressivism and organized interest groups reflect the changing political expectations of many Americans and their new political choices?

The Reform of Politics, the Politics of Reform

- How did city and state reforms reflect new expectations for political parties and government?

Roosevelt, Taft, and Republican Progressivism

- What constraints did Roosevelt face and how did he choose to deal with them?
- What were the outcomes for the role of the federal government in the economy and for the power of the presidency?

Wilson and Democratic Progressivism

- How did choices by Wilson and the Democrats influence the role of the federal government in the economy and the power of the presidency?

Progressive in Perspective

- Was progressivism successful?
- What are your criteria for judging success?
- What lasting outcomes of progressivism affect modern American politics?

INTRODUCTION

E **xpectations**
C **onstraints**
C **hoices**
O **utcomes**

"Nothing is done in this country as it was done twenty years ago," wrote President Woodrow Wilson in 1913. He exaggerated only slightly. The late 1890s and first 20 years of the twentieth century—years historians call the Progressive era—were a time when "reform was in the air," as one small-town journalist later recalled. In 1912, Walter Weyl, a former settlement house worker, described the state of American politics this way:

> We are in a period of clamor, of bewilderment, of an almost tremulous unrest. We are hastily revising all our social conceptions. We are hastily testing all our political ideals.

Weyl's description, overstated as it was, reflected the widespread popular *expectation* for change. Reform was "in the air" almost everywhere, and many different individuals and groups joined the crusade, often with quite different *expectations*. The variety of competing organizations seeking to reform politics could—and did—produce nearly as much clamor and bewilderment as Weyl described.

At the dawn of the new century, however, few Americans could have anticipated the *extent* of change that lay just ahead. Most probably *expected* a continuation of nineteenth-century political patterns, in which parties dominated politics and government's role in the economy was limited largely to stimulating economic development through the tariff and land policies. At the same time, however, many Americans also believed that something should be done to curb the power of the new industrial corporations and to correct the problems of the cities.

Progressivism took shape through many *choices* by voters and political leaders. Most decisions were specific to a particular election or legislative proposal, but a more basic *choice* loomed behind many of them: should government play a larger role in the lives of Americans? This question lay behind debates over regulation of railroads in 1906 and regulation of banking in 1913, as well as behind proposals to prohibit alcoholic beverages and to limit working hours of women wage earners in factories. Time after time, Americans chose a greater role for government. Many times, in fact, all agreed on the need for greater government intervention, and the only *choices* were about the form intervention would take. As they gave government more power, Americans also sought to make it more responsive to ordinary citizens. *Constrained* by nineteenth-century patterns of political decision making, Americans sometimes impatiently cast them aside by putting stricter limits on political parties and by introducing ways for people to participate more directly in politics—such as the direct primary and the initiative and referendum.

The *constraints* imposed by traditional values of private property and individualism proved more hardy. Although progressives imposed restrictions on the rights of private property, few Americans responded to calls by socialists to eliminate it. Although some reformers proposed to limit individual liberties in the name of morality, a more lasting outcome proved to be the breakdown of separate spheres for men and women in politics.

The *outcome* of the political changes of the Progressive era, following on the heels of the political realignment of the 1890s, was a revamped pattern of politics, significantly different from that of the nineteenth century. The long-term changes in the structure and function of government wrought during these decades fundamentally altered American politics and government in the twentieth century. The Progressive era essentially gave birth to many aspects of modern American politics.

CHRONOLOGY

Reform in the Progressive Era

1889	Pingree elected Detroit mayor
1895	Anti-Saloon League formed *U.S. v. E. C. Knight*
1896	McKinley elected
1897	Jones elected Toledo mayor
1898	South Dakota adopts initiative and referendum Spanish-American War
1900	First city commission, Galveston, Texas La Follette elected Wisconsin governor McKinley reelected
1901	Socialist Party of America formed McKinley assassinated Roosevelt becomes president
1902	Muckraking journalism begins Oregon adopts initiative and referendum Antitrust action against Northern Securities Company Roosevelt intervenes in coal strike Newlands Act
1903	Women's Trade Union League formed Du Bois's *Souls of Black Folk* Elkins Act Expedition Act
1904	Steffens's *The Shame of the Cities* Tarbell's *History of Standard Oil* Roosevelt elected
1905	Niagara Movement Industrial Workers of the World organized
1906	Sinclair's *The Jungle* Hepburn Act Pure Food and Drug Act Meat Inspection Act
1907	Financial panic

1908	*Muller v. Oregon* Race riot in Springfield, Illinois First city-manager government, Staunton, Virginia Taft elected
1909	First "red-light abatement" law Payne-Aldrich Tariff
1910	Washington approves woman suffrage Mann Act National Association for the Advancement of Colored People formed Johnson elected California governor Wilson elected New Jersey governor Revolt against Cannonism Taft fires Pinchot
1911	Triangle fire
1912	Progressive ("Bull Moose") party formed Wilson elected
1913	Congressional Union formed Sixteenth and Seventeenth Amendments Underwood Tariff Federal Reserve Act
1914	Clayton Antitrust Act Federal Trade Commission Act Panama Canal completed
1915	National Birth Control League formed
1916	Montana elects Rankin first woman in Congress Adamson Act Wilson reelected Brandeis appointed to Supreme Court
1917	U.S. enters WWI

Progressivism: Organizing for Change

● How did progressivism and organized interest groups reflect the changing political expectations of many Americans and their new political choices?

During the Progressive era, politics dramatically expanded to embrace a wide range of concerns, raised by a complex assortment of groups and individuals. In the swirl of proponents and proposals, more than ever before, politics came to reflect the interaction of organized interest groups.

Progressivism

Regardless of their specific cause, among reformers of the **Progressive era**, organization was indispensable for success. By revolutionizing travel and communication, the railroad, telegraph, and telephone had encouraged some people to think in regional or national terms. These technologies also eased the way for citizens to form organizations to express their common concerns and promote their common interests. Manufacturers, farmers, merchants, teachers, lawyers, and many others all established or revitalized their own associations to advance their interests. Such organizations to protect and advance a common economic interest were probably the most typical. Organized interest groups increasingly looked to government for help. Merchants' associations and farmers' groups, for example, pushed for laws to regulate railroad freight rates.

Not all groups were organized to promote their own economic interests. Some expected to foster the interests of ethnic, racial, or gender groups. Some had humanitarian goals—to end child labor or promote racial harmony, for example. Others promoted prohibition, blaming alcohol for immorality and poverty.

Such organized interest groups grew out of many separate strands of social and economic development and often evolved over a quarter-century or more. These groups now entered the political arena to advocate an eclectic mixture of reforms. Some reformers hoped to restrain big business, and others were concerned about corruption in urban politics and the power of party bosses. Humanitarian groups raised concerns about victims of industrialization. Some middle-class and upper-class Americans, frightened by labor strife and political unrest during the 1890s, hoped to use government to stabi-

lize the social order. Some wanted to do so by suppressing unions, but others tried to address what they saw as the causes of social unrest—brutal poverty and irresponsible wealth. New professionals, graduating from recently transformed universities, confidently sought the authority to apply their technical knowledge and shape a different future. Organized women emerged onto the political scene as a major force, advocating a variety of social reforms and demanding for themselves the right to vote. Still other groups promoted other causes. Despite such diversity, most groups had at least one feature in common. They shared an optimism that responsible citizens, assisted by technical know-how and operating through government, could accelerate "progress"—the improvement of the human situation. By 1910, many had started calling themselves "progressives."

The term *progressivism* signifies three related developments: (1) the emergence of new concepts of the purposes and functions of government, (2) changes in government policies and institutions, and (3) the political agitation that produced those changes. A *progressive*, then, was a person involved in one or more of these activities. The many individuals and groups all promoting their own visions of change made progressivism a complex political phenomenon. There was no one progressive movement. To be sure, an organized **Progressive party** appeared in 1912 and sputtered for a brief time after, but it failed to capture the allegiance of all those who called themselves progressives. Although there was no typical progressive, many aspects of progressivism reflected concerns of the urban middle class, and especially of urban middle-class women.

Progressivism appeared at every level of government: local, state, and federal. And progressives promoted a wide range of new government activities: regulation of business, moral revival, consumer protection, conservation of natural resources, educational improvement, tax reform, and more. In all these ways, they brought government more directly into the economy and more directly into the lives of most Americans.

Progressive era A period of reform in the late nineteenth and early twentieth century.

Progressive party Party formed in 1912 with Theodore Roosevelt as its candidate for president; it disintegrated when Roosevelt lost the election.

Women and Reform

Organizations formed by or dominated by women burst upon politics during the Progressive era. By 1900 or so, a new ideal for women had emerged from women's colleges and clubs and from discussions on national lecture circuits and in the press. The New Woman stood for self-determination rather than unthinking acceptance of roles prescribed by the cult of domesticity and separate spheres. By 1910, this fresh attitude, sometimes called **feminism,** was accelerating the transition from the nineteenth-century women's movement for suffrage, to the twentieth-century struggle for equality and individualism.

Women's increasing control over one aspect of their lives is evidenced in the birthrate, which fell steadily throughout the nineteenth and early twentieth century as couples chose (or, perhaps, women alone chose) to have fewer children. In the early nineteenth century, many women used abortion to end unwanted pregnancies, but that option became illegal after midcentury. By the end of the century, state and federal laws also banned information about contraception. As a result, women or couples seeking to prevent conception often had to rely on word of mouth or advertising for pills or devices that only hinted at their use.

In the Progressive era, some women began to challenge such restrictive laws. **Margaret Sanger,** a nurse practicing among the poor of New York City, became convinced that too-large families contributed to poverty and damaged the mental and physical health of women. And she saw that women died after botched abortions. By 1914, Sanger also concluded, "Women cannot be on an equal footing with men until they have full and complete control over their reproductive function." In 1916, she went to jail for informing women about *birth control,* a term she originated. The year before Sanger's arrest, in 1915, a group of women (not including Sanger) formed the National Birth Control League to seek the repeal of laws that barred contraceptive information.

Other women also formed organizations to advance specific causes. Some, like the settlement houses, were oriented to service. The National Consumers' League (formed in 1890) and the Women's Trade Union League (1903) tried to improve the lives of working women. Such efforts received a tragic boost in 1911 when fire roared through the Triangle Shirtwaist Company's clothing factory in New York City, killing 146 workers—nearly all

♦ Margaret Sanger is seen here in 1916, leaving court after being charged with distributing birth control information illegally. During the Progressive Era, women worked to remove legal barriers to obtaining information on preventing conception. *Smith College Collection, Smith College.*

women—who were trapped in a building with no outside fire escapes and with exit doors locked to deter workers from taking breaks. The public outcry produced a prominent state investigation and, in 1914, a new state factory safety law.

Some states passed laws specifically to protect working women. In *Muller v. Oregon* (1908), the Supreme Court approved the constitutionality of one such law, limiting women's hours of work. Louis Brandeis, a lawyer working with the Consumers' Union, defended the law on the grounds that women were "in general weaker than men in muscular strength and in nervous energy" and

---

feminism   The conviction that women are and should be the social, political, and economic equals of men.

Margaret Sanger   Birth-control advocate who believed that birth-control information was essential to help women escape poverty and who disobeyed government laws against its distribution.

Muller v. Oregon   Supreme Court case in 1908 in which the Court upheld an Oregon law that limited the hours of employment for women.

◆ Women marched in support of suffrage in New York City in 1910. This part of the march featured women wearing academic robes to symbolize their educational accomplishments, thereby dramatizing the injustice of being denied the ballot. Other marches also demonstrated the extent of support for woman suffrage. *Schlesinger Library, Radcliffe College.*

needed special protection because of their social roles as mothers. Such arguments ran contrary to the New Woman's rejection of separate spheres and ultimately raised questions for women's drive for equality. At the time, however, the decision was widely hailed as a vital and necessary protection for women wage earners. By 1917, all but nine states had laws restricting women's working hours.

Although prominent in reform causes, most women could neither vote nor hold office. Support for suffrage grew, however, as more women recognized the need for political action to bring social reforms. By 1896, four western states had extended the vote to women. Then came the doldrums, from 1896 to 1910, when no state approved extension of the franchise. Finally, in 1910, Washington approved female suffrage and seven more western states followed over the next five years. In 1916, a western state dissolved another separate sphere when **Jeannette Rankin** of Montana—born on a ranch, educated as a social worker, experienced as a suffrage campaigner—became the first woman elected to the House of Representatives. Suffrage scored few victories outside the West, however.

Convinced that only a federal constitutional amendment would gain the vote for all women, the **National American Woman Suffrage Association, (NAWSA),** led by Carrie Chapman Catt and Anna Howard Shaw, developed a national organization geared to lobbying in Washington. Alice Paul advocated public demonstrations and civil disobedience, tactics she learned from English suffragists while she was a settlement house worker there from 1907 to 1910. In 1913, Paul and her followers formed the Congressional Union, to pursue their more militant strategies. Some white suffragists tried to build an interracial movement for suffrage—NAWSA, for example, condemned lynching in 1917—but most white suffragists feared that attention to other issues would weaken their position.

Despite the predominantly white and middle-class cast of its leaders, the cause of woman suffrage ignited a mass movement during the 1910s, mobilizing young, old, rich, poor, black, and white women of all socioeconomic classes. Opponents of woman suffrage had long argued that voting would bring women into the male sphere, make them subject to the same corrupting influences as men, and thereby render them unsuitable as guardians of the moral order. But some suffrage advocates now turned the domesticity argument to their favor, claiming that, instead of politics corrupting women, women would purify politics, making them more morally righteous and family-oriented. Others, especially feminists, argued that women should vote because they deserved full equality with men. The broad-based suffrage movement could embrace both the

---

Jeannette Rankin   Montana reformer and pacifist who in 1916 became the first woman elected to Congress; she worked to pass the woman suffrage amendment and to protect women in the workplace.

National American Woman Suffrage Association   Organization formed in 1890 that united the two major women's suffrage groups at that time.

former, who argued that women were morally superior to men, and the latter, who argued that women were essentially similar to men. Such unity was unlikely to continue, though, once suffrage was accomplished.

Moral Reform

Causes other than suffrage stirred women to action during the Progressive era. Women were prominent as well in new organizations intended to bring moral reform. Their primary target was alcohol, which the reformers called Demon Rum. The temperance movement dated to at least the 1820s, but initially most temperance advocates focused on persuading *individuals* to give up strong drink. By the late nineteenth century, however, they looked increasingly to *government* to control individual behavior, by prohibiting the production, sale, or consumption of alcoholic beverages. Many saw prohibition as a progressive reform, enlisting government to safeguard the public interest. Few Progressive era efforts could claim as many women activists as prohibition.

The drive against alcohol developed a broad base during the Progressive era. Some old-stock Protestant churches— notably the Methodists—termed alcohol one of the most significant obstacles to a better society. Adherents of the Social Gospel (see page 554) viewed prohibition as one of several social reforms needed to save the victims of industrialization and urbanization. Others, appealing to concepts of domesticity, emphasized the need to protect the family and home from the destructive influence of alcohol on husbands and fathers. At the same time, scientists related alcohol to certain diseases and discovered alarming aspects to the **narcotic** and **depressive** qualities of the drug. Sociologists added studies demonstrating—just as prohibitionists claimed—unmistakable links between liquor and prostitution, venereal disease, poverty, crime, and broken families. Other evidence pointed to alcohol as contributing to industrial accidents and inefficiency on the job.

Earlier, prohibitionists had organized into either the Prohibition party or the Women's Christian Temperance Union. After its formation in 1895, however, the **Anti-Saloon League** became the model for successful interest group politics. Proudly describing itself as "the Church in action against the saloon," it usually operated through the large **old-stock** Protestant denominations. The League focused much of its antagonism against the saloon,

attacking it as the least defensible element in the liquor industry. Reformers viewed saloons as corrupting not only individual patrons—such as men who neglected their families—but politics as well. Saloons, where political cronies struck deals and mingled with neighborhood voters, had long been identified with the party machines that dominated many large cities.

The League endorsed only politicians who opposed Demon Rum, regardless of their party or stand on other issues. As the prohibition cause demonstrated its growing political clout, increasing numbers of politicians lined up against the saloon. At the same time, the League also promoted statewide referendums to ban alcohol. Between 1900 and 1917, voters in nearly half of the states adopted prohibition, including nearly all of the West and the South. Elsewhere, many towns and rural areas voted themselves "dry" under **local option laws.**

Opposition to prohibition came especially from immigrants—and their American-born descendants—from Ireland, Germany, and southern and eastern Europe. Unlike many old-stock Protestant denominations, Catholics, Lutherans, German Calvinists, and Jews did not regard the use of alcohol as inherently sinful. For them, beer or wine was an accepted part of social life, and they opposed prohibition as an effort by old-stock Protestants to impose their moral views on others. "Personal liberty" became the slogan for these "wets." Companies that produced alcohol, especially beer brewers, also organized in opposition to the prohibitionists and subsidized some associations, especially the German American Alliance, in an effort to build a political coalition against the "dry" crusade.

The drive against alcohol, ultimately successful at the national level (see page 718), was by no means the only target for moral reformers. Throughout the

---

narcotic A drug that reduces pain and induces sleep or stupor.

depressive Tending to lower someone's spirits and to lessen activity.

Anti-Saloon League Political lobby for temperance founded in 1893, which organized through churches and offered its endorsement to politicians who favored prohibition.

old-stock People whose families had been in the United States for several generations.

local option laws A state law that permitted an individual town or city to decide, by an election, whether liquor sales would be banned there.

nineteenth century, many cities had tried to regulate prostitution. During the Progressive era, reformers—many of them women—tried to eliminate prostitution completely through state and federal legislation. Beginning in Iowa in 1909, states passed "red-light abatement" laws designed to close down brothels. In 1910, Congress passed the **Mann Act,** making it illegal to take a woman across a state line for "immoral purposes." Other campaigns to regulate individual behavior—to ban gambling or make divorces more difficult to obtain, for example—also represented attempts to use the power of government to control disturbing aspects of America's social front.

Racial Issues in the Progressive Era

Whereas women's issues and moral reform often took prominent places during the Progressive era, racial issues were usually more remote. Despite widely expressed concerns for social justice, only a few white progressives actively opposed disfranchisement and segregation in the South (see pages 563–564). Indeed, southern white progressives often took the lead in enacting discriminatory laws. Journalist Ray Stannard Baker was one of the few white progressives to address the plight of African-Americans. In his book, *Following the Color Line,* Baker asked: "Does democracy really include Negroes as well as white men?" For most white Americans, the answer appeared to be no.

Lynchings and violence continued as a fact of life for African-Americans. Between 1900 and World War I, lynchings claimed more than 1,100 victims, mostly in the South but many in the Midwest. The same years also saw several race riots in which whites attacked blacks. In 1906, Atlanta erupted into a riot as whites attacked African-Americans at random, killing four, injuring many more, and destroying many homes. In 1908, in Springfield, Illinois (where Abraham Lincoln had made his home), a mob of whites lynched two black men, injured others, destroyed black-owned businesses, and dispersed only when five thousand troops from the state militia appeared. In North and South alike, little effort was made to prosecute the leaders of such mobs.

During the Progressive era, some African-Americans dared to pose alternatives to the accommodationist leadership of Booker T. Washington. W. E. B. Du Bois, the first African-American to receive a

◆ An unknown photographer captured this lynching on film and preserved all its brutality and depravity. Although there are many such photographic records of lynch mobs, local authorities nearly always claimed that they were unable to determine the identity of those responsible for the murder. *The Picture Cube.*

Ph.D. from Harvard, wrote some of the first scholarly studies of African-Americans. He emphasized the contributions of black men and women, disproved racial stereotypes, and urged African-Americans to take pride in their accomplishments. A professor at Atlanta University after 1897, Du Bois used his book *Souls of Black Folk* (1903) to criticize Washington (see Individual Choices: W. E. B. DuBois). He argued moreover that African-Americans should struggle for their rights "unceasingly," and, "if they fail, die trying." "The hands of none of us are clean," he vowed, speaking to both whites and blacks, "if we bend not our energies to a righting of these great wrongs."

Realizing that few politicians cared about their situation, some African-American leaders organized in support of black rights. In 1905, Du Bois and others met secretly in Canada, near Niagara Falls, and drafted demands for racial equality—

Mann Act   Law passed by Congress in 1910 designed to suppress prostitution. It made it illegal to transport a woman across state lines for immoral purposes.

including civil rights and equality in job opportunities and education—and an end to segregation. The Springfield riot so shocked some white progressives that in 1909 they called a bi-racial conference, including members of the **Niagara Movement,** to seek ways to improve race relations. In 1910, they formed a new organization, the **National Association for the Advancement of Colored People (NAACP),** destined to provide important leadership in the fight for black equality. Du Bois served as the NAACP's director of publicity and research.

Challenging Capitalism: Socialists and Wobblies

Many progressive organizations reflected middle-class and upper-class concerns, such as businesslike government, prohibition, and greater reliance on experts. Not so the Socialist Party of America (SPA), formed in 1901. Proclaiming themselves the political arm of workers and farmers, the Socialists argued that industrial capitalism had produced "an economic slavery which renders intellectual and political tyranny inevitable." They rejected many progressive proposals as inadequate to resolve the nation's problems. Instead they called for an end to "the making of goods for profit" and for a cooperative commonwealth in which workers would share in the ownership and control of the means of production.

The Socialists' best known national leader was Eugene V. Debs, leader of the Pullman strike (see page 503) and virtually the only person able to unite the many socialist factions, ranging from theoretical **Marxists** completely opposed to capitalism to municipal reformers seeking only city-owned gas, electric, water, and streetcar systems. Strong among immigrants, some of whom had become socialists in their native lands, the SPA also took in Christian Socialists (who drew their inspiration from religion rather than from Marx), farmers, and trade union activists. In addition, the party attracted support from some of the intellectuals who sought comprehensive social change, including W. E. B. Du Bois, Margaret Sanger, and Upton Sinclair.

In 1905, a variety of radicals, including socialists, organized the Industrial Workers of the World (IWW). IWW organizers boldly proclaimed "We have been naught, we shall be all," as they set out to organize the unskilled and semiskilled workers at the bottom of the socioeconomic structure. They aimed at the armies of **sweatshop** workers of east-

♦ This design appeared originally on a "stickerette," a small poster (2½" x 3") with glue on the back. When the glue was moistened, the poster could be stuck on a fence post or inside a box car (where migratory workers often traveled). Wobblies sometimes called the stickerettes "silent agitators." *Courtesy Labor Archives and Research Center, San Francisco State University.*

ern cities, the **migrant workers** who followed western crops, southern sharecroppers, women workers, African-Americans, the "new" immigrants from southern and eastern Europe. These were the workers usually ignored by the American Federation of Labor with its emphasis on skilled workers, most of whom were white males.

IWW members, called Wobblies, carried small posters with IWW slogans that they stuck up on telephone poles in poor neighborhoods or in boxcars where migratory workers stole rides from one harvest to the next. They also carried little red song-

---

Niagara Movement Civil Rights movement that began in 1905 with the meeting at Niagara Falls of W. E. B. Du Bois and others interested in ending segregation and racial inequality in the United States.

National Association for the Advancement of Colored People Biracial civil rights organization founded in New York City in 1910, which worked to end segregation and discrimination in the United States.

Marxist A believer in the ideas of Karl Marx and Friedrich Engels.

sweatshop A shop or factory in which employees work long hours at low wages under poor conditions.

migrant workers Laborers who travel from one area to another in search of work.

Fighting for Equality

W. E. B. Du Bois

A brilliant young intellectual, W. E. B. Du Bois had to choose between leading the quiet life of a college professor or challenging Booker T. Washington's claim to speak on behalf of all African-Americans. Schomburg Center for Research in Black Culture, New York Public Library, Astor, Lenox and Tilden Foundations.

In 1904 and 1905, William Edward Burghardt Du Bois moved toward a difficult choice. Should he, or should he not, challenge the leadership of Booker T. Washington, the "Wizard of Tuskegee," the most powerful African-American in the nation? In the decade after his Atlanta Compromise address (pages 562–563), Washington emerged as head of a "Tuskegee Machine." His access to northern white philanthropists made him the chief channel for donations to African-American institutions. And his access to leaders of the Republican party gave him a hand in influencing many, if not most, African-American political patronage appointments, North and South alike. Du Bois, by contrast, was a college professor with few connections to funds or politics but well known and highly respected among black intellectuals.

Born in Great Barrington, Massachusetts, an area with a very small black population, Du Bois experienced little racial hostility before leaving home. At Fisk University, in Nashville, Tennessee, however, he encountered both the constraints of racism and the African-American culture of the South. He completed his undergraduate studies at Harvard, graduated with honors, then studied in Germany and wrote a doctoral dissertation on the suppression of the African slave trade to the United States. In

books that put new words to well-known tunes to sing of their troubles.

> *Are you poor, forlorn and hungry?*
> *Are there lots of things you lack?*
> *Is your life made up of misery?*
> *Then dump the bosses off your back.*
> (to the tune of "Take It To the Lord in Prayer")

The Wobblies objective was simple: when most workers had joined the IWW, they would call a general strike, labor would refuse to work, and capital-

ism would collapse. The general strike even appeared in their songs.

> *If the workers take a notion,*
> *They can stop all speeding trains,*
> *Every ship upon the ocean,*
> *They can tie with mighty chains,*
> *Every wheel in the creation,*
> *Every mine and every mill,*
> *Fleets and armies of the nation,*
> *Will at their command stand still.*

1895, he became the first African-American to receive a Ph.D. from Harvard.

Du Bois then taught at the college level and undertook research and scholarly writing. By the early twentieth century, however, he had chosen to do more than research and teach. In his third book, *Souls of Black Folk* (1903), he challenged Washington's accommodationist approach and insisted that African-Americans should never acquiesce in the surrender of their rights. He also presented the concept of *double consciousness*, by which he meant that African-Americans had both an African identity and an American identity and needed to be aware of both parts of their cultural heritage. He argued that the "talented tenth"—the African-American intellectual elite—had special leadership obligations. Refuting Washington's claim that African-Americans should start at the bottom, Du Bois insisted instead that denial of educational opportunities for the talented tenth constrained all African-Americans.

Although the book created a sensation among African-American intellectuals and some white philanthropists, Washington's first response was to invite Du Bois to Tuskegee, apparently to coopt him into the Tuskegee Machine. Du Bois, however, held back, weighing his choices against the potential for retribution that Washington could bring to bear against his opponents. By late 1904, however, Du Bois determined to challenge Washington directly, and early in 1905 he charged that Washington had bought and paid for much of the support he received from the black press. The next important step, in July 1905, was formation of the Niagara Movement. This body was to be the organizational vehicle for mobilizing African-Americans for an assault both on white supremacy and on Washington's accommodationism. Proclaiming that "persistent manly agitation is the way to liberty," the new organization chose Du Bois as its general secretary. Despite a promising beginning, the movement failed to thrive. In 1910, what was left of the Niagara Movement was transformed into the NAACP, and Du Bois became editor of its journal, *The Crisis*. About the same time, Du Bois briefly joined the Socialist Party of America. He continued to espouse socialist ideas, and the experience of World War I moved him further toward anti-imperialism and pacifism.

Du Bois's uncompromising leadership in the struggle for civil rights and his voluminous writings on both current events and black history made him probably the single most influential African-American intellectual of the twentieth century. By the end of his long life, he concluded that America would never accomplish racial equality. In 1961, he joined the Communist party and accepted citizenship in Ghana, then a socialist nation. There he died during the night of August 27, 1963, the day before one of the greatest civil rights gatherings in American history (see page 910). In announcing Du Bois's death to the huge crowd in Washington, D.C., Roy Wilkins, executive secretary of the NAACP, noted that "at the dawn of the twentieth century his was the voice calling you to gather here today in this cause."

The IWW did organize a few dramatic strikes and demonstrations and even scored a few significant victories. One Wobbly strike by textile workers in Lawrence, Massachusetts, gained national attention. But more often, they met brutal suppression by local authorities and rarely made lasting gains for their members.

The Wobblies claimed a few victories, but the SPA counted considerably more. Hundreds of cities and towns—including Milwaukee, Wisconsin; Reading, Pennsylvania; and Berkeley, California— elected Socialist mayors or council members. Socialists also won election to state legislatures in several states. Districts in New York City and Milwaukee sent Socialists to the national House of Representatives. Most Americans, however, had no interest in eliminating private property. Most progressive reformers looked aghast at the Socialists and sometimes tried to undercut their appeal with reforms that addressed some of their concerns but stopped short of challenging capitalism. The violence sometimes directed against the Wobblies proved a forecast of the experience of radicals during World War I, when most extremist groups were ruthlessly suppressed.

The Reform of Politics, the Politics of Reform

● How did city and state reforms reflect new expectations for political parties and government?

Progressivism emerged at all levels of government as cities elected reform-oriented mayors and states swore in progressive governors. Such reformers sometimes hoped only to make government more honest and efficient. Other times they sought basic changes in the structure and function of government, to make it more responsive to the needs of America's urban, industrial society. In their quest for change, reformers sometimes found themselves in conflict with the entrenched leaders of political parties. In response, some reformers dedicated themselves to limiting the power of political parties.

Exposing Corruption: The Muckrakers

Journalists played an important role in preparing the ground for reform. Although mass-circulation newspapers and yellow journalism had emerged in the 1890s, magazines and journals changed more slowly. By the early 1900s, however, magazine publishers discovered that their sales boomed when they fed the public's taste for dramatic exposés of scandal—political corruption, corporate wrongdoing, or other offenses. Those who practiced this provocative journalism acquired the name **muckrakers** when President Theodore Roosevelt, in 1906, compared them to "the Man with the Muck-rake," a character in John Bunyan's classic allegory *Pilgrim's Progress*. Roosevelt intended the comparison as a rebuke, but the journalists accepted the label with pride.

Although not the first to run exposés of government and business, *McClure's Magazine* led the surge in muckraking journalism that developed after 1902. That October, *McClure's* began a series in which **Lincoln Steffens** revealed corruption in city governments. The January 1903 issue carried Steffens's installment on Minneapolis, the first of a series by **Ida Tarbell** on Standard Oil's sordid past, and a piece by Ray Stannard Baker revealing cor-

ruption and violence in labor unions. Sales of *McClure's* boomed, and other monthlies copied the muckraking style, serving up accounts on the defects of patent medicines, fraud in the insurance industry, the horrors of child labor, and more.

Muckraking extended from periodicals like *Collier's, Cosmopolitan,* and *American Magazine* to books. Both Steffens and Tarbell collected their articles in book form (*The Shame of the Cities,* 1904; *The History of the Standard Oil Company,* 1904). Other examples of muckraking included David G. Phillips's 1906 *The Treason of the Senate,* initially a series in *Cosmopolitan* depicting the Senate as a bastion of big business, and Gustavus Myers's *The History of Great American Fortunes* (1910), emphasizing the devious means by which they were attained.

The most famous muckraking book, however, was a novel—*The Jungle* by **Upton Sinclair** (1906). *The Jungle* exposed in disgusting detail the very real shortcomings of the meat-packing industry. Sinclair, a socialist, hoped his readers would recognize that the offenses portrayed in his book were the result of industrial capitalism. He described in chilling detail the afflictions of packinghouse workers, from severed fingers to tuberculosis and blood poisoning. He shocked the nation when he wrote of men who "fell into the vats; and when they were fished out, there was never enough left of them to be worth exhibiting—sometimes they would be overlooked for days, till all but the bones of them had gone out to the world as Durham's Pure Leaf Lard!"

Finley Peter Dunne, a political humorist, claimed that he hadn't "been able to eat anything more nourishing than a cucumber" since reading Sinclair's book and advised, "If you want to reduce your butcher's bills, buy *The Jungle*." President Roosevelt appointed a commission to investigate and its report confirmed Sinclair's charges. Pressured by

---

muckrakers   Journalists in the Progressive era who wrote investigative articles exposing corruption in city government, business, and industry.

Lincoln Steffens   Muckraking journalist and managing editor of *McClure's* magazine best known for revealing political corruption in city governments.

Ida Tarbell   Journalist in the Progressive era whose exposé on the Standard Oil Company revealed its ruthless business ethics.

Upton Sinclair   Socialist writer and reformer whose novel *The Jungle* helped bring about government regulation of meat-packing and other industries.

♦ Upton Sinclair's novel, *The Jungle* (1906), prompted a range of responses. One was new federal legislation to inspect meatpacking—including the use of a stamp such as this one for condemned meat. Another was the defense of the meatpacking industry by such people as Rev. J. R. Day (inset), criticized here in *Collier's*, a muckraking magazine. *Chicago Historical Society.*

Roosevelt and the public, Congress passed the **Pure Food and Drug Act,** which banned impure or mislabeled food and drugs, and the **Meat Inspection Act,** which required federal inspection of meat packing, a move the industry itself welcomed to reassure nauseated consumers. Sinclair, however, was disappointed that his revelations had only prodded meatpackers to reform rather than converting readers to socialism. "I aimed at the public's heart," Sinclair later complained, "and by accident I hit it in the stomach."

Reforming City Government

In the early twentieth century, muckrakers, especially Lincoln Steffens, helped to focus public concern on city government. By the time of Steffens's first article in 1902, however, advocates of reform had already won office and brought changes to some cities, and municipal reformers soon appeared in many other cities.

Municipal reformers urged honest and efficient government, and many—perhaps most—also argued that corruption and inefficiency were inevitable without major changes in the structure of city government. Usually **city councils** consisted of members elected from **wards** that roughly corresponded to neighborhoods. Most voters lived in middle-class and working-class wards, which therefore dominated most city councils. Reformers, however, condemned the ward system as producing city council members unable to see beyond the needs of their own blocks to the problems of the city as a whole. They pointed to support for political bosses and machines in poor immigrant neighborhoods and concluded, correctly, that the ward leaders' devotion to voter needs kept the machine in power despite its corruption. They argued that citywide elections, with all city voters choosing from one list of candidates, would result in council members with broader perspectives—men with citywide business interests, for example—and would undercut the ward leaders and their machines.

James Phelan of San Francisco provides an example of an early structural reformer. Son of a pioneer banker, he entered politics just as the organization of Boss Chris Buckley fell into disarray. Equally at

---

Pure Food and Drug Act 1906 law that discouraged the use of dyes and preservatives in foods; it forbade the sale of impure or improperly labeled food and drugs.

Meat Inspection Act 1906 law requiring federal inspection of meat packing; it was the result of Upton Sinclair's exposé of unsanitary conditions in the industry.

city council A body of representatives elected to govern a city.

ward A division of a city or town, especially an electoral district, for administrative or representative purposes.

home in the worlds of politics, business, and the arts, Phelan attacked corruption in city government and won election as mayor in 1896. He then led in adopting a new charter that strengthened the office of mayor and required citywide election of supervisors, San Francisco's term for councilmen.

Some municipal reformers proposed more fundamental changes in the structure of city government. Eventually new forms of city government emerged, notably the **commission system** and the **city-manager plan.** Both reveal prominent traits of progressivism: a distrust of political parties and a desire for expertise and efficiency. The commission system first developed in Galveston, Texas, after a hurricane and tidal wave nearly destroyed it in 1900. The governor appointed five businessmen to run the city, and they attracted widespread attention for their efficiency in administering city government in time of crisis. Within two years, more than two hundred communities had adopted a commission system. Typically all the city's voters elected the commissioners, and each commissioner then took charge of a specific city function as a way to encourage effective and efficient management. The city-manager plan had similar objectives, based on adapting the administrative structure of the corporation to city government. It featured a professional city manager (similar to a corporate executive) who was appointed by an elected city council (similar to a corporate board of directors) to handle much of municipal administration. Staunton, Virginia, tried such a system in 1908 but attracted little attention. In 1913 a serious flood led the citizens of Dayton, Ohio, to adopt a city-manager plan and other cities then followed.

Most municipal reforms focused on changing the structure of city government to bring honest, efficient, effective city administration, but a few went beyond structural reform to advocate social reform. Hazen Pingree, for example, a successful and socially prominent businessman, attracted national attention as mayor of Detroit. Elected in 1889 as an advocate of honest, efficient government, he soon began to criticize the city's gas, electric, and streetcar companies for overcharging customers and providing poor service. The depression of 1893 led him to address the needs of the unemployed with such measures as work projects and community gardens. Another prosperous manufacturer, Samuel "Golden Rule" Jones, won election as mayor of Toledo, Ohio, in 1897. He boasted of conducting his factory on the Golden Rule—do unto others as you would have them do unto you—and brought the same standard

to city government. Under his leadership, Toledo acquired free concerts, free public baths, kindergartens (childcare centers for working mothers), and the eight-hour workday for city employees. Phelan, Pingree, Jones, and a few others went so far as to advocate city ownership of utilities.

The Progressive era also saw city governments take up **city planning.** Throughout most of the nineteenth century, urban growth had been largely unplanned, driven primarily by a market economy. Early planning efforts sprang from a desire for beautification, but functional concerns soon took priority. Cities recognized the need to establish separate zones for residential, commercial, and industrial use (first in Los Angeles in 1904 and 1908) and to develop efficient transportation systems to reduce traffic congestion. And occasionally cities acted to improve substandard housing in city slums. In 1907, Hartford, Connecticut, set up one of the first city planning commissions, charged with planning on a continuing basis. The emergence of city planning represents an important transition in thinking about government and the economy, for it emphasized expertise and presumed greater government control over use of private property.

Saving the Future

Just as city planning represented the emergence of a new profession with important implications for local government, so the Progressive era also saw other professions develop that were to have an impact on the whole social fabric. In public health, mental health, social work, education, and related areas, professionals worked to reshape government—especially at city and state levels—to solve the problems of an urban, industrial, multiethnic society. At the most basic, their objective was to use scientific and social scientific knowledge to control social forces and thereby to define the future. As

---

commission system   System of city government in which all executive and legislative power is vested in a small elective board, usually composed of five members.

city-manager plan   System of city government under which a small council, chosen on a nonpartisan ballot, hires a city manager who exercises full executive authority.

city planning   The practice of planning urban development by regulating the location of transportation, public buildings, recreational facilities, and zoning.

♦ The Progressive Era saw the rise of a number of new professions, as reformers sought to use medical, scientific, and social scientific knowledge to change society. This photograph shows a New York City rat catcher, a public health worker, busily engaged in his work. *Library of Congress.*

Walter Lippmann, a rising young journalist, put it in 1914, their goal was "mastery."

The public schools presented an important arena in which professionals sought change. In the cities, especially, graduates of recently established university programs for the preparation of teachers and school administrators began to seek greater control over education. Stressing the challenges of educating multiethnic urban students—many of whom did not speak English—and preparing them for a complex and technological society, professional educators pushed for greater centralization in school administration. They particularly pushed to reduce the role of local, usually elected, **school boards** and elected school superintendents who presented no particular professional qualifications for their positions beyond the ability to win elections. Professional educators also began to rely on the recently developed intelligence tests as a way of identifying children unable to perform at average levels and to isolate them in special classes.

Advances in medical knowledge, together with efforts by the American Medical Association to raise the standards of medical colleges and to restrict access to the profession, improved the professional status of physicians. Scientific discoveries helped to transform hospitals from charities that provided minimal help for the poor into centers for dispensing the most up-to-date care to all who could afford it. Current knowledge about disease and health, often developed in research universities, together

with the facilities of the modernized hospitals, seemed to present an opportunity to reduce disease on a significant scale. Physicians helped to launch public health programs for eradication of hookworm in the South, **tuberculosis** in the slums, and venereal disease. In the process, public health emerged as a new medical field, combining the knowledge of the medical doctor with insight of the social scientist and, often, with the skills of the corporate manager.

Other emerging professional fields that carried important implications for public policy included mental health and social work. Mental health professionals—psychiatrists and psychologists—tried to transform the nineteenth-century asylums from places for confining the mentally ill into places where they could be treated and perhaps cured. They tried, too, to address the larger social context that seemed to cause mental breakdown. Social workers often found themselves allied with public health and mental health professionals in their efforts to bring greater governmental control over urban health and safety codes.

Reforming State Government

As reformers launched changes in various cities and as new professionals considered ways to improve society, **Robert M. La Follette** pushed Wisconsin state government to the forefront of reform. A Republican, he entered politics soon after graduating from the University of Wisconsin. Elected to Congress in 1884, 1886, and 1888, he lost in the Democratic sweep of 1890. He later claimed that in 1891 U.S. Senator Philetus Sawyer, leader of the state Republican organization, asked him to deliver a bribe. Sawyer denied it and blocked La Follette politically throughout the 1890s. La Follette was finally elected governor in 1900, after Sawyer's death. The long battle with Sawyer, he later said, convinced him of the need for reform.

school board   A local board of policymakers that oversees a city or town's public schools.

tuberculosis   An infectious disease that attacks the lungs, causing coughing, fever, and weight loss; it was common and often fatal in the nineteenth and early twentieth centuries.

Robert M. La Follette   Governor of Wisconsin at the turn of the century, who instituted a series of reforms including direct primaries, tax reform, and anticorruption measures.

As governor, La Follette soon ran into opposition from conservative members of his own party who held sway in the state legislature. Conservatives defeated La Follette's proposals to regulate railroad rates and replace party nominating conventions with the **direct primary.** Intensely committed to his proposals, La Follette threw himself into an energetic campaign to elect a state legislature that would support reform. Short in stature, with bristling gray hair, he earned the nickname "Fighting Bob" as he traveled the state speaking wherever a crowd gathered, holding forth for an hour or two hours or more, explaining the issues, and asking for support. Most of his favored candidates won and, in the process, La Follette built a strong political following among Wisconsin's farmers and urban wage earners. The political organization he built not only elected reformers to the state legislature but also reelected La Follette as governor in 1902 and 1904.

La Follette then led the way to a wide range of reform legislation designed to limit both corporations and political parties. Acclaimed as a "laboratory of democracy," Wisconsin adopted a direct primary, set up a commission to regulate railroad rates, increased taxes on railroads and other corporations, enacted a merit system for hiring and promoting state employees, and limited the activities of lobbyists. In many of his efforts, La Follette drew on the expertise of faculty members at the University of Wisconsin. These reforms and reliance on experts came to be called the **Wisconsin Idea.** La Follette won election to the U.S. Senate in 1905 and was reelected until his death in 1925.

La Follette's success prompted imitators elsewhere. In 1901, Iowans elected Albert B. Cummins governor, and Cummins launched a campaign against railroad corporations that paralleled La Follette's. He, too, went on to the Senate. Self-proclaimed reformers won office in other states as well but only a few matched La Follette's success in achieving passage of such an impressive list of legislation or in winning the allegiance of so many voters.

California came to progressivism relatively late, but, once in power, progressives there produced a volume of reform that rivaled the Wisconsin Idea. California reformers accused the Southern Pacific railroad of running a powerful political machine that controlled the state by dominating the Republican party. In 1906 and 1907, a highly publicized investigation revealed widespread bribery in San Francisco government. The ensuing trials made famous one of the prosecutors, Hiram W. Johnson. Reform-minded Republicans persuaded Johnson to run for governor in 1910. He conducted a vigorous campaign and won.

Stubborn and principled, Johnson proved to be an uncompromising foe of corporate influence in politics. As governor, he pushed the legislature to adopt an array of reforms—regulation of railroads and public utilities, restrictions on political parties, protections for labor, and conservation. Progressives in the legislature arranged a public vote on woman suffrage and California voters approved the measure. Johnson showed more sympathy for labor than did most progressive reformers. He appointed union leaders to state positions and supported a variety of measures to benefit working people, including an eight-hour day law for women, **workers' compensation,** and restrictions on child labor. These and other improvements pushed California to the front of the reform movement. California progressives in both parties vied with each other, however, in the vehemence of their attacks on Asian immigrants and Asian Americans. In 1913, Johnson and the progressive Republicans pushed through a law that prohibited Asian immigrants from owning land in California.

California progressives worked to limit the influence of political parties. By 1913, California exceeded all other states in the range of offices that were nonpartisan, including all judges, school administrators, and local and county officials. Only members of the federal Congress, a few statewide officers, and members of the state legislature ran for office as party candidates. Even for those offices, progressives modified the primary to reduce the significance of the party label.

Like La Follette, Johnson carved out a career in national politics after serving as governor. In 1912, he was vice-presidential candidate for the underdog Progressive party. Reelected governor in 1914, he won election to the U.S. Senate in 1916 and was reelected until his death in 1945.

---

direct primary   A primary in which the voters who identify with a party choose that party's candidates directly through an election.

Wisconsin Idea   The program of political reforms sponsored by Robert La Follette in Wisconsin, which were designed to decrease political corruption and foster direct democracy.

workers' compensation   Payments that employers are required by law to award to workers injured on the job.

The Decline of Parties and Rise of Interest Groups

Though California represents the extreme in weakening political parties, nearly all states took steps in that direction. City and state reformers charged that party bosses and their machines manipulated nominating conventions, managed public officials, and controlled law enforcement. They claimed, too, that bosses, in return for payoffs, used their influence on behalf of powerful interests, especially companies that did business with city or state government. Articles by muckrakers and a few highly publicized bribery trials convinced many voters that the reformers were correct. The mighty party organizations that had dominated politics so completely during the nineteenth century now found themselves under attack on every side.

Reforms intended to increase the power of the individual voter and to reduce the power of political party organizations sprouted nearly everywhere. State after state adopted the direct primary, and most reformers also sought to introduce or strengthen the merit system so as to reduce the number of state positions filled through patronage. In most states, judgeships, school board seats, and educational offices were made nonpartisan.

A number of states also chose to adopt the initiative and referendum. Adopted first in South Dakota in 1898, the initiative and referendum gained national attention after they were approved in Oregon in 1902. Oregon reformers led by William U'Ren, an unassuming former Populist who became a progressive Republican, quickly employed the initiative to create new laws. The publicity they received caused the initiative and referendum to be called the **Oregon System.** Some states also adopted the **recall,** under which voters could petition for a special election to remove a public official from office. The direct primary, initiative and referendum, and recall are sometimes classed together as "direct democracy" because they removed intermediate steps between the voter and final political decisions.

One outcome of the switch to direct primaries and direct election of United States senators was a new style of campaign. Candidates now appealed directly to voters rather than to party leaders and convention delegates. Whereas nineteenth-century party leaders had often insisted on informal **term limits,** voters returned the same candidates to office again and again. Individual candidates built up their own organizations (separate from party organizations) to win renomination and reelection, and they ran for office on their previous records and personal attributes not their party identification. As campaigns focused more on individual candidates rather than on party positions, advertising supplanted the armies of party retainers who had mobilized voters in the nineteenth century. Without party efforts to get out the vote, voter turnout began to fall. The emergence of so many new channels for political participation, however, created the illusion of a vast outpouring of public involvement—even though the proportion of those exercising their right to vote steadily dropped.

Political participation opened up not only through the instruments of direct democracy, but also through organized **interest groups.** As the power of political parties and party leaders faded, organized interest groups became more involved in politics as the most direct way to advance their specialized concerns. Such organized groups cooperated with each other when their political objectives coincided, as when merchants and farmers both favored regulation of railroad rates. Other times, they found themselves in conflict, perhaps over tariff policy. The many groups that advocated change sometimes fought among themselves over which reform goals were most important and how best to achieve those goals. More and more groups took up the tactics of the Anti-Saloon League: pressuring individual candidates for office to commit themselves to the group's stand on issues and then urging their members to vote only for candidates who supported the group's goals. In 1904, for example, the National Association of Manufacturers (NAM) targeted and defeated two key prolabor members of Congress, one in the House and one in the Senate. The American Federation of Labor (AFL) responded in 1906 with a similar strategy and managed to elect six union members to the House of Representatives.

Oregon System   Name given to the initiative and referendum, first used widely in state politics in Oregon after 1902.

recall   Procedure by which voters can seek to remove an elected official from office, submitting a petition to bring the matter to a public vote.

term limit   A limit on the number of times one person can be elected to the same political office.

interest group   A coalition of people working on behalf of a particular cause, such as an item of legislation, a particular industry, or a special segment of society.

Organized interest groups also focused greater attention on the legislative process. When Congress was in session, interest groups retained the services of one or more full-time representatives, or **lobbyists,** in Washington. Lobbyists urged congressmen to support their group's position on pending legislation, reminded senators and representatives of the electoral power of the group, and arranged campaign support for those who voted in keeping with the group's positions. Similar patterns developed with state legislatures.

Thus, as political parties receded from the dominant position they once occupied, organized interest groups moved in. Some elected officials came to see themselves less as loyal members of a political party and more as mediators among competing interest groups. Pushed one way by the AFL and the other by the NAM, under opposing pressure from the Anti-Saloon League and liquor interests, some politicians responded by counting the number of voters each group could influence in their districts and voting in the way likely to lose the fewest votes in the next election.

Roosevelt, Taft, and Republican Progressivism

● What constraints did Roosevelt face and how did he choose to deal with them?

● What were the outcomes for the role of the federal government in the economy and for the power of the presidency?

The American public came to identify Theodore Roosevelt with progressivism more than any other single person. Elected vice president in 1900, he became president in 1901 after the assassination of President William McKinley. The 42-year-old Roosevelt was the youngest president in the nation's history. His buoyant optimism and energy fascinated Americans as much as his bristling mustache, pince-nez glasses, and prominent front teeth delighted cartoonists.

Roosevelt later wrote, "I cannot say that I entered the Presidency with any deliberately planned and far-reaching scheme of social betterment." In seven years, however, he changed the nation's domestic policies more than any president since Lincoln, and made himself a legend in the process. One visitor to the United States reported that the most exciting things he had seen were "Niagara Falls and the President, . . . both great wonders of nature!"

Roosevelt: Asserting the Power of the Presidency

Roosevelt was unlike most politicians of his day. Wealthy thanks to his inheritance and his writings, he saw politics as a duty he owed the nation rather than as an opportunity for personal advancement. He defined his political views in terms of character, morality, hard work, and patriotism rather than in the stale phrases of party rhetoric. Uncertain whether to call himself a "radical conservative" or a "conservative radical," he considered political power a tool to achieve an ethical and socially stable society. Confident in his own personal principles, he did not hesitate to wield the fullest possible powers of the presidency. As president, he later explained, "I did not care a rap for the mere form and show of power. I cared immensely for the use that could be made of the substance." Roosevelt used not only all possible powers of the presidency, but also the office itself as what he called a "bully pulpit," to gain attention for his message of character and responsibility.

In his first message to Congress, in December 1901, Roosevelt sounded a theme that he was to repeat throughout his political career: the growth of powerful corporations was "natural," but some of them exhibited "grave evils" that the law needed to overcome. Most previous presidents had taken the view that delivering such a firm message to Congress was all that they could or should do—but not Roosevelt. Roosevelt later explained that "when I became President, the question as to the *method* by which the United States Government was to control the corporations was not yet important. The absolutely vital question was whether the Government had power to control them at all." He set out to establish that power.

The chief obstacle to the exercise of power over the new corporations was the Supreme Court decision in *U.S. v. E. C. Knight* (1895), preventing the Sherman Anti-Trust Act from being used against manufacturing monopolies. Roosevelt soon found

---

lobbyist   A person who tries to influence the opinions of legislators or other public officials for or against a specific cause.

U.S. v. E. C. Knight   Supreme Court ruling in 1895 that the Sherman Anti-Trust Act did not prohibit manufacturing monopolies; it seriously impaired the enforcement of antitrust laws.

◆ President Theodore Roosevelt's distinctive face attracted photographers and cartoonists, and he was often shown with a big grin. He loved fun, and a friend of his once observed that "You must always remember that the President is about six." *Brown Brothers.*

an opportunity to challenge the *Knight* decision. Some of the nation's most prominent business leaders—J. P. Morgan, the Rockefeller interests, and railroad magnates James J. Hill and Edward H. Harriman—joined forces to create the Northern Securities Company. Their enterprise consolidated the three largest railroads north and west of Chicago and set up a railroad monopoly in the Northwest. The *Knight* case had involved manufacturing, but the Northern Securities Company dealt in interstate transportation. If any industry could satisfy the Supreme Court that it fit the language of the Constitution authorizing Congress to regulate interstate commerce, the railroads could. In February 1902, Roosevelt advised Attorney General Philander C. Knox to seek dissolution of the Northern Securities Company for violating the Sherman Act. Wall Street leaders condemned Roosevelt's action as "beyond comprehension," but most Americans responded positively. For the first time, they witnessed a serious federal challenge to the ever-increasing might of powerful corporations. In 1904, the Supreme Court agreed that the Sherman Act could be applied to the

Northern Securities Company and ordered it dissolved.

Bolstered by this confirmation of federal power, Roosevelt launched additional antitrust suits and gloried in his reputation as a **trustbuster.** In all, Roosevelt initiated more than forty antitrust actions, though not all were successful. He never regarded the trustbusting route as the best way to regulate the economy, however. Large corporations, in Roosevelt's view, were natural, inevitable, and potentially beneficial. He thought it made more sense to regulate them than to break them up, so he used trustbusting selectively. Companies that met Roosevelt's standards of character and public service—and acknowledged the supremacy of the presidency—had no reason to fear antitrust action. Acknowledging the power of the president sometimes meant informal understandings between Roosevelt and corporate heads. For example, in 1907, in the midst of a financial panic, officials of U.S. Steel first secured Roosevelt's consent before taking over the Tennessee Coal and Iron Company, arguing that the takeover would stabilize the industry.

Roosevelt's willingness to take bold action did not stop at reining in the trusts. In time of crisis, he felt, "it is the duty of the President to act upon the theory that he is the steward of the people, and . . . to assume that he has the legal right to do whatever the needs of the people demand, unless the Constitution or the laws explicitly forbid him to do it." A year after he took office, he found himself preparing to exercise that power as a result of a strike by coal miners.

In June 1902, **anthracite** coal miners went on strike in Pennsylvania, seeking higher wages, an eight-hour workday, and other contract changes. Mine owners refused to negotiate or even to meet with representatives of the **United Mine Workers,** led by president John Mitchell. The railroads of the coal-mining region owned the mines, and J. P. Morgan held a significant stake in the railroads. The

trustbuster   Label applied to Theodore Roosevelt and others who sought to prosecute or dissolve business trusts.

anthracite   Type of coal that contains high levels of carbon and burns with a clean flame; widely used for heating homes and businesses in the early twentieth century.

United Mine Workers   Union of coal miners organized in 1890.

president of the Reading Railroad, George F. Baer, led the mining companies. When urged to negotiate with the union, Baer wrote in reply,

The rights and interests of the laboring men will be protected and cared for—not by the labor agitators, but by the Christian men to whom God in his infinite wisdom has given control of the property interests of this country.

Baer's claim to God-given control failed to impress the miners, much of the public, or Roosevelt.

As cold weather approached and coal prices edged upward, public concern grew because many people heated their homes with coal. In early October, Roosevelt called both sides to Washington, where he urged them to submit their differences to arbitration. The owners haughtily refused and instead insisted that the army be used against the miners, just as Cleveland had broken the Pullman strike ten years before. Roosevelt, now angry, considered them "insolent" and so "obstinate" as to be both "utterly silly" and "well-nigh criminal."

Believing that "great crises" required "immediate and vigorous executive action," Roosevelt began preparations to use the army to dispossess the mine owners and reopen the mines. He also sent Secretary of War Elihu Root to talk with J. P. Morgan. The threat of military intervention apparently led Morgan to convince the companies to accept arbitration. Although the mine owners still disputed the composition of the arbitration panel appointed by Roosevelt, the president got most of what he wanted. The arbitration board granted the miners higher wages and a nine-hour workday but denied their other objectives. Mining companies were permitted to raise their prices to cover the increased costs. No president before had ever intervened in a strike by treating a union as equal to the owners, let alone threatening to use the army on the side of labor. The coal strike settlement represented what Roosevelt liked to call a **Square Deal,** in which each side received fair treatment.

The Square Deal in Action: Creating Federal Economic Regulation

Roosevelt's trustbusting and settlement of the coal strike brought him great popularity across the country. In 1903, Congress approved several measures he requested or endorsed: the Expedition Act, to speed up prosecution of antitrust suits; creation of a cabinet-level Department of Commerce and Labor, including a Bureau of Corporations to investigate corporate activities; and the **Elkins Act,** which amended the Interstate Commerce Act by setting punishments for railroads that paid rebates. When Roosevelt sought election in 1904, he won by one of the largest margins up to that time, securing more than 56 percent of the popular vote. Conservatives had taken control of the Democratic party and named the party's presidential candidate, expecting to attract enough support from conservatives to defeat Roosevelt. Alton B. Parker, their drab nominee, took only 38 percent in one of the Democrats' worst showings ever.

Elected in his own right, with such a powerful demonstration of public approval, Roosevelt now set out to implement meaningful regulation. The railroads, largest of the nation's big businesses, formed his target. He, and reformers in Congress, wanted to move beyond the relatively uncontroversial Elkins Act to the question of rates. In Roosevelt's year-end message to Congress in 1905, he asked them to pass laws regulating railroad rates, opening financial records of railroads to government inspection, and increasing governmental power in strikes involving interstate commerce. At the same time, the attorney general initiated suits against some of the nation's largest corporations, and muckrakers (some of them friends of Roosevelt) launched exposés of railroads and attacks on Senate conservatives. Although he had to compromise from time to time with conservative Republicans, Roosevelt accomplished most of his agenda. On June 29, 1906, Congress passed the **Hepburn Act,** which allowed the Interstate Commerce Commission (ICC) to establish maximum railroad rates and extended ICC authority to other forms of transportation. The act also limited railroads' ability to issue free passes, a practice reformers had long considered bribery. The next day, on June 30, Congress approved the Pure Food and Drug Act and the Meat

---

Square Deal   Phrase used by Theodore Roosevelt to describe the effort to deal fairly with all.

Elkins Act   1903 law that supplemented the Interstate Commerce Act of 1887 by penalizing railroads that paid rebates.

Hepburn Act   1906 law that authorized the Interstate Commerce Commission to fix maximum railroad rates and extended ICC authority to other forms of transportation.

Inspection Act, as the aftermath to Sinclair's stomach-turning revelations. Congress also passed legislation defining employer liability for injured workers in the District of Columbia and on the interstate railroads.

Regulating Natural Resources

An outspoken proponent of strenuous outdoor activities, Roosevelt took great pride in establishing five national parks and more than fifty wildlife preserves, to save what he called "beautiful and wonderful wild creatures whose existence was threatened by greed and wantonness." Preservationists, such as John Muir of the Sierra Club, applauded the creation of such parks and refuges, condemned any violation of the scenic majesty of nature, and urged that wilderness areas be kept forever safe from developers. For Roosevelt, however, setting aside parks and wildlife refuges formed a relatively minor element in his understanding of conservation.

For Roosevelt and **Gifford Pinchot,** his chief adviser on natural resources, conservation involved not preserving wild and beautiful lands but carefully planning the use of federally owned resources. Pinchot, trained in scientific forestry in Europe, delighted in his title as Chief Forester. Combining recent scientific and technical information with a managerial outlook, Pinchot worked with Roosevelt to conserve timber and grazing resources by withdrawing large tracts of federal land from public sale or use. By maintaining close federal management of these lands, they hoped to provide for the needs of the present and still leave resources for the future. While president, Roosevelt withdrew nearly 230 million acres from public sale, more than quadrupling the land under federal protection.

Roosevelt's attitude toward western water clearly reveals his definition of conservation. He strongly supported the National Reclamation Act of 1902. Known as the Newlands Act, it set aside proceeds from sale of federal lands in sixteen western states to finance irrigation projects. The act established a commitment later expanded many times: the federal government had the responsibility for constructing western dams, canals, and other facilities that made agriculture possible in areas of slight rainfall. Thus water, perhaps the single most important resource in the arid West, was to be managed. Far from preserving the western landscape, federal water projects profoundly transformed it, vividly illustrating the vast difference between the preservation of

◆ In 1903, at Yosemite National Park, Theodore Roosevelt met with John Muir, a leading advocate for the preservation of wilderness. While Roosevelt made important contributions to the preservation of parks and wildlife refuges, he was more interested in the careful management of national resources, including federal lands. *Culver Pictures, Inc.*

wilderness advocated by Muir and the careful management of productive resources that motivated Pinchot and Roosevelt.

Taft's Troubles

Soon after Roosevelt won the election of 1904, he announced that he would not seek another term in 1908. By 1908, he may have regretted this statement, but he kept his word. He remained immensely popular, however, and virtually named his successor

---

Gifford Pinchot Head of the Bureau of Forestry from 1898 to 1910, who helped begin the conservation movement.

◆ This cartoon blames President William Howard Taft, hand-picked successor of Theodore Roosevelt (peeking in the window), for the Republican party's many political tangles during Taft's presidency. In fact, Roosevelt did leave Taft a divided party, but Taft contributed to further divisions. *Theodore Roosevelt Collection.*

when the Republican national convention nominated William Howard Taft. A graduate of Yale and former federal judge, Taft had served as governor of the Philippines before joining Roosevelt's cabinet as secretary of war in 1904.

William Jennings Bryan, still leader of the progressive wing of the Democratic party, faced no serious opposition in winning his party's nomination for the third time. Roosevelt's popularity and his endorsement of Taft overcame a lackluster Republican campaign. Taft won just under 52 percent of the vote and Republicans kept control of the Senate and the House. Soon after turning the reins of office over to Taft, Roosevelt set off to hunt big game in Africa.

Roosevelt had been Taft's mentor in politics, but Taft's approach was far more restrained than his predecessor's. Unlike Roosevelt, Taft hated campaigning and disliked conflict. He often took a legalistic approach to the presidency that appeared timid when compared to Roosevelt's boldness. But Taft worked to demonstrate his support for Roosevelt's Square Deal. His attorney general initiated some ninety antitrust suits in four years, twice as many as during Roosevelt's seven years. And Taft approved several efforts to strengthen regulatory agencies, as in 1910 when Congress extended the power of the Interstate Commerce Commission to cover most communication companies.

Taft's administration also saw two constitutional amendments. Reformers had long considered the income tax as the fairest means of raising federal revenues. With support from Taft, the **Sixteenth Amendment,** permitting a federal income tax, won ratification by enough states to take effect in 1913. By contrast, Taft took no position on the **Seventeenth Amendment,** proposed in 1912 and adopted shortly after he left office in 1913. It changed the method of electing U.S. senators from election by state legislatures to direct election by the voters of the state, another long-time goal of reformers, who claimed state legislatures had been swayed by corporate influence and even outright bribery.

Roosevelt had handed Taft a Republican party divided by battles over the Hepburn Act and other presidential actions. Divisions between conservatives and progressives continued and, after 1909, Taft increasingly sided with the conservatives. That year, he called a special session of Congress to reform the tariff. However, the resulting **Payne-Aldrich Tariff** retained high rates on most imports. Disappointed, Taft nonetheless signed the bill to avoid antagonizing powerful Republicans in Congress. When Republican progressives—mostly from midwestern farm states that would have benefited from lower tariffs—protested, Taft became defensive, alienating them even more by calling it "the best bill that the Republican party ever passed."

The battle within the Republican party intensified when Republican progressives attacked the highhanded way that Joseph Cannon, Speaker of the House of Representatives since 1902, used his power to support conservatives. "Uncle Joe" Cannon, known for his profanity and poker playing, used the Speaker's power not just to support conservative issues but also to stifle efforts by progressives. Initially favorable to attempts by Republican progressives to replace Cannon, Taft backed off when he realized that the progressives lacked the votes, and he then made his peace with Cannon. A small band of Republican progressives tried to trim the Speaker's power in 1909 but lost. In 1910, ignoring Taft, George W. Norris led Republican progres-

Sixteenth Amendment Constitutional amendment ratified in 1913 that gives the federal government the right to establish an income tax.

Seventeenth Amendment Constitutional amendment ratified in 1913 that authorizes the direct popular election of U.S. senators.

Payne-Aldrich Tariff Tariff bill in 1909 that began as a Republican attempt to reduce tariffs but that ultimately retained high tariffs on most imports.

sives in a "revolt against Cannonism" that gained the support of the Democrats and permanently reduced the power of the Speaker.

A dispute over conservation further widened Republican divisions. Taft kept Gifford Pinchot as head of the Forest Service. But Pinchot charged that Taft's secretary of the Interior, **Richard A. Ballinger,** had weakened the conservation program and favored corporate interests by opening lands previously designated as reserves. Taft determined that Ballinger had not violated any laws. In fact, he concluded that Ballinger was reversing actions of Pinchot and Roosevelt's secretary of the interior that had exceeded their legal authority. Pinchot persisted, however, and publicly aired other charges against Ballinger. Taft, who considered Pinchot "a radical and a crank," fired him early in 1910. An investigation by Congress cleared Ballinger, but the affair further estranged Taft from congressional progressives and distracted from his generally strong record on conservation. By 1912, when Taft faced reelection, the Republican party was in serious disarray and he faced opposition from most progressive Republicans.

Wilson and Democratic Progressivism

● How did choices by Wilson and the Democrats influence the role of the federal government in the economy and the power of the presidency?

"We stand at Armaggedon," thundered former president Theodore Roosevelt in 1912, invoking the Biblical prophecy of a final battle between good and evil. "And," he continued, "we battle for the Lord." He soon bolted the Republican party to run for president as the candidate of the newly formed Progressive party. The Democratic presidential candidate that year was Woodrow Wilson who, like Roosevelt, claimed to be the true voice of progressivism. Roosevelt and Wilson, however, presented quite different proposals for dealing with big business and attacked each other's right to claim the title "progressive." They agreed only that William Howard Taft, the incumbent president and the Republican candidate, was not a progressive at all.

The presidential election of 1912 marks a moment when Americans actively and seriously debated their future. All three nominees were well educated and highly literate: Theodore Roosevelt graduated from Harvard in 1880, William Howard Taft, Yale, 1878, and Woodrow Wilson, Princeton, 1879. Roosevelt and Wilson were authors of respected books on American history and politics. They approached politics with a sense of destiny and purpose. And none was afraid to talk frankly to the American people about their ideas for the future.

Debating the Future: The Election of 1912

As the hapless Taft watched the Republican party unravel, Theodore Roosevelt was traveling abroad, first hunting in Africa and then hobnobbing with European leaders. When he returned in 1910, he had already met with the indignant Pinchot and other former associates. He then undertook a speaking tour and, without criticizing Taft, proposed a broad program of reform that he labeled the **New Nationalism.** Roosevelt did not openly question Taft's reelection, but other Republican progressives began to do so. In the 1910 congressional elections, Republican candidates fared badly, plagued both by divisions within their party and by an economic downturn. For the first time since 1892, Democrats won a majority in the House of Representatives. Democrats also won a number of governorships, including Woodrow Wilson in New Jersey.

By early 1911, many Republican progressives looked to Robert La Follette as their candidate to wrest the Republican nomination from Taft. Roosevelt, however, found La Follette too radical and thought him irresponsible in his attacks on corporations. Roosevelt criticized Taft, sometimes in public, for failing to maintain Republican unity, for his approach to conservation, and for his antitrust policies, which seemed to ignore Roosevelt's distinctions based on behavior rather than size. One suit, against U.S. Steel over its acquisition of Tennessee Coal and Iron, implied that Roosevelt either had been fooled into aiding the growth of a monopoly or had purposely done so (see page 655).

Richard A. Ballinger Taft's secretary of the interior accused of hampering conservation efforts and favoring corporate interests; a congressional investigation exonerated him, but he failed to regain public confidence.

New Nationalism Program of labor and social reform that Theodore Roosevelt advocated in 1910; he made an unsuccessful bid to regain the presidency using this platform in 1912.

◆ In 1912, former President Theodore Roosevelt broke with the Republican party and launched a new party, the Progressive party. Progressives took the Bull Moose as their symbol, from Roosevelt's boast that he was as strong as a bull moose. The Democrats nominated Woodrow Wilson, the progressive governor of New Jersey. *Museum of American Political Life, University of Hartford.*

In February 1912, Roosevelt announced he would oppose Taft for the Republican presidential nomination. Thirteen states had established direct primaries to select delegates to the national nominating convention, and Roosevelt enjoyed great popularity at the primary polls, winning 278 delegates to 48 for Taft and 36 for La Follette. Elsewhere, however, Taft had all the advantages of an incumbent president in control of the party machinery. At the Republican nominating convention, many states sent contesting delegations, one pledged to Taft and one to Roosevelt. Taft's supporters controlled the **credentials committee** and gave most of the contested seats to delegates supporting their man. Roosevelt's delegates walked out, claiming that Taft had stolen the nomination. The remaining delegates nominated Taft on the first ballot.

Roosevelt's angry supporters regrouped to form a third party: the Progressive party, nicknamed the **Bull Moose party** after Roosevelt's boast that he was "as fit as a bull moose." The delegates sang "Onward, Christian Soldiers" and issued a platform based on the New Nationalism, including tariff reduction, regulation of corporations, a minimum wage, an end to child labor, woman suffrage, and the initiative, referendum, and recall. Women were more prominent at the Progressive convention than at any presidential nominating session since the Populists'. They helped draft platform planks—especially those dealing with labor—and Jane Addams addressed the convention to second the nomination of Roosevelt.

When the Democratic convention opened, delegates were overjoyed, certain that the Republican split gave them their best chance at the presidency in twenty years. The nomination was hotly contested, and the convention took 46 ballots to nominate Woodrow Wilson, the governor of New Jersey who had earned a reputation as a progressive. Their platform attacked monopolies and called for limits on campaign contributions by corporations, a single term for the president, and major tariff reductions. Where Roosevelt called his program the New Nationalism, Wilson labeled his the **New Freedom.**

Much of the attention in the campaign focused on Roosevelt's and Wilson's views on big business. Roosevelt continued to maintain that the behavior of corporations was the problem, not their size. Before winning the nomination, Wilson criticized big business but had not developed a proposal for dealing with it. After his nomination, he met with Louis Brandeis, a Boston attorney and leading critic of corporate consolidation. Brandeis convinced Wilson to center his campaign on the issue of big business and to offer a significantly different solution than Roosevelt's. Where Roosevelt and the Progressives promised regulation, Wilson depicted monopoly itself as the most serious problem, not the misbehavior of individual corporations. Breaking up monopolies and restoring competition, he argued, would benefit consumers through better products and lower prices. He also pointed to what he considered the most serious flaw in Roosevelt's proposals for regulation: as long as monopolies faced regulation, they would continually and naturally seek to control the regulator—the federal government. Only antitrust actions, Wilson argued, could protect democracy from this threat.

Taft, the Republican nominee, claimed a stronger record as a trustbuster than Roosevelt, but he was clearly the most conservative of the candidates. Eugene V. Debs, the Socialist candidate, rejected both regulation and antitrust actions and argued instead for government ownership of monopolies. The real

---

credentials committee Party convention committee that settles disputes arising when rival delegations from the same state demand to be seated.

Bull Moose party Popular name given to the Progressive party in 1912 as a tribute to its candidate Theodore Roosevelt.

New Freedom Program of reforms advocated by Woodrow Wilson during his 1912 presidential campaign, including lowering tariffs, revising the monetary system, and prosecuting trusts.

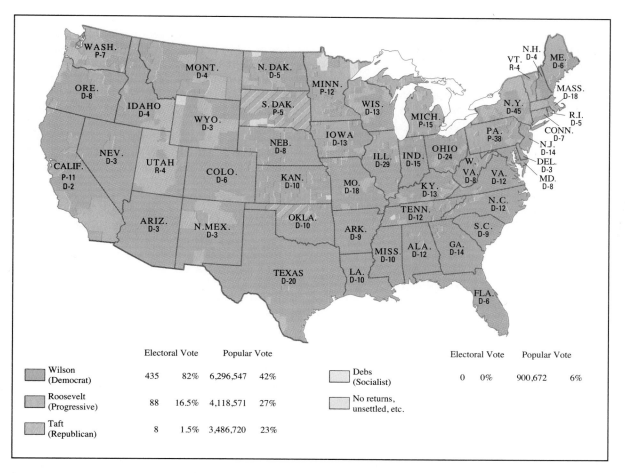

	Electoral Vote		Popular Vote				Electoral Vote		Popular Vote	
Wilson (Democrat)	435	82%	6,296,547	42%		Debs (Socialist)	0	0%	900,672	6%
Roosevelt (Progressive)	88	16.5%	4,118,571	27%		No returns, unsettled, etc.				
Taft (Republican)	8	1.5%	3,486,720	23%						

◆ **MAP 21.1 Election of 1912, by Counties**   The presidential election of 1912 was complicated by the campaign of former President Theodore Roosevelt running as a Progressive. Roosevelt's campaign split the usual Republican vote without taking much away much of the usual Democratic vote. Woodrow Wilson, the Democratic candidate, carried many parts of the West and Northeast that Democratic candidates rarely won.

contest, however, was between Roosevelt and Wilson. In the end, Wilson received most of the usual Democratic vote and won with 42 percent of the total. Democrats also won sizable majorities in both houses of Congress. Roosevelt and Taft split the traditional Republican vote, 27 percent for Roosevelt and 23 percent for Taft. Debs, with but 6 percent, did come in first in some counties and in some city precincts (see Map 21.1).

Wilson and Reform, 1913–1914

Born in Virginia in 1856, Woodrow Wilson grew up in the South during the Civil War and Reconstruction. His father, a Presbyterian minister, impressed on him lessons in morality and responsibility that remained with him his entire life. After a brief and disappointing experience with practicing law, Wilson earned a Ph.D. in political science from the Johns Hopkins University. His first book, *Congressional Government*, presented a critical study of federal lawmaking. A professor at Princeton University after 1890, he proved a popular lecturer but struck many as cold and uncomfortable when dealing with people. He became president of Princeton in 1902 and initiated educational reforms that brought him national attention.

In 1910, New Jersey Democrats needed a respectable candidate for governor. Conservative Democratic leaders thought Wilson had the perfect qualifications: he was known to be an anti-Bryan Democrat and a good public speaker. He won the nomination and the election. As governor, he suddenly embraced reform, shocking the conservatives who had nominated him. In two years as governor, he led the legislature to adopt many progressive measures, including a direct primary, a corrupt practices act, workers' compensation, and regulation of railroads and public utilities. His record won support from many Democratic progressives, including Bryan, when he sought the 1912 presidential nomination.

Wilson firmly believed in party government and an active role for the president in policymaking. He set out to work closely with Democrats in Congress and succeeded to such an extent that, like Roosevelt, he changed the nature of the presidency itself. Confident in his abilities as a public speaker and firmly believing that a persuasive orator could change people's views, he went to the Capitol to address Congress in person, the first president since John Adams to do so.

Wilson focused first on tariff reform, tying his party's longtime opposition to the protective tariff to the argument that high tariff rates helped to create monopolies by reducing competition. Despite the opposition of many manufacturers, Congress passed the Underwood Tariff in October 1913, establishing the most significant reductions since the Civil War. To offset the subsequent federal revenue losses, the **Underwood Act** also initiated an income tax, recently authorized by the Sixteenth Amendment.

The next matter facing Wilson and the Democrats was reform of the banking system. The national banking system dated to 1863 but periodic economic problems, such as the **Panic of 1907,** made evident the system's shortcomings. Chief among these, it had no real center to provide direction and no way to adjust the **money supply** to the needs of the economy. In 1913, a congressional investigation also revealed the high degree of concentration of power in the hands of the few investment bankers with vast corporate control. For Wilson and Democrats in Congress, the crucial question was that of control. Conservatives, led by Carter Glass of Virginia, joined with bankers in favoring a system that minimized governmental regulation. Progressive Democrats, especially William Jennings Bryan (now Wilson's secretary of state) and Louis Brandeis, favored strong federal control.

In December 1913, Wilson approved the **Federal Reserve Act,** establishing twelve regional Federal Reserve Banks. These were "banker's banks," places where banks kept their reserves. All national banks were required to belong to this Federal Reserve System, and state banks were invited to join. The debate over control ended in compromise. The participating banks exercised significant control over the twelve district banks, but the district banks were regulated and supervised by the Federal Reserve Board, a new federal agency with members chosen by the president. In his appointments, Wilson named men sympathetic to banking, choices that puzzled and outraged progressives but reassured the banking community that the "Fed" posed no threat. The Federal Reserve Act stands as the most important domestic act of the Wilson administration, for it still provides the framework for regulating the nation's banking system.

In 1914, Congress passed the **Clayton Antitrust Act,** which prohibited specified business practices, including **interlocking directorates** among large companies that could be proven to reduce competition. It also exempted farmers' organizations and unions from antitrust prosecution under the Sherman Act. The antitrust sections in the final version of the Clayton Act, however, provided little basis for breaking up big corporations. One senator claimed that the bill started out as "a raging lion with a mouth full of teeth" but ended up as "a tabby cat with soft gums." The weakening of the Clayton Act partly reflected a change of course by Wilson. Instead of breaking up big business, Wilson now moved closer to Roosevelt's position that regulation

Underwood Act   1913 law that substantially reduced tariffs and made up for the lost revenue by providing for a small graduated income tax.

Panic of 1907   Minor depression brought about by a stock market collapse and several bank failures, which showed the need for banking reform.

money supply   The amount of money in the economy, such as cash and the contents of checking accounts.

Federal Reserve Act   1913 law establishing twelve federal reserve banks to hold the cash reserves of commercial banks.

Clayton Antitrust Act   1914 law banning such monopolistic business practices as price fixing and interlocking directorates; it also exempted farmers' organizations and unions from prosecution under antitrust laws.

interlocking directorate   Situation in which the same individuals sit on the boards of directors of various "competing" companies in one industry.

had more potential for protecting small businesses. Wilson agreed to the transformation of the Clayton Act into what amounted to lackluster regulation, and he energetically supported passage of the **Federal Trade Commission Act,** also passed in 1914, a regulatory measure designed to prevent unfair methods of business competition.

Wilson and Social Reform

Many progressives applauded the record of the Wilson administration in reforming the tariff, establishing the Federal Reserve System, and passing the Clayton Act. On the other hand, they found his appointees to the Federal Trade Commission and the Federal Reserve Board disappointing for their sympathies with business and banking. Early in the Wilson administration, Congress fulfilled a Democratic campaign promise by creating a separate department of labor. As secretary of labor, the president appointed William Wilson (not a relative), a Congressman who was a union member and a close associate of Samuel Gompers, president of the American Federation of Labor. Beyond that support for labor, Wilson did little to appeal to progressives who favored social reform. He considered efforts to outlaw child labor unconstitutional and was not convinced of the need to amend the Constitution for woman suffrage.

During his first year in office, Wilson drew sharp criticism from some northern social reformers when his appointees began to institute racial segregation in several federal agencies. A southerner by birth and heritage, Wilson undoubtedly believed in segregation. Even though he resisted the most extreme racists in his party, he appointed adamant segregationists to many federal positions. His position on racial issues was always determined in part by the need to work closely with southern Democrats in Congress. At a cabinet meeting shortly after Wilson took office, the postmaster general (a southerner) proposed racial segregation of all federal employees. No cabinet member objected, and several federal agencies began to segregate African-Americans. In the South, some Wilson appointees even began to fire African-Americans from federal jobs, and one announced that "a Negro's place is in the cornfield," not in federal employment. Wilson was surprised at the swell of protests, not just from African-Americans but also from some white progressives in the North and Midwest. He never designated a change in policy, but the process of segregating federal facilities thereafter slowed greatly.

Late in 1914, Wilson announced that he was satisfied and would seek no further reforms. In part, this reflected his underlying conservatism and opposition to social reform. Early in 1916, however, he reversed direction in anticipation of the coming election. Wilson had received fewer than half the popular votes in 1912, and he won the White House only because of the split among Republicans. He joined Democratic progressives in Congress, therefore, in pushing measures intended to secure their claim as the true voice of progressivism and to capture the loyalty of all progressive voters.

As a first step, Wilson nominated **Louis Brandeis** for the Supreme Court. Brandeis's reputation as a staunch progressive and critic of business aroused intense opposition from conservatives. Brandeis would be the first Jewish member of the Court, and some opposition to his confirmation carried anti-Semitic overtones. The Senate vote on the nomination was close, but he was confirmed with support from a few progressive Republicans. Wilson followed up the Brandeis nomination with support for a number of reform measures—improved credit facilities for farmers, workers' compensation for federal employees, and a law to eliminate child labor. Under threat of a national railroad strike, Congress also passed and Wilson signed the **Adamson Act,** securing an eight-hour workday for railroad employees.

Wilson's shift toward the social reformers may have been a significant factor in the election. His support for organized labor gave him strong backing among unionists, and labor's votes probably provided Wilson's victory in certain states, especially California. In states where women could vote, they seem to have supported Wilson in disproportionate numbers, probably because he backed issues of interest to women, such as outlawing child labor and keeping the nation out of war. In a very close election, Wilson won with 49 percent of the popular vote to 46 percent for Charles Evans Hughes, a moderately progressive Republican.

Federal Trade Commission Act   1914 law that outlawed unfair methods of competition in interstate commerce, and created a commission appointed by the president to investigate illegal business practices.

Louis Brandeis   Lawyer and reformer who opposed monopolies and defended individual rights; in 1916 he became the first Jewish justice on the Supreme Court.

Adamson Act   1916 law passed at the urging of the railway unions, establishing an eight-hour workday on all interstate railroads.

Progressivism in Perspective

- Was progressivism successful?
- What are your criteria for judging success?
- What lasting outcomes of progressivism affect modern American politics?

The Progressive era began with efforts at municipal reform in the 1890s, and sputtered to a close during World War I. Some politicians who called themselves progressives remained in prominent positions afterward, and progressive concepts of efficiency and expertise continued to guide government decision making. But the war diverted public attention from reform, and by the end of the war political concerns had changed. By the mid-1920s, too, many of the major leaders of progressivism had passed from the political stage.

The changes of the Progressive era transformed American politics and government. Before the Hepburn Act and the Federal Reserve Act, the federal government's role in the national economy consisted largely of instituting land-grant subsidies and protective tariffs. After the Progressive era, the federal government became a significant and permanent player in the economy, regulating a wide range of economic activity. The income tax, first treated almost as a joke, quickly became the most significant source of federal funds, without which it is impossible to imagine the activities that the federal government has assumed during the course of the twentieth century—from vast military expenditures to social welfare to support for the arts. Since at least the 1930s, the income tax has also been understood to have the potential to serve directly as an instrument of social policy, by which the federal government can redistribute income.

The decline of political parties and emergence of political campaigns based largely on personality and advertising accelerated in the second half of the twentieth century under the impact of television and public opinion polling. Organized pressure groups have proliferated and become ever more influential. Women's participation in politics has continued to increase, especially in the last third of the twentieth century.

The assertion of presidential authority by Roosevelt and Wilson, though not echoed in the administrations of their immediate successors, reappeared in the presidency of Franklin D. Roosevelt (1933–1945). Theodore Roosevelt, Woodrow Wilson, and Franklin Roosevelt transformed Americans' expectations regarding the office of the presidency itself.

Throughout the nineteenth century, Congress dominated the making of domestic policy. During the twentieth century, however, Americans came to expect domestic policy to flow from forceful executive leadership in the White House.

Perhaps the most instructive legacy from progressivism is the understanding that reforms rarely fulfill all the expectations of their **proponents.** Some advocates of prohibition, for example, predicted that crime and poverty would diminish once alcohol was banned. Prohibition, however, helped give birth to organized crime, as the makers of illegal liquor began to cooperate among themselves rather than engage in cutthroat competition. Those who reduced the power of political parties hoped to destroy political machines and bosses. Some such organizations proved highly resilient however, adapting themselves to new conditions and continuing—not as before, but continuing nonetheless—with a significant role in politics. So the Progressive era taught America that even the most well-intended reforms are not cure-alls.

Finley Peter Dunne, the leading political humorist of the Progressive era, voiced a cynical view of reform when observed that "a man that would expect to train lobsters to fly in a year is called a lunatic; but a man that thinks men can be turned into angels by an election is called a reformer and remains at large." But the lesson from the sometimes disappointing outcome of progressive reforms is not to avoid change. Americans have tinkered with the structure and function of their government repeatedly and will continue to do so. Such changes are normal parts of American politics. As Dunne wrote, reform was like housecleaning, and he quoted this conversation between a woman who ran a boardinghouse and one of her lodgers:

"I don't know what to do," says she. "I'm worn out, and it seems impossible to keep this house clean. What is the trouble with it?"

"Madam," says my friend Gallagher, . . . "the trouble with this house is that it is occupied entirely by human beings. If it was a vacant house, it could easily be kept clean."

Thus, Dunne concluded about progressive reform, "The noise you hear is not the first gun of a revolution. It's only the people of the United States beating a carpet."

---

proponent   One who argues in support of something.

SUMMARY

Progressivism, a phenomenon of the late nineteenth and early twentieth centuries, refers to new concepts of government, to changes in government that made those concepts reality, and the political process by which change occurred. Those years marked a time of far-reaching political transformation, brought about through many *choices* by groups and individuals, who approached politics with fresh but often quite different *expectations*. Organized interest groups became an important part of this process. Women broke through previous *constraints* to take a more prominent role in politics, and succeeded in gaining the suffrage in several states. The Anti-Saloon League was the most successful of a number of organizations that *chose* to reshape government to enforce their moral standards. Some African-Americans *chose* to fight the *constraints* of segregation and disfranchisement, looking to W. E. B. Du Bois for leadership. Socialist and radicals in the Industrial Workers of the World saw capitalism as the source of many problems, but few Americans *chose* their radical solutions.

Political reform took place at every level, from cities to states to the federal government. Muckraking journalists exposed corruption, wrongdoing, and suffering, thereby alerting many Americans to the need for change. Municipal reformers introduced modern methods of city government in a quest for efficiency and expertise. Some *chose* to use government to remedy social problems by employing the expertise of new professions such as public health and social work. Reformers also *chose* to attack the power of party bosses and machines by reducing the role of political parties through the reforms that comprised direct democracy.

At the federal level, Theodore Roosevelt set the pace for progressive reform. He *chose* to challenge judicial *constraints* on federal authority over big business and advocated other forms of economic regulation. The *outcome* was an increase in the federal government's power within the economy. He also *chose* to regulate the use of natural resources. His successor, William Howard Taft, failed to maintain Republican party unity and eventually sided with conservatives against progressives.

In 1912, Roosevelt *chose* to form a new political party, the Progressives, making that year's presidential election a three-way contest. Roosevelt called for regulation of business whereas Wilson, the Democrat, favored breaking them up through antitrust action. Wilson won the election but soon *chose* regulation over antitrust actions. He presided over the creation of the Federal Reserve System of regulating banking nationwide. As the 1916 election approached, Wilson also pushed for social reforms, including restrictions on child labor, in an effort to unify all progressives behind his leadership.

Progressive reforms have had a profound impact on American politics throughout the twentieth century. In many ways, the *outcome* of the Progressive era was the origin of modern American politics.

E xpectations

C onstraints

C hoices

O utcomes

SUGGESTED READINGS

Chambers, John Whiteclay, II. *The Tyranny of Change: Americans in the Progressive Era, 1890–1920.* 2nd ed. (1992).

A concise overview of American life during the Progressive era.

Lewis, David Levering. *W. E. B. Du Bois: Biography of a Race, 1868–1919* (1993).

A powerful biography of Du Bois that delivers on its promise to present, as well, the "biography of a race" during the Progressive era.

Link, Arthur S., and Richard L. McCormick. *Progressivism* (1983).

A thorough survey of progressivism, including the views of historians.

Roosevelt, Theodore. *An Autobiography* (1913, abridged ed. rpt. 1958).

Roosevelt's account of his actions sometimes needs to be taken with a grain of salt but nevertheless provides insight into Roosevelt, the person.

Sinclair, Upton. *The Jungle.* Intro. by James R. Barrett. (1988).

This socialist novel about workers in Chicago's packinghouses is a classic example of muckraking.

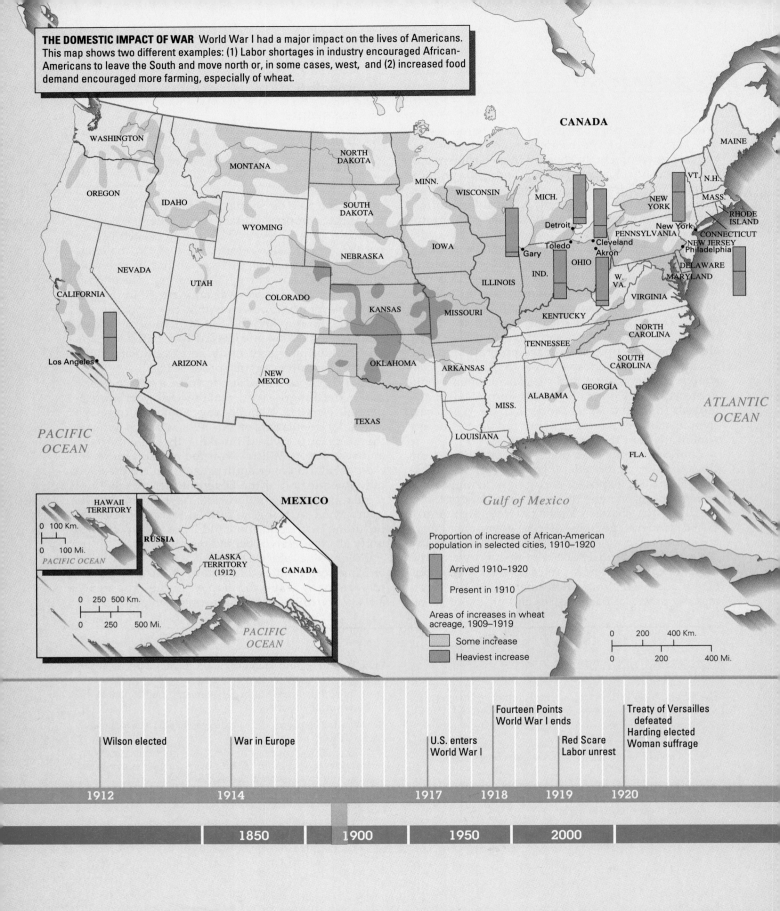

THE DOMESTIC IMPACT OF WAR World War I had a major impact on the lives of Americans. This map shows two different examples: (1) Labor shortages in industry encouraged African-Americans to leave the South and move north or, in some cases, west, and (2) increased food demand encouraged more farming, especially of wheat.

CANADA

WASHINGTON

OREGON

IDAHO

MONTANA

NORTH DAKOTA

MINN.

WISCONSIN

MICH.

Detroit

MAINE

VT. N.H.

NEW YORK

MASS.

RHODE ISLAND

New York

CONNECTICUT

NEW JERSEY

Philadelphia

PENNSYLVANIA

SOUTH DAKOTA

WYOMING

NEVADA

UTAH

COLORADO

NEBRASKA

IOWA

ILLINOIS

IND.

OHIO

Toledo

Gary

Cleveland

Akron

W. VA.

VIRGINIA

DELAWARE

MARYLAND

CALIFORNIA

KANSAS

MISSOURI

KENTUCKY

NORTH CAROLINA

Los Angeles

ARIZONA

NEW MEXICO

OKLAHOMA

ARKANSAS

TENNESSEE

SOUTH CAROLINA

GEORGIA

ALABAMA

MISS.

TEXAS

LOUISIANA

FLA.

ATLANTIC OCEAN

PACIFIC OCEAN

MEXICO

Gulf of Mexico

HAWAII TERRITORY

0 100 Km.
0 100 Mi.

PACIFIC OCEAN

RUSSIA

ALASKA TERRITORY (1912)

CANADA

0 250 500 Km.
0 250 500 Mi.

PACIFIC OCEAN

Proportion of increase of African-American population in selected cities, 1910–1920

Arrived 1910–1920

Present in 1910

Areas of increases in wheat acreage, 1909–1919

Some increase

Heaviest increase

0 200 400 Km.
0 200 400 Mi.

Wilson elected

War in Europe

U.S. enters World War I

Fourteen Points
World War I ends

Red Scare
Labor unrest

Treaty of Versailles defeated
Harding elected
Woman suffrage

1912

1914

1917

1918

1919

1920

1850

1900

1950

2000

22.

America and the World, 1913–1920

Inherited Commitments and New Directions

- In what ways did existing foreign policy commitments constrain Wilson's choices?
- How did Wilson seek to establish new directions in international relations?

From Neutrality to War: 1914–1917

- What were Wilson's expectations regarding American neutrality?
- What constraints did he face in seeking to maintain neutrality?
- What choices did he make in an effort to do so?

The Home Front

- What constraints hindered the United States' contribution to the Allied war effort?
- What choices did the federal government make in mobilizing the economy and society in support of the war?
- What was the outcome?

Americans "Over There"

- Why did Wilson choose to keep the AEF as separate as possible from the troops of the other Allies?

Wilson and the Peace Conference

- What were Wilson's expectations regarding peace?
- What constraints did he face in realizing those objectives?
- What choices did he make, and what was the outcome?

Trauma in the Wake of War

- How did Americans' expectations change as a result of the outcome of the war and the events of 1919?
- How did these new expectations affect their choice in the 1920 presidential election?

INTRODUCTION

On June 28, 1914, a Serbian terrorist killed Archduke Franz Ferdinand, heir to the throne of Austria-Hungary, and his wife Sophie. They were visiting Sarajevo, in Bosnia-Herzegovina, which the Austrians had recently annexed against the wishes of the neighboring kingdom of Serbia. To punish the assassinations, Austria first consulted with its ally, Germany, then made stringent demands on Serbia. Serbia sought help from Russia, which was allied with France. Tense diplomats invoked elaborate, interlocking alliance systems. Huge armies began to move. By August 4, most of Europe was at war.

Earlier, Theodore Roosevelt had probably voiced the *expectations* of many Americans when he claimed in 1899 that war had become practically obsolete among what he called the world's "civilized" nations. As president, Roosevelt helped to shape Americans' expectations of security when he argued that the best way to preserve peace was by *choosing* to develop naval and military strength. Given such *expectations*, many Americans were shocked, saddened, and repelled in August 1914 when the leading "civilized" nations of the world—all of whom had been busily accumulating arsenals for the previous two decades— lurched into war.

When Europeans *chose* war in August 1914, the United States had already taken a major role in world affairs, in part the result of *choices* made between 1898 and 1908. In that decade, America had acquired the Philippines and the Panama Canal, come to dominate the Caribbean and Central America, and pursued an active and continuing involvement in the balance of power in eastern Asia. All three presidents of the Progressive era—Theodore Roosevelt, William Howard Taft, and Woodrow Wilson—agreed wholeheartedly that the United States should exercise a major role in world affairs. And they disagreed only slightly about the nature of the American presence in Latin America, the Pacific, and eastern Asia. Despite such long-term and far-reaching commitments, in 1914 the United States was the only large, industrial nation that had *chosen* not to tie into the elaborate network of treaties and understandings among the powers of Europe and Asia. During the first years of the war Woodrow Wilson *chose* to try to maintain U.S. neutrality.

E xpectations
C onstraints
C hoices
O utcomes

When Wilson entered the White House in 1913, he *expected* to spend most of his time dealing with domestic issues. As a political scientist, he had mostly studied domestic politics, and his winning presidential campaign in 1912 had focused primarily on domestic issues. Although well-read on international affairs, he brought to the White House neither significant international experience nor carefully considered foreign policies. For secretary of state, he *chose* William Jennings Bryan, who also had devoted most of his political career to domestic matters and had little experience that qualified him as the nation's foreign policy chief. Both Wilson and Bryan were devout Presbyterians, sharing a confidence that God had a plan for humankind and that all people shared a basic bond. Both hoped too—idealistically and perhaps naively—that their foreign policy *choices* might make the United States a model among nations for the peaceful settlement of international disputes. Neither man *expected* that they and the nation were soon to face difficult *choices* over a war so immense and so horrible that—no matter who was victorious—its *outcome* would be a profoundly altered world.

The United States and World Affairs

1912 Wilson elected

1913 Huerta takes power in Mexico
Wilson denies recognition to Huerta
Bryan proposes cooling-off treaties

1914 U.S. Navy occupies Veracruz
War breaks out in Europe
U.S. neutrality declared
Stalemate on the western front
Bryan-Chamorro Treaty
Panama Canal completed

1915 German U-boat sinks the *Lusitania*
United States occupies Haiti

1915–1920 Great Migration

1916 U.S. troops pursue Villa into Mexico
National Defense Act
Virgin Islands purchased
Congress promises Philippine independence
Sussex pledge
United States occupies Dominican Republic
Wilson reelected

1917 Wilson calls for "peace without victory"
American troops leave Mexico
Germany resumes submarine warfare
Czar overthrown in Russia
United States declares war on Germany
Committee on Public Information
War Industries Board
Selective Service
Espionage Act
Race riot in East St. Louis
Government crackdown on IWW
Bolsheviks seize power in Russia
Russia withdraws from war
Secret treaties published
Railroads placed under federal control

1917–1918 Union membership rises sharply
Lynchings increase

1918 Wilson presents Fourteen Points
Germans launch major offensive
War Labor Board appointed
Sedition Act
U.S. troops in northern Russia and Siberia
Successful Allied counteroffensive
Republican majorities in Congress
Armistice in Europe

1918–1919 Worldwide influenza epidemic
Civil war in Russia
Rampant U.S. inflation

1919 Versailles peace conference
Prohibition approved
Seattle general strike
Communists seize power in Hungary
Urban race riots
Wilson suffers stroke
Boston police strike
Senate defeats Versailles Treaty

1919–1920 Steel strike
Red Scare
Palmer raids

1920 Senate defeats Versailles Treaty again
Woman suffrage approved
Harding elected

1921 Sacco-Vanzetti convictions

Inherited Commitments and New Directions

• In what ways did existing foreign policy commitments constrain Wilson's choices?

• How did Wilson seek to establish new directions in international relations?

When Woodrow Wilson entered the White House, he first fixed his foreign policy attention on the three areas of greatest American involvement: Latin America, the Pacific, and eastern Asia. There, he tried to balance the anti-imperialist principles of his Democratic party against the **interventionist** commitments of his Republican predecessors. He marked out some new directions, but in the end he not only accepted but actually extended most previous commitments.

Anti-Imperialism, Intervention, and Arbitration

Wilson's party had criticized many of the foreign policies of McKinley, Roosevelt, and Taft, especially imperialism. Secretary of State Bryan was a leading anti-imperialist who had faulted Roosevelt's "Big Stick" approach to foreign affairs. "The man who speaks softly does not need a big stick," Bryan said, adding that "if he yields to temptation and equips himself with one, the tone of his voice is very likely to change." Wilson shared Taft's commitment to American commercial expansion, but he criticized dollar diplomacy for using the State Department to advance the interests of particular companies.

During the Wilson administration, the Democrats' long adherence to anti-imperialism produced two measures. In 1916, Congress established a bill of rights for residents of the Philippine Islands and promised them independence—but failed to specify a date. The next year, Puerto Rico became a U.S. territory and its residents became U.S. citizens. Thus the Democrats wrote into law a limited version of the anti-imperialism they had proclaimed for more than twenty years.

Democrats had also criticized Roosevelt's actions in the Caribbean, but in the end Wilson intervened more in Central America and the Caribbean than had any other administrations during any other comparable eight-year period. Regarding Nicaragua, where Taft had used marines to prop up the rule of President Adolfo Días, Wilson wanted to revise a proposed treaty to give the United States even more authority within that country. Senate Democrats rejected his efforts, reminding Wilson and Bryan of their party's opposition to further protectorates. Even so, the **Bryan-Chamorro Treaty** of 1914 gave the United States significant concessions, including the right to build a canal through Nicaragua.

In Haiti, which owed a staggering debt to foreign bankers, the dictatorial president ordered many of his opponents put to death in 1915. When a mob then tore him apart, Wilson sent in American marines. A treaty followed, making Haiti a protectorate in which American forces controlled nearly all aspects of government until 1933. Wilson sent marines into the Dominican Republic in 1916, and U.S. naval officers took control there until 1924. In 1916, too, the United States agreed to buy the Virgin Islands from Denmark for $25 million.

Although Wilson made few changes in previous policies regarding the Caribbean, he enthusiastically encouraged efforts by Bryan to promote arbitration of international disputes. Roosevelt's and Taft's secretaries of state had tried to promote international arbitration, but their efforts had foundered on the Senate's refusal to yield any degree of its role in foreign relations. Learning from those failures, Bryan drafted a model arbitration treaty and first obtained its approval from the Senate Foreign Relations Committee. The State Department then distributed the proposal—called "President Wilson's Peace Proposal"—to the forty nations that maintained diplomatic relations with the United States. Negotiations produced thirty treaties, all of which featured a cooling-off period for disputes, typically a year, during which the nations agreed not to go to war and instead to seek outside fact-finding and arbitration. For Wilson the arbitration treaties marked the beginning of a process by which he eventually sought to redefine international relations, substituting rational negotiations and arbitration for raw power.

---

interventionist Tending to interfere in the affairs of another sovereign state.

Bryan-Chamorro Treaty 1914 treaty under which Nicaragua received $3 million in return for granting the United States exclusive rights to a canal route and a naval base.

Wilson and the Mexican Revolution

In Mexico, however, Wilson faced choices which led him into brazen power politics. **Porfirio Díaz** had ruled Mexico as a dictator for a third of a century, supported by the great landholders, the church, and the military. By the early twentieth century, discontent was brewing among nearly everyone else—peasants, workers, and intellectuals. Rebellion broke out in the south, led by **Emiliano Zapata,** and in the north, led by Pascual Orozco and Francisco "Pancho" Villa. Mobs took to the streets demanding that Díaz resign. He did so in 1911. Francisco Madero, member of a wealthy landowning family but with a reputation as a leading proponent of reform, assumed the presidency to great acclaim, but proved incapable of uniting the country. Discontent rolled across Mexico, as peasant armies calling for *tierra y libertad* ("land and liberty") attacked the mansions of great landowners. Conservatives feared Madero as a reformer at the same time that Zapata and the radicals dismissed him as too timid. Conservative forces launched an uprising in Mexico City in February 1913, working with the commander of the army, **General Victoriano Huerta.** Huerta took control of the government and had Madero executed.

Most European governments quickly extended diplomatic recognition to Huerta because his government clearly held power in Mexico City, but Taft—about to hand over the presidency—left that matter to his successor. Thus, soon after his inauguration, Wilson had to choose. American companies with investments in Mexico, especially mining and oil, urged recognition because they considered Huerta most likely and able to protect their holdings against the radicals. Wilson, however, considered Huerta a murderer and vowed "not to recognize a government of butchers."

Wilson announced that his choice came because Huerta's regime did not rest on the consent of the governed. Adding such a moral dimension to diplomatic recognition constituted a new element in American foreign policy. Previous American presidents had extended diplomatic recognition to all governments in power as simple acknowledgment of their existence. Labeled as "missionary diplomacy," Wilson's denial of recognition implied that the United States bore the moral responsibility to discriminate between pure and impure governments. Telling one visitor, "I am going to teach the

South American republics to elect good men," Wilson engaged in what he called "watchful waiting," seeking an opportunity to act against Huerta. In the meantime, anti-Huerta forces in northern Mexico, led by Venustiano Carranza, began to make significant gains.

In April 1914, Wilson found an excuse to intervene when Mexican officials in Tampico arrested a few American sailors who had come ashore. The city's army commander immediately released them and apologized. Wilson, however, used the incident to justify ordering the navy to occupy **Veracruz,** the leading Mexican port. Veracruz also happened to be the major source of governmental revenue, from customs, and the landing point for most governmental military supplies. The occupation cost more than a hundred Mexican lives and turned many Mexicans against Wilson for violating their national sovereignty over a petty dispute. Huerta, however, facing the steady advance of Carranza's armies and deprived of munitions and customs revenues, fled the country in mid-July. Wilson withdrew the last American forces from Veracruz in November.

Carranza succeeded Huerta as president and Wilson officially recognized his government. Carranza faced armed opposition, however, from **Pancho Villa** in northern Mexico. When Villa suffered serious defeats, he apparently decided his best hope for defeating Carranza was to incite a war between the Carranza government and the United States. Villa's men murdered several Americans in Mexico and then, in March 1916, raided across the border and

---

Porfirio Díaz Mexican soldier and politician who became president after a coup in 1876 and governed the country until 1911.

Emiliano Zapata Mexican Indian revolutionary who led a peasant revolt demanding agrarian reforms from 1910 until his death in 1919.

General Victoriano Huerta Mexican general who overthrew the president, Francisco Madero, in 1913, and established a military dictatorship until forced to resign in 1914.

Veracruz The major port city of Mexico, located in east central on the Gulf of Mexico; in 1914, Wilson ordered the U.S. Navy to occupy the port.

Pancho Villa Mexican bandit and revolutionary who led a raid into New Mexico in 1916, which prompted the U.S. government to send troops into Mexico in unsuccessful pursuit.

killed several Americans in Columbus, New Mexico. After securing reluctant approval from Carranza, Wilson sent an expedition of nearly 7,000 men, commanded by General John Pershing, into Mexico to punish Villa. Villa deftly evaded the American troops, all the while drawing them ever deeper into Mexico. Carranza now became alarmed, protesting the size of the expedition and the distance it had invaded. When a clash between Mexican government forces and American soldiers produced deaths on both sides, Carranza asked Wilson to withdraw the American troops. Wilson refused. Villa now doubled behind the American army and raided into Texas, killing more Americans. When Wilson sent more men into Mexico, Carranza insisted that all the American forces be withdrawn. Wilson still refused. Only when he expected that America might soon be drawn into war with Germany, in early 1917, did he order the troops to withdraw, leaving a deep reservoir of Mexican resentment and even hatred toward the United States.

From Neutrality to War: 1914–1917

- What were Wilson's expectations regarding American neutrality?
- What constraints did he face in seeking to maintain neutrality?
- What choices did he make in an effort to do so?

At first, Americans paid only passing attention to the assassinations at Sarajevo. The nations of Europe, however, began methodically—sometimes regretfully, sometimes enthusiastically—to activate their intricate alliance networks. When Europe plunged into war, Wilson and all Americans faced difficult choices.

The Great War in Europe

Europe's great powers—Britain, France, Germany, Austria-Hungary, and Russia—had avoided armed conflict with each other since 1871, when Germany had humiliated France in the brief Franco-Prussian War. During those years, however, competition for world markets and colonies encouraged nations to accumulate arms and seek allies. European diplomats had constructed two major alliance systems by 1907. The **Triple Entente** linked Britain, France, and Russia. Britain was also allied with Japan. The

◆ When Francisco "Pancho" Villa and his forces raided New Mexico and killed several American citizens, President Woodrow Wilson sent an American military force into Mexico to punish him. Led by General John J. Pershing (shown here), the expedition was unsuccessful in capturing Villa. *Culver Pictures, Inc.*

Triple Alliance of Germany, Austria-Hungary, and Italy stood in opposition.

As European nations formed their alliance networks, most European governments also encouraged their citizens to identify strongly with their nation, thereby cultivating the intense patriotism known as *nationalism*. Among the peoples of central Europe, particularly within the ethnically diverse empires of Austria-Hungary, Russia, and Turkey, a different sort of nationalism fueled aspirations for independence among the various cultural or linguistic groups. Those ethnic antagonisms and aspirations were especially powerful in the **Balkan peninsula**.

Triple Entente   Informal alliance that linked France, Great Britain, and Russia in the years before World War I.

Triple Alliance   Alliance that linked Germany, Italy, and Austria-Hungary in the years before World War I.

Balkan peninsula   Region of southeast Europe bounded by the Adriatic, Aegean, and Black seas; once ruled by Turkey, it included a number of relatively new and sometimes unstable states.

Imperialism and nationalism spawned an unprecedented arms build-up and an increasingly professionalized military officer corps. By 1900, most European powers had instituted universal military service. Technological advances produced powerful weapons like the machine gun. Military planners quickly adapted automobiles and airplanes, too, for their own purposes. Germany had the most powerful army in Europe and, in 1898, launched a naval construction program designed to make its navy as powerful as Britain's.

Thus, the events at Sarajevo occurred in the midst of an arms race between rival alliances. The assassinations themselves grew out of conflict between Austria-Hungary and Serbia. Austria-Hungary, whose empire included a number of restive **Slavic** ethnic groups, feared that Serbia might form the nucleus of a strong Slavic state on its south. Russia, alarmed over Austrian expansion in the Balkans, presented itself as the protector of Serbia. Called "the powder keg of Europe," the Balkans lived up to their explosive nickname in 1914.

Austria first assured itself of Germany's backing, then declared war on Serbia. In turn, Russia confirmed France's support and began the ponderous process of mobilizing in support of Serbia. Rather than wait for Russia to marshal its army, Germany declared war on Russia on August 1 and on France two days later. German strategists planned to bypass French defenses along the Franco-German border by moving through neutral Belgium (see Map 22.1). The Germans expected to knock France out of the war quickly, as they had done in 1871, and then turn their full power against Russia. When the Belgians refused permission for German troops to cross their territory, Germany declared war on Belgium. Britain entered the conflict in defense of Belgium on August 4. Eventually Germany and Austria-Hungary combined with Bulgaria and Turkey to form the Central Powers. Italy abandoned its Triple Alliance partners and joined Britain, France, Russia, Rumania, and Japan to make up the Allies.

At first, Secretary of State Bryan took a hopeful view of the war. "It may be," he suggested, "that the world needed one more awful object lesson to prove conclusively the fallacy of the doctrine that preparedness for war can give assurance for peace." Sir Edward Grey, Britain's foreign minister, was far less optimistic. At twilight on August 3, 1914, he mourned to a friend, "The lamps are going out all over Europe. We shall not see them lit again in our lifetime." Grey proved a more accurate prophet than Bryan.

The Germans had expected to roll through Belgium, a small and militarily weak nation. The Belgians, however, resisted long enough for Britain and France to position their troops to block the Germans. Instead of the quick knockout blow the Germans had anticipated, the armies settled into defensive lines over the **western front**—475 miles of French countryside, extending from the English Channel to the Alps (see Map 22.1). By the end of 1914, the troops had dug elaborate networks of trenches, separated from each other by a desolate **no man's land** filled with coils of barbed wire, where any movement brought a burst of machine gun fire. As the war progressed, terrible new weapons—poison gas, aerial bombings, tanks—took many thousands of lives but failed to break the deadlock.

American Neutrality

Wilson's initial reaction to the European conflagration revealed his own deep religious beliefs. He wrote to his closest adviser, Edward House, on August 3, of his confidence that "Providence has deeper plans than we could possibly have laid for ourselves." The next day, he announced that the United States was not committed to either side and was to be accorded all neutral rights. The death of his wife, Ellen, on August 6, briefly diverted the grief-stricken Wilson from the war. Then, on August 19, he spoke to the nation, urging Americans to be "neutral in fact as well as in name . . . impartial in thought as well as in action." He hoped not only that America would remain outside the conflict, but that he, head of the most powerful neutral, might serve as the peacemaker.

Wilson's hopes for peace proved unrealistic. Most of the warring nations wanted to gain territory, and only a decisive victory could deliver such a prize. The longer they fought, the more territory they coveted to satisfy their losses. So long as they saw a chance of winning, they had no interest in the appeals of Wilson or other would-be peacemakers.

Slavic   Relating to the Slavs, a linguistic group that includes Poles, Czechs, Slovaks, Slovenes, Serbs, Croats, and Bosnians, as well as Russians and Ukrainians.

western front   The line of battle between the Allies and Germany in World War II, which was located in French territory.

"no man's land"   The field of battle between the lines of two opposing, entrenched armies.

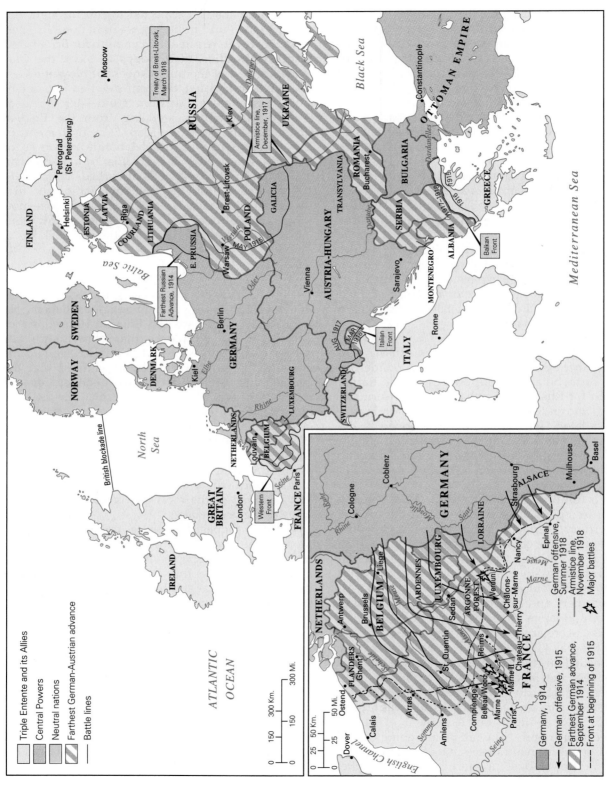

◆ **MAP 22.1 The War in Europe, 1914–1918** This map identifies the members of the two great military coalitions: the Central Powers and the Allies. Notice how much territory Russia lost by the Treaty of Brest-Litovsk as compared to the armistice line (the line between the two armies when Russia sought peace).

◆ The "western front" was a maze of trenches in which opposing armies faced each other across a no-man's land of barbed wire and machine gun fire. Much of the time, troops waited in their trenches, enduring rain, snow, heat, and boredom. When the Germans began to use poison gas, gas masks became standard issue for Allied soldiers. *Trench: Imperial War Museum. Gas mask: Collection of Colonel Stuart S. Corning, Jr.*

Wilson's hope that Americans could remain impartial was also unrealistic. American socialists probably came the closest. They condemned all the warring nations for seeking imperial spoils at the expense of the working class that filled the trenches. Most Americans probably sided with the Allies. England had cultivated American friendship since at least the mid-1890s. A shared language and culture joined the upper classes in both countries, while trade and finance united many members of their business communities. Memories of French assistance during the American Revolution fueled enthusiasm for France. And the martyrdom of Belgium aroused American sympathy. Allied propagandists also worked hard to generate anti-German sentiment in America, publicizing—and sometimes exaggerating—German atrocities in Belgium and portraying the war as a conflict between civilized peoples and brutal **Huns.**

Not all Americans sympathized with the Allies. Nearly eight million of the 97 million people in the United States had one or both parents from Germany or Austria. And not surprisingly, many of them disputed the depictions of their cousins as bloodthirsty barbarians. Ethnic loyalties also influenced some Americans not directly tied to the warring countries. Many of the five million Irish-Americans, for example, hated the English who ruled their

ancestral homeland and held no sympathy for them in the war.

Neutral Rights and German U-Boats

Wilson and Bryan agreed on the need to keep American interests separate from those of either side in the European conflict. Although both men continued to believe that the United States should remain neutral, they developed different approaches for carrying out that policy. Perhaps even their definitions of *neutrality* differed. Bryan proved willing to sacrifice neutral rights if insistence on those rights posed the prospect of conflict with one of the belligerents. Wilson stood firm on maintaining all traditional rights of neutral nations, a posture that proved more favorable to the Allies. For example, Bryan initially opposed loans to **belligerent** nations as incompatible with neutrality. Wilson first agreed,

---

Hun   Disparaging term used to describe Germans during World War I; the name came from a warlike tribe that invaded Europe in the fourth and fifth centuries.
belligerent   A nation formally at war.

hoping to starve the war financially. But once it became clear that the ban hurt the Allies more than the **Central Powers,** Wilson modified it to permit buying goods on credit. Finally, he dropped the ban on loans, partly because neutrals had always been permitted to lend to belligerents and partly because the freeze endangered the stability of the American economy.

Traditional neutral rights also included freedom of the seas: neutrals could trade with all belligerents. However, European powers quickly recognized the war as a struggle for survival in which new technologies rendered many neutral rights obsolete. Wilson soon found himself in conflict with both sides over the rights of neutral ships, as both sides turned to naval warfare to break the deadlock on the western front.

In command of the seas during the war's first months, Britain began to redefine neutral rights by announcing a blockade not only of German ports, but also of neutral ports from which goods could reach German markets. Britain also expanded traditional definitions of **contraband** to include anything that might give even indirect aid to an enemy—eventually including even cotton and food. Britain also took liberties with the traditional right of "visit and search," which enabled belligerent nations to stop and search neutral ships for contraband. Insisting that large, modern ships could not be searched at sea, Britain escorted neutral ships to port, thus imposing costly delays.

Germany responded by declaring a blockade of the British Isles, to be enforced by its submarines, called **U-boats.** U-boats were relatively fragile, and even a lightly armed merchant ship stood a reasonable chance of sinking one that surfaced and ordered the ship to stop in the traditional manner. Consequently, submarines struck from below the surface, without the warning dictated by traditional rules of naval warfare. When Britain began disguising its ships with neutral flags, Germany countered that neutral flags no longer guaranteed protection from U-boat attacks. Whereas Wilson issued token reprimands over Britain's practices, he strongly denounced those of Germany. Because they involved taking human lives, he considered Germany's assaults on neutrality of a different order than Britain's, which involved only property.

On February 10, 1915, Wilson warned that the United States would hold Germany to "strict accountability" for its actions and would do whatever was necessary to "safeguard American lives and property and to secure to American citizens the full enjoyment of their acknowledged rights on the high seas." On May 7, 1915, a German U-boat torpedoed the British passenger liner *Lusitania,* which sank so quickly that few passengers survived—1,198 died, including 128 Americans. Americans reacted with shock and horror. When Bryan learned that the *Lusitania* carried rifle cartridges and other contraband, he urged restraint in drafting a message to Germany. Wilson, however, prepared a protest message that stopped just short of demanding an end to submarine warfare against unarmed merchant ships. When the German response was noncommittal, Wilson composed an even stronger ultimatum. Bryan feared the words would lead to war, and he resigned as secretary of state rather than sign it.

Robert Lansing, Bryan's successor, was outspoken in favor of the Allies. Where Bryan had counseled restraint, Lansing urged a show of strength. As other U-boat attacks followed that on the *Lusitania,* Wilson continued to protest. But he knew that most Americans opposed going to war over the issue. The sinking of the unarmed French ship *Sussex* in March 1916, injuring several Americans, led Wilson to warn Germany that if unrestricted submarine warfare did not stop, "the United States can have no choice" but to sever diplomatic relations. (Usually this measure was the last step before declaring war.) Germany responded with the *Sussex* **pledge,** promising that U-boats would no longer strike merchant vessels without warning, provided the United States would convince the Allies to obey "international law." Wilson accepted the pledge but did little to persuade the British to change their tactics.

America's economic ties to the Allies grew as the war progressed. The British blockade stifled Americans' trade with the Central Powers, which fell from

---

Central Powers   In World War I, the coalition of Germany, Austria-Hungary, Bulgaria, and the Ottoman empire.

contraband   Goods prohibited by law or treaty from being imported or exported.

U-boat   A German submarine (in German, *Unterseeboot*).

Lusitania   British passenger liner torpedoed by a German submarine in 1915; more than one thousand drowned, including 128 Americans, bringing the United States closer to war with Germany.

Sussex pledge   German promise in 1916 to stop sinking merchant ships without warning, if the United States would compel the Allies to obey "international law."

around $170 million in 1914 to almost nothing two years later. Meanwhile, trade with Britain and France more than offset this decline. American companies sent $756 million in exports to those two nations in 1914 and $2.7 billion in 1916. American companies exported $6 million worth of explosives in 1914 and $467 million in 1916. Even more significant was the nation's transformation from a debtor to a **creditor nation.** By April 1917, American bankers had loaned more than $2 billion to the Allied governments.

Deeply convinced that the best way to keep the United States neutral was to end the war, Wilson sent Edward M. House to London and Berlin early in 1916 to sound out the British and Germans on the possibility for peace. Wilson directed that House should present proposals for peace, **disarmament,** and a league of nations to maintain peace in the future. Receiving no encouragement from either the British or the Germans, House concluded that neither side wanted a negotiated end to the war. Discouraged, Wilson yielded to the increasing numbers of Americans who sought "preparedness," which amounted to a military build-up. In the summer of 1916, Congress passed the **National Defense Act,** more than doubling the size of the army, and appropriated the largest naval expenditures in the country's peacetime history.

The Election of 1916

By agreeing to preparedness, Wilson took control of an issue that might otherwise have helped the Republicans in the 1916 presidential campaign. The Democrats nominated Wilson for a second term and campaigned on his progressive domestic record, his support for preparedness, and his success in keeping the nation out of war. Democrats frequently repeated their most popular campaign slogan, "He kept us out of war." Wilson, however, was troubled by that emphasis, knowing that it was dependent on Germany's continued commitment to its *Sussex* pledge.

Republicans nominated Charles Evans Hughes, a Supreme Court justice and former governor of New York who had a reputation as a progressive. Leading a party divided between progressives and conservatives, Hughes tried to avoid alienating either and sometimes ended up antagonizing both. He also avoided taking a clear position on preparedness and neutrality, hoping to keep support from German-American organizations upset with Wilson's harshness toward Germany and from others

who pressed for maximum assistance for the Allies. As a result, he failed to present a compelling alternative to Wilson. Hughes made other errors too, as in California where he slighted unions and Senator Hiram Johnson, both powerful forces. Wilson narrowly carried California.

The contest was very close, in part because most voters still identified with the Republicans, and Wilson could win only by getting support from some of them. First election reports—from eastern and midwestern states—were so strongly for Hughes that some Democrats conceded defeat. But Wilson won by uniting the always-Democratic South with the West, much of which was Republican and progressive. He also received significant backing from unions, socialists, and women in states where women could vote. In the end, Wilson received 49.4 percent of the vote to 46.2 percent for Hughes.

The Decision for War

After the election, Wilson tried again to end the war by asking the belligerents to state their terms for ending the fighting as the first step toward a peace conference at which he might preside. Germany was considering a return to unrestricted submarine warfare even though such an action might bring the United States into the war on the Allies' side. Hoping to cultivate Wilson, Germany announced its support for a peace conference but refused to specify terms, because it still expected to gain huge territories in Europe and Africa. Lansing and House, both deeply committed to the Allies, secretly undercut Wilson's initiative with Britain and France, expecting that Germany would then resume unrestricted submarine warfare and that the United States would enter the war on the side of the Allies.

Still hoping to secure a peace conference, Wilson spoke to the Senate in late January and presented his views on the best way to achieve and preserve peace. The galleries were packed and hushed as he

---

creditor nation   A nation is considered a creditor if the total of all loans received by its residents from all sources outside the nation is *less* than the total of all loans made to outsiders.

disarmament   The reduction or abolition of a nation's military forces or weaponry.

National Defense Act   1916 law enlarging the army, strengthening the national guard, and providing for an officers' reserve corps.

eloquently called for a league of nations to keep peace in the future and to replace the old balance-of-power concept with "a community of power." He urged that the only lasting peace would be a "peace without victory" and a "peace among equals" in which neither side exacted gains from the other. He called for government by consent of the governed, freedom of the seas, and reductions in armaments. The speech received an enthusiastic welcome from most Democrats and progressives—except for Theodore Roosevelt, who wanted to fight. Wilson's real audience, he admitted privately, was "the *people* of the countries now at war." He won praise from left-wing opposition parties in France and Britain and from the Russian government, which was reeling from severe losses and eager to find any way out. But the British, French, and German governments had no interest in "peace without victory."

In Germany, the initiative passed to those who wanted to break the western front stalemate by resuming unrestricted submarine warfare. Germany announced it would do so on February 1, 1917. Germany knew this move was likely to bring the United States into the war but gambled on being able to throttle the British and French war machine before American troops could reinforce them. Wilson, accordingly, broke off diplomatic relations with Germany on February 3, 1917. The U-boats began immediately to take a devastating toll on British shipping.

On March 1, Wilson released a decoded message from German foreign minister **Arthur Zimmermann** to the German minister in Mexico. Writing on January 16, Zimmermann proposed that, if the United States went to war with Germany, Mexico should ally itself with Germany and attack the United States. As its reward, when Germany won the war, Mexico was to recover its "lost provinces" of Texas, New Mexico, and Arizona. The British intercepted the message and, on February 24, gave it to American representatives. Zimmermann's suggestions outraged Americans, and the public outcry lent support to Wilson's proposal to arm American merchant ships for protection against the U-boats. Not everyone agreed that arming merchant ships was the best way to protect them. A few senators, mostly progressives, blocked the measure, arguing that a safer strategy was to keep merchant ships out of the war zone. Wilson then authorized merchant ships to be armed on his own.

Between February 3 and March 21, German U-boats sank six American ships, backing Wilson into a corner. The only way he could avoid war now was

◆ This photograph, released shortly after the nation went to war in 1917, is titled "Our Answer to the Kaiser—3,000 of America's Millions Eager to Fight for Democracy." *Picture Research Consultants.*

to back down from his previous insistence on "strict accountability." He did not retreat. On April 2, 1917, Wilson spoke to a special session of Congress and asked for a declaration of war (see Voices: Wilson's War Message). Previously, he had concentrated on neutral rights and only occasionally spoken of larger concerns, such as his proposal for a league of nations. Now he thought that the nation was unlikely to go to war solely to protect American commerce with the Allies, and he was probably unwilling himself to seek war unless he could justify it in more noble terms. In fact, his major objective in going to war seems to have been to put the United States, and himself, in a position to demand the sort of peace he had outlined to the Senate in January.

In asking for war, Wilson tried to unite Americans in a righteous, progressive crusade. He condemned German U-boat attacks as "warfare against mankind" and defined American war aims idealisti-

---

Arthur Zimmermann   German foreign minister who proposed in 1917 that if the United States declared war on Germany, Mexico might become a German ally and win back Texas, Arizona, and New Mexico.

cally. "The world must be made safe for democracy," he pleaded. He repeated his terms from January, promising that the United States would fight for democracy, self-government, "the rights and liberties of small nations," and a league of nations to "bring peace and safety to all nations and make the world itself at last free."

Not all members of Congress agreed that war was necessary and not all were ready to join Wilson's crusade to make the world safe for democracy. During the four days of debate that ensued, Senator George W. Norris, a progressive Republican from Nebraska, best voiced the arguments of the opposition. The nation, he claimed, was going to war "upon the command of gold" to "preserve the commercial right of American citizens to deliver munitions of war to belligerent nations." Against the opposition of Norris, Robert La Follette, and four others, eighty-two Senators voted to declare war on Germany. Jeannette Rankin of Montana, the first woman to serve in the House of Representatives, was among those who said no when the House voted 373 to 50 for war. In December, Congress also declared war against Austria-Hungary.

The Home Front

- What constraints hindered the United States' contribution to the Allied war effort?
- What choices did the federal government make in mobilizing the economy and society in support of the war?
- What was the outcome?

Historians have called World War I the first "total war" because long-term, modern warfare demanded mobilization of an entire society and economy. The war altered nearly every aspect of the economy, as the progressive emphasis on expertise and efficiency produced unprecedented centralization of economic decision making. Mobilization extended beyond war production to the people themselves, their attitudes toward the war, and their response to the need for labor.

Mobilizing the Economy

The war was so dependent on a fully developed industrial economy that each warring country sought to organize the entire nation around supplying the war machine. In the United States, shortages of military supplies, railway transportation snarls, and serious delays in military equipment deliveries led to increased federal direction over manufacturing, food and fuel production, and transportation. The American experience in this regard was not unusual and, if anything, was less extreme than in other nations because the United States entered the war later. Even so, the extent to which the federal government exercised direct control over the economy during the first World War I has never been matched.

Although unprecedented, much of the government intervention was also voluntary. Business enlisted as a roughly equal partner with government and supplied its cooperation and expertise. Many prominent entrepreneurs even volunteered their full-time services for a dollar a year. Much of the wartime centralization of economic decision making came through new agencies composed of government officials, business leaders, and prominent citizens.

The **War Industries Board (WIB)** was established in 1917 to oversee production of war materials. At first, it had only limited success in mobilizing industrial productivity. Then, in early 1918, Wilson appointed Bernard Baruch, a successful Wall Street speculator, to head the board. By pleading, bargaining, and sometimes threatening, Baruch usually managed to persuade companies to do what he wanted: set and meet production quotas, allocate raw materials, develop new industries, and make the entire economy more efficient. Confrontation was sometimes necessary—Baruch once threatened steel company executives with a government takeover—but he accomplished most WIB goals without coercing corporate America. Under WIB prompting, industrial production increased by 20 percent.

Efforts to conserve fuel included the first use of **daylight savings time.** To make rail transportation more efficient, the federal government consolidated the country's railroads and ran them as a single system, but without removing them from private ownership. The government took over the telegraph and

---

War Industries Board   Board headed by Bernard Baruch that coordinated American production during World War I, setting production quotas, fixing prices, and allocating raw materials.

daylight saving time   Setting of clocks one hour or more ahead of standard time to provide more daylight at the end of the workday during late spring, summer, and early fall.

The United States Goes to War

Wilson's War Message

With the failure of Wilson's 1917 effort to convince the European belligerents to submit to a peace conference, and with the Germans' resumption of unrestricted submarine warfare, Wilson and his entire cabinet reluctantly chose for the nation to go to war against Germany. On April 2, 1917, Wilson addressed a joint session of Congress and requested that the House and Senate declare war on Germany. When he returned to the White House following his speech, Wilson said to his secretary, "My message today was a message of death for our young men. How strange it seems [for them] to applaud that."

The present German submarine warfare against commerce is a warfare against mankind. It is a war against all nations. American ships have been sunk, American lives taken, in ways which it has stirred us very deeply to learn of, but the ships and people of other neutral and friendly nations have been sunk and overwhelmed in the waters in the same way. There has been no discrimination. The challenge is to all mankind. The choice we make for ourselves must be made with a moderation of counsel and a temperateness of judgment befitting our character and motives as a nation. We must put excited feeling away. Our motive will not be revenge or the victorious assertion of the physical might of the nation, but only the vindication of right, of human right, of which we are only a single champion. . . .

There is one choice we cannot make, we are incapable of making: we will not choose the path of submission and suffer the most sacred rights of our Nation and our people to be ignored or violated. The wrongs against which we now array ourselves are no common wrongs; they cut to the very roots of human life. . . .

We are glad, now that we see the facts with no veil of false pretense about them, to fight thus for the ultimate peace of the world and for the liberation of its peoples, the German peoples included: for the rights of nations great and small and the privilege of men everywhere to choose their way of life and of obedience.

The world must be made safe for democracy. Its peace must be planted upon the tested foundations of political liberty. We have no selfish ends to serve. We desire no conquest, no dominion. We seek no indemnities for ourselves, no material consumption for the sacrifices we shall freely make. We are but one of the champions of the rights of mankind. We shall be satisfied when those rights have been made as secure as the faith and the freedom of nations can make them.

Supporters Had This to Say

■ Mr. President, you have expressed in the loftiest manner the sentiments of the American people.   *Senator Henry Cabot Lodge, of Massachusetts, speaking to Wilson immediately after the war message.*

■ If that message was right, everything he has done for two years and a half is fundamentally wrong.   *Lodge, letter to a friend, April 23, 1917.*

■ I cannot vote against a resolution which commits this Government to no other proposition than warring against those who war against us. . . . I join no crusade; I seek or accept no alliances; I obligate this Government to no other power. I make war for my countrymen and their rights, for my country and its honor.   *Senator William Borah of Idaho, during debate on the declaration of war, April 4, 1917.*

■ We should stand for whatever good things [Wilson] does. I stand by him in these matters and stand most actively by him against the La Follette-German-socialism-pacificsm combination. . . . But what is perfectly impossible, what represents really nauseous hypocrisy, is to say that we have gone to war to make the world safe for democracy. *Theodore Roosevelt, letter to a friend, August 3, 1917.*

Opponents Had This to Say

■ There are many honest, patriotic citizens who think we ought to enter this war and who are behind the President. I think such people err in judgment and to a great extent have been misled . . . by the almost unanimous demand of the great combination of wealth that has a direct financial interest in our participation in the war. . . . [Voting to go to war] will make millions of our countrymen suffer, and the consequences of it may well be that millions of our brethern must shed their lifeblood, millions of broken-hearted women must weep, millions of children must suffer with cold, and millions of babes must die from hunger, and all because we want to preserve the commercial right of American citizens to deliver munitions of war to belligerent nations.   *Senator George W. Norris of Nebraska, during debate on the declaration of war, April 4, 1917.*

■ The Socialist party . . . can have no concern in any ruling class war. . . . It is morally bound to stand squarely against every war [except] the war of the world's enslaved and exploited workers against the world's enslaving and exploiting masters.   *Eugene V. Debs, letter to a friend, April 11, 1917.*

♦ Once the nation went to war, all aspects of the economy were mobilized, including food. Farmers were encouraged to raise more, with the slogan "Wheat Will Win the War." Housewives were urged to conserve food, as in this poster that directly connected American food conservation to the suffering of the Allies. *Museum of the City of New York. Gift of John W. Campbell.*

telephone system under a similar arrangement and also set in motion a huge shipbuilding program to expand the merchant marine.

The National War Labor Board, created to mediate labor disputes, endorsed **collective bargaining** and gave some support for an eight-hour workday in return for a no-strike pledge from labor. Many unions secured contracts that brought significant wage increases, and union membership boomed from 2.7 million in 1916 to more than 4 million by 1919. Most established labor leaders fully supported the war. Samuel Gompers, president of the AFL, called it "the most wonderful crusade ever entered upon in the whole history of the world."

One crucial American contribution to the Allied victory was food, for the war had severely disrupted much of European agriculture. Food Administrator **Herbert Hoover,** a prominent mining engineer who had skillfully directed the relief program in Belgium, promoted increased production and conservation of food, urging families to conserve food through Meatless Mondays and Wheatless Wednesdays and to plant "war gardens" to raise some of their own food. Farmers also brought large areas under cultivation for the first time. (The chapter opening map indicates the expansion of wheat growing.) As a result, food shipments to the Allies tripled.

Some progressives urged that the Wilson administration pay for the war by taxing wartime profits and earnings of corporations. That did not happen, but taxes—especially the relatively new income

♦ This poster encouraged Americans to buy Liberty bonds (that is, loan money to the government) by emphasizing the image of the vicious and brutal Hun. This was part of a larger process of demonizing the people of the Central Powers that extended to condemning the music of Beethoven and the writings of Goethe. *Collection of Robert Cherny.*

tax—did account for almost half of the $33 billion that the United States spent on the war between April 1917 and June 1920. The government borrowed the rest, most of it through four **Liberty Loan** drives in 1917 and 1918, when rallies, parades, and posters carried the message to all patriotic Americans that they should buy "Liberty bonds." Groups like the Red Cross and the YMCA also offered the public opportunities to donate time and energy in support of American soldiers. Wilson himself raised

> **collective bargaining** Negotiation between the representatives of organized workers and their employer to determine wages, hours, and working conditions.
>
> **Herbert Hoover** U.S. food administrator during World War I known for his proficient handling of relief efforts; he was elected president in 1928, only to see the country enter a major depression.
>
> **Liberty Loan** One of a series of four bond issues floated by the U.S. Treasury Department from 1917 to 1919 to help finance World War I.

funds for the Red Cross by selling wool from sheep that grazed on the White House lawn—not only as replacements for gardeners drafted into the military, but also as a lesson in using every possible resource to expand production.

Mobilizing Public Opinion

Not all Americans fully supported the war. Some German-Americans were reluctant to see their sons sent to war against their cousins. Some Irish-Americans took little interest in saving Britain, especially after the English brutally suppressed an attempt at Irish independence in 1916. In a special national convention, the Socialist party voted its opposition to American participation in the war. Socialist candidates greatly increased their share of the vote in several cities in 1917—to 22 percent in New York City and 34 percent in Chicago—suggesting that their antiwar stance attracted significant numbers of voters.

To mobilize public opinion in support of the war, Wilson created the Committee on Public Information (CPI), headed by George Creel. Once a muckraking journalist, Creel set out to sell the war to the American people. He succeeded in reaching (if not convincing) almost every American. The **Creel Committee** eventually counted 150,000 lecturers, writers, artists, actors, and scholars championing the cause and whipping up hatred of the "Huns." Social clubs, movie theaters, and churches all joined what Creel called "the world's greatest adventure in advertising." Most of those serving with the Creel Committee did so as "Four-Minute Men"—that is, they were ready to make a four-minute speech anytime and anywhere a crowd gathered. The legions delivered 755,190 speeches to roughly 300 million people in 5,000 towns.

The fierce patriotism kindled by military exploits overseas and fanned by the Creel Committee sometimes sparked extreme measures against those considered "slackers" and "Kaiserites." "Woe to the man or group of men that seeks to stand in our way in this day of high resolution," warned Wilson. "He who is not with us, absolutely and without reserve of any kind," proclaimed former president Theodore Roosevelt, "is against us, and should be treated as an alien enemy." Zealots across the country took up the cry. Some states prohibited the use of foreign languages in public as "Americanization" drives sought to persuade immigrants to give up their native cultures. German books were removed from libraries and sometimes publicly burned. Some communities banned the music of Bach and Beethoven and dropped German classes from their schools. Even words with German connections became objectionable: sauerkraut became "liberty cabbage," German measles were renamed "liberty measles," and dachshunds trotted as "liberty pups." Sometimes mobs hounded people with German names and occasionally attacked or even lynched people suspected of antiwar sentiments.

Civil Liberties in Time of War

German-Americans suffered the most from the wartime hysteria, but pacifists, socialists, and other radicals also became targets for government and vigilante repression. Congress passed the **Espionage Act** in 1917 and the **Sedition Act** in 1918, prohibiting interference with the draft and outlawing criticism of the government, the armed forces, or the war effort and specifying large fines and long prison terms for violators. Officials arrested some 1,500 people for violating the Espionage and Sedition acts, including Eugene V. Debs, leader of the Socialist party.

The government often applied these laws broadly. One passage in the Espionage Act gave the postmaster general the power to decide what could pass through the nation's mails. By the war's end, the Post Office Department had denied mailing privileges to some four hundred periodicals, including, at least temporarily, such mainstream publications as the *Saturday Evening Post* and *The New York Times*.

Those who voiced dissenting opinions found they could not rely on the courts for protection. When opponents of the war challenged the Espionage Act as unconstitutional, the Supreme Court ruled that freedom of speech was never absolute.

Creel Committee The U.S. Committee on Public Information (1917–1919), headed by journalist and editor George Creel, that used films, posters, pamphlets, and news releases to mobilize American public opinion in favor of World War I.

Espionage Act 1917 law that mandated severe penalties for anyone found guilty of interfering with the draft or encouraging disloyalty to the United States.

Sedition Act 1918 law that supplemented the Espionage Act by extending the penalty to anyone deemed to have abused the government in writing.

Just as no one has the right to shout "Fire" in a crowded theater, said Justice Oliver Wendell Holmes, Jr., so in time of war no one has a constitutional right to say anything that might endanger the security of the nation. The Court also upheld the Sedition Act in 1919, by a vote of 7 to 2.

Although the Industrial Workers of the World (IWW) avoided making a public pronouncement against the war, most Wobblies probably opposed it, providing an excuse to employers and other opponents. IWW members and leaders came under relentless attack by both government officials and vigilantes. In July 1917, in Bisbee, Arizona, for example, managers of local copper mines, law enforcement officials, and deputized citizens staged an early morning roundup of more than 1,100 IWW members and suspected members, marched them at gunpoint into railroad boxcars, transported them over 100 miles into the desert, and abandoned them. In September 1917, Justice Department agents raided IWW offices throughout the West and arrested the union's leaders, who were sentenced to jail terms of up to twenty-five years and to fines totaling millions of dollars. Deprived of its leaders and virtually bankrupted, the IWW never recovered.

A few Americans protested the abridgment of civil liberties. One group formed the Civil Liberties Bureau—forerunner of the American Civil Liberties Union, or ACLU—under the leadership of Roger Baldwin. Most Americans, however, did not object to the repression. Many others who were sympathetic to the victims kept silent. Jane Addams, who had been viciously maligned herself for expressing her pacifist views before the war, would not sign the Civil Liberties Bureau's appeal for funds, explaining that "I am obliged to walk very softly in all things suspect."

The grounds for suppressing civil liberties were not limited to espionage and sedition. To discourage prostitution, General Pershing instructed his troops that "sexual intercourse is not necessary for good health, and complete continence is wholly possible." Federal officials soon concluded that such testimonials were not enough. They launched the American Plan, under which the military arrested any woman found within the "pure zone," that is, anywhere within 5 miles of a military establishment. The civil rights of arrested women could be suspended, and those with venereal disease could be sentenced to a detention facility or hospital until cured. By the war's end, 15,520 women had served sentences. Still, when it came to keeping soldiers healthy, the American Plan proved as unsuccessful

♦ Jane Addams, on the right, worked actively to keep the United States from going to war and drew harsh criticism for her efforts. Once war was declared, she kept her opinions to herself. *Jane Addams Memorial Collection, Special Collections, The University Library, The University of Illinois at Chicago.*

as Pershing's moral instruction. So, by the end of the war, the army was giving out millions of condoms as more reliable protection—and coincidentally providing the most widespread governmental sex education program up to that time.

Changes in the Workplace

American labor's wartime experience was characterized by intense activism and remarkable productivity. Union membership almost doubled, and a significant number of women were among the surge of new cardholders. In addition, unions benefited from the encouragement that the **National War Labor Board** gave to collective bargaining between unions and companies as the most effective way to keep labor peace. The board also stepped in and

---

National War Labor Board   Board appointed by President Wilson in 1918 to act as court of last resort for labor disputes.

helped to settle labor disputes through mediation. Never before had a federal agency interceded this way. Nonetheless, many workers felt that their purchasing power failed to keep pace with increases in prices.

Demands for increased production at a time when millions of men were marching off to war opened opportunities for women in many fields. Employment of women in factory, office, and retail jobs had increased before the war, but the war certainly accelerated those trends. Many women's wartime jobs returned to male hands at the war's end, but in office work and some retail positions, especially, women continued to predominate after the war.

Most women who worked outside the home were young and single, making the sex-segregated world of the nineteenth century even less the norm than before. Some middle-class women who now entered the paid labor force not only gave up their home-bound roles but also rejected their parents' standards of morality and behavior. They adopted instead the less restricted lifestyles that had long been experienced by many wage-earning, working-class women. One commentator observed, "For the first time in the memory of man, girls from well-bred, respectable middle-class families broke through these invisible chains of custom and asserted their right to a nonchalant, self-sustaining life of their own."

The Great Migration and White Reactions

The war also had a great impact on African-American communities. Until the war, about 90 percent of all African-Americans lived in the South, 75 percent in rural areas. By 1920, perhaps as many as 500,000 had moved north in what has been called the **Great Migration.** The largest proportional increases in the African-American population came in the industrial cities of the Midwest. Gary, Indiana, showed one of the greatest gains—1,284 percent between 1910 and 1920. New York City, Philadelphia, and Los Angeles also attracted many blacks. (See the chapter opening map for further information.) Several factors combined to stimulate and feed this migration. T. Arnold Hill of Chicago's Urban League attributed the exodus to the brutality of southern life. "Every time a lynching takes place in a community down South," he pointed out, "colored people will arrive in Chicago within two weeks." Economic disaster in the South was another impetus. In 1915 and 1916,

◆ Labor shortages attracted new people into the labor market and opened up some jobs to women and members of racial minorities. In May 1918, these women worked in the Union Pacific Railroad freight yard in Cheyenne, Wyoming. Most of them seem delighted to have their picture taken in their work clothes. *Wyoming State Museum.*

southern farmers alternately battled drought and severe rains and fought the **boll weevil** throughout.

Still another significant factor in the Great Migration was the sharp decline in European immigration caused by the war, at a time when American industry desperately needed more workers. The wartime labor needs of northern cities attracted hundreds of thousands of African-Americans seeking better jobs and higher pay. A laundress or cook in the North could earn $1.50 to $2 a day plus carfare and meals, almost as much as for a week's work in the South. Many industrial jobs paid $3 a day, compared to 50 cents for picking cotton. The impact on some southern cities was striking. Jackson, Mississippi, for example, was estimated to have lost half of all working-class African-Americans, and a quarter to a third of black business owners and professionals. Two of the largest black churches in Jackson lost 40

Great Migration   Mass movement of black people from the rural South to the urban North during World War I; about a half-million people relocated.

boll weevil   Small beetle of the southern United States that infests cotton plants and whose larvae hatch in and damage cotton bolls.

♦ Labor shortages and high wages drew African-Americans from the rural South to the industrial North. This suitcase is part of an exhibit on the Great Migration at the Smithsonian Institution. The Bible recalls the central role of churches in southern black communities and the new, northern black churches created by migrants. *Poster: Library of Congress; articles: Smithsonian Institution.*

percent of their congregations, and two-thirds of the remaining families said good-bye to some members.

The war heightened racial tensions in the South because some whites resented the new options available to blacks. For example, black women who received money from their men in uniform or in wartime jobs sometimes found that they no longer needed farm work. In Pine Bluff, Arkansas, city officials tried to extend the nation's "work or fight" rule, under which anyone not aiding the war effort by either working or fighting could be arrested, to black women who refused to work in the cotton fields. African-American women leaving other jobs were also harassed. A woman in Jackson, Mississippi, quit her job as cook for a white family when her carpenter husband began making enough money to support them both. The same day, two policemen informed her that they would arrest her for vagrancy if she did not return to her job. In Vicksburg, Mississippi, a mob tarred and feathered two black women who quit their jobs. Lynchings continued: lynch mobs killed at least thirty-eight African-Americans in 1917 and fifty-eight in 1918, most of them in the South.

Severe wartime racial conflicts erupted in several cities on the northern end of the Great Migration trail. The worst race riot in American history swept through the industrial city of East St. Louis, Illinois, on July 2, 1917. Thousands of African-American laborers, most from the South, had settled in the city during the previous two years. A least thirty-nine of them perished in the riot, and six thousand found themselves homeless. Incensed that such brutality could occur so soon after the nation's moralistic entrance into the war, W. E. B. Du Bois charged, "No land that loves to lynch 'niggers' can lead the hosts of Almighty God." He and the NAACP soon led a parade of ten thousand people through **Harlem** in a silent protest.

Americans "Over There"

● Why did Wilson choose to keep the AEF as separate as possible from the troops of the other Allies?

With the declaration of war, the United States needed to mobilize quickly for combat in a distant part of the world. The navy was already large and powerful after nearly three decades of shipbuilding, and the preparedness measures of mid-1916 had further strengthened U.S. sea power. The army, however, was tiny compared to those contesting in Europe. Millions of men and thousands of women had to be enlisted or drafted, trained, supplied, and transported to Europe.

Harlem A section of New York City in the northern part of Manhattan, which became one of the largest black communities in the United States.

Mobilizing for Battle

Almost immediately the navy was able to strike back successfully at the German fleet. The navy's convoy technique, in which several ships traveled together under the protection of destroyers, helped to cut shipping losses in half by late 1917. By the following spring, the U-boat ceased to pose a significant danger.

The army, however, was not ready for action in April 1917—the combined strength of the U.S. Army and the National Guard stood at only 372,000 men. Many men volunteered but not enough. Congress therefore rushed into law the **Selective Service Act** in May, requiring men aged 21 to 30 (later extended to 18 to 45) to register with local boards to determine who was to be called to duty. Not everyone agreed that this conscription, usually called "the draft," was the best way to raise troops. Some, including members of Congress, objected to the draft as undemocratic. One opponent claimed, "There is precious little difference between a conscript and a convict." The law exempted those who opposed war on religious grounds, but such **conscientious objectors** were sometimes badly treated. Nonetheless, no draft riots like those of the Civil War years broke out. In fact, World War I witnessed few public demonstrations of opposition to the draft. For the most part, Americans accepted the draft as both efficient and fair. Eventually, 24 million men registered and 2.8 million were drafted—about 72 percent of the entire army. By the end of the war, the combined army, navy, and marine corps counted 4.8 million members.

No women were drafted, but some women chose to serve in the military. Almost 13,000 women joined, mostly in clerical capacities, in the navy and marines, making the first time women were permitted to hold full military rank and status. The army, however, considered enlisting women a "most radical departure" and refused to do it. Women could serve in the Army Corps of Nurses, which enrolled nearly 18,000 women but denied them army rank, pay, or benefits. When army headquarters in France requested uniformed women for clerical and telephone duties, the War Department instead sent women civilians or uniformed men. Even so, personnel shortages seemed about to force the "radical departure" just as the war ended. At least 5,000 civilian women served in various capacities in France, sometimes near the front lines, the largest number through the Red Cross, which helped to staff hospitals and rest facilities.

◆ The army and navy segregated African-Americans into separate units, and the navy limited black units to service functions. In the army, however, some black units were trained for combat, including this machine gun company equipped with Lewis machine guns in the 8th Illinois Infantry. *Collection of William Gladstone.*

Nearly 400,000 African-Americans served during World War I. Almost 200,000 served overseas, nearly 30,000 on the front lines. Emmett J. Scott, an African-American and former secretary to Booker T. Washington, became special assistant to the secretary of war with responsibilities for insuring the uniform application of the draft and for the morale of African-Americans, military and civilian alike. His appointment brought praise from both whites and blacks. Black soldiers were nonetheless treated as second-class citizens. They marched in segregated **Jim Crow** units in the army, were limited to food service in the navy, and were excluded from the marines altogether. More than 600 African-Americans earned commissions as officers, but they were trained in separate camps and the army was reluctant to commission too many. White officers commanded most black troops.

> **Selective Service Act**   1917 law establishing compulsory military service for men aged 21 to 30.
>
> **conscientious objector**   Person who on the basis of religious or moral principles refuses to bear arms or participate in military service.
>
> **Jim Crow**   Name for any laws or forms of organization that discriminate against blacks; probably derived from a minstrel-show stock character named Jim Crow.

"Over There"

By mid-1918, it seemed that Allied troops all along the western front had taken up a tune by the popular American composer George M. Cohan.

> *Over there, over there,*
> *Send the word, send the word over there,*
> *The Yanks are coming, the Yanks are coming,*
> *And we won't come back 'til it's over over there.*

A few Yanks—troops of the **American Expeditionary Force (AEF)**—arrived in France in June 1917, commanded by General John J. Pershing, recently returned from Mexico. Most American troops, however, were still to be drafted, supplied, trained, and transported across the Atlantic.

As the first American troops began to trickle into France, the Central Powers seemed close to victory. French offensives in April 1917 had failed, and a British summer effort in Flanders resulted in enormous casualties but little gain. The Italians suffered a major defeat late in the year. A Russian drive in midsummer proved disastrous, and, in November, Russia withdrew from the war. As German-Russian peace talks began, German troops moved from east to west. Hoping to win the war before many American troops arrived, the Germans planned a massive spring offensive for 1918.

The German offensive came in Picardy with sixty-four divisions smashing into the point where the French and British lines, under separate commands, joined. The Germans pushed forward, even as the desperate Allies created a Supreme Command to overcome problems of coordination. AEF units were hurried to the front to block the German advance. In mid-May, an AEF officer described trench life in this letter to his sister:

> We have to lay low all day to escape observation. . . . At nine P.M. we emerge and do various work all night: digging trenches, wiring, carrying ammunition, burying the dead. . . . It is scary . . . when the shelling begins, the rockets and flares all along the near horizon lighting up the weird scene, the Boche flashlights [German searchlights] simulating the aurora, the everlasting crack and roar of our own artillery . . . and the whine of the innumerable shells passing overhead, the sputtering of the machine guns, and in the midst of it all the persistent singing of a nightingale down in the ravine.

By late May, the Germans had moved down the **Marne River** to within 50 miles of Paris. French offi-cials considered evacuating the capital, and all available troops were rushed to that area. AEF units fought bravely and effectively. At Chateau-Thierry and at Belleau Woods, they took 8,000 casualties during a month-long battle over a single square mile of wheat field and woods. Of 310,000 AEF troops who fought in the Marne region, 67,000 were killed or wounded.

Throughout the war, Wilson held the United States apart from the Allies, referring to this country as an Associated Power, rather than one of the Allies, and trying as much as possible to keep American troops separate. This distinction stemmed partly from his distrust of Allied war aims, but more from his wish to make the American contribution to victory as prominent as possible in order to maximize the American influence in peacemaking.

The Allies launched a counteroffensive in July, as fresh American troops continued to pour into France, topping the million mark that month. The American command insisted on being assigned its own sector of the front, and in September Pershing successfully launched a stunning one-day offensive against the St. Mihiel **salient** (see Map 22.1). One AEF private concisely summarized his day at St. Mihiel: "We shot Germans, captured Germans and a lot of freight cars loaded with supplies and beer, so I have drank Dutch beer . . . I lost some mighty good pals." AEF forces then joined a larger Allied offensive in the Meuse-Argonne region, the last major assault of the war and one of the fiercest battles in American military history. In the Argonne forest on October 8, Corporal Alvin York, virtually alone and armed with only a rifle and pistol, managed to kill twenty-five German soldiers, eliminate thirty-five enemy machine guns, and take 132 prisoners—and to become the most heroic figure of the war (see Individual Choices: Alvin York). By then, the German general staff was pleading with their government to seek an armistice. Fighting ended on the eleventh hour of the eleventh day of the eleventh month of

---

American Expeditionary Force   American army commanded by General John J. Pershing that served in Europe during World War I.

Marne River   River in northeast France that was the site of pivotal fighting in World War I, including a successful French and American counterattack on German forces in July 1918.

salient   Battle line that projects closest to the enemy.

1918. By then, more than two million American soldiers were in France, giving the Allies an advantage of about 600,000 men.

When the clamor of celebration replaced the din of battle across the battered French countryside, thirty-two nations, including the United States, had entered the war against Germany or the other Central Powers. Nearly 9 million men in uniform died: Germany lost 1.8 million, Russia 1.7 million, Austria-Hungary 1.2 million, the British Empire 908,400. France lost 1.4 million, including *half* its men between the ages of 20 and 32. More than 20 million combatants suffered wounds, producing many permanent disabilities. American losses were small in comparison— 115,000 men, including 48,000 killed in action. Millions of people worldwide, including civilians, died from starvation and disease, especially during a global **influenza** epidemic in 1918 and 1919 that killed 500,000 Americans.

Among the American casualties were African-Americans. Some Americans, though, tried to hide the presence in Europe of African-American soldiers. Many black units were assigned to menial tasks behind the lines, although some saw action. Even so, some white Americans, including some military officers, worried that experiences in France might cause African-American soldiers to resist segregation at home. In August 1918, AEF headquarters confidentially requested that the French maintain separation between the races and that they not prominently commend black units. The French ignored the request, awarding the **Croix de Guerre** to several all-black units that had distinguished themselves in combat and presenting awards to individual soldiers for acts of bravery and heroism. When the Allies staged a grand victory parade down Paris's Champs Elysées, the British and French contingents included all races and ethnicities, but American commanders permitted no African-American troops to march.

Wilson and the Peace Conference

- What were Wilson's expectations regarding peace?
- What constraints did he face in realizing those objectives?
- What choices did he make, and what was the outcome?

When the war ended, Wilson hoped that the peace treaty would not contain the seeds of future wars. He hoped, too, to create an international organization to keep the peace. Most of the Allies, however, had more interest in grabbing territory and punishing Germany.

Bolshevism, the Secret Treaties, and the Fourteen Points

In March 1917, war-weary, hungry Russians overthrew their Czar. In November, the **Bolsheviks** seized power from the more moderate prime minister, Alexander Kerensky. Soon renamed Communists, the Bolsheviks condemned capitalism and imperialism and sought to destroy them. The Bolshevik leader, **Vladimir Lenin,** immediately began peace negotiations with the Central Powers. Despite Germany's harsh and humiliating terms, Lenin saw no choice but to accept. By the **Treaty of Brest-Litovsk,** in March 1918, Russia surrendered vast holdings—Finland, the Baltic provinces, parts of Poland and the Ukraine—making up a third of Russia's population, half its industries, fertile agricultural land, and a quarter of its territory in Europe.

In December 1917, the Bolsheviks tried to demonstrate that the war was nothing more than a scramble for imperial spoils. They published secret treaties, made before and during the war, by which the Allies agreed to take colonies and territories from the Central Powers and to divide those spoils among themselves. These exposés strengthened Wilson in his intent to separate American war aims from those of the Allies and in his efforts to impose his war objectives on them.

On January 8, 1918, Wilson spoke to Congress about those war objectives. Elaborating on the goals he had first presented nearly a year before, he di-

---

influenza   Contagious viral infection characterized by fever, chills, and muscular pain, which swept across the world in an unusually deadly strain in 1918 and 1919.

Croix de Guerre   French military decoration for bravery in combat; in English, "the Cross of War."

Bolsheviks   Communists who seized power in Russia in November 1917.

Vladimir Lenin   Leader of the Bolsheviks, and of the Russian Revolution in 1917, and head of the USSR until 1924.

Treaty of Brest-Litovsk   Humiliating 1918 treaty by which Germany permitted Russia to withdraw from the war in return for surrendering vast territories in central Europe.

The Choice to Fight

Alvin York

Alvin York, a devout Christian, had to choose between his moral compunctions about killing and his sense of obligation to his country. This photograph was taken in 1919, the year York was promoted to sergeant and received the Congressional Medal of Honor, as well as similar awards from many of the Allies for his exploits in battle. Brown Brothers.

Long before Alvin York won the nation's admiration for his amazing demonstration of bravery and coolness under fire on October 8, 1918, he underwent a personal crisis of conscience over his choice to fight. Born in the Cumberland Mountains of Tennessee in 1887, York was raised in a backwoods community where people expected to secure food for their tables through skill with their hunting rifles. York grew up with guns, remembering that his father "threatened to muss me up right smart if I failed to bring a squirrel down with the first shot or hit a [wild] turkey in the body instead of [shooting] its head off." From his youth, red-haired Alvin York was highly proficient with both rifle and pistol.

As a young man, York was known for his drinking, carousing, recklessness, and sometimes violent behavior. He put all that behind him when he became a born-again Christian in 1915 and joined a small fundamentalist church. He took his new faith seriously, and his commitment posed difficult choices for him when the war came.

I loved and trusted old Uncle Sam and I have always believed he did the right thing. But I was

rectly challenged the secret treaties and tried to seize the initiative in defining a basis for peace. He stressed that American war objectives derived from "the principle of justice to all peoples and nationalities, and their right to live on equal terms of liberty and safety with one another, whether they be strong or weak." Wilson presented fourteen specific objectives, soon called the **Fourteen Points.** Points one through five provided a general context for lasting peace: no secret treaties, freedom of the seas, reduction of barriers to trade, reduction of armaments,

and adjustment of colonial claims based partly on the interests of colonial peoples. Points six through thirteen addressed particular situations: return of territories France had lost to Germany in 1871 and

Fourteen Points President Wilson's program for maintaining peace after World War I, which called for arms reduction, national self-determination, and a league of nations.

worried clean through. I didn't want to go and kill. I believed in my bible. And it distinctly said "THOU SHALT NOT KILL." And yet old Uncle Sam wanted me. And he said he wanted me most awful bad. And I jest didn't know what to do. I worried and worried. I couldn't think of anything else. My thoughts just wouldn't stay a hitched.

York chose to seek exemption from the draft as a conscientious objector but was refused. Called to active duty, he made "good friends" with his new rifle and excelled at target practice. Deeply troubled about the morality of war, however, he shared his concern with his battalion commander, Major Edward Buxton, who spent long hours discussing the Bible with York and trying to convince him that a good Christian might morally choose to go to war. Buxton recognized York's sincerity, however, and offered him the choice of noncombatant duty if he decided he could not kill on the battlefield. After struggling with his religious beliefs, York finally decided not only that he could fight in good conscience but that he was doing the Lord's work in helping bring peace.

His choice made, he arrived with his unit on the front lines in France in late June 1918, took part in the attack on the St. Mihiel salient in September, and was then dispatched to the Meuse-Argonne sector. Part of a sixteen-man unit sent to take out some enemy machine guns, York—now a corporal—helped to capture a small group of Germans. Then a sudden burst of machine-gun fire killed or wounded nine members of his unit, including his sergeant. York was closest to the enemy gun. While the six surviving Americans remained with the prisoners, York coolly practiced his mountaineer's marksmanship, killing fourteen or so Germans as they trained machine-gun fire in his direction and tried to determine his position. When six Germans charged him with fixed bayonets, he dropped them all with his pistol. He then captured the German lieutenant in command and had him call upon his men to surrender. York shot those who resisted. Prisoners in tow, York and other members of his unit moved from position to position, using the German lieutenant to order each to surrender. Credited with killing twenty-five enemy soldiers and silencing thirty-five machine guns, York and the six other Americans marched 132 prisoners back to their stunned commanding officer. The next day, York returned to the area searching for survivors. There he knelt and prayed for the souls of the dead, including those he had killed.

Promoted to sergeant and given national attention by an article in the *Saturday Evening Post*, York received the Congressional Medal of Honor, the Croix de Guerre, and similar awards from many of the other Allies. Still, the blessings of his contemporaries were not enough to settle the matter. Toward the end of his life, confined to bed, Alvin York pressed his son, a minister, for assurance that God would accept the choice he had made and the action he had taken in the Argonne forest.

Source: Adapted from David D. Lee, *Sergeant York: An American Hero* (Lexington: University Press of Kentucky, 1985), chs 1–3.

---

self-determination in central Europe and the Middle East. The fourteenth point called for "a general association of nations" that could afford "mutual guarantees of political independence and territorial integrity to great and small states alike."

The major Allies reluctantly accepted Wilson's Fourteen Points as a basis for discussion but expressed little enthusiasm for them. The Germans were more interested. When they asked for an end to the fighting, they specified that their request was based on the Fourteen Points.

The World in 1919

In December 1918, Wilson sailed for France—the first time that an American president in office had gone to Europe, and the first time that a president had personally taken part in negotiations with other world leaders. Wilson brought along some two hundred experts on European history, culture, ethnology, and geography. In France, Italy, and Britain, huge welcoming crowds paid homage to the great "peacemaker from America."

Delegates to the peace conference assembled amid far-reaching change. The Austro-Hungarian empire had crumbled, producing the new nations of Poland, Czechoslovakia, Yugoslavia, and the republics of Austria and Hungary. In Germany, **Kaiser Wilhelm** had **abdicated** and a republic was being formed. In January 1919, Berlin witnessed an unsuccessful communist uprising. Amidst the ruins of the Russian empire, Finland, Estonia, Latvia, Lithuania, and other regions were asserting their independence. The Turkish empire was collapsing, too, as Arabs revolted with aid from Britain and France. Throughout Europe and the Middle East, national self-determination and government by the consent of the governed—part of Wilson's design for the postwar world—seemed to be stumbling into reality. Nor were the British and French colonial empires immune, for both faced growing independence movements among their many possessions.

In Russia, in 1919, civil war raged between the Bolsheviks' Red Army and their "White" (anti-Communist) opponents. When the Bolsheviks left the war, the Allies had pushed Wilson to join them in intervening in Russia, ostensibly to protect war supplies from falling into German hands but actually to aid the foes of Bolshevism. In mid-1918, Wilson included American troops in Allied expeditions to northern Russia and eastern Siberia. In Siberia, his cooperation was primarily to head off a Japanese grab of territory. The American troops remained in northern Russia until May 1919, and in eastern Siberia until early 1920, fueling Bolshevik suspicions of American objectives.

Wilson at Versailles

The peace conference opened on January 18, 1919, just outside Paris, at the glittering **Palace of Versailles,** once home to French kings. Representatives attended from all the nations that had declared war against any of the Central Powers, but major decisions were made by the Big Four: Woodrow Wilson of the United States, David Lloyd George of Britain, Georges Clemenceau of France, and Vittorio Orlando of Italy. Germany was excluded. Terms of peace were to be imposed, not negotiated. Russia, too, was absent, on the grounds that it had withdrawn from the war earlier and made a separate peace with Germany. Russia may have been barred from Versailles, but the specter of Bolshevism was all too present at the proceedings, affecting decisions about eastern Europe especially. Even as the Big Four moved to conclude their deliberations, a

♦ Many of the crucial decisions at Versailles were made by the Big Four: seated from left to right, Vittorio Orlando of Italy, David Lloyd George of Great Britain, Georges Clemenceau of France, and Woodrow Wilson of the United States. This photo was taken in December 1919. *The Granger Collection (detail).*

communist government seized power in Hungary, to be overthrown by an invading Rumanian army that summer.

Wilson learned at the outset that the European leaders were far more interested in pursuing their own national interests than in implementing his Fourteen Points. Clemenceau, nicknamed "the Tiger," carried painful memories of Germany's humiliating defeat of France in 1871 and wanted to so disable Germany that it could never again invade his nation. Lloyd George agreed in principle with many of Wilson's proposals but came to Paris with his own agenda—a mandate from British voters for exacting heavy **reparations** from Germany. Orlando insisted on reaping all the territorial gains promised when Italy joined the Allies in 1915. Other war aims had been spelled out in the secret treaties. Japan, Britain, and France planned to divide Germany's colonies. Britain and France were to acquire much of

Kaiser Wilhelm II German emperor who had worked to create the great military machine and system of alliances that precipitated the outbreak of World War I.

abdicate To formally relinquish a high office.

Palace of Versailles Magnificent estate near Paris built by Louis XIV in the seventeenth century, where the treaty ending World War I was signed in 1919.

reparations Payments required from a defeated nation as compensation to the victors for damage or injury during a war.

Turkey's Middle East holdings. And Rumania and Serbia expected territory at the expense of Austria-Hungary. In addition, the European Allies all feared the spread of Bolshevism into western Europe.

Facing the insistent and acquisitive Allies, Wilson had no choice but to compromise. He did secure the creation of a **League of Nations.** Rather than a "peace without victory," however, the treaty instead imposed harsh victors' terms. A War Guilt clause forced Germany to accept the blame for starting the war. Other provisions required Germany to pay the Allies $5 billion in reparations and to surrender all its colonies, Alsace-Lorraine (which Germany had taken from France in 1871), and other European territories. (Map 22.2 indicates these changes.) To prevent further aggression, the treaty deprived Germany of its navy and merchant marine and limited its army to 100,000 men. German representatives signed on June 28, 1919.

Wilson reluctantly agreed to the massive reparations but insisted that colonies taken from Germany should not go to the Allies. Called **mandates,** they would instead be governed by one of the Allies on behalf of the League of Nations. Most mandates were intended to move toward self-government and independence. In nearly every case, however, the mandate went to the nation slated to receive the territory under the secret treaties. Britain and France, for example, received mandates for Turkey's former territories in the Middle East. Wilson blocked Italy's most extreme territorial demands but gave in on others. The peace conference recognized the new nations of central Europe, thereby creating a so-called "quarantine zone" between Russian Bolshevism and western Europe. But the treaty ignored other matters of self-determination. No one gave a hearing to people—from Ireland to Vietnam—seeking the right of self-determination in colonies held by one of the victorious Allies. Japan failed to secure a statement supporting racial equality.

In the end, Wilson compromised on nearly all of his Fourteen Points, but every compromise intensified his commitment to the League of Nations. The League, he still hoped, would resolve future controversies without war and would also solve the problems created by the compromises he had reluctantly accepted. Even so, the Allies finally agreed to include the **League Covenant** in the treaty only after Wilson threatened to make a separate peace with Germany. He was especially pleased with Article 10 of the League Covenant—he called it the League's "heart"—which specified that League members would protect each other's independence and terri-tory against external attacks and would take joint economic and military action against aggressors.

The Senate and the Treaty

While Wilson was in Paris, opposition to his plans was taking shape at home. The Senate, controlled by Republicans since the 1918 election, had to approve any treaty. In response to the concerns of some senators, Wilson had added several provisions to the League Covenant. Where McKinley had included three senators (two Republicans and one Democrat) in his delegation to negotiate the Treaty of Paris in 1898, however, Wilson's delegation to Versailles included no senators and no prominent Republicans.

Faced with the treaty, the Senate split into three groups. **Henry Cabot Lodge,** chairman of the Senate Foreign Relations Committee, led the largest faction, called *reservationists* after the reservations, or amendments, to the treaty that Lodge developed. Chief among Lodge's misgivings was his concern that Article 10 might be used to commit American troops to war without congressional approval. A smaller group, mostly Republicans, earned the name *irreconcilables* because they opposed any American involvement in European affairs. A third Senate group, mostly Democrats, supported the president and his treaty.

Wilson decided to appeal directly to the people. In September 1919, he undertook an arduous speaking tour—9,500 miles with speeches in twenty-nine cities. Huge crowds came to hear his usual eloquent arguments, but the effort proved too demanding for his fragile health. He collapsed in Pueblo, Colorado, on September 25, and returned to Washington. Soon after, he suffered a serious stroke.

Half-paralyzed and weakened, Wilson remained in seclusion and carried on few of his duties. Lodge

---

League of Nations   A world organization proposed by President Wilson and founded in 1920; it worked to promote peace and international cooperation.

mandate   A territory that the League of Nations authorized one of its member nations to govern, with the understanding that the region would move toward self-government.

League Covenant   The constitution of the League of Nations, which was incorporated in the Versailles Treaty in 1919.

Henry Cabot Lodge   Massachusetts senator who led Congressional opposition to the Versailles Treaty and the League of Nations.

Boundaries of German, Russian, and Austro-Hungarian empires in 1914

Areas lost by Austro-Hungarian Empire

Areas lost by Russian Empire

Areas lost by German Empire

Areas lost by Bulgaria

Areas lost by Ottoman Empire

Demilitarized Zones

Boundaries of 1926

Areas controlled under mandates from the League of Nations, 1920

NORWAY

Oslo

SWEDEN

Stockholm

FINLAND

Helsinki

Leningrad (St. Petersburg)

Tallinn

ESTONIA

North Sea

GREAT BRITAIN

DENMARK

Copenhagen

Baltic Sea

Riga LATVIA

Memel

LITHUANIA

Vilnius

Volga

RUSSIAN EMPIRE
(Became Union of Soviet Socialist Republics, 1922)

NETHERLANDS
Amsterdam

GERMANY

Danzig
POLISH CORRIDOR

EAST PRUSSIA

Brussels

BELGIUM

RUHR
Cologne

Berlin

Elbe

Oder

POLAND

Warsaw

Ural

Paris

LUX.

Weimar

Frankfurt

Rhine

Prague

Vistula

Kiev

Don

Seine

FRANCE

LORRAINE

Strasbourg

CZECHOSLOVAKIA

GALICIA

Dnieper

ALSACE

Loire

Geneva

Bern
SWITZ.

Vienna

S. TYROL

AUSTRIA

Budapest

BESSARABIA

Caspian Sea

Locarno

Milan

Po

Venice

Trieste

HUNGARY

Genoa

Rapallo

Zagreb

CROATIA

ROMANIA

Bucharest

Rhône

Corsica

ITALY

YUGOSLAVIA

Belgrade

Danube

Black Sea

Batum

Baku

Rome

SERBIA

Kars

Sardinia

Naples

MONTENEGRO
(To Yugoslavia 1921)

BULGARIA
Sofia

Istanbul
(Constantinople)

Tabriz

ALBANIA

GREECE

Ankara

TURKEY

PERSIA
(IRAN)

Sicily

Izmir
(Smyrna)

Athens

Annexed
by Turkey
1939

Aleppo

TUNISIA
(French)

Crete

Cyprus
(Gr.Br.)

SYRIA
(French Mandate)

Euphrates

Tigris

Baghdad

Mediterranean Sea

Beirut

Damascus

IRAQ
(MESOPOTAMIA)
(British Mandate)

Kut el Amara

LIBYA
(Italian)

PALESTINE
(British Mandate)
Jerusalem

Amman

TRANSJORDAN
(British Mandate)

Basra

KUWAIT
(Gr. Br.)

Cairo

Suez Canal

NEUTRAL
ZONES

EGYPT
(Independent 1922)

NEJD
(SAUDI ARABIA)

Nile

Red Sea

Riyadh

0   200   400 Km.

0   200   400 Mi.

Medina

MAP 22.2 Postwar Boundary Changes in Central Europe and the Middle East This map shows the boundary changes in Europe and the Middle East that resulted from the defeat of the four large, multiethnic empires—Austria-Hungary, Russia, Germany, and the Ottoman Empire.

proposed that the Senate accept the treaty with fourteen reservations, his retort to the Fourteen Points. Some of them were minor, but other amendments took aim squarely at Article 10 by permitting Congress to block action to fulfill League commitments, especially those involving military force. Wilson, however, refused to compromise. His refusal produced a deadlock, in which the president's supporters opposed the treaty with the Lodge reservations, and Lodge's supporters opposed it without the reservations. The irreconcilables opposed it either way. On November 19, 1919, the Senate defeated the treaty with the Lodge reservations by votes of 39 to 55 and 41 to 50. It then defeated the original version of the treaty by 38 to 53. The treaty with reservations came to a vote again in March 1920. By then, some treaty supporters had concluded that the League could be never approved without Lodge's reservations, so they joined the reservationists to produce a vote of 49 to 35. Approval, however, required a two-thirds majority of those voting. Enough Wilson loyalists—following their stubborn leader's order not to compromise—joined the irreconcilables to defeat the treaty once again. The United States would not join the League of Nations.

Legacies of the Great War

Roosevelt, Wilson, and most other prewar leaders had projected the progressive mood of optimism and confidence. Wilson invoked this tradition in claiming that the United States was going to war to make the world "safe for democracy." One of his most optimistic supporters even described it as the "war to end war," a holy struggle to eliminate war for all time. Just as progressives defined their domestic policies in terms of progress, democracy, and social justice, so Wilson had tried to invest his foreign policy with similar enlightened values and expectations. In doing so, however, he had fostered unrealistic expectations that world politics might be transformed overnight.

Americans who believed that rational, civilized people had outgrown war found the conflict a disillusioning experience. For some, wartime suppression of civil liberties called into question their belief in the inevitability of progress. Many Americans became disenchanted, especially, by the contrast between Wilson's lofty idealism and the Allies' cynical opportunism at Versailles. The war to make the world safe for democracy turned out to be a chance for Italy to grab Austrian territory and for Japan to seize German concessions in China. Ironically, the

"war to end war" spun off several wars in its wake. Rumania invaded Hungary in 1919, Poland invaded Russia in 1920, the Russian civil war continued until 1921, and Greece and Turkey battled until 1923.

In the end, the war and its peace conference left unresolved many problems. Wilson's elevation of self-government and **self-determination** encouraged aspirations for independence throughout the colonial empires retained by the Allies. Some of the new nations of central Europe, supposedly based on ethnic self-determination, actually included different and sometimes antagonistic ethnic groups. Above all, the war and the treaty helped to produce economic and political instability in much of Europe, making it a breeding ground for totalitarian and nationalistic movements that were eventually to bring on another world war.

Trauma in the Wake of War

● How did Americans' expectations change as a result of the outcome of the war and the events of 1919?

● How did these new expectations affect their choice in the 1920 presidential election?

The United States began to demobilize almost as soon as French church bells pealed for the **Armistice.** The military immediately discharged more than 600,000 men, and by November 1919 nearly the entire force of four million men and women was out of uniform. Industrial demobilization occurred even more quickly, as officials canceled war contracts with no more than month's notice. The year 1919 saw not only the return of the troops from Europe, but also raging inflation, massive strikes, bloody race riots, widespread fear of radical **subversion,** violations of civil liberties, and passage of an unenforceable law to prohibit alcohol.

"HCL" and Strikes

Inflation—described in newspapers as "HCL" for "High Cost of Living"—was the most pressing single problem Americans faced after the war. Between

> **self-determination**   The freedom of a given people to determine their own political status.
> **Armistice**   An agreement to stop fighting.
> **subversion**   Efforts to undermine or overthrow an established government.

1913 and 1919, the average American family saw its cost of living double. Such inflation contributed to labor unrest. When the Armistice ended the no-strike pledge taken by unions, they made wage demands to maintain wartime gains and to keep up with the soaring cost of living. In 1919, however, management was ready for a fight.

After the war, some companies determined to return labor relations to prewar patterns. They blamed wage increases won by organized labor for the rise in prices, and connected strikes and unions to "dangerous foreign ideas" from Bolshevik Russia. In February 1919, Seattle's Central Labor Council called out all the city's unions in a five-day general strike to support striking shipyard workers. The walkout revived fears of the IWW, and Seattle's mayor inflamed such alarms by claiming the strike was a Bolshevik plot. Boston's police struck in September 1919 after the city's police commissioner fired nineteen policemen for joining an AFL union. Governor **Calvin Coolidge** refused to negotiate and instead activated the state guard to maintain order and break the union. "There is no right to strike against the public safety by anybody, anywhere, anytime," he proclaimed, and his statement won him the Republican nomination for vice president in 1920. No polls measured public opinion on strikes and unions in 1919, but by midyear it was clear that conservative political leaders had joined with business figures in an effort to roll back the union gains of the war years.

The largest and most dramatic labor conflict in 1919 came against the United States Steel Corporation. Most steelworkers had not had a recognized union since the 1892 Homestead strike. Steel companies often hired recent immigrants, intentionally keeping the work force divided by language and culture. Many steelworkers put in twelve-hour days and, when they changed shifts, sometimes slogged through twenty-four hours in the mills without rest. Wages had not increased as fast as inflation—nor as fast as company profits. When, in 1919, the AFL launched an ambitious unionization drive in the steel industry, many steelworkers responded eagerly.

The men who ran the steel industry firmly refused to deal with the new organization in any way. So the workers went on strike in late September, demanding union recognition, collective bargaining, the eight-hour workday, and higher wages. U.S. Steel, however, blamed the strike on radicals. Company guards protected strikebreakers, and military forces commanded by General Leonard Wood moved into Gary, Indiana, to help round up what they called "the Red element." By January 1920, after eighteen workers had been killed and hundreds beaten, the strike was over and the unions ousted. An investigation by the Interchurch World Movement concluded that the industry's "effective mobilization of public opinion against the strikers through charges of radicalism" was among the leading causes of the strikers' defeat.

Red Scare

The steel industry's charges of Bolshevism to discredit strikers came at a time when many government and corporate leaders decried the dangers of Bolshevism at home and abroad. In late April, thirty-four bombs addressed to prominent Americans—including J. P. Morgan, John D. Rockefeller, and Supreme Court Justice Oliver Wendell Holmes—were discovered in various post offices after the explosion of two others addressed to a senator and to the mayor of Seattle. In June, bombs in several cities damaged buildings and killed two people. Although the work of a few anarchists, the explosions set off a panic over a nationwide, radical conspiracy to overthrow the government.

With President Wilson still bedridden, Attorney General A. Mitchell Palmer organized an anti-Red campaign, hoping to enhance his own chances for the 1920 presidential nomination in the process. "Like a prairie fire," Palmer claimed, "the blaze of revolution was sweeping over every American institution." In August 1919, he appointed **J. Edgar Hoover,** a young lawyer, to head a new antiradical division in the Justice Department, the predecessor of the Federal Bureau of Investigation. In November, Palmer launched the first of what came to be called the **Palmer raids** to arrest suspected radicals. Authorities rounded up some five thousand people

---

Calvin Coolidge Massachusetts governor and conservative Republican who became Harding's vice president in 1921; he served as president from 1923 to 1929.

J. Edgar Hoover Official appointed to head a new antiradical division in the Justice Department in 1919, which eventually became the Federal Bureau of Investigation.

Palmer raids A series of government attacks on individuals and organizations in 1919 and 1920, carried out in a climate of anticommunist hysteria to search for political radicals.

between November and January 1920. Although officials found only a few firearms and no explosives, the raids led to the **deportation** of several hundred aliens whose only offense was some tie to a radical organization.

In May 1919, a group of veterans formed the American Legion, which not only lobbied on behalf of veterans but also condemned radicals, endorsed the deportations, and committed itself "to foster and perpetuate a one hundred percent Americanism." The Legion signed up a million members by the end of the year. Some of its branches soon gained a reputation for vigilante action against suspected radicals.

State legislatures joined in with antiradical measures of their own, including criminal **syndicalism** laws—measures designed to outlaw the IWW by making nearly every aspect of its ideology illegal. The Nebraska legislature even prohibited the public display of red flags. In January 1920, the assembly of the New York state legislature expelled five members elected as Socialists, solely because of their party affiliation. However, when a wide range of respected public figures denounced the assembly action as undemocratic, public opinion regarding the **Red Scare** began to shift. With the approach of May 1, the major day of celebration for socialists and communists alike, Palmer issued dramatic warnings for the public to be on guard against radical activity. Be prepared, he predicted, for attacks on government officials, a general strike, more bombings. When nothing happened, many concluded that the radical threat may have been overstated.

As the Red Scare sputtered to an end, in May 1920, police in Massachusetts arrested **Nicola Sacco and Bartolomeo Vanzetti,** both Italian-born anarchists, and charged them with robbery and murder. Despite inconclusive evidence and the accused men's protestations of innocence, a jury found them guilty and they were sentenced to death. While appeals delayed their execution, many Americans became convinced that the two had been convicted because of their political beliefs and Italian origins. Further, many doubted that they had received a fair trial because of the nativism and antiradicalism that infected the judge and jury. Over loud protests at home and abroad, both men were executed in 1927.

Race Riots and Lynchings

The racial tensions of the war years continued into the postwar period. Black soldiers encountered more acceptance and less discrimination in Europe than they had ever known at home. In May 1919 the NAACP journal *Crisis* expressed what the more militant returning soldiers felt.

We return. We return from fighting. We return fighting. Make way for Democracy! We saved it in France, and by the Great Jehovah, we will save it in the U.S.A., or know the reason why.

Some whites, North and South, greeted homecoming black troops with furious violence intended to restore the state of race relations that had prevailed before 1917. Mobs in Mississippi, Georgia, Arkansas, Florida, and Alabama lynched ten returning black soldiers, some still in uniform. Mobs lynched more than seventy blacks in the first year after the war and burned eleven victims alive.

Rioting also struck outside the South. In July, violence reached the nation's capitol, where white mobs, many of them soldiers and sailors, attacked blacks throughout the city for three days, killing several. Unprotected, the city's African-Americans resorted to organizing their own, sometimes armed, defense. A few days later, in Chicago, whites threw rocks at a young African-American swimming near a Lake Michigan beach usually used by whites. The youth drowned, and many blacks concluded the death was from being hit on the head by a stone. For nearly two weeks in late July, war raged between white and black mobs, despite peacekeeping efforts by the militia after the fourth day. The rioting caused thirty-eight deaths (fifteen white, twenty-three black) and more than five hundred injuries. More than a thousand families—nearly all black—were burned out of their homes. In Omaha, in September, a mob tried to hang the mayor when he bravely stood between them and a black prisoner

---

deportation Expulsion of an undesirable alien from a country.

syndicalism A radical political movement that advocated using strikes to bring industry under the control of its workers.

Red Scare Wave of anticommunism in the United States in 1919 and 1920, which included a government crackdown that focused on foreigners and labor unions.

Nicola Sacco and Bartolomeo Vanzetti Italian anarchists convicted in 1921 of the murder of a Braintree, Massachusetts, factory paymaster and theft of a $16,000 payroll; in spite of public protests on their behalf, they were electrocuted in 1927.

accused of rape. Police were able to save the mayor but not the prisoner.

By the end of 1919, race riots had flared in more than two dozen places. The year saw not only rampant lynchings but also the reappearance of the Ku Klux Klan (see page 721). Attempting to capture the militant spirit African-Americans displayed in these confrontations, poet **Claude McKay** wrote "If We Must Die," which so impressed Senator Henry Cabot Lodge that he inserted it into the *Congressional Record*.

> *If we must die, let it not be like hogs*
> *Hunted and penned in an inglorious spot*
> *O kinsmen! we must meet the common foe!*
> *Though far outnumbered let us show us brave,*
> *And for their thousand blows deal one deathblow!*
> *What though before us lies the open grave?*
> *Like men we'll face the murderous, cowardly pack,*
> *Pressed to the wall, dying, but fighting back!*

As W. E. B. Du Bois observed, black veterans "would never be the same again. You cannot ask them to go back to what they were before. They cannot, for they are not the same men."

The Election of 1920

Republicans confidently expected to regain the White House in the 1920 election. The Democrats had lost their congressional majorities in the 1918 elections, and the postwar confusion and disillusionment often focused on Wilson. One reporter described the stricken president as the "sacrificial whipping boy for the present bitterness."

The reaction against Wilson almost guaranteed election of any competent Republican nominee. Several candidates attracted significant support, notably former Army Chief of Staff General Leonard Wood, Illinois governor Frank Lowden, and California's Senator Hiram Johnson. However, no candidate could muster a majority of the convention delegates. Harry Daugherty, campaign manager for Senator **Warren G. Harding** of Ohio, foresaw such a deadlock months earlier. He also predicted it would be broken by a compromise candidate, chosen at about "eleven minutes after two o'clock on Friday morning," by about "fifteen or twenty men, bleary-eyed and perspiring profusely from the heat." And so it was. A group of party leaders, mostly senators, met late at night in a smoke-filled hotel room and picked Harding. Even some who supported him were unenthusiastic, one faintly praising him as

"the best of the second-raters." For vice president, the Republicans nominated Calvin Coolidge, the Massachusetts governor who broke the Boston police strike. The Democrats also suffered severe divisions and took forty-four ballots to choose James Cox, the governor of Ohio, as their presidential candidate. For vice president, they nominated Wilson's assistant secretary of the navy, Franklin D. Roosevelt, a remote cousin of Theodore Roosevelt.

Usually described as good-natured and likable—and sometimes as bumbling—Harding had published a small-town newspaper in Marion, Ohio, until his wife Florence and some of his friends urged him to enter politics. He eventually won election to the Senate. Unhappy with his marriage, Harding apparently found contentment with a series of mistresses. The press knew something of Harding's liaisons but, as was the usual practice, never reported them.

More of an uproar came, however, over suspicions that Harding was part African-American. A professor at Ohio's Wooster College reported that Harding's great-grandmother, Elizabeth Madison, was black, and that his great-grandfather, George T. Harding was part black. The rumor spread rapidly and in no time became the juiciest campaign story. One reporter in Cincinnati asked Harding outright, "Do you have any Negro blood?" Harding replied mildly, "How do I know, Jim? One of my ancestors may have jumped the fence." The charge, and Harding's response to it, apparently did not hurt his cause.

The election was a Republican landslide, with Harding winning thirty-seven of the forty-eight states and 60 percent of the popular vote—the largest popular majority up to that time. Wilson had hoped the election might be a "solemn referendum" on the League of Nations. But it proved more a response to the disappointments of the Wilson years—a war launched with the loftiest ideals that turned sour in the halls of Versailles, the high cost of living, the strikes and riots of 1919, and similar frustrations and anxieties. Americans, it seemed, had had enough idealism and sacrifice for a while.

Claude McKay   Jamaican-born poet and novelist whose 1928 novel *Home to Harlem* was the first bestseller by a black author in the United States.

Warren G. Harding   Ohio politician and Republican who was elected president of the United States in 1920; his administration was marred by corruption and scandal.

SUMMARY

E xpectations
C onstraints
C hoices
O utcomes

Woodrow Wilson took office *expecting* to focus on domestic policy, not foreign affairs. He fulfilled some Democratic party commitments to anti-imperialism, but *chose* to intervene extensively in the Caribbean. He also *chose* to intervene in Mexico, but was *constrained* from fully accomplishing his objetives.

When war broke out in Europe in 1914, Wilson proclaimed the United States to be neutral, and most Americans agreed. German submarine warfare and British restrictions on commerce, however, *constrained* traditional *expectations* for neutrality. Wilson secured a German pledge to refrain from unrestricted submarine warfare. He was reelected in 1916 on the platform that "he kept us out of war." Shortly after he won reelection, however, the Germans violated their pledge, and Wilson *chose* to ask for war against Germany.

The war brought new *expectations* in nearly every aspect of the nation's economic and social life. To overcome *constraints* of inefficiency, the federal government *chose* to develop a high degree of centralized economic planning. Fearing that opposition to the war might pose a *constraint* on full mobilization, the Wilson administration *chose* to mold public opinion and to secure new laws that *constrained* some civil liberties. When the federal government *chose* to back collective bargaining, unions registered important gains. And when labor shortages threatened to *constrain* the war effort, more women and African-Americans *chose* to enter the industrial workforce. One outcome of the labor shortage was that many African-Americans chose to move to northern and midwestern industrial cities.

Germany *chose* to launch a major offensive in early 1918, *expecting* to achieve victory before American troops could make a difference. However, the AEF was able to take a significant part in breaking the German advance. The *outcome* was that the Germans requested an armistice.

In his Fourteen Points, Wilson expressed his *expectations* for peace. *Constrained* by opposition from the Allies, Wilson *chose* to compromise at the peace conference, but still expected that the League of Nations would be able to maintain the peace. Fearing the *constraints* that League membership might place on the United States, enough senators opposed the treaty to defeat it. The *outcome,* thus, was that the United States did not become a member of the League.

In the United States, the immediate *outcome* of the war was disillusionment, and a year of high prices, costly strikes, a Red Scare, and race riots and lynchings. In 1920, the nation returned to its Republican preference when it elected Warren G. Harding, a mediocre conservative, to the White House.

SUGGESTED READINGS

Clements, Kendrick A. *The Presidency of Woodrow Wilson* (1992).

> More than half of this recent account of Wilson's presidency is devoted to foreign policy matters and the war.

Friedel, Frank. *Over There: The Story of America's First Great Overseas Crusade.* Rev. ed. (1990).

> A vivid survey of American participation in the fighting in Europe, with many firsthand accounts.

Lewis, Sinclair. *Main Street* (1920, rpt. 1961).

> An absorbing novel about a woman's dissatisfaction with her life and her decision to work in Washington during the war.

Link, Arthur S. *Woodrow Wilson: Revolution, War, and Peace* (1979).

> A concise introduction to Wilson's role in and thinking about foreign affairs.

Remarque, Erich Maria. *All Quiet on the Western Front.* A. W. Wheen, trans. (1930, rpt. 1982).

> The classic and moving novel about World War I, seen through German eyes.

Tuchman, Barbara W. *The Guns of August* (1962, rpt. 1976).

> A popular and engaging account of the outbreak of the war, focusing on events in Europe.

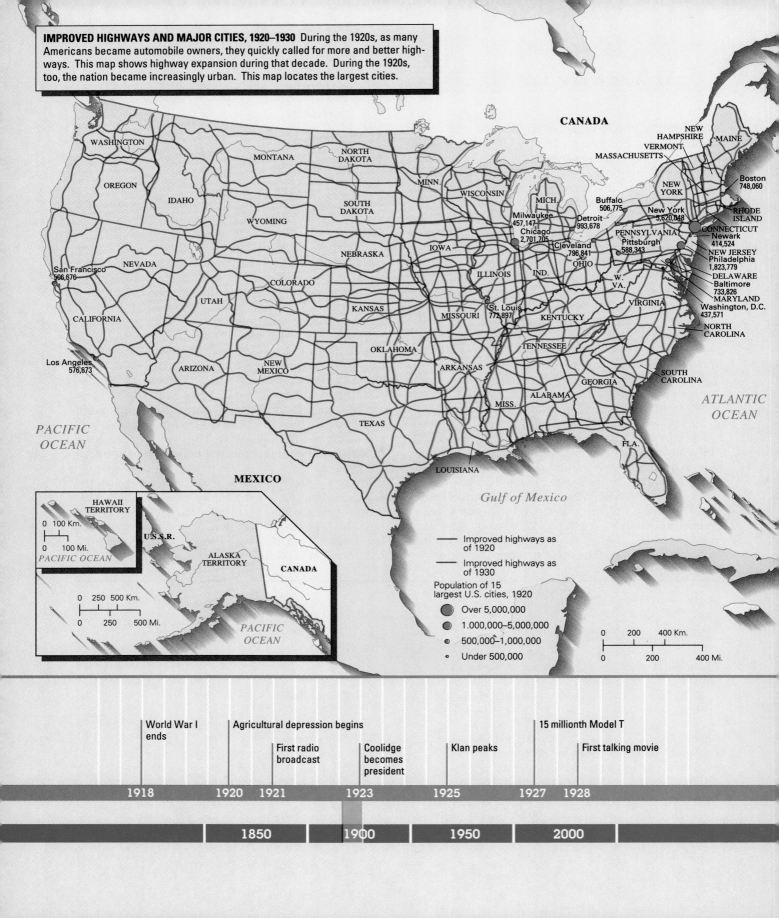

IMPROVED HIGHWAYS AND MAJOR CITIES, 1920–1930 During the 1920s, as many Americans became automobile owners, they quickly called for more and better highways. This map shows highway expansion during that decade. During the 1920s, too, the nation became increasingly urban. This map locates the largest cities.

CANADA

WASHINGTON
OREGON
IDAHO
MONTANA
NORTH DAKOTA
SOUTH DAKOTA
WYOMING
NEVADA
UTAH
COLORADO
CALIFORNIA
ARIZONA
NEW MEXICO
NEBRASKA
KANSAS
OKLAHOMA
TEXAS
MINN.
WISCONSIN
IOWA
MISSOURI
ARKANSAS
LOUISIANA
MICH.
ILLINOIS
IND.
KENTUCKY
TENNESSEE
MISS.
ALABAMA
GEORGIA
OHIO
W. VA.
VIRGINIA
NORTH CAROLINA
SOUTH CAROLINA
FLA.

NEW HAMPSHIRE
MAINE
VERMONT
MASSACHUSETTS
NEW YORK
RHODE ISLAND
CONNECTICUT
PENNSYLVANIA
NEW JERSEY
DELAWARE
MARYLAND

San Francisco 506,676
Los Angeles 576,673
Milwaukee 457,147
Chicago 2,701,705
Detroit 993,678
Cleveland 796,841
St. Louis 772,897
Buffalo 506,775
New York 5,620,048
Pittsburgh 588,343
Newark 414,524
Philadelphia 1,823,779
Baltimore 733,826
Washington, D.C. 437,571
Boston 748,060

PACIFIC OCEAN

ATLANTIC OCEAN

MEXICO

Gulf of Mexico

HAWAII TERRITORY
0 100 Km.
0 100 Mi.
PACIFIC OCEAN

U.S.S.R.
ALASKA TERRITORY
CANADA
PACIFIC OCEAN
0 250 500 Km.
0 250 500 Mi.

—— Improved highways as of 1920
—— Improved highways as of 1930

Population of 15 largest U.S. cities, 1920
● Over 5,000,000
● 1,000,000–5,000,000
● 500,000–1,000,000
• Under 500,000

0 200 400 Km.
0 200 400 Mi.

World War I ends

Agricultural depression begins

First radio broadcast

Coolidge becomes president

Klan peaks

15 millionth Model T

First talking movie

| 1918 | 1920 | 1921 | 1923 | 1925 | 1927 | 1928 |

| 1850 | 1900 | 1950 | 2000 |

The 1920s, 1920–1928

Prosperity Decade

- What new economic choices opened for consumers during the 1920s? What new choices opened for business?
- What were some outcomes of these choices?

The "Roaring Twenties"

- What new expectations and choices shaped American society in the 1920s?
- How did they reflect or contribute to the important social changes of the period?

Traditional America Roars Back

- How did some Americans try to restore traditional social expectations and values during the 1920s?
- What were the outcomes of their choices?

Race, Class, and Gender in the 1920s

- During the 1920s, what expectations and constraints influenced choices faced by American Indians, Mexicans, working people, women, and homosexuals?
- What were the outcomes of their choices?

The Politics of Prosperity

- What were the expectations of the Republican administrations of the 1920s?
- What were their resulting policy choices?

INTRODUCTION

E xpectations
C onstraints
C hoices
O utcomes

Called the "Jazz Age" and the "Roaring Twenties," the decade of the 1920s sometimes seems to be a swirl of conflicting images. Prohibition marked an ambitious effort to preserve the values of nineteenth-century America at the same time "the flapper" was flaunting the liberation of women from previous *constraints*. The booming stock market promised prosperity to all with money to invest at the same time thousands of farmers were abandoning the land because they could not survive financially. Business leaders celebrated the expansion of the economy at the same time many wage earners in manufacturing endured the destruction of their unions and their legal protections. White-sheeted armies of the Ku Klux Klan marched as self-proclaimed defenders of Protestant American values and white supremacy at the same time African Americans were creating an impressive flowering of cultural expression in art, literature, and music. The values of big business reigned supreme in politics at the same time the economy was lurching toward a collapse that few anticipated.

In the 1920s, business turned as never before to focus on the consumer. Americans suddenly found themselves facing a range of consumer *choices* beyond all previous *expectations*, as they were deluged with a flood of new products within the purchasing power of most families—automobiles, radios, electric household appliances of every description, trendy fashions in clothing and household furnishings, innovative products for personal hygiene, and many others. More and more Americans began to purchase on credit as installment-plan buying swept the nation, shattering old *constraints* about paying cash and avoiding debt. By the mid-1920s, it seemed as though much of the nation had *chosen* to borrow money and go on an extended buying binge.

Not everyone shared in the *expectations* bred by the consumer culture of postwar America. The poorest farmers and wage earners were *constrained* from doing so by their economic situation. Some others *chose* not to. Disillusioned with the "war to end war" and scornful of the widespread infatuation with consumer buying, many intellectuals became alienated from American culture. They bemoaned their "botched civilization" but conceived no alternative other than complaint and despair.

Dissatisfied with the choices that faced them in the United States, some *chose* to move to Paris—or England or elsewhere in Europe—to escape what they saw as the emptiness of American life. For them, modern America had become a spiritual and cultural waste land, committed to little more than consumption of standardized material goods.

Few Americans shared the gloom of such intellectuals. For most, the 1920s were a time of glittering *expectations,* when they cast aside old *constraints* and made bold new *choices*. Many revealed an unfettered optimism as they picked out their new radio, signed papers to buy a new automobile on the installment plan, and, perhaps, speculated on the stock market. For them, the immediate *outcome*—new car, new radio, new styles—seemed to fulfill the rosy expectations bred by advertising and the alluring consumer culture.

This optimism fed into an expansive popular culture that seemed to reflect a nation-wide "age of excess." Radio and movies popularized nationwide tastes, trends, and "heroes" as never before, as entertainment became big business. Led primarily by youths of white middle-class background, many young people *chose* to flaunt behavior that defied the values of their parents' generation.

Some Americans never shared in those outcomes, however, and all were unprepared for the long-term *outcome* of economic collapse that lay ahead. Like the shiny new roadsters that filled the advertising in popular magazines, the economy roared along at high speed, fueled by easy credit and consumer spending, virtually unregulated. It carried most Americans with it—until the economic engine sputtered and seemed to die in 1929.

America in the 1920s

1908	Ford introduces Model T General Motors formed
1912	Wilson elected
1914	Universal Negro Improvement Association founded War breaks out in Europe
1915	Griffith's *Birth of a Nation* Ku Klux Klan revived
1917	U.S. enters World War I
1918	World War I ends
1920	Eighteenth Amendment (Prohibition) takes effect Nineteenth Amendment grants women the vote Lewis's *Main Street* Harding elected Esch-Communs Act American Legion's *Shadows of the West*
1920–1921	Nationwide recession Agricultural depression begins
1921	Temporary immigration quotas First commercial radio broadcasts *Halitosis* sells Listerine Farm Bloc formed
1922	Lewis's *Babbitt* Cather's *One of Ours* Eliot's *The Waste Land* Louis Armstrong joins King Oliver's jazz ensemble Conference for Progressive Political Action formed
1923	Harding dies Coolidge becomes president Garvey convicted of mail fraud Toomer's *Cane* American Indian Defense Association formed

1923–1925	Harding administration scandals revealed
1924	National Origins Act Coolidge elected First disposable handkerchiefs Wheaties marketed as "Breakfast of Champions" Crossword puzzle fad Full citizenship for American Indians
1925	Scopes trial Barton's *The Man Nobody Knows* Fitzgerald's *The Great Gatsby* Locke's *The New Negro* Ku Klux Klan claims 5 million members Klan leader convicted of murder One automobile for every three residents in Los Angeles Chrysler Corporation formed
1926	Railway Labor Act Florida real-estate boom collapses Hemingway's *The Sun Also Rises* Ederle swims English Channel
1927	Coolidge vetoes McNary-Haugen bill Lindbergh's transatlantic flight 15 millionth Model T sold Ellington conducts jazz at Cotton Club
1928	Coolidge vetoes McNary-Haugen again First commercial talking motion picture *Confederacion de Uniones Obreras Mexicanas* formed Ford introduces Model A Communist Party forms Trade Union Unity League
1931	Allen's *Only Yesterday* Capone convicted and imprisoned

Prosperity Decade

- What new economic choices opened for consumers during the 1920s? What new choices opened for business?
- What were some outcomes of these choices?

By 1920, the industrialization of America was substantially achieved—the foundations of the modern corporate economy were in place, controlled by large industrial corporations run by professional managers. After a difficult but short adjustment at the end of the war, the economy completed an important shift. Until then, U.S. production efforts had been dominated by railroads, steel, heavy equipment manufacturing, and similar industries, few of which made products for sale to the average consumer. During in the 1920s, though, the rise of the automobile industry dramatized the new prominence of **consumer goods** industries. This significant change in direction carried implications for advertising, banking, and even the stock market.

The Economics of Prosperity

The end of the war brought cancellation of orders for war supplies from ships to uniforms. At the same time, large numbers of recently discharged military and naval personnel swelled the ranks of job seekers. Such postwar conditions have often brought on a recession or depression. At the end of World War I, however, there was no immediate economic collapse, thanks in part to pent-up demand. Given wartime shortages and overtime pay, many Americans had been earning more than they could spend. At the end of the war, their eagerness to spend helped to delay the postwar slump until 1920 and 1921. Then production fell sharply: the **Gross National Product (GNP)** dropped by only 4.3 percent between 1919 and 1920, but by 8.6 percent between 1920 and 1921. During the war, unemployment affected only about 1 percent of the work force. The jobless rate increased to 5 percent in 1920 and 12 percent in 1921. Among workers who kept their jobs, many worked fewer hours, and some took pay cuts. In manufacturing, workers' earnings averaged $26 a week in 1920 and only $21 in 1922. One bright spot was that decreased earnings, unemployment, and declining demand halted the rampaging inflation of 1918 and 1919. In fact, consumer prices fell by 10 percent from 1920 to 1921, led by a 24 percent drop in the price of food.

The economy quickly rebounded after 1921. The GNP increased by 16 percent between 1921 and 1922, a bigger jump than during the booming war years. By 1923, unemployment had fallen to 2 percent and remained between 2 and 5 percent through 1929. By 1922, most manufacturing workers were again working full-time, and their average weekly paycheck grew from $21 in 1922 to $24 in 1925 to nearly $25 in 1929. Paychecks went up slightly for workers in manufacturing and some other industries, but increased productivity meant that prices for most manufactured goods remained stable or even went down. Declining prices for agricultural products brought lower prices for food and clothing. Thus, many Americans seemed better off by 1929 than in 1920: they earned about the same and they paid somewhat less for necessities. (Figure 23.1 presents a summary of paycheck tendencies for workers in manufacturing.)

Targeting Consumers

In 1931, journalist Frederick Lewis Allen, wrote *Only Yesterday,* a popular and often perceptive history of the 1920s. In it, he noted that "business had learned as never before the immense importance to it of the ultimate consumer. Unless he could be persuaded to buy and buy lavishly, the whole stream of six-cylinder cars, super-heterodynes [radios], cigarettes, rouge compacts, and electric ice-boxes would be dammed at its outlet." In short, persuading Americans to consume an array of products became crucial to keeping the economy healthy.

The marketing of Listerine demonstrates the rising importance of creative advertising. Listerine had been devised as a general antiseptic, but in 1921 Gerard Lambert devised a more persuasive—and profitable—approach when he plucked the obscure term *halitosis* from a medical journal. Through aggressive advertising using the word, he fostered anxieties about the impact of bad breath on popularity and made millions by selling Listerine to combat the offensive condition. Also in 1921, the General Foods company invented Betty Crocker to give its baking products a womanly, domestic image. In 1924, General Mills first advertised Wheaties as the "Breakfast of Champions," thereby tying consump-

---

consumer goods   Products such as food and clothing that directly satisfy human wants.

Gross National Product   The total market value of all goods and services produced by a nation during a specified period.

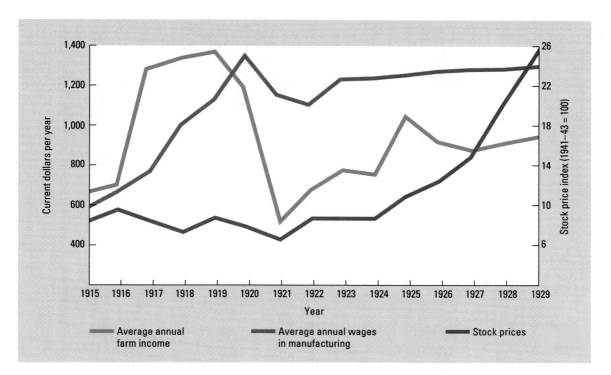

◆ **FIGURE 23.1 Economic Indicators, 1915–1929** This figure presents three measures of economic activity for the period covering World War I and the 1920s. Farm income and wages should be read on the left-hand scale; stock prices should be read on the right-hand scale.
Note: Incomes are in current dollars, not adjusted for changes in purchasing power.
Source: U.S. Department of Commerce, Bureau of the Census, *Historical Statistics of the United States, Colonial Times to 1970,* Bicentennial Edition, 2 vols. (Washington, D.C.: U.S. Government Printing Office, 1975), I: 483, 170; II: 1004.

tion of cold cereal to success in sports. Americans responded by buying those products and others with similarly creative pitches. "We grew up founding our dreams on the infinite promises of American advertising," later wrote Zelda Sayre Fitzgerald, writer and wife of novelist F. Scott Fitzgerald. "I still believe that one can learn to play the piano by mail," she added, "and that mud will give you a perfect complexion."

Changes in fashion also encouraged increased consumption and, therefore, economic growth. The popularity of short hair styles for women, for example, led to the development of hair salons and stimulated sales of the recently invented **bobby pin.** Cigarettes became more fashionable after World War I, as soldiers had found them easier to carry and smoke than pipes or cigars. Cigarette advertisers also began to target women. The American Tobacco Company advised women to "Reach for a Lucky instead of a sweet" to attain a fashionably-slim figure. Style and technology combined to invent disposable products, thereby promoting regu-

lar, recurring consumer buying of throw-away items. Kotex, the first manufactured disposable sanitary napkin, appeared on the market in 1921, its production made possible by technological advances in the processing of wood cellulose fiber. In 1924, the same technology produced the first disposable handkerchief, later known as Kleenex.

Technological advances contributed in other ways to the growth of consumer-oriented manufacturing. In 1920, about one-third of all residences had electricity. By 1929, electrical power had reached most urban homes (but fewer than 10 percent of rural homes). As the number of residences with electricity increased, advertisers stressed the time and labor that housewives could save by using electrical appliances—vacuum cleaners, washing machines,

> **bobby pin** Small metal hair clip with ends pressed tightly together, designed for holding short or "bobbed" hair in place.

irons, toasters, and more. Between the postwar years of 1919 to 1921 and the end of the decade, consumer expenditures for household appliances grew by more than 120 percent as such products flowed into American homes.

This increased consumption contributed to a change in people's spending habits. Before the war, most urban families expected to pay cash for most of what they bought, but in the 1920s many retailers adopted the installment plan: "Buy now, pay later." And many consumers listened, choosing to take home their new radio today and worry about paying for it tomorrow. By the late 1920s, about 15 percent of all retail purchases came through the installment plan, including most furniture, phonographs, washing machines, and refrigerators. Charge accounts in department stores also became popular, and **finance companies** grew rapidly.

The Automobile: Driving the Economy

The automobile, more than any other single product, epitomized the consumer-oriented economy of the 1920s. Although automobiles had been built in Germany and France in the late nineteenth century, they remained a luxury until American entrepreneurs found ways to bring prices within the budgets of most families. **Henry Ford,** a former mechanic, scored the greatest success by developing a mass-production system that drove down production costs. Other companies jostled with Ford for the patronage of American car buyers and, by the late 1920s, about 80 percent of the world's registered vehicles were in the United States. By then, America's roadways sported nearly one automobile for every five people.

Ford built his success on the **Model T,** introduced in 1908. For many Americans, a Model-T Ford was their first middle-class dream come true, and families came to love their ungraceful but reliable "Tin Lizzies," so-called for their lightweight metal bodies. By 1927, Ford had produced more than 15 million of them, dominating the market by selling the largest possible number of cars at the lowest possible price. "Get the prices down to the buying power," Ford ordered. And his dictatorial management combined with technological advances and high worker productivity to bring the price of a new Model T as low as $290 by 1927. Cheap to buy, run, and maintain, the Model T made Henry Ford into a folk hero—and a wealthy one. By 1925 Ford turned

"How did he ever get the money to buy a car"

♦ Henry Ford constantly worked to reduce car prices on his cars. He also promoted installment buying, promising in this ad that "with even the most modest income, [every family] can now afford a car of their own." This ad also encouraged impulse buying: "You live but once and the years roll by quickly. Why wait for tomorrow for things that you rightfully should enjoy today?" *Library of Congress.*

out nine thousand cars a day with a *daily* profit of some $25,000.

Not only streamlined production, but also competition helped to keep prices low for middle-class cars. Other automobile companies challenged Ford's predominance, notably General Motors (GM), founded by William Durant in 1908, and

---

finance company   Business that makes loans to clients based on some form of collateral, like a new car, thus allowing a form of installment buying when sellers do not extend credit.

Henry Ford   Inventor and manufacturer who founded the Ford Motor Company in 1903 and pioneered mass production in the auto industry.

Model T   Lightweight automobile produced by Ford from 1908 to 1927 and sold at the lowest possible price, on the theory that an affordable car would be more profitable than an expensive one.

♦ Ford pioneered the automobile assembly line as a way to reduce both costs and dependence on skilled workers. During the 1920s, he paid the highest wages in Detroit, but he required complete obedience from his employees, even to the point of prohibiting whistling while working. *From the Collections of Henry Ford Museum & Greenfield Village.*

Chrysler Corporation, created by Walter Chrysler in 1925. GM and Chrysler adopted some of Ford's techniques but also emphasized comfort and style, both missing in the purely functional Model T. Ford finally ended production of the Model T in 1927 and, the next year, introduced the Model A, which incorporated some of the smarter features promoted by his chief competitors.

Ford's company also provides an example of efforts by American businesses to reduce labor costs by improving labor efficiency. In the process, however, work on Ford's assembly line became a thoroughly **dehumanizing** experience. He prohibited his workers from talking, sitting, smoking, singing, or even whistling while working. As one critic put it, workers were only to "put nut 14 on bolt 132, repeating, repeating, repeating until their hands shook and their legs quivered." However, Ford paid his workers more than any of his competitors— enough that they, too, could afford a Model T. Workers thus came to enjoy some types of consumer buying previously restricted to middle- and upper-income groups.

The automobile came to symbolize not only the ability of many Americans to acquire material goods but also technology, progress, and the freedom of the open road. The industry worked to promote this heady image. One car salesman remarked in 1926, "When I sold a car, I sold it with the honest conviction that I was doing the buyer a favor in helping him to take his place in a big forward movement."

The automobile industry in the 1920s often led the way in promoting new sales techniques. Installment buying became so widespread that, by 1927, two-thirds of all American automobiles were sold on credit. The largest companies kept prices low on models aimed at middle-income Americans. Ford's Model T had emphasized no-frills reliability, but after 1928 he tended to follow GM in introducing new models every year. This practice enticed owners to trade in their cars to keep up with the latest fashions in design, color, and optional features. Dozens of small auto makers closed down when they could not compete with the low prices and yearly models offered by the Big Three. By 1929, Chrysler, Ford, and GM made 83 percent of all cars manufactured in the country. The industry had become **oligopolistic.**

Changes in Banking and Business

Just as Ford led the way in bringing automobiles within reach of most Americans, **A. P. Giannini** did the same for banking. The son of Italian immigrants, Giannini founded the Bank of Italy in 1904 as a bank for shopkeepers and workers in the Italian neighborhood of San Francisco. Called the greatest innovator in twentieth-century American banking, Giannini not only based his bank on ordinary people, but also began to open branches throughout California, near people's homes and workplaces. Until then, most banks had only one location, in the center of a city, and had limited their services to businesses and substantial citizens with hefty accounts. Giannini significantly broadened the base of banking by encouraging working people to open small checking and savings accounts and to borrow for such investments as car purchases. In the process, his bank— later renamed the Bank of America—became the third largest in the nation by 1927.

dehumanizing   That which deprives of human qualities, such as individuality, by rendering a task mechanical and routine.
oligopolistic   Describes a market condition in which sellers are so few that the actions of any one of them can affect prices and practices throughout the industry.
A. P. Giannini   Italian-American banker who changed the banking industry by opening multiple branches and encouraging the use of banks for small accounts and loans.

Giannini's bank survived as a relic of family management in a new world of modern corporations with large bureaucracies. Ownership and control continued to grow apart as salaried managers came to run most big businesses. Large integrated corporations, such as GM, Du Pont, and General Electric, typically organized themselves into divisions. For instance, GM established separate divisions for its five car lines, each with distinct production, sales, advertising, and operations departments.

Although the number of corporations increased steadily, from 345,600 in 1920 to 518,700 in 1930, a great corporate merger wave also accelerated as the 1920s progressed—1922 saw 309 mergers, 1929 counted 1,245. These mergers continued earlier patterns toward greater economic concentration. By 1930, 5 percent of American corporations received 85 percent of all net corporate income, up from 78 percent in 1921.

Business giants like Henry Ford emerged as popular and respected figures and were widely viewed as socially responsible trustees of the public interest. In 1925, in a book entitled *The Man Nobody Knows*, Bruce Barton (later founder of a leading advertising agency) suggested that Jesus Christ could best be understood as a chief executive who "had picked up twelve men from the bottom ranks of business and forged them into an organization that conquered the world." Portraying Jesus' parables as "the most powerful advertisements of all time," Barton's book led the nonfiction best-seller lists for two years.

"Get Rich Quick"—The Speculative Mania

More than ever before, the stock market captured people's fancy as a certain route to riches. Stock market speculation—buying a stock and expecting to make money by selling it at a higher price—ran rampant. Articles in popular periodicals proclaimed that everyone could participate and get rich in no time, even with a small investment. By 1929, some 4 million Americans owned stock, equivalent to about 10 percent of American households.

Just as Americans bought their cars and radios on the installment plan, so some hastened to buy stock on credit, expecting to sell it at an enormous profit, pay off the debt, and be wealthy. The secretary of treasury and the Federal Reserve Board cooperated with an **easy-money policy** that permitted investors to buy on credit. It was possible to purchase stock listed at $100 a share with as little as $10 down and the other $90 on margin; that is, the other $90 was owed to the stock broker. If the stock advanced to $150, the investor could sell, pay off the broker, and still gain a profit of $50 (500 percent!) on the $10 investment. The propaganda promoting stock speculation rarely mentioned that, if the stock fell to $50, the investor would still owe $90 to the broker, even though sale of the stock would bring only $50. Actually, fewer than 1 percent of those who bought stocks did so on margin, and the size of the margin rarely exceeded 45 or 50 percent. A larger number of people bought stocks using borrowed money, however, and that carried the same potential for disaster as buying on margin.

Driven partly by real economic growth and partly by speculation, stock prices rose higher and higher. Standard and Poor's index of common stock prices tripled between 1920 and 1929. The New York Stock Exchange sold 236 million shares in 1923 and 1,125 million in 1928. As long as the market stayed **bullish**—meaning that prices kept going up—prosperity, it seemed, would never end. (Figure 23.1 shows stock prices.)

Easy-money policies, stock speculation, and the ever-rising stock prices and corporate dividends of the 1920s sometimes encouraged the creation of peculiar corporate structures, based less on selling actual goods or services than on the expectation of continued dividends. Samuel Insull created a vast empire of electrical utilities companies. Much of the structure of Insull's enterprise—and others like it—consisted of holding companies, which existed solely to own stock in another company, which often existed primarily to own stock of yet another company. Even Insull admitted that he was not sure how it all worked. The entire structure rested on the **operating companies'** dividends which in turn enabled the holding companies to pay dividends on their bonds. Any interruption in the dividends from the operating companies was likely to bring the collapse of the entire network, swallowing up the investment of speculators.

---

easy-money policy   The Federal Reserve's strategy for encouraging banks to extend credit; it involves lowering interest rates charged to banks and reducing the cash reserves banks are required to store.

bullish   Characterized by rising stock market prices.

operating company   Company that exists to sell a product or service, as opposed to a holding company that exists only to own other companies, including operating companies.

Although the stock market held the nation's attention as the most popular path to instant riches, other speculative opportunities abounded. One of the most prominent was the Florida land boom. The mania was fed by rapid growth in the population of Florida, especially Miami, which swelled from 30,000 people in 1920 to more than 75,000 five years later. People poured into Florida, attracted by the climate, the beaches, and the ease of travel from the cities of the chilly Northeast (either by train or automobile). Speculators large and small began to buy land—almost any land—amid slick predictions that it would boom in value. By 1925, according to one observer, "the whole city [of Miami] had become one frenzied real-estate exchange." Stories circulated of land that had increased in value by 1500 percent over ten years. Like stocks, land was bought on credit with the intention of reselling it at a quick profit. The boom began to falter early in 1926, however, as the population influx slowed, and it collapsed when a hurricane slammed into Miami in September 1926. By 1927, many speculators faced bankruptcy.

Agriculture: Depression in the Midst of Prosperity

Prosperity never extended to agriculture. Farmers by and large did not recover from the postwar recession and struggled to survive financially throughout the 1920s. Many had expanded their operations during the war in response to government demands for more food. Between 1914 and 1920, exports of farm products had nearly quadrupled. After the war, as European farmers resumed production, the glut of agricultural goods on world markets caused prices to fall. Exports of farm products tumbled by half within a few years of the end of the war. Throughout the 1920s, American farmers produced more than the domestic market could absorb.

Prices fell as a consequence of this **overproduction.** When adjusted for inflation, corn and wheat prices never rebounded to their prewar levels. Even in current dollars, corn and wheat sold for about half what they brought during the war. The average farm's net income for the years 1917 to 1920 had ranged between $1,196 and $1,395 per year. This fell to a dreadful $517 in 1921, then slowly began to rise but never reached the levels of 1917 to 1920 until World War II. Although farm income fell, farmers' mortgage payments more than doubled from prewar levels, partly because of debts incurred to ex-

pand production during the war. Tax increases, the cost of tractors and trucks—now necessities on most farms—and growing costs for fertilizer and other supplies bit further into farmers' meager earnings. (Figure 23.1 compares farm income with other economic indicators for the 1920s.)

Throughout the 1920s, farmers pressed the government for help. In 1921, farm organizations worked with a bipartisan group of senators and representatives to form a congressional **Farm Bloc** that promoted legislation to assist farmers. The Bloc enjoyed a substantial boost in the 1922 elections, when distraught farmers across the Midwest turned out conservatives and elected candidates who voiced sympathy for farmers' problems. Congress passed a few assistance measures in the early 1920s, but none addressed the central problems of overproduction and low prices. In the mid-1920s, proposals to tackle these two key issues invariably met presidential vetoes.

Legislative efforts did not stanch the hemorrhaging of the farm economy. The average value of an acre of farmland, in constant dollars, fell by more than half between 1920 and 1928. Farmland was actually less valuable in 1928 than in 1912! Hundreds of thousands of people left farms each year in the 1920s. The outcome was easy to predict: the number of farms declined, and the proportion of farmers in the total population fell from 30 percent to 25 percent. The prosperity decade was nearly the opposite for rural America.

The "Roaring Twenties"

● What new expectations and choices shaped American society in the 1920s?

● How did they reflect or contribute to the important social changes of the period?

"The world broke in two in 1922 or thereabouts," wrote the novelist Willa Cather, and she indicated her distaste for much that came after. F. Scott Fitzgerald, another novelist, agreed with the date but embraced the change. He thought 1922 marked

---

overproduction   Production that exceeds consumer need or demand.

Farm Bloc   Bipartisan group of senators and representatives formed in 1921 to promote legislation to assist farmers.

"the peak of the younger generation," who initiated an "age of miracles" and "age of art." He recognized, however, that it also became an "age of excess." For most Americans, evidence of sudden and dramatic social change was on all sides, from automobiles, radios, and movies to a new youth culture and an impressive cultural outpouring by African Americans in northern cities.

The Automobile and American Life

During the 1920s, the automobile profoundly changed American patterns of living. Highways significantly shortened the traveling time from cities to rural areas, for example, thereby reducing the isolation of farm life. One farm woman, when asked why her family had an automobile but not indoor plumbing, responded, "Why, you can't go to town in a bathtub." Trucks allowed farmers to take more products to market more quickly and conveniently than ever before. In the fields, tractors saved weeks' worth of time. Farmers no longer had to use pastures and hayfields to raise food for the horses and mules being replaced by trucks and tractors, so they converted them to crops or added more cattle, thereby contributing further to overproduction. The spread of gasoline-powered farm vehicles also reduced the need for human farm labor and so stimulated migration to urban areas.

If the automobile changed rural life, it made an even more profound impact on life in the cities. Cities continued to grow. The 1920 census, for the first time, recorded more Americans living in urban areas than in rural ones. The automobile freed suburban developments from their dependence on commuter rail lines. Suburbs mushroomed, with most of the growth in the form of single-family houses. From 1922 through 1928, construction began on an average of 883,000 new homes each year, many of them in the new suburbs. New home construction rivaled the auto as a major driving force behind economic growth. The automobile began to undermine streetcars. Streetcar usage in fact peaked at 15.7 billion trips nationwide in 1923, then began a steady decline. Many considered it a sign of progress for people to abandon streetcars in favor of automobiles.

A look at Los Angeles shows the automobile's pervasive impact on urban life. From 1920 to 1930 the population of Los Angeles County more than doubled, from fewer than 1 million to 2.2 million.

♦ In this photo from the mid-1920s, Culver City boasts of its 1,011 percent growth. Culver City was a Los Angeles suburb, and its growth was fueled both by the automobile and motion pictures industries. A major movie studio, Pathe, was located down the street to the right. *Security Pacific National Bank Photograph Collection/Los Angeles Public Library.*

This expansion occurred after automobile ownership began to multiply, and Los Angeles became the first large city organized around the auto. By 1925 Los Angeles counted one automobile for every three residents, twice the national average. The auto made it possible for Angelenos to live farther from work than ever before. In the 1920s, Los Angeles developed the greatest ratio of single-family residences and the lowest urban population density in the United States. By 1930 about 94 percent of all residences in Los Angeles were single-family homes, an unprecedented figure for a major city. The first modern supermarket (for so-called one-stop shopping) appeared in Los Angeles. So did the first large shopping district designed for the automobile. The *Los Angeles Times* put it this way in 1926: "Our forefathers in their immortal independence creed set forth 'the pursuit of happiness' as an inalienable right of mankind. And how can one pursue happiness by any swifter and surer means . . . than by the use of the automobile?"

By the late 1920s, the automobile had also begun to demonstrate its ability to strangle urban traffic. Detroit introduced the first traffic lights in 1920 and they spread rapidly to other large cities, but traffic congestion continued to worsen. By 1926, cars in the evening rush hour in Manhattan crawled along at less than three miles per hour—slower than a person could walk.

A Homogenized Culture Searches for Heroes

As the automobile cut traveling times and as more people moved to urban areas, restrictive immigration laws were closing the door to immigrants from abroad. These factors, together with the new technologies of radio and film, began to **homogenize** the culture—that is, to make it more uniform by breaking down cultural differences based on region or ethnicity.

In 1921, the first commercial radio broadcasting station opened. Within six years, 681 were operating. By 1930, 40 percent of all households had radio sets. By the mid-1920s, too, most towns of any size boasted at least one movie theater. Movie attendance increased rapidly, from a weekly average of 40 million people in 1922 to 80 million in 1929. The equivalent of two-thirds of the total population went to the cinema every week! As Americans all across the country tuned into the same radio broadcast, and families in rural villages as well as urban neighborhoods laughed or wept at the same movie, radio and film did their part in homogenizing American life. In the process, the profit potential in movie admission fees and radio advertising revenues pushed forward a burgeoning entertainment industry.

Radio and film joined newspapers and magazines—the media—in prompting national trends and fashions as Americans pursued one fad after another. In 1923, the opening of the fabulous tomb of the Egyptian pharaoh Tutankhamen led to a passion for things Egyptian. Crossword puzzle books captured the attention of many Americans in 1924, and the card game contract bridge did the same in 1926. Such fads, in turn, created markets for new consumer goods, from Egyptian-styled furniture to folding card tables to crossword dictionaries.

The media also contributed to the development of national sports heroes. In the 1920s, as Frederick Lewis Allen observed, sports "had become an American obsession." Baseball had long been the preeminent national sport, and radio now began to broadcast baseball games nationwide. Boxing and college football vied with baseball for national favor and for spectators' dollars. Most Americans were familiar with the exploits of such baseball greats as Lou Gehrig, Ty Cobb, and Babe Ruth, as well as box-

ers like Jack Dempsey and Gene Tunney and golfers like Bobby Jones. Gertrude Ederle won national acclaim in 1926 when she not only became the first woman to swim the English Channel but did so two hours faster than any previous man. Fame extended even to race horses, notably Man o' War.

The rapid spread of movie theaters created a new category of fame—the movie star. Charlie Chaplin, Buster Keaton, Harold Lloyd, and others brought laughter to the screen. Tom Mix was the best known of those introducing the western as a rugged dramatic genre. Sex, too, sold movie tickets and made stars of Theda Bara, the **vamp,** and Clara Bow, the "It" girl, whose publicists not only said she had "it" but also insisted that no one had to ask what "it" was. Rudolph Valentino soared to fame as a male sex symbol, with his most famous film, *The Sheik,* set in a fanciful Arabian desert. The stunning success of *The Sheik* led young men to call themselves "sheiks" and their dates "shebas." Several women committed suicide after Valentino's sudden death in 1926. "Valentino had silently acted out the fantasies of women all over the world," claimed screen star Bette Davis, adding "A whole generation of females wanted to ride off into a sandy paradise with him."

The greatest popular hero of the 1920s, however, was neither an athlete nor an actor but a small-town airmail pilot named **Charles Lindbergh.** Aviation was, at the time, barely out of its infancy. The Wright brothers' first flight got off the ground in 1903, but the earliest regular airmail deliveries in the United States, between New York City and Washington, D.C., began only in 1918, and night flying did not become routine until the mid-1920s. There had been a few transatlantic flights between 1919 and 1926, but the longest nonstop flight was San Diego to New York, 2,500 miles.

Lindbergh, in 1927, decided to collect the prize of $25,000 offered by a New York hotel owner to the pilot of the first successful nonstop flight between New York and Paris—a distance of 3,500 miles. His plane, *The Spirit of St. Louis,* was a stripped-down, one-engine craft, built for one occupant. In a sleepless, 33½-hour flight, Lindbergh earned both the

---

homogenize   To make something uniform throughout.

vamp   A woman who uses her sexuality to entrap and exploit men.

Charles Lindbergh   American aviator who made the first solo transatlantic flight in 1927 and became an international hero.

◆ Charles Lindbergh chose photo settings in which he was alone with his plane, thereby emphasizing the individual nature of his flights. This photo was taken before his solo flight across the Atlantic. *Culver Pictures, Inc.*

◆ Rudolph Valentino, the leading male movie star of the 1920s, is shown outfitted as a desert sheik, a role he played in *The Sheik* and *Son of the Sheik.* He died in 1926, at age 31, from complications following removal of his appendix. *Son of the Sheik* was released to his adoring fans after his death. *Culver Pictures, Inc.*

$25,000 and the adoration of crowds on both sides of the Atlantic. In Paris, 100,000 people streamed onto the landing field to greet him. In an age devoted to materialism and dominated by a corporate mentality, Lindbergh's accomplishment seemed to proclaim that old-fashioned individualism, courage, and self-reliance could still triumph over adversity.

Alienated Intellectuals

Lindbergh went to Paris to win a prize and became a living legend. Other Americans, too, went to Paris and other European cities in the 1920s, but for a different reason. They left to escape what they considered the America's dull conventionalism and dangerous materialism. Whether living abroad or in New York City, many American writers bemoaned what they saw as the shallowness, greed, and homogenization of American life. In Willa Cather's *One of Ours* (1922), for example, the sensitive and romantic main character dies in the war and thereby escapes the stifling emptiness of the postwar triumph of technological materialism.

Sinclair Lewis and **H. L. Mencken** were among the leading critics of mainstream values. Lewis,

in *Main Street* (1920) and *Babbitt* (1922), presented small-town, middle-class existence as not just boring but stifling. Title character George F. Babbitt was Lewis's version of a typical suburban businessman—a real-estate salesman, member of the Boosters' Club and Good Citizens' League—who speaks in clichés and buys every gadget on the market. Lewis's scathing depiction put a new word into the dictionary of American English: *Babbitt,* a materialistic, narrow-minded, and complacent businessman. H. L. Mencken, the influential editor of *The American Mercury,* relentlessly pilloried the "booboisie," jeered at all politicians (reformers and conservatives alike), and celebrated only those writers who shared his distaste for most of American life.

Sinclair Lewis Novelist who satirized middle-class America in works such as *Babbitt* (1922) and who became the first American to win a Nobel Prize for literature.

H. L. Mencken Editor and critic who founded *The American Mercury* and who wrote essays of scathing social criticism.

Other writers, too, expressed a rejection of traditional values, a disillusionment with postwar society, and a search for self. Some turned to seeking pleasure and excitement. Edna St. Vincent Millay captured this spirit of rebellion and pleasure seeking in 1920.

> *My candle burns at both ends;*
> *It will not last the night;*
> *But ah, my foes, and oh, my friends—*
> *It gives a lovely light!*

F. Scott Fitzgerald, in *The Great Gatsby* (1925), revealed the dark side of the hedonism of the 1920s, as he portrayed the pointless lives of wealthy pleasure seekers and their careless disregard for life and values. The novel is presented through the eyes of Nick Carraway, a young midwesterner who moves to New York to find his fortune but becomes so disillusioned by the novel's end that he returns home to the Midwest. Ernest Hemingway, in *The Sun Also Rises* (1926), depicted jaded and disillusioned **expatriates** who go to Spain to see the bull fights in an effort to introduce some excitement into their lives. Just as the love between two of the major characters, Jake Barnes and Brett Ashley, can never be fulfilled physically because a war wound left Jake impotent, so the novel's dominant tone is one of frustration, futility, and suffering.

Others took the theme of hopelessness even further. **T. S. Eliot,** a poet who had fled America for England in 1915, published *The Waste Land* in 1922, in which he presented a grim view of the barrenness of modern life, where a search for meaning yielded "the empty chapel, only the wind's home." Some writers moved beyond despair to predict the end of western civilization. Joseph Wood Krutch, in 1929, concluded that "ours is a lost cause," that modern civilization was so decadent that it could not rejuvenate itself, and that we could only wait to be overthrown by barbarians, as Rome had been in its day.

Renaissance Among African-Americans

Krutch's fear of the imminent end of western civilization and the more general attitude of despair and disillusionment were limited largely to white writers and intellectuals. Such views were little reflected in the striking outpouring of literature, music, and art by African-Americans in the 1920s.

Many blacks moved to northern cities in the 1920s, continuing patterns begun earlier. Harlem

By the time this 1923 photo was taken, F. Scott Fitzgerald had soared to fame as author of two novels and two collections of short stories, most of them depicting the hedonistic youth culture of the Jazz Age. Zelda, a writer, too, was best known as the beautiful and tormented wife of the handsome author. *Papers of F. Scott Fitzgerald, Manuscript Division. Department of Rare Books and Special Collections, Princeton University Libraries.*

emerged as a large, predominantly black neighborhood in New York City. It quickly became a symbol of the new, urban life of African-Americans. The term **Harlem Renaissance,** or Negro Renaissance, describes a literary and artistic movement in which black artists and writers insisted on the value of black culture and used African and African-Ameri-

---

F. Scott Fitzgerald   Fiction writer who captured the Jazz Age in such novels as *The Great Gatsby* (1925).

expatriate   A person who has taken up residence in a foreign country or renounced his or her native land.

T. S. Eliot   American poet who settled in England and whose long poem *The Waste Land* (1922) chronicled the barrenness of modern life.

Harlem Renaissance   Literary and artistic movement in the 1920s, centered in Harlem, in which black writers and artists described and celebrated African-American life.

Choosing to Live in Harlem

Langston Hughes

Langston Hughes, an acclaimed author, chose to spend his life and career among African-Americans, celebrating black people in his writing and developing opportunities for other black artists to cultivate their creativity. This portrait by Winold Reiss was taken in 1925, when Hughes, in his early twenties, had already become a significant figure in the Harlem Renaissance. National Portrait Gallery, Smithsonian Institute/Art Resource, NY.

In the late 1940s, Langston Hughes bought a house on East 127th Street, in central Harlem. He could have afforded a house in a wealthy suburb if he had wished, but he chose Harlem. It symbolized other choices he had made throughout his writing career, for he chose to write for and about African Americans.

Born in Joplin, Missouri, in 1902, he lived for a time with his grandmother, Mary Langston, from whom he learned lessons in social justice. He began to write poetry in high school, briefly attended college, then chose to work and travel in Africa and Europe. He continued writing poetry, some of which won prizes from African-American journals.

Hughes had become a significant figure in the Harlem Renaissance by 1925, sometimes reading his poetry to the musical accompaniment of jazz or the blues. Some of his work then presented images from black history, like "The Negro Speaks of Rivers" (1921). Other works, like "Song for a Dark Girl" (1927), vividly depicted the constraints of racism.

Way Down South in Dixie
(Break the heart of me)
They hung my black young lover
To a cross roads tree.

can traditions to shape an abundance of literature, painting, and sculpture. Alain Locke, in 1925, published *The New Negro*, a collection of work by these writers. In the introduction, Locke argued that African Americans were "achieving something like a spiritual emancipation" and that, henceforth, the nation "must reckon with a fundamentally changed Negro." Black actors, notably Paul Robeson, began to appear in serious theaters and earn acclaim for their abilities. Earlier black writers, notably Locke, James Weldon Johnson, and Claude McKay, encouraged and guided the novelists and poets of the Renaissance.

Among the movement's poets, **Langston Hughes** became the best known. His poetry rang with the

---

Langston Hughes   Poet of the Harlem Renaissance whose work, inspired by the rhythms of jazz and the blues, dealt with the joys and sorrows of African-Americans.

Way Down South in Dixie
(Bruised body high in air)
I asked the white Lord Jesus
What was the use of prayer.

Way Down South in Dixie
(Break the heart of me)
Love is a naked shadow
On a gnarled and naked tree.

Other poems looked to the future with an expectation for change and for new choices, as in "I, Too" (1925).

I, too, sing America.

I am the darker brother.
They send me
To eat in the kitchen
When company comes,
But I laugh,
And eat well,
And grow strong.

Tomorrow
I'll sit at the table
When company comes.
Nobody'll dare
Say to me,
"Eat in the kitchen,"
Then.
Besides
They'll see
How beautiful I am
And be ashamed.

I, too, am America.

In the early 1930s, as the Harlem Renaissance waned and the Depression deepened, Hughes, like other American intellectuals, turned to socialism. He traveled again and began writing short stories and plays. Few theaters at that time would stage works by or about African-Americans, and few hired African-American actors. Hughes, therefore, chose to use his prestige and his time to create black theater companies in Harlem, Los Angeles, and Chicago.

Hughes's writings poured forth in a near-torrential stream. By the end of his life, in 1967, he had produced ten volumes of poetry; sixty-six short stories; some twenty plays, musicals, and operas; two autobiographical volumes; more than a hundred published essays, both serious and humorous; and several novels, histories, and children's books. The outcome of his devotion to writing and his choice to focus on the African-American experience was not only that Hughes established a prominent place for himself among American authors of his time. Also, and perhaps more significant, he helped to define the Harlem Renaissance, and he greatly encouraged the development of African-American poetry, fiction, drama, and other writing.

voice of the people, as he sometimes used folk language to convey powerful images. His subject, as for many Harlem artists, was often the black experience (see Individual Choices: Langston Hughes). Zora Neale Hurston came from a poor southern family, won a scholarship to Barnard College, and began her long writing career with several short stories in the 1920s. Jean Toomer's novel *Cane* (1923) has been praised as "the most impressive product of the Negro Renaissance." In it, Toomer, the grandson of P. B. S. Pinchback, combined poetry and prose to produce sketches and short stories dealing with African-Americans in rural Georgia and Washington, D.C.

The Renaissance included **jazz,** which was becoming a central element in distinctly American

jazz   Style of music developed in America in the early twentieth century, characterized by strong, flexible rhythms and improvisation on basic melodies.

♦ Zora Neale Hurston, whose long and prolific writing career began during the Harlem Renaissance, grew up in an all-black town in Florida. She studied anthropology with Franz Boas, one of the leading figures in that field, and her writings included both fiction and ethnography. *The Beinecke Rare Book and Manuscript Library, Yale University.*

♦ Louis Armstrong, born in 1900, first began to play the trumpet in New Orleans but emerged as a leading innovator in jazz after 1924, when he joined Fletcher Henderson's orchestra in New York. Some of his recordings from the 1920s are among the most original and imaginative contributions to jazz. *Frank Driggs Collection.*

music. Jazz developed in the early twentieth century, drawing from several patterns in African-American music, particularly the blues and ragtime (see page 569). Created and nurtured by African-American musicians in southern cities, especially New Orleans, jazz had been introduced to northern and white audiences by 1917. It became so popular that the 1920s have been called the Jazz Age. Jazz also began to influence leading white composers, notably George Gershwin, whose *Rhapsody in Blue* (1924) brought jazz into the symphony halls. Some attacked the new sound, however, claiming it excited "the basic human instincts" and encouraged people to abandon their self-restraint, especially with regard to sex. Despite—or because of—such condemnation, the wail of the saxophone became as much a part of the 1920s as the roar of the automobile and the flicker of the movie projector.

Louis "Satchmo" Armstrong emerged as a leading jazz innovator whose trumpet playing could transform the most ordinary tune into something original and compelling. He performed in some of the top jazz groups, beginning in 1922 with King Oliver's ensemble in Chicago and later in New York with Fletcher Henderson's orchestra. Bessie Smith, the "Empress of the Blues," was the outstanding vocalist of the decade. The great black jazz musicians of the 1920s—Armstrong, Henderson, Ferdinand

"Jelly Roll" Morton, Smith, and others—drew white audiences into black neighborhoods to hear them. As increasing numbers of whites went "slumming" to Harlem, the area came to be associated with exotic nightlife and glittering jazz clubs, of which the Cotton Club was best known. There Edward Kennedy "Duke" Ellington came in 1927, to lead the club band until 1931, and there he began to develop the works that made him a respected twentieth-century American composer.

The sparkle of the Cotton Club seemed remote from the experience of most African Americans, but one Harlem black leader affected black people throughout the country and beyond. **Marcus Garvey,** born in Jamaica, advocated a form of **black separatism.** His organization, the Universal Negro Improvement Association (UNIA), founded in 1914, stressed racial pride, the importance of Africa, and racial solidarity across national boundaries. After World War I, UNIA offices appeared in many black urban ghettos. Garvey supporters argued that

---

Marcus Garvey   Jamaican black nationalist active in America in the 1920s.

black separatism   Doctrine of cultural separation of blacks from white society.

whites would always be racist. Therefore, they contended, blacks from around the world needed to assist Africans in overthrowing colonial rule and building a strong African state, which would develop in prestige and power to become a symbol of black accomplishment. Garvey established a steamship company, the **Black Star Line,** which he hoped would carry American blacks to Africa, and he tried to promote other black economic enterprises. The UNIA message of racial pride and solidarity attracted wide support among blacks in the United States—especially in the cities—and also in the Caribbean and in Africa.

Black integrationist leaders, however, condemned UNIA for its separatism. The NAACP, especially W. E. B. Du Bois, editor of *Crisis,* took the lead among African Americans in opposing Garvey, arguing that the first task facing blacks was integration and equality in the United States. Garvey and Du Bois each labeled the other a traitor to his race.

Federal officials eventually charged Garvey with irregularities in his fund-raising for the Black Star Line, and he was convicted of mail fraud in 1923. He spent two years in jail and then was deported to his native Jamaica. Garvey continued to lead UNIA in exile and the organization persisted, but most of the local organizations lost members and influence.

"Flaming Youth"

Although African-Americans created jazz, those who danced to it, in the popular imagination of the 1920s, were white—a male college student, clad in a swank raccoon-skin coat with a hip flask of illegal liquor in his pocket, and his female counterpart, the uninhibited **flapper** with bobbed hair and a daringly short skirt. This stereotype of "flaming youth," the title of a popular novel, reflected startling changes among many white, college-age youths of middle- or upper-class background.

The prosperity of the 1920s allowed many middle-class families to send their children to college. On the eve of World War I, just over 3 percent of the population aged 18 to 24 were enrolled in college. By 1930, that proportion had more than doubled. Larger increases came among women than among men. In 1916, 30 percent of all bachelor's degrees went to women, but in 1930, women received 40 percent. On campus, students reshaped colleges into youth centers, where football games and dances assumed as much significance as examinations and term papers.

♦ On the one hundred fiftieth anniversary of the Declaration of Independence, *Life* presented this cover parodying the famous painting, the "Spirit of '76," by depicting the "Spirit of '26"—an uninhibited flapper, a jazz saxophonist and drummer, and banners with the snappy sayings of the day. The caption reads: "One Hundred and Forty-three Years of LIBERTY and Seven Years of PROHIBITION." *Harvard College Library.*

For some young women—especially college students but also others from urban backgrounds—the changes of the 1920s seemed especially dramatic. Called "flappers" for the flapping sound made by their fashionably unfastened galoshes, young women scandalized their elders by skirts that stopped at the knee, stockings rolled below the knee, short hair often dyed black, and generous amounts of rouge and lipstick. Many observers assumed that the outrageous look reflected outrageous behavior, and that suddenly young women were ignoring the insistence of their parents' generation on chastity. In fact, women's sexual activity outside marriage had begun to increase before the war, especially among working-class women and radicals. In the 1920s, such changes began to affect college and high school students, most of them from middle-class families. About half of the women who

Black Star Line Steamship company founded by Marcus Garvey to carry blacks to Africa; Garvey was convicted of mail fraud in connection with its finances and imprisoned in 1923.

flapper Name given in the 1920s to a young woman with short hair and short skirts who discarded old-fashioned standards of dress and behavior.

came of age during the 1920s had intercourse before marriage, a marked increase from prewar patterns.

Such changes in behavior were often linked to the automobile. It brought greater freedom to young people, for behind the wheel they had no chaperone and could go where they wanted. Sometimes they went to one of the many **speakeasies.** Before Prohibition, few women who valued their reputation entered saloons. Prohibition, however, seemed to glamorize drinking. Now men and women alike went to speakeasies, to drink and smoke together, and to dance to popular music derived from jazz. While some adults criticized the frivolities of the young, others emulated them, launching the first American youth culture. F. Scott Fitzgerald later called the years after 1922 "a children's party taken over by elders."

Traditional America Roars Back

- How did some Americans try to restore traditional social expectations and values during the 1920s?
- What were the outcomes of their choices?

Many Americans, while embracing some changes of the 1920s—from cars and electrical appliances to movies and crossword puzzles—nonetheless felt threatened by the pace of change and the upheaval in social values that often seemed centered in the cities. Some historians have seen the 1920s as a cultural battleground between rural and urban values, but this explanation is too simplistic. Rural people often embraced the changes of the Roaring Twenties, and city-dwellers often gave full support to efforts to preserve traditional values. In nearly every case, these efforts to stop the tide of change dated to the prewar era, as some Americans sensed even then a threat to their way of life from immigration or new patterns of thought and behavior. In the 1920s, however, several such movements came to fruition at the same time as Fitzgerald's age of excess.

Prohibition

Prohibition came to epitomize the cultural struggle to preserve white, old-stock Protestant values in the face of challenge. Spearheaded by the Anti-Saloon League (see page 643), prohibition advocates gained strength throughout the Progressive era. They con-

vinced Congress to pass a temporary prohibition measure in 1917, as a war measure to conserve grain. A more important victory for the "dry" forces came late that year, when Congress adopted and sent to the states the **Eighteenth Amendment,** prohibiting the manufacture, sale, or transportation of alcoholic beverages. Intense and single-minded lobbying by dry advocates persuaded three-fourths of the state legislatures to ratify, and the amendment took effect in January 1920. It was, in some ways, the last gasp of the reforming zeal that had generated much of progressivism.

Many Americans simply ignored the Eighteenth Amendment from the beginning, and it grew less popular the longer it lasted. By 1926, a poll indicated that only 19 percent of Americans supported Prohibition, 50 percent wanted it modified, and 31 percent favored outright **repeal.** Nonetheless, Prohibition remained the law, if not the reality, from 1920 until 1933, when the Twenty-first Amendment finally repealed it. Even after 1933, some states continued to ban alcohol within their borders.

Prohibition did reduce drinking and it apparently produced a decline in drunkenness and in the number of deaths from alcoholism. It was probably most effective among those groups and in those areas that had provided its greatest support. It was never well enforced anywhere, however, and was pretty much ignored in most cities. Congress never provided enough money for more than token federal enforcement, and most city police didn't even try because of the immensity of the task and the press of other duties. New York State admitted the impossibility of enforcing Prohibition by repealing its enforcement act in 1923. That same year, a federal agent visited major cities to see how long it took to get an illegal drink: it took only 35 seconds in New Orleans, 3 minutes in Detroit, and 3 minutes 10 seconds in New York City.

Prohibition produced unintended consequences. Whereas neighborhood saloons had often functioned as social centers for working-class and lower-middle-class men, the new speakeasies were often

---

speakeasy A place for the illegal sale and consumption of liquor during Prohibition.

Eighteenth Amendment Amendment to the Constitution ratified in 1919 forbidding the manufacture, sale, or transportation of alcoholic beverages.

repeal Annulment of an official act; repeal of a constitutional amendment requires a new amendment.

more glamorous, attracting an upper- and middle-class clientele, women as well as men. **Bootlegging**—production and sale of illegal beverages—flourished. Some bootleggers brewed only small amounts of beer and sold it to their neighbors. In the cities, however, the thirst for alcohol provided criminals with a fresh and lucrative source of income, part of which they used to buy influence in city politics and protection from police.

Congress provided funds for only about two thousand enforcement agents nationwide. By contrast, in Chicago, **Al Capone**'s gang alone counted nearly a thousand members and, in 1927, took in more than $100 million—$60 million of it from bootlegging. The scar-faced Capone realized such huge gains in part by systematically eliminating the competition, something he accomplished through violence unprecedented in American cities. Gang warfare raged in Chicago throughout the 1920s, producing some five hundred slayings. Despite Capone's undoubted role in murders, bootlegging, and other illegal activities, his extensive political influence kept him immune from local prosecution. Only in 1931 did federal officials finally convict him of income-tax evasion and send him to prison.

The blood-drenched gangs of Chicago had their counterparts elsewhere, as other gangsters—many of recent immigrant background, including Italians, Irish, Germans, and Jews—followed similar bullet-riddled paths to wealth. Profits from bootlegging not only provided bribes to police and political officials but also bought fast cars and submachine guns for gang warfare. The gangs found other sources of easy money, too, including gambling, prostitution, and **racketeering.** Through racketeering they gained power in some labor unions. Some Americans regarded these developments as the result of Prohibition—a policy that the federal government was unwilling either to enforce or to repeal. For other Americans, however, the gangs, killings, and corruption confirmed their long-standing distrust of cities and immigrants, and they clung to the vision of a dry America as the best hope for renewing traditional values.

Fundamentalism and the Crusade Against Evolution

Another effort to maintain traditional values came with the growth of fundamentalist Protestantism. **Fundamentalism** emerged from a conflict between Christian modernism and **orthodoxy.** Where modernists tried to reconcile their religious beliefs with modern science, fundamentalists rejected anything incompatible with a literal reading of the Scriptures and argued that the Bible's every word is the revealed word of God. The fundamentalist movement grew throughout the first quarter of the twentieth century, led by such figures as Billy Sunday, a baseball player turned evangelist.

In the early 1920s, some fundamentalists focused especially on **evolution** as contrary to the Bible. Biologists and geologists cite the theory of evolution to explain how the world and living things have developed over millions of years, but the Bible states that God created the world and all living things in six days. Thus, fundamentalists saw in evolution not just a challenge to the Bible's account of creation, but also a challenge to religion itself.

William Jennings Bryan, the former Democratic presidential candidate and secretary of state, fixed on the evolution controversy after 1920. Until his death, he provided fundamentalists with their greatest champion. His energy, eloquence, and enormous following—especially in the rural South—guaranteed that the issue received wide attention. "It is better," Bryan wrote, "to trust in the Rock of Ages than to know the age of rocks; it is better for one to know that he is close to the Heavenly Father than to know how far the stars in the heavens are apart." Bryan played a central role in the most famous of the disputes over evolution—the **Scopes trial.**

---

bootlegging   Illegal production, distribution, or sale of liquor.

Al Capone   Italian-born American gangster who ruthlessly ruled the Chicago underworld until he was imprisoned for tax evasion in 1931.

racketeering   Commission of crimes such as extortion, loansharking, bribery, and obstruction of justice in the course of illegal business activities.

fundamentalism   An organized, evangelical movement originating in the United States in the 1920s in opposition to liberalism and secularism.

orthodoxy   Traditional or established doctrine of faith.

evolution   The central organizing theorem of the biological sciences, which holds that organisms change over generations, mainly as a result of natural selection; it includes the concept that humans evolved from nonhuman ancestors.

Scopes trial   Trial in 1925 in which a high school biology teacher was prosecuted for teaching evolution in violation of Tennessee law; it raised issues concerning the place of religion in American education.

In March 1925, the Tennessee legislature passed a law making it illegal for any public school teacher to teach evolution. When the **American Civil Liberties Union (ACLU)** offered to defend a teacher willing to present a test case against the law, John T. Scopes, a young biology teacher in Dayton, Tennessee, accepted. Bryan volunteered to assist the local prosecutors, who faced an ACLU defense team that including the famous attorney **Clarence Darrow.** Bryan claimed that the only issue was the right of the people to regulate public education in the interest of morality, but Darrow insisted he was there to prevent "bigots and ignoramuses from controlling the education of the United States."

The court proceedings were carried nationwide, live, via radio. Toward the end of the trial, in a surprising move, Darrow called Bryan to the witness stand as an authority on the Bible. By examining him on the Bible and modern science, Darrow hoped to demonstrate the problems of requiring classroom teachers to adhere to the logic of the Bible. Under Darrow's withering questioning, Bryan revealed that he knew little about findings in archaeology, geology, and linguistics that cast doubt on Biblical accounts, and he also admitted, to the dismay of many fundamentalists, that he did not always interpret the words of the Bible literally. "Bryan was broken," one reporter wrote. "Darrow never spared him. It was masterful, but it was pitiful." Bryan died a few days later.

Scopes was found guilty, but the Tennessee Supreme Court threw out his sentence on a technicality, preventing appeal. The Tennessee law remained in force until 1968, and constraints on teaching evolution still exist in places.

Nativism and Immigration Restriction

Prohibition and laws against teaching evolution represent efforts to use government to define individual behavior and beliefs. Laws designed to restrict immigration had a similar origin, resulting in major part from nativist antagonism against immigrants, especially those from southern and eastern Europe who had come to the United States in ever-increasing numbers before the war (see pages 558–560). After the war the flood resumed, with 430,000 immigrants in 1920 and 805,000 in 1921, more than half from southern and eastern Europe.

Since the 1890s, some groups had urged Congress to cut off immigration, but earlier efforts met either Congressional indifference or presidential vetoes. However, the disquieting presence of so many German-Americans during the war with Germany, the Red Scare and fear of foreign radicalism, and the continued influx of poor immigrants at a time of growing unemployment all combined in 1921 to win greater support for restriction. The result was an emergency act to limit immigration from any country to 3 percent of the number of people from that country living in the United States at the time of the 1910 census.

The act of 1921 slowed the arrival of immigrants, but advocates of restriction considered it only a stop-gap measure. A permanent law, the **National Origins Act** of 1924, limited total immigration to 150,000 people each year, with quotas for each country based on 2 percent of the number of white Americans whose ancestors came from that country, based for the time being on the 1890 census. The law thus attempted to freeze the ethnic composition of the nation. Its intent was to stop immigrants from southern and eastern Europe, who, nativists argued, made less desirable citizens than people from northern and western Europe. The law completely excluded Asians, upsetting relations with Japan, but it permitted unrestricted immigration from Canada and Latin America.

Throughout the 1920s, nativism and discrimination flourished, sometimes taking violent forms. In West Frankfort, Illinois, for example, during three days in August 1920, rioting townspeople beat and stoned Italians, pulling them out of their homes, and setting the houses on fire. Nativist-inspired discrimination was more subtle. Exclusive eastern colleges placed quotas on the number of Jews admitted each year, and some companies refused to hire Jews. In 1920, Henry Ford, in the *Dearborn Independent* magazine for Ford dealers, began to accuse international Jewish bankers of controlling the American econ-

---

American Civil Liberties Union Private organization founded in 1920 that donates its services in cases involving individual rights.

Clarence Darrow Lawyer known for his defense of unpopular causes; his merciless cross-examination of Bryan in the Scopes trial made the argument against evolution look weak.

National Origins Act 1924 law establishing quotas that discouraged immigration from southern and eastern Europe and encouraged immigration from Scandinavia and western Europe; it also prohibited Asian immigration.

omy. He soon broadened his attack to suggest an international Jewish conspiracy to control not only banking but virtually everything from baseball to Bolshevism. The published accusations continued until Aaron Sapiro, an attorney, sued Ford for libel and challenged him to prove his claims. In 1927, Ford retracted his charges and apologized.

The Ku Klux Klan

Nativism, anti-Catholicism, anti-Semitism, and fear of radicalism all contributed to the spectacular growth of the Ku Klux Klan in the early 1920s. The original Klan, created during Reconstruction to intimidate former slaves, had long since died out. D. W. Griffith's hugely popular film, *The Birth of a Nation,* released in 1915, glorified the old Klan and focused attention on efforts to resurrect it. Formed by William Simmons, a small-time salesman and organizer for fraternal orders, the new Klan portrayed itself as a patriotic order devoted to America, Protestant Christianity, and white supremacy.

Growth came slowly, to only 5,000 members by 1920. Then new recruiting technique offered local organizers $4 of every $10 initiation fee. This incentive combined with the postwar wave of nativism and antiradicalism to produce rapid growth. Frederick Lewis Allen described its appeal this way:

> Its white robe and hood, its flaming cross, its secrecy, and the preposterous vocabulary of its ritual could be made the vehicle for all that infantile love of hocus-pocus and mummery, that lust for secret adventure, which survives in the adult whose lot is cast in drab places. Here was a chance to dress up the village bigot and let him be a Knight of the Invisible Empire.

Declaring itself to be the defender of old-fashioned Protestant morality, the Klan attacked Catholics, Jews, immigrants, and blacks, along with bootleggers, corrupt politicians, and gamblers. Feeding on the insecurities of the early 1920s, the Klan attracted as many as 5 million members nationwide by 1925. In rural areas, the Klan's terror was sometimes carried out by **nightriders,** who roved country roads under cover of darkness to carry out beatings, kidnappings, torture, brandings, floggings, and even murder.

The Klan was strong not only in the South but also in the Midwest, West, and Southwest, and it mushroomed in towns and cities as well as rural areas. The organization participated actively in local

♦ This image is from a Ku Klux Klan pamphlet published in the mid-1920s, when the Klan claimed as many as five million members nationwide. The Klan portrayed itself as defending traditional, white, Protestant America against Jews, Catholics, and African-Americans. *Private collection.*

politics, with its leaders sometimes exerting powerful political influence in communities and in state governments, most notably Texas, Oklahoma, Oregon, and Indiana. In Oklahoma, the Klan led a successful impeachment campaign against a governor who tried to restrict their nightriding. In Oregon, the Klan claimed responsibility for a 1922 law aimed at eliminating Catholic schools, but the Supreme Court eventually ruled the law unconstitutional.

Although Klan members in 1923 hailed themselves as "the return of the Puritans in this corrupt, and jazz-mad age," extensive corruption underlay the Klan's self-righteous rhetoric. Some Klan leaders joined primarily for the profits, both legal (from recruiting) and illegal (mostly from political payoffs). And some lived personal lives in stark contrast to the morality they preached. In 1921, Simmons's chief publicity agents were revealed to be living together without being married. In 1925, D. C. Stephenson, Grand Dragon of Indiana and one of the most prominent Klan leaders, was convicted of second-degree murder after the death of a woman who accused him of raping her. When the governor refused to pardon him, Stephenson produced records that proved the corruption of the governor,

---

nightriders Bands of masked white men associated with the Ku Klux Klan who roamed rural areas at night, terrorizing and murdering blacks.

a member of Congress, the mayor of Indianapolis, and other officials endorsed by the Klan. Thereafter, Klan membership fell sharply, not only because of the Stephenson episode but also factional disputes and further evidence of fraud and corruption.

Race, Class, and Gender in the 1920s

- During the 1920s, what expectations and constraints influenced choices faced by American Indians, Mexicans, working people, women, and homosexuals?
- What were the outcomes of their choices?

The "spiritual emancipation" that Alain Locke ascribed to the Harlem Renaissance, on the one hand, and the terror of Klan nightriders, on the other, represent polar extremes for race relations in the 1920s. For most people of color, the reality of their daily lives fell somewhere in between. For working people, the 1920s represented what Irving Bernstein, a labor historian, has termed "the lean years," when many gains from the Progressive era and World War I were lost and when unions remained largely on the defensive. For women, the 1920s opened with a political victory in the form of suffrage, but the unity developed in support of that measure soon broke down.

Race Relations: North, South, and West

Race relations changed little during the 1920s. Terror against African-Americans continued after the rioting and bloodshed of 1919 (see page 697). In 1921, nine whites and twenty-one blacks were killed and several hundred injured in racial fighting in Tulsa, Oklahoma. In 1925, a mob of whites attacked the home of a black physician soon after he moved into a white Detroit neighborhood. In Mississippi in 1929, two thousand people watched a lynch mob burn an accused black rapist, but a coroner's jury found the man's death due to "unknown causes."

The NAACP tried to secure a federal anti-lynching law throughout the 1920s but southern legislators defeated them each time, arguing against any federal interference in the police power of the states. As part of its efforts to combat lynching, the NAACP tried to educate the public by publicizing crimes against blacks. A typical handbill presented the disgraceful record.

◆ African-Americans intensified their efforts to put an end to lynching. This protest parade was held in Washington, D.C., in 1922. The NAACP's efforts to secure a federal antilynching law, however, were repeatedly defeated by southerners in Congress. *UPI/Bettmann.*

THE SHAME OF AMERICA. . . . Do you know that the United States is the Only Land on Earth where human beings are BURNED AT THE STAKE? . . . In Four Years, 1918–1921, Twenty-Eight People Were Publicly BURNED BY AMER-ICAN MOBS. . . 3,436 People Lynched 1889 to 1922.

Discrimination and violence were not directed only at blacks, Jews, and Italians. In the West and Southwest, the most frequent victims of racism were American Indians and those of Asian and Latino descent.

Californians had long advocated exclusion of Asian immigrants and had led the way among western states in passing a series of laws discriminating against Asian immigrants and Asian-Americans. Westerners, especially Californians, had also compiled a lengthy record of violence and discriminatory legislation aimed at Asians (see pages 529–533). Senator James D. Phelan, leader of the California Democratic party, based his unsuccessful reelection campaign in 1920 almost entirely on what he depicted as the dire threat from Japan. *Shadows of the West,* a film produced by the California American Legion in 1920, borrowed from *Birth of a Nation* to portray Japanese-Americans as spies and sex fiends preying on innocent white girls, whose only hope of rescue was the American Legion. In 1920, California voters voted by 3 to 1 to approve an initiative forbidding Asian immigrants to own or lease land in

California, an effort to close the loopholes in a 1913 law (see page 652). Some California nativists also sought a constitutional amendment to remove citizenship from Americans of Asian descent.

Beginnings of Change in Federal Indian Policy

In the early 1920s, American Indians experienced an intensification of previous allotment and assimilationist policies (see pages 533–534). Resistance to those policies, however, sometimes succeeded and laid the basis for a significant shift in federal policy in the 1930s. In the administration of President Warren G. Harding, Interior Secretary Albert Fall tried to lease parts of reservations to white developers and especially to extinguish the Pueblo Indians' title to sizable lands along the Rio Grande. Opposition to Fall's schemes came both from assimilationist-oriented reformers and from some who had begun to question assimilation. Fall's proposals were either dropped or modified. Efforts to reverse directives from the Bureau of Indian Affairs (BIA) intended to suppress Indian religious ceremonies were not so successful.

The Pueblo land question led directly to the organization of the **American Indian Defense Association (AIDA),** created in 1923 by John Collier, an eastern social worker, to support the Pueblos. Collier and the AIDA soon emerged as the leading voice calling for changes in federal Indian policy. Their goals were an end to land allotments, better health and educational services on the reservations, creation of tribal governments, and tolerance of Indian religious ceremonies and other customs. In sum, they proposed a major policy change, from assimilation to recognition of Indian cultures and values.

The political pressure applied by the AIDA and similar groups, as well as political efforts by Indians themselves, secured several new laws favorable to Indians. One measure, in 1924, extended full citizenship to all Indians—about one-third of the total—who were still not citizens. Some had been reluctant to accept citizenship for fear of losing their tribal rights, so the law included provisions specifically protecting those rights. In 1926, Secretary of the Interior Hubert Work ordered a comprehensive study of Indian life. Completed in 1928, the report described widespread poverty and health problems among Indians, demonstrated the lack of adequate health care and education on the reservations, and condemned allotment as the single most important cause of Indian hardship.

Mexicans in California and the Southwest

California and the Southwest, home to Mexican and Mexican-American families since the region was part of Mexico (see pages 533–534), attracted growing numbers of Mexican immigrants in the 1920s. Many Mexicans went north to escape the revolution and civil war that devastated their nation from 1910 into the 1920s. Nearly one Mexican in ten may have fled to the United States between 1910 and 1930, nearly 700,000 of them legally and probably as many more illegally. More than half went to Texas, but by the mid-1920s, increasing numbers arrived in California. Between 1920 and 1930, the Mexican population of Los Angeles more than doubled. Including undocumented immigrants and those missed by census takers, it may have expanded as much as fivefold. Southern California and south Texas also experienced large increases in their Anglo populations during the same years.

Population changes in southern California and south Texas came as the agricultural economies of those regions also changed. In south Texas, some cattle ranches were converted to farms, especially for cotton, but for fruit and vegetables too. The 1920s saw dramatic increases in commercial production and sale of fruit and vegetables, as fewer people raised their own but more people ate them. By 1925, the Southwest produced 40 percent of the nation's fruits and vegetables, crops that were highly labor intensive. In the late 1920s, Mexicans made up 80 to 85 percent of farm laborers in southern California and south Texas. These changes in population and economy reshaped relations between Anglos and Mexicans.

In south Texas, many Anglo newcomers cared little about the accommodations worked out between ranch owners—mostly Anglo—and Mexicans in the late nineteenth century. Looking on Mexicans as a "partly colored race," white settlers tried to import elements of southern black-white relations—sharecropping, disfranchisement, and segregation.

American Indian Defense Association Organization founded in 1923 to defend the rights of American Indians; it pushed for an end to allotment and a return to tribal government.

◆ Throughout California and the southwest, as the number of Latino residents grew, so too did their organizations—including civil rights organizations, political groups, labor unions, social associations, and mutual-benefit societies. This banner graced the meeting hall of one such organization in the late 1920s or early 1930s. *The Oakland Museum.*

Disfranchisement was relatively unsuccessful, but schools and other social institutions were segregated in several areas despite Mexican opposition. Efforts organized through the League of United Latin American Citizens (LULAC) occasionally halted discrimination by business—but only occasionally.

In California, Mexican workers' efforts to organize and strike for better pay and working conditions often sparked violent opposition. Strikes involving thousands of workers in the early 1920s were broken quickly and brutally. They began organizing on a larger scale in 1928, with formation of the *Confederacion de Uniones Obreras Mexicanas*, an umbrella group for various unions in southern California. Local authorities arrested and often beat strikers, and growers' armies of private guards beat or kidnapped them. Leaders found themselves subject to deportation. Nonetheless, Mexican labor had become vital to agriculture, and growers adamantly opposed any proposals to restrict immigration from Mexico. The landowners made certain that the revised quota law permitted unlimited immigration from the Western Hemisphere.

Labor on the Defensive

Difficulties in establishing unions among Mexican workers mirrored a larger failure of unions in the 1920s. When unions tried to recover lost purchasing power by striking in 1919 and 1920, they nearly all failed. After 1921, business took advantage of the conservative political climate to challenge Progressive era legislation benefiting workers. The Supreme Court responded by limiting workers' rights, voiding laws that eliminated child labor, and striking down minimum wages for women and children.

Many companies undertook anti-union drives. Arguing that unions were no longer necessary and had become either corrupt or radical, some employers used the term **American Plan** to describe their refusal to recognize unions as representing employees. At the same time, many companies initiated an approach known as "welfare capitalism." The strategy was to provide workers with benefit programs like insurance, retirement pensions, cafeterias, paid vacations, and stock purchase plans. Such innovations stemmed both from genuine concern about workers' well-being and from the expectation that such improvements would increase productivity and discourage unionization.

Only the railroad unions made significant gains in the 1920s. At the end of the war, railroads were under federal management. The **Esch-Cummins Act** of 1920 restored private ownership but railroad unions disliked the law's provisions for labor relations. They took a leading role in forming the Conference for Progressive Political Action (CPPA) in 1922. The CPPA, in turn, initiated efforts to create a revamped, Progressive party in 1924. The **Railway Labor Act** of 1926 was primarily a response to these political activities. It drew on wartime experiences (see page 682) to establish collective bargaining for railroads, with a board of mediation to intervene if the parties could not agree. By giving the railway unions most of their demands, the act effectively removed them from politics.

The gains of the railroad unions were unique. The 1920s marked the first period of prosperity since the

---

American Plan   Term used by some employers in the 1920s to describe their policy of refusing to negotiate with unions.

Esch-Cummins Act   1920 law restoring railroads to private ownership after World War I and setting up an official Railway Labor Board to mediate disputes.

Railway Labor Act   1926 law that replaced the Railway Labor Board with a board of mediation only loosely connected with the federal government.

1830s when union membership declined, falling from 5 million in 1920 to 3.6 million in 1929, a 28 percent decline at a time when the total work force increased by 15 percent. The slide was the outcome of a number of factors: hostile government policies, welfare capitalism, the American Plan, and lost strikes, among others. Prohibition devastated once-strong unions of brewery workers and bartenders. Some unions suffered from internal battles. For example, the International Ladies' Garment Workers' Union lost two-thirds of its members during power struggles between Socialists and Communists.

The Communists sought influence and power within other unions, but the **American Communist Party (CP)** never gained the number of supporters characteristic of the Socialist party before World War I. In 1919, the two predecessors to the CP claimed fifty to sixty thousand members. After a decade that included the Red Scare, deportations, and several internal conflicts, the CP counted only 9,300 members. Always closely tied to the Communist leadership of the Soviet Union, the CP labored strenuously to organize workers throughout the 1920s. William Z. Foster, leader of the unsuccessful steel strike in 1919, formed the Trade Union Education League (TUEL) in 1920, joined the CP, and tried in his words to "bore from within"—that is, to radicalize AFL unions through the TUEL. In 1928, in response to prompting from the **Comintern,** American CP leaders created the Trade Union Unity League (TUUL) to challenge the AFL with new, separate unions. The TUUL tried to organize the unskilled, people of color, women, and others outside AFL craft unions, but had little success.

Changes in Women's Lives

The attention given to the flapper in accounts of the 1920s should not conceal important changes in the nature of women's gender roles during those years. Significant changes occurred in two areas: the size and structure of the family, and politics.

Marriage among white middle-class women and men came increasingly to be valued as a companionship between two partners. Although the ideal of marriage was often expressed in terms of man and woman taking equal responsibility for a relationship, the actual responsibility for the smooth functioning of the family typically fell on the woman. In the 1920s, however, many women increased their control over decisions about childbearing.

Usually in American history, prosperity has brought increases in the birthrate. In the 1920s, however, changing social values together with more options for birth control resulted in fewer births. The average woman who reached her child-bearing years during and immediately after the Civil War gave birth to more than five children, and one woman in seven then had ten children or more. In contrast, women who came of child-bearing age in the 1910s and 1920s were distinctive in three ways when compared with women of both earlier and later time periods: (1) they had fewer children on the average, (2) more of them chose to have no children at all, and (3) far fewer had very large families (see Figure 23.2).

The declining birthrate in the 1920s reflected, in part, some degree of success for earlier efforts to secure wider availability of birth-control information and devices. More women used diaphragms rather than relying on the males to use condoms. Margaret Sanger continued to carry the banner in the battle to extend birth-control information (see page 641), and she persuaded more doctors to join her efforts. As the birth control movement gained the backing of male physicians, it became a more respectable, middle-class reform movement. The American Medical Association, the New York Academy of Medicine, and the New York Obstetrical Society in 1925 declared their support for birth control, and the Rockefeller Foundation began to fund medical research into contraception methods. Nonetheless, until 1936, federal law restricted public distribution of information about contraception.

Although the lives of many middle-class women lightened with the introduction of labor-saving devices such as vacuum cleaners and electric irons, working-class women still spent long days struggling to maintain families with thrifty economizing. As before, these women and sometimes their children often worked outside the home, not because they sought fulfilling careers, but because the family needed the additional income. The proportion of women working for wages remained quite stable during the 1920s, at about one in four. The proportion of married women working for wages increased, though, from 23 percent of the female labor force in 1920 to 29 percent in 1930.

American Communist Party Party organized in 1919. Its object was to destroy capitalism.

Comintern International association of Communist political parties in all countries, headquartered in the Soviet Union.

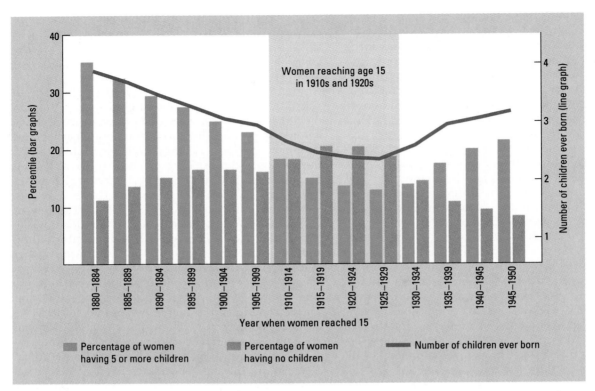

◆ **FIGURE 23.2 Changing Patterns of Childbearing Among Women** This figure depicts three different choices regarding family size: (1) the number of children born to women ever married, (2) the percentage of women having large families, and (3) and the percentage of women having no children at all.

Note: Child-bearing ages are considered to be between 15 and 45.

Sources: For women born in 1914 and before, Series B42–48, Percent Distribution of Ever-Married Women (Survivors of Birth Cohorts of 1835–39 to 1920–24) by Race and By Number of Children Ever Born, as Reported in Censuses of 1910, 1940, 1950, 1960, and 1970, U.S. Bureau of the Census, *Historical Statistics of the United States, Colonial Times to 1970,* Bicentennial Edition, 2 vols. (Washington, D.C.: U.S. Government Printing Office, 1975), I:53. For women born in 1916 and after, Table 270, Children Ever Born and Marital Status of Women by Age, Race, and Spanish Origin: 1980, U.S. Bureau of the Census, *1980 Census of Population: Detailed Population Characteristics: United States Summary,* (Washington, D.C.: U.S. Government Printing Office, 1984), p. 1–103.

Perhaps the most publicized event in women's lives was national woman suffrage. In June 1919, by a narrow margin, Congress proposed the **Nineteenth Amendment,** to enfranchise women over 21, and sent it to the states for ratification. After a grueling, state-by-state battle, ratification came in August 1920, enabling women to participate in the 1920 election.

As women began to participate in the political mainstream, the unity of the suffrage movement quickly disintegrated in squabbles over the proper political role for women. Both major political parties soon modified the structure of their national committees to provide that each state be represented by a national committeeman and a national committeewoman, and both parties welcomed women as vot-

> **Nineteenth Amendment** Amendment to the Constitution in 1920 that prohibited federal or state governments from restricting the right to vote on account of sex.

ers. Some suffrage activists, however, joined the League of Women Voters, a nonpartisan group committed to social and political reform. The Congressional Union, led by Alice Paul (see page 642), converted itself into the National Woman's Party and, after 1923, focused its efforts largely on securing an **Equal Rights Amendment** to the Constitution. The League of Women Voters disagreed, arguing that such an amendment would endanger laws that provided special rights and protections for women. In the end, woman suffrage did not dramatically change either women or politics.

Development of Gay and Lesbian Subcultures

In the 1920s, gay and lesbian subcultures became more established and, in some cities, including New York, Chicago, New Orleans, and Baltimore, relatively open. *The Captive*, a play about lesbians, opened in New York in 1926, and some movies included unmistakable references to gays or lesbians. Novels with gay and lesbian characters circulated in the late 1920s and early 1930s. By the late 1920s, some nightclub acts included material about gays and lesbians in performances intended for audiences that were largely heterosexual.

A relatively open gay and lesbian community emerged in Harlem, mostly of African-Americans. Some popular blues singers referred to gay men and lesbians in songs, and some prominent figures of the Renaissance were gay or bisexual. In the early 1930s, the nation's largest gay and lesbian event was the annual Hamilton Lodge drag ball in Harlem, and at the height of its popularity, as many as 7,000 revelers and spectators of all races attended.

At the same time, however, more and more psychiatrists and psychologists were labeling homosexuality a **perversion.** Shortly before World War I, as the work of Sigmund Freud became well known, the view that homosexuality was physiological in origin was replaced by a different explanation. Most psychiatrists and psychologists now labeled homosexuality a sexual disorder that required a cure, though no "cure" ever proved viable. Thus, Freud may have been a liberating influence with regard to heterosexual relations, but proved harmful for same-sex relations.

This new characterization of homosexuality had a number of social ramifications. For example, in 1919, during a U.S. Navy investigation at Newport,

Rhode Island, officers recruited enlisted men to investigate homosexuals. Throughout most of the investigation, however, no one referred to recent medical and psychological studies on same-sex relationships. When the navy accused a local minister of homosexual behavior based on ambiguous evidence, the Senate Naval Affairs Committee intervened, held hearings in 1921, and condemned the initial investigation. Afterward, the navy and army continued previous practices, making little effort to prevent homosexuals from enlisting and taking disciplinary action only against behavior that clearly violated the law.

The late 1920s and early 1930s, however, brought increased suppression of gays and lesbians. New state laws gave police greater authority to crack down on them as a group and all open expressions of their identity and culture. In 1927, New York police raided *The Captive* and other plays with gay or lesbian themes, and the New York legislature banned all such plays. In 1929 Adam Clayton Powell, a leading Harlem minister, launched a highly publicized campaign against gays. Motion-picture studios instituted a morality code that, among its wide-ranging provisions, prohibited any depiction of homosexuality. The end of prohibition after 1933 brought increased regulation of businesses selling liquor, and local authorities used this regulatory power to close establishments that tolerated gay or lesbian customers. Thus, by the late 1930s, many gays and lesbians were forced to become more secretive about their sexual identities.

The Politics of Prosperity

- What were the expectations of the Republican administrations of the 1920s?
- What were their resulting policy choices?

Sooner or later, nearly all the social and economic developments of the 1920s found their way into politics, from highway construction to Prohibition, from immigration restriction to teaching evolution, from farm prices to lynching. After 1918, the Repub-

---

Equal Rights Amendment Constitutional amendment first proposed by the National Woman's Party in 1923, giving women in the United States equal rights under the law.

perversion A sexual practice considered abnormal or deviant.

licans returned to the majority role they had exercised from the mid-1890s to 1912, and they continued as the unquestioned majority party throughout the 1920s. Progressivism largely disappeared, although a few veterans of earlier struggles, led by Robert La Follette and George Norris, persisted in their vigil to limit corporate power. The Republican administrations of the 1920s, instead, shared a faith in the ability of business to establish prosperity and thereby to benefit the American people. To those in power, government was the partner of business, not its regulator.

Harding's Failed Presidency

Warren G. Harding looked like a president—handsome, gray-haired, dignified, warm, and outgoing—but he displayed little intellectual depth below the charming surface. For some positions, he named the most respected leaders of his party. His cabinet was well above the average in ability, including Charles Evans Hughes for secretary of state, Andrew Mellon for secretary of the treasury, and Herbert Hoover for secretary of commerce. Harding, however, was most at home in a smoke-filled room, drinking whiskey and playing poker with friends. He gave hundreds of government jobs to his cronies and political supporters. They betrayed his trust and turned his administration into one of the most corrupt in American history. As their misdeeds began to come to light, Harding put off taking action until after an expedition to Alaska. During his return trip, on August 2, 1923, he died when a blood vessel burst in his brain.

The full extent of corruption became clear after Harding's death. Interior Secretary Fall had accepted huge bribes from oil companies for leases on government oil reserves at Elk Hills, California, and **Teapot Dome,** Wyoming. Attorney General Harry Daugherty and others had accepted bribes to approve the sale of government-held property for less than its value, and Daugherty may also have been involved in protecting bootleggers. The head of the Veterans Bureau had swindled the government out of more than $200 million. In all, three cabinet members resigned, four officials went to jail, and five men committed suicide. As if the corruption were not enough, in 1927 Nan Britton published a book revealing that she had been Harding's mistress, had his child, and carried on trysts with him in the White House. Not until 1964 did evidence appear that Harding had also maintained a long-term love affair with a married neighbor in Marion, Ohio.

In 1924, the Democrats tried to capitalize on the Republicans embarrassment over the Teapot Dome scandal. They received little response because the death of Harding brought Calvin Coolidge to the presidency, and Coolidge's personal honesty and morality were unquestioned. *Collection of David J. and Janice L. Frent.*

The Three-way Election of 1924

When Harding died, Vice President Calvin Coolidge was visiting his father's farm in Vermont. Fortunately for the Republican party, the new president exemplified the honesty, virtue, and sobriety associated with rural New England. In 1924, Republicans quickly chose Coolidge as their candidate for president.

The Democratic convention, however, sank into a long and bitter deadlock. Since the Civil War, the party had had two major wings—southerners, mostly Protestant and committed to white supremacy, and northerners, often city-dwellers and of recent immigrant descent, including many Catholics. In 1924, the Klan was approaching its peak membership. With its attacks on Catholics, Jews, immigrants, and urban decadence, it exercised significant influence among many Democratic delegates from the South and Midwest. Northern Democrats that year tried to nominate **Al Smith** for president. Highly popular as governor of New York,

Teapot Dome Government-owned Wyoming oil field that Interior Secretary Albert B. Fall leased to private developers in return for a bribe, causing one of the scandals that disgraced the Harding administration.

Al Smith Democratic New York governor who ran unsuccessfully for president in 1928; his Catholicism and his desire to repeal Prohibition were both political liabilities.

Smith epitomized urban America. Catholic and the son of immigrants, he was everything the Klan—and most of the southern convention delegates—hated. His chief opponent for the nomination, William G. McAdoo of California, boasted progressive credentials but had done legal work for an oil company executive tainted by the Elk Hills scandal. After nine hot days of stalemate and 103 ballots, the exhausted Democrats turned to a compromise candidate, John W. Davis. Davis had served in the Wilson administration and then became a leading corporate lawyer. All in all, the convention seemed to confirm the observation of the contemporary humorist Will Rogers: "I belong to no organized political party. I am a Democrat."

Americans committed to progressivism found little attractive in either Coolidge or Davis and welcomed the independent candidacy of Senator Robert M. La Follette of Wisconsin. La Follette was nominated as a Progressive, at a convention that expressed the concerns of the CPPA (organized by unions in 1922, see page 724), hard-pressed farmers, and an assortment of reformers dating back as far as the Populist party of the 1890s. The La Follette Progressives attacked big business and embraced collective bargaining, reforms of the political process, public ownership of railroads and water power resources, and a public referendum on questions of war and peace. La Follette became the first presidential candidate ever to be endorsed by the American Federation of Labor. The Socialist Party of America threw him their support as well.

Republican campaigners largely ignored Davis and focused on portraying La Follette as a dangerous radical. Coolidge himself claimed the key issue was "whether America will allow itself to be degraded into a communistic or socialistic state or whether it will remain American." Coolidge won with nearly 16 million votes and 54 percent of the total, as voters seemed to champion the **status quo.** Davis held onto most traditional Democratic voters, especially in the South, receiving 8 million votes and 29 percent. La Follette carried only his home state of Wisconsin but garnered almost 5 million votes, 17 percent, and did well both in urban working-class neighborhoods and in the rural Midwest and Northwest (see Map 21.1).

The Politics of Business

If the voters wanted Coolidge to continue as before, he did not disappoint them. Resolved to limit government and content to let problems work them-

♦ This cartoon depicts Coolidge playing the praises of big business. Big business, dressed like a flapper, responds by dancing the Charleston with wild abandon and singing a paraphrase of a popular song, "Yes Sir, He's My Baby." *Library of Congress.*

selves out, Coolidge tried to reduce the significance of the presidency—and succeeded. Having once announced that "the business of America is business," he believed that the free market and free operation of business leadership would best sustain economic prosperity for all. As president, he set out to prevent government from interfering in the operation of business.

The Coolidge administration's firm commitment to an unfettered market economy meant the executive had little sympathy for proposals to use the federal government to assist the faltering farm economy. Congress tried to address the related problems of low prices for farm products and persistent agricultural surpluses with the **McNary-Haugen bill.** This law would have created federal price supports

status quo The existing condition or state of affairs.
McNary-Haugen bill Farm relief bill that provided for government purchase of crop surpluses during years of large output; it was vetoed by Coolidge in 1927, and again in 1928.

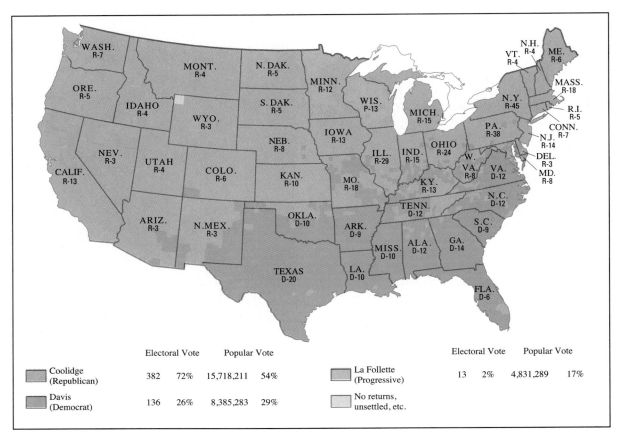

	Electoral Vote	Popular Vote		Electoral Vote	Popular Vote
Coolidge (Republican)	382 72%	15,718,211 54%	La Follette (Progressive)	13 2%	4,831,289 17%
Davis (Democrat)	136 26%	8,385,283 29%	No returns, unsettled, etc.		

◆ **MAP 23.1 Election of 1924, by County**   The presidential election of 1924 was complicated by the campaign of Senator Robert La Follette of Wisconsin, who ran as a Progressive. As you can see, much of his support came from Republicans living in the north
central and northwestern regions where the agricultural economy was most hard hit.

and authorized the government to buy farm surpluses and sell them abroad at prevailing world
prices. After long effort, the Farm Bloc finally
pushed the bill through Congress in 1927, only to
have Coolidge veto it. The same thing happened in
1928.

Andrew Mellon, an aluminum magnate and one
of the wealthiest men in the nation, served as secretary of the treasury throughout the Republican administrations of the 1920s. Widely acclaimed by
Republicans and business leaders as the greatest
secretary of the treasury since Alexander Hamilton,
Mellon secured substantial tax cuts for the wealthy
and for corporations. He argued that high taxes on
the very affluent stifled the economy and that tax
cuts at those levels would result in economic benefits to all as a result of the "productive investments"
that the wealthy would make. Herbert Hoover, sec-

retary of commerce during both the Harding and
Coolidge administrations, urged Coolidge to regulate the increasingly wild use of credit, which inflated stock values and produced rampant stock
market speculation, but Coolidge refused. The easy-
money policy encouraged speculators to buy stock
on borrowed money and promoted stock market
speculation (see page 708).

Coolidge cut federal spending and staffed Washington's agencies with people who shared his distaste for government. Unlike Harding, Coolidge
found honest and competent appointees. Like Harding, he named probusiness figures to regulatory
commissions and put conservative, probusiness
judges in the courts. The *Wall Street Journal* described the outcome: "Never before, here or anywhere else, has a government been so completely
fused with business."

SUMMARY

The 1920s were a decade of prosperity: unemployment was low, GNP grew steadily, and many Americans fared well. Sophisticated advertising campaigns created bright *expectations,* and installment buying freed consumers from the old *constraints* of having to pay cash. Many consumers did *choose* to buy more and to buy on credit— stimulating manufacturing and an expansion of personal debt. Easy credit and *expectations* of continuing prosperity also helped to loosen *constraints* on speculation. Fueled by many individual *choices,* the stock market climbed higher and higher. Agriculture, however, did not share in this prosperity.

As *expectations* changed during the Roaring Twenties, Americans experienced significant social change. The automobile, radio, and movies broke down old *constraints* on travel and communication and, abetted by immigration restriction, produced, as one *outcome,* a more homogeneous culture. Many American intellectuals, however, *chose* to reject the consumer-oriented culture. During the 1920s, African-Americans produced an outpouring of significant art, literature, and music. Some young people *chose* to reject traditional *constraints* and one outcome was a so-called youth culture.

Not all Americans embraced change. Some *chose,* instead, to try to maintain or restore earlier cultural values. The *outcomes* were mixed. Prohibition was largely unsuccessful. Fundamentalism grew and prompted a campaign against teaching evolution. Nativism helped produce significant new restrictions on immigration. The Ku Klux Klan, committed to nativism, traditional values, and white supremacy, experienced nationwide growth until 1925, but membership declined sharply thereafter.

E **xpectations**
C **onstraints**
C **hoices**
O **utcomes**

Discrimination and occasional violence continued to *constrain* the lives of people of color. Federal Indian policy had long stressed assimilation and allotment, but some groups *chose* to promote different policies based on respect for Indian cultural values. Immigration from Mexico greatly increased the Latino population in California and the Southwest, and some Mexicans working in agriculture tried, unsuccessfully, to organize unions. Nearly all unions faced strong opposition from employers, and only the railroad unions made significant gains during the twenties.

Some older *expectations* and *constraints* regarding women's roles broke down as women gained the right to vote and exercised more control over the *choice* to have children. An identifiable gay and lesbian subculture emerged, especially in cities.

Politics became less prominent. Warren G. Harding was a poor judge of character, and some of his appointees lived by graft and disgraced their chief. Harding and his successor, Calvin Coolidge, both *expected* that government should act as a partner with business, and they made *choices* that minimized regulation and encouraged speculation. With some exceptions, progressive reform disappeared from politics, and efforts to secure federal assistance for farmers fizzled. One *outcome* was a federal government that was strongly conservative, staunchly probusiness, and absolutely unwilling to intervene in the economy.

SUGGESTED READINGS

Allen, Frederick Lewis. *Only Yesterday: An Informal History of the Nineteen-Twenties* (1931, rpt. 1964).
    Filled with anecdotes that bring the decade to life.

Fitzgerald, F. Scott. *The Great Gatsby* (1925).
    A fictional portrayal of high living and pleasure seeking among the wealthy of New York.

Huggins, Nathan Irvin. *Harlem Renaissance* (1971).
    Thorough and thoughtful, this work places the Harlem Renaissance into the larger context of race relations in the 1920s.

Leuchtenburg, William E. *The Perils of Prosperity, 1914–1932.* Rev. ed. (1993).
    A comprehensive yet readable account by a leading historian.

The Smithsonian Collection of Classic Jazz. 5 compact disks (1987).
    An outstanding collection that reflects the development of American jazz, with annotations and biographies of performers.

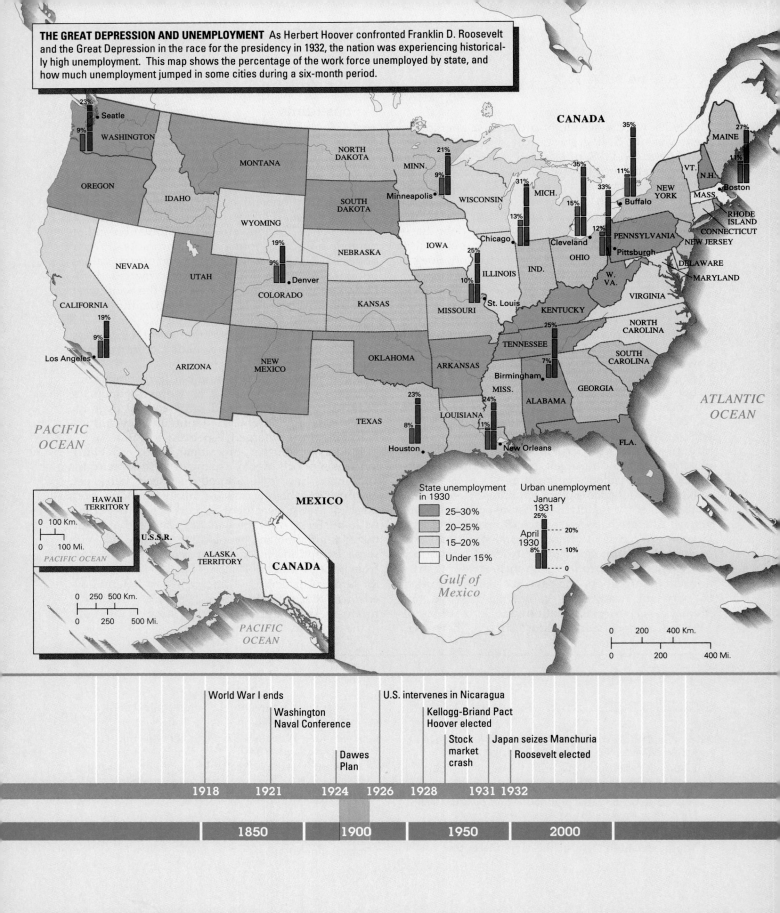

THE GREAT DEPRESSION AND UNEMPLOYMENT As Herbert Hoover confronted Franklin D. Roosevelt and the Great Depression in the race for the presidency in 1932, the nation was experiencing historically high unemployment. This map shows the percentage of the work force unemployed by state, and how much unemployment jumped in some cities during a six-month period.

CANADA

23% Seattle
9% WASHINGTON
OREGON
MONTANA
NORTH DAKOTA
MINN.
21%
9% Minneapolis
WISCONSIN
13% Chicago
31% MICH.
35%
35% Cleveland
15%
12%
33% Buffalo
11%
PENNSYLVANIA
Pittsburgh
OHIO
IND.
27% MAINE
11%
VT.
N.H.
NEW YORK
MASS. Boston
RHODE ISLAND
CONNECTICUT
NEW JERSEY
DELAWARE
MARYLAND
W. VA.
VIRGINIA
IDAHO
SOUTH DAKOTA
WYOMING
19%
9% Denver
COLORADO
NEBRASKA
IOWA
25%
10% St. Louis
ILLINOIS
MISSOURI
KANSAS
KENTUCKY
25% TENNESSEE
7% Birmingham
NORTH CAROLINA
SOUTH CAROLINA
NEVADA
UTAH
CALIFORNIA
19%
9% Los Angeles
ARIZONA
NEW MEXICO
OKLAHOMA
ARKANSAS
MISS.
24%
11% New Orleans
ALABAMA
GEORGIA
23%
8% Houston
TEXAS
LOUISIANA
FLA.

CANADA

PACIFIC OCEAN

ATLANTIC OCEAN

HAWAII TERRITORY
0 100 Km.
0 100 Mi.
PACIFIC OCEAN

U.S.S.R.

ALASKA TERRITORY

MEXICO

CANADA

PACIFIC OCEAN

Gulf of Mexico

0 250 500 Km.
0 250 500 Mi.

State unemployment in 1930
☐ 25–30%
☐ 20–25%
☐ 15–20%
☐ Under 15%

Urban unemployment
January 1931
25% — 20%
April 1930 — 10%
8% — 0

0 200 400 Km.
0 200 400 Mi.

World War I ends

Washington Naval Conference

Dawes Plan

U.S. intervenes in Nicaragua

Kellogg-Briand Pact
Hoover elected

Stock market crash

Japan seizes Manchuria

Roosevelt elected

1918   1921   1924   1926   1928   1931 1932

1850   1900   1950   2000

From Good Times to Hard Times, 1920–1932

The Diplomacy of Prosperity

- How did the strength of the American economy, along with America's desire to remain unconstrained in foreign affairs shape the choices in U.S. foreign policy during the 1920s?

The Failure of Prosperity

- What weaknesses constrained the American economy, making a mockery of Hoover's expectation that poverty would soon be eliminated?

Government and Economic Crisis

- Why were Hoover's choices in dealing with the problems created by the Depression neither appreciated nor effective?

Depression America

- What economic and social constraints and choices did the Depression generate for industrial workers, minorities, and women?

INTRODUCTION

E **xpectations**

C **onstraints**

C **hoices**

O **utcomes**

As the decade of the Roaring Twenties drew toward its close, the United States seemed to have reached new levels of success. American prosperity bloomed, fueling much of the world's economic growth. Representing the world's strongest economic power and most abundant source of capital, American business interests invaded Europe, Asia, the Middle East, and Latin America. At the same time, the United States government *chose* to avoid a direct role in world politics. In place of collective security and participation in international organizations, American policymakers from Harding to Hoover *expected* indirect and private means to promote American interests and a stable and peaceful world.

Domestically, the Republican presidents of the twenties *chose* to rely less on governmental supervision and more on unfettered American business to build a prosperous and stable America. For Herbert Clark Hoover, the Great Engineer and Humanitarian, the outlook in 1928 seemed bright. He *expected* to be elected president and to guide the continued growth of American and world prosperity through noncoercive and cooperative means. He was confident that domestic poverty would nearly disappear and international peace would prevail. The pattern already had been set, and Hoover was sure, and he believed that all he needed to do was fine-tune the process.

This chapter examines the failure of these *expectations,* as a worldwide *constraint*—the Great Depression—made a mockery of prosperity, presidential leadership, and the quest for a cooperative world.

Hoover *chose* to face the decline of the economy with the principles and policies that he had *expected* would produce continued growth. He found, however, that they only heightened disillusionment and individual hardship. Confronted with dismal realities, Hoover altered policy, but his new *choices* failed to change the course of either the Depression or the public's harsh image of him. As individuals and society responded to the Depression, many, like Hoover, questioned their long-held values and *choices* and revised their *expectations,* especially about the role of government. By 1932 it was obvious that the Depression had thwarted Hoover's hopes and ruined his political career. The American people *chose* change, and the *outcome* was the election of a president pledged to activism—Franklin D. Roosevelt—and a Democratic Congress.

The Depression also revealed the weaknesses of the *expectations* and *choices* that had governed American foreign policy throughout the 1920s. The *constraints* of economic failure dashed hopes of basing peace and international stability on economic growth and voluntary agreements. The *outcome* was an increasingly dangerous world, as nations moved to protect and promote their own economic goals at the expense of others and, in the case of Japan, of world peace.

The Diplomacy of Prosperity

● How did the strength of the American economy, along with America's desire to remain unconstrained in foreign affairs shape the choices in U.S. foreign policy during the 1920s?

Two realities shaped American foreign policy in the 1920s: the rejection of Woodrow Wilson's internationalism following World War I and the continuing quest for economic expansion by American business. President Warren Harding, soon after being elected, dismissed any American role in the League of Nations and refused to accept officially the

Treaty of Versailles. Anxious to restore normal relations with Germany and other defeated Central Powers, the administration and Congress passed a joint resolution that simply declared the war to be over. Harding's secretary of state, Charles Evan Hughes, who had run against Wilson in 1916 and was one of the most respected members of the Republican party, then quickly concluded separate

Treaty of Versailles   Treaty that ended World War I, which was signed at Versailles in France in 1919.

A New Era

1918	World War I ends
1920	Harding elected president
1921–1922	Washington Naval Conference Nine Power Pacts
1922	Fordney-McCumber Tariff
1923	France occupies the Ruhr Harding dies in office Coolidge becomes president
1924	Coolidge elected president Dawes Plan U.S. forces withdraw from Dominican Republic
1926	United States intervenes in Nicaragua
1927	Stimson negotiates the Peace of Titiapa Sandino begins guerilla war in Nicaragua
1928	Kellogg-Briand Pact Stock market peaks Hoover elected president First talking motion picture Model A Ford introduced
1929	Agricultural Marketing Act (Farm Board) Stock market crash
1930	Trujillo seizes power in Dominican Republic Hawley-Smoot Tariff
1931	Japan seizes Manchuria United States announces Stimson Doctrine Mexican repatriation Scottsboro Nine convicted
1932	32,000 U.S. businesses fail U.S. forces begin withdrawal from Nicaragua Glass-Steagall Banking Act Reconstruction Finance Corporation RCF begins emergency relief Farmers Holiday Association founded Bonus March Roosevelt elected president
1933	4,000 U.S. banks fail Unemployment reaches 25 percent Japan withdraws from League of Nations
1934	U.S. forces withdraw from Haiti Sandino murdered by Somoza
1936	Somoza becomes president of Nicaragua

peace treaties with the Central Powers. Hughes also supported efforts by American banks and corporations to expand their business activities around the world. International economic changes caused by the Great War had made American businesses not only the world's major producers but the world's major bankers as well, and throughout the 1920s American businesses helped to shape the global economy by lending money to other nations.

Because neither Harding nor Coolidge had any expertise or interest in foreign affairs, they deferred making and implementing policy to their secretaries of state: Hughes and Frank Kellogg—nicknamed "nervous Nellie" because of a nervous twitch. Both were capable men interested in developing American business and influence abroad through what many historians have called "independent internationalism." Independent internationalism had two central thrusts: avoiding political and international responsibilities—sometimes called **isolationism**—and expanding economic opportunities overseas. As secretary of commerce, Herbert Hoover was equally involved in promoting American business activities worldwide. In Asia, the Commerce and State departments encouraged private American investments in Japan and China. In the Middle East, the United States worked hard to overcome British

> **isolationism** A national policy of avoiding political or economic entanglements with other countries.

opposition and provide openings for American oil companies seeking drilling rights in Iran, Iraq, the Persian Gulf region, and Saudi Arabia. Successes in Asia and the Middle East were limited, but efforts to expand the American economic position in Latin America and Europe were quite successful.

The United States and Latin America

Throughout Latin America, but especially in Central America and the Caribbean, the United States's influence was projected by the Monroe Doctrine, direct American investments, control of the Panama Canal, and, when necessary, the use of direct armed intervention (see Map 24.1). When President Harding took office in 1921, the United States had troops stationed in Panama, Haiti, the Dominican Republic, and Nicaragua. During the presidential campaign, Harding had criticized Wilson's "bayonet rule" in Haiti and the Dominican Republic as too costly and had expressed his intention to end the American occupation of those adjoining nations. But the withdrawal of American troops proceeded slowly as neither Harding, Coolidge, nor Hoover wanted the removal of American troops to leave behind footholds for anti-American governments. To ensure continued American influence and local governments that could keep order, Americans maintained controls over national finances and installed American-trained national guards to act as each nation's police force. With such precautions in place, American troops left the Dominican Republic in 1924, Nicaragua in 1932, and Haiti in 1934 (see Map 24.1). In the Dominican Republic and in Haiti, the United States held onto control of the customhouse and import tax revenues until the 1940s.

When American troops withdrew from the Dominican Republic and Haiti, they left better roads, improved sanitary systems, governments favorable to the United States, and well-equipped national guards. But years of occupation had not advanced educational systems, national economies, or the standard of living for most native people. In Haiti, social divisions were made worse by American-imposed segregation and favoritism toward the minority, lighter-colored **mulattos** who were given charge of the economic and political structure. Nor did the United States promote the cause of democracy, favoring not freedom but stability, enforced as needed by the national guard and authoritarian rulers. In 1930, Rafael Trujillo, an American-trained officer of

the national guard, seized power in the Dominican Republic and declared himself dictator. He would rule the country brutally until his death in 1961.

In Nicaragua, American marines had protected the conservative pro-American government in power since 1911. But as American forces left, political turmoil and civil war broke out. By mid-1926, President Coolidge had reintroduced American forces to protect the government and sent special envoy Henry L. Stimson to negotiate a truce. Stimson worked to carve out an agreement between the two major warring groups that included the formation of a provisional coalition government and free election to be held later. The **Peace of Titiapa** that followed ended most of the fighting, leaving only followers of Augusto Sandino continuing the war. Sandino, who characterized himself as a nationalist whose primary goal was to see Nicaragua free of American influence, rejected the Peace of Titiapa. Between 1927 and 1932, he successfully carried on a guerilla war against the government and American forces. In fact, he vowed to maintain his fight until not one American soldier remained in Nicaragua. Throughout Latin America, his resistance earned him many admirers who saw the United States as an imperial power wielding its military, political, and economic might to control Latin Americans. Between 1932 and 1934, the United States withdrew its forces from Nicaragua, leaving behind an American equipped and trained National Guard to maintain order. As the last U.S. Marine left, the Nicaraguan president Juan Bautista Sacasa and his nephew and commander of the *Guardia Nacional* **Anastasio Somoza,** arranged a peace conference with the rebel. After a farewell dinner, Somoza ordered Sandino and his aides seized and executed. Somoza next turned against Sacasa and in 1936 using the guard as a political weapon, ensured his own election as president. Anastasio Somoza ruled either directly or through puppet presidents until his assassination in 1956. His family would remain in power until 1979, when rebels calling themselves the Sandinistas—af-

---

mulatto   A person of mixed black and white ancestry.

Peace of Titiapa   Agreement negotiated by U.S. Secretary of State Henry L. Stimson in 1927 that sought to end factional fighting in Nicaragua.

Anastasio Somoza   General who established a military dictatorship in Nicaragua in 1934, deposed his uncle to become president in 1936, and ruled the country for two decades, amassing a personal fortune and suppressing all opposition.

CANADA

UNITED STATES

ATLANTIC OCEAN

Ottawa

San Francisco

Washington, D.C.

| Roosevelt's Good Neighbor Policy, 1933 |

| U.S. upholds right of intervention at Pan American Conference, 1928 |

| U.S. troops, 1917–1922
U.S. investors dominate sugar industry
Revolution of 1933
U.S. abrogates Platt Amendment, 1934
Batista era, 1934–1959 |

| U.S. troops, 1915–1934
Financial supervision, 1916–1941 |

MEXICO

Gulf of Mexico

Miami

THE BAHAMAS

Nassau

Guantánamo

| U.S. financial supervision, 1905–1941
U.S. troops withdrawn, 1924
Trujillo era, 1930–1961 |

| Constitution of 1917 challenges U.S. interests
Nationalization of foreign oil companies, 1938
U.S.-Mexico agreement settles oil dispute, 1942 |

Havana **CUBA**

DOMINICAN REP.

San Juan

VIRGIN IS. (US,UK)

Mexico City

JAMAICA

HAITI

PUERTO RICO (US)

| U.S. colony since 1917 |

Belmopan   Kingston

BELIZE

Port-au-Prince   Santo Domingo

Caribbean Sea

| U.S. colony
Jones Act grants U.S. citizenship, 1917 |

GUATEMALA

HONDURAS

Guatemala   Tegucigalpa

EL SALVADOR   San Salvador

NICARAGUA

Managua

| U.S. invasion, 1924
United Fruit Company active |

San José   Panama

COSTA RICA

Caracas

VENEZUELA

Georgetown
Paramaribo

GUYANA

SURINAM

Cayenne

PANAMA

FRENCH GUIANA (FR.)

| U.S. financial supervision, 1911–1924
U.S. military occupation, 1912–1925
U.S. war against Sandino, 1926–1933
Somoza era, 1936–1979 |

Bogatá

COLUMBIA

| U.S. oil investments |

| U.S. control of Canal Zone
Declaration of Panama, 1939 |

ECUADOR

Quito

BRAZIL

PERU

Lima

La Paz

Brasília

BOLIVIA

| U.S. copper interests |

PACIFIC OCEAN

CHILE

PARAGUAY

Asunción

Santiago

Buenos Aires

URUGUAY

Montevideo

ARGENTINA

| U.S. votes for nonintervention pledge at Pan American Conference, 1936 |

0   500   1000 Km.

0   500   1000 Mi.

♦ **MAP 24.1 The United States and Latin America, 1919–1939**   As this map shows, between the two world wars, the United States continued to play an active role in promoting its interests throughout Central and South America and the Caribbean. In some cases, as in Nicaragua in the 1920s, this included military intervention, but during the 1920s and the terms of Hoover and Roosevelt, political and economic pressures replaced military force as the primary means to protect U.S. interests.

♦ During the 1920s, American businesses greatly expanded their operations overseas. In Latin America, corporations such as United Fruit Company oversaw a wide-range of enterprises, from running shiplines to growing bananas. Here, recently picked bananas begin their journey from the field to American homes. *Benson Latin American Collection, University of Texas at Austin.*

ter their hero Sandino—drove the Somozas out of Nicaragua.

Elsewhere in Latin America, the 1920s saw American interventions of another sort—not military but commercial. Throughout Central America, American firms like the United Fruit Company purchased thousands of acres of land for plantations on which to grow tropical fruits, especially bananas. In Venezuela and Colombia, American oil companies, with State Department help, successfully negotiated profitable contracts for drilling rights, pushing aside European oil companies like Royal Dutch Shell and British Petroleum. American investment in Colombia rose from $2 million in 1920 to $124 million by 1929.

Oil also played a key role in American relations with Mexico and nearly led to armed American intervention. Following the Mexican revolution (see pages 671–672), the Mexican Constitution of 1917 limited foreign ownership and Mexico moved to **nationalize** all of its subsurface resources, including oil (see Map 24.1). The United States, supported by American businessmen, objected strongly, especially to the nationalization of oil. By 1925, American oil men and some within the Coolidge administration were calling for military action to protect American oil interests in northern Mexico from "Bolshevism." To resolve the dispute, Coolidge sent Dwight W. Morrow—a college friend—as ambas-

sador to Mexico with instructions "to keep us out of war with Mexico." Morrow, who understood Mexican nationalism and pride, had learned some Spanish and clearly appreciated Mexico and its people. He and his family lived in a Mexican-style home and shopped in open air markets. He cultivated a personal relationship with Mexican president Plutarco Calles, often over social breakfasts. Together they reached a compromise that reduced tensions, recognized Mexican sovereignty over its oil, and effectively delayed Mexico's nationalization of existing oil properties until 1938.

America and the European Economy

World War I had shattered most of Europe physically and economically, while the United States had climbed during wartime to unprecedented economic heights—emerging as the world's leading creditor nation. At the same time, the United States sought to expand exports and restrict imports. High tariffs inched higher throughout the 1920s. In 1922, the **Fordney-McCumber Tariff** set records in protective rates for most industrial goods imported into the United States. The effect was not only to limit European imports but also to forestall Europe's ability to acquire the dollars needed to repay their war debts to the United States. And repay the debts they must, declared both presidents Harding and Coolidge. As leaders from Britain, France, and Italy begged the United States to forgive their war debts, Coolidge reportedly replied "They hired the money didn't they," and demanded full payment with interest.

As Harding and Coolidge sought debt repayment, Secretary of State Hughes and Secretary of Commerce Hoover worked to expand American economic interests in Europe, especially Germany. They believed that if Germany recovered economically and was able to pay its $33 billion war reparations, other European nations would recover as well and be able to repay their war debts. With Hughes's and Hoover's encouragement, over $4 billion in American investments flowed into Europe, dou-

---

nationalize To convert an industry or enterprise from private to governmental ownership and control.

Fordney-McCumber Tariff 1922 law that raised tariff rates to record levels, fostering the growth of monopolies and provoking foreign tariff reprisals.

bling the total American investment there by the end of decade. General Motors purchased Opel, a German automobile firm. Ford built the largest automobile factory outside of the United States in England and constructed a tractor factory in the Soviet Union.

Even with the infusion of American business capital, Germany could not keep up with its reparations burden, and in 1923 failed to make its payments to France and Belgium. France responded by sending troops to occupy the **Ruhr Valley** of Germany, a key economic region, igniting an international emergency. Hoping to help resolve the crisis, Hughes sent Chicago banker Charles G. Dawes to Europe to negotiate a plan to restore the payments and renew progress toward economic stability. Under the **Dawes Plan,** American bankers loaned $2.5 billion to Germany for economic development, while the Germans promised to pay $2 billion in reparations to the Europeans. The Europeans, in turn, paid $2.5 billion in war debts to the United States. This circular flow of capital was the butt of jokes at the time, but the remedy worked fairly well until 1929 when the Depression ended nearly all loans and payments.

Independent internationalism emphasized the positive results of economic diplomacy and growth, but American policymakers also understood that, on some questions, international cooperation was the only means to achieve American goals and solve specific international problems. On those matters, the United States would cooperate with other nations, sign treaties, and play an active role, but only with the understanding that compliance was voluntary. One such thorny issue was disarmament. The destruction caused by World War I had spurred postwar pacifism and calls for disarmament. Reducing the means to wage war would not only reduce the number of weapons but also eliminate what many considered wasteful military spending from national budgets. Moreover, if governments cut military spending, they could then lower taxes. In the United States support for arms cuts was widespread and vocal, as proponents pressed Harding to trim military budgets and take the initiative in world disarmament efforts. In early 1921, Senator William E. Borah of Idaho suggested an international conference to reduce the size of the world's navies. Fearing that cumbersome naval expenditures would prevent tax cuts, Secretary of the Treasury Andrew Mellon and many congressmen strongly supported the idea. In November 1921, Harding invited the major naval powers to Washington for discussions on reducing "the crushing burdens of military and naval establishments."

But lessening the tax burden was not the sole motivating factor. Other reasons for naval disarmament reflected specific American concerns in Asia. Between 1900 and 1920, American naval strength had climbed from fourth in the world to a first-place tie with Britain. At the same time, Japan's navy had become the world's third strongest. As the Great War ended, American and British politicians had no desire to expand their navies, but Japan seemed inclined to continue its naval build-up. Americans also worried about growing Japanese pressures on China that could endanger Chinese territory and the Open Door that allowed the United States to trade throughout the country. To deal with the Japanese, Harding and Hughes were willing to reject isolationism and host two conferences: one to limit the size of navies, the other—composed of all the Asian powers except China—to ensure the status quo in China. If successful, the meetings could move the world closer to disarmament, limit Japanese naval expansion, and protect China.

As the naval powers assembled, Hughes shocked delegates with a radical proposal that called for participants to scrap more than 200 tons of warships, primarily battleships. He also called for a ten-year ban on naval construction and for limits to the size of navies, based on a ratio of tonnage, that would keep the Japanese behind the British and American navies. Hughes put forth a ratio of 5 to 5 to 3 for the United States, Britain, and Japan—with lesser naval powers like Italy and France receiving even smaller ratios. "Cadillac, Cadillac, Ford," one observer quipped. Hughes's plan generated immediate favor among the American public and most of the nations attending—but not Japan. The Japanese called the ratio a national insult and demanded equality. The conference dragged on for two months, but finally the Japanese agreed—as Hughes had known they would. Prior to the conference, the United States had broken the Japanese **diplomatic code** and had

> **Ruhr Valley**   Region surrounding the Ruhr River in northwestern Germany, which contained many major industrial cities and valuable mines.
>
> **Dawes Plan**   Plan for collecting World War I reparations from Germany, which scheduled annual payments and stabilized German currency by reorganizing the Reichsbank under Allied supervision.
>
> **diplomatic code**   Secret code in which diplomatic messages are transmitted.

◆ In an era of isolationism, the United States hosted its first major international conference, the Washington Naval Conference, to limit the naval arms race and protect its interests in China. At the center of the conference was Secretary of State Charles Evan Hughes (pictured here), who shocked everyone by asking for major reductions in naval strength. *Brown Brothers.*

intercepted secret messages from Tokyo instructing the Japanese delegates to resist inequality but then to concede if Hughes held firm. When the conference ended in February 1922, nine treaties were generated among the participating nations. The United States, Britain, Japan, France, and Italy agreed in a naval armaments treaty to build no more **capital ships** for ten years and abide by the 5 to 5 to 3 ratio of such ships. A British observer commented that Hughes had sunk more British ships in one speech "than all the admirals of the world have sunk in . . . centuries." In other agreements, the powers agreed to prohibit the use of poison gas and not attack one another's Asian possessions. The **Nine Power Pact,** concluded at the same time, affirmed support for the sovereignty and territorial boundaries of China and guaranteed equal commercial access to China—the Open Door. Hughes rightfully considered the two meetings successful, although critics complained that the agreements included no provisions for enforcement and that smaller naval ships, including submarines, were not even considered. As it turned out, the **Washington Naval Conference** was the only successful disarmament conference of the 1920s. Other attempts to reduce naval and land forces had mixed outcomes. After a failure in 1927 to limit the number of certain smaller naval vessels, Britain, the United States, and Japan established a series of ratios—similar to those of the Washington Naval Conference—for cruisers and destroyers at the 1930 London Conference. That was the last positive stroke. Thereafter, competition reigned: by the mid-thirties, Japan's demands for naval equal-

ity ended British and American cooperation and spurred renewed naval construction by all three powers.

Many Americans and Europeans applauded the achievements of the Washington conference but wanted to go even further. They sought total disarmament and a repudiation of war. In 1923, Senator Borah introduced a resolution in the Senate to outlaw war. It failed but the idea remained active, and in 1927, French Foreign Minister Aristide Briand hoped to use the concept to establish a treaty of friendship with the United States. He suggested a French-American pact to formally outlaw war between them, privately hoping that such an agreement would commit the United States to aid France if attacked. Secretary of State Kellogg wanted to avoid any such American commitment and deflected the proposal by suggesting a multinational

---

capital ships   The Navy's primary warships; defined by the Washington Conference as any ship over 10,000 tons, using guns with an 8-inch bore.

Nine Power Pact   Agreement signed in 1922 by Britain, France, Italy, Japan, the United States, China, the Netherlands, Portugal, and Belgium to recognize China and affirm the Open Door policy.

Washington Naval Conference   International conference held in Washington, D.C., in November 1921 through December 1922; it produced a series of agreements to limit naval armaments and prevent conflict in the Far East.

statement opposing war. By expanding the number of nations involved, Kellogg removed any hint of an American commitment to aid any nation under attack. Briand was left no choice but to agree and the Pact of Paris, or the **Kellogg-Briand Pact,** was signed on August 27, 1928, by the United States and fourteen other nations, including Britain, France, Germany, Italy, and Japan. Each renounced war "as an instrument of national policy" and promised to settle their disputes by peaceful means. They invited others to sign the resolution, and eventually sixty-four nations did, expressing an almost universal hope for world peace. But the pact included no enforcement provisions and nearly every **signatory** maintained its right to defend itself and its possessions.

By the end of 1928, American independent internationalism seemed to be a flourishing success. American business investments and loans were fueling an expansive world economy and adding to American prosperity. Avoiding entangling alliances, the United States had acted to protect its Asian and Pacific interests against Japan while promoting the idealism of world disarmament and peace. In Latin America, it had moderated its interventionist image by withdrawing American troops in the Caribbean, not applying force in Mexico, and trying to mediate a peace among warring factions in Nicaragua (see Map 24.1). It appeared that foreign policies based on economic expansion and noncoercive diplomacy were establishing a promising era of cooperation and peace in world affairs.

The Failure of Prosperity

● What weaknesses constrained the American economy, making a mockery of Hoover's expectation that poverty would soon be eliminated?

In August 1927, Calvin Coolidge called reporters from his vacation spot in South Dakota and told them, "I do not choose to run in 1928." Expected to be an easy winner in the 1928 race for the presidency, Coolidge's announcement stunned both the country and his party. Secretary of Commerce Herbert Hoover immediately declared his candidacy. And he seemed the ideal person for the job, representing what most believed was best about America: individual effort and honestly earned success.

A Quaker farm boy from Iowa, born in 1874 and orphaned while a child, Hoover had grown up among thrifty, self-sufficient farmers who believed

that hard work was the only way forward. He worked his way through Stanford University, earning a degree in geology. After graduation he took jobs in Australia and China, working, as he put it, "like a dog." He formed his own mining engineering company in 1908, and by 1914 he had offices in London, Petrograd, Paris, New York, and San Francisco. *Fortune* estimated that he and his wife Lou Henry Hoover, also a Stanford graduate, were worth more than $4 million dollars. Having reached the top in business, Hoover wanted to apply his belief in hard work and sound planning to public service. So when the Great War broke out, he offered his organizational skills and energy to help provide relief to Belgium through the Committee for the Relief of Belgium. Called by some the Great Humanitarian, Hoover traveled across wartorn Europe seeking funds and materials for Belgium. "This man is not to be stopped anywhere under any circumstance," the Germans noted on his passport. When the United States entered the war, President Wilson named him to head the U.S. Food Administration. By war's end, Hoover was an international hero. Considering politics, he discussed the possibility of becoming a Democratic presidential candidate with New York governor Franklin D. Roosevelt, but eventually declared himself a Republican. When Coolidge chose not to run for re-election, Hoover, in his first race for any elected political office, at once became the strongest contender for the presidency.

The 1928 Election

Receiving the Republican nomination, before thousands of supporters gathered in the Stanford football stadium, Hoover sounded the theme of this candidacy: American prosperity. "We in America today are nearer to the final triumph over poverty than ever before. . . . The poorhouse is vanishing among us," he boldly announced. The Democrats nominated Al Smith, four-time governor of New York. Like Hoover, Smith was a self-made man. But unlike his opponent who had gone to Stanford, Smith had received his education on the streets of the

---

Kellogg-Briand Pact Treaty signed in 1928 by fifteen nations, including Britain, France, Germany, the United States, and Japan, renouncing war as a means of solving international disputes.

signatory One who has signed a treaty or other document.

♦ The 1928 presidential election offered Americans a clear choice in candidates. In one corner was Al Smith, product of the streets of New York, Roman Catholic, and opposed to prohibition. Opposing him was Iowa-born Herbert Hoover, the "Great Engineer and Humanitarian," a self-made millionaire, and a proven administrator. Although he gave only seven campaign speeches, Hoover won easily. *Collection of David J. and Janice L. Frent.*

Lower East Side of New York City. Smith had entered politics as part of Tammany Hall, the Democratic machine that ran New York City, and quickly proved to be an able politician. As a reform-minded, progressive governor, Smith had streamlined government, improved governmental efficiency, and supported legislation to set a minimum wage and maximum hours of work and to establish state ownership of hydroelectrical plants.

Despite his progressive record, Smith ran a conservative campaign that allowed Republicans to make him the main issue of the 1928 contest. Opponents attacked his Catholic religion, his big-city background, his opposition to Prohibition, his Tammany connections, and even his New York accent. Anti-Catholic sentiment burned hotly in many parts of the country, often fanned by the remnants of the Klan, whose fiery crosses marked the route of Smith's campaign train in some areas. Evangelist Billy Sunday called Smith supporters "damnable whiskey politicians, bootleggers, crooks, pimps and businessmen who deal with them," and a Methodist bishop ominously predicted that Smith would not "get within gunshot of the White House." For many voters, the choice seemed between a candidate who represented hard work and the pious values of small-town, old-stock, Protestant America and one who represented urban upheaval, machine politics, foreigners, and Catholics.

Hoover won easily, with 58 percent of the popular vote, as an unusually large number of Americans went to the polls. He owed his victory in large part to the prosperity that Republicans claimed as their accomplishment, although Smith's religion and position against Prohibition cost him substantial support in the South. Balancing those losses, though, were Democratic gains in northern cities. Their

large Catholic populations responded to Smith's candidacy with unprecedented numbers at the polls voting Democratic. In 1920 and 1924, the twelve largest cities had voted Republican, but in 1928 only one, Los Angeles, voted heavily Republican. Smith won the other eleven, including New York, Cleveland, St. Louis, Milwaukee, and San Francisco. As the nation became more urban, the strength of Democrats in cities surfaced as a potential political advantage.

Herbert Hoover became the first president born west of the Mississippi River, and he came to the presidency with some definite ideas about how the nation and its foreign affairs should be run. More than Harding and Coolidge, he meant to be an active president, creating a "New Day" for America at home and overseas. Hoover's goal was to promote economic and social growth through the concept of **associationalism**—the voluntary cooperation among otherwise competing groups. The role of government among business and other components of society was to promote cooperation without resorting to punitive measures like antitrust laws. He believed that once government, especially the federal government, stepped in to solve society's problems directly, the people gave up their freedom and the government became the problem. Of course, Hoover recognized that problems existed and that the federal government had a responsibility to help find solutions. The key word for Hoover,

---

associationalism President Hoover's belief that the government could foster economic and social progress by promoting voluntary cooperation among competing groups and interests.

TABLE 24.1	DROP IN AGRICULTURE PRICES, 1928–1932		
	1928	**1929**	**1932**
Wheat	$1.37/bushel	$1.02/bushel	.37/bushel
Cotton	.19/lb	.17/lb	.07/lb
Corn	.92/bushel	.91/bushel	.31/bushel
Beef	9.45/100lb	9.55/100lb	4.35/100lb

Source: U.S. Department of Commerce, *Historical Statistics of the United States, Colonial Times to 1970,* Part 1 (Washington, D.C.: U.S. Government Printing Office, 1975), pp. 510–511, 517, 519.

though, was *help.* The government should help—but not solve. In foreign affairs, he and his secretary of state Henry L. Stimson, would tread a similar path, following closely the economic and noncoercive policies that had characterized the 1920s.

Origins of the Depression

When Herbert Hoover took office, ever-rising stock prices, shiny new cars, and rapidly expanding suburbs seemed to verify Hoover's observation about "the final triumph over poverty." But behind the rush for radios, homes, and vacuum cleaners lay several economic weaknesses. The prosperity of the 1920s depended in large part on a few major industries such as construction, automobiles, and consumer goods. Other important sectors of the economy, textiles, railroads, steel, and iron, for example—barely made a profit, while farming and mining suffered steady losses. As farmers watched demand for their goods shrink year after year, they also saw their income and property values decline to about half of their wartime highs (see Table 24.1). Caught in an economic squeeze of lower profits and increasing production costs, hundreds of thousands of people left farms throughout the twenties. Others turned to government for help. The most popular remedy was incorporated in the twice-vetoed Mc-Nary-Haugen bill, which called for the federal government to buy farm surpluses so as to maintain agricultural production and profits (see pages 729–730). By the end of 1928, agriculture was approaching an economic crisis.

But agriculture's troubles were only part of a growing economic distress. By 1929, even the boom industries were showing signs of weakness. New construction starts had fallen from 11 to 9 billion units between 1926 and 1929. Furniture companies, expecting an unlimited market for new furniture, had by 1927 produced far too many goods, and some plants the next year were cutting their labor force to shave production costs. A similar story held for many makers of smaller consumer goods, especially household appliances. In the automobile industry, sales fluctuated from year to year with slight drops coming in 1926 and 1927, but sales rebounded to record levels in 1928 and 1929.

The slowdown of the economy as Hoover assumed office was the consequence of overproduction, poor distribution of income, and too much credit buying. For the upper and middle classes and for many industrial workers, the 1920s had been a decade of prosperity. Corporate profits had risen 62 percent, and dividends, 65 percent. Wages had increased nearly 11 percent while prices on many popular consumer goods had fallen. National income had jumped from $65 to $83 billion, and total savings had soared from $15 to $35 billion. Still, many others, especially minorities and those living in rural areas, had enjoyed no increase in wages or savings. The only increase they experienced was in prices. As Hoover assumed the presidency, over 70 percent of all American families lived on less than what the Brookings Institute determined to be an income that provided an adequate standard of living—$2,500 a year. At the other end of the scale, the nation had 513 families with annual incomes exceeding $1 million. Few people, however, took notice of the wide gap between those who had much money and those who had little, probably because it was obscured by a generally higher standard of living. Most of the population were fairly comfortable, but at what cost? They exhausted nearly all of their monthly incomes—and what they could put on credit—on food, housing, and an appealing assortment of consumer products. For the nearly three-fourths of the population who spent all they earned, any change in credit policy or paycheck could spell economic hard times.

The Stock Market Plunge

Credit contributed significantly to consumer buying, added to the vision of American prosperity, and helped to generate the boom in the stock market through buying on the margin (see page 708). The desire to invest in the stock market fed a speculative fervor that pushed stock prices higher and higher, until by 1929 the price of many stocks had little relationship to the dividends the stocks paid or the actual worth of the company they represented. Finally in the fall of 1929, the realities of wages, credit, inflated stock prices, and the slowing American economy collided.

When Americans awoke on the morning of Thursday, October 24, 1929, no one realized they would experience one of those days that would change their lives and their nation. It was business as usual as men and women prepared to go to work. In the Midwest, people braced themselves against a frigid, unseasonable ice and snow storm. Across the country Americans followed the lurid story of millionaire theater owner Alexander Pantangas, on trial for assaulting a 17-year-old dancer who had wanted to audition for his show. (He was found guilty.) Not being shareholders, most Americans hardly noticed the rise and fall of stock prices on Wall Street.

Despite the lack of public concern, the events that occurred in the New York Stock Exchange on October 24, 1929, would have profound consequences for all Americans. On that morning, later called **Black Thursday,** the bottom suddenly fell out of the stock market. Immediately, no one wanted to buy stocks while everyone clamored to sell. As buyers failed to materialize, the selling price and the value of stocks plummeted. By 11:30, the ticker tape that relayed stock prices across the nation ran nearly two and a half hours behind, further contributing to the sense of panic. By noon, millions of stocks had been sold as the stock exchange became a frenzied sea of waving arms, raised fists, and screaming voices. Winston Churchill, who happened to be visiting the New York Stock Exchange, observed that in the face of disaster there was "surprising calm and orderli-

ness" as those on the floor were "offering each other enormous blocks of securities at a third of their old prices and half of their present value." In brokerage offices across the country, brokers rushed to place sell orders. No refuge was untouched by the panic: in the mid-Atlantic, aboard the passenger liner *Berengaria,* Helena Rubenstein watched stock prices fall and finally sold her fifty thousand shares of Westinghouse Company. She had lost more than $1 million.

As the Exchange closed for lunch, New York's financial leaders hurriedly met to deal with the panic and try to restore confidence. They concluded that to reverse the market's plunge they needed to show that prices would be supported. On almost the same day twenty-two years earlier, in 1907, New York bankers had stopped a panic and thwarted a possible depression by pooling funds to buy stocks. Now they hoped to repeat history. Led by the bank of J. P. Morgan, financial leaders put together a buying fund of nearly $50 million. Rumors soon expanded the figure to between $100 and $240 million. The bankers then told Richard Whitney, vice chairman of the Exchange, to use the fund to buy stocks as soon as the market reopened.

At 1:30, then, Whitley jauntily marched onto the floor and announced that he was buying ten thousand shares of steel at 205—ten points higher than the existing market price. Amid cheers, others quickly joined the buying drive. At the end of the day, the ticker tape recorded the last transaction four hours after the Exchange had closed. Nearly half of the $6 billion lost in the morning had been recovered. A record 12,894,650 shares had been traded and confidence seemed to have been restored.

On Monday, October 28, prices dropped again. But this time no rescuer appeared to stabilize them. Bankers and Wall Street leaders, having already committed $50 million, were hesitant to add to their bailout. On Black Tuesday, October 29, prices plunged drastically and continued to fall throughout November. Between early September and mid-November, *The New York Times* **industrials** fell from 469 to 22l. Quality stocks likewise plummeted—RCA from 101 to 28, Montgomery Ward from 138 to

---

Black Thursday October 24, 1929, when the stock market fell dramatically in what proved to be the beginning of the crash.

industrials Industrial stocks chosen as indicators of trends in the economy.

♦ On "Black Thursday," October 24, 1929, the entire nation suddenly became aware of Wall Street. The collapse of the stock market historically signals the beginning of the greatest depression in American history. Despite the efforts of Hoover and Roosevelt, it was only the economic activity generated by World War II that revived the economy.
Black Thursday: UPI/Bettman Archives; NYT headline: Picture Research Consultants.

49, Union Carbide from 138 to 59. Hundreds of brokers and speculators were ruined. By mid-November, stories circulated of New York hotel clerks asking guests whether they wanted rooms for sleeping or jumping.

What had caused the greatest depression in American history? Then and now, economists disagree—there is no simple, uniform explanation. Since 1927, the overall economy had been slowing down and unemployment had been inching upward, resulting in decreasing consumption. But few manufacturers noticed the trend and most continued to produce more goods. The surplus of goods might have not been critical if they could have been sold overseas or if prices had been lowered. But neither of these correctives took place. With two hundred major corporations controlling over half of the nation's wealth and dominating the production of most goods, there was little competitive pressure to lower prices substantially. Nor was the overseas market willing to take up the surplus left by the shrinking American market. In 1929, Hoover wanted to stimulate trade by lowering some tariffs as much as 50 percent, but most Republicans wanted higher not lower tariffs. The final product, the **Hawley-Smoot Tariff,** passed in June 1930—af-

ter the great crash—was a victory for American economic nationalism but a catastrophe for world trade. Angered by American actions, twenty-three foreign governments, in turn, raised their tariffs on American goods, further stifling world trade. By 1932, American exports had fallen to their lowest level since 1905, two years later the value of international trade had dropped over forty percent. Rather than protect national economies, the high tariffs only furthered the spread of the global depression. With fewer goods being sold, businesses faced declining profits and slashed production. More and more employers laid off workers and anticipated bankruptcy.

Stock prices continued downward. *The New York Times* industrials sank to 58 by mid-1932. United States Steel fell from a pre-crash high of 262 to a low of 22. General Motors dropped to 73, then to 8. Many companies did not survive. Between 1929 and 1933, ninety thousand businesses failed, corporate

---

Hawley-Smoot Tariff   1930 law passed in response to the Depression, setting the highest tariff rates in U.S. history and thus undermining world trade.

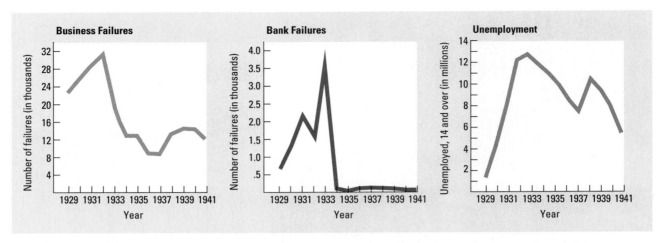

◆ **FIGURE 24.1 Charting the Economics of the Depression** Between 1929 and 1933, there was an expanding number of unemployed people seeking work, and banks and businesses closing their doors. By 1933, over 4,000 banks had failed, unemployment had reached 24.9 percent, and over 100,000 firms had closed. As the New Deal began, not only did the statistics improve, but there was for most Americans a feeling of hope and improvement.

profits fell 60 percent, and nine thousand banks closed (see Figure 24.1). As banks collapsed, depositors lost $2.5 billion. As the money supply shrank, dropping by a third between 1930 and 1933, expenditures for goods plummeted by 45 percent. Purchases of automobiles dropped by 75 percent. At the same time, unemployment rose from 3 percent in 1929, to 9 percent in 1930, to 25 percent in 1933 (see the chapter-opening map). As the downward spiral of economic contraction and the stock market continued, nearly everyone in the nation felt its effects—the depression was becoming the **Great Depression.**

Government and Economic Crisis

● Why were Hoover's choices in dealing with the problems created by the Depression neither appreciated nor effective?

Within the Hoover administration, the immediate response to the plunge in stock prices was not gloom and doom, but guarded optimism. Secretary of the Treasury Mellon thought the drop would strengthen the market and cleanse the economy of inflated values. He believed the government should just let the economy heal itself. Hoover disagreed. He was unwilling to sit idle and let the economy fail

without exerting any effort to reverse the slide. Government, he believed, needed to play some, even if only a limited, role. As the stock market declined and the money supply shrank, Hoover called leaders of banking, industry, and labor together. He pleaded with employers not to cut wages or production or to lay off workers. He exhorted unions not to demand higher wages. At the same time, he assured the public that the economy was sound and would soon improve. These efforts worked for only a short time.

When cheerleading and voluntary action failed to improve the worsening situation, public pressure grew for the federal government to take more direct action. Hoover continued to make optimistic speeches but also began to lean toward a more direct government involvement. In December 1929, he asked Congress, along with state and local governments, to increase spending for the construction of **public works** projects, including highways, govern-

---

Great Depression The years 1929 to 1941 in the United States, during which the economy was in a severe decline and millions of people were out of work.

public works Construction projects such as highways and dams, financed by public funds and carried out by the government.

ment facilities, and **Boulder Dam.** Federal, state, and local governments doubled their spending on public works but the investment had little immediate impact. The economy continued to worsen. Over the next two years Hoover would greatly expand the role of government in responding to the Depression, but increasingly a majority of Americans blamed him and his administration for the hardships they faced. A popular jingle went

> *Mellon pulled the whistle*
> *Hoover rang the bell*
> *Wall Street gave the signal*
> *And the country went to hell.*

By the end of 1932, workers' income had dropped 40 percent and unemployment had raced to an alarming 25 percent. Small industrial towns were especially hard hit. Donora, Pennsylvania, for instance, had only 277 jobs for its population of over 14,000. Many, like Donora's future baseball great Stan Musial, left home seeking greener pastures, moving from one community to another looking for work. Most would be unsuccessful. Ed Paulson left his hometown in Montana to find work. Arriving in San Francisco, he heard of a job and at 5:00 A.M. dashed to the job site, only to find more than "three thousand men, carpenters, cement men, guys who knew machinery and everything else" were already there. Paulson continued to roam the country looking for work, developing a "coyote mentality." "You were a predator," he said. "You had to be. The coyote is crafty. . . . We were coyotes in the Thirties, the jobless." Private, state, and local charities and relief agencies vainly tried to meet the needs of the millions out of work and in need. Bread lines and soup kitchens did their best to feed the growing army of hungry and displaced Americans. But the numbers were too overwhelming. Across the country, shantytowns bitterly named **"Hoovervilles"** housed the homeless.

When the stock market crashed, agriculture was already in a depression. Drought in the Mississippi Valley soon spread throughout the South and Midwest. It would last a decade. Adding to the misery of farmers, swarms of grasshoppers ate their way across the nation's midsection. Between grasshoppers and drought, the land was laid bare as winds whipped up huge clouds of dust, sometimes stretching more than 200 miles across and 7,000 to 8,000 feet high. Tidal waves of dust descended on the Midwest, and winds blew what had once been midwestern **topsoil** more than halfway across the Atlantic (see Map 24.2). In 1938, the worst year for dust

♦ The Great Depression produced large-scale unemployment, reaching 25 percent in 1933. This picture, titled "Unemployed," painted by Reginald Marsh effectively captured the despair of men and women seeking jobs. *"Unemployed" by Reginald Marsh, 1932. Library of Congress.*

storms, over 850 million tons of topsoil were lost to erosion. Dust hung in the air and filtered into homes, covering clothing, furniture, food, everything. One reporter observed that an "uncorked jug placed on a sidewalk two hours . . . [was] found to be half filled with dust." Hoover, moved by the plight of farmers, within a month of taking office asked Congress to create a national farm board. The board would help stabilize prices by buying agricultural products on the open market. Although

---

Boulder Dam   Dam on the Colorado River between Nevada and Arizona, which was renamed in honor of Hoover.

"Hooverville"   Crudely built camp set up by the homeless on the fringes of a town or city during the Depression.

topsoil   Surface layer of the soil, in which crops grow.

♦ **MAP 24.2 The Dust Bowl** Throughout the 1930s, sun and wind eroded millions of acres of crop land, sending tons of topsoil into the air, generating tidal waves of dust—and the Dust Bowl. This map shows the regions most affected by the Dust Bowl and loss of population, and Route 66, which many chose to travel, hoping that it would lead to a better life in California.

conservatives attacked the plan as a leap into socialism, Congress passed the **Agricultural Marketing Act** in May. The Farm Board was initially successful in supporting farm prices. The world price of wheat sank to nearly $.55 in February, 1931, but because the Farm Board had bought over 257 million bushels—one fourth of the world supply—the American price held steady at $.80 a bushel. But by the end of 1931, the Farm Board, running short of funds, could no longer provide economic support. Agricultural prices inevitably tumbled downward, forcing more farmers into bankruptcy.

As declining farm prices, drought, and dust destroyed farmers' hopes, many turned to direct action. The **Farmers' Holiday Association,** led by Milo Reno, formed in the Midwest and called on farmers to destroy their products and to resist **foreclosures** (see Individual Choices: Milo Reno).

"When you took a man's horse and his plow away, you denied him food, you just convicted his family to starvation," recalled one farmer, who added that the "people were desperate." Angry and frequently armed, farmers used their numbers and threats of violence to ensure that foreclosed properties were

> **Agricultural Marketing Act** 1929 law that created the Farm Board to stabilize farm prices by buying crop surpluses; the price support program ended in 1931.
>
> **Farmers' Holiday Association** Farmers' organization led by Milo Reno of Iowa, which organized a strike in the summer of 1932 to protest the drastic decline in farm income.
>
> **foreclosure** Confiscation of a property by the bank when mortgage payments are delinquent.

sold at auction to their previous owners for a fraction of their value. One such "penny auction," returned Walter Crozier's farm in Haskins, Ohio, for a high bid of $1.90. Other farmers burned their corn, killed their livestock, and dumped milk and eggs onto the arid ground. A judge who was notorious for foreclosing on farms was hauled "out of his court and . . . had a rope around his neck, and . . . the rope over a limb of a tree before . . . somebody had sense enough to stop the thing before it got too far," remembered one farmer. Critics of the agrarian protest linked it with "international Jews, the IWW, Socialists, and Communists" and blamed the unrest on **outside agitators.** But in fact the protesters were home-grown and simply wanted government support for the farmer. Democrats joyfully blamed Hoover and the Farm Board for the deepening problems and promised change.

Hoover's Final Efforts

By December 1931, succumbing to political pressure and a still worsening economy, Hoover moved in a new direction, promoting more direct federal involvement in dealing with the Depression. He asked Congress for banking reforms, financial support for home mortgages, the creation of the **Reconstruction Finance Corporation (RFC),** and higher taxes to pay for it all. Congress responded with the **Glass-Steagall Banking Act,** which increased bank reserves to encourage lending, and the Federal Home Loan Act, which allowed home owners to remortgage their homes at lower rates and payments. But it was through the RFC that Hoover intended to fight the Depression by pumping money into the economy. Using federal funds, the RFC was to provide loans to banks, savings and loans, railroads, insurance companies, and large corporations to prevent their collapse and encourage expanded operations. Hoover and his advisers believed the money would "trickle down" to workers and the unemployed through higher wages and new jobs. It was an unprecedented effort by the federal government to intervene directly in the private sector and stimulate the economy. Conservatives called it "an experiment in socialism." Senator Burton Wheeler (Democrat from Montana) warned that RFC handouts would create a welfare state with loans and credits eventually being given to nearly everyone. Within five months of operation, the RFC had loaned over $805 million mostly to large businesses, but little relief and less money seemed to be trickling down to workers. Liberal critics labeled the program "welfare for the rich," and insisted that Hoover do more for the poor and unemployed through **direct relief** payments and more public works projects.

Hoover opposed direct federal relief, the "dole," for several basic reasons. He believed that it would be too burdensome for the federal budget and that relief should instead be distributed by private organizations and local government. "Where people divest themselves of local government responsibilities," he explained, "they at once lay the foundation for the destruction of their liberties." He and others also were convinced the dole would erode the work ethic and bring about a class of idle Americans who would rather live on relief than work. Still, in the spring of 1932, it was getting harder and harder for Hoover to resist Congressional and public pressure to provide assistance. Finally, Hoover agreed to create the Emergency Relief Division within the RFC and provide $300 million to loan states for relief. Like other RFC efforts, actual relief spending did not match the potential. Headed by a conservative board of directors, the RFC loaned money too cautiously. Further, states whose budgets were already overstrained hesitated to increase their debt by borrowing more. Consequently, by the end of 1932, the RFC had spent only 10 percent of its relief fund.

The patience of many Americans seemed at an end by the summer of 1932. The Farmers' Holiday movement was spreading across the Midwest, and thousands of veterans, the Bonus Expeditionary Force, were making their way toward Washington. The **Bonus Army,** twenty thousand unemployed veterans of the Great War, headed to the capital to

---

outside agitator   Term applied to a radical organizer who instigates protests in an area or industry where he or she does not belong.

Reconstruction Finance Corporation   Organization to promote economic recovery established at Hoover's request in 1932; it provided emergency financing for banks, life insurance companies, railroads, and farm mortgage associations.

Glass-Steagall Banking Act   1932 law that expanded credit through the Federal Reserve System in order to counteract foreign withdrawals and domestic hoarding of money.

direct relief   Payments directly to the poor and unemployed.

Bonus Army   Unemployed World War I veterans who marched to Washington in 1932 to demand early payment of a promised bonus; Congress refused and protesters who remained were evicted by the army.

Choosing Confrontation

Milo Reno

In 1918 Milo Reno chose to become a spokesman for the farmer and organized the Farmers' Holiday Association. In 1933, he chose to reject Roosevelt's agricultural recovery program, and lost support of most farmers, who supported the president. State Historical Society of America.

Born in 1866, Milo Reno was raised in the heartland of Populism and enthusiasm for William Jennings Bryan. Ordained as a Cambellite minister by Oskalossa College, Reno chose to give up the ministry to pursue his true calling—organizing farmers for political action. He joined the Farmers' Union in 1918, dominating it until his death in 1936, and was the driving force behind the Farmers' Holiday Association. Wearing a ten-gallon hat and flaming red necktie, Reno captured farmers' hearts with evangelical-style speeches that combined simple explanations, personalized enemies, Biblical quotes, and farm wisdom.

In 1932, he claimed that Hoover's farm policies were driving hard-working, decent people from the land, and in August, he called for a farmers' strike. "Stay home, buy nothing, sell nothing," he commanded the farmers, to force change and break "the grip of Wall Street and international bankers on government." Farmers across Iowa and neighboring states heeded his call, refusing to sell their products. Others exceeded it, erecting barricades across highways to prevent farmers' products from reaching processors. Outside Sioux City and other midwestern towns, farmers armed with clubs and

lobby for the Wright-Patman bill, which stipulated early payment of their veterans' bonus, originally scheduled to be paid in 1945. Against the warnings of advisers, Hoover allowed the Bonus Marchers to enter the District of Columbia and even ensured that tents, clothing, medicine, and food were available as the marchers set up their Hooverville across from Congress in Anacostia Flats.

Hoover respected the veterans' right to assemble and lobby, but when the Senate rejected the Patman bill, the president thought the marchers should go home. He even provided loans to cover the cost of

leaving. Over half of the Bonus Marchers left, but nearly ten thousand stayed behind at Anacostia Flats or in condemned buildings within Washington. When the police attempted to clear the buildings, nearly five thousand veterans and eight hundred police clashed. Two Bonus Marchers were killed. As the police withdrew, Hoover turned to the army to evict the squatters. Army Chief of Staff General Douglas MacArthur was ready. He had marshaled a force of four troops of cavalry, four companies of infantry, six tanks, and several mounted machine guns for the unpleasant task. Us-

pitchforks clashed with truck drivers and hastily dispatched sheriff's deputies. By mid-August over eighty picketers had been arrested, and fearful of further violence and arrests, Reno called a "temporary halt" to the strike.

With the barricades the strike had received national news coverage focused on the distress of farmers—and politicians had responded. Midwest governors listened to Farmers' Holiday spokesmen and pushed Hoover for increased support for farmers. Presidential candidate Franklin D. Roosevelt emphasized that Democrats promised farm prices "in excess of cost." Reno, like millions of other Americans, saw in Roosevelt a chance for hope, cheered his election, and waited anxiously for the New Deal to begin.

As Roosevelt assumed office, Reno and the Farmers' Holiday movement—now claiming ninety thousand members—continued to attract national attention by stopping farm foreclosures and forcing "penny auctions." Again, direct action seemed to work as many companies halted foreclosures and ten states even passed foreclosure "moratorium laws." But with Roosevelt in office, farmers were also receiving less and less public support for their activism. Many politicians and journalists now linked their movement with communism. Reno was faced with a hard choice. Should he continue direct action or support Roosevelt's agriculture program?

Responding to negative public opinion, Reno asked farm activists to pull back from confrontation and give Roosevelt time to implement his farm programs. Still, Reno had

doubts. He disliked Henry A. Wallace as secretary of agriculture, considered Roosevelt an "enigma," and was angry when the New Deal's agriculture program—the Agriculture Adjustment Act—did not include cost-of-production provisions. He told a friend, "I have no faith whatever in the gestures that are being made by the administration. It is simply the same old tactic to hand the people a little measure of relief to suppress rebellion, with no intention of correcting a system that is fundamentally wrong."

In October 1933, Reno made a difficult decision but one he believed necessary. Roosevelt, he was sure, was taking the nation down the wrong path that would eventually "crush all . . . independence and liberty . . . setting up a bureaucratic, autocratic, dictatorial government." He renewed the call for a strike and stated that a third political party was the only possible solution "to clean up the stinking mess" in Washington. The strike call was largely ignored by farmers, who had begun to trust Roosevelt's promise of federal support. The momentum of the farmers' protest had vanished, consumed by the spread of the federal government into agricultural affairs.

Increasingly out of touch with most farmers, Reno fell into periods of depression and heavy drinking until, stricken with influenza in March 1936, he checked into a sanitarium. "Tell them I'm really sick," he said. Milo Reno died on May 5, 1936.

---

ing sabers, rifles, tear gas, and fixed bayonets, the army drove the veterans from the abandoned buildings and then proceeded to Anacostia Flats. Hoover had given orders to leave the Bonus Marchers at Anacostia Flats alone, but MacArthur ignored his commander-in-chief. In the one-sided fight that ensued, veterans and their families were driven off and their huts and tents set afire. Over one hundred veterans were injured in the melee, but rumors quickly swelled the number and added several deaths, including a baby who reportedly died from the tear gas. The rumors intensified the public's angry reaction. What slim chance Hoover had for reelection certainly died at the "Battle of Anacostia Flats." On hearing of the forced eviction of the marchers, the governor of New York, Franklin D. Roosevelt crowed, "This will elect me."

Franklin D. Roosevelt

As Americans sought to adapt to the economic crisis and reacted to the spectacle of U.S. Army tanks chasing unarmed men and women, many looked to the Democratic party for leadership and a change.

◆ After the Bonus Marchers were evicted from their "Hooverville" in Washington in 1932, Hoover said, "Thank God we still have a government that knows how to deal with a mob." But in the battle between Bonus Marchers and the police and army troops, many Americans sided with the marchers, further hurting Hoover's slim chances for reelection. *Culver Pictures, Inc.*

◆ Held upright by heavy steel leg braces that the public rarely saw, Franklin D. Roosevelt accepted the Democratic's party's nomination for the presidency and promised the American people a New Deal. Compared to a dreary Hoover, the cheerful Roosevelt provided hope to expectant Americans and received their votes, swamping Hoover in the 1932 election. *UPI/Bettman Archives.*

Throughout the early months of 1932, **Franklin D. Roosevelt** had campaigned for the Democratic presidential nomination, saying that government needed to be concerned about the "forgotten man" who, through no fault of his own, suffered from the Depression.

Born into wealth and privilege, Roosevelt had attended elite schools popular with America's aristocracy: Groton Academy, Harvard University, and Columbia Law School. Neither academically nor athletically gifted, Roosevelt was nonetheless popular. With a recognizable name (Theodore Roosevelt was his fifth cousin), family wealth, and influential connections, Roosevelt easily entered New York politics in 1910, winning a seat in the New York legislature. Tall, handsome, charming, glib, and willing to work with Tammany Hall, Roosevelt moved up the political ladder quickly. In 1920, he was selected James Cox's running mate, and even though Cox was defeated, many observers saw Roosevelt's career still climbing. The climb seemed suddenly over in 1921, however, when Roosevelt was stricken with polio. Paralyzed from the waist down, Roosevelt might have retired from politics and become a forgotten man himself. But he and his wife Eleanor were determined to overcome his handicap. For two years, Roosevelt worked hard to advance from bedridden invalid to barely mobile. He was never able to walk except with the aid of heavy steel leg braces and crutches. At the same time, Eleanor Roosevelt toiled tirelessly to keep his political career alive. It was largely through her efforts that he got the opportunity to deliver the nominating speech for Al Smith at the 1924 Democratic convention. Making his return to the political battlefield, Roosevelt ran for governor of New York. Smith lost in a Hoover landslide, but Roosevelt won.

As governor, Roosevelt too faced the Depression, but unlike Hoover, he saw nothing wrong with governmental activism to deal with economic disaster. He was one of the few governors to mobilize his state's limited resources to help the unemployed and poor. Although he made little headway against the Depression, his efforts projected an image of a more caring and energetic leader than Hoover. His

---

Franklin D. Roosevelt New York governor elected President in 1932 with the promise of a New Deal for the American people; he was to lead the country through the Depression and World War II.

brave struggle to overcome polio combined with his effectiveness as governor and his cheery disposition earned him a reputation as the champion of the "forgotten man" and made him the logical candidate for the presidency. Hoover's apparent lack of leadership when confronted by declining wages and profits and 11 million unemployed people made Roosevelt the next president.

The 1932 Election

Roosevelt was nominated on the fourth ballot, over Al Smith and Speaker of the House John Nance Garner of Texas. Traditionally, candidates did not attend the convention and accepted the nomination from their homes. Showing his dynamic flair, Roosevelt broke that tradition and immediately flew to Chicago to accept the nomination in person. In his acceptance speech, the nominee emphasized two points: he was a man of action who promoted change, and his health was good and his paralysis in no way hindered his capacity for work. Roosevelt also established the theme for the coming campaign. Pointing to his tradition-breaking trip to the convention, he emphatically announced that he and the Democratic party had no fear of breaking "all foolish traditions." He closed by promising a "new deal for the American people." In writing the speech, neither Roosevelt nor his advisers had placed any emphasis on the phrase "new deal," but the media quickly focused on it, handing Roosevelt a clever, symbolic slogan for his campaign: the **New Deal.** Although the acceptance speech offered no concrete solutions to the problems plaguing the country, it stirred the desire for hope and change.

Roosevelt selected Garner as his vice-presidential nominee. Garner was a good choice and his name on the ballot helped to heal east-west, north-south, urban-rural splits within the party. During the campaign, Roosevelt tried to avoid any commitments and policies that might offend voters or blocs among the Democrats. Like most politicians, he promised all things to all people. He supported direct federal relief while promising to balance the budget, but mostly he went on stressing hope and the prospect of change. Hoover, trying to overcome his opponent's popularity, emphasized their philosophical differences. He claimed that the campaign, "more than a contest between two men," was "a contest between two philosophies of government." Few people seemed to care, and Roosevelt continued to use his sharpest campaign tools: his dynamic energy and contagious optimism.

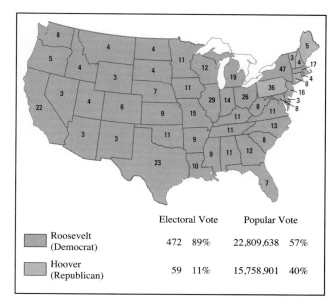

	Electoral Vote		Popular Vote	
Roosevelt (Democrat)	472	89%	22,809,638	57%
Hoover (Republican)	59	11%	15,758,901	40%

◆ **MAP 24.3 Election of 1932**   In the election of 1932, Herbert Hoover not only faced Franklin D. Roosevelt but the Great Depression. With many Americans blaming Hoover and the Republicans for the economic catastrophe and with Roosevelt promising a New Deal, the outcome was not close. Roosevelt won 42 of 48 states.

The election was a huge success for the Democratic party and Roosevelt. Across the nation, people voted for Democrats—for state and local officials, for Congress, and most importantly, for president. Roosevelt won in a landslide, burying Hoover with 22.8 million votes, 57.4 percent of over 39.7 million votes cast. Hoover carried only six states (see Map 24.3). The rest belonged to Roosevelt. Roosevelt and the American people now had to wait four months, until the March 4, 1933 inauguration, before the New Deal could begin.

The Diplomacy of Depression

When Hoover entered the presidency, the world—like the nation—appeared stable and peaceful. Hoover intended to follow the foreign policies of his predecessors, using economic and noncoercive

> **New Deal**   Roosevelt's program for attacking the problems of the Depression, which included relief for the poor and unemployed, efforts to bring about economic recovery, and reform of the nation's financial system.

means to protect American interests and promote world prosperity. Since the days of Theodore Roosevelt, Latin Americans had accused the United States of being a "new Rome," of creating an empire based on money rather than territory. When Hoover took office in 1929, Latin Americans were adamant in opposing the Roosevelt Corollary (see page 631) and demanding the withdrawal of American troops from Haiti and Nicaragua (see Map 24.1). Hoover promised to respect and not intervene in Latin American affairs and continued the process of removing troops. He also made public a memorandum written by Assistant Secretary of State J. Reuben Clark that stated that the Monroe Doctrine did not give the United States the right to intervene in Latin American affairs. To American investors and bankers, Hoover let it be known that they should not expect the government to come to their rescue when they found themselves or their investments threatened. Overall during Hoover's administration, relations between Latin America and the United States improved greatly.

Elsewhere, however, Hoover's efforts to promote prosperity and peace abroad came to little. And at home, increasingly larger and vocal numbers of Americans denounced even a cooperative role for the United States in world affairs. As the Depression became entrenched, so did isolationism. Most Americans were far more concerned about keeping their jobs and homes than about international affairs. Many, including Hoover, blamed a major part of the country's economic woes on the Europeans. Republican Senator George W. Norris of Nebraska publicly linked his state's farm foreclosures with the events spawned by the Europeans and the Great War. He urged the United States to look out for its own interests and let Europe be damned. Others agreed, including most Republicans. Unfortunately, like the Depression, world problems would not go away.

If most Americans reacted to the Depression by spurning foreign involvements, the opposite was true in Japan. Japan relied heavily on international trade for its economic growth and its food supply, and as the Depression and shrinking world trade weakened their economy, calls arose among the Japanese for their government to protect national interests. Rejecting most Western values and free trade, many nationalists advocated a Japanese sphere of influence, or empire, and looked hungrily toward Manchuria.

Situated north and west of Japanese-controlled Korea, Manchuria was rich in iron and coal, ac-

counted for 95 percent of Japanese overseas investment, and also supplied large amounts of vital foodstuffs to the island nation. Most important, the Japanese maintained a military presence in Manchuria to help the Chinese authorities keep order and to protect Japanese interests. Conflict was increasing between the Japanese military authorities in Manchuria and Jiang Jieshi's (Chiang Kai-shek) government, which was seeking to reassert Chinese control there. In September 1931, fearful of growing Chinese power, a small group of young, anti-Western Japanese army officers executed a plan to establish Japanese rule over the region. Members of the Japanese Manchurian Army, the Guandong, blew up a section of track of the Southern Manchurian Railroad and blamed the Chinese. Then, without informing the government of Japan, the Guandong used this ruse as an excuse to attack Chinese forces and take control of the province (see Map 24.4).

World reaction was one of shock and eventual condemnation, but little else. The League of Nations sheepishly called for peace and appointed a committee to investigate the conflict. Neither the United States nor Great Britain, the two major Pacific naval powers, wanted to become involved in an Asian war. From Washington, Secretary of State Stimson asked on September 24 that the Chinese and Japanese governments halt the fighting, and when that failed, he denounced the Japanese for their aggression. As Japan won control of the province, the United States invoked the **Stimson Doctrine,** implementing the policy of nonrecognition, which meant ignoring Japan's control over its newly created puppet state of **Manchukuo.** In American eyes, Manchuria remained a part of China.

The Japanese had violated the Nine Power Pact, the Kellogg-Briand Pact, and principles of the League of Nations, but the ensuing barrage of spoken and written protests did nothing to deter their aggression. World leaders would run out of stationery penning their protests, American humorist Will Rogers sarcastically noted, before Japan would run out of soldiers. In Japan, the successful conquest of Manchuria magnified the power of pro-imperial

---

Stimson Doctrine Declaration by the U.S. Secretary of State in 1932 that the United States would not recognize Manchuko or any other arrangement that threatened China's independence.

Manchukuo Puppet state established by Japan in 1932 and not recognized by the United States.

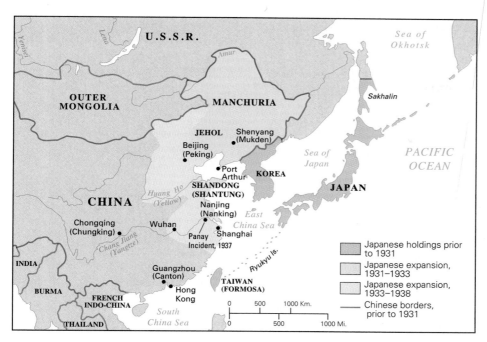

◆ **MAP 24.4 Japanese Expansion, 1931–1938** As this map indicates, in 1931 at China's expense, Japan began to expand its empire in East Asia. Although other nations condemned Japanese aggression, they took no direct action, and Japan continued to occupy more and more of China, forcing the Chinese government to move its capital to Chiongoing (Chungking).

and anti-Western groups. In 1933, the Japanese government, dominated by militant nationalists, withdrew from the League of Nations. When Franklin Roosevelt ran for the presidency in 1932, the world was a much different place than in 1928. The cheery optimism of a prosperous world at peace had dissipated. In its place were serious concerns about the global depression and the possibility of other wars.

Depression America

● What economic and social constraints and choices did the Depression generate for industrial workers, minorities, and women?

As Americans contemplated the presidential race in November 1932, however, it was not the problems in Manchuria that they considered. Most of their concerns were much closer to home—the rout of the Bonus Marchers and how three years of the Great Depression had affected their own lives. For the Depression had touched every American, forcing changes in lifestyle, thought, and politics. Poverty was no longer reserved for those viewed as lazy or

unworthy—it was no longer relegated to remote areas and inner cities. Now poverty dragged down blue- and white-collar workers, and even a few of the once-rich.

Families in the Depression

Average annual income dropped 35 percent between 1929 and 1933, from $2,300 to $1,500. Although income rose after 1933, nagging fears of cuts in wages or loss of work remained. To help those facing economic "insecurity," magazines and newspapers provided useful hints and "Depression recipes" that stretched budgets and included nutritional information. According to trained home economists, a careful shopper and creative cook could feed a family of five on as little as $8.00 a week (see Tables 24.2 and 24.3). This was comforting news for those with that much to spend on food a week, but for many families and for relief agencies $8.00 a week for food was beyond possibility. New York City, which paid out the highest amount in assistance, provided only $2.39 a week for each family.

TABLE 24.2 CONSUMER PRICES, 1931

Food		Other goods	
Rye Bread	$ .05 a loaf	Eastman Camera	$ 6.95
Apples	.25 for 4 lbs	Philco Baby Grand Radio	79.95
Bananas	.19 for 4 lbs	Sears Refrigerator	139.50
Round Steak	.28 a pound	Men's Dress Shirt	.50
Chicken Broilers	.39 a pound	DeSoto Six (Automobile)	695.00
Ground Beef	.29 for 2 lbs		
Shredded Wheat	.19 cents for 2 boxes		
Clorox	.16 cents a bottle		
Cigarettes	.27 cents for 2 packs		
Coffee	.69 cents for 2 lbs		
Butter	.59 cents for 2 lbs		
Sugar	1.25 for 25 lbs		
Flour	.79 for 25 lbs		
Lifebouy Soap	.25 for 4 cakes		
Milk	.10 for a quart		

Source: Observer Reporter (Washington, PA), July, 1931.

Many people worried about basic survival, but some looked beyond the individual and were uneasy about the impact of the Depression on society. They suspected that the Depression was causing a decline in family values and morality. Pointing to the drifters uprooted by hard times, to families without fathers, and to reports of increasing abortions and premarital and deviant sexual activities, they forecast the end of American civilization. Their fears were unfounded. The vast majority of Americans clung tightly to traditional family values and emphasized family unity. Church attendance rose during the Depression, and the number of divorces declined. The percentage of people getting married dropped slightly, and the nation's birthrate fell during the thirties. But marriages were only delayed, not put off entirely, and the lower birthrate resulted from economic fears and increased availability of birth control devices, especially condoms and diaphragms. One could even order contraceptives through the Sears, Roebuck mail-order catalog. Moralists decried an increasing abortion rate, but in fact the estimated number of abortions remained steady. Abortions were illegal and the number of abortions is unknown, but the number of abortion-related deaths—a known statistic—remained about nine thousand per year throughout the Depression. Studies also indicated that sexual activity, rather than becoming more varied and promiscuous, actually decreased.

Nor did the Depression tear many families apart. In fact, economic necessity kept families at home playing board games and cards, reading, and listening to the radio. "Monopoly" was introduced, allowing players to fantasize about becoming a millionaire and laugh about going broke. To save money, many women sewed, baked bread, and canned, reaffirming traditional female roles. Outside of the house, dances and movies provided inexpensive ways of spending time while escaping from daily problems. An estimated 65 percent of the population saw a movie once a week. The official censor of Hollywood movies, **Will Hays,** ensured that films portrayed conventional, traditional values and morals.

But not all families remained stable and united. Unemployed males, especially fathers, often felt shame for their economic problems. Suicides increased, as did the number of men and women admitted to state mental hospitals. Some families ex-

Will Hays Organizer in 1922 of the Motion Picture Producers and Distributors of America, through which the movie industry censored itself.

TABLE 24.3   DEPRESSION MENU, 1932

Breakfast	Lunch	Dinner
Oatmeal with milk	Macaroni and cheese	Salmon croquettes
Scrambled eggs	Cole slaw	Creamed potatoes
Toast	Corn bread	Stewed tomatoes
Milk	Baked apples	Bread
Coffee	Milk	Milk
Cost $1.72		

Source: Susan F. West, "Low Cost Diets Planned According to Different Standards," *Journal of Home Economics* (February 1932): 113–118.

perienced a change in traditional roles as women and children replaced husbands and fathers as breadwinners. A social worker wrote, "I used to see men cry because they didn't have a job. . . . They were belittled before the eyes of their families and they couldn't take it . . . lowering the pride of manhood." John Boris, a Slavic immigrant, after working loyally for Ford for fourteen years, was among the 91,000 workers that the automaker laid off. He was devastated by the dismissal: "Last July, I was a good man," he lamented. "I ain't a man now." Boris lost his home and his dignity, but he survived by living with relatives, supported by his children. He never recovered his job at Ford or his sense of pride.

Boris was fortunate to be able to stay with family members, but others, unable to provide support, deserted their homes and took to the road. Many rode the rails—"hobos" hitching rides in box cars, living in shantytowns, begging and scrounging for food and supplies along the road. Estimates in 1932 placed the number of homeless migrants between 1 and 2 million.

Included in the so-called migration of despair were thousands from rural areas, especially parts of Texas, Arkansas, and Oklahoma that were hard hit by **dust bowl** storms. Forced from their farms by dust, debt, and landlords, many families—like the **"Arkies" and "Okies"** characterized in John Steinbeck's *Grapes of Wrath*—loaded their meager possessions on their **jalopies** and trekked toward California. By the end of the decade, California's population had jumped by over a million people. Some migrants found jobs but most continued to wander, looking for new opportunities.

African-Americans in the Depression

As the 1930s began, most African-Americans lived in the rural South, making less than $200 a year. The onslaught of the Depression only intensified the economic and social difficulties they faced. As agricultural prices shrank, especially for cotton, black sharecroppers, farmhands, and tenants farmers were evicted. Many migrated to urban areas. Harlem's black population more than doubled during the thirties. But cities provided no cure for the pains of unemployment and poverty. As jobs grew scarce, whites demanded and got those jobs previously held by minorities, who were fired to make room. Urban black unemployment ran 20 to 50 percent higher than for whites. Nationally, over 2 million African-Americans, or 50 percent of the black population, were out of work or on relief.

African-American women, especially in northern cities, also saw significant drops in employment even though they held low-paying and low-status jobs. In Chicago, Cleveland, and Philadelphia between 1929 to 1940, the decline in employment

---

dust bowl   Name given to the Great Plains region devastated by drought and dust storms during the 1930s.

"Arkies and Okies"   Name applied to dispossessed sharecroppers from Arkansas and Oklahoma, both black and white, who migrated to California during the Depression.

jalopy   An old, rundown truck or car.

♦ Dorothea Lange became one of the most famous photographers of the Depression. Her photo of a migrant mother and her children at a migrant camp in Nipomo, California captured the human tragedy of the Depression. Seeking jobs and opportunities, over 350,000 people traveled to the state, most finding few opportunities. *Library of Congress.*

♦ In one of the most controversial cases of the decade, nine African-American men, the Scottsboro Nine, shown here with one of their lawyers, were convicted of raping two white women. Eight were sentenced to death by an all-white jury, but in 1937 after a series of appeals and retrials, only five were sentenced to jail. Four of the five were paroled in 1944, the fifth man had successfully escaped to Michigan. *Brown Brothers.*

among black women averaged 22.6 percent as white women and men pushed them out of the labor force. Working or not, many African-American women found that the Depression brought a surprising social gain. Merchants, especially in the South, competing for fewer and fewer shopper dollars, for the first time allowed African-American women to try on clothes before buying them. However, such benefits hardly offset the sinking wages and rising racial hostility.

Racial violence and injustice increased during the Depression as whites used violence and intimidation to drive blacks from jobs and maintain social dominance. In Harlem, low wages and limited relief funds combined with existing racial tensions to spark a race riot in 1935 that cost four lives and millions of dollars in damage. In the South, lynchings of blacks continued. In 1931, the nation's attention was drawn to Scottsboro, Alabama, where nine

black men were arrested and charged with raping Victoria Price and Ruby Bates, both white prostitutes. Although there was no physical evidence of the men's guilt, a jury of white males did not question the testimony of white women and quickly found the **Scottsboro Nine** guilty. Eight were sentenced to death, but the ninth, a minor, escaped the death penalty. Years of appeals and retrials followed, with the Supreme Court twice ordering new trials. None of the accused was ever acquitted, but by 1950 all were free. The state dropped charges against four in 1935, four others received early

Scottsboro Nine Nine African-Americans convicted of raping 2 white women in a freight train in Alabama in 1931; their case became famous as an example of racism in the legal system.

◆ Adding to racial prejudices, the Depression provided a reason to remove unwanted Mexico aliens from the United States. In Los Angeles, special trains took Mexicans to San Diego where they were returned to Mexico. An estimated 425,000 Mexicans were repatriated between 1929 and 1934. *Los Angeles Public Library.*

paroles, and one escaped to Michigan, where the governor refused to return him. Although the Supreme Court and other liberal groups and individuals championed the Scottsboro defendants, the 1930s saw little effort to challenge the reality of segregation and discrimination faced by America's nonwhite minorities.

Mexican-Americans in the Depression

Like African-Americans, Latinos found that the Depression only aggravated white hostility and made a hard life harder. Since 1914 the Latinos, largely Mexican, population of the United States had grown rapidly, not only in California and the Southwest but in the Midwest as well. In 1910 only about seven hundred Latinos lived in Illinois, but as industries recruited Mexican workers, the population grew to over four thousand, nearly half living in the Chicago area. Squeezing out a meager living, most Mexican nationals and Mexican-Americans filled menial jobs, worked in the fields, and farmed small plots of land. Many lived on the margin even in good times, but the Depression forced them and many others into deeper poverty. At the same time it inflamed racial hostility.

Anglos not only demanded that Mexican and Mexican-American workers be fired to provide jobs for whites, they wanted Mexicans out of the country altogether. In many cities, including Los Angeles, the economics of relief encouraged the return of Mexicans to Mexico. It was cheaper to send Mexican aliens back than to provide relief for them. In many instances, private, municipal, and state agencies gave free transportation to the border for those willing to return. Throughout the nation, the United States Immigration Bureau worked with local authorities and private agencies to send illegal aliens, especially Mexicans, back to their native countries. The lack of jobs, together with Anglo pressure and Mexican government encouragement, convinced more than seventy thousand to return to Mexico between 1929 and 1930. In Los Angeles, Immigration Bureau sweeps of Mexican-American communities started in 1931, significantly adding to the pressure on the Mexican population to leave. The district director of immigration for Los Angeles bragged that thousands of Mexicans had been scared out of the city. In truth, in 1931 and 1932, nearly ten thousand Mexicans and Mexican-Americans, mostly children born in the United States of Mexican parents, boarded special trains from Los Angeles bound for Mexico. Nationally, the number of returned Mexican aliens jumped to over 138,500, and by 1937, half a million Mexicans had left the United States. Those Latinos who remained in the United States faced intense social and economic discrimination. Jobs were scarce and pay was pitiful. On the farms of California, an estimated 2.36 workers vied for every job, and whites, including those fleeing the dust bowl, were replacing Mexican laborers. As farm wages dropped and work conditions deteriorated, Mexican-American agricultural unions organized strikes. In a few cases, the unions won small pay raises, but usually the growers, supported by local authorities and public opinion, easily broke the strikes. A California deputy sheriff stated the case bluntly.

We protect our farmers here in Kern County. They are our best people. . . . They keep the county going. They put us in here and they can put us out again, so we serve them. But the Mexicans are trash. They have no standard of living. We herd them like pigs.

In another instance, a group of farmers surrounded a Mexican-American workers' meeting and opened fire with pistols and rifles, killing three.

For those Mexican-American families who found work in the fields, the average wage in 1935 was $289 a year, about a third of what the government described as a subsistence budget. Clearly, the $8.00 a week that popular magazines suggested for food expenses was far beyond the means of the majority of Mexican-Americans. Government relief programs were of little help because many Mexican-Americans, fearing deportation, avoided government agencies. Those who did apply frequently received lower benefits than Anglos or were denied entirely.

Women in the Depression

While African-Americans and Latinos found their already low status declining, some women were discovering new opportunities. More women, especially white women, entered the work force than ever before. But employment patterns were uneven. More jobs were available at the bottom of the occupational levels. Thus women holding primarily low-paying and low-status service jobs were less likely to be laid off than men holding industrial jobs. But at higher-level jobs in the professions, gender worked against women. The number of women in the professions, especially teaching, declined from 14.2 to 12.3 percent during the Depression. No matter what the job level, women workers encountered hostility. Public opinion polls consistently found

that most people, including women, believed that men not women should have what jobs there were. Women were accused of stealing jobs from men. Opinion was especially hostile toward married women who worked, and many companies and local governments made it a policy not to employ married women. A survey of fifteen hundred school districts found that 77 percent did not hire married women as teachers and 63 percent fired women when they married. In 1931, New England Telephone, the Northern Pacific Railway, and the Norfolk and Western Railway were among those businesses that dismissed a majority of their married female employees. By 1932, 2 million women were out of work. In 1933, an estimated 145,000 women were homeless, wandering across America, adding to the concerns that family and moral values were eroding.

For many rural women the Depression took away a major avenue to new status: migration to the city. Throughout the 1920s, an increasing number of rural women, white and black, had deserted farm life and moved to urban areas, taking domestic and other service jobs. But during the 1930s, such jobs in the cities became scarce, and many women were forced to remain on the farm. Too frequently foreclosures and drought destroyed farm life. Rural women like Ma Joad, heroically depicted in the *Grapes of Wrath*, had to adapt to life on the road as over 2.5 million farm families were forced to migrate seeking farmland and work.

Among women who did enter the work force, few found that bringing home the paycheck changed either their status or their role within the family. Husbands still maintained authority and dominance in the home. Rarely did even unemployed husbands help with household chores. One husband agreed to help with the laundry, but refused to go outside and hang the wash for fear that neighbors might see him doing woman's work. Still, as wives and mothers if not as workers, women were praised as pillars of stability in a changing and perilous society. Reflecting on her own steadiness, one woman remembered,

I did what I had to do. I seemed to always find a way to make things work. . . . Women just seem to know where they can save or where they can help, more than a man. . . . My husband got very despondent . . . he'd say you can't have this and you're not getting that, and I don't want to hear about this. . . . A woman, like I said, can take more. I always said that she can stand more pain.

SUMMARY

E xpectations
C onstraints
C hoices
O utcomes

In the period from 1928 to 1932, the United States underwent major changes of lasting impact—few that anyone expected as Hoover entered the Oval Office in 1929. Hoover assumed the presidency a heroic figure, widely regarded as well qualified to direct the course of the nation. *Expectations* were high that further growth in the economy would enhance prosperity and the quality of American life. The onslaught of the Depression quickly changed Hoover's and the nation's fortunes. The flaws that *constrained* the economy, largely hidden by the apparent prosperity of the 1920s, were soon exposed as banks and businesses closed. The economic collapse originated in part from internal weaknesses in the economy and the government's *choices* to promote easy money and to encourage speculation.

More than any previous president, Hoover *chose* to expand the role of the federal government to meet the nation's needs in the economic crisis. He initiated a series of measures, including the Reconstruction Finance Corporation, by which the federal government tried to stimulate the economy. But Hoover's philosophy of limited government still *constrained* the effort. The *outcome* was that the economy continued to worsen, and many not only held Hoover responsible but believed him callous to the hardships facing many Americans. By 1932, most Americans had lost their faith in Hoover, Republicans, and American business. With altered *expectations* about the role of government, voters *chose* to

put their faith instead in Franklin D. Roosevelt and his promise of a New Deal.

The Depression affected the lives of all Americans, rich or poor. Everyone had to adjust their values and lifestyles to meet the economic and psychological crisis, but industrial workers and minorities faced extra burdens of discrimination and loss of status. Although many Americans had to make difficult *choices* that disrupted their lives, the *outcome* was that society generally remained stable as most people learned to cope with the Great Depression as best they could.

The Depression also made a mockery of Hoover's *expectations* about a prosperous and peaceful world. During the 1920s, the United States had *chosen* a path of independent internationalism that stressed voluntary cooperation among nations, while at the same time enhancing private American economic opportunities around the world. Although relations with Latin America improved under Hoover, elsewhere an *outcome* of the world-wide depression was international instability, as symbolized by Japan's invasion of Manchuria. *Constrained* by economic worries, however, more and more Americans withdrew into isolationism.

SUGGESTED READINGS

Bird, Carolyn. *The Invisible Scar* (1966).
    An excellent study of how people responded to the impact of the Depression.

Macaulay, Neill. *The Sandino Affair* (1985).
    An examination of Nicaraguan affairs and the American role in Central America through the eyes of Augusto Sandino.

Nash, Gerald D. *The Crucial Era: The Great Depression and World War II, 1929–1945* (1992).
    A comprehensive and straightforward history of the period.

Terkel, Studs. *Hard Times: An Oral History of the Great Depression* (1970).
    A classical example of how oral histories can provide the human dimension to history.

Thomas, Gordon, and Max Morgan-Witts. *The Day the Bubble Burst: The Social History of the Wall Street Crash of 1929* (1979).
    A view of the American economy and the stock market crash as experienced by selected individuals.

Wilson, Joan Hoff. *Herbert Hoover: Forgotten Progressive* (1970).
    A positive evaluation of the life of Herbert Hoover that stresses his accomplishments as well as his limitations.

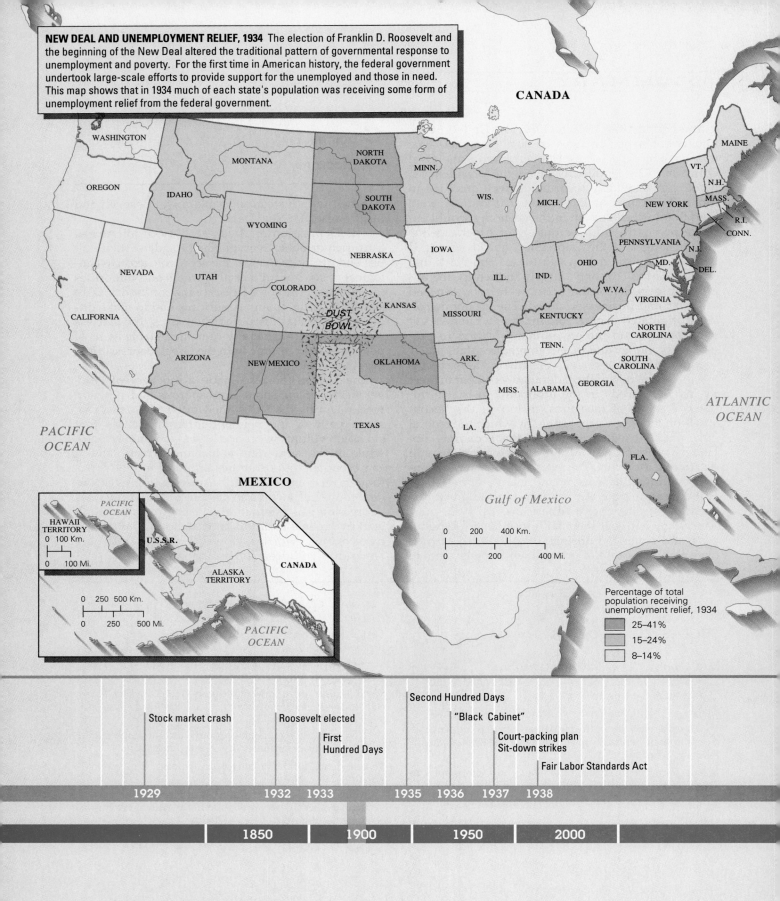

NEW DEAL AND UNEMPLOYMENT RELIEF, 1934 The election of Franklin D. Roosevelt and the beginning of the New Deal altered the traditional pattern of governmental response to unemployment and poverty. For the first time in American history, the federal government undertook large-scale efforts to provide support for the unemployed and those in need. This map shows that in 1934 much of each state's population was receiving some form of unemployment relief from the federal government.

CANADA

WASHINGTON
OREGON
MONTANA
IDAHO
NORTH DAKOTA
MINN.
MAINE
VT.
N.H.
WYOMING
SOUTH DAKOTA
WIS.
MICH.
NEW YORK
MASS.
R.I.
CONN.
NEVADA
UTAH
COLORADO
NEBRASKA
IOWA
PENNSYLVANIA
N.J.
OHIO
MD.
DEL.
CALIFORNIA
DUST BOWL
KANSAS
ILL.
IND.
W.VA.
VIRGINIA
MISSOURI
KENTUCKY
NORTH CAROLINA
ARIZONA
NEW MEXICO
OKLAHOMA
ARK.
TENN.
SOUTH CAROLINA
MISS.
ALABAMA
GEORGIA
TEXAS
LA.
FLA.

ATLANTIC OCEAN

PACIFIC OCEAN

MEXICO

Gulf of Mexico

PACIFIC OCEAN

HAWAII TERRITORY
0   100 Km.
0   100 Mi.

U.S.S.R.
ALASKA TERRITORY
CANADA

0   250 500 Km.
0   250 500 Mi.

PACIFIC OCEAN

0   200   400 Km.
0   200   400 Mi.

Percentage of total population receiving unemployment relief, 1934

25–41%
15–24%
8–14%

Stock market crash
Roosevelt elected
First Hundred Days
Second Hundred Days
"Black Cabinet"
Court-packing plan
Sit-down strikes
Fair Labor Standards Act

1929   1932 1933   1935 1936 1937 1938

1850   1900   1950   2000

The New Deal, 1932–1940

A New President, a New Deal

- How did public and political expectations and constraints shape Roosevelt's choices during the First Hundred Days?

Opposition and Change

- What were the sources of opposition to Roosevelt's First Hundred Days?
- What was the outcome of Roosevelt's response to his critics?

The New Deal and Society

- In what ways did the New Deal change society so as to provide better opportunities and offer more choices to those who found their road to success obstructed on account of gender, race, and poverty?

The New Deal Winds Down

- What constraints and choices led to the end of the New Deal following the 1936 election?

INTRODUCTION

E xpectations

C onstraints

C hoices

O utcomes

The Depression defeated Hoover and brought to the presidency an individual who would dominate American history for the next thirteen years: Franklin D. Roosevelt. The economic problems and the failure of Republican responses, gave Roosevelt unparalleled opportunities to reshape the federal government's relationship to the country. And, Roosevelt had few qualms about using the power of the government to combat the Depression and reform society.

Americans' *expectations* created opportunities for Roosevelt, but he faced serious *constraints* as well. Roosevelt and the New Deal existed within a political and ideological context. Crisis or not, there were limits on how much the president could change and how much he wanted to change. To many on the political left, Roosevelt's election offered the perfect chance to reform society to achieve social justice for all and to restructure American capitalism to make it more humane and responsive to government planning and controls. But Roosevelt had no intention of abandoning capitalism or restructuring American society. Eleanor Roosevelt, more socially liberal than her husband, reflected, "I'm the agitator; he's the politician." And, as a politician, Roosevelt knew that the nature of two-party politics and the southern wing of the Democratic party loomed as constraints to any significant shift toward the political left. Indeed, many conservatives of both parties *chose* to oppose any form of government activism and expansion of federal power. Another obstacle was the lack of precedent: no one knew what kinds of intervention would work on the reeling economy. Even among Roosevelt's advisers there was disagreement on the nature of programs and the extent and type of governmental activism.

Roosevelt's *choices* were thus shaped by both public and political *expectations* and *constraints* as they intersected with the economic and social needs caused by the Depression. The *outcome* was the New Deal, which witnessed a barrage of legislation along three paths: economic recovery; relief for the victims of the Depression; and reforms to better regulate the economic sector. The outcome, as it emerged over the next six years, was to change the definition of *liberalism* and the responsibilities and power of the federal government. Roosevelt would be revered and hated, but no one could deny his impact.

In 1933, riding a wave of popular support, Roosevelt seemed to face few political *constraints* as he moved to initiate the First Hundred Days of the New Deal. A year later that tide had changed. Inside and outside of government many who had given Roosevelt a freehand in 1933 were now beginning to oppose him and his programs. Conservatives condemned economic and business controls and federal spending as excessive government. Liberals called for fewer compromises with business, increased spending, and more programs for workers, minorities, the poor, and the unemployed. With his popularity confirmed by the 1934 elections, Roosevelt *chose* to consider new approaches that placed a stronger emphasis on people than on business recovery. The *outcome* was a Second Hundred Days of legislation passed in 1935 and 1936.

The New Deal expanded not only the functions of government but also the ranks of those voting Democratic. New Deal programs attracted women, minorities, and blue-collar workers, who thus *chose* to support Roosevelt and his party. The president's overwhelming victory in 1936 verified the party's increased strength and raised the possibility of a third hundred days that would further expand the government's social programs. Such *expectations* quickly evaporated, however, *constrained* by the growing power of conservative political opposition and Roosevelt's own tactical errors. By 1938, the New Deal was sputtering to an end. It had not rescued the economy, but it had profoundly changed the role and function of government. The long-term *outcome* of the New Deal was that the federal government, especially the executive branch, emerged as the most powerful and important level of government in the nation. Before the 1930s, people looked to local, county, and state government for help. After the New Deal, people looked to Washington for assistance. New interest groups had emerged. Government and politics would never be the same.

Out of Depression

1929   Stock market crash

1932   Roosevelt elected president
Reno forms Farmers' Holiday Association
32,000 U.S. businesses fail

1933   Dust bowl begins
4,000 U.S. banks fail
National Bank Holiday
First Fireside Chat
13 million Americans (25%) unemployed
First Hundred Days: AAA, TVA, NIRA, CCC
Twenty-first Amendment
Home Owners Loan Act

1934   Long's Share the Wealth plan
Coughlin forms National Union for Social
   Justice
Indian Reorganization Act
Securities and Exchange Act
American Liberty League established
Townsend movement begins

1935   Second Hundred Days: WPA, Social Secu-
   rity Act, Wagner Act
Rural Electrification Administration formed
National Youth Administration created
Long assassinated
Committee of Industrial Organization
   established
NRA ruled unconstitutional in *Schecter*
   case

1936   AAA ruled unconstitutional in *Butler* case
FDR re-elected president
"Black Cabinet" established

1937   Sit-down strikes begin
Republic Steel strike
Court-packing plan
"Roosevelt's recession"

1938   Fair Labor Standards Act
AAA re-established
10.4 million Americans unemployed
Welles's broadcast of "War of the Worlds"
Republican victories in congressional
   elections

1939   Anderson's concert at Lincoln Memorial
Steinbeck's *The Grapes of Wrath*

1940   Wright's *Native Son*

A New President, a New Deal

● How did public and political expectations and constraints shape Roosevelt's choices during the First Hundred Days?

In the four months between the presidential election and the day Roosevelt took office, fate seemed to be playing a cruel joke on the nation. To many, Franklin D. Roosevelt was the leader who could fight the Depression and restore prosperity. Yet the nation had to wait, from November to March, until he could act. In those winter months, many more people lost homes and jobs, more banks and facto- ries closed their doors, more families suffered and lost hope. Still, Roosevelt's election brought hope and, from all appearances, it seemed that Roosevelt and his advisers were ready and able to combat the Depression. During the campaign and after, Roosevelt had surrounded himself with a number of advisers labeled the **Brain Trust** by the press. Com-

Brain Trust   Group of specialists in law, economics, and social welfare who, as advisers to President Roosevelt, helped develop the social and economic principles of the New Deal.

♦ Franklin and Eleanor Roosevelt and their son James pose before going to the White House on Inauguration Day, March 4, 1933. With soaring unemployment, businesses and banks closing, and farmers protesting, Roosevelt told the American people they had "nothing to fear but fear itself," and began to restore people's confidence in the government and nation by promising quick action in fighting the Depression. *UPI/Bettmann Archives.*

posed of professors, lawyers, and journalists like Rexford Tugwell, Adolf A. Berle, Jr., Raymond Moley, and Felix Frankfurter, the mere existence of the Brain Trust convinced many people that Roosevelt was working on a program to end the Depression and restore prosperity.

In reality, neither Roosevelt nor his advisers had a coherent plan. His advisers were deeply divided over what was best for the American economy. A number of advisers, led by Columbia professors Tugwell and Moley, believed the concentration of American business in fewer and fewer hands was inevitable and favorable. Like Theodore Roosevelt they applauded big business as efficient, economical, and, with the proper controls, beneficial. Their solution to the economic crisis was corporate regulation and public planning done by an energetic executive branch. Except for Tugwell, those supporting the national planning approach had little concern for the still "forgotten man."

Felix Frankfurter represented another faction within the Brain Trust. He disagreed about the benefits derived from the concentration of business and centralization of planning. Frankfurter and his "little dogs" distrusted big business and wanted more competition, along with social programs to help those most harmed by the Depression. Despite their differences, the Brain Trust agreed on a number of basic ideas which gave shape to the New Deal. They believed the origins and dynamics of the Depression were rooted within the United States and that it therefore required internal solutions. They also asserted the necessity of federal action and had little fear in using it.

Roosevelt had no strong economic convictions and relished his advisers' debates, but in the end he made up his own mind, for reasons he rarely shared. He would do what seemed expedient and would discard whatever did not work or cost too much, politically or socially.

Bank Holiday

As Roosevelt's inauguration approached, the nation faced a severe banking crisis. Unable to collect debts owed and drained by too many investments in the sinking stock market, many banks had gone out of business since the crash, leaving depositors penniless. In 1932, 1,456 banks had failed and by March 1933, the entire banking system seemed ready to collapse. The public's dwindling confidence in banks caused a growing number of **runs** on banks as depositors demanded their money—money most banks did not have—forcing them to close their doors. By March 4, Inauguration Day, nearly all the country's banks were either closed or operating under severe restrictions. The governors of all forty-eight states had declared their state banks closed until further notice. With banks unable to operate, the economy of the United States was stiffening with paralysis. Few presidents had ever faced such an immediate crisis, and the country waited anxiously to see how the new chief executive would respond.

---

run A panic which depositors fearful of bank failure demand to withdraw their money, thus forcing the bank to close.

On Inauguration Day, Franklin D. Roosevelt spoke reassuring words to the American public and let the nation know that he was going to take action. Millions listened to the radio as the president calmly stated that Americans had "nothing to fear but fear itself," and that despite the incompetence of business leaders, the American economy was sound and would revive. But, he stressed, the nation would not revive by merely talking about it. "We must act quickly," he cautioned, telling the public that he intended to ask Congress for sweeping powers to deal with the crisis.

It was a comforting speech but would have amounted to nothing unless supported by action. On March 6, Roosevelt made his first move. He announced a national **Bank Holiday** that closed all the country's banks. At nearly the same time, he called a special session of Congress. Three days later, as freshmen congressmen were still finding their seats, the president presented Congress with a request for an Emergency Banking Bill. Without even seeing a written version of the bill, Democrats and Republicans responded almost immediately, giving Roosevelt what he wanted in less than four hours. Drafted partly by holdover Hoover officials, the **Emergency Banking Act** allowed the Federal Reserve to examine banks and certify those that were sound. It also allowed the Federal Reserve and the Reconstruction Finance Corporation (which had outlasted Hoover) to support the nation's banks by providing funds and buying stocks of preferred banks.

On Sunday evening, March 12, in the first of his so-called **Fireside Chats,** in a soothing and confident tone, Roosevelt told Americans that they had nothing to fear and that the federal government was solving the banking crisis. Federal banking officials were going to inspect banks, he announced, and those banks determined to be sound would be allowed to reopen. Banks would be safe again. "I can assure you," he joked, "it is safer to keep your money in a reopened bank than under the mattress." Over 60 million Americans listened to the speech, and most believed in the president. When banks in the twelve Federal Reserve cities reopened on Monday, customers appeared to deposit rather than withdraw money. Within a month, certainly before examiners could inspect many banks, nearly 75 percent of the nation's banks were operating again. Roosevelt's quick and effective action in dealing with the banking crisis established a positive national mood. The New Deal was under way. Over the next one hundred days, the new president would sign fifteen major pieces of legislation. The legislation, Roosevelt explained in another Fireside Chat, was moving along three paths: relief, recovery, and reform. Actual legislation almost always overlapped the three tracks, as in ending Prohibition.

Supporting the repeal of the Eighteenth Amendment, which had instituted Prohibition, Roosevelt called on Congress to approve a Beer and Wine Act permitting the manufacture, sale, and consumption of wine and beer with a 3.2 percent alcohol content. Congress quickly passed it on March 22. With a tax of $5 a barrel, the act provided only a small amount of revenue but greatly boosted public morale. Later that year, in December, the **Twenty-first Amendment** repealed Prohibition altogether.

The stock market crash, the Depression, and the banking crisis indicated to New Dealers that reforms were needed to prevent abuses in the banking and stock market industries. Completing Roosevelt's promise during the banking crisis, in June 1933, Congress passed the Glass-Steagall Banking Act, which reorganized the banking and financial system, gave new powers and responsibilities to the Federal Reserve System, and created the **Federal Deposit Insurance Corporation (FDIC).** The FDIC provided federal insurance for accounts of less than $5,000, and within six months over 97 percent of all commercial banks had joined the FDIC program, providing safety to millions of customers. Reforms for the stock market came first in May 1933 with the Federal Security Act, which required companies to

---

Bank Holiday   Temporary shutdown of banks throughout the country by executive order of President Roosevelt in March 1933, until government authorities could examine each bank's condition to determine its soundness.

Emergency Banking Act   1933 law that permitted sound banks in the Federal Reserve System to reopen and allowed the government to supply funds to support private banks.

Fireside Chats   Radio talks in which President Roosevelt promoted New Deal policies and reassured the nation.

Twenty-first Amendment   Amendment to the Constitution in 1933 that repealed the Eighteenth Amendment and thus brought Prohibition to an end.

Federal Deposit Insurance Corporation   Created by the Glass-Steagall Banking Act of 1933, it insured deposits up to a fixed sum in member banks of the Federal Reserve System.

provide information about their economic condition to stock buyers, and second with the creation of the **Securities and Exchange Commission (SEC)** in June 1934, which regulated stock market activities, including the setting of margin rates. Public approval for the reforms was high: "Let the seller beware," applauded supporters.

Seeking Agricultural Recovery

As Roosevelt assumed office, the plight of farmers appeared near disaster. The Farmers' Holiday Association threatened to call a farmers' strike across the nation unless Congress acted to restore farm profits. Roosevelt and his advisers were ready to respond. And helping the farmer went beyond mere economics. Roosevelt believed that the family farm was an essential part of American life and needed to be saved. Politically, he was aware that a successful farm program would help tie the Farm Bloc to him and the Democratic party. The goal was to raise farm prices through national planning to a point of **parity,** where the relationship between the cost of farming and the prices farmers' received matched that of the profitable years prior to World War I. Reducing rural poverty would be a by-product—recovery, not relief, was the goal. New Dealers, especially Secretary of Agriculture Henry A. Wallace, were convinced that neither individual farmers nor state governments could solve the problem without direct help from the federal government. A one-time Republican, Wallace had broken with traditional Republican programs for farmers and advocated direct government involvement, supporting both McNary-Haugen bills. By 1932, Wallace was convinced that the nation's economic problems could not be solved without first resolving the problem of agriculture overproduction and farm profits. The challenge was to convince farmers to modify farming methods and cut production. On March 12, the administration introduced the **Agricultural Adjustment Act (AAA)**—it was passed three months later on May 12.

The central part of the act, the Domestic Allotment Plan, encouraged farmers to reduce production by paying them not to plant. Focusing on seven basic commodities, a national planning board determined the amount of agricultural production needed to raise farm prices and set the amount to be removed from production. The board then allocated to states specific reductions for wheat, cotton, field corn, rice, tobacco, hogs, and milk and milk products. State boards divided production cuts among participating farmers and compensated them for lost crops and livestock. The money for paying farmers not to plant was generated by a special tax on the industrial food processors.

Because the AAA was not approved until May, after spring sowing, hundreds of acres of corn and tobacco crops already planted had to be plowed under. Likewise, farmers had to destroy thousands of hogs and dairy cows and huge quantities of milk and milk products. In the Midwest the continuing drought made it easier for ranchers and wheat and corn farmers take land out of production, accounting for more than 90 percent of the reduction of wheat crops in 1934. Many, especially those concerned about the hungry, shuddered at the waste, criticized the plan, and pressed for the surplus food to be made available for the needy. Others complained that the Agricultural Adjustment Act primarily benefited the large-scale producer and that small farmers did not have enough land to remove from cultivation to gain from the program. They also pointed out that in many cases sharecroppers and tenant farmers were evicted when landlords selected land to take out of production to meet AAA reduction quotas.

Although large amounts of land were removed from production, in many cases production did not drop. Farmers tended to take their least productive lands out of cultivation and used more scientific farming methods to actually grow more on fewer acres. To ensure true crop reduction, in 1934, Congress passed two additional acts—the Bankhead Cotton Control Act and the Kerr-Smith Tobacco Control Act—that levied special taxes on cotton and tobacco farmers who exceeded their quota for production.

Because the Agricultural Adjustment Act took time to implement, in October 1933, Roosevelt initiated the Commodity Credit Corporation to rescue

---

Securities and Exchange Commission Bipartisan agency created by Congress to license stock exchanges and supervise their activities, including the setting of margin rates.

parity The fair value of something compared to its market value.

Agricultural Adjustment Act 1933 law that sought to reduce overproduction by paying farmers to keep land fallow; it was struck down by the Supreme Court in 1936.

♦ Unable to get adequate prices for their crops, farmers were destroying their crops and killing their livestock. Milo Reno's Farmers' Alliance and other farmer organizations called for swift government action to protect the family farm. Here, more than twenty thousand farmers march in St. Paul, Minnesota demanding tax relief and a halt to evictions. *Minnesota Historical Society.*

many farmers financially. Financed through the Reconstruction Finance Corporation, the **Commodity Credit Corporation** lent money to farmers participating in the domestic allocation program based on the price of their crop. If the price rose higher than that borrowed against, the farmers could sell their crops, pay back the loan, and make a profit. If the price fell so that farmers could not repay the loan, the government kept the crops. Nonpayment did not, however, prevent the farmer from taking out another loan the following year. Seized agricultural commodities provided the government with food that was distributed to the needy through a series of relief agencies.

By 1935, recovery in the agricultural sector had clearly started (see Figure 25.1). Farm prices were rising and the purchasing power of farmers was increasing. Farmer support for the agricultural programs remained high even as the Supreme Court in 1936 declared the Agricultural Adjustment Act unconstitutional in *Butler v. the United States.* The Court ruled that the federal government could not set production quotas and that the special tax on food processing was illegal.

Quickly, the Roosevelt administration pushed the Soil Conservation and Domestic Allotment Act through Congress to circumvent the Court's decision. Working through the **Soil Conservation Service,** established in April 1933, the act used general funds to pay farmers for cutting back on soil-depleting crops like cotton, tobacco, and wheat, and adopting better conservation methods. Finally, in 1938, Congress approved a second Agricultural Adjustment Act that re-established the principle of federally set commodity quotas, acreage reductions, and parity payments.

The combination of drought and governmental policies took sizable amounts of land out of production, stabilized farm prices, and saved farms. From 1932 to 1939, farm income more than doubled, and the government had provided over $4.5 billion in aid to farmers, more direct help than it would give to any other economic group. Initially regarded by the administration as short-term measures to re-energize agriculture, the second AAA and the Commodity Credit Corporation became accepted solutions to farm problems. The policies would contribute to stable agricultural prices, frequently higher than the world market price, for over fifty

Commodity Credit Corporation   Government agency authorized to lend money to farmers using their crops as collateral.

Butler v. the United States   1936 Supreme Court ruling that declared the Agricultural Adjustment Act invalid on the grounds that it overextended the powers of the federal government.

Soil Conservation Service   Agency established by Congress for the prevention of soil erosion; by paying farmers to cut back on soil-depleting crops, the government also addressed the problem of overproduction.

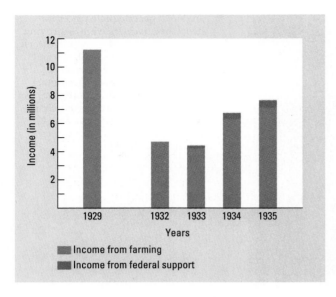

◆ **FIGURE 25.1 Farm Income, 1929–1935** Prices for farm products fell rapidly as the Depression set it (see Table 24.1), but by 1933, with support from New Deal programs like the Agricultural Adjustment Act, some farm incomes were rising. Note, however, that some of the increase was a direct result of government payments. *Source:* U.S. Department of Commerce, *Historical Statistics of the United States, Colonial Times to 1970* (2 parts) (Washington, D.C.: U.S. Government Printing Office), pp. 483–484, part 1.

years. Equally important, Roosevelt's farm programs significantly changed the relationship between agricultural producers and the federal government, linking the government inescapably to the farmers' future.

Seeking Industrial Recovery

With the AAA in place, Roosevelt and his advisers addressed the problem of industrial recovery but disagreed about the best means to promote industrial and business growth. The Tugwell-Moley group favored national economic planning and controls to stabilize production, prices, employment, and wages. Frankfurter's faction opposed a national plan and preferred an industry-by-industry approach. In Congress, Democratic liberals were pushing in yet another direction, calling for massive **public works** programs and a 30-hour work week. Fearful of losing the initiative, Roosevelt asked Moley to mesh congressional ideas with those of the administration. The result was the **National Industrial Recovery Act (NIRA).** Introduced in Congress on May 15, 1933, it was approved a month later. A

relief as well as a recovery plan, the NIRA offered something for everyone and quickly earned widespread support from business, labor, the unemployed, and community leaders. In a two-part offensive, the Public Works Administration (PWA) was given $3.3 billion to put people to work immediately, while the National Recovery Administration (NRA) provided programs to restart the nation's industrial engine and create permanent jobs. Both were viewed as only temporary, lasting only until the nation's economy was stronger.

Roosevelt called it the "most important and far reaching legislation passed by the American Congress," and he expected business and labor leaders, consumers, and government officials to work together on planning boards to promote industrial growth. The NRA was, Roosevelt explained in a Fireside Chat, a "partnership in planning, and a partnership to see that the plans are carried out." To achieve their goals, the boards developed "industrial codes" that set limits on prices, production, and wages. In turn, the government suspended antitrust laws for two years. Roosevelt selected General Hugh Johnson to command the NRA, but placed Secretary of the Interior **Harold Ickes** in charge of the PWA. Meticulous and always watchful for corruption and inefficiency, Ickes moved slowly to provide PWA jobs, exerting pressure on Johnson to implement the national recovery program.

Johnson, nicknamed "Old Iron Pants," had impressive experience in organizing industry to confront a crisis. During World War I, he had headed the War Industries Board (see page 679), which had mobilized American industries for the war effort. Now he relished a similar opportunity to wage war against the Depression. He tackled the project with the vigor of a missionary spreading the faith. He immersed himself in promoting the NRA, forming the planning boards, and drafting the codes for the nation's major industries. The blue eagle was selected

public works Construction projects, such as highways or dams, financed by public funds and carried out by the government.

National Industrial Recovery Act 1933 law establishing the National Recovery Administration to supervise industry and the Public Works Administration to create jobs.

Harold Ickes Secretary of the interior under Roosevelt and Truman and director of the Public Works Administration; he was an efficient administrator who opposed racial discrimination.

♦ The National Recovery Administration was Roosevelt's main vehicle to restore industrial recovery during his First One Hundred Days. Headed by General Hugh Johnson, the NRA's goal was to mobilize management, workers, and consumers under the symbol of the Blue Eagle; establish national production codes; and get America moving again. *Collection of David J. and Janice L. Frent.*

as the symbol of the NRA and "We Do Our Part" as its motto. Johnson exhorted the American public,

Nothing can stop the President's program, nothing will even hamper the President's program. . . . The power of this people, once aroused and united in a fixed purpose, is the most irresistible force in the world.

Business supported the NRA because it allowed **price-fixing,** which raised prices and profits. Labor was attracted by codes in Section 7a that gave workers the right to organize and bargain collectively, outlawed child labor, and established minimum wages and maximum hours of work. Labor organizers used Section 7a to promote unionism, calling it the Magna Carta of labor. Although representing consumers, workers, businesspeople, and governmental officials, the boards were dominated by business elements, who were invariably the best organized and prepared.

Johnson's zealous efforts were remarkably successful. Nearly overnight, the blue eagle appeared everywhere as Americans promised to do their part. Within six months, the National Recovery Administration had written 557 specific codes covering industries of every size. By the beginning of 1935, over seven hundred industries operated under codes and over 2.5 million workers were covered.

But almost from the beginning, there was growing dissatisfaction with the NRA. The program, which had started out as something for everyone, in practice had little for anybody. Critics soon dubbed it the "National Run Around." Because the boards were dominated by business, they emphasized profit returns rather than market expansion or wage increases. Workers complained that too many codes instituted low wages and often ignored wages for blacks and women entirely. They also complained that employers frequently violated the negotiated wage, hour, and unionization provisions of the codes. By 1934, New York's Democratic senator Robert Wagner was considering specific legislation to provide a more enduring support for worker rights than the NRA, which was only a temporary measure to deal with the effects of the Depression. Consumers also lost faith in the blue eagle as prices rose without any corresponding growth in wages or jobs. Farmers complained that NRA-generated price increases on products they used ate up any AAA benefits they received. Within the administration, Tugwell and others, angered by business activities and the level of price-fixing and profits, wanted tougher anti–price-fixing and monopoly provisions. Even businesses, including those benefiting from the NRA, complained about mountains of paper work, criticized Section 7a, and feared further restrictions on their business practices. To nearly everyone's relief, on May 27, 1935, the Supreme Court declared the NRA unconstitutional in *Schechter Poultry Corporation v. the United States.* Noting that the Schechter Corporation, located in Brooklyn, was a local business and not involved in interstate commerce, the high court determined that the Constitution did not permit the government to set national codes or set wages and hours in local plants. The PWA remained in place, but with the NRA gone, Roosevelt was forced to consider other means to rekindle the economy.

TVA and REA

Perhaps the most innovative and successful recovery program of the New Deal was the **Tennessee Valley Authority (TVA).** The goal was to showcase federally directed regional planning and develop-

---

price-fixing   A government's or industry's artificial setting of commodity prices.
Tennessee Valley Authority   Independent public corporation created by Congress in 1933 and authorized to construct dams and power plants in the Tennessee Valley region—Tennessee, North Carolina, Kentucky, Virginia, Mississippi, Georgia, and Alabama.

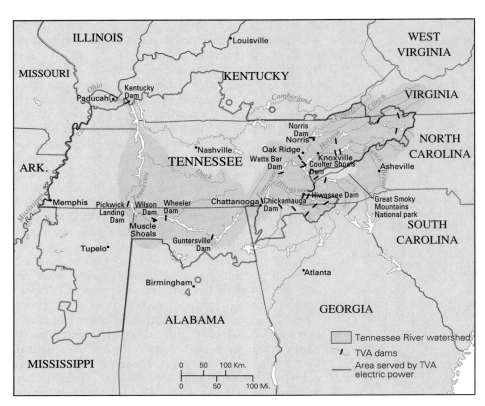

◆ **MAP 25.1 The Tennessee Valley Authority** One of the most ambitious New Deal projects was developing the Tennessee Valley by improving waterways, building hydroelectric dams, and providing electricity to the area. This map shows the various components of the TVA and the region it changed.

ment of a rural and impoverished region. The Tennessee River and its **tributaries** ran through seven states, including some of the most economically disadvantaged areas of the nation. The river basin offered great potential for development of vitally needed flood controls and nitrates, river navigation, and hydroelectric power. Passed midway through Roosevelt's First Hundred Days, the TVA cut across the lines of recovery, relief, and reform. At the center of the plan was harnessing the river system of the Tennessee Valley region through the construction of flood-control systems and hydroelectric dams (see Map 25.1). The first benefit was new jobs, but chief outcome was the long-term economic development of the region. Five existing dams were refurbished and twenty new ones constructed.

The TVA involved much more than building dams, though. The project brought seasonal flooding more under control and made hundred of miles of river and lakes more navigable. The TVA also provided regional planning and economic vitaliza-

tion. Its directors, especially David Lilienthal, used the AAA and other government agencies to improve agriculture while the TVA provided electricity through federally owned and operated hydroelectric systems. Only 2 percent of the homes and farms in the region had electricity in 1933. Twelve years later the number of electrified homes had reached 75 percent. The drop in cost of electricity from $.10 to $.03 attracted businesses like Monsanto Chemical and American Aluminum to the area.

Although many hailed the TVA for its flood controls and economic renewal, others criticized the authority for its racial policies. The TVA duplicated local racial attitudes by accepting segregation, excluding African-Americans from many jobs and paying lower wages to the few it hired. Private util-

> **tributary** A river or stream that flows into a larger river.

ity companies and conservatives also opposed the idea of a government-owned agency operating factories and power companies, calling the practice socialism. Such conservative opposition was largely responsible for Congress's failure to approve seven more proposed TVA-like projects in 1937.

The TVA's electrification program nevertheless became a precedent for a nationwide effort. Utility companies had argued that rural America was too isolated and poor to make service profitable, and only about 30 percent of farms had electricity in the early thirties. In 1935, the Roosevelt administration committed itself to the electrification of rural America through the **Rural Electrification Administration (REA).** By creating, financing, and working with rural and farmer electrical cooperatives, the REA bypassed and overcame most of the opposition from private utilities and state power commissions. The impact was tremendous. By 1945, electricity flowed to 45 percent of rural homes and farms, and by 1951, 90 percent of America's farms had electricity. The availability of electricity in rural America was one of the most important social and economic changes that took place during the New Deal. Running water, the availability of household products, improved education, health, and sanitation—all these lessened the drudgery of farm life and promoted the diversification of agriculture.

Remembering the "Forgotten Man"

Recovery was only one thrust of Roosevelt's three-part offensive against the Depression. He had campaigned on the slogan of helping the "forgotten man," his metaphor for the men and women facing unemployment and poverty. In March 1933, unemployment was at a historic high: 25 percent of the population, nearly 12 million people. In industrial states like New York, Ohio, Pennsylvania, and Illinois unemployment pushed 33 percent. Recognizing that state and private relief sources were unable to cope with the Depression, Roosevelt accepted federal responsibility. During his First Hundred Days, he proposed and Congress enacted four major relief programs (see Table 25.1). All were seen as temporary measures, but they did establish a new role for the federal government (see chapter-opening map).

The first was the **Civilian Conservation Corps (CCC),** passed on March 31, 1933. Patterned after the military, the CCC established over 2,650 army-style camps to house and provide a healthy, moral environment for unemployed, urban males aged 18 to 25. Within months the program had enrolled over 300,000 men, paying them $30 a month, $25 of which they had to send home. By 1941, enrollment was over 2 million men. The federally clothed, housed, fed, and paid "Conservation Army" swept across the nation building, developing, and improving national park facilities, cutting out roads and **firebreaks,** erecting telephone poles, digging irrigation ditches, and planting trees. But the CCC was not for everyone—those selected had to be male and, especially until after 1936, primarily white and from an urban area. The Civilian Conservation Corp thus touched only a small percentage of those needing relief. To provide a wider range of relief programs, the Roosevelt administration created the Federal Emergency Relief Administration (FERA) in May, and the Public Works Administration (PWA)—as part of the NIRA—in June 1933. The FERA was headed by **Harry Hopkins,** a former social worker and relief organizer, and was funded with $500 million to give to states for their relief efforts. Hopkins and his staff soon discovered that some states did not make very good use of these grants and showed little compassion for the poor. Oregon's governor, for example, opposed payments to anyone able-bodied enough to work and thought that the feeble-minded and aged asking for aid should instead be chloroformed. Despite such obstacles, by 1935, the FERA was spending over $300 million a year on relief measures.

Although much of the FERA's funds went to states, Hopkins instituted several programs to meet particular needs. One program opened special centers to provide housing, meals, and medical care for many of the homeless roaming the nation. In the program's first year of operation, as many as 5 mil-

---

Rural Electrification Administration   Government agency established in 1936 for the purpose of loaning money to rural cooperatives to start power plants that would bring electricity to isolated farms.

Civilian Conservation Corps   Organization created by Congress in 1933 to hire young, unemployed men for conservation work, such as planting trees, digging irrigation ditches, and caring for national parks.

firebreak   Strip of cleared or plowed land used to stop the spread of a fire.

Harry Hopkins   Head of several New Deal agencies, first organizing emergency relief and then public works; he remained a close adviser to Roosevelt during World War II.

TABLE 25.1 RELIEF, RECOVERY, REFORM, 1933–1938

Relief	Recovery	Reform
1933		
Civilian Conservation Corp (CCC)	Emergency Banking Relief Act	Beer and Wine Revenue Act
Federal Emergency Relief Act (FERA)	Tennessee Valley Authority Act (TVA)	Banking Act, 1933 (guaranteed deposits)
Home Owners Refinancing Act (HOLC)	Agricultural Adjustment Act (AAA)	Federal Securities Act
Public Works Administration (PWA)	National Recovery Administration (NRA)	Glass-Steagall Banking Act
Civil Works Administration (CWA)		
1934		
National Housing Act	Gold Reserve Act	Securities and Exchange Act
Federal Housing Administration (FHA)		Reciprocal Trade Agreements
1935		
Frazier-Lemke Farm Bankruptcy Act		National Labor Relations Act
Resettlement Administration		Rural Electrification Administration
National Youth Administration (NYA)		Social Security Act
Works Progress Administration (WPA)		Public Utility Holding Company Act
Soil Conservation and Domestic Act		Revenue Act
1937		
Farm Security Administration		U.S. Housing Authority
1938		
	Second Agricultural Adjustment Act	Fair Labor Standards Act

lion people received care. Ed Paulson was one. Riding the rails, he and other hobos were pulled off a train in Omaha and forced into trucks by deputies. "You're not going to jail," they told him. "You're going to the transient camp." There, Paulson was deloused, given a bath, a bed, and "a spread with scrambled eggs, bacon, bread, coffee, and toast." He recalled years later, "We ate a great meal. We thought we'd gone to heaven." In other programs, over half a million people attended literacy classes and 1 million people received free vaccinations and immunizations.

The Public Works Administration, directed by Ickes, paid $.45 an hour for unskilled labor and $1.10 for skilled workers, regardless of race, and eventually provided over $4 billion to state and local governments for more than 34,000 projects, including construction of sidewalks and roads, schools, and

◆ Here, Civilian Conservation Corp workers plant seedlings to reforest a section of forest destroyed by fire. Before its demise in 1942, the CCC enrolled over 2.75 million young men. In addition to its work in conservation, the CCC also taught around thirty-five thousand men how to read and write. *CCC badge: Collection of David J. and Janice L. Frent; CCC workers: UPI/Bettmann.*

community buildings. Ickes wanted PWA projects that were socially and economically desirable, but not all fulfilled his criteria. Urban bosses used PWA and other relief monies to make jobs for political supporters, and many communities often ignored their poorest neighborhoods when spending PWA funds. One Texas town on the Mexico border used PWA money to hire Mexican-Americans to plant palm trees along the main street and paint Protestant churches, while making no effort to improve the town's barrio—where the workers lived—or to paint Catholic churches.

In November 1933, as high unemployment continued despite the CCC, FERA, and PWA, Roosevelt established the **Civil Works Administration (CWA)** to provide nearly 4 million immediate jobs, especially during the winter of 1933–1934. Rapidly instituted, the CWA was administered directly by the federal government. CWA workers, like PWA workers, participated in a wide variety of work programs and were paid from $.30 to $.50 an hour for unskilled labor, $1.00 to $1.20 for skilled work. Critics complained of "make-work" projects that wasted money, but overall CWA funds were well spent. The CWA built over half a million miles of roads and forty thousand schools. It paid the salaries of over fifty thousand rural schoolteachers. Despite its success, Roosevelt ended the CWA in February 1934, when the immediate crisis was over. The PWA and FERA could now fill the need for

relief, and the CWA had turned out to be more expensive than expected—in its short existence it had disbursed over $1 billion—and had generated considerable political opposition from state and local politicians.

Not all relief programs were aimed at the homeless and poor. Two aided homeowners. The Home Owner's Loan Corporation (HOLC), passed in May 1933, permitted homeowners to **refinance** their mortgages at lower interest rates through the federal government. Before it stopped making loans in 1936, the HOLC had refinanced 1 million homes, including 20 percent of all mortgaged urban homes. The National Housing Act, passed in June 1934, created the still active **Federal Housing Administration (FHA),** which provides federally backed loans for home mortgages and repairs.

Civil Works Administration   Emergency unemployment relief program in 1933 and 1934, which hired 4 million jobless people for federal, state, and local work projects.

refinance   To pay off an old mortgage with the proceeds of a new mortgage obtained at a lower interest rate.

Federal Housing Administration   Agency created in 1934 to help homeowners finance repairs and to stimulate residential construction through federal mortgages.

Opposition and Change

● What were the sources of opposition to Roosevelt's First Hundred Days?

● What was the outcome of Roosevelt's response to his critics?

The New Deal had begun with almost total support in Congress and among the people. That support did not last. As proposals flowed from the White House, opposition soon emerged. By mid-1933, most Republicans were actively opposing New Deal legislation, objecting to relief programs, federal spending, and increased governmental controls over business. By 1934, American politics had found new vitality. Conservatives fumed that Roosevelt threatened free enterprise, if not capitalism itself. They deplored the president's attack on the gold standard, which many considered the foundation of world capitalism. Conservatives thought it bad enough when Roosevelt pulled the nation off the gold standard in April 1933, but in January 1934 he nationalized gold deposits in Federal Reserve banks and devalued the gold value of the dollar to $.59. To warn the country about Roosevelt and his "baloney dollars," conservatives became increasingly vocal in their attacks on the president and the New Deal. The Hearst newspaper chain instructed its editors to expose the New Deal as a "raw deal" and to warn the public that Roosevelt planned to "Soak the Successful" and lead the nation into socialism. In August 1934, a coalition of anti-Roosevelt and anti–New Deal Democrats and Republicans joined forces with many leaders of American business to form the **American Liberty League (ALL),** dedicated to mobilizing political opposition against Roosevelt. By 1935, ALL was the center of conservative opposition to Roosevelt and claimed nearly 150,000 supporters, including many Democrats. According to the Liberty League, in addition to the NRA being unconstitutional, the AAA constituted "fascist control" of agriculture, and relief meant the "end of democracy." As a *New Yorker* cartoon indicated, for many of the rich—whose names dotted the roster of the ALL—*Roosevelt* had become a nasty word.

Populist Voices

For the majority of the American people, however, Roosevelt and the New Deal still spelled hope and faith in the future. State elections held in 1934 found Democrats friendly to Roosevelt gaining overwhelming victories, winning twenty-six of thirty-

♦ By 1934, Roosevelt's political honeymoon with Congress and the nation was over and the New Deal became the object of criticism. This political cartoon shows one of the common conservative complaints against Roosevelt and the New Dealers—that they were more interested in the "experiment" of government intervention than in the patient. *FDR Library.*

five contested Senate races and nine additional seats in the House of Representatives. The segment of the Republican party most opposed to the New Deal was virtually wiped out, while liberal Democrats arrived in Washington anxious to expand relief and social programs even further. Supported by congressional Democrats and public opinion throughout 1934, Roosevelt continued to add to the New Deal and became less willing to cooperate with conservatives and business. The president was also aware that economic recovery was not progressing as projected. Unemployment had been reduced, yes, but primarily through government work programs, which still supported nearly 8 million households, or 22 percent of the population. Encouraged by elec-

---

American Liberty League   Conservative organization that existed between 1934 and 1940 to oppose the New Deal.

tion results and angry at business elements and conservatives for their dissent, Roosevelt was ready to switch approaches to fighting the Depression. Pushing Roosevelt toward a new approach was the unexpected grassroots criticism that the New Deal was not doing enough to help the "forgotten man." The nation seemed especially interested in the views and activities of three outspoken critics: Father Charles Coughlin, Senator Huey Long, and Dr. Francis Townsend.

At three o'clock every Sunday afternoon, **Father Charles Coughlin,** a Roman Catholic priest, used the radio to reach out to nearly 30 million Americans with a mix of anti-communism, anti-elitism, and populist political and economic arguments. In his thick Irish brogue, Coughlin had lashed out at Hoover and anyone else who opposed relief. "God would have been condemned for giving manna in the desert because it was a dole," he told his audience. Throughout 1932 and 1933, the "radio priest" of Royal Oak, Michigan, strongly supported Roosevelt and the New Deal. But by mid-1934, he had turned his influential radio voice first against the National Recovery Administration and then against the whole New Deal and Roosevelt himself. In November, he formed the National Union for Social Justice, calling it the "people's lobby," to promote politicians and legislation that would help the masses. Coughlin advocated a guaranteed annual income, the redistribution of national wealth, tougher antimonopoly laws, and the nationalization of banking. Within a year the organization claimed more than 5 million members and showed that Father Coughlin's influence was reaching far beyond his regular audience of blue-collar urban workers.

Coughlin was not alone in broadcasting that Roosevelt was not doing enough for the "forgotten man." In the Senate, **Huey Long** of Louisiana, another one-time supporter, hotly criticized the president. Heavyset, known for his red hair and purple shirts, Long had achieved power in Louisiana by attacking big money and promising to help poor whites. As governor, he had built roads, schools, and hospitals, provided free textbooks, and imposed new taxes on oil companies and the wealthy. Developing a similar, anti-elitist plan for the nation in 1934, he broke with Roosevelt and advocated a **Share the Wealth** plan. It called for the federal government to provide every American family with an annual check for $2,000, a home, car, radio, and a college education for each child. The plan would be funded by having incomes over $1 million taxed at 100 percent and by inheritance laws that would make it nearly impossible to inherit more than $5 million. Crying "Soak the Rich!" Share the Wealth societies mushroomed around the nation, soon enrolling over 4 million followers.

By 1936, Democratic leaders feared that Long was considering a run for the presidency, which, if he joined forces with Father Coughlin to form a third party, might pull several million votes away from Roosevelt. Prospects of a third party soared when **Francis Townsend,** a third popular spokesman for the poor, particularly the elderly, appeared willing to join with Long and Coughlin. A public health doctor in Long Beach, California, Townsend, nearly 70, was well aware of the elderly's extreme plight. Ignored by work programs and frequently denied relief because they owned property, the elderly were among those most cruelly hit by the Depression. Retired by a budget-cutting city, Dr. Townsend advocated a federal, old-age pension plan. He wanted the government to provide every American age 60 and over with a monthly $200 pension check. To qualify for the check, individuals would be required not to work and to spend the money within the month. Townsend proposed a national sales tax of 2 percent on business transactions to finance the payments. Thousands of clubs were created in support of Townsend's idea, with an estimated membership of several million, including sixty members of Congress.

The growing popularity of Long, Coughlin, and Townsend reflected the frustration of a large segment of the American population, largely blue-collar and lower-middle-class, who believed that after nearly two full years of the New Deal, government

---

Father Charles Coughlin   Roman Catholic priest whose influential radio addresses in the 1930s at first emphasized social justice but eventually became anti-Semitic and pro-fascist.

Huey Long   Louisiana governor, then U.S. senator, who ran a powerful political machine and whose advocacy of redistribution of income was gaining him a national political following at the time of his assassination in 1935.

Share the Wealth   Movement that sprang up around the nation in the 1930s urging the redistribution of wealth through government taxes or programs; its slogan was "Every man a king."

Francis Townsend   California physician who proposed the Townsend Plan in 1933, under which ever retired person over sixty would be paid a $200 monthly pension to be spent within the month.

was still doing too little to help them. Long's and Townsend's programs were attractive because they would aid people, not businesses, and would push the country toward recovery by promoting consumption—a position also being strongly recommended by several of Roosevelt's advisers, particularly Felix Frankfurter and Harry Hopkins.

Rise of Labor

Long's and Townsend's plans were designed to fight the Depression by expanding the amount of money in the hands of consumers. With more money in circulation, they reasoned, people would buy more goods, which would drive up demand and generate economic growth. Federal jobs and relief payments were one method of putting money into the hands of people, but a better and longer lasting way was to raise wages. To raise and protect wages, the NRA had incorporated workers' rights into its industrial codes. Although the NRA itself did not always protect and increase wages, union organizers had used workers' rights under Section 7a of the codes to support calls for higher wages and unionization. "President Roosevelt wants you to join the union," was a common plug used by labor organizers in recruiting workers. In the coal fields of West Virginia, union organizer Jesse Aquino invoked the image of a prolabor president not only to attract workers to the union but to save his own life. While he was speaking to a group of miners, a company guard thrust a gun into his back. Believing he would be killed, Aquino repeatedly reminded the guard of Roosevelt's support for workers and unions. Evidently not wanting to go against the president's wishes, the guard finally holstered his gun and moved away.

Workers responded positively to organizers like Aquino, and by mid-1934, unions were growing and becoming more militant. There were over 1,800 strikes in 1934, involving more than 1.5 million workers—union membership doubled that year. The rise of organized labor was especially pronounced in the mass-production industries—John L. Lewis's United Mine Workers union, for example. When the leadership of the American Federation of Labor discouraged industry-wide unionization in 1935, a minority element formed the Committee of Industrial Organization (CIO) to continue organizing industrial unions. Unionization drives were launched in the automobile, rubber, and electrical industries. The CIO also took an active political stance, pushing workers to support only those politicians who were friends of labor. In 1938, the CIO completed its break from the AFL and formed an independent labor organization: the **Congress of Industrial Organization.**

The Second Hundred Days

Responding to the growing pressures to modify the New Deal and showing his irritation with business leaders, Roosevelt announced a change in priorities in his 1935 State of the Union address. The administration would now focus more on people than on business, and New Deal programs would target underconsumption rather than low production and profits. He asked Congress to provide more work relief, to develop an old-age and unemployment insurance program, and to pass legislation regulating holding companies and utilities. During the period dubbed the Second Hundred Days, a solidly Democratic and largely liberal Congress responded with a series of acts. In April 1935, Congress allocated nearly $5 billion for relief to be divided among the CCC, PWA, FERA, and the newly created **Works Progress Administration (WPA).**

Roosevelt named Hopkins to head the WPA, whose goal was to provide jobs as quickly as possible. The WPA established a maximum 140-hour work month with wages based on skill level, gender, race, and geography. That is, wages varied from area to area and were usually higher than relief payments but lower than local wages, except for nonwhites and women, whose WPA wages generally exceeded local wages. Between 1935 and 1938, the WPA employed over 2.1 million people a year. Most did manual labor, building roads, schools, and public buildings, but the WPA employed professional and white-collar workers as well. In Georgia, the WPA not only built but also staffed 145 new libraries.

But librarians were not the only professionals aided by the New Deal: teachers, writers, artists, actors, photographers, composers, and musicians

Congress of Industrial Organizations Labor organization established in 1938 by a group of powerful unions that left the AFL to unionize workers by industry rather than by trade.

Works Progress Administration Agency established in 1935 and headed by Harry Hopkins, which hired the unemployed for construction, conservation, and arts programs.

◆ The Works Progress Administration not only built roads and buildings, but provided employment for writers and artists. Artist Ben Shahn painted *The Riveter with Electric Drill* in 1938 for the lobby of the Bronx Central Post Office in New York. *National Museum of American Art, Washington D.C./Art Resource, NY. Courtesy the Art Gallery University of Maryland at College Park.*

were among other professionals who benefited from New Deal programs. Historians conducted numerous oral interviews, wrote state and local histories and guide books, and produced a significant study of slavery based on their research. The WPA's Writers Project provided Jewish novelist and future Pulitzer Prize winner Saul Bellow with his first literary job—writing short biographies—and allowed African-American author Richard Wright to write his highly acclaimed *Native Son*. Professional theater groups toured towns and cities performing Shakespearean and other plays. By 1939, an estimated 30 million people had watched WPA productions that included known actors like Orson Welles, John Housman, and Arlene Francis.

The art programs were designed primarily to help artists, but they were also conceived as a way to elevate the public's awareness of art—"Art for the Millions"—and to promote positive themes and im-

ages of American society, especially the importance of the farmer, the worker, the common man. This concept was especially evident in the federally sponsored mural project, in which government-funded artists created over 2,500 murals and 100,000 paintings, most for public buildings. Artist Ben Shahn's mural in the Bronx Post Office, *Worker with Electric Drill*, provided a heroic portrait of those who built America and were its strength. Abstract expressionist Jackson Pollock received $7,800 from the WPA and produced paintings now worth more than half a million dollars. Some people objected to artists and writers receiving aid—art was not real work, they argued. But, Hopkins responded, "Hell, they've got to eat just like other people."

The WPA also made special efforts to help women, minorities, and students and young adults. Prodded by Eleanor Roosevelt, the WPA employed between 300,000 and 400,000 women a year. Although some were hired as teachers and nurses, the majority, especially in rural areas, worked on sewing and canning projects. WPA efforts to ensure African-American employment thrived in the northeastern states but stalled in the South. The **National Youth Administration (NYA),** directed by Aubrey Williams, was an especially successful venture that provided aid for college and high school students and programs for young people not in school. In 1936, over 200,000 students were receiving aid and several education-work programs had been established. Mary McLeod Bethune, an African-American educator, directed the NYA's Office of Negro Affairs, and through determination and constant, skillfully applied pressure, she obtained support for black schools and colleges and increased African-American enrollments in vocational and recreational programs (see Individual Choices: Mary McLeod Bethune).

More dramatic than the Works Progress Administration was passage of the **Social Security Act** of 1935. Whereas the WPA was a temporary expedient to reduce unemployment, the establishment of a federal, old-age and survivor insurance program

National Youth Administration   Program established by executive order in 1935 to provide employment for young people and to help needy high school and college students continue their education.

Social Security Act   1935 law that created systems of unemployment, old-age, and disability insurance, and provided for child welfare.

Resisting Prejudice

Mary McLeod Bethune

Mary McLeod Bethune chose to devote her life to helping African-Americans become "full citizens." A woman of great drive and ability, she started a school for African-American girls in 1904. She openly opposed the Klan in her community, and in 1944 became the first African-American woman to hold a high-ranking government position. "Mary McLeod Bethune" by Betsy Graves Reyneau. National Portrait Gallery, Smithsonian Institute / Art Resource, NY.

In 1904 Mary McLeod Bethune made a choice that would alter her life. She established a private school for African-American girls in Daytona, Florida, with nothing more than $1.50 and her strong will and faith. She rented a frame two-story house for $11 a month, and on October 4, with boxes and crates serving as desks and chairs for five students, opened the Daytona Literary and Industrial School for Training Negro Girls. She and the school soon became an important part of Daytona and its African-American community—and a target for those who wished to keep blacks in a submissive role. In 1907, she chose to openly oppose the Klan candidate for mayor and rallied African-American voters for his opponent. Exhorting the black community to "Eat your bread without butter, but pay your poll tax. Don't be afraid of the Klan! Quit running! . . . Look every man straight in the eye and make no apology to anyone because of race or color. When you see a burning cross, remember the Son of God who bore the heaviest cross of all."

When over one hundred Klansmen surrounded their school one evening, Bethune's students raised their voices in a hymn. The Klansmen retreated into the dark. The following day, the black community's vote helped defeat the Klan candidate. Bethune was proud: her efforts to instill "self-control, self-respect, self-reliance and race pride" had borne fruit not only among her students but throughout the African-American community. For Mary Bethune it was also a start of a larger, national

was to be permanent modification of the government's role in society. Only 15 percent of workers were covered by any sort of pension plan, and many of those plans no longer functioned in 1935. The primary force behind the Social Security Act was **Frances Perkins,** the first woman cabinet member, who accepted the position of secretary of labor with

the understanding that the administration would pass some type of old-age pension system. In 1934,

> **Frances Perkins** Industrial reformer who, as Roosevelt's secretary of labor from 1933 to 1945, was the first woman cabinet member.

role that would make her a major spokesperson for African-Americans.

The fifteenth of seventeen children, Mary McLeod was born to ex-slaves in 1875 and was the only one of her family to receive an education. Her schooling began at a local freedman's school operated by Presbyterian missionaries, and from the beginning, she was infused with the idea that education was the path to improvement and opportunity for blacks. After the missionary school, she graduated from Scotia Seminary in 1894, and enrolled at the Mission Training School of the Moody Bible Institute in Chicago. Her "greatest desire" was to do "great work . . . in dark Africa." But after a year of study, the only African-American at Moody was told that there were no openings for black missionaries in Africa. Disappointed, she chose to return home to make helping African-Americans her goal. Over the next decade, she taught at several southern schools for black children, until she moved to Daytona to open her own school, which in 1923 merged with Cookman Institute of Jacksonville (a private, Methodist-sponsored school for black males) to become Bethune-Cookman Collegiate Institute. In 1929, the school was accredited as a junior college, becoming Bethune-Cookman College.

By the time of the merger, Mary McLeod Bethune was widely recognized as an effective organizer, a respected educator, a gifted speaker, and an African-American leader. She had served as the president of the National Association of Colored Women (NACW), an office that at the time was the highest national position an African-American woman could hold. After serving on several national organizations and committees, in December 1935, she formed the National Council of Negro Women to focus on issues facing African-American women at the national level. Catching the attention of the Roosevelts, she was soon named to an advisory board of the National Youth Administration (NYA).

At a meeting of the board, Bethune told how the $15 and $20 checks the NYA provided meant economic salvation to many southern black families. "We are bringing life and spirit to those many thousands who for so long have lived in darkness," she exclaimed. In her presentation, Bethune had wanted to make her listeners, including the president, "cry." And afterward, teary-eyed Roosevelt promised to do his best. Doing his best included offering Bethune a position, created just for her, within the NYA—the Office of Minority Affairs. "I'm afraid you'll have to do it," explained NYA's director Aubrey Williams. "This is the first such post created for a Negro woman in the United States." She would hold position until 1944, when Congress killed the NYA.

Her presence in the NYA, combined with her access to the White House, made her a powerful spokesperson for what she termed her "long-suffering people." "It's about time that white folks recognize that Negroes are human, too, and will not much longer stand to be the dregs of the work force," she told her New Deal colleagues. Within the New Deal, she assured that black administrators were hired to run NYA programs, provided opportunities for over six hundred thousand black youth in NYA programs, organized the "Black Cabinet," whose very existence focused government and society's attention on racial issues, and convinced the administration to support two conferences on African-American problems. Bethune left government service in 1944 but carried on her choice to work for civil rights until her death in Daytona Beach in 1955.

encouraged by the popularity of Dr. Townsend's plan, Perkins chaired the Committee on Economic Security to draft a social security bill. Passed by Congress in August 1935, the Social Security Act had three sections.

The most controversial part of the legislation created the social security system. Conservatives called it socialistic and insisted it would remove the incentive to work. As approved by Congress in August, social security provided a pension plan for retirees 65 or older, who would receive initial payments ranging from $10 to $85 a month, depending on how much the worker paid into the system. The more a worker paid into the system, the larger his or her

◆ Passage of the Social Security Act in 1935 created a new role for the federal government, providing benefits to retired, disabled and unemployed workers. Since 1935 that role has greatly expanded. *Library of Congress.*

pension. The program would begin in 1937 when a new tax (FICA) would be collected from workers and employers. Not all workers were covered, however. Many occupations, including domestic and agricultural laborers, were exempt. Compared to Townsend's dream and many existing European systems, U.S. social security was limited and conservative. Nonetheless, it represented a major leap in government's responsibility for the welfare of society.

Another, less controversial section of the bill established a federally supported system of unemployment compensation at the state level funded by a new federal tax levied against employers. Within two years, every state was part of the system, paying the jobless between $15 and $18 a week in unemployment compensation and supplying support to over 28 million people. A third section of the Social Security Act made federal funds available to states for aid to families with dependent children and the disabled. In 1934, twenty-four states already had legislation that provided pensions to the blind, and forty-five states officially supported single-parent, female-headed families (under Aid to Dependent Children, or ADC). But the ravages of the Depression and lack of funds resulted in only about a fourth of those states actually providing funds, leav-

ing nearly 3.8 million needy, female-headed families helplessly impoverished.

Another change in the role of government was emphasized by the National Labor Relations Act, passed in July 1935. Largely the work of Senator Robert Wagner, and generally called the **Wagner Act,** it strengthened the union movement by putting the power of government behind the workers' right to organize and to bargain with employers for wages and benefits. It created the National Labor Relations Board to ensure workers' rights, to conduct elections for union representatives, and to prevent unfair labor practices like firing or **blacklisting** workers for union activities. Roosevelt's support for the Wagner Act helped clinch labor support for himself and the Democrats. By 1936, union contributions to the Democratic party were among the largest.

The combination of the Wagner Act and the Social Security Act reduced the credibility of those who called Roosevelt too conservative. Similar political goals were evident in other acts of the Second Hundred Days. When considering tax reforms, Roosevelt's adviser Raymond Moley suggested that they "steal Long's thunder" by placing higher taxes on inheritance and gifts, raising income-tax rates for the wealthy, and instituting a graduated income tax for corporations. Roosevelt agreed and asked Congress for the Revenue Act of 1935. Conservatives, the business community, and the wealthy all blasted the tax changes, but among workers and the not-so-wealthy, the law was clearly popular. The final product, passed in August 1935, raised taxes on those making over $50,000 and boosted corporate, estate, and gift taxes. Largely symbolic, the new tax structure did little to redistribute wealth. In fact, from 1933 to 1939, the wealthiest 1 percent increased their personal wealth 2.3 percent, controlling 30.6 percent of the nation's wealth. Still, Roosevelt's tax measures further angered business interests and conservatives as did other reform acts of his Second Hundred Days, like the Banking Act and the Public Utilities Holding Company Act. Both provided more governmental controls and enhanced the

Wagner Act 1935 law that defined unfair labor practices and protected unions against such coercive measures as the blacklist and company unions.

blacklisting Practice of keeping records of workers known to belong to unions so that anti-union businesses would not inadvertently hire them.

government's ability to conduct fiscal policy—and in the process raised conservative cries of a New Deal dictatorship.

Other acts reasserted Roosevelt's support for the "forgotten man." To help small farmers, sharecroppers, and tenant farmers, the **Resettlement Administration** (RA) and the Farm Mortgage Moratorium Act were passed. The latter, introduced by William Lemke of North Dakota and initially opposed by Roosevelt, allowed federal courts to reduce the debts of farmers to that equal to their property value and to establish a schedule for repayment. It also provided a three-year **moratorium** against farm seizures for farmers who had court permission. Headed by Brain Truster Rexford Tugwell, the RA tried to resettle marginal farmers on better land. It also established planned communities outside Washington, Milwaukee, and Cincinnati, and communal farms in Arizona, Missouri, and Arkansas. Although both acts helped only a small percentage of those in need, along with the WPA, social security, and the Wagner Act, they emphasized Roosevelt's concern for the common man just in time for the 1936 presidential election.

The New Deal and Society

● In what ways did the New Deal change society so as to provide better opportunities and offer more choices to those who found their road to success obstructed on account of gender, race, and poverty?

The Depression had made a shambles of the optimism of the 1920s. Just as the Depression had an impact on every segment of society, so too did Roosevelt and the New Deal. In 1933, society looked to Roosevelt for hope and change, and he rose to the occasion. He projected a presidency and a government that cared and worked for the "forgotten man" and redefined liberalism. Secretary of Agriculture Henry A. Wallace spoke of new "liberal" values that established a government responsible for balancing the social and economic needs of society.

Through his Fireside Chats and prolific legislation, Roosevelt personalized the presidency and the New Deal. It was not uncommon for people to credit Roosevelt directly for their betterment. "Mr. Roosevelt saved our home," and "The President found me a job," were commonly heard sentiments across the nation. Roosevelt's image as a concerned public official renewed the public's trust in government and the American political system. This confi-

dence found expression in such popular movies as *Mr. Smith Goes to Washington* and *Mr. Deeds Goes to Town*. In both films, honest, self-sacrificing citizens assume leadership and improve the conditions of life for all.

Popular Culture

Movies and radio, the most popular form of entertainment throughout the thirties, provided a break from the worries of Depression life. On a national average, 60 percent of the people saw a movie a week. *Gone with the Wind, The Wizard of Oz,* and dozens of musicals like *Top Hat* and *Broadway Melody* afforded a brief escape from the gloom of the daily routine. Movies offered not only escape, though. Some also reflected the social and political changes generated by the Depression and the New Deal. As Roosevelt entered the White House, the musical *Golddiggers of 1933* delighted audiences with its cheerful music, lavish sets, and attractive, young chorus line. But the show also contained social commentary and reflected the public's hope for change. In one scene, unemployed men march across the stage while the lead singer asks,

Remember my forgotten man,
You put a rifle in his hand,
You sent him far away,
You shouted, "Hip Hooray!"
But look at him today.

Romantic comedies were also popular, but they too could look seriously at the troubles of the times. A favorite plot involved romance between people of opposite economic and social backgrounds. A delighted audience would laugh at the problems created by the couple's social differences and the meddling of their snobby, class-conscious relatives and friends. In the end, good sense and love prevailed, honest virtues were rewarded, and different social classes found a common ground. "Cops-and-robbers" films remained popular but underwent a slight change. Before the New Deal, famous stars

---

Resettlement Administration   Agency established in 1935 to resettle poor families on new farms or in new communities and to make loans enabling sharecroppers to buy their own land.

moratorium   Suspension of an ongoing or planned activity.

♦ Throughout the Depression, the most popular form of entertainment was the movies, providing escape from daily hardships into a prosperous world of fantasy. At twenty cents a ticket, movies attracted as many as seventy-five million people a week. In this photo, taken at a movie theatre in San Diego, children display door prizes given during the matinee. *San Diego Historical Society, Photograph Collection.*

frequently played heroic but doomed gangsters. But as the New Deal became part of the American experience, those big names were increasingly cast as brave government officials who brought villains to justice. James Cagney became an FBI agent in *G-Men*; Humphrey Bogart was a crusading district attorney in *Crime School* and *Marked Woman*; and even Edward G. Robinson became a respectable good guy in *Bullets or Ballots*. All three actors had achieved fame playing tough guys, usually convicts or conmen. Such character changes reflected a more positive vision of government than ever before and renewed emphasis in Hollywood's **production codes,** which stressed uplifting themes like honesty and courage.

Radio was even more popular than the silver screen, with nearly 90 percent of American households having at least one radio. Like movies, radio provided escape from the "De-repression," as the Depression was frequently called on the "Amos 'n' Andy Show." When the "Amos 'n' Andy Show," radio's most popular broadcast from 1928 to 1932, began to lose its audience, an estimated 20 to 25 percent of listeners turned off their sets, forcing programmers to scramble for new shows and fresh talent. That year the radio introduced comedians—

commonly called "gloom chasers"—like the Marx Brothers, George Burns and Gracie Allen, and Jack Benny to the American public. Singers Al Jolson and Bing Crosby also crooned their first songs over the radio in 1932, joining Rudy Valle and Eddie Cantor who had begun a year earlier. In 1934, radio fueled an amateur craze with the "Original Amateur Hour." Few contestants ever became professional entertainers, but the audience loved the idea that an ordinary person could walk in off the street and, with a little luck and boldness, become a success. When amateur programs began to fade in 1937, radio turned to quiz shows that allowed the common person to show uncommon knowledge and skill. Keeping pace in popularity with comedians, amateur shows, and quiz programs were crime fighters like the Shadow, the Green Hornet, Dick Tracy, the Lone Ranger and Tonto, and Sergeant Preston of the

---

production code Standards adopted by Hollywood film production companies to govern the content of movies; their goal was to avoid any material considered immoral or indecent and thus make movies acceptable to mainstream audiences.

Yukon Mounted Police. These heroes proved again and again that truth, justice, honor, and courage always prevailed. Although both movies and radio provided hours of entertainment and escape from the everyday life, radio also played a key role in providing information about world and national events. News commentators like Walter Winchell drew their faithful audiences, and the president's fireside chats frequently attracted over 20 percent of radio listeners. An equally popular program was Eleanor Roosevelt's spot on the "Vanity Fair" program. Perhaps radio's biggest ever impact occurred when Orson Welles merged news with entertainment in his 1938 Halloween broadcast of the "War of the Worlds," a science-fiction story of a Martian invasion of New Jersey. Welles presented the tale in such a newscast manner that millions of Americans believed that earth had actually been invaded. Obviously, panic followed.

Movies and radio rarely criticized American politics and society. On the other hand, many novelists certainly intended their works as social criticism. Michael Gold, a young Communist writer, urged other writers and artists to produce works criticizing society and politics so as to further revolutionary change. Many responded by stressing the immorality of capitalism and the inequities caused by racism and class differences. But few advocated an end to capitalism or the downfall of democracy. Instead they emphasized the plight of workers, minorities, and the poor in American society. They found heroes among those who refused to break under the strain of the Depression and the inhumanity of the nation's materialism. Erskine Caldwell's *Tobacco Road*, John Steinbeck's *The Grapes of Wrath*, and Richard Wright's *Native Son* described "losers" in society but showed that their misery was not of their own making but society's fault. In these and similar novels, authors assailed the rich and powerful, praised the poor's noble humanitarian spirit and their sense of fair play and equality, and stressed social morality and responsibility.

Although many feared that the Depression would add to the ranks of those who rejected American social, economic, and political values, the main thrust of the popular culture was to affirm traditional American values. Popular themes expressed faith that the long-term effects of democracy would allow the integrity of the nation's people and leaders to emerge. As one American wrote to Eleanor Roosevelt, the United States would be an ideal place again if only the "people would work together for the common good." That the New Deal was working for the common good, of course, was exactly the image that the president sought to project.

A New Deal for Minorities and Women

President Roosevelt was not alone in fostering the idea of a caring government. Perhaps even more than the president, Eleanor Roosevelt was sensitive to the needs of average Americans, especially minorities and women. The first truly active First Lady, she crisscrossed the country meeting, listening to, and talking with coal miners, waitresses, farmers, housewives—a cross-section of American society. Those who missed her personal visits could read her daily newspaper column, "My Day," or write her. And thousands did write, generally describing their hardships and asking for help. It was not uncommon for her to receive as much personal mail as the president. Rarely able to provide any direct assistance, Eleanor Roosevelt's replies emphasized hope and explained changes being made by the New Deal. Within the White House, she was a constant goad to her husband and New Dealers not to neglect the poor, women, and minorities.

Eleanor Roosevelt took the lead in supporting women and African-Americans. She publicly and privately worked to reduce discrimination in the government and throughout the country. In 1933, she helped to convene a special White House conference on the needs of women, and with the help of Perkins, Ellen Woodward, and other women in the administration, labored to ensure that women received more than just token consideration from New Deal agencies and the Democratic party. She made herself especially available to women as a source of information, inspiration, and help. Her outspoken support helped Democratic women to organize their own division within the party and to lobby for more important roles for women in the party and the government. Mary "Molly" Dewsom, a Democratic politician and head of the Women's Division of the Democratic National Committee, noted, "When I wanted help on some definite point, Mrs. Roosevelt gave [me] the opportunity to sit by the President at dinner and the matter was settled before we finished our soup."

Promoting women journalists, she held news conferences just for women reporters. And because women were banned from the National Press Club and its annual Gridiron feast, she helped to create the "Gridiron Widow's party," which recognized

Giving Her a Lift to Town · · · · · · · · ·   —By Knott

♦ President Franklin D. Roosevelt campaigned on helping the "forgotten man." As shown in this political cartoon, as First Lady, Eleanor Roosevelt did not forget women. She worked diligently to ensure that they benefited from the New Deal and had access to government and the Democratic Party. *Franklin D. Roosevelt Library.*

the important work of women journalists. With Eleanor Roosevelt as role model and supporter, the New Deal provided more opportunities for women in government and politics than at any previous time in American history.

Eleanor Roosevelt was just as determined to affirm the equality and the significant contributions of African-Americans. Working with black educators and administrators like Mary Bethune of the National Youth Administration, she sought to generate new opportunities for blacks. In 1939, she graphically demonstrated her commitment to racial equality when the Daughters of the American Revolution refused to allow renowned black opera singer Marian Anderson to sing at their concert hall in Washington, D.C. In a highly visible protest, Eleanor Roosevelt resigned her membership in the DAR and helped arrange a larger, public concert on the steps of the Lincoln Memorial. Marian Anderson's perfor-

mance before Lincoln's statue attracted more than 75,000 people.

Eleanor Roosevelt's support for equality and better treatment for African-Americans was welcomed, but most black leaders perceived that the existing patterns of prejudice, discrimination, and segregation remained untouched by the New Deal. A political realist, Roosevelt recognized the key role of white southern Democrats in Congress and the Democratic party, and so he retreated from promoting civil rights legislation, even an antilynching law. When black leaders complained, he admitted, "If I come out for the antilynching bill now, they will block every bill I ask Congress to pass. . . . I just can't take that risk."

Nonetheless, the New Deal and the Roosevelts brought about some positive changes in favor of racial equality. Several African-Americans were appointed throughout the government, and in August 1936, Mary Bethune organized African-Americans within the administration into a **"Black Cabinet"** that acted as a semiofficial advisory commission on racial relations. "Let us forget the particular office each one of us holds," she said, "and think how we might . . . get over to the masses the things that are being done and the things that need to be done. We must think in terms as a 'whole' for the greatest service of our people." Among the most pressing need for African-Americans, the "Black Cabinet" concluded, was access to relief and jobs. In northern cities, black unemployment ran from 50 to 90 percent, and it was not uncommon for African-Americans routinely to be denied relief by state and local agencies. Fortunately, Ickes and Hopkins were proponents of racial equality and used the PWA, CWA, and WPA to provide African-Americans relief and jobs. The WPA alone supported nearly 1 million African-American families and, in northern cities, nearly eliminated discrimination from its programs.

Not every New Deal administrator or agency was as committed to equality as Hopkins and the WPA. The Civilian Conservation Corps and the Tennessee Valley Authority openly practiced segregation and discrimination, and even within the PWA and WPA many federal administrators frequently found antiblack attitudes too great to overcome. African-

"Black Cabinet"   Members of the Roosevelt administration organized by Mary McLeod Bethune into a semiofficial advisory committee on racial issues.

♦ When the Daughters of the American Revolution denied renowned opera singer Marian Anderson the use of Constitution Hall for a concert because of her race, Eleanor Roosevelt arranged a public concert using the Lincoln Memorial as the stage. The Easter concert drew over seventy-five thousand people. *National Portrait Gallery, Smithsonian Institution, Art Resource, NY.*

American skilled workers were almost always given unskilled, lower-paying public works jobs, and the Texas state legislature mandated that women, especially minority women, were to be trained only in cooking, cleaning, and sewing. Even in the best of cases, federal support was not enough to help more than a segment of the black population. In Cleveland, for example, 40 percent of PWA jobs were reserved for African-Americans, but black unemployment and poverty still remained high. Plans to tear down slums and build low-income housing projects in most cases underwent local revisions and resulted in segregated, middle-income housing instead. Slums merely changed address.

Still, by 1938, New Deal programs were providing nearly 30 percent of the African-American population with some federal relief, often over the opposition of local authorities. Most African-Americans praised Roosevelt and promised their political support. "The WPA came along and Roosevelt came

to be a god. . . . You worked, you got a paycheck, and you had some dignity." By 1934, in northern cities and wherever African-Americans could vote, blacks were bolting from the Republican party and enlisting in the Democratic party. In the 1936 presidential election, Roosevelt would carry every black ward in Cleveland and receive nearly 90 percent of the nation's black vote.

Mexican-Americans benefited from the New Deal in much the same way as African-Americans—indirectly. In San Antonio, for instance, 30 percent of blacks and 29 percent of Mexican-Americans were on relief. Agencies like the PWA and WPA not only included Mexican-Americans but paid wages that usually exceeded what they received in the **private sector.** The WPA paid $8.54 a week for unskilled labor, whereas Mexican-Americans received an average of $6.02 or less a week from private employers. New Deal legislation also helped union organizers trying to assist Latino workers throughout the West and Southwest. San Antonio's Mexican-American pecan shellers, mostly women, were among the lowest paid workers in the country, earning less than $.04 per pound of shelled pecans, making an annual wage of less than $180. In 1934, 1935, and again in 1938, local union activist "Red" Emma Tenayuca and CIO representatives led the pecan shellers in strikes, finally gaining higher wages and union recognition in 1938. In the fields of central California, however, Mexican-American unions had little success in protecting the interests of farm workers, although strikers were often helped by federal relief agencies supplying food and clothing. Like African-Americans, most Hispanics became poorer during the thirties but recognized in Roosevelt a compassionate president. And where they were permitted to vote, they deserted the Republican party voted Democratic.

For the most part, Mexican-Americans and African-Americans benefited only indirectly from the New Deal, but that was not the case for American Indians, who had two champions in Secretary of the Interior Ickes and Commissioner of Indian Affairs John Collier. Both opposed existing Indian policies, which since 1887 had sought to destroy the reservation system and obliterate Indian cultures.

private sector Businesses run by private citizens rather than by the government.

At Collier's urging, Congress passed the **Indian Reorganization Act** in 1934. The act returned land and community control to tribal organizations, thereby reaffirming the reservation system. It provided Indian self-rule on the reservations and prevented individual ownership of tribal lands. To improve the squalid conditions of most reservations and to provide jobs, Collier organized a CCC-type agency solely for Indians and ensured that other New Deal agencies played a part in improving Indian lands and providing jobs. He also tried to promote American Indian culture. Working with tribal leaders, Collier took measures to protect, preserve, and encourage Indian customs, languages, religions, and folkways. Reservation school curricula incorporated Indian languages and traditions, and American Indians could once more openly and freely exercise their religions. Although it was a positive effort, Collier's New Deal for Indians did little to truly improve their standard of living. Funds were too few, and problems created by years of poverty and government neglect were too great. At best, Collier's programs slowed the pace of a long-running economic decline and allowed American Indians to regain some control over their culture and society.

The New Deal Winds Down

● What constraints and choices led to the end of the New Deal following the 1936 election?

By the presidential election year of 1936, the Second Hundred Days had effectively reasserted Roosevelt's leadership and popularity. The prospects of a successful Republican or third-party challenge to Roosevelt was remote. Huey Long had died, the victim of an assassin's bullet. Another Louisianan, Gerald L. K. Smith, took up Long's populist standard but hardly matched the colorful "Kingfish" in popularity or flair. Smith joined forces with Coughlin and Townsend to form a third party, the Union party, but it never posed a threat to Roosevelt. Nor did the Socialist or Communist parties mount any noticeable opposition. The Depression had caused more people to flirt with Marxism, and membership in the Communist party by 1936 had mushroomed to between fifty and sixty thousand from only seven thousand in 1930. But, as in the Socialist party, many of its members left disenchanted soon after joining, and both parties were torn by constant internal disputes over whether to support Roosevelt

and the New Deal. Neither party comprised a threat to Roosevelt or the American system.

The Republican party was hardly more of a worry. In a less than enthusiastic convention, Republicans nominated the only available man, **Alfred Landon** of Kansas. Hoover was willing to try the presidency again, but not even the most optimistic Republican believed that people would forgive the party if it nominated him. Congress was void of suitable candidates, leaving only governors, which left only Landon, who had been the only Republican governor reelected in 1934. Landon had an impressive record as governor, having cut taxes and streamlined the administration. Landon accepted most New Deal programs in principle—aligning work and relief programs in Kansas with federal New Deal agencies—objecting primarily to their inefficient administration. But most Republicans wanted him to attack Roosevelt and the New Deal as destroying the values of America. Reluctantly, Landon agreed, gaining support from the Liberty League, which announced that the election presented a choice between the "clean, pure, fresh air of free America, and the foul breath of Communistic Russia."

Roosevelt followed a politically wise path, reminding voters of the New Deal's achievements and stressing his support for the "forgotten man." He attacked big business, the "economic royalists" who wanted to rule like kings over the people. The tactics worked and Roosevelt won in a landslide. Landon carried only two states, Maine and Vermont, an achievement that earned him a woeful eight electoral votes.

The Democratic victory in 1936 demonstrated not only the personal popularity of Roosevelt but also the realignment of political forces around the concept of an activist New Deal government that could foster social and economic gains. Prior to 1930, only two major interest groups successfully influenced government: big business and the South. With Roosevelt and the New Deal, other interest groups—some new like the CIO and some old like agri-

---

Indian Reorganization Act   1934 law that ended Indian allotment and returned surplus land to tribal ownership; it also sought to encourage tribal self-government and improve economic conditions on reservations.

Alfred Landon   Kansas governor who ran unsuccessfully for president in 1936.

culture—were recognized as parts of the political spectrum and wooed by the Democratic party through legislation. Workers, farmers, women, minorities, the aged, and those on relief now competed with the South and business interests for government favor and legislation. The result was that the unemployed, workers—especially organized labor—and farmers voted Democratic and expected further legislation to match their needs. Applauding relief policies that did not automatically discriminate and largely symbolic actions and appointments, African-Americans deserted the party of Lincoln and voted for Roosevelt. The political challenge for Roosevelt and future Democrats was to keep as many interest groups as possible within the fold. By 1936, Roosevelt had lost widespread support from business elements, but as the 1936 election showed, that loss was more than offset by his ability to keep the rest of the coalition intact. Roosevelt recognized the political importance of those who cast their vote for him and the New Deal, and he promised a government intent on seeking "social justice" and further legislation to bring it to pass.

His second inaugural address, sometimes referred to as the "One-third speech," raised expectations that there would be a third one hundred days. "I see millions of families trying to live on incomes so meager that the pall of family disaster hangs over them day by day," he announced. "I see one-third of a nation ill-housed, ill-clad, ill-nourished." The words seemed to promise new legislation aimed at helping the poor and the working class. But the Third Hundred Days failed to materialize.

Roosevelt and the Supreme Court

Instead of promoting new social legislation, Roosevelt pitched his popularity against the Supreme Court—and lost. The president's anger at the high court had been growing since the Schechter case, as the Court continued to nullify New Deal legislation. It ruled in the *Butler* case (1936) that the AAA was unconstitutional and wreaked havoc with many other New Deal concepts. A quota plan for the oil industry, the Railroad Retirement Act, a New York law establishing a minimum wage for women—all were declared illegal. As 1937 began, legal challenges to the Wagner Act and the Social Security Act were on the Court's docket, and Roosevelt feared the Court was going to undo much of the Second Hundred Days' legislation. The president believed that before he could proceed with new programs, he

must protect what had already been passed. To alter the political philosophy of the Court, Roosevelt wanted to appoint enough new justices to ensure it would have a pro–New Deal majority.

Without consulting congressional leaders or even his closest advisers, Roosevelt presented a plan to reorganize the Court to Congress in early February 1937. Claiming that the Court was overburdened and that its elderly judges could not meet the demands of the office, he asked for additional justices to help carry the judicial load. His goal was a new justice for every one over age 70 who had served more than ten years on the court. Although changing the size of the Supreme Court was within the powers of Congress, many thought Roosevelt's action threatened the checks and balances of government as established by the Constitution. He had made a major political miscalculation with his **Court-packing plan,** and many Democrats whose loyalty was shaky because of their reservations about the New Deal now welcomed the opportunity to join with Republicans and say no to Roosevelt.

Still aglow from his election victory, Roosevelt ignored the growing opposition and pressed on. To gain public support, he told political adviser Jim Farley, "All I have to do is to devise a better speech." Roosevelt's case weakened further, however, when Court decisions failed to attack the New Deal. In a series of split, 5-to-4 decisions, the Supreme Court upheld Washington state's minimum wage law, the Wagner Act, and the social security system. Even Roosevelt's supporters in Congress now questioned the need to enlarge the Court. The president's position collapsed completely in May when conservative Justice Willis van Devanter announced his retirement. By July, Roosevelt realized that no speech could stem the tide of opposition to his court plan and conceded defeat. He dropped the issue and took solace in appointing Hugo Black, a southern New Dealer, to the Court. Before Roosevelt died in 1945, he would have the opportunity to appoint eight other justices and ensure a Supreme Court that would approve of and expand the role of government.

Despite the Court's favorable decisions, Roosevelt had lost a great deal. He had squandered his

---

Court-packing plan   Roosevelt's unsuccessful proposal in 1937 to increase the number of Supreme Court justices; it was an effort to circumvent Supreme Court hostility to the New Deal.

political assets in trying to win a hopeless cause and lost control over conservative southern Democrats. Having safely broken with Roosevelt on the Court issue, many Democrats—mainly from the South— found it possible, even popular, to oppose other Roosevelt initiatives. The election of 1936 had formed a strong Democratic coalition of northerners and southerners, liberals and conservatives, but the Court fight had weakened that bloc and produced a new conservative grouping composed of Republicans, business interests, and southern Democrats. Consequently, a Third Hundred Days was now impossible. The New Deal was slowing to a crawl.

Sit-down Strikes

It was not just the Court-packing scheme that weakened Roosevelt's political control. Higher taxes, including the social security tax, burdened voters with the cost of the New Deal. Labor strife, too, dampened enthusiasm for the New Deal, especially as the CIO continued to organize workers and call for political support. In March 1936, the CIO supported workers striking against the rubber industry in Akron, the home of the three major producers of tires and rubber products: Firestone, Goodyear, and Goodrich. Wanting recognition of their union and higher wages, workers stopped work and refused to leave the factory, launching one of the first major **sit-down strikes** in the United States. By making it very difficult to remove them from company property, strikers denied the employer access to the factory and thus prevented the use of **strikebreakers.** These advantages were somewhat offset by the public's general view that such tactics were too radical and amounted to illegal seizure of company property. But when the rubber industry quickly agreed to most of the strikers' demands, it seemed clear that the benefits of sit-down strikes outweighed the negatives.

Encouraged by the Akron results, Walter Reuther and other leaders of the **United Automobile Workers (UAW)** planned a sit-down strike against General Motors, the largest of the Big Three automakers. The situation for automobile workers had deteriorated steadily during the Depression. In 1928, over 435,000 workers were employed. By 1933, the number was only 244,000. Wages had dropped from an average of $33 to $20 a week. To prevent unions from organizing, the industry had formed company associations and paid thousands of dollars to agents to spy on and disrupt union activities. Chrysler alone paid $72,000 for such infiltrators in 1935.

In planning the General Motors strike, the UAW focused on car body plants in Cleveland, Ohio, and Flint, Michigan. Because most General Motors plants received car bodies from Cleveland and Flint, successful strikes in those plants would eventually shut down most of GM's assembly lines. The sit-down strike began on November 30, 1936, when Flint workers took over the factory. To dislodge the strikers, GM authorities cut off heat in 16-degree weather and tried to block deliveries of food and other supplies. When the blockade did not work, on January 11, 1937, company guards and city police armed with guns, clubs, and tear gas, attacked the factory. The strikers fought back. Police cars were overturned outside the plant, while inside strikers turned fire hoses and homemade slingshots that flung 2-pound door hinges against their attackers. Frustrated, the guards and police opened fire. Fourteen workers and 37 police were injured—but the strikers held their ground. GM then asked Governor Frank Murphy to send in state militia units to remove the strikers, but when the liberal Democrat refused, the company settled with the UAW. After forty-four days, the strikers left the Fisher Body plant to the cheers of assembled workers. Weeks later, Chrysler gave in to sit-down strikers and also recognized the UAW. In March, United States Steel accepted the steelworkers' union without a strike. Throughout 1937, labor staged more than 4,700 strikes—and won over 80 percent of them. Union membership soared. *Time* observed, "Sitting down has replaced baseball as the national pastime."

Despite the successes, not all union efforts were effective. In Ohio, the National Guard broke through **picket lines** and shielded strikebreakers, allowing several steel mills to continue operation. In

---

sit-down strike   Strike in which workers refuse to leave their place of employment until their demands are met.

strikebreaker   Temporary workers hired by employers to substitute for striking workers; they were often mercenary thugs who courted violence with the strikers.

United Automobile Workers   Union of workers in the automobile industry, which used sit-down strikes in 1936 and 1937 to end work speed-ups and win recognition for the fledgling labor organization.

picket line   Procession of strikers or protesters that blocks the entrance to a place of business to prevent its operation.

◆ In 1936 these workers from the Fisher Body Plant in Flint, Michigan used a new tactic in the United Autoworkers strike against General Motors—the sit-down strike. Workers took over the plant and held it against all attempts to reclaim it for forty-four days, until GM agreed to negotiate a settlement. In 1939 the Supreme Court declared the sit-down strike illegal. *Library of Congress.*

Chicago, the police staunchly protected Republic Steel from strikers and, on Memorial Day 1937, attacked a rally of workers and their families. Among those attending the rally, ten were killed, nearly ninety were wounded, and sixty-seven were arrested. Ford and many of the smaller steel companies, including Republic, successfully resisted unionization until 1941.

As strikes spread and violent incidents multiplied, unions did not fare well in public opinion. Many equated strikes and labor militancy with radicalism and pointed to the seemingly large numbers of socialists and communists within the labor movement. Critics also blamed unions for most of the strike-related violence and considered sit-ins illegal. In 1939, the Supreme Court agreed, declaring sit-down strikes unconstitutional.

The End of New Deal Legislation

By 1937, Roosevelt and New Deal legislation faced an increasingly hostile political environment. Responding to Roosevelt's Court-packing plan and sometimes-alarming union activities, a growing number of moderates, including many Democrats, joined conservatives in viewing Roosevelt as too radical and antibusiness. The economy seemed steady, industrial outputs had reached their 1929 level, and unemployment had fallen to 14 percent. Thus many joined Secretary of the Treasury Henry Morganthau in arguing that the administration should reduce governmental activism, which he asserted was unpopular and hampered further recovery. Morganthau recommended that Roosevelt cut back relief programs, balance the budget, and allow business a freer hand in shaping the economy. Roosevelt agreed. He cut government spending and closed down many federal job programs. Nearly 1.5 million workers were released from the WPA alone. Unemployment rapidly soared to 19 percent and recovery collapsed. Republicans cheerfully called it "Roosevelt's recession."

Roosevelt's liberal advisers called for a resurrection of the New Deal, with more government controls and spending. The WPA rehired those dropped from the rolls and Roosevelt took aim at big business. He appointed Assistant Attorney General Thurmond Arnold to undertake a vigorous antitrust campaign. Within five years Arnold had filed 230 suits, winning a majority of them. Roosevelt attempted to marshal liberal forces to provide new legislation. But the political mood had changed since 1933, and a coalition of conservative forces in Congress blocked passage of most of Roosevelt's requested programs. Hopkins observed that most Americans were now "bored with the poor, the unemployed, and the insecure."

Prodded by a strong agricultural lobby, Congress did enact a second Agricultural Adjustment Act that used general revenue funds to pay farmers to reduce production. And, in June, congressional New Dealers overcame strong opposition to pass the **Fair Labor Standards Act.** The act established an initial maximum work week of forty-four hours, set a minimum wage of $.25 an hour, and outlawed child labor (under age 16). With its minimum wage provision, the Fair Labor Standards Act was especially beneficial to unskilled, nonunion, and minority workers. It was also the last piece of New Deal legislation (see Table 25.1). By the November 1938 congressional elections, "Roosevelt's recession" was ending, 3.3 million people were still receiving federal aid, and the public's mood had become decidedly conservative and opposed to further New Deal–type legislation. During the elections, Roosevelt actively campaigned for liberal candidates but saw few victories. The new Congress was more conservative and determined to oppose any of the president's "socialistic" ideas. Roosevelt recognized political reality and asked for no new domestic programs. The New Deal was over.

The New Deal's Impact

By 1939, the economy was recovering, reaching the point where it had been in 1929 and 1937. But the "recovery" was not the result of Roosevelt's New Deal. New Deal programs had in fact failed to achieve recovery, largely because Roosevelt, like Hoover, never spent enough money to generate rapid economic growth. It was spending connected with the outbreak of another world war that would propel the American economy to new levels of prosperity. Yet despite the New Deal's failure to promote economic recovery, it had changed the country and its people. It ended the fear generated by the Depression and encouraged a return to a stable and orderly society and economy well within traditional American values. Equally important, it had altered the basic relationships between government and society and between government and the economy.

Evaluations of the New Deal are numerous and generally reflect attitudes about the proper role of government in society. Conservatives, during the New Deal and since, argue that the positive legacy of the New Deal is an illusion. Government intervention, they say, was the problem rather than the solution because it undermined individualism and free enterprise, creating an expensive and overbearing government. Liberals, as expected, praise Roosevelt and the New Deal for effectively balancing the needs of the economy with those of society. From the liberal viewpoint, the New Deal promoted stable economic growth and contributed to the overall health of American society. More radical, leftist critics of the New Deal focus on missed opportunities and what the New Deal failed to accomplish. They point out that the same groups who held power and wealth before the New Deal were still in control afterward, and, they contend, that Roosevelt made no effort to combat racism or economic inequalities. Roosevelt, they argue, faced few political or social constraints and could have made more significant social and economic changes, but chose not to do so.

Whether viewed as good or bad, one point is undeniable: during the New Deal the federal government became almost a literal "Uncle" Sam. Before the New Deal, the federal government had remained aloof and remote from the lives of most Americans, but by 1939, it had assumed new and expanded responsibilities and practices. Institutions created by Roosevelt still regulate the nation's banking and financial systems. The economic health of agriculture continues to rely on a series of price-support and loan programs started by the New Deal. The Wagner Act remains the overseer of labor-management relations. With social security, the federal government accepted the principle of governmental responsibility for the economic welfare of the elderly. Although relief agencies were eliminated over the years that followed, the belief in governmental responsibility for the needy remained part of the American memory and experience. The combination of the Depression and the New Deal had altered people's choices and expectations: people now looked to the federal government and the president for leadership, for legislation, and for solutions not only to the nation's problems but, increasingly, to social, local, and regional problems as well.

Fair Labor Standards Act 1938 law that established a minimum wage and a maximum work week and forbade labor by children under 16.

SUMMARY

E xpectations
C onstraints
C hoices
O utcomes

The Great Depression brought Franklin D. Roosevelt to power amid widespread *expectations* that he would initiate a major shift in the nature of government. Through a variety of programs—the New Deal—Roosevelt's administration *chose* to use the federal government to try to regenerate economic growth, aid millions of Americans in need, and institute reforms that further regulated the economy and ensured a more equitable society. Although never a specific overarching plan, the New Deal attacked the Depression on three fronts—recovery, relief, and reform.

The First Hundred Days witnessed a barrage of legislation—in most of which Roosevelt *chose* to deal with immediate problems of unemployment and economic collapse. In 1935, assailed by both liberals and conservatives, Roosevelt *chose* to respond with a second burst of legislation—the Second Hundred Days—that focused more on social legislation and putting people to work—concerns for the "common man"—than on business-oriented recovery. The overwhelming Democratic victory in 1936 confirmed the popularity of Roosevelt and the changes brought by his New Deal, and raised *expectations* of further social and economic regulatory legislation.

A Third Hundred Days, however, never materialized. The Court-packing scheme, an economic downturn, labor unrest, and growing conservatism generated more political *constraints* than New Deal forces could overcome. The *outcome* was that the New Deal wound down after 1937.

The New Deal opened doors for those frequently ignored by government and blocked from achieving the American dream. Farmers, blue-collar workers, women, and minorities, all—in varying degrees—had their New Deal, leaving each with stronger *expectations* about government's role in promoting their interests and enhancing their ability to participate in politics.

The New Deal never restored the economy, but its *outcome* was a profound shift in the nature of government and in society's *expectations* about the federal government's role. After the New Deal, neither the economy, nor society, nor government and politics would ever be the same.

SUGGESTED READINGS

Bergman, Andrew. *We're In the Money: Depression America and Its Films* (1971).

An interesting look at the movie industry and how it reflected the Great Depression.

Fine, Sidney. *Sit-Down: The General Motors Strike of 1936–1937* (1969).

Using the United Auto Workers' strike against General Motors, Fine examines the industrial union movement and the use of the sit-down strike.

Blackwelder, Julia Kirk. *Women of the Depression: Caste and Culture in San Antonio, 1929–1939* (1984).

A tightly focused study on Mexican-American, African-American, and Anglo women in the world of San Antonio during the Depression.

Leuchtenberg, William. *Franklin D. Roosevelt and the New Deal* (1983).

A comprehensive, classic account of how Roosevelt directed the nation from his 1932 election until 1941.

Steinbeck, John. *The Grapes of Wrath* (1939).

A classic novel about the survival of the Joad family during the Depression, later turned into an award winning film.

Sitkoff, Harvard. *A New Deal for Blacks* (1978).

A review of how African-Americans benefited from and otherwise affected by the New Deal and the Roosevelts.

Ware, Susan. *Holding Their Own: American Women in the 1930s* (1982).

An examination of the impact of the Depression on the lives and lifestyles of women.

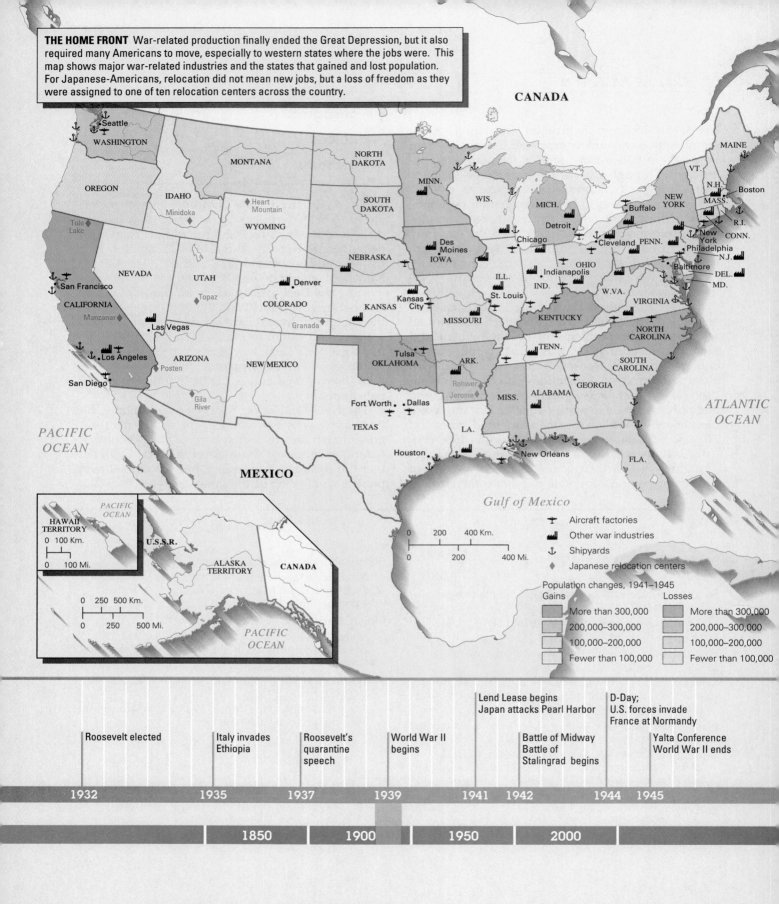

THE HOME FRONT War-related production finally ended the Great Depression, but it also required many Americans to move, especially to western states where the jobs were. This map shows major war-related industries and the states that gained and lost population. For Japanese-Americans, relocation did not mean new jobs, but a loss of freedom as they were assigned to one of ten relocation centers across the country.

CANADA

WASHINGTON
Seattle
OREGON
IDAHO
MONTANA
NORTH DAKOTA
SOUTH DAKOTA
MINN.
WIS.
MICH.
MAINE
VT.
N.H.
MASS.
Boston
Buffalo
NEW YORK
R.I.
CONN.
New York
Heart Mountain
Minidoka
WYOMING
Des Moines
IOWA
Detroit
Chicago
Cleveland
PENN.
Philadelphia
N.J.
DEL.
MD.
Baltimore
OHIO
Indianapolis
Tule Lake
NEVADA
UTAH
NEBRASKA
ILL.
IND.
W.VA.
VIRGINIA
San Francisco
Topaz
Denver
COLORADO
KANSAS
Kansas City
MISSOURI
St. Louis
KENTUCKY
NORTH CAROLINA
CALIFORNIA
Manzanar
Las Vegas
Granada
ARIZONA
Posten
NEW MEXICO
OKLAHOMA
Tulsa
ARK.
TENN.
SOUTH CAROLINA
Los Angeles
San Diego
Gila River
Fort Worth
Dallas
Rohwer
Jerome
MISS.
ALABAMA
GEORGIA
TEXAS
Houston
LA.
New Orleans
FLA.

PACIFIC OCEAN

MEXICO

ATLANTIC OCEAN

Gulf of Mexico

HAWAII TERRITORY
PACIFIC OCEAN
0   100 Km.
0   100 Mi.

U.S.S.R.
ALASKA TERRITORY
CANADA
PACIFIC OCEAN
0   250   500 Km.
0   250   500 Mi.

0   200   400 Km.
0   200   400 Mi.

✈ Aircraft factories
🏭 Other war industries
⚓ Shipyards
◆ Japanese relocation centers

Population changes, 1941–1945

Gains	Losses
More than 300,000	More than 300,000
200,000–300,000	200,000–300,000
100,000–200,000	100,000–200,000
Fewer than 100,000	Fewer than 100,000

Roosevelt elected

Italy invades Ethiopia

Roosevelt's quarantine speech

World War II begins

Lend Lease begins
Japan attacks Pearl Harbor

Battle of Midway
Battle of Stalingrad begins

D-Day;
U.S. forces invade France at Normandy

Yalta Conference
World War II ends

1932   1935   1937   1939   1941 1942   1944 1945

1850   1900   1950   2000

America's Rise to World Leadership, 1933–1945

Roosevelt and Foreign Policy

- What foreign policy constraints did Roosevelt face before 1939?
- How did they shape America's foreign policy choices from 1932 to the outbreak of World War II?

The Road to War

- What measures did Roosevelt take between 1935 and December 1941 to help defeat Hitler and to constrain Japanese aggression?

America Responds to War

- What new opportunities did women and minorities encounter on the home front as they responded to the war?

Waging World War

- What strategic choices and constraints did Roosevelt and Truman confront in making the decisions that shaped the course of the war against Germany and Japan?

INTRODUCTION

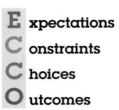

E xpectations
C onstraints
C hoices
O utcomes

In September 1939, Germany invaded Poland, starting the second world war. By the end of the war in 1945, the United States stood as an international military and economic giant—the one true superpower—anxiously hoping to direct world affairs. The leap from the isolationism of the 1920s to internationalism was the *outcome* of war and of the leadership of Franklin D. Roosevelt.

When Roosevelt assumed office in 1933, the cheery optimism of a prosperous world at peace that had greeted Hoover was gone. The Depression had altered *expectations* about international stability and had contributed to global economic and political changes that had altered international relationships. By 1933, three nations seemed intent on changing the international system and willing to *choose* military conquest if necessary to achieve their goals. Japan, seeking an empire in Asia, had annexed Manchuria and was threatening China. In Germany, the Depression had helped Adolf Hitler and the National Socialist (Nazi) Party gain political dominance amid promises of restoring Germany's military and diplomatic prowess. Having seized power in 1922, Benito Mussolini used nationalism, imperial designs, and military power to tighten his control over Italy. Roosevelt faced the events in Asia and Europe as an internationalist and as a politician. He wanted the country to take a more active role in world affairs, but he was *constrained* by strong isolationist views in Congress and among the public. In addition, he understood that American economic recovery was his first priority and that, at least in the short term, he might have to reject international cooperation in favor of more immediate American interests.

Between 1933 and 1939, Roosevelt wrestled with two problems: how to improve U.S. economic and political positions abroad while protecting economic and political interests at home. For Roosevelt and others who wanted to expand the nation's international role, the *outcome* was an unhappy one that in general deferred to Congress's and the public's *choices* regarding American interests. As Hitler aimed his armies at Poland, a majority of Americans appeared determined to avoid involvement in Europe even if that choice resulted in the defeat of France and England. The onslaught of war, however, allowed Roo-

sevelt to chart a path away from neutrality. He *chose* to help defeat Hitler by providing economic and military assistance to Britain, and to seek to *constrain* Japanese expansion by using trade restrictions. Japan's attack on Pearl Harbor in December 1941 not only drew the United States into World War II but created a series of new *choices* for Roosevelt.

The war not only altered American foreign and military policy but also managed to do what the New Deal had not—restore American prosperity. An *outcome* of the United States becoming the "arsenal of democracy" was full recovery and full employment as well as cooperation among business, labor, and government on a scale unparalleled during the New Deal. Over 15 million Americans marched off to war. Those remaining at home faced new opportunities and *constraints*. An already mobile society became even more mobile as Americans *chose* to move to take war-related jobs, especially on the West Coast. The *outcome* for women and minorities was mixed: they experienced greater opportunities, but they also were *expected* by most to give up their new opportunities once the war was over.

For presidents Roosevelt and Harry S Truman, defeating the Axis powers required not only mobilizing America's resources but making strategic decisions that shaped the course and outcome of the war. Faced with manpower and logistical *constraints*, Roosevelt *chose* to allocate most of the nation's resources to defeat Hitler first, agreeing with Winston Churchill to invade North Africa and Italy before invading France. In the Pacific, the victory at Midway gave the United States naval and air superiority and allowed American forces to close the circle on Japan. By the end of May 1945, Hitler's Third Reich was in ruins and American forces were on the verge of victory over Japan. Roosevelt had died, and facing the prospect of huge casualties with an invasion of Japan, Truman chose instead to use the atomic bomb. The *outcome* was the surrender of Japan and the beginning of a new age of atomic power with the United States at the forefront.

A World at War

1931	Japan occupies Manchuria
1932	Roosevelt elected
1933	London Economic Conference Machado resigns as president of Cuba United States recognizes Soviet Union Hitler and Nazi party take power in Germany
1934	Batista assumes power in Cuba Engelbrech and Hanighen's *Merchants of Death*
1935	Italy invades Ethiopia First Neutrality Act
1936	Spanish Civil War begins Germany reoccupies the Rhineland Second Neutrality Act
1937	Japan invades China Roosevelt's quarantine speech *Panay* attacked by Japanese aircraft Third Neutrality Act
1938	Austria annexed by Germany
1939	Munich Conference Germany invades Czechoslovakia Ribbentrop-Molotov Nonaggression Pact World War II begins as Germany invades Poland Soviets invade Poland "Cash-and-Carry" Act
1940	Soviets invade Finland and Baltic nations Germany occupies most of western Europe Tripartite Pact signed Economic sanctions against Japan Roosevelt re-elected president Selective Service Act Destroyers-for-bases agreement
1941	Lend-Lease begins Fair Employment Practices Commission created U.S. forces occupy Greenland and Iceland

	Atlantic Charter Germany invades Soviet Union U.S. war ships attacked by U-boats Japan attacks Pearl Harbor United States enters World War II
1942	War Production Board created Japanese conquer Philippines Japanese-Americans interned Battles of Coral Sea and Midway Manhattan Project begins Congress of Racial Equality founded U.S. troops invade North Africa
1943	U.S. forces capture Guadalcanal Soviets defeat Germans at Stalingrad Smith-Connally Act Detroit race riot U.S. forces invade Italy Tehran Conference
1944	D-day: U.S. forces invade France at Normandy and reach the Rhine G.I. Bill Roosevelt re-elected president U.S. forces capture Philippines Soviet forces liberate eastern Europe Battle of the Bulge

1945	Yalta Conference
	Roosevelt dies
	Truman becomes president
	Soviets capture Berlin
	Germany surrenders
	Iwo Jima and Okinawa captured by U.S.
	   forces
	Potsdam Conference
	Atomic bombs dropped on Hiroshima and
	   Nagasaki
	Japan surrenders

Roosevelt and Foreign Policy

- What foreign policy constraints did Roosevelt face before 1939?
- How did they shape foreign policy choices from 1932 to the outbreak of World War II?

Until Franklin Roosevelt ran for the presidency, he was an internationalist who had supported the Wilsonian image of an America active in world affairs. But as presidential candidate Roosevelt, he stated his opposition to American participation in the League of Nations and other world organizations and generally tried to avoid making foreign policy statements. Instead, he concentrated on domestic issues—the New Deal and economic recovery. Yet at heart Roosevelt remained an internationalist who believed that international cooperation would create a better world.

Soon after taking office, he sent Secretary of State Cordell Hull, who was well known for his economic internationalism and opposition to protective tariffs, to the London Economic Conference. As Hull worked to help shore up international currencies to facilitate world trade, Roosevelt demonstrated another aspect of his foreign policy—ignoring the State Department and making foreign policy decisions from the White House. Focusing on the immediate needs of the American economy, Roosevelt retreated from economic cooperation and lowering tariffs. Without informing Hull, he publicly withdrew support for using the dollar and an international gold standard to stabilize worldwide currencies. Hull was humiliated at this change in policy and watched as, without American support, the economic conference collapsed. It was not to be the last time that Roosevelt would conduct foreign policy without consulting or considering Hull or the State Department. "I'm sure that Hull doesn't know half of what goes on," remarked presidential adviser Rexford Tugwell. Still, Hull managed some policy successes a year later when Congress and Roosevelt approved the **Reciprocal Trade Agreements Act** and the establishment of the **Import-Export Bank.** The Reciprocal Trade law allowed the president to lower some tariffs by as much as 50 percent if the benefiting nations gave the United States most-favored-nation trading status. The Import-Export Bank allowed the government to lend money to foreign nations for the purpose of buying American goods. Initially, neither act had much economic impact, but over time both became central parts of American economic policy.

The Good Neighbor Policy

In Latin America, Roosevelt built on the improving relations already begun by Hoover by stressing his support of international rather than unilateral actions. He promised that the United States would be the "good neighbor" and would respect Latin American views and interests and not interfere in Latin American affairs. His promise was soon tested in Cuba, where the actions of President Gerado "the Butcher" Machado fed political unrest and revolution. To stabilize Cuba in the summer of 1933, Roosevelt sent special envoy Sumner Welles to encourage Machado to resign. He succeeded, but Welles considered the new government of Ramon Grau San Martin too radical and recommended using American military force to overthrow Grau. Although Roosevelt approved of "friendly" political intervention, he refused to send in the marines. Instead, the United States refused to recognize the Cuban government as legitimate while Welles searched for a local solution. Welles found his man in **General Fulgencio Batista,** who overthrew Grau and installed a government acceptable to the United States. The United States recognized the new government, rescinded the Platt Amendment, and signed a favorable trade agreement. Batista, who was the real power in Cuba, would control the island nation until 1958.

Watching American actions in Cuba, many Latin Americans questioned the reality of Roosevelt's **Good Neighbor Policy,** and pressed for U.S. agreement in opposing all forms of foreign intervention. At the Seventh Pan American conference in Montevideo, Uruguay, while Welles was involved in reshaping the Cuban government, Secretary of State

---

Reciprocal Trade Agreements Act   1934 law authorizing the president to lower tariffs on imports from nations that gave the United States trading status equal to the most favorable terms given to other nations.

Import-Export Bank   Bank established by the U.S. government to lend money to foreign nations that wished to buy American goods.

General Fulgencio Batista   Dictator who ruled Cuba from 1934 through 1958; his corrupt authoritarian regime was overthrown on New Year's Day, 1959, by Fidel Castro's revolutionary movement.

Good Neighbor Policy   Phrase used to describe Roosevelt's Latin American policy, which was based on the belief that the United States had no right to intervene in Latin American affairs.

Hull appeared to accept a statement banning all forms of foreign intervention. But before Latin Americans could rejoice, he added that despite supporting the principle of **nonintervention,** the United States maintained the right to intervene according to international law, especially to protect American citizens. At subsequent Pan American conferences in 1936 and 1938, however, the United States went further and rejected all reasons for foreign armed intervention.

Roosevelt's commitment to nonintervention was tested when in 1938, Mexico's president **Lázaro Cárdenas** nationalized foreign-owned oil properties. American oil interests quickly called on the United States to take action against Mexico to protect their property and profits. Hull supported the oil companies and sent inflammatory messages to the Mexican government demanding the return of "American property." Rather than deliver the harsh dispatches, U.S. Ambassador Josephus Daniels modified them to avoid offending the Mexican government. Reporting directly to Roosevelt, Daniels recommended accepting Mexico's actions and negotiating a fair payment to American companies. "We are strong. Mexico is weak. It is always noble for the strong to be generous and generous and generous," he told the president. Roosevelt took Daniels's advice. The United States recognized Mexico's right to control its own oil, and in 1941 the United States and Mexico agreed on monetary compensation to American oil companies. By the end of his first administration, Roosevelt had vastly improved the United States' image and position of leadership throughout Latin America.

Roosevelt and Isolationism

While Roosevelt was improving the image of the United States in Latin America, tensions were increasing in Europe and Asia. In Germany, Adolph Hitler rejected the democratic system that had brought him to power in 1933. Expanding the German military and promising to re-establish a German empire, Hitler by 1935 had ruthlessly instituted a **dictatorship.** Having conquered Manchuria (see page 796), the Japanese spoke openly of establishing a larger Japanese sphere of influence, the **"Greater East Asian Co-prosperity Sphere,"** and increased pressure on China (see Map 24.4). Resting uneasily between the Japanese and the Germans, the Soviet Union, led by Joseph Stalin, sought to improve relations with the United States, western European states, and China. Roosevelt, seeking trade possibili-

ties and hoping to stiffen Soviet resolve in the face of possible Japanese and German expansion, also sought improved relations. Although the United States granted recognition of the Soviet Union in November 1933, the Soviets had too little credit to buy American goods, and the United States was not willing to provide credit. Thus a decade of distrust and suspicion remained as neither nation tried to bridge the ideological gap that separated them.

Within the United States, Roosevelt's decision to establish relations with the Soviets increased protests that Roosevelt meant to abandon isolationism and embrace Wilsonian internationalism, dragging the country into the global tensions. By 1934, isolationists were in full cry, even repudiating U.S. entry into World War I. H. C. Engelbrech and F. C. Hanighen (*Merchants of Death*) and George Seldes (*Iron, Blood, and Profits*) concluded that the "true origins" of the war were profits and British propaganda, not idealistic goals. A congressional investigation chaired by Senator Gerald P. Nye of North Dakota determined that America's entry into the war had been the product of arms manufacturers, bankers, and war profiteers—"the merchants of death." Novelists like Ernest Hemingway (*A Farewell to Arms*, 1929) and John Dos Passos (*Three Soldiers*, 1921) added to antiwar and isolationist sentiments with their powerful stories depicting the senseless horror of war. As college students called for arms limitations and peace, a Gallup poll revealed that 67 percent of Americans believed that the nation's intervention in World War I had been wrong.

By 1935, tensions in Asia and Europe combined with American isolationism to generate neutrality laws that many hoped would prevent American involvement in future foreign wars. In August 1935, Congress passed the **Neutrality Act of 1935** pro-

---

nonintervention Refusal to interfere, especially in the affairs of another nation.

Lázaro Cárdenas Mexican president from 1934 to 1940, who distributed land to peasants, instituted social reforms, and nationalized foreign-owned oil properties.

dictatorship State or government controlled by a tyrant, or absolute ruler.

Greater East Asian Co-prosperity Sphere Plan proposed by Japan to create an economic and defensive union in East Asia, using force if necessary.

Neutrality Act (1935) Congressional resolution prohibiting arms shipments to nations at war and authorizing the president to warn U.S. citizens against traveling on belligerents' vessels.

hibiting the sale of arms and munitions to any nation at war. It also permitted the president to warn Americans traveling on ships of belligerent nations that they sailed at their own risk. If Roosevelt opposed the legislation, announced Senator Key Pittman, he was "riding for a fall." Anxious to see the Second Hundred Days successfully through Congress, Roosevelt gave up his preference for discriminatory neutrality and accepted political reality. Isolationist Senator Hiram Johnson of California cheered the act as the means to keep the United States "out of European controversies, European wars, and European difficulties."

Many Americans felt the 1935 Neutrality Act came just in time as the two leading **fascist** nations of Europe, Italy, and Germany, sought to overturn the international status quo through aggressive action. Hitler had announced his decision to break the military restrictions imposed by the Treaty of Versailles, and Benito Mussolini's Italian troops invaded the African nation of Ethiopia on October 3. Roosevelt immediately announced American neutrality toward the Ethiopian conflict, denying the sale of war supplies to either side. The arms embargo had little effect on Italy, whose modern army overpowered the nineteenth-century-style soldiers of Ethiopia's emperor **Haile Selassie.** Aware that Italy was buying an increasing amount of American nonwar goods, including coal and oil, Roosevelt asked Americans to apply a "moral embargo" on Italy. The request had no effect. American trade continued as did Italian victories. On May 9, 1936, Italy formally annexed Ethiopia.

The end of the Italian-Ethiopian war did not reduce international tensions. In March, German troops violated the Treaty of Versailles by occupying the **Rhineland,** and in July, civil war broke out in Spain. Roosevelt responded by proclaiming that the remilitarization of the Rhineland was of no concern to the United States and then left on a planned fishing trip. Most Americans agreed that Hitler's actions in the Rhineland, a part of Germany, were of no concern to the United States. But public opinion was sharply divided about the conflict in Spain. Liberals and leftists supported the Spanish government's **Republican** forces. Conservatives and most Catholics supported the rebels led by the fascist general **Francisco Franco.** Even though they might support one side or the other, however, most Americans believed that the United States should avoid any active role in the civil war and agreed when Roosevelt applied the neutrality acts to both sides. At the same time, Congress modified the neutrality laws to require absolute noninvolvement in civil wars and to forbid making loans to countries at war—whether victim or aggressor.

While the United States, Britain, and France remained neutral in the Spanish civil war, Italy and Germany actively aided Franco, taking the opportunity to test their military capability. German and Italian planes, tanks, and infantry troops augmented Franco's soldiers in attacks on Republican forces and towns. On April 26, 1937, German planes brutally bombed the Basque city of Guernica with a tremendous loss of civilian lives. Facing better equipped and larger armies, the Republican forces fought bravely but were forced to surrender city after city. What little support the government received came from the Soviet Union and from individuals and leftist groups in Europe and the United States. With the fall of Madrid in March 1939, Franco defeated the last Republican forces and ended the civil war. Over one hundred thousand Italian and ten thousand German soldiers had helped Franco establish his harsh dictatorship over Spain, which lasted for thirty-six years.

With the Italian conquest of Ethiopia, German remilitarization, and war in Spain as background, both American political parties entered the 1936 elections as champions of neutrality. Roosevelt told an audience at Chautauqua, New York, that he hated war and if it came to "the choice of profits over peace, the nation will answer—must answer—'We choose peace.' " Alf Landon and the Republicans were equally adamant that they were the real party of peace and isolationism. Roosevelt easily defeated Landon (see page 788) and with strong public

---

fascism   A political system and dictatorship that glorifies the state, nation, and race over individual liberties and rights.

Haile Selassie   Emperor of Ethiopia, whose country fell to Mussolini's Italian forces in 1935.

Rhineland   Region of western Germany along the Rhine River, which under the terms of the Versailles Treaty was to remain free of troops and military fortifications.

Republican   In Spain, a left-wing political group that won national elections in 1936 but was prevented from carrying out its programs by a military rebellion and the outbreak of civil war.

Francisco Franco   Fascist general whose rebel forces defeated the Republicans in the Spanish Civil War (1936–1939); he ruled as dictator of Spain until his death in 1975.

♦ Painted by Pablo Picasso in 1937 to attack the "brutality and darkness" of war, *Guernica* commemorates the destruction of the Spanish town of Guernica, where, in one night, bombs from fascist planes killed over a 1000 people and destroyed the village. *Guernica by Pablo Picasso, 1937. © 1995 Artists Rights Society (ARS), New York/SPADEM, Paris.*

support, approved the 1937 **Neutrality Act.** It required warring nations to pay cash for all "nonwar" goods and to carry them away on their own ships, and barred Americans from sailing on belligerents' ships. For Roosevelt, who disliked the inflexibility of strict neutrality, the new act provided a small victory. It allowed him to determine which nations were at war and which goods were nonwar goods. The president therefore wrote the "cash-and-carry" list.

Roosevelt used that provision in late July 1937, following a Japanese invasion of northern China. Ignoring reality and protests, he refused to recognize that China and Japan were at war and allowed American trade to continue with both nations. Hoping that isolationist views had softened, on October 5, Roosevelt suggested that the United States and other peace-loving nations should **quarantine** "bandit nations" that were contributing to "the epidemic of world lawlessness." The so-called quarantine speech was applauded in many foreign capitals, but not in Berlin, Rome, or Tokyo, and not at home. Within the United States, it only heightened cries for isolationism while Japan continued gobbling up Chinese territory (see Map 24.4). On December 12, 1937, Japanese aircraft strafed and bombed the American gunboat *Panay* and two Standard Oil tankers. Two Americans died and nearly fifty others were wounded. Roosevelt was outraged and wanted to take some retaliatory action, but public opinion and Congress insisted otherwise. Within forty-eight hours of the *Panay* bombing, isolationists

in the House of Representatives pushed forward a previously proposed constitutional amendment drafted by Louis Ludlow of Indiana that would require a public referendum before Congress could declare war. Public opinion polls indicated that 70 percent of Americans supported the idea. Only after Roosevelt had expended a great deal of political effort did the House vote 209 to 188 to return the amendment to committee, effectively killing it. Understanding that there was no support for any action against Japan, Roosevelt accepted Japan's apology and payment of damages for the *Panay*.

The Road to War

● What measures did Roosevelt take between 1935 and December 1941 to help defeat Hitler and to constrain Japanese aggression?

World peace was crumbling fast as 1938 started. The fighting in China and Spain raged on with increased intensity. From Berlin, Hitler pronounced his intentions to unify all German-speaking lands and create a new German empire, or *Reich*. Austria,

---

Neutrality Act (1937)   Law that required warring nations to pay cash for "nonwar" goods and barred Americans from sailing on their ships.

quarantine   To isolate, in this case politically and economically.

♦ **MAP 26.1 German and Italian Expansion, 1933–1942** By the end of 1942, the Axis nations of Italy and Germany, through conquest and annexation, had occupied nearly all of Europe. This map shows the political and military alignment of Europe as Germany and Italy reached the limit of their power.

Hitler's homeland, was the first target and in an *Anschluss* was merged with Germany. Hearing only mild protests from other nations, Hitler confidently moved to incorporate other questionably German-speaking areas into the Reich. He turned next to the German population of the Sudeten region of western Czechoslovakia, demanding its annexation to Germany. With a respectable military force and defense treaties with France and the Soviet Union, the Czechoslovakian government was prepared to resist. War loomed in September 1938, as German troops massed along the Sudeten border and as the Czechs appealed for help to defend their nation. Neither France nor the Soviet Union nor Britain, however, wanted a confrontation with Hitler. And when Hitler claimed he wanted only what was Germany's by right and vowed that he would seek no territory beyond the Sudetenland, they were willing to compromise. On September 30, Britain's prime minister **Neville Chamberlain** met with Hitler in

> *Anschluss* Political union, especially the one absorbing Austria into Nazi Germany in 1938.
>
> **Neville Chamberlain** British prime minister who pursued a policy of appeasement toward the fascist regimes of Europe before World War II.

Munich and accepted Germany's annexation of the Sudetenland (see Map 26.1). Without British and French support, the Czechs had no option but to concede the loss of territory. Chamberlain returned smiling to England promising "peace in our time." Roosevelt wired his congratulations to the prime minister.

The policy of **appeasement** did not end Hitler's aggressive policies, however. Within Germany, Hitler stepped up the persecution of the country's Jewish population. Germany was home to nearly half a million Jews, who since Hitler's rise to power had suffered increasing discrimination and harassment. In 1938, Hitler launched government-sponsored violence against the German-Jewish population. Synagogues and Jewish businesses and homes were looted and destroyed. Detention centers—concentration camps—at Dachau and Buchenwald soon confined over fifty thousand Jews. Thousands of German and Austrian Jews fled to other countries. Many applied to enter the United States, but most were turned away. American anti-Semitism was strong, and the State Department, citing immigration requirements that no one be admitted to the country who would become "a public charge," routinely denied entry to German Jews whose property and assets had been seized by the German government. Despite thousands of applications between 1933 and 1939, the State Department implemented the immigration laws so strictly that nearly three-fourths of the 27,400-person quota for Germany and Austria went unfilled. Roosevelt regretted this rebuff of Jewish immigrants, but with little public interest in changing immigration rules, he did nothing more than offer sympathetic words to those wanting to allow more Jewish émigrés to enter America.

Not only was Hitler persecuting German Jews, but he was also pressuring Poland to cede territory to Germany that contained large German populations. Convinced that Hitler was a threat to humanity, Roosevelt sounded a dire warning to Americans in his 1939 State of the Union address. "Events abroad have made it increasingly clear to the American people that the dangers within are less to be feared than dangers without," he warned. "This generation will nobly save or meanly lose the last best hope of earth." Quickly, events seemed to verify Roosevelt's prediction of danger. Hitler ominously concluded a military alliance with Italy, "the pact of steel," invaded and seized what remained of Czechoslovakia, and demanded that Poland turn over to Germany the **Danzig corridor** that connected Poland to the Baltic Sea. British and French

◆ In September 1939, Germany introduced the world to a new word and type of warfare, *blitzkrieg*—lightening war. Combining the use of tanks, aircraft, and infantry, German forces quickly overran first Poland then most of Western Europe. This picture shows a German victory parade in Warsaw, Poland. *Hugo Jaeger/LIFE Magazine.* © *Time Warner Inc.*

officials, unwilling to appease Hitler any longer, pledged to protect Poland. Meanwhile, unable to conclude an agreement with the British and the French, the Soviet Union had reached a secret, last-minute agreement with Germany—the **Ribbentrop-Molotov Nonaggression Pact** of August 23, 1939—which divided Poland between them. No longer worried about a Soviet attack, Hitler invaded Poland on September 1, 1939. Two days later, Britain and France declared war on Germany. Buckling under new **blitzkrieg** tactics that emphasized movement and maneuver, Polish forces collapsed. Within a matter of days, German troops had overrun nearly all of Poland. On September 17, Soviet forces seized the eastern parts of Poland as agreed on in the Soviet-German nonaggression pact (see Map 26.1). World War II had begun.

---

appeasement   Policy of granting concessions to potential enemies to maintain peace.

Danzig corridor   Territory adjoining the city of Danzig, which connected Poland with the Baltic Sea and which Germany demanded from Poland in 1939.

Ribbentrop-Molotov Nonaggression Pact   Secret 1939 agreement in which Germany and the Soviet Union pledged not to fight one another and arranged to divide Poland after the invasion.

blitzkrieg   Sudden, swift military offensive that allowed Germany to defeat Poland in a matter of days.

Roosevelt and American Neutrality

As Europe rushed into war, in the United States there was little desire to come to the aid of Poland, Britain, or France. Congressional and public isolationism remained strong. Just weeks before the invasion of Poland, a poll taken by *Fortune* magazine revealed that 54 percent of those asked believed that no international question was important enough to involve the United States in a war. Sixty-six percent opposed the United States going to war to save France and Britain from defeat by an unnamed dictatorship. Roosevelt had a different view. He was determined to do everything possible, short of war, to help those nations opposing Hitler.

When Germany invaded Poland, the president proclaimed the United States neutral but emphasized that he could not ask Americans to be neutral in their thoughts. He called Congress into special session and announced that he would enforce neutrality restrictions that prevented loans to warring nations and kept Americans out of combat zones. But he also asked that the cash-and-carry policy of the Neutrality Act of 1937 be modified to allow the sale of any goods, including arms, to any nation, provided the goods were paid for in cash and carried away in ships belonging to the purchasing country. A "peace bloc" argued that the request was a ruse to aid France and Britain and would certainly drag the nation into the war. They vowed to fight the request "from hell to breakfast." With the rapid collapse of Poland providing the president with needed votes, Congress passed the **Neutrality Act of 1939** in November. Any nations could now buy weapons from the United States. But, Roosevelt calculated, with German ships denied access to American ports by the British navy, only Britain and France would be able to obtain American supplies.

To protect merchant ships approaching American ports and to aid the British navy, Roosevelt established a 300-mile neutrality zone around the Western Hemisphere, excluding Canada and other British and French possessions. With the U.S. Navy patrolling to enforce the decree, warships of the belligerent nations were forbidden in the zone. If the navy happened to sink any German submarines, Roosevelt joked to his cabinet, he would respond like "the Japs do, 'So sorry. Never do it again.' Tomorrow we sink two."

As Roosevelt shaped American neutrality, Hitler mopped up Polish resistance, announced he had no further territorial desires in Europe, and quietly readied his armies for an attack on the west in the spring. Not so secretly, the Soviets continued their expansion by incorporating the Baltic republics (Latvia, Estonia, and Lithuania) into the Soviet Union and invading Finland. In March 1940, Finland surrendered and Hitler unleashed his forces on Denmark and Norway. Unprepared for such a move, two more nations fell under Nazi domination. On May 10, the German offensive against France began with an invasion of Belgium and the Netherlands. On May 26, Belgian forces surrendered, while the outnumbered and nearly surrounded French and British troops began their remarkable evacuation to England from the Belgian port of Dunkirk (see Map 26.1). That 350,000 British and French forces avoided total defeat at Dunkirk was the only bright spot in an otherwise dismal showing by Britain and France. On June 10, Mussolini entered the war on Germany's side and invaded France from the southeast. Twelve days later, France surrendered.

Germany and Italy, called the **Axis powers,** controlled almost all of western and central Europe, leaving Britain to face the seemingly invincible German army and air force alone. England's new prime minister, the feisty **Winston Churchill,** however, pledged never to surrender until the Nazi scourge was destroyed. On August 8, the **Battle of Britain** began with the German air force heavily bombing targets throughout England in preparation for an invasion of the island. In mid-September London and other cities came under attack. Defending Britain against more than 2,600 German bombers and fighters, outnumbered eight to one, was the Royal Air Force (RAF). Outfighting the German *Luftwaffe,* British pilots shot down over 1,700 German planes and forced Hitler to call off his planned invasion.

Neutrality Act (1939) Law repealing the arms embargo and authorizing cash-and-carry exports of arms and munitions even to belligerent nations.

Axis powers Coalition of nations that opposed the Allies in World War II, first consisting of just Germany and Italy, and later joined by Japan.

Winston Churchill Prime minister who led Britain through World War II; he was known for his eloquent speeches and his refusal to give in to the Nazi threat.

Battle of Britain Series of air battles between British and German planes fought over Britain from August to October 1940, during which English cities suffered heavy bombing.

◆ Hitler ordered the German airforce to attack British cities in an effort to break the will of the British people. London, like the British people, suffered tremendous damage but withstood the onslaught. By the end of 1942, the small British airforce was winning the battle against Germany for the air space over Britain. *Library of Congress.*

"Never have so many owed so much to so few," Churchill declared.

Even before the fall of France, Churchill had turned to Roosevelt for aid. He needed forty or fifty destroyers and a huge number of aircraft. Roosevelt promised to help. He asked American industry to produce over fifty thousand planes a year, lobbied Congress to increase the military budget, and ordered National Guard units to active federal duty. The president argued that with American support Britain could defeat the Axis without America having to enter the conflict. Even so, isolationists bitterly denounced Roosevelt for pushing the nation toward war. As both parties prepared for the 1940 presidential election, opinion polls on American foreign policy showed public confusion. Ninety percent of those asked hoped the United States would stay out of the war, but 70 percent approved giving Britain the destroyers, and 60 percent wanted to support England, even if the choice led to war.

Roosevelt pressed his support for Britain. In September, he signed the **Burke-Wadsworth Act,** creating the first peacetime military draft in Ameri-

can history, and by executive order, he exchanged fifty old, mothballed destroyers for ninety-nine-year leases over British military bases in Newfoundland, the Caribbean, and British Guiana. By the end of the year, Congress had approved over $37 billion for military spending, more than the total cost of World War I.

In the 1940 presidential election, the Republicans nominated **Wendell Willkie** of Indiana, a public utilities executive and ex-Democrat. Initially Willkie was politically much like Roosevelt. He accepted the bulk of the New Deal, opposing only its inefficiency and expense. He also supported aid to Britain and increased military spending. With little to distinguish himself from Roosevelt, Willkie relied on his own personality and simple honesty, and the nation's widespread opposition to Roosevelt's running for a third term. With their candidate trailing in the preference polls, Republican leaders convinced Willkie to present himself as the peace candidate and to attack Roosevelt for pushing the nation into war. Willkie's popularity surged upward, forcing Roosevelt to affirm more strongly his commitment to peace. "Your boys," the president promised American mothers, "are not going to be sent into any foreign wars." The election results demonstrated solid personal support for Roosevelt, who won easily, but not for the Democratic party, which lost three Senate seats to the Republicans.

The Battle for the Atlantic

As Roosevelt knew, the destroyers-for-bases deal was only a temporary solution to Britain's growing shortage of cash. By December 1940, Churchill had asked Roosevelt for loans to pay for supplies and for help to protect merchant ships from German submarines. Roosevelt agreed, and knowing that both requests would face tough congressional and public opposition, he turned to his powers of persuasion. In his December Fireside Chat, he told his audience that a strong England was America's best defense against Germany. If England fell, Hitler would attack the United States next. He urged the people to make the nation the "arsenal of democracy" and to

---

Burke-Wadsworth Act 1940 law creating the first peacetime draft in American history and providing for the training of 1.2 million troops.

Wendell Willkie Business executive and Republican presidential candidate who lost to Roosevelt in 1940.

supply Britain with all the material help it needed to defeat Hitler. He then presented Congress with the **Lend-Lease bill,** which would allow the president to lend, lease, or in any way dispose of war materials to any country considered vital to American security. The request drew the expected fire from isolationists. Senator Burton K. Wheeler called it a military Agricultural Adjustment Act that would "plow under every fourth American boy." Supporters countered with "Send guns, not sons." Despite isolationist opposition, the bill passed easily on March 11, 1941, and the 60-year-old president breathed a sigh of relief. American merchant ships were also permitted to carry supplies to England.

The Lend-Lease Act made American supplies available to Britain without cost, but was it too late? To many, it appeared that Germany was on the brink of another series of victories. In the Atlantic, German submarines were sinking so much cargo and so many irreplaceable ships that not even Britain's minimal needs were reaching ports. In March 1941, Churchill warned Roosevelt that Germany's foes could not afford to lose the battle for the Atlantic. In response, Roosevelt ordered the American Atlantic fleet to prepare for action, sent part of the Pacific fleet to the Atlantic, and extended the neutrality zone to include Greenland. By the summer of 1941, the neutrality zone, patrolled by the United States Navy, overlapped Hitler's Atlantic war zone. It was only a matter of time until American and German ships confronted each other.

Meanwhile, German forces plowed into Yugoslavia and Greece, heading toward the Mediterranean and North Africa. From Berlin, agents warned that Hitler was preparing for an invasion of the Soviet Union. The nonaggression pact of 1939 had served its purpose and now was ignored. Hitler planned to crush the Soviets with the largest military force ever assembled on a single front: 2,700 planes, 3,350 tanks, 3.3 million men divided into 142 divisions. On June 22, German forces, supported by Finnish, Hungarian, Italian, and Romanian armies, opened the eastern front. Few believed that the Soviet army would last more than three months, and several, including Missouri Senator Harry S Truman, saw a ray of hope in the bloody fighting between the fascists and the communists. "Let the Nazis and the Communists so weaken each other that the democracies will soon gain the upper hand or at least will be released from their dire peril," wrote the American ambassador to Japan Joseph Grew. Yet despite initial crushing victories in which German soldiers surrounded Leningrad and advanced within miles

of Moscow, by November it was becoming clear that the Soviets were not going to collapse. Claiming he would join even with the devil to defeat Hitler, Churchill made an ally of Stalin, while Roosevelt extended credits and lend-lease to the Soviet Union.

In May, as Hitler prepared to invade Russia, the *Robin Moor* became the first American merchant ship sunk by a German submarine. With the number of American naval ships protecting convoys growing, the inevitable encounter between warships took place on September 4, 1941. The U.S.S. *Greer* had been tracking the German submarine *U-652* for several hours, directing a British plane in dropping **depth charges.** The German captain, believing the depth charges had come from the ship and not knowing it was American, fired two torpedoes at it. Both missed. The *Greer* counterattacked, dropping its own depth charges. The *U-652* eluded the attack and escaped westward.

Claiming that the destroyer was only carrying mail to Iceland and that the attack was totally unprovoked, Roosevelt obtained congressional permission to arm American merchant ships, to use the navy to convoy ships all the way to England, and to implement an "SOS"—sink on sight—policy allowing American ships to attack German or Italian warships. By the fall of 1941, the U.S. Navy was unofficially at war with Germany and taking casualties. On October 17, the U.S.S. *Kearney* was damaged while protecting a convoy, with seven seamen killed. Two weeks later, the U.S.S. *Reuben James* was sunk, with 115 deaths. On November 13, Congress rescinded all neutrality laws.

With the battle for the Atlantic reaching a turning point, Roosevelt and Churchill met secretly off the coast of Newfoundland (the Argentia Conference, August 9–12, 1941). They discussed strategies, supplies, and future prospects. For the first time, both leaders sensed some room for optimism. More ships were getting safely across the Atlantic, and reports from Russia indicated that the German offensive was killing more Germans than Russians. But Roosevelt's main concern at the meeting was more political than strategic. He wanted to develop a political

---

Lend-Lease bill 1941 law providing that any country whose security was vital to U.S. interests could receive arms and equipment by sale, transfer, or lease from the United States.

depth charge Explosive designed for detonation at a preset depth under water and used against submarines.

♦ From the beginning of World War II, Roosevelt was determined to help defeat the forces of fascism. Meeting with Churchill, on board a cruiser off the coast of Newfoundland in August 1941, the two leaders signed the Atlantic Charter as a prelude to the United States waging war against Germany. *FDR Library.*

base to support America's entry into the war by announcing principles that would draw distinctions between the open, multilateral world of the democracies and the closed, self-serving world of fascist expansion. He and Churchill produced the **Atlantic Charter,** which set forth the Wilsonian goals of self-determination, freedom of trade and the seas, no territorial gains, and the establishment of a "permanent system of general security" in the form of a new world organization. Churchill agreed they were worthy goals but reminded Roosevelt that Britain could not fully accept the goals of self-determination and free trade within the commonwealth and British empire. Roosevelt, who saw the Atlantic Charter as a domestic tool and not a blueprint for foreign policy, had no objection to the prime minister's exceptions.

Facing Japan

Throughout 1941, President Roosevelt had to balance Britain's desperate needs with those of his own military, who pressed the administration for more equipment to strengthen American positions in the Pacific. Since 1937, Japanese troops had seized more and more of coastal China while the United States did little but protest. By 1940, popular sentiment favored not only beefing up American defenses in the Pacific but also using economic pressure to slow Japanese aggression. In July 1940, Roosevelt acted and placed some restrictions on Japanese-American trade, forbidding the sale and shipment of aviation fuel and scrap iron. Many Americans believed the action was too limited and pointed out that Japan was still allowed to buy millions of gallons of American oil, which was being used to "extinguish the lamps of China."

In September 1941, the situation in East Asia worsened. Knuckling under to German and Japanese pressure, the **Vichy** French government allowed Japanese troops to enter French Indochina (see Map 26.2), while Japan signed a defense treaty with Germany and Italy. Roosevelt promptly increased American forces in the Philippines and increased trade restrictions—all scrap metals were included, but still not oil. Within the Japanese government of Prime Minister Fumimaro Konoye, there were opposing views on how to react to the growing American hostility and economic sanctions. Those seeking to avoid war succeeded in getting pro-West Admiral Kichisaburo Nomura appointed as ambassador to the United States in February 1941. Nomura was instructed to resolve existing difficulties without giving up territorial gains. Discussions began almost immediately with Secretary of State Cordell Hull but resulted in little success because Hull demanded Japan's withdrawal from Indochina and China. At the same time, other Japanese leaders, especially within the military, argued that war was unavoidable unless Japan found a way to break the "circle of force" being created to deny its interests and place in the world. High on the Japanese navy's list of objectives was control over Malaysia and the Dutch East Indies (Indonesia)—sources of vital raw materials, including oil. Seizing those regions, they concluded, would probably involve fighting the United States.

By September, the Hull-Nomura talks had accomplished nothing, and for Minister of War Hideki Tojo, the choice had become simple: either submit to

---

Atlantic Charter   Joint statement issued by Roosevelt and Churchill in 1941 to formulate the postwar aims of the United States and Britain, including international economic and political cooperation.

Vichy   City of central France that was the capital of unoccupied France from 1940 to 1942; the Vichy government continued to govern French territories and was sympathetic to the fascists.

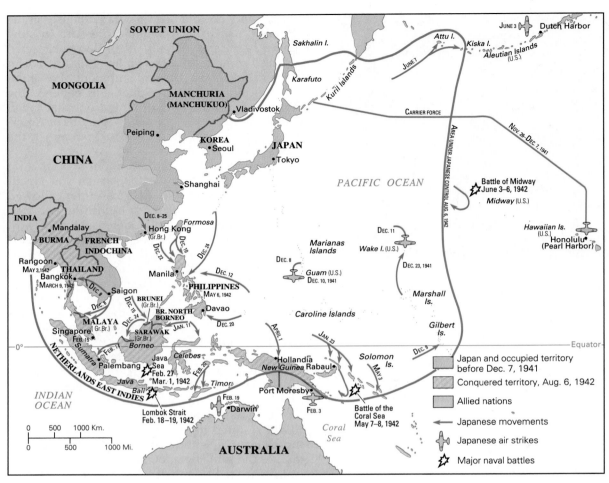

◆ **MAP 26.2 Japanese Advances, December 1941–1942**   Beginning on December 7, 1941, Japanese forces began carving out a vast empire, the East Asian Co-prosperity Sphere, by attacking American, British, Dutch, and Australian forces from Pearl Harbor to the Dutch East Indies. This map shows the course of Japanese expansion until the critical naval battles of the Coral Sea and Midway in the spring of 1942 that halted Japanese advances in the Pacific.

American demands, giving up the achievements of the last ten years and accepting a world order defined by the United States, or safeguard the nation's honor and achievements by initiating a war. Nomura's negotiations could continue through November, and if the United States agreed to stop its aid to China, not to expand its military presence in the Pacific or East Asia, and to resume full trade, then war could be avoided. But if the Americans did not concede to these three demands, Japan would begin military operations in the first week in December. Naval aircraft would strike the American fleet at Hawaii while the army would invade the Philippines, Malaya, Singapore, and the Dutch East Indies.

American officials, having earlier broken the major Japanese military and diplomatic codes, were aware of the December deadline. America too prepared for war, but Japan moved first. On November 26, Admiral Isoroku Yamamoto dispatched part of the Japanese fleet, including six aircraft carriers, toward Hawaii. American observers, however, focused on the activity of a larger part of the Japanese fleet, which joined troop ships in sailing on December 5 toward the South China Sea and the Gulf of Siam.

Pearl Harbor

The Japanese planned to attack the American fleet anchored at **Pearl Harbor** a scant thirty minutes after their formal declaration of war, which was to be delivered at 1:00 P.M. (Washington time) on December 7. However, the formal declaration was nearly fifty minutes late, by which time President Roosevelt was already receiving reports about the attack on Pearl Harbor. At 7:49 A.M. (Hawaii time) Japanese planes struck. By 8:12 along Battleship Row seven battleships of the American Pacific fleet were aflame, sinking, or badly damaged. Eleven other ships had been hit, nearly two hundred American aircraft had been destroyed, and 2,500 Americans had lost their lives. Fortunately, U.S. aircraft carriers were on maneuvers in the Pacific and not at Pearl Harbor, and Admiral Chuichi Nagumo decided to withdraw without launching further attacks that would have targeted the important support facilities—repair shops, dry docks, and oil storage tanks. These incurred only light damages.

The attack on Pearl Harbor, however, was only a small part of Japan's strategy. Elsewhere that day, Japanese planes struck Singapore, Guam, the Philippines, and Hong Kong. Everywhere, British and American positions in the Pacific and East Asia were being overwhelmed. Roosevelt declared the unprovoked, sneak attack on Pearl Harbor made December 7, 1941, "a day which will live in infamy" and asked Congress for a declaration of war against Japan. Only the vote of Representative Jeanette Rankin of Montana, a pacifist, kept the December 8 declaration of war from being unanimous. Three days later, Germany and Italy declared war on the United States. Americans were angry, full of fight. And in England Churchill "slept the sleep of the saved and thankful." He knew that with the economic and human resources of the United States finally committed to war, the Axis would be "ground to powder."

America Responds to War

- What new opportunities did women and minorities encounter on the home front as they responded to the war?

The attack on Pearl Harbor unified the nation as no other event had done. Afterward, it was almost impossible to find an isolationist. Even Colonel Charles Lindbergh, once a vocal isolationist who had admired Hitler and visited him in Germany, called on the nation to unite and build a strong enough

◆ Roosevelt called it a "Day of Infamy"—December 7, 1941, when Japanese planes bombed Pearl Harbor, Hawaii, without warning and before a formal declaration of war. In this photo, U.S. navy planes are being destroyed on the ground. A total of 2,403 Americans died in the attack that sunk or damaged most of the American Pacific fleet that was anchored at Pearl Harbor. *National Archives.*

military force to whip the Axis. The popularity of Lindbergh's view was evident as thousands of young men rushed to enlist, especially in the navy and marines. On December 8, in New York City, the navy recruiting station was besieged by 1,200 applicants, some of whom had waited outside the doors all night. Eventually over 16.4 million people would serve in the armed forces during World War II, including over 350,000 women who served in the military in a variety of noncombat roles.

Included among volunteers for military service and the massive mobilization of the draft were many homosexuals. Even though the military service had an official policy of not enlisting homosexuals, *Newsweek* complained that too many "inverts managed to slip through" a screening process that asked only if a person was a homosexual and looked for obvious effeminate behavior. In the military, many gays and lesbians discovered they could manage both military and personal needs, and that the military generally tolerated them—provided they

> **Pearl Harbor**   American naval base in Hawaii bombed by Japanese planes on December 7, 1941, in an attack that prompted the United States to declare war on Japan.

were not caught in a sexual act. In a circular letter sent to military commanders, the surgeon general's office asked that homosexual relationships be tolerated as long as they did not disrupt the unit.

The shock of Japan's attack on Pearl Harbor not only brought men and women to recruiting stations but raised fears of further attacks, especially along the Pacific coast. On the night of December 7 and throughout the next week, West Coast cities reported enemy planes overhead and practiced blackouts. Phantom Japanese planes were spotted above San Francisco and Los Angeles. In Seattle, crowds hurled rocks at an offending blue neon light that defied the blackout and then, venting both fear and rage, rioted across the city. The Rose Bowl game between Oregon State and Duke was moved from Pasadena to Duke's stadium in Durham, North Carolina. Stores everywhere removed "made in Japan" goods from shelves. Alarm and anger were focused especially on Japanese-Americans. Rumors circulated wildly that they intended to sabotage factories and military installations, in order to pave the way for the invasion of the West Coast. Within a week, the FBI had arrested 2,541 citizens of Axis countries: 1,370 Japanese, 1,002 Germans, and 169 Italians. Attorney General Francis Biddle announced that he did not believe it would be necessary to arrest more. Biddle soon changed his mind as anti-Japanese hysteria spread.

Japanese-American Internment

The feelings against Japanese-Americans were a product of long-standing racist attitudes and an immediate reaction to the war. Of the nearly 125,000 Japanese-Americans in the country, about three-fourths were **Nisei,** those born in the United States. The remaining, **Issei,** were officially citizens of Japan, although nearly all had lived in the United States for over eighteen years. Beginning in 1924, American law barred Japanese from entering the United States and denied those already living in the country the right to become naturalized citizens.

Fueling the hatred following Pearl Harbor were the actions of General John L. De Witt, Commanding General of the Western Defense District. On December 7, he had seen Japanese planes over San Francisco where none existed, and he believed that everyone of Japanese heritage was a threat. Except for individual cases, the nation need not worry about Americans of Italian or German ancestry, he pronounced, but the Japanese were a different matter. "We must worry about the Japanese all the

♦ In February 1942, President Roosevelt signed an order sending all Japanese-Americans living on the West Coast to internment camps. This photo shows a young boy, with a chocolate bar and comic books, awaiting transportation to one of the ten camps. *FDR Library.*

time," De Witt stated, "until he is wiped off the map." Unable to discover any acts of espionage or sabotage, California Attorney General Earl Warren somehow concluded that a plot existed nonetheless, and it was only a matter of time until "zero hour," when the enemy within would carry out its sinister plans. Echoing its anti-Japanese actions in the 1880s, California moved to "protect" itself. Japanese-Americans were fired from state jobs and had their law and medical licenses revoked. Banks froze Japanese-American assets, stores refused service, and loyal citizens vandalized Nisei and Issei homes and businesses.

Although some doubted the reality of any threat from the Japanese-American community, no one came forward to speak on their behalf or to protest the growing cry that those of Japanese ancestry be relocated away from the coast. President Roosevelt was no exception. On February 19, 1942, he signed **Executive Order #9066,** which allowed the military

---

Nisei A person born in America of parents who emigrated from Japan.

Issei A Japanese immigrant to the United States.

Executive Order #9066 Order of President Roosevelt in 1942 that authorized the removal of "enemy aliens" from military areas and that was used to isolate Japanese-Americans in internment camps.

to remove anyone deemed a threat from official military areas. When the entire West Coast was declared a military area, the eviction of the Japanese-Americans from the region began. By the summer of 1942, over 110,000 Nisei and Issei had been transported to ten **internment camps** (see chapter-opening map). When tested in court, the internment order was twice upheld by the Supreme Court in *Hirabayshi v. United States* (1943) and in *Korematsu v. United States* (1944).

The orders to relocate gave Japanese-Americans almost no time to prepare. Families had to pack the few personal possessions they were allowed to take and to store or **liquidate** the rest of their property, including homes and businesses. Some had two weeks, others had two days, but it did not matter. Finding storage facilities was nearly impossible and most families had to sell their possessions at ridiculously low prices. "It is difficult to describe the feeling of despair and humiliation experienced," one man recalled, "as we watched the Caucasians coming to look over all our possessions and offering such nominal amounts knowing we had no recourse but to accept whatever they were offering." A twenty-six room hotel was sold for $500; a pickup truck went for $25; farms sold for a fraction of what they were worth. When denied a few additional days to harvest his strawberry crop, one bitter farmer plowed it under. The FBI promptly arrested him for sabotage. Japanese-American families lost an estimated $810 million to $2 billion in property and possessions. Decades later in 1988, and after several lawsuits on behalf of victims, a semiapologetic federal government paid $20,000 in compensation to each of the surviving sixty thousand internees.

If having to dispose of a lifetime of possessions almost overnight was not bad enough, the process of internment produced a feeling of helplessness and isolation. Tags with numbers were issued to every family to tie to luggage and coats—no names, only numbers. "From then on," wrote one woman, "we were known as family #10710." Going to the camp, she had lost her identity, dignity, and privacy. Despite signs reading "Welcome to Manzanar" or "Welcome to Rohwer," the Nisei and Issei knew that they were surrounded by barbed wire and watched over by guards in towers mounted with machine guns pointing inward. Photographers were not allowed to take pictures of the wire or the guard towers. In camp, families and individuals were assigned to apartments of 20 by 25 feet in long barracks of plywood covered with tar paper. An average of eight people were assigned to each apartment. Cots, straw-filled mattresses, and three army blankets were furnished each person. Between rows of barracks were communal bathrooms and eating areas. Within each camp, the internees were expected to create a community complete with farms, shops, and small factories. And within a remarkably short period of time, they did. Making the desert bloom, the camp at Manzanar by 1944 was producing over $2 million worth of agricultural products.

Some internees were able to leave the camps by working outside, supplying much-needed labor, especially for farm work. Others volunteered for military service, the other escape route from the camps. Japanese-American units served in both the Pacific and European theaters, the most famous being the four-thousand-man 422nd Combat Team that saw action in Italy, France, and Germany. The men of the 422nd would be among the most decorated in the Army (see Individual Choices: Daniel Ken Inouye).

Aware of rabidly anti-Japanese public opinion, Roosevelt waited until after the 1943 elections to allow internees who passed a loyalty review to go home. A year later, the camps were empty, each internee being given train fare home and $25. Returning home, the Japanese-Americans discovered that nearly everything was gone. Stored belongings had been stolen. Land, homes, and businesses had been seized by the government for unpaid taxes. Quietly demonstrating their ongoing loyalty, Japanese-Americans began to re-establish their homes and businesses, denied even an apology from the government.

Mobilizing the Nation for War

When President Roosevelt made his first Fireside Chat following Pearl Harbor, "Dr. New Deal" became "Dr. Win the War." He called on Americans to produce the goods necessary for victory—factories were to run twenty-four hours a day, seven days a week. Gone was every trace of the antibusiness attitude that had characterized much New Deal rhetoric, and in its place was the realization that only big business could produce the vast amount of

---

internment camps Camps where over 110,000 Japanese-Americans living in the West were isolated on the grounds that they were "enemy aliens" dangerous to U.S. security.

liquidate To convert assets into cash.

Fighting for Democracy

Daniel Ken Inouye

Like many Americans, World War II changed Daniel Inouye's expectations and life. He chose to temporarily abandon his plans to become a physician and enlist in the army. While fighting in Europe, he suffered serious wounds, which effectively ended his medical career. After the war, he chose to enter politics in order to achieve "full citizenship" for Hawaiians and Japanese-Americans. He is now Hawaii's senior senator. Courtesy of the office of U.S. Senator Daniel Inouye.

On December 7, 1941, as the Japanese bombed Pearl Harbor, 17-year-old Daniel Ken Inouye rushed to a Red Cross aid station to care for the first American civilian casualties of World War II. Like many other Japanese-Americans, or Nisei, he wanted to enlist, but that choice was impossible. Nisei were being discharged from the armed forces, not enlisted, and on the mainland, Japanese-Americans were being interned. Internment did not occur in Hawaii, however, where other Hawaiians supported freedom for Japanese-Americans, who represented 40 percent of the population. Still, Inouye knew, "No matter how hard we worked . . . there would always be those who would look at us and think—and some would say it aloud—'Dirty Jap.' "

In September 1942, the Nisei got their chance to serve, as volunteers were being accepted for the newly created 422nd Regimental Combat Team. Inouye tried to enlist but was turned down because of his student status in the pre-med program at the University of Hawaii and his work with the Red Cross. He chose to quit both and became the second-to-last man to be assigned to the 422nd. Training in Mississippi, he and other Nisei were told they would have to fight not only the enemy but "prejudice and discrimination," as well, and that the best way to deal with both foes was to be exemplary soldiers who conducted themselves with honor.

armaments and supplies needed. Roosevelt forgave past transgressions and welcomed big business back into the heart of government. With Americans stepping forward to enlist, many corporate executives left their companies and flocked to Washington to take "dollar-a-year" jobs, contributing their business skills to help the war effort. Few saw any conflict of interest in the **dollar-a-year men** award-

ing million-dollar contracts to the corporate world they had just left. Eighty-two percent of government contracts during the war went to the nation's top

> **dollar-a-year men** Corporate executives who volunteered for government jobs to help the war effort.

Those who survived would "have a chance to make a world where every man is a free man and the equal of his neighbor." It was a patriotic speech, but to Inouye and other Nisei the words were prophetic.

Serving with the 422nd, Inouye experienced the carnage of battle, earning a battlefield commission as a second lieutenant. In the final days of the European war, his platoon was pinned down by German machine-gun fire from three bunkers. Not waiting for the Germans "to get us all," Inouye dashed forward. Wounded in the leg and stomach, he silenced two of the enemy positions. Then, crawling to within 10 feet of the third machine gun, he rose to throw a grenade, but a German fired first, shattering Inouye's right arm. "It dangled there," still holding the live grenade, he remembered. Throwing the grenade with his left hand, Inouye destroyed the last emplacement. For his actions, he received the nation's second highest award for valor, the Distinguished Service Cross, and spent two years recovering from his wounds and learning to live with only one arm. He concluded that a medical career was out and turned to politics.

Inouye returned to Hawaii, married, completed his education—including law school—and dove into Hawaiian politics. War had changed him and many Hawaiians, especially the Japanese-Americans: "We didn't want to go back to the plantations." "The 422nd was very much a part of what was happening," he reasoned. We were "heirs of an alien culture and very much expected—and, I suppose, expecting—to resume our unobtrusive minority. . . . But the army had given us a taste of full citizenship. . . . The feeling was infectious. It spread to the old folks. . . . They walked tall and proud."

Part of an energized Democratic party, Inouye ran for territorial office in 1954 and won easily. After Hawaii's admission to statehood in 1959, he was elected by an overwhelming margin to the House of Representatives, moving to the Senate in 1962. In Congress, Inouye emerged as an advocate of civil rights and American foreign and military policy. He kept a low, even bland, public profile, but was effective in getting legislation passed. It was his low profile that earned him a spot on the Senate Select Committee that investigated the Watergate coverup (see pages 961–962) in 1973. Not fooled by his quiet demeanor, a White House adviser said that Inouye's name should be pronounced " 'Ain't no way,' for no way he's going to give us anything but problems." The observation proved correct. During the televised hearings, Inouye's public approval rating rose to 84 percent—even as Bob Haldeman's lawyer called him a "fat Jap."

In 1987, Inouye chaired the Senate's investigation of the Reagan administration's illegal arms sales to the Contra rebels in Nicaragua (see page 990). As in the Watergate hearings, it became clear that Inouye disliked those who abused their power. Concluding the Iran-Contra hearings, he condemned the administration's actions as a "chilling . . . disregard for the rule of law." To him, the defendants' assertions that national survival in a "dangerous world" justified going beyond the limits of the law were nothing more than "an excuse for autocracy." As a Japanese-American, who was raised in "respectable poverty" and who felt the sting of discrimination, as a World War II veteran and a U.S. Senator who had fought for democracy, Inouye was pleased to announce that, in the United States, "the people still rule."

hundred corporations. In fact, three corporations received over 17 percent of all contracts, General Motors alone getting 8 percent. Small companies received very little of the $240 billion paid out by the U.S. government, and during the war over half a million small businesses collapsed.

By 1942, one-third of all American production was geared to the war, and the government was al-

locating millions of dollars to improve production and to build new plants in vital industries like aluminum and synthetic rubber. By the end of the war, the United States had pumped over $320 billion into the American economy and the final production amounts exceeded almost everyone's expectations: U.S. manufacturers had built over 300,000 aircraft, 88,140 tanks, and 86,000 warships. "Sir Launchalot,"

Henry J. Kaiser, had dramatically improved methods of shipbuilding—incorporating the use of many **prefabricated** sections—and had cut the time it took to build a merchant ship from about three hundred days prior to the war to an average of eighty days in 1942.

As the nation's economy began to retool to become the arsenal of democracy, Roosevelt acted to provide government direction and planning. His first step was to establish an **Office of Price Administration (OPA)** to control prices and inflation. In January 1942, as American economic mobilization took new meaning in the light of Pearl Harbor, Roosevelt expanded the power of the federal government and the executive branch by establishing the War Production Board (WPB) and the War Labor Board (WLB). Working together, these boards plus the OPA were to coordinate and plan production, establish the allotment of materials, and ensure harmonious labor relations. At first, however, the OPA, the WLB, and the WPB did not create a smoothly working economy. By the fall of 1942, confused priorities and guidelines, added to unregulated and soaring food prices, were creating a public outcry and labor unrest. To give the government still more control, in September, Congress passed the Stabilization Act, which expanded the powers of the OPA and regulated agricultural prices. In turn, Roosevelt created a new umbrella agency—the Office of Economic Stabilization (OEO)—to better coordinate prices, rents, and wages. He appointed former Supreme Court Justice James F. Byrnes as its chief.

Armed with extensive powers and the president's trust, Byrnes became known as the "Assistant President," the second most powerful man in the country. "If you want something done, go see Jimmie Byrnes," became the watchword. Almost immediately, Byrnes and the new director of the OPA, Chester Bowles, set maximum prices and froze wages and rents at their March 1942 levels. To deal with scarce commodities, Bowles and Byrnes expanded the existing rationing system, adding gasoline, tires, butter, sugar, cheese, and meat. By the end of 1942, most Americans had a ration book stocked with a confusing array of different colored and valued coupons that limited what they could buy and eat. Still, despite all government efforts and public opposition, a strong black market thrived. The right amount of money could buy nearly any item, no matter how restricted.

In May 1943, Roosevelt further expanded governmental planning and direction over the economy by establishing the **Office of War Mobilization**

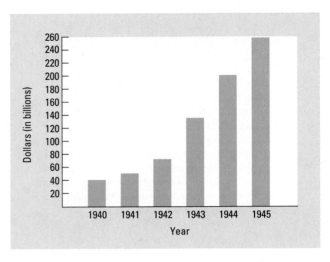

♦ **FIGURE 26.1 The Cost of War, 1940–1945**   As the United States fought to defeat the Axis nations, its national debt soared. Rather than further raise taxes, the government chose to borrow about 60 percent of the cost, adding to a $259 billion national debt.

and naming Byrnes as its director. The "Assistant President" managed a far-flung economic empire of policies and programs coordinating production, procurement, transportation, and distribution of civilian and military supplies. By mid-1943, production was booming, jobs were plentiful, wages and family incomes were rising, and inflation was under control—held to around 8 percent. Even farmers were climbing out of debt as farm income had tripled since 1939.

While the nation grappled with producing goods for both the home front and the fighting front, Roosevelt tackled the problem of financing the war. Initially, he was determined to fund as much as possible out of existing taxes, but as war costs raced toward a total of $321 billion, it became necessary to raise taxes, placing an increasing burden on businesses and the more affluent (see Figure 26.1). Those making $500,000 or more a year paid 88 percent in

---

prefabricated   Manufactured in advance, especially in standard sections for easy shipment and assembly.

Office of Price Administration   Agency established by executive order in 1941 to set prices for critical wartime commodities.

Office of War Mobilization   Umbrella agency headed by James Byrnes to coordinate the production, procurement, and distribution of civilian and military supplies.

Don't Let That Shadow Touch Them
Buy **WAR BONDS**

♦ Using the threat to children that fascism posed, this American war bond poster asked patriotic Americans to protect their children by buying war bonds. *National Archives.*

taxes. Corporate taxes averaged 40 percent, with a 90 percent tax on excess profits. The 1942 Revenue Act also slapped everyone making more than $645 a year with a special "victory tax" of 5 percent and expanded the number of people paying personal income taxes from 13 to 50 million. The tax changes from 1940 to 1945 moderately altered the basic distribution of wealth by reducing the percentage of income held by the wealthy.

Increased tax revenues funded about half of the total cost of the war. To finance the rest, the government borrowed from the people and itself. The national debt jumped from $40 billion to $260 billion by 1945. The most publicized borrowing effort encouraged the purchase of **war bonds.** Movie stars and other celebrities asked Americans to "do their part" and buy bonds, especially Series E bonds worth $25 and $50. The public responded by purchasing over $40 billion of individual bonds, but the majority of bonds—$95 billion—were sold to corporations and financial institutions. Still, buying individual bonds made many Americans feel that they were helping the war effort.

The war brought an end to the Depression and created full employment. With the formation of the War Labor Board, Roosevelt sought to prevent labor disputes while at the same time protecting the needs of the worker. To prevent strikes and keep down labor costs, the WLB adopted a formula that allowed workers a maximum 15 percent increase in wages above January 1941 salary levels. Although most workers and unions accepted this cap on wages as a patriotic duty, others, looking at living costs and corporate profits doubling, did not. In 1943, John L. Lewis and his United Mine Workers went out on strike. An angry president threatened to seize the mines and jail Lewis. Congress passed, over Roosevelt's veto, the **Smith-Connally War Labor Disputes Act** (June 1943) that gave the president the right to seize and operate any strike-bound plant or operation deemed vital for war production. Eventually, the parties reached a compromise that kept the 15 percent formula but established special circumstances to exceed the cap. Other strikes broke out during the war, but war production was never in jeopardy and most workers' wages rose during the war. Higher wages, Roosevelt's veto of the Smith-Connally Act, and support for a wartime president—all these kept labor loyal to Roosevelt as he prepared for the 1944 presidential race.

Wartime Politics

As Roosevelt mobilized the nation for war, Republicans and conservative Democrats moved to bury what was left of the New Deal. The congressional elections of November 1942 indicated that Roosevelt and liberal Democrats were facing hard political times. People secure in wartime jobs were no longer as concerned about the social welfare programs of the New Deal. They griped about higher taxes, rents, and prices; about the scarcity of goods to buy, especially the limits on gasoline and meat; and about government inefficiency. And they aimed their complaints at Roosevelt and Democrats. Early military defeats in the Pacific added to the dissatisfaction. Consequently, many Americans who had once supported the New Deal and voted Democratic either decided not to vote or voted Republican in 1942. Bolstered by Republican victories, business-oriented publications like *Fortune* and the *Wall Street Journal* sounded the attack on remaining New Deal social welfare agendas. Congress was not far behind,

war bond   Bonds sold by the government to finance the war effort.

Smith-Connally War Labor Disputes Act   1943 law authorizing the government to seize plants in which labor disputes threatened war production; it was later used to take over the coal mines.

axing the CCC, WPA, and NYA and drastically reducing the budgets of several other government agencies.

To keep the social image of the New Deal alive during the election year of 1944, Roosevelt called for a **G.I. Bill** of Rights and a commitment to achieving "freedom from want." In June, the G. I. Bill became law. It guaranteed a year's unemployment compensation for veterans while they looked for "good" jobs, provided economic support if they chose to go to school, and offered low interest home loans.

Republicans nominated Governor Thomas Dewey of New York as their 1944 presidential candidate. Responding to the conservative tone of the nation, Roosevelt allowed party conservatives to drop the liberal Henry Wallace as vice president and selected the moderately conservative Truman from Missouri in his place. Roosevelt campaigned on a strong wartime economy, his record of leadership, and, by November 1944, a successful war effort. Dewey had little with which to attack Roosevelt except suggestions of inefficiency and waste in the government and the argument that Roosevelt was too old and quarrelsome for the job. A Republican-inspired "whispering campaign" hinted that Roosevelt was close to death. As it turned out, voters were less concerned with Roosevelt's age (62) than they were with Dewey's youth (42) and the New Yorker's obvious arrogance. Dewey could "strut sitting down," one critic observed. Roosevelt's winning totals, although not as large as in 1940, were still greater than pollsters had predicted and proved that FDR could still generate widespread support.

A People at Work and War

Within sixteen days of Pearl Harbor, nearly 600,000 men were in uniform. But still more were needed and there were not enough volunteers. Turning to the draft, or Selective Service, the United States conscripted over 10 million during the war, most serving in the army. In the initial legislation, men aged 20 to 44 were eligible for **induction,** but later the ages were lowered to 18 and 38. Those drafted were required to serve until the war was over. By 1945, the U.S. military had gone from a "third-rate" force to one with over 9 million people in uniform.

At home the call-up and need to manufacture the goods necessary to win the war had begun to change everyday life. Cotton, silk, gasoline, and items made of metal, including hair clips and safety pins, became increasingly scarce. The War Production Board established fashion rules to conserve cotton and wool. Garment-makers eliminated vests and shirt cuffs and narrowed the lapels on men's suits. The amount of fabric in women's skirts was also reduced, and the two-piece bathing suit was introduced as "patriotic chic." People turned thermostats down to 65 degrees. Families collected scrap metals, paper, and rubber to be recycled for the war effort and grew **victory gardens** to support the war. For entertainment, Americans turned to comic books and cheap paperback novels, especially mysteries, and continued to watch movies in increasing numbers. The public loved *Holiday Inn* (1942), with its popular song "White Christmas" sung by Bing Crosby, and Humphrey Bogart and Ingrid Bergman in *Casablanca* (1942). When people complained about shortages and inconveniences, more would challenge, "Don't you know there's a war on?"

One sure sign there was a war on was that people were moving and taking new jobs as never before. Prior to the war nearly 3.8 million Americans were unemployed, but by the end of 1942 a severe labor shortage existed. To fill the gaps in the work force, employers increasingly turned to those excluded prior to the war: women and minorities. Even the Nisei were allowed to leave their relocation camps if their labor was needed. To reach new jobs, Americans relocated—between 1941 and 1945, 15 million Americans packed up and left home. Two hundred thousand people, many from the rural south, headed for Detroit, but more went west, where defense industries beckoned. Shipbuilding and the aircraft industry sparked boomtowns that could not keep pace with the growing need for local services and facilities. Once a small retirement community, San Diego, California, mushroomed into a major military and defense industrial city almost overnight. Nearly 55,000 people flocked there each year of the war, with thousands living in small travel trailers leased by the federal government for $7 a month. Mobile, Alabama; Norfolk, Virginia; Seattle, Washington; Denver, Colorado—all experienced similar rapid growth (see chapter opening map).

G.I. Bill 1944 law that provided financial and educational benefits for American veterans after World War II; *G.I.* stands for "government issue."

induction Formal admission to military service.

victory garden Small plot cultivated by a patriotic citizen during World War II to supply household food and allow farm production to be used for the war effort.

With the expanding populations, war industrial cities experienced massive problems providing homes, water, electricity, and sanitation. Crime flourished. Marriage, divorce, family violence, and juvenile delinquency rates soared. Visiting Mobile, John Dos Passos wrote, "a trailer army had filled all the open lots," while backyards, chicken coops, and packing-crate sheds were cluttered with people. "Hot beds" were available at $2.50 for twelve hours. The flood of people also brought other disturbing social problems, some familiar and some new. With its huge naval base and nearly twelve thousand sailors and soldiers looking for a good time, Norfolk was regarded as a major sin city. Police estimated the number of prostitutes working in alleys, taxis, clubs, and restaurants at between two and three thousand.

Contributing to the old problem of prostitution was the new problem posed by many unsupervised teenage children. Juvenile crime increased dramatically during the war, much of it blamed on lockout and latchkey children whose working mothers left them unsupervised. Mobile authorities speculated that two thousand children a day skipped school, some going to movies but most just hanging out looking for something to do.

Particularly worrisome to authorities were those nicknamed "V-girls." Victory girls were young teens, sometimes called "khaki-wacky teens," who hung around gathering spots like bus depots and drugstores to flirt with GIs and ask for dates. Wearing "sloppy-joe" sweaters, hair ribbons, bobby sox, and saddle shoes, their young faces thick with makeup and bright red lipstick, V-girls traded sex for movies, dances, and drinks. Seventeen-year-old Elvira Taylor of Norfolk took a different approach—she became an "Allotment Annie." She simply married the soldiers, preferably pilots, and collected their monthly **allotment checks.** Eventually, two American soldiers at an English pub showing off pictures of their wives discovered they had both married Elvira! It turned out she had married six servicemen.

Women and Minorities in Wartime

Lockout children and V-girls were a product of wartime changes, one of those changes being a workplace that hired more and more women. Throughout 1941 and 1942, employers did not actively recruit women, preferring to hire white males. But as the labor shortage deepened, they

◆ Over 350,000 women served in the military during the war, including Lt. Hazel Ying Lee, a Women's Airforce Service Pilot. WASPs flew "non-combat," ferrying planes and supplies across the United States and Canada. Already an experienced pilot in China, Lt. Lee is seated here in the cockpit of a trainer. Lt. Lee died in 1943, when her plane crashed. *Texas Woman's University.*

turned to women and minorities to work the assembly lines. The federal government applauded the move and conducted an emotional campaign suggesting that women could shorten the war if they left the home and went to work. The image of Rosie the Riveter became the symbol of the patriotic woman doing her part. As more jobs opened, women did fill them—some because of patriotism, but most because they wanted both the job and the wages. Leaving home, Peggy Terry worked in a munitions plant and considered it "an absolute miracle. . . . We made the fabulous sum of $32 a week. . . . Before, we made nothing." By 1944, 37 percent of all adult women were working, almost 19.4 million (see Figure 26.2). Of these, the majority (72.2 percent) were married and over half were 35 or older.

Despite the patriotic appeal and image, not all was rosy at work. Male workers resented and harassed women, who were generally paid lower wages than men and constantly reminded that their jobs were temporary. Employers and most men expected that when the war was over, women would

---

allotment check   Check that a soldier's wife received from the government, amounting to a percentage of her husband's pay.

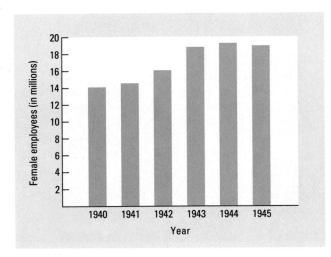

♦ **FIGURE 26.2 Working Women, 1940–1945** As men went to war, the nation turned increasingly to women to fill vital jobs. With government's encouragement, the number of women working swelled from 14 million to nearly 20 million. With the war's end, however, many of the 20 million women chose to leave the workplace and return home.

happily return to their traditional roles at home. Without adequate childcare and nursery facilities, worried about abandoning traditional family roles and their families, some women found it difficult to balance family needs and work. With regrets, many gave up their jobs.

For large numbers of women, the war had provided only a brief opportunity to enter the work force. When the war ended, women were among the first fired to make room for returning veterans. At that point, the government reversed itself and crowed that patriotism lay at home with the family. By the summer of 1945, three-fourths of the women working in shipyards and the aircraft industry had been released from their jobs. In Detroit, the automobile industry executed a similar cut in women workers, from 25 to 7.5 percent. Those who managed to remain at work were frequently transferred to less attractive, poorly paying jobs. For women, the war experience was a mixed one. They became more aware of their potential and ability. But when the war was over, many were required to sacrifice their newly discovered potential for traditional American values that kept women less than equal.

Like the war experiences of women, those of minorities were mixed. New employment and social opportunities existed, but they were accompanied by increased racial and ethnic tensions and

the knowledge that, when war ended, the opportunities were likely to vanish. Initially, the war provided few opportunities for African-Americans. Shipyards and other defense contractors wanted white workers. **Closed shop** agreements between white-only AFL unions and employers even squeezed black skilled workers out of existing jobs. Sometimes when African-American workers were hired, white unions responded with job actions. North American Aviation Company spoke for the aircraft industry when, in early 1942, it announced that it would not hire blacks "regardless of their training."

The antiblack bias began to change by mid-1942 as businesses felt pressure from the worsening labor shortage, especially in the West, the growing unwillingness of African-Americans to be denied the equality and rights due all Americans, and the efforts of the federal government. In California, these pressures dissolved the color line by the end of 1942. West Coast shipyards were the first to integrate. Lockheed Aircraft then broke the color barrier in August. Word soon spread to the South that blacks could find work in California, and between the spring of 1942 and 1945, over 340,000 African-Americans moved to Los Angeles alone. Overall, nearly 400,000 African-Americans abandoned the South for the West. Thousands of others went north to cities like Chicago and Detroit.

The growing availability of jobs for African-Americans was not just the result of labor needs, it was also the product of increased pressure on government from African-American leaders. Many black leaders agreed with **A. Philip Randolph,** leader of the powerful Brotherhood of Sleeping Car Porters union. In early 1941, he declared that without direct pressure from the black population, Roosevelt and the government would never provide legal, social, or economic justice for blacks. Randolph proposed that African-Americans march en masse on Washington to demand equality in jobs and the armed forces. In June, fearing that over 100,000 African-Americans were prepared to descend on Washington, Roosevelt signed a law that created the Fair Employment Practices Committee (FEPC)

closed shop Business or factory in which workers are required to be union members.

A. Philip Randolph African-American labor leader who organized the 1941 march on Washington that pressured Roosevelt to issue an executive order banning discrimination in defense industries.

and forbade racial job discrimination by the government and companies holding government contracts. Although the FEPC was not always willing or successful in promoting job equality, by 1945, 9 percent of the work force was African-American. Black wages, still only about 65 percent those of white males, rose from an average of $457 to $1,976 a year. Across the nation, blacks supported the "Double V" campaign: victory over racist Germany and victory over racism at home. Membership of the NAACP and Urban League increased as both turned to public opinion, the courts, and Congress to attack segregation, lynching, and discrimination. In 1942, the newly formed **Congress of Racial Equality (CORE)** adopted the sit-in tactic to attempt to integrate public facilities. Successes were minor but still noteworthy. Led by James Farmer, CORE integrated some public facilities in Chicago and Washington, although it failed in the South, where many CORE workers were badly beaten. In 1944, the Supreme Court ruled in *Smith v. Allwright* that Texas could not use the "all white primary" to deny African-Americans the right to vote. This decision changed the law, but whites soon found other ways to keep blacks from the polls in Texas and throughout the South. Meanwhile, a survey of some white southerners showed that they preferred a Nazi victory to racial equality.

In the North, patterns of hostility, discrimination, and violence hardened as the population of African-Americans increased. Jobs at Ford and Chrysler paid $5 a day, but suitable wages hardly compensated for white hostility. White workers went on strike when three black workers were promoted, harping, "We'd rather see Hitler and Hirohito win than work beside a nigger on the assembly line." Similar attitudes existed in Detroit's schools and stores, where real estate and property-owner associations ensured that blacks were tightly restricted to certain residential areas. A violent confrontation occurred when African-American families tried to move into the federally constructed Sojourner Truth housing development. Eventually, Michigan's governor had to deploy National Guard soldiers to protect the families as they moved in. A Justice Department examination reported, "White Detroit seems to be a particularly hospitable climate for native fascist-type movements."

With racial hatred and violence just below the surface in Detroit, it took only a small incident to set off a major confrontation. The match was struck on a hot summer Sunday—June 20, 1943—as blacks and whites tried to escape the heat at Belle Island

Park on the Detroit River. A series of small fights broke out that escalated and spread beyond the park. Feeding on long-standing fears and tensions, rumors of whites murdering blacks sent an African-American mob rampaging through the black district. The rioters smashed windows and looted white-owned stores, and some among them beat to death a milkman and a doctor, both white. By the early morning of June 21, a white reaction was under way, with marauding whites assaulting and killing blacks. A 16-year-old white youth bragged, "There were about two hundred of us in cars. We killed eight of 'em." Federal troops finally arrived and managed to restore order by noon, but not before twenty-five blacks and nine whites were dead. African-Americans and some other observers blamed the riot on the lack of equality and democracy for blacks and the long-standing patterns of white abuse against blacks in the city. Racial violence continued with 242 outbreaks in forty-seven cities during 1943. Roosevelt regretted the riots, but he ignored the basic sources of racial conflict and offered no positive steps to reduce tensions between blacks amd whites.

The opportunities and realities of African-Americans in uniform matched those of black civilians. Prior to 1940, blacks served at the lowest ranks and in the most menial jobs in a segregated army and navy. The Army Air Corp and the Marines Corps refused to accept blacks at all. Compounding the problem, most in the **noncommissioned** and officer ranks openly agreed with Secretary of War Henry L. Stimson when he said, "Leadership is not embedded in the negro race." President Roosevelt created the FEPC, but as commander-in-chief of the armed forces, he made no effort at all to integrate the military. Blacks and civil rights supporters, including Eleanor Roosevelt, strongly disagreed with this posture and lobbied hard for changes. In April 1942, Secretary of the Navy James Forrestal permitted black noncommissioned officers in the U.S. Navy, although blacks would wait until 1944 before being commissioned as officers. With only a small number of African-American officers, in 1940 the army

---

Congress of Racial Equality Civil rights organization founded in 1942 and committed to using nonviolent techniques such as sit-ins to end segregation.

noncommissioned officer Enlisted member of the armed forces, such as a corporal or sergeant, who has been promoted to a rank conferring leadership over others.

began to encourage the recruitment of black officers and promoted **Benjamin O. Davis** from colonel to general. By the beginning of 1942, the Army Air Corps had an all-black unit, the 99th Pursuit Squadron, and eventually would commission six hundred African-Americans as pilots.

Higher ranks and better jobs for a few still did not disguise the fact that for most blacks, even officers, military life was often demeaning and brutal and almost always segregated. In Indiana, over a hundred black officers were arrested for trying to integrate the officers' club. Across the country, blacks objected to the Red Cross's practice of segregating its blood supply. In Salinas, Kansas, German prisoners could eat at any local lunch counter and go to any movie theater, but their black guards could not. One dismayed soldier wrote, "The people of Salinas would serve these enemy soldiers and turn away black American GIs. . . . If we were . . . in Germany, they would break our bones. As 'colored' men in Salinas, they only break our hearts." In truth, many black soldiers had bones broken and their lives taken on the home front. As in the civilian world, blacks in the military resisted discrimination and called on Roosevelt and the government for help. But their complaints accomplished little.

Latinos, too, found new opportunities during the war while encountering continued segregation and hostility. Like other Americans, Latinos, almost invariably called "Mexicans" by their fellow soldiers, rushed to enlist as the war started. More than 300,000 Latinos served—the highest percentage of any ethnic community—and seventeen won the nation's highest award for valor, the Medal of Honor. Although they faced some institutional and individual prejudices in the military, unlike African-Americans and most Nisei, Latinos served in integrated units and generally faced less discrimination in the military than in society.

For those remaining at home there were more jobs available, but still Latinos worked almost always as common laborers and agricultural workers. In the Southwest, it was not until 1943 that the FEPC attempted to open semiskilled and skilled positions to Mexican-Americans. Gains thus made came only with increased Anglo hostility and, on numerous occasions, with the clear understanding that when the war was over, the new opportunities would vanish and Mexican-Americans would be relegated to their "proper place."

Jobs drew Mexican-Americans to cities, creating a serious shortage of farm workers. After having deported Mexicans during the Depression (see pages 759–760), the government had to ask Mexico to supply agricultural workers. Mexico agreed but insisted that the contracts for the *braceros* (Spanish for "helping arms") workers must ensure fair wages and adequate housing, transportation, food, and medical care. In practice, the contracts and guarantees were little help. Ranchers and farmers commonly paid low wages and provided barely livable facilities.

By 1940 Los Angeles had the largest urban population of people of Mexican heritage outside of Mexico City. The city also had a shameful history of discrimination in housing, jobs, and education when it came to the African-American and Mexican-American population. Blacks and Latinos could use the public swimming pool only on Wednesdays, after which it was drained and cleaned. The average Mexican-American family earned slightly more than $800 a year, well below the government-established $1,130-a-year minimum standard for a family of five.

Many young Mexican-Americans, known as *pachucos*, expressed their rejection of Anglo culture and values by wearing "zoot suits"—a long jacket with wide lapels and padded shoulders over pleated trousers, pegged and cuffed at the ankle—topped off by a pancake hat and gold chains. In the summer of 1943 in Los Angeles, tensions between Anglos and Mexican-Americans were running high, incited by newspaper articles highlighting a Mexican crime wave and depicting the "zooters" as dope addicts, draft dodgers, and terrorists. Anglo mobs, including several hundred servicemen, descended on East Los Angeles for three successive nights. They dragged zoot suiters out of movies, stores, even houses, beating them, and tearing apart their clothes. When the police acted, it was to arrest Mexican-Americans—over six hundred youths were taken into "preventive custody." The riot lasted a week until authorities set a strict curfew that was enforced by civilian and military police. Afterward, the Los Angeles city council outlawed the wearing of zoot suits.

Although they received the least from American society and frequently faced discrimination, Ameri-

---

Benjamin O. Davis Army officer who, in 1940, became the first black general in the U.S. Army.

braceros Mexican nationals who worked on U.S. farms beginning in 1942 because of the labor shortage during World War II.

◆ Secure communications on the battle field are a necessity, and no communications were more secure than those provided by the code-talkers—American Indians, who spoke in their native languages. Here Henry Bake, Jr. and George H. Kork, Navahos, "talk code" in the jungle of Bougainville in the Solomon Islands. *National Archives.*

Waging World War

● What strategic choices and constraints did Roosevelt and Truman confront in making the decisions that shaped the course of the war against Germany and Japan?

In December 1941, within the United States, 4 million people were unemployed, another 7.5 million were earning less than the minimum wage of $.40 an hour, and ongoing economic and ethnic differences continued to divide society. To many, the outbreak of war promised a reversal of those trends, generating national unity and a sense of purpose as well as a return of prosperity. *Time* magazine commented that the attack on Pearl Harbor was "a reverse earthquake that in one terrible jerk shook everything disjointed, distorted, askew back into place." Public opinion polls showed nearly total support for Roosevelt's decisions to declare war on Japan, Germany, and Italy and for the noble purpose of the struggle: a **pluralistic** American democracy waging war against "the evil pagan forces of strife, injustice, treachery, immorality, and slavery."

The Japanese attack also convinced most Americans that defeating Japan should be the country's first priority. The navy too was pushing hard for a Japanese-first strategy, but, to Churchill's relief, Roosevelt still considered victory in Europe as the first priority. Both leaders believed that Hitler was the most dangerous enemy. In late April 1942, Soviet foreign minister V. M. Molotov arrived in Washington also anxious to confirm Roosevelt's commitment to the Europe-first strategy. Further, Molotov asked for increased lend-lease supplies and a second front in western Europe to force the withdrawal of some of the 3.3 million Germans fighting in the Soviet Union. Establishing a western front would require an Allied invasion across the English Channel separating Britain and continental Europe. Roosevelt promised more lend-lease materials and a second front sometime in 1942. Roosevelt's commitment to the European theater of operations cemented what was called the Grand Alliance between the United States, Great Britain,

can minorities took advantage of new job opportunities and served gallantly during the war in the military. So it was with the American Indian. Many Indians eagerly supported war efforts, realizing that they offered both individual and tribal opportunities. At least 25,000 Indians served in the military. Among the most famous were three hundred Navahos who served as **code talkers** for the Marine Corps, using their native language as a secure means of communication. Although often called "chief," the American Indian, unlike other minorities, met little discrimination in the military. For most, military life and wages compared favorably to reservation life, and like many other soldiers, Indians found the travel and experiences of the military positive and educational. Once the war was over, the 1944 G.I. Bill provided many American Indians with their first chance to go to college.

During the war, not only the military but also jobs and higher wages lured over 40,000 American Indians away from their reservations. Mostly unskilled, these wartime workers boosted their families' average income from $400 a month in 1941 to $1,200 in 1945. Many of those who left the reservation assimilated into American culture and never returned to the old patterns of life.

code talkers   Navaho Indians serving in the U.S. Marines who communicated by radio in their native language so the enemy could not interpret messages.

pluralistic   Relating to a nation or society in which numerous distinct ethnic, religious, or cultural groups coexist.

and the Soviet Union to defeat Hitler and to establish a lasting peace following the war.

The British, however, vigorously opposed a cross-channel invasion so soon: it was too risky, and not nearly enough troops or supplies would be available within a year. Instead, the British promoted the idea of an Allied landing in western North Africa—Operation Torch. This would be an easier, safer venture that would also help the British army fighting in western Egypt. The U.S. chiefs of staff opposed the plan, but Roosevelt agreed to it— the American people needed a sign that the United States was taking the offensive. Head of the Joint Chiefs of Staff, General George C. Marshall cynically observed that "the leader of a democracy needed to keep the people entertained." To command American forces in Europe and North Africa, Marshall selected General **Dwight David Eisenhower** over 366 more senior general officers. Eisenhower, who had been serving on Marshall's staff in the war planning division, had impressed the chief of staff with his planning and organizational ability.

As work began on plans for the invasion of North Africa in 1942, the course of the war seemed to darken for the Allies. German forces under General Erwin Rommel were advancing toward Egypt and the Suez Canal. A renewed German offensive was penetrating deeper into the Soviet Union. In the Atlantic, German U-boats were sinking ships at an appalling rate. In the Pacific, Japanese successes continued. In May, commanding general Douglas MacArthur fled by sea as the last American forces in the Philippines surrendered. Japanese forces also captured Singapore and the Dutch East Indies and were establishing bases on New Guinea and the Solomon Islands. General Patrick Hurley admitted, "We were out-shipped, out-planed, out-manned, and out-gunned by the Japanese" (see Map 26.2).

Halting the Japanese Advance

Despite the commitment to the North Africa campaign, Roosevelt and military planners decided to move against the Japanese offensive in the Pacific as well. For reasons more psychological than military, U.S. military planners agreed to try to bomb Japan by flying sixteen medium-range bombers (B-25s) from an aircraft carrier. The Doolittle raid, led by Major General James H. Doolittle on April 18, 1942, took off from the *Hornet*, 650 miles from Tokyo, dropped a few bombs on the city, and flew on to China. Cheering this daring raid, Americans were

determined to take the action to the Japanese. The first major action in the Pacific occurred on May 7, when the Navy reported a "victory" at the **Battle of the Coral Sea** (see Map 26.3). "Magic," the code name for deciphering Japanese codes, had alerted American forces that Japan was preparing to invade Port Moresby, New Guinea, a step that would threaten Australia. The aircraft carriers *Lexington* and *Yorktown* intercepted the invasion fleet, and in the air-to-ship battle that followed, the *Lexington* was damaged and had to be sunk. But the Japanese also lost a carrier and had another damaged. More important, the invasion fleet turned back.

The Battle of the Coral Sea stopped the Japanese thrust toward the south, but a second part of Admiral Yamamoto's plan was to seize **Midway Island** and draw the American fleet into a major battle. Again alerted by Magic, the carriers *Hornet, Enterprise,* and *Yorktown* lay in wait northeast of Midway (see Map 26.3). The engagement on June 4, 1942, changed the course of the war in the Pacific. The battle was several hours old when a flight of thirty-seven undetected American dive-bombers surprised the Japanese carriers in the middle of re-arming and refueling their planes. The result was cataclysmic. Their decks cluttered with planes, fuel, and bombs, the Japanese carriers suffered staggering casualties and damage. Three sank immediately, a fourth later in the battle. Although the *Yorktown* too went down, the carriers and the air superiority of the Japanese had been destroyed. Hundreds of superb Japanese pilots had perished. The United States, with its greater industrial and population base, now held the upper hand. Between 1942 and 1945, Japan would launch six new aircraft carriers; the United States would put fourteen to sea.

With the victories at Coral Sea and Midway, the next step was to begin the task of retaking lost territory. To resolve disputes between the army and navy, commanders selected two avenues of attack.

Dwight David Eisenhower Supreme commander of Allied forces in Europe during World War II, who planned the D-day invasion; he later became president of the United States.

Battle of the Coral Sea Major U.S. victory in the Pacific in May 1942, which prevented the Japanese from invading New Guinea and thus isolating Australia.

Midway Island Strategically located island in the Pacific that the Japanese navy tried to capture in June 1942; naval intelligence warned American forces of the Japanese plans, and they repulsed the attack.

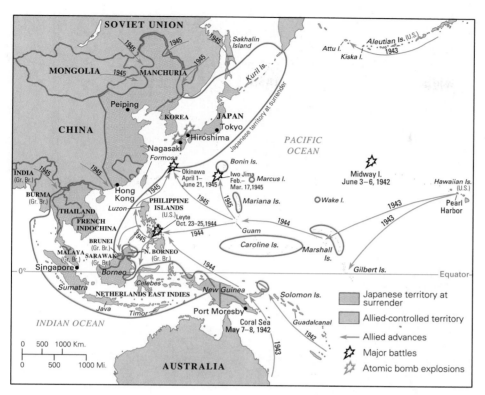

♦ **MAP 26.3 Closing the Circle on Japan, 1942–1945** Following the Battle of Midway, with the invasion of Guadalcanal (August 1942), American forces began the costly process of island hopping. This map shows the paths of the American campaign in the Pacific, closing the circle on Japan. After the Soviet Union entered the war and Hiroshima and Nagasaki were destroyed by atomic bombs, Japan surrendered on August 15, 1945.

General MacArthur and the army would take primary responsibility for an offensive beginning in New Guinea and advancing toward the Philippines from the south. The navy, under the direction of Admiral Chester Nimitz, would seize selected islands and atolls in the Solomon, Marshall, Gilbert, and Mariana island groups, approaching the Philippines from the east. Eventually, both forces would join for the final attack on Japan. On August 7, soldiers of the 1st Marine Division waded ashore on **Guadalcanal Island** in the Solomons. Japan, considering the invasion to be "the fork in the road that leads to victory for them or for us," furiously defended the island. Fierce fighting dragged on for the next six months, but in early February, Japan withdrew its last troops from Guadalcanal. By early 1943, American and Australian forces were also driving the Japanese forces out of southeastern New Guinea. The road to victory in the Pacific was now in American hands.

The Tide Turns in Europe

In Europe, too, the Allies began to meet with some success, although at great cost. By late 1942, as American marines sweated in the jungles of Guadalcanal, British and American forces were closing in on Rommel's Afrika Corps (see Map 26.4). After halting Rommel's advance at El Alamein, a British offensive led by General Bernard Montgomery drove the German "Desert Fox" westward out of Egypt toward Tunisia. To the west, British and American forces landed in Morocco and Algeria, in Operation Torch. Although inexperienced, American forces weathered a sharp defeat at the Kasserine

Guadalcanal Island   Pacific island that was the site of the first major U.S. offensive action in the Pacific. In November 1942, U.S. troops finally secured the island from the Japanese.

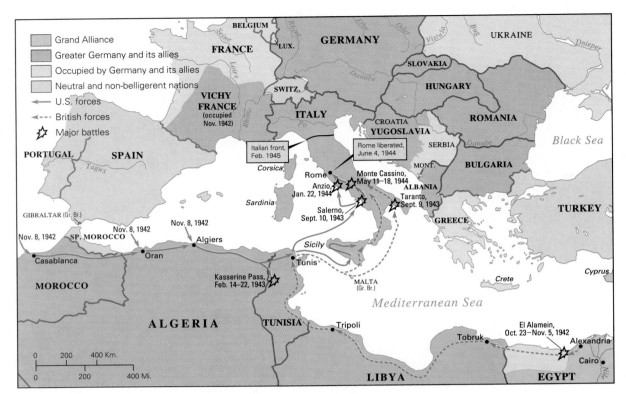

◆ **MAP 26.4 The North African and Italian Campaigns**   Having rejected a cross-channel attack on Hitler's "Atlantic Wall," British and American forces in 1942 and 1943 invaded North Africa and Italy, where victory seemed more assured. This map shows the British and American advances across North Africa and the invasions of Sicily and Italy. German forces fought stubbornly in Italy, slowing Allied advances up the peninsula. By February 1945, Allied forces were still advancing toward the Po Valley.

Pass and then under General **George S. Patton** overcame stiff resistance to link up with Montgomery. Caught between two Allied armies, the last German forces in North Africa surrendered on May 13, 1943.

German losses in North Africa were light compared with those in Russia. As American troops landed at Casablanca in Morocco, Soviet and German forces were locked in a titanic struggle. Germany's 1942 summer offensive had made dramatic gains, especially in southern Russia where the Germans reached the Volga River and turned southward into the Caucasus region. But Stalingrad stood in the way of further advances. Bitter fighting quickly reduced the city to rubble, but the Soviets stood fast. A Russian soldier wrote,

We have fought for fifteen days for a single house with mortars, grenades, machine guns, and bayonets . . . by the third day fifty-four German corpses are strewn in the cellars, on the landings, and the

staircases . . . imagine Stalingrad; eighty days and eighty nights of hand-to-hand struggle. . . . Stalingrad is no longer a town. By day it is an enormous cloud of burning, blinding smoke; it is a vast furnace lit by the reflection of flame. . . . Animals flee this hell; the hardest storms cannot bear it for long; only men endure.

From August through November, the German 6th Army fought to take the city—after November, it fought to survive. On February 2, 1943, after a three-month Soviet counteroffensive in the dead of winter, the German 6th Army surrendered, having lost over 140,000 men. The number of Soviet losses was probably just as large, but figures have never been

George S. Patton   American general who commanded troops in North Africa, Sicily, and Europe in World War II and who was known as a brilliant tactician.

released. As German strength in Russia ebbed, Soviet strength grew. Although it was hard to predict in February, the tide of the war had turned in Europe. Soviet forces would continue to grind down the German army all the way to Berlin (see Map 26.5).

In February, however, Stalin knew only that the **Battle of Stalingrad** had cost the Russians dearly and that German strength was still formidable. To ease the pressure on his forces, the Soviet leader again demanded that the Allies engage the enemy on a second front in western Europe. Again, he would be disappointed. Churchill had already met with Roosevelt at Casablanca (January 14–24, 1943) and once more overcame American recommendations for a cross-channel attack. Roosevelt agreed instead to invade Sicily and Italy, targets that Churchill called the "soft underbelly of the Axis." General Albert Wedemeyer expressed the U.S. military reaction: "We lost our shirts . . . we came, we listened, and we were conquered." To placate Stalin, who was told in May that there would be no second front in the west in 1943, Roosevelt and Churchill promised an increased flow of supplies and pronounced the principle of "unconditional surrender," promising they would make no separate peace with Hitler that would allow him to continue fighting the Soviets.

The invasion of **Sicily**—Operation Husky—took place in early July, and in a month the Allies controlled the island (see Map 26.4). In response, the Italians overthrew Mussolini, installed a new government under General Pietro Badoglio, and immediately opened negotiations with Britain and the United States to change sides. Italy surrendered unconditionally on September 8, just hours before American troops landed at Salerno in Operation Avalanche. Immediately, German forces assumed the defense of Italy. German troops also raided Mussolini's prison and freed him, taking the Italian dictator to German-controlled northern Italy where they proclaimed him ruler of Italy. The "soft underbelly" of the Axis turned out to be far from soft. Strong German defenses halted the American advance just north of Salerno, along the Gustav line, dominated by the hilltop abbey-fortress of Monte Cassino. Not until late May 1944 did Allied forces finally break through the German defenses. On June 4, U.S. General Mark Clark's forces entered Rome. Two days later, the world's attention turned toward Normandy along the west coast of France. The second front demanded by Stalin had, at long last, begun (see Map 26.5).

Approval for the cross-channel attack was assured at a Big Three summit meeting in Tehran (November 27 to December 1, 1943). In the Iranian capital, Roosevelt and Churchill met with Stalin to discuss strategy and to consider the process of establishing a postwar settlement. Roosevelt arrived wanting two agreements from the Soviets: to establish Soviet support for a new world organization and to obtain a Soviet commitment to declare war against Japan. The president asserted that he could handle that "old buzzard" Stalin and throughout their meetings believed he worked well with the Soviet dictator. Discussions of the world organization were only preliminary, but Roosevelt left with the impression that Stalin would participate fully in international affairs following the war. Of more immediate importance were military discussions. The three agreed on plans to coordinate a Soviet offensive with the Allied landings at Normandy, and Stalin pledged he would declare war on Japan once the European war was over.

The invasion of Normandy, Operation Overlord—**D-day**—was the grandest **amphibious** assault ever assembled: 6,483 ships, 1,500 tanks, and 176,000 men. Opposing the Allies were thousands of German troops behind the Atlantic Wall they had constructed along the coast to stop such an invasion. Those in charge of the landing knew they would have to "blast our way onshore" and get a good foothold before the Germans could "bring up sufficient reserves to turn us out." On D-day, June 6, 1944, American forces landed on Utah and Omaha beaches, while British and Canadian forces hit Sword, Gold, and Juno beaches (see Map 26.5). In the air, 12,000 British and American planes overwhelmed the 169 German fighter aircraft facing them. At the landing sites, German resistance varied: the fiercest fighting was at Omaha Beach, where

---

Battle of Stalingrad   Battle over the Russian city of Stalingrad, which was besieged by the German army in 1942 and recaptured by Soviet troops in 1943.

Sicily   Large island in the Mediterranean, west of Italy, which the Allies conquered in July 1943 as a first step to invading Italy.

D-day   Allied invasion of Europe on June 6, 1944, which was carried out by transporting tanks and soldiers from England across the Channel to Normandy; *D-day* is short for "designated day."

amphibious   Designating a military operation involving the landing of assault troops on a shore from seaborne transports.

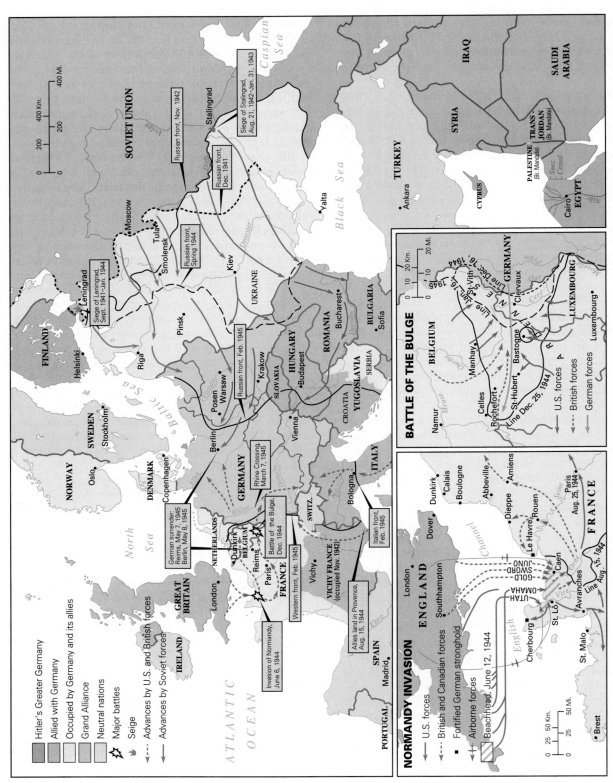

◆ **MAP 26.5 The Fall of the Third Reich**   In 1943 and 1944, the war turned in favor of the Allies. On the Eastern front, Soviet forces drove German forces back toward Germany. On June 6, 1944, D-Day, British, Canadian, and American forces landed on the coast of Normandy to begin the liberation of France. This map shows the course of the Allied armies as they fought their way toward Berlin. On May 7, Germany surrendered.

♦ On June 6, 1944, in the largest sea-to-land invasion, American, British, and Canadian forces stormed ashore against Hitler's "Atlantic Wall" in Normandy to begin the liberation of France. At Omaha and Utah beaches, American forces encountered heavy resistance before driving the Germans back from the sea. In the days following the invasion, over 1.5 million troops crossed the English channel to land in France. *Texas Woman's University.*

the American 1st Division suffered heavy casualties. By nightfall, the invaders had repulsed the German counterattacks and all five beaches were secure. After a week of attacks and counterattacks, the five beaches finally were linked, and British and American forces coiled to break through the German positions blocking the road to the rest of France. On July 25, American forces under General Omar Bradley pierced the stubbornly held German defensive lines at St.-Lô and rumbled toward Paris and the German border. The Allies liberated Paris on August 23, and by early November, took Aachen on the west side of the Rhine River, the first German city to fall. From November to March, American forces consolidated and regrouped for the final assault on Germany across the Rhine (see Map 26.5).

While the British and Americans advanced across France, Allied bombers and fighter-bombers were doing what they had been doing since the spring of 1942: bombing German-held Europe night and day. Vital industries and transportation systems were destroyed by what at times seemed to be around-the-clock bombing. Nor were German cities and civilians spared. In one of the worst raids, during the night of February 13–14, 1945, three flights of British and American bombers set **Dresden** aflame, creating a firestorm that killed over 135,000 civilians. Nearly 600,000 German civilians would die in Allied air raids, with another 800,000 injured.

Stresses Within the Grand Alliance

As Allied forces moved eastward toward the Rhine, the Soviets advanced rapidly westward, pushing the last German troops from Russia by the end of June. Behind Germany's retreating eastern armies, the Soviets occupied parts of Poland, Rumania, Bulgaria, Hungary, and Czechoslovakia. Following the Red Army came Soviet officials and eastern European Communists who had lived in exile in the Soviet Union before and during the war. The Soviet goal was to establish new eastern European governments that would be "friendly" to the Soviet Union. A Communist Lublin government (named after the town where the government was installed) was established in Poland, while in Rumania and Bulgaria "popular front" governments, heavily influenced by local and returning Communist party members, took command. Only Czechoslovakia and Hungary managed to establish non-Communist–dominated governments as the German occupation collapsed. Britain and the United States eyed the political changes in eastern Europe with suspicion.

On February 4, 1945, the Big Three met at the Black Sea resort of **Yalta** amid growing apprehension about Soviet territorial and political goals in eastern Europe. In the United States, many conservatives feared any expansion of Soviet power and influence and considered Stalin another Hitler. Confident that he could work with Stalin, Roosevelt arrived at Yalta fully aware of America's negotiating strengths and weaknesses. First and foremost, he needed a Soviet declaration of war on Japan and support for the new **United Nations.** Both were necessary to usher in peace and international stability. He also wanted the Soviets to show some willingness to modify their controls over eastern Europe. Stalin's diplomatic goals were basic to the Soviet Union's postwar needs: Western acceptance of a

Dresden   Industrial city in eastern Germany, which was almost totally destroyed when it was firebombed by the Allies in 1945.

Yalta   Site in the Crimea of the last meeting, in 1945, between Roosevelt, Churchill, and Stalin; they discussed the final defeat of the Axis powers and the problems of postwar occupation.

United Nations   International organization established in 1945 to maintain peace among nations and foster cooperation in human rights, education, health, welfare, and trade.

◆ As allied armies fought their way closer to Berlin, Roosevelt, Churchill, and Stalin met at the Black Sea resort of Yalta, in February 1945, to discuss military strategy and postwar concerns. Among the most important issues were the Polish government, German reparations, and the formation of the United Nations. Two months later, Roosevelt died and Harry S Truman assumed the presidency. *National Archives.*

Soviet sphere of influence in eastern Europe, the weakening of Germany, the economic restoration of the Soviet Union, and indications from Britain and America that any postwar international system would be based on Big Three cooperation.

Roosevelt's and Stalin's views on Germany seemed nearly parallel. To prevent Germany from ever again posing a military threat to its neighbors, they desired to divide their enemy into smaller, weaker states. Churchill disagreed, saying that the dismemberment of Germany would be too harsh and disruptive. He also opposed the Soviet request for at least $20 million in German reparations to help rebuild the Soviet Union. Unable to agree on the future of Germany, the Big Three postponed further discussions until their next meeting.

The question of which Polish government represented Poland, however, could not be put off. The Soviet Union supported the Lublin government as the only legitimate government of postwar Poland. Roosevelt and Churchill supported a London-based government-in-exile, considered the Lublin govern-

ment to be a puppet of the Soviet Union, and hoped to establish a Polish government that could hold free and honest elections. Their goal matched the ideals of the Atlantic Charter but not the **geopolitics** of the Soviet Union. Stalin believed that the London-based government would be hostile to the Soviet Union and argued that Soviet security demanded a friendly government in Poland. After considerable acidic haggling, the powers agreed on a compromise phrased in language that covered many sins. Admiral William Leahy, one of Roosevelt's primary advisers, ruefully noted that the language was so vague that its meaning could be "stretched from Yalta to Washington" without breaking. Roosevelt agreed, but he realistically concluded that it was the best he could do for Poland at the moment. On the related issue of Soviet influence throughout eastern Europe, Roosevelt fared little better. The Yalta Conference left control over eastern Europe firmly in Soviet hands. Although Roosevelt failed to get more than cosmetic agreements on eastern European issues, he did accomplish his two major goals. Stalin promised to enter the war against Japan within three months of Germany's surrender and to support the formation of the United Nations.

Roosevelt was extremely tired and seriously ill with high blood pressure and a bad heart throughout the Yalta meetings. Nevertheless, he negotiated and played the diplomatic game on a par with Churchill and Stalin and consistent with his goals and resources. Believing that there could be no postwar stability and security without Soviet cooperation, Roosevelt permitted Stalin to keep what he already had, or could easily take. Short of ending friendly relations with the Soviet Union, Roosevelt had no means to reduce Soviet power in eastern Europe or to prevent the Soviets from declaring war on Japan and taking whatever they wanted in East Asia. Roosevelt hoped that his good will would encourage Stalin to respond in kind, maintaining at least a semblance of representative government in the nations of eastern Europe and continuing to cooperate with the United States. Publicly and privately, both Stalin and Roosevelt were pleased with the results and were buoyed by the "spirit of Yalta." Only Churchill, who feared growing Soviet influence, left Yalta in a gloomy mood.

---

geopolitics Government policy based on the influence of geographic and political factors on national interests.

Hitler's Defeat

With his forces crumbling in the east, Hitler approved a last-ditch attempt to halt the American advance. Taking advantage of bad weather that grounded Allied aircraft, German forces launched an attack through the Ardennes Forest that pushed back the Americans and drove fifty miles into Belgium. If successful, the attack would have split American forces and significantly delayed further British and American advances. It was a desperate gamble that depended on surprise, the weather, and rapid movement to overrun American positions. The gamble failed. Although surprised by the attack, not all American forces were pushed aside. At Bastogne, a critical crossroads, the 101st Airborne Division refused to retreat, and when invited to surrender, General A. C. McAuliffe simply told the Germans, "Nuts." After ten days, the weather improved, the German offensive slowed and halted, and a relief column reached Bastogne. The **Battle of the Bulge** delayed Eisenhower's westward assault only briefly but cost Germany valuable reserves and equipment (see Map 26.5). Ultimately, it merely hastened the end of the war. The war was also winding down in Italy. By the end of 1944, British and American forces had taken Florence and most of northern Italy. When German armies began to surrender in April 1945, Italian partisans captured Mussolini and hanged him.

On March 7, 1945, American forces crossed the Rhine at Remagen and began to battle their way into the heart of Germany. In Berlin, Hitler and the German High Command waited for the end. American and British troops were moving steadily eastward toward Berlin, while Soviet forces were dangerously close to Berlin's eastern suburbs. Russian soldiers began the bloody, house-to-house conquest of the city on April 22. Three days later, American and Soviet infantrymen shook hands at the Elbe River 60 miles south of Berlin. Unwilling to be captured, on April 30, Hitler committed suicide and had aides burn his body. On May 8, 1945, German officials surrendered. The war in Europe was over.

Although Roosevelt had worked since 1939 to ensure Hitler's defeat, he did not live to see it. On April 12, while relaxing and recovering from the strains of the presidency and Yalta, he died of a massive cerebral hemorrhage at Warm Springs, Georgia. Nor did Roosevelt live to know the full horror of what came to be called the **Holocaust.** World War II was a total war that counted among its casualties millions of civilians. All sides bombed

♦ At concentration camps like Buchenwald, Bergen-Belsen, and Auschwitz, advancing Allied troops faced the horrors of Hitler's "final solution"—the effort to exterminate Europe's Jews. Over six million Jews died in such camps. This picture shows starving survivors of the camp at Wobbelin being taken to hospitals for medical attention. *National Archives.*

cities and their civilian occupants ruthlessly, but no such horror could match what advancing Allied armies found as they fought their way toward Berlin. In 1941, the Nazi political leadership decided on what was called the **Final Solution** to rid German-occupied Europe of Jews. In concentration camps, Jews, along with homosexuals, gypsies, and the mentally ill, were brutalized, starved, worked as slave labor, and systematically exterminated. At Auschwitz, Nazis used gas chambers—disguised as showers—to execute twelve thousand victims a day. When the camps and their remaining inmates were

---

Battle of the Bulge Battle in December 1944 that was the last major Axis counteroffensive against Allied invasion of Europe; German troops gained territory in France but were eventually driven back.

Holocaust Genocide of European Jews systematically carried out by the Nazis during World War II.

Final Solution German plan to destroy the Jews by isolating them in concentration camps and committing mass executions; by the end of the war, the Nazis had killed 6 million Jews.

liberated in 1945, 6 million Jews had been slaughtered in the death camps, nearly two-thirds of prewar Europe's Jewish population.

Closing the Circle on Japan

Victory in Europe—**V-E Day**—touched off parades and rejoicing in the United States, but it was too early to demobilize and return to normal. Japan still had to be defeated. Although Europe was getting first priority, American forces had managed to build on their 1942 victories and take the offensive in the Pacific. Japan's defensive strategy was simple: force the United States to invade a seemingly endless number of islands and atolls in the Pacific before it could launch an attack against Japan. With each speck of land costing the Americans dearly in lives and materials, the Japanese hoped that pressure would build in the United States for a negotiated settlement. The strategy was based on wrong assumptions. After Pearl Harbor, few Americans would accept anything less than the total defeat of Japan, and, equally important, the American military realized that it had to seize only the most strategic of islands. With carriers providing mobile air superiority, the Americans could bypass and isolate many Japanese-held islands.

Throughout 1943, General MacArthur advanced up the northern coast of New Guinea, while the navy and marines fought their way through the Solomon Islands. By mid-1944 having bypassed Japanese bases on Rabaul and Kavieng, MacArthur was ready to fulfill his promise to return to the Philippines. At the same time, far to the northeast, the U.S. Navy and the Marines Corps were establishing a foothold in the Gilbert Islands, where on November 21, 1943, marines fought their way ashore on "bloody Tarawa." Tarawa was defended by five thousand well-entrenched Japanese troops—nearly all of them would fight to the death. The victorious marines suffered nearly three thousand casualties. After equally bitter fighting, U.S. forces took Kwajalein and Eniwetok in the western Marshall Islands in February 1944 (see Map 26.3).

With the Gilbert and Marshall islands neutralized, Admiral Nimitz approached Guam and Saipan in the Mariana Islands. The Japanese rushed a fleet with nine carriers to halt the American invasion of Saipan. Warned of their approach, Admiral Marc Mitscher turned his fifteen carriers to intercept. When the "Great Marianas' Turkey Shoot"—or the Battle of the Philippine Sea—ended on June 20, 243 of 373 Japanese planes had been shot down and

three Japanese carriers were sunk. On Saipan itself, the Japanese defenders, including 22,000 Japanese civilians, expended all their ammunition and then committed suicide rather than surrender. Marines next seized the nearby islands of Tinian (August 1) and Guam (August 11). By July 1944, the southern and eastern approaches to the Philippines were in American hands. From airfields on Tinian, Saipan, and Guam, long-range American bombers, the B-29s, began devastating raids against the homeland of Japan. In October, with an overwhelming superiority of men, guns, and supplies, American forces landed on Leyte in the center of the Philippine archipelago. Again, the Japanese navy acted to halt the invasion, and with the same results. In the largest naval battle in history, the **Battle of Leyte Gulf** (October 23–25, 1944), American naval forces shattered what remained of Japanese air and sea power. On October 23, wading ashore with an escort of subordinates and at least one photographer, General MacArthur returned to the Philippines.

After the Battle of Leyte Gulf, the full brunt of the American Pacific offensive bore down on Okinawa and Iwo Jima in the Ryukyu Islands, only 750 miles from Tokyo. To defend the islands, Japan resorted to a new tactic: the *kamikaze*—suicide attacks in explosive-laden airplanes. The American assault on Iwo Jima began on February 19. Japanese soldiers had honeycombed the small island with tunnels and fortified positions and would sooner die than surrender. Iwo Jima was the worst experience faced by U.S. Marines in the war, and a warning of what lay ahead on Okinawa. Virtually all of the 21,000 Japanese defenders died, while American losses approached one-third of the landing force: 6,821 dead and 20,000 wounded.

On **Okinawa,** American forces landed unopposed on April 1, and quickly secured the northern part of the island. But five days later, they began to take heavy losses along Japanese defensive lines on

---

V-E Day Official end of the war in Europe on May 8, 1945, following the unconditional surrender of the German armies.

Battle of Leyte Gulf Largest naval battle in history, which occurred in the Philippines in October 1944 as American naval forces crushed Japanese air and sea power.

Okinawa Pacific island that U.S. troops captured in the spring of 1945 after a grueling battle in which over a hundred thousand Japanese soldiers, unwilling to surrender, were killed.

the south end of the island. At sea, nine hundred Japanese planes, including three hundred kamikazes, rained terror and destruction on the American fleet. Five thousand American sailors died and several ships were lost or badly damaged. Throughout May and June, the Japanese air onslaughts continued but became weaker each month as Japan ran out of planes and pilots. By the end of June, Okinawa was in American hands, but at a fearful price: 12,000 Americans, 110,000 Japanese soldiers, and 160,000 Okinawan and Japanese civilians dead.

Entering the Nuclear Age

Okinawa proved a painful warning for those planning the invasion of Japan. Fighting for their homeland, the Japanese could be expected to resist until death. American casualties would be extremely high, perhaps as many as a million. But by the summer of 1945, the United States had an alternative to invasion: a new and untried weapon—the atomic bomb. The **A-bomb** was the product of years of British-American research and development, the **Manhattan Project.** From the beginning of the war, science had played a vital role by developing and improving the tools of combat. Among the outcomes were radar, sonar, flamethrowers, rockets, and a variety of other useful and frequently deadly products. But the most fearsome and secret of projects was the effort, started in 1941, to construct a nuclear weapon. Between then and 1945, the Manhattan engineers, led by J. Robert Oppenheimer and Edward Teller, controlled a chain reaction involving uranium and plutonium to create the atomic bomb. By the time Germany surrendered, the project had cost over $2 billion, but the bomb had been born. When it was tested at Alamogordo, New Mexico, on July 16, the results were spectacular. In the words of General Leslie Groves,

> *The effect could well be called unprecedented, magnificent, beautiful, stupendous and terrifying. . . . The whole country was lighted by a searing light. . . . Thirty seconds after the explosion came . . . the air blast . . . followed almost immediately by the strong, sustained, awesome roar which warned of doomsday and made us feel that we puny things were blasphemous to dare tamper with the forces heretofore reserved to The Almighty.*

Word of the successful test was quickly relayed to Truman, who had assumed the presidency when Roosevelt died in April. Truman was meeting with Churchill and Stalin at Potsdam.

Truman had traveled to Potsdam with a new secretary of state, James F. Byrnes. Before leaving for Germany, they agreed not to tell Stalin any details about the atomic bomb (although both knew about a Soviet spy ring within the Manhattan project) and to use the bomb as quickly as possible against Japan. Using the atomic bomb, Truman and Byrnes hoped, would serve two purposes. It would force Japan to surrender without an invasion, and it would impress the Soviets and, just maybe, make them more amenable to American views.

Soon after his arrival at Potsdam, Truman met privately with Stalin and achieved his primary goal. The Soviet dictator promised to enter the Japanese war in mid-August. Later, in a major understatement, Truman informed Stalin that the United States had a new and powerful weapon to use against Japan, never mentioning that it was an atomic bomb. Stalin appeared disinterested and told Truman to go ahead and use the weapon. Then, with Prime Minister Clement Attlee, who had replaced Churchill, Truman released the **Potsdam Declaration,** which called upon Japan to surrender by August or face total destruction. The declaration reflected two developments: one Japan knew about, the other it was soon to learn. Prior to and during the Potsdam meeting, Japanese officials had asked the "neutral" Soviets to ask the Americans if they would consider negotiating a Japanese surrender. Stalin brought the message to Truman, and all agreed to reject the idea and insist on unconditional surrender. In the Potsdam Declaration, the Japanese could read the rejection of their overture, but they had no way of knowing that the utter destruction referred to in the declaration meant using the A-bomb.

On July 25, Truman ordered the use of the atomic bombs as soon after August 3 as possible, provided the Japanese did not surrender (See Voices: The Dropping of the Atomic Bomb). Moral reasons for

---

A-bomb The first nuclear weapon, which used a chain reaction involving uranium and plutonium to create an explosion of enormous destructive force.

Manhattan Project Scientific research effort to develop an atomic bomb begun in 1942 and carried on in a secret community of scientists and workers near Oak Ridge, Tennessee.

Potsdam Declaration The demand for Japan's unconditional surrender, made after the July 1945 Potsdam Conference attended by Truman, Churchill, Attlee and Stalin.

The Dropping of the Atomic Bomb

The Atomic Age Begins

At 8:15 A.M. the Enola Gay dropped the first atomic bomb on the Japanese city of Hiroshima. Over 100,000 people died and another 100,000 were injured. Three days later the United States exploded a second atomic bomb over Nagasaki, killing about sixty thousand Japanese. On August 14, Japan surrendered— the atomic age had been born. At the time, nearly everyone applauded the use of the atomic bomb to end the war. But, choices had been made. Was it necessary to use the atomic bomb to force the surrender of Japan? What would be the consequences of the new atomic age? Here is part of Harry S Truman's address to the American people on the use of the atomic bomb, August 6, 1945.

Sixteen hours ago an American airplane dropped one bomb on Hiroshima, an important Japanese army base. That bomb had more power than 20,000 tons of TNT.

The Japanese began the war from the air at Pearl Harbor. They have been repaid many fold. And the end is not yet. With this bomb we have now added a new and revolutionary increase in destruction to supplement the growing power of our armed forces. In their present form these bombs are now in production and even more powerful forms are in development.

It is an atomic bomb. It is a harnessing of the basic power of the universe. The force from which the sun draws its power has been loosened against those who brought war to the Far East. . . . Beginning in 1940, before Pearl Harbor, scientific knowledge useful in war was pooled between the United States and Great Britain. . . . Employment during peak construction numbered 125,000 and over 65,000 individuals are even now engaged in operating the plants. Many have worked . . . for two and a half years. Few know what they have been producing. . . . We have spent two billion dollars on the greatest scientific gamble in history—and won.

But the greatest marvel is not the size of the enterprise, its secrecy, nor its cost, but the achievement of scientific brains in putting together infinitely complex pieces of knowledge held by many men in different fields of science into a workable plan. . . . What has been done is the greatest achievement of organized science in history.

We are now prepared to obliterate more rapidly and completely every productive enterprise the Japanese have above ground in any city. We shall destroy their docks, their factories, and their communications. Let there be no mistake; we shall completely destroy Japan's power to make war.

It was to spare the Japanese people from utter destruction that the ultimatum of July 26 was issued at Potsdam. Their leaders promptly rejected that ultimatum. If they do not accept our terms they may expect a rain of ruin from the air, the like of which has never been seen on this earth. . . .

Supporters Had This to Say

■ To extract a genuine surrender from the Emperor and his military advisers, they must be administered a tremendous shock which would carry convincing proof of our power to destroy the Empire. Such an effective shock would save many times the number of lives, both American and Japanese that it would cost. In the middle of July, 1945, the intelligence section of the War Department . . . estimated Japanese military strength as follows: in the home islands, slightly under 2,000,000; in Korea, Manchuria, China . . . and Formosa, slightly over 2,000,000 . . . the total estimated strength of about 5,000,000 men. . . . [With a] total U.S. military and naval force . . . of 5,000,000 men . . . we estimated that . . . the major fighting would not end until the later part of 1946 at the earliest . . . [and] that such an operation might cost over a million casualties to American forces . . . enemy casualties would be much larger than our own. *Henry L Stimson, "The Decision to Use the Atomic Bomb,"* Harper's *(1947).*

■ We should not give the Japanese any warning . . . we should seek to make a profound psychological impression on as many of the inhabitants as possible . . . that the most desirable target would be a vital war plant employing a large number of workers and closely surrounded by workers' houses. *Minutes of the Interim Committee, May 31, 1945.*

Opponents Had This to Say

■ The military advantages and the saving of American lives, achieved by the sudden use of atomic bombs against Japan, may be outweighed by the ensuing loss of confidence and wave of horror and repulsion, sweeping over the rest of the world, and perhaps dividing even the public opinion at home. *Franck Committee Report, June 11, 1945.*

■ Japan was already defeated . . . dropping the bomb was completely unnecessary. . . . It was my belief that Japan was, at that very moment, seeking some way to surrender with a minimum loss of "face." *Dwight David Eisenhower,* The White House Years: Mandate for Change, 1953–1956 *(1963).*

■ It is my opinion that the use of this barbarous weapon at Hiroshima and Nagasaki was of no material assistance in our war against Japan. The Japanese were already defeated and ready to surrender because of the effective sea blockade and the successful bombing with conventional weapons. *Admiral William D. Leahy, Truman's chief of staff in 1945,* I Was There *(1950).*

◆ On August 6, 1945, the world entered the atomic age with the destruction of the city of Hiroshima by an atomic bomb. The blast left few buildings standing in a city that once housed 250,000 people, leaving about 130,000 of them dead. Robert Oppenheimer, one of the leading atomic scientists, said, "I am become Death, Destroyer of Worlds." *National Archives.*

TABLE 26.1	WAR DEAD
Country	**Dead**
Soviet Union	13.5 million
China	7.4 million
Poland	6.0 million
Germany	4.6 million
Japan	1.2 million
Britain and Commonwealth	430,000
United States	220,000

not using the bomb had never been seriously considered. Massive American bombing raids against Japanese cities already had killed and wounded tens of thousands of Japanese civilians. The losses at Iwo Jima and Okinawa, along with growing distrust of Stalin, had only strengthened Truman's belief that both military and diplomatic benefits would come from ushering in the nuclear age.

On the island of Tinian, B-29s were readied to carry the two available bombs to targets in Japan—a third was waiting to be assembled. The first bomb, "Little Boy," was dropped from a B-29 bomber named the *Enola Gay* over Hiroshima at 9:15 A.M. on August 6. Japan's eighth largest city, **Hiroshima** had a population of over 250,000 and had not to that point suffered heavy bombing. In the atomic blast and fireball, almost a hundred thousand Japanese were killed or terribly maimed. Another hundred thousand would eventually die from the effects of radiation. The United States announced that unless the Japanese surrendered immediately, they could "expect a rain of ruin from the air, the like of which has never been seen on this earth."

In Tokyo, peace advocates in the Japanese government again sought to use the Soviets as an intermediary. They wanted some guarantee that Emperor Hirohito would be allowed to remain as emperor and a symbol of Japan. The Soviet response was to declare war and to advance into Japanese-held Manchuria on August 8, exactly three months after V-E day. On August 9, as a high-level Japa-

nese council considered surrender, a second atomic bomb, "Fat Man," destroyed **Nagasaki**. Nearly sixty thousand people were killed. Although some within the Japanese army argued for continuing the fight, Emperor Hirohito, watching the Red Army slice through Japanese forces in China and afraid of losing more cities to atomic attacks, made the final decision. Japan must "bear the unbearable," he said, and surrender. On August 14, Japan officially surrendered, and the United States agreed to leave the position of emperor intact.

World War II was over, but much of the world now lay in ruins. Some 50 million people, military and civilian, had been killed (see Table 26.1). The United States was spared most of the destruction. It had suffered almost no civilian casualties, and its cities and industrial centers stood intact. In many ways, in fact, the war had been good to the United States. It had decisively ended the Depression, and although some economists predicted an immediate postwar recession, the overall economic picture was bright. Government regulation and planning for the economy that had their beginning in the New Deal took root during the war. As the war ended, only a few wanted a return to the laissez-faire–style government that had characterized the 1920s. Big government was here to stay, and at the center of big government was a powerful presidency ready to direct and guide the nation.

Hiroshima   Japanese city that became the target on August 6, 1945, of the first atomic bomb used in World War II.

Nagasaki   City in western Japan devastated on August 9, 1945, by the second atomic bomb used in World War II.

SUMMARY

E **xpectations**
C **onstraints**
C **hoices**
O **utcomes**

Franklin Roosevelt *chose* to promote better relations with Latin America and succeeded. But elsewhere the international situation grew steadily worse and expectations of conflict increased. Japan had seized Manchuria in 1931 and in 1937 invaded China, while Mussolini and Hitler were seeking to expand their nations' power and territory. In the lengthening shadow of world conflict, the majority of Americans still *chose* to maintain isolationism. Wanting to take a more active role in world affairs, Roosevelt found himself *constrained* by isolationist sentiment—characterized by a set of neutrality acts—and by his own *choice* to fight the Depression at home first. Even as Germany invaded Poland in September 1939, the majority of Americans were still anxious to remain outside the conflict. Roosevelt, however, was determined to provide all necessary aid to those nations fighting Germany and Italy.

Roosevelt also *chose* to increase economic and diplomatic pressure on Japan to halt its conquest of China and occupation of Indochina. But the pressure only heightened the crisis, convincing many in the Japanese government that the best *choice* was to attack the United States before it grew in strength. Japan's attack on Pearl Harbor on December 7, 1941, brought a fully committed American public and government into World War II.

Mobilizing the nation for war ended the Depression and increased government intervention in the economy. Another *outcome* of the war was a range of new *choices* for women and minorities in the military and the workplace. For Japanese-Americans, however, the *outcome* was the loss of freedom and property, as anti-Japanese sentiment caused the government to *choose* a policy of internment.

Fighting a two-front war—in Europe and the Pacific—American planners *chose* to give first priority to defeating Hitler. The British and American offensive to recover Europe began in North Africa and expanded to Italy in 1943 and to France in 1944. By the beginning of 1945, Allied armies were threatening Nazi Germany from the west and the east, and on May 8, 1945, Germany surrendered.

In the Pacific theater, the victory at Midway in mid-1942 gave American forces naval and air superiority over Japan and allowed the use of carrier task forces to begin tightening the noose around Japan. Worried about casualties if American troops had to invade Japan, Truman *chose* to use the atomic bomb to hasten Japan's surrender. Indeed, the outcome of victory in the war was that the United States had become economically, spiritually, and militarily stronger than when the war started. And many confident Americans *expected* the postwar years to begin "America's Century."

SUGGESTED READINGS

Blum, John Morton. *V Was for Victory* (1976).
A good introduction to society and politics during the war.

Calvocoressi, P., Wint, G., Pritchard, J. *Total War* (1989).

Keegan, John. *The Second World War* (1990).
Two excellent one-volume works that summarize the military and diplomatic aspects of World War II.

Dallek, Robert. *Franklin D. Roosevelt and American Foreign Policy, 1932–1945* (1979).
An excellent, balanced study of Franklin Roosevelt's foreign policy.

Daniels, Roger. *Concentration Camps, USA* (1971).
An in-depth and compassionate look at the internment of Japanese-Americans.

Gluck, Sherna B. *Rosie the Riveter Revisited: Women, the War, and Social Change* (1987).
An important work examining the changes that took place among women in society during the war.

Jonas, Manfred. *Isolationism in America* (1966).
A solid examination of the varieties of isolationist attitudes in the United States, especially in the 1930s.

Spector, Ronald. *Eagle Against the Sun* (1988).
One of the most well-written general accounts of the war in the Pacific.

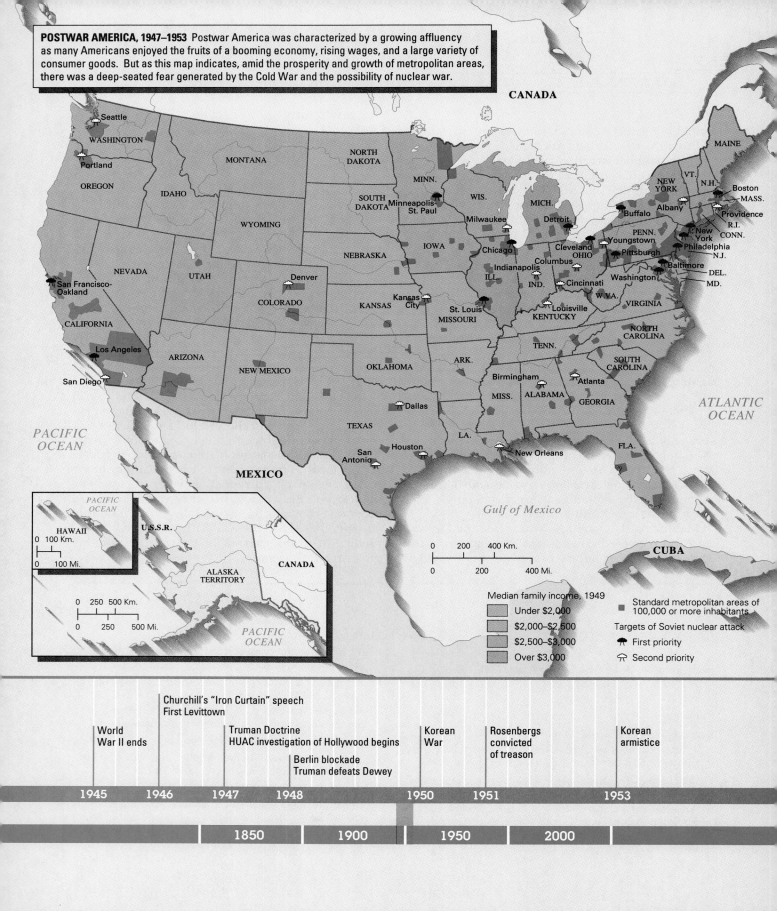

POSTWAR AMERICA, 1947–1953 Postwar America was characterized by a growing affluency as many Americans enjoyed the fruits of a booming economy, rising wages, and a large variety of consumer goods. But as this map indicates, amid the prosperity and growth of metropolitan areas, there was a deep-seated fear generated by the Cold War and the possibility of nuclear war.

CANADA

WASHINGTON
Seattle
Portland
OREGON
MONTANA
IDAHO
WYOMING
NEVADA
UTAH
CALIFORNIA
San Francisco-Oakland
Los Angeles
San Diego
ARIZONA
NEW MEXICO
COLORADO
Denver
NORTH DAKOTA
SOUTH DAKOTA
NEBRASKA
KANSAS
OKLAHOMA
TEXAS
San Antonio
Houston
Dallas
MINN.
Minneapolis-St. Paul
IOWA
Kansas City
MISSOURI
St. Louis
ARK.
LA.
New Orleans
WIS.
Milwaukee
ILL.
Chicago
MICH.
Detroit
IND.
Indianapolis
KENTUCKY
Louisville
TENN.
MISS.
ALABAMA
Birmingham
GEORGIA
Atlanta
OHIO
Columbus
Cincinnati
Cleveland
Youngstown
PENN.
Pittsburgh
W. VA.
VIRGINIA
NORTH CAROLINA
SOUTH CAROLINA
FLA.
Buffalo
NEW YORK
Albany
VT.
N.H.
MAINE
Boston
MASS.
Providence
R.I.
CONN.
New York
Philadelphia
N.J.
Baltimore
DEL.
MD.
Washington

CANADA
MEXICO
PACIFIC OCEAN
ATLANTIC OCEAN
Gulf of Mexico
CUBA

0   200   400 Km.
0   200   400 Mi.

Inset:
PACIFIC OCEAN
HAWAII
0   100 Km.
0   100 Mi.
U.S.S.R.
ALASKA TERRITORY
CANADA
PACIFIC OCEAN
0   250   500 Km.
0   250   500 Mi.

Legend:

Median family income, 1949
- Under $2,000
- $2,000–$2,500
- $2,500–$3,000
- Over $3,000

■ Standard metropolitan areas of 100,000 or more inhabitants

Targets of Soviet nuclear attack
- First priority
- Second priority

Timeline:

Churchill's "Iron Curtain" speech
First Levittown

World War II ends

Truman Doctrine
HUAC investigation of Hollywood begins

Berlin blockade
Truman defeats Dewey

Korean War

Rosenbergs convicted of treason

Korean armistice

1945   1946   1947   1948   1950   1951   1953

1850   1900   1950   2000

Truman and Cold War America, 1945–1952

The Cold War Begins

- How did America's expectations regarding world affairs affect the foreign policy choices of the Truman administration between 1946 and 1952?

The Korean War

- As the North Koreans invaded South Korea, what choices and constraints did Truman confront when considering policy options?

Homecomings and Adjustments

- What constraints did Truman face in implementing his domestic programs?
- How did they influence his choices?

Cold War Politics

- What constraints and choices did the Cold War place on American politics and society?

INTRODUCTION

E xpectations
C onstraints
C hoices
O utcomes

When World War II ended, most Americans hoped for a bright future. The Great Depression was over, the war had reignited American industry, creating jobs and prosperity, and the United States stood as the world's most powerful economic and military power. Many Americans, especially returning veterans, looked forward to living the "American dream," which included owning a home, a car, and a variety of consumer products designed to make life easier. More than ever before, women and minorities shared in *expectations* for greater opportunity—trusting that the new economic and social openings created during the war would extend into the postwar era.

Although everyone hoped for postwar economic growth and prosperity, political conservatives anticipated the demise of the New Deal. They argued that the liberalism of the New Deal was no longer necessary and that society and the economy should revert to traditional norms. They sought to place *constraints* on the economic and social gains made by minorities, women, and workers, which, they held, threatened business growth and social stability. Unions, they asserted, had become too powerful and must be restrained. Women, conservatives—along with many other Americans—argued, should give up their jobs and greater independence and return full-time to the roles of wife and mother. For African-Americans and other minorities, it was an old story, "last hired, first fired," as they were dismissed from many wartime jobs.

Which direction would the nation *choose:* the path of the liberal New Deal or a more conservative one? Would President Harry S Truman, *choose* to expand on New Deal progressivism? Would he provide support for minorities, workers, and women in their quests for continued opportunity? Or would he buckle under the conservative opposition that had halted Roosevelt in 1938? The outcome that emerged from the "politics of the possible" pleased neither ardent liberals nor staunch conservatives. It reflected what some called the "vital center"—an acceptance of, and even some expansion on, existing governmental activism, but little political or public support for adding new programs.

Truman also faced *choices* in shaping a new international system out the ashes of the war. Isolationism had virtually vanished amid the wreckage of Pearl Harbor and Hiroshima, leaving the United States as the major world power. The *Los Angeles Times* expressed the *expectations* of most Americans: that the United States would lead the postwar world because it had "no other direct interest" except a lasting, just peace. Seeking this lasting peace, between 1945 and 1952, Truman tried to forge the structure of postwar world affairs, but the *outcome* was not what most expected. By the end of 1947, American and Soviet leaders had made *choices* that ended their wartime cooperation and produced a bitter rivalry. The outcome, the Cold War, polarized the world, expanded America's global role, and added a new force in American society—the fear of the Soviet Union and communism. When North Korea invaded South Korea, Truman *chose* to commit American troops to halt Communist aggression. At home, the activities of anti-Communists like Senator Joseph McCarthy exposed a dark side of American politics and society, one less tolerant of change and liberalism.

Despite economic growth and increased prosperity, American society began to seem less stable and unified, clouding some Americans' *expectations* for a bright future. Labor unions clashed with employers, many women and minorities found their expectations thwarted, and the Korean War—which most people had believed would end in a quick American victory—dragged on in stalemate. The *outcome,* by the end of Truman's second term, was widespread political dissatisfaction and a general desire for change. Conservatives like Senator Robert Taft, and even some moderates, blamed America's problems on Truman and New Deal liberalism. Both, in their opinion, followed "a policy of appeasing the Russians abroad and of fostering Communism at home."

CHRONOLOGY

From World War to Cold War

1945 U.S. forces advance toward Berlin
Soviets advance across Eastern Europe
Yalta Conference
FDR's death
Truman becomes president
United Nations formed
Germany surrenders
Potsdam Conference
U.S. drops atomic bombs
Japan surrenders

1946 Employment Act
Kennan's "Long Telegram"
Churchill's "Iron Curtain" speech
Iran crisis
Railroad and coal miners strikes
Construction begins on first Levittown

1947 Truman Doctrine
Truman's employee loyalty program
Taft-Hartly Act
House Un-American Activities Committee
begins investigation of Hollywood
Jackie Robinson joins the Brooklyn
Dodgers
Marshall Plan announced
To Secure These Rights issued
Rio Conference (Rio Pact)

1948 Communist coup in Czechoslovakia
State of Israel founded
Western zones of Germany unified
Berlin blockade begins
Congress approves Marshall Plan
Truman defeats Dewey

1949 North Atlantic Treaty Organization created
Berlin blockade lifted
Peekskill riot
West Germany created
National Housing Act
Soviet Union explodes atomic bomb
Communist forces win civil war in China
Hiss convicted of perjury

1950 Hydrogen bomb project announced
McCarthy's announcement of Communists
in the State Department
NSC-68
Korean War begins
Rosenbergs arrested for treason
Inchon landing
North Korean forces retreat from South
Korea
U.S. forces cross into North Korea; China
enters Korean War

1951 McArthur relieved of command
Korean War armistice talks begin
Rosenbergs convicted of treason
Dennis et al. v. U.S.

1952 Hydrogen bomb tested

1953 Korean War armistice signed

The Cold War Begins

● How did America's expectations regarding world affairs affect the foreign policy choices of the Truman administration between 1946 and 1952?

Germany, Italy, and Japan had been defeated, and the world hoped that an enduring peace would follow war's end. But could the cooperative relationship of the victorious Allies continue into the post-war era without a common enemy to bind them together? Suspicion and distrust had already occurred when Britain and the United States objected to the pro-Soviet governments established by the Soviet Union in Eastern Europe. Franklin D. Roosevelt, who believed he could work with the Soviets, had deemed Soviet cooperation more important than the composition of Soviet-sponsored governments, but it was Harry S Truman now who directed American foreign policy and had the responsibility of shaping the postwar world. And Truman had a different attitude. It was his opinion that "the Soviet Union needs us more than we need them."

When Roosevelt died on April 12, 1945, Truman was left to face the imposing job of finishing the war and creating the peace. Winning the war was mostly a matter of following existing policies and listening to the military planners, but formulating a new international order required new ideas and policies. In facing this formidable task, the new president counted on his common sense and what he believed would be best for the country. Truman loved history and the idea that great individuals shaped it. Lazy men caused trouble, he wrote, and those who "worked hard had the job of rectifying their mistakes." Truman was determined to be a decisive, hard-working president. He had read history; now he would shape it. A plaque on his desk proclaimed, "THE BUCK STOPS HERE."

Truman and the Soviets

Truman and other American leaders identified two overlapping paths to peace: international cooperation and **deterrence** based on military strength. Drawing on the lessons of the war, they concluded that the United States must continue to field a strong military force with bases in Europe, Asia, and the Middle East. But deterrence alone could not guarantee peace and a stable world. Policy makers needed to address the underlying causes of war. Examining the origins of World War II, Americans blamed first the Depression, second the isolationism that had brought men like Hitler to power, and third the governments that had appeased the tyrants' aggressive actions. An isolationist America, an ineffective League of Nations, and a weak-kneed Britain and France had allowed Mussolini, Hirohito, and Hitler to embark on a global war that had cost millions of lives and billions of dollars. To prevent history from repeating itself, a strong world organization, a determination not to appease aggressors, and a prosperous world economy were necessary. These had been the ideals of the Atlantic Charter (see page 807), and most Americans saw them as universal values on which to construct peace. However, if international cooperation failed, the United States should rely on its military strength and exercise its global responsibilities to ensure peace.

Not all nations accepted the American vision for peace and stability. Having different political and economic systems and historical experiences—two invasions from Western Europe in forty years—the

Soviets advanced goals that seemed to oppose American ones. They too relied on military deterrence, but they also wanted to be treated as a major power, to have Germany reduced in power, and to see "friendly" governments in neighboring states, especially in Eastern Europe. When World War II ended, many Americans were especially worried about Soviet actions in Eastern Europe. There, it seemed, the Soviets were unwilling to allow an open political and economic system, contradicting American democratic and capitalistic principles. At the Tehran and Yalta conferences (pages 825 and 827), Roosevelt had generally acquiesced to Soviet influence in Eastern Europe and, in return, had received Soviet support for the establishment of the United Nations (UN) and pledges of continued cooperation with the United States.

Roosevelt had presented the idea of a new world organization to Churchill during their meeting that had produced the Atlantic Charter. In the fall of 1944, the Big Four (the United States, the Soviet Union, Britain, and China) mapped out the basic organization of the United Nations at the **Dumbarton Oaks** conference. At Yalta, Roosevelt, Stalin, and Churchill further refined their agreements on the United Nations, finally permitting a meeting in San Francisco (April 1945) to write a charter for the new world organization. The United Nations charter established a weak **General Assembly,** composed of all the world's nations, that could discuss issues but would have no authority to create or execute policies. Decisions were to be made by a smaller, executive-type **Security Council** composed of the Big Five (now including France) as permanent members, and six other nations elected for two-year terms. The Security Council would establish and im-

---

deterrence   Measures taken by a state, often including a military build-up, to discourage another state from attacking it.

Dumbarton Oaks   Conference in Washington, D.C., at which representatives of China, Britain, the USSR, and the United States drew up a blueprint for the charter of the United Nations.

General Assembly   Assembly of all members of the United Nations, which debates issues but neither creates nor executes policy.

Security Council   Executive agency of the United Nations, which includes five permanent members (China, France, Russia, Britain, and the United States) and six members chosen by the General Assembly for two-year terms.

In July 1945, Truman met with Stalin and Churchill at Potsdam on the outskirts of Berlin. Meeting with Churchill and Stalin for the first time, Truman was surprised that the Soviet leader was shorter than he, and thought Churchill talked too much, giving him "a lot of hooey." Later, Truman wrote, "you never saw such pig-headed people as are the Russians." Here, Stalin and Truman (*left*) and advisers Byrnes and Molotov (*right*) pose for photographers. *Truman Library*.

plement policies and would have the power to apply economic and military pressure against aggressor nations. Each of the Big Five was given a veto over Security Council decisions to ensure that the council could not interfere with their national interests. The United Nations represented the concept of peace through world cooperation, but its structure clearly left the future of peace in the hands of the major powers, particularly the United States and the Soviet Union. In July, the Senate approved the United Nations charter and American membership by a vote of 89 to 2. Truman believed that the choice of New York City as the site of the permanent United Nations headquarters proved that the center of western civilization and power had transferred from Western Europe to the United States.

When Truman became president, he had virtually no preparation or understanding of past American foreign policies. As Senator Truman, he had very limited knowledge of diplomatic and military affairs, and as vice president, Roosevelt had not confided in him on either issue. In fact, when he took office, he knew nothing about the Yalta Conference or the atomic bomb. Immediately, he sought experienced advisers, especially on how to deal with the Soviets. Ambassador to the Soviet Union W. Averell Harriman and Admiral William Leahy, one of Roosevelt's military and diplomatic advisers, pictured the Soviet advance into eastern and central Europe as threatening peace and western civilization. Truman agreed, noting that Soviet actions in Poland

and Rumania violated proper behavior, the principles of the Atlantic Charter, and the Yalta agreements.

Determined to be decisive, Truman quickly confronted Soviet foreign minister V. M. Molotov and berated the Soviet Union for not fulfilling its Yalta promises to allow self-determination in Eastern Europe. At nearly the same time, lend-lease goods en route to the Soviet Union and Britain were abruptly stopped. Although Truman moderated his toughness toward the Soviets during the next few months, it was clear that Truman was less willing to consider Soviet "needs" than Roosevelt had been. In July 1945, Truman had his only face-to-face meeting with Stalin at the Potsdam Conference. As a meeting to begin the shaping of the postwar world, Potsdam accomplished little. The United States expressed concern about the lack of democracy in Eastern Europe but accepted Soviet promises of change in the future. Truman found Stalin tough, not unlike political bosses in American cities, and was more convinced than ever that the Soviets were a major obstacle to world stability. He also discovered he disliked **summit** diplomacy—nothing ever got accomplished, he said, except talk. Potsdam was the last international conference Truman would attend.

---

summit   Conference of the highest-ranking officials of two or more governments.

♦ Alerting the public about the dangers of an aggressive, expansionist, and Communist (Red) Soviet Union was an important part of Truman's Cold War policy. This map from the New York *Daily News* is one example of how these dangers were reinforced in the public mind. Look at how the size (note state of New York in box for comparison) and unrelenting expansion of the Soviet state, whose goal was world dominance, were presented. *Collection of Michael Barson/Past Perfect.*

By early 1946, Truman was "tired of babying the Soviets" and believed that the United States had gone more than halfway to meet Soviet requests. It was now up to the Soviets to prove their peaceful intentions, and it did not appear that the Russians were interested in meeting the United States halfway. The Soviet press warned of "capitalist encirclement" and accused the United States of poisoning Soviet-American relations. In Eastern Europe, every indication suggested that the Soviets were tightening their controls over Poland, Rumania, and Hungary, by denying their peoples political and civil freedoms. On February 9, 1946, Stalin asserted that future wars were inevitable because of "present capitalist conditions," which most American observers saw as proof of Soviet hostility. Secretary of the Navy James Forrestal, a long-time anti-Communist, distributed a private study that concluded the Soviets were committed to "global, violent, **proletarian** revolution." Supreme Court Justice William O. Douglas called Stalin's speech "A Declaration of World War III." The War Department and navy officials agreed, and the Joint Chiefs of Staff recommended a foreign policy that would support nations threatened by Soviet hostility. The State Department was less alarmed, but it too concluded that the Soviets were following an "ominous course."

Anxious to confirm Soviet intentions, the State Department asked George Frost Kennan, the **chargé d'affaires** in Moscow, to evaluate Soviet policy. He described Soviet totalitarianism as internally weak. Soviet leaders, he said, held Communist ideology secondary to remaining in power. To rule, Soviet leaders relied on fear, repression, and resistance to a foreign enemy. To stay in control, Soviet leaders needed Western capitalism to serve as that enemy, Kennan wrote. Therefore, they could not afford to reach meaningful, long-lasting agreements with the West. He recommended a policy of **containment,** facing the Soviet Union with strength and meeting head-on any attempted expansion of Soviet power. His eight-thousand-word report, the "Long Telegram," immediately flowed through Washington's official circles and was praised as a well-written, understandable, expert explanation of Moscow's behavior. Soon thereafter, Truman adopted a policy designed to "set will against will, force against force, idea against idea . . . until Soviet expansion is finally worn down."

Fear of Soviet expansion quickly became a bipartisan issue, with Democrats and Republicans each trying to educate the public about the Soviet

---

proletarian Relating to the working class, especially industrial wage laborers.

chargé d'affair A high-ranking member of an embassy, frequently the highest ranking career diplomat of the mission.

containment Policy of checking the expansion or influence of a hostile power by such means as strategic alliances or the support of weaker states in areas of conflict.

threat—ending any possibility of a return to isolationism—and to convince the public that the United States must resist Soviet **globalism.** In February, as Kennan's telegram circulated, Republican Senator Arthur Vandenberg of Michigan asked from the Senate floor, "What is Russia up to now?" To a standing ovation from the Senate gallery, he answered his own question: Russia was up to no good and America needed to stop compromising and start standing up for what was right and just.

The most sensational warning, however, came from Winston Churchill on March 5, 1946, at Westminster College in Fulton, Missouri. With President Truman sitting beside him, the former prime minister of England warned the audience about Soviet expansionism and stated that an **"iron curtain"** had fallen across Europe. He called for a "fraternal association of the English-speaking peoples" to halt the Russians. Truman thought it was a wonderfully eloquent speech and would do "nothing but good." Churchill, *Time* magazine pronounced, had spoken with the voice of a "lion."

As Churchill gave his address, it appeared that an "American lion" was needed in Iran. During World War II, the Big Three had stationed troops in Iran to ensure the safety of lend-lease materials going by that route to the Soviet Union. The troops were to be withdrawn by March 1946, but as that date neared, Soviet troops remained in northern Iran. Suddenly, on March 2, reports flashed from northern Iran that Soviet tanks were moving toward Tehran, the Iranian capital, as well as Iraq and Turkey. Some believed that war was imminent. Britain and the United States sent harshly worded telegrams to the Soviets and petitioned the United Nations to consider an Iranian complaint against the Soviet Union. War did not break out. The Soviet tanks never approached Tehran, Iraq, or Turkey, and Soviet forces soon evacuated Iran. The crisis was diffused, but it had convinced many Americans that the Soviets were aggressive and would retreat only when confronted with firmness.

Throughout the rest of 1946, the United States hardened its resolve in Europe. Postwar credits and loans were determined on the basis of ideology and geography. Secretary of State James Byrnes explained, "I am convinced we must help our friends in every way and refrain from assisting those who . . . are opposing the principles for which we stand." Thus Britain received a $3.8 billion loan and France a $650 million loan, but loans to the Soviet Union and Czechoslovakia were killed. In Germany, the United States merged its occupation zone first with the British and then with the French zones and then promised that American troops would remain as long as necessary to protect the German people. By the end of 1946, public opinion showed concern about the possibility of Soviet aggression. *Woman's Home Companion* reported that 3.6 million women believed war with Russia would come within fifteen years.

The Division of Europe

Kennan had provided the form and justification for containment, but it was left to Truman to determine how to implement the policy—how to set apart and use American resources to construct a political, economic, and if necessary, military wall around the Soviet Union. As the crisis in Iran receded, events in Europe assumed first priority. Throughout western and southern Europe, economic and social turmoil was adding to the popularity of **leftist** and Communist groups, who argued that the future of Europe rested on socialism and closer relations with the Soviet Union. In the eastern Mediterranean, Turkey especially was being pressured by the neighboring Soviets to permit some degree of Soviet control over the Dardanelles, the straits that link the Black Sea to the Mediterranean. Nearby, Greece was torn by a civil war between Communist-backed rebels and the British-supported conservative government (see Map 27.1).

On March 12, 1947, Truman stood before Congress and proclaimed that the world was divided into two opposing camps—the free and the unfree—and that "nearly every nation must choose between alternative ways of life." It was the duty of the United States, he said, "to support free people" who resisted subjugation "by armed minorities or by outside pressure." Truman asked Congress for $400 million in aid for Greece and Turkey. The speech was the result of a British request. Britain could no

---

globalism   National geopolitical policy in which the entire world is regarded as the appropriate sphere for a state's influence.

"iron curtain"   Name given to the military, political, and ideological barrier established between the Soviet bloc and Western Europe after World War II.

leftist   Holding various liberal or radical political beliefs, often resting on a sympathy with the working class and a conviction that government should provide for the basic needs of its people.

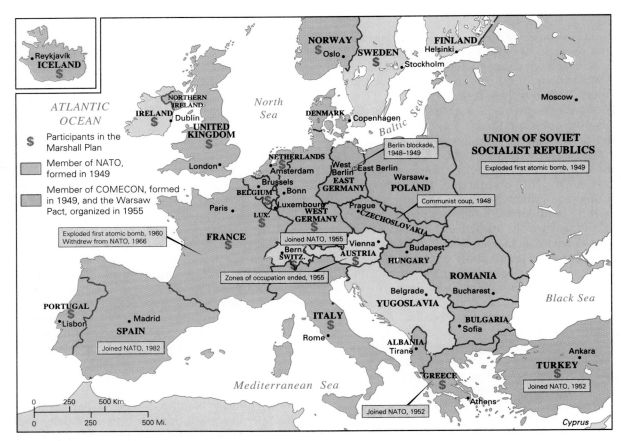

♦ **MAP 27.1 Cold War Europe**   Following World War II, Europe was divided by what Winston Churchill called the "Iron Curtain," that separated most of the continent politically, economically, and militarily between an eastern bloc (the Warsaw Pact) led by the Soviet Union and a western bloc (NATO) supported by the United States. This postwar division of Europe lasted until the collapse of the Soviet Union in early 1990s.

longer provide economic and military aid for Greece and Turkey and in February had asked for the United States to assume that support. The Truman administration was eager to take on the "job of world leadership with all of its burdens and all of its glory." The central question, however, was whether he could persuade a penny-pinching Congress and the American public that a free Greece and Turkey were vital to American and world security.

Secretary of State **George Marshall** and Assistant Secretary of State **Dean Acheson** explained to a select group of senators from both parties that all Communist activities were directed from Moscow and warned that Greece was on the brink of collapse. A Communist victory there would endanger neighboring states and eventually the entire eastern Mediterranean and Middle East. The Soviets were

on the move, Acheson told the senators, and would triumph unless the United States stepped forward and stopped them. Impressed, Senator Vandenberg suggested that to win congressional and public support, Truman needed to "scare the hell" out of the country. The president took the advice, and in his

---

George Marshall   Chief of staff of the U.S. Army during World War II, who became Truman's secretary of state in 1947 and worked to rebuild the economy of Western Europe.

Dean Acheson   Diplomat who took over as secretary of state in 1949; he helped formulate U.S. policy in Korea and advocated a firm stand against Soviet aggression in the Berlin crisis.

The present time," stated a War Department official, "but they are just one of the keys on the keyboard of this world piano."

♦ In many people's views, Truman's decision to support Greece and Turkey and his announcement of the Truman Doctrine (March 1947) represented the transfer of world responsibility from Great Britain to the United States. In Truman's words, "The free peoples of the world look to us for support in maintaining their freedoms."

Truman Doctrine speech of March 12, he offered an ideological, black-and-white view of world politics that blamed almost every threat to peace and stability on an unnamed villain, the Soviet Union. In the speech, Truman implied a national commitment to an activist world role in supporting freedom, but privately to Eleanor Roosevelt, he was more precise: "If the Greek-Turkish land bridge between the continents is one point at which our democratic forces can stop the advance of Communism . . . then this is the place to do it, regardless of whether or not the terrain is good." The terrain was good. With American support Turkey resisted Soviet pressure and retained control over the straits, and the Greek government was able to defeat the Communist rebels in 1949.

The Truman administration had asked Congress only for $400 million in aid for Greece and Turkey, but officials admitted among themselves that the request was just the beginning. "It happens that we are having a little trouble with Greece and Turkey at

On June 5, 1947, in a commencement address at Harvard, Secretary of State Marshall uncovered the keyboard and offered Europe a program of economic aid: the **Marshall Plan.** The United States had already loaned nearly $9 billion to Western European nations, but more was needed to ward off a possible European economic collapse. Not only had the war destroyed thousands of homes, farms, and factories, but nature too bombarded Britain and the continent after the war. A drought and an extremely bitter winter had, by 1947, brought Europe close to social and economic chaos. Because of rapidly diminishing supplies of fuel and food, millions could not heat their homes and were existing on less than 1,200 calories a day. Feeding on the social and economic turmoil, Communist and Socialist parties were gaining in popularity and strength. Italian Communists represented a third of the electorate, whereas in France nearly a quarter voted Communist. European prosperity had to be restored if only to deny leftists their points of attack. And the United States was the only nation with the resources to do it. Fearful of a recession at home, American business was more than ready to sell Europe an abundance of goods and services. But without dollars or credit, Europeans could not buy American offerings. The solution, American planners concluded, was to provide Europeans with credit that would both rebuild Europe and ensure a long-term market for American products.

For the Truman administration, the question was not whether to provide Western Europe with aid, but whether to include the Soviets and Eastern Europeans. To allow the Soviets and their satellites to participate seemed contrary to the intent of the Truman Doctrine. Would a Congress that had just spent $400 million to keep Greece and Turkey out of Soviet hands be willing to provide millions of American dollars to the Soviet Union? If it excluded the

Truman Doctrine   Anti-Communist foreign policy enunciated by Truman in 1947, which called for military and economic aid to countries whose political stability was threatened by communism.

Marshall Plan   Program to foster economic recovery in Western Europe in the postwar period through massive amounts of U.S. financial aid, which began in 1948.

Soviets, however, the United States might seem to be encouraging the division of Europe, an image the State Department wanted to avoid. Chaired by Kennan, the State Department planning staff recommended that the United States take "a hell of a big gamble" and offer economic aid to all Europeans. Kennan believed that the Soviets' unwillingness to cooperate economically and politically with capitalists would keep them from taking part. Thus, when Marshall spoke at Harvard, he invited all Europeans to work together and write a program "designed to place Europe on its feet economically."

Britain and France accepted the American offer within two weeks and called for a meeting in Paris of all interested parties on June 26, 1947. To nearly everyone's surprise—and worry—a Soviet delegation of nearly a hundred advisers arrived. Had the gamble failed? It was soon clear that it had not. Soviet foreign minister Molotov rejected a British- and French-written proposal for an economically integrated Europe, joint economic planning, and a requirement to purchase mostly American goods. At first the Marshall Plan looked like a "tasty mushroom," commented one Soviet official, but on closer examination it turned out to be a "poisonous toadstool." Unwilling to participate in any form of economic integration with non-Communist Europe, the Soviets and the Eastern Europeans left the conference. Molotov blasted the Marshall Plan, condemning it for violating national sovereignty, forcing the division of Europe, and allowing for the re-industrialization of Germany. Attracted by the prospect of American aid, sixteen other nations stayed in Paris and drafted a European recovery program. Completed on September 22, the plan called for four years of American assistance amounting to over $20 billion. In December, Truman asked Congress for $17 billion. Without such a program, he said, the iron curtain might soon rest on the Atlantic shore. Congress gave its consent in 1948, but not until it had cut the total to $12.5 billion.

The Marshall Plan produced far-reaching consequences for countries both east and west of the iron curtain. In Germany, the United States moved to unify the western zones into a political and economic whole. Western European countries were informed that if they were to receive full American aid, they would have to purge Communist elements from their governments. The Soviet sphere responded in kind with a hardening of Communist influence and control over Eastern Europe. In July 1947, Moscow announced its Molotov Plan, a move to incorporate Eastern European economies into the Soviet system. Non-Communist elements were expelled from the Hungarian government, and in September, the Soviet Union formed the Communist Information Bureau (Cominform) to ensure Soviet direction of Europe's Communist parties. As Congress debated funding the Marshall Plan in February 1948, the Soviets engineered a **coup** in Czechoslovakia and installed a Communist government. The death of political freedom in Czechoslovakia proved to many Americans the hostile intent of the Soviets. "We are faced with exactly the same situation with which Britain and France were faced in 1938 and 1939 with Hitler," Truman announced. But unlike France and Britain in 1938, the United States meant to mobilize its full resources to contain Soviet power and to maintain an armed peace.

With "sovietization" taking place in Eastern Europe, the United States, Britain, and France moved to unify their German occupation zones into a West German state and to integrate it into the framework of Western Europe. In March 1948, the United States announced that Germany's western zones, called Trizonia, were eligible for Marshall Plan aid, were to hold elections to select delegates to a constitutional convention, and would use a standard currency. The meaning of these actions seemed clear: a West German state was being formed.

Faced with the prospect of a pro-Western, industrialized, and eventually remilitarized Germany, Stalin reacted. On April 1, 1948, after asking for a Four Powers meeting to discuss Germany, the Soviets briefly denied entry from the West to the city of Berlin—the old German capital, which lay entirely within the Soviet occupational zone and which also was divided into zones controlled by the Four Powers (see Map 27.2). On June 23, ignoring Soviet objections, officials issued the new currency in the western zones of Berlin. The following day, the Russians blockaded all land traffic to and from Berlin and shut off the electricity to the city's western zones. With a population of over 2 million, West Berlin lay isolated 120 miles inside the Soviet zone of Germany. The Soviet goal was to force the West either to abandon the creation of West Germany or to face the loss of Berlin. Americans viewed the blockade simply as further proof of Soviet hostility and were determined not to retreat. Churchill af-

coup Sudden overthrow of a government by a small group of people in or previously in positions of authority.

♦ When the Soviets blockaded the western zones of Berlin, in one of the first confrontations of the Cold War, the United States replied by staging one of the most successful logistical feats of the twentieth century, Operation Vittles, in which vital supplies were flown into the city. After 321 days and more than 272,000 U.S. missions, the Soviets lifted the blockade, without explanation, permitting land access to the divided city in May 1949.

♦ **MAP 27.2 Cold War Germany** This map shows how Germany and Berlin were divided into occupation zones. Meant as temporary divisions, they became permanent, transformed by the Cold War into East and West Germany. In 1948, with the Berlin airlift, and again in 1961, with the erection of the Berlin Wall, Berlin became the flash point of the Cold War. With the end of the Cold War, the division of Germany also ended. In 1989, the Berlin Wall was torn down, and in 1990 the two Germanies were unified.

firmed the West's stand. We want peace, he stated, "but we should by now have learned that there is no safety in yielding to dictators, whether Nazi or Communist." The prospect of war loomed.

Having decided to stay in Berlin, American strategists confronted the question of how to stand fast without starting a shooting war. Although some in the army recommended fighting their way across the Soviet zone to the city. Truman chose another option, one that would not violate Soviet occupied territory or any international agreements. In November 1945, the Allies, including the Soviet Union, had agreed to maintain three air corridors to Berlin from the West, providing no legal right for Soviet interference with air traffic. Marshalling a massive effort of men, supplies, and aircraft, British and Americans flew through these corridors to three Berlin airports on an average of one flight every three minutes. To drive home to the Soviets the depth of American resolve, Truman ordered a wing of B-29 bombers, the "atomic bombers," to Berlin. Although these planes carried no atomic weapons, the general impression was that their presence deterred the likelihood of Soviet aggression.

The **Berlin airlift** was a tremendous victory for the United States. The unceasing flow of aircraft and

> **Berlin airlift** Response to the Soviet blockade of West Berlin in 1948, in which American and British planes made continuous flights to deliver supplies and keep the city open.

supplies testified not only to America's economic and military power but also to American resolve to contain Soviet power and protect Europe. The crisis bore other fruit, too: almost all congressional opposition to the Marshall Plan and the creation of West Germany was now swept away, and those who had protested a permanent military commitment to Western Europe were now silenced. Truman followed the Berlin action with a call for an American military alliance with Western Europe. And by April 1949, negotiations to create the **North Atlantic Treaty Organization (NATO)** were completed (see Map 27.1). Finding no diplomatic gain from the blockade, the Soviets ended it in May 1949 without explanation. Two months later, Congress approved American entry into NATO. Membership in the alliance ensured that American forces would remain in the newly created West Germany and that Western Europe would be eligible for additional American economic and military aid. The Mutual Defense Assistance Act passed in 1949 provided $1.5 billion in arms and equipment for NATO member nations—by 1952, 80 percent of all American assistance to Europe was military aid.

A Global Presence

American foreign policy from 1945 to 1950 focused on rebuilding Western Europe and containing Soviet power, but American policy did not ignore the rest of the world. Called one part humanitarianism and one part imperialism by a British official, U.S. foreign policy worked to expand American economic and political interests in Latin America, the Middle East, and Asia. To the south, the Truman administration rejected requests from Latin Americans for a Marshall Plan–style program. Instead, it encouraged private firms to develop the region through business and trade. To ensure that the Western Hemisphere would remain under the American eagle's wing, however, the United States, in the Rio Pact of 1947, encouraged Latin Americans to join with the United States and accept the concept of collective security and the establishment of a regional organization—the **Organization of American States**—to coordinate defense, economic, and social concerns.

In the Middle East, fear of future oil shortages led the United States to promote the expansion of American petroleum interests. In Saudi Arabia, Kuwait, and Iran, the goal was to replace Britain as the major economic and political influence. At the same time, the United States became a powerful

supporter of a new Jewish state. Truman's support for such a nation to be created out of **Palestine** arose from several considerations—moral, political, and international. As early as August 1945, he had asked that at least 100,000 displaced European Jews be allowed to migrate to Palestine, then under British rule. Considering the Nazi terror against Jews, he believed that the Jews should have their own nation—a view strongly advocated by a well-organized, pro-Jewish lobbying effort across the United States.

In May 1947, Britain announced it no longer had the resources or the desire to maintain control over Palestine. The stage was therefore set for the United Nations to divide the region into two nations: one Arab and one Jewish. When the United Nations voted to **partition** Palestine into Arab and Jewish states on May 14, 1948, Truman recognized the nation of Israel within fifteen minutes. And when war quickly broke out between the surrounding Arab states—who refused to accept partition—and Israel, Truman and most Americans applauded the victories of Israeli armies.

If Americans were pleased with events in Latin America and the Middle East, Asia provided several disappointments. Under American occupation, Japan's government had been reshaped into a democratic system and placed safely within the American orbit, but success in Japan was offset by diplomatic setbacks in China and Korea. During World War II, the **Nationalist Chinese** government of Jiang Jieshi (Chiang Kai-shek) and the Chinese Com-

---

North Atlantic Treaty Organization Alliance formed in 1949 that included most of the nations of Western Europe and North America; its mutual defense agreement was a basic element in the effort to contain communism.

Organization of American States An international organization composed of most of the nations of the Americas, including the Caribbean, which deals with the mutual concerns of its members. Cuba is not currently a member.

Palestine Region on the Mediterranean that was a British mandate after World War I; the U.N. partitioned the area in 1948 to allow for a Jewish and a Palestinian state.

partition To divide a country into separate, autonomous nations.

Nationalist Chinese Supporters of Jiang Jieshi, who fought the Communists for control of China in the 1940s; in defeat they retreated to Taiwan in 1949, where they set up a separate government.

munists under Mao Zedong (Mao Tse-tung) had moderated their hostility toward each other to fight the Japanese. But when the war ended, old suspicions and animosities quickly resurfaced. In late 1945, General Marshall traveled to China to try to arrange a coalition government between Mao and Jiang, but the effort failed and the truce between the two forces collapsed. By February 1946, civil war flared in China and several American supporters of Jiang recommended that the United States increase its economic and military support for the Nationalist government. Especially vocal in promoting the cause of the Nationalists was the "China Lobby," led by *Time-Life* publisher Henry R. Luce, a long-time friend of Jiang. Luce and others argued that the civil war in China was as important as the one that threatened Greece and that Asia was threatened by Soviet power as much as Europe. Truman and Marshall were of a different opinion. Although dreading a Communist success in China, they blamed the corrupt and inefficient Nationalist government under Jiang for the China's political and economic turmoil, and questioned whether Jiang could ever effectively rule the country. Both Truman and Marshall were willing to continue some political, economic, and military support, but neither Truman nor Marshall wanted to pull Jiang's "chestnuts out of the fire" by committing American power to an Asian war. Providing more aid would be like "throwing money down a rat hole," Truman told the cabinet. Faced with a more efficient and popular opponent, unable to mobilize the Chinese people and resources, and without increased American support, Jiang's forces steadily lost the civil war. In 1949, Jiang's army disintegrated and the Nationalist government fled to the island of Formosa (Taiwan).

Conservative Democrats and Republicans labeled the rout of Jiang as a humiliating American defeat and complained that the administration was too soft on communism. To quiet critics and to protect Jiang, Truman refused to recognize the People's Republic of China on the mainland and ordered the U.S. 7th Fleet to waters near Taiwan. Increasingly, Truman was feeling pressure to expand the containment policy to areas beyond Europe. The pressure intensified in late August 1949, when the Soviets detonated their own atomic bomb, shattering the American nuclear monopoly. Suddenly, it seemed to many Americans that the United States was losing the Cold War. From inside and outside the administration came calls for a more global and aggressive policy against communism. David Lilienthal, one of Truman's atomic advisers and head of the Atomic Energy Commission, recommended building a **hydrogen bomb.** A joint Pentagon–State Department committee, headed by Paul Nitze, concluded that the Soviets were driven by "a new fanatic faith, antithetical to our own" whose objective was to dominate the world. The group further speculated that the Soviets would be able to launch a nuclear attack on the United States as early as 1954. The committee's report, **National Security Council (NSC)** Memorandum #68, stated that compromises and negotiations with the Soviets provided no security and called for global containment and a massive build-up of American military force. In fact, NSC-68 called for an almost 400 percent increase in military spending for the next fiscal year, which would have raised military expenditures to nearly $50 billion.

Truman studied the report but hesitated to implement its recommendations. He worried about the impact of such large-scale military production on domestic goods manufacturing. A separate report concluded that the projected mobilization of industry for the Cold War would reduce automobile construction by nearly 60 percent and that the production of radios and television sets might fall to zero. He eventually agreed to a "moderate" $12.3 billion military budget for 1950 that included building the hydrogen bomb. Supporters of NSC-68, however, won the final argument on June 24, 1950, when North Korean troops stormed across the **38th parallel.**

The Korean War

● As the North Koreans invaded South Korea, what choices and constraints did Truman confront when considering policy options?

When World War II ended, Soviet forces occupied Korea north of the 38th parallel and American forces remained south of it (see Map 27.3). As with

---

hydrogen bomb   Explosive weapon of enormous destructive power fueled by the fusion of the nuclei of various hydrogen isotopes.

National Security Council   Executive agency established in 1947 to coordinate the strategic policies and defense of the United States; it includes the president and four cabinet members.

38th parallel   Negotiated dividing line between North and South Korea, which was the focus of much of the fighting in the Korean War.

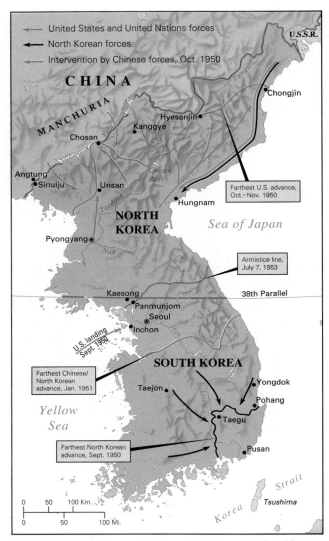

◆ **MAP 27.3 The Korean War, 1950–1953** Seeking to unify Korea, North Korean forces invaded South Korea in 1950. To protect South Korea, the United States and the United Nations intervened. After driving North Korean forces northward, Truman sought to unify Korea under South Korea. But as United Nations and South Korean forces pushed toward the Chinese border, Communist China intervened, forcing UN troops to retreat. This map shows the military thrusts and counterthrusts of the Korean War as it stalemated roughly along the 38th parallel.

trusteeship might last as long as twenty-five years. Most Koreans felt otherwise and quickly began pressing Soviet and American authorities for immediate independence. Across Korea, "People's Committees" sprang into existence promoting political, social, and economic changes. Although Communist influence in these nationalistic committees was limited, the American commander, General John Hodge, a tough anti-Communist with little understanding of Korean affairs, saw them as part of a worldwide Communist movement directed from Moscow. He instinctively supported Korean political conservatives led by **Syngman Rhee**. Finding no American support for a joint Soviet-American trusteeship, north of the 38th parallel the Soviets quickly backed Korean Communists led by **Kim Il-Sung**. By mid-1946, the division of Korea appeared more permanent than temporary.

In 1949, believing Korea to be of little political or strategic importance, the Soviet and American governments withdrew their forces, leaving behind two hostile regimes, each claiming to be Korea's rightful government. Using force to promote their nationalistic claims, both Koreas launched raids across the border. Neither side gained much ground, but within a year over 100,000 Koreans had lost their lives in the conflict, and both sides had expanded their military capabilities.

On June 25, 1950, Kim Il-Sung launched a full-scale invasion of the south. Apprised of the invasion, Truman reconsidered strategic priorities and quickly announced that Korea was, after all, a region vital to American interests that needed protection from Communist aggression. In Truman's and most Americans' minds, Moscow had directed the invasion. The wisdom of NSC-68's recommendations for a global, military-backed campaign of containment was undeniably confirmed.

The UN Responds to Communist Aggression

Within days, the South Korean army (ROK) was fleeing before stronger, better equipped North Ko-

Germany, the division of Korea was expected to be temporary, with the United States and the Soviet Union working to create a reunited Korean nation. Many Americans, though, including President Roosevelt, had little confidence in Korean political abilities and had projected that the Soviet-American

> **Syngman Rhee** Korean politician who became president of South Korea in 1948; his dictatorial rule ended in 1960, when he was forced out of office into exile.
>
> **Kim Il-Sung** Installed by the Soviets as leader of North Korea. He served as premier from 1948 to 1972, when he became president until his death in 1994.

rean forces. Immediately, the United States asked the UN Security Council to intervene. The Security Council called for a cease-fire and asked member nations to provide assistance to South Korea. To blunt the invasion, Truman ordered **General Douglas MacArthur** to commit American naval and air units south of the 38th parallel. Two days later, as North Koreans captured the South Korean capital of Seoul, the Security Council approved an international military force to defend South Korea—that is, to push the invaders back into North Korea and restore peace. General MacArthur was named commander of the United Nations forces. As a member of the Security Council, the Soviet Union could have blocked the actions with its veto, but at the time of the invasion the Russians were boycotting the council for its refusal to recognize the People's Republic of China. The Soviets returned to the Security Council in August.

Although the public's support of Truman's decision to intervene was over 70 percent of those polled, there was no rush to arms as in World War II. National Guard and reserve forces had to be called to active duty to fill the ranks, and the draft was instituted to ensure a monthly quota of fifty thousand soldiers. General Lewis B. Hershey, head of the Selective Service, noted, "Everyone wants out; nobody wants in." Within the military, the war sped the integration of African-Americans into previously all-white combat units. On July 1, the first American soldiers, officially under United Nations control, arrived in Korea. Fearful that a congressional declaration of war against Korea might expand the conflict to involve the Chinese and Russians, Truman never sought one. American troops served in Korea under United Nations resolutions and followed Truman's orders as commander-in-chief. For the record the war was called the Korean Conflict, a "police action" to defeat a "bandit raid." Few in Congress objected, and with little dissent the House and Senate approved large-scale expansions of the military and its budget.

The infusion of American troops had not halted the North Korean advance, and by the end of July, North Korean forces occupied most of South Korea. United Nations forces, including nearly 122,000 Americans and the whole South Korean army, held the southeastern corner of the peninsula—the **Pusan perimeter**—and prepared for an offensive. The tide was about to turn in the war. In a bold maneuver, that required precise timing and coordination, on September 15, seventy thousand American forces landed at Inchon, near Seoul, nearly 200 miles north

♦ After liberating South Korea, United Nations and American troops advanced north, nearly to the Chinese border, until massive numbers of Chinese troops pushed them back toward the 38th parallel. In this picture, battle-weary Marines dig in along a road in their retreat from the Changjin Reservoir—the road dubbed "Nightmare Alley." *Keystone Press.*

of the Pusan defensive perimeter. It was a brilliant tactical move that surprised the enemy and not only threatened North Korean supply and communication lines but also could cut off the retreat of North Korean troops. The next day, the United Nations forces along the Pusan perimeter began their advance. Ten days later, forces advancing north from Pusan joined forces driving east from Inchon. Their army collapsing, the North Koreans fled back across

General Douglas MacArthur Commander of Allied forces in the South Pacific during World War II and of U.N. forces in Korea until a conflict over strategy led Truman to dismiss him.

Pusan perimeter Area near the city of Pusan in South Korea, which was the center of a beachhead held by U.N. forces in 1950.

the 38th parallel. **Seoul** was liberated on September 27, and United Nations forces had achieved the purpose of the police action. The bandits were beaten, the South Korean government was saved, and the 38th parallel was again a real border.

Seeking to Liberate North Korea

But restoring the conditions that had prevailed before the invasion was not enough for the United States. MacArthur, Truman, and most Americans now wanted to unify the peninsula under South Korean rule. Bending under American pressure, the United Nations approved the new goal on October 7. MacArthur had a green light to "liberate" North Korea from Communist rule (see Map 27.3).

An invasion seemed safe. North Korean forces were in disarray and intelligence sources discounted the possibility of either Soviet or large-scale Chinese intervention. By mid-October, United Nations forces were moving quickly northward toward the Korean-Chinese border at the Yalu River. The Chinese threatened intervention if the invaders approached the border, and some UN units had already encountered some Chinese "volunteer" troops. Anxious that the Chinese might move in force, Truman flew to Wake Island to confer with MacArthur. The United Nations' commander was supremely confident. If Chinese forces did cross the border, he explained, they could not number more than thirty thousand and American air power would slaughter them. Truman, less than convinced, ordered MacArthur to use only South Korean forces in approaching the Yalu River. The overconfident general bridled at being constrained by his civilian commander, however, and on November 24, in violation of his orders, MacArthur moved American, British, and Korean forces to within a few miles of the Yalu. He also publicly promised to have victorious American soldiers home by Christmas. Two days later, nearly 300,000 Chinese soldiers entered the Korean Conflict.

In the most brutal fighting of the war, with their distinct bugles blowing, the Chinese attacked in waves, hurling grenades, taking massive casualties, and encircling and nearly trapping several American and South Korean units. MacArthur had believed that vastly superior American air and fire power would deal with any Chinese invaders. But his calculations had not foreseen the hundreds of thousands of Chinese soldiers involved, nor the bitter winter weather, nor night battles that severely limited the role of American aircraft. Across northern Korea, UN forces fell back in bitter combat, including the U.S. 1st Marine Division, which was nearly surrounded at the Chosin Reservoir. The marines battled their way to the port of Hamnung by leap-frogging units to clear the road in front of them. During the Communist offensive, American casualties exceeded twelve thousand, but the Chinese lost over three times as many, lending grim proof to General O. P. "Slam" Smith's statement about the "retreat" from Chosin: "Gentlemen, we are not retreating. We are merely advancing in another direction."

Within three weeks, the North Koreans and Chinese had shoved the United Nations forces back to the 38th parallel. During the retreat, General MacArthur asked for permission to bomb bridges on the Yalu River and Chinese bases across the border. He also urged a naval blockade of China and the possible use of Nationalist Chinese forces against the mainland. Believing such an escalation could lead to World War III, Truman allowed only the Korean half of the bridges to be bombed and flatly rejected MacArthur's other suggestions. In the face of the new military reality, Truman abandoned the goal of a unified pro-Western Korea and sought a negotiated settlement to end the conflict that would leave two Koreas (see Map 27.3).

The decision was not popular. Americans wanted victory. Encouraged by public opinion polls and vocal Republican critics of Truman, in March and April 1951, MacArthur publicly took exception to the limitations his commander-in-chief had placed on him. He put it simply: there was "no substitute for victory." Already dissatisfied with MacArthur's arrogance, Truman used the general's direct challenge to presidential power as grounds to fire him. Replaced by General Matthew Ridgway on April 11, 1951, MacArthur returned to the states and received a hero's welcome, including a ticker-tape parade down New York's Fifth Avenue. Only a quarter of those asked supported the president's decision to recall the popular general. Jokes circulated about ordering a "Truman beer"—"one without a head." Across the country some called for Truman's impeachment and MacArthur's nomination for president. Congressional hearings to investigate the

---

Seoul Capital of South Korea, which suffered extensive damage during its occupation by Communist forces in 1950 and 1951.

conduct of the war followed in June 1951, with MacArthur testifying that an expanded war could achieve victory. The administration responded by projecting fears of a nuclear world war and effectively made the case for a limited war and the need for civilian authority over the military.

In the face-off between MacArthur and Truman, neither won. Polls showed Truman's public approval rate continuing to fall, reaching a dismal 24 percent by late 1951. At the same time, MacArthur's hopes for a presidential candidacy collapsed as most Americans feared his aggressive policies might result in World War III. By the beginning of 1952, frustrated by the war, the vast majority of Americans were simply tired of it, calling it "useless," and wanted it over. As public opinion turned against both Truman and the war in mid-1951, the Korean front stabilized along the 38th parallel. Four Power peace talks, seating the United States and South Korea against China and North Korea, had begun on July 10 amid sharp and ugly fighting. The negotiations did not go smoothly. For two years, the powers postured and argued about prisoners, cease-fire lines, and a multitude of lesser issues. Meanwhile, soldiers fought and died over scraps of territory. Over 125,000 UN casualties resulted during the two years of peace negotiations. When the **cease-fire** finally was concluded by the Eisenhower administration on July 26, 1953, the Korean Conflict had cost over $20 billion and 33,000 American lives.

The "hot war" in Korea had far-reaching military and diplomatic results for the United States. The expansion of military spending envisioned by NSC-68 had proceeded rapidly following the North Korean invasion. In Europe, Truman moved forward with plans to rearm West Germany and Italy, and, in the name of anticommunism, improved relations with Spain's fascist dictator, Francisco Franco. Throughout Asia and the Pacific, a large American presence was made permanent. In 1951, the United States concluded a settlement with Japan that kept American forces in Japan and Okinawa. The Australian-New Zealand-United States (ANZUS) treaty of 1951 promised American military protection to Australia and New Zealand, at the same time the United States was increasing its military aid and commitments to Nationalist China and French **Indochina**. The containment policy that George F. Kennan had envisioned to protect only Western Europe had expanded to incorporate—formally and financially—East Asia and the Pacific. Kennan had objected to the growing number of commitments, but his arguments were more than offset by those stressing the

global struggle against the forces of communism. According to the philosophy of the day, a Communist victory anywhere threatened the national security of the United States.

Homecomings and Adjustments

- What constraints did Truman face in implementing his ~mestic programs?
- How did they influence his choices?

In September 1944, the War Department had announced that as soon as the war against Germany was over, demobilization would begin—the "boys" would start coming home. Germany had hardly surrendered when soldiers' wives across the nation organized "Bring Daddy Back" clubs and began flooding Washington with letters demanding a speedier return of their husbands. In the Pacific, soldiers sent letters and telegrams to their congressmen saying, "No boat; no vote." Despite protests from the military and the State Department, and against Truman's own better judgment, by November 1.25 million GIs were returning home each month wanting to rediscover family, jobs, and the American way of life—the American dream. Of course, that American dream differed from person to person, but in general it centered around Franklin D. Roosevelt's 1944 Economic Bill of Rights: the right to a decent job, to sufficient food, shelter, and clothing, and to financial protection during unemployment, illness, and old age. Armed with the G.I. Bill that provided low-interest home loans and a year's unemployment compensation (see page 816), returning veterans were eager to begin civilian life.

Initially, in 1945 and 1946, not enough homes were available for the reunited families. The nation faced a massive housing shortage, especially in California and major cities. Streetcars were converted into homes in Chicago, grain silos became apartments in North Dakota, and across the country families doubled up. Of course, most desired to live

---

cease-fire   A truce that brings an end to fighting.

Indochina   French colony in southeast Asia, which included the present-day states of Vietnam, Laos, and Cambodia; it began fighting for its independence in the mid-twentieth century.

◆ As World War II ended, Americans flocked to the suburbs, creating a demand for new housing—a demand matched by developers of planned communities like Levittown. In 1949, on one day alone, over 1400 people signed contracts for their dream homes, some of which included automatic dishwashers and built-in televisions. *Joe Scherschel, LIFE Magazine © Time Warner, Inc.*

in the charming "dream homes" advertised in popular magazines, by mid-1946, developers like William Levitt were supplying mass-produced, prefabricated houses—the suburban **tract house**—to meet the demand. Using building techniques developed during the war, Levitt boasted that he could construct a house on an existing concrete slab in sixteen minutes. Standardized, with few frills, his homes cost slightly less than $8,000, a very attractive price to many returning soldiers.

The first Levittown sprang up in Hempstead, Long Island, soon to be followed by others in Pennsylvania and New Jersey. In California and along the West Coast, Henry Kaiser built homes using the same efficient methods he had used to build ships during the war. Most suburban developments were built for the "typical" American family—white, middle-class, and Christian. African-Americans, Jews, and other minorities were not welcome. Although the 1948 Supreme Court decision of **Shelly v. Kraemer** made it illegal for developers and real estate agents to restrict housing, the decision had little impact. Banks rarely made home loans to minorities trying to buy in a white neighborhood, and realtors still abided by the Realtors Code of Ethics, which called it unethical to permit the "infiltration of inharmonious elements" into a neighborhood. Across the nation, less than 5 percent of the nation's suburban neighborhoods provided nonwhites access to the American dream house. In the San Francisco Bay area, of the more than 100,000 homes built between 1945 and 1950, less than 1 percent were sold to nonwhites.

Cozy homes were only part of postwar expectations. Veterans expected jobs, too, and that the workers—especially married women—who had been hired while they "fought for democracy" would now relinquish those jobs. A fall 1945 *Fortune* poll discovered that 57 percent of women and 63 percent of men believed that married women should not work. Psychiatrists and marriage counselors argued that men wanted feminine and submissive wives, not fellow workers. Fashions, like Christian Dior's "New Look," lowered skirts and accented waists and breasts to emphasize femininity.

Many women accepted the role of contented wife and homemaker, but not all. When one ex-GI husband informed his wife that she could no longer handle the finances because it was not "woman's work," she indignantly reminded him that she had successfully balanced the checkbook for four years and that his return did not make her suddenly stupid. Reflecting such tensions and too many hasty wartime marriages, the divorce rate jumped dramatically. Twenty-five percent of all marriages were ending in divorce in 1946, and by 1950 over a million GI marriages had broken apart.

---

tract house   One of numerous houses of similar design built on a plot of land.

Shelly v. Kraemer   1948 Supreme Court ruling that barred developers and real estate agents from creating whites-only housing but that had little immediate impact.

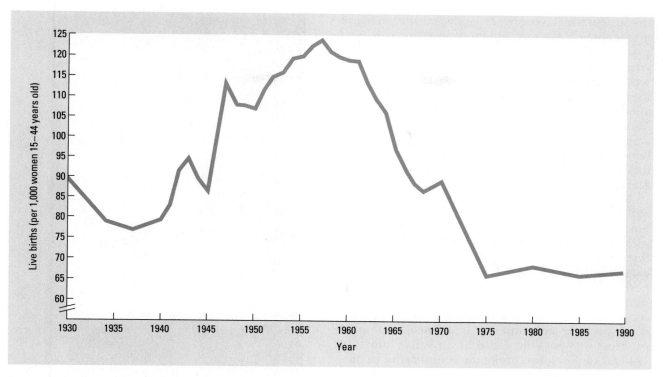

♦ **FIGURE 27.1 Birthrate, 1930–1990** Between 1946 and 1957, rebounding from the low
birthrate of the Depression, families choose to have more children. This period is often
called the "Baby Boom." Since the 1960s, the birthrate has slowed, and since the 1970s,
it has remained fairly constant.

Despite the growing divorce rate, however, marriage was more popular than ever: two-thirds of the population was married by 1950, and having children. From a Depression level of under 19 per 1,000, the birthrate rose to over 25 per 1,000 within two years of the war (see Figure 27.1). The so-called **baby boom** had arrived—and would last for nearly twenty years. The baby boom did not occur merely because soldiers returned home, however. A variety of other forces contributed as well. Fear of "male scarcity" caused by war losses encouraged some women to choose marriage earlier than later, but more important, there was a new attitude toward marriage. Increasingly, marriage was seen as ideal for younger people as many women's magazines and marriage experts championed the idea that men should marry at around age 20 and women at age 18 or 19.

Like women, nonwhites found that "fair employment" vanished as employers favored white males once the war was over. The skilled and industrial jobs that had opened to Latinos and African-Ameri-

cans during the war became scarce by 1946. In 1943, over a million African-Americans were employed in the aircraft industry but by 1950, the number had shrunk to 237,000. The decline was less marked in the automobile, rubber, and shipbuilding industries, but minority job levels dropped as many of the skilled and higher-paying positions routinely were denied to nonwhites.

Mexican-Americans too found themselves limited to unskilled, menial jobs, despite their rapidly growing numbers in urban areas. Discrimination, denial of educational opportunities, and language barriers combined to trap a majority of Mexican-Americans as common laborers. Throughout the Southwest and West, the pattern of Mexican-American migration to urban areas continued to heighten

baby boom   Sudden increase in the birthrate that occurred in the United States after World War II and lasted from 1947 to 1961.

the agricultural labor shortage. Mechanization made up for some of the loss, but more workers were necessary and Mexico was the logical source. In 1947, when Mexico pressed for higher wages and better working conditions for those Mexicans working in the *bracero* program (see page 820), the United States allowed American farmers to contract directly for Mexican workers with virtually no restrictions on wages and working conditions. The result was that between 1947 and 1950 nearly twice as many undocumented Mexican workers were recruited than had worked under the *bracero* program.

Nonwhite Americans at the end of World War II still lived in a distinctly segregated world. From housing to jobs, from health care to education, white society continued to deny nonwhites full participation in the American dream. Still, African-Americans and Latinos looked eagerly toward the postwar period. Notwithstanding ongoing segregation and discrimination, minorities had achieved social and economic gains during the war, and despite immediate postwar adjustments, it seemed that more progress was possible. Reflecting a better future, in 1945 Jackie Robinson broke the color barrier in professional baseball when he signed with Branch Rickey of the Brooklyn Dodgers to play for the Dodgers' farm team, the Montreal Royals. The first African-American player in the previously all-white major leagues, Robinson joined the Dodgers in 1947 and that season was voted the National League's Rookie of the Year. A popular opinion poll named him the second most popular man in the country, after singer Bing Crosby.

Having fought for democracy, minorities were more determined than ever not to return to the old ways. Latino and African-American leaders, supported by returning black and Mexican-American veterans, insisted that democracy be practiced at home. W. E. B. Du Bois stated that the real problems facing the United States came not from Stalin and Molotov but from racists like Mississippi's Senator Theodore Bilbo and Congressman John Rankin. "Internal injustice done to one's brother," Du Bois warned, "is far more dangerous than the aggression of strangers from abroad." When the Anglos of Three Rivers, Texas, refused to bury war hero Felix Longoria in the city cemetery, Latino veterans protested to Washington. Wanting to avoid a civil rights confrontation, the Truman administration agreed to bury Longoria in Arlington National Cemetery. In 1948, Mexican-American veterans organized the G.I. Forum in Corpus Christi and with other Latino organizations protested the segre-

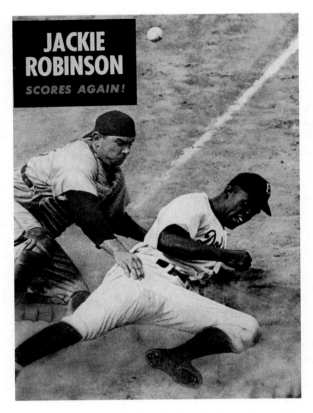

◆ Jackie Robinson broke the color barrier in major league baseball in 1947, when he joined the Brooklyn Dodgers. An All-American in football and baseball at UCLA, after serving as a lieutenant in the army during the war, Robinson played with the Kansas City Monarchs of the Negro American Baseball League until signed by the Dodgers in 1945. Moved from the minors to the majors in 1947, he earned "Rookie of the Year" honors and later was inducted into the Baseball Hall of Fame. *Collection of Michael Barson/Past Perfect.*

gation of Latino schoolchildren. Although many of the court cases they filed against several school districts were won, including the Supreme Court 1948 *Delgado* ruling that Latin Americans should not be segregated, "Mexican ward schools" remained throughout the Southwest. Still, changes were taking place and minorities hoped that President Truman would protect and extend the benefits acquired during the war.

Truman and Liberalism

When Roosevelt died, many wondered if Truman would continue the Roosevelt–New Deal approach to domestic policies. Would he work to protect the social and economic gains that labor, women, and minorities had earned during the Depression and the war? Would the government continue to play a key role in managing the economy? In January 1945, New Deal liberals had introduced a full-employment bill requiring the government to guarantee jobs. Would Truman follow through on such proposals or would he reverse the New Deal's course? Close Roosevelt adviser Samuel Rosenman noted that conservatives and some of Truman's friends were predicting that the new president was "going to be quite a shock to those who followed Roosevelt—that the New Deal is as good as dead . . . and that the 'Roosevelt nonsense' was over."

Conservatives were disappointed. Emphasizing his New Deal roots, on September 6, President Harry S Truman presented to Congress what one Republican critic called an effort to "out–New Deal the New Deal." The president asked the legislature for a twenty-one point program to re-energize the New Deal. He wanted to continue governmental controls over the economy, especially on prices, and to renew the **Fair Employment Practices Committee (FEPC).** He recommended an expansion of social security coverage and benefits, an increase in the minimum wage to $.65 an hour, and the development of additional housing programs and Tennessee Valley–style projects. Truman also advised Congress that he would soon ask for a national health system to ensure medical care for all Americans.

The expanded New Deal that Truman projected never fully developed. Republicans, conservative Democrats, business leaders, and a variety of conservative groups were determined to prevent it. They argued that an advancing New Deal would lead to the development of a socialistic state that would eventually destroy private enterprise. These same opponents had successfully contained the New Deal in 1937, and as the war ended in 1945, they set their sights on squelching any further expansion of the welfare state and federal management of the economy. To promote their political views, conservatives and big business embarked on a campaign to persuade the American public of the dangers of "New Deal socialism" and to sell the benefits to everyone of a return to business-directed free enterprise. The National Association of Manufacturers spent nearly $37 million on such propaganda in one year. "Public sentiment is everything," wrote an officer of Standard Oil. "He who molds public sentiment goes deeper than he who enacts statutes or pronounces decisions."

Warning that Truman's program involved too much government, threatened free enterprise, and endangered existing class and social relations, conservatives flatly rejected nearly all of his programs. Conservatives in Congress, with surprisingly little opposition from the White House, either killed or significantly modified nearly all of Truman's twenty-one proposals. FEPC faded away. The liberal full-employment act was revised: it called on the government to promote maximum employment but any requirement to create jobs was axed. Price, wage, and rent controls that Truman insisted would ease the country through its conversion to a peacetime economy were in time re-established by Congress in the summer of 1946, but they did little to halt spiraling inflation and demands for higher wages.

As prices rose—25 percent during the first eighteen months after the war—most workers' incomes fell. The lack of overtime and the lower wages decreased buying power nearly 30 percent. Labor logically wanted 30 percent more in wages. A government study recommended less, an 18.5 percent raise, but with an oversupply of workers, employers saw little need to offer any increased wages at all. Nearly 4.5 million workers went on more than five thousand strikes to protect jobs and purchasing power. Congress and state and local governments responded with antilabor measures designed to weaken unions and end strikes. "Right to work" laws banned compulsory union membership and in some cases provided legal and police protection for those crossing picket lines during strikes. Other laws restricted boycotts and secondary, sympathy strikes or promoted the **open shop** and company-organized workers' associations. Even Truman squared off against the railroad and coal miners' unions. When locomotive engineers struck in late May 1946, Truman asked Congress for power to draft striking workers into the army. The railroad strike was soon settled and the "draft strikers" bill never passed, but Truman still faced an ever-aggressive John L. Lewis and 400,000 United Mine Workers. Demanding higher wages, the UMW went on

---

Fair Employment Practices Committee   Committee established by executive order in 1941 to curb racial discrimination in war industries; in 1946 a bill for a permanent FEPC was killed by a southern Democrat filibuster.

open shop   Business or factory in which workers are employed without having to join a union; unlike a closed shop, which requires union membership.

♦ Workers march in New York City in support of unions, the FEPC, and worldwide worker solidarity. As the war ended, business and government assumed a more hostile attitude toward organized labor—many claiming that unions were socialistic or communistic. The outcome of this attitude were laws, including the Taft-Hartley Act, that restricted union activities as well as a decline in union membership. *UPI/Bettmann Archives.*

strike in April 1946. Considering Lewis "a Hitler at heart, a demagogue in action, and a traitor in fact," the president seized the mines, ordered miners back to work, and applauded when a federal court fined Lewis and the union $3.5 million. When the miners finally returned to work on December 7, Truman took personal satisfaction in the victory: "Lewis folded up on Saturday," he wrote in his diary. "He is, as all bullies are, as yellow as a dog pound pup. He cannot face the music when the tune is not to his liking. On the front under shellfire he'd crack up."

The strikes, soaring inflation rates, and divisions within Democratic ranks fit the Republican party's prescription for a 1946 election bonanza. "Had Enough?" Republican candidates asked the voters. Voters responded affirmatively, filling both houses of the 80th Congress with anti-Truman and anti–New Deal forces. Undeterred by Republican successes during the congressional elections, a bold Truman opened the new year by proposing a near repeat of his 1945 program. As expected, Congress ignored Truman's domestic proposals and focused on passing a tax cut and anti-union legislation. The **Taft-Hartley Act,** passed in June 1947 over Truman's veto, was a clear victory for management over labor. It banned the closed shop, prevented industry-wide collective bargaining, and legalized state-sponsored "right to work" laws. Echoing Truman's actions in the coal strike, the law also empowered the president to use a court injunction to force striking workers back to work for an eighty-day cooling-off period. Privately, Truman liked the Taft-

Hartley Act and had cast his veto knowing it would be overridden. "So we're going to have a pretty good law on the books in spite of my veto," he told one official, "and if I veto it, I'm going to hold labor support in the election next year." In December, a tax cut was also passed over Truman's veto.

Truman's position on civil rights was cautious but generally supportive. Blacks applauded his call for the continuation of the FEPC but were disappointed that he had done little to prevent its termination. African-Americans and liberals, including Eleanor Roosevelt, organized a protest in Washington, their placards demanding "Speak, Speak, Mr. President," to prod Truman and Congress into confronting the raising tide of racial violence. Admitting that he did not know how bad conditions were for blacks, Truman agreed in December 1946 to create a Committee on Civil Rights to examine race relations in the country. The committee was a product of Truman's belief in equality, pressure from blacks and liberals, and hints that many northern blacks might vote Republican.

In October 1947, the committee presented a lengthy report, *To Secure These Rights,* stressing the racial inequalities in American society and calling on the government to take steps to correct the im-

---

Taft-Hartley Act 1947 law banning closed shops, permitting employers to sue unions for broken contracts, and requiring unions to observe a cooling-off period before striking.

balance. Among its recommendations were the establishment of a permanent Commission on Civil Rights, the enactment of antilynching laws, and the abolition of the poll tax (see page 562). It also called for integration of the U.S. Armed Forces and support for integrating housing programs and education. Truman asked Congress in February 1948 to act on the commission's recommendations, but he himself provided no direction or legislation. Nor did the White House make any effort to fully integrate the armed forces until black labor leader A. Philip Randolph once again threatened a march on Washington. Faced with the prospect of an embarrassing mass protest only months before the 1948 election, Truman issued an executive order asking the military to integrate its forces. The navy and air force complied, but the army resisted until high casualties in the summer of 1950 in Korea forced the integration of black replacements into previously white combat units. Despite his caution, Truman had done more in the area of civil rights than any president since Lincoln, a record that ensured African-American and liberal support for his 1948 bid for the presidency.

The 1948 Election

Republicans had high expectations in 1948. Republican candidates had done well in congressional elections and Truman's approval ratings remained low. To take on Truman the Republicans chose New York's governor **Thomas E. Dewey**. In his loss to Roosevelt in 1944, he had earned a respectable 46 percent of the popular vote. And prospects looked very good for Dewey in 1948. Not only was the Republican party strong and Truman's popularity weak, but the Democrats were mired in bitter infighting over the direction of domestic policy. Many Democratic liberals and minorities were dissatisfied that Truman had not worked harder to sell his New Deal–type programs to the public and to push them through Congress. These dissenters hoped to replace him on the ballot with General Dwight David Eisenhower or Supreme Court Justice William O. Douglas. Liberal and foreign policy critic Henry A. Wallace was another alternative. Neither option developed. Eisenhower and Douglas were not interested in unseating Truman, and Wallace's criticisms of the containment policy were apparently too pro-Soviet for most Americans. Grudgingly, minorities and liberals marched into line behind Truman, writing a strong New Deal–style party platform that included a civil rights plank.

♦ Many considered Harry S Truman's 1948 victory over Thomas E. Dewey a major political upset—nearly all of the major polls had named the Republican an easy winner. Here Truman holds up the *Chicago Tribune's* incorrect headline announcing Dewey's triumph. *UPI/Bettmann Archives.*

Many southerners, after losing the fight to exclude civil rights from the platform, walked out of the convention waving Confederate flags. Unwilling to support a Republican, southern Democrats met in Birmingham and organized the **Dixiecrat party,** nominating South Carolina's governor J. Strom Thurmond for president. Wallace's supporters also deserted Truman, forming the Progressive party and naming Wallace as their candidate.

With the Democratic party so splintered and public opinion polls showing a large Republican lead, Dewey, not known for his charm or speaking ability, conducted a low-key campaign almost devoid of debate on issues and contact with the public. Running for his political life, on the other hand, Truman

Thomas E. Dewey New York governor who twice ran unsuccessfully for president as the Republican candidate, the second time against Truman in 1948.

Dixiecrat party Party organized in 1948 by southern delegates who refused to accept the civil rights plank of the Democratic platform, they nominated Strom Thurmond of South Carolina for president.

states. Wallace carried none as Truman's veto of the Taft-Hartley Act and his position on civil rights had indeed kept labor, northern liberals, and minorities loyal to the party. Black voters in Los Angeles, Chicago, and Cleveland played key roles in adding California, Illinois, and Ohio to Truman's electoral votes. His victory was made even sweeter when most of the West and Midwest voted Democratic. With Congress once again solidly in Democratic hands, Truman hoped that in 1949 he would be able to succeed with his domestic program, which he called the **Fair Deal.** In his inaugural address, Truman again held up the images of the New Deal, calling on government to ensure that all Americans received a "fair share" of the American dream. As in 1945, he asked for increases in social security, public housing, and the minimum wage. He proposed the repeal of the Taft-Hartley Act and the institution of a national health program, and he gave civil rights and federal aid to education a place on the nation's agenda. Rewarding farmers for their role in his victory, Truman submitted the Brannan Plan, which included federal benefits for small farmers.

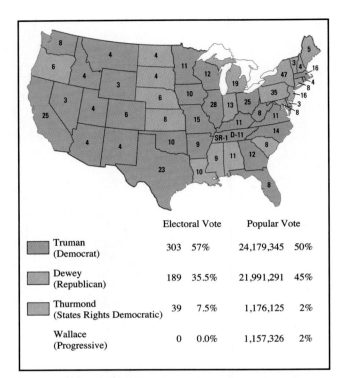

		Electoral Vote		Popular Vote	
Truman (Democrat)		303	57%	24,179,345	50%
Dewey (Republican)		189	35.5%	21,991,291	45%
Thurmond (States Rights Democratic)		39	7.5%	1,176,125	2%
Wallace (Progressive)		0	0.0%	1,157,326	2%

◆ **MAP 27.4 Election of 1948** In the 1948 presidential election, Harry S Truman confounded the polls and analysts by upsetting his Republican opponent Thomas Dewey, earning 50 percent of the popular vote and 57 percent of the electoral vote.

crossed the nation by train, making hundreds of speeches that stressed the gains made under the progressive policies of Democrats. He attacked the "do nothing" 80th Congress and its business allies. He told one audience, "Wall Street expects its money to elect a Republican administration that will listen to the gluttons of privilege first and not to the people at all." Truman also emphasized the bipartisan nature of his foreign policy and his expertise in dealing with the Soviet-engineered coup in Czechoslovakia and the Berlin blockade. Comparing himself to Dewey, Truman projected the image of a man who had more experience and the guts to stand up to Stalin.

Confounding the pollsters, Truman defeated Dewey (see Map 27.4). His margin of victory was the smallest since 1916—slightly over 2 million votes. Nevertheless, Truman's victory was a triumph for Roosevelt's New Deal coalition. Despite the Dixiecrat candidate, most southerners did not abandon the party, and Thurmond carried only four southern

Cold War Politics

● **What constraints and choices did the Cold War place on American politics and society?**

Congress responded favorably to Truman's programs in areas already well established by the New Deal: a $.65 minimum hourly wage, funds for low- and moderate-income housing, and increases in social security coverage and payments. New proposals going beyond the scope of the New Deal, however, failed to generate the necessary support and encountered entrenched, organized opposition. Attacks on the Fair Deal were based on a time-honored objection: too much government intrusion. But in 1949 this objection found renewed energy and meaning in the growing national fear of communism. The American Medical Association attacked the idea of a national health system by stressing its "Communistic" nature and claiming it would result in worse health care. Conservatives emphasized the

Fair Deal President Truman's plan for legislation on civil rights, fair employment practices, and educational appropriations.

"Communist" nature of government intervention in education. Civil rights legislation was held captive by the southern wing of the party, who called the FEPC part of a Communist conspiracy to undermine American unity. Agribusiness leaders and conservatives attacked the Brannan Plan as a socialistic, class-orientated attack on agriculture. One of Truman's aides wrote that "the consuming fear of communism" fostered a widespread belief that change was subversive and that those who supported change were Communists or **fellow-travelers.**

Responding to fears of Communists within the government and rumors that Republicans might gain political support by calling for legislation to ensure loyalty among government workers, Truman moved to beef up the existing loyalty program. Nine days after his Truman Doctrine speech (March 1947), the president issued Executive Order 9835, establishing the Federal Employee Loyalty Program. Accordingly, after a hearing a federal employee could be fired if "reasonable grounds" existed for believing he or she was disloyal in belief or in actions. Attorney General Tom Clark provided a lengthy list of subversive organizations, and government administrators were instructed to screen their employees for questionable loyalties. Soon more than just screening was taking place: supervisors and workers also began to accuse each other of "un-American" thoughts and activities. Between 1947 and 1951, almost three thousand federal employees were forced to resign, and another three hundred were discharged on the basis of disloyalty. In almost every case, the accused had no right to confront the accusers or to refute evidence. Few of those forced to leave government service were Communists. Fewer still were threats to American security. Truman's loyalty program, despite all the discharges, did little to calm internal fears. Instead it intensified a growing hysteria about an "enemy within."

The Red Scare

Among those stepping forward to protect the nation from the insidious enemy within, none were more vicious than the **House Un-American Activities Committee (HUAC)** and **Joseph McCarthy,** Wisconsin's Republican senator. Working with FBI Director J. Edgar Hoover, HUAC announced in 1947 its intention to root out communism within the government and society. Targeting State Department officials, New Dealers, labor activists, entertainers,

writers, educators, and those with known liberal philosophies, the panel would examine their philosophies and backgrounds. Adding to the fear that Communist agents were active in the United States, FBI Director Hoover proclaimed that there was one American Communist for every 1,814 loyal citizens. Joining in the hysteria, Attorney General Clark cried that Communists were everywhere, "in factories, offices, butcher shops, on street corners, in private businesses—and each carries with him the germs of death for society."

HUAC made its first Cold War splash with its investigation of Hollywood. An enticing target for the headline hunting committee, sure to attract national attention, the movie industry was known to be full of New Deal liberals and Communists. The committee's goals were to remove those with liberal, leftist viewpoints from the entertainment industry and thus to ensure that the mass media promoted American capitalism and traditional American values. Just as World War II had required mobilization of the film industry, committee supporters reasoned, the Cold War necessitated that movies continue to promote the "right" images. With much fanfare, HUAC called Hollywood notables to testify about Communist influence in the industry. Many of those called used the opportunity to strut their patriotism and denounce communism. Ronald Reagan—actor and president of the Screen Actors Guild—denounced Communist methods that "sucked" people into carrying out "red policy without knowing what they are doing" and testified that the Conference of Studio Unions was full of Reds. Not all witnesses were cooperative. Some who were or had been members of the Communist party, including the "Hollywood Ten," took the Fifth Amendment and lashed out at the activities of the committee. Soon labeled "Fifth Amendment Communists," ten were jailed for contempt of Congress and blacklisted by

---

fellow-traveler   Person who sympathizes with or supports the beliefs of the Communist party, without being a member.

House Committee on Un-American Activities   Congressional committee that investigated suspected Communists during the McCarthy era and that Richard Nixon used to advance his career. Created in 1938.

Joseph McCarthy   Senator who began a Communist witch hunt in 1950 that lased until his censure by the Senate in 1954.

♦ Having been investigated by the House Un-American Activities Committee, Hollywood joined the Cold War, producing films that presented wholesome American values and the evils of Communism. *The Red Menace* (1949) claimed to show how the Communists infiltrated American society by preying on the idealistic and disillusioned. At the end of the film, a Texas sheriff nicknamed, Uncle Sam, promised to make things "all right." *Collection of Michael Barson/Past Perfect.*

the industry. President of the Motion Picture Association Eric Johnson announced that no one would be hired who did not cooperate with the committee and that there would be no more films like *The Grapes of Wrath* or *Tobacco Road*, featuring the hardships of poor Americans or "the seamy side of American life." Hollywood soon produced a new code—*A Screen Guide for Americans*—that demanded, "Don't Smear the Free Enterprise System"; "Don't Deify the Common Man"; "Don't Show That Poverty Is a Virtue." Moviemakers responded positively, even producing movies like *Iron Curtain* and *I Was a Communist for the FBI* that exposed the "true evil nature" of communism and the "enemy within."

Anticommunism was in vogue, proving to be a useful weapon for a variety of causes. Manufacturers, including tobacco giant R. J. Reynolds, conducted a massive campaign to inform the nation about the communistic nature of unions, especially the CIO. The multimillion dollar ad blitz successfully harnessed patriotism and anti-Red hysteria both to defeat the CIO's efforts—"Operation Dixie"—to unionize southern industry and to break existing unions throughout the country. Conforming to the anti-Red consensus and protecting itself from further attack after the passage of the Taft-Hartley Act, the CIO expelled eleven unions for having Communist leaders and members. Southerners used anticommunism to fight the civil rights movement. Neighborhoods and communities organized "watch groups" to protect themselves from the subversion of communism. These watch groups screened books, movies, and public speakers, and they questioned teachers and public officials, seeking to ban or dismiss those considered suspect. In Peekskill, New York "loyal" Americans attacked the concert of singer, actor, and activist Paul Robeson, turning it into a riot (see Individual Choices: Paul Robeson). A library in Indiana removed *Robin Hood* from its shelves because it glorified robbing from the rich and giving to the poor.

Just before the election of 1948, HUAC focused on spies within the government, bringing forth a number of informants who had once been Soviet agents and were now willing to name other Americans who allegedly had sold out the United States. The most sensational revelation came from one of the editors of *Time*, repentant ex-Communist named Whittaker Chambers. Chambers accused Alger Hiss of being a Communist. A New Deal liberal and one-time State Department official who had been with Roosevelt at Yalta, Hiss was the perfect target for conservatives and the committee. At the time of the accusation, Hiss was president of the Carnegie Endowment for International Peace.

At first Hiss denied even knowing Chambers, but under questioning by HUAC members, especially Congressman Richard M. Nixon, Hiss admitted an

Alger Hiss State department official accused in 1948 of being a Communist spy; in a climate of anti-Communist hysteria, he was convicted of perjury and sent to prison.

◆ A member of the House Un-American Activities Committee, Congressman Richard M. Nixon gained a national audience by leading the investigation into the allegations that Alger Hiss, one-time New Dealer and State Department official, was a spy for the Soviet Union in the 1930s. In this picture Nixon displays the headline proclaiming Hiss's perjury conviction. The important thing, Nixon later stated, was "we got across the point that Hiss was a spy, a liar, and a Communist." *UPI/Bettmann Archives.*

acquaintance with Chambers in the 1930s, but denied he was or had been a Communist. When Hiss sued for libel, Chambers escalated the charges by stating that Hiss had passed State Department secrets to him in the 1930s. Chambers even produced rolls of microfilm, hidden in a pumpkin, and showed typed copies of the stolen documents—the notorious Pumpkin Papers. In a controversial and sensationalized trial, Hiss was found guilty of **perjury** (the statute of limitations on espionage having expired) and sentenced to five years in prison.

As the nation followed the Hiss case, news of the Communist victory in China and the Soviet explosion of an atomic bomb heightened American fears. In many people's minds, such Communist successes could only have occurred with help from American traitors. Congressman Harold Velde proclaimed, "The Russians undoubtedly gained three to five years in producing the atomic bomb because our government from the White House down has been sympathetic toward the views of Communists and fellow-travelers, with the result that it has been infiltrated by a network of spies. . . . Plainly Congress must act now unless we want to welcome a second Pearl Harbor with open arms." Congress responded

by passing, over Truman's veto, the **McCarran Internal Security Act.** It required all Communists to register with the attorney general and made it a crime to conspire to establish a totalitarian government in the United States. The following year the Supreme Court upheld the Smith Act in *Dennis et al. v. U.S.*, ruling that membership in the Communist party constituted conspiring to overthrow the American government and that no specific act of treason was necessary for conviction.

Congressman Velde's observation about spies seemed proven in February 1950, when English authorities arrested nuclear scientist Klaus Fuchs for passing technical secrets to the Soviet Union. A physicist, Fuchs had worked at Los Alamos, New Mexico, on the American atomic bomb project.

---

perjury   Deliberate giving of false testimony under oath.

McCarran Internal Security Act   1951 law requiring Communists to register with the U.S. Attorney General and making it a crime to conspire to establish a totalitarian government in the United States.

Speaking Out

Paul Robeson

Paul Robeson was a brilliant African-American actor, opera singer, and civil rights activist. By choosing to support Communism, whose principles he thought would further the cause of social equality in this country, he sacrificed his career and everything else for which he had worked. National Portrait Gallery, Smithsonian Institute/Art Resource, NY.

Paul Leroy Bustill Robeson was exceptional at nearly everything he did. A scholar-athlete, he earned several varsity letters and was named an All-American in football before graduating Phi Beta Kappa from Rutgers in 1919—only its third black graduate. He attended Columbia School of Law and played professional football on weekends to cover living expenses. In 1922, Robeson took his first acting role in a play staged by the Harlem YMCA. He received his law degree the following year, but believing he could do more for African-Americans as an actor than a lawyer, he returned to the theater as an actor and concert singer. Working with playwright Eugene O'Neill, Robeson was cast as the lead in the Broadway production of O'Neill's *The Emperor Jones* and in his controversial new play about interracial marriage, *All God's Chillun Got Wings*. Critics wrote rave reviews and Robeson was soon one of the most sought-after actors in the United States and Britain. But more than an entertainer, he was an activist—choosing to advocate equal rights, especially for blacks. "The artist must elect to fight for freedom or for slavery. I have made my choice," he explained.

In fighting for freedom, Paul Robeson walked picket lines for striking workers, demonstrated against lynchings and segregation, and refused to work on any stage that practiced segregation. In 1939, he announced

Fuchs named an American accomplice, Harry Gold, who in turn named David Greenglass, an army sergeant at Los Alamos. Greenglass then claimed that his sister Ethel and her husband Julius Rosenberg, current or former members of the Communist party, were part of the Soviet atomic spy ring. The prosecution alleged that the information obtained and passed on by the Rosenbergs was largely responsible for the successful Soviet atomic bomb. The Rosenbergs claimed innocence, but based on testimony of Gold and Greenglass, they were convicted of espionage and executed in 1953.

Joseph McCarthy and the Politics of Loyalty

Feeding on the furor over the enemy within, Senator Joseph McCarthy of Wisconsin emerged at the forefront of the anticommunist movement. McCarthy

he would no longer act in movies because the film industry did not allow him to show "the life or express the . . . interests, hopes, and aspirations of the struggling people from whom I come." Also in the 1930s, he spoke out loudly against fascism, entertaining Republican troops in Spain and raising money for Jewish refugees from Nazism. In 1934, he visited the Soviet Union and was impressed with Soviet social equality. "I feel like a human being for the first time. . . . Here I am not a Negro but a human being." He told Soviet filmmaker Sergei Eisenstein, "Here . . . I walk in full human dignity."

Despite his activism and his support of liberal causes and the Soviet Union, Robeson's popularity continued to soar, as he performed before thousands in the United States and Europe and broke racial barriers everywhere. In 1942, he became the first African-American in modern American theater to be cast as Othello. During World War II, he campaigned for war bonds and toured the European theater in the first integrated USO show. But not everyone was tolerant. Even as he patriotically pushed war bonds, the FBI listed his name on its Detain Communist List (DetComList).

With the onset of the Cold War, Robeson's views, especially his refusal to condemn the Soviet Union and its policies, became unacceptable to most Americans and effectively ended his artistic career. Considering him a Communist, the mayor of Peoria, Illinois, canceled his concert in 1947. And in 1949, over a hundred fans were injured in Peeksill, New York, when an anti-Robeson, anti-Communist mob attacked those who came to hear him. The Peeksill riot was a direct outcome of his statement that blacks would not fight against the Soviet Union "on behalf of those who have oppressed us for generations." From over $100,000 in 1946, his income fell to under $6,000 by 1949.

Considering Robeson an undesirable representative of the country, the State Department took away his passport in 1950. For the next eight years, Robeson was a prisoner in the United States until the Supreme Court upheld his right as a citizen to travel. Free again, he left for Europe. He also published his autobiography, *Here I Stand*, proclaiming that civil rights should become a mass movement, independent of whites, and urging blacks to become aware of their African heritage.

Ill, he returned from Europe in 1963 and retired in virtual seclusion. By the seventies, however, Paul Robeson was again popular, recognized and appreciated for his great talents and—despite great personal costs—his advocacy of civil and social rights. At a Carnegie Hall celebration of his 75th birthday, Coretta King, widow of slain civil rights leader Martin Luther King, Jr. (see page 887), remarked that Robeson "had been buried alive because . . . he had tapped the . . . wells of latent militancy among blacks." Unable to attend the gala affair, Robeson sent a simple message from the lyrics of "Old Man River," a song he had sung in the 1936 musical *Show Boat*:

"You can be sure that in my heart I go on singing:
But I keeps laughin' instead of cryin';
I must keep fightin' until I'm dyin'
And Ol' Man River, he just keeps rollin' along!"

entered the public arena as a candidate for Congress following World War II. Running for the Senate in 1946, he invented a glorious war record for himself that included the nickname "Tail-gunner Joe" and several wounds—even walking with a fake limp—to help him win the election. As a senator, he was regarded by some as among the worst in Washington—available to lobbyists, without principles, and absent most of the time. In February 1950, he was looking for an issue on which to focus in his re-election bid. After conferring with friends, he settled on the internal Communist threat as an issue "with sex appeal."

The senator tried his gambit first in Wheeling, West Virginia. He announced to a Republican women's group that the United States was losing the Cold War because of traitors within the government. After naming several of them, he claimed to know of 205 Communists working in the State Department. In Denver, en route to his next speech in

Salt Lake City, the senator told a few curious reporters that in reality he had a list of "207 bad risks" in the State Department but that the list was in his baggage on the plane. As he crossed the country, McCarthy changed the number of people on his list but continued to hammer away at security risks, traitors that he could prove existed in the State Department. In Salt Lake City, the number was reduced to "57 card-carrying members of the Communist party," who actually made policy within the State Department. At the Reno airport, he faced a large crowd of reporters anxious for proof. He produced no names and no list for the reporters.

McCarthy's accusations were quickly examined by a Senate committee and shown to be at best inaccurate. When the chair of the committee, Democrat Millard Tydings, pronounced McCarthy a hoax and a fraud, the Wisconsin senator countered by accusing Tydings of questionable loyalty. During Tyding's 1950 re-election campaign, McCarthy worked for his defeat, spreading false stories and pictures that supposedly showed connections to American Communists, including a faked photograph showing the Democrat talking to Earl Browder, head of the American Communist party. When Tydings lost by forty thousand votes, McCarthy's stature swelled. Republicans and conservative Democrats rarely opposed him and frequently supported his wild accusations. The Senate's most powerful Republican, Robert Taft, slapped McCarthy on the back saying, "Keep it up, Joe," and sent him the names of State Department officials who merited investigation. Taft encouraged him, "If one case doesn't work out, bring up another."

The outbreak of the Korean War and the reversals at the hands of the Chinese only increased the senator's popularity. The nation was ripe for McCarthy's aggressive style and he quickly emerged as a national hero. Supported by Republican political gains in the 1950 elections, **McCarthyism** became a powerful political and social force. Politicians flocked to the anti-Communist bandwagon, making it ever more difficult for Truman to push his Fair Deal. Federal Trade Commissioner John Carson despaired that liberals "were on the run" and that reactionaries were "winning the fight."

By 1952, Truman's popularity was almost nonexistent: only 24 percent of those asked approved of his presidency. The Korean Conflict was stalemated, and Republicans were having a field day attacking "cowardly containment" and calling for victory in Korea. The Fair Deal was dead and Truman had

lost control over domestic policy. Compounding his problems, a probe of organized crime by a congressional committee chaired by Senator **Estes Kefauver** had found scandal, corruption, and links to organized crime within the government. Presidential aide Harry Vaughan and other administration appointees were accused of accepting gifts and selling their influence. When Truman lost the opening presidential primary in New Hampshire to Kefauver, he withdrew from the race, leaving the Democrats with no clear choice for a candidate. As in 1948, Republicans looked to the November election with great anticipation. At last, they were sure, voters would elect a Republican president—someone who, in Thomas Dewey's opinion, would "save the country from going to Hades in the handbasket of paternalism-socialism-dictatorship."

McCarthyism Attacks on suspected Communists in the early 1950s by Joseph McCarthy and others, which were often based on unsupported assertions and carried out without regard for basic liberties.

Estes Kefauver Tennessee legislator who chaired a series of Senate hearings that exposed nationwide crime syndicates with links to state and local political

---

SUMMARY

E xpectations
C onstraints
C hoices
O utcomes

People hoped that the end of World War II would usher in a period of international cooperation and peace. This *expectation* vanished as the world entered a period of armed and vigilant suspicion called the Cold War. To protect the country and the world from Soviet expansion, the United States *chose* to assume a primary economic, political, and military role around the globe. The *outcome* was Truman's containment policy. First applied to Western Europe, it eventually included Asia as the Cold War became a hot war in Korea. By 1952, with the "loss" of China and the stalemate in Korea, Americans turned against Truman's foreign policy. Many thought that the United States was losing the Cold War and that containment was not a strong enough policy to defeat communism and protect American interests.

At home the Cold War had its impact as well, acting as a *constraint* on the expansion of liberalism. Many, moderates and conservatives alike, *chose* to use the fear of communism to promote their own political, social, and economic interests. They attacked liberals, unions, and civil rights advocates as radicals, fellow-travelers, and Communists. Economic prosperity also reduced public support for further growth of the New Deal as postwar Americans turned their attention toward enjoying the "good life." Politically the *outcome* was that although some existing New Deal–style programs—social security,

a minimum wage, and farm supports—grew in scope, initiatives, like civil rights and national health care, that would have enlarged the federal government's domestic role were rejected.

As Americans adjusted to postwar life, one of the major *outcomes* was a re-emphasis on home and family. Women experienced strong social pressure to give up their wartime jobs and responsibilities and take up "domestic" life. Marriages and births rose as many Americans *chose* to move to suburbs. While jobs and homeownership multiplied for white males and white families seemed poised to achieve the American dream, minorities found that the *constraints* of discrimination ended or limited many of the economic and social gains they had made during the war. Although pushed out of the work force or into lesser jobs, and still living in a socially segregated society, many non-whites, joined by some white women, *chose* to resist being cast in customary roles.

SUGGESTED READINGS

Bernstein, Barton. *Politics and Policies of the Truman Administration* (1970).

An excellent collection of essays on the Truman administration from a generally critical point of view.

Gaddis, John L. *The United States and the Origins of the Cold War* (1972).

A comprehensive and balanced view of the origins of the Cold War.

Hastings, Max. *The Korean War* (1987).

A short and readable study of the military dimension of the Korean War.

McCullough, David. *Truman* (1992).

A highly acclaimed, readable biography of Truman.

Reeves, Thomas. *The Life and Times of Joe McCarthy* (1982).

A solid, but critical study of Joseph McCarthy and his role in the Red Scare.

Theoharis, Athan. *Seeds of Repression: Harry S. Truman and the Origins of McCarthyism* (1971).

An examination of the causes of the Red Scare and Truman's role in contributing to it.

Tygiel, Jules. *Baseball's Great Experiment: Jackie Robinson and his Legacy* (1983).

Reflections on the life and decisions that brought Jackie Robinson to break the color barrier in professional baseball.

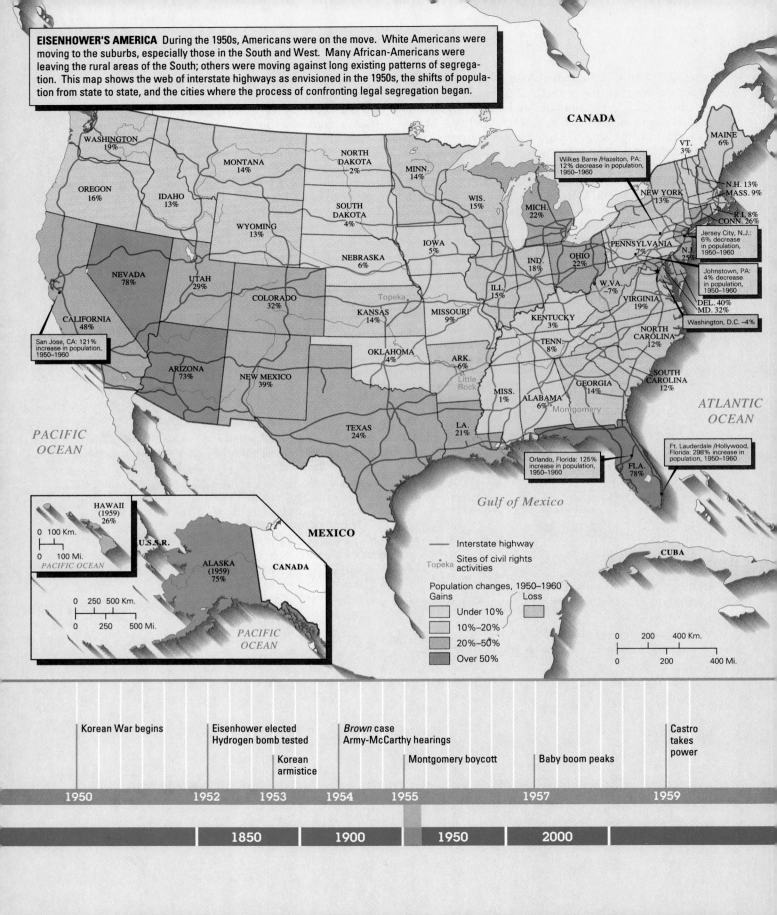

EISENHOWER'S AMERICA During the 1950s, Americans were on the move. White Americans were moving to the suburbs, especially those in the South and West. Many African-Americans were leaving the rural areas of the South; others were moving against long existing patterns of segregation. This map shows the web of interstate highways as envisioned in the 1950s, the shifts of population from state to state, and the cities where the process of confronting legal segregation began.

CANADA

WASHINGTON 19%
MONTANA 14%
NORTH DAKOTA 2%
MINN. 14%
MAINE 6%
VT. 3%

OREGON 16%
IDAHO 13%
SOUTH DAKOTA 4%
WIS. 15%
MICH. 22%
NEW YORK 13%
N.H. 13%
MASS. 9%
R.I. 8%
CONN. 26%

WYOMING 13%
IOWA 5%
PENNSYLVANIA 7%
N.J. 25%

NEVADA 78%
UTAH 29%
COLORADO 32%
NEBRASKA 6%
IND. 18%
OHIO 22%
W.VA. –7%
VIRGINIA 19%
DEL. 40%
MD. 32%

CALIFORNIA 48%
KANSAS 14%
MISSOURI 9%
ILL. 15%
KENTUCKY 3%
NORTH CAROLINA 12%
Topeka

ARIZONA 73%
NEW MEXICO 39%
OKLAHOMA 4%
ARK. –6%
TENN. 8%
Little Rock
GEORGIA 14%
SOUTH CAROLINA 12%

TEXAS 24%
MISS. 1%
ALABAMA 6%
LA. 21%
Montgomery
FLA. 78%

Wilkes Barre /Hazelton, PA: 12% decrease in population, 1950–1960

Jersey City, N.J.: 6% decrease in population, 1950–1960

Johnstown, PA: 4% decrease in population, 1950–1960

Washington, D.C. –4%

San Jose, CA: 121% increase in population, 1950–1960

Orlando, Florida: 125% increase in population, 1950–1960

Ft. Lauderdale /Hollywood, Florida: 298% increase in population, 1950–1960

ATLANTIC OCEAN

PACIFIC OCEAN

Gulf of Mexico

CUBA

HAWAII (1959) 26%
0   100 Km.
0   100 Mi.
PACIFIC OCEAN

U.S.S.R.
MEXICO

ALASKA (1959) 75%
CANADA
0   250   500 Km.
0   250   500 Mi.
PACIFIC OCEAN

— Interstate highway

Topeka   Sites of civil rights activities

Population changes, 1950–1960
Gains   Loss

Under 10%
10%–20%
20%–50%
Over 50%

0   200   400 Km.
0   200   400 Mi.

Korean War begins | 1950
Eisenhower elected
Hydrogen bomb tested | 1952
Korean armistice | 1953
Brown case
Army-McCarthy hearings | 1954
Montgomery boycott | 1955
Baby boom peaks | 1957
Castro takes power | 1959

1950   1952   1953   1954   1955   1957   1959

1850   1900   1950   2000

28

Quest for Consensus, 1952–1960

The Best of Times

- During the 1950s, what expectations reflected the American dream and which ones conflicted with it?

- What choices were people making as they tried to fulfill their expectations?

Politics of Consensus

- What constraints did Eisenhower and other Republicans encounter in trying to roll back the New Deal, and how did the outcome reflect what Eisenhower called the "middle path"?

Seeking Civil Rights

- How did African-American leaders choose to attack *de jure* segregation in American society during Eisenhower's administration?

Eisenhower and a Hostile World

- What expectations and constraints lay behind Eisenhower's foreign policy choices, and how did the New Look differ from Truman's foreign policy?

INTRODUCTION

E xpectations
C onstraints
C hoices
O utcomes

In 1952, Republicans represented change. A victory by Dwight David Eisenhower would end twenty years of Democratic control of the White House and would, many Republicans believed, reverse two "dangerous" trends: creeping socialism in the form of the New Deal and appeasement of communism in the guise of containment. Most people in the nation *expected* an Eisenhower presidency and a Republican Congress to end the Korean War, to re-emphasize individual freedoms, to reduce government intervention in social and economic affairs, to expand prosperity by supporting capitalism, and to win some victories in the Cold War. But most of all, Americans *expected* to enjoy their lives to the fullest, in the strongest, most democratic, and most prosperous nation in the world.

The United States of the 1950s seemed to justify this expectation. The country was experiencing one of the longest periods of sustained economic growth in its history, one that—in most people's opinion—offered every citizen an opportunity to live free from the fear of economic want. This affluent America matched the image of a gentle and quiet president who presided over a prosperous nation composed of families that *chose* a stable, suburban life in which the husband worked and the wife raised their children.

For a large segment of the population, this America was real, but there was another America—one with constraints that narrowed the *choices* available. Prosperity did not touch all Americans. Nor were all Americans, even those in the suburbs, leading happy, stable, or fulfilling lives. Many men and women were dissatisfied with their roles as husband and father, wife and mother, and *chose* other forms of social and personal expression. An increasing number of wives entered the work place by choice or, more often, by necessity. Dissatisfaction also seemed to strike American youths, many of whom chose to reject the values of suburban culture, turning to the driving rhythms of rock 'n' roll and displaying antisocial behavior. At the same time, intellectual and cultural critics condemned the sameness and lack of vitality of the suburban culture. The *outcome* was an American society growing fragmented by economic and social realities that fed into differing *expectations*.

For minorities in 1950, the *constraints* against achieving the American dream appeared insurmountable. Poverty, prejudice, and segregation remained the norm. But some groups nurtured *expectations* of change that would open new *choices*. By mid-decade, armed with a renewed commitment and a Supreme Court decision, African-Americans were tearing down barriers that blocked their access to the American dream. The *outcome* was a civil rights movement that attacked existing social and legal restrictions and forced government, political parties, and society to confront long-standing contradictions in the country's democratic image.

Like the decade of the 1950s itself, President Eisenhower was more complex than people commonly realized at the time. On the surface "Ike" seemed to live up to the popular joke: "What happens when you wind up an Eisenhower doll?"— "Absolutely nothing!" But the real Eisenhower was an effective behind-the-scenes leader who recognized that a political and social consensus accepted the structure of government as shaped by the New Deal. Faced with this *constraint* on any effort to dismantle New Deal–style programs, he *chose* to modify them by cutting spending and reducing government regulations where possible.

In foreign policy, Eisenhower made similar *choices*. He chose to maintain the basic strategy of containment, placing new areas of the globe under an American nuclear umbrella. *Constrained* by his desire to balance the budget, he adopted the New Look, stressing use of atomic weapons, the air force, alliances, and covert activities as foreign policy tools. Thus, responding to political and international constraints established by the Great Depression, World War II, and the Truman years, Eisenhower shaped an *outcome* built on existing patterns of domestic and foreign policy rather than initiate new ones.

CHRONOLOGY

The Fifties

1948 Kinsey's *Sexual Behavior in the Human Male*

1950 Korean War begins
Riesman's *The Lonely Crowd*

1951 Salinger's *Catcher in the Rye*
Mattachine Society formed
Freed's "Moondog's Rock 'n' Roll Party"

1952 Eisenhower elected president
Eisenhower visits Korea
Hydrogen bomb tested

1953 Korean armistice at Panmunjom
Mossadeq overthrown in Iran
Stalin dies
McCarthy investigates USIA and Voice of America
Kinsey's *Sexual Behavior in the Human Female*
Termination policy for American Indians implemented
Warren appointed chief justice
Father Knows Best debuts on television
Playboy published

1954 *Brown v. Board of Education*
St. Lawrence Seaway Act
Federal budget balanced
Rosenbergs executed for treason
Army–McCarthy hearings
Arbenz overthrown in Guatemala
Quemoy-Matsu crisis
Nasser assumes power in Egypt
Battle of Dienbienphu
Geneva Agreement (Vietnam)
SEATO founded

1955 Murder of Emmett Till
Montgomery bus boycott
Salk vaccine approved for use
AFL-CIO merger
Warsaw Pact
McDonald's opens in California
Blackboard Jungle debuts
Geneva Summit
Eisenhower's Open Skies proposal

1956 Federal (Interstate) Highway Act
Gayle et al. v. Browser
Southern Christian Leadership Conference formed
Eisenhower re-elected
Suez crisis
Soviets invade Hungary
Ginsburg's *Howl*
Metalious's *Peyton Place*
Presley's "Heartbreak Hotel" recorded

1957 Little Rock crisis
Civil Rights Act
Baghdad Pact
Eisenhower Doctrine
Sputnik I launched
Kerouac's *On the Road*
Shute's *On the Beach*
Baby boom peaks at 4.3 million births

1958 Demonstrators attack Nixon in Latin America
Berlin crisis
U.S. troops to Lebanon
Second Quemoy-Matsu crisis
CENTO formed
National Defense Education Act
NASA established
Nuclear test moratorium

1959 Castro overthrows Batista in Cuba
Alaska and Hawaii become states
Khrushchev visits United States
Cooper v. Aaron

1960 Soviets shoot down U-2 and capture pilot
Paris Summit

The Best of Times

• During the 1950s, what expectations reflected the American dream and which ones conflicted with it?

• What choices were people making as they tried to fulfill their expectations?

According to *Reader's Digest,* in 1954 the average American male stood 5 feet 9 inches tall and weighed 158 pounds. He liked brunettes, baseball, bowling, and steak and french fries. In seeking a wife he could not decide if brains or beauty was more important, but he definitely wanted a wife who could efficiently run a home. The average female was 5 feet 4 inches tall and weighed 132 pounds. She preferred marriage to career, but she wanted to remove the word *obey* from her marriage vows. Both were enjoying life to the fullest, according to the *Digest,* and buying more of nearly everything. The economy appeared to be bursting at the seams, providing jobs, good wages, a multitude of products, and profits.

The nation's "easy street" was a product of big government, big business, and an expanding population. World War II and the Cold War had created military-industrial-governmental linkages that primed the economy through government spending. National security needs by 1955 accounted for half of the U.S. budget, equaling 17 percent of the gross national product, and exceeded more than the total net incomes of all American corporations. The connection between government and business went beyond spending, though. Government officials and corporate managers moved back and forth in a vast web of jobs and directorships. Few saw any real conflict of interests. Eisenhower's cabinet was said to be composed of "eight millionaires and a plumber," and the plumber, Secretary of Labor Martin P. Durkin, soon resigned. Frequently, cabinet positions and regulatory agencies were staffed by people from the businesses to be regulated. Secretary of Defense Charles E. Wilson had been the president of General Motors and voiced the common view: "What was good for our country was good for General Motors and vice versa."

Direct military spending was only one aspect of governmental involvement in the economy. Federal research and development (R&D) funds flowed into colleges and industries, producing not only new scientific and military technology but a variety of marketable consumer goods. Polyester fabrics—dacron, orlon, and rayon—had begun as wartime innovations but soon were converted into textiles for civil-

◆ In the popular culture of the 1950s, one of the most memorable events in any young person's life was the high school prom. Here, on this cover of the *Saturday Evening Post,* painted in 1957 by Norman Rockwell, is a young man in his tuxedo and a young woman in her prom dress having an after-prom milkshake at the local diner. Is that Dad behind the counter? *Courtesy of the Norman Rockwell Family Trust and Curtis Archives.*

ian clothing. Teflon and "silly putty" were products of aircraft research. On an international level, American foreign aid programs provided billions of dollars with which foreign countries bought American goods.

Technological advances, especially in the field of automation, also increased profits and productivity. Profits doubled between 1948 and 1958, with 574 of the largest corporations making nearly 53 percent of all business income. At the same time, over 4,000 mergers took place. In the steel, automobile, and aircraft industries, fewer workers used new technology to produce more goods, contributing to an overall decline in the industrial work force. Faced with these diminishing numbers, organized labor showed almost no growth as union membership remained at about 16 million workers. Agricultural and white-collar workers remained unorganized, and unions made little effort to organize the economically booming Sunbelt. Instead, they focused on getting better pensions, cost-of-living raises, and paid vacations for their members. Another consequence of declining union rolls was the merger of the AFL and the CIO in 1955 under the leadership of George Meany. But membership continued to fall and within four years unionized workers had dropped from 35.5 percent in 1950 to 31.4 percent of the work force by 1955.

Despite the downturn in union membership and industrial jobs, for most Americans, jobs and good wages were available—especially in an expanding number of white-collar jobs. Except for brief **recessions** in 1953 and 1958, when unemployment reached 8 percent, employment remained around 95 percent throughout the 1950s. On average, industrial wages rose from about $55 a week in 1950 to $72 in 1960. But not everyone benefited from the growing economy. Expanding opportunities in management and sales went almost exclusively to whites. Unemployment for minorities remained at about 10 percent, and their wages failed to keep pace with inflation. Those able to reach the fruits of prosperity, however, could enjoy the comfortable lifestyle associated with the American dream.

Suburban and Consumer Culture

During the fifties, the popular and common images of American life were the suburb and prosperity. People wanted to live in the suburbs, and between 1945 and 1960 business and government promoted the building of over 14 million single-family homes. All levels of government helped, some by passing legislation and others by pouring money into projects that made suburbs possible. The Veteran's Administration and Federal Housing Administration (FHA) (see page 775) underwrote thousands of loans for single-family homes. **Zoning laws** were changed to ease construction of tract housing developments and shopping centers. States, counties, and communities spent millions of dollars on thousands of miles of roads to connect the workplaces, schools, parks, and shopping centers to suburban homes. Along with the streets went water systems, electricity, and sewer systems. On the national level, the **Federal Highway Act** of 1956 provided $32 billion over thirteen years to build a national highway system. Originally projected to involve 41,000 miles of federal highway, by 1980 there were 33,796 miles of interstate open to traffic, but the cost had nearly tripled.

As Americans sought the pleasant life of suburbia, the urban core deteriorated at an accelerating rate. Shrinking tax bases, eroded by departing homeowners, businesses, and shoppers, made it increasing difficult for cities to afford to maintain services, buildings, and mass transportation. Increased automobile traffic damaged roads, left railroad stations largely deserted and in disrepair, and added to

First it warms your heart... *(That Thunderbird Styling!)*

Then it reads your mind... *(That Trigger-Torque Power!)*

'55 **Ford**

◆ In the 1950s, American society was shaped by the automobile. From the bursting suburbs, Americans took to roads and freeways, going to shopping malls, drive-in restaurants, the very first McDonald's, and to ever-popular drive-in movies. Cars were both status symbols and necessities, as the American people ordered their days—and nights—around the car. *Collection of Picture Research Consultants.*

noise and air pollution. Programs to rebuild homes in cities rarely succeeded in meeting the needs of the poor who increasingly made up the urban core's population.

The automobile industry benefited from and contributed to the development of both roads and suburbs. By 1960, 75 percent of all Americans had at least one car, increasing the pressure on governments and businesses to consider the needs of automobile owners. Stores had to include parking lots and easy access to roads and highways as part of their planning. New industries arose to service the needs of automobile-borne consumers—amusement parks like Disneyland, miniature golf courses, drive-in theaters, and fast-food restaurants. McDonald's, franchised in San Bernardino, California in 1955 by

---

recession   A decline in the economy that is less severe than a depression.

zoning laws   Local regulations that limit particular types of buildings, such as residences, businesses, or factories, to specified sections of a city or town.

Federal Highway Act   1956 law appropriating $32 billion for the construction of federal and interstate highways.

TABLE 28.1   CONSUMER PRICES, JULY 1955

Food		Other	
Rye Bread	$ .20 a loaf	Kodak Brownie camera	$ 13.65
Apples	.19 for 2 pounds	Portable, B & W 14-inch	
Bananas	.15 a pound	television set	120.00
Round steak	.70 a pound	Refrigerator	519.95
Chicken fryers	.49 a pound	Oldsmobile 88 automobile	2381.62
Wheaties	.43 for two boxes	"Scrabble" game	2.39
Clorox	.19 a bottle		
Coffee	.91 a pound		
Instant coffee	1.49 for 6 ounces		
Margarine (oleo)	.45 for 2 pounds		
Sugar	.49 for 5 pounds		
Flour	.95 for 10 pounds		
Frozen orange juice	1.00 for 8, 6 ounce cans		
Frozen fishsticks	.39 for 8 ounces		
Lifebuoy soap	.28 for 3 cakes		
Milk	.23 a quart		

Source: *Observer-Reporter*, Washington, PA, July 1955.

entrepreneur Ray Kroc, sold a standardized hamburger for 15 cents and changed the eating habits of America.

The suburban market was a result of expanding purchasing power made possible by higher wages and ready credit. Why pay cash when consumer credit was available? The Diner's Club credit card made its debut in 1950 and was soon followed by American Express and a host of other plastic cards. Credit purchases leaped from $8.4 billion in 1946 to over $44 billion in 1958. To enjoy the "good life," Americans were not only buying "necessities" like washing machines, cars, and televisions, but an ever-expanding array of other products: high fidelity record players and records, patio furniture, and toys and recreational equipment (see Table 28.1). Many of these non-essential items, and even some of the basic goods, incorporated a new dimension of marketing—**planned obsolescence,** in which a product is designed to be discarded and replaced by a newer model within a short period of time. The automobile industry was especially good at changing styles or adding gadgets to cars every few years to encourage people to trade in their old model for a new and better one.

To sell their products, Madison Avenue continued to use images of youth, glamour, sex appeal, and sophistication. In the forefront of the advertising onslaught was the tobacco industry, persuading people that smoking cigarettes was a stylish way to relax from the rigors of work and family. In one television commercial, Fred Flintstone and Barney Rubble, two Stone Age cartoon characters, escape housework and their nagging wives by slipping behind the house to enjoy a cigarette. When medical reports surfaced about health risks connected to smoking, the tobacco giants intensified their advertising and stressed that new, longer, filtered cigarettes were milder and posed no health hazard. Cigarette advertising increased 400 percent between 1945 and 1960, whereas advertising in general increased "only" a little more than 250 percent.

Family Culture

With or without Madison Avenue ads, many Americans were sure that they were living in the best of all possible times. At the center of those feelings lay the economy, the home, the family, and the church. Religion, with an emphasis on family life, enjoyed a new popularity in the 1950s, reflecting President Eisenhower's view that "everybody

---

planned obsolescence   Practice of designing consumer goods to last or be fashionable for only a short time, guaranteeing purchase of a replacement.

should have a religious faith." Church attendance rose to 59.5 percent in 1953, a historic high. Religious leaders were rated as the most important members of society, with those who used television to reach huge audiences among the most respected and popular. None were more esteemed than the reverends Billy Graham and **Norman Vincent Peale** and Catholic bishop Fulton J. Sheen. They and others captivated millions with messages that were full of positive, religious, patriotic, and anti-Communist pronouncements. In 1954, Peale was named one of the nation's ten most successful salesmen. In spirit with the times, Congress added "under God" to the Pledge of Allegiance in 1954, and "In God We Trust" to all American currency in 1955. Not all church leaders were pleased with being regarded as salesmen. Some theologians and philosophers like Reinhold Neibuhr and Paul Tillich worried that the public's rush to religion was for the wrong reasons—that churches were guilty of softening their theology to attract parishioners and that Americans selected their churches more on the basis of the music and activities than the religious teaching.

Filling the churches and homes were increasingly affluent families of the fifties. After the disruptions of Depression and war, family took on a renewed importance. The divorce rate slowed and the numbers of marriages and births climbed—the baby boom continued (see page 855). The popular image of the ideal place for women was in the home raising children. Those not anxious to rush into wedded bliss were suspected of being homosexual, emotionally immature, too involved in a career, or just irresponsible. Career women frequently were thought of as neurotic and masculine, whereas wives and mothers were considered content. For guidance on how to raise babies and children, millions of Americans turned to Dr. Benjamin Spock's popular book *Baby and Child Care.* A mother's love and positive parental examples were seen as keys to raising healthy and well-adjusted children. Strict rules and corporal punishment were to be avoided. Equally widespread was the view that, to ensure proper sex identity among children, boys should participate in sports and outdoor activities, and girls should be complimented on their dress and hair and given opportunities to develop domestic skills. Toy guns and doctor bags were for boys; dolls, tea sets, and nurse kits were for girls. As in the case of their parents, fitting in—being part of the group—was important, as was membership in such social organizations as the Boy Scouts and Girl Scouts. At college, many students became part of the **silent generation,** enjoying

♦ "No jingles to write . . . no boxtops to mail!"—just enter and win a chunk of the American dream, as the "new and improved" Wheaties offered everyone a chance to enjoy life to the fullest in the "great outdoors" by winning the products in this picture. From a 16-foot boat, to golf clubs, and charcoal brazier, what family's life would not be enriched by owning these symbols of affluent America? *Collection of Picture Research Consultants.*

the social life of college that centered around fraternities and sock hops, and hoping for corporate jobs and marriage after graduation. A college dean described the perfect student as one who had "an 80 or 85 average . . . and plenty of extracurricular activities." This educator had little use for the "brilliant introvert."

The home was the center of "togetherness," a term defined in 1954 by *McCall's* as the modern partnership of husbands and wives who shared housework and shopping and catered to their children's needs and desires. Popular television shows like *Leave It to Beaver* (1957) and *Father Knows Best* (1953) reflected that togetherness and presented the ideal middle-class family. The TV families were always white, living in all white neighborhoods, with hard-working fathers and attractive, savvy mothers who always knew the right steps to take to solve the weekly problem. Their children, who usually numbered between two and four, did well in school,

Norman Vincent Peale   Minister who told his congregations that positive thinking could help them overcome all their troubles in life.

silent generation   Name applied to the young people who came of age in the 1950s because of their perceived complacency and lack of political involvement.

were not overly concerned about the future, and provided the usually humorous dilemmas that Mom's common sense and sensitivity untangled. Reality, however, rarely matched *McCall's* or television's images.

Another View of Suburbia

Unlike the wives shown on television, more and more married women were working, many even though they had young children. Some desired careers, but the majority worked to ensure their family's existing **standard of living.** The percentage of middle-class women working rose from 7 percent in 1950 to 25 percent in 1960, most finding jobs in part-time or sales clerk and clerical positions that paid low wages and provided few benefits (see Figure 28.1). Women represented 46 percent of the banking work force—filling most secretary, teller, and receptionist slots—but held only 15 percent of upper-level positions.

Nor were all homemakers happy. Togetherness was more of an ideal than a reality. A study of husband and wife cooperation found that of eighteen household chores, men were willing to lock up at night, do yard work, and make repairs—leaving fifteen other routine tasks to the woman. Other surveys discovered that more than one-fifth of suburban wives were unhappy with their marriages and lives. Many women complained of the drudgery and boredom of housework and the lack of understanding and affection from their husband. Women were also more sexually active than generally thought, shattering the image of loyal wife and mother. **Alfred Kinsey**'s research on women's sexuality, *Sexual Behavior in the Human Female* (1953), indicated that a majority of American women not only had had sexual intercourse before marriage, but that 25 percent were having affairs while married.

Men also showed signs of being less than satisfied with the popular role of suburban Dad. In 1953, Hugh Hefner first published *Playboy,* urging men to break away from the boring middle-class, husband-father image and cater to their own pleasures. The growing popularity of *Playboy* and other "men's magazines" signaled that many men were, in thought if not in practice, rejecting togetherness. Reflecting the shadier side of middle-class life in fiction, the best-selling novel *Peyton Place* by Grace Metalious (1956) set America buzzing over the licentious escapades of the residents of a quiet town in traditionally staid New England. Hollywood kept pace with stars like **Marilyn Monroe.** In a series of movies starting in 1952, the "blonde bombshell" was repeatedly cast in slightly dumb but very sexy roles, in which she was usually romanced by slightly older, more worldly men. A newspaper was relieved to find that, after returning from acting in England, she had not changed, that she was still "the same . . . love goddess that millions of American men have dreams of sharing a small island with."

Monroe and other sex symbols in the movies and men's magazines represented a minor threat to the image of family, community, and nation. Homosexuality, however, was another matter. In many people's minds, it threatened the moral and social fabric of the society. Kinsey's 1948 study of male sexuality shocked readers by claiming that nearly 8 percent of the population lived a gay lifestyle and that a much larger percentage of the male population had experienced some sort of homosexual experience. Not only was homosexuality widespread, according to Kinsey, but it existed throughout American society. To those observing the homosexual community, his findings were clearly reflected in a more open gay subculture that centered around gay bars in every major city.

In a postwar society that emphasized the traditional family and feared internal subversion, homosexuals represented a double threat. After a government official admitted in 1950 that many of those dismissed from the government were homosexuals, the Republican national chairman warned that "sexual perverts . . . have infiltrated our Government" and were "as dangerous as . . . Communists." A Senate investigating committee concluded that because of sexual perversions and lack of moral fiber, one homosexual could "pollute a Government office." Responding to such views, the Eisenhower administration barred homosexuals from most government jobs. Taking their cue from the federal government, state and local authorities intensified their efforts to control and, if possible, purge homo-

---

standard of living Level of material comfort as measured by the goods, services, and luxuries currently available.

Alfred Kinsey Biologist whose studies of human sexuality attracted great attention in the 1940s and 1950s, especially for his conclusions on infidelity and homosexuality.

Marilyn Monroe American actress who became an icon, famous for her blonde hair, her sex appeal, and her vulnerability; she died in 1962, at the age of 36.

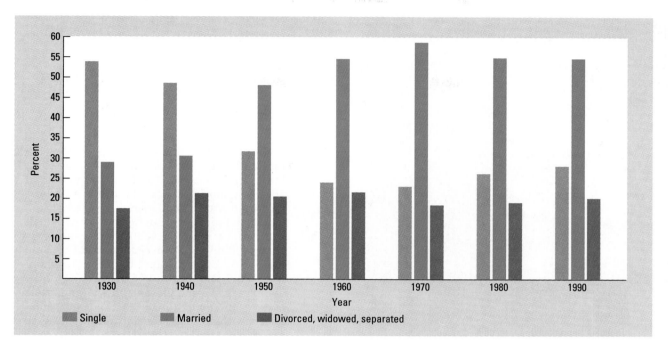

◆ **FIGURE 28.1 Working Women, 1930–1990**   This figure shows the percentage of women in the work force from the Great Depression through 1990. While the number of women who fall into the category of divorced, widowed, and separated has remained fairly constant, there has been a significant shift in the number of single and married women in the work force, with the number of single women declining as the number of married women increased.   *Source:* U.S. Department of Commerce, *Historical Statistics of the United States, Colonial Times to 1970,* Vol. I (Washington, D.C.: U.S. Government Printing Office, 1970), pp. 20–21, 131–132; and U.S. Department of Commerce, *Statistics of the United States, 1993* (Washington, D.C.: U.S. Government Printing Office, 1993), pp. 74, 399.

sexuals from society. **Vice squads** made frequent raids on gay and lesbian bars and newspapers frequently listed the names, addresses, and employers of those arrested. In response to the virulent attacks, many took extra efforts to hide their homosexuality, but some organized to confront the attacks. In Los Angeles, Henry Hay formed the Mattachine Society in 1951 to fight for homosexual rights, claiming that gays were an oppressed minority. In San Francisco in 1955, Del Martin and Phyllis Lyon organized a similar organization for lesbians, the Daughters of Bilitis.

Gay and lesbian lifestyles appeared to the majority of Americans to reject traditional values of family and community and therefore could be dismissed and even suppressed. But there were others whose critiques of American society were difficult to reject. Several respected writers and intellectuals

claimed that the suburban and consumer culture was destructive—stifling diversity and individuality in favor of conformity. Mass-produced homes, meals, toys, fashions, and the other trappings of suburban life created a gray sameness about Americans. Sociologist David Riesman in *The Lonely Crowd* (1950) argued that, unlike earlier generations, postwar Americans were "outer-directed"—less sure of their values and morals, while overly concerned about fitting into a group. Peer pressure had replaced individual thinking. William Whyte's *Organization Man* (1955) examined a Chicago suburb and

vice squad   Police unit charged with the enforcement of laws dealing with such crimes as gambling and prostitution.

Rejecting Consensus

Allen Ginsberg

Allen Ginsberg was born in Paterson, New Jersey. He graduated from Columbia University, moved to San Francisco, and took a job doing market research. Dissatisfied with his traditional lifestyle, he chose to abandon it. He stopped working and started writing poetry. Eventually he became one of the leading "Beat" poets and voices of his generation. Robert Kelley LIFE Magazine © Time Warner Inc.

In the mid-fifties, Allen Ginsberg left New York for California. "I had passed one session of my life," he remembered, "and it was time to start all over again." In the San Francisco area, he took a job with a small market-research firm and explored poetry, but he was not personally satisfied. He sought psychotherapy—and psychiatrist Philip Hicks asked him what he would like to do. "Doctor, I don't think you're going to find this very healthy," Ginsberg responded, "but I really would like to stop working forever . . . and do nothing but write poetry and have leisure to spend the day outdoors and go to museums and see friends. And I'd like to keep living with someone—maybe even a man—and explore relationships." Hicks said, "Do it." Making his choice, Ginsberg established a long-term relationship with Peter Orlovsky, retired from work, and wrote his first long-lined poem "Howl."

In 1956, "Howl"—a semi-autobiographical cry of outrage and despair against a destructive and abusive society that worships Moloch, the god of materialism and conventionality—exploded on American society.

> *Moloch whose mind is pure machinery!*
> *Moloch whose blood is running money!*
> *Moloch whose fingers are ten armies!*
> *Moloch whose heart is a cannibal dynamo!*
> *Moloch whose love is endless oil and stone!*
> *Moloch whose soul is electricity and banks!*

found the same lack of individuality and independence. He claimed that workplace action verbs like *control, compel,* and *force* had been replaced by consensus nouns like *communication* and *teamwork*. Both authors urged readers to resist being packaged like cake mixes and reassert their individualities. Serious literature also highlighted a sense of alienation from the conformist society. Much of Sylvia Plath's poetry and her novel *The Bell Jar* (1963) reflect many of those forces, especially as they affected women torn between the demands of society and the quest for individual freedom. Parallel themes were central to many contemporary novels, including Saul Bellow's *Henderson the Rain King* (1959), Sloan Wilson's *The Man in the Grey Flannel Suit* (1955), and J. D. Salinger's *Catcher in the Rye* (1951), whose hero Holden Caulfield concludes that the major features of American life are all phoney.

At the end of the poem, Ginsberg celebrates his victory over Moloch's control of his conventional identity.

"Howl" not only rejected traditional American values but immediately became a target of censorship by San Francisco authorities, who claimed that the poem was obscene and pornographic. Almost as soon as it was published, San Francisco police arrested its publisher, Lawrence Ferlinghetti, and sought to confiscate existing copies of the poem. In the obscenity trial that followed, a parade of respected poets and literary critics testified that the poem had merit, forcing the judge to declare it was not obscene. The poem and the furor over it promptly established a virtually unknown author as a leading Beat poet.

An opponent of social norms, Ginsberg believed it was necessary to save the nation by rejecting conventionality and calling on the people to discover their true spirits. Interviewed by the *Village Voice* in 1959, Ginsberg argued that recent history was "a vast conspiracy to impose . . . a level of mechanical consciousness" on humankind, and that the "suppression of contemplative individuality" was nearly complete. Fortunately, according to Ginsberg, "a few individuals, poets, have had the luck and courage . . . to glimpse something new through the crack of mass consciousness" and "have entered the world of Spirit" to battle "an America gone mad with materialism, a police-state America, a sexless and soulless America."

Ginsberg became the model for Beat writers—writing in the language of the streets about unliterary topics—and fulfilled the popular expectations of the "hipster" Beatnik. As the fifties dissolved into the sixties, Ginsberg and his Haight-Ashbury apartment became a center of the counterculture. He coined the term "flower power," while advocating spirituality and individual freedom induced by using psychedelic drugs and practicing Oriental philosophies and Buddhism. Opposed to the war in Vietnam (see Chapter 30), he asked antiwar protestors to demonstrate for peace, but peacefully, arguing that flowers, bells, and chants would overcome jeers and oppression. In 1967, he organized the first "Gathering of the Tribes for a Human Be-In" in San Francisco, the first of hundreds of counterculture festivals to follow.

As a poet, Ginsberg has chosen to write about his political and social concerns, attacking what he describes as the evil forces in society. In 1973, his *The Fall of America, 1965–1971* presented Moloch in the guise of the war in Vietnam, nuclear energy, threats to the environment, and America's rampant materialism—and won the National Book Award. From the obscenity trial to prestigious literary awards, the outcome of Allen Ginsberg's choice has been a literary Horatio Alger story, from a "dirty" Beat poet—a hipster predicted to self-destruct—to one of the country's best and best-known modern poets and "the biographer of his time."

More extreme were the **Beats,** or "beatniks," a group of often controversial artists, poets, and writers. Allen Ginsberg (*Howl*, 1956) and Jack Kerouac (*On the Road*, 1957) graphically denounced American materialism and sexual **repression**—according to Ginsberg, "that mass-produced self they keep trying to shove down your throat"—and glorified a freer, natural life with little social or self-restriction (see Individual Choices: Allen Ginsberg). Although

Beats   Group of American writers, poets, and artists in the 1950s, including Jack Kerouac and Allen Ginsberg, who rejected traditional middle-class values and championed nonconformity and sexual experimentation.

repression   Strict control that prevents the natural development or expression of impulses like the sex drive.

some college students found the beatnik critique of "square America" meaningful, most Americans rejected their message and condemned their lifestyles. In an article in *Life* (1959), Paul O'Neil described them as being smelly, dirty people in beards and sandals, who were "sick little bums" and "hostile little females." Few in number, Beats hardly worried most Americans, except as contributors to the growing numbers of "JD's"—juvenile delinquents—and to the swelling popularity of rock 'n' roll music.

The Trouble with Kids

Juvenile delinquency was not new to American society, especially among the urban poor, but in the 1950s many observers saw an alarming new style of delinquency among many white, middle-class, suburban teens. To most parents, the violent crime associated with inner-city gangs was not as much troublesome as teenage disrespect for adults and teens running amok in cars in pursuit of amusement, which often involved alcohol and sex. One study of middle-class delinquency concluded that the automobile not only allowed teens to escape adult controls but also provided "a private lounge for drinking and for petting or sex episodes."

The problem with kids also seemed wedded to music—**rock 'n' roll.** Some sociologists argued that the music of the lower classes, especially African-Americans, in which rock 'n' roll had its roots, glamorized behavior that led to crime and alienation. The assumed connection between rock 'n' roll and delinquency was cemented when **Chuck Berry** incorporated "Shake, Rattle, and Roll" and other rock songs into the 1955 movie *The Blackboard Jungle.*

In 1951, Cleveland disc jockey Alan Freed coined the name "rock 'n' roll." He had noticed that white teens were buying rhythm and blues (R&B) records popular among African-Americans, but he also knew that few white households would listen to a radio program playing "black music." Freed decided to change the name to rock 'n' roll and play the less sexually suggestive of the R&B records. His radio program, "Moondog's Rock 'n' Roll Party," was a smash hit. Quickly the barriers between "black music" and "white music" began to blur with white singers copying and modifying R&B songs to produce **cover records.** Cover artists like Pat Boone and Georgia Gibbs sold millions of records that avoided suggestive lyrics and were heard on hundreds of radio stations that had refused to play the original black artists. By mid-decade, African-American artists like Chuck Berry, Little Richard,

◆ The 1950s saw the rise of a youth subculture as the first wave of baby boomers reached their teen years. Hollywood rushed to meet the new market with a number of inexpensively made movies that featured teens, cars, and rock'n'roll—*Rock Baby Rock It* typifies this type of movie. Note the "way-out" fashions and the football mural on the wall of the teen hang-out. *Michael Barson Collection/Past Perfect.*

and Ray Charles were successfully "crossing over" and being heard on "white" radio stations. At the same time, white artists, including 1956's most dynamic star, **Elvis Presley,** were making their own contributions to rock 'n' roll. From Tupelo, Mississippi, Elvis Aron Presley blended strains of gospel, country, and R&B into an original musical form that quickly rocked the nation. Beginning with "Heartbreak Hotel" in 1956, in two years, he recorded fourteen gold records, appeared on the prestigious *Ed Sullivan Show* on television, and drove his audiences into frenzies with sexually suggestive movements

---

rock 'n' roll   Style of music that developed out of rhythm and blues in the 1950s, with a fast beat and lyrics that appealed to teenagers.

Chuck Berry   African-American rock musician and composer whose songs chronicled teenage experiences and sentiments and who helped establish rock and roll in the 1950s.

cover record   A new version of a song already recorded by an original artist.

Elvis Presley   Rock 'n' roll musician from a poor white family in Mississippi, who gained immense popularity with songs that incorporated the driving beat and frank sexuality of rhythm and blues.

that earned him the nickname "Elvis the Pelvis." Blaming Elvis and rock 'n' roll music for a decline in morals, if not civilization, a Catholic Youth Center newspaper asked readers to "smash" rock 'n' roll records because they promoted "a pagan concept of life." But such opponents were waging a losing battle. Like Elvis, rock 'n' roll surged in popularity and by the end of the decade, Dick Clark's weekly television show featuring teens dancing to rock 'n' roll music, *American Bandstand,* was one of the nation's most-watched and accepted programs.

Politics of Consensus

● What constraints did Eisenhower and other Republicans encounter in trying to roll back the New Deal, and how did the outcome reflect what Eisenhower called the "middle path"?

In 1952, Republicans expected finally to end the Democrats' twenty-year monopoly on the White House. The lingering war in Korea, revelations of government corruption, and the soft-on-communism label had sunk Truman's popularity to 23 percent. Truman toyed with the idea of running again, but after Estes Kefauver (see page 866) won the New Hampshire primary, he decided to retire. Eventually, Democrats nominated Illinois governor **Adlai E. Stevenson,** who not only carried Truman's political handicaps but added his own. Recently divorced, Stevenson was widely regarded as too intellectual and too liberal.

Crying "It was time for a change," Republicans selected the politically inexperienced General Dwight David Eisenhower. "Ike" appeared to be the perfect candidate. He was well known, revered as a war hero, and carried the image of an honest man being thrust into public service. In truth, Eisenhower wanted to be president and, supported by moderate Republicans, had skillfully outmaneuvered conservative Senator Robert Taft of Ohio for the nomination. Eisenhower chose Richard M. Nixon of California as the vice-presidential candidate. Nixon was young and had risen rapidly in the party through his outspoken anticommunism and his aggressive role in the investigation of Alger Hiss (see page 862).

The Republican campaign took two paths. One concentrated on the popular image of Eisenhower. "Spot commercials" were introduced on television and aired in the middle of popular shows like *I Love Lucy.* Featuring Ike's smile and stressing his

◆ In this picture, the triumphant Republican nominees for the White House pose with smiles and wives—Pat Nixon and Mamie Eisenhower. Seen as a statesman and not a politician during the campaign, Eisenhower worked hard to ensure his nomination over Robert Taft, and then chose Richard Nixon to balance the ticket because he was a younger man, a westerner, and a conservative. *UPI Bettmann Archives.*

honesty, integrity, and "American-ness," the ads proved to be extremely effective. Public appearances were much the same. Eisenhower crusaded for high standards and good government and posed as another George Washington. A war-weary nation applauded his promise to go to Korea "in the cause of peace." If anyone could bring peace, maybe even victory, people thought, it was Ike. The second campaign path was taken by McCarthy, Nixon, and others, who brutally attacked the Democrats' Cold War and New Deal record. They proudly boasted that there were "no Communists in the Republican Party," that the containment policy was cowardly, and that a Republican administration would roll back communism. The liberal spending of the Democrats would be stopped and the New Deal dismantled.

The campaign was almost without drama, the only tense moment coming when it was asserted on "Meet the Press" that Nixon had accepted gifts

Adlai E. Stevenson   Illinois governor who became the Democratic candidate for president in both 1952 and 1956 but lost both times to Eisenhower.

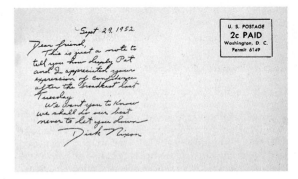

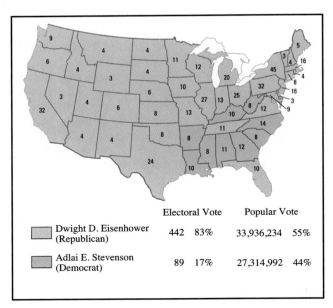

♦ Nixon was almost dropped from the 1952 ticket by Eisenhower when allegations surfaced about a secret fund used to pay personal expenses. But, because of the widespread public support he received following his "Checkers speech," Eisenhower kept him on the ticket. This picture shows the postcard Nixon mailed thanking those who showed their support following the speech. *Collection of David J. & Janice L. Frent.*

♦ **MAP 28.1 Election of 1952**   Dwight David Eisenhower and the Republicans swept into office in 1952. Leading the ticket, Eisenhower swamped his Democratic opponent Adlai Stevenson with 83 percent of the electoral vote and 55 percent of the popular vote. Republicans also won majorities in both houses of Congress. In the 1956 presidential election, Eisenhower beat Stevenson by even larger margins, but Democrats regained majority status in Congress.

from and used a secret cash fund provided by California business friends. While Eisenhower considered dropping him from the ticket, Nixon used television to explain his side of the story and rally public opinion. In the "Checkers speech," a teary-eyed Nixon denied the fund existed, contended that his was just an average American family and that the only gift they had ever received was a puppy, Checkers. His daughter loved the puppy, Nixon stated, and he would not make her give it back, no matter what that choice did to his career. It was an overly sentimental speech, but it worked—Nixon stayed on the ticket.

With a smile as powerful as FDR's grin, Eisenhower buried Stevenson in popular and electoral votes (see Map 28.1). Ike's broad political coattails ensured a Republican majority in Congress. The 1956 election would be a repeat of 1952, with Eisen-

hower again swamping Stevenson. But in 1956, it was Eisenhower's victory alone as Democrats maintained their 1954 majorities in both houses of Congress.

Ike or General Eisenhower?

The presidential victory of 1952 placed in office two Eisenhowers: one public, one private. The public Eisenhower was Ike, a warm, friendly, slightly bumbling, grandfather figure. He was the personification of calm and stability in a nation seeking soothing, consensus-type solutions. He seemed an almost absentee president, often leaving the government in the hands of Congress and his cabinet while he played golf or bridge. The other Eisenhower strongly believed that he was the only man capable of directing the United States and had no intention of being an absentee president. He oversaw the formation and the implementation of most policies, but he did so from behind the scenes in what has been labeled the "hidden-hand presidency." In military fashion, the private Eisenhower relied on his staff to provide a full discussion of any issue. We had a "good growl," he would say after especially heated cabinet talks. Willing to let subordinates receive credit and praise for policy, Eisenhower expected them to shoulder blame and responsibility as well. He was impressed by successful business people, and the majority of his cabinet and other appointments were drawn from the ranks of business. Few had political connections or any governmental administrative experience.

The two Eisenhowers coexisted—one an intelligent and forceful president working to implement policy, the other a mask constructed to protect Eisenhower politically and to project an aura of tranquillity. When Press Secretary Jim Hagerty worried that in press conferences the private Eisenhower might be forced to answer a tough question, the president dismissed his anxiety "If that question comes," he chuckled, "I'll just confuse them."

The Middle Path

Eisenhower called himself a modern Republican and labeled his approach "dynamic conservatism." He wanted to follow a "middle course" that was "conservative when it comes to money and liberal when it comes to human beings." The president's first priority was the budget, and he considered the balanced budgets of 1954 and 1960 as two of his greatest achievements. Facing Truman's projected deficits for 1952 and 1953, Eisenhower knew it was necessary to end the war in Korea and make substantial cuts in the defense budget.

Seeking to resolve the Korean Conflict and to fulfill his campaign pledge, President-elect Eisenhower flew to Korea in December 1952 for a three-day visit. South Korean president Syngman Rhee and U.S. commander General Lucius Clay anxiously awaited the opportunity to promote their strategy for escalating the war to achieve victory. Eisenhower ignored their plans, however, and chose instead to visit the front line to get a real feel for the war. By the time the commander-in-chief left Korea on December 5, he was convinced that the war could not be won and that a negotiated peace was the only solution. The problem was how to persuade the North Koreans and Chinese that such a settlement would be in their best interests.

To prod the Communists, Eisenhower used the aggressive images of liberation that had been part of his election campaign. Through public and private channels, he and Secretary of State **John Foster Dulles** implied that the United States would escalate the war and use atomic weapons unless a negotiated settlement was soon reached. By July 1953, the "atomic diplomacy" had worked. A truce signed at Panmunjom ended the fighting, brought home almost all the troops, left a Korea divided by a **demilitarized zone (DMZ)**, and allowed Eisenhower to cut the military budget.

Even as Eisenhower flew home from Korea, he was contemplating other ways to reduce military spending. The answer, he decided, was to reshape the tactics of containment. Called the **New Look,** Eisenhower's policy emphasized atomic weapons and air power and thus permitted reduction of more expensive conventional forces. Despite much foot-dragging and opposition from the military and legislators from both parties, Eisenhower prevailed: the federal budget was balanced in 1954. As the budget came into balance, Eisenhower worked to stimulate the economy by approving a new tax structure that reduced income taxes and increased business deductions.

The changes in taxes reflected Eisenhower's second priority—to return the direction of the economy to the business community and to reduce federal controls. The end of the Korean conflict meant the end of wartime controls over the economy, but Eisenhower wanted to go much further. Using budget justifications, he wanted to reverse the "creeping socialism" of the New Deal by removing or at least reducing federal regulations. High on his list of government programs to reverse were those involving American Indians, energy, and agriculture.

A series of acts between 1953 and 1954, made without American Indian input, eliminated federal economic support to tribes and liquidated selected reservations. Critics blasted this "termination policy" as an attack on American Indian culture and

---

John Foster Dulles   Secretary of state under Eisenhower, who called for massive retaliation with nuclear weapons to deter Soviet aggression.

demilitarized zone   Area from which military forces, operations, and installations are prohibited.

New Look   National security policy under Eisenhower that called for reductions in the size of the army, development of tactical nuclear weapons, and build-up of strategic air power employing nuclear weapons.

◆ One of Eisenhower's goals was to reduce federal spending and controls. In line with this policy, he tried to turn Indian affairs over to the states and liquidate federal services and reservations. Between 1954 and 1960, sixty-one tribes were affected. This picture shows a 4-year-old Tuscarora boy protesting state and federal policies that attacked Indian rights. *Wide World.*

society. As federal policies were implemented, Native Americans increasingly fell under less protective state laws, while economic and other pressures encouraged American Indians to sell tribal lands and leave their reservations. By 1960, nearly one-half of American Indians had abandoned their reservations, and most tribes were economically and socially worse off than before Eisenhower took office.

Reversing New Deal policies, Eisenhower also returned to state and private hands federally owned or controlled energy sources, and he instructed Secretary of Agriculture Ezra Taft Benson to reduce farm subsidies. Although successful in removing many federal controls over energy, Eisenhower faced bitter opposition in trying to modify agriculture policy. A strong bipartisan Farm Bloc ensured that the Agricultural Act of 1954 contained only small modifications of Roosevelt's policy (see page

768). Lower payment rates were approved, but because payments were based on production levels, which continued to grow, the total cost of federal subsidies steadily rose.

Eisenhower's "middle path" produced budget cuts and reduced federal involvement, and the economy flourished except for a period in 1957 and 1958 when the nation slipped into a brief recession. But he did not discard New Deal programs altogether, nor prevent government-sponsored building projects, nor shrink the size of government. Eisenhower created a new cabinet post—Health, Education, and Welfare—directed by Oveta Culp Hobby, who had commanded the WACs during World War II and was also a millionaire. During his two terms, 7 million more Americans became qualified for social security and 4 million more received unemployment payments. The minimum wage rose from $.75 to $1.00 an hour. But Eisenhower's liberal nature had limits. After the **polio** vaccine developed by **Jonas Salk** was declared effective in 1955, Eisenhower strongly agreed with Secretary Hobby and the American Medical Association that the government should not get directly involved in inoculating the public because it would be socialistic. Eisenhower also vetoed housing projects, public works bills, and antipollution proposals as inappropriate for the federal government.

When Eisenhower increased government spending, his rationale was generally based on national economic and security needs. He pushed the St. Lawrence Seaway project (1954), which committed American support in building a sea lane to connect the Great Lakes with the Atlantic, on the grounds that it would benefit the nation by increasing trade. He approved the Federal Highway Act (1956) to meet the needs of an automobile-driven nation and to provide the military with a workable transportation network. Following the Soviet launching of the space satellites *Sputnik I* (1957) and *Sputnik II*

---

polio Acute viral infection that usually struck children and often caused partial or total paralysis; it was common in the United States until the development of the Salk vaccine.

Jonas Salk American microbiologist who developed the first effective vaccine against polio in 1954.

Sputnik I Satellite launched by the Soviet Union in 1957; the first successful launch of an artificial satellite by any nation, it marked the beginning of the space race.

(1958), Eisenhower quoted national security needs to support spending more federal money on education.

The successful orbiting of the Soviet satellites created a multilevel panic across the nation. Not only was the nation vulnerable to missiles and bombs launched from the Soviet Union and now possibly from Soviet satellites in space, but *Sputnik* appeared to underscore basic weaknesses in the American educational system. American schools, many critics argued, stressed soft subjects and social adjustment rather than hard subjects: science, languages, mathematics. *Sputnik* spurred Eisenhower and Congress to approve grants to schools developing strong programs in those subjects. Similarly, Congress cited national defense when it established the **National Defense Student Loans** for college students.

The Problem with McCarthy

During the 1952 presidential campaign, Senator Joseph McCarthy had taken a prominent role in attacking Democrats as being soft on communism. With Ike in the White House and Republicans controlling Congress, many Republicans including Eisenhower hoped that McCarthy would quietly disappear. But McCarthy enjoyed the spotlight and relished his power, and he had no intention of fading from view. He continued his search for subversives, ripping through the State Department, the Voice of America, and the **United States Information Agency (USIA)**. Government workers thought to be security risks were discharged or pressured to resign, and the USIA cleaned its library shelves of questionable titles, including those by Mark Twain. Although few of the individuals McCarthy attacked were guilty of any form of disloyalty, the agitation helped to rid the government of Democratic-appointed officials and allowed their replacement with faithful Republicans.

But when McCarthy, furious at the army for drafting his aide David Schine, threatened to expose army favoritism toward known Communists, anti-McCarthy forces in Congress, quietly supported by Eisenhower, concluded that it was time to silence the senator. Charging that he was trying to blackmail the U.S. Army, the Senate investigated McCarthy. The American Broadcasting Company's telecast of the 1954 **Army-McCarthy hearings** allowed over 20 million viewers to see McCarthy's ruthless bullying firsthand. Public and congressional opposition to the senator rose, and when the army's lawyer Joseph Welch asked the brooding

◆ At the heart of the Red Scare was Senator Joseph McCarthy and his staff of Roy Cohn (*left*) and David Schine (*right*). They used inquisition-style tactics to destroy opponents and bolster their own power. Schine's induction into the army set up the final confrontation between McCarthy and the army and eventually with Congress and the American public. *Eve Arnold/Magnum.*

McCarthy, who had accused Welch's cocounsel of being a homosexual, "Have you no sense of decency?" the nation burst into applause. Several months later, with Republicans evenly divided, the Senate voted 67 to 22 to censure McCarthy's "unbecoming conduct." Drinking heavily, rejected by his colleagues, and ignored by the media, McCarthy died in 1957. But McCarthyism, refined and tempered, remained for years a potent political weapon against liberal opponents.

National Defense Student Loans   Loans established by the U.S. government in 1958, designed to encourage the teaching and study of science and modern foreign languages.

United States Information Agency   Agency established by Congress in 1953 to distribute information about U.S. culture and political policies and gain support for American international goals.

Army-McCarthy hearings   1954 congressional investigation of allegations that McCarthy had tried to get special treatment from the U.S. Army for an aide; the televised hearings revealed McCarthy's villainous nature and ended his popularity.

Seeking Civil Rights

● How did African-American leaders choose to attack *de jure* segregation in American society during Eisenhower's administration?

The average American depicted by *Reader's Digest* lived in suburbia, had white skin, and belonged to the middle class. This was not the world of the nation's racial minorities, most of whom faced poverty, degradation, and segregation. Legal, or *de jure,* segregation existed not only in the South but in the District of Columbia and several western and midwestern states. Discrimination and *de facto* segregation were nationwide realities. Politically, neither party wanted to risk its unity by championing the cause of minorities too actively. Aware of Democratic and Republican apathy, African-American leaders were determined on their own to attack the racial inequalities in America.

Changes had occurred, but most African-Americans regarded them as minor tokens, indicating no real shift in white America's racial views. The NAACP had by 1952 won cases permitting African-American law and graduate students to attend white colleges and universities, even though the concept of "separate but equal," established in 1896 by the Supreme Court ruling in *Plessy v. Ferguson* (see page 563), remained intact. Cities like Atlanta, Birmingham, and Montgomery had more black voters and had even hired African-Americans for their police forces. But throughout the country, African-Americans still occupied the lowest rungs of the social ladder and worked at the most menial jobs. United Nations diplomat **Ralph Bunche** exemplified the frustration of black Americans: after winning the Nobel Peace Prize in 1950 for negotiating a cease-fire between the Arab states and Israel, he turned down a position as undersecretary of state because he refused to subject his family to the segregation of Washington, D.C. Nonetheless, from the delta of the Mississippi to the White House, African-Americans were committed to enlarging their civil and political rights.

The *Brown* Decision

A step toward change came in 1954 when the Supreme Court considered the arguments of NAACP lawyer **Thurgood Marshall** in *Brown v. The Board of Education, Topeka, Kansas.* The *Brown* case had started four years earlier, when Oliver Brown sued to allow his daughter to attend a nearby white school rather than the black school across town. The Kansas courts had rejected his suit, pointing out that the availability of a school for African-Americans fulfilled the Supreme Court's separate-but-equal ruling. The NAACP appealed. In addressing the Supreme Court, Marshall held that the basic concept of "separate but equal" was inherently unequal. He used statistics to show that black schools were separate and unequal when it came to finances, quality and number of teachers, and physical and educational resources. But going beyond the cold statistics he read into the record a psychological study indicating that black children educated in a segregated environment suffered from low self-esteem. He stressed that segregated educational facilities, even if physically similar, could never yield equal products.

In 1952, a divided Court was unable to make a decision, but two years later the Court heard the case again. Now sitting as chief justice was Eisenhower appointee **Earl Warren,** the Republican former governor of California, regarded by most as legally conservative. Eisenhower was shocked when Warren read the unanimous decision that decreed "separate educational facilities are inherently unequal." The Court had made school segregation illegal under the Fourteenth Amendment, but it had avoided the larger issue of society-wide segregation. In 1955, in a second *Brown* decision, the Court provided enforcement guidelines. The high Court did not expect segregated schools to change overnight but wanted school districts to begin the

---

de jure   According to or brought about by law.

de facto   Existing in practice, though not officially established by law.

Ralph Bunche   African-American diplomat and mediator of international disputes who was awarded the Nobel Peace Prize in 1950 for his work on the UN Palestine Commission.

Thurgood Marshall   Civil rights lawyer who argued thirty-two cases before the Supreme Court and won twenty-nine of them; he became the first African-American on the Supreme Court in 1967.

Brown v. The Board of Education, Topeka, Kansas   1954 Supreme Court ruling that separate educational facilities for different races were inherently unequal.

Earl Warren   Chief justice of the Supreme Court from 1953 to 1969, under whom the Court issued decisions protecting civil rights, the rights of criminals, and First Amendment rights.

process of integration and to proceed with "all deliberate speed." The justices instructed lower federal courts to monitor progress according to this vague guideline.

The Court's decision raised a loud cry of protest from white southerners, who vowed to resist segregation by using all means possible. Virginia passed a law closing any integrated school. Southern Congressmen, in what was called the **Southern Manifesto,** proudly pledged to oppose the *Brown* ruling. Consequently, "all deliberate speed" amounted to a snail's pace. By 1965, only about 2 percent of all southern schools were integrated.

Southern white reactions to the *Brown* case confirmed to African-Americans that efforts to undo existing social traditions and controls would be met with strong opposition, even violence. An incident in August 1955 brought home exactly how far some were willing to go to halt threats to "tradition." **Emmett Till** was a teenager from Chicago visiting relatives in Mississippi. One day he broke "tradition" by approaching and speaking to a white girl without being asked. For his actions, that evening he was tortured and murdered. Roy Bryant and J. W. Milam were brought to trial and admitted to killing Till. An all-white jury acquitted both men. The verdict was not unexpected, but what was a surprise, and an indication of the changes taking place in the South, was that black eyewitnesses bravely testified at the trial, despite threats against their lives.

The Montgomery Bus Boycott

In Montgomery, Alabama, African-Americans were aware of the Till murder, but they were determined to confront another form of white social control: the manner of segregation used on the city bus line. The bus company practiced "rolling segregation." This scheme required African-American passengers to take seats behind white riders and, if necessary, to give up seats and stand so that whites could sit. In this humiliating game of musical chairs, black Americans always lost—and some bus drivers played the game with an abusive glee.

On December 1, 1955, **Rosa Parks** refused to give up her seat on the bus so that a white man could sit. At 42, Mrs. Parks, a high school graduate who earned $23 a week as a seamstress, had not boarded the bus with the intention of disobeying the law, although she strongly opposed the bus company's policy and had been involved in efforts to fight it. That afternoon, the humiliation of the demand to move was suddenly too much. She refused and was arrested.

Hearing of her arrest, local African-American leaders Jo Ann Robinson and Edward Nixon felt they had found the right person to contest rolling segregation. Rosa Parks was committed enough to withstand white pressure and able to draw popular support. African-American community leaders called for a boycott of the buses to begin on the day of Mrs. Parks' court appearance. Accordingly, they submitted a list of proposals to the city and bus officials calling for courteous drivers, the hiring of black drivers, and a more equitable system of bus seating, although they did not insist on an end to separate seating.

On December 5, 1955, the night before the boycott was to begin, nearly four thousand people filled and surrounded Holt Street Baptist Church to hear **Martin Luther King Jr.,** the newly selected leader of the boycott movement—now called the Montgomery Improvement Association. New to Montgomery, King was young (26), had a small child and too much to do. At first, he hesitated to become involved in the boycott but finally agreed to lead the action because he firmly believed that the church had a social justice mission and that violence and hatred, even when considered justified, brought only ruin. In shaping his evening's speech, Martin Luther King faced the problem of how to balance disobedience with peace, confrontation with civility, and rebellion with tradition. He succeeded. His words electrified the crowd and tugged at the experiences, hopes, and pride of those listening. "We are here this evening," he announced, "to say to those who

---

Southern Manifesto Statement issued by one hundred southern congressmen in 1954 after the *Brown v. Board of Education* decision, pledging to oppose desegregation.

Emmett Till African-American teenager from Chicago who was killed in Mississippi in 1955 and whose confessed murderers were acquitted by an all-white jury.

Rosa Parks Black seamstress who refused to give up her seat to a white man on a bus in Montgomery, Alabama, in 1955, triggering a bus boycott that stirred the civil rights movement.

Martin Luther King, Jr. Ordained Baptist minister, brilliant orator, and civil rights leader committed to nonviolence who led many important protests of the 1950s and 1960s; he was assassinated in Tennessee in 1968.

♦ Seen by many as the beginning of the civil rights movement, the Montgomery bus boycott brought its young leader, Martin Luther King, Jr. to the nation's attention. Here African-Americans walk to work rather than ride the segregated city buses. The boycott lasted 361 days and ended with the Supreme Court ruling that segregated buses were illegal. *Greg Villet, LIFE Magazine © Time Warner Inc.*

have mistreated us so long that we are tired—tired of being segregated and humiliated, tired of being kicked about by the brutal feet of oppression." He asked the crowd to boycott the buses. The "tools of persuasion" had to be supported with the "tools of coercion," he stated, urging his listeners to protest with love and, when confronted with violence, to "bless them that curse you." He promised that if they protested "courageously, and yet with dignity and Christian love, when the history books are written in the future, somebody will have to say, 'There lived a race of people, of black people, of people who had the moral courage to stand up for their rights. And thereby they injected a new meaning into the veins of history and civilization.'"

On December 6, Rosa Parks was tried, found guilty, and fined $10, plus $4 court costs. She appealed. Bus and city administrators met with boycott leaders but refused to budge on hiring and rolling segregation. The boycott, 90 percent effective, stretched into days, weeks, and finally months. Police wrote baskets full of traffic tickets for those involved in the car pools that provided transportation for the boycotters. Insurance companies cancelled automobile coverage and acid was poured on car pool cars. On January 30, 1956, a stick of dynamite was thrown onto King's front porch, destroying it and almost injuring King's wife and a friend.

Even in the face of personal attack and growing white hostility, King remained calm, reminding supporters to avoid violence and maintain the boycott. On February 1, attorney Fred Grey arguing in federal court challenged the legality of all segregated buses. At nearly the same time, a white Montgomery grand jury issued an injunction against the boycott and indicted 115 of its leaders, including King. All were tried and sentenced without a jury. However, as the boycott approached its anniversary, the Supreme Court ruled in *Gayle et al. v. Browser* (1956), that the city's and bus company's policy of segregation was unconstitutional. "Praise the Lord. God has spoken from Washington, D.C.," cried one boycotter.

Even though it took the Supreme Court to force the integration of the bus line, the 381-day boycott had been tremendously successful in establishing conditions for change. The traditional white view that African-Americans accepted segregation had been shattered, and a pattern of nonviolent resistance had been initiated. In King, a leader had emerged determined to build on the energy generated by the boycott to fight segregation throughout American society. Within weeks, he and other black leaders had formed a new civil rights organization, the **Southern Christian Leadership Conference (SCLC)**. King and the SCLC were nationally visible, but across the South thousands of unseen African-Americans were drawing heart from *Brown* and Montgomery. They too were willing and eager to take to the streets and use the federal courts to achieve equality.

Ike and Civil Rights

As the press covered the Montgomery boycott, from the White House came either silence or carefully selected platitudes. When asked, Eisenhower gave elusive replies: "I believe we should not stagnate . . . I plead for understanding, for really sympathetic consideration of a problem . . . I am for moderation, but I am for progress; that is exactly what I am for in this thing." Personally, Eisenhower believed that government, especially the executive branch, had little role in integration. Max Rabb, the president's adviser on minority affairs, thought that "Negroes

Southern Christian Leadership Conference Group formed by Martin Luther King, Jr., and others after the Montgomery bus boycott; it became the backbone of the civil rights movement in the 1950s and 1960s.

were being too aggressive." On a political level, cabinet members and Eisenhower were disappointed in the low number of blacks who had voted Republican in 1952 and 1956.

But not all within the administration were so unsympathetic toward civil rights. Attorney General Herbert Brownell drafted the first civil rights legislation since Reconstruction. It passed Congress after a year of political maneuvering, having gained the support of Democratic majority leader Lyndon B. Johnson. A moderate law, it provided for the formation of the U.S. Commission on Civil Rights and opened the possibility of using federal suits to ensure voter rights.

While both political parties were carefully dancing around civil rights, African-Americans made it more and more difficult for politicians to avoid stepping on the issue. For Eisenhower, the unavoidable finally came over the effort to integrate Central High School in **Little Rock,** Arkansas. Central High was scheduled to be integrated starting in 1957. Opposing integration were the parents of the school's students and Governor Orval Faubus, who ordered National Guard troops to surround the school and prevent desegregation. He said the action was to protect the students and to ensure order. But his claim rang hollow to Elizabeth Eckford, one of the nine integrating students. National guardsmen blocked her path as she walked toward Central High amid jeers from a hostile mob roaring, "Lynch her! Lynch her!" Spat upon by the crowd, she retreated to her bus stop. Central High remained segregated.

For three weeks the National Guard prevented the black students from enrolling. On September 14, Eisenhower thought he had convinced Faubus to allow the blacks to attend classes, but back in Little Rock, the governor maintained his segregationist stance. When, on September 20, a federal judge ordered the integration of Central High School, Faubus complied and withdrew the National Guard. Eisenhower, relieved that the crisis was over, cooked steaks that evening and played bridge with close friends while vacationing in Newport, Rhode Island.

The crisis was not over. Segregationists were still determined to block integration and were waiting for the black students on Monday, September 23, 1957. When they discovered that the nine had slipped into the school unnoticed, the mob rushed the police lines and battered the school doors yelling, "Lynch the niggers!" Inside the school, Melba Pattillo Beals thought, "We were trapped. I'm going to die here, in school." Hurried into the prin-

◆ As Elizabeth Eckford approached Little Rock's Central High School, the crowd began to hurl curses, yelling "Lynch her! Lynch her!" and a national guardsman blocked her entrance into the school with his rifle. Terrified, she retreated down the street away from the threatening mob. A week later, with army troops protecting her, Elizabeth Eckford finally attended—and integrated—Central High School. *Frances Miller, LIFE Magazine © Time Warner Inc.*

cipal's office, the students were loaded into cars and warned to duck their heads. School officials ordered the drivers to "start driving, do not stop. . . . If you hit somebody, you keep rolling, 'cause [if you stop] the kids are dead."

With the black students safely away, the crowd's rampage quieted. Integration had lasted almost three hours. The following morning angry throngs began looting and burning part of the city and the mayor asked for federal troops. Faced with insurrection and believing that Faubus had violated his trust, Eisenhower, on September 24, nationalized the Arkansas National Guard, dispatched 1,000 troops

Little Rock   Capital of Arkansas, where Eisenhower sent federal troops in 1957 to protect black students entering an all-white high school and to end rioting by segregationist mobs.

of the 101st Airborne Division to Little Rock, and returned to Washington. Speaking to the nation, the president emphasized that he had sent the federal troops not to integrate the schools but to uphold the law and to restore order. It was a distinction lost on most white southerners, who fumed as soldiers protected the nine integrating students for the rest of the school year.

Still Faubus resisted. The following school year (1957–1958), the city closed its high schools rather than integrate them. To prevent such actions, the Supreme Court ruled in *Cooper v. Aaron* (1959) that an African-American's right to attend school could not "be nullified openly and directly by state legislators or state executive officials nor nullified indirectly by them by evasive schemes for segregation." Little Rock's high schools reopened and integration slowly spread to the lower grades. But in Little Rock, as in many other communities, many white students fled the integrated public schools to attend private ones that were beyond the reach of the federal courts. Federal power had been used to uphold integration in Little Rock, but meaningful integration of schools was still years away. Although Eisenhower had signed a Civil Rights Act, critics argued that he had provided little political or moral leadership and that such leadership was critical if the nation was to commit itself to civil rights.

Eisenhower and a Hostile World

● What expectations and constraints lay behind Eisenhower's foreign policy choices, and how did the New Look differ from Truman's foreign policy?

Eisenhower provided little command on civil rights because he questioned the basic role of the executive branch in promoting integration and because he felt ill at ease with the issue. But when it came to foreign affairs, he had no such misgivings. He firmly believed that foreign policy was the almost exclusive territory of the executive branch and that he was eminently qualified to direct it. In surveying the world scene, he and Secretary of State John Foster Dulles believed the Soviet Union and communism were implacable enemies of America and in fact of civilization. They affirmed that the United States held a moral responsibility to protect the world from communism and to speed the demise of Soviet power. During the 1952 campaign, Dulles, a master

of provocative speech and imagery fashioned to woo voters, condemned containment as "appeasement" and promised a global "roll-back" of communism and the liberation of captive peoples. Dulles's language made good campaign rhetoric, but President Eisenhower quickly dismissed *liberation* and *roll-back* as too provocative. Instead, he sought a modification of Truman's containment that would be less expensive and would move the nation away from confrontation, while weakening the Soviet Union and ending the Cold War.

The New Look

In a series of sometimes fierce cabinet and staff discussions, the New Look took shape. It was a policy that relied on cheaper nuclear deterrence, an enhanced arsenal of nuclear weapons and delivery systems, and the threat of **"massive retaliation"** to protect American international interests. In explaining the shift to more atomic weapons, Nixon stated, "Rather than let the communists nibble us to death all over the world in little wars, we will rely . . . on massive mobile retaliation." Secretary of Defense Wilson quipped that the policy sought "more bang for the buck" (see Map 28.2). Demonstrating the country's nuclear might, the United States exploded its first hydrogen bomb in November 1952. Although the New Look was sold to the public as more positive than Truman's defensive containment policy, insiders recognized that it was marred by several flaws.

The central problem was where the United States should draw the massive retaliatory line. What if the enemy calls our bluff? "How do you convince the American people and the U.S. Congress to declare war?" asked one planner. The answer was to make the bluff so convincing that it would never be called. The key was psychological: convince aggressors that the United States would strike back, raining nuclear destruction not only on the attackers but also on the Soviets and Chinese, who would obviously be directing the aggression. This policy drew

> *Cooper v. Aaron*   1959 Supreme Court ruling that barred state authorities from interfering with desegregation either directly or through strategies of evasion.
>
> **"massive retaliation"**   Term used by John Foster Dulles in a 1954 speech implying that the United States was willing to use nuclear force in response to Communist aggression anywhere in the world.

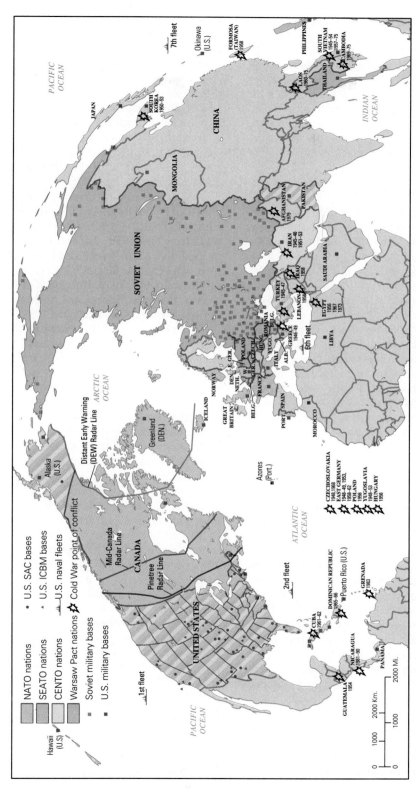

◆ **MAP 28.2 The Global Cold War** During the Cold War, both the United States and the Soviet Union faced each other as enemies. The United States attempted to construct a ring of containment around the Soviet Union and its allies, while the Soviets worked to expand their influence and power. This map shows the nature of this military confrontation—the bases, alliances, and flash-points of the Cold War.

the label of **brinksmanship,** because it required the administration to take the nation to the verge of war and trust that the opposition would back down. To convince the world of this daring boldness, Dulles and Eisenhower indulged in dramatic speeches aimed at drawing lines and stressing that atomic weapons were as usable as conventional ones. It was necessary "to remove the taboo" from using nuclear weapons, Dulles informed the press. Eisenhower publicly maintained that circumstances could exist that would require the use of atomic weapons, and that he would evaluate each crisis before making a decision to "go nuclear." Privately, he was much more restrained in his willingness to apply of American power. He recognized that areas under Communist control could not be liberated and that a thermonuclear war would allow for no winners. Despite the emphasis placed on brinksmanship, Eisenhower sought solutions to international problems that would not push the nation to the edge of war.

To make the idea of "going nuclear" and the possibility of World War III less frightening, the administration introduced efforts related to surviving an atomic war. With proper planning, officials emphasized, survival was possible. Public and private underground **fallout shelters**—well stocked with food, water, and medical supplies—could, it was claimed, provide safety against an atomic attack. A 32-inch-thick slab of concrete, *U.S. News and World Report* reported, could protect people from an atomic blast "as close as 1,000 feet away." Across the nation, civil defense drills were established for factories, offices, businesses, and schools, including "duck-and-cover" drills in schools. Teachers would shout "Drop!" and students would immediately get into a kneeling or prone position with their hands placed behind their necks and faces covered. Some school districts also issued identification "dog tags" to their students. While educators and government agencies worked to convince the public it could survive a nuclear war, movies and novels showed the horror of nuclear death and destruction. Nevil Shute realistically portrayed the extinction of humankind in *On the Beach* (1957), while in *Them!* (1954) and dozens of other B-movies, giant ants and other hideous creatures mutated by atomic fallout threatened the world.

Seeking ways to avoid a nuclear solution to international problems, Eisenhower and Dulles emphasized alliances and covert operations. Alliances would clearly mark areas protected by the American nuclear umbrella and deter Soviet adventurism.

They would also protect the United States from being drawn into limited, "brushfire" wars. When insurrections or small conflicts broke out, the ground forces of regional allies, perhaps supported with American naval and air strength, would deal with them. Reflecting existing tensions in Asia, Eisenhower concluded bilateral defense pacts with South Korea (1953) and Taiwan (1955), and a multilateral agreement, the Southeast Asia Treaty Organization (SEATO, 1954), that linked the United States, Australia, Thailand, the Philippines, Pakistan, New Zealand, France, and Britain. In the Middle East, the United States joined Britain, Iran, Pakistan, Turkey, and Iraq in the Baghdad Pact in 1957, later called the Central Treaty Organization (CENTO) when Iraq withdrew in 1959. In Europe, the United States helped to rearm West Germany and welcomed it into NATO. The Soviet bloc responded to the latter move with the formation of a military alliance between Eastern European nations and the Soviet Union, the **Warsaw Pact,** in 1955.

Alliances helped to draw lines of containment and provided a means to combat brushfire wars, but there were many places where neither the bludgeon of brinksmanship nor the support of alliances would work. Alliances were not possible where governments were either neutral or hostile to the United States. And brinksmanship did little to persuade many underdeveloped peoples that Western-style capitalism and representative government were superior to Communist-style state planning and authoritarian rule. In most developing countries, capitalism appealed most to that small percentage of the population who controlled wealth and property. Communist ideology, on the other hand, called for nationalistic social revolutions, which appealed to the poor who believed themselves to be exploited by the elite. Referring to the problem in terms of past policies, Dulles told congressmen: "In the old days we used to be able to

---

brinksmanship   Practice of seeking to win disputes in international politics by creating the impression of being willing to push a highly dangerous situation to the limit.

fallout shelter   Underground shelter stocked with food and supplies that was intended to provide safety in case of atomic attack; fallout refers to the nuclear particles falling through the atmosphere.

Warsaw Pact   Alliance for mutual defense made in 1955 by the USSR and the nations of Eastern Europe, which was the Soviet bloc's answer to NATO.

let South America go through the wringer of bad times . . . but the trouble is, now, when you put it through the wringer, it comes out red." To prevent social change from "coming out red," Eisenhower relied on economic and political pressures and the **Central Intelligence Agency.** It seemed a never-ending task. "While we are busy rescuing Guatemala or assisting Korea and Indochina," Eisenhower observed, the Communists "make great inroads in Burma, Afghanistan, and Egypt."

Turmoil in the Middle East

Eisenhower was especially concerned about the Middle East, where Arab nationalism fired by anti-Israel and anti-Western attitudes posed a serious threat to American interests. Egypt and Iran offered the greatest challenges. Egyptian leader Colonel **Gamal Nasser** and Iranian Prime Minister Mohammed Mossadegh were attempting to expel British influence from their nations and grasp control over their valuable resources—the Suez Canal in Egypt and oil in Iran. Eisenhower could either cooperate with the nationalist movements, trying to pull them toward more Western-American goals, or he could oppose the nationalists and promote conservative pro-Western governments.

Although suspicious of Nasser, Eisenhower hoped to woo him with loans, cash, arms, and an offer to help build the **Aswan Dam** on the Nile. "We should look for a way of getting an assurance from Nasser, if we do this, that he will go along with a Western orientation," wrote one Eisenhower adviser. At first Nasser seemed interested in bettering relations with the West, but eventually he rejected the American efforts, in large part because of American efforts to push an Egyptian-Israeli peace and closer ties with Britain. As Nasser resisted American lures and bought Soviet-bloc weapons, Eisenhower concluded that he was an "evil influence" in the region. Some within the administration suggested that Nasser be killed, but Eisenhower rejected that option—there was, he explained, no suitable replacement.

Instead, Eisenhower turned to economic pressures, and in July 1956, Dulles announced the cancellation of the Aswan Dam project. Days later, claiming the need to finance the dam, Nasser nationalized the Anglo-French–owned **Suez Canal,** through which the majority of European-bound oil passed. Resisting American pressures to negotiate, Israel, France, and Britain resorted to military action to regain control of the canal. On October 29, Israeli forces sliced through the Sinai toward Egypt. Two days later, French and British forces began bombing Egyptian targets and landed their forces in the canal zone on November 3.

Eisenhower was furious. He disliked Nasser, but he could not approve of armed aggression. Standing up to the West would enhance Nasser's influence in the Arab world and could provide the Soviets with a real foothold in the Middle East. Joined by the Soviets, who were threatening armed intervention on behalf of Egypt, Eisenhower sponsored a UN General Assembly resolution (November 2, 1956) calling for an end to the fighting, the removal of foreign troops from Egyptian soil, and the assignment of a United Nations peacekeeping force there. Faced with worldwide opposition and intense pressure from the United States—including a threat to withhold oil shipments—France, Britain, and Israel withdrew their forces. Nasser regained control of the canal and, as Eisenhower had feared, emerged from the crisis the uncontested leader of those opposing Western influence in Arab countries. There was also a growing Soviet presence in Egypt, building the Aswan Dam and equipping and training the army. Elsewhere in the Middle East, Eisenhower had better luck.

Nasser's actions forced the Eisenhower administration to construct a Middle Eastern anti-Soviet alliance with the northern tier of Middle Eastern states: Turkey, Iraq, Pakistan, and Iran. The first three nations harbored no strong anti-British or anti-Western sentiments, but Iran was a different matter. There, Prime Minister Mossadegh had nationalized British-owned oil properties and was unlikely to join the United States and Britain in an anti-Soviet alliance. Eisenhower considered him to be "neurotic and periodically unstable" and, along

---

Central Intelligence Agency   Agency established by Congress in 1947 to gather data and organize intelligence operations in foreign countries; it is responsible solely to the President.

Gamal Nasser   Prime minister and president of Egypt in the late 1950s; he was an Arab nationalist who sought to return valuable foreign-owned resources to Egyptian control.

Aswan Dam   Dam on the Nile River in Egypt, which was intended to provide electric power and stop seasonal flooding; construction finally began in 1960.

Suez Canal   Canal running through Egypt from Mediterranean to the Red Sea, which was under French and British control until 1955, when it was nationalized by Egypt.

◆ Implementing the Eisenhower Doctrine, American forces landed troops in Lebanon in July 1958, as the U.S. 6th fleet patrolled off the coast. In this picture, water skiiers enjoy the warm waters of the eastern Mediterranean as American forces take up positions. American forces landed and withdrew without incident, American forces in 1983 were not so lucky. *Hank Walker, LIFE Magazine © Time Warner Inc.*

try controlled by internationalism" (a term by which Eisenhower referred to the forces of communism). Congress agreed in March 1957, establishing the so-called **Eisenhower Doctrine** and providing $200 million in military and economic aid to improve military defenses in the nations of the Middle East.

It did not take long for Eisenhower to use his powers. When Jordan's King Hussein was threatened by an internal revolt, the White House announced Jordan was "vital" to American interests, moved the 6th Fleet into the eastern Mediterranean, and supplied over $10 million in aid. King Hussein put down the revolt, dismissed parliament and all political parties, and instituted authoritarian rule. In 1958, when Lebanon's Christian president Camile Chamoun ignored his country's constitution and ran for a second term, opposition leaders—including nationalistic, anti-West Muslim elements—rebelled. Chamoun requested American intervention and Eisenhower committed nearly 15,000 troops to protect the pro-American government. The U.S. Army arrived at the Beirut airport amid hordes of tourists while U.S. Marines waded ashore in full battle gear as beachgoers watched from the sand. The American forces left in three months—after Chamoun, with American approval, had stepped down and been replaced by General Faud Chehab. Eisenhower had demonstrated his willingness to protect American interests but had done little to resolve the problems faced by Lebanon and the rest of the Middle East.

A Protective Neighbor

During the 1952 presidential campaign, Eisenhower had charged that Truman had followed a "Poor Neighbor policy" toward Latin America, allowing

with the British, favored forcing him from power. Eisenhower gave the CIA the green light to overthrow the Iranian leader and replace him with pro-Western General Fazlollah Zahedi and Shah **Mohammed Reza Pahlevi.** On August 18, 1953, a mass demonstration funded and orchestrated by the CIA toppled the Mossadegh government and brought General Zahedi to power. American money flowed into Iran to support the new government—$900,000 immediately from a CIA safe and $45 million more within a month. A thankful Iranian government joined the anti-Soviet Baghdad Pact in 1956 and CENTO in 1959.

With the northern tier safely under American influence, Eisenhower redoubled his effort to contain Nasser's **Pan-Arab movement** and an expanding Soviet presence in the region. The goal was to encourage and support conservative, West-leaning governments. To protect Arab friends from Communist-nationalist rebellions, Eisenhower asked Congress for permission to commit American forces if requested to resist "armed attack from any coun-

---

Mohammed Reza Pahlevi   Iranian ruler who received the hereditary title of shah from his father in 1941 and who helped oust the militant nationalist Mohammed Mossadegh in 1953.

Pan-Arab movement   Attempts to political unify the Arab nations of the Middle East that arose stressing freedom from Western control and opposition to Israel.

Eisenhower Doctrine   Policy under Eisenhower of providing military and economic aid to Arab nations in the Middle East to help defeat Communist-nationalistic rebellions.

economic problems and popular uprisings to develop that had been "skillfully exploited by the Communists." As president, Eisenhower intended to reverse that trend by offering anti-Communist Latin American governments—including dictatorships—economic, political, and military support. He was most concerned about Guatemala, disapproving of the reformist president, Jocobo Arbenz, who had instituted agrarian reforms by nationalizing thousands of acres of land, much of it owned by the American-based United Fruit Company. These radical actions convinced the administration to use the CIA to remove Arbenz. Organizing a rebel army in Honduras, the CIA supplied Guatemalan Colonel Carlos Castillo Armas with "wads of dollar bills" and arms to overthrow the elected government. Colonel Armas launched the effort to "liberate" Guatemala on June 18, 1954 and within two weeks a new, pro-American government was installed in Guatemala City. On July 8, 1954, a military **junta** named Colonel Armas president.

Eisenhower had created a pro-American government in Guatemala, but little was done to reduce social and economic inequalities, blunt the cry for revolution, or foster good will toward the United States among Latin Americans. When Vice President Nixon toured Lima, Peru in 1958, his car was stoned and demonstrators spat on him. In Caracas, Venezuela, after being pelted with eggs, Nixon's limousine was almost turned over by an angry mob before he was able to speed safely away. Nixon called the demonstrators "Communist thugs" and refused to be intimidated.

As Nixon toured Latin America, Fulgencio Batista, who had controlled Cuba through the 1940s and 1950s, was warding off a rebellion led by **Fidel Castro.** The corrupt and dictatorial Batista had become an embarrassment to the United States, and many Americans believed that Castro could be a pro-American leader who would reform Cuba. By 1959, rebel forces had control of the island and Eisenhower watched closely to see which direction Castro would take. By midyear many of Castro's economic and social reforms seemed to endanger American investments and interests. In truth, it would have been impossible for anyone to make *any* economic changes without affecting American interests, which controlled 40 percent of Cuba's sugar industry, 90 percent of Cuba's telephone and electric companies, 50 percent of its railroads, and 25 percent of its banking. In addition, 70 percent of Cuba's imports came from the United States. Concerned

about Castro's political leanings, Washington tried to push Cuba in the right direction by applying economic pressures. In February 1960, Castro reacted to the American arm-twisting by signing an economic pact with the Soviet Union. Eisenhower was seething. Castro was a "madman . . . going wild and harming the whole American structure." In March, Eisenhower approved a CIA plan to prepare an attack against Castro. Actual implementation of the effort to overthrow the Cuban leader, however, would have to be approved by Eisenhower's successor.

The New Look in Asia

When Eisenhower took office, Asia was the focal point of cold war tensions. Fighting continued in Korea, and in Indochina the Communist **Viet Minh** were fighting a "war of national liberation" against the French. From Communist mainland China, Mao Zedong broadcast that the United States was a "paper dragon" unable to defend its interests, and in early September 1954, the Communist Chinese began to shell several Nationalist-held islands only a few miles from the Chinese mainland, including the larger islands of Quemoy and Matsu. Were the attacks part of a plan to seize Taiwan? If fighting broke out and threatened Taiwan, Eisenhower told the military, it would not be a brushfire war but "the threshold of World War III." Having assailed the Democrats for losing China to the Communists, Republicans were now determined to protect Taiwan but were unsure about the importance of the offshore islands that were "wading distance" from mainland China.

Unwilling to draw a line to protect Quemoy and Matsu, Dulles and Eisenhower decided to "keep the Chinese guessing." They hoped that tough talk, supported with atomic threats, would be enough to persuade the Chinese Communists not to invade.

---

junta Group of military officers ruling a country after seizing power.

Fidel Castro Cuban revolutionary leader who overthrew the corrupt regime of dictator Fulgencio Batista in 1959 and established a socialist state.

Viet Minh Vietnamese army made up of Communist and other nationalist groups, which fought the French from 1946 to 1954 in order to win independence from French rule.

When asked if the United States would use atomic weapons to defend the region, Eisenhower said that he saw no reason to not use atomic weapons "exactly as you would use a bullet or anything else." Beginning in the fall of 1954 and into 1955, and again in 1958, the nation faced the prospect of war in the Formosa Straits that separated Taiwan from China. Tough talk worked. In both instances, the Chinese stopped their shelling. Most Americans credited the threat to use nuclear weapons with forcing the Communists to back down.

Indochina was a different type of problem. There, Ho Chi Minh and the Viet Minh rebels had been fighting French colonial forces since 1946. Truman had supported France in its efforts to re-establish colonial rule and defeat communism (see page 845), and American policy remained unchanged under Eisenhower. By 1954, the United States was paying nearly 78 percent of war's cost, had dispatched more than three hundred advisers to Vietnam, and watched the French military position there worsen. Describing the **domino theory,** Eisenhower warned that if Indochina fell to Communism, the loss "of Burma, of Thailand, of the [Malay] Peninsula, and Indonesia" would certainly follow, endangering Australia and New Zealand.

In Vietnam, the Viet Minh forces led by General Vo Nguyen Giap, having encircled the French fortress at **Dienbienphu,** launched murderous attacks on the beleaguered garrison. Fearing a French defeat would encourage the French government to negotiate a settlement at an international conference in Geneva, Eisenhower said, "My God, we must not lose Asia," and transferred forty bombers and detailed two hundred air force mechanics to bolster the French in Vietnam. The French—and some in the administration—wanted a more direct American role, but Eisenhower, believing that "no military victory is possible in that kind of theater," rejected such options. When, after a fifty-five-day siege, Dienbienphu fell on May 7, 1954, Eisenhower was left no option but to try and salvage a partial victory at Geneva.

There was no victory at Geneva either. The **Geneva Agreement** "temporarily" partitioned Vietnam along the 17th parallel and created the neutral states of Cambodia and Laos. The two Vietnams were to hold elections to unify the nation within two years, and neither was to enter into military alliances or allow foreign bases on their territory. American strategists called the settlement a "disaster"—half of Vietnam was lost to communism—and showing its opposition, the United States refused to

sign the agreements. To save South Vietnam, Eisenhower rushed advisers and aid to the government of Prime Minister Ngo Dinh Diem to ensure an anti-Communist South Vietnam. With American blessings, Diem ignored the Geneva-mandated unification elections, repressed his political opposition, and in October 1955, staged a **plebiscite** that created the Republic of Vietnam and elected him president. The predicament of Vietnam was just beginning (see Chapters 29 and 30).

The Soviets and Cold War Politics

Throughout the world, Eisenhower feared and opposed the spread of Communist influence. He also realized that deterrence was only one tactic to limit Soviet power and avoid nuclear confrontation. A second way was to improve American-Soviet relations, reduce the expanding arms race, and limit points of conflict. Personally, this was a difficult approach for Dulles and Eisenhower. Both men questioned any Soviet commitment to peace and willingness to keep agreements. Politically, both knew that adversaries in the military and Congress and among the public would condemn any softening of American policy toward the Soviets. Still, growing Soviet nuclear capabilities and the death of Stalin in 1953 provided the need and the opportunity for reducing tensions. Soon after Stalin's death, the new Soviet leader, Georgii Malenkov, called for "peaceful coexistence." Dulles dismissed the suggestion. But Eisenhower, with an eye on world opinion, called on the Soviets to demonstrate openly a change of policy and their willingness to cooperate with the West. Malenkov complied. He agreed to consider

---

domino theory   Notion that if one nation comes under Communist control, then neighboring nations will also fall to the Communists.

Dienbienphu   Site of a French military post in northwest Vietnam that fell to the Viet Minh in May 1954, after a fifty-five-day siege, prompting the French to agree to partition Vietnam.

Geneva Agreement   Truce signed at Geneva in 1954 by French and Viet Minh representatives, dividing Vietnam along the 17th parallel; the North became Communist and the South had a French-backed government.

plebiscite   Special election that allows people to either approve or reject a particular proposal.

◆ In this cartoon, Soviet Premier Khrushchev and President Eisenhower sit atop the negotiating table, balanced precariously on the tip of a nuclear warhead. Having tested their first H-bombs in 1953, both superpowers had an impressive array of nuclear weapons aimed at each other by 1960. Some observers spoke of the MAD (mutually assured destruction) strategy that ensured that there would be no winners in a nuclear World War III. © *1959 Newsweek, Inc. All rights reserved. Reprinted by permission/Bob Engle.*

some form of on-site inspection to verify any approved arms reductions. Eisenhower responded by asking the Soviets in December 1953 to join him in the **"Atoms for Peace" plan** and to work toward universal disarmament.

Both countries were by now testing hydrogen, **thermonuclear** bombs, hundreds of times more powerful than atomic bombs. And world concern was growing not only about the threat of nuclear war but about the dangers of radiation from the testing. Throughout 1954, worldwide pressures grew for a summit meeting to deal with the "balance of terror." In 1955, Eisenhower accepted a meeting with the new Soviet leadership of Nikolai Bulganin and **Nikita Khrushchev,** who had replaced Malenkov. Eisenhower expected no resolution of the two major issues—disarmament and Berlin (see pages 846–847)—and instead saw the meeting largely in public relations terms. He intended to make a bold disarmament initiative, called the Open Skies proposal, that would earn broad international support.

In a dramatic presentation, highlighted by a sudden thunderstorm that momentarily blacked out the conference room, Eisenhower asked the Soviets to share information about military installations and to permit aerial reconnaissance to verify peaceful intentions and reduce tensions while work began on general disarmament. Bulganin voiced official interest, but Khrushchev, speaking privately, called the proposal a "very transparent espionage device."

Eisenhower recognized that Khrushchev now represented the real power in the Soviet Union and that his response meant rejection of the proposal. He was correct, and the Geneva summit went as expected: the Americans and Soviets agreed to disagree. Nonetheless, Eisenhower was pleased. His Open Skies proposal was popular, and the meeting had generated a "spirit of Geneva" that reduced East-West tensions without appeasing the Communist foe. Besides, he knew that the United States would soon have in service a new high-altitude jet, the U-2, that could safely fly above Soviet antiaircraft missiles while taking close-up photographs of Soviet territory. It was Cold War gamesmanship at its best.

The spirit of Geneva quickly vanished when Soviet forces invaded Hungary in November 1956 to put down a nationalistic, anti-Soviet revolt. In October, many Hungarians, including part of the army, had tried to expel Soviet forces and institute political and social reforms. As Soviet tanks and troops invaded, the nationalists appealed to the United Nations and the world for help. Many Americans expected the United States to support the Hungarian freedom fighters, but no aid was sent. Facing a crisis in Egypt and seeing no way to help the Hungarians without risking all-out war, the administration could only watch as the Soviets crushed the revolt.

After the Hungarian crisis, Soviet-American relations rapidly cooled and rivalry intensified. Khrush-

---

"Atoms for Peace" plan   Proposal by Eisenhower to the United Nations in 1953 that the United States and other nations cooperate in the development of peaceful uses of atomic energy.

thermonuclear   Relating to the fusion of atomic nuclei at high temperatures or to weapons based on fusion, as distinct from those based on fission.

Nikita Khrushchev   Soviet premier who denounced Stalin in 1956 and improved the USSR's image abroad; he was deposed in 1964 for his failure to improve the country's economy.

chev emerged as a wily leader who, like Eisenhower, sought to gain global support for Soviet policies, especially in the Third World. During Eisenhower's administration, nearly thirty Asian and African nations gained their independence from colonial rule. As in Latin America, many of the new governments sought social and economic changes that threatened the property-holding classes and foreign interests. Khrushchev invariably promised such countries Soviet economic aid. Reflecting on these problems, CIA director Allen Dulles lamented to Eisenhower that they faced "the spirit of revolution . . . a revolt of the have-nots, particularly in Latin America, Asia, and Africa."

Khrushchev also sought to gain favorable world opinion by calling for a ban on nuclear weapons testing. Having finished a round of nuclear explosions, Khrushchev offered to halt testing if the Americans did also. Eisenhower rejected the proposal, but not wanting to lose in the arena of world opinion, he called for a comprehensive treaty to eliminate all nuclear weapons and their construction. Playing the same game, Khrushchev accepted. Discussions began, but they quickly stalemated on the issue of **verification**—neither superpower trusted the other. Both sides continued to develop new missiles, explode more nuclear tests, and call for banning nuclear weapons. In March 1958, following another series of Soviet H-bomb tests, Khrushchev announced a voluntary moratorium on further testing. The world praised his initiative, putting pressure on the United States to do likewise. The U.S. military said it needed more tests, but Eisenhower and Dulles, believing it was "intolerable" to allow the Soviets to gain such positive world opinion, called for a meeting to consider international controls and a permanent end to nuclear testing. Khrushchev agreed to meet in Geneva—and then rushed to test the latest nuclear devices. An orgy of testing followed as each nation raced to improve its weapons before the meeting. When the last Soviet test was over on November 3, a voluntary moratorium went into effect that lasted for three years.

Eisenhower was pleased. The two superpowers were talking, not testing, and world public opinion was optimistic. The optimism soon dissipated, however, when discussions on a permanent test ban again bogged down on the issue of verification. Negotiations became even more difficult when a Cold War crisis over Berlin reemerged. It had started in November 1958, when the Soviets announced they intended to sign a treaty with East Germany that would terminate the West's right to occupy West Berlin. For Eisenhower, retreat from Berlin was unthinkable, and supported by the British and French, he declared that the Western Allies would remain. As American and NATO forces made plans for the defense and resupply of their zones of the city, many feared that confrontation over Berlin could trigger World War III. Faced with unflinching Western determination, Khrushchev announced a permanent delay in the treaty. The crisis was over.

To recover world opinion and smooth relations with the West, Khrushchev visited the United States. In September 1959, Eisenhower welcomed the Soviet premier to Camp David, the presidential retreat in Maryland, during Khrushchev's twelve-day tour of the country. The Camp David conference produced no agreements, but the two leaders announced that both would attend a Five Power summit in Paris in May and that Eisenhower would later visit the Soviet Union.

Neither event fully materialized. On May 1, 1960, an American U-2 spy plane was shot down over the Soviet Union, and its pilot, Francis Gary Powers, was captured. At first, the United States feebly denied the nature of the flight, saying the U-2 was only a weather plane that had strayed from its Turkish flight plan. Khrushchev then showed pictures of the plane's wreckage and presented Major Powers, clearly proving the American spy mission. With both leaders in Paris, Eisenhower took full responsibility but refused to apologize for such flights, which he contended were necessary to prevent a "nuclear Pearl Harbor." Khrushchev withdrew from the summit and Eisenhower cancelled his trip to the Soviet Union. The Cold War thaw was over.

Eisenhower returned home a hero, having stood up to the Soviets. But public support was temporary. The loss of the U-2, Soviet advances in missile technology and nuclear weaponry, and a Communist Cuba only ninety miles from Florida provided the Democrats with strong reasons to claim that the Republicans and Eisenhower had been deficient in meeting Soviet threats. In 1960, turning the Republicans' own tactics of 1952 against them, Democrats cheerfully accused their opponents of endangering the United States by being too soft on communism.

---

verification In disarmament, the methods of inspection that allow each nation to assure that the others are abiding by agreements.

SUMMARY

E **xpectations**
C **onstraints**
C **hoices**
O **utcomes**

"Had enough?" Republicans had asked voters in 1952, offering the *choice* of a new vision of domestic and foreign policy—stripping down the New Deal and rolling back communism. Americans answered by electing Eisenhower. With Ike in the White House, the 1950s spawned popular, if flawed, images of America that reflected the *expectations* of many whose lives centered around affluent suburbs and a growing consumer culture. The images were partially true. Many white, middle-class Americans fulfilled their expectations by moving to the suburbs and living the American dream. Many other Americans faced *constraints* on achieving the dream, however, and prosperity and stability did not extend to all Americans.

Economic realities, social prejudice, and dissatisfaction *constrained* many Americans and led to *choices* contradicting the popular imagery. More married women chose to enter the workforce. Many men and women behaved contrary to the supposed norms of family and suburban culture, while teens and young adults turned to forms of expression that seemed to reject or criticize established norms and values. The *outcome* was that even in affluent suburbia, society and culture were less stable than they appeared. And while Eisenhower spoke about a social and political consensus, African-Americans chose to reshape the nation's social and political agenda. The *outcome* was that racial equality became an issue that neither society nor government could ignore.

Although promising change, in practice, Eisenhower *chose* foreign and domestic policies that continued the basic patterns established by Roosevelt and Truman. Republican beliefs, anticommunism, and budget concerns allowed reductions in some domestic programs, but the public acceptance of existing federal responsibilities *constrained* any large-scale dismantling of the New Deal. The New Look relied on new tactics, but Cold War foreign policies did not change significantly. Using alliances, military force, and covert activities, Eisenhower continued containment and expanded American influence in southern Asia and the Middle East. Meanwhile, relations with the Soviet Union deteriorated with the launching of *Sputnik*, another Berlin crisis, Castro's victory in Cuba, and the U-2 incident.

SELECTED READINGS

Ambrose, Stephen E. *Eisenhower: The President* (1984).
A generally positive and well-balanced biography of Eisenhower as president by one of the most respected historians of the Eisenhower period.

Burk, Robert F. *The Eisenhower Administration and Black Civil Rights* (1984).
An insightful examination of federal policy and the civil rights movement.

Devine, Robert A. *Eisenhower and the Cold War* (1981).
A solid and brief account of Eisenhower's foreign policy, especially toward the Soviet Union.

Diggins, John Patrick. *The Proud Decades: America in War and Peace, 1941–1960* (1988).
A short, well-written, and well-researched examination of the postwar period.

Garrow, David J. *Bearing the Cross* (1986).
An in-depth description of the development of the civil rights movement and Martin Luther King Jr.'s role.

Halberstam, David. *The Fifties* (1993).
A positive interpretative view of the 1950s by a well-known journalist and author, especially recommended for its description of famous and not-so-famous people.

Kaledin, Eugenia. *Mothers and More: American Women in the 1950s* (1984).
A thoughtful look at the role of American women in society during the 1950s.

Miller, Douglas T., and Marion Novak. *The Fifties: The Way We Really Were* (1977).
An interesting and useful—and often quoted—description of American society during the 1950s.

Salt of the Earth (1954)
An interesting movie about Mexican-American miners and their wives during a strike, with a cast and production crew composed of several people accused of being Communists by the HUAC.

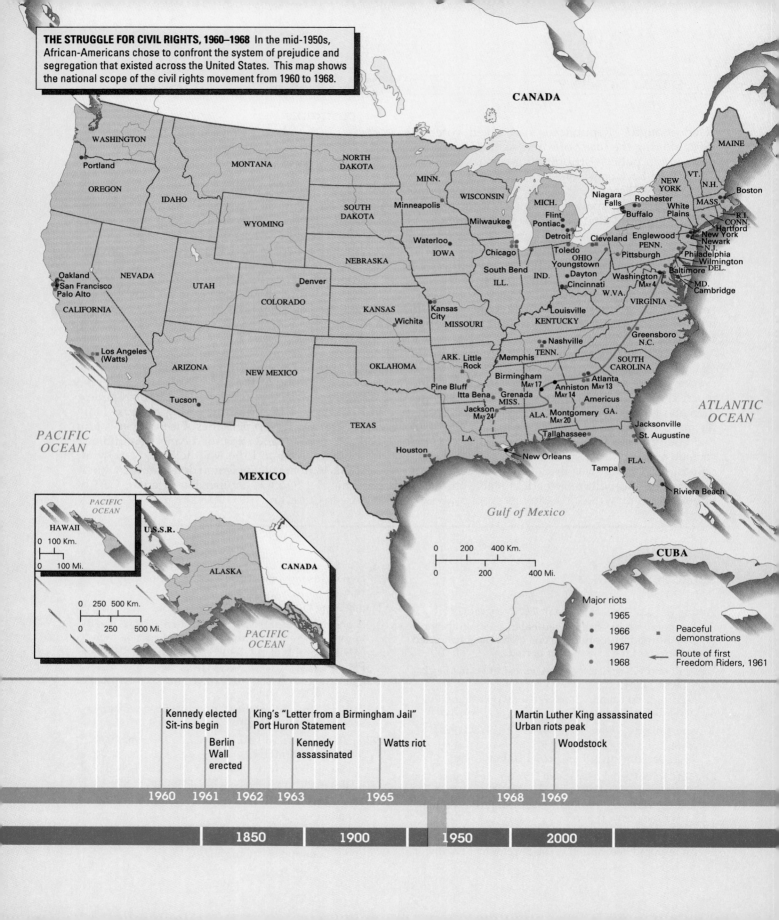

THE STRUGGLE FOR CIVIL RIGHTS, 1960–1968 In the mid-1950s, African-Americans chose to confront the system of prejudice and segregation that existed across the United States. This map shows the national scope of the civil rights movement from 1960 to 1968.

CANADA

WASHINGTON
Portland
OREGON
IDAHO
MONTANA
NORTH DAKOTA
SOUTH DAKOTA
WYOMING
NEBRASKA
MINN.
Minneapolis
WISCONSIN
MICH.
Milwaukee
Waterloo
IOWA
Chicago
ILL.
MAINE
VT.
N.H.
NEW YORK
MASS.
Boston
Niagara Falls
Rochester
White Plains
Buffalo
R.I.
CONN.
Hartford
New York
Englewood
Newark
N.J.
Flint
Pontiac
Detroit
Cleveland
PENN.
Pittsburgh
Toledo
OHIO
Youngstown
South Bend
IND.
Dayton
Cincinnati
Philadelphia
Wilmington
DEL.
Baltimore
Washington
MAY 4
MD.
Cambridge
W.VA.
VIRGINIA

Oakland
San Francisco
Palo Alto
NEVADA
UTAH
COLORADO
Denver
CALIFORNIA
Los Angeles
(Watts)
ARIZONA
Tucson
NEW MEXICO
KANSAS
Wichita
Kansas City
MISSOURI
Louisville
KENTUCKY
Nashville
TENN.
Memphis
ARK. Little Rock
Pine Bluff
Itta Bena
Grenada
MISS.
Jackson
MAY 24
LA.
Houston
OKLAHOMA
TEXAS
Birmingham
MAY 17
Anniston
MAY 14
Montgomery
MAY 20
ALA.
Americus
GA.
Greensboro
N.C.
SOUTH CAROLINA
Atlanta
MAY 13
Tallahassee
Jacksonville
St. Augustine
FLA.
Tampa
Riviera Beach
New Orleans

PACIFIC OCEAN

MEXICO

Gulf of Mexico

ATLANTIC OCEAN

CUBA

0   100 Km.
0   100 Mi.
PACIFIC OCEAN
HAWAII
U.S.S.R.
ALASKA
CANADA
0   250   500 Km.
0   250   500 Mi.
PACIFIC OCEAN

0   200   400 Km.
0   200   400 Mi.

Major riots
• 1965
• 1966
• 1967
• 1968
■ Peaceful demonstrations
← Route of first Freedom Riders, 1961

Kennedy elected
Sit-ins begin

King's "Letter from a Birmingham Jail"
Port Huron Statement

Martin Luther King assassinated
Urban riots peak

Berlin Wall erected

Kennedy assassinated

Watts riot

Woodstock

1960   1961   1962   1963   1965   1968   1969

1850   1900   1950   2000

CHAPTER

Great Promises, Bitter Disappointments, 1960–1968

JFK and the New Frontier

- What expectations and constraints did Kennedy face in establishing his domestic New Frontier?
- How did Kennedy's approach to civil rights differ from Eisenhower's?

Flexible Response

- What choices and expectations shaped Kennedy's Cold War foreign policies?
- How did his policies contribute to the Cuban missile crisis?

Beyond the New Frontier

- How did Johnson's Great Society expand on the New Deal?
- How did the outcome of the Great Society's programs contribute to increased disillusion and social tensions?

Confronting America

- How did the expectations of African-Americans change as the Civil Rights movement changed from a primarily southern movement confronting legal discrimination to a national movement combating poverty and social prejudice?

INTRODUCTION

E xpectations

C onstraints

C hoices

O utcomes

Running for the presidency, John F. Kennedy symbolized a new beginning and promised an interventionist government that many *expected* would provide a better society for all Americans. He energized the nation, raising expectations especially among the poor and minorities that he would press for solutions to end poverty and discrimination. But Kennedy faced political *constraints* in the form of conservatives in Congress who objected to an expansion of liberal programs and civil rights legislation. As a result, during his three years in office Kennedy achieved only part of his goals. Constrained by Republican and southern Democratic opposition, Kennedy *chose* to delay civil rights legislation and to not press forward with aid to education and health care. The *outcome* was a domestic record of legislation that expanded on existing programs but did not chart new paths of social policy.

Kennedy also vowed to intensify the global struggle against communism, especially in developing nations. To defeat communism, Kennedy *chose* to loosen past military budget constraints, funding both an arms race and a space race with the Soviet Union. Yet, despite Kennedy's vigor and emphasis on winning the Cold War, the *outcome* was not a safer and less divided world. The erection of the Berlin Wall, the Cuban missile crisis, and events in Vietnam symbolized heightened tension.

Building on Kennedy's legacy, Lyndon Johnson *chose* to create the largest expansion of New Deal–style legislation since the Depression. John-

son's Great Society waged a war on poverty and discrimination, promoted education, and created a national system of health care for the aged and poor. But Johnson also faced *constraints*. Conservatives opposed the Great Society's social and political goals, while some moderates and even a few liberals objected to its cost and the ineffectiveness of many programs. An expanding and increasingly unpopular war in Vietnam also added *constraints* to Johnson's domestic program and power as president.

By 1968, growing social and political turmoil was contributing to the rejection of liberal policies. The optimistic *expectations* Kennedy had inspired were declining amid the apparent divisions and excesses of American society. Within the civil rights movement, Black Power leaders *chose* confrontation over compromise. Urban riots and violence drove wedges between African-American leaders and some white supporters. The emergence of a youth-centered counterculture that *chose* to reject traditional social and moral values and stressed personal freedoms also worked to fragment American society. The *outcome* was that a decade that began with great optimism ended much differently. By 1968, few Americans *expected* that the federal government could ensure a positive future.

JFK and the New Frontier

• What expectations and constraints did Kennedy face in establishing his domestic New Frontier?

• How did Kennedy's approach to civil rights differ from Eisenhower's?

Republicans had every reason to worry as the 1960 presidential campaign neared. The last years of the 1950s had not been kind to the Republican party. The Cold War seemed to be going badly as the Soviets downed an American spy plane over the Soviet Union, launched *Sputnik* into space, and supported Castro in Cuba. Domestically, there seemed little or

no direction from the White House or from Republicans in Congress to deal with the problems of the country: civil rights, a weak economy that in 1960 tumbled into another recession, and a soaring national debt that had reached $488 billion by 1960. Democratic victories in the congressional elections of 1958 signaled that Democrats were again the majority, if not the dominant, party. Vice President Richard Nixon speculated that for a Republican presidential victory to occur, the "candidate would have to get practically all Republican votes, more than half of the independents—and, in addition, the votes of 5 to 6 million Democrats." A Republican victory would have been difficult even for Eisen-

CHRONOLOGY

New Frontiers

1960	Kennedy elected president
	Sit-ins begin
	Boynton v. Virigina
	Birth-control pill marketed
1961	Bay of Pigs invasion
	Alliance for Progress
	Peace Corps formed
	Berlin Wall erected
	Vienna summit
	Shephard rides *Mercury* capsule into space
	Freedom rides begin
	SNCC formed
1962	*Baker v. Carr*
	Engle v. Vitale
	Glenn orbits Earth
	Cuban missile crisis
	Meredith enrolls at the University of Mississippi
	King's "Letter from a Birmingham Jail"
	SDS's Port Huron Statement
	Harrington's *The Other America*
1963	Limited Test Ban Treaty
	Kennedy assassinated; Johnson becomes president
	Gideon v. Wainright
	March on Washington
	Equal Pay Act
	Diem assassinated

1964	Civil Rights Act
	Freedom Summer in Mississippi
	War on Poverty begins
	Economic Opportunity Act
	Johnson elected president
	Escobedo v. Illinois
	Griswold v. Connecticut
	Berkeley Free Speech Movement
1965	Malcolm X assassinated
	Watts riot
	Selma march
	Voting Rights Act
	Medicaid and Medicare
	Elementary and Secondary Education Act
	Immigration Act
1966	Carmichael announces Black Power
	Black Panther party formed
	Model Cities Act
	Miranda v. Arizona
1967	Ginsberg organizes first "be-in"
	Urban riots in one hundred twenty-seven cities
1968	Martin Luther King, Jr., assassinated
	Urban riots in one hundred sixty-eight cities
	Kerner Commission Report
	Vietnam peace talks begin in Paris
	Fair Housing Act

hower, whose health and age, and the **Twenty-second Amendment,** prevented him from running for a third term.

On the Democratic side loomed **John Fitzgerald Kennedy,** a youthful, vigorous senator from Massachusetts who had run a successful primary campaign—beating Hubert Humphrey and Lyndon B. Johnson—and gained a first ballot nomination. Kennedy, a Harvard graduate, came from a wealthy, Catholic Massachusetts family. Some worried about his young age (43) and lack of experience, and others worried about his religion—no Catholic had ever been elected president. To lessen these possible liabilities, Kennedy had astutely added the politi-

cally savvy Senate majority leader **Lyndon Baines Johnson** of Texas to the ticket, called for a new gen-

Twenty-second Amendment Amendment to the Constitution in 1951 that limited presidents to two terms in office.

John Fitzgerald Kennedy Massachusetts senator elected president in 1960, who established the Peace Corps and forced Khrushchev to remove Soviet missiles from Cuba; he was assassinated in 1963.

Lyndon Baines Johnson Senate majority leader who became Kennedy's vice president in 1961, and president when Kennedy was assassinated in 1963.

◆ The 1960 presidential race was the closest in recent history, with many people believing that the outcome hinged on the public's perception of the candidates during their nationally televised debates. The majority of viewers believed that Kennedy won the debates and looked more in control and presidential than Nixon. Kennedy won the election by fewer than 120,000 votes. *UPI/Bettmann Archives.*

eration of leadership, and emphasized that those who were making religion an issue were bigots. Drawing on the legacy of Franklin Roosevelt, he challenged the nation to enter a **New Frontier,** to improve the overall quality of life of all Americans, and to re-energize American foreign policy to stand fast against the Communist threat.

Facing Kennedy was Eisenhower's vice president, Richard M. Nixon. Trying to distance himself from the image of Eisenhower's elderly leadership, Nixon promised a forceful, energetic presidency and emphasized his executive experience and history of anticommunism (see page 851). He, too, promised to improve the quality of life, support civil rights, and defeat international communism. Several political commentators called the candidates "two peas in a pod" and speculated that the election would probably hinge on appearances more than issues.

Trailing in the opinion polls and hoping to give his campaign a boost, Nixon agreed to televised debates with Kennedy. He was proud of his debating skills and thought he could adapt them successfully to radio and television. Kennedy seized the opportunity, recognizing that the candidate who appeared more calm and knowledgeable—more "presidential"—would "win" the debate. Before the camera's eye, in the war of images, Nixon made a

poor impression. Having been ill, he appeared tired and haggard. He looked at Kennedy and not the camera whenever answering questions—a good debating technique but a disastrous television tactic. Worst of all, he seemed to sweat. In contrast, Kennedy appeared fresh and confident, facing the television camera and the television audience while speaking. The differences in appearance were critical. Unable to see Nixon, the radio audience believed he won the debates, but to the 70 million television viewers the winner was the self-assured and sweat-free Kennedy.

The televised debates helped Kennedy, but victory rested in his ability to hold the Democratic coalition together, maintaining southern Democratic support while wooing African-American and liberal voters. The Texan Johnson used his political clout to keep the South largely loyal even as Kennedy blasted the lack of Republican leadership on civil rights. Martin Luther King, Jr., had been arrested for civil rights activities in Atlanta, and in a

New Frontier Program for social and educational reform put forward by John F. Kennedy; though charismatically presented, it was resisted by Congress.

grand gesture, Kennedy telephoned Coretta Scott King to express his concern about her husband's jailing. Kennedy's brother Robert used his influence to get King freed, convincing even the staunchest Protestant black ministers, including Martin Luther King, Sr., to overlook Kennedy's religion and endorse him—and every vote was critical. When the ballots were counted, Kennedy had scored the narrowest of victories. Nixon had carried more states, 25 to 21, but Kennedy had a narrow margin over Nixon in popular votes and had won the electoral count, 303 to 219. (The independent southern candidate Harry Byrd earned 15 electoral votes.) Despite voting irregularities in Chicago, Illinois, and Texas, Nixon did not contest the election (see Map 29.1).

The New Frontier

The weather in Washington was frigid when Kennedy gave his inaugural address, but his speech fired the imagination of the nation. Speaking in idealistic terms, avoiding any mention of specific programs, he promised to march against "the common enemies of man: tyranny, poverty, disease, and war itself." He asked all Americans to participate, exhorting them to "ask not what your country can do for you—ask what you can do for your country."

Kennedy's staff and cabinet kept up the image of change and activism. Recruiting from businesses and universities, he appointed men and women whom one reporter dubbed the "best and the brightest." Rhodes scholars and Harvard professors were prominent, including historian Arthur Schlesinger, economist John Kenneth Galbraith (both personal advisers), McGeorge Bundy (national security director), and Dean Rusk (secretary of state). Ford Motor Company's president, Robert McNamara, was tapped for secretary of defense. In a controversial move, Kennedy gave the position of attorney general to his younger brother Robert. John Kennedy praised his choices as men with "know-how," experienced in solving problems. Not everyone, however, was convinced. Referring to the lack of political background among appointees, Speaker of the House Sam Rayburn remarked that he would "feel a whole lot better . . . if just one of them had run for sheriff once."

Rayburn had noted a critical point. Kennedy and his staff wanted to be activists, leading the nation along new paths of liberalism, but Congress was likely to be an obstacle. Democrats had lost twenty-one seats in the House in the 1960 election and since 1937 many congressional Democrats had voted with

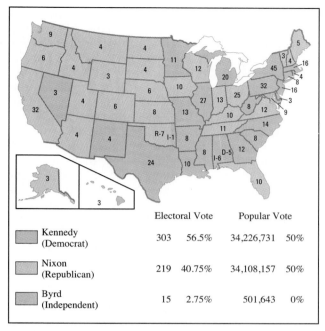

	Electoral Vote		Popular Vote	
Kennedy (Democrat)	303	56.5%	34,226,731	50%
Nixon (Republican)	219	40.75%	34,108,157	50%
Byrd (Independent)	15	2.75%	501,643	0%

◆ **MAP 29.1 Election of 1960** Although Richard Nixon won in more states than John F. Kennedy, in the closest presidential election in the twentieth century, Kennedy defeated his Republican opponent by a slim eighty-four electoral votes and fewer than nineteen thousand popular votes.

Republicans to prevent any notable expansion of the New Deal. It would be "very difficult" to pass controversial legislation, Kennedy told his staff, and so he decided to delay civil rights and social legislation and instead concentrate on shaping foreign policy and improving the economy.

To spur economic recovery, Kennedy turned to "new economics" as advocated by Walter Heller, his chairman of the Council of Economic Advisers, and called for more government spending and business and income-tax cuts. The defense budget was the first beneficiary, growing by almost 20 percent ($6 billion). Kennedy also asked Congress for a modest domestic program that included increases in social security coverage and benefits and in the minimum wage, an extension of unemployment insurance, a housing and **urban renewal** bill, and aid to educa-

---

urban renewal Effort to revitalize rundown city centers by providing federal funding for the construction of apartment houses, office buildings, and public facilities.

tion. By the autumn of 1961, Congress had passed all but the education bill and tax cuts. Meanwhile, the economy was also rebounding from the "Eisenhower recession" as unemployment fell by 2 percent from a 1960 high of 7 percent.

The booming economy, however, created a new problem: inflation. Fearful of slowing economic growth, Kennedy established informal price and wage guidelines for businesses and labor unions. Most accepted the president's formulas, but in early 1962 United States Steel and a few other steel makers raised their prices above Kennedy's ceiling. He took it as a personal insult and lashed out at U.S. Steel. Announcing that the new price was not in the public interest, he told the Federal Trade Commission and FBI to investigate the steel maker for possible **price fixing** and other fraudulent business practices, and he threatened to reduce its government contracts. Facing an angry president and being undersold by other steel companies, Roger Blough, president of U.S. Steel, retreated and lowered prices. Kennedy gloried in the victory but allowed steel prices to rise the following year. As 1962 ended, the White House boasted that the economy was strong and that forty of fifty-four bills had been passed in the first 170 days of Kennedy's administration. When liberals complained about the lack of civil rights legislation and new social programs, Kennedy hid behind the Republican–southern/conservative Democratic coalition. "There is no sense in raising hell and then not being successful," he told them. He promised a liberal package for 1963 and 1964, including a civil rights bill and programs to attack poverty.

Civil Rights and the Kennedys

During the campaign, Kennedy had promised "moral leadership" and executive action in support of civil rights, and African-American leaders looked forward to a more interventionist federal government. But once in office, Kennedy moved cautiously. He did appoint several blacks to high office and district courts, including Thurgood Marshall to the United States Circuit Court, but civil rights advocates were far from satisfied. They noted that several of his judicial appointments went to recognized segregationists, including Harold Cox of Mississippi, who once, in court, had referred to African-Americans as "niggers" and "chimpanzees," and that there was no immediate civil rights legislation. Despite his campaign pledge to do so immediately, Kennedy did not lift his pen to ban segregation in

◆ As Kennedy took office, the sit-in movement was spreading across the South as students from colleges and universities sought to integrate places of public accommodation. In this picture, whites harass students from Tougaloo College as they "sit-in" at a Woolworth lunch counter in Jackson, Mississippi. *State Historical Society of Wisconsin.*

federal housing until November 1962, and a civil rights bill was not forthcoming until 1963. But civil rights activism was a grass roots movement, not a product of federal action, and activists continued to confront segregation. They resolved, if necessary, to force governmental action.

Even as Kennedy assumed office, a new wave of black activism was striking at segregation in the South in the form of **sit-ins** and boycotts. The sit-ins began when four freshmen at Carolina A&T in Greensboro, North Carolina, decided to integrate the public lunchcounter at the local Woolworth's store. On February 1, 1960, they entered the store, sat down at the counter, and ordered a meal. A black waitress told them she could not serve them, but still they sat and waited for service. Soon, people were passing by, hurling insults or giving encouragement, but no one tried to remove or arrest them. When the store closed, they were unserved

> **price fixing** Illegal mutual agreements among competing firms to hold prices at a certain level; the price is usually somewhat inflated so that all firms will make larger profits.
>
> **sit-in** The act of occupying the seats or an area of a segregated establishment to protest racial discrimination.

but energized by their confrontation with segregation. They returned to campus as heroes and the next day twenty A&T students sat at the lunch-counter demanding service. By the end of the week, similar sit-ins had spread throughout the South.

Begun by students, the sit-ins remained largely a student movement supported by the more established civil rights groups, especially the Congress of Racial Equality (CORE) and King's Southern Christian Leadership Conference (SCLC). In April 1961, the **Student Nonviolent Coordinating Committee (SNCC, "snick")** was formed to coordinate the dramatically increasing sit-in activities as the number of sit-ins and boycotts of stores, recreational facilities, libraries, bus and train stations, and lunchrooms that segregated or refused to serve African-Americans. Over seventy thousand people protested for integrated public facilities in more than one hundred forty cities, including some outside the South, in Nevada, Illinois, and Ohio. Many of those participating in demonstrations were like Alice Walker, young college students (see Individual Choices: Alice Walker). In some cities, including Greensboro, equal service was achieved with a minimum of resistance, but particularly in the deep South, whites resisted violently to protect segregation. In Orangeburg, South Carolina, protesters were blasted with high-pressure fire hoses and arrested. Overall, thousands of "sit-in-ers" were beaten and jailed, but many saw jail as just another place to protest. CORE leader Thomas Gaither called for a "jail-in."

Sharing headlines with those "sitting-in" were the **freedom riders.** Prior to Kennedy taking office, the Supreme Court had ruled in *Boynton v. Virginia* that all interstate buses, trains, and terminals be desegregated. CORE's James Farmer planned a series of "freedom rides" to force integration on southern bus lines and stations. Farmer knew that riders would meet with opposition, creating a crisis and putting pressure on the executive branch to uphold the Court's decision. The first buses of freedom riders left Washington, D.C., in May 1961, headed toward Alabama and Mississippi. The freedom riders expected trouble. Governor John Patterson of Alabama had announced that integration would come only over his "dead body." In Anniston, Alabama, a mob of angry whites attacked the buses, smashing their windows and setting them on fire and severely beating several freedom riders. The savagery continued at Birmingham, with one freedom rider needing 53 stitches to close his head wound. When asked why no police were at the station to protect the riders, the Birmingham public safety commis-

◆ Anniston, Alabama was the end of the line for this bus of freedom riders. As riders got off the bus, they were pelted by stones and savagely beaten by a white mob. The bus was fire-bombed and its tires slashed. A second bus continued on to Montgomery. *UPI/Bettmann Archives.*

sioner Eugene "Bull" Connor explained that it was a holiday—Mother's Day.

As Farmer had predicted, the violence forced the federal government to respond. Hoping to avoid further bloodshed, Justice Department official John Seigenthaler obtained state and local protection for the riders through Alabama. But as the buses approached Montgomery, the police and National Guard escorts mysteriously vanished, leaving the freedom riders to face a large and violent crowd alone. "There are no cops," John Doar of the Justice Department phoned Robert Kennedy. "It's terrible." The brutal attack left many freedom riders injured, including federal agent Seigenthaler, who was beaten unconscious when he rushed to help a female rider. After an hour of terror, the police finally arrived and restored order.

A livid attorney general deputized local federal officials as marshals and ordered them to escort the freedom riders to the state line, where Mississippi

> **Student Nonviolent Coordinating Committee** Organization formed to give young blacks a greater voice in the civil rights movement; it initiated black voter registration drives and freedom rides.
>
> **freedom riders** Civil rights protestors who rode buses throughout the South in 1961 to press for integration in bus terminals.

Choosing Activism

Alice Walker

Alice Walker was the first African-American woman to receive the Pulitzer Prize for literature. Choosing to merge her life with her art, she has stressed the dignity and survival of the oppressed. Moving beyond civil rights and feminism, she has chosen to advocate freedom, justice, and dignity for humans and nonhumans alike. George Steinmetz

In 1961, at age 17, Alice Malsenior Walker enrolled at Spelman College in Atlanta. Born in Eatonton, Georgia, in 1944, the youngest of eight children, she was the daughter of sharecroppers who earned only $300 a year. Despite their poverty, the Walkers instilled in their children a strength of character based on proud dignity and hope based on ability. It was to emphasize human dignity and to promote a society based on abilities that Alice Walker chose to become an activist, making justice and equality a central theme in her life and writings. Encouraged by historians Howard Zinn and Staughton Lynd, she and other Spelman students took to the streets of Atlanta on weekends demonstrating for an end to segregation and for black equality. We were "young and burst with fear and determination to change our world," she recalled.

Dissatisfied with Spelman's conservatism and the dismissal of Zinn for his radical views and civil rights activities, she transferred to the largely white, liberal, all-women Sarah Lawrence College, in New York. She majored in English, continued her civil rights activism—participating in King's March on Washington—and traveled to Africa to discover her spiritual self. She returned in the fall of 1964, pregnant and suicidal. Recovering from an abortion, she

forces would take over. Battered and bloodied, the riders continued to the state capital, Jackson. There they were peacefully arrested for violating Mississippi's recently passed **public order laws.** The jails quickly filled as more freedom riders arrived and were arrested. The nation waited for the administration to act. Finally, in September 1961, the Interstate Commerce Commission declared it would uphold the Court's decision prohibiting segregation. Faced with direct federal involvement, most state and local authorities grudgingly accepted the desegregation of bus and train terminals.

A year later **James Meredith** integrated the University of Mississippi. Meredith, an air force veteran

public order laws Laws passed by many southern communities to discourage civil rights protests; they allowed the police to arrest anyone suspected of intending to disrupt public order.

James Meredith Black student admitted to University of Mississippi under federal court order in 1962; in spite of rioting by racist mobs, he finished the year and graduated in 1963.

wrote her first volume of poetry, *Once* (published in 1968). Like nearly all her writings, the poems reflected her life and her understanding of the African-American experience.

Graduating in 1965, she moved to Mississippi, the "heart of the civil rights movement," and merged her activism with writing, winning the *American Scholar's* essay contest for her personal account of the civil rights movement in Mississippi. She also married Melvyn Leventhal, a Jewish civil rights lawyer—challenging Mississippi's laws against interracial marriage. "Love, politics, work—it was a mighty coming together," she explained. There she registered African-American voters and taught black history and writing. In 1969, Walker published her first novel, *The Third Life of Grange Copeland*.

She "escaped" Mississippi to the East Coast, teaching, lecturing, working as a contributing editor for *Ms.* magazine, and writing—winning critics' praise and national awards. Drawing on her experiences, she extended her themes beyond civil rights and focused on the plight of African-American women, who were considered inferior by most male civil rights and radical activists. Her "womanist" views—a term she used to describe black feminism—drew attention and condemnation, as women became central characters in her writings. In *You Can't Keep a Good Woman Down* (1981), she asserted that African-American women were among the nation's "greatest heroes," oppressed beyond recognition not only by whites but also by black men. Comments about her views on race and women increased with the publication of her third and most praised novel, *The Color Pur-*

ple. Although a best seller that won her the first Pulitzer Prize given to an African-American woman, Walker received bitter criticism for her portrayal of African-Americans in the novel. Many people objected to her characters using what she called black folk language and her depiction of black men who abused and brutalized women. In a positive review, one critic noted that her works could be followed "as an ongoing narrative of an African-American woman's emergence from the voiceless obscurity of poverty and racial and sexual victimization to become a reshaper of culture and tradition."

In her actions and more recent works, *The Temple of My Familiar* and *Living by the Word*, Walker's range of activism and efforts to reshape culture and tradition have extended beyond African-Americans to encompass world issues, environmental and nuclear destruction, and oppressed people around the globe. She champions change that will be brought about by "alternative Americans," people of all colors who recognize where they came from, who they are, and where they can go. About American history, she wrote that there have been "ancestors we have been encouraged to avoid, not to praise, not to know. This alone tells us much. In the America we are building, they laid many a foundation. In the America that will be, they will have an honored place."

and student at a black college, heard Kennedy's inaugural speech and decided to transfer to Mississippi, knowing that Governor Ross Barnett had vowed to go to jail before allowing blacks to enroll. Robert Kennedy sent five hundred federal marshals to guard Meredith, hoping a show of force would prevent violence. The tactic did not work. Thousands of white students and nonstudents attacked Meredith and the marshals. Two people were killed and 166 marshals were wounded before 5,000 army troops arrived and restored order. Protected by federal forces, Meredith finished the year, and in May,

the University of Mississippi had its first African-American graduate.

"Old Miss" was but one victory as the sit-ins and boycotts continued. Martin Luther King, Jr., and the SCLC focused their attention on overturning segregation in Birmingham, Alabama. The civil rights movement must go forward or die, King told reporters, and Birmingham was the "point of no return." Organizers pushed an economic boycott of stores and planned a series of protest marches demanding the integration of Birmingham's businesses. King also expected a violent white reaction

◆ On August 28, 1963, one-quarter of a million people gathered in Washington, D.C. to support racial equality. Martin Luther King, Jr. electrified the crowd by saying "I have a dream that my four little children will one day live . . . where they will not be judged by the color of their skin but the content of their character." *Francis Miller, LIFE Magazine © Time Warner Inc.*

to force federal intervention and raise national support. On Good Friday, 1963, he led the first march and along with others was quickly arrested. From his cell, using smuggled paper and pen, he wrote a nineteen-page "letter" defending his confrontational tactics and aimed at those who denounced his activism in favor of patience. The "Letter from a Birmingham Jail" called for immediate and continuous, peaceful civil disobedience. Freedom was "never given voluntarily by the oppressor," King asserted, but "must be demanded by the oppressed." Smuggled out of jail and read aloud in churches and printed in newspapers across the nation, the letter rallied support for King's efforts in Birmingham.

On May 3, young and old alike filled the streets of Birmingham and confronted "Bull" Connor's police, who attacked the marchers with nightsticks, attack dogs, and high-pressure fire hoses. Television caught it all, including the arrest of over 1,300 battered and bruised children. Connor's brutality not only horrified much of the American public but caused many Birmingham blacks to reject the tactic of **nonviolence.** To many it appeared that the South was teetering on the verge of a race war, as on the following day, many African-Americans fought the police with stones and clubs. Fearing more violence, King and Birmingham's business element met on May 10, 1963, and white business owners agreed to hire black salespeople. Neither the agreement nor King's pleading, however, halted the violence, and

two days later President Kennedy ordered three thousand troops to Birmingham to maintain order and to uphold the integration agreement. Reflecting on the outcomes, King observed, "The sound of the explosion in Birmingham reached all the way to Washington."

Indeed, the sound had reached the White House and helped Kennedy conclude that the time had come to fulfill his campaign promise to make civil rights a priority. In June 1963, speaking to Congress and the nation, he made civil rights an immediate moral issue. In strong words, he announced that America could not be truly free "until all its citizens were free" and that he would send Congress civil rights legislation that would mandate integration in places of public accommodation. The speech did little to convince Congress to pass the civil rights bill, however. To pressure Congress to act on the bill, King and other civil rights leaders organized a march on Washington.

The August 28 **March on Washington** exceeded all expectations. It was the largest crowd to assem-

---

nonviolence   Doctrine of rejecting violence in favor of peaceful tactics as a means of gaining political objectives.

March on Washington   Meeting of a quarter of a million civil rights supporters in Washington in 1963, at which Martin Luther King, Jr., delivered his "I Have a Dream" speech.

ble in American history, with over 250,000 people. King capped the day with an address that electrified the throng. He promised to continue the struggle until justice flowed "like a mighty stream," and he warned about a "whirlwind of revolt" if black rights were denied. "I have a dream," he offered, "that even Mississippi could become an oasis of freedom and justice" and that "all of God's children, black men and white men, Jews and Gentiles, Protestants and Catholics, will be able to join hands and sing . . . 'Free at last! Free at last! Thank God almighty, we are free at last!'"

Nationally, the march and reactions to white violence against African-Americans worked in favor of civil rights legislation. The civil rights bill cleared the House Judiciary Committee with bipartisan support and by November, as Kennedy left for a campaign trip to Dallas, it was near passage in the House of Representatives. But the massive outpouring of support for civil rights did not translate into a better climate in the South. Within weeks of King's "I Have a Dream" speech, four young girls attending Sunday School died when their Birmingham church was bombed. Civil rights advocates had few illusions. Civil rights laws would help give African-Americans legal protection on paper, but it would not shield them from racial hatred and violence.

Flexible Response

● What choices and expectations shaped Kennedy's Cold War foreign policies?

● How did his policies contribute to the Cuban missile crisis?

If Kennedy was slow to bring federal power to bear on civil rights, he, like Eisenhower, had no reluctance to use executive power when it came to foreign policy—and like Franklin Roosevelt, he intended to direct foreign policy from the White House. He wanted to make a difference and do it quickly. "Let's not worry about four years from now," he told his advisers. "What do we do tomorrow?" To accomplish his activist goals, Kennedy relied on a circle of close advisers, principally Robert Kennedy, McGeorge Bundy, Robert McNamara, and Walter Rostow—"action intellectuals" who were willing to take risks to meet whatever challenges the United States faced, from the arms race, to the space race, to winning the allegiance of Third World countries.

To back up his foreign policies, Kennedy released the military from budget constraints imposed by

Eisenhower. Military spending should not be "bound by arbitrary budget ceilings," Kennedy told Congress. Quickly, the Pentagon began a build-up of both nuclear and conventional forces. Space exploration also received a new priority. The United States seemed to have fallen alarmingly behind in the so-called **space race** when, in April 1961, the Soviets hurled the first human being, **cosmonaut** Yuri Gagarin, into space. The American Mercury program, also designed to send an astronaut into space, had suffered several setbacks. Therefore, Kennedy informed Congress, immediate funding was needed not only to catch up with the Soviets but to beat them to the moon by the end of the decade. Congress agreed and funded the Apollo project, which reached its goal in 1969.

But the country's Cold War challenges were not limited to racing against Soviet arms development and space exploration. An equally important confrontation had been shaping up in the developing regions of the globe. In the Third World, the key problems remained economic inequalities, nationalism, and revolution. Kennedy focused on two strategies, military and economic, to win the "hearts and minds" of emerging nations. Special military units, like the Green Berets, were trained to deal with insurgency, able to live off the countryside while gaining the people's trust. Working with friendly governmental forces, they would help defeat the anti-American foes and provide stability. A multifaceted economic approach was to include direct governmental aid and increased private investment, along with the personal involvement of American volunteers in the **Peace Corps,** composed mostly of idealistic college-age men and women who were eager to help the people of developing nations.

Latin America posed a special problem. The inability of this region of dominant American influence to develop economically, socially, and politically, and the presence of a Communist regime in Cuba, seemed to many in the world to expose a

---

space race   Competition between the United States and the USSR to develop space technology; the Soviets launched the first manned space flight in 1961, but in 1969 the United States put the first man on the moon.

cosmonaut   A Soviet astronaut.

Peace Corps   Program established by President Kennedy in 1961 to send young American volunteers to other nations as educators, health workers, and technicians.

weakness in the American system. Kennedy intended to deal with both issues. First he would remove Fidel Castro by proceeding with the Eisenhower administration's plans to topple the Cuban leader (see pages 895–896). In March 1960, the Central Intelligence Agency had begun training Cuban exiles and mercenaries for an invasion of Cuba—Operation Pluto. In January 1961, the newly elected president gave the operation his approval—although there was growing concern that such a raid would not be strong enough to remove Castro.

The invasion of Cuba began on April 17, 1961. Over 1,400 Cuban exiles landed at the **Bay of Pigs,** a swampy area nearly 80 miles from the mountains that were to be their refuge if the attack did not go smoothly. It did not. The predicted uprisings in support of the invaders did not occur, and within three days, Castro's forces had captured or killed most of the invading force. Kennedy took responsibility for the fiasco but indicated no regrets for his aggressive policy and the violation of Cuban territory, vowing to continue the "relentless struggle" against Castro and communism.

To blunt the growing appeal of Castroism, and to show Latin Americans that the United States was still their best and most powerful friend and neighbor, Kennedy announced a sweeping foreign aid package, the **Alliance for Progress.** He proposed over $20 billion in aid to show that "liberty and progress walk hand in hand." In return, Latin American nations were to introduce land and tax reforms and commit themselves to improving education and their overall standard of living. Action fell short of promises. The United States granted far less than proposed, and Latin American governments implemented few reforms and frequently squandered the aid, much of which ended up in the pockets of government officials. Throughout the 1960s in Latin America, the gap between rich and poor widened as did the number of military dictatorships.

To try to recapture some of the "can-do" image deflated by the Bay of Pigs disaster, Kennedy sought an opportunity to stand toe to toe with the Soviets. Soviet leader Nikita Khrushchev and Kennedy, wanting to test each other's mettle, agreed to meet in Vienna in early June 1961 to discuss Berlin, Laos, and a nuclear test ban treaty. The results of their talks were mixed. After his first private meeting with the Soviet leader, Kennedy was shaken and angry. He thought that Khrushchev had bullied him and that his response had been feeble. In following meetings, Kennedy stood his ground more firmly, stressing that the United States would remain true to its international commitments, especially in Berlin. Khrushchev was unmoved and maintained a December deadline for Allied withdrawal from Berlin.

Returning home, determined not to appear weak under increasing Soviet pressure against Berlin, Kennedy asked for large increases in military spending and called 51,000 reservists to active duty. Some within the administration advocated the use of force if the East Germans or the Soviets interfered with Western access to or control of West Berlin. Meanwhile Khrushchev, appearing in military uniform, bellicosely reaffirmed Moscow's commitment to wars of national liberation, and he renewed atmospheric atomic bomb testing. American testing started shortly thereafter. To some it appeared that Kennedy and Khrushchev were moving to the brink of war over Berlin.

In August, the Soviets and East Germans added a new point of confrontation by erecting a wall between West and East Berlin to choke off the flow of refugees fleeing East Germany and Eastern Europe. Although the Wall challenged Western ideals of freedom, it did not directly threaten the West's presence in West Berlin and so required no military response by the United States. When Khrushchev announced that he no longer cared about the December deadline, the crisis faded, leaving only the Wall—and those who died trying to cross it—as a stark reminder of where Soviet and American interests collided.

Far more serious than the Berlin crisis was the possibility of nuclear confrontation over Cuba in October of 1962. On October 14, an American U-2 spy plane flying over the island discovered that medium-range nuclear missile sites were being built there. Launched from Cuba, such missiles would drastically reduce the time the United States had to launch a counterattack on the Soviet Union. Clearly, the missiles in Cuba were unacceptable to Kennedy, who decided on a showdown with the Soviets and organized a small crisis staff.

Bay of Pigs Site of an invasion of Cuba in 1961 by Cuban exiles and mercenaries sponsored by the CIA, which was crushed within three days and which embarrassed the United States.

Alliance for Progress Program proposed by Kennedy in 1961, through which the United States provided aid for social and economic programs in Latin American countries.

U.S. IMPOSES ARMS BLOCKADE ON CUBA ON FINDING OFFENSIVE-MISSILE SITES; KENNEDY READY FOR SOVIET SHOWDOWN

◆ After America announced a quarantine around Cuba to prevent any further delivery of weapons by the Soviet Union, the world watched as American warships tracked and confronted Soviet cargo ships headed for Cuba. Fortunately, the Soviets respected the quarantine and agreed to withdraw their nuclear missiles from Cuba. Some consider this "victory" over the Soviets to be Kennedy's finest moment. *Headline: Copyright © 1962 by the New York Times Company; U.S. and Russian ships: UPI/Bettmann Archives.*

Negotiations were out of the question until the missiles were removed or destroyed. The military offered a series of recommendations ranging from a military invasion to a "surgical" air strike to destroy the missiles. All were rejected as too dangerous, possibly inviting a Soviet attack on West Berlin or American nuclear missile sites in Turkey. President Kennedy, supported by his brother, decided to blockade Cuba until Khrushchev met the U.S. demand to remove the missiles. On Monday, October 22, Kennedy went on television and radio to inform the public of the missiles and his decision to quarantine Cuba. With one hundred eighty American warships ready to stop Soviet ships carrying supplies for the missiles, army units converged on Florida. The **Strategic Air Command** kept a fleet of nuclear-bomb-carrying B-52s in the air at all times. On Wednesday, confrontation, and perhaps war, seemed imminent as two Soviet freighters and a Russian submarine approached the quarantine line. Robert Kennedy recalled, "We were on the edge of a precipice with no way off." His anxiety was echoed around the world.

The Soviet vessels, however, stopped short of the blockade. Khrushchev had decided not to test Kennedy's will. On October 26, he sent a message through NBC's John Scali that the Soviet Union was ready to remove the missiles from Cuba if the United States publicly announced it would not invade the island. Relieved, Robert Kennedy told Scali that the United States and the Soviet Union had stood "eyeball to eyeball" and that the Soviets "had blinked first." More diplomatic maneuvering followed, but the basis of a solution had been found. The United States publicly pledged not to invade Cuba, and Khrushchev ordered the removal of the missiles. In a nonpublicized, separate agreement, the United States also agreed to remove its missiles from Turkey.

Kennedy basked in the victory. In a contest of wills he had bested Khrushchev. But he also recognized how near the world had come to nuclear war and that it was time to improve Soviet-American relations. A "hot line" telephone link was established

---

Strategic Air Command   Air force agency formed in 1946 to control America's long-range nuclear strike force.

between Moscow and Washington to allow direct talks in case of another East-West crisis. In a major foreign policy speech in June 1963, Kennedy suggested an end to the Cold War and offered that the United States, as a first step toward improving relations, would halt its nuclear testing. By July, American-Soviet negotiations produced the **Limited Test Ban Treaty,** which forbade those who signed to conduct nuclear tests in the atmosphere, in space, and under the seas. Underground testing, with its verification problems, was still allowed. By October 1963, one hundred nations had signed the treaty, although the two newest atomic powers, France and China, refused to participate and continued to test in the atmosphere.

Vietnam

Berlin, Cuba, and nuclear weapons were not the only hot points. Southeast Asia represented one of the most significant challenges that faced the United States. In early 1961, the major Indochina crisis involved Laos, a small landlocked nation to the west of Vietnam. Communist insurgents, the Pathet Lao, were winning a civil war. Dissuaded by Eisenhower from involving American troops, Kennedy sought and achieved a diplomatic solution. With Soviet approval, by July 1962, a neutral government was installed in Laos.

Almost immediately Laos was replaced as a trouble spot by South Vietnam. South Vietnamese president **Ngo Dinh Diem** was losing control of his nation. In the countryside, South Vietnamese Communist rebels, the **Viet Cong,** controlled a large portion of both land and people, having battled Diem's troops (the Army of the Republic of Vietnam, or ARVN) to a standstill. Military advisers argued that the use of American troops was necessary to turn the tide. Kennedy was more cautious. "The troops will march in, the bands will play," he said privately, "the crowds will cheer; and in four days everyone will have forgotten. Then we will be told we have to send in more troops. It's like taking a drink. The effect wears off and you have to take another." The South Vietnamese forces would have to continue to do the fighting, but the president agreed to send more "advisers." By November 1963, the United States had sent $185 million in military aid and had committed 16,000 advisers to Vietnam—compared with only a few hundred in 1961.

The Viet Cong were only part of the problem. Diem's administration was unpopular and out of touch with the majority of South Vietnamese. A Ro-

◆ In 1963 Buddhist monks protested the harsh regime of South Vietnamese President Ngo Dinh Diem. Some, like this young priest, committed ritual suicide by fire. Demonstrations like these helped to convince the Kennedy administration that the Diem government was too unstable and needed to be replaced. In November 1963 the army overthrew and murdered Diem. *UPI/Bettmann Archives.*

man Catholic whose family had lived in the north and had been French officials and minor landholders, Diem was no believer in republican forms of government or society. He ruled through a hand-picked, largely Catholic, bureaucracy whose loyalty to Diem was the key to advancement. Everywhere there appeared political opposition to his rule, from Buddhists, crime bosses, political reformers, and his own military. With American support and direction, Diem cracked down on his opponents. Reformers, rival officers, and protesting Buddhists were jailed, tortured, and killed. Protesting Diem's rule, on June 10, 1963, a Buddhist monk set himself on fire. Other **self-immolations** followed. To the shock

---

Limited Test Ban Treaty   Treaty signed by the United States, the USSR, and nearly one hundred other nations in 1963, banning nuclear weapons tests in the atmosphere, in outer space, or under water.

Ngo Dinh Diem   President of South Vietnam in 1954 who jailed and tortured opponents of his rule and who was assassinated in a coup in 1963.

Viet Cong   Vietnamese Communist rebels in South Vietnam.

self-immolation   Suicide by fire as an act of sacrifice to a cause.

of many Americans, Diem's sister-in-law, Madame Nhu referred to the protests as "Buddhist barbecues" and "the barbecue show." To Kennedy and his advisers, Diem and his inner circle had become liabilities, and the administration secretly informed several Vietnamese generals that it would approve of a change of government. The army acted on November 1, killing Diem and creating a new military government. However, the change of government brought neither political stability nor improvement in the South Vietnamese army's capacity to fight the Viet Cong.

Death in Dallas

In late 1963, with his civil rights bill and $13.5 billion tax cut in limbo in Congress, a mushrooming military commitment in Vietnam, and an economy that had turned sluggish, Kennedy began to prepare for the 1964 presidential race. Watching his popularity drop to under 60 percent by September, he decided to visit Texas in November to try and heal divisions within the Texas Democratic party. There he was assassinated on November 22, 1963. Strong evidence suggested that Lee Harvey Oswald fired the fatal shots. Oswald was captured quickly by police, but the next day a local nightclub owner and gambler, Jack Ruby, stepped out of a crowd, and shot him to death in the basement of the police station. Many wondered if Kennedy's assassination was the work of Oswald alone or part of a larger conspiracy. To dispel rumors, the government hastily formed a commission headed reluctantly by Chief Justice Earl Warren to investigate the assassination and determine if others were involved. The commission hurriedly examined most, but not all, of the available evidence and announced that Oswald was a psychologically disturbed individual who had acted alone—that there were no other gunmen nor any conspiracy. Most Americans willingly accepted the findings.

Kennedy's assassination traumatized the nation. Many people, in their anguish, soon canonized the fallen president as a brilliant, innovative chief executive who combined vitality, youth, and good looks with forceful leadership and good judgment. Lyndon B. Johnson, sworn in as president as he flew back to Washington on the plane carrying Kennedy's body, did not appear to be cut from the same cloth. Kennedy had attended the best eastern schools, enjoyed the cultural and social life associated with wealth, and liked to surround himself

◆ As millions watched on television, the final scenes of this national tragedy unfolded as Jackie, Caroline, and John-John watched the flag-draped casket carrying the slain president pass on its way to Arlington National Cemetery. *John S. Boyer © National Geographic Society.*

with intellectuals. Johnson, a product of public schools and a state college of education, distrusted intellectuals. Raised in the hill country of Texas, his passion was politics. He entered the national scene as a New Deal Democrat and soon became a political force in Washington. By 1960, his congressional experiences were unrivaled: he had served from 1937 to 1948 in the House of Representatives, and from 1949 to 1961 in the Senate, where he had been Senate majority leader. Johnson knew how to wield political power and get things done in Washington. He was famous for his "treatment," in which he would overpower people by putting his face inches from theirs, sometimes grabbing their lapels, and overwhelming them with a barrage of facts, fictions, humor, and threats. Political columnists Roland Evans and Robert Novak wrote that it was "an almost hypnotic experience and rendered the target stunned and helpless."

Beyond the New Frontier

- How did Johnson's Great Society expand on the New Deal?
- How did the outcome of the Great Society's programs contribute to increased disillusionment and social tensions?

Five days after Kennedy's death, Johnson asked Congress for "no memorial oration or eulogy," other than the passage of Kennedy's civil rights bill. At the same time, Johnson applied the "treatment" to several politicians and, in February, Kennedy's tax cut was approved. The civil rights bill moved more slowly, especially in the Senate, where it faced a stubborn southern filibuster. Johnson traded political favors for Republican backing to silence the fifty-seven-day filibuster, and the **Civil Rights Act of 1964** became law on July 2. The law made it illegal to discriminate for reasons of race, religion, or gender in places and businesses that served the public. Putting force behind the law, Congress established a federal Fair Employment Practices Committee (FEPC) and empowered the executive branch to withhold federal funds from institutions that violated the act.

Johnson had passed two major landmarks of the New Frontier, but he was unwilling merely to reflect Kennedy's image. He intended to have a domestic program as ambitious as his political passion. A Johnson-led **Great Society** would declare war on racial injustice and poverty. In 1962, Michael Harrington had alerted the public to wide-scale poverty in America with his book *The Other America*. Harrington's study projected that one-fifth of the population, 35 million people, lived in poverty. A government study established the poverty line for an urban household of four at $3,130, and $1,925 for a rural family. Using those figures, nearly 34.6 million Americans lived in poverty, with almost 40 percent (15.6 million) under the age of 18.

Johnson's assault against poverty was to be fought on two fronts: expanding opportunities and improving the social environment. He believed that state and local governments were unable or politically unwilling to take the action necessary to break the cycle of poverty. Therefore, he projected a huge expansion of federal responsibility, funds, and power in the area of social welfare. Special efforts would be made to provide education and job training, especially for the young. "Our chief weapons will be better schools . . . better training, and better job opportunities to help more Americans, especially young Americans, to escape from squalor and misery." The Manpower and Development Training Act, Job Corps, Head Start, and the Work Incentive Program all aimed at providing new educational and economic opportunities for the disadvantaged. In 1964, the Job Corps enrolled unemployed teens and young adults (16 to 21) needing job skills, while the Volunteers in Service to America (VISTA) served as a Peace Corps for the United States, sending young, service-minded, mostly middle-class men and women to work in regions of poverty. In 1965, Head Start reached out to prekindergarten children to provide disadvantaged preschoolers an opportunity to gain important thinking and social skills. The Office of Economic Opportunity (OEO) was created in 1964 to coordinate much of the War on Poverty, including ambitious and innovative Community Action Programs (CAP). CAP allowed the disadvantaged to deal with their local problems, especially those involving housing and jobs. Although many community groups were mobilized under CAP, the program was never as effective as projected. Poor local leadership and rivalries with other agencies over funds and turf frequently disabled its efforts. CAP did, however, energize many communities, generate local agencies like Legal Aid, and breed new community leaders who took their place in the political structure.

Conservative Response

Johnson's Great Society offered a tempting political target to the Republicans and **Barry Goldwater,** the Republican presidential nominee in 1964. Senator Goldwater of Arizona had risen on a wave of conservative and ultraconservative ideology, the **New Right,** that was cresting through the Republican party. Intellectually led by William F. Buckley and the *National Review,* the New Right decried many of

---

Civil Rights Act of 1964   Law that barred segregation in public facilities and forbade employers to discriminate on the basis of race, religion, sex, or national origin.

Great Society   Program called for by Lyndon Johnson in 1965, which included plans to reduce poverty, protect civil rights, and fund education.

Barry Goldwater   Conservative Republican and senator from Arizona who ran unsuccessfully for president in 1964.

New Right   Conservative movement that opposed the political and social reforms of the 1960s, demanding less government intervention in the economy and a return to traditional values.

♦ Considered by Eisenhower to be a conservative when he was appointed to the Supreme Court, Chief Justice Earl Warren became one of the most consistent supporters of judicial activism, using the Court to promote social justice and expand the rights of individuals, thus angering many staunch conservatives. Here in the New Mexico desert, this sign reflects the divided loyalties the Court and Warren received. *Paul Conklin.*

the political and social changes taking place in society. According to these conservatives, traditional American values of localism, self-help, and individualism were being destroyed by a New Deal–style, national welfare state. Rabidly anti-Communist groups like the John Birch Society made McCarthy-like denouncements of liberal American politicians and programs. But Democrats were not the only target of conservatives. The Supreme Court, they argued, had violated its constitutional role and actively promoted liberal political and social causes. The John Birch Society went so far as to demand the impeachment of Chief Justice Earl Warren.

From the mid-1950s through the 1960s, the Supreme Court under Warren handed down one decision after another that angered conservatives. To them, the Court seemed to be forcing the liberal agenda of individual rights, social justice, and equality down society's throat. The high Court not only had promoted civil rights but had also expanded the rights of individuals, often at the expense of state authority. In *Yates v. US* (1957), the Court's decision released fourteen officials of the

American Communist party who had been imprisoned for publicly advocating the overthrow of the American government. The Court decided that verbal statements, unless accompanied by actions, did not constitute a crime. In *Gideon v. Wainright* (1963), *Escobedo v. Illinois* (1964), and *Miranda v. Arizona* (1966), the Court's rulings declared that all defendants had a right to an attorney, even if the state had to provide one, and that anyone who was arrested had to be informed of the right to remain silent and to have an attorney present during questioning (the *Miranda* warning). The New Right argued that these and other decisions tipped the scale of justice too much in favor of the criminal at the expense of society. Conservatives believed that the Warren Court's actions also threatened traditional values by allowing the publication and distribution of sexually explicit materials (in *Jacobvellis v. Ohio*, 1963) and by forbidding prayers (*Engel v. Vitale*, 1962) and the reading of the Bible (*Abington v. Schempp*, 1963) in public schools. Disturbing to many, including a minority on the Court, was the 1964 *Griswold v. Connecticut* decision that overturned Connecticut's laws forbidding the sale of contraceptives, arguing that individuals have a right to privacy that the state cannot abridge. Much less controversial was the *Baker v. Carr* ruling in 1962 that established the goal of making congressional districts "as nearly as practicable" equal in population—"one person, one vote."

Shaping the Great Society

To the New Right, Johnson's Great Society programs and the Warren Court's judicial activism fit the same mold. Both advocated social legislation and values that rewarded people the conservatives characterized as lazy and immoral at the expense of hard-working, solid American families. Plain-spoken and direct, Goldwater offered most conservatives a chance to reassert their brand of traditional values and patriotic ideals. He had voted against the Civil Rights Act and against censuring McCarthy. He opposed "Big Government" and New Deal–style programs. On the world stage, Goldwater promised a more intense anti-Communist crusade. Where Johnson promised not to Americanize the war in Vietnam—"American boys," Johnson swore, would not "do the fighting for Asian boys"—Goldwater stood for "victory over communism" and was willing to commit American troops in Vietnam and even use nuclear weapons against Communist nations, including Cuba and North Vietnam, if necessary.

In the war of slogans and television spots, Johnson's ads scored more points. One memorable Goldwater slogan, "In your heart you know he's right," was modified by Democrats who added, "Yeah, far right!" and "In your guts you know he's nuts." Another Johnson ad suggested that a trigger-happy Goldwater would lead the nation into a nuclear holocaust. In a lopsided election, American voters supported liberalism over conservatism and chose containment over incinerating Communists. Although Goldwater did well in the deep South, he received less than 10 percent of the electoral vote and only 38.4 percent of the popular vote. Over forty new Democratic legislators followed Johnson to Washington, D.C., swelling the Democratic majority in the House of Representatives.

Having beaten Goldwater, Johnson pushed forward legislation to enact his Great Society. Between 1965 and 1968, over sixty programs were put in place. Most of these sought to provide better economic and social opportunities by removing social and economic barriers thrown up by health, education, region, and race. The Appalachian Regional Development Act (1965), Public Works and Development Act (1965), and Model Cities Act (1966) focused on developing economic growth in cities and long-depressed regional areas. An Omnibus Housing Bill (1965) provided $8 billion for constructing low- and middle-income housing and supplementing low-income rent programs. In a related move, the cabinet position of Secretary of Housing and Urban Development (HUD) was created. Mass transit laws (1964 and 1966) provided needed funds for the nation's bus and rail systems, and consumer protection legislation established new and higher standards for product safety and truth in advertising. First Lady "Ladybird" Johnson's beautification program turned national attention to the environment, while the National Wildlife Preservation Act (1964) and the Clean Water Restoration Act (1966) were among the first conservation projects since Theodore Roosevelt. Immigration laws also underwent major modification, dropping the racial and ethnic discrimination that had been established in the 1920s, by setting a uniform yearly limit on immigration from any one nation.

At the top of Johnson's priorities, however, were health and education. Above all, he wanted those two "coonskins on the wall." The Elementary and Secondary Education Act (1965) was the first general educational funding act by the federal government. It granted more than a billion dollars to public and parochial schools for textbooks, library materi-

als, and special education programs. Poorer and rural school districts were supposed to receive the highest percentage of federal support. But, as with many of the Great Society's programs, application fell short of intention, and much of the money went to more affluent suburban school districts. Johnson's biggest "coonskin" was the Medical Care Act (1965) which established **Medicaid** and **Medicare.** Administered within the social security structure, Medicare helped the elderly cover their medical costs. For those on welfare, Medicaid provided funds to states to provide free health care.

Despite the flood of legislation, by the end of 1965 many Great Society programs were underfunded and diminishing in popularity. Antipoverty reformers and black leaders asked for more funds—a domestic Marshall Plan—but the dollars never came. An expanding American war in Vietnam, white backlash to urban riots, and partisan politics were forcing reductions in the budget of the **War on Poverty** and changing the administration's priorities. Still, by 1970 the Great Society had contributed to an almost 10 percent decrease in the number of people living below the poverty line and a one-third drop in the infant mortality rate. Between 1963 and 1968, African-American unemployment fell nearly 42 percent while average family income rose 53 percent.

Confronting America

● How did the expectations of African-Americans change as the Civil Rights movement changed from a primarily southern movement confronting legal discrimination to a national movement combating poverty and social prejudice.

The decade of the 1950s created a powerful image of a suburban, affluent, and stable American society, a pretty picture that was reflected in popular maga-

---

Medicaid   Program of health insurance for the poor, which was established in 1965 and which provided states with funding to buy health care for people on welfare.

Medicare   Program of health insurance for the elderly and disabled, which was established in 1965 and under which the government paid the bills for health care supplied by private doctors and hospitals.

War on Poverty   Program proposed by Lyndon Johnson in 1964, which aimed to help Americans escape poverty through education, job training, and community development.

zines, movies, and in the minds of those who classified themselves as part of the middle class (see pages 873–875). Although that image mirrored part of the American reality, it was an incomplete and flawed picture. Throughout the decade, it was clear that there were many Americans who neither matched the popular image nor accepted it. African-Americans and other minorities called for equality and the end of second-class citizenship, many women were disillusioned with their roles as mother and housewife, and an increasing number of young people faulted society's emphasis on materialism and tradition. These and other groups saw the election of John F. Kennedy and his call for change and social activism as providing a new set of social choices. With Kennedy and Johnson in the White House, there was the expectation among many activists that government would no longer stand on the sideline or oppose social change but would support it. Activists were also realistic: without a grassroots demand for change, they knew, even a socially liberal government was unlikely to act. Nowhere was this more clearly evident than in the continuing quest by African-Americans for civil and political rights. During Kennedy's administration, African-Americans had continued to rely on their own efforts to combat segregation and discrimination, while begging, encouraging, prodding, and even forcing the federal government to act. They were determined to keep the same pressure on Johnson.

Freedom Now

Reflecting Johnson's own desires and responding to African-American and liberal desires, early in the new administration (1965), the president advanced on the issue of civil rights by signing an Executive Order that required government contractors to ensure nondiscrimination in jobs. He also appointed the first African-American cabinet member, Secretary of Housing and Urban Development Robert Weaver; the first African-American woman federal justice, Constance Baker Motley; and the first black on the Supreme Court, Thurgood Marshall. Blacks applauded the president's actions but realized that large pockets of active opposition to civil rights continued to infect government and society. Civil rights leaders therefore wanted to push voting rights as the next step in achieving equality. For nearly one hundred years, most southern whites had viewed voting as a function for whites only, and through their control of the ballot had maintained their political power and a segregated society. Hoping to pull

♦ The summer of 1964 was called "Freedom Summer," as hundreds of civil rights volunteers—many of them college students—converged on Alabama and Mississippi to conduct voter registration drives, often facing violent opposition. Many were beaten, some were jailed, and some lost their lives, but as Anne Moody wrote in her autobiography, *Coming of Age in Mississippi*, "threats did not stop them." *Art and Artifacts Division, Schomburg Center for Research in Black Culture, the New York Public Library, Astor, Lenox, and Tilden Foundations.*

the federal government behind their efforts to expand black political and social rights, civil rights leaders targeted Alabama and Mississippi.

The result was "the **Freedom Summer** of 1964." Led by SNCC's Bob Moses, whites and blacks went to Mississippi to open "Freedom Schools" and to encourage African-Americans to register to vote. The Freedom Schools taught basic literacy and black history, stressed black pride and achievements. They also tutored African-Americans on the Mississippi

---

Freedom Summer Effort by civil rights groups in Mississippi in the summer of 1964 to register black voters and cultivate black pride.

◆   The fifty-mile Freedom March from Selma to Montgomery, Alabama caught the attention of a world-wide audience as blacks and whites marched in solidarity through jeers, threats, and violence by those opposing racial change. In this picture Reverend Martin Luther King, Jr., and Coretta Scott King (center) join with children and others in singing freedom songs as they finished the march. *Matt Herron.*

voter literacy test. As in several southern states, all answers, including "a reasonable interpretation" of a section of the state constitution and a description of "the duties and obligations of citizenship," had to satisfy a white registrar. Confronting this obstacle took a massive effort, and white hostility made the work dangerous. "You talk about fear," one Freedom Summer organizer told recruits, "It's like the heat down there, it's continually oppressive. You think they're rational. But, you know, you suddenly realize, they want to kill you." Civil rights violence in Mississippi occurred almost daily from June through August of 1964. There were over thirty-five shooting incidents; thirty buildings, many of them churches, were bombed; and six Freedom Summer workers were murdered while hundreds were beaten and arrested. But the crusade registered nearly sixty-thousand new African-American voters.

Although the 1964 Civil Rights Act had made discrimination illegal; clearly it was still practiced throughout much of the South, and civil rights leaders were just as clearly determined to eliminate it. Change would occur, Martin Luther King told reporters, because nonviolent demonstrators would go into the streets to exercise their constitutional rights and be attacked by racists, "unleashing violence against them." Seeing the violence, King ex-

plained, "Americans of conscience in the name of decency" would demand federal intervention and legislation, and under public pressure, the administration would intervene and initiate "remedial legislation." King and other civil rights leaders selected Selma, Alabama, as their target, because the white community there, and its sheriff Jim Clark, vehemently opposed integration. Clark could not have fit the negative image of the southern segregationist better. Pot-bellied, he wore mirrored sunglasses and a helmet and carried a swagger stick. His temper was short and he had sworn never to integrate.

As expected, Sheriff Clark confronted protesters, arresting nearly two thousand before King called for a **freedom march** from Selma to Montgomery to increase the pressure. On March 7, 1965, hundreds of freedom marchers faced fifty Alabama state troopers and Clark's mounted officers at Pettus Bridge. After ordering the marchers to halt, the state troopers fired tear gas and charged. As marchers fled

---

freedom march   Civil rights march from Selma to Montgomery, Alabama, in March 1965; the violent treatment of protesters by local authorities helped stir national opinion in favor of the civil rights.

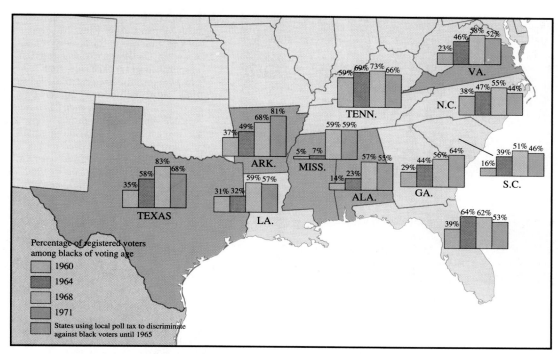

♦ **MAP 29.2 African-Americans and the Southern Vote, 1960–1971** An important part of the civil rights movement was to reestablish the African-American vote that had been stripped away in the South following Reconstruction. Between 1960 and 1971, with the outlawing of the poll tax and other voter restrictions, African-American voter participation rose significantly across the South.

back to Selma, Clark's men chased them down, wielding rubber tubing wrapped with barbed wire. Television coverage of the onslaught stirred nationwide condemnation of Clark's tactics and support for King and the marchers. Johnson told Governor George Wallace that he would not tolerate any further interference with the march. When 25,000 resumed the march on March 25, they were escorted by the National Guard.

Johnson also used the violence in Selma to pressure Congress to pass his voting rights bill, which he had proposed during his 1965 State of the Union address. Approved in August, the 1965 **Voting Rights Act** banned a variety of methods that states used to deny blacks the right to vote, including Mississippi's literacy test (See Map 29.2). In Selma, 60 percent of qualified African-American voters registered, voted, and stopped Sheriff Clark's bid for reelection.

By the end of 1965, federal legislation had confirmed what the Supreme Court had implied in the *Brown* decision: official, *de jure* segregation was illegal in the United States. But equality depended on more than laws. Many other ways remained to deny

minorities an equal place in America. Neither the 1964 Civil Rights Act nor the 1965 Voting Rights Act guaranteed justice, removed oppressive poverty, provided jobs, or ensured a higher standard of living. *De facto* discrimination and prejudice remained, and African-American frustrations—born of raised expectations, poverty, prejudice, violence—soon changed the nature of civil rights protest and ignited northern cities.

By 1964, more than half of the nation's black population lived in northern cities. More were arriving every year, over 1 million in the 1960s. Nearly all were poor and unskilled. They entered a society with shrinking job opportunities and growing problems. Unskilled jobs were declining and urban black unemployment was high, while social services, despite Great Society programs, were too meager and

> **Voting Rights Act** 1965 law that suspended literacy and other voter tests and authorized federal supervision of registration in places where tests had been used.

♦ In 1965 the nonviolence associated with Martin Luther King, Jr., gave way to violence in the streets of Los Angeles. The Watts riot was the first of many summer race riots that swept across the nation from 1965 to 1968. "Burn Baby Burn" quickly became a rallying cry for many urban African-Americans as they protested against economic and social inequality. Thirty-four people died in the Watts riot before police and national guardsmen restored order. *Co Rentmeester, LIFE Magazine © Time Warner Inc.*

often too mean-spirited to provide adequate support. In New York City, a protester's sign spelled out the reality of civil rights for northern blacks: "I'd eat at your lunchcounter—if only I had a job." Poverty and false hopes led to increased violence and crime while largely white police forces were seen by African-Americans as suppressors rather than protectors. James Baldwin observed that the police were "the force of the white world" and moved through black neighborhoods "like occupying soldier in a bitterly hostile country." By the mid-1960s, the nation's cities were primed for racial violence. Minor race riots occurred in Harlem and Rochester, New York, during the summer of 1964, but it was the 1965 Watts riot that shook the nation.

Watts did not look like most ghettoes. It was a community of largely single-family homes and duplexes, many with garages that housed family cars. The fairly new buildings were usually well maintained. There was little open discrimination in Los Angeles, no restrictions on voting, public transportation, or eating at lunchcounters. Los Angeles was among the nation's leaders in public assistance programs, spending more than $500 million a year. But outward appearances were deceptive. The 50-square-mile area called Watts was home to more than 250,000 African-Americans, more than four times the people per block than in the rest of the city. Male unemployment was 34 percent and almost two-thirds of the residents were on public assistance. Schools were overcrowded and a bureaucratic maze choked city services. The mayor of Los

Angeles, Sam Yorty, disapproved of federal anti-poverty programs that interfered with his control and had prevented $20 million of federal aid from being used. The nearly all-white L.A. police force (of 205 officers assigned to Watts only 5 were black) had earned a reputation for racism and brutality. Police Chief William Parker disliked "Communists" and civil rights leaders because he felt that, like criminals, they undermined respect for law and order. In this climate, Officer Lee Minikus stopped Marquette Frye for drunk driving on August 11, 1965. What started as a simple arrest soon mushroomed into a major riot. A crowd of onlookers gathered as more police arrived and as Frye and Minikus began to scuffle. The police charged through the crowd of about 150 bystanders using nightsticks, and word quickly rushed through Watts that the police were attacking innocent people. The Watts riot followed, as many residents pelted the police with stones and bottles and vented their frustrations and anger by looting and setting fire to cars and stores. When firemen and police arrived to restore order and put out the flames, they had to dodge snipers' bullets and **Molotov cocktails.** Thirty-six hours later, Los An-

Watts Predominantly black neighborhood of Los Angeles where race riots in August 1965 did $200 million in damages and took the lives of 28 blacks.

Molotov cocktail Makeshift bomb made of a bottle filled with gasoline.

geles authorities called for the California National Guard. It took 14,000 ill-equipped guardsmen, with no riot training, together with over 1,000 police and 800 sheriff's deputies to calm the storm. The costs were high: 34 dead, including 28 African-Americans, more than 900 injured, and over $45 million in property destroyed. The police arrested 4,000 rioters and convicted 350 of felonies and nearly 1,500 others for various misdemeanors. The rest were released.

The Watts riot shattered the complacency of many northern whites who had supported civil rights in the South while ignoring the plight of the inner cities. It also demonstrated a gap between the attitudes of northern blacks and those of many civil rights leaders. In 1964, King had received the Nobel Peace Prize, but in 1965, when he spoke to the people of Watts after the rioting, he discovered they had little use for his "dreams." He was shouted down and jeered. "Hell, we don't need no damn dreams," one skeptic remarked. "We want jobs." Watts was only the beginning. More deadly urban riots followed, and a new, militant approach to racial and economic injustices erupted: the **Black Power** movement.

The new voices of Black Power called on blacks to seek power through solidarity, independence, and, if necessary, violence. African-Americans needed to use the same means as whites, argued one veteran of the battle to integrate Mississippi: "If he pose with a smile, meet him with a smile, and if he pose with a gun, meet him with a gun." Many in SNCC and CORE agreed. SNCC's leader, Bob Moses, by the winter of 1965, had had too much of clubs, dogs, threats, and jails. Emotionally spent, he resigned, changed his name, and moved north. The new leadership led by **Stokely Carmichael** exalted Black Power: "I'm not going to beg the white man for anything I deserve," he announced. "I'm going to take it." SNCC and CORE quickly changed from biracial, nonviolent organizations to Black Power resistance movements.

The cry of "Black Power!" had established roots in inner cities across the nation. Among those receptive to a more militant approach were the **Black Muslims** (the Nation of Islam) founded by Elijah Muhammad in the 1930s. The Black Muslim movement attracted mostly young males and demanded adherence to a strict moral code that prohibited the use of drugs and alcohol. Preaching black superiority and independence from an evil white world, Black Muslims looked to the black community for regeneration and improvement. With little under-

standing of Black Muslim goals of self-improvement, most whites focused solely on the group's hostility toward whites and considered the movement a threat to peace and order. By the early 1960s, there were nearly a hundred thousand Black Muslims, but most whites were concerned with only one: **Malcolm X.**

By the age of 20, Malcolm Little's life of hard drugs, pimping, and burglary had put him in prison. Behind bars, his intellectual abilities blossomed. He devoured the prison library, took correspondence courses, and converted to the Nation of Islam—becoming Malcolm X. On his release in 1952, he quickly became one of the Black Muslims' most powerful and respected leaders. A mesmerizing speaker, he proclaimed the ideals of black nationalism and separatism. He rejected integration with a white society that, he said, emasculated blacks by denying them power and personal identity. "Our enemy is the white man!" he roared. But in 1964, he re-evaluated the policy of rejecting cooperation with whites and other civil rights groups. Although still a black nationalist, he admitted that to achieve their goals Black Muslims needed to cooperate with other groups, including some whites. He broke with Elijah Muhammad and the defection cost him his life. On February 21, 1965, three Black Muslims assassinated him in Harlem. After his death, Malcolm X's *Autobiography*, chronicling his personal triumph over white oppression, became a revered guide for many blacks.

Malcolm X represented only one model for urban blacks. Others pursued direct action against white power and advocated violence, nearly drowning out the nonviolent voice of King. Huey P. Newton

---

Black Power Movement beginning in 1966 that rejected the nonviolent, coalition-building approach of traditional civil rights groups and advocated black control of black organizations.

Stokely Carmichael Civil rights activist who led SNCC and who coined the term "black power" to describe the need for blacks to use militant tactics to force whites to accept political change.

Black Muslims Popular name for the Nation of Islam, an African-American religious group founded by Elijah Muhammad, which professed Islamic religious beliefs and emphasized black separatism.

Malcolm X Black activist who advocated black separatism as a member of the Nation of Islam; in 1963 he converted to orthodox Islam and two years later he was assassinated.

◆ Born Malcolm Little in Omaha, Nebraska, Malcolm X became a Black Muslim and one of the most recognized African-American nationalists' leaders. Known for his fiery words, he condemned white exploitation and preached separatism for African-Americans. Assassinated in 1963 by members of the Nation of Islam, he is shown here with the leader of the Nation of Islam, Elijah Mohammed in 1961. *Eve Arnold/Magnum.*

and Bobby Seale, in October 1966, organized the **Black Panthers** in Oakland, California. Although they pursued community action, like developing school lunch programs, they were more noticeable for adopting Mao Zedong's adage that "power flows from the barrel of a gun." The Black Panthers were well armed. Their willingness to use violence frightened many, but some applauded the militance and urged others to follow suit. New SNCC leader H. Rap Brown told listeners to grab their guns, burn the town down, and shoot the "honky." The summer of 1967 seemed to bring Brown's words to life. Over seventy-five major riots took place, the deadliest occurring in Detroit and Newark, resulting in a nationwide total of eighty-seven dead and over 16,300 arrested.

Finally, after a third year of urban riots, Johnson created a special commission chaired by Governor Otto Kerner of Illinois to investigate their causes. The committee's report, issued in March 1968, put the primary blame on the racist attitudes of white America. The study described two Americas, one white and one black, and concluded:

Pervasive discrimination and segregation in employment, education, and housing have resulted in the continuing exclusion of great numbers of Negroes from the benefits of economic progress.

The Kerner Commission believed the solution to the riots and America's racial problem was a "compassionate, massive and sustained" commitment "backed by the resources of the most powerful and richest nation on this earth."

Just a month later, a new wave of riots spread across the United States following the assassination of Martin Luther King, Jr., by a white racist. King had worked hard to regain his leadership of the civil rights movement since the Watts riot and the emergence of Black Power. Shifting from legal rights to economic rights, he had become a champion of the black urban **underclass,** criticizing the capitalistic

---

Black Panthers   Black revolutionary party founded in 1966, which accepted violence as a means of social change; many of their leaders were killed in confrontations with police or sent to prison.

underclass   Term identifying the lowest economic class, with the implication that its members are so disadvantaged by poverty that they have little or no chance to move upward economically.

◆ In 1968 the world turned its attention to the Olympic games in Mexico City, where spectacle of sport was supposed to take precedence over national and international conflicts. But, even in the Olympic stadium, the divisions in American society were evident as 200-meter winners Tommie Smith and John Carlos raised their fists in a salute to Black Power while on the medal platform. Both athletes had their medals taken away as a result of their political statement. *UPI/Bettmann Archives.*

system that relegated millions to poverty. Still an advocate of nonviolence, King called for mass demonstrations to compel economic and social justice. King was in Memphis supporting striking black sanitation workers when, on April 4, 1968, he was gunned down by James Earl Ray. Spontaneously, African-Americans took to the streets in over 125 cities. Sections of Washington, D.C., itself were engulfed in flames.

As American cities burned and cries of "Burn, Baby, Burn," and "Black Power!" emerged from the smoke, a white backlash occurred. Many Americans, fearful of Black Power advocates and increased urban violence, backed away from supporting civil rights. Republican politicians were especially vocal. Governor of California Ronald Reagan argued the "riff-raff" theory of urban prob-

lems: "mad dogs" and "lawbreakers" were the sole cause of the trouble. Governor Spiro Agnew of Maryland blamed activists like H. Rap Brown and urged that he be jailed. Senator Everett Dirksen and House leader Gerald Ford suspected a Red conspiracy. Most Americans applauded as police cracked down on the Black Panthers, arresting or killing its membership. As the 1968 political campaign began, law and order replaced the Great Society and the War on Poverty as the main issue. The backlash was in part a result of white dread of Black Power and a reaction to the violence of the urban riots, but it was also a reaction to fears that traditional American society was being torn apart at the seams. As alarming to many Americans as the revolution that was reshaping African-American attitudes was the growing tendency of the nation's youth—including white, middle-class young people—to confront and reject traditional social and political values.

The Challenge of Youth

High school and college-aged students were among the most active social groups during the decade of the sixties. The first wave of "baby boomers"(see page 855) were now young adults, and they were going to college in record numbers. In 1965, over 40 percent of the nation's high school graduates were attending college, a leap of 13 percent from 1955 and of nearly 30 percent since World War II. Graduate schools, too, swelled in size and churned out Ph.D.s—over half of all doctorates awarded from the Civil War until 1970 were conferred during the 1960s. Although the majority of young adults maintained the typical quest for family, a good-paying job, and a house in the suburbs, as the decade progressed, some took up social concerns and personal fulfillment as alternative values. The civil rights movement, the fear of nuclear destruction, and Kennedy's idealistic imagery inspired many youths to think first of improving the human community. By the middle of the decade, the image of America's young adults had changed: they were active and would be heard, no longer apathetic or self-absorbed, merely seeking jobs, homes, and the suburban lifestyle. The transformation was especially true among those attending colleges and universities.

On college campuses across the nation, many students—often encouraged by professors—began to question the role of the university and the goal of education. Particularly at huge institutions like the University of California at Berkeley and at Los An-

SEPTEMBER 1967
PRICE $1

COLLEGE ISSUE

If you think the war in Vietnam is hell, you ought to see what's happening on campus, baby. *see page 89*

♦ "We're in a time that's divorced from the past," wrote author Norman Mailer, and from Berkeley to Harvard Yard, college campuses were becoming battle grounds of the social, cultural, and political changes that were sweeping the nation. Whether participating in the counterculture or Freedom Summer, or opposing the war in Vietnam or college restrictions, in the 1960s it appeared that America's youth demanded new values and attitudes. *Michael Barson Collection/Past Perfect.*

conformity. Education was designed to meet the needs of administrators and teachers, not students. Reflecting Goodman's view, many students demanded freedom of expression and a new, more flexible attitude from college administrators and faculty.

Campus activists confronted a broad spectrum of issues, from those directly related to campus life to those dealing with the nation and the world. Denouncing course requirements and restrictions on dress, behavior, and living arrangements, students insisted on more personal choices in selecting courses and pursuing lifestyles. By the end of the decade, many colleges and schools had relaxed or eliminated dress codes. Long hair was accepted for males, and casual clothes like faded blue jeans and shorts were common dress for both sexes on most college campuses. Colleges also lifted dorm curfews and other residence requirements. Some dorms became co-ed. Academic departments reduced the number of mandatory courses, allowing students more options in their educational program, and pass/fail grades were instituted. The "open" and liberal arts major, students argued, had as much value as the pre-med or business major. Learning for its own sake was as important as "arbitrarily given" grades or **vocational** or professional training. By the beginning of the 1970s, many colleges and even some high schools had introduced programs in nontraditional fields like African-American, Native American, and women's studies. Although it remained popular, the "Greek system" of fraternities and sororities declined in reputation and importance on many campuses.

Setting their sights beyond the campus community, some student activists urged that the campus should be a haven for free thought and a marshaling ground for efforts to change society significantly. At the University of Michigan in the early 1960s, Tom Hayden and Al Haber broke new ground in campus consciousness when they organized **Students for a Democratic Society (SDS).** Hayden wanted to throw off the "silent generation" label and harness student energy to attack complacency and indifference in American society. SDS members insisted that Americans recognize that their affluent nation

geles and the University of Michigan, students complained that humanism and concern for individuals were missing from education. Known by matriculation numbers instead of names, students were stuffed into courses based on impersonal evaluation tests and taught by professors or teaching assistants who preferred to be in the lab or library. Education seemed sterile, more like an assembly line producing a standardized product than an effort to create an independent, thinking individual. Paul Goodman, in *Growing Up Absurd,* argued that schools destroyed natural creativity and replaced it with a highly structured system that stressed order and

vocational   Providing training in a special skill to be pursued in a trade.

Students for a Democratic Society   Left-wing student organization founded in 1960 to criticize American materialism and call for social justice.

was also a land of poverty and want, that the **military-industrial complex** dominated the economy and society, and that business and government chose to ignore social inequalities. In 1962, SDS issued its Port Huron Statement, which maintained,

> *The search for truly democratic alternatives to the present, and a commitment to social experimentation with them, is a worthy and fulfilling human enterprise, one which moves us and, we hope, others today.*

Hayden argued that the country should allocate its resources according to social need and strive to build "an environment for people to live in with dignity and creativeness."

SDS and other activist groups believed that most college administrators and faculty members opposed the idea of the campus as a base for social criticism and activism. Throughout the decade, students clashed with college authorities in struggles over what kind of forum the college should represent. The earliest major confrontation occurred at Berkeley in 1964 and became a model for those that followed.

At Berkeley, activists led by Mario Savio protested **Establishment** repression when the administration tried to prevent students from using a plaza on campus to recruit supporters and solicit funds for various social and political causes, including the civil rights movement. Fresh from the Freedom Summer, Savio demanded freedom of speech and political activism on campus. Claiming that the university was not fulfilling its moral obligation to provide an open forum for education and free thought, Savio asked students and faculty to disrupt the university's activities: to jam the gears, to bring the machine to its knees, so that students could be unleashed. Over six thousand students responded, seizing campus sites, including the administration building, boycotting classes, and yelling and chanting what many consider vulgar four-letter words. Savio and two other organizers were arrested, expelled, tried for inciting a riot, and sentenced to four months in jail—but Chancellor Clark Kerr and the administration agreed to allow freedom of expression, including political literature, on campus.

The Berkeley Free Speech Movement encouraged other campus organizers to assert their right to address social and political issues. Student activists in growing numbers focused their attention on civil rights, the environment, and social and sexual norms. By the late sixties, though, their loudest protests opposed American foreign policy, the military-industrial complex, and the war in Vietnam. As the next chapter will show, opposition to the war in Vietnam and the draft would further expand the number of student activists and increase pressure on the Johnson administration to modify its policies.

Aside from politics, the youth movement's discontent with social and cultural norms found expression in what was labeled the **counterculture.** As the New Left rejected political standards and values, so also many young people spurned the traditional moral and social values of their parents and the fifties. "Don't trust anyone over 30," was the motto of the young generation. Counterculture thinking rejected conformity and glorified freedom of the spirit and self-knowledge. A large number of teens and young adults began to accuse American society of being "plastic" in its materialism and disregard for change, and they sought ways to express their dissatisfaction. Music was one of the most prominent forms of defiance. Some musicians, like Bob Dylan and Joan Baez, challenged society with protest and antiwar songs aimed at specific problems. Folk music and protest rock, however, were only a small part of the music challenge. For the majority, rock 'n' roll, which took a variety of forms, remained dominant. Performers like the **Beatles,** an English group that exploded on the American music scene in 1964, were among the most popular, sharing the stage with such other British imports as the Rolling Stones and the Animals, whose behavior and songs depicted a life of pleasure and lack of social restraints. Other musicians, like the Grateful Dead and Jimi Hendrix, turned rock 'n' roll into a new form of music, psychedelic **acid rock,** whose swirls of sound and lyrics acclaimed a drug culture and attacked social conventions.

---

military-industrial complex   Term first used by Eisenhower to describe the arms industry; in the 1960s it was used by radicals to describe all those in power who benefited from U.S. militarism.

Establishment   The established social order, or the group that holds most of the power and influence in a society.

counterculture   A culture with values or lifestyles in opposition to those of the established culture.

Beatles   English rock group that gained international fame in 1962 and disbanded in 1970; they were known for the intelligence of their lyrics and their sophisticated instrumentation.

acid rock   Rock music having a driving, repetitive beat and lyrics that suggest psychedelic drug experiences.

The message of much music of the sixties was wrapped up in drug use—"get high" or "stoned"—reflecting a view that drugs offered another way to be free of the older generation's values. Todd Gitlin, president of SDS, thought that "to get access to youth culture," a person "had to get high." For many in the sixties generation, marijuana, or "pot," was the primary means to get high. Marijuana advocates claimed that it was nonaddictive and that, unlike the nation's traditional drug—alcohol—it reduced aggression and heightened perception. Thus, they argued, marijuana contributed to the counterculture's ideals of peace, serenity, and self-awareness. A more dangerous and unpredictable drug also popular with some of the counterculture was LSD, lysergic acid diethylamide. LSD, or "acid," was a hallucinogenic drug that altered the user's perceptions of reality and had originally been developed for interrogation purposes by government agencies like the CIA. Harvard psychology professor **Timothy Leary** used the drug and argued for its widespread consumption. He believed that by "tripping" on LSD people could free themselves—"blow their minds," "turn on, tune in, and drop out"—of the rat race that was American society. Although most youths did not use them, drugs offered some within the counterculture and the nation a new experience that many believed was liberating. Drugs also proved to be self-destructive and deadly, contributing to the deaths of several counterculture figures, including musicians Jimi Hendrix, Jim Morrison, and Janis Joplin.

Another realm of traditional American values the counterculture overturned was sex. Some young people appalled their parents and society by questioning and rejecting the values that placed restrictions on sexual activities. Sex was a form of human expression, they argued, and if it felt good, why stifle it? A new openness about sexuality and a relaxation of the stigma on extramarital sex turned out to be a significant legacy of the sixties. But the philosophy of **free love** also had a negative side as increased sexual activity contributed to a rapid rise in cases of venereal disease. The notion of free love also exposed women to increased sexual assault as some men chose to assume that all "liberated" women desired sexual relations.

Perhaps the most colorful and best-known advocates of the counterculture and its ideals were the **Hippies.** Seeking a life of peace, love, and self-awareness—governed by the law of "what feels good" instead of by the rules of traditional behavior—Hippies tried to distance themselves from society. They flocked in large numbers to northern California, congregating especially in the Haight-Ashbury neighborhood of San Francisco, where they frequently carried drug abuse and free love to excess. Elsewhere, some Hippie groups, abandoned the "old-fashioned" nuclear family and lived together as extended families on communes. Hippies expressed their nonconformism in their appearance, favoring long unkempt hair and ratty blue jeans or long flowered dresses. Although the number of true Hippie dropouts was small, their style of dress and grooming greatly influenced young Americans.

The influence of the counterculture peaked, at least in one sense, in the summer of 1969, when an army of teens and young adults converged on **Woodstock,** New York, for the largest free rock concert in history. For three days, through summer rains and deepening mud, more than four hundred thousand came together in a temporary open-air community, while many of the most popular rock 'n' roll bands performed day and night. Touted as three days of peace and love, sex, drugs, and rock 'n' roll, Woodstock symbolized the power of counterculture values to promote cooperation and happiness.

The spirit of Woodstock was fleeting. For most people, at home and on campus, the communal ideal was impractical, if not unworkable. Nor did the vast majority of young people who took up some counterculture notions completely reject their parents' society. Most stayed in school and continued to participate in the society they were criticizing. To be sure, the counterculture had a lasting impact on American society—on dress, sexual attitudes, music, and even personal values—but it did not reshape America in its image.

Timothy Leary　Harvard professor and counterculture figure who advocated the expansion of consciousness through the use of drugs such as LSD.

free love　Popular belief among members of the counterculture in the 1960s in having sexual activity with as many partners as they liked.

Hippies　Members of the counterculture in the 1960s who rejected the competitiveness and materialism of American society and searched for peace, love, and individual autonomy.

Woodstock　Free rock concert in Woodstock, New York, in August 1969, which attracted 400,000 people and was remembered as the classic expression of the counterculture.

SUMMARY

E xpectations
C onstraints
C hoices
O utcomes

The *outcome* of Kennedy's election was a wave of renewed optimism and liberalism. Kennedy's call for a more responsible society and government was at the heart of his New Frontier and of Johnson's Great Society as well. Kennedy raised *expectations*, but faced political *constraints*, and it was Johnson's Great Society that greatly expanded the role of government in social affairs. Heightened expectations were clearly visible among the African-Americans who looked to Kennedy, and later to Johnson, for legislation to end segregation and discrimination. As Kennedy took office, African-American leaders *chose* to launch a series of sit-ins and freedom marches designed to keep the pressure on American society and the government. Kennedy responded by introducing a civil rights act in 1963 that was finally passed in 1964—after his assassination.

In foreign policy, Kennedy *chose* to expand the international struggle against communism. Confrontations over Berlin and Cuba, a heightened arms race, and an expanded commitment to Vietnam were *outcomes* accepted as part of the United States' global role and passed intact to Johnson.

As president, Johnson *chose* to expand on the slain president's New Frontier. The 1964 Civil Rights Act, the 1965 Voting Rights Act, and Great Society legislation, were designed to wage war on poverty and discrimination, while providing federal aid to education and creating a national system of health insurance for the poor and elderly. But by 1968, the growing societal and political divisions constrained liberalism. Despite legal and political gains, many African-American activists *chose* to become more militant in their demands for social and economic equality. The nation's youth too seemed unwilling to accept the traditional values of society, and they demanded change. Disturbed by the turmoil, conservatives and many moderate Americans chose to oppose government programs that appeared to favor the poor and minorities at their expense. The *outcome* was that a decade that had begun with great promise produced for many, disappointment and disillusionment.

SELECTED READINGS

Bernstein, Irving. *Promises Kept: John F. Kennedy's New Frontier* (1991).

A brief and balanced account of Kennedy's presidency that nonetheless presents a favorable report of the accomplishments and legacy of the New Frontier.

Berschloss, Michael. *The Crisis Years: Kennedy and Khrushchev, 1960–1963* (1991).

A strong narrative account of the Cold War during the Kennedy administration and the personal duel between the leaders of the two superpowers.

Carson, Clayton. *In Struggle: SNCC and the Black Awakening of the 1960s* (1981).

A useful study that uses the development of SNCC to examine the changing patterns of the civil rights movement and the emergence of black nationalism.

Gitlin, Tidd. *The Sixties: Years of Hope, Days of Rage* (1987).

A readable and impressionistic examination of the political and cultural changes that occurred throughout the 1960s.

Kearns, Doris. *Lyndon Johnson and the American Dream* (1977).

An effective study of how Johnson's background and values shaped his career and the Great Society.

Wolfe, Tom. *The Electric Kool-Aid Acid Test* (1968).

A classic account of the dimensions of the counterculture.

Easy Rider (1969) and *The Graduate* (1967) are two period films that critique traditional social and cultural norms and provide a glimpse of the "values" of the 1960s.

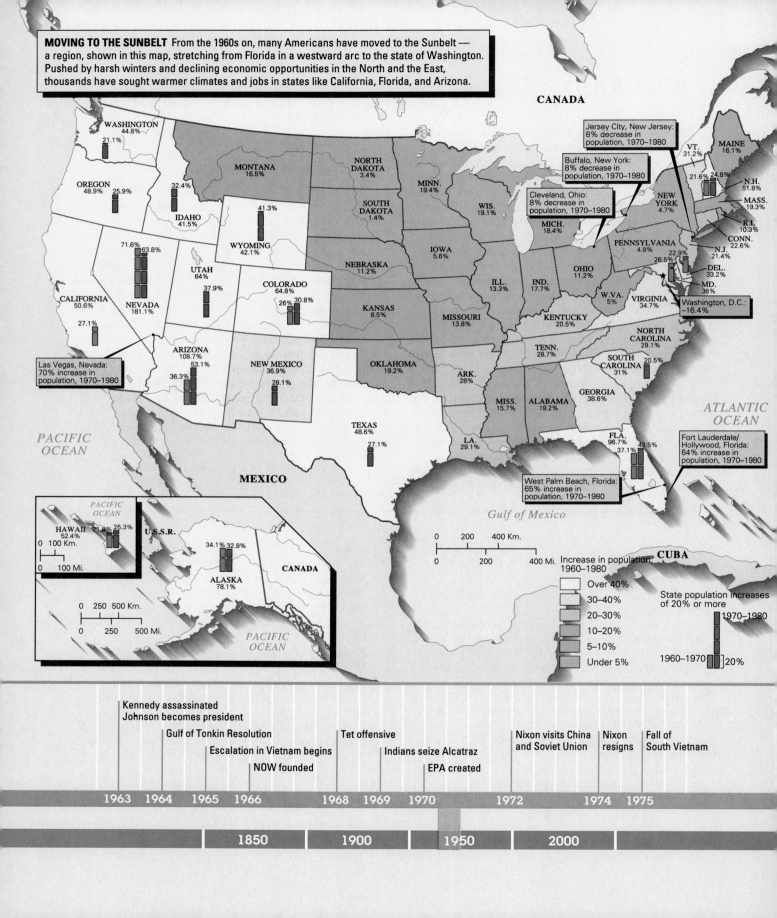

MOVING TO THE SUNBELT From the 1960s on, many Americans have moved to the Sunbelt — a region, shown in this map, stretching from Florida in a westward arc to the state of Washington. Pushed by harsh winters and declining economic opportunities in the North and the East, thousands have sought warmer climates and jobs in states like California, Florida, and Arizona.

CANADA

WASHINGTON
44.8%
21.1%

OREGON
48.9% 25.9%

IDAHO
32.4%
41.5%

MONTANA
16.5%

NORTH
DAKOTA
3.4%

SOUTH
DAKOTA
1.4%

WYOMING
41.3%
42.1%

NEBRASKA
11.2%

MINN.
19.4%

WIS.
19.1%

IOWA
5.6%

CALIFORNIA
50.6%

NEVADA
71.6% 63.8%
181.1%

UTAH
64%
37.9%

COLORADO
64.8%
26% 30.8%

KANSAS
8.5%

MISSOURI
13.8%

ILL.
13.3%

IND.
17.7%

MICH.
18.4%

OHIO
11.2%

27.1%

ARIZONA
108.7%
36.3% 53.1%

NEW MEXICO
36.9%
28.1%

OKLAHOMA
19.2%

ARK.
28%

KENTUCKY
20.5%

W.VA.
5%

TENN.
28.7%

Las Vegas, Nevada:
70% increase in
population, 1970–1980

TEXAS
48.6%
27.1%

LA.
29.1%

MISS.
15.7%

ALABAMA
19.2%

GEORGIA
38.6%

NORTH
CAROLINA
29.1%
20.5%

SOUTH
CAROLINA
31%

PENNSYLVANIA
4.8%

NEW
YORK
4.7%

VERMONT
VT.
31.2%
21.6%

MAINE
16.1%
24.8%

N.H.
51.8%

MASS.
19.3%

R.I.
10.3%

CONN.
22.6%

N.J.
21.4%
22.9%
26.5%

DEL.
33.2%

MD.
36%

VIRGINIA
34.7%

Jersey City, New Jersey:
8% decrease in
population, 1970–1980

Buffalo, New York:
8% decrease in
population, 1970–1980

Cleveland, Ohio:
8% decrease in
population, 1970–1980

Washington, D.C.:
–16.4%

Fort Lauderdale/
Hollywood, Florida:
64% increase in
population, 1970–1980

West Palm Beach, Florida:
65% increase in
population, 1970–1980

FLA.
96.7%
37.1% 43.5%

PACIFIC
OCEAN

MEXICO

ATLANTIC
OCEAN

Gulf of Mexico

PACIFIC
OCEAN

HAWAII
52.4% 21.8% 25.3%

0   100 Km.
0   100 Mi.

U.S.S.R.

34.1% 32.8%

ALASKA
78.1%

CANADA

0   250 500 Km.
0   250 500 Mi.

PACIFIC
OCEAN

0   200   400 Km.
0   200   400 Mi.

CUBA

Increase in population,
1960–1980

Over 40%
30–40%
20–30%
10–20%
5–10%
Under 5%

State population increases
of 20% or more

1970–1980

1960–1970   20%

Kennedy assassinated
Johnson becomes president

Gulf of Tonkin Resolution

Escalation in Vietnam begins

NOW founded

Tet offensive

Indians seize Alcatraz

EPA created

Nixon visits China
and Soviet Union

Nixon
resigns

Fall of
South Vietnam

1963   1964   1965   1966   1968 1969 1970   1972   1974   1975

1850   1900   1950   2000

America Under Stress, 1960–1975

Johnson and the World

- What expectations led Johnson to choose the policy of escalation of America's role in Vietnam?
- What was the military outcome of his decision?

Confronting the American Dream

- Why did women, Latinos, and American Indians choose to become more confrontational in seeking equality in American society?

Nixon and the Balance of Power

- How did Nixon's foreign policy choices differ from those sought by traditional Republican conservatives?

Nixon and Politics

- How did Nixon's choices in dealing with the economy and environment reflect his pragmatic conservatism?

INTRODUCTION

E xpectations
C onstraints
C hoices
O utcomes

The sixties began with a wave of optimism and confidence in the ability of the national government to improve society and promote American interests abroad. In 1963, those *expectations,* combined with Kennedy's assassination and Johnson's political skill, provided the new president an opportunity to create his Great Society. In foreign affairs, Johnson had less ambitious expectations. He seemed content to continue Kennedy's policies as he understood them, especially in Vietnam, where he was determined that the United States not be beaten by the Communists of a "two-bit" nation like North Vietnam. Unsophisticated about foreign policy, Johnson was not going to appear weak in any context.

But an array of *constraints* blocked any dramatic increase in the American military role in South Vietnam, which many regarded as necessary to defeat the Communists. Sudden major escalation would be expensive, could weaken support for Johnson's domestic program, and might drive the Chinese and the Soviets to increase their support of North Vietnam. To the president, the best *choice* seemed a carefully controlled, gradual escalation of American force, which would convince the North Vietnamese that the cost of the war was too high. The administration *expected* the North Vietnamese would then abandon their efforts to conquer South Vietnam, and an American-supported South Vietnam would win the war.

The strategy failed miserably. North Vietnam *chose* to meet escalation with escalation, until many Americans turned against both the war and Johnson. In 1968, watching opposition to the war mount, Johnson *chose* to break the momentum of escalation and started peace negotiations with North Vietnam. Unexpectedly, he also announced his withdrawal from the presidential campaign. The 1968 Democratic convention symbolized the *outcome* of Johnson's presidency—a divided nation and an end to liberal optimism.

Republicans rallied behind Richard Nixon, who, they said, would provide the leadership necessary to restore national unity and global prestige and reassert the traditions and values that had made the nation strong. Nixon's call for unity played on the uneasy *expectations* of a society that was fragmented by the Vietnam war and by sharp demands from an array of social groups seeking political, economic, and social changes. After the mid-1960s, the African-American civil rights movement competed with active feminist, Latino, and American Indian groups for government and public recognition, but conservative and most moderate Americans declined to support their calls for change.

Despite their claims of wanting to bring the nation together, Nixon and Republicans *chose* to inflame social divisions to ensure their victories in 1968 and in 1972. They *expected* to construct a solid political base around a Silent Majority, composed largely of middle-class, white Americans living in suburbs, the South, and the West, who were tired of social reform. Promising a new, pragmatic conservatism that accepted legitimate government activism, Nixon's first administration achieved generally successful *outcomes.* He improved relations with the Soviet Union and People's Republic of China and withdrew American forces from Vietnam. Domestically, his policy choices showed surprising flexibility, expanding some Great Society programs and using Keynesian policies to confront inflation and a sluggish economy.

Despite his successes, Nixon was not satisfied. He wanted his political enemies destroyed, which contributed to the illegal activities surrounding the Watergate break-in. Watergate's *outcomes* included not only the unprecedented resignation of a president but a nationwide wave of disillusionment with politics and government.

CHRONOLOGY ▪▪▪▪▪▪▪▪▪▪▪▪▪▪▪▪▪▪▪▪▪▪▪▪

From Camelot to Watergate

1960 Kennedy elected president

1961 Berlin Wall erected

1962 SDS's Port Huron Statement
Cuban Missile Crisis
Chavez forms National Farm Workers
Association
King's "Letter from a Birmingham Jail"

1963 Report of the Presidential Commission on
the Status of Women
Friedan's *The Feminine Mystique*
La Raza Unida formed in Texas
Kennedy assassinated
Johnson becomes president
16,000 U.S. advisers in South Vietnam

1964 Johnson elected president
Civil Rights Act
Gulf of Tonkin Resolution

1965 Voting Rights Act
U.S. air strikes against North Vietnam
begin
American combat troops arrive in South
Vietnam
Anti-Vietnam "teach-ins" begin
Dominican Republic intervention
National campaign for farm workers

1966 National Organization for Women founded

1967 Antiwar march on Washington

1968 Tet offensive
My Lai massacre
Peace talks begin in Paris
Johnson withdraws from presidential race
Robert Kennedy assassinated
Nixon elected president
Mexican-American student walk-outs
American Indian Movement founded

1969 American Indians occupy Alcatraz
First American troop withdrawals from
Vietnam
Secret bombing of Cambodia
Nixon Doctrine
Deloria's *Custer Died for Your Sins*
Alexander v. Holmes
Burger appointed to Supreme Court

1970 Cambodian invasion
Kent State and Jackson State killings
Anti-Vietnam march on Washington
Clean Air and War acts
Earth Day observed
Environment Protection Agency created
Strike-for-Equality parade
Blackmum appointed to Supreme Court

1971 *Pentagon Papers*
Nixon enacts price and wage freeze
Swann v. Charlotte-Mecklenburg
Rehnquist and Powell appointed to
Supreme Court

1972 Revenue Sharing Act
Watergate break-in
Nixon re-elected president
Nixon visits China and Soviet Union
SALT I treaty
Bombing of North Vietnam resumes

1973 Allende overthrown in Chile
Watergate hearings
Vietnam peace treaty
War Powers Act
"Second battle of Wounded Knee"

1974 Nixon resigns
Ford becomes president
Apodaca elected governor of New Mexico
Castro elected governor of Arizona

1975 South Vietnam government falls to North
Vietnamese

Johnson and the World

- What expectations led Johnson to choose the policy of escalation of America's role in Vietnam?
- What was the military outcome of his decision?

Suddenly thrust into the presidency by Kennedy's assassination, Lyndon Baines Johnson moved quickly and effectively to breathe life into Kennedy's domestic program and to launch his own more extensive Great Society. Johnson was comfortable dealing with domestic issues and politics. But foreign affairs were a different matter. He had scant experience with the world beyond the United States. His grasp of United States foreign policy was superficial, as was his knowledge of geography and his desire to understand other societies. When he traveled overseas, it was as a "tourist," demanding king-sized beds and taking a supply of Cutty Sark whiskey wherever he went. Put simply, Johnson saw the world in black and white: the free world on one side, and Communist hostility and aggression on the other. When questioned about the realism of his view, he usually hardened his position—what some called his "Alamo syndrome"—and lashed out at those challenging his perspective. In 1964, in Johnson's opinion, the Communist menace seemed especially ominous in Latin America and Vietnam.

In Latin America, Castro cast a huge shadow, and Johnson was determined to halt its growth. Under his leadership, there would be no further erosion of American power in the region. Revising the focus of Kennedy's policy (see pages 911–912), Assistant Secretary of State Thomas Mann told Latin American leaders that first and foremost the United States wanted order and stability, and that political, social, and economic reforms were no longer a central requirement. This revised perspective, labeled the **Mann Doctrine,** resulted in increasing amounts of American military equipment and advisers provided to regimes trying to suppress disruptive, opposition—"Communist" elements within their borders. The new policy led to direct military intervention in the Dominican Republic. There, supporters of deposed, democratically elected president Juan Bosch rebelled against a repressive, pro-American regime. Johnson and his advisers decided that the pro-Bosch coalition was Communist-dominated, asserted the right to protect the Dominican people from an "international conspiracy," and sent in 22,000 American troops to restore order. The troops left the island in mid-1966, after monitoring national elections that elected Joaquin Balaguer, a conserva-

tive, pro-American candidate, as president. Johnson claimed to have saved a free nation from communism, but many Latin Americans only saw an example of Yankee arrogance and intrusive power.

The Americanization of Vietnam

Latin America was not the only region in which Johnson believed American interests were threatened by communism. A more direct challenge existed in South Vietnam, where by the winter of 1963 and 1964, the Viet Cong, supported by men and supplies from North Vietnam, appeared to be winning the war and the ineffective South Vietnamese army teetered on the verge of collapse. American advisers saw little hope for improvement. Captain Edwin Shank, a military adviser who flew combat missions in South Vietnam, found South Vietnamese soldiers to be "stupid, ignorant . . . [and] a menace." He believed that the war could be won only by American forces.

Shank, who was shot down and killed on a secret bombing mission in May 1964, was not alone in his harsh assessment. Throughout the chain of command there was agreement that to stabilize Vietnam and turn the tide of battle, a larger American combat role was required. Johnson agreed, but just then, he also had Goldwater and Congress to worry about. To expand the American combat role in Vietnam during an election year was not politically wise. The solution, Johnson concluded, was to try and delay escalation at least until after the passage of the civil rights bill and, he hoped, after the presidential election. But planning began immediately.

The **Joint Chiefs of Staff,** Secretary of Defense Robert McNamara, and the National Security Council proposed using American air power against industrial and commercial targets in North Vietnam. They believed that North Vietnamese leader Ho Chi Minh would choose to withdraw support from the Viet Cong rather than watch his nation's economic future go up in smoke. Without support from the

---

Mann Doctrine U.S. policy outlined by Thomas Mann during the Johnson administration, calling for stability in Latin America rather than economic and political reform.

Joint Chiefs of Staff Military advisory group to the president that consists of the chiefs of the U.S. Army, U.S. Navy, and U.S. Air Force and the commandant of the U.S. Marine Corps.

North, they reasoned, the Viet Cong could be defeated by an American-equipped and -advised South Vietnamese army (ARVN). The need for large numbers of American ground forces would consequently be limited. **General William Westmoreland,** commander of American forces in Vietnam, disagreed, insisting that the inept ARVN could never defeat the Viet Cong. American ground forces *were* necessary, he argued. Johnson chose a "tit-for-tat" policy of reacting to Viet Cong aggression by the limited bombing of North Vietnam, while telling Hanoi that continued aggression would result in heavier air attacks. This strategy made the most political sense. Facing election and concerned about implementation of the Great Society, he did not want to be the president who sent American soldiers to die in the jungles of Southeast Asia. Acting only in response to Viet Cong assaults would also help disarm critics accusing Johnson of intentionally broadening the war.

While planning continued, the administration began generating public support for a larger American role in defending South Vietnam. Encouraged by the White House and the **Pentagon,** throughout the spring and summer of 1964, newspapers and magazines printed articles and stories stressing the Communist threat to South Vietnam, Southeast Asia, and the Pacific. Fixed on the domino theory (see page 896), the White House awaited a chance to ask Congress for permission to use whatever force necessary to defend South Vietnam.

The chance came in August 1964 off the coast of North Vietnam. On August 1, North Vietnamese torpedo boats skirmished with the American destroyer *Maddox* in the Gulf of Tonkin (see Map 30.1). On August 4, experiencing rough seas and poor visibility, radar operators on the *Maddox* and another destroyer, the *C. Turner Joy,* concluded that the patrol boats were making another attack. Confusion followed. Both ships fired wildly at targets shown only on radar screens. At one point, the *Maddox* almost fired on the *C. Turner Joy.* Within hours, officers on both ships concluded that the radar blips had not been attacking vessels and informed Washington. Hearing the corrected reports, Johnson joked that the sailors had probably been shooting at flying fish. Still, he implemented his reactive policy and told the nation that Communist attacks against "peaceful villages" in South Vietnam had been "joined by open aggression on the high seas against the United States of America." On August 7, he submitted to Congress a resolution, drafted earlier, asking approval "to take all necessary steps, including

the use of armed force" to aid South Vietnam. The **Gulf of Tonkin Resolution** was, in Johnson's terms, "like Grandma's nightgown, it covered everything." Public opinion polls showed strong support for the president and only two senators opposed the resolution, Wayne Morse of Oregon and Ernest Gruening of Alaska.

The Gulf of Tonkin Resolution gave Johnson the freedom to take whatever measures he wanted in Vietnam, but he remained cautious and limited bombings to the August retaliatory air strikes. Before deciding on further action, Johnson conferred with his advisers. Reports from the field concluded that the Viet Cong was continuing to win the battle for land while the South Vietnamese government remained unstable and unpopular. Nearly all of Johnson's advisers agreed that two moves were needed to win the war: commit American combat troops and bomb North Vietnam. To do nothing, McNamara warned, was the "worst course of action" and would "lead only to a disastrous defeat."

Johnson listened to his "wise men," approving a policy to bomb North Vietnam and the supply routes to South Vietnam, while using a small number of American troops to protect American airfields. Before unleashing American air power, however, Johnson wanted a clear cause, another enemy provocation. He was told that he would not have to wait long because incidents were like streetcars—they came around every few minutes. On February 7, one such streetcar pulled into the American base at Pleiku: the Viet Cong attacked, killing eight Americans.

Operation Rolling Thunder, the air assault on North Vietnam, began on March 2, 1965. On March 8, the 3rd Marine Division arrived to take up positions around the American base at Danang. By July, American planes were flying over nine hundred missions a week and a hundred thousand American ground forces had reached Vietnam. Near their

---

General William Westmoreland   Commander of all American troops in Vietnam from 1964 to 1968.

Pentagon   United States military establishment, so named because its central offices are located in a five-sided building in Arlington, Virginia, called the Pentagon.

Gulf of Tonkin Resolution   Resolution passed by Congress in 1964 authorizing the president to take any measures necessary to repel attacks against the U.S. forces in Vietnam.

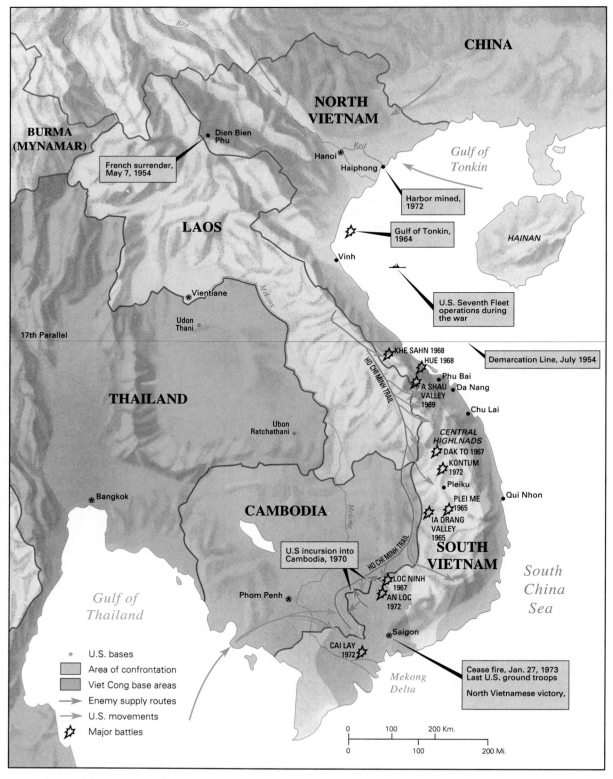

CHINA

NORTH
VIETNAM

BURMA
(MYNAMAR)

Dien Bien
Phu

French surrender,
May 7, 1954

Hanoi
Haiphong

Red

Gulf of
Tonkin

HAINAN

LAOS

Harbor mined,
1972

Gulf of Tonkin,
1964

Vinh

U.S. Seventh Fleet
operations during
the war

Vientiane

Udon
Thani

17th Parallel

THAILAND

KHE SAHN 1968
HUE 1968

Phu Bai
Da Nang

Demarcation Line, July 1954

A SHAU
VALLEY
1969

Chu Lai

Ubon
Ratchathani

CENTRAL
HIGHLNADS
DAK TO 1967

KONTUM
1972

Pleiku

Qui Nhon

Bangkok

CAMBODIA

PLEI ME
1965

IA DRANG
VALLEY
1965

SOUTH
VIETNAM

South
China
Sea

U.S incursion into
Cambodia, 1970

LOC NINH
1967
AN LOC
1972

Gulf of
Thailand

Phom Penh

HO CHI MINH TRAIL

Saigon

CAI LAY
1972

Cease fire, Jan. 27, 1973
Last U.S. ground troops

North Vietnamese victory,

Mekong
Delta

- U.S. bases
  Area of confrontation
  Viet Cong base areas
  → Enemy supply routes
  → U.S. movements
  ✪ Major battles

| 0 | 100 | 200 Km. |
| 0 | 100 | 200 Mi. |

MAP 30.1 The Vietnam War, 1954–1975   Following the French defeat at Dienbienphu, the
United States became increasingly committed to defending South Vietnam. This map
shows some of the major battle sites of the Vietnam War from 1954 to the fall of Saigon and
the defeat of the South Vietnamese government in 1975.

In 1964 Johnson and his advisers concluded that the United States must commit its resources to defeat Communism in South Vietnam. In 1968, Johnson's advisers advised the president that victory in Vietnam could not be obtained through military means and that the United States should look for a negotiated settlement. Johnson agreed in both cases. Here, Johnson meets with his Vietnam advisers, including Robert McNamara, General Earle Wheeler, Clark Clifford, Walt Rostow, Richard Helms, and Dean Rusk. *Lyndon B. Johnson Library.*

bases, American infantry and armored units patrolled aggressively, searching out the enemy. Johnson's strategy soon showed its flaws. As the United States escalated the war, so too did the enemy, including committing units of the North Vietnam army (NVA) in South Vietnam. General Westmoreland and others now insisted that victory required taking the offensive, which necessitated even more American soldiers. Reluctantly, Johnson gave the green light. Vietnam had become an American war.

Westmoreland's plan was to use overwhelming numbers and firepower to destroy the enemy. In the first major American offensive, a large-scale sweep of the Ia Drang Valley in November 1965, men of the 1st Air Cavalry, supported by air strikes, forced North Vietnamese units to retreat into Cambodia. The brutal hand-to-hand fighting left three hundred Americans and an estimated three thousand enemy soldiers dead. Westmoreland and Johnson were pleased—they could live with such lopsided results. *Time* magazine named Westmoreland "Man of the Year" for 1965.

Such "victories" continued, but they were less than they appeared. Throughout 1966 and 1967, both sides continued to escalate. The Viet Cong and North Vietnamese suffered heavy loses of men and supplies, but their determination and ability to continue the struggle were unbroken. American aircraft rained bombs on North Vietnam and supply routes south, especially the **Ho Chi Minh trail,** but arms and provisions still moved. In the fall of 1967, Westmoreland informed Washington that the enemy was "largely confined to the periphery of South Vietnam" and that half of the enemy's forces were no longer capable of combat. At the same time, he asked for more soldiers, and the American presence increased to 542,000.

Unknown to Westmoreland, North Vietnamese leaders were planning an immense campaign that would totally discredit his assessment of their military situation. Aimed at capturing South Vietnamese cities, the offensive began during the Vietnamese new year holiday of Tet in January 1968. The Viet Cong struck forty-one cities throughout South Vietnam, including the capital Saigon. In some of the bloodiest fighting of the war, American and South Vietnamese forces moved to recapture lost cities and villages. It took twenty-four days of bitter fighting to oust the Viet Cong from the old imperial city of Hue, leaving the city in ruins and costing over 10,000 civilian, 5,000 Communist, 384 South Vietnamese and 216 American lives (see Map 30.1).

The **Tet offensive** was a military defeat for North Vietnam and the Viet Cong. It provoked no popular uprising against the South Vietnamese government, the Communists held no cities or provincial capitals, and they suffered staggering losses in men and material. Over forty-thousand Viet Cong were killed. Tet was, nonetheless, a "victory" for the North Vietnamese in that it seriously weakened American support for the war. Coming amid official pronouncements of "victory just around the corner," Tet destroyed the administration's credibility and intensified a growing antiwar movement.

Ho Chi Minh trail   Main infiltration route for North Vietnamese soldiers into South Vietnam; it ran through Laos and Cambodia.

Tet offensive   Viet Cong and North Vietnamese offensive against South Vietnamese cities in January 1968; a military defeat for North Vietnam, it nevertheless undermined U.S. support for the war.

♦ Unlike previous American wars, Vietnam was a war without fixed front lines. At the isolated outpost at Khe Sanh, fewer than six thousand American Marines fought to hold back thirty to forty thousand North Vietnamese regulars for seventy-seven days, killing or wounding more than ten thousand of the enemy. Within weeks after the siege, the United States withdrew from the area. *Robert Ellison/Black Star.*

The Antiwar Movement

Throughout 1964, there was widespread support for an American role in Vietnam. Most Americans accepted the domino theory and claims that horrible reprisals against non-Communists would follow a Communist victory. Those opposing the war were of little concern to the White House, which dismissed them as leftists or pacifists. A year later, little had changed except the largely college-based opposition to the war was more outspoken. The University of Michigan held the first Vietnam "teach-in" to mobilize opposition to American policy on March 24, 1965. In April, Students for a Democratic Society (SDS) organized a protest march of about fifteen thousand in front of the White House.

Those opposing the war fell into two major types—and they rarely agreed on anything other than that the war should be ended. Pacifists and radical liberals on the political left opposed the war for moral and ideological reasons. Others, as the American military commitment grew, opposed the war for more pragmatic reasons—the draft, the loss of lives and money, and the inability of the United States to either defeat the enemy or create a stable, democratic South Vietnam. In 1966, high school students hardly mentioned Vietnam or the draft as a problem facing their lives. Three years later, 75 per-

cent of those polled listed both as major worries. By 1967, the draft and the possibility of being sent to Vietnam was becoming a concern of many college students, who often took the lead in opposing the war and the draft. A University of Michigan student complained that if he was drafted and spent two years in the army, he would lose over $16,000 in income. "I know I sound selfish," he explained, "but . . . I paid $10,000 to get this education." Yet college students and graduates were not the most likely to be drafted. Far more often, those who were drafted and sent to Vietnam were poorly educated, low-income whites and minorities—men President Eisenhower once called "sitting ducks" for the draft.

But low-income youth and minorities were not the bulk of those who were swelling the antiwar movement. Rather it was America's middle class, especially college students, who participated in a "Stop-the-Draft Week" in October 1967. That week, over 10,000 demonstrators blocked the entrance of an induction center in Oakland, California, while over 200,000 people staged a massive protest march in Washington against "Lyndon's War."

Until 1967, Johnson was barely concerned about the antiwar movement. Press and television coverage continued to be positive, emphasizing American successes and clinging to the domino theory. Public opinion polls found that the nation stood behind Johnson's efforts to save South Vietnam, while Barry Sadler's patriotic *Ballad of the Green Berets* lit up popular music charts. But as antiwar numbers increased in 1967, Johnson responded with **Operation Chaos,** in which federal agents infiltrated, spied on, and tried to discredit antiwar groups.

The Tet offensive served to broaden and intensify antiwar sentiments even further. The highly respected CBS news anchor Walter Cronkite had supported the war, accepting the rosy optimism that had spewed forth from official sources, but Tet changed his mind. Unable to match the administration's claims of impending victory with the fierce Communist offensive, he went on a personal fact-finding tour of Vietnam. On his return, Cronkite announced that there would be no victory in Vietnam and that the United States should make peace. "If I have lost Walter Cronkite, then it's over. I have lost Mr. Average Citizen," Johnson lamented.

> **Operation Chaos** FBI operation ordered by President Johnson that infiltrated the antiwar movement in the United States in the hope of discrediting it.

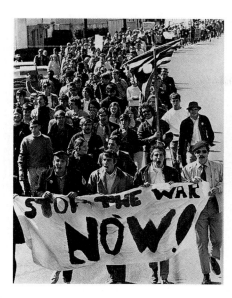

◆ As the American role in Vietnam escalated, so, too, did the antiwar movement in the United States. In October 1967, over one hundred thousand people marched in Washington, D.C., protesting the war. Here, college students from New Orleans, like hundreds of thousands of others, demonstrated against the war during the 1969 Moratorium Day march. Nixon was privately pleased that more did not participate and planned a week of National Unity celebration in response. *Wide World.*

Johnson also found opposition to American policy within his own circle of advisers—Undersecretary of State George Ball, Ambassador to South Vietnam Henry Cabot Lodge, and Secretary of War Robert McNamara left the administration over its war policy. Secretary of State Rusk and new Secretary of Defense Clark Clifford argued that military victory was impossible and that the Americanization of the war needed to be reversed. According to Clifford,

> *I could not find out when the war was going to end. . . . I could not find out whether the new requests for men and equipment were going to be enough, or whether it would take more and, if more, how much; I could not find out how soon the South Vietnamese forces would be ready to take over. . . .*

Clifford concluded that after four years of "enormous casualties" and "massive destruction from our bombing" there was no lessening of "the will of the enemy." Thus, following Tet, when Westmoreland called for more troops, most of Johnson's "wise men" urged sending fewer troops and seeking instead a diplomatic end to the war.

The 1968 Presidential Campaign

As Johnson prepared for the 1968 presidential race and rethought his Vietnam policy, rumors circulated that 200,000 more Americans were being sent to Vietnam. In New Hampshire, benefiting from such rumors, was Minnesota senator **Eugene McCarthy,** who was running a presidential primary campaign based largely on opposition to the Vietnam War. At the heart of his New Hampshire campaign were hundreds of student volunteers who, deciding to "go clean for Gene," knocked on thousands of doors and distributed bales of flyers and pamphlets touting their candidate and condemning the war.

Expecting no real challenge to his renomination, the president's name had not even been placed on the nation's earliest presidential primary (March 18), in New Hampshire. But with the furor over Tet strengthening McCarthy's antiwar candidacy, Johnson's political advisers suddenly feared that the challenge could make the war the central issue of the campaign and might in fact threaten the president's renomination. Consequently, a **write-in campaign** was quickly organized for Johnson, who succeeded in beating McCarthy, winning 48 percent of the vote—6 percent ahead of McCarthy. But political commentators called McCarthy the real winner—Johnson had not won big enough. Adding to Johnson's political worries, New York senator **Robert Kennedy** also proclaimed his candidacy and opposition to the war in Vietnam. The war had become the critical issue in the campaign and a major liability to Johnson.

On March 31, 1968, a haggard-looking president delivered a major televised speech, changing his Vietnam policy. The United States would seek a political settlement through negotiations with the Viet Cong and North Vietnamese. The escalation of the ground war was over, and steps would be taken to

---

Eugene McCarthy   Senator who opposed the Vietnam War and who made an unsuccessful bid for the 1968 Democratic nomination for president.

write-in campaign   An attempt to elect a candidate not registered or listed on the ballot; voters are urged to write in the candidate's name on the ballot themselves.

Robert Kennedy   Attorney general during the presidency of his brother John F. Kennedy; he was elected to the Senate in 1964 and was campaigning for the presidency when he was assassinated in 1968.

◆ Violence erupted during the 1968 Democratic National Convention in Chicago. Using nightsticks, police in the "Battle for Michigan Avenue" charged into the crowd of protestors near the Conrad Hilton Hotel. The violent confrontations in Chicago did little to heal the divisions in the Democratic party or help Hubert Humphrey's chances for election. *Demonstration: UPI/Bettmann Archives; campaign button: Collection of David J. and Janice L. Frent.*

ensure that the South Vietnamese took a larger role in the war. The bombing of North Vietnam above the 20th parallel would end, with a complete halt of the air war to follow the start of negotiations. At the end of his speech, Johnson calmly made this announcement: "I have concluded that I should not permit the presidency to become involved in the partisan divisions that are developing in this political year. . . . Accordingly, I shall not seek, and I will not accept, the nomination of my party for another term as president." Listeners were shocked. Lyndon B. Johnson had thrown in the towel. Although he later claimed that his fear of having a heart attack while in office was the primary reason for his decision not to run, nearly everyone agreed that the Vietnam War had ended Johnson's political career.

Negotiations with North Vietnam began in Paris in May and proceeded nowhere. Still, Johnson halted the bombing of North Vietnam in October and hoped that the talks would allow him to withdraw American troops and would eliminate the war as a political issue. Instead, the antiwar movement intensified as protesters redoubled their efforts to mobilize opposition to the war. Thus the war remained the critical issue within the Democratic political race, which had grown to three with the entry of Vice President **Hubert H. Humphrey.** McCarthy campaigned against the war and the "imperial presidency." Kennedy opposed the war but not executive and federal power, and he called on the government to meet the needs of the poor and minorities. Standing by Johnson's peace efforts, Humphrey relied on party regulars and White House clout and emphasized civil rights and labor issues. While Kennedy and McCarthy battled for public opinion and primary victories, Humphrey captured the nonprimary delegations, knowing that there were enough nonprimary delegates to the national convention to win the nomination without winning a single primary.

By June, Kennedy was winning the primary race, drawing heavily from minorities and urban Democratic voters. In the critical California primary, Kennedy gained a narrow victory over McCarthy, 46 to 41 percent, but the victory was all too short. As the winner left his election headquarters, he was shot in the head by Sirhan Sirhan, a Jordanian immigrant. Kennedy died the next day.

Kennedy's assassination stunned the nation. It also ensured Humphrey's nomination. McCarthy continued his campaign but was unable to generate much support among party regulars. By the time of the national convention in Chicago in August, Humphrey had enough pledged votes to assure his nomination, but the convention was nevertheless dramatic. Inside and outside the convention center, antiwar and anti-establishment groups demonstrated for McCarthy, peace in Vietnam, and social justice. In the streets of Chicago, radical factions within the Students for a Democratic Society promised physical confrontation. The so-called **Yippies** (the Youth International Party) led by Abbie Hoffman and Jerry Rubin threatened to contami-

---

Hubert H. Humphrey Vice president under Lyndon Johnson who won the Democratic nomination for president in 1968 but lost the election to Richard Nixon.

Yippies Counterculture group that inflamed the protests that disrupted the Democratic National Convention in Chicago in 1968.

nate the water supply with drugs and bragged of confronting the police, whom they called "pigs." Chicago's mayor Richard Daley was determined to maintain order. Inside the convention, delegates argued and screamed support for their positions. Outside, protesters threw eggs, bottles, rocks, and balloons filled with water, ink, and urine at the police, who responded with tear gas and nightsticks. On August 28, the police went berserk before television cameras, viciously and indiscriminately attacking protesters and bystanders alike. The violence in Chicago's streets overshadowed Humphrey's nomination and acceptance speech, as it would much of his campaign. "Dump the Hump" became a popular slogan as antiwar activists tried to disrupt Humphrey's campaign appearances.

Many Americans were disgusted by the chaos in Chicago and saw it as typical of the general disruption that was plaguing the nation. **George Wallace,** the Democratic governor of Alabama, appealed to this sentiment when he left the Democratic party and ran for president as the American Independent party's candidate. The conservative Wallace opposed federal civil rights legislation and took a dim view of antiwar protesters and welfare recipients. He aimed his campaign at southern whites, blue-collar workers, and lower-income white Americans, all of whom deplored the "loss" of traditional American values and society. On the campaign trail, Wallace took special glee in attacking the counter-culture and the "rich-kid" war protesters, who avoided serving in Vietnam while the sons of working-class Americans died there. Calling for victory in Vietnam, Wallace agreed with his vice-presidential candidate General Curtis LaMay that the United States should bomb North Vietnam "back to the Stone Age." Two months before the election, Wallace commanded 21 percent of the vote according to national opinion polls. "On November 5," he confidently predicted, "they're going to find out there are a lot of rednecks in this country."

Wallace's support indicated widespread disapproval of liberalism, disruptions at home, and impotence abroad. The Republican candidate, Richard Nixon also intended to tap the general dissatisfaction but without fanning the hostility of the Wallace campaign. He and Spiro Agnew, his vice-presidential running mate, focused the campaign on the need for effective international leadership, national unity, law and order, and support for the traditional American values of honesty, decency, and hard work. On Vietnam he announced during the New Hampshire Republican primary that he would "end

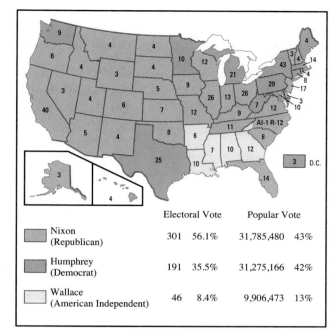

	Electoral Vote		Popular Vote	
Nixon (Republican)	301	56.1%	31,785,480	43%
Humphrey (Democrat)	191	35.5%	31,275,166	42%
Wallace (American Independent)	46	8.4%	9,906,473	13%

◆ **MAP 30.2 Election of 1968**   In winning the 1968 election against Hubert Humphrey, Richard Nixon received fewer popular votes than he did in 1960, when he won more than 34 million votes. But in the all-important electoral vote, Nixon easily defeated his Democratic rival. As they did in the 1960 election, some Southerners opted for a third choice, unwilling to vote for a Republican or a liberal Democrat. The third choice was George Wallace.

the war and win the peace" but refused to comment further, saying he was afraid of upsetting the delicate discussions in Paris. Instead, he embraced the law-and-order issue, campaigning loudly against pot, pornography, protesters, and permissiveness. Nixon glided smoothly through the primaries, easily won the nomination at an orderly convention, and rolled up a huge public opinion lead against his Democratic rival.

As election day neared, Humphrey was gaining support, but it was not enough. Nixon won with a comfortable margin in the electoral college, although receiving only 43.4 percent of the popular vote (see Map 30.2). Conservatives were pleased. Combined, Nixon and Wallace attracted almost 57

George Wallace   Conservative Alabama governor who opposed desegregation in the 1960s and who ran unsuccessfully for the presidency as an independent in 1968 and 1972.

percent of the vote, which conservatives said indicated wide public support for an end to liberal social programs and a return to traditional values. They believed that a major political realignment was being led by **Middle Americans,** many living in the **Sunbelt,** who attended church regularly, and encouraged their children to be patriotic.

Confronting the American Dream

● Why did women, Latinos, and American Indians choose to become more confrontational in seeking equality in American society?

Part of Nixon's appeal in 1968, and again in 1972, was that he and his supporters visualized a nation that was composed largely of traditional, white, middle-class families. He projected a government that would enact legislation to meet the needs of the so-called Silent Majority rather than to promote social experimentation and cater to minorities. The explosion of the civil rights movement during the 1960s had not only spread African-American activism to all parts of the nation, but it also contributed to the growth of other groups demanding equal rights and access to the American dream. Joining the counterculture and antiwar and youth movements were women's rights, Mexican-American, and Native American movements. To some Americans, the "sudden" emergence of these trends signaled a fragmentation of American society that needed to be controlled.

The Women's Rights Movement

For women, the 1950s had been a paradox. Popular social images and ideals pictured women as best fulfilled and most happy at home raising children and running the household. Although this scenario held true for many women, a growing number were less satisfied with their lives and work opportunities. As the 1960s began, more women were entering the work force, having fewer children, and getting divorced. Many women complained that gender stereotyping denied them access to profitable career jobs, a position affirmed by the Kennedy administration's 1963 report of the Presidential Commission on the Status of Women, which showed in stark statistics that women constituted a social and economic underclass. Compared to white men, women worked for less pay (on average 40 percent that of a

◆ Assigned to do an article for her fifteenth college reunion, Betty Friedan (shown here with her daughter Emily) found that she was not alone in being disappointed with her career options. The outcome was a larger work, the *Feminine Mystique* (1963) and the rebirth of the feminist movement. In 1966, she became the leader of the National Organization for Women (NOW). *Radcliffe College Archives, Schlesinger Library.*

man), were more likely to be fired or laid off, and had little success in reaching top career positions. Nor was it just in the workplace that women faced discrimination. Throughout the country divorce, credit, and property laws generally favored men, and in three southern states, women were not allowed to serve on juries.

To some women, the role of housewife itself symbolized oppression. **Betty Friedan** was one who concluded the chores of the housewife amounted to a form of servitude that prevented women from achieving their full potential. As a young woman, she had dropped out of a psychology doctoral pro-

> **Middle Americans**   Part of the U.S. middle class considered average in income and education and moderately conservative in values and attitudes.
>
> **Sunbelt**   Region of the United States that extends from Washington, D.C., to Florida and from Texas to California and the Pacific coast; during the sixties, its population grew dramatically because of its climate and economic opportunities.
>
> **Betty Friedan**   Feminist who wrote *The Feminine Mystique* in 1963 and helped found the National Organization for Women in 1966.

gram to get married, bear children, and keep a sub-urban home. In her 1963 best seller, *The Feminine Mystique*, she pondered the question of why she—and, according to several studies, thousands of other women—were not satisfied. After reviewing the responsibilities of the housewife (making beds, grocery shopping, driving children everywhere, preparing meals and snacks, and pleasing her husband), she asked: "Is this all?" She concluded it was not enough. Women needed to overcome the "feminine mystique" that promised them fulfillment through the domestic arts. She called on women to set their own goals and seek careers outside the home. Her book, combined with the presidential report, provided new perspectives for women and contributed to a renewed women's movement. Also producing more activism was the passage of the 1964 Civil Rights Act, with the inclusion of **Title VII.** The original version of the civil rights bill excluded sex as a form of discrimination, but Representative Martha Griffiths (Democrat from Michigan) joined with conservative Democrat Howard Smith of Virginia to add the word *sex* to the act—she to strengthen the bill, he to kill it. As finally approved, Title VII prohibited discrimination on the basis of race, religion, creed, national origins, or sex.

Many women and liberals hoped Title VII would begin a serious effort by government to provide gender equality. But when the Equal Employment Opportunity Commission, established to support the law, and the Johnson administration showed little interest in dealing with gender discrimination, proponents organized to promote women's interests and to press the government to enforce Title VII. Many organizers, like Mary King and Casey Hayden of the Student Nonviolent Coordinating Committee (see page 907), were experienced civil rights activists and anxious to push women's rights. In "the black movement," one woman civil rights worker wrote, "I had been fighting for someone else's oppression and now there was a way I could fight for my own freedom and I was going to be much stronger than I ever was." The most prominent woman's organization to emerge was the **National Organization for Women (NOW)** formed in 1966. With Betty Friedan as president, NOW launched an aggressive campaign to draw attention to sex discrimination and to redress wrongs. It sued EEOC for not upholding the law and 1,300 corporations for gender discrimination. It demanded an Equal Rights Amendment to the Constitution and pushed for easier access to birth-control devices and the right to have an abortion.

NOW's membership grew rapidly, from about 300 in 1966 to 175,000 in 1968. But the movement was larger than NOW's membership and political agenda. Women in droves attended **consciousness-raising** sessions and other grassroots gatherings to promote women's issues. Calls arose for new social and sexual codes for women. Some rejected high-heel shoes, bras, and any of the trappings associated with a male-defined image of feminine sexuality and desirability. NOW's 1970 Strike-for-Equality parade demonstrated the growing mass appeal of the woman's movement when fifty thousand supporters marched down New York City's Fifth Avenue.

As within the African-American civil rights movement, divisions developed. Many women, while supporting equal opportunities and rights, rejected the label *feminist* and what they believed was the movement's bias toward career and working women. At the other extreme, some went further than NOW and called for a complete redefinition of the traditional institutions of family and marriage. Marriage was "slavery," "legalized rape," and "unpaid labor," according to radical feminist Ti-Grace Atkinson. Still, despite the internal differences, by the end of the seventies, a general feminist critique of American society had succeeded in convincing many Americans that women should pursue goals and aspirations beyond the traditional roles of wife, mother, and homemaker. By the late seventies, women's rights issues, in particular the Equal Rights Amendment and abortion rights, became a major issue in society and politics (see pages 998–1001).

The Emergence of Chicano Power

Beginning in the 1960s, Mexican-Americans also organized to assert their social and political rights. As the 1960s began, Mexican-Americans were largely an invisible minority (see Map 30.3). Outside the

---

Title VII   Provision of the Civil Rights Act of 1964 that guaranteed women legal protection against discrimination.

National Organization for Women   Women's rights organization founded in 1966 to improve educational, employment, and political opportunities for women and to fight for equal pay for equal work.

consciousness-raising   Related to achieving greater awareness of the nature of a political or social issue through group therapy or group interaction.

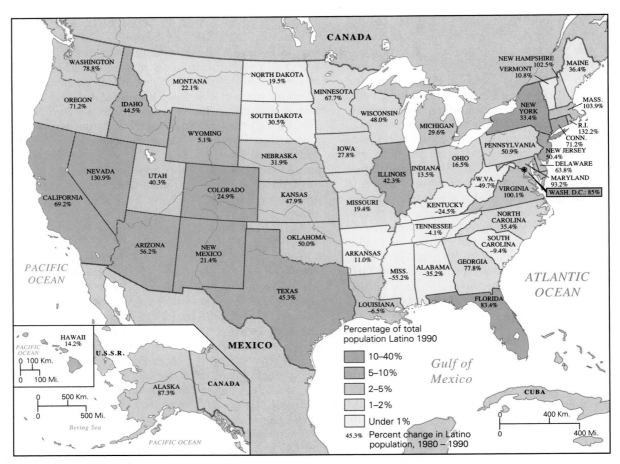

MAP 30.3 Changing Latino Population At one time, the great majority of Latinos were Mexican-American, located in the Southwest. In the 1990s, Latinos reside in nearly every major city and include Cubans, Puerto Ricans, and others from throughout the Caribbean, Central and South America. Growing rapidly, the Latino population is projected to become the largest minority in the country by the year 2000, perhaps 12 percent of the total population.

Southwest, few Americans were aware of or concerned with their place in American society. Prevailing stereotypes portrayed them as docile, if not lazy, and ridiculed them as poorly educated, unskilled people who spoke English badly. Statistically, Mexican-Americans were near society's lowest levels of income and education.

Throughout the 1940s and 1950s, organizations like the League of Latin American Citizens and the GI Forum (see page 853) had made minor gains, mostly fighting legal segregation, but little had changed for most Mexican-Americans. The New Frontier and the Great Society had revived hopes as organizations began to pressure American society to recognize the needs of the Latino population. In

1963, the Mexican-American majority in Crystal City, Texas, stunned the region by toppling the established Anglo political machine and electing an all Mexican-American slate to the city council. The Crystal City vote was, for many Mexican-Americans, a revolutionary act, the beginning of the end of political and social segregation. Across south Texas, Mexican-Americans banded together to form *El Partido Raza Unida* (The United People Party) to spread the political "revolution" throughout Texas. The passage of the 1965 Voting Rights Act and Johnson's War on Poverty added more impetus. In Colorado in 1965, Rodolfo "Corky" Gonzales formed the Crusade for Justice to work for social justice for Mexican-Americans there, to integrate Colorado's schools, and to foster pride in Mexican heritage. In New Mexico, Reies Lopez Tijerina demanded that Mexican-Americans enjoy the rights promised under the Treaty of Guadalupe Hidalgo that ended the Mexican-American War, including land grants, and formed the *Alianza Federal de Mercedes* (the Federal Alliance of Land Grants). Throughout the Southwest, the activism of Mexican-Americans frightened those supporting the status quo. Texas Governor Dolph Briscoe typified conservative sentiment when he denounced the *La Raza Unida* movement, saying the "Communist" *La Raza Unida* aimed to create a "little Cuba" in south Texas.

Briscoe was wrong. The Mexican-American movement was a local one, born of poverty and oppressive segregation. Reflecting the grassroots character of the movement was the important role that youths played. Many Mexican-American teens and young adults adopted the term **Chicano** to stress their unwillingness to accept the dictates of Anglo society and to distinguish themselves from the more **accommodationist** Mexican-Americans they called *Tio Tacos*. Although many Mexican-Americans disapproved, the term Chicano was soon applied to Mexican-Americans who promoted their heritage and rights. In schools, Chicanos demanded better teachers, support systems, integration, and Mexican-American (Latino) studies programs. During the 1967–1968 academic year, Raul Ruiz mobilized Mexican-American students in Los Angeles: "If you are a student you should be angry! You should demand! You should protest! You should organize for a better education! This is your right! This is your life!" He called for students to walk out of class and picket schools that did not meet demands.

In the small south Texas town of Ed Couch-Elsa, where the average education level for Mexican-Americans was 3.5 years of schooling, Mexican-American students walked out of the high school in November 1968. Supported by their parents and most of the Mexican-American community, the students demanded dignity, respect, and an end to "blatant discrimination against Mexican-American students in the schools." For one thing, corporal punishment in the form of spankings was common for speaking Spanish on school grounds outside of Spanish class, and students wanted it stopped. The school board, blaming "outside agitators" for the unrest, suspended over 150 students and finally expelled 20. But changes took place. The board agreed not to discourage the speaking of Spanish and to incorporate a Mexican-American heritage program into the curriculum. An extremely poor school dis-

trict, Ed Couch-Elsa was limited in its efforts to improve the curriculum or educational environment, but under pressure from the Mexican-American community, other school districts, including Los Angeles, implemented Mexican-American studies and bilingual programs, hired more Mexican-American teachers and counselors, and adopted programs to meet the special needs of migrant farm worker children who moved from one school to another during picking season. By the 1970s, calls for bilingual education had become an important educational reform focus for the Latino community.

Before and during the 1960s, nearly one-third of all Mexican-Americans worked at **stoop labor** in the fields—picking onions, carrots, grapes, and other perishable crops—and were deprived of most basic needs: education, housing, wages, health care. Trapped at the bottom of the occupation ladder, unskilled and uneducated farm laborers were ignored by society and all levels of government. They were not covered under minimum wage or labor laws, and established unions had made no effort to organize agricultural labor. Finally, in 1962, **Cesar Chavez** created the **National Farm Workers Association (NFWA)** to seek higher wages, better working and living conditions, and dignity for migrant workers (see Individual Choices: Cesar Chavez). When Chavez called a strike against the grape growers of central California in 1965, NFWA had reached 1,700 members. He demanded a wage of $1.40 an hour and asked the public to support the farm workers by buying only union-picked grapes. With varying degrees of success, the boycott and

---

Chicano   Term adopted by many Mexican-Americans during the late 1960s to describe their ethnic identity; it was associated with the promotion of Mexican-American heritage and rights.

accommodationist   Compromising with or adapting to the viewpoint of the opposition.

stoop labor   Field labor that involves constant bending, usually to pick fruits and vegetables.

Cesar Chavez   Labor organizer who founded the National Farm Workers Association; he believed in nonviolence and used marches, boycotts, and fasts to bring moral and economic pressure to bear on growers.

National Farm Workers Association   Migrant workers' union organized by Cesar Chavez in 1962, which used a series of boycotts to force California growers to recognize the union and improve wages and working conditions.

La Causa

Cesar Chavez

Cesar Chavez organized the first successful farm workers union in America in 1961, the United Farm Workers Association. Choosing to confront opponents by using the nonviolent tactics of the Civil Rights movement, Chavez sought to give power and dignity to Mexican-American workers. Bob Fitch/Black Star.

"Viva la huelga!" With these words, in September 1965, Cesar Chavez chose to strike (*huelga*) against the grape growers in the central valley of California. Although a new organization, the National Farm Workers Association (NFWA) mobilized more than 2,700 workers and activists, carrying red banners bearing the black thunderbird, to picket vineyards and to encourage other workers not to pick grapes. The strike was the beginning of a five-year effort to force California agribusiness to pay higher wages, provide better working conditions, and to give farm workers some control over their employment.

Chavez knew what it meant to be a migrant worker, to be trapped at the bottom of economic and social ladder—without choices. "The work is backbreaking, it is temporary, and it still leaves us almost at the bottom, standing ahead only of even more destitute farm workers in other states." The "whole fight, if you're poor, and if you're a minority group," Chavez believed, "is economic power." But the strike was about more than wages—the average farm laborer earned about $1,350 a year—it was *La Causa*, a matter of respect and dignity.

Chavez also knew what it meant to have little control over one's life. During the Depression, he had watched helplessly as his family was evicted from their Arizona farm and as bulldozers demolished their home. His parents

strike continued for five years until most of the major growers accepted unionization and improved wages and working conditions.

Meanwhile, Chavez had become a national figure, attracting public and political support for the farm workers' movement. Unionization of agricultural workers under the NFWA and other unions, including the Teamsters, was most successful in California, where a 1975 law required growers to

recognize and bargain with farm worker unions. In other states efforts to unionize farm workers were less successful.

As Mexican-Americans and other Latinos became more organized and vocal in their demands for a fairer share of the American dream, both political parties began to reach out to moderate Mexican-American leaders to woo them and the growing Hispanic vote. New Mexico's Manuel Lujan, a Re-had moved to California and became migrant workers, never able to break the cycle of poverty. Education was, Chavez recalled, a "nightmare" to migrant children rather than a possible escape route. School was little more than a succession of classes ruled over by Anglo teachers with little concern about the Spanish-speaking migrant children, who were frequently absent helping parents pick crops and who would soon move on to another school.

Seeking other choices, Chavez joined the navy in 1944. But two years later, without vocational or educational training, he returned to the fields. Chavez's expectations changed dramatically when two social activists, Father Donald McDonnell and Fred Ross, recruited him as a community organizer for the Community Service Organization (CSO), which was trying to mobilize poor communities for social and political change. In 1962, Chavez left CSO and with $1,200 he formed the United Farm Workers Association (UFWA).

During the five-year strike against the grape growers, as traditional union activities like picket lines failed to work, Chavez chose other means. Stressing nonviolence, he mobilized public opinion behind the plight of the workers with marches and mass rallies. He also fasted—one time refusing to eat for twenty-five days—and called on consumers to boycott fruits and vegetables not picked by union hands. "Alone," he explained, "the farm workers have no economic power, but with the help of the public, they can develop the economic power to counter that of the growers."

Chavez's energy and persistence along with an effective consumer boycott—an estimated 12 percent of the public refused to buy nonunion grapes—finally brought the grape growers to the bargaining table in 1970. Growers agreed to upgrade wages, offer some health benefits, and improve the conditions of work—including providing portable toilets and restricting the use of pesticides.

Success faded quickly, as the union was soon involved in another tougher strike against lettuce growers, confronting not only growers but a hostile rival union, the Teamsters, which also claimed to represent agricultural workers. After five months of struggle, with over 3,500 arrests, numerous beatings, and two deaths, Chavez recalled the pickets, emphasized *La Causa*, and turned to political activism—pushing voter registration and passage of laws to protect migrants' rights. The outcome was a 1975 California law that gave farm workers the right to choose union representation by secret ballot and guaranteed protection from employer reprisals. United Farm Workers membership again shot upward, reaching nearly 50,000 in the late 1970s, but internal divisions, economic recessions, and a growing antiunion climate combined in following years to reduce its numbers and influence. Chavez was saddened but not surprised, concluding that "the work for social change and against social injustice is never ended." Still working and fasting for social justice, Chavez died in April 1993.

Note: The United Farm Workers went through several names as it evolved: United Farm Workers Association (UFWA or UFW) 1961; National Farm Workers Association (NFWA) 1965; United Farm Workers Organizing Committee (UFWOC) 1966; and United Farm Workers of America (UFW) 1972.

publican, was elected to Congress, joining several Mexican-American Democrats in the House of Representatives. In 1974, Democrats Jerry Apodaca and Raul Castro were elected governors of New Mexico and Arizona. Henry Cisneros was elected mayor of San Antonio, and Federico Pena became the mayor of Denver in 1981. Both became members of President Clinton's cabinet in 1993. In 1987, Latinos were elected mayors in sixty-seven cities.

Yet despite the success stories like Lujan and Cisneros, the majority of Mexican-Americans have not achieved social or economic equality. Economically, although there have been some gains—the number of Latino households making $50,000 grew 234 percent between 1972 and 1984—as a whole the Mexican-American population remains one of the poorest minorities in the United States (see Table 30.1). "Often the father works two jobs and the mother

TABLE 30.1 WHITES, AFRICAN-AMERICANS, AND LATINOS, 1992

	Whites	African-Americans	Latinos
Average income	$30,513	$18,676	$22,330
Female-headed households	11.4%	47.8%	19.1%
High school education	80.5%	66.7%	51.3%
College	22.5%	11.5%	9.7%
Unemployment	6.9%	12.4%	10.0%
Below poverty	12.1%	31.9%	28.1%

Source: Congressional Quarterly Researcher, Oct. 30, 1992, p. 936.

one," recounted one researcher, "and they just can't make ends meet." Lack of economic success also impacts on education. Without the prospect of jobs, there is less incentive for Latino children to stay in high school. The Hispanic dropout rate was 45 percent nationwide in 1990, exceeding rates for blacks and whites.

American Indian Activism

American Indians, too, have asserted their rights with new vigor since the 1960s. The 1950s had been oppressive years for Indians, with the federal government pursuing a termination program designed to reduce or eliminate Indian reservations. Although the program actually eliminated few reservations or tribal units, federal policies encouraged more than 35,000 American Indians to leave their reservations and move to urban areas, where the government believed they could find jobs and a higher standard of living. Few urban Indians found anything but discrimination, poverty, and disease (see Map 30.4).

Indians on and off reservations organized and called for changes in white attitudes and new federal and state policies. Increasingly militant Indian leaders demanded the protection and restoration of their ancient burial grounds, along with fishing and timber rights. Museums were asked to return for proper burial the remains and bones of dead Indians on display. The National Indian Youth Council called for "Red Power," for Indians to use all means possible to resist further loss of Indian lands, rights, and traditions. Vine Deloria's popular *Custer Died*

for Your Sins (1969) informed readers that Indians had a culture and society of their own and asked "only to be freed of cultural oppression." "The white does not understand the Indian," he wrote, "and the Indian does not wish to understand the white." The central issue was not equality and assimilation, Deloria and other American Indian leaders explained, but Indian self-determination, especially in the control of reservations. As one leader explained, there was a difference between equality and sameness. They wanted economic prosperity and opportunity but on terms that would ensure their continued tribal and cultural existence.

In the 1960s, Kennedy and Johnson provided some change, ending the termination program and advocating self-rule and cultural pluralism for American Indians. Nixon continued the process by placing Indians in top-level positions within the Bureau of Indian Affairs and expanding federal programs. Four years later, Congress passed the **Indian Self-Determination and Education Assistance Act,** which gave tribes control and operation of many federal programs on their reservations. On the issue of lost lands, American Indians pressed their claims, with little prospect of success. Still, some Indian victories have occurred. In 1972, the Passamaquoddy and Penobscot tribes in Maine sued to have over

---

Indian Self-Determination and Cultural Assistance Act 1974 law giving Indian tribes control over federal programs carried out on their reservations and increasing their control of reservation schools.

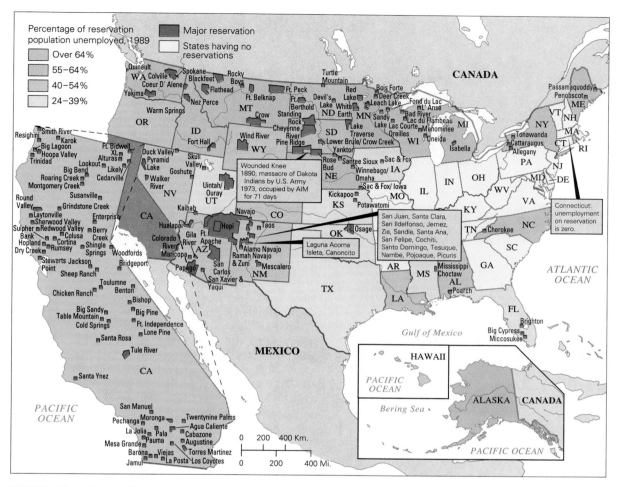

MAP 30.4 American Indian Reservations   In the seventeenth century, American Indians roamed over an estimated 1.9 billion acres, but by 1990 that area had shrunk to about 46 million acres spread across the United States. This area constitutes the federal reservation system. Comprising about one percent of the population, American Indians are among the most impoverished people in society, facing a life expectancy of about twenty fewer years than the average non-American Indian. This map shows the location of most of the federal Indian reservations, and highlights the high unemployment found on nearly every reservation. (*Note:* California is enlarged to show the many small reservations located there.)

12.5 million acres returned to the tribe that they claimed had been illegally seized by the state. They settled in 1980 for 300,000 acres and the establishment of a $27 million trust fund for the tribes. Also in 1980, the Supreme Court decided that the federal government owed over $106 million to the Sioux for taking the Black Hills of South Dakota in the 1870s.

Indian leaders applauded these efforts but lamented the slow pace of change, continued to complain about corruption and inefficiency in the BIA, and insisted that too much of reservation life was still controlled by the BIA and federal authorities. In the 1980s, the Reagan administration prompted more protests when it slashed more than one-third from federal assistance programs for Indians and suggested that the tribes look to the private sector to recoup losses from federal sources. Indian activist Vine Deloria called Reagan's "gospel of reliance on the private sector . . . absurd when applied to reservations, where the only private enterprise has been the non-Indian trader."

American Indians have also protested federal and state regulations that restrict gambling on reservations. By 1990, many tribes, like many states,

♦ In 1973, two hundred Sioux organized by the American Indian Movement (AIM) took over Wounded Knee, South Dakota, the site of the 1890 massacre, holding out for seventy one days against state and federal authorities. The confrontation ended after one protester was killed and the government agreed to examine the treaty rights of the Oglala Sioux. In this picture, AIM leader Russell Means received a blessing and symbolic red paint during the siege. *Dirck Halstead, TIME Magazine.*

were turning to gambling as sources of revenue and jobs, by operating "high-stakes" bingo games and Las Vegas–style casinos. The Supreme Court had opened the door to reservation gambling in 1982 and 1987 by ruling that if states allowed bingo and other forms of gambling, the state must also allow reservations within the state to run their own games. Despite court decisions and new legislation, the issues surrounding tribal sovereignty and federal and state controls continue to remain complex and unclear, with state and federal courts increasingly deciding issues of jurisdiction on a case-by-case basis.

Although some American Indian leaders turned to Washington and the courts to assert Indian rights, others took more direct action. In 1968, the Chippewas organized the **American Indian Movement (AIM)** to dramatize police brutality toward Indians in Minneapolis and to demand social justice for urban Indians. In the same year, a group of San Francisco Indian activists seized **Alcatraz Island,** offering to buy the federally owned island for $24 in beads and cloth, the amount that Dutch settlers paid the Manhattan Indians in 1626 for Manhattan Island. They held the island until 1971, when federal authorities, without bloodshed, retook control. Also in 1971, AIM directed the "Trail of Broken Treaties" march on Washington, and occupied the offices of the Bureau of Indian Affairs for several days. Two years later, AIM leaders Russell Means and Dennis Banks organized the armed occupation of Wounded Knee, South Dakota, the site of the 1890 massacre of the Sioux by the Army (see Map 30.2). AIM militants controlled the town for seventy-one days before surrendering to federal authorities. Although drawing international attention, the "second battle of Wounded Knee" failed to change federal policy, although Congress did agree to hold hearings on Indian needs and problems. In 1992, American Indian activists again received national and international notice with their opposition to the celebration of the 500th anniversary of Columbus' "discovery" of the "New World." Some claimed that the explorer should be held responsible for bringing slavery and disease to the Americas and destroying advanced and functioning native Indian cultures.

Nixon and the Balance of Power

● How did Nixon's foreign policy choices differ from those sought by traditional Republican conservatives?

During the 1968 presidential campaign, Nixon had promised to work for national unity, promoting minority rights and a new style of conservatism that accepted the basic role of government in domestic affairs. He presented himself as a controlled, pragmatic, and statesmanlike politician who could bal-

---

American Indian Movement   Militant Indian movement organized to demand social justice for urban Indians.

Alcatraz Island   Rocky island in San Francisco Bay that was occupied in 1969 by Native American activists who demanded that it be made available as a cultural center.

♦ In the Oval Office, Richard Nixon confers with his closest advisers, nicknamed by the press as the "Germans": Henry Kissinger, John Erlichman, and Bob Haldeman. Yet, Nixon remained aloof from even these advisers. For instance, he never knew how many children his Chief-of-Staff Haldeman had, nor did he care to ask. *Nixon Presidential Materials Project.*

ance liberal and conservative views and chart a middle course not unlike that of Eisenhower. In foreign affairs, he expected to achieve an honorable peace in Vietnam and re-establish American leadership in world affairs. Although he worked hard to shed his negative images, like the nickname "Tricky Dick," there remained the Nixon that was reclusive, inarticulate, and vindictive. And it was the latter characteristics that were reflected in his administrative style. Rather than work with Congress or his cabinet, he relied almost exclusively on a few personal advisers. For domestic affairs, he leaned on "the Germans," H. R. "Bob" Haldeman and John Ehrlichman, neither of whom had ever held a major political office. For international affairs, he turned to Harvard professor **Henry Kissinger,** his national security adviser.

A respected expert on foreign and military policy, Kissinger wielded an ego that matched his intellect, and he, like Nixon, wanted to restructure Cold

War policies, to break free of the constraints imposed by ideology and morality. Together they sought new policies based on "realistic" geopolitical values that stressed a combination of strength and flexibility in an ever-changing international balance of power. The Soviet Union was their number one agenda item, and Nixon believed that the America's military advantage over the Soviets was rapidly narrowing. Because there was little chance of persuading Congress to support the efforts needed to regain clear military superiority, Nixon concluded that it was necessary to improve relations with the Communist **superpower.** He and Kissinger recognized that the expanding Soviet-Chinese split, which had developed in the 1960s, offered the most promising diplomatic possibilities for changing the balance of Cold War power.

Vietnamization

The Soviets may have been the most important agenda item, but Nixon and Kissinger also knew that Vietnam was the most immediate problem. It dominated and shaped nearly all other issues: the budget, public and congressional opinion, foreign policy, and domestic stability. The Republicans needed a solution to Vietnam before moving ahead on other issues. The war was in a new phase, **de-escalation** and negotiation, and many Americans wanted the immediate removal of American troops. Nixon dismissed these calls for a "bug out." Not only would such a policy be politically unpopular in Middle America, but it would, Nixon believed, create a global collapse of confidence in American foreign policy. "A nation cannot remain great, if it betrays its allies and lets down its friends," Nixon explained. The central problem was to find a means to protect South Vietnam, encourage the North Vietnamese to negotiate, and allow the gradual withdrawal of American forces. Nixon's solution was

Henry Kissinger German-born American diplomat who was national security adviser and secretary of state under President Nixon; he helped negotiate the cease-fire in Vietnam.

superpower Term applied to the United States and the USSR in the Cold War period because both were powerful and heavily armed nations that dominated their allies in international politics.

de-escalation Decreasing the size, scope, or intensity of a war.

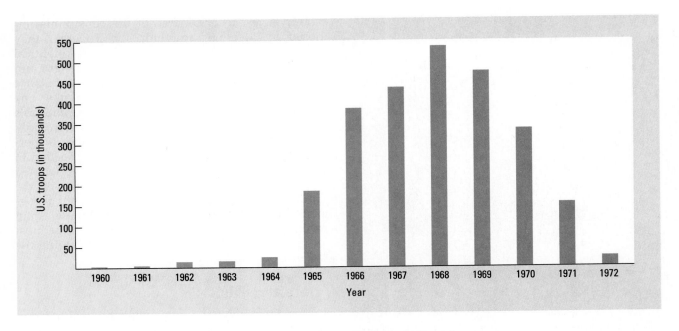

◆ **FIGURE 30.1 Troop Levels by Year**   For America, the Vietnam War went through two major phases: the "Americanization" of the war from 1960 to 1968, and the "Vietnamization" from 1969 to 1972.

Vietnamization, reducing the American role while enhancing South Vietnam's military capability. Nixon believed that with a change in the "color of bodies" and American soldiers coming home, large-scale opposition to the war would soon fade away. "I'm not going to end up like LBJ," he informed his advisers.

Vietnamization began in the spring of 1969, when Nixon announced that 25,000 American soldiers were coming home and that the South Vietnamese were assuming a larger role in the fighting. By the end of the year, American forces in Vietnam had declined by over 110,000 (see Figure 30.1). Expanding on the theme of limiting American involvement, the president issued the **Nixon Doctrine:** countries warding off communism would have to shoulder the bulk of the military burden, with the United States providing political and economic support and limited naval and air support.

Vietnamization, however, was only a part of Nixon's strategy. The other element in the "peace plan" was to increase the economic, diplomatic, and military pressure on North Vietnam to end the war and to accept the existence of South Vietnam. This, Nixon hoped, would be done two ways: getting the Soviets and Chinese to reduce their support for North Vietnam, and increasing the bombing inside South Vietnam and beginning the bombing against enemy bases across the border in Cambodia and Laos. In March 1969, Nixon ordered the heavy bombardment of Communist sanctuaries inside Cambodia, Operation MENU. Fearful of public and political reactions, the administration tried to keep the operation a secret, falsifying air force records and denying all rumors and stories about any such strikes. When Operation MENU ended in 1973 over 383,800 tons of bombs had been dropped in Cambodia. The intense assault was also part of a "madman strategy" Nixon designed to convince the North Vietnamese to negotiate. Nixon said he wanted Hanoi "to believe that I've reached the point where I

> **Vietnamization**   Policy announced by Nixon in which the United States scaled back its involvement in Vietnam, returning to its earlier role of helping Vietnamese forces fight their own war.
>
> **Nixon Doctrine**   Nixon's policy of requiring countries threatened by communism to shoulder the bulk of the military burden, with the United States mainly offering political and economic support.

◆ On the morning of March 16, 1968, American soldiers entered the hamlet of My Lai and massacred over two hundred women, children, and old men. The army successfully covered up the massacre until November 1969. Later Lt. William Calley was found guilty of mass murder and court martialed. An official evaluation by an army commander commented that some of the units "were little better than organized bands of thugs, with the officers eager participants in the body-count game." *Ron Haeberle, LIFE Magazine © Time Warner, Inc.*

might do anything to stop the war." "We'll just slip the word," Nixon told his advisers, "that 'for God's sake, you know Nixon. . . . We can't restrain him when he's angry—and he has his hand on the nuclear button.'"

The strategy did not work. The North Vietnamese appeared unconcerned about Nixon's "madness," the increased bombing, or decreasing support from China and the Soviet Union. They still believed that victory was only a matter of patiently waiting until America's will to pay the price of the war disappeared. Consequently, talks between Kissinger and the North Vietnamese in Paris produced only bitter feelings. Nor did American opposition to the war fade away, as Nixon hoped. In November 1969, over 250,000 antiwar protesters, in the largest single demonstration of the war, paraded past the White House calling for an end to the conflict. Adding fuel to the antiwar cause, news of American atrocities at **My Lai** came to light in 1970. In March 1968, Lieutenant William Calley's platoon had "wasted" the small village, killing over two hundred men, women, and children. The massacre and other revelations about the behavior of American troops seemed to many to offer uncontestable proof that the Vietnam War was immoral and was unraveling the moral fiber of American soldiers—resulting in drugs, dementia, and mindless slaughter. By 1968,

studies done of the army, even those conducted by the military, found morale among all ranks in the military had reached a dangerously low level, and some observers worried that the army could disintegrate from within.

Adding to public disillusionment about Vietnam was the publication of the *Pentagon Papers,* a collection of official documents gathered by former Defense Department researcher **Daniel Ellsberg** that showed that government officials had deceived the American public about conditions in Vietnam from the 1950s.

Neither the size of the march on Washington, the uproar over My Lai, nor the 1971 release of the *Pentagon Papers* dissuaded Nixon, who plotted further

---

My Lai   Site of a massacre of five hundred South Vietnamese villagers by U.S. infantrymen in 1969, an event that added to antiwar sentiment in the United States.

Pentagon Papers   Classified government documents on the policy decisions that led to U.S. involvement in Vietnam, which were leaked to *The New York Times* in 1971.

Daniel Ellsberg   Former Defense Department aide who was indicted for the theft of government property after he arranged for the publication of the *Pentagon Papers.*

♦ On May 4, 1970, Ohio National Guard troops opened fire on a crowd of Kent State students, protesting the American incursion into Cambodia, killing four of them. Here, a student screams in horror as she hovers over the body of one of the dead students. In outrage, campuses throughout the nation closed and students flocked to Washington to protest the war. *John Filo.*

"madness" and deceit. In 1970, he ordered American troops to cross the border into Cambodia and destroy North Vietnamese and Viet Cong headquarters and supply areas. He told the public that the incursion was not to widen the war but to hasten its end and achieve a just peace. Had we not invaded Cambodia, he argued, the United States would seem "like a pitiful, helpless giant," and the free world would be threatened everywhere.

The Cambodian invasion involved nearly eighty thousand American and South Vietnamese troops and destroyed large amounts of supplies. But it failed to defeat the enemy or stop the flow of supplies from North Vietnam. It also generated loud protests across the United States, especially on college campuses. At Kent State University on May 4, 1970, the Ohio National Guard fired on protesters, killing four and wounding eleven. At Jackson State University in Mississippi, police killed two students during another demonstration. Outraged students responded by shutting down over a hundred campuses as again thousands of antiwar demonstrators marched through Washington. An angry Senate repealed the Gulf of Tonkin Resolution and forbade the further use of American troops in Laos or Cambodia. Still, despite the furor over the Cambodian

incursion, the antiwar movement was finally ebbing. As Nixon had predicted, with American soldiers returning home, opposition to the war shrank and more Americans supported the administration's quest for an honorable peace.

By the end of 1971, Kissinger and Nixon were frustrated. Despite their public claims to the contrary, they knew Vietnamization was not progressing well and there seemed no sign of a settlement in Paris. There, the North Vietnamese refused to consider any settlement that did not replace South Vietnamese president Nguyan Van Thieu and his government with a coalition that included the Communist National Liberation Front—conditions rejected by the United States. Then in March 1972, Communist forces drove toward Saigon as South Vietnamese forces tottered on the brink of collapse. Livid at the Communist offensive, Nixon responded with force. "I'm going to show the bastards," he told Kissinger. "Unless they deal with us I'm going to bomb the hell out of them." He ordered massive bombing raids against North Vietnam and Communist forces in South Vietnam. By mid-June 1972, American air power had stalled the offensive and enabled ARVN forces to regroup and drive back the North Vietnamese. With their cities under almost

TABLE 30.2	THE VIETNAM GENERATION, 1964–1975	
	Men	**Women**
Total Military Service	8,700,000	250,000
Served in Vietnam	2,700,000	6,431
Killed in Vietnam	46,000	9
Wounded	300,635*	
Missing in action	2,330	—
Draft resistors (estimate)	570,000	—
Accused	210,000	—
Convicted	8,750	—

*Combined men and women
Source: Department of Defense and Veterans Administration.

continuous air attacks, the North Vietnamese became more flexible in negotiations. By October, with both sides offering some concessions, a peace settlement was ready. "Peace is at hand," Kissinger announced.

Thieu, however, rejected the plan, and reluctantly, Nixon supported Thieu and ordered Linebacker II: the Christmas bombing of Hanoi and North Vietnam. The bombing had two goals: to put additional pressure on Hanoi and to convince Thieu that the United States would use its air power to protect South Vietnam. After eleven days, the bombings stopped and Washington advised Thieu that if he did not accept the next peace settlement, the United States would leave him to fend for himself. Thieu thereupon accepted a peace settlement that did not differ significantly from the one offered in October. Nixon and Kissinger proclaimed peace with honor, and Kissinger shared the 1973 Nobel Peace Prize with his North Vietnamese counterpart.

The peace settlement imposed a cease-fire, required the removal of all American troops (only 24,000 now remained in South Vietnam) but not North Vietnamese troops, and promised the return of American prisoners of war. The peace terms permitted the United States to complete its military and political withdrawal, but the pact did little to ensure the continued existence of Thieu's government or South Vietnam. The cease-fire, everyone expected, would be temporary. When Haldeman asked

Kissinger how long the South Vietnamese government could last, Kissinger answered, "If they're lucky, than can hold out for a year and a half."

As expected, the cease-fire soon collapsed. North Vietnam continued to funnel men and supplies to the south, but substantial American air and naval support for South Vietnam never arrived. Neither Congress nor the public was anxious to help Thieu's government. Instead, Congress cut aid to South Vietnam and in November 1973 passed the **War Powers Act.** The law was designed to prevent executive decisions from involving the United States in a war by requiring the president to inform Congress within forty-eight hours of the deployment of troops overseas and to withdraw them within sixty days if Congress failed to authorize the action. In March 1975, North Vietnam began its final campaign to unify the country. A month later, North Vietnamese troops entered Saigon as a few remaining Americans and some South Vietnamese were evacuated by helicopter—some from the roof of the American embassy. The Vietnam War ended as it had started, with Vietnamese fighting Vietnamese (see Table 30.2).

War Powers Act   1973 law that set a sixty-day limit on presidential commitment of U.S. troops to hostilities abroad unless Congress authorized continued action.

Modifying the Cold War

Ending the Vietnam War was a political and diplomatic necessity for Nixon and Kissinger, essential to their goal of redefining the Cold War. In his first inaugural address, Nixon urged that an "era of confrontation" give way to an "era of negotiation." To this end, he pursued *détente,* a policy that reduced tensions with the two Communist superpowers. China was the key to the Nixon-Kissinger strategy. The Soviets and Chinese had already engaged in several bloody clashes along their border, and the Chinese feared a border war. Believing that better relations with the United States would help deter Soviet aggression, the Chinese were ready to open diplomatic discussions with Nixon. From Nixon's perspective, American friendship with the Chinese would encourage the Soviets to improve their relations with the United States, leading to *détente.* Sending a signal to China, Nixon lowered restrictions on trade, and in April 1971, the Chinese responded by inviting an American ping-pong team to tour China. A few months later, Kissinger secretly flew to Beijing to meet with Premier Zhou Enlai. The result would, as Kissinger phrased it, "send a shock wave around the world": Nixon was going to China. In February 1972, Nixon arrived in Beijing, met with Communist party chairman Mao Zedong and Zhou, and suddenly the "Red Chinese" were no longer the enemy but "hard-working, intelligent . . . and practical" friends. The Cold War was thawing a little in the East.

Nixon's China policy, as hoped, contributed to improved relations with the Soviet Union. Kissinger followed his secret visit to China with one to Moscow, where he discussed improving relations with President **Leonid Brezhnev.** Nixon flew to Moscow in May 1972 and told Brezhnev, "I know that my reputation is one of being a very hard-line, Cold War–oriented, anti-Communist," but that he now believed that the two nations should "live together and work together." Needing to reduce military spending, develop the Soviet domestic economy, and increase American trade, Brezhnev agreed. The meeting was a success. Brezhnev obtained increased trade with the West, including shipments of American grain, and the superpowers announced a **Strategic Arms Limitation agreement (SALT I)** that restricted antimissile sites and established a maximum number of **intercontinental ballistic missiles (ICBMs)** and submarine-launched missiles (SLBMs) for each side. It seemed as if *détente* had arrived and that Nixon was reshaping world affairs.

In efforts to redirect the Cold War, Nixon became the first president to visit China, meeting with Mao Zedung and Zhou Enlai in 1972. With regard to Chinese–Soviet relations, Nixon confided to Zhou that if Moscow marched either East or West, he was ready to "turn like a cobra on the Russians." Nixon's visit to China began the process of normalizing relations with the People's Republic of China that was finalized under Carter. *John Dominis, LIFE Magazine © Time Warner, Inc.*

But not all that Nixon and Kissinger did in foreign affairs differed from traditional Cold War policy. In Latin America, Nixon followed closely in Johnson's footsteps, working to isolate Cuba and prevent any additional Communist-style leaders

---

détente   Relaxing of tensions between the superpowers in the early 1970s, which included increased diplomatic, commercial, and cultural contact.

Leonid Brezhnev   President of the Soviet Union from 1977 to his death in 1982, who worked to foster *détente* with the United States during the Nixon era.

Strategic Arms Limitation agreement   Agreement between the United States and the USSR in 1972 to limit both offensive nuclear weapons and the antiballistic missile systems that protected against them.

intercontinental ballistic missiles   Missiles that can travel from one continent to another.

from gaining power. Borrowing from Eisenhower's foreign policy, he used covert operations to destabilize and disrupt the socialist-Marxist government of **Salvador Allende** in Chile. He told the CIA in 1970 to squeeze the Chilean economy "until it screamed" while funneling money to opposition groups. Three years later the Chilean economy was in shambles with food riots, inflation over 100 percent, and endless strikes. Finally the military moved, and on September 11, 1973, Allende was killed when Chilean armed forces stormed and bombed the presidential palace. Kissinger denied any direct American role in the coup and quickly recognized the repressive military government of General Augusto Pinochet, who promptly reinstated a free market economy.

Nixon and Politics

• How did Nixon's choices in dealing with the economy and environment reflect his pragmatic conservatism?

In his foreign policy, Nixon followed new paths in dealing with the Chinese and Soviets that did not reflect traditional Republican views. This was also true in many of his domestic programs. Nixon believed that Republicans needed to be more pragmatic. They needed to emphasize a conservatism that did not automatically reject social responsibility and executive activism.

Pragmatic Conservatism

Nixon called for a style of conservatism, a **New Federalism,** that embraced the uses of federal power while eliminating useless governmental machinery and making programs more responsive to state and local government. His **Revenue Sharing Act** reflected the new approach. The government would continue to raise revenue through its broad tax base, but it would release more of the money to state and local governments and reduce the amount of federal controls and restrictions on how they spent it. Some Republicans disliked the plan because it did not reduce federal spending, but in October 1972, the act passed Congress. Before the program was ended in 1986, state and local governments had received over $83 billion in revenue sharing funds, reversing the flow of responsibility and political power for the first time since the Great Depression.

Nixon also wanted to redirect the flow of money and responsibility in the welfare system. Unlike

many staunch conservatives, Nixon was not opposed to welfare, but he and his adviser on the issue, Daniel Patrick Moynihan, believed the existing welfare system robbed people of their self-esteem, contributed to the break-up of nuclear families, and punished people for working. His proposal for welfare reform, the Family Assistance Plan (FAP), sought to balance work and welfare but was quickly attacked by conservatives and liberals alike and defeated in the Senate in 1969 and 1971. After its second defeat, Nixon lost interest: "I did not want to be in a losing fight with conservatives over FAP in an election year."

Although the Family Assistance Program had failed, Nixon did not abandon what he saw as the political need for federal social responsibility. Without fanfare, his administration increased welfare support and approved legislation that enhanced the regulatory powers of the federal government. Food stamps became more accessible, the elderly and handicapped received direct federal support, and social security, Medicare, and Medicaid payments were increased. Nixon also supported subsidized housing for low- and middle-income families and expanded the Job Corps. He signed the **Twenty-sixth Amendment** giving 18-year-olds the right to vote, and his administration oversaw the formation of the Occupational Safety and Health Administration (OSHA) and the **Environmental Protection Agency (EPA).**

Nixon's support for these domestic social programs arose not only from his belief in their importance but also from his understanding of politics. He believed that the Republican party could not afford

---

Salvador Allende   Chilean president who was considered the first democratically elected Marxist head of government; he was killed in a CIA-backed coup in 1973.

New Federalism   Nixon's policy of accepting the existence of government social programs but seeking to trim waste and increase the power of state and local governments.

Revenue Sharing Act   Five-year program established in 1972 to distribute large amounts of federal tax revenues to state and local governments to use as they saw fit.

Twenty-sixth Amendment   Amendment to the Constitution in 1971 lowering the voting age from 21 to 18.

Environmental Protection Agency   Agency created in 1970 to consolidate all major government programs combatting pollution.

to ignore social needs and public concerns in the name of conservatism. The environmental issue was a case in point. When Nixon took office in 1969, the environment was not a major issue. Few Americans thought about ecology. Almost overnight, however, the environment became a serious public issue. The ever-present Los Angeles smog, an oil slick off Santa Barbara, California, the declaration that Lake Erie was ecologically dead, and growing mountains of garbage everywhere provided graphic reminders of the ecological dangers facing the nation. Less than 6 percent of the world's population, environmentalists complained, Americans consumed 40 percent of the globe's resources and created 50 percent of the world's trash. During the second celebration of Earth Day, April 1970, nearly every community in the nation and over ten thousand schools and two thousand colleges hosted some type of Earth Day activities. There was also a national call for governmental action to improve environmental quality.

Nixon was not an environmentalist, but he recognized a new national agenda topic. Seizing the opportunity, two days after Earth Day 1970, he proposed the creation of the Environmental Protection Agency. He also signed Clean Air and Clean Water acts that directed the EPA to establish limits on the amount of pollutants that business and industry could dump into the air and water. Conservatives complained that the standards placed too great a burden on business, whereas liberals objected that the guidelines did not go far enough to protect the environment. But few could deny that Nixon had moved quickly to expand government regulations in an area in which most people agreed a need existed.

When Nixon took office, most people also thought the economy was a primary concern. Johnson had left a budget deficit of nearly $25 billion, huge at the time, and a climbing rate of inflation. Nixon's initial response was to cut spending, increase interest rates, and try to balance the budget. He succeeded in balancing the budget in 1969, but other results were unexpected. Inflation continued to rise even as economic growth slowed, a new phenomenon soon dubbed **"stagflation."** By 1971, the economy was in its first recession since 1958. Unemployment and bankruptcies increased, but inflation still climbed, approaching 5.3 percent. Joyous Democrats quickly blamed Nixon and "Nixonomics." Fearing that the economy would erode Republican support and urged on by Secretary of Treasury John Connally, Nixon radically shifted his approach. "I am now a

◆ On April 22, 1970, the nation celebrated the first national Earth Day. Part of the ecology movement, Earth Day emphasized the things that ordinary people could do to improve the environment. A few days later Nixon created the Environment Protection Agency. *Ken Regan, Camera Five.*

Keynesian," he announced in April 1971, asking for increased federal spending to boost recovery and wage and price controls to stall advancing inflation. Conservatives were shocked and complained bitterly at the betrayal of their values. "American fascism arrived on April 15, 1971," stated one conservative Republican. The public and the economy responded positively, however, as inflation and unemployment declined. At the end of ninety days,

"stagflation"   Persistent inflation combined with stagnant consumer demand and relatively high unemployment.

Nixon replaced the wage and price freeze with recommended guidelines, but without federal restrictions, wages and prices began to climb again.

Nixon's battle with inflation was a losing one, in part because of economic events over which he had no control. A global drought pushed up farm prices, while Arab nations raised oil prices and limited oil sales in response to the devaluation of the American dollar and continued United States support for Israel. Following the October 1973 Arab-Israeli Yom Kippur War, Arab nations instituted an oil boycott of the United States that, before it was over in 1974, nearly doubled gasoline prices and forced many Americans to wait in long lines to gas up their cars. Some areas of the country even instituted fuel oil and gasoline rationing. Increases in food and oil prices pushed the 1974 inflation rate over 10 percent. That same year, 85 percent of those asked said not only that the economy was the nation's most pressing problem but also that they expected it to get worse.

Law and Order and Southern Politics

During the 1968 campaign, Nixon had presented himself as the law-and-order candidate who would use the resources and power of government to combat crime. But once in office, the administration seemed more interested in using the law-and-order theme for political purposes than attacking street crime. An aide to Attorney General John Mitchell, Kevin Phillips, argued in *The Emerging Republican Majority* that the future of the Republican party rested on drawing support from people living in suburbs, working-class neighborhoods, the South, and the Sunbelt. In those areas, Phillips asserted, there was little sympathy for student activists, antiwar protesters, welfare recipients, or civil rights advocates. Nixon hoped to link those groups with lawlessness and tap existing public resentment of them for political gain. Matching the political strategy, Mitchell approved of a full range of actions against Nixon's "enemies."

Throughout Nixon's first term, administration officials had waged war against student, antiwar, and civil rights activists. Zealously, vice president **Spiro Agnew** denounced antiwar protesters for aiding the enemy and ruining the nation's social and patriotic values and condemned the press for being too lib-

eral. Supported by others, he called for the Silent Majority to reject "the nattering nabobs of negativism" and for authorities to take back the campuses and reassert strict controls. The White House also employed more direct tactics. The Justice Department, often acting illegally, used **wiretaps** and preventive detention against opponents and infiltrated groups viewed as the administration's enemies.

As part of the ongoing "southern strategy"—Nixon's efforts to lock up the once solidly Democratic South for Republicans—the administration opposed busing to achieve school integration, worked to slow down integration in other areas, and sought to put a southerner on the Supreme Court. Finding a friendly attitude in the White House, Mississippi officials in 1969 asked that the court-ordered integration of several school systems be postponed. Mitchell agreed and the Justice Department petitioned the Supreme Court for a delay. At the same time, the administration lobbied Congress for a revision of the 1965 Voting Rights Act that would have weakened southern compliance. Neither effort was successful. Congress rejected changes to the Voting Rights Act and, in October, the Supreme Court unanimously decreed in *Alexander v. Holmes* that it was "the obligation of every school district to terminate dual school systems at once." The White House suffered another loss in 1971 when the Court reaffirmed the use of busing to achieve integration in a North Carolina case, *Swann v. Charlotte-Mecklenburg*. In both cases, the Nixon administration criticized the decisions but agreed to "carry out the law." Nixon eased the process by adding federal monies to schools going through court-ordered integration. By 1973, most African-American children in the South attended integrated public schools. Nixon lost in the effort to slow down the process of integration, but he won politically among white southerners, who increasingly looked to the Republican party to support their interests.

A second part of Nixon's southern strategy was to alter the geographical and ideological composi-

---

Spiro Agnew Vice president under Richard Nixon, who resigned in 1973 amid charges of illegal financial dealings during his governorship of Maryland.

wiretap Concealed listening or recording device used to monitor communications.

tion of the Supreme Court. He wanted a more conservative Court that would more narrowly interpret the Constitution and move away from the social interventionist nature of the Warren Court—and for political reasons, he wanted to appoint a southerner. His first opportunity came in 1969 when Chief Justice Earl Warren retired. Nixon nominated federal judge Warren Burger. Although not a southerner, Burger was a conservative who, as a respected judge, would be easily confirmed by the Senate.

Almost immediately, liberal Justice Abe Fortas resigned, giving Nixon a second chance to alter the Court. Burger's nomination had been based on his judicial decisions, but the next appointment was clearly political. Without much consideration of his background, Nixon selected Clement Haynesworth of South Carolina. Haynesworth had a history of antilabor and anti–civil rights statements and decisions that raised predictable trouble in the Senate. Democrats and several Republicans joined forces to deny his confirmation.

The rejection incensed Nixon, who was determined to force a southerner down the Senate's throat. His second choice was worse than the first. Not only was G. Harrold Carswell of Florida opposed to civil rights and labor, but his ratings as a lawyer and judge were below average. Making the best of a bad situation, one Republican defender pointed out that there were "lots of mediocre judges" and that mediocre people should have a representative on the Court. As before, a coalition of Republicans and Democrats rejected Carswell. On his third try, Nixon stopped looking for a southerner and selected Harry Blackmun, a conservative from Minnesota. Blackmun was confirmed easily. In 1971, Nixon appointed two more justices, Lewis Powell of Virginia (finally a southerner) and William Rehnquist of Arizona, creating a more conservative and less interventionist Supreme Court.

An Embattled President

By the end of Nixon's first term, Republicans had every reason to gloat. Nearly 60 percent of those asked in national opinion polls approved of Nixon's record. The efforts on behalf of southern whites had ensured growing support in what had once been the "solid Democratic South." The law-and-order campaign was supported by Middle America while protesters and activists were losing strength and support. The economy, although still a worry, seemed under control with unemployment dropping and inflation held in check. Diplomatically, Nixon had scored major successes: the opening of relations with China, *détente* with the Soviets, the reduction of American forces in Vietnam, and the possibility of a peace agreement in Paris. The continued disarray of the Democratic party only added to Republican confidence. Yet despite Republican confidence, the Oval Office was plagued by a seige mentality. Nixon was convinced that he was surrounded by enemies: Democrats, social activists, liberals, most of the press, and even some within his own staff and party. Repeatedly, he spoke about "screwing" his domestic enemies before they got him. He kept an "enemies list" and stepped up wiretaps and infiltration, and he used the FBI, the Internal Revenue Service, and other government organizations to intimidate and punish his opposition. As the 1972 election neared, Nixon was determined to not only win but to smash his opposition.

The Democrats had not found party unity following the 1968 campaign, and the 1972 primary fights between Hubert Humphrey, George Wallace, Edmund Muskie, and **George McGovern** only compounded the divisions. The liberal McGovern of South Dakota won the nomination, but the party remained fractured. To many Democrats, McGovern appeared out of touch with the majority of the party, too liberal and too much a candidate of the counterculture and radicals. George Wallace again bolted the party to run as a third-party candidate on the American Independent ticket. Wallace's candidacy was brief, ending on May 15, when Arthur Bremer shot and paralyzed him. Facing Nixon, McGovern ran a poor, boring campaign that continued to lose supporters even as the election neared. In the November election, Nixon buried him in an electoral avalanche, winning every state except Massachusetts.

But Nixon wanted more than a victory. Throughout the campaign, he and his campaign staff were obsessed with humiliating the Democrats, securing a Republican Congress, and reconstituting a party that would lead to Republican victories for decades. To achieve this objective, Nixon's staff and the campaign

George McGovern South Dakota senator who opposed the Vietnam War and was the Democratic candidate for president in 1972 defeated by Nixon.

◆ As the Watergate investigation uncovered a host of "dirty tricks" and other unethical and illegal activities by the Nixon Administration, cartoonist Edward Sorell drew the "Watergate Shootout," showing Nixon, Mitchell, and others involved in the Watergate scandal as a band of mobsters holding off the police. *"Watergate Shootout" by Edward Sorell. Collection of Byron Dobell.*

managers of the **Committee to Re-elect the President (CREEP),** directed by **John Mitchell,** were willing to step outside the normal bounds of election behavior. The administration already had gone after enemies, using tactics that ranged from unethical to illegal, and during the campaign they turned to a Special Investigations Unit, the "Plumbers," to disrupt the Democrats. The Plumbers had used illegal surveillance and even burglary to investigate sources of suspected leaks of sensitive materials, like the *Pentagon Papers,* and under ex-FBI agent G. Gordon Liddy and former CIA operative E. Howard Hunt, they conducted "dirty tricks" against the Democrats. Seeking inside information on the opposition, CREEP approved sending burglars into the Democratic National Headquarters office in the **Watergate** building to copy documents and tap phones.

There on June 17, 1972, a security guard detected the burglars and notified the police, who arrested five men carrying "bugging" equipment. Officials soon determined that they worked for Hunt and Liddy. CREEP and the White House immediately denied any connection to the burglars and worked to contain the investigation of the break-in. As Nixon "categorically" denied that anyone in the White House was involved, Mitchell and White

House staffers destroyed documents that indicated the opposite and arranged payments to those arrested in return for their silence. The FBI was encouraged to limit its investigation. The furor passed and the Watergate break-in had little apparent effect on the public or the election.

Nixon began his second term claiming a clear mandate for his policies. From the outside it appeared that the Nixon administration had a clear field to promote its agenda. But within the White House, concern simmered over one possible con-

---

Committee to Re-elect the President   Nixon's campaign committee in 1972, which enlisted G. Gordon Liddy and others to spy on the Democrats and break into the offices of the Democratic National Committee.

John Mitchell   Nixon's attorney general, who eventually served four years of prison time for his part in the Watergate scandal.

Watergate   Washington apartment complex that housed the Democratic party's national headquarters; it gave its name to the scandal over the Nixon administration's involvement in a break-in at those headquarters and the president's part in the cover-up that followed.

straint—the approaching trial of the Watergate burglars. If the truth about Watergate was discovered, the Nixon administration might disintegrate. Not directly involved in the covert actions against the Democrats, Nixon knew soon after the Watergate break-in that White House officials were implicated, and the president approved of efforts to hide their connection. "I want you all to stonewall it," he told John Mitchell. "Cover it up."

But as the trial approached, the cover-up began to unravel. Before being sentenced for the break-in, James McCord, who led the burglary team, informed Judge John J. Sirica that key Republicans were involved in planning the operation and that the burglars had been paid to keep quiet. *Washington Post* reporters Bob Woodward and Carl Bernstein, investigating the suspicious payments, found a path leading to the White House, John Mitchell, and CREEP. Amid growing publicity and suspicions of White House involvement, the Senate convened a special committee to investigate the break-in, chaired by a Democrat, Senator Sam Ervin, Jr., of North Carolina. Among those called before Sirica's court and Ervin's committee, White House staffer John Dean testified that top White House officials, including Nixon, were involved in the cover-up. By May 1973, Nixon had fired Dean and watched Haldeman and Ehrlichman resign.

The cover-up further fell apart with testimony that Nixon had secretly recorded Oval Office conversations, including those with Dean. Responding to public pressure, Nixon appointed Archibald Cox as special Justice Department prosecutor to investigate Watergate, promising full cooperation. But when Cox demanded Oval Office tapes, Nixon ordered him fired. Following the October 20, 1973, **"Saturday Night Massacre,"** Nixon's popularity shrank to 30 percent and calls for his resignation or impeachment intensified. Adding to Nixon's troubles were accusations he had improperly taken tax deductions and that Vice President Agnew was guilty of income-tax evasion and influence peddling. "I am not a crook," Nixon announced as both denied any wrongdoing. Nevertheless, Agnew was convicted of incorrect tax reporting and accepting a bribe, and the Internal Revenue Service concluded that Nixon had made errors in his deductions and owed the government an additional half million dollars. Agnew resigned and as Nixon, using the new Twenty-fifth Amendment, named Congressman Gerald R. Ford of Michigan vice president, a newly formed House of Representatives Judiciary Committee considered grounds for impeachment.

In March 1974, the grand jury investigating the Watergate break-in indicted Mitchell, Haldeman, and Ehrlichman, and named Nixon as an "unindicted co-conspirator." Under tremendous pressure, Nixon released to the House Judiciary Committee transcripts of selected tapes. Even without the real tapes, the outcome was devastating. Not only did the transcripts contradict some official testimony, but Nixon's profane language, callousness, and apparent lack of moral values shocked many Americans. By the end of July, the House Judiciary Committee had charged Nixon with three impeachable crimes: obstructing justice, abuse of power, and denying subpoenas. Nixon's remaining support evaporated and once-loyal Republicans told him that he could either resign or face impeachment. Nixon resigned on August 9, 1974, making Gerald Ford an unelected president. Eventually, twenty-nine people connected to the White House were convicted of crimes related to Watergate and the 1972 campaign.

"Saturday Night Massacre" Events on October 20, 1973, when Nixon ordered the firing of Watergate special prosecutor Archibald Cox and ended up firing those who refused to carry out his order.

SUMMARY

E xpectations

C onstraints

C hoices

O utcomes

President Johnson *chose* to continue Kennedy's commitment to save South Vietnam from communism. The *outcome*, through a series of planned escalations, was an Americanized war in Vietnam. The *expectation* that American superiority would defeat Ho Chi Minh's Communists proved false and disastrous for Johnson and the nation. The military, economic, and political *constraints* associated with Vietnam cost Johnson his presidency and compounded the divisions in American society.

It was not just the debate over the war that divided the nation. By 1968, the country was aflame with riots in urban centers and an increasing number of groups seeking better social, economic, and political *choices*. Those advocating social reforms also encountered growing *constraints* generated by a resurgence of conservatism. In 1968, Nixon *chose* to emphasize dissatisfaction with Johnson's war and the Great Society and the concerns about a fragmented society to win the presidency.

As president, Nixon *chose* to escape the quagmire of Vietnam by implementing Vietnamization. *Expecting* to restructure international relations, he *chose* to promote *détente*, working to improve relations with the Soviet Union and China. At home, Nixon *chose* an uneven course, switching between maintaining governmental activism and reducing the power of government and intervention in society and the economy. Politically, he sought a broader base for the Republican party by pursuing a southern strategy that diminished federal support for civil rights and appointed a southerner to the Supreme Court. Despite Nixon's domestic and foreign policy successes, however, his desire to crush opposition eventually led to the Watergate scandal. *Expecting* impeachment, the president *chose* to resign. The *outcome* of the Johnson years and Watergate was a nation with low expectations for politics and government, caught in a feeling of drift, disillusionment, and disunity.

SUGGESTED READINGS

Caputo, Philip. *Rumor of War* (1986).

An excellent personal account of one person's changing perspectives on the war in Vietnam. From his experiences as a young marine officer in Vietnam to an experienced journalist covering the final days in Saigon, Caputo's views frequently reflected those of the American public.

There are several usable films about the American experience with Vietnam, from the PBS series on Vietnam to feature films like *Platoon, Apocalypse Now,* and *The Deer Hunter.*

Deloria, Jr., Vine. *Behind the Trail of Broken Treaties* (1974).

An examination of U.S. government policies toward Native Americans by a leading Indian activist.

Echols, Alice. *Daring to be Bad* (1989).

An insightful and interesting account of the radical dimension of the women's movement.

Kutler, Stanley. *The Wars of Watergate* (1990).

A detailed account of the events surrounding the Watergate break-in and the hearings that led to the resignation of Nixon.

McQuaid, Kim. *The Anxious Years: American in the Vietnam-Watergate Era* (1989).

A brief and solid overview of the 1960s.

Roberts, Robert. *Where the Dominoes Fell* (1990).

A brief, well-written history of America's role in Vietnam.

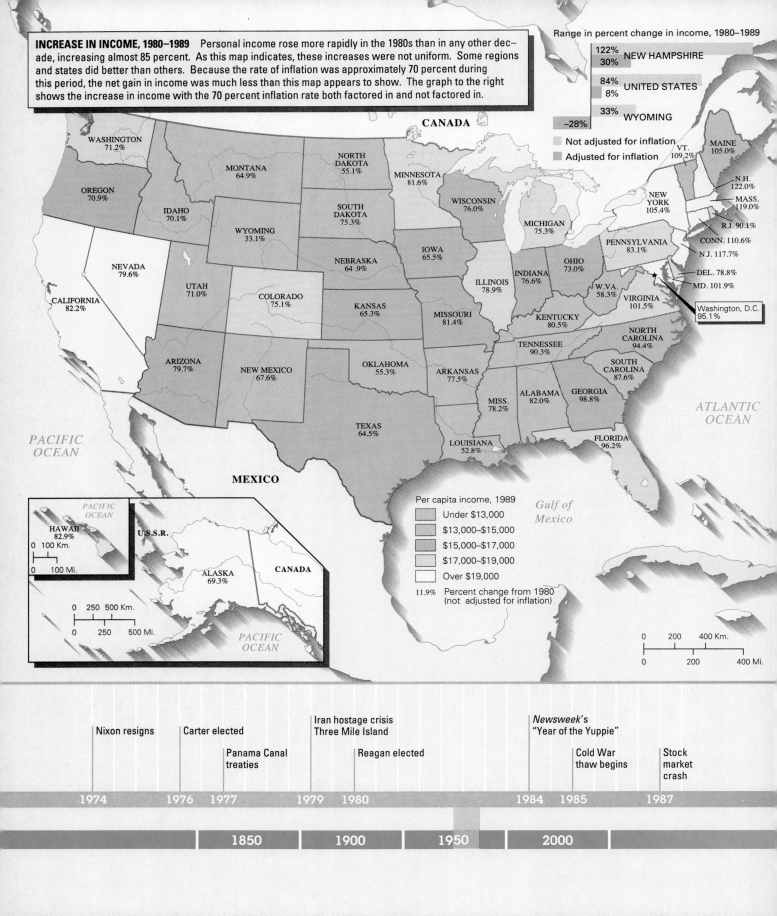

INCREASE IN INCOME, 1980–1989   Personal income rose more rapidly in the 1980s than in any other dec–ade, increasing almost 85 percent. As this map indicates, these increases were not uniform. Some regions and states did better than others. Because the rate of inflation was approximately 70 percent during this period, the net gain in income was much less than this map appears to show. The graph to the right shows the increase in income with the 70 percent inflation rate both factored in and not factored in.

Range in percent change in income, 1980–1989

122% / 30%	NEW HAMPSHIRE
84% / 8%	UNITED STATES
33% / –28%	WYOMING

Not adjusted for inflation
Adjusted for inflation

CANADA

WASHINGTON 71.2%
OREGON 70.9%
MONTANA 64.9%
IDAHO 70.1%
NORTH DAKOTA 55.1%
MINNESOTA 81.6%
WISCONSIN 76.0%
MICHIGAN 75.3%
WYOMING 33.1%
SOUTH DAKOTA 75.3%
IOWA 65.5%
NEVADA 79.6%
UTAH 71.0%
NEBRASKA 64.9%
ILLINOIS 78.9%
INDIANA 76.6%
OHIO 73.0%
PENNSYLVANIA 83.1%
NEW YORK 105.4%
CALIFORNIA 82.2%
COLORADO 75.1%
KANSAS 65.3%
MISSOURI 81.4%
KENTUCKY 80.5%
W.VA. 58.3%
VIRGINIA 101.5%
ARIZONA 79.7%
NEW MEXICO 67.6%
OKLAHOMA 55.3%
ARKANSAS 77.5%
TENNESSEE 90.3%
NORTH CAROLINA 94.4%
SOUTH CAROLINA 87.6%
TEXAS 64.5%
MISS. 78.2%
ALABAMA 82.0%
GEORGIA 98.8%
LOUISIANA 52.8%
FLORIDA 96.2%

MAINE 105.0%
VT. 109.2%
N.H. 122.0%
MASS. 119.0%
R.I. 90.1%
CONN. 110.6%
N.J. 117.7%
DEL. 78.8%
MD. 101.9%
Washington, D.C. 95.1%

CANADA

PACIFIC OCEAN

ATLANTIC OCEAN

MEXICO

Gulf of Mexico

Per capita income, 1989

	Under $13,000
	$13,000–$15,000
	$15,000–$17,000
	$17,000–$19,000
	Over $19,000

11.9%   Percent change from 1980 (not adjusted for inflation)

Inset:
PACIFIC OCEAN
HAWAII 82.9%
0 100 Km.
0 100 Mi.

U.S.S.R.
ALASKA 69.3%
CANADA
0 250 500 Km.
0 250 500 Mi.
PACIFIC OCEAN

0 200 400 Km.
0 200 400 Mi.

Timeline:

Nixon resigns	Carter elected		Iran hostage crisis Three Mile Island			*Newsweek*'s "Year of the Yuppie"	
		Panama Canal treaties		Reagan elected		Cold War thaw begins	Stock market crash
1974	1976	1977	1979	1980		1984	1985	1987

1850	1900	1950	2000	

Facing Limits, 1974–1986

Politics of Uncertainty
- What choices did Ford and Carter make in an effort to improve the American economy?
- How did the constraints they faced shape the outcome?

Carter's Foreign Policy
- Compare Carter's expectations with the outcomes of his foreign policies.
- How did his choices reflect new views of America's role in world affairs?

Enter Ronald Reagan—Stage Right
- What expectations influenced Americans who chose to vote for Reagan?
- How did his social and domestic policies both reflect those expectations and alter expectations?

Asserting World Power
- What expectations shaped the choices Reagan's administration made in implementing American foreign policy?

INTRODUCTION

Although Gerald Ford was praised for his honesty, few expected him to provide challenging leadership that would solve the serious problems facing the nation. Serving out Nixon's term of office, Ford did little to implement or build on Nixon's policies or improve an economy suffering from stagflation—both stagnation and inflation (see page 958). To some people's surprise, however, he defeated party rivals and was renominated in 1976.

As the nation celebrated its 200th birthday and television showed 30-second clips of proud moments in American history, few *expected* the next few years to reflect the nation's greatness. *Constraints* on American success seemed to loom everywhere. The sluggish economy, the failure in Vietnam, and Watergate had eliminated what remained of the hopeful, crusading spirit that President Kennedy had generated. Less optimistic expectations pushed Americans to seek different political *choices*. The economy responded to neither liberal nor conservative policy choices, and the liberalism that had attacked racism and poverty was out of vogue, challenged by more fiscal and socially conservative choices favoring less government involvement and more traditional values. Many expected the *outcome* would be a new conservative majority that would restructure public policy. Even James Earl Carter, the Democratic candidate for the presidency in 1976, based a large part of his political message on personal and moral choices rather than on an expansive social agenda.

Carter argued that certain *constraints* made it impossible for the U.S. government to solve every problem facing the nation. He appealed to a national belief in morality and urged sacrifice to open new *choices* for policies that would help America solve domestic and world problems. His *expectations*, however, ran aground on the hard realities of politics and public opinion. As president, Carter failed to support his calls for sacrifice and morality with an effective domestic or foreign policy. Many Americans believed that his policies were partially responsible for the *constraints* that he was warning them about. They argued that the main constraint was not the nation's limited capabilities but Carter's misguided policies and a federal government that stifled individual choices.

E xpectations
C onstraints
C hoices
O utcomes

Opposing Carter, the 1980 Republican candidate for president, Ronald Reagan, won popular approval by promoting the *expectation* of a renewed America, powerful and prosperous. He attacked liberal economic and social policies and re-emphasized a Cold War–style foreign policy that would "stand tall" against the Soviet "evil empire." When Reagan left office in 1989, many people believed that he had fulfilled his promises. The *outcome* was that the economy seemed vitalized and government was redirected away from costly social programs. Many Americans felt that business had been freed of many needless government controls; traditional social and family values had been properly reasserted; and the Cold War had been all but won.

Not everyone agreed that Reagan's *choices* had produced a favorable *outcome*, however. Critics argued that his choices had placed too much emphasis on wealth and too little on the needs of minority groups, the less well off, and the poor. Others pointed to serious flaws in the economy—including a massive national debt—and a growing imbalance in trade between the United States and the rest of the world and predicted an economic decline in the immediate future. They argued that the Reagan administration had sold the nation only an illusion of strength and prosperity, but had not overcome the real *constraints* and limits that remained.

CHRONOLOGY

New Directions, New Limits

1974 Nixon resigns
Gerald Ford becomes president and
pardons Nixon
Brezhnev-Ford summit at Vladivostok

1975 Fall of South Vietnam
Helsinki summit
Jackson-Vanik Amendment

1976 Jimmy Carter elected president

1977 Department of Energy created
Panama Canal treaties
SALT I treaty expires

1978 Camp David accords
Revolution in Iran topples the Shah
United States recognizes People's Republic of China

1979 Ayatollah Khomeini assumes power in Iran
Nuclear accident at Three Mile Island, PA.
Egyptian-Israeli peace treaty signed in
Washington, D.C.
SALT II treaty signed in Vienna
Hostages seized in Iran
Soviet Union invades Afghanistan

1980 Carter applies sanctions against Soviet
Union
SALT II withdrawn from Senate
Carter Doctrine
Chrysler bailout
Iran-Iraq War begins
Ronald Reagan elected president

1981 Iran releases American hostages

Economic Recovery Tax Act
Sandra Day O'Connor appointed to
Supreme Court

1982 Garn–St. Germain Act
United States sends Marines to Lebanon

1983 SDI funded
United States invades Grenada
Marine barracks in Beirut destroyed

1984 Reagan re-elected
Charles Murray's *Losing Ground*
Withdrawal of U.S. forces from Lebanon
Boland Amendment
Newsweek's "Year of the Yuppie"

1985 Graham-Rudman-Hollings Act
Mikhail Gorbachev assumes power in Soviet Union
Antonin Scalia appointed to Supreme Court
Secret arms sales to Iran in exchange for
hostages
Gorbachev-Reagan summit in Geneva

1986 U.S. bombing raid on Libya
Gorbachev-Reagan summit in Iceland

1987 Iran-Contra hearings
Stock market crash
Anthony Kennedy appointed to Supreme
Court

1988 Intermediate Nuclear Force Treaty
U.S. warship shoots down Iranian passenger jet
Terrorists blow up a Pan American jet over
Scotland

Politics of Uncertainty

● What choices did Ford and Carter make in an effort to improve the American economy?

● How did the constraints they faced shape the outcome?

Gerald Ford brought to the White House a personality very different from Richard Nixon's. An expe-

rienced congressman, Ford had been appointed vice president when Nixon named him to replace Spiro

> **Gerald Ford** Michigan congressman who became vice president under Nixon in 1973 after Vice President Agnew resigned; Ford became president in 1974 when Nixon resigned.

Agnew (see page 959). Nixon was innovative, suspicious, and arrogant. Ford appeared humble, trustworthy, and personally conservative—an administrative president. Responding to the consequences of Watergate, he sought to establish cordial relations with Congress and to restore the people's faith in government. Acknowledging his unique political position and personal attributes, he joked that he was a Ford and not a Lincoln.

Most political observers believed that, given Ford's desire to overcome the legacy of Watergate and work with Congress, he would enjoy a political honeymoon with Congress that few presidents had experienced. Those expectations faded rapidly.

An Interim Presidency

Soon after taking office in 1974, Ford pardoned Nixon for any crimes the former president might have committed. The pardon was unpopular, unleashing public and congressional protests. Showing that Ford's political honeymoon was indeed short-lived, Democrats opposed Ford's policies to deal with the economic problems of inflation, recession, and the federal deficit. He wanted to cut spending, raise interest rates, and cut business taxes. Democrats confronted the president by introducing legislation to create jobs and increase spending for social and educational programs. When the Democratic-sponsored bills passed Congress, Ford vetoed them and conducted a public opinion campaign to mobilize support for his program. His vetoes were successful—thirty-seven vetoes in two years—but his publicity campaign, based on the slogan "Whip Inflation Now" (WIN), was a flop. The consequence of the pardon, rising inflation and unemployment, and thousands of unused WIN buttons was a sharp drop in Ford's popularity and a political stalemate.

Ford fared only slightly better in his foreign policies. With little knowledge about or experience in foreign affairs, he relied heavily on Henry Kissinger—who by then held the key positions of national security adviser and secretary of state. With Kissinger on board, Ford continued Nixon's policies, including Vietnamization, arms limitation, and détente (see page 956). Trying to maintain the thaw in the Cold War, in November 1974 Ford traveled to Vladivostok, a Soviet city located on the Sea of Japan, to meet with Soviet Premier Leonid Brezhnev where some progress was made on negotiations to limit the number of strategic weapons available to each side. Having made some progress in improving Soviet-American relations at Vladivostok,

◆ Without ceremony, the replacing of Richard Nixon's picture with that of President Gerald Ford at an American embassy reflected one of the most unusual events in the history of the presidency—the resignation of the president and the succession of a vice president who had not been elected to that office. Ford was appointed to the vice presidency by Nixon when Spiro Agnew resigned from that office. *Wide World.*

Ford next met with Brezhnev and leaders from thirty-three other nations in Helsinki, Finland. As a result of the August 1975 negotiations the United States officially recognized the boundaries of Europe established after World War II, and in a gesture toward better East-West relations, Brezhnev and the Eastern-bloc leaders agreed to respect an extensive list of **human rights.** The Helsinki agreements quickly came under fire as human rights violations continued throughout the Eastern bloc and the Soviet Union. Seeking to assert leadership in foreign policy and to support human rights in the Soviet Union, Congress passed the Jackson-Vanik Amendment. It required that the Soviets allow more Jewish immigration from the Soviet Union before

---

human rights Basic rights and freedoms to which all human beings are entitled, including the right to life and liberty, freedom of thought and expression, and equality before the law.

the United States granted trade agreements. Reading the political climate, Ford promptly backed away from the policy of détente with the Soviets and adopted a more traditional Cold War attitude.

Ford's efforts to maintain Nixon's pledges of economic and military support for South Vietnam (see page 955) also met with congressional opposition. When North Vietnamese forces seized Saigon in April 1975, Ford blamed Congress for the Communist victory. Most Americans, however, had little concern and were happy that the conflict was no longer an American war. On a more positive note, Kissinger successfully worked to end an Israeli-Arab war and to improve relations between Israel and Egypt.

During a conflict in June 1967 called the Six-Day War, Israel had soundly defeated Egyptian and Syrian forces and seized considerable territory (see Map 31.1). Vowing to recapture lost territory, Egypt and Syria attacked Israel on Yom Kippur, October 6, 1973. At the same time, Arab states within the **Organization of Petroleum Exporting Countries (OPEC)** embargoed the sale of oil to the United States in support of the Arab cause (see page 959). After initial Arab victories, Israeli forces drove the invaders back into Arab territory and even crossed the Suez Canal into Egypt. Supporting a U.N. cease-fire, Kissinger flew back and forth from one enemy capital to another seeking to negotiate the removal of Israeli forces from Arab territory. His so-called shuttle diplomacy continued from 1973 until September 1975, when Israel and Egypt signed an agreement whereby Israeli troops withdrew from some occupied areas and Egypt resigned from the anti-Israeli Arab coalition.

The Bicentennial Election and Jimmy Carter

Against the background of the bicentennial celebration of American independence, Ford and his record seemed especially mediocre. From within his own party, he faced a stiff challenge from California governor Ronald Reagan and the Republican right wing. Reagan ran a spirited campaign and proved to be an effective speaker and organizer. At the Republican National Convention the final tally was close, but Ford gained the nomination by 117 votes and faced a largely unknown Democratic opponent: **Jimmy Carter.**

James Earl Carter had no national exposure and, except for being governor of Georgia, had little po-

litical experience. But people in 1976 were fed up with politics and politicians, and Carter's lack of political experience was a decided advantage. He presented himself as the nonpolitician candidate who, armed with common sense, honesty, and morality, would heal the wounds of Watergate and Vietnam. A wealthy peanut farmer from a small town in Georgia, a **born-again** Christian, more at home in blue jeans than in a three-piece suit, Carter seemed the ideal candidate for the time. Overcoming less well organized opponents, Carter sailed toward the Democratic party's nomination, winning almost by default on the first ballot.

As Ford and Carter squared off, public opinion polls showed that people liked Ford but thought he was ineffective. Thus "Jimmy who?" took a commanding lead. In a lackluster campaign, the candidates were vague on issues but expansive on smiles and photo sessions. Ford managed to close the gap between himself and Carter, but on election day, with less than 54 percent of the eligible voters bothering to cast ballots, Carter received 297 electoral votes to Ford's 240.

Brimming with enthusiasm and plans for new choices in domestic and international problems, Carter arrived in Washington in January 1977. He stressed that he was an outsider, free of political debts and untouched by the politics of Washington and the lure of special interests and political deals. He pledged an administration of honesty, simplicity, and hard work. Promoting his image as a simple farmer, Carter took the oath of office wearing a plain blue business suit. His message to the people was without frills. "We must simply do our best," he stated, to generate a "new spirit . . . of individual sacrifice for the common good." Portraying himself as the people's president, Carter delivered Roosevelt-style "fireside chats" (see page 767) on radio and television and held "phone-ins" that gave people a chance to talk with their president. The public

---

Organization of Petroleum Exporting Countries (OPEC)   Economic alliance of oil-producing countries, mostly Arab, formed in 1960; in 1973, OPEC members placed an embargo on the sale of oil to countries allied with Israel.

Jimmy Carter   Georgia governor elected president on the Democratic ticket in 1976; he worked to foster peace in the Middle East and called for energy conservation in the United States.

born-again   Having renewed a commitment to Jesus Christ as one's personal savior.

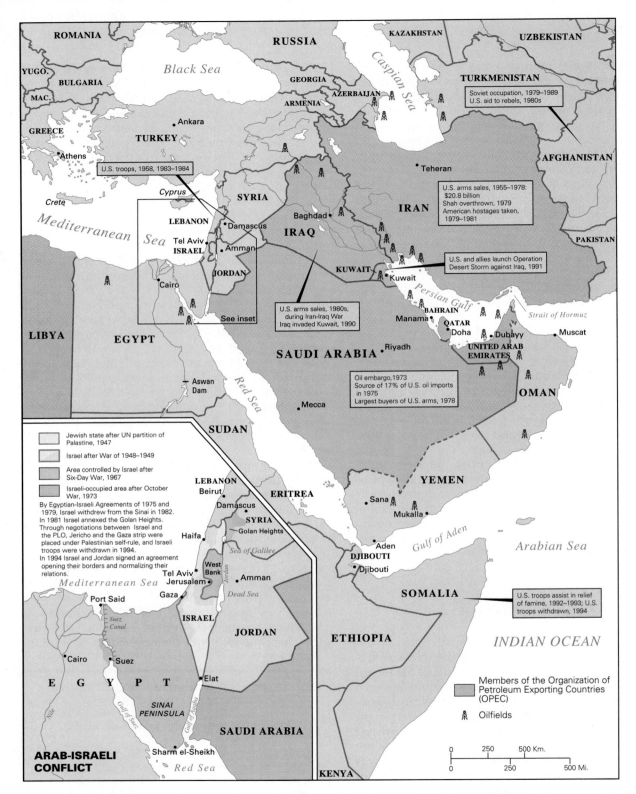

MAP 31.1 The Middle East From 1946 to present, the Middle East has tested U.S. foreign policy as the United States has tried to balance strong support for Israel and its need for oil from the Arab states. To support its interests in this volatile region, the United States had funneled large amounts of financial and military aid to the area and used overt and covert force to shape regional governments. In 1993 and 1994, agreements signed in Washington between Israel and the Palestine Liberation Organization and between Israel and the kingdom of Jordan have reduced tensions in the region.

welcomed Carter's open, informal presidency and his pledge never to lie to the American people—refreshing changes from previous presidents.

But not everyone was charmed—some saw trouble behind the folksy image. Could Carter, the outsider, play the insiders' game of political give-and-take? Did he have the political flexibility, expertise, and muscle to control Democratic politicians and attract Republicans? Another question mark was Carter's staff and appointees. Most of them were Georgia friends, new to the federal government and aloof toward congressional Democrats. "I busted my butt for Carter," one Democrat complained, "and there's nobody I know who got an appointment." Responding to such complaints, members of Carter's staff proudly stated that they, the outsiders, included more minorities and women than ever before and that the time for new faces in Washington's bureaucracy was long past. Soon, communications between the White House and congressional Democrats almost vanished.

Largely ignored by the president and his staff, Democratic congressional leaders flew into a rage when Carter presented his first budget, which axed eighteen pet projects that would have provided jobs and revenue for home districts. Angry Democrats joined with gleeful Republicans to attack the budget, forcing Carter to restore many of the cuts. Democratic representative Dan Rostenkowski of Illinois observed: "I don't see this Congress rolling over and playing dead. . . . Carter is going to set up his priorities and we are going to set up ours. We'll see where we go from there." The battle over the budget established a pattern. Congress and President Carter frequently marched in different directions. Consequently, by mid-1977, most of Carter's proposals were buried in Congress, and some Democrats and political observers were complaining about a lack of presidential wisdom, leadership, and inspiration. Criticism increased when allegations of financial mismanagement forced the president's close friend and adviser Bert Lance to give up his post as director of the Office of Management and Budget in September 1977. The Lance affair further eroded public trust in Carter's judgment and leadership and raised questions about the administration's claim of honesty.

Domestic Priorities

Carter faced two major domestic problems: a sluggish economy and high energy costs due to dependence on foreign sources of oil. He concluded that the economy could not improve until the United States stopped consuming more energy than it produced—the nation was importing about 60 percent of its oil. Solving the energy imbalance was the "moral equivalent of war," Carter told the American people, and the only road to economic recovery. Arguing that small, individual energy savings would result in a huge national saving, he asked Americans to stop wasting energy by lowering thermostats, wearing sweaters, and using public transportation. Turning to Congress, he pushed both conservation as well as increases in domestic production, and he offered 113 energy proposals as legislation, including the creation of a cabinet-level Department of Energy, support for research and development of fuels other than oil, and special regulations and taxes to prevent the energy industry from reaping excess profits.

Lobbyists for automobile, oil, gas, and other industries immediately tried to steer Congress away from conservation, regulation, and taxes. They advocated increased oil production, which they said, would also create jobs. With new fields along Alaska's ecologically delicate North Shore supplying large quantities of oil, many people had a hard time believing that there was an **energy crisis,** and Congress passed only fragments of Carter's plan—creating the Department of Energy in 1977, approving some incentives for conservation, and deregulating the natural gas industry.

When oil prices rose in 1978, forced upward by a revolution in Iran, Congress reconsidered Carter's program. By 1980, support and funds for **alternative fuels** (including nuclear energy) and an excess-profits tax on the oil and gas industry had been passed. But congressional support for Carter's vision of the long-term energy problem was shallow, and Congress made no real effort to develop a comprehensive plan to achieve energy independence. In 1980, with a Republican administration coming in, Congress backed away from energy conservation, stressed increasing production of natural gas, coal, oil, and nuclear energy, and eased regulations on energy producers.

---

energy crisis   Vulnerability to energy shortages due to dwindling fossil fuels, wasteful energy consumption, and potential embargoes by oil-producing countries.

alternative fuels   Sources of energy other than coal, oil, and natural gas; alternative energy sources include solar, geothermal, hydroelectric, and nuclear energy.

Since the 1950s, nuclear power advocates had been arguing that nuclear energy was the energy of the future. It was cheap, plentiful, and, they claimed, environmentally safe. In the 1970s, they pointed to years of safe operation at nuclear plants and called for larger and more powerful plants that would produce all the energy the nation needed. Opponents argued that nuclear energy was expensive and potentially dangerous to people and the environment. *The China Syndrome, Silkwood,* and other movies warned that irresponsible management of nuclear power plants made radioactive leaks, **meltdowns,** and other catastrophes likely. On March 28, 1979, the dire predictions seemed to come true. A nuclear power plant at **Three Mile Island** in central Pennsylvania had a serious accident that released a cloud of radioactive gas and nearly caused a meltdown. It took two weeks to shut down the reactor, and over a hundred thousand people were evacuated from the surrounding area. Amid the fears and investigations that the Three Mile Island accident aroused, over thirty energy companies canceled nuclear building projects, and the government was forced to write stronger regulations.

With nuclear energy questionable as an alternative source of cheap, clean fuel, natural gas, oil, and coal remained the primary sources of American energy. Conservationists cautioned that these resources existed in limited quantities and that their production and use polluted the environment. It was time, they argued, for Americans to change their lifestyles, to conserve more and make do with less. Some even suggested that the era of American affluence was over. Others disagreed—including Ronald Reagan, the 1980 Republican candidate for the presidency. Reagan argued that there was no energy crisis, only the crisis caused by too much government.

During the 1976 campaign, the Democrats had used a "misery index" to remind voters about inflation and unemployment under Nixon and Ford. Many Democrats expected Carter to make the economy, especially the reduction of unemployment, his top priority. But Carter gave energy his primary attention, and his economic program was barely more interventionist than Ford's and less so than Nixon's.

To stimulate the economy and reduce unemployment, Carter asked for tax reforms, the **deregulation** of transportation industries (trucking, railroads, and airlines), and passage of his energy program. He tried to use tighter credit and higher interest rates to curb inflation. Like Ford, he asked workers and producers to hold the line on wages and prices,

and he rejected wage and price controls and the use of federal funds to create jobs. These measures failed to satisfy many congressional Democrats, who introduced bills increasing the minimum wage and instituting cost-of-living raises for federal **entitlement programs.**

Neither congressional nor presidential programs succeeded, however, and by 1980 inflation was at 14 percent—the highest rate since 1947. With unemployment at nearly 7.6 percent, Carter's "misery rating" exceeded Ford's and his popularity was lower than Ford's. Carter assumed part of the blame, saying that he had not provided enough leadership. But he also said that a large part of the nation's woes arose from the public's unwillingness to sacrifice, which weakened the nation's ability to overcome its problems. Most people, however, rejected the notion of a national malaise and blamed the president for the nation's difficulties.

The stagflation troubling the American economy was largely the product of a changing world economy over which presidents had little control. The booming economies of West Germany, Japan, Korea, and Taiwan cut into American markets—reducing American profits and prosperity. The skyrocketing cost of petroleum products not only added to inflation and unemployment but threatened the nation's industrial base, which depended on the availability of inexpensive fuel. In the new global economy, many American industries were unable to match the production costs, retail prices, or quality of goods produced overseas. Japanese goods, once the joke of international commerce, were gobbling up the electronics industry and cutting deeply into the American automobile market. Korea and Taiwan were taking huge bites out of the American textile and clothing markets. Many of the nation's primary industries (iron and steel, rubber, automobiles and their parts, clothing, coal), especially those lo-

---

meltdown Severe overheating of a nuclear reactor core, resulting in the melting of the core and the escape of radiation.

Three Mile Island Site of a nuclear power plant near Harrisburg, Pennsylvania; an accident at the plant in 1979 led to a partial meltdown and the release of radioactive gases.

deregulation Removal of government regulations from an industry.

entitlement programs Government programs that provide benefits to a particular group, such as the elderly, the disabled, and poor families.

cated in the Great Lakes region, were forced to cut back production, lay off workers, and even close plants.

In 1978, the giant Chrysler Corporation tottered on the brink of bankruptcy. Carter, facing a stalled economy and soaring unemployment, agreed to help Chrysler, and in 1980 Congress underwrote a $1.5 billion private loan for the automobile maker. Critics called the Chrysler bailout welfare for the rich, but supporters argued that the loan saved jobs. Even with the loan, Lee Iacocca, Chrysler's new chief executive officer, slashed production, closed sixteen plants, and dismissed nearly half of Chrysler's labor force of 111,000. With new models, effective advertising, and more efficient production, by 1984 Chrysler was making more than $2.4 billion in profits, and Iacocca was a national hero—the manager willing to make tough and unpopular decisions to save a company. Chrysler's success, however, was the exception. From the Great Lakes to the Northeast, a **rust belt** spread over the once-vibrant industrial center of the United States. Many corporations moved overseas or to the South and West, where production costs—primarily for labor and heating—were lower and governments were willing to provide economic incentives to attract industry.

Carter's Foreign Policy

● Compare Carter's expectations with the outcomes of his foreign policies.

● How did his choices reflect new views of America's role in world affairs?

Carter's foreign policy was as controversial as his domestic policy. He said that American foreign policy had been preoccupied by an "inordinate fear of communism" and was too European centered. He took special pride in advocating a foreign policy that would safeguard human rights, fight poverty, and promote economic and social development—especially in the nations of the so-called **Third World**—as well as stress traditional East-West power politics. His foreign policy advisers reflected both sides of this balance.

Zbigniew Brzezinski, Carter's national security adviser, focused on the Soviet Union and Europe. An uncompromising cold warrior, Brzezinski looked for chances to, as one inside observer noted, "stick it to the Russians." He neither cared about nor understood the Third World outside of its Cold War context. He worried that Carter's emphasis on hu-

man rights might weaken pro-American but abusive regimes in South Korea, Nicaragua, and the Philippines.

Cyrus Vance, Carter's secretary of state, was more diplomatic and broad-minded than Brzezinski. Vance recognized Cold War constraints but wanted to follow policies that focused on human issues and economic development. Clashes between him and Brzezinski were expected, but Carter believed he could bridge the gap between his advisers' personalities and perspectives.

A Good Neighbor and Human Rights

Latin America seemed to Carter and Vance the best place to sound a new tone in American policy and move away from the Cold War perspective that had colored U.S. relations with Latin America. Carter wanted the United States to abandon its "paternalism" and instead fashion policies that considered each Latin American nation's internal priorities. Carter believed that Panama and the Panama Canal presented an excellent opportunity to chart a new course for U.S. policy in Latin America.

The Panama Canal Zone lay like an affluent foreign occupied island within Panama. To Panamanians it was an everyday reminder of the inequalities between themselves and the United States. When Carter took office, negotiations to turn control of the canal over to Panama had been stalled for years. Carter assigned the canal a high priority, wanting to show Latin Americans that the United States could recognize their needs even at the expense of its own interests. Within a year, two treaties were written that returned ownership and control of the canal to Panama by 1999 and guaranteed the neutrality of the canal.

Carter was pleased, but the American public was not. Nearly 80 percent of those asked opposed giv-

rust belt Industrialized region containing older factories that are barely profitable or that have been closed.

Third World Underdeveloped or developing countries of Latin America, Africa, and Asia.

Zbigniew Brzezinski National security adviser who favored Cold War confrontations with the Soviet Union.

Cyrus Vance Secretary of state who wanted the United States to defend human rights and further economic development in the Third World.

ing up the canal. Opponents argued that the canal was built and operated by the United States and should remain that way forever. Ronald Reagan labeled the agreement outright appeasement, and conservative Republican senator Jesse Helms of North Carolina promised to kill it in the Senate. He failed, but only barely.

After being amended to make clear the responsibility of the United States to intervene if the canal were threatened by an outside force, the Senate passed the treaties in 1977 by one vote over the necessary two-thirds majority. As a result, Panama will have complete control of the canal and the Canal Zone after 1999.

Carter also hoped to promote a policy against human rights abuses, especially in Latin America, where many governments secured their power by ruthlessly suppressing their own people. Conservatives complained that letting human rights drive policy might undermine pro-American governments, especially in Nicaragua and El Salvador.

In Nicaragua, the autocratic Somoza family had ruled with an iron hand since the 1930s, with few complaints from Washington (see page 737). Under Anastasio Somoza, who had held power since 1967, corruption and oppression had reached new heights by mid-1970 and had stirred opposition from nearly all sides in Nicaragua. The **Sandinista Liberation Front,** a largely Marxist-led organization conducting a guerrilla war to oust Somoza's regime, had gained the support of most Nicaraguans. Carter considered Somoza a liability and began to reduce aid, stopping all direct military and economic aid to Nicaragua in early 1979. With his National Guard disintegrating, Somoza fled to Paraguay in July, taking much of the nation's treasury.

The Sandinistas, led by **Daniel Ortega,** assumed power, promised free elections, and invited Western businesses to return to Nicaragua. Hoping that Ortega would adopt moderate reform programs, in September, Carter asked Congress for $75 million in aid for the new government. But as Congress debated the request, the Nicaraguan government became more radical and **autocratic.** By the time Congress approved the aid in 1980, the Sandinistas had canceled elections, hardened their control over the nation, and entered into trade arrangements with the Soviet Union—a choice that, in the opinion of many Americans, clearly placed Nicaragua within the Soviet bloc.

Republicans and other conservatives attacked Carter's human rights policy for destroying a pro-American leader and allowing a Communist gov-

ernment to be established in Central America. Republican presidential candidate Ronald Reagan denounced the Communist "takeover" of Nicaragua and the Sandinistas' effort to export revolution to neighboring El Salvador, Guatemala, and Honduras. Reagan called for support for the rebel **Contras** fighting the Sandinistas in the jungles of Nicaragua. Many of the Contras were former supporters or soldiers of Somoza and had vowed to overthrow Ortega and restore "democracy." Responding to the restrictions on human rights and on democracy in Nicaragua and to the political pressure at home, Carter stopped all aid to the Ortega government in early 1981.

Conservatives also called for more American support for El Salvador. There the newly created government of **José Napoleón Duarte** faced threats from both the left and the right. On the left were Farabundo Martí National Liberation Front (FMLN) guerrillas, who occupied more and more territory. On the right were elements within the military and officials linked to traditional ruling families, who used terrorism to eliminate opposition figures. Carter almost cut off military and economic aid when right-wing death squads murdered reform advocate Archbishop Oscar Romero as he said mass. But FMLN victories prodded Carter to send millions of dollars in equipment and credit to Duarte.

As the election of 1980 neared, Carter's program for human rights and economic development in Latin America lay in ruins. The constraints of Cold War politics and traditional U.S.–Latin American relations had forced him to break ties with Nicaragua and disregard murder and torture in El Salvador. His one triumph, the canal treaties, was unpopular at home.

Sandinista Liberation Front Leftist guerrilla movement that overthrew the corrupt regime of Anastasio Somoza in Nicaragua in 1979.

Daniel Ortega Sandinista leader who helped establish the revolutionary government that replaced the Somoza regime in 1979 and who served as president of Nicaragua from 1984 to 1990.

autocratic Having unlimited power or authority; despotic.

Contras Nicaraguan rebels, many of them former followers of Somoza, fighting to overthrow the Sandinista government.

José Napoleón Duarte Moderate civilian named to head the government of El Salvador in 1980.

The Camp David Accords

Carter credited his success in Panama with his ability to take a new approach to an old issue. He believed that such a tactic would also generate movement in the Middle East toward a peace settlement between Israel and its Arab neighbors (see Map 31.1). To this end, Carter broke with earlier American positions. He called for an international peace conference that would include the Soviets, and he suggested making concessions to the Palestinians. Palestinians—Arabs who had been living in Palestine when Israel was formed (see page 848)—demanded the creation of a Palestinian state free of Israeli rule. Loosely organized by the **Palestine Liberation Organization (PLO),** they resorted to terrorism, civil disobedience, and political action to undermine Israeli power.

Concluding that there could be no resolution to Arab-Israeli hostility until the Palestinian issue was resolved, Carter called for Israel to return occupied territories in exchange for Arab pledges of secure borders, and he supported the formation of a Palestinian "homeland." Arab leaders cautiously accepted the idea, but Israel's Prime Minister Menachem Begin rejected it. Although Begin's position seemed to end any chance for an international conference, Egypt's president Anwar Sadat flew to Israel to open a dialogue for peace. Carter supported Sadat's initiative by flying to Cairo.

Sadat's "Aswan formula" nearly matched Carter's views, and the two leaders became personal friends. Unwilling to allow the peace initiative to die, Carter invited Sadat and Begin for talks at the presidential retreat at Camp David in Maryland. Surprisingly, both agreed and arrived in September 1978.

Sadat and Begin did not get along well, and Carter shuttled between the two leaders, pleading, threatening, and stressing his personal commitment to both nations. He and Begin frequently exchanged harsh words. "He was angry," Carter explained, "and so was I." Still, Carter carefully negotiated two agreements. Israel agreed to withdraw from the Sinai and work toward a resolution of the Palestinian problem. Egypt and Israel also pledged to conclude a bilateral peace treaty in which Egypt recognized Israel's right to exist and Israel returned the Sinai to Egypt.

Many within Israel and Egypt, as well as the other Arab states, immediately attacked the agreements. By November 1978, the **Camp David accords** were falling apart. Carter blamed "provocative ac-

♦ One of President Carter's greatest triumphs was the signing of the 1978 peace accords between President Anwar Sadat of Egypt *(left)* and Prime Minister Menachem Begin of Israel *(right).* The agreement followed days of personal diplomacy by Carter at the Camp David presidential retreat. Both Sadat and Begin received the Nobel Peace Prize for their efforts. *Jimmy Carter Presidential Library.*

tions" by Begin, who after returning to Israel had resumed his earlier position that Israel would not deal with the Palestinians. Chances for a regional peace had vanished, but Carter rushed to save the Egyptian-Israeli peace treaty. Again, he managed to pull Begin and Sadat together. And, in a ceremony at the White House on March 26, 1979, acting as a proud midwife, Carter watched as Begin and Sadat signed the first peace treaty between an Arab state and Israel. Sadat and Begin received Nobel Peace prizes, and Carter's popularity soared. But the glow of success was fleeting. Arab leaders, Palestinians, and many Egyptians bitterly condemned both the treaty and Sadat (who was assassinated in 1981) and reaffirmed their commitment to the destruction of Israel.

Palestine Liberation Organization   Political and military organization of Palestinians originally dedicated to opposing the state of Israel through terrorism and other means.

Camp David accords   Treaty, signed at Camp David in 1978, in which Israel agreed to return territory captured from Egypt in the Six-Day War and Egypt agreed to recognize Israel as a nation.

The Collapse of Détente

The Panama Canal treaties and the Camp David accords marked successes in Carter's foreign policy. The president hoped that his efforts to deal with the Soviet Union would bring similar positive results, but his behavior toward the Soviet Union was inconsistent. Although he wanted to increase cooperation and promote détente, he irritated the Soviets with his attempts to encourage reform within the Soviet Union and his denunciations of Soviet violations of human rights. The differing views of Vance and Brzezinski called attention to the inconsistency, and inner-circle debates over Soviet policy were prolonged and intense. The final product reflected a dual approach of cooperation and competition.

The most immediate Soviet-American issue that Carter faced was the still-unfinished **SALT II** treaty —a pressing need because SALT I had expired in October 1977. Rather than try to get President Ford's treaty through Congress, Carter decided to negotiate even deeper cuts in nuclear weapons. Showing the inconsistency of his policy, Carter sent Secretary of State Vance to Moscow to begin SALT discussions and at the same time publicly announced support for Soviet dissidents, which offended the Soviets. Vance received a chilly welcome. Soviet premier Brezhnev scorned the American SALT proposal as "unconstructive and one sided . . . harmful to Soviet security."

Throughout 1977 and 1978, Carter's policy seemed more competitive than cooperative. He urged construction of new high-tech weapons and the improvement of long-range missile systems. U.S. recognition of the People's Republic of China on January 1, 1979, and National Security Adviser Brzezinski's visit to China were designed both to put more pressure on the Soviets and to improve American-Chinese relations. Still, despite chilly relations, the strategic arms limitation discussions continued, and an agreement was reached in July 1979. As with Ford's treaty, few in the United States liked the results. Some argued that more reductions were needed. A growing majority, however, believed that the agreement was too favorable to the Soviets and opened, according to Ronald Reagan, an American "window of vulnerability." They demanded more, not less, military spending. Then in December, with the Senate vote on SALT II approaching, news flashed that the Soviet Union had invaded neighboring Afghanistan.

A Muslim country bordering the southern part of the Soviet Union, Afghanistan had a pro-Soviet government but a large number of anti-Soviet elements, including many fundamentalist Muslims. The pro-Soviet leadership seemed to be losing control, and the Soviets feared that under another government Afghan fundamentalists might stir unrest among Muslims in the southern republics of the Soviet Union itself. Claiming that the Afghan government had asked for help, Brezhnev sent in eighty thousand Soviet troops and occupied Afghanistan.

Calling the invasion the "gravest threat to peace since 1945," Carter reinstated registration for the draft for all 18-year-old males, withdrew the SALT II agreements from the Senate, halted grain shipments to the Soviet Union, and announced an American boycott of the 1980 Moscow Olympics. He also announced the **Carter Doctrine:** any nation that attempted to take control of the **Persian Gulf** would "be repelled by any means necessary, including the use of force." The Soviet invasion of Afghanistan ended Carter's ambiguous Soviet policy. He now called for military superiority and a renewed arms race.

In Afghanistan, the Soviets quickly were engulfed in a vicious guerrilla war with an American-supported Afghan resistance, the **mujahedeen.** In a Vietnam-like scenario, the Soviet government sent more and more Soviet forces into Afghanistan, increasing economic and political problems at home.

The Iranian Revolution

Brezhnev's decision to intervene in Afghanistan and Carter's announcement of the Carter Doctrine were more than responses just to events in Afghanistan. Both leaders were also reacting to the 1978 revolution in Iran, which had toppled the pro-American ruler, Shah Reza Pahlavi, and created a new force in

---

SALT II Agreement between the United States and the Soviet Union in 1979 to limit the numbers of strategic nuclear missiles in each country; Congress never approved the treaty.

Carter Doctrine Carter's announced policy that the United States would use force to repel any nation that attempted to take control of the Persian Gulf.

Persian Gulf Arm of the Arabian Sea that includes the ports of several major oil-producing Arab countries, including Iran, Saudi Arabia, Kuwait, and Iraq.

mujahedeen Afghan resistance, supplied with arms by the United States, that fought the Soviets after the invasion of Afghanistan in 1979.

♦ In November 1979, Iranians seized the American embassy in Teheran and took seventy-one people hostage. Blind-folded and handcuffed, the hostages were paraded through the streets as crowds jeered. Held over a year, the hostages were released as Ronald Reagan was being sworn in as president. *UPI/Bettmann Archives.*

Middle East politics: **Islamic fundamentalism.** The United States had lost a military ally in the shah, one that had been counted on to defend the Persian Gulf. And Brezhnev faced the presence of an expansionary religious movement that threatened to topple the weak Soviet-sponsored regime in Afghanistan and infect Muslims living within the Soviet Union.

Since Eisenhower, the United States had supported the shah as a barrier to Soviet influence in the region and a supplier of oil. The shah had received billions of dollars in American weapons and aid, but his regime had become increasingly repressive. Among those opposing the shah's rule was a Shiite Muslim sect that condemned not only the shah but also the contamination of Iranian culture and society by Western ideas and values. The Shiite opposition was led by ayatollahs, religious leaders whose central figure was **Ruhollah Khomeini.** Khomeini returned to Iran from exile in Paris in February 1979, when an alliance between the Shiites and the Iranian military forced the shah to flee. In a brief struggle for power, the Ayatollah Khomeini won, setting in motion a repressive fundamentalist Islamic revo-

lution that attacked the United States as the main source of evil in the world.

Carter ended economic and military aid to Iran, ordered Americans home, and reduced the embassy staff. On October 22, the exiled shah, who was dying, entered a New York hospital to receive cancer treatments. Amid warnings of Iranian reprisals, on November 4 an angry mob stormed the American embassy in Tehran and took the staff hostage. Sixty-six Americans were paraded through the streets and subjected to numerous abuses as the Iranians demanded the return of the shah for trial. The press quickly dubbed the crisis "America Held Hostage," and television accounts flooded American homes.

Carter weighed the conflicting options identified by his advisers. Brzezinski wanted to use military force to free the hostages, even if doing so cost all of their lives. Vance argued for negotiation, hoping that Iranian moderates would find a way to free the hostages. Carter sided with Vance and through the PLO was able to negotiate freedom for thirteen hostages, mostly women and African-Americans. As further discussions failed, American frustration and anger grew, and Carter's popularity ratings fell to near 30 percent. It was time to "lance the boil," concluded Brzezinski, and in April 1980, Carter agreed and ordered a military rescue mission.

The operation was a disaster. Flying to a desert base south of Tehran, the American forces were struck by a violent dust storm that caused vital equipment, including three helicopters, to malfunction. With Iranian forces headed toward the American base, Carter scratched the mission. Vance, who had opposed the operation, resigned, and Carter's popularity dropped another 10 points.

Diplomatic efforts through the Canadians and the Algerians eventually resulted in an agreement in late 1980 to release the hostages. By that time the shah had died of cancer, and Iran was at war against Iraq and needed assets that Carter had frozen. On January 20, 1981, the hostages reached freedom, ending 444 days of captivity. On the same day, Ronald Reagan took office as president.

Islamic fundamentalism   Movement calling for the replacement of western secular values and attitudes with traditional Islamic values and an orthodox Muslim state.

Ruhollah Khomeini   Iranian Shiite leader who was exiled for his opposition to the shah but returned to Iran on the shah's downfall in 1979 and established a new constitution giving himself supreme powers.

Enter Ronald Reagan— Stage Right

• What expectations influenced Americans who chose to vote for Reagan?

• How did his social and domestic policies both reflect those expectations and alter expectations?

According to Republicans in 1980, Carter's failure to free the hostages was typical of his administration's ineptness. Inflation had reached 12.4 percent, and unemployment was near 8 percent. Confident of victory in 1980, Republicans claimed that Carter was incapable of maintaining either American honor abroad or prosperity at home. **Ronald Reagan,** a movie actor turned conservative politician, offered voters a clear alternative to Carter and the Democrats.

Impressed in 1964 with Reagan's popular appeal and his speeches for Barry Goldwater (see page 916), conservative Republicans groomed him to run for governor of California. Reagan presented himself as a nonpolitician, defeated the incumbent governor, Edmund "Pat" Brown, and quickly emerged as one of the nation's most popular conservatives. After failing to unseat Ford for the Republican presidential nomination in 1976, Reagan easily outran CIA Director George Bush four years later to become the Republican candidate. Reagan named Bush his running mate. Liberal Republican John Anderson protested his party's turn to the right by running as an independent.

In his campaign for the presidency Reagan denounced "big government" and Carter's failure to provide prosperity. He argued that the federal government had grown too large and powerful, restricting individual rights and free enterprise with its burdensome regulations and interference. Reagan promised to reduce the role of government and lower taxes, freeing American ingenuity and competitiveness. Across the country taxes had become a hot issue. In 1978, California had led a tax revolt by passing **Proposition 13,** which placed a limit on property taxes.

A smooth and effective campaigner who communicated a sense of confidence and good feeling, Reagan quipped: "A recession is when your neighbor loses his job. A depression is when you lose yours. A recovery is when Jimmy Carter loses his." Correct policies and effective leadership, he argued, would make the country prosperous again. To the audience of dissatisfied Americans who were angry at

◆ A former movie star and host of television shows, Ronald Reagan used television and radio very effectively to outline his visions of American domestic and foreign policies. Because of his communication style, he was called "the great communicator." *UPI/Bettmann Archives.*

inefficient government, too much government intervention, and too many taxes, Reagan presented himself as the "citizen politician, speaking out for the ideas, values, and common sense of everyday Americans." His conservative agenda called for more power for the individual and less power for the federal government. A vote for Reagan, his supporters claimed, would restore American pride, power, and traditions—and make Americans feel good about themselves and the nation again.

Reagan's message was welcome news not only to those who routinely voted Republican but also to many voters who had once been part of the Democratic party. While civil rights and Nixon's "southern strategy" (see page 959) were pulling many southern whites into the Republican camp, the Democrats' continued support for minority and women's rights, affirmative action and abortion, and increased spending for social programs convinced a growing number of voters from the suburbs and blue-collar workers—especially Catholics—to support Republican candidates. Further

---

Ronald Reagan   Thirty-fifth President; succeeded Jimmy Carter.

Proposition 13   Measure adopted by referendum in California in 1978 cutting local property taxes by more than 50 percent.

contributing to Republican popular and electoral totals were men and women mobilized by the New Right, the growing number of people moving to the sun belt, and young voters attracted by the economic goals and social stability promised by Republicans. Except for the size of Reagan's majority and how many Republicans his presidential coattails would carry into office, the outcome of the election of 1980 was never in doubt.

The Jimmy Carter who succeeded in turning back a strong challenge from Democratic senator Edward Kennedy of Massachusetts seemed a different candidate from the Jimmy Carter of 1976. Not only could he not run as an anti-Washington candidate, but he seemed older and pessimistic—his once-prominent smile and flashing teeth replaced by a look of sadness. His call for public sacrifice seemed to underline his inability to solve the nation's problems, and his presidential campaign floundered as Reagan's soared. Reagan promised pride and power. Carter appeared to offer only further decline from economic and diplomatic world leadership.

When the voting ended, Reagan had 51 percent of the popular vote compared to 41 percent for Carter and 7 percent for Anderson. Reagan's electoral count was even more impressive, 91 percent: 489 to 49. Republicans gained twelve seats and held a majority in the Senate. Thirty-three more Republicans sat in the House of Representatives, narrowing the Democratic majority. It appeared that a new conservative era was beginning.

The Moral Majority and the New Right

Reagan's campaign pulled vital support from the New Right, which now sought a role in shaping domestic policy. A loosely knit alliance that combined political and social conservatives, the New Right organized itself around opposition to practices and policies associated with the social and cultural changes spawned during the 1960s and 1970s. Charles Murray's *Losing Ground* (1984) argued that Johnson's Great Society had caused people to lose their will to work and had encouraged destructive behavior. The New Right's social agenda promoted the movement's views of correct family and moral values, condemning abortion, pornography, and homosexuality in particular. To mobilize support, the New Right pioneered the effective political use of direct mail campaigns that targeted specific segments of the population.

Liberal educational reforms, Murray charged, and the New Right stressed, had diluted the curriculum, and schools had retreated from teaching solid middle-class work and moral habits. As a result, according to Murray and the New Right, public schools were not preparing children to function successfully in the real world, and education needed to focus on the basics: reading, writing, arithmetic, and traditional values.

Education was just one problem. The New Right declared that liberal views threatened "to destroy everything that is good and moral here in America." Reagan said that he agreed.

Highly visible among New Right groups were evangelical Christian sects, many of whose ministers were **televangelists**—preachers who used radio and television to spread the gospel of the "religious Right." With donations that exceeded a billion dollars a year, they did not hesitate to mix religion and politics. Jerry Falwell's **Moral Majority** promoted a conservative revolution on more than five hundred television and radio stations and embraced Ronald Reagan. Reaching millions of Americans, Falwell called on his listeners to wage political war against politicians whose views on the Bible, homosexuality, prayer in school, abortion, and communism were too liberal. Although many of the television evangelists were sincere in their goals and ministries, some were susceptible to the lure of wealth and power that accompanied the medium. Sex scandals, financial excesses, and abuses of personal power had weakened the electronic ministry's impact on society and politics by the 1990s. In the most publicized scandal, Jim Bakker, who with his wife Tammy Faye Bakker had run the *Praise the Lord* radio and television shows and enterprises and had earned millions of dollars, was denounced for forcing women of his church to have sex with him. He was also found guilty of fraud and conspiracy and sentenced to prison in 1987.

As a whole, the New Right easily survived the scandals because its organization rested on much

---

televangelist   Protestant evangelist minister who conducts television broadcasts; many such ministers used their broadcasts as a forum for defending conservative values.

Moral Majority   Right-wing religious organization, led by televangelist Jerry Falwell, that had an active political lobby in the 1980s on issues such as opposition to abortion and to the Equal Rights Amendment.

♦ In the 1970s and into the 1990s, the "electronic church" developed an audience of over 100 million viewers. With fancy, high-tech showmanship, televangelists like Jerry Falwell pictured here, damned liberalism, feminism, sex education, homosexuality, and the teaching of evolution, while demanding a return to traditional Christian values and prayer in school. Praising the power of the modern, media pulpit, Falwell stated, "You can explain the issues. . . . And you can endorse candidates, right there in church on Sunday morning." *Steve McCurry/Magnum Photos.*

more than televangelism. Sophisticated political organizations like the Conservative Political Action Committee and the Heritage Foundation continued to mobilize support and raise money for conservative causes. Before the end of the 1980s, the New Right took credit not only for electing Reagan but for defeating several prominent liberal Democrats—including Senator Birch Bayh of Indiana and Senator George McGovern of South Dakota—and for stopping the Equal Rights Amendment and weakening the right to choose an abortion (see pages 998–1001).

Reaganism

Reagan brought to the White House two distinct advantages over Nixon, Ford, and Carter. He had a clear and simple vision of the type of America he wanted and an unusual ability to convey that image to the American public. Called the "Great Communicator" by the press, Reagan and his staff expertly used imagery and the media. Reagan presented images and visions, but he did not create the policies to bring them about. Secretary of Treasury Donald Regan once commented, "The President's mind is not cluttered with facts." A hands-off president, Reagan delegated authority to the cabinet and executive

staff and made little effort to initiate, direct, or control policy. He set the grand agenda. His lieutenants assumed the blame when policies failed or could not overcome opposition.

Reagan rode to the presidency on a wide domestic platform promising not just prosperity and less government but also morality. During the campaign, he had tapped the New Right's political strength on issues of family and gender by declaring his opposition to "indolence, promiscuity, easy abortion, and casual attitudes toward marriage and divorce." Conservatives were anxious to apply their vision of order to society and to dismantle the welfare state. In his inauguration address, however, Reagan virtually ignored their social agenda and hit hard at the need to end the economic crisis of inflation, high interest rates, and unemployment.

Reagan's chief of staff James A. Baker wanted no repetition of Carter's failure with Congress and was determined to cultivate both Republican and Democratic support for Reagan's economic policies. The administration's economic formula to restore the economy was deceptively simple: increase military spending and reduce taxes and government restrictions, allowing American business to rediscover economic growth. "If we can do that the rest will take care of itself," Baker argued.

Budget Director David Stockman was a believer in **supply-side economics**—the idea that lowering taxes will increase revenue from taxation by increasing the amount of money available for investments. Stockman fashioned a tax package and budget that reduced income and corporate taxes and slashed federal spending on social programs. The **Economic Recovery Tax Act,** passed in 1981, cut income and most business taxes by an average of 25 percent; upper income levels received the largest tax reduction. Stockman later admitted that "none of us really understand what's going on" or what to expect and that the tax act was really a "Trojan Horse" to help the rich. Conservative Democrats in the House joined with Republicans to cut $25 billion from social programs, including food stamps, Aid to Fami-

> **supply-side economics** Theory that reducing taxes on the wealthy and increasing the money available for investment will stimulate the economy and eventually benefit everyone.
>
> **Economic Recovery Tax Act** Law, passed by Congress in 1981, that cut income taxes by 25 percent across the board and further reduced taxes on the wealthy.

lies with Dependent Children, and jobs and housing programs. Reagan also ended Nixon's federal revenue-sharing programs (see page 957) and reduced the amount of federal monies paid to the states for Medicare and Medicaid programs. To halt inflation, Federal Reserve chairman Paul Volker pushed interest rates upward, reducing the money supply.

Cutting taxes and domestic spending was only part of the Reagan agenda for economic growth. Another aim of **Reaganomics** was to free businesses and corporations from restrictive regulations. Appointees to regulatory agencies were selected because of their support of deregulation and business. At first, this approach was most visible in the area of environmental regulations. Secretary of Interior James Watt sought to open federally controlled land, coastal waters, and wetlands to mining, lumber, oil, and gas companies—a policy strongly supported in the West, where the economy partially depended on such industries. The Environmental Protection Agency, under Anne Gorsuch Burford, delayed and weakened enforcement of federal guidelines for reducing air and water pollution and the cleanup of toxic waste sites (see Map 31.2).

Wanting to help business by reducing the power of labor unions, Reagan set an example when the nation's air-traffic controllers' union called a strike for higher wages and better working conditions. Reagan promptly fired the strikers and used military personnel to replace them until new air-traffic controllers could be trained.

Reagan took office during the worst recession since the Great Depression, but he was optimistic that his policies would restore prosperity. The economy's initial response, however, was not positive. Higher interest rates and the recession forced inflation downward, from 14 percent in 1980 to 4 percent by 1982, but economic growth and jobs failed to materialize. Unemployment continued to rise, climbing over 10 percent, and small businesses and farms faced bankruptcy in increasing numbers. The **trade deficit,** the amount by which imports exceed exports, skyrocketed from $31 to $111 billion, and the federal deficit swelled alarmingly, pushed by declining tax revenues and more military spending. Reagan called for patience, saying that his economic programs eventually would show effects.

Suddenly in 1983, the recession ended. With inflation at 4 percent, unemployment dropped to 7.5 percent. Many economists and Republicans praised the administration's policies for the recovery. Others said that the recovery had less to do with Reagan's policies than with increases in world trade

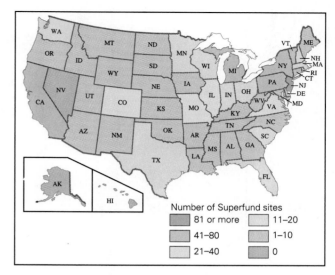

◆ **MAP 31.2 Superfund Clean-up Sites**   Americans generate trash—more than three-and-a-half pounds for every person, every day. In addition, the United States produces nearly three hundred tons of hazardous waste every year, and about eight out of ten Americans live near one of more than twenty-two thousand toxic waste sites. In the 1980s, Congress provided funds—Superfunds—for the clean-up of some of the worst and most health-threatening sites. This map shows that hazardous waste sites exist in nearly every state, as well as the location of the major Superfund sites.

and the lowering of oil prices. Critics also pointed out that the national "recovery" was selective. The West Coast was doing well, but the rust belt was still rusting. Critics argued that serious weaknesses in the economy still existed—specifically, the federal deficit, imbalance of trade, the continuing decline of the dollar, and a lack of new industrial jobs. But most Americans paid little attention to the economic debate and sought to make the most of the renewed prosperity.

The new prosperity, however, did not reach everyone, as the Reagan theory had predicted it would. The impact of smaller appropriations and higher qualifications for welfare reduced the number of people on federal welfare rolls, and the num-

---

Reaganomics   Economic beliefs and policies of the Reagan administration, including the belief that tax cuts for the wealthy and deregulation of industry will benefit the economy.

trade deficit   Amount by which imports exceed exports.

Leading the Computer Revolution

Bill Gates

In 1974, Bill Gates made an eventful choice. Along with a friend from high school, Paul Allen, the Harvard sophomore decided to create an operating system for a new development in the computer world—the personal computer. The system worked, and Gates left Harvard and formed the Microsoft Company, creating MS DOS and software packages for what soon became the personal computer revolution. Twelve years later, his systems dominated the computer world, and he has become the country's richest billionaire. UPI/Bettmann Archives.

In December 1974, Bill Gates, a sophomore at Harvard, and his high school friend Paul Allen claimed that they could write a computer program for a new personal computer, the Altair 8080, which came unassembled and cost $397. Neither Gates nor Allen had seen the computer or the microchip that made the Altair run, but they were positive that the advent of personal computing was the beginning of a new era in information processing. "We realized that the revolution" had started, Gates recalled, and "there was no question of where life would focus." Gates and Allen chose to be a part of the revolution.

Having read only sketchy information about the Altair 8080, Gates and Allen invaded the Harvard computer lab and worked day and night for eight weeks. Ignoring his classes and sometimes sleeping at the keyboard, Gates modified the computer language BASIC to fit the Altair. Having no idea if the program would work—"If we had read the book wrong . . . we were hosed," Allen recalled. He then flew to New Mexico to demonstrate the program. Fortunately, the program worked, and Gates and Allen were on the cutting edge of the computer revolution. Allen stayed to work for the computer company. Gates finished his academic year at Harvard. Then, over the objections of his parents, he chose to drop

ber living in poverty increased. Reduced federal support for a variety of state and local social and economic programs forced state and local governments to eliminate or limit programs and to raise taxes. By the end of Reagan's first term, the reduction in the number of poor brought about by President Johnson's War on Poverty had vanished. Their numbers swelled by reductions in federal housing programs, the homeless became symbols of an econ-omy that liberals called unfair. Democrats attacked Reaganomics for catering to the rich and ignoring the poor.

The Power of Money

Reagan's support for American business and opposition to government restrictions placed an emphasis on success, profits, and individual gain. While

out of Harvard and join Allen. At 19, he and Allen formed Microsoft, a company to write software for personal computers. Microsoft made Gates, at age 31, the youngest billionaire in America.

Gates's obsession with computers began in 1968, when his high school in Seattle arranged computer time on a local company's machine. "We were off in our own world," he remembered, "Nobody quite understood the thing but I wanted to figure out exactly what it could do." At the age of 13, he was "hired" by the company—paid with computer time—to find bugs in the system. Three years later, with Allen, Gates formed a company to analyze automobile traffic data by computer. They made about $20,000 until the government offered to analyze the traffic for no cost.

In 1980, their expectations rising, Gates and Allen agreed to design an operating system to run the software for IBM's entry into the personal computing field. IBM was already a giant in large business and institutional computers, and it was expected that IBM's personal computers would greatly expand the popularity and uses of personal computers. In 1980, each computer company wanted to capture and keep users by having a unique operating system to run software. IBM wanted Microsoft to formulate a new, exclusive system. Gates and Allen began by buying an existing system— QDOS, the "quick and dirty operating system"—and then modified it. Within a year, they had created, in great secrecy, Microsoft DOS (MSDOS).

IBM's personal computers became the industry's leader and were soon being cloned by other companies. Gates chose to offer MSDOS to other companies. At first, IBM was reluctant to share "their" system, but both companies benefited. By the 1990s, only two major operating systems still existed for personal computers: Apple and MSDOS. Microsoft had become the industry giant and Gates the country's richest man.

Looking toward the twenty-first century, Gates continues to seek better and innovative applications for personal computers, telecommunications, and information processing. His newest challenge is to more effectively integrate multimedia and communication systems with an interactive software package. Still pursuing his choice to be at the forefront of a revolution, Gates looks confidently toward a bright future. "We are going to create the software," he says, "that puts a computer on every desk and in every home." A billionaire, Paul Allen left Microsoft in 1983 and has since invested in and worked to develop companies in the high technology, communications, and information delivery fields.

---

some argued that the new business culture was based on a "greed factor," others disagreed, pointing to the creations of many new business opportunities, especially in the communications and electronics fields. In those two fields, technological developments—miniaturization, satellite transmission, the videocassette recorder (VCR), and computers—affected almost every segment of American society, from the office to homes to schools. With Apple and IBM leading the way, personal computers restructured the process of handling information and offered new choices and opportunities for nearly everyone. Accompanying the development of computers were individuals like Bill Gates, America's youngest billionaire, who developed software and programs for the seemingly ever-expanding computer and telecommunications fields (see Individual Choices: Bill Gates).

With inflation under control and the economy growing, many Americans considered income the primary sign of success and social worth. In 1974, only 46 percent of college freshmen and high school seniors had listed being "financially successful" as the first priority in their lives. Twelve years later, in 1986, 73 percent of college freshmen put being "very well off financially," and 63 percent of high school seniors listed making "lots of money," as their first priorities. But making "lots of money" was possible only for a few.

Aided by tax cuts and other government actions, the wealthiest 1 percent of Americans saw their slice of the economic pie grow from 8.1 to 15 percent. The majority of American workers and families during the same period lost income. Still, newspapers, magazines, television, and movies were full of stories about people making millions. Income-conscious college graduates hoping to become highly paid, aggressive professionals eagerly applied to law, business, and other postgraduate schools. *Newsweek* declared 1984 the year of the **Yuppie**—a young, upwardly mobile urban professional, the leading edge of the new economy and new economic vitality.

Above Yuppies on the new ladder of economic success were merger artists and financial wizards like Donald Trump, T. Boone Pickens, and Ivan Boesky—a financier who argued that greed was not a bad thing and that the greedy should not feel guilty. Trump, who proclaimed himself the king of the "megadeal," commanded national attention for both his business ventures and his social life. His ghost-written books, *Trump: The Art of the Deal* and *Trump: Surviving at the Top*, glorified him as the master of manipulating the economic system for personal gain.

Symbolizing the carnivorous business culture was a seemingly ever-climbing stock market and speculators, many of whom took advantage of government deregulation to sell **junk bonds** to finance **leveraged buyouts.** Riding the crest of the speculative boom, barons of buyouts and junk bonds amassed vast fortunes, and huge business conglomerates gobbled up smaller and economically vulnerable companies. "Buy high, sell higher," *Fortune* magazine proclaimed. *Money* magazine, whose circulation leaped from 800,000 in 1980 to 1.85 million in 1987, forecast in 1986 that the American people were confident about the continued growth of stocks and mutual funds over the next year.

But not everyone was so optimistic. Social critics like author Tom Wolfe complained of a "Me Gener-ation" and compared what they saw as the negative values of the late 1970s and 1980s—apathy, self-indulgence, and materialism—to the values of the previous decade—social commitment, self-denial, and valuing the quality of life. Many economists and others voiced fears of a recession and warned that many mergers and much of the stock market's climb rested on a weak foundation of shaky credit and fast profits. Such credit and profits, they argued, were related neither to actual economic growth nor to an increase in real buying power and wages.

On "Black Monday," October 19, 1987, their fears came true when the stock market dropped 508 points, losing 22 percent of its value in the largest single decline in American history. Images of the 1929 Crash and the Great Depression reared up (see Chapter 24). The Reagan administration was shaken, but the Federal Reserve quickly acted to lower interest rates and pump money into the economy. The Fed's action stopped the panic selling, and the stock market turned slowly upward again. But some warned that the stock market still did not reflect real economic health and argued that more trouble lay ahead.

They soon had additional evidence when the savings and loan system began edging toward collapse. Deposits in **savings and loan associations (S&Ls)** are insured by the federal government through the FSLIC (Federal Savings and Loan Insurance Corporation), and, until 1982, government regulations permitted S&Ls to lend money only for single-family homes. In that year, the Reagan administration lifted nearly all restrictions on lending by S&Ls (the Garn–St. Germain Act), and many S&L operators jumped quickly into speculative transactions. Soon, S&L loans began to finance risky ventures such as office buildings, shopping malls, and junk bonds. Losses were covered by the FSLIC. It was a no-lose

---

Yuppie   Young urban resident with a well-paid professional job and a materialistic lifestyle.

junk bond   Corporate bond having a high yield and high risk.

leveraged buyout   Use of a target company's asset value to finance the debt incurred in acquiring the company.

savings and loan associations   Financial institutions originally founded to provide home mortgage loans; deregulation during the Reagan era allowed them to speculate in risky ventures and led to many S&L failures.

situation for the S&L operators—"Heads I win, tails FSLIC loses"—and many S&L directors quickly made themselves wealthy by brokering their depositors' money into multi-million-dollar investment deals.

Corruption, bad loans, poor judgment, and a slowing economy soon pricked the S&L bubble. As the stock market slumped and real estate values slipped in 1987, it was clear that many S&Ls were losing vast sums of money. Some started to close their doors. Charles Keating, president of Lincoln Savings and Loan in California, lost more than $2.6 billion of depositors' money. To keep his operation from being investigated, he made sizable "political" contributions to several senators. Eventually convicted of fraud, Keating was not alone in bending and breaking the law. He and scores of others left the S&L industry in ruins, with the federal government responsible for providing more than $500 billion to cover the losses.

By the late 1980s, the financial boom was fading along with the reputations of many who had fallen victim to the greed factor. Donald Trump's credit-based empire was crumbling—he had to sell his airline and most of his real estate to pay creditors. Boesky, named "crook of the year" by *Fortune,* was arrested for **insider trading** (he had earned over $50 million in illegal profits) and was sentenced to three years in prison.

Insider deals and crooks seemed to abound within the Reagan administration as well. Secretary of Interior James Watt and Attorney General Edwin Meese had received money and favors in return for using their influence with government agencies to help some businesses gain lucrative contracts and avoid government regulations. Both resigned their positions. They were not alone. Over a hundred members of the Reagan administration were found guilty of unethical and illegal behavior. Reagan was untouched by the scandals, and his popularity remained high. Some called him the "Teflon President" because no criticism seemed to stick to him.

Reagan's Second Term

Throughout the presidential campaign of 1984, Republicans credited Reagan's leadership and policies for renewed prosperity, restored military superiority, and "standing tall" against communism throughout the world. Using the theme "Morning in America," Reagan's re-election campaign projected a new day of economic expansion, morality, and national power. Reagan and Bush, as front runners, avoided specific issues while announcing that big-govern-

ment liberalism was dead. Opinion polls indicated that Reagan would have an easy re-election.

Still, a number of Democrats believed that they could successfully challenge the president. They maintained that Reagan's economic policies and recovery helped only the rich and were a disaster for everyone else. They blamed the president for increases in the deficit, unrestrained military spending, hostility toward social programs, and not caring about minorities, the poor, and the environment. The Democrats, however, could unite on neither a standard-bearer nor the best approach to challenging Reagan.

Leading the group of Democratic candidates were former vice president **Walter Mondale** of Minnesota and Senator Gary Hart of Colorado. Adding zest to the primary campaign was the candidacy of Reverend Jesse Jackson, a Baptist minister and African-American leader—the first serious African-American to seek nomination to the presidency. Although Jackson had little chance of winning, he forged the **Rainbow Coalition,** hoping to generate increased political activity by the nation's less well off and ensure that the Democratic platform supported minorities, small farmers, and workers.

After a divisive primary season that did more to divide than unite Democrats, Mondale won the presidential nomination. He called for revitalizing social programs and sought to reforge the traditional Democratic coalition. He also selected Geraldine Ferraro, a congresswoman from New York, to be his vice-presidential candidate. Many people applauded Mondale for selecting a woman, but others complained that Ferraro was not the best-qualified woman for the position, noting that she had little political experience. The outcome was that neither Mondale's nor Ferraro's candidacy healed the divisions within the Democratic party or generated much enthusiasm.

President Reagan won an overwhelming victory, taking 59 percent of the popular vote and carrying

---

insider trading   Trading of stocks by someone who has access to confidential information about the companies involved.

Walter Mondale   Minnesota senator who was vice president under Jimmy Carter and ran unsuccessfully for president on the Democratic ticket in 1984.

Rainbow Coalition   Supporters of African-American leader Jesse Jackson in his bid for the presidency in 1984; the name reflected Jackson's goal of forging a coalition of people of all races.

◆ In 1984, Geraldine Ferraro, a Congresswoman from New York, made history by being the first woman nominated by a major political party to run for the vice presidency. She and Democratic presidential candidate Walter Mondale lost, however, winning only thirteen electoral votes—those from Minnesota and the District of Columbia. *Smithsonian Institution, Division of Political History.*

every state except Mondale's Minnesota. A postelection analysis showed that all that remained of the once-powerful Democratic voting machine were the poor, African-Americans, and Hispanics. A majority of organized labor, women, Catholics, white southerners, farmers, and the middle and upper classes all had voted for Reagan's Republican vision of "Morning in America."

A growing cloud, however, hung over Reagan's American morning: the soaring budget deficit. During his first administration, the annual deficit had gone from $73.8 billion to over $200 billion. Although controlling and reducing the deficit had bipartisan support, how to do it remained a very partisan issue. Most Democrats took the view that cuts in military spending were necessary to reduce the national debt. They argued that a large part of the deficit came from military spending, which had risen from $164 billion in 1980 to $228 billion in 1985. Conservatives and Republicans hotly denied that military spending was the primary cause of the growing debt and blamed uncontrolled and wasteful social programs.

In late 1985, an unusual coalition of Republicans and Democrats passed the **Gramm-Rudman-Hollings Act,** which established a maximum debt level and ordered across-the-board cuts if the budget failed to match the level set. Though agreeing in principle with cutting the budget, both Congress and the White House found ways to circumvent the law. The intent of the act was further reduced in 1986, when the Supreme Court permitted exceptions to automatic budget cuts. Consequently, de-

spite all the posturing and support for balancing the budget, neither the White House nor Congress made any significant effort to cut federal spending or raise taxes to halt the expanding deficit.

By 1989, federal expenditures had climbed to $1,065 billion a year, and the national debt stood at nearly $3 trillion, with a $200 million annual interest payment. If spread evenly across the country, every American would owe about $5,000. And most worrisome, the nation owed more and more money to foreign investors, especially German and Japanese interests, and it continued to import more goods than it exported. By 1990, nearly 20 percent of the national debt was owed to foreign investors, and the once-largest creditor nation—the United States—had become the world's largest debtor nation.

Although the Reagan administration proved unable to solve the problem of the budget deficit and the imbalance in trade, it continued to attack the **welfare state,** reducing the budgets of many social programs. Conservatives applauded Reagan's cuts in domestic social programs but continued to be disappointed in the lack of legislation to restore prayer in school, make abortion illegal, and fulfill other aims of their domestic agenda. Reagan continued to speak out against abortion and bans on prayer in school, but it became clear that major changes in the law would have to come through the judiciary rather than through the White House and Congress. Reagan had made it clear that when given the opportunity he would appoint federal judges who would work to restore conservative values and reverse liberal decisions in civil and criminal rights that, in Reagan's mind, promoted crime and a general decline in American morality.

The Rehnquist Court

The first president since Eisenhower to serve two full terms, Reagan had an opportunity to name many federal justices who would support the social, economic, and political views of the New Right. By the end of his eight years in office, he had appointed

---

Gramm-Rudman-Hollings Act Law, passed by Congress in 1985, that set targets for eliminating the federal budget deficit by 1990; the targets were never met.

welfare state Social system in which government assumes primary responsibility for citizens' welfare, paying for health care, education, employment, and social security.

nearly half of all sitting federal district and appeals judges, most without controversy. His appointments to the Supreme Court were another matter. Reagan wanted Supreme Court justices who would reject judicial activism—the use of judicial power to legislate liberal social values—and practice **judicial restraint,** deferring to the views of Congress, the presidency, and the states on legislation and policy.

Reagan's first Supreme Court appointment, in 1981—Sandra Day O'Connor, the first woman appointed to the Court—raised little opposition (see page 1000). Although she had a conservative record and personally opposed abortion, her gender and high marks as a judge pleased many liberals and even some feminists. Reagan's second appointment opportunity occurred when Chief Justice Warren Burger retired in 1985. The administration promoted Justice William Rehnquist to the position of chief justice and named Antonin Scalia to the Court. Scalia encountered some opposition from liberal senators concerned about his views on civil rights and abortion, but he had a reputation as an accomplished legal scholar with sound judgment, and he was confirmed. Reagan's third nomination, two years later, however, raised a storm of opposition. His choice, Robert Bork, many believed to be an inflexible conservative **ideologue.**

Strongly supported by the New Right, Bork was well known for his opposition to abortion and to liberal activism in general. After bitter and partisan Senate hearings, Bork's appointment was rejected 58 to 42. Quickly, Reagan presented Douglas Ginsburg for the position. Almost as quickly, Ginsburg withdrew from consideration when it became known that he had used marijuana and may have violated conflict-of-interest procedures as a judge. Anthony M. Kennedy, Reagan's third choice, was approved with little controversy in 1987.

Most believed that the O'Connor, Scalia, and Kennedy appointments would allow the Rehnquist Court to support the values championed by Reagan and the New Right, and the expected new slant of the Supreme Court was soon evident. By 1989 the Court had restricted criminal rights, approved the reinstatement of the death penalty, and weakened affirmative action applications. In that year the Court upheld, in *William L. Webster v. Reproduction Health Services,* a Missouri law restricting free access to abortion. It was a good beginning, and conservatives expected that the combination of conservatives in the White House, Congress, and Supreme Court would ensure the expansion of their social and political agenda.

Asserting World Power

● What expectations shaped the choices Reagan's administration made in implementing American foreign policy?

Reagan's victories in 1980 and 1984 resulted not only from his views on domestic issues but from public support for his views on the role of the United States in world affairs. Throughout the 1980 presidential campaign, the Republicans had hammered at Carter's ineffective foreign policy and at slipping American prestige in the world. They had promised to re-establish the United States as the pre-eminent world leader. To accomplish that goal, Reagan believed it was necessary to overcome what he termed the "Vietnam syndrome," which made American leaders politically unwilling to use force to defend U.S. interests. Reagan and most Republicans believed that the Vietnam War had been a "noble cause" that was lost through political weakness rather than force of arms. As president, Reagan promised no lack of resolve and a strong military to support American interests. The crusade against communism was the core of his policy.

Reagan shaped the context and imagery of foreign policy. But he had little knowledge or interest in the complexities of international affairs and left to his foreign policy staff the setting of specific policies. General Alexander Haig, Reagan's first secretary of state, quickly recognized that the president would not be steering the "ship of state" and attempted to assert his control over foreign policy. Brash, arrogant, and self-promoting, Haig soon discovered that Secretary of Defense Caspar Weinberger, CIA Director William Casey, and some members of the White House staff sought to fulfill the same role, but without upstaging Reagan as Haig seemed to do. In 1982, Reagan replaced Haig with George Shultz, a close and loyal friend who, together with Casey, quickly became the driving force behind Reagan's foreign policy. Using overt and covert means, Shultz and Casey pursued an aggressive anti-Communist strategy without interference from other branches of government.

judicial restraint Refraining from using the judiciary as a forum for implementing social change but instead deferring to Congress, the president, and the consensus of the people.
ideologue Person who advocates a particular ideology.

Cold War Renewed

At the center of Reagan's view of the world was his hostility toward the Soviet Union. He told a gathering of evangelical Protestants that the Soviet Union was an "evil empire" and the "focus of evil in the modern world" and that it would "commit any crime, . . . lie . . . cheat" to achieve world conquest. America's grand role was to act as global peacekeeper and the defender of global freedom against the expansion of communism. The main objective of Reagan's foreign policy was the containment of the "evil empire" through an interventionist policy committed to defeating the forces of communism wherever they existed. Large increases in the military budget were necessary, Reagan argued, to back up the nation's diplomacy and to close the "window of vulnerability" that Carter had created by allowing the Soviets to pull ahead in the arms race.

With almost no dissent, Congress funded Reagan's military budget, agreeing to increase the overall defense budget. More funds were available for nuclear weapons and new aircraft, including the B-1 bomber and technologically advanced Stealth fighters and bombers. The navy was enlarged; the army received more tanks and helicopters. By far, the most innovative and controversial program called for a new system of defense against Soviet missiles: the **Strategic Defense Initiative (SDI)**. Star Wars, as SDI was dubbed, was at the top of Reagan's military priorities.

According to some sources, physicist Edward Teller, who had spoken to Reagan about developing a defense system that would use X-ray lasers to blast incoming Soviet missiles, had planted the idea for SDI. Reagan, who had starred in a 1950s science fiction movie that had depicted such a weapon, was immediately smitten by the idea. In March 1983, he asked Congress to fund the building of a defense system that would use lasers to make nuclear weapons "obsolete." Between 1983 and 1989, Congress provided over $17 billion for Star Wars research amid complaints that the concept was conceptually and technologically flawed. Critics pointed out that even if the system could work and was 95 percent effective, the 5 percent of Soviet warheads that would hit the United States would still destroy the nation, if not civilization.

Reagan's military spending added over $100 billion a year to the federal budget, contributing greatly to the deficit. By 1985 a million dollars was being spent on weapons every minute, but the outcome was not a more efficient or productive system.

In several arms industries the greed factor was at work, and production and quality control actually fell. Test results were falsified and costs artificially inflated. With billions of dollars available, government and industry officials padded their expense accounts and exchanged bribes and kickbacks. Billion-dollar cost overruns became commonplace. Critics loudly opposed the military shopping spree, arguing that it wasted money being denied social programs and hurt Soviet-American relations. But their complaints had little effect on Congress or the public, which seemed ready to accept the U.S. role as global sheriff and the costs it required.

The Middle East

Stretching from North Africa to Afghanistan, the Middle East presented the Reagan administration with a complex series of problems that, except for Afghanistan, resisted being explained as Communist aggression. In Afghanistan, the CIA continued to supply the mujahedeen, whom Reagan called "freedom fighters," with arms to use against Soviet and Afghan forces. Elsewhere in the Middle East, problems involving Arab nationalism, Arab-Israeli disputes, and terrorism could not so readily be understood in a Cold War context.

As Reagan assumed office, Yassir Arafat's Palestine Liberation Organization had increased its raids against Israel, and shadowy militant Islamic groups had begun a campaign of terrorism against Israel and its Western supporters. In Lebanon and throughout the Mediterranean region, terrorists kidnapped Americans and Europeans, hijacked planes and ships, and attacked airports and other public places. Reagan linked the terrorists to Communist organizations, the PLO, and various Arab nations and threatened reprisals against those accused unless they stopped supporting terrorism. With Secretary of State Haig's encouragement, Israel invaded neighboring southern Lebanon in 1982 to halt terrorist attacks and to suppress the PLO. As Israeli forces drove north and approached the capital city of Beirut, all semblance of internal stability in Lebanon collapsed, and a smoldering civil war between Christians and Muslims raged anew.

Strategic Defense Initiative   Research program designed to create an effective defense against nuclear attack; President Reagan asked Congress to fund SDI in 1983.

♦ Like Eisenhower twenty years before, President Reagan in 1983 committed American troops to Beirut, Lebanon as part of a peace-keeping operation. This intervention, however, was not successful. In October, terrorists blew up the Marine's barracks, killing 240 soldiers. "Too few to fight and too many to die," said one Congressional critic, as four months later Reagan withdrew the remaining American forces from the war-torn nation. *UPI/Bettmann Archives.*

As part of an international peacekeeping effort, the United States sent nearly two thousand Marines to Beirut, where they quickly became a target for Muslim terrorists. In April 1983, terrorists attacked the American embassy in Beirut and killed sixty-three people. In October, a suicide driver rammed a truck filled with explosives into the Marine barracks at the Beirut airport, killing 241 Marines. Reagan denounced the terrorist attack, defended the Marines' presence in Beirut, and quietly made plans for their removal. In January 1984, the United States withdrew its forces from Lebanon, leaving Israel in control of southern Lebanon, Syrian forces occupying much of central Lebanon, and a civil war still raging. In Lebanon there were no victories nor were there easy solutions.

Nor were there easy solutions in protecting American interests in the Persian Gulf region. Iran and Iraq had gone to war in 1980, making the Persian Gulf part of the battlefield. The war created two problems for American foreign policy: to protect vital shipments of oil and to ensure that neither Iran nor Iraq emerged from the war with the power to dominate the region. Secretly using third parties, the Reagan administration provided money and weapons to both sides. When Iranian forces attacked several oil tankers in 1986, American warships began escorting and protecting all oil tankers

in the gulf. Clashes between American and Iranian forces occurred, and in 1988 the U.S.S. *Vincennes* mistakenly shot down an Iranian airliner, killing 290 passengers. When the **Iraq-Iran War** ended in 1988, it had cost over 2 million lives, and American intelligence concluded that neither Iran nor Iraq could immediately threaten other countries in the region. There were, however, worrisome reports of Iraqi chemical and nuclear weapons research.

To counterbalance Iran and Iraq, the United States supplied Saudi Arabia with more military hardware, including sophisticated radar detection planes, tanks, and fighter aircraft. Stores of American military supplies were also buried in the Saudi desert in case of future need.

Further west, in North Africa, Reagan faced off against the person he called the "mad dog of the Middle East": **Moamar Qaddafi,** the vehemently anti-American ruler of Libya. Reagan denounced Libya as a "rogue" nation that actively supported the PLO and terrorist groups and, through its manufacture of chemical weapons, constituted a threat to its neighbors and the region.

In April 1986, terrorists bombed a disco popular among American troops in West Berlin, wounding several and killing an American soldier. American intelligence tied Qaddafi to the terrorists, and Reagan ordered a reprisal raid. American navy and air force planes bombed several targets in Libya, including Qaddafi's quarters, killing one of his daughters. The United States had showed Qaddafi "that we could get people close to him," bragged one official.

The majority of Americans cheered the daring raid, although Qaddafi remained in power and terrorism continued. What seemed important to most Americans was that the United States had responded to terrorism. The White House continued to keep the pressure on Libya, calling for the economic and political isolation of Qaddafi, particularly after investigations suggested that Libya had aided the terrorists who blew up a Pan American airliner over Lockerbie, Scotland, in December 1988, murdering over 250 people.

Iraq-Iran War   War between Iran and Iraq that broke out in 1980 over control of a disputed waterway and ended in 1988 with more than 2 million dead.

Moamar Qaddafi   Libyan political leader who seized power in a military coup in 1969 and imposed socialist policies and Islamic orthodoxy on the country.

Central America and the Caribbean

It was hard to fit Middle Eastern problems into a Cold War context, but things seemed more black and white in Central America and the Caribbean (see Map 31.3). The area was closer to the United States, and Reagan thought that any hint of Communist influence justified American action. In the southern Caribbean, Reagan focused on the tiny island of **Grenada,** where a Marxist government had ruled since independence from Britain in 1979.

In October 1983, the radical New Jewel Movement took control of Grenada in a coup. The Reagan administration immediately expressed concern about the new government, the construction of a large airport runway by Cuban "advisers," and the potential threat to about five hundred Americans attending medical school on the island. On October 25, Reagan ordered American forces to invade Grenada and remove the "brutal gang of thugs" that ruled. More than two thousand American soldiers quickly overcame minimal opposition, brought home the American students, and installed a pro-American government on Grenada. The administration basked in the light of public approval. Though small in scale, the Grenada operation implied that the "Vietnam syndrome" no longer restricted American foreign policy.

Determined to uphold his campaign pledge to defeat communism in Central America, Reagan provided billions in monetary and military support for the El Salvadoran government and the Contra "freedom fighters" in Nicaragua. Although the public and Congress strongly supported Reagan's invasion of Grenada, his efforts in Central America stirred considerable opposition. Some critics were disturbed by reports of human rights violations by "death squads" linked to the Salvadoran military. Many feared that Central America would become another Vietnam, with American troops following the aid and advisers already being sent. When the press uncovered large-scale American covert aid to the Contras, including the CIA's mining of Nicaraguan harbors in 1984, Congress passed legislation drafted by Representative Edward Boland that allowed only humanitarian aid to the Contras. Reagan and CIA Director Casey strongly opposed what came to be called the **Boland Amendment** and sought ways to work around it.

In the fall of 1985, the White House believed it had found a way to arm the Contras without Congress's knowledge and at the same time to gain the release of some American hostages held in Lebanon. Despite the U.S. trade embargo with Iran, national security advisers Robert McFarlane and John Poindexter, working with the CIA, arranged for the secret sale of arms to Iran. In return, Iran agreed to use its influence with terrorist groups in Lebanon to secure the release of American hostages. The cash that Iran paid for the arms was to be routed to the Contras, allowing them to purchase supplies and weapons.

When the press broke word of the so-called arms-for-hostages deal fourteen months later, there were calls for official investigations to determine the extent of the operation and the White House's involvement in it. A special White House commission, led by former Texas senator John Tower, and a congressional committee began separate investigations in 1987. Both uncovered that the CIA and the National Security Council had acted independently, without the knowledge or approval of Congress, and that members of both organizations had lied to Congress to keep their operation secret. McFarlane, Poindexter, and NSC aide Oliver North were found guilty of violating a variety of federal laws and were sentenced to prison terms. Although neither investigation uncovered proof that Reagan knew of the operation, it was clear that some of his closest aides were deeply involved, and the scandal damaged his image and that of his presidency.

Reagan and Gorbachev

Reagan made no attempt to improve relations with the Soviet superpower during the first three and a half years of his administration. Suddenly, without warning, Reagan changed course during the first weeks of his second term. He called for the resumption of arms limitation talks, and when Soviet leader Konstantin Chernenko died in March 1985, he invited Chernenko's successor, **Mikhail S. Gorbachev,** to the United States.

Grenada   Country in the West Indies that achieved independence from Britain in 1974 and was invaded briefly by U.S. forces in 1983.

Boland Amendment   Motion, approved by Congress in 1984, that barred the CIA from using funds to give direct or indirect aid to the Nicaraguan Contras.

Mikhail S. Gorbachev   Soviet leader who came to power in 1985; he introduced political and economic reforms and then found himself presiding over the breakup of the Soviet Union.

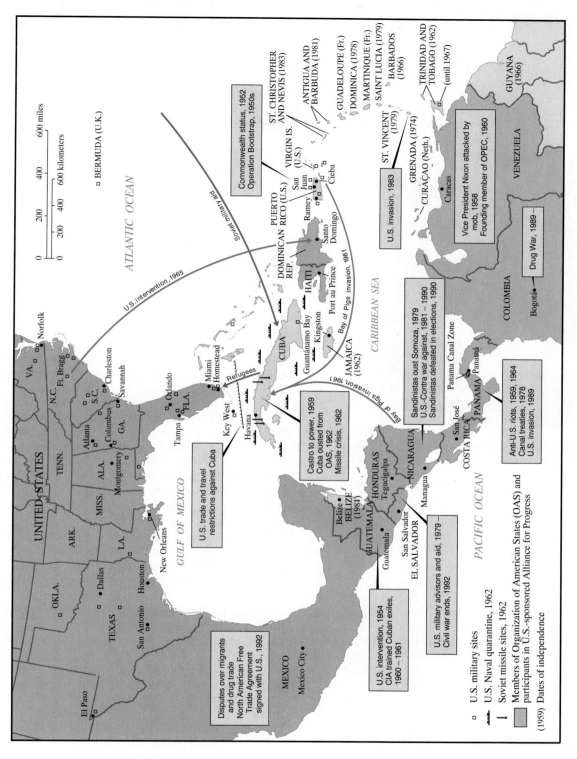

MAP 31.3 The United States and Central America and the Caribbean Geographical nearness, important economic ties, security needs, and the drug trade have continued to make Central America and the Caribbean a critical region for American interests. This map shows some of the American economic, military, and political actions taken in the region since the end of World War II.

The following labels appear on the map:

ATLANTIC OCEAN

BERMUDA (U.K.)

600 miles
600 kilometers
0 200 400 600

Soviet military aid

Commonwealth status, 1952
Operation Bootstrap, 1950s

ST. CHRISTOPHER AND NEVIS (1983)
ANTIGUA AND BARBUDA (1981)
GUADELOUPE (Fr.)
DOMINICA (1978)
MARTINIQUE (Fr.)
SAINT LUCIA (1979)
BARBADOS (1966)
TRINIDAD AND TOBAGO (1962)
(until 1967)
GUYANA (1966)
ST. VINCENT (1979)
GRENADA (1974)
CURAÇAO (Neth.)

VIRGIN IS. (U.S.)
PUERTO RICO (U.S.)
San Juan
Ramey
Cieba

U.S. invasion, 1983

Vice President Nixon attacked by mob, 1958
Founding member of OPEC, 1960

VENEZUELA
Caracas

U.S. intervention, 1965

DOMINICAN REP.
Santo Domingo
HAITI
Port au Prince
Bay of Pigs invasion, 1961

CARIBBEAN SEA

COLOMBIA
Bogotá
Drug War, 1989 –

Norfolk
VA.
N.C. Ft. Bragg
Charleston
S.C. Savannah
Columbus GA.
Atlanta
ALA.
Montgomery
MISS.
TENN.
UNITED STATES
ARK.
OKLA.
Dallas
TEXAS
San Antonio
Houston
El Paso

Orlando
FLA.
Tampa
Miami
Homestead
Key West
Havana
New Orleans
GULF OF MEXICO

CUBA
Guantánamo Bay
Kingston
JAMAICA (1962)

Refugees

Castro to power, 1959
Cuba ousted from OAS, 1962
Missile crisis, 1962

U.S. trade and travel restrictions against Cuba

Bay of Pigs invasion, 1961

Sandinistas oust Somoza, 1979
U.S.-Contra war against, 1981 – 1990
Sandinistas defeated in elections, 1990

Panama Canal Zone
PANAMA
Panamá

Anti-U.S. riots, 1959, 1964
Canal treaties, 1978
U.S. invasion, 1989

San José
COSTA RICA
NICARAGUA
Managua
HONDURAS
Tegucigalpa
GUATEMALA
Belize
BELIZE (1981)
Guatemala
San Salvador
EL SALVADOR
PACIFIC OCEAN

U.S. military advisors and aid, 1979 –
Civil war ends, 1992

U.S. intervention, 1954
CIA trained Cuban exiles, 1960 – 1961

Disputes over migrants and drug trade
North American Free Trade Agreement signed with U.S., 1992

MEXICO
Mexico City

□ U.S. military sites
□ U.S. Naval quarantine, 1962
⊥ Soviet missile sites, 1962
▨ Members of Organization of American States (OAS) and participants in U.S.-sponsored Alliance for Progress
(1959) Dates of independence

◆ After declaring the Soviet Union an "evil empire" responsible for nearly all the world's problems, President Reagan reversed course in 1988 and opened productive discussions with Soviet reformer Mikail Gorbachev. The outcome was an intermediate-range nuclear-forces treaty that helped to end the Cold War as well as to reduce the overall number of nuclear missiles. Here, the two superpower leaders pose in front of the St. Basil cathedral in Moscow. *UPI/Bettmann Archives.*

Gorbachev was different from previous Soviet leaders—younger and committed to change. He was determined to breathe new life into the Soviet economy, which was stagnating under the weight of military spending and government inefficiency and corruption. He also wanted to institute reforms that would provide more political and civil rights to the Soviet people. British prime minister Margaret Thatcher called him "charming" and someone with whom the West could work to improve East-West relations.

Gorbachev declined Reagan's invitation but agreed to a summit meeting in Geneva in November 1985. Meeting for the first time, the two leaders at first jousted with each other. Reagan condemned the Soviets for human rights abuses, their involvement in Afghanistan, and their aid to Communist factions fighting in Angola and Ethiopia. Gorbachev attacked American military policies, especially the

proposed development of SDI. Later, when Gorbachev showed an interest in Hollywood and Reagan responded with stories about film making and movie stars, their relationship improved. The two leaders left Geneva with a growing fondness for each other.

Shortly after the summit, Gorbachev announced two new policies: **perestroika** and **glasnost.** Reagan and Gorbachev met again in October 1986 in Reykjavik, Iceland, and the Soviet leader shocked American participants by suggesting a 50 percent reduction of strategic weapons over a five-year period and, less surprisingly, the nondeployment of SDI for ten years. Without consulting his advisers, Reagan responded that the two powers should eliminate all strategic missiles within ten years but allow the development of SDI. The summit ended without an agreement, to the relief of American advisers who considered Reagan's idea of eliminating all nuclear missiles to be dangerous to national security.

Still, Soviet-American negotiations on arms limitations continued with new optimism. By December 1987, as Gorbachev prepared to visit the United States, negotiators reached an agreement that eliminated Soviet and American intermediate-range missiles from Europe. Reagan and Gorbachev signed the **Intermediate Nuclear Force Treaty** in Washington during their December summit.

Throughout 1988, Soviet-American relations continued to improve. Gorbachev withdrew Soviet forces from Afghanistan, the Senate approved the Intermediate Nuclear Force Treaty, and Reagan visited Moscow. To many it seemed as if the Cold War was over and a new era of international relations was unfolding. Liberals applauded the changes, calling on Washington to make further concessions, including the scrapping of SDI. But many conservatives still believed the Soviets could not be trusted and quietly criticized Reagan for working to improve relations.

---

perestroika Organizational restructuring of the Soviet economy and bureaucracy that began in the mid-1980s.

glasnost Official policy of the Soviet government under Gorbachev emphasizing freedom of thought and candid discussion of social problems.

Intermediate Nuclear Force Treaty Treaty, signed in 1987 by Reagan and Gorbachev, that provided for the destruction of all U.S. and Soviet medium-range nuclear missiles and for verification with on-site inspections.

SUMMARY

E xpectations
C onstraints
C hoices
O utcomes

The years between Nixon's resignation and Reagan's retirement were ones of changing *expectations*. During the presidencies of Ford and Carter, the nation seemed beset with *constraints* that limited its domestic prosperity and international status. The policy *choices* made by Ford and Carter neither recaptured the people's faith in the nation nor established national goals. In his foreign policy, Carter chose to de-emphasize Cold War relationships and give more attention to human rights and Third World problems. The *outcome*, many believed, was a weakened American world position.

Reagan rejected Carter's notion that Americans must sacrifice to overcome the limits facing the nation. He argued that the only *constraint* on American greatness was excessive government regulation and interference in society. He promised to reassert American power and renew the offensive in the Cold War. As president, Reagan *chose* a conservative program to restore the nation's values, honor, and international prestige. He fulfilled many conservative *expectations* by reducing support for some social programs, easing and eliminating some government regulations, and exerting American power around the world—altering the structure of Soviet-American relations. Supporters claimed that the *outcome* of Reagan's choices was a prosperous nation that faced few *constraints*. They applauded Reagan's view that his administration had chosen to "change a nation, and instead . . . changed a world."

SUGGESTED READINGS

Bialer, Seweryn, and Mandelbaum, Michael, eds. *Gorbachev's Russia and American Foreign Policy* (1988).

An excellent account of the changes taking place in the Soviet Union and the role of the superpowers in ending the Cold War.

Bill, James A. *The Lion and the Eagle* (1988).

A well-written and insightful examination of American relations with Iran and the Iranian crisis.

Burroughs, Bryan, and Helyar, John. *Barbarians at the Gate: The Fall of RJR Nabisco* (1990).

A novel-like account—that became a made-for-television movie—of hostile takeovers, leveraged buyouts, and the politics of greed that revolved around the Nabisco company.

Cannon, Lou. *President Reagan: The Role of a Lifetime* (1992).

The most complete and detailed account of the Reagan presidency from a generally positive perspective.

Kaufman, Burton. *The Presidency of James Earl Carter, Jr.* (1993).

A well-balanced account and analysis of Carter's presidency and the changing political values of the 1970s.

Schaller, Michael. *Reckoning with Reagan* (1992).

A brief but scholarly analysis of the Reagan administration and the society and values that supported the Reagan revolution.

White, F. Clinton. *Why Reagan Won: A Narrative History of the Conservative Movement, 1964–1981* (1980).

A balanced account of the rise of the conservative movement that culminated in Reagan's election.

Wolfe, Tom. *Bonfire of the Vanities* (1987).

A best-selling novel—made into a movie—about the inside world of financial deals and the quest for power and wealth.

The movie *Wall Street* (1988) provides another example of financial wheeling and dealing and Yuppies in search of wealth and power.

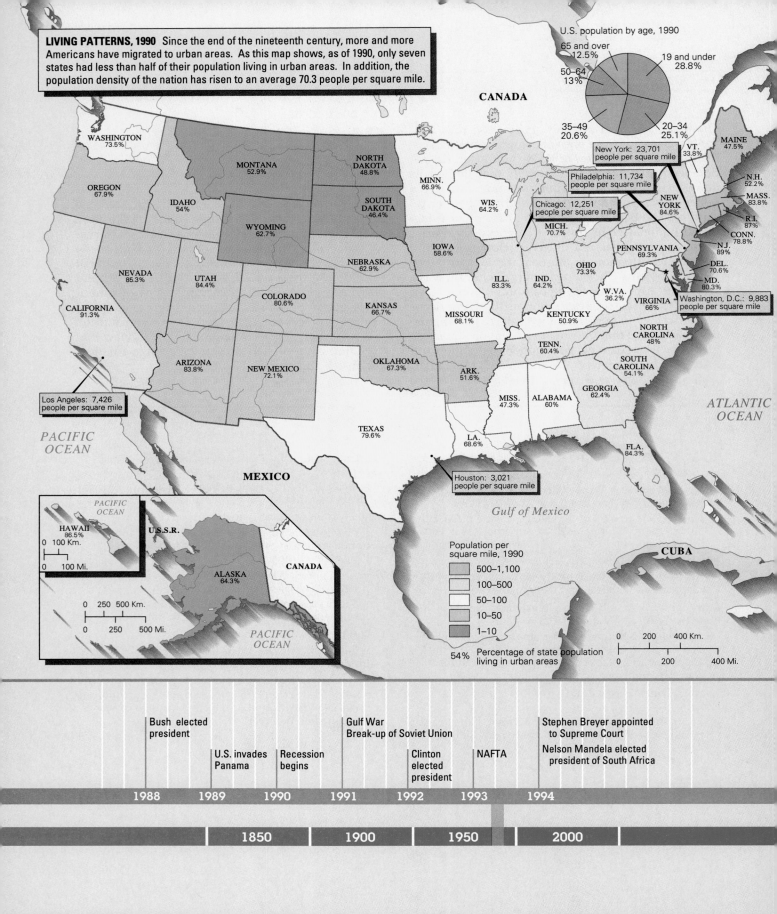

LIVING PATTERNS, 1990 Since the end of the nineteenth century, more and more Americans have migrated to urban areas. As this map shows, as of 1990, only seven states had less than half of their population living in urban areas. In addition, the population density of the nation has risen to an average 70.3 people per square mile.

CANADA

U.S. population by age, 1990

65 and over 12.5%
50–64 13%
35–49 20.6%
20–34 25.1%
19 and under 28.8%

WASHINGTON 73.5%
OREGON 67.9%
IDAHO 54%
MONTANA 52.9%
NORTH DAKOTA 48.8%
SOUTH DAKOTA 46.4%
WYOMING 62.7%
NEVADA 85.3%
UTAH 84.4%
CALIFORNIA 91.3%
COLORADO 80.6%
ARIZONA 83.8%
NEW MEXICO 72.1%
NEBRASKA 62.9%
KANSAS 66.7%
OKLAHOMA 67.3%
TEXAS 79.6%
MINN. 66.9%
WIS. 64.2%
IOWA 58.6%
MISSOURI 68.1%
ARK. 51.6%
MICH. 70.7%
ILL. 83.3%
IND. 64.2%
OHIO 73.3%
KENTUCKY 50.9%
TENN. 60.4%
MISS. 47.3%
ALABAMA 60%
LA. 68.6%
GEORGIA 62.4%
W.VA. 36.2%
VIRGINIA 66%
NORTH CAROLINA 48%
SOUTH CAROLINA 54.1%
FLA. 84.3%
PENNSYLVANIA 69.3%
NEW YORK 84.6%
MAINE 47.5%
VT. 33.8%
N.H. 52.2%
MASS. 83.8%
R.I. 87%
CONN. 78.8%
N.J. 89%
DEL. 70.6%
MD. 80.3%

New York: 23,701 people per square mile
Philadelphia: 11,734 people per square mile
Chicago: 12,251 people per square mile
Washington, D.C.: 9,883 people per square mile
Los Angeles: 7,426 people per square mile
Houston: 3,021 people per square mile

PACIFIC OCEAN
ATLANTIC OCEAN
Gulf of Mexico
MEXICO
CUBA

PACIFIC OCEAN
HAWAII 86.5%
0 100 Km.
0 100 Mi.

U.S.S.R.
ALASKA 64.3%
CANADA
0 250 500 Km.
0 250 500 Mi.
PACIFIC OCEAN

Population per square mile, 1990
500–1,100
100–500
50–100
10–50
1–10

54% Percentage of state population living in urban areas

0 200 400 Km.
0 200 400 Mi.

Bush elected president
U.S. invades Panama
Recession begins
Gulf War Break-up of Soviet Union
Clinton elected president
NAFTA
Stephen Breyer appointed to Supreme Court
Nelson Mandela elected president of South Africa

1988 1989 1990 1991 1992 1993 1994

1850 1900 1950 2000

Making New Choices, 1986–1994

A Divided Society

- How did the introduction of moral and social values into American politics change political and social choices, especially for women and homosexuals?

Poverty and Race

- What constraints and choices do new immigrants and minorities face in seeking to find social and economic equality?

Bush and a New International Order

- What new foreign policy choices does the United States face as a result of the collapse of the Soviet Union?

- How did economic and social problems constrain and shape American politics for President Bush?

Calls for Change: The Election of Clinton

- The election of President Clinton was the outcome of what expectations?

<table>
<tr><td>

┌─────────────────────────────────┐
│ **INTRODUCTION** │
└─────────────────────────────────┘

</td><td>

E xpectations
C onstraints
C hoices
O utcomes

</td></tr>
</table>

Before the election of 1992, many people *expected* the central issue of the campaign and perhaps of the 1990s would be the social and cultural divisions within American society. Whose values would prevail? There seemed little *expectation* that either side was willing to compromise.

On one side were liberals, women, homosexuals, racial and ethnic minorities, and others who demanded a larger slice of the American economic and political pie and major changes in American values and attitudes. They saw government as a prime force in reshaping American society, both economically and culturally. Support for the Equal Rights Amendment, affirmative action, and bans on anti-gay legislation were seen as means to ensure the federal government's role in combating job and legal discrimination based on gender, color, and lifestyle.

On the other side were conservatives, led by the New Right. They argued that the changes demanded by liberals would destroy the basic value system of the nation and result in dysfunctional families, crime, violence, and other forms of immoral behavior. Many of the social problems of American society, they argued, looking to Reagan and Bush to support their cause, would be solved by a return to traditional two-parent family values.

As liberal and conservative choices clashed and as economic growth slowed in 1988, Vice President George Bush ran for the presidency. Public opinion polls showed widespread dissatisfaction with the country's direction but no consensus about what was wrong or how to fix it. The economy—unemployment and the possibility of recession—was the most commonly mentioned problem, but it generated only a 12 percent response. With polls showing little or no consensus, Bush promised a "kinder, gentler nation" that would show more concern for minorities, the poor, education, and the environment. Easily defeating Democratic candidate, Michael Dukakis, Bush assumed the presidency but had little desire to implement change. Domestically, the best *choice* was to do less.

Bush focused, instead, on foreign policy. Taking office as the Soviet Union shattered, he charted foreign policy in a new international setting: the United States was now the only superpower and faced fewer *constraints* abroad than at home. The president cautiously supported democratic change in the Soviet Union and Eastern Europe and *chose* to commit American military force in Panama, Kuwait, and Somalia. Unlike his lackluster domestic policy, his foreign policy generated widespread praise and support.

As the 1992 presidential election campaign started, many expected that foreign policy successes would ensure Bush's re-election. His opponents—the Democratic governor of Arkansas Bill Clinton and an independent businessman from Texas, H. Ross Perot—had no foreign policy expertise or any real experience in setting national policy. But the *expectation* that experience would triumph faded quickly when it became obvious that the public was most interested in economic and domestic issues. The *outcome* of the campaign was a victory for Clinton, who promised to be supportive of social needs while making the *choices* necessary to control the federal budget and reduce the national debt.

A Divided Society

● How did the introduction of moral and social values into American politics change political and social choices, especially for women and homosexuals?

When Ronald Reagan retired from the presidency in 1989, the United States was divided by social outlook and cultural politics. Many people worried that America had become a nation of interest groups clamoring for rights and power and that a sense of national identity and purpose was rapidly fading.

Liberals argued that social and cultural pluralism, which emphasized tolerance and the belief in democracy, was under fire from narrow-minded conservatives seeking to reassert the social influence

CHRONOLOGY ■■■■■■■■■■■■ ■■

New Expectations, New Directions

1968	Stonewall Riot
1972	Equal Rights Amendment begins ratification process
1973	*Roe v. Wade*
1974	Busing confrontation in Boston
1976	Hyde Amendment restricts federally funded abortions
1978	*Regents of the University of California v. Bakke*
1980	Ronald Reagan elected president *Harris v. McRae*
1981	Beginning of AIDS epidemic in the United States Sandra Day O'Connor appointed to Supreme Court Economic Recovery Tax Act
1982	Equal Rights Amendment fails to win ratification
1986	Howard Beach incident
1988	George Bush elected president
1989	*Webster v. Reproductive Health Service* Chinese government represses democracy movement in Tiananmen Square Berlin Wall pulled down U.S. invades Panama Bush summit with Gorbachev on Malta

1990	Recession begins Sandinistas defeated in Nicaraguan elections Clean Air Act Iraq invades Kuwait Germany unified Bush and Congress agree on tax increase Americans with Disabilities Act
1991	Breakup of the Soviet Union Gorbachev resigns Persian Gulf War Clarence Thomas appointed to Supreme Court
1992	Riots in south-central Los Angeles U.S. troops sent to Somalia Bill Clinton elected president *Planned Parenthood of Southeastern Pennsylvania v. Casey*
1993	North American Free Trade Agreement passed Clinton introduces national health package Ruth Bader Ginsburg appointed to Supreme Court
1994	Withdrawal of U.S. troops from Somalia Nelson Mandela elected president of South Africa Stephen Breyer appointed to Supreme Court Crime bill passed

of white middle- and upper-class male Americans. Conservatives charged that liberal attitudes and programs had made victims of middle-class Americans, who worked hard, saved their money, and believed in strong, traditional family values. Conservatives argued that the middle class was being overtaxed to pay for expensive social programs and that liberals were attacking the rights and values of the middle class in an effort to advance minority rights and opportunities.

Most conservatives had hoped the election of Ronald Reagan signaled a shift in American values

and politics and the retreat of liberalism. But the majority of Americans still described themselves politically as being "middle-of-the-road," holding both liberal and conservative values.

Whose Values?

At the center of the value dispute were long-standing issues, such as the place in American society of women and racial and ethnic minorities, and newer concerns about the structure and nature of personal relationships. Some of the cultural conflict was an offshoot of the civil rights movement. People also pointed to the women's movement, the counterculture, and the **sexual revolution.** These movements, they claimed, had undermined family togetherness by advocating that everyone should seek personal fulfillment by doing "your own thing."

The sexual revolution had been brought about by the baby-boomers as they reached college age and young adulthood in the 1960s. Surveys of college students in the 1960s revealed that casual sex was increasingly common and that on many campuses nearly 75 percent of women and men were sexually active. By 1970 more than half of those surveyed said they approved of premarital sex and cohabitation outside of marriage. Marriage, though still the norm, had lost some of its importance. Many people chose to remain single well into their twenties. Children, when they arrived, were fewer in number than they had been in earlier decades. As couples limited their families to an average of two children, the United States reached zero population growth during the 1970s.

By the 1970s, divorce rates were increasing, pushed upward by changes in attitudes toward marriage by both men and women. In the late 1950s and into the 1960s, men had led the escape from marriage commitments, but by the 1970s women unwilling to stay within an unsatisfactory marriage were initiating an increasing number of divorces. As attitudes toward marriage and divorce changed, divorce laws also changed. **No-fault divorce** allowed spouses to dissolve their marriage because of so-called irreconcilable differences. By the end of the 1980s, 50 percent of all those who married eventually divorced, and the number of households headed by single women, many with children, was growing rapidly.

Keeping pace with society's openness about sex, industry and advertising agencies found new and more explicit ways to use sexuality in their products and ads, especially those aimed at singles and "liberated" people. The first singles bar opened in New York City in 1964, and within five years there was a large industry catering to the needs of "swinging singles." A cigarette company tapped into the women's movement with its slogan "You've Come a Long Way, Baby." The television networks aired shows that transformed the supposedly typical 1950s family—white, suburban, mother as housewife—into many variations. Each program's commercials were aimed at specifically targeted audiences with certain age, gender, ethnic, and income-level characteristics.

Television shows in a typical week in 1976 featured African-American households (*The Jeffersons, Sanford and Son,* and *Good Times*), a single Latino (*Chico and the Man*), several single working women (*Laverne and Shirley, The Mary Tyler Moore Show,* and *Rhoda*), divorced women raising children (*Alice* and *One Day at a Time*), and a variety of normal and not-so-normal white families (*All in the Family, Happy Days,* and *The Waltons*).

By the 1980s, sexual content and eroticism had become standard fare in movies and television. The two appeared in combination on the new medium of cable television, which boasted of late-night adult programming and The Playboy Channel. In 1987 it was estimated that over sixty-five thousand sexual references were broadcast each year on prime-time television programs. During the day, sex and sex-related issues became more daring and numerous on the soaps, and talk-show hosts probed their guests for intimate details about their sex lives. There was also an expanding market in increasingly sexually explicit materials ranging from magazines, books, and X-rated films to clothing and sexual aids. Critics asserted that much of the sexual revolution debased and exploited women, but others argued that it freed women from traditional roles and standards.

Women and Changing Values

For many women, especially upper-middle-class women, Betty Friedan's *The Feminine Mystique* had opened the door to a new self-awareness, and by the late 1960s some had channeled this awareness into a full attack on sexism in American society and culture (see pages 942–943). Unprecedented numbers of women were working, and many were angered by the gap between their abilities and earnings and by the treatment they received on the job. In August 1970, over fifty thousand women marched in New York, calling not only for new laws to ensure equal pay and equal access to jobs and credit but also for changes in social values related to gender and gender roles.

Responding to the experiences and demands of women both at home and at work, the women's movement began to emphasize not only equality of

---

sexual revolution Dramatic change in attitudes toward sex; it began in the 1960s, as more and more Americans considered premarital sex acceptable.

no-fault divorce Divorce granted without the need to establish wrongdoing by either party.

◆ By the 1970s, the woman's movement was calling for more economic and social choices for women and for an Equal Rights Amendment. By 1990, the effort to ratify ERA had failed, but more and more women were running for, and being elected to, office than ever before, causing some to call 1992 the "Year of the Woman." *ERA rally: Arthur Grace/Sygma; button: Picture Research Consultants.*

jobs, wages, and opportunities but also modifications in the culture of gender throughout American society. Included in the latter category were women's rights to control their own bodies and sexuality (abortion rights), the removal of restrictions on the behavior of consenting adults, and the right of women to reject unwanted sex and **sexual harassment.** To help achieve these goals, the National Organization for Women (NOW) and other women's groups in 1967 called for an **Equal Rights Amendment (ERA)** and recognition of a woman's right to reproductive self-determination, which included unlimited access to abortion and birth control. By 1971, half of all women asked complained of sex discrimination, and three-fourths thought that it was necessary to confront men about gender issues, including basic male attitudes. Otherwise, they believed, "nothing would be done."

Many states responded to the changing social values and to pressure from women's groups. They modified laws to reduce or eliminate gender discrimination within the law and the marketplace. Some states liberalized their abortion laws to allow women to seek legal abortions. In 1972, Congress drafted an Equal Rights Amendment and sent it to the states for ratification. ERA advocates argued that it was needed to eliminate laws and restrictions at the state and local levels that blocked the achievement of women's equality. They pointed out that ERA would also transfer the responsibility of ensuring equality from individuals and state governments to the federal government. At first, ratification of ERA appeared almost certain.

Thirty-three of the thirty-eight states needed for ratification approved by 1974, and a 1973 Gallup poll showed that nearly 78 percent of Americans supported the amendment. But opposition stiffened, and only two more states voted approval before the 1978 deadline for ratification expired. Congress granted an extension of the deadline until 1982, but it did no good. Conservative forces, making ERA a symbol for activities and values that they said threatened traditional family values, mounted an effective "STOP-ERA" movement and prevented any additional states from approving the proposed amendment. In 1982, the Equal Rights Amendment remained three votes short of ratification.

Instrumental in defeating the amendment were over 130 conservative organizations that blamed the philosophy behind ERA for destroying American values and the family. **Phyllis Schlafly** and other STOP-ERA leaders changed the meaning of equal rights in the minds of many Americans. Rather than openly opposing women's rights, Schlafly labeled ERA as a means to alter the "role of the American woman as wife and mother" and to destroy the American family. The changed definition attracted

---

sexual harassment   Unwanted and offensive sexual advances or sexually derogatory or discriminatory remarks.

Equal Rights Amendment   Proposed constitutional amendment giving women equal rights under the law; Congress approved it in 1972, but it failed to achieve ratification by the required thirty-eight states.

Phyllis Schlafly   Leader of the movement to defeat the Equal Rights Amendment; Schlafly believed that the amendment threatened the domestic role of women.

◆ Ever since the controversial *Roe v. Wade* decision in 1973, opponents of abortion have asked the Supreme Court, lobbied Congress, and demonstrated to ban abortions. In January 1990, with President Bush's encouragement, thousands of participants in the March for Life rallied outside the White House, demanding an end to abortions. Some radical pro-life supporters have even advocated violence against and murder of those performing abortions as a moral choice in the "war" against abortion. *Reuters Bettmann.*

many who were increasingly uneasy about the growing sexual openness of American society and the debate over abortion.

In 1973, in a 5-to-2 decision, the Supreme Court in **Roe v. Wade** invalidated a Texas law that prevented abortions. Justice Harry Blackmun, writing for the majority, held that "the right to privacy" gave women the freedom to choose to have an abortion during the first three months of pregnancy. The controversial ruling struck down abortion laws in forty-six states that had made it nearly impossible for women to have an abortion except in cases of rape and to save the life of the mother. As the number of legal abortions rose from about 750,000 in 1973 to nearly a million and half by 1980, so too did opposition.

Although most public opinion polls indicated that a majority of Americans favored giving women the right to choose an abortion, Catholics, Mormons, some Orthodox Jews, and many Protestant churches worked with conservative groups to organize a "Right to Life" campaign to oppose abortion rights

on moral and legal grounds. The **Right to Life movement** easily merged with the conservative critique of American society and liberalism. Responding to conservative and anti-abortion pressure, Congress in 1976 passed the Hyde Amendment, which prohibited the use of federal Medicaid funds to pay for abortions. The Supreme Court upheld this position in 1980 in *Harris v. McRae*. As President Reagan appointed Sandra Day O'Connor and other conservative justices to the Supreme Court, many people expected the Court to eventually overturn *Roe v. Wade* (see Individual Choices: Sandra Day O'Connor; see also Voices). But instead, in 1992, in *Planned Parenthood of Southeastern Pennsylvania v. Casey*, the Court confirmed a woman's right to have an abortion, although it did assert that in some cases the state could modify that right. The decision did little to quiet the controversy as the nation entered the 1992 presidential season.

The *Casey* decision was a disappointment to nearly all conservative and anti-abortion advocates. They had expected the presence of Bush appointee Justice Clarence Thomas to finally tip the scales against abortion. In 1991, Thomas, a conservative and an African-American, had been selected to fill the seat of Thurgood Marshall, also an African-American. Liberals disliked Thomas's conservative views and objected to his low American Bar Association ratings as a lawyer and judge but otherwise found little reason to reject his candidacy—until the press revealed that Anita Hill, a University of Oklahoma law professor, had privately accused him of sexual harassment.

Appearing at Thomas's Senate confirmation hearings, Hill testified that a decade earlier, while she was working for Thomas at the Department of Education's Office of Equal Employment Opportunity, he had pressured her for dates and told her pornographic stories and tales of his sexual abilities. Thomas denied her allegations and lashed back at her and at her supporters. The hearing "is a high-tech lynching for uppity blacks," Thomas angrily charged. Hill was lying, he said. The judge was lying, she said. The Senate hearings became a national

Roe v. Wade Supreme Court ruling in 1973 that women have an unrestricted right to abort a fetus during the first three months of pregnancy.

Right to Life movement Anti-abortion movement that favors a constitutional amendment to prohibit abortion; it grew increasingly militant during the 1980s and 1990s.

television spectacle. Public opinion was divided. A slight majority believed Thomas's denials rather than Hill's accusations. More women than men supported Hill.

The Senate confirmed Thomas in a close vote, but the hearings focused national attention on the issue of sexual harassment and the lack of women in government at all levels, especially in Congress. At the time of the hearing, one public opinion poll revealed that 42 percent of women had been sexually harassed at work or knew someone who had been. Responding to Hill's appearance before the all-male Senate committee, women's organizations stepped up campaigns against sexual harassment and intensified their efforts to promote women candidates for the 1992 elections. As the nation braced for those elections, many observers expected that the culture wars would be a major issue that the candidates would have to confront.

Gay Rights: Progress and Resistance

Women were not the only group asking society to reconsider America's traditional views of gender. Homosexuals too were demanding equality. Since the 1950s, organizations like the Daughters of Bilitis and the Mattachine Society (see page 877) had worked quietly to promote new attitudes toward homosexuality. Nevertheless, in most states homosexual activities remained against the law, and most homosexuals remained "in the closet," unknown to society at large. Then in the late 1960s, groups promoting gay and lesbian rights and gay liberation openly confronted American society, demanding an end to social values and laws that discriminated against homosexuals.

The spark for the movement was a police raid in June 1968 on the Stonewall Inn, a gay bar in the Greenwich Village section of New York City. Gays fought back and were soon joined by other members of the community in what has come to be called the Stonewall Riot. One outcome of the riot was that gays and lesbians borrowed tactics from the women's and civil rights movements, formed activist groups, and demanded equality. Because visibility was a major tool and goal of the movement, gays and lesbians demonstrated in support of their lifestyles.

Throughout the 1970s, the gay liberation movement expanded and pressured government at all levels to end restrictions against homosexuals in employment, housing, and the military. Success

came slowly. Polls indicated confusing views held by the "straight" public. The majority of Americans considered homosexuality wrong. But by the mid-1970s a slight majority of Americans opposed job discrimination based on sexual orientation and seemed willing to show more toleration of gay lifestyles. Responding to gay rights pressure in 1973, the American Psychiatric Association ended its classification of homosexuality as a mental disorder. In 1984, the United States Conference of Mayors called for legal protection of homosexual rights at all levels of government.

The growing toleration of gays in the United States and the gains made by the gay liberation movement did not end legal or political discrimination or physical attacks. The Reagan administration equated homosexuality with disease and denied entry into the United States to any "self-professed homosexuals." The New Right and Moral Majority campaigned actively against the rights of homosexuals. Evangelical minister Jerry Falwell called on his followers to "stop gays *dead* in their perverted tracks." And in 1986, Pope John Paul II instructed American bishops to stop supporting gay rights efforts and labeled homosexuality a "moral disorder." Although by 1986, twenty-six states had decriminalized sexual relationships between consenting adults, only seven states and about 110 communities by 1993 had prohibited social and economic discrimination against homosexuals. In the remaining forty-three, or under federal law, no legal recourse existed for those fired from their jobs because of their sexual preference.

As the 1992 presidential election neared, the majority of gays and lesbians supported the candidacy of Democrat Bill Clinton rather than that of Republican George Bush. Bush had gained some support from the gay community during his presidency because he increased funding for AIDS research and signed into law a bill calling for the study of **hate crimes**, including attacks on homosexuals. But in 1992, in response to the right wing of the Republican party, Bush backed away from gay rights. He opposed antidiscriminatory legislation for homosexuals and applauded when several speakers at the Republican National Convention attacked gays as being abnormal and immoral. In contrast, Clinton openly supported gay antidiscrimination legislation,

hate crime Crime motivated by racial, ethnic, or sexual prejudice.

Choosing an Independent Path

Sandra Day O'Connor

In September 1981, Sandra Day O'Connor became the first woman to be appointed to the Supreme Court. Appointed by President Ronald Reagan for her conservative views, she has steadily chosen her own course, defying easy categorization. The outcome has been her gravitation toward the center of judicial opinion. When asked how she would like to be remembered, she answered as "a good judge." Tom Zimberoff/Sygma.

On July 7, 1981, President Ronald Reagan announced that his choice to replace Supreme Court justice Potter Stewart was "a person for all seasons": Sandra Day O'Connor. The 102nd justice appointed to the Court, she was the first woman nominated and the first confirmed.

Reagan's choice drew conflicting responses. Many within the conservative wing of the Republican party bitterly objected to O'Connor. They reminded the president that she favored abortion rights and the Equal Rights Amendment. They pointed out that he had run on a platform promising that judges appointed by the Reagan administration would "respect family values and the sanctity of human life." Some liberals applauded Reagan for nominating a woman, but were nonetheless suspicious of any Reagan appointee. After all, O'Connor believed in judicial restraint, the idea that the Court should defer to Congress, the president, and public consensus to resolve controversial social and political questions.

The nomination was quickly approved by the Senate Judiciary Committee and confirmed by the Senate. On September 26, 1981, Sandra Day O'Connor became associate justice of the Supreme Court.

The daughter of an Arizona rancher, Sandra Day attended Stanford University, receiving a B.A. in economics and in 1952 a law degree. She graduated third in her law class, behind fellow Arizonian William Rehnquist, who by 1981 was

the right of homosexuals to be in the armed forces, and more funding to fight the AIDS epidemic.

The AIDS Controversy

The antigay opposition was strengthened not only by the Reagan administration's attitude but by a growing fear of **acquired immune deficiency syndrome (AIDS),** a disease that spread through a portion of the gay community and was at first regarded primarily as a "gay disease." Fear of AIDS was critical in a 1985 decision by Massachusetts voters to reject a homosexual bill of rights. Patrick Buchanan, conservative writer and Republican presidential

also an associate justice of the Supreme Court. In 1952 she married John O'Connor. Despite high graduating rank and a Stanford law degree, Sandra Day O'Connor had difficulty finding a job as an attorney with a private law firm. A company in Los Angeles offered her a legal secretary's position, which she declined. Unable to land a job with a private firm, she worked as a county deputy attorney in northern California while her husband finished his law degree at Stanford. After he had graduated and received his commission in the army, she resigned from her job and joined him in Frankfurt, Germany, where she worked as a civilian lawyer for the army.

In 1957 the O'Connors returned to the United States and settled in the Phoenix area. Two years later, following the birth of the first of three sons, Sandra Day O'Connor opened her own law firm with a friend. In 1960, when her second son was born, she stopped working to become a full-time mother. Doing volunteer work, she became active in Republican politics and served on a statewide committee on marriage and the family in 1965. That year, recognizing her skills as an organizer and a lawyer, the governor appointed her an assistant attorney general for Arizona. "I wanted a family and . . . I wanted to work," she recalled.

During her first five years on the Court, O'Connor most often voted with the conservative bloc but frequently issued an independent opinion. In her opinions, she chose to emphasize two recurring themes: her belief that states are equal partners with the national government within the federal system and that courts should not play an active role in shaping social and political values.

With the arrival of other justices appointed by Reagan and by George Bush, the Court in 1990 became more activist in the name of conservatism and rewrote several earlier liberal decisions. Conservatives hoped that the Court, with its conservative agenda, would move forward to reverse positions on abortion, separation of church and state, free speech, and affirmative action. As the Court became increasingly activist, Justice O'Connor's position shifted slightly away from the conservative bloc and toward the center. During the 1990–1991 session, she frequently was the swing vote in 5-to-4 decisions. One observer of the Court commented, "As O'Connor goes, so goes the Court."

By the end of the 1991–1992 session, she was regarded as a leading member of a centrist bloc, which also included justices Anthony Kennedy and David Souter. In perhaps the most controversial decision of the Court's calendar, *Planned Parenthood of Southeastern Pennsylvania v. Casey* (1992), she co-authored the majority decision, which reaffirmed the right of women to seek an abortion, while criticizing the constitutional argument in the *Roe v. Wade* decision. Writing for the majority, O'Connor explained her choice, "Some of us as individuals find abortion offensive to our most basic principles of morality, but that cannot control our decision. Our obligation is to define the liberty of all, not to mandate our own moral code."

As the Supreme Court enters a new era under the Clinton administration and with the appointment of the second woman justice—Ruth Bader Ginsburg—many observers expect the O'Connor center will be strengthened. But the same observers have difficulty predicting how O'Connor herself will vote, except to say that because of her open-minded conservative approach and lack of an overarching ideology that could predetermine her decision, she will continue to guide her choices in judging each case based on its own merits.

candidate in 1992, argued that homosexuals had violated nature and that AIDS was nature's way of getting even.

AIDS was first discovered in the United States in 1981. Within ten years, over 195,700 cases had been reported; over 97,000 Americans had died of the always fatal disease; and 1.5 million were estimated

acquired immune deficiency syndrome Gradual and eventually fatal breakdown of the immune system caused by the virus HIV; AIDS is transmitted by exchanging body fluids through means such as sex or blood transfusions.

Roe v. Wade

Justice Blackmun's Decision

In 1969, Norma McCorvey, a divorced high school dropout with a 5-year-old daughter, unsuccessfully sought an abortion in Texas. She gave birth to a daughter and gave her up for adoption. Working with lawyers Sarah Weddington and Linda Coffee to protect her identity, McCorvey became Jane Roe, and in a case against Henry Wade, the criminal district attorney for Dallas, Texas, she challenged the state's abortion law. A three-judge federal appeals district court listened to the arguments and found in favor of Roe: the Texas law was unconstitutional. Wade appealed to the Supreme Court, and on January 23, 1973, Justice Harry Blackmun handed down the majority decision that changed the nation's abortion laws.

The Texas statutes under attack here are typical of those that have been in effect in many States for approximately a century. . . .

We forthwith acknowledge our awareness of the sensitive and emotional nature of the abortion controversy, of the vigorous opposing views, even among physicians, and of the deep and seemingly absolute convictions that the subject inspires. . . . Our task . . . is to resolve the issue by constitutional measurement, free of emotion and of predilection.

The principal thrust of appellant's attack on the Texas statutes is that they improperly invade a right, said to be possessed by the pregnant woman, to choose to terminate her pregnancy. . . .

Three reasons have been advanced to explain historically the enactment of criminal abortion laws. . . . These laws . . . discourage illicit sexual conduct. . . . A second reason is concerned with abortion as a medical procedure. . . . A State's real concern . . . was to protect the pregnant woman, . . . to restrain her from submitting to a procedure that placed her life in serious jeopardy. . . . The third . . . is the State's interest . . . in protecting prenatal life. Some of the argument . . . rests on the theory that a new human life is present from the moment of conception. . . .

This right of privacy . . . is broad enough to encompass a woman's decision whether or not to terminate her pregnancy. The detriment that the State would impose upon the pregnant woman by denying this choice altogether is apparent. . . .

We, therefore, conclude that the right of personal privacy includes the abortion decision, but that this right is not unqualified and must be considered against important state interests in regulation. . . .

To summarize and to repeat:

1. A state criminal abortion statute of the current Texas type, that excepts from criminality only a *life-saving* procedure on behalf of the mother, without regard to pregnancy state and without recognition of the other interests involved, is violative of the Due Process Clause of the Fourteenth Amendment.

(a) For the stage prior to approximately the end of the first trimester, the abortion decision and its effectuation must be left to the medical judgment of the pregnant woman's attending physician.

(b) For the stage subsequent to approximately the end of the first trimester, the State, in promoting its interests in the health of the mother, may, if it chooses, regulate the abortion procedure in ways that are reasonably related to maternal health.

(c) For the stage subsequent to viability, the State in promoting its interest in the potentiality of human life may, if it chooses, regulate, and even proscribe, abortion except where it is necessary in appropriate medical judgment, for the preservation of the life or health of the mother. . . . *Roe v. Wade 410 U.S. 113, 93 S. Ct 705 (1973).*

Supporters Had This to Say

■ Abortion . . . has become a focal point for . . . conflict between the ethic of patriarchal authoritarianism and the ethic of courage. . . . Women are saying that because there is ambiguity surrounding the whole question and because a sexually hierarchial society is stacked against women, abortion is not appropriately a matter of criminal law. . . . Women—many of them victims also of economic and racial oppression—have just begun to cry out publicly about their rights over their own bodies. . . . Women are making explicit the dimension that traditional morality and abortion legislation simply have not taken into account: the reality of their existence as an oppressed caste of human beings. *Mary Daly*, Commonweal, *(February 4, 1972), 418–419.*

■ I think women who are young, and those not so young, today must be able to choose when to have a child, given the necessities of their jobs. They will indeed join their mothers, who remember the humiliations and the dangers of back-street butcher abortions, in a march of millions to save the right of legal abortions. *Betty Friedan*, New York Times Magazine, *Nov 3, 1985.*

■ When the day comes that the decision to bear a child for all women is a moral choice . . . then and only then, the human liberation of women will be a reality. *Beverly Wildung Harrison*, Our Right to Choose *(1983).*

Opponents Had This to Say

■ In his dissent, Justice William Rehnquist wrote the following:

I have difficulty in concluding . . . that the right of 'privacy' is involved in this case.

The decision here to break pregnancy into three distinct terms and to outline the permissible restrictions that State may impose in each one . . . partakes more of judicial legislation than it does of a determination of the intent of the drafters of the Fourteenth Amendment.

The fact that a majority of States . . . have had restrictions on abortion for at least a century is a strong indication . . . that the asserted right to an abortion is not so rooted in the traditions and conscience of our people as to be ranked as fundamental.

To reach its result, the Court necessarily has had to find within the scope of the Fourteenth Amendment a right that was apparently completely unknown to the drafters of the Amendment. *Roe v. Wade, 410 U.S. 113, 93 S. Ct 705 (1973).*

■ We stand in danger of becoming an abortion culture—one which . . . sanctions . . . death . . . for the convenience of the ruling class. An abortion culture is built on individualism, the rights of the strongest individuals to thrive. *Editorial from* Commonweal *(February 16, 1973), 435–436.*

◆ In 1987, the San Francisco-based Names Project started to make quilts in remembrance of those who had died of AIDS. In 1992, the quilt, containing twenty-six thousand names and covering over fifteen acres, was displayed before the Capitol. Even though the quilt made a strong impact, it still represented only one-sixth of those who had died of the disease. *Matt Herron.*

to be infected by HIV (human immunodeficiency virus), the virus that causes AIDS. Initially, because the majority of those with the illness were either homosexuals or intravenous drug users, official and public response to the disease was restrained. But as the number of AIDS victims increased and included more and more non-drug-using heterosexuals, research and educational efforts were expanded and given national coverage.

As public knowledge and fear of AIDS increased, controversy flared about the best means to prevent the spread of disease and soon became part of the political battle over values. Claiming to be "realists," many recommended "safe sex," emphasizing the use of condoms as a means to reduce the possibility of getting the disease. Television ads used prominent movie and sports figures to advocate the use of condoms, especially by teens, a high-risk population. Some advocated that high schools provide students with free condoms and information about AIDS and other sexually transmitted diseases. Others disagreed. They argued that free condoms would encourage sexual activity; and they promoted abstinence, fidelity in marriage, and traditional moral values as the only behavior that would prevent AIDS.

Contributing to the public's awareness of the threat of AIDS were revelations by Earvin "Magic" Johnson and Arthur Ashe, two well-known and respected athletes, that they had tested positive for the HIV virus. Ashe—one-time U.S. Open tennis champion—contracted the disease from HIV-infected blood during a heart bypass operation. Johnson—a world and Olympic champion basketball player—caught the disease through heterosexual activity.

Johnson admitted being "naive" about AIDS and told the public, "Here I am saying it can happen to anybody." Both men became spokesmen for AIDS research and prevention. In 1991, President Bush appointed Johnson to the National Commission on AIDS. A year later, Johnson publicly resigned from the commission in disagreement over its policy. "I cannot in good conscience continue to serve on a commission whose important work is so utterly ignored," he told Bush and the public.

Poverty and Race

● What constraints and choices do new immigrants and minorities face in seeking to find social and economic equality?

Gender and family values were not the only issues that tore at the fabric of American society. Other, older issues related to poverty, race, and ethnicity—prejudice, discrimination, equality—continued to divide American society.

Racial and Economic Frustrations

By the 1970s, a majority of African-Americans were experiencing decreasing opportunities and continuing white hostility—despite some noticeable economic, social, and political gains, especially by middle-class African-Americans. An economic window of opportunity was closing, and the widespread support for civil rights generated by the post–World War II economic boom and the civil rights movement was ending. New groups and issues—women, Latinos, gays, Asian immigrants—were competing for government programs and support, and a sluggish economy and reduced government spending combined to limit opportunities and increase competition and prejudice. An increasing number of white Americans, reacting to urban riots, cries for Black Power, and what they saw as special treatment of minorities at the expense of the white majority, believed that most minorities no longer needed special programs. **Affirmative action** and busing to achieve school integration came under fire by many white Americans.

Despite opposition from the Nixon White House, the Supreme Court in 1971 reaffirmed the use of busing to achieve racial integration of public schools. The decision was resisted not only in the South but in many communities across the nation (see page 959).

In Boston, a 1974 court order to use busing to integrate city schools brought not only loud protests from politicians but also violence and the movement of whites out of the city. Buses carrying African-American students into South Boston were pelted with rocks. Eventually, over twenty thousand white students left the public schools, and African-American and Latino students were in the majority in the system by 1976.

Throughout the 1980s and into the 1990s, busing for integration continued to be a point of contention between liberals and conservatives. Opponents of busing applauded the Reagan and Bush administrations as they backed away from court-ordered busing. "We aren't going to compel children who don't want to have an integrated education to have one," said one Reagan official in the Justice Department's division on civil rights. By 1992, five conservative justices appointed by Reagan and Bush were serving on the Supreme Court and the Bush administration was siding with antibusing forces. In a case involving DeKalb County, Georgia, the Supreme Court declared in 1992 that busing should not be used to integrate schools segregated by de facto housing patterns.

Affirmative action also came under increasing attacks during the 1970s and 1980s. By the late 1960s, as the economy slowed, a growing number of middle-class and blue-collar whites believed that affirmative action programs limited their job and educational opportunities and constituted preferential treatment for minorities and **reverse discrimination.**

Believing himself a victim of reverse discrimination, Allan Bakke sued the University of California system. Bakke claimed that the School of Medicine at the University of California at Davis had accepted black students less qualified than he and had denied him admission because of his color—white. In 1978, in *Regents of the University of California v. Bakke,* the Supreme Court decided in Bakke's favor and ruled that the university should admit him to the medical school. The Court did not totally reject color and gender as considerations for hiring, but the *Bakke* decision weakened support for affirmative action. The retreat from affirmative action continued during the 1980s as the Reagan administration actively opposed affirmative action and **racial quotas,** calling them a "racial spoils system."

Amid the decline in society's and the government's support for civil rights and pluralism, racial discrimination and violence increased. White Power groups became more visible and violent. Hate crimes, including physical attacks on African-Americans and gays, became more common. The Aryan Nation, the Ku Klux Klan, and other groups held rallies to promote "white rights" and proclaim their hatred of blacks, Latinos, gays, Asians, feminists, and others they said threatened white civilization. Between 1980 and 1986, according to Justice Department estimates, racist attacks jumped from less than a hundred to more than 270 a year.

One such attack took place in 1986 at Howard Beach, in the Queens section of New York City. Three African-American youths who wandered into the predominately white neighborhood after their car broke down were severely beaten by a group of white teens. "We own the turf," one white boy bragged. Michael Griffith escaped from the beating but, while running from the whites, was struck by a car and died. A year later, three of the white youths were convicted of manslaughter.

A more violent expression of racial and economic frustration occurred in April 1992 in south-central Los Angeles. For five days African-Americans and Latinos rioted over the acquittal of three white Los Angeles policemen accused of excessive violence (one policeman was found guilty) in the beating of

---

affirmative action   Policy that seeks to redress past discrimination through active measures to ensure equal opportunity, especially in education and employment.

reverse discrimination   Discrimination against members of a dominant group; it results from policies established to correct discrimination against members of minority groups.

racial quota   An allotment based on race.

♦ After the death of Martin Luther King, Jr., Reverend Jessie Jackson emerged as one of the nation's most prominent African-American leaders. He heads the Rainbow Coalition, an anti-poverty organization, and sought the presidency on the Democratic ticket in 1984 and in 1988. Here he speaks to students of Manual Arts High School in South Central Los Angeles just prior to the riots sparked by the decision handed down in the Rodney King civil rights trial. *UPI/Bettmann Archives.*

Rodney King, an African-American, a year earlier. Caught on videotape by an eyewitness, four policemen had clubbed, kicked, and beaten King into submission. For many African-Americans the policemen's actions were simply further proof of white and especially police racism. When an all-white jury returned the verdict, mobs of African-Americans and Latinos took to the streets. They set fires and looted businesses, many belonging to Korean merchants who they believed had been overcharging them. The outcome of the riot was the death of sixty people and over $850 million in damages.

New Immigrants

As American society became less tolerant and government less supportive of social programs, a new wave of immigrants from Asia, Latin America, and the Caribbean arrived. Legally allowed to enter the United States by the Immigration Act of 1965, Asians by 1990 represented only 3 percent of the American population, but their numbers were growing fast—doubling during the 1980s. Most came as families and tended to cluster in ethnic communi-

ties. Some were highly educated, had marketable skills, and found economic success as engineers, medical professionals, and owners of small businesses. Chang-Lin Tien was such a success. Born in China, he became a professor of mechanical engineering and eventually chancellor of the University of California at Berkeley in 1990.

The success of Asian-Americans—they are among the nation's most prosperous and best-educated minority (19.7 percent of the Harvard 1991 freshman class)—has caused them to be classified as a "model minority." But this stereotype ignores many, including many from what once was Indochina, who arrive with few possessions, little education, and few skills, are mired in poverty, and have great difficulty assimilating into American society. The model-minority stereotype, many Asian-Americans charge, provides a rationale for denying access to special programs and aid that benefit other immigrants and minorities. Some Asian-American students believe that many universities, under pressure from whites and from non-Asian minority groups, have established quotas to limit the admission of Asians to professional and graduate programs. Many Korean and other Asian-American store owners, especially in the inner city, say that their success has increased hostility among Latinos and African-Americans. Many of the stores looted and set afire during the 1992 Los Angeles riot were owned by Asians. Despite Asians' success and assimilation into American society, concluded one Asian-American activist, "there is a stereotype that Asians are foreigners even though they've been here for many generations."

Immigrants from Latin America, the Caribbean, and Mexico also faced negative stereotypes as they entered the country. A 1991 Gallup poll found that 64 percent of Americans favored limits on immigration and 69 percent believed that there were too many Latinos in the country. Another public opinion poll indicated that old stereotypes of Latinos as "lazy" and "unpatriotic" were still held by the non-Latino population. Prejudice and the lack of unskilled jobs keep Latinos at the bottom of the economic and social ladder. "There is a growing schism between poor Latinos, on the one hand, and middle-class Latinos on the others," noted one Latino leader.

> **Rodney King** African-American whose beating by Los Angeles police officers was captured on videotape; the acquittal of the officers in 1992 triggered rioting in which sixty people were killed.

♦ In many cities, as the economy slowed and the vitality of inner cities collapsed, the lack of jobs, services, and choices have contributed to increasingly unsafe neighborhoods, where drugs, youth gangs, and violence, including homicide, are commonly found. Commenting on the relationship between opportunities and gang membership, a Chicago criminologist explained, "They've got turf. That's all they've got." *Steve Liss, TIME Magazine © Time Warner.*

Despite families working two and three jobs, he concluded, "the ladder isn't there" for newer immigrants and other poor Latinos.

Adding to the overall rate of poverty and hostility faced by Latinos is the issue of illegal immigration, primarily from Mexico. In 1986, trying to stem the flow of illegal immigrants into the United States, the **Immigration Reform and Control Act** outlawed the hiring of illegal aliens and strengthened controls to prevent illegal entry into the United States. The act also offered amnesty to illegal aliens who could provide documented proof that they had been in the United States before January 1, 1982. The law, however, did little to reduce the number of Mexicans and other Latin Americans trying to enter the United States, most of them seeking jobs.

The Urban Crisis

Hostile whites and declining support for civil rights were not the only problems that minorities faced. Throughout the 1970s and 1980s a stagnant and shifting economy deepened poverty and heightened racial and ethnic tension, especially in the nation's cities. It was in the inner cities that the new immigrants competed with other poor Americans for fewer and fewer jobs and resources. One sociologist warned that to say immigrants and the poor will

"make their way—as they always have—is no longer tenable. The soup is getting watered down."

The Reagan years provided mixed economic results for the nation. Among the economic winners were defense industries and new corporations connected to computer, electronic, and the healthcare industries. Some Americans enjoyed wider economic opportunities, higher incomes, and a rising standard of living. The majority, however, believed that their slice of the economic pie was dwindling. Industrial jobs that paid high wages and provided retirement and medical benefits were declining, and service and part-time jobs that paid low wages and provided almost no benefits were increasing.

Half of the new jobs created in 1980s paid less than $12,675 a year—the government-set poverty level for a family of four—although an estimated 31.5 million (12.8 percent of the population) lived in poverty. For minorities the economic facts were worse. African-Americans represented 30 percent, Latinos 26 percent, and whites 10 percent of those existing below the poverty line. As job opportunities shrank in the inner cities, African-Americans and other minorities increasingly relied on welfare, especially Aid to Families with Dependent Children (AFDC), and on the drug economy in order to exist.

Also noticeable among the statistics of impoverished Americans was the number of households headed by women and the number of single mothers. One outcome of changes in the attitudes of women and society toward divorce, parenting, and sex was that in the early 1990s an estimated 31.1 percent of women who were heads of households lived in poverty. The poverty rate among single parents or African-Americans was about 10 percent higher.

Contributing to what some have described as the "feminization of poverty" was the continuing gap between men's income and women's income. In 1992, women working full-time earned on average 76 cents for every dollar earned by men. Also contributing to the impoverishment of women were new trends in divorce settlements, which reduced the amount of economic support provided by former husbands. Awards of alimony became less frequent. And child support payments, when ordered,

> **Immigration Reform and Control Act**   Law, passed by Congress in 1986, that prohibits the hiring of illegal aliens and offered amnesty and legal residence to any who could prove they had entered the country before January 1, 1982.

were likely to be too small to be of much help. Also the enforcement of child support orders was lax. In 1990, for example, over a fourth of spouses, mostly men, who owed child support paid nothing.

Poverty was widespread, but was most noticeable in urban areas, where competition for diminishing goods and services led to increases in social violence and tension. Throughout the 1970s and 1980s, cities continued to undergo population shifts. People who could do so—including many middle-class African-Americans, Latinos, and other minorities—moved to more affluent and safer suburban, integrated neighborhoods. Those left behind not only were poor but faced increasing decay and violence, for police forces and social safety nets were shrinking. The departure of business and industry from the inner cities also shrank the urban **tax base** and eliminated jobs. Jobs that paid more than the minimum wage were replaced with lower-paying service and part-time jobs. Feeling the effects of shrinking tax revenues and reductions in support from the state and federal government, social agencies and programs to aid the inner-city poor faced higher costs and greater responsibilities. Between 1978 and 1990 federal support for low-income housing fell from over $32 billion to less than $10 billion. And between 1970 and 1992, the purchasing power of AFDC benefits declined 42 percent.

Every American city seemed to have increasing numbers of homeless people. Their presence overwhelmed private and public efforts to provide housing, food, and basic services. By 1987, there were at least half a million homeless. They were a cross section of the nation's poor: 46 percent single men, 36 percent families with children, 14 percent single women, 4 percent unaccompanied children. Fifty-one percent were African-American, 35 percent white. An estimated 40 percent suffered from serious mental illness.

For the homeless and for others living in America's cities, high unemployment, reduced social programs, racism, drugs, and crime produced frustration and despair. Half of black schoolchildren never finished high school, urban African-American unemployment hovered around 60 percent, and the leading cause of death for black males under the age of 35 was murder.

Chicago's largest housing project, Robert Taylor Homes, provides an example of the destructive nature of inner-city life. In 1984, the Robert Taylor project had a population of more than 26,000 people, an average family income of less than $5,000 a year, and an unemployment rate of nearly 47 percent.

Nearly 90 percent of Robert Taylor families were headed by a woman. Within the project, nearly 10 percent of Chicago's murders, rapes, and aggravated assaults took place. In such an environment, the chances for normal development are small, and the lure of crime is high.

For some urban youths, one way to escape poverty and a feeling of isolation and quickly gain riches and power was to join a gang and turn to crime, especially drug selling. In 1980, only ten cities had serious gang problems. By 1990, the number of cities with gang-related problems was 125 and growing. What accounts for the rapid increase in gangs and gang members? Lack of jobs and community programs and the expansion of the drug trade, especially the selling of **crack cocaine,** are major factors. One expert on gangs noted that "gangs don't have membership drives" and that "kids drift toward gangs . . . where there are no programs." Turning to the streets for recreation, identity, and jobs, children under the age of 10 earn hundreds of dollars a day standing lookout, and older dealers, from 10-upward, can make thousands of dollars a day selling drugs.

As violence increased and buildings deteriorated, sections of many major cities and many inner-city schools took on the appearance of war zones. By 1991, a fourth of all urban school districts had installed metal detectors to try to prevent students from bringing weapons to school. Outside and inside schools, in disputes over drug deals, over turf, and over the wearing of the wrong "colors," gang-related murders mushroomed. Constrained by shrinking resources, police and community groups became less and less effective against the growing crime and violence. The police complained about legal restrictions on their activities, supported gun control measures, and joined with the public to press for harsher penalties for people involved in crime and especially for those connected with the drug trade.

Responding to public concerns, Reagan and Bush announced a war on drugs and made support for law enforcement a special priority. By 1987, federal authorities were spending nearly $15 billion per year to reduce the flow of drugs into the United

---

tax base   Sources of tax revenue available to a government.

crack cocaine   Highly potent form of cocaine that is smoked through a glass pipe and is extremely addictive.

States and to identify and arrest not only drug dealers but users. Many companies, government agencies, and even schools instituted compulsory or voluntary drug testing to detect drug users. Arrested drug dealers seemed to fill jails to overflowing. As the 1990s began, official figures showed some progress. The total amount of drug use was down—especially casual use by the middle class. Yet the official figures also indicated that the actual availability of illegal drugs stayed fairly constant, even after the U.S. invasion of Panama in 1989 (see page 1016).

Despite some signs of declining drug use and the high visibility of the Reagan-Bush war on drugs, critics argued that the best way to eliminate the flow of drugs into the United States was to confront the social, economic, and psychological problems that caused people to turn to drugs. They argued that more funds needed to be spent on education instead of on interdiction and that more effort was needed to deal with the underlying causes of drug use and sales, especially in the inner cities among minorities.

After leaving office, C. Everett Koop, Reagan's surgeon general, remarked that when he looked back, "the things I banged my head against were all poverty." Many liberals and social activists argued that eliminating poverty would eventually solve most of the nation's social problems. Conservatives, however, disagreed. They contended that the cause of poverty and other social problems was not a lack of opportunity but the "tradition" of the "free ride" of welfare. Conservatives asserted that the liberal welfare system had spawned an "epidemic of family breakdown" that destroyed traditional family values and the value of work and encouraged people not to work and women to become "welfare mothers." "Why experiment with new anti-poverty programs," asked Kate O'Beirne of the conservative Heritage Foundation, "when the most important indicator of poverty is whether there are two parents at home?"

Bush and a New International Order

- What new foreign policy choices does the United States face as a result of the collapse of the Soviet Union?
- How did economic and social problems constrain and shape American politics for President Bush?

"It's not been a great year," Nancy Reagan said about 1987. Despite the apparent thaw in the Cold War, for the first time in the Reagan administration, a combination of events had dented the image of Reagan and Republican leadership. The stock market collapse in October and the Iran-Contra revelations (see pages 984 and 990) created the impression that the administration was not in control of events or of itself and that the president had little grasp of what was happening. Suddenly, the popularity ratings of the "Teflon President" were lower than usual. Republicans, however, were not overly concerned and expected the conservative Reagan agenda to continue to attract voters, defeat Democrats, and strengthen the nation.

Bush Assumes Office

As Republicans got ready for the 1988 election, the torch of Reaganism seemed likely to be passed on to Reagan's vice president, **George Bush.** Bush had devoted many years to public service and had held several important posts under presidents Nixon and Ford: ambassador to the United Nations, chairman of the Republican National Committee, ambassador to China, and director of the Central Intelligence Agency. During World War II, he had been a fighter pilot and was awarded the Distinguished Flying Cross.

Bush won most of the Republican primaries, easily shaking off challenges from Senator Robert Dole of Kansas and televangelist Marion (Pat) Robertson. Dole and Robertson, but especially Robertson, claimed that Bush was not a true Reagan, New Right conservative and that they would do a better job than he of continuing Reagan's domestic and social policies. After gaining the Republican nomination, in an effort to ensure active New Right support, Bush shocked the nation by selecting as his running mate a young, conservative, and virtually unknown Indiana senator, J. Danforth Quayle.

Several contenders jumped into the race for the Democratic presidential nomination, eager to confront Bush, whom they considered a faint shadow of Reagan. Repeat candidates Gary Hart and Jesse Jackson (see page 985), along with first-timers Governor Michael Dukakis of Massachusetts and Delaware senator Joseph R. Biden seemed the strongest contenders. "Character" questions forced Hart and Biden to withdraw from the race; Jackson stayed in

> **George Bush** Politician and diplomat who was vice president under Ronald Reagan and was later elected president of the United States.

George Bush for President

Paid for by George Bush for President
733 15th Street, N.W. • Suite 800 • Washington, D.C. 20005 • (202) 842-1988

♦ In 1988 and again in 1992, the Republican ticket of Bush and Quayle emphasized traditional family values as a cure for many of the social problems the nation faced. In this picture, President Bush poses with his family in front of their estate in Kennebunkport, Maine. *Collection of David J. and Janet L. Frent.*

the race, attracting support especially among minorities. Dukakis pulled steadily ahead in the delegate count, and by the time of the Democratic National Convention he was the only viable candidate. Once nominated, Dukakis, who had no national political experience, selected long-time senator Lloyd Bentsen of Texas as his running mate.

The 1988 campaign, dominated by television commercials, was dull. Both candidates lacked flair and style and were unable to energize the voters. Dukakis ignored most social and international issues and focused on his personal integrity and success in revitalizing the economy of Massachusetts. Bush fought to overcome the so-called wimp factor—suggestions by Democrats and some Republicans that he was not a strong leader. Proclaiming his patriotism and pointing to his years of experience, Bush promised to fight drugs and crime, to take special interest in education and the environment, and not to raise taxes. "Read my lips, no new taxes," he said.

The war of television commercials concentrated on **negative campaigning,** which aimed at discrediting the opponent rather than addressing issues and policies. Republican ads were very effective and put Dukakis on the defensive. One focused on Willie Horton, an African-American convicted of murder and imprisoned in Massachusetts, Dukakis's home state. While out of prison on a weekend pass, Horton had raped a white woman. Lee Atwater, Bush's campaign manager, said that by the time he was through running the Horton ad, the public would believe that Horton was Dukakis's running mate.

By November, Republican negative campaigning, falling unemployment and inflation, and im-

proved relations with the Soviet Union placed Bush ahead in the opinion polls. He won election easily, with 79.2 percent of the electoral vote and 54 percent of the popular vote, and became the first sitting vice president to be elected president since Martin Van Buren in 1836. Although Bush trounced Dukakis, the victory was not as sweet as Bush hoped it would be. His **political coattails** and conservative issues seemed to have little effect. The Democrats were the majority party in both houses of Congress.

Bush announced that he wanted to concentrate on domestic problems, but his own preferences and international events dictated that foreign affairs would consume most of his attention. The world was changing rapidly, and Bush considered the management of international relations to be one of his strengths. "Watch and learn, maybe I'll turn out to be a Teddy Roosevelt," he told a friend.

Bush thought that his view of the world was realistic. He was inclined to focus on immediate problems and base solutions on rigorous evaluations of needs and resources. Secretary of State James Baker III, a close friend of Bush and a Washington insider, shared the president's approach to foreign policy. He too preferred to tackle problems at hand rather than speculate about problems over the horizon.

negative campaigning Presenting a political opponent as weak, dishonest, or untrustworthy instead of addressing basic political issues.

political coattails The result of voters casting their votes for all members of a political party based on voting for one particular member, generally the highest ranking candidate on the ticket.

The difficulty for both men was that the most pressing international problem was both short- and long-term. The end of the Cold War and the seeming collapse of communism in Eastern Europe and in the Soviet Union required the formulation of short- and long-term policies.

The Winds of Democracy

The Communist world from Nicaragua to China was being torn apart by political and economic changes. Within the Soviet Union, Mikhail Gorbachev's policies of glasnost and perestroika (see page 992) were producing political and religious freedom, reducing censorship and repression, and starting the privatization of business and the development of a capitalist-style economy. Soviet armed forces were being withdrawn from Afghanistan and Eastern Europe (see Map 32.1).

The Bush administration cautiously voiced support for Gorbachev's efforts, and in December 1989 Bush met with Gorbachev on the island of Malta in the Mediterranean Sea. Gorbachev declared that the Cold War was over. Bush more prudently stated that they were working toward "a lasting peace." Later, Gorbachev visited Washington and signed agreements to improve trade and reduce chemical weapons and the size of conventional and nuclear arsenals. He was cheered in the United States and around the world, but at home his popularity fell as the Soviet economy continued its downward spiral and as divisions among the Soviet Union's nationalities intensified. Attacked by people wanting more reform and by hard-line Communists who feared any reform, Gorbachev asked the United States, Japan, and Western Europe to provide economic support to prevent "chaos and civil wars" in the Soviet Union.

Unable to slow the rush toward reform, the hardliners on August 19, 1991, attempted a coup. They confined Gorbachev and his family in his vacation home along the Black Sea. Declaring a state of emergency, the coup leaders outlawed all political parties. In Moscow, **Boris Yeltsin,** leader of the Russian Republic, declared the coup illegal and called on the Russian people to resist. Over 150,000 Muscovites surrounded the Russian parliament building to defend Yeltsin and reform. Faced with popular opposition in Moscow and other cities, the coup collapsed within seventy-two hours. Released from captivity, Gorbachev announced that he was again in control of the Soviet Union, but he was commanding a sinking ship of state.

By 1992, there was no Soviet Union to command. All that remained of the Soviet Union was a weak federation, the **Commonwealth of Independent States.** Power rested not with Gorbachev, who soon retired from office, but with the independent republics and especially with Yeltsin, the president of the Russian Republic.

The collapse of the Soviet Union both simplified and complicated U.S. foreign and military policies. The threat of war with the Soviet Union was gone, but the new relationship between the United States and the former Soviet Union was not yet determined. Bush recognized the independent republics and Yeltsin as the spokesman for the Russian Republic and for the Commonwealth. In June 1992, Yeltsin visited Washington to ask for American and Western economic support. He also announced that Russia was ready to eliminate nearly all of its land-based strategic missiles but could not speak for the other republics. Bush embraced Yeltsin, applauded his arms reduction proposal, promised increased economic support, and hoped that Yeltsin could bring some stability to what had once been the Soviet Union.

Yeltsin, however, could barely provide stability for Russia, let alone end the civil wars that had broken out among religious and ethnic groups throughout the Commonwealth of Independent States. Within Russia, Yeltsin used military force to remove his political opponents from the Russian parliament building in October 1993. By then, Bill Clinton was president, but American policy was still on the path established by Bush. The United States backed Yeltsin in the hope that he could provide stability and democracy.

Even before the Soviet Union collapsed, communism was in retreat throughout Eastern Europe. In December 1988, Gorbachev announced that the Soviet Union would no longer intervene to prevent political opposition in Eastern Europe. Within a year, Poland had a new constitution, a free-market economy, and a non-Communist government. In 1989,

---

Boris Yeltsin   Russian parliamentary leader who was elected president of the new Russian Republic in 1991 and promised increased democratic and economic reforms.

Commonwealth of Independent States   Weak federation of the former Soviet republics replaced the Soviet Union in 1992 and soon gave way to total independence of the member countries.

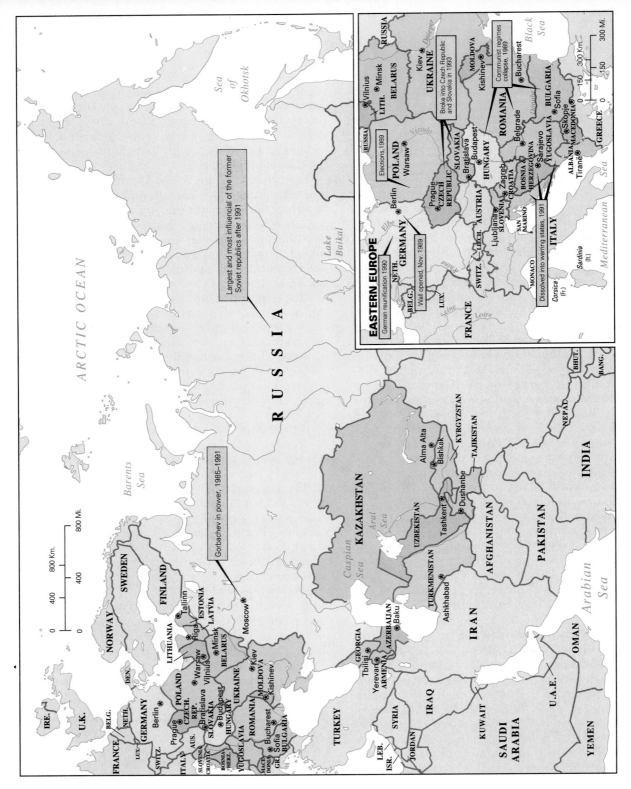

◆ MAP 32.1 The Fall of Communism As the Soviet Union collapsed and lost its control over the countries of Eastern Europe, the map of Eastern Europe and Central Asia changed. The Soviet Union disappeared into history, replaced by fifteen new national units. In Eastern Europe, West and East Germany merged, Czechoslovakia divided into two nations, and Yugoslavia broke into five feuding states.

◆ After the Soviet Union's collapse, Boris Yeltsin, the president of the Russian Republic, emerges as the ex-Soviet Union's most powerful leader. In June 1992, President Bush met with Yeltsin. Giving his characteristic "thumbs-up" sign, Bush remarked that their meeting began "a new era" in post–Cold War, East–West relations. *UPI/Bettmann Archives.*

workers in Berlin tore down the **Berlin Wall.** As the wall crumbled, so too did the Communist governments of East Germany, Hungary, Bulgaria, Czechoslovakia, and Rumania. By the end of 1990, a unified Germany existed, and the Baltic states—Latvia, Estonia, and Lithuania—had declared their independence from the Soviet Union.

The Bush administration applauded the changes, hoping that they would generate free market economies and stable and democratic governments. In some nations there was peaceful movement toward both; in others there was increased regional and ethnic conflict. Yugoslavia collapsed in 1991, and its major ethnic groups began a series of brutal and bloody conflicts in an effort to carve out individual republics and autonomous regions. By 1994 over a hundred thousand people had died, many of them in **Bosnia,** where Muslims fought better-armed Christian Serbs and Croats who were trying to dismember the Bosnian republic. The United States joined with European and United Nations agencies to provide humanitarian aid for Bosnia and to encourage an end to the carnage, but with little success.

The breeze of democracy was not limited to Eastern Europe or Communist countries. In the People's Republic of China, in Central America, and in South Africa similar movements were taking place.

Chinese university students sought an end to the authoritarian policies of Deng Xiaoping. Prodemocracy protesters took to the streets in Beijing and other Chinese cities, demanding political, economic, and civil freedoms. They filled the massive expanse of **Tiananmen Square** in Beijing, erecting a "Goddess of Liberty" statue that looked like the Statue of Liberty. Rather than relinquishing power, however, on June 4, 1989, China's leaders resorted to force. Police and army forces brutally cleared the square and arrested many leaders of the democracy movement. Thousands were killed or injured as the movement for democracy across China was crushed. President Bush condemned the violent repression but resisted demands for sanctions against China. He argued that harsh action toward China would further isolate the Chinese leadership and make it even more brutal.

Although Bush's policy toward China stirred criticism, his policies toward South Africa and Central America drew praise for supporting democratic change. In South Africa the goal was to end **apartheid** and encourage the all-white South African government to share political power with black South Africans. In 1988, after South African President P. W. Botha brutally repressed anti-apartheid demonstrations, Congress, over Reagan's veto, had instituted **economic sanctions.** As president, Bush supported the sanctions and applauded the willingness of South Africa's new president, F. W. de Klerk, to work with Nelson Mandela and other black Africans to end apartheid. As progress was made ending apartheid and establishing a mul-

---

Berlin Wall   Wall that the Communist East German government built in 1961 to divide East and West Berlin; it was torn down in 1989 as the Cold War ended.

Bosnia   Region of the former Yugoslavia; its major city is Sarajevo.

Tiananmen Square   City square in Beijing where army forces attacked student protesters in 1989, crushing the pro–democracy movement in China.

apartheid   Official policy of racial segregation in South Africa; its outcome was political, legal, and economic discrimination against blacks and other people of color.

economic sanctions   Trade restrictions that several nations acting together impose on a country that has violated international law.

tiracial political system in South Africa, the sanctions were lifted. In 1993, Mandela and de Klerk were awarded the Nobel Peace Prize, and in April 1994 South Africa held its first multiracial free elections, electing Mandela president.

In Central America, Bush broke with Reagan's policies (see page 990) by reducing aid to the Contras and encouraging negotiations that would end the brutal fighting in Nicaragua and El Salvador (see Map 31.3). His actions contributed to the acceptance of the **Contadora Plan,** a formula for peace in Nicaragua negotiated by a coalition of Central American nations. The Contras agreed to halt their military operations, and the Ortega government initiated political and civil reforms and held free elections. In the February 1990 Nicaraguan elections, opposition candidate Violeta de Chamorro defeated Daniel Ortega. Although friction and occasional confrontation between Sandinista and Contra supporters continued, the peaceful change in government effectively ended a bitter struggle that had destroyed the economy and killed over thirty thousand people.

In El Salvador, American-supported peace negotiations also ended a civil war. Antigovernment rebels agreed to a cease-fire and to participate in future elections. Bush proudly boasted that American efforts in both El Salvador and Nicaragua helped to produce more democratic governments.

Protecting American Interests Abroad

By mid-1991, almost everyone agreed that the Cold War was over. The Soviet Union and Soviet communism had collapsed. The United States stood alone as the sole superpower. Liberals and many moderate Democrats called for a "peace dividend," monies taken from the military budget and allocated for social programs. But Bush resisted any reductions in America's global responsibilities and any sizable cuts in the military budget. The world was still a dangerous place, he warned, and needed the military and economic strength of the United States. A civil war in what had been Yugoslavia, Third World nations mired in poverty, ongoing tensions in the Middle East, and the daily flow of illegal drugs into the United States, all demanded a strong, activist U.S. foreign policy.

Bush had made drugs a key issue during his presidential campaign and had promised a crackdown on the flow of drugs into the United States. The majority of the public applauded the president's tough

talk against the gangsters who poured poison into American society and cheered when Bush ordered American forces into Panama in December 1989 to arrest Panamanian dictator **Manuel Noriega** on drug-related charges. Once praised by Reagan and Bush, General Noriega by 1988 was an embarrassment. Implicated in the torture and murder of his political enemies, he was actively involved in the transshipment of Colombian drugs to the United States. Claiming that Noriega was guilty of drug trafficking and that the United States had the right to arrest him, Bush ordered American forces to invade Panama in Operation Just Cause.

Within seventy-two hours, American forces were in charge of the country and had Noriega surrounded in the Vatican embassy. American casualties were light (only twenty-three had lost their lives). The number of Panamanians who died exceeded three thousand, almost all civilians. Noriega surrendered on January 10, 1989, was found guilty in a Miami courtroom of drug-related offenses, and was sentenced to prison in 1992.

Little changed in Panama, however. It remained a major route in the smuggling of drugs into the United States. And some American officials charged that members of the Panamanian government were still deeply involved.

General Noriega represented a minor threat to American interests. By the fall of 1990, however, President Bush faced a much more serious threat from **Saddam Hussein,** the authoritarian ruler of Iraq. Hussein claimed that the oil-rich sheikdom of Kuwait was waging economic war against Iraq and that the annexation of Kuwait was necessary for Iraqi security (see Map 32.2). Kuwait was a friendly supplier of oil to the United States, Japan, and Europe. And for years Iraq had been receiving economic and military aid from the United States as a counterweight against neighboring Iran. Believing the United States would not intervene, Hussein invaded and quickly overran Kuwait in early August 1990.

Contadora Plan   Pact signed by the presidents of five Central American nations in 1987; it called for cease-fires in conflicts in the region and for democratic reforms.

Manuel Noriega   Panamanian dictator who was captured by U.S. invasion forces in 1989 and taken to the United States to be tried for drug trafficking.

Saddam Hussein   Iraqi ruler who annexed Kuwait in 1990, triggering the Gulf War.

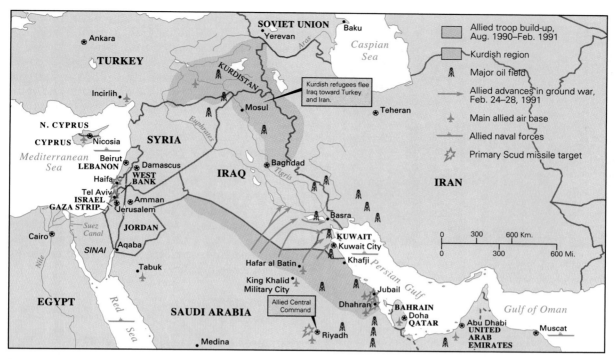

♦ **MAP 32.2 The Gulf War** On August 2, 1990, Iraq invaded Kuwait, threatening Saudi Arabia and the Persian Gulf region. In response, the United States and other nations formed an international coalition to restore Kuwaiti independence. In January 1991, the coalition forces of Operation Desert Storm began to attack the forces of Saddam Hussein. The outcome was the destruction of most of the Iraqi army and Kuwait liberation, but Saddam Hussein maintained control of Iraq.

Many worried that Hussein intended to control the Persian Gulf region's oilfields and thus gain control of over 40 percent of the world's supply of oil. Within hours of the invasion, Bush warned, "This [action] will not stand," and he organized the United Nations response. A multinational force of over 700,000, including 500,000 Americans, was sent to Saudi Arabia to protect Saudi Arabia and to convince Iraq to withdraw from Kuwait. Nearly 80 percent of the American public supported Operation Desert Shield to protect Saudi Arabia, but at first only a minority approved invading Iraq or Kuwait to restore the status quo.

Many Americans, including most congressional Democrats, believed that the economic sanctions imposed by the United Nations were the best means to force Iraq to leave Kuwait. Bush, however, concluded that the sanctions were ineffective, and he worked within the United Nations to set a deadline of January 15, 1991, for Iraqi withdrawal from Kuwait. As the deadline approached, many Americans worried that a long, Vietnam-like struggle faced the United States even though Bush confidently promised a short and successful war.

Eighteen hours after the deadline expired, Iraq had made no move to withdraw from Kuwait. So aircraft of the United Nations coalition began devastating attacks on Iraqi positions in Kuwait and on Iraq itself. American public support immediately rallied behind the **Gulf War.** For nearly forty days a high-tech air attack pounded the Iraqis as United Nations ground forces prepared to push Saddam Hussein's forces out of Kuwait. Hussein had promised that the ground war would be the "mother of all battles," and concerns about casualties among the coalition forces were high. According to estimates of Iraqi strength, coalition and Iraqi ground forces were nearly equal, numbering around 545,000. Neverthe-

Gulf War War in the Persian Gulf region in 1991 triggered by the Iraqi invasion of Kuwait; a U.S.-led coalition defeated Iraqi forces and freed Kuwait.

♦ In Operation Desert Storm, regarded by many as Bush's most successful action as president, United Nations forces led by the United States successfully pushed back the Iraqi army and liberated Kuwait. With burning oil wells as a background, American troops cross the desert in their "humvee." At the end of the war, in which an estimated 100,000 Iraqis died, Bush exclaimed, "By God, we've kicked the Vietnam syndrome once and for all." *Bruno Barbey/Magnum Photos.*

less, General Norman Schwarzkopf, coalition force commander, was confident of victory and ridiculed the Iraqi leader's military ability: Saddam is "neither a strategist, nor is he schooled in the operational arts, nor is he a tactician, nor is he a general, nor is he a soldier. Other than that he is a great military man."

The ground offensive, called Operation Desert Storm, started the night of February 23 as Arab forces and American marines assaulted the Iraqi defenses along Kuwait's southern border. At the same time, miles to the west, in an end-run nicknamed the "Hail Mary pass," American, French, and British forces slashed into the Iraqi desert unopposed and unnoticed, cutting off Saddam Hussein's armies in Kuwait from any northward retreat into Iraq. In Kuwait, thousands of demoralized Iraqi soldiers, many of whom had gone without food and water for days, surrendered to advancing coalition forces. Within a hundred hours of the start of the ground offensive, coalition forces mopped up the remaining resistance.

Kuwait was liberated, rebellion broke out in Iraq, and the Iraqi army was thoroughly humiliated. Estimates of Iraqi losses ranged from 70,000 to 115,000 killed. The United States lost fewer than 150. It was the "mother of all victories," quipped Americans as President Bush's popularity soared to over 90 percent. Some, less euphoric, speculated that the offen-

sive had ended too soon and should have continued until all, or nearly all, of the Iraqi army had been destroyed and Saddam ousted from power.

By the summer of 1991, the United States could claim victory in two wars, the Gulf War and the Cold War, and was clearly the diplomatic and military leader of the world. Riding a wave of popularity and foreign policy successes, the White House looked hopefully toward the forthcoming presidential campaign. Many people expected that experience and foreign policy triumphs would ensure Bush's re-election. But Bush's foreign policy triumphs and popularity were surprisingly short-lived. A year later, Saddam Hussein remained firmly in power and was still a potential threat to the Persian Gulf region, and the American public seemed much more concerned about the economy than about foreign policy.

A Kinder, Gentler Nation at Home?

Bush entered the White House in 1989 promising a "kinder, gentler nation," an administration concerned about the nation's social problems. Noting that during the Reagan years public concern for the poor seemed nearly to have vanished and that further fragmentation of American society had occurred, some praised Bush for his rediscovery of social issues. Others pointed out that he had promised not to increase taxes—"Read my lips, no new taxes"—and had frequently reminded listeners that more government and money were not always the best solutions to the country's ills. Thomas Foley, Democratic Speaker of the House of Representatives, noted that concerns about costs dominated the White House and Congress more than thoughts about social programs. He suspected that there would be little real change and that Bush's domestic programs would march down the same path as Reagan's.

Foley was basically correct. Bush faced more constraints than Reagan. He was not an effective communicator and seemed to lack vision. He faced Democratic majorities in the House and Senate and had little influence over the New Right within the Republican party. He believed in a passive government and liked talking to people over the phone rather than face to face. Bush's domestic policy goal was to manage the presidency and ensure his own re-election—to, as he put it, avoid "stupid mistakes" and "see that government doesn't get in the way." Neither he nor his staff, headed by the abrasive John

Sununu, believed that there was not anything wrong with America, its society, or its economy. Bush even announced to his adviser, "We don't need to remake society."

By the end of his first year in office, Bush and his advisers were confident they were doing well. They pointed to successful legislation that protected disabled Americans against discrimination (the Americans with Disabilities Act) and reduced smokestack and auto emissions and acid rain (the Clean Air Act). Bush also noted that under his administration the minimum wage had risen from $3.35 to $4.25 an hour and more funding had been provided for the Head Start program. Only two problem areas seemed to exist: the economy and his broken pledge on taxes.

In mid-1990, in part because of oil-price increases caused by Iraq's invasion of Kuwait, the nation entered into a recession. The recession, plus the growing national deficit, had convinced Bush to work with Congress to raise taxes, despite his "no new taxes" pledge. Bush believed that by 1992 the recession would be over, the national debt would be reduced, and voters would happily re-elect him.

The recession, however, deepened through 1991 and into 1992, and Bush looked less and less like a successful and efficient manager of the nation. Any bipartisanship that had existed in 1989 quickly disappeared. Like Gerald Ford, President Bush used the veto to block Democratic-sponsored legislation. When House Majority Leader Richard Gephardt was asked to define Bush's domestic program, he icily commented that it was "the veto pen."

Bush believed that recessions usually lasted from six to sixteen months and fixed themselves. But the 1990 recession lasted longer than he expected, for several reasons. There was a slowing of the world economy, and one result of it was that fewer American goods were being sold overseas. A restructuring of the American economy forced many businesses to declare bankruptcy or downsize, releasing both blue-collar and white-collar workers. Between July 1990 and July 1993, over 1.9 million people lost their jobs, and 63 percent of American corporations cut their staffs. IBM and General Motors were among those that faced huge losses and dismissed thousands of workers. "I don't see the United States regaining a substantial percentage of the jobs lost for five to ten years," said one chief executive.

Sharply rising federal spending and the ever-increasing deficit contributed to the length and depth of the recession. Despite Bush's pledges to hold down federal spending and reduce the deficit, during his term the budget skyrocketed, reaching $1.5 trillion in 1992. At the same time, family income dropped below 1980 levels, to $37,300 from a 1980 high of $38,900. Consumers, caught between increasing unemployment, falling wages, and inflation, saw personal savings and confidence in the economy shrink.

How did Bush respond to the economic slide? He voiced confidence in the ability of the American economy to rebound, and he relied on raising interest rates to lower inflation. He also sought to increase American sales overseas by eliminating trade barriers. Negotiations went forward to establish a North American free trading zone with Mexico and Canada and to eliminate Japanese barriers to American trade, but these negotiations had little impact on the economy. As the recession wore on, Democrats called for tax cuts on the middle class, for increased and extended unemployment benefits, and for other social programs. Bush responded with the veto and by asking for reductions in **capital gains** taxes. The result was political gridlock.

As 1992 began, public opinion polls gave Bush his lowest approval rating ever—around 40 percent. He then announced that improving the economy was his major priority. Positioning himself as an agent of change, he said to journalist David Frost, "I will do what I have to do to be re-elected." But no consistent recovery plan—or re-election strategy—ever emerged. To defeat his Democratic opponent in 1992, Bush counted on his experience, especially his foreign policy expertise. But increasingly Bush appeared politically vulnerable, for voters' interest in foreign policy generally extended no further than its effect on their pocketbooks.

Calls for Change: The Election of Clinton

● The election of President Clinton was the outcome of what expectations?

The election of 1992 was unusual because of the candidacies of billionaire **H. Ross Perot** and baby-

---

capital gains Profit made from selling assets such as securities and real estate.

H. Ross Perot Texas billionaire who used large amounts of his own money to run as an independent candidate for president in 1992.

boomer **Bill Clinton,** the use of television talk shows as a campaign tool, and the number of women and minorities running for office. Change was in the air.

In mid-1991 Bush was basking in the afterglow of Operation Desert Storm and the fall of communism and enjoying an 88 percent approval rate. Most prominent Democrats expected that the president would easily win re-election, so they chose not to compete for their party's presidential nomination. As a result, the door was opened for less well known Democratic candidates: Governor Bill Clinton of Arkansas; Senator Tom Harkin of Iowa; Senator Bob Kerrey of Nebraska; Paul Tsongas, a former senator from Massachusetts; and Jerry Brown, a former governor of California. Each claimed to be a Washington outsider who would deviate from politics-as-usual. Better funded and organized, and focusing steadily on the economy, Clinton emerged as the front-runner and easily won the Democratic party's nomination. Breaking with the tradition of geographically balancing the ticket, he selected Senator Albert Gore of Tennessee, another baby-boomer, as his running mate.

Unable to run on the strength of his domestic record, Bush solidified his support from the New Right by adopting Vice President Dan Quayle's call for family values, and he stressed his presidential experience and knowledge of world affairs. He blamed the Democratic-controlled Congress for the political gridlock that had thwarted his efforts to institute change. He called Clinton a "tax and spend Democrat" and warned that the Arkansas governor's lack of experience, especially in foreign and military affairs, would ruin the country. Late in the campaign, he called Clinton and Gore "bozos" and said that his dog Millie knew more about foreign policy than Clinton did.

Calling himself a new kind of Democrat, Clinton presented an economic plan that included increased taxes for the wealthy, programs to rebuild the nation's transportation and industrial base, and a strong commitment to a national healthcare program. Unlike Bush, Clinton embraced government activism and never appeared to tire of making public appearances. Surviving Bush's ads attacking his character, personal life, avoidance of the draft during the Vietnam War, and lack of experience, Clinton steadily emphasized the economy and the need for a national system of healthcare. To keep the campaign focused on core issues, James Carville, Clinton's top political strategist, tacked a reminder above his desk: "Change vs. more of the same. The economy, stupid. Don't forget healthcare."

◆ More than in any other presidential election, the candidates, especially H. Ross Perot, used television to sell themselves. Perot appeared on several talk shows and sponsored "info-mercials," while Bill Clinton amazed many people with his appearance on the Arsenio Hall Show, playing the saxophone. *Wide World.*

The 1992 campaign also saw the emergence of a third-party candidate. H. Ross Perot offered to use as much as $100 million of his own money if his supporters could get his name on the presidential ballots in all fifty states. Perot's announcement in February 1992 on the cable news-talk program *Larry King Live* drew immediate support from many Americans who were disenchanted with both political parties and their candidates.

While the competing Democratic candidates and President Bush and his Republican challengers plowed their way through the primaries, Perot used television and radio appearances to present simple and straightforward messages. The politicians had messed up the nation, and control needed to be returned to the people, he declared. "It's time to take out the trash and clean up the barn," he told listeners. The deficit was the foremost problem, he said, and he promised to shrink it.

By June, one opinion poll showed the feisty Texan leading with 39 percent of the voters. Then, without warning, in July he withdrew from the race. But by October he was back, running more infomercials on national television, promising to fix Amer-

Bill Clinton Arkansas governor who was elected president in 1992; he promised to seek compromises to break congressional gridlock and improve the economy.

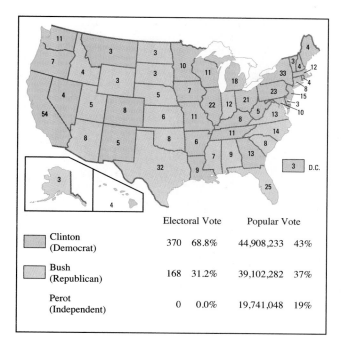

	Electoral Vote		Popular Vote	
Clinton (Democrat)	370	68.8%	44,908,233	43%
Bush (Republican)	168	31.2%	39,102,282	37%
Perot (Independent)	0	0.0%	19,741,048	19%

◆ **MAP 32.3 Election of 1992** Bill Clinton received almost 69 percent of the electoral votes—almost double the electoral votes received by George Bush. Nevertheless, Clinton received only 43 percent of the popular vote—the lowest popular vote percentage since Wilson's victory in 1912 over Theodore Roosevelt and William Taft. Third party candidate Ross Perot drew votes from both Democrats and Republicans in equal numbers and had no impact on the electoral vote.

◆ After facing strong Congressional and public opposition over the budget and NAFTA, President Clinton had an easier time in his efforts to appoint Ruth Bader Ginsburg to the Supreme Court. A moderate, Ginsburg is expected to strengthen the centrists on the Court. *UPI/Bettmann.*

ica's problems, and blasting his opponents' (especially Bush's) weaknesses. However, he never regained the momentum he had had in June.

The campaign culminated in three televised debates among Bush, Perot, and Clinton in September and October. An estimated 88 million people watched the third debate, in which Bush was most successful. Few, however, thought that Bush won any of the debates. Although both Bush and Perot gained in the public opinion polls, neither could overtake the front-running Clinton. William Jefferson Clinton won the election with 43 percent of the popular vote. Bush received 37.4 percent and Perot 18.9 percent. In the all-important Electoral College, Clinton received 370 votes, 100 more than he needed to win (see Map 32.3).

On election day, voters gave Clinton a chance to implement the changes he had promised during the campaign. But the 1992 election signaled change in other ways as well. Across the nation, women and minorities were elected in larger numbers than ever

before. The number of women in the House of Representatives nearly doubled—from 28 to 47—and the number in the Senate tripled—from 2 to 6. More minorities were elected to Congress than ever before. President Clinton promised to appoint more minorities and women to the judiciary, the cabinet, and other federal offices. Fulfilling his promise to appoint women, in 1993 Clinton named Ruth Bader Ginsburg to the Supreme Court. In 1994, he appointed Stephen Breyer. It was also expected that Hillary Rodham Clinton, the president's wife, would be an influential adviser and would be incorporated into the formal policy-making system. This expectation was confirmed when the president appointed her to chair the committee charged with drafting a national healthcare plan. With these and other changes in mind, some called 1992 the "Year of the Woman."

The growing presence of women and minorities in politics and Clinton's social advocacy during the campaign generated expectations of a new social agenda that would reject the social policies of the Reagan and Bush administrations. Within the White

House, however, the focus was not on a social agenda but on an economic one. Clinton gave highest priority to winning congressional approval of the **North American Free Trade Agreement (NAFTA),** which aimed to eliminate trade barriers among the United States, Canada, and Mexico over a fifteen-year period, and to his plans to reduce the deficit and stimulate the economy. He also promised to introduce a comprehensive health plan as soon as possible. Social and foreign policy issues were expected to intrude, but the hope was that they would not distract from the immediate legislative goals. Clinton was anxious to begin, to make changes. "I want to get something done," he told a press conference, "I want to do things."

The spirit was willing, but halfway through his first year in office, many people wondered whether Clinton had the ability to get things done. By June 1993, public opinion polls showed him receiving only a 36 percent approval rating, and *Newsweek* was calling Clinton's leadership efforts "slow motion" and the "road to indecision." Inexperience took its toll on his efforts to deal with complex foreign policy issues and translate campaign promises into legislation.

Despite his desire to implement domestic programs, Clinton had to grapple with foreign policy problems involving Bosnia and **Somalia.** In both cases, Clinton and his foreign policy staff—including Secretary of State Warren Christopher—appeared indecisive.

In Somalia, in the period between Bush's decision to deploy American forces to provide humanitarian aid in 1992 and Clinton's assumption of office, the goal of United Nations and U.S. forces had expanded to include the establishing of a stable foundation for a political settlement. The change in mission led to hostilities with some Somali political groups. In October 1993, when a firefight cost the lives of seventeen Americans, many members of Congress and of the general public demanded that Clinton remove American forces from Somalia. Responding to this pressure, Clinton withdrew all American troops by April 1994.

Finding a popular solution to the Somali problem was simple in comparison with the complexities facing Clinton in Bosnia. During the campaign, Clinton had chided Bush for not promoting peace in Bosnia more assertively. Once in office, however, he found support for an assertive policy in Bosnia to be highly controversial. As the carnage increased, Clinton inched forward, finally approving limited military options to encourage negotiations between the

♦ Named to lead the healthcare effort, Hillary Rodham Clinton quickly became the leading spokesperson for national medical coverage. Speaking before the American Medical Association, which has traditionally opposed government-controlled medical programs, she emphasized that the medical community needed to work with the government to keep healthcare costs down. *UPI/Bettmann Archives.*

warring factions and to support United Nations peacekeeping and relief efforts. In March and April 1994, American aircraft shot down four Serbian jets over Bosnia and bombed Serbian Bosnian targets. But many questioned Clinton's choice and willingness to commit American forces and wondered whether increased military pressure would lead to any real progress toward peace. A pessimistic Senator Richard Lugar of Indiana concluded there was little that could prevent the Serbs from taking what they wanted.

While administration critics charged that the president's foreign policy lacked substance and leadership, supporters complained that his domestic style was not much better. The president, they argued, showed little commitment to principle and

North American Free Trade Agreement Agreement approved in 1993 that eliminated most tariffs and other trade barriers between the United States, Canada, and Mexico.

Somalia East African country that civil war and drought plunged into famine in 1992, prompting the United Nations to send troops to distribute food and attempt to restore order.

was too willing to compromise. He had promised to end discrimination against homosexuals in the military. But in the face of strong opposition from Congress, the military, and sizable segments of the public—who claimed that allowing avowed homosexuals into the military would weaken and perhaps destroy military effectiveness—Clinton chose to compromise. The result was a compromise that required the armed forces to stop asking about sexual preference as long as gays and lesbians in the service refrained from homosexual activities. The new policy failed to please either those who advocated the exclusion of gays from the military or gay rights activist who wanted total equality.

In the eyes of many, Clinton's retreat from his commitment to gays was duplicated by his lack of firmness on the budget-economy bill. Faced with opposition from Republicans led by Senate Minority Leader Bob Dole and from many Democrats—who one political observer noted seemed to have no fear of opposing their president—Clinton cut political deals with almost anyone or any group to gain support for the bill. Despite the compromises, the budget-economy bill needed the tie-breaking vote of Vice President Gore to pass in the Senate. Still, Clinton's supporters and some political analysts saw passage of the bill as an indication of the president's ability to work within the system and to make compromises without undermining the central thrust of his legislation. They argued that the budget, though different from the one Clinton had introduced, was still a major departure from the economic policies of Reagan and Bush. It did cut spending and the deficit, and it did raise taxes.

The budget bill was followed by a fight over NAFTA. Most Democrats, Perot, and organized labor were in opposition. "This is the big domino," said one of Clinton's top advisers. "If we lose, then everyone will say our first year was a failure—nothing else we did will matter. If we win, all the dominoes fall the other way." Clinton won, and with momentum provided by the NAFTA victory and the passage in December 1993 of the **Brady bill,** which mandated a five-day waiting period before a handgun could be purchased, Clinton's forces expected that 1994 would see passage of legislation that would reduce crime, provide a national healthcare system, and reform the welfare system.

In Memphis and Los Angeles in November 1993, he had outlined his approach to the problems associated with poverty and the inner cities. He called for government-supported national security, consisting of personal security and job and health secu-

rity. But he also stated that "unless we deal with the ravages of crime and drugs and violence, and unless we recognize that it's due to the breakdown of the family, the community and the disappearance of jobs; and unless we say some of this cannot be done by government . . . none of the other things we seek to do will ever take us where we need to go." In his 1994 State of the Union address, Clinton continued to stress that what he called the "journey of renewal" for America runs not only through the White House and Congress but also through every American community and home. He pledged an administration committed to changing welfare and healthcare and providing additional support against crime and violence. He warned, however, that even enormous government efforts would amount to nothing unless "the American people . . . want to change from within."

"Let's be honest," he stated, our "problems go way beyond the reach of government." But he was optimistic that Americans could put aside their political and social differences and work together to forge a renewed community of opportunity, equality, and world unity.

> **Brady bill** Law, passed by Congress in 1993, that established a five-day waiting period for handgun purchases.

SUMMARY

E xpectations
C onstraints
C hoices
O utcomes

During the two decades leading up to 1988, varied, often conflicting *expectations* and *choices* confronted Americans, as activist groups from everywhere on the political spectrum promoted their points of view. Racial and ethnic minorities, gays, and women were among those insisting that government remove discriminatory laws and practices and provide more economic and social opportunities. Conservatives and many moderates argued that too many government programs were already providing special opportunities for minorities and the disadvantaged. Opposed to homosexuality, abortion, and what they considered as secular values, they claimed that American society was too permissive, too preoccupied with sex and violence, and too tolerant of immorality and what they termed "alternative lifestyles." They advocated less government interference in economic matters and policy choices that stressed "traditional values."

Also widening the divisions within society was the arrival of large numbers of immigrants from Latin America and Asia. Hoping to experience the American dream, they encountered an economy offering limited *choices,* especially for people with few skills and little education. Tension among minorities grew as competition for jobs and government assistance programs intensified amid the Reagan administration's reductions of funding for many federal programs. As the social safety net shrank and economic opportunities declined, the *outcome* was that crime, violence, and drug usage became epidemic in many urban areas, and some inner cities looked more like battlegrounds than like communities. Conservatives blamed the crisis of the inner cities on the lack of values and irresponsibility of inner-city residents. Liberals blamed the lack of jobs and educational opportunities.

The Bush administration *chose* to do little to lessen the divisions within American society or to strengthen the economy. President Bush focused much of his attention on foreign affairs. As the Soviet Union and communism in Eastern Europe collapsed, Bush gained public approval for *choosing* to act in Panama and the Persian Gulf. His foreign policy successes, however, highlighted the weaknesses in his domestic policy.

Facing Bush in the presidential election, Clinton overcame personal and political *constraints* by focusing on domestic policy. He stressed that he would support changes in American society and improve the economy. But he did not win the election so much as Bush lost it. His first year in office provided *expected* images of indecisiveness and weak leadership, especially in foreign affairs. But his *choices* also showed signs of effective leadership, winning the passage of the budget and NAFTA. In surveying the future, Clinton offered optimism and hope. He urged Americans to recognize that government could not solve all the nation's ills. But he promoted the *expectation* that ordinary Americans, through their own *choices,* could restore community and family and national well-being. The *outcome* would be a stronger nation and a force for good in a world undergoing "profound and rapid" change.

SUGGESTED READINGS

Congressional Quarterly's Research Reports.
    A valuable monthly resource for information and views on issues facing the United States and the world.

Daniels, Roger. *Coming to America* (1990).
    A solid analysis of the new immigrants seeking a place in American society; especially effective on Asian immigration.

Duffy, Michael, and Goodgame, Don. *Marching in Place: The Status Quo Presidency of George Bush* (1992).
    An insightful but critical analysis of the Bush presidency.

Garrow, David J. *Liberty and Sexuality: The Right to Privacy on the Making of Roe v. Wade* (1994).
    An in-depth and scholarly account of the origins and impact of *Roe v. Wade* and the legal and political issues dealing with privacy, gender, and abortion.

Oye, Kenneth A., et al., eds., *Eagle in a New World* (1992).
    A useful and thoughtful collection of essays on the role of the United States in the post–Cold War world.

Schwartzkopf, H. Norman. *It Doesn't Take a Hero* (1992).
    The U.S. role in the Gulf War as seen through the eyes of the American commander.

Shilts, Randy. *And the Band Played On: Politics, People and the AIDS Epidemic* (1987).
    A compelling book on the AIDS epidemic and the early lack of action by society; written by a victim of AIDS.

Terkel, Studs. *The Great Divide* (1988).
    An interesting and informative collection of oral interviews that provide a personal glimpse of changes recently taking place in American society.

Bibliography

Chapter 15 Reconstruction: High Hopes and Broken Dreams, 1865–1877

Herman Belz, *Emancipation and Equal Rights: Politics and Constitutionalism in the Civil War Era* (1978); Michael Les Benedict, *The Impeachment and Trial of Andrew Johnson* (1973); David Warren Bowen, *Andrew Johnson and the Negro* (1989); Albert E. Castel, *The Presidency of Andrew Johnson* (1979); Vincent P. DeSantis, *Republicans Face the Southern Question* (1959); John Hope Franklin, *Reconstruction: After the Civil War* (1961); John Hope Franklin and Alfred A. Moss, Jr., *From Slavery to Freedom: A History of Negro Americans*, 6th ed. (1988); Herbert G. Gutman, *The Black Family in Slavery and Freedom* (1976); Harold M. Hyman and William M. Wiecek, *Equal Justice Under Law: Constitutional Development, 1835–1875* (1982); Jacqueline Jones, *Labor of Love, Labor of Sorrow: Black Women, Work and the Family, from Slavery to the Present* (1985); Mark Krug, *Lyman Trumbull: Conservative Radical* (1965); William S. McFeely, *Grant: A Biography* (1981); Martin E. Mantell, *Johnson, Grant, and the Politics of Reconstruction* (1973); Eric L. McKitrick, *Andrew Johnson and Reconstruction* (1960; reprint, 1988); James M. McPherson, *Ordeal by Fire: Reconstruction* (1982); Milton Meltzer, *Thaddeus Stevens and the Fight for Negro Rights* (1967); David Montgomery, *Beyond Equality: Labor and the Radical Republicans, 1862–1872* (1967); Michael Perman, *Reunion Without Compromise: The South and Reconstruction, 1865–1868* (1973); Keith I. Polakoff, *The Politics of Inertia: The Election of 1876 and the End of Reconstruction* (1973); Roger L. Ransom and Richard Sutch, *One Kind of Freedom: The Economic Consequences of Emancipation* (1977); Kenneth M. Stampp, *The Era of Reconstruction, 1865–1877* (1965); Hans Louis Trefousse, *Andrew Johnson: A Biography* (1989); Hans Louis Trefousse, *Impeachment of a President: Andrew Johnson, the Blacks, and Reconstruction* (1975); Allen W. Trelease, *White Terror: The Ku Klux Klan Conspiracy and Southern Reconstruction* (1971); Vernon Lane Wharton, *The Negro in Mississippi: 1865–1890* (1965; reprint, 1974); Forrest G. Wood, *The Era of Reconstruction, 1863–1877* (1975); C. Vann Woodward, *Reunion and Reaction: The Compromise of 1877 and the End of Reconstruction*, rev. ed. (1956); C. Vann Woodward, *Origins of the New South, 1877–1913* (1951).

Chapter 16 Survival of the Fittest: Entrepreneurs and Workers in Industrial America, 1865–1900

Ralph Andreano, ed., *The Economic Impact of the Civil War*, rev ed. (1967); Paul Avrich, *The Haymarket Tragedy* (1984); Robert V. Bruce, *1877: Year of Violence* (1959); David F. Burg, *Chicago's White City of 1893* (1976); Vincent P. Carosso, *The Morgans: Private International Bankers, 1854–1913* (1987); Alfred D. Chandler, Jr., with Takashi Hikino, *Scale and Scope: The Dynamics of Industrial Capitalism* (1990); Alfred D. Chandler, Jr., *The Essential Alfred Chandler: Essays Toward a Historical Theory of Big Business*, ed. by Thomas K. McCraw (1988); Alfred D. Chandler, ed., *The Railroads: The Nation's First Big Business* (1965); Thomas C. Cochran, *American Business in the Twentieth Century* (1972); Thomas C. Cochran and William Miller, *The Age of Enterprise: A Social History of Industrial America*, rev. ed. (1961); Carl N. Degler, *In Search of Human Nature: The Decline and Revival of Darwinism in American Social Thought* (1991); Leon Fink, *Workingmen's Democracy: The Knights of Labor and American Politics* (1983); Robert Fogel, *Railroads and American Economic Growth* (1965); John A. Garraty, *The New Commonwealth, 1877–1890* (1968); Peter George, *The Emergence of Industrial America: Strategic Factors in American Economic Growth Since 1870* (1982); Louis M. Hacker, *The World of Andrew Carnegie: 1865–1901* (1968); Robert L. Heilbroner, *The Economic Transformation of America* (1977); Richard Hofstadter, *Social Darwinism in American Thought* (1944); Matthew Josephson, *The Robber Barons: The Great American Capitalists, 1861–1901* (1934; reprint, 1962); Alice Kessler-Harris, *Out to Work: A History of Wage-Earning Women in the United States* (1982); Edward Chase Kirkland, *Industry Comes of Age: Business, Labor, and Public Policy, 1860–1897* (1961); Harold C. Livesay, *Andrew Carnegie and the Rise of Big Business* (1975); David Montgomery, *Workers' Control in America* (1979); Daniel Nelson, *Managers and Workers: Origins of the New Factory System in the United States, 1880–1920* (1975); Allan Nevins, *Study in Power: John D. Rockefeller, Industrialist and Philanthropist*, 2 vols. (1953); Robert Rydell, *All the World's a Fair: Visions of Empire at American International Expositions, 1876–1916* (1984); Nick Salvatore, *Eugene V. Debs: Citizen and Socialist* (1982); Fred A. Shannon, *The Farmer's Last Frontier: Agriculture, 1860–1897* (1945); Stephan Thernstrom, *Poverty and Progress: Social Mobility in a Nineteenth Century City* (1964); Harold G. Vatter, *The Drive to Industrial Maturity: The U.S. Economy, 1860–1914* (1975).

Chapter 17 Conflict and Change in the West, 1865–1902

Albert Camarillo, *Chicanos in a Changing Society: From Mexican Pueblos to American Barrios in Santa Barbara and Southern California, 1848–1930* (1979); Sucheng Chan, *Asian Californians* (1991); Stuart Daggett, *Chapters on the History of the Southern Pacific* (1922, reprint, 1966); Sarah Deutsch, *No Separate Refuge: Culture, Class, and Gender on an Anglo-Hispanic Frontier in the American Southwest, 1880–1940* (1987); Everett Dick, *The Sod-House Frontier, 1854–1890* (1954); Robert R. Dykstra, *The Cattle Towns* (1968); Allen F. Davis, *American Heroine: The Life and Legend of Jane Addams* (1973); John D'Emilio and Estelle B. Freedman, *Intimate Matters: A History of Sexuality in America* (1988); Peter Gammond, *Scott Joplin and the Ragtime Era* (1975); John A. Garraty, *The New Common-*

wealth, 1877–1890 (1968); William H. Gerdts, *American Impressionism* (1984); Lynn D. Gordon, *Gender and Higher Education in the Progressive Era* (1990); David F. Greenberg, *The Construction of Homosexuality* (1988); Wesley S. Griswold, *A Work of Giants: Building the First Transcontinental Railroad* (1962); Richard Griswold del Castillo, *The Los Angeles Barrio, 1850–1890* (1979); Frederick E. Hoxie, *A Final Promise: The Campaign to Assimilate the Indians, 1880–1920* (1984); William Issel, and Robert W. Cherny, *San Francisco, 1865–1932: Politics, Power, and Urban Development* (1986); [Hinmatonyalatkit] Joseph, "An Indian's View of Indian Affairs," *North American Review*, 128 (1879), 412–433; William L. Kahrl, *Water and Power: The Conflict over Los Angeles' Water Supply in the Owens Valley* (1982); Richard E. Lingenfelter, *The Hardrock Miners: A History of the Mining Labor Movement in the American West, 1863–1893* (1974); Albro Martin, *James J. Hill and the Opening of the Northwest* (1976); Carey McWilliams, *Factories in the Field: The Story of Migratory Farm Labor in California* (1935, 1939; reprint, 1971); Douglas Monroy, *Thrown Among Strangers: The Making of Mexican Culture in Frontier California* (1990); Sandra L. Myres, *Westering Women and the Frontier Experience, 1800–1915* (1982); Victor G. Nee and Brett de Barry Nee, *Longtime Californ': A Documentary History of an American Chinatown* (1972, 1973; reprint, 1986); Rodman Paul, *The Far West and the Great Plains in Transition, 1859–1900* (1988); Donald Pisani, *From the Family Farm to Agribusiness: The Irrigation Crusade in California and the West, 1850–1934* (1984); Leonard Pitt, *The Decline of the Californias: A Social History of the Spanish-Speaking Californians, 1846–1890* (1971); Earl Pomeroy, *The Pacific Slope: A History of California, Oregon, Washington, Idaho, Utah, and Nevada* (1965); Francis Prucha, *The Churches and the Indian Schools, 1888–1912* (1979); Francis Prucha, *American Indian Policy in Crisis: Christian Reformers and the Indian, 1865–1900* (1975); Glenda Riley, *The Female Frontier: A Comparative View of Women on the Prairie and the Plains* (1988); Fred A. Shannon, *The Farmer's Last Frontier: Agriculture, 1860–1897* (1945); Ronald Takaki, *Strangers from the Different Shore* (1989); Robert M. Utley, *The Indian Frontier of the American West, 1846–1890* (1984); Walter Prescott Webb, *The Great Plains* (1931); Donald Worster, *Rivers of Empire:*

Water, Aridity, and the Growth of the American West (1985).

Chapter 18 The New Social Patterns of Urban and Industrial America, 1865–1917

Edward L. Ayers, *The Promise of the New South: Life After Reconstruction* (1992); Karen J. Blair, *The Clubwoman as Feminist: True Womanhood Redefined, 1868–1914* (1980); John E. Bodnar, *The Transplanted: A History of Immigrants in Urban America* (1985); Ruth Bordin, *Frances Willard: A Biography* (1986); George Chauncy, *Gay New York* (1994); George Cotkin, *Reluctant Modernism: American Thought and Culture, 1880–1900* (1992); Lawrence Arthur Cremin, *American Education: The Metropolitan Experience, 1876–1980* (1988); Thomas J. Curran, *Xenophobia and Immigration, 1820–1930* (1975); Roger Daniels, *Coming to America: A History of Immigration and Ethnicity in American Life* (1990); David C. Hammack, *Power and Society: Greater New York at the Turn of the Century* (1982); Louis R. Harlan, *Booker T. Washington: The Making of a Black Leader, 1856–1901* (1972); Kenneth T. Jackson, *Crabgrass Frontier: The Suburbanization of the United States* (1985); Jonathan Ned Katz, ed., *Gay American History: Lesbians and Gay Men in the U.S.A.: A Documentary History*, rev. ed. (1992); A. T. Lane, *Solidarity or Survival? American Labor and European Immigrants: 1830–1924* (1987); James B. Lane, *Jacob A. Riis and the American City* (1974); Lawrence W. Levine, *Highbrow/Lowbrow: The Emergence of Cultural Hierarchy in America* (1988); Eric H. Monkkonen, *America Becomes Urban: The Development of U.S. Cities and Towns, 1780–1980* (1988); Regina Markell Morantz-Sanchez, *Sympathy and Science: Women Physicians in American Medicine* (1985); H. Wayne Morgan, ed., *Victorian Culture in America, 1865–1914* (1973); Bernard B. Perlman, *Painters of the Ashcan School: The Immortal Eight* (1979); Lewis O. Saum, *The Popular Mood of America, 1860–1890* (1990); Thomas J. Schlereth, *Victorian America: Transformations in Everyday Life, 1876–1915* (1991); Robert A. Slayton, *Back of the Yards: The Making of a Local Democracy* (1986); Louise L. Stevenson, *The Victorian Homefront: American

Thought and Culture, 1860–1880* (1991); Jon C. Teaford, *The Unheralded Triumph: City Government in America, 1870–1900* (1984); David Ward, *Cities and Immigrants: A Geography of Change in Nineteenth Century America* (1971); Ida B. Wells-Barnett, *Crusade for Justice: The Autobiography of Ida B. Wells*, edited by Alfreda M. Duster (1970).

Chapter 19 Political Stalemate and Political Upheaval, 1868–1900

Walter Dean Burnham, *Critical Elections and the Mainsprings of American Politics* (1970); Gene Clanton, *Populism: The Humane Preference in America, 1890–1900* (1991); Paolo E. Coletta, *William Jennings Bryan*, 3 vols. (1964–1969); Carl N. Degler, *The Age of the Economic Revolution, 1876–1900*, 2d ed. (1977); Justus D. Doenecke, *The Presidencies of James A. Garfield and Chester A. Arthur* (1981); Milton Friedman and Anna Jacobson Schwartz, *A Monetary History of the United States, 1867–1960* (1963); John A. Garraty, *The New Commonwealth, 1877–1890* (1968); Paul W. Glad, *McKinley, Bryan, and the People* (1964, rpt. 1991); Lewis L. Gould, *The Presidency of William McKinley* (1980); Samuel P. Hays, "Political Parties and the Community-Society Continuum," in W. N. Chambers and W. D. Burnham, eds., *The American Party Systems: Stages of Political Development*, 2d ed. (1975); John D. Hicks, *The Populist Revolt: A History of the Farmers' Alliance and the People's Party* (1931); Charles Hoffman, *The Depression of the Nineties: An Economic History* (1970); Ari Hoogenboom, *Outlawing the Spoils: A History of the Civil Service Reform Movement* (1961); Ari Hoogenboom, *The Presidency of Rutherford B. Hayes* (1988); Stanley L. Jones, *The Presidential Election of 1896* (1964); Paul Kleppner, *The Third Electoral System, 1853–1892: Parties, Voters, and Political Cultures* (1979); Richard L. McCormick, *The Party Period and Public Policy: American Politics from the Age of Jackson to the Progressive Era* (1986); Robert C. McMath, Jr., *American Populism: A Social History, 1877–1898* (1993); Horace Samuel Merrill, *Bourbon Leader: Grover Cleveland and the Democratic Party* (1957); H. Wayne Morgan, *William McKinley and His America* (1963); Allan Nevins, *Grover Cleveland: A Study in*

Courage (1932); Nell Irvin Painter, Standing at Armageddon: The United States, 1877–1919 (1987); Norman Pollack, ed., The Populist Mind (1967); Carlos A. Schwantes, Coxey's Army: An American Odyssey (1985); Theda Skocpol, Protecting Soldiers and Mothers: The Politics of Social Provision in the United States (1992); Stephen Skowronek, Building a New American State: The Expansion of National Administrative Capacities, 1877–1920 (1982); Homer E. Socolofsky and Allan B. Spetter, The Presidency of Benjamin Harrison (1987); Richard E. Welch, Jr., The Presidencies of Grover Cleveland (1988); R. Hal Williams, Years of Decision: American Politics in the 1890s (1978).

Chapter 20 Becoming a World Power: America and World Affairs, 1865–1913

Robert L. Beisner, Twelve Against Empire: The Anti-Imperialists, 1898–1900 (1968); Richard H. Collin, Theodore Roosevelt: Culture, Diplomacy, and Expansion (1985); Justus D. Doenecke, The Presidencies of James A. Garfield and Chester A. Arthur (1981); Willard B. Gatewood, Black Americans and the White Man's Burden, 1898–1903 (1975); Lewis L. Gould, The Presidency of Theodore Roosevelt (1991); Lewis L. Gould, The Presidency of William McKinley (1980); John A. S. Grenville, and George Berkeley Young, Politics, Strategy, and American Diplomacy: Studies in Foreign Policy, 1873–1917 (1966); David Healy, U.S. Expansionism: The Imperialist Urge in the 1890s (1970); Ari Hoogenboom, The Presidency of Rutherford B. Hayes (1988); Jerry Israel, Progressivism and the Open Door: America and China, 1905–1921 (1971); Paul M. Kennedy, The Samoan Tangle: A Study in Anglo-German– American Relations, 1878–1900 (1974); Walter LaFeber, Inevitable Revolutions: The United States in Central America, rev. ed. (1993); Gerald F. Linderman, The Mirror of War: American Society and the Spanish-American War (1974); T. J. McCormick, China Market: America's Quest for Informal Empire (1967); Alfred Thayer Mahan, The Influence of Seapower upon History, 1660–1783 (1890, rpt. 1957); C. Roland Marchand, The American Peace Movement and Social Reform, 1898–1918 (1972); Ernest R. May, American Imperialism: A Speculative Essay (1968); Ernest R. May, Imperial Democracy:

The Emergence of America as a Great Power (1961, rpt. 1973); H. Wayne Morgan, America's Road to Empire: The War with Spain and Overseas Expansion (1965); H. Wayne Morgan, ed., The Gilded Age, rev. ed. (1970); H. Wayne Morgan, William McKinley and His America, (1963); Thomas J. Osborne, "Empire Can Wait": American Opposition to Hawaiian Annexation, 1893–1898 (1981); Thomas G. Paterson and Stephen G. Rabe, eds., Imperial Surge: The United States Abroad, the 1890s–Early 1900s (1992); Bradford Perkins, The Great Rapprochement: England and the United States, 1895–1914 (1968); Dexter Perkins, A History of the Monroe Doctrine (1963); Milton Plesur, America's Outward Thrust: Approaches to Foreign Affairs, 1865–1900 (1971); Julius W. Pratt, Expansionists of 1898 (1936); Emily S. Rosenberg, Spreading the American Dream: American Economic and Cultural Expansion, 1890–1945 (1982); Homer E. Socolofsky and Allan B. Spetter, The Presidency of Benjamin Harrison (1987); E. Berkeley Tompkins, Anti-Imperialism in the United States: The Great Debate, 1890–1920 (1970); Richard E. Welch, Jr., The Presidencies of Grover Cleveland (1988); Richard E. Welch, Jr., Response to Imperialism: The United States and the Philippine-American War, 1899–1902 (1979); William Appleman Williams, The Roots of the Modern American Empire (1969); Marilyn Blatt Young, The Rhetoric of Empire: American China Policy, 1895–1901 (1968).

Chapter 21 The Progressive Era, 1900–1917

Paula Baker, "The Domestication of Politics: Women and American Political Society, 1780–1920." American Historical Review 89 (1984): 620–647; Jack S. Blocker, Jr., Retreat from Reform: The Prohibition Movement in the United States, 1890–1913 (1976); John Morton Blum, The Republican Roosevelt, 2d ed. (1977); Ruth Bordin, Women and Temperance: The Quest for Power and Liberty, 1873–1900 (1980); Kendrick A. Clements, The Presidency of Woodrow Wilson (1992); Melvyn Dubofsky, We Shall Be All: A History of the Industrial Workers of the World (1969); Louis Filler, The Muckrakers (1976); Noralee Frankel and Nancy S. Dye, eds., Gender, Class, Race, and Reform in the Progressive Era (1991); Linda Gordon, Woman's Body,

Woman's Right: Birth Control in America, rev. ed. (1990); Lewis L. Gould, The Presidency of Theodore Roosevelt (1991); Louis R. Harlan, Booker T. Washington: The Wizard of Tuskegee, 1901–1915 (1983); Samuel P. Hays, Conservation and the Gospel of Efficiency: The Progressive Conservation Movement, 1890–1920 (1959); Samuel P. Hays, American Political History as Social Analysis (1980); Ari and Olive Hoogenboom, A History of the ICC: From Panacea to Palliative (1976); Alice Kessler-Harris, Out to Work: A History of Wage-Earning Women in the United States (1982); Gabriel Kolko, The Triumph of Conservatism: A Reinterpretation of American History, 1900–1916 (1963); Arthur S. Link, Woodrow Wilson, 5 vols. (1947–1965); Richard Coke Lower, A Bloc of One: The Political Career of Hiram W. Johnson (1993); Richard L. McCormick, The Party Period and Public Policy: American Politics from the Age of Jackson to the Progressive Era (1986); Michael E. McGerr, The Decline of Popular Politics: The American North, 1865–1928 (1986); Manning Marable, W. E. B. Du Bois: Black Radical Democrat (1986); Sally M. Miller, Victor Berger and the Promise of Constructive Socialism, 1910–1920 (1973); George E. Mowry, The Era of Theodore Roosevelt and the Birth of Modern America, 1900–1912 (1958); Spencer C. Olin, California's Prodigal Sons; Hiram Johnson and the Progressives, 1911–1917 (1968); Daniel Rodgers, "In Search of Progressivism." Reviews in American History 10 (Dec. 1982): 113–132; Nick Salvatore, Eugene V. Debs: Citizen and Socialist (1982); Stanley K. Schultz, Constructing Urban Culture: American Cities and City Planning, 1880–1920 (1989); Melvin I. Urofsky, Louis D. Brandeis and the Progressive Tradition (1981); Robert H. Wiebe, The Search for Order, 1877–1920 (1967); William H. Wilson, The City Beautiful Movement (1989).

Chapter 22 America and the World, 1913–1920

Lloyd E. Ambrosius, Woodrow Wilson and the American Diplomatic Tradition: The Treaty Fight in Perspective (1987); Arthur E. Barbeau and Florette Henri, The Unknown Soldiers: Black American Troops in World War I (1974); W. J. Breen, Uncle Sam at Home: Civilian Mobilization, Wartime Federalism, and the Council of National De-

fense, 1917–1919 (1984); David Brody, *Labor in Crisis: The Steel Strike of 1919* (1965); John Whiteclay Chambers II, *To Raise an Army: The Draft Comes to Modern America* (1987); Kendrick A. Clements, *William Jennings Bryan: Missionary Isolationist* (1982); Edward M. Coffman, *The War to End All Wars: The American Military Experience in World War I* (1986); Jean Conner, *The National War Labor Board* (1983); John Milton Cooper, Jr., *The Vanity of Power: American Isolationism and World War I* (1969); Robert D. Cuff, *The War Industries Board: Business-Government Relations During World War I* (1973); Patrick Devlin, *Too Proud to Fight: Woodrow Wilson's Neutrality* (1974); Robert H. Ferrell, *Woodrow Wilson and World War I, 1917–1921* (1985); Lloyd C. Gardner, *Wilson and Revolutions, 1913–1921* (1976); Mark T. Gilderhus, *Diplomacy and Revolution: U.S.-Mexican Relations Under Wilson and Carranza* (1977); Maurine Weiner Greenwald, *War and Work: The Impact of World War I on Women Workers in the United States* (1980); Edward Haley, *Revolution and Intervention: The Diplomacy of Taft and Wilson in Mexico, 1910–1917* (1970); David M. Kennedy, *Over Here: The First World War and American Society* (1980); Thomas J. Knock, *To End All Wars: Woodrow Wilson and the Creation of the League of Nations* (1992); David D. Lee, *Sergeant York: An American Hero* (1985); Arthur S. Link, *Woodrow Wilson: Revolution, War, and Peace* (1979); C. Roland Marchand, *The American Peace Movement and Social Reform, 1898–1918* (1972); Ernest R. May, *The World War and American Isolation, 1914–1917* (1959); Arno J. Mayer, *Politics and Diplomacy of Peacemaking: Containment and Counterrevolution at Versailles, 1918–1919* (1967); Paul L. Murphy, *World War I and the Origin of Civil Liberties in the United States* (1979); Robert K. Murray, *Red Scare: A Study in National Hysteria, 1919–1920* (1955, rpt. 1964); Robert E. Quirk, *An Affair of Honor: Woodrow Wilson and the Occupation of Veracruz* (1962); Ruth Rosen, *The Lost Sisterhood: Prostitution in America, 1900–1918* (1982); Francis Russell, *A City in Terror, 1919: The Boston Police Strike* (1975); William M. Tuttle, *Race Riot: Chicago in the Red Summer of 1919* (1970); Stephen Vaughn, *Holding Fast the Inner Lines: Democracy, Nationalism, and the Committee on Public Information* (1980); James Weinstein, *The Decline of Socialism in America; 1912–1925* (1967, rpt. 1984); William C. Widenor, *Henry Cabot Lodge and the Search for an American Foreign Policy* (1980).

Chapter 23 The 1920s, 1920–1928

William J. Barber, *From New Era to New Deal: Herbert Hoover, the Economists, and American Economic Policy, 1921–1933* (1985); Daniel H. Borus, ed., *These United States: Portraits of America from the 1920s* (1992); David Burner, *The Politics of Provincialism: The Democratic Party in Transition, 1919–1932* (1968); Paul A. Carter, *The Twenties in America*, 2d ed. (1987); E. David Cronon, *Black Moses: The Story of Marcus Garvey and the Universal Negro Improvement Association*, 2d ed. (1969); Lyle W. Dorset, *Billy Sunday and the Redemption of Urban America* (1991); Martin Bauml Duberman, *Paul Robeson: A Biography* (1989); Martin Bauml Duberman, Martha Vicinus, and George Chauney, Jr., eds., *Hidden From History: Reclaiming the Gay and Lesbian Past* (1989); Larry Engelmann, *Intemperance: The Lost War Against Liquor* (1979); Richard Wightman Fox and T. J. Jackson Lears, eds., *The Culture of Consumption: Critical Essays in American History, 1880–1980* (1983); Linda Gordon, *Woman's Body, Woman's Right; Birth Control in America*, rev. ed. (1990); Ellis W. Hawley, *The Great War and the Search for a Modern Order: A History of the American People and their Institutions, 1917–1933* (1979); Edward Jablonski, *Gershwin* (1987); Kenneth T. Jackson, *The Ku Klux Klan in the City, 1915–1930* (1967); Harvey Klehr and John Earl Haynes, *The American Communist Movement: Storming Heaven Itself* (1992); David L. Lewis, *When Harlem Was in Vogue* (1981); Robert S. Lynd and Helen M. Lynd, *Middletown* (1929); Roland Marchand, *Advertising the American Dream: Making Way for Modernity, 1920–1940* (1985); Robert K. Murray, *The Politics of Normalcy: Governmental Theory and Practice in the Harding-Coolidge Era* (1973); Gerald D. Nash, *A. P. Giannini and the Bank of America* (1992); James S. Olson and Raymond Wilson, *Native Americans in the Twentieth Century*, (1984); Arnold Rampersad, *The Life of Langston Hughes*, 2 vols. (1986, 1988); Arthur M. Schlesinger, Jr., *The Crisis of the Old Order, 1919–1933* (1957); Arnold Shaw, *The Jazz Age: Popular Music in the 1920's* (1987); Robert Sobel, *The Great Bull Market: Wall Street in the 1920s* (1968); Ferenc Szasz, *The Divided Mind of Protestant America, 1880–1930* (1982); Jerry R. Tompkins, *D-Days at Dayton* (1965); Eugene R. Trani and David L. Wilson, *The Presidency of Warren G. Harding* (1977); Bernard A. Weisberger, *The Dream Maker: William C. Durant, Founder of General Motors* (1979); Robert H. Zieger, *American Workers, American Unions, 1920–1985* (1986).

Chapter 24 From Good Times to Hard Times, 1920–1932

Anthony J. Badger, *The New Deal: The Depression Years, 1933–1940* (1989); Francisco E. Balerman, *In Defense of La Raza: The Los Angeles Mexican Consulate and the Mexican Community, 1929–1936* (1982); Michael Bernstein, *The Great Depression: Delayed Recovery and Economic Change in America, 1929–1939* (1988); Julia Kirk Blackwelder, *Women of the Depression: Caste and Culture in San Antonio, 1929–1939* (1984); David Burner, *Herbert Hoover: The Public Life* (1978); Dan T. Carter, *Scottsboro* (1969); Warren I. Cohen, *Empire Without Tears: America's Foreign Relations, 1921–1933* (1987); Charles DeBenedetti, *Origins of the Modern American Peace Movement, 1915–1929* (1978); Paula Elder, *Governor Alfred E. Smith: The Politician as Reformer* (1983); Ethan Ellis, *Republican Foreign Policy, 1921–1933* (1968); Milton Friedman and Anna Schwartz, *The Great Contraction, 1929–1933* (1965); John Kenneth Galbraith, *The Great Crash, 1929* (1961); John Garraty, *The Great Depression* (1987); Cheryl L. Greenberg, *"Or Does It Explode?" Black Harlem in the Great Depression* (1991); David Hamilton, *From New Day to New Deal: American Farm Policy from Hoover to Roosevelt, 1928–1933* (1991); Lois Rita Helmbold, "Beyond the Family Economy: Black and White Working-Class Women During the Great Depression," *Feminist Studies*, 13 (Fall 1987); Abraham Hoffman, *Unwanted Mexican Americans in the Great Depression: Repatriation Pressures, 1929–1939* (1974); A. Iriye, *After Imperialism: The Search for New Order in the Far East, 1921–1931* (1965); Charles Kindelberger, *The World in Depression* (1974); Donald L. Lisio, *Hoover, Blacks, and Lily-Whites* (1985); Robert S. McElvaine, *The Great Depression, 1929–1941* (1984); James S. Olson, *Herbert Hoover and the Reconstruction Finance Corporation, 1931–1933* (1977); Emily Rosenberg, *Spreading the American Dream* (1982); Louis Schraf, *To Work and to Wed: Female Employment and the Great Depression* (1980); John Shover, *Cornbelt Rebellion: The Farmers' Holiday Association* (1965); Bernard Sternsher, ed., *Hitting Home: The Great Depression in Town and Country* (1989); Peter Timim, *Did Monetary Forces Cause the Great Depression* (1976); Susan Ware, *Holding Their Own: American Women in the Thirties* (1982); Joan Hoff Wilson, *American Business and Foreign Policy, 1920–1933* (1968); Donald Worster, *Dust Bowl: The Southern Plains in the 1930s* (1979).

Chapter 25 The New Deal, 1932–1940

Ann Banks, ed., *First Person America* (1980); John Barnard, *Walter Reuther and the Rise of the Auto Workers* (1983); Irving Bernstein, *A Caring Society: The New Deal, The Worker, and the Great Depression* (1985); Gary D. Best, *Pride, Prejudice, and Politics: Roosevelt Versus Recovery, 1933–1938* (1990); Roger Biles, *A New Deal for the American People* (1991); Roger Biles, *The South and the New Deal* (1992); Alan Brinkley, *Voices of the Protest: Huey Long, Father Coughlin, and the Great Depression* (1982); William U. Chandler, *The Myth of the TVA: Conservation and Development in the Tennessee Valley, 1933–1983* (1984); Kenneth S. Davis, *FDR: Into the Storm, 1937–1940: A History* (1993); Kenneth S. Davis, *FDR: The New Deal Years, 1933–1937* (1986); Sidney Fine, *Sit-Down: The General Motors Strike of 1936–1937* (1969); Steve Fraser and Gary Gerstle, eds., *The Rise and Fall of the New Deal Order, 1930–1980* (1989); James Gregory, *American Exodus: The Dust Bowl Migration and the Okie Culture in California* (1989); Lawrence C. Kelley, *The Assault on Assimilation: John Collier and the Origins of Indian Policy Reform* (1983); Joseph Lash, *Eleanor and Franklin* (1972); Roy Lubove, *The Stuggle for Social Security* (1968); Robert S. McElvaine, ed., *Down and Out in the Great Depression: Letters from the Forgotten Man* (1983); Patrick J. Maney, *The Roosevelt Presence: A Biography of Franklin Delano Roosevelt* (1992); George McJimsey, *Harry Hopkins* (1987); Jerre Mangione, *The Dream and the Deal: The Federal Writers' Project, 1935–1943* (1972); David Milton, *The Politics of U.S. Labor: From the Great Depression to the New Deal* (1980); James T. Patterson, *Congressional Conservatism and the New Deal* (1967); Richard H. Pells, *Radical Visions and American Dreams: Culture and Social Thought in the Depression Years* (1973); Kenneth Philip, *John Collier's Crusade for Indian Reform, 1920–1945* (1977); Theodore Saloutos, *The American Farmer and the New Deal* (1982); Lois Schraf, *Eleanor Roosevelt: First Lady of American Liberalism* (1987); Harvard Sitkoff, ed., *Fifty Years Later: The New Deal Evaluated* (1985); Elaine M. Smith, "Mary McLeod Bethune and the National Youth Administration," in Marbel E. Deutrich and Virginia C. Purdy, eds., *Clio Was A Woman: Studies in the History of American Women* (1979); Nancy J. Weiss, *Farewell to the Party of Lincoln: Black Politics in the Age of FDR* (1983).

Chapter 26 America's Rise to World Leadership, 1933–1945

Stephen E. Ambrose, *D-Day, June 6, 1944* (1994); Allen Berube, *Coming Out Under Fire: The History of Gay Men and Women in World War II* (1990); Dorothy Borg and Shumpei Okamoto, eds., *Pearl Harbor as History* (1973); David Brinkley, *Washington Goes to War* (1988); Dominic J. Capeci, Jr., *Race Relations in Wartime Detroit: The Sojourner Truth Housing Controversy of 1942* (1984); Wayne Cole, *Roosevelt and the Isolationists* (1983); John Costello, *Virtue Under Fire: How World War II Changed Our Social and Sexual Attitudes* (1985); John D'Emilio, *Sexual Politics, Sexual Communities* (1983); Henry L. Feingold, *The Politics of Rescue: The Roosevelt Administration and the Holocaust, 1938–1945* (1970); Lloyd Gardner, *Economic Aspects of New Deal Diplomacy* (1964); Irwin F. Gellman, *The Good Neighbor Diplomacy: United States Policies in Latin America, 1933–1945* (1979); Susan Hartmann, *The Homefront and Beyond: American Women in the 1940s* (1982); Waldo H. Heinrichs, Jr., *Threshold of War* (1988); Akira Iriye, *Power and Culture: The Japanese-American War, 1941–1945* (1981); Peter Irons, *Justice at War* (1984); Clayton R. Koppes and Gregory D. Black, *Hollywood Goes to War: How Politics, Profits, and Propaganda Shaped World War II Movies* (1987); Nelson Lichtenstein, *Labor's War at Home: The CIO in World War II* (1983); Gerald D. Nash, *The American West Transformed: The Impact of the Second World War* (1985); William O'Neill, *A Democracy at War: America's Fight at Home and Abroad in World War II* (1993); Richard Polenberg, *War and Society: The United States, 1941–1945* (1972); Richard Rhodes, *The Making of the Atomic Bomb* (1987); Ronald Schaffer, *Wings of Judgement: American Bombing in World War II* (1985); Martin Sherman, *A World Destroyed* (1975); Gaddis Smith, *American Diplomacy During the Second World War* (1965); Mark Stoler, "A Half Century of Conflict: Interpretations of World War II Diplomacy," *Diplomatic History* 18 (Summer 1994): 375–403; Susan C. Taylor, *Jewel of the Desert: Japanese American Internment at Topaz* (1994); Studs Terkel, *The Good War: An Oral History of World War Two* (1984); Jonathan Utley, *Going to War with Japan* (1985); Harold G. Vetter, *The U.S. Economy in World War II* (1985); Donald Watt, *How War Came* (1989); Theodore A. Wilson, ed., *D-Day, 1944* (1993); Allen E. Winkler, *Home Front U.S.A.: America During World War II* (1986); David S. Wyman, *The Abandonment of the Jews* (1984); Neil A. Wynn, *The Afro-American and the Second World War* (1975).

Chapter 27 Truman and Cold War America, 1945–1952

Jack S. Ballard, *The Shock of Peace: Military and Economic Demobilization after World War II* (1983); William C. Berman, *The Politics of Civil Rights in the Truman Administration* (1970); Dorothy Borg and Waldo Heinrichs, eds., *Uncertain Years: Chinese-American Relations, 1947–1950* (1980); Paul Boyer, *By the Bomb's Early Light: American Thought and Culture at the Dawn of the Atomic Age* (1985); Richard M. Dalfiume, *Desegregation of the U.S. Armed Forces* (1969); Robert J. Donovan, *The Tumultuous Years: the Presidency of Harry S Truman, 1949–1953* (1982); Robert J. Donovan, *Conflict and Crisis: The Presidency of Harry S Truman, 1945–1948* (1977); Robert Griffith, *The Politics of Fear: Joseph R. McCarthy and the Senate* (1987); John L. Gaddis, *Strategies of Containment* (1982); Herbert J. Gans, *The Levittowners*

(1967); William S. Graebner, *The Age of Doubt: American Thought and Culture in the 1940s* (1991); Alonzo Hamby, *Beyond the New Deal: Harry S Truman and American Liberalism* (1973); John Halliday and Bruce Cummings, *Korea: The Unknown War* (1987); Susan Hartman, *Truman and the 80th Congress* (1971); Gregory Herken, *The Winning Weapon* (1981); Michael Hogan, *The Marshall Plan* (1987); Kenneth T. Jackson, *Crabgrass Frontiers: the Suburbanization of the United States* (1985); Landon Y. Jones, *Great Expectations: America and the Baby Boom Generation* (1980); Donald Katz, *Home Fires: An Intimate Portrait of One Middle-Class Family in Postwar America* (1992); Walter LaFeber, *America, Russia, and the Cold War, 1945–1990* (1990); Melvyn Leffler, *A Preponderance of Power* (1991); Norman D. Markowitz, *The Rise and Fall of the People's Century: Henry A. Wallace and American Liberalism, 1941–1948* (1973); Allen J. Matusow, *Farm Policies and Politics in the Truman Years* (1967); Eaine Tyler May, *Homeward Bound: American Families in the Cold War Era* (1988); William O'Neil, *American High: The Years of Confidence, 1945–1960* (1986); David M. Oshinsky, *A Conspiracy So Immense: The World of Joseph McCarthy* (1983); Thomas G. Paterson, *On Every Front: The Making and Unmaking of the Cold War* (1992); Gary W. Reichard, *Politics as Usual* (1988); Michael Schaller, *Douglas MacArthur: The Far Eastern General* (1989); Michael Schaller, *The American Occupation of Japan: The Origins of the Cold War in Asia* (1985); Athan Theoharis and John S. Cox, *The Boss: J. Edgar Hoover and the Great American Inquisition* (1988); Stephen Whitfield, *The Culture of the Cold War* (1987).

Chapter 28 Quest for Consensus, 1952–1960

Charles C. Alexander, *Holding the Line* (1985); H. W. Brands, Jr., *Cold Warriors* (1988); Wini Breines, *Young, White, and Miserable: Growing Up Female in the Fifties* (1992); Taylor Branch, *Parting the Water: America in the King Years, 1954–1963* (1988); Larry W. Burt, *Tribalism in Crisis: Federal Indian Policy, 1953–1961* (1982); Paul Carter, *Another Part of the Fifties* (1983); Willard W. Cochrane and Mary E. Ryan, *American Farm Policy, 1948–1973*

(1976); John D'Emilio, and Estelle B. Freedman, *Intimate Matters: A History of Sexuality in America* (1988); Michael N. Danielson, *The Politics of Exclusion* (1976); Robert A. Devine, *Blowing in the Wind: The Nuclear Test Ban Debate* (1978); Robert A. Devine, *The Sputnik Challenge* (1993); Barbara Ehrenreich, *Hearts of Men* (1983); Robert Fishamn, *Bourgeois Utopias* (1987); Donald I. Fixico, *Termination and Relocation: Federal Indian Policy, 1945–1970* (1986); Lloyd Gardner, *Approaching Vietnam* (1988); Fred I. Greenstein, *The Hidden-Hand Presidency* (1982); Robert Griffith, "Dwight D. Eisenhower and the Corporate Commonwealth," *American Historical Review*, 87 (February, 1982): 87–122; Richard G. Hewlett and Jack M. Hall, *Atoms for Peace and War* (1989); Alice Kessler-Harris, *Out to Work: A History of Wage-Earning Women in the United States* (1982); Richard Kluger, *Simple Justice* (1975); Paul A. C. Koistinen, ed., *The Military Industrial Complex: A Historical Perspective* (1980); Nicholas Lemann, *The Promised Land* (1991); George Lipsitz, *Time Passages: Collective Memory and American Popular Culture* (1991); Victory Marchetti and John D. Marks, *The CIA and the Cult of Intelligence* (1974); Richard H. Pells, *The Liberal Mind in a Conservative Age* (1983); Stephen G. Rabe, *Eisenhower and Latin America* (1988); Mark H. Rose, *Interstate* (1979); John W. Sloan, *Eisenhower and the Management of Prosperity* (1991); Jane Smith, *Patenting the Sun: Polio and the Salk Vaccine* (1990); John Tytell, *Naked Angels: The Lives and Literature of the Beat Generation* (1976).

Chapter 29 Great Promises, Bitter Disappointments, 1960–1968

Vaughn Bornet, *The Presidency of Lyndon B. Johnson* (1983); David Burner, *John F. Kennedy and a New Generation* (1988); David Chalmers, *And the Crooked Places Made Straight: The Struggle for Social Change in the 1960s* (1991); Noam Chomsky, *Re-thinking the Kennedy Myth* (1991); Morris Dickstein, *Gates of Eden: American Culture in the Sixties* (1977); David Garrow, *Protest at Selma: Martin Luther King and the Voting Rights Act of 1965* (1978); Raymond Gartoff, *Reflections on the Cuban Missile Crisis* (1989); James Giglio, *The*

Presidency of John F. Kennedy (1991); Henry Hurt, *Reasonable Doubt* (1985); David Knapp and Kenneth Polk, *Scouting the War on Poverty: Social Reform in the Kennedy Administration* (1971); Sar A. Levitan and Robert Taggert, *The Promise of Greatness* (1976); Richard D. Mahoney, *JFK: Ordeal in Africa* (1983); Allen Matusow, *The Unraveling of America: A History of Liberalism in the 1960s* (1984); James Miller, "Democracy Is in the Streets"— *From Port Huron to the Siege at Chicago* (1987); Charles Murray, *Losing Ground: American Social Policy, 1950–1980* (1984); Herbert Parmet, *JFK: The Presidency of John F. Kennedy* (1983); Thomas Paterson, *Confronting Castro: The United States and the Triumph of the Cuban Revolution* (1994); Thomas Paterson, ed., *Kennedy's Quest for Victory: American Foreign Policy, 1961–1963* (1989); Thomas C. Reeves, *President Kennedy: Profile of Power* (1994); Theodore Roszak, *The Making of the Counterculture* (1969); Thomas Schoenbaum, *Waging Peace and War: Dean Rusk in the Truman, Kennedy, and Johnson Years* (1988); Bernard Schwartz, *Super Chief: Earl Warren and His Supreme Court* (1983); John E. Schwartz, *America's Hidden Success: A Reassessment of Twenty Years of Public Policy* (1983); Jay Stevens, *Storming Heaven: LSD and the American Dream* (1987); James Sundquist, *Politics and Policy: The Eisenhower, Kennedy and Johnson Years* (1968); Barbara L.Tischler, ed., *Sights on the Sixties* (1992); Irwin Unger, *The Movement: A History of the Amerian New Left, 1959–1972* (1974); Melvin Urofsky, *The Continuity of Change: The Supreme Court and Individual Liberties, 1953–1986* (1991); William L. Van Deburg, *New Day in Babylon: The Black Power Movement and American Culture, 1965–1975* (1992); Robert Weisbrot, *Freedom Bound: A History of America's Civil Rights Movement* (1991).

Chapter 30 America Under Stress, 1960–1975

Rodolfo F. Acuna, *Community Under Seige: A Chronicle of Chicanos East of the Los Angeles River, 1945–1975* (1984); Stephen Ambrose, *Nixon: The Triumph of the Politician, 1962–1972* (1990); Larry Berman, *Lyndon Johnson's War* (1989); Cole Blasier, *Hovering Giant* (1974); Larry Cable, *Unholy Grail* (1991); Peter Caroll, *It*

Seemed Like Nothing Happened (1982); Vine Deloria, Jr., *Custer Died for Your Sins* (1969); Philip L. Geyelin, *Lyndon B. Johnson and the World* (1966); H. R. Haldeman, *The Haldeman Diaries: Inside the Nixon White House* (1994); Seymour Hersh, *The Price of Power: Kissinger in the Nixon White House* (1983); Ole R. Holdsti and James Rosenau, *American Leadership in World Affairs: Vietnam and the Breakdown of Consensus* (1984); William G. Hyland, *Mortal Rivals: Superpower Relations from Nixon to Reagan* (1987); Richard Krickus, *Pursuing the American Dream: White Ethnics and the New Populism* (1976); Kim McQuaid, *The Anxious Years: America in the Vietnam and Watergate Era* (1989); Marguerite V. Marin, *Social Protest in an Urban Barrio: A Study of the Chicano Movement, 1966–1974* (1991); George D. Moss, *Vietnam: An American Ordeal* (1994); Carlos Munoz, Jr., *Youth, Identity, Power: The Chicano Movement* (1989); Richard Nixon, *RN: The Memoirs of Richard Nixon* (1978); Herbert Parmet, *The World and Richard Nixon* (1990); William Quandt, *Decade of Decision* (1977); A. James Reichley, *Conservatives in an Age of Change* (1981); Neil Sheehan, *A Bright Shining Lie: John Paul Vann and America in Vietnam* (1988); Melvin Small, *Johnson, Nixon, and the Doves* (1988); Ronald Spector, *After Tet: The Bloodiest Year in Vietnam* (1992); Steven J. Spiegel, *The Other Arab-Israeli Conflict: Making America's Middle East Policy from Truman to Reagan* (1985); Bob Woodward and Carl Bernstein, *All the President's Men* (1974); Daniel Yergin, *The Prize* (1991).

Chapter 31 Facing Limits, 1974–1986

Sidney Blumenthal, *The Rise of the Counter-Establishment* (1986); John A. Booth and Thomas W. Walker, *Understanding Central America* (1989); Paul Boyer, ed., *Reagan as President* (1990); Connie Bruck, *The Predator's Ball: The Junk Bond Raiders and the Man Who Staked Them* (1988); Robert O. Crummey, ed., *Reform in Russia and the USSR* (1989); Paul Dukes, *The Last Great Game* (1989); Carol Felsenthal, *The Sweetheart of the Silent Majority* (1981); Betty Glad, *Jimmy Carter* (1980); William E. Griffth, ed., *Central and Eastern Europe: The Opening Curtain* (1989); Samuel P. Hays, *Beauty, Health, and Permanence: Environmental Politics in the United States, 1955–1985* (1987); Michael J. Hogan, *The Panama Canal in American Politics* (1986); Haynes Johnson, *Sleepwalking Through History: America in the Reagan Years* (1991); Charles O. Jones, *The Trusteeship Presidency: Jimmy Carter and the United States Congress* (1988); Harold H. Koh, *The National Security Constitution* (1990); Walter LaFeber, *The Panama Canal* (1989); Robert S. Leiken, ed., *Central America: Anatomy of Conflict* (1984); Robert C. Liberman and Robert Wuthnow, eds., *The New Christian Right* (1983); John Osborne, *The White House Watch: The Ford Years* (1977); John Palmer and Elizabeth Sawmill, eds., *The Reagan Record* (1984); William B. Quandt, *Camp David* (1986); Itamar Rabinovich, *The War for Lebanon, 1970–1983* (1984); Richard Reeves, *A Ford, Not a Lincoln* (1975); T. S. Reid, *The Chip* (1985); Herman Schwartz, *Packing the Courts: The Conservative Campaign to Rewrite the Constitution* (1988); Robert Scheer, *With Enough Shovels* (1982); Charles E. Shepard, *The Rise and Fall of Jim Baker* (1989); Laurence H. Shoup, *The Carter Presidency and Beyond* (1980); Allan P. Sindler, *Bakke, DeFunis, and the Minority Admissions* (1978); Philip Slater, *Earthwalk* (1974); Gaddis Smith, *Morality, Reason, and Power* (1986); James B. Stewart, *Den of Thieves* (1991); Strobe Talbot, *Deadly Gambits* (1984); E. Fuller Torrey, *Nowhere to Go: the Tragic Odyssey of the Homeless Mentally Ill* (1988); John Kenneth White, *The New Politics of Old Values* (1988); John Woodridge, *The Evangelicals* (1975).

Chapter 32 Making New Choices, 1986–1994

Deborah Amos, *Lines in the Sand* (1992); Frank Bean and Marta Tienda, *The Hispanic Population of the United States* (1988); Colin Campbell and Bert A. Rockman, eds., *The Bush Presidency: First Appraisals* (1991); James D. Cockcroft, *Outlaws in the Promised Land* (1986); Ruth Colker, *Abortion and Dialogue: Pro-Choice, Pro-Life, and American Law* (1992); Maria Costa, *Abortion: A Reference Handbook* (1991); E. J. Dionne, *Why Americans Hate Politics* (1992); Michael Duffy and Daniel Goodgame, *Marching in Place: The Status Quo Presidency of George Bush* (1992); Leslie W. Dunbar, ed., *Minority Report: What Has Happened to Blacks, Hispanics, American Indians, and Other Minorities in the Eighties* (1984); Barbara Ehrenreich, *The Worst Years of Our Lives* (1990); Lawrence Freedman and Efraim Karsh, *The Gulf Conflict, 1990–1991* (1993); Nathan Glazer, ed., *Clamor at the Gates: The New American Immigration* (1986); Carl C. Hodge and Cathy J. Nolan, eds., *Shepherd of Democracy?* (1992); James D. Hunter, *Culture Wars: The Struggle to Define America* (1991); Michael Katz, *The Undeserving Poor: From the War on Poverty to the War on Welfare* (1989); Jonathan Kozol, *Rachael and Her Children: Homeless Families in America* (1988); John Longone, *AIDS: The Facts* (1988); Donald J. Mabry, ed., *The Latin American Narcotics Trade* (1992); Michael Nelson, ed., *The Elections of 1992* (1993); Robert Reich, *The Work of Nations: Preparing Ourselves for Twenty-First Century Capitalism* (1991); Farley Reynolds and Walter R. Allen, *The Color Line and the Quality of Life in America* (1987); Hilda Scott, *Working Your Way to the Bottom: The Feminization of Poverty,* (1985); Peter Scott and Jonathan Marshall, *Cocaine Politics: Drugs, Armies, and the CIA in Central America* (1991); Ruth Sildel, *Women and Children Last* (1986); William J. Wilson, *The Truly Disadvantaged* (1987); Bob Woodward, *Agenda* (1994).

Documents

When, in the course of human events, it becomes necessary for one people to dissolve the political bonds which have connected them with another, and to assume, among the powers of the earth, the separate and equal station to which the laws of nature and of nature's God entitle them, a decent respect to the opinions of mankind requires that they should declare the causes which impel them to the separation.

We hold these truths to be self-evident: That all men are created equal; that they are endowed by their Creator with certain unalienable rights; that among these are life, liberty, and the pursuit of happiness; that, to secure these rights, governments are instituted among men, deriving their just powers from the consent of the governed; that whenever any form of government becomes destructive of these ends, it is the right of the people to alter or to abolish it, and to institute new government, laying its foundation on such principles, and organizing its powers in such form, as to them shall seem most likely to effect their safety and happiness. Prudence, indeed, will dictate that governments long established should not be changed for light and transient causes; and accordingly all experience hath shown that mankind are more disposed to suffer, while evils are sufferable, than to right themselves by abolishing the forms to which they are accustomed. But when a long train of abuses and usurpations, pursuing invariably the same object, evinces a design to reduce them under absolute despotism, it is their right, it is their duty, to throw off such government, and to provide new guards for their future security. Such has been the patient sufferance of these colonies; and such is now the necessity which constrains them to alter their former systems of government. The history of the present King of Great Britain is a history of repeated injuries and usurpations, all having in direct object the establishment of an absolute tyranny over these states. To prove this, let facts be submitted to a candid world.

He has refused his assent to laws, the most wholesome and necessary for the public good.

He has forbidden his governors to pass laws of immediate and pressing importance, unless suspended in their operation till his assent should be obtained; and, when so suspended, he has utterly neglected to attend to them.

He has refused to pass other laws for the accommodation of large districts of people, unless those people would relinquish the right of representation in the legislature, a right inestimable to them, and formidable to tyrants only.

He has called together legislative bodies at places unusual, uncomfortable, and distant from the depository of their public records, for the sole purpose of fatiguing them into compliance with his measures.

He has dissolved representative houses repeatedly, for opposing, with manly firmness, his invasions on the rights of the people.

He has refused for a long time, after such dissolutions, to cause others to be elected; whereby the legislative powers, incapable of annihilation, have returned to the people at large for their exercise; the state remaining, in the mean time, exposed to all the dangers of invasions from without and convulsions within.

He has endeavored to prevent the population of these states; for that purpose obstructing the laws for naturalization of foreigners; refusing to pass others to encourage their migration hither, and raising the conditions of new appropriations of lands.

He has obstructed the administration of justice, by refusing his assent to laws for establishing judiciary powers.

He has made judges dependent on his will alone, for the tenure of their offices, and the amount and payment of their salaries.

He has erected a multitude of new offices, and sent hither swarms of officers to harass our people and eat out their substance.

He has kept among us, in times of peace, standing armies, without the consent of our legislatures.

He has affected to render the military independent of, and superior to, the civil power.

He has combined with others to subject us to a jurisdiction foreign to our constitution, and unacknowledged by our laws, giving his assent to their acts of pretended legislation:

For quartering large bodies of armed troops among us;

For protecting them, by a mock trial, from punishment for any murders which they should commit on the inhabitants of these states;

For cutting off our trade with all parts of the world;

For imposing taxes on us without our consent;

For depriving us, in many cases, of the benefits of trial by jury;

For transporting us beyond seas, to be tried for pretended offenses;

For abolishing the free system of English laws in a neighboring province, establishing therein an arbitrary government, and enlarging its boundaries, so as to render it at once an example and fit instrument for introducing the same absolute rule into these colonies;

For taking away our charters, abolishing our most valuable laws, and altering fundamentally the forms of our governments;

For suspending our own legislatures, and declaring themselves invested with power to legislate for us in all cases whatsoever.

He has abdicated government here, by declaring us out of his protection and waging war against us.

He has plundered our seas, ravaged our coasts, burned our towns, and destroyed the lives of our people.

He is at this time transporting large armies of foreign mercenaries to complete the works of death, desolation, and tyranny already begun with circumstances of cruelty and perfidy scarcely paralleled in the most barbarous ages, and totally unworthy the head of a civilized nation.

He has constrained our fellow-citizens, taken captive on the high seas, to bear arms against their country, to become the executioners of their friends and brethren, or to fall themselves by their hands.

He has excited domestic insurrection among us, and has endeavored to bring on the inhabitants of our frontiers the merciless Indian savages, whose known rule of warfare is an undistinguished destruction of all ages, sexes, and conditions.

In every stage of these oppressions we have petitioned for redress in the most humble terms; our repeated petitions have been answered only by repeated injury. A prince, whose character is thus marked by every act which may define a tyrant, is unfit to be the ruler of a free people.

Nor have we been wanting in our attentions to our British brethren. We have warned them, from time to time, of attempts by their legislature to extend an unwarrantable jurisdiction over us. We have reminded them of the circumstances of our emigration and settlement here. We have appealed to their native justice and magnanimity; and we have conjured them, by the ties of our common kindred, to disavow these usurpations, which would inevitably interrupt our connections and correspondence. They, too, have been deaf to the voice of justice and of consanguinity. We must, therefore, acquiesce in the necessity which denounces our separation, and hold them, as we hold the rest of mankind, enemies in war, in peace friends.

We, therefore, the representatives of the United States of America, in General Congress assembled, appealing to the Supreme Judge of the world for the rectitude of our intentions, do, in the name and by the authority of the good people of these colonies, solemnly publish and declare, that these United Colonies are, and of right ought to be, FREE AND INDEPENDENT STATES; that they are absolved from all allegiance to the British crown, and that all political connection between them and the state of Great Britain is, and ought to be, totally dissolved; and that, as free and independent states, they have full power to levy war, conclude peace, contract alliances, establish commerce, and do all other acts and things which independent states may of right do. And for the support of this declaration, with a firm reliance on the protection of Divine Providence, we mutually pledge to each other our lives, our fortunes, and our sacred honor.

JOHN HANCOCK
and fifty-five others

Articles of Confederation

Whereas the Delegates of the United States of America in Congress assembled did on the fifteenth day of November in the Year of our Lord One Thousand Seven Hundred and Seventy seven, and in the Second Year of the Independence of America agree to certain articles of Confederation and perpetual Union between the States of Newhampshire, Massachusetts-bay, Rhodeisland and Providence Plantations, Connecticut, New York, New Jersey, Pennsylvania, Delaware, Maryland, Virginia, North-Carolina, South-Carolina and Georgia in the Words following, viz. "Articles of Confederation and perpetual Union between the states of New-hampshire, Massachusetts-bay, Rhodeisland and Providence Plantations, Connecticut, New-York,

New-Jersey, Pennsylvania, Delaware, Maryland, Virginia, North-Carolina, South-Carolina and Georgia.

Article I   The Stile of this confederacy shall be "The United States of America."

Article II   Each state retains its sovereignty, freedom and independence, and every Power, Jurisdiction and right, which is not by this confederation expressly delegated to the United States, in Congress assembled.

Article III   The said states hereby severally enter into a firm league of friendship with each other, for their common defence, the security of their Liberties, and their mutual and general welfare, binding themselves to assist each other, against all force offered to, or attacks made upon them, or any of them, on account of religion, sovereignty, trade, or any other pretence whatever.

Article IV   The better to secure and perpetuate mutual friendship and intercourse among the people of the different states in this union, the free inhabitants of each of these states, paupers, vagabonds and fugitives from Justice excepted, shall be entitled to all privileges and immunities of free citizens in the several states; and the people of each state shall have free ingress and regress to and from any other state, and shall enjoy therein all the privileges of trade and commerce, subject to the same duties, impositions and restrictions as the inhabitants thereof respectively, provided that such restriction shall not extend so far as to prevent the removal of property imported into any state, to any other state of which the Owner is an inhabitant; provided also that no imposition, duties or restriction shall be laid by any state, on the property of the united states, or either of them.

If any Person guilty of, or charged with treason, felony, or other high misdemeanor in any state, shall flee from Justice, and be found in any of the united states, he shall upon demand of the Governor or executive power, of the state from which he fled, be delivered up and removed to the state having jurisdiction of his offence.

Full faith and credit shall be given in each of these states to the records, acts and judicial proceedings of the courts and magistrates of every other state.

Article V   For the more convenient management of the general interests of the united states, delegates shall be annually appointed in such manner as the legislature of each state shall direct, to meet in Congress on the first Monday in November, in every year, with a power reserved to each state, to recal its delegates, or any of them, at any time within the year, and to send others in their stead, for the remainder of the Year.

No state shall be represented in Congress by less than two, nor by more than seven Members; and no person shall be capable of being a delegate for more than three years in any term of six years; nor shall any person, being a delegate, be capable of holding any office under the united states, for which he, or another for his benefit receives any salary, fees or emolument of any kind.

Each state shall maintain its own delegates in a meeting of the states, and while they act as members of the committee of the states.

In determining questions in the united states, in Congress assembled, each state shall have one vote.

Freedom of speech and debate in Congress shall not be impeached or questioned in any Court, or place out of Congress, and the members of congress shall be protected in their persons from arrests and imprisonments, during the time of their going to and from, and attendance on congress, except for treason, felony, or breach of the peace.

Article VI   No state without the Consent of the united states in congress assembled, shall send any embassy to, or receive any embassy from, or enter into any conference, agreement, or alliance or treaty with any King, prince or state; nor shall any person holding any office of profit or trust under the united states, or any of them, accept of any present, emolument, office or title of any kind whatever from any king, prince or foreign state; nor shall the united states in congress assembled, or any of them, grant any title of nobility.

No two or more states shall enter into any treaty, confederation or alliance whatever between them, without the consent of the united states in congress assembled, specifying accurately the purposes for which the same is to be entered into, and how long it shall continue.

No state shall lay any imposts or duties, which may interfere with any stipulations in treaties, entered into by the united states in congress assembled, with any king, prince or state, in pursuance of any treaties already proposed by congress, to the courts of France and Spain.

No vessels of war shall be kept up in time of peace by any state, except such number only, as shall be deemed necessary by the united states in congress assembled, for the defence of such state, or its trade; nor shall any body of forces be kept up by any state, in time of peace, except such number only, as in the judgment of the united states, in congress assembled, shall be deemed requisite to garrison the forts necessary for the defence of such state; but every state shall always keep up a well regulated and disciplined militia, sufficiently armed and accoutred, and shall provide and constantly have ready for use, in public stores, a due number of field pieces and tents, and a proper quantity of arms, ammunition and camp equipage.

No state shall engage in any war without the consent of the united states in congress assembled, unless such state be actually invaded by enemies, or shall have received certain advice of a resolution being formed by some nation of Indians to invade such state, and the danger is so imminent as not to admit of a delay, till the united states in congress assembled can be consulted: nor shall any state grant commissions to any ships or vessels of war, nor letters of marque or reprisal, except it be after a declaration of war by the united states in congress assembled, and then only against the kingdom or state and the subjects thereof, against which war has been so declared, and under such regulations as shall be established by the united states in congress assembled, unless such state be infested by pirates, in which case vessels of war may be fitted out for that occasion, and kept so long as the danger shall continue, or until the united states in congress assembled shall determine otherwise.

Article VII When land-forces are raised by any state for the common defence, all officers of or under the rank of colonel, shall be appointed by the legislature of each state respectively by whom such forces shall be raised, or in such manner as such state shall direct, and all vacancies shall be filled up by the state which first made the appointment.

Article VIII All charges of war, and all other expences that shall be incurred for the common defence or general welfare, and allowed by the united states in congress assembled, shall be defrayed out of a common treasury, which shall be supplied by the several states, in proportion to the value of all land within each state, granted to or surveyed for any Person, as such land and the buildings and improvements thereon shall be estimated according to such mode as the united states in congress assembled, shall from time to time direct and appoint. The taxes for paying that proportion shall be laid and levied by the authority and direction of the legislatures of the several states within the time agreed upon by the united states in congress assembled.

Article IX The united states in congress assembled, shall have the sole and exclusive right and power of determining on peace and war, except in the cases mentioned in the sixth article—of sending and receiving ambassadors—entering into treaties and alliances, provided that no treaty of commerce shall be made whereby the legislative power of the respective states shall be restrained from imposing such imposts and duties on foreigners, as their own people are subjected to, or from prohibiting the exportation or importation of any species of goods or commodities whatsoever—of establishing rules for deciding in all cases, what captures on land or water shall be legal, and in what manner prizes taken by land or naval forces in the service of the united states shall be divided or appropriated.—of granting letters of marque and reprisal in times of peace—appointing courts for the trial of piracies and felonies committed on the high seas and establishing courts for receiving and determining finally appeals in all cases of captures, provided that no member of congress shall be appointed a judge of any of the said courts.

The united states in congress assembled shall also be the last resort on appeal in all disputes and differences now subsisting or that herafter may arise between two or more states concerning boundary, jurisdiction or any other cause whatever; which authority shall always be exercised in the manner following. Whenever the legislative or executive authority or lawful agent of any state in controversy with another shall present a petition to congress, stating the matter in question and praying for a hearing, notice thereof shall be given by order of congress to the legislative or executive authority of the other state in controversy, and a day assigned for the appearance of the parties by their lawful agents, who shall then be directed to appoint by joint consent, commissioners or judges to constitute a court for hearing and determining the matter in question: but if they cannot agree, congress shall name three persons out of each of the united states, and from the list of such persons each party shall alternately strike out one, the petitioners beginning, until the number shall be reduced to thirteen; and from that number not less than seven, nor more than nine names as congress shall direct, shall in the presence of congress be drawn out by lot, and the persons whose names shall be so drawn or any five of them, shall be commissioners or judges, to hear and finally determine the controversy, so always as a major part of the judges who shall hear the cause shall agree in the determination: and if either party shall neglect to attend at the day appointed, without shewing reasons, which congress shall judge sufficient, or being present shall refuse to strike, the congress shall proceed to nominate three persons out of each state, and the secretary of congress shall strike in behalf of such party absent or refusing; and the judgment and sentence of the court to be appointed, in the manner before prescribed, shall be final and conclusive; and if any of the parties shall refuse to submit to the authority of such court, or to appear to defend their claim or cause, the court shall nevertheless proceed to pronounce sentence, or judgment, which shall in like manner be final and decisive, the judgment or sentence and other proceedings being in either case transmitted to congress, and lodged among the acts of congress for the security of the parties concerned: provided that every commissioner, before he sits in judgment, shall take an oath to be administered by one of the judges of the supreme or superior court of the state, where the cause shall be tried, "well and truly to hear and determine the matter in question, according to the best of his judgment, without favour, affection or hope of reward:" provided also that no state shall be deprived of territory for the benefit of the united states.

All controversies concerning the private right of soil claimed under different grants of two or more states, whose jurisdictions as they may respect such lands, and the states which passed such grants are adjusted, the said grants or either of them being at the same time claimed to have originated antecedent to such settlement of jurisdiction, shall on the petition of either party to the congress of the united states, be finally determined as near as may be in the same manner as is before prescribed for deciding disputes respecting territorial jurisdiction between different states.

The united states in congress assembled shall also have the sole and exclusive right and power of regulating the alloy and value of coin struck by their own authority, or by that of the respective states—fixing the standard of weights and measures throughout the united states.—regulating the trade and managing all affairs with the Indians, not members of any of the states, provided that the legislative right of any state within its own limits be not infringed or violated—establishing and regulating post-offices from one state to another, throughout all the united states, and exacting such postage on the papers passing thro' the same as may be requisite to defray the expences of the said office—appointing all officers of the land forces, in the service of the united states, excepting regimental officers.—appointing all the officers of the naval forces, and commissioning all officers whatever in the service of the united states—making rules for the government and regulation of the said land and naval forces, and directing their operations.

The united states in congress assembled shall have authority to appoint a committee, to sit in the recess of congress, to be denominated "A Committee of the States," and to consist of one delegate from each state; and to appoint such other committees and civil officers as may be necessary for managing the general affairs of the united states under their direction—to appoint one of their number to preside, provided that no person be allowed to serve in the office of president more than one year in any term of three years; to ascertain the necessary sums of Money to be raised for the service of the united states, and to appropriate and apply the same for defraying the public expences—to borrow money, or emit bills on the credit of the united states, transmitting every half year to the respective states an account of the sums of money so borrowed or emitted,—to build and equip a navy—to agree upon the number of land forces, and to make requisitions from each state for its quota, in proportion to the number of white inhabitants in such state; which requisition shall be binding, and thereupon the legislature of each state shall appoint the regimental officers, raise the men and cloath, arm and equip them in a soldier like manner, at the expence of the united states, and the officers and men so cloathed, armed and equipped shall march to the place appointed, and within the time agreed on by the united states in congress assembled: But if the united states in congress assembled shall, on consideration of circumstances judge proper that any state should not raise men, or should raise a smaller number than its quota, and that any other state should raise a greater number of men than the quota thereof, such extra number shall be raised, officered, cloathed, armed and equipped in the same manner as the quota of such state, unless the legislature of such state shall judge that such extra number cannot be safely spared out of the same, in which case they shall raise, officer, cloath, arm and equip as many of such extra number as they judge can be safely spared. And the officers and men so cloathed, armed and equipped, shall march to the place appointed, and within the time agreed on by the united states in congress assembled.

The united states in congress assembled shall never engage in a war, nor grant letters of marque and reprisal in time of peace, nor enter into any treaties or alliances, nor coin money, nor regulate the value thereof, nor ascertain the sums and expences necessary for the defence and welfare of the united states, or any of them, nor emit bills, nor borrow money on the credit of the united states, nor appropriate money, nor agree upon the number of vessels of war, to be built or purchased, or the number of land or sea forces to be raised, nor appoint a commander in chief of the army or navy, unless nine states assent to the same: nor shall a question on any other point, except for adjourning from day to day be determined, unless by the votes of a majority of the united states in congress assembled.

The congress of the united states shall have power to adjourn to any time within the year, and to any place within the united states, so that no period of adjournment be for a longer duration than the space of six Months, and shall publish the Journal of their proceedings monthly, except such parts thereof relating to treaties, alliances or military operations as in their judgment require secresy; and the yeas and nays of the delegates of each state on any question shall be entered on the Journal, when it is desired by any delegate; and the delegates of a state, or any of them, at his or their request shall be furnished with a transcript of the said Journal, except such parts as are above excepted, to lay before the legislatures of the several states.

Article X The committee of the states, or any nine of them, shall be authorised to execute, in the recess of congress, such of the powers of congress as the united states in congress assembled, by the consent of nine states, shall from time to time think expedient to vest them with; provided that no power be delegated to the said committee, for the exercise of which, by the articles of confederation, the voice of nine states in the congress of the united states assembled is requisite.

Article XI Canada acceding to this confederation, and joining in the measures of the united states, shall be admitted into, and entitled to all the advantages of this union: but no other colony shall be admitted into the same, unless such admission be agreed to by nine states.

Article XII All bills of credit emitted, monies borrowed and debts contracted by, or under the authority of congress, before the assembling of the united states, in pursuance of the present confederation, shall be deemed and considered as a charge against the united states, for payment and satisfaction whereof the said united states, and the public faith are hereby solemnly pledged.

Article XIII Every state shall abide by the determinations of the united states in congress assembled, on all questions which by this confederation are submitted to them. And the Articles of this confederation shall be inviolably observed by every state, and the union shall be perpetual; nor shall any alteration at any time hereafter be made in any of them; unless such alteration be agreed to in a congress of the united states, and be afterwards confirmed by the legislatures of every state.

AND WHEREAS it hath pleased the Great Governor of the World to incline the hearts of the legislatures we respectively represent in congress, to approve of, and to authorize us to ratify the said articles of confederation and perpetual union. Know Ye that we the under-signed delegates, by virtue of the power and authority to us given for that purpose, do by these presents, in the name and in behalf of our respective constituents, fully and entirely ratify and confirm each and every of the said articles of confederation and perpetual union, and all and singular the matters and things therein contained: And we do further solemnly plight and engage the faith of our respective constitutents, that they shall abide by the determinations of the united states in congress assembled, on all questions, which by the said confederation are submitted to them. And that the articles thereof shall be inviolably observed by the states we respectively represent, and that the union shall be perpetual. In Witness whereof we have hereunto set our hands in Congress. Done at Philadelphia in the state of Pennsylvania the ninth Day of July in the Year of our Lord one Thousand seven Hundred and Seventy-eight, and in the third year of the independence of America.

Constitution of the United States of America and Amendments*

Preamble

We the people of the United States, in order to form a more perfect union, establish justice, insure domestic tranquillity, provide for the common defense, promote the general welfare, and secure the

* Passages no longer in effect are printed in italic type.

blessings of liberty to ourselves and our posterity, do ordain and establish this Constitution for the United States of America.

Article I

Section 1 All legislative powers herein granted shall be vested in a Congress of the United States, which shall consist of a Senate and a House of Representatives.

Section 2 The House of Representatives shall be composed of members chosen every second year by the people of the several States, and the electors in each State shall have the qualifications requisite for electors of the most numerous branch of the State Legislature.

No person shall be a Representative who shall not have attained to the age of twenty-five years, and been seven years a citizen of the United States, and who shall not, when elected, be an inhabitant of that State in which he shall be chosen.

Representatives and direct taxes shall be apportioned among the several States which may be included within this Union, according to their respective numbers, *which shall be determined by adding to the whole number of free persons, including those bound to service for a term of years and excluding Indians not taxed, three-fifths of all other persons.* The actual enumeration shall be made within three years after the first meeting of the Congress of the United States, and within every subsequent term of ten years, in such manner as they shall by law direct. The number of Representatives shall not exceed one for every thirty thousand, but each State shall have at least one Representative; *and until such enumeration shall be made, the State of New Hampshire shall be entitled to choose three, Massachusetts eight, Rhode Island and Providence Plantations one, Connecticut five, New York six, New Jersey four, Pennsylvania eight, Delaware one, Maryland six, Virginia ten, North Carolina five, South Carolina five, and Georgia three.*

When vacancies happen in the representation from any State, the Executive authority thereof shall issue writs of election to fill such vacancies.

The House of Representatives shall choose their Speaker and other officers; and shall have the sole power of impeachment.

Section 3 The Senate of the United States shall be composed of two Senators from each State, *chosen by the legislature thereof,* for six years; and each Senator shall have one vote.

Immediately after they shall be assembled in consequence of the first election, they shall be divided as equally as may be into three classes. The seats of the Senators of the first class shall be vacated at the expiration of the second year, of the second class at the expiration of the fourth year, and of the third class at the expiration of the sixth year, so that one-third may be chosen every second year; *and if vacancies happen by resignation or otherwise, during the recess of the legislature of any State, the Executive thereof may make temporary appointments until the next meeting of the legislature, which shall then fill such vacancies.*

No person shall be a Senator who shall not have attained to the age of thirty years, and been nine years a citizen of the United States, and who shall not, when elected, be an inhabitant of that State for which he shall be chosen.

The Vice-President of the United States shall be President of the Senate, but shall have no vote, unless they be equally divided.

The Senate shall choose their other officers, and also a President *pro tempore,* in the absence of the Vice-President, or when he shall exercise the office of President of the United States.

The Senate shall have the sole power to try all impeachments. When sitting for that purpose, they shall be on oath or affirmation. When the President of the United States is tried, the Chief Justice shall preside: and no person shall be convicted without the concurrence of two-thirds of the members present.

Judgment in cases of impeachment shall not extend further than to removal from the office, and disqualification to hold and enjoy any office of honor, trust or profit under the United States: but the party convicted shall nevertheless be liable and subject to indictment, trial, judgment and punishment, according to law.

Section 4 The times, places and manner of holding elections for Senators and Representatives shall be prescribed in each State by the legislature thereof; but the Congress may at any time by law make or alter such regulations, except as to the places of choosing Senators.

The Congress shall assemble at least once in every year, and such meeting *shall be on the first Monday in December, unless they shall by law appoint a different day.*

Section 5 Each house shall be the judge of the elections, returns and qualifications of its own members, and a majority of each shall constitute a quorum to do business; but a smaller number may adjourn from day to day, and may be authorized to compel the attendance of absent members, in such manner, and under such penalties, as each house may provide.

Each house may determine the rules of its proceedings, punish its members for disorderly behavior, and with the concurrence of two-thirds, expel a member.

Each house shall keep a journal of its proceedings, and from time to time publish the same, excepting such parts as may in their judgment require secrecy; and the yeas and nays of the members of either house on any question shall, at the desire of one-fifth of those present, be entered on the journal.

Neither house, during the session of Congress, shall, without the consent of the other, adjourn for more than three days, nor to any other place than that in which the two houses shall be sitting.

Section 6 The Senators and Representatives shall receive a compensation for their services, to be ascertained by law and paid out of the treasury of the United States. They shall in all cases except treason, felony and breach of the peace, be privileged from arrest during their attendance at the session of their respective houses, and in going to and returning from the same; and for any speech or debate in either house, they shall not be questioned in any other place.

No Senator or Representative shall, during the time for which he was elected, be appointed to any civil office under the authority of the United States, which shall have been created, or the emoluments whereof shall have been increased, during such time; and no person holding any office under the United States shall be a member of either house during his continuance in office.

Section 7 All bills for raising revenue shall originate in the House of Representatives; but the Senate may propose or concur with amendments as on other bills.

Every bill which shall have passed the House of Representatives and the Senate, shall, before it become a law, be presented to the President of the United States; if he approve he shall sign it, but if not he shall return it with objections to that house in which it originated, who shall enter the objections at large on their journal, and proceed to reconsider it. If after such reconsideration two-thirds of that house shall agree to pass the bill, it shall be sent, together with the objections, to the other house, by which it shall likewise be reconsidered, and, if approved by two-thirds of that house, it shall become a law. But in all such cases the votes of both houses

shall be determined by yeas and nays, and the names of the persons voting for and against the bill shall be entered on the journal of each house respectively. If any bill shall not be returned by the President within ten days (Sundays excepted) after it shall have been presented to him, the same shall be a law, in like manner as if he had signed it, unless the Congress by their adjournment prevent its return, in which case it shall not be a law.

Every order, resolution, or vote to which the concurrence of the Senate and House of Representatives may be necessary (except on a question of adjournment) shall be presented to the President of the United States; and before the same shall take effect, shall be approved by him, or being disapproved by him, shall be repassed by two-thirds of the Senate and House of Representatives, according to the rules and limitations prescribed in the case of a bill.

Section 8 The Congress shall have power

To lay and collect taxes, duties, imposts, and excises, to pay the debts and provide for the common defense and general welfare of the United States; but all duties, imposts and excises shall be uniform throughout the United States;

To borrow money on the credit of the United States;

To regulate commerce with foreign nations, and among the several States, and with the Indian tribes;

To establish an uniform rule of naturalization, and uniform laws on the subject of bankruptcies throughout the United States;

To coin money, regulate the value thereof, and of foreign coin, and fix the standard of weights and measures;

To provide for the punishment of counterfeiting the securities and current coin of the United States;

To establish post offices and post roads;

To promote the progress of science and useful arts by securing for limited times to authors and inventors the exclusive right to their respective writings and discoveries;

To constitute tribunals inferior to the Supreme Court;

To define and punish piracies and felonies committed on the high seas and offenses against the law of nations;

To declare war, grant letters of marque and reprisal, and make rules concerning captures on land and water;

To raise and support armies, but no appropriation of money to that use shall be for a longer term than two years;

To provide and maintain a navy;

To make rules for the government and regulation of the land and naval forces;

To provide for calling forth the militia to execute the laws of the Union, suppress insurrections, and repel invasions;

To provide for organizing, arming, and disciplining the militia, and for governing such part of them as may be employed in the service of the United States, reserving to the States respectively the appointment of the officers, and the authority of training the militia according to the discipline prescribed by Congress;

To exercise exclusive legislation in all cases whatsoever, over such district (not exceeding ten miles square) as may, by cession of particular States, and the acceptance of Congress, become the seat of government of the United States, and to exercise like authority over all places purchased by the consent of the legislature of the State, in which the same shall be, for erection of forts, magazines, arsenals, dockyards, and other needful buildings; — and

To make all laws which shall be necessary and proper for carrying into execution the foregoing powers, and all other powers vested by this Constitution in the government of the United States, or in any department or officer thereof.

Section 9   The migration or importation of such persons as any of the States now existing shall think proper to admit shall not be prohibited by the Congress prior to the year 1808; but a tax or duty may be imposed on such importation, not exceeding $10 for each person.

The privilege of the writ of habeas corpus shall not be suspended, unless when in cases of rebellion or invasion the public safety may require it.

No bill of attainder or ex post facto law shall be passed.

No capitation, or other direct, tax shall be laid, unless in proportion to the census or enumeration herein before directed to be taken.

No tax or duty shall be laid on articles exported from any State.

No preference shall be given by any regulation of commerce or revenue to the ports of one State over those of another; nor shall vessels bound to, or from, one State, be obliged to enter, clear, or pay duties in another.

No money shall be drawn from the treasury, but in consequence of appropriations made by law; and a regular statement and account of the receipts and expenditures of all public money shall be published from time to time.

No title of nobility shall be granted by the United States: and no person holding any office of profit or trust under them, shall, without the consent of the Congress, accept of any present, emolument, office, or title, of any kind whatever, from any king, prince, or foreign state.

Section 10   No State shall enter into any treaty, alliance, or confederation; grant letters of marque and reprisal; coin money; emit bills of credit; make anything but gold and silver coin a tender in payment of debts; pass any bill of attainder, ex post facto law, or law impairing the obligation of contracts, or grant any title of nobility.

No State shall, without the consent of Congress, lay any imposts or duties on imports or exports, except what may be absolutely necessary for executing its inspection laws: and the net produce of all duties and imposts, laid by any State on imports or exports, shall be for the use of the treasury of the United States; and all such laws shall be subject to the revision and control of the Congress.

No State shall, without the consent of Congress, lay any duty of tonnage, keep troops or ships of war in time of peace, enter into any agreement or compact with another State, or with a foreign power, or engage in war, unless actually invaded, or in such imminent danger as will not admit of delay.

Article II

Section 1   The executive power shall be vested in a President of the United States of America. He shall hold his office during the term of four years, and, together with the Vice-President, chosen for the same term, be elected as follows:

Each State shall appoint, in such manner as the legislature thereof may direct, a number of electors, equal to the whole number of Senators and Representatives to which the State may be entitled in the Congress; but no Senator or Representative, or person holding an office of trust or profit under the United States, shall be appointed an elector.

The electors shall meet in their respective States, and vote by ballot for two persons, of whom one at least shall not be an inhabitant of the same State with themselves. And they shall make a list of all the persons voted for, and of the number of votes for each; which list they shall sign and certify, and transmit sealed to the seat of government of the United States, directed to the President of the Senate. The President of the Senate shall, in the presence of the Senate and House of Representatives, open all the certificates, and the votes shall then be counted. The person having the greatest number of votes shall be the Presi-

dent, if such number be a majority of the whole number of electors appointed; and if there be more than one who have such majority, and have an equal number of votes, then the House of Representatives shall immediately choose by ballot one of them for President; and if no person have a majority, then from the five highest on the list said house shall in like manner choose the President. But in choosing the President the votes shall be taken by States, the representation from each State having one vote; a quorum for this purpose shall consist of a member or members from two-thirds of the States, and a majority of all the States shall be necessary to a choice. In every case, after the choice of the President, the person having the greatest number of votes of the electors shall be the Vice-President. But if there should remain two or more who have equal votes, the Senate shall choose from them by ballot the Vice-President.

The Congress may determine the time of choosing the electors and the day on which they shall give their votes; which day shall be the same throughout the United States.

No person except a natural-born citizen, *or a citizen of the United States at the time of the adoption of this Constitution,* shall be eligible to the office of President; neither shall any person be eligible to that office who shall not have attained to the age of thirty-five years, and been fourteen years a resident within the United States.

In cases of the removal of the President from office or of his death, resignation, or inability to discharge the powers and duties of the said office, the same shall devolve on the Vice-President, and the Congress may by law provide for the case of removal, death, resignation, or inability, both of the President and Vice-President, declaring what officer shall then act as President, and such officer shall act accordingly, until the disability be removed, or a President shall be elected.

The President shall, at stated times, receive for his services a compensation, which shall neither be increased nor diminished during the period for which he shall have been elected, and he shall not receive within that period any other emolument from the United States, or any of them.

Before he enter on the execution of his office, he shall take the following oath or affirmation:—"I do solemnly swear (or affirm) that I will faithfully execute the office of the President of the United States, and will to the best of my ability preserve, protect and defend the Constitution of the United States."

Section 2   The President shall be commander in chief of the army and navy of the United States, and of the militia of the several States, when called into the actual service of the United States; he may require the opinion, in writing, of the principal officer in each of the executive departments, upon any subject relating to the duties of their respective offices, and he shall have power to grant reprieves and pardons for offenses against the United States, except in cases of impeachment.

He shall have power, by and with the advice and consent of the Senate, to make treaties, provided two-thirds of the Senators present concur; and he shall nominate, and by and with the advice and consent of the Senate, shall appoint ambassadors, other public ministers and consuls, judges of the Supreme Court, and all other officers of the United States, whose appointments are not herein otherwise provided for, and which shall be established by law: but Congress may by law vest the appointment of such inferior officers, as they think proper, in the President alone, in the courts of law, or in the heads of departments.

The President shall have power to fill up all vacancies that may happen during the recess of the Senate, by granting commissions which shall expire at the end of their next session.

Section 3   He shall from time to time give to the Congress information of the state of the Union, and recommend to their consideration such measures as he shall judge necessary and expedient; he may, on extraordinary occasions, convene both houses, or either of them, and in case of disagreement between them, with respect to the time of adjournment, he may adjourn them to such time as he shall think proper; he shall receive ambassadors and other public ministers; he shall take care that the laws be faithfully executed, and shall commission all the officers of the United States.

Section 4   The President, Vice-President and all civil officers of the United States shall be removed from office on impeachment for, and on conviction of, treason, bribery, or other high crimes and misdemeanors.

Article III

Section 1   The judicial power of the United States shall be vested in one Supreme Court, and in such inferior courts as the Congress may from time to time ordain and establish. The judges, both of the Supreme and inferior courts, shall hold their offices during good behavior, and shall, at stated times, receive for their services a compensation which shall not be diminished during their continuance in office.

Section 2 The judicial power shall extend to all cases, in law and equity, arising under this Constitution, the laws of the United States, and treaties made, or which shall be made, under their authority;—to all cases affecting ambassadors, other public ministers and consuls;—to all cases of admiralty and maritime jurisdiction;—to controversies to which the United States shall be a party;—to controversies between two or more States;—*between a State and citizens of another State;*—between citizens of different States;—between citizens of the same State claiming lands under grants of different States, and between a State, or the citizens thereof, and foreign states, citizens or subjects.

In all cases affecting ambassadors, other public ministers and consuls, and those in which a State shall be party, the Supreme Court shall have original jurisdiction. In all the other cases before mentioned, the Supreme Court shall have appellate jurisdiction, both as to law and fact, with such exceptions, and under such regulations, as the Congress shall make.

The trial of all crimes, except in cases of impeachment, shall be by jury; and such trial shall be held in the State where said crimes shall have been committed; but when not committed within any State, the trial shall be at such place or places as the Congress may by law have directed.

Section 3 Treason against the United States shall consist only in levying war against them, or in adhering to their enemies, giving them aid and comfort. No person shall be convicted of treason unless on the testimony of two witnesses to the same overt act, or on confession in open court.

The Congress shall have power to declare the punishment of treason, but no attainder of treason shall work corruption of blood, or forfeiture except during the life of the person attainted.

Article IV

Section 1 Full faith and credit shall be given in each State to the public acts, records, and judicial proceedings of every other State. And the Congress may by general laws prescribe the manner in which such acts, records, and proceedings shall be proved, and the effect thereof.

Section 2 The citizens of each State shall be entitled to all privileges and immunities of citizens in the several States.

A person charged in any State with treason, felony, or other crime, who shall flee from justice, and be found in another State, shall on demand of the executive authority of the State from which he fled, be delivered up, to be removed to the State having jurisdiction of the crime.

No person held to service or labor in one State, under the laws thereof, escaping into another, shall, in consequence of any law or regulation therein, be discharged from such service or labor, but shall be delivered up on claim of the party to whom such service or labor may be due.

Section 3 New States may be admitted by the Congress into this Union; but no new State shall be formed or erected within the jurisdiction of any other State; nor any State be formed by the junction of two or more States, or parts of States, without the consent of the legislatures of the States concerned as well as of the Congress.

The Congress shall have power to dispose of and make all needful rules and regulations respecting the territory or other property belonging to the United States; and nothing in this Constitution shall be so construed as to prejudice any claims of the United States, or of any particular State.

Section 4 The United States shall guarantee to every State in this Union a republican form of government, and shall protect each of them against invasion; and on application of the legislature, or of the executive (when the legislature cannot be convened), against domestic violence.

Article V

The Congress, whenever two-thirds of both houses shall deem it necessary, shall propose amendments to this Constitution, or, on the application of the legislatures of two-thirds of the several States, shall call a convention for proposing amendments, which, in either case, shall be valid to all intents and purposes, as part of this Constitution, when ratified by the legislatures of three-fourths of the several States, or by conventions in three-fourths thereof, as the one or the other mode of ratification may be proposed by the Congress; provided *that no amendments which may be made prior to the year one thousand eight hundred and eight shall in any manner affect the first and fourth clauses in the ninth section of the first article;* and that no State, without its consent, shall be deprived of its equal suffrage in the Senate.

Article VI

All debts contracted and engagements entered into, before the adoption of this Constitution, shall be as valid against the United States under this Constitution, as under the Confederation.

This Constitution, and the laws of the United States which shall be made in pursuance thereof; and all treaties made, or which shall be made, under the authority of the United States, shall be the supreme law of the land; and the judges in every State shall be bound thereby, anything in the Constitution or laws of any State to the contrary notwithstanding.

The Senators and Representatives before mentioned, and the members of the several State legislatures, and all executive and judicial officers, both of the United States and of the several States, shall be bound by oath or affirmation to support this Constitution; but no religious test shall ever be required as a qualification to any office or public trust under the United States.

Article VII

The ratification of the conventions of nine States shall be sufficient for the establishment of this Constitution between the States so ratifying the same.

Done in Convention by the unanimous consent of the States present, the seventeenth day of September in the year of our Lord one thousand seven hundred and eighty-seven and of the Independence of the United States of America the twelfth. In witness whereof we have hereunto subscribed our names.

GEORGE WASHINGTON
and thirty-seven others

Amendments to the Constitution*

Amendment I

Congress shall make no law respecting an establishment of religion, or prohibiting the free exercise thereof; or abridging the freedom of speech, or of the press; or the right of the people peaceably to assemble, and to petition the government for a redress of grievances.

Amendment II

A well-regulated militia being necessary to the security of a free State, the right of the people to keep and bear arms shall not be infringed.

Amendment III

No soldier shall, in time of peace, be quartered in any house without the consent of the owner, nor in time of war, but in a manner to be prescribed by law.

Amendment IV

The right of the people to be secure in their persons, houses, papers, and effects, against unreasonable searches and seizures, shall not be violated, and no warrants shall issue but upon probable cause, supported by oath or affirmation, and particularly describing the place to be searched, and the persons or things to be seized.

Amendment V

No person shall be held to answer for a capital, or otherwise infamous crime, unless on a presentment or indictment of a grand jury, except in cases arising in the land or naval forces, or in the militia, when in actual service in time of war or public danger; nor shall any person be subject for the same offense to be twice put in jeopardy of life or limb; nor shall be compelled in any criminal case to be a witness against himself, nor be deprived of life, liberty, or property, without due process of law; nor shall private property be taken for public use without just compensation.

Amendment VI

In all criminal prosecutions, the accused shall enjoy the right to a speedy and public trial, by an impartial jury of the State and district wherein the crime shall have been committed, which district shall have been previously ascertained by law, and to be informed of the nature and cause of the accusation; to be confronted with the witnesses against him; to have compulsory process for obtaining witnesses in his favor, and to have the assistance of counsel for his defense.

Amendment VII

In suits at common law, where the value in controversy shall exceed twenty dollars, the right of trial by jury shall be preserved, and no fact tried by a jury shall be otherwise reexamined in any court of the United States, than according to the rules of the common law.

Amendment VIII

Excessive bail shall not be required, nor excessive fines imposed, nor cruel and unusual punishments inflicted.

* The first ten Amendments (the Bill of Rights) were adopted in 1791.

Amendment IX

The enumeration in the Constitution, of certain rights, shall not be construed to deny or disparage others retained by the people.

Amendment X

The powers not delegated to the United States by the Constitution, nor prohibited by it to the States, are reserved to the States respectively, or to the people.

Amendment XI

[Adopted 1798]

The judicial power of the United States shall not be construed to extend to any suit in law or equity, commenced or prosecuted against one of the United States by citizens of another State, or by citizens or subjects of any foreign state.

Amendment XII

[Adopted 1804]

The electors shall meet in their respective States, and vote by ballot for President and Vice-President, one of whom, at least, shall not be an inhabitant of the same State with themselves; they shall name in their ballots the person voted for as President, and in distinct ballots the person voted for as Vice-President, and they shall make distinct lists of all persons voted for as President, and of all persons voted for as Vice-President, and of the number of votes for each, which lists they shall sign and certify, and transmit sealed to the seat of government of the United States, directed to the President of the Senate;—the President of the Senate shall, in the presence of the Senate and House of Representatives, open all the certificates and the votes shall then be counted;—the person having the greatest number of votes for President shall be the President, if such number be a majority of the whole number of electors appointed; and if no person have such majority, then from the persons having the highest numbers not exceeding three on the list of those voted for as President, the House of Representatives shall choose immediately, by ballot, the President. But in choosing the President, the votes shall be taken by States, the representation from each State having one vote; a quorum for this purpose shall consist of a member or members from two-thirds of the States, and a majority of all the States shall be necessary to a choice. And if the House of Representatives shall not choose a President whenever the right of choice shall devolve upon them, before *the fourth day of March* next following, then the Vice-President shall

act as President, as in the case of the death or other constitutional disability of the President.

The person having the greatest number of votes as Vice-President shall be the Vice-President, if such number be a majority of the whole number of electors appointed; and if no person have a majority, then from the two highest numbers on the list the Senate shall choose the Vice-President; a quorum for the purpose shall consist of two-thirds of the whole number of Senators, and a majority of the whole number shall be necessary to a choice. But no person constitutionally ineligible to the office of President shall be eligible to that of Vice-President of the United States.

Amendment XIII

[Adopted 1865]

Section 1 Neither slavery nor involuntary servitude, except as a punishment for crime whereof the party shall have been duly convicted, shall exist within the United States, or any place subject to their jurisdiction.

Section 2 Congress shall have power to enforce this article by appropriate legislation.

Amendment XIV

[Adopted 1868]

Section 1 All persons born or naturalized in the United States, and subject to the jurisdiction thereof, are citizens of the United States and of the State wherein they reside. No State shall make or enforce any law which shall abridge the privileges or immunities of citizens of the United States; nor shall any State deprive any person of life, liberty, or property, without due process of law; nor deny to any person within its jurisdiction the equal protection of the laws.

Section 2 Representatives shall be apportioned among the several States according to their respective numbers, counting the whole number of persons in each State, excluding Indians not taxed. But when the right to vote at any election for the choice of Electors for President and Vice-President of the United States, Representatives in Congress, the executive and judicial officers of a State, or the members of the legislature thereof, is denied to any of the male inhabitants of such State, being twenty-one years of age and citizens of the United States, or in any way abridged, except for participation in rebellion, or other crime, the basis of representation therein shall be reduced in the proportion which the number of such male citizens shall bear to the whole number of male citizens twenty-one years of age in such State.

Section 3 No person shall be a Senator or Representative in Congress, or Elector of President and Vice-President, or hold any office, civil or military, under the United States, or under any State, who, having previously taken an oath, as a member of Congress, or as an officer of the United States, or as a member of any State legislature, or as an executive or judicial officer of any State, to support the Constitution of the United States, shall have engaged in insurrection or rebellion against the same, or given aid or comfort to the enemies thereof. Congress may, by a vote of two-thirds of each house, remove such disability.

Section 4 The validity of the public debt of the United States, authorized by law, including debts incurred for payment of pensions and bounties for services in suppressing insurrection or rebellion, shall not be questioned. But neither the United States nor any State shall assume or pay any debt or obligation incurred in aid of insurrection or rebellion against the United States, or any claim for the loss or emancipation of any slave; but all such debts, obligations, and claims shall be held illegal and void.

Section 5 The Congress shall have power to enforce, by appropriate legislation, the provisions of this article.

Amendment XV
[Adopted 1870]

Section 1 The right of citizens of the United States to vote shall not be denied or abridged by the United States or by any State on account of race, color, or previous condition of servitude.

Section 2 The Congress shall have power to enforce this article by appropriate legislation.

Amendment XVI
[Adopted 1913]

The Congress shall have power to lay and collect taxes on incomes, from whatever source derived, without apportionment among the several States, and without regard to any census or enumeration.

Amendment XVII
[Adopted 1913]

Section 1 The Senate of the United States shall be composed of two Senators from each State, elected by the people thereof, for six years; and each Senator shall have one vote. The electors in each State shall have the qualifications requisite for electors of [voters for] the most numerous branch of the State legislatures.

Section 2 When vacancies happen in the representation of any State in the Senate, the executive authority of such State shall issue writs of election to fill such vacancies: Provided, that the Legislature of any State may empower the executive thereof to make temporary appointments until the people fill the vacancies by election as the Legislature may direct.

Section 3 This amendment shall not be so construed as to affect the election or term of any Senator chosen before it becomes valid as part of the Constitution.

Amendment XVIII
[Adopted 1919; Repealed 1933]

Section 1 After one year from the ratification of this article the manufacture, sale, or transportation of intoxicating liquors within, the importation thereof into, or the exportation thereof from the United States and all territory subject to the jurisdiction thereof, for beverage purposes, is hereby prohibited.

Section 2 The Congress and the several States shall have concurrent power to enforce this article by appropriate legislation.

Section 3 This article shall be inoperative unless it shall have been ratified as an amendment to the Constitution by the legislatures of the several States, as provided by the Constitution, within seven years from the date of the submission thereof to the States by the Congress.

Amendment XIX
[Adopted 1920]

Section 1 The right of citizens of the United States to vote shall not be denied or abridged by the United States or by any State on account of sex.

Section 2 The Congress shall have power to enforce this article by appropriate legislation.

Amendment XX
[Adopted 1933]

Section 1 The terms of the President and Vice-President shall end at noon on the 20th day of January, and the terms of Senators and Representatives at noon on the 3rd day of January, of the years in which such terms would have ended if this article had not been ratified; and the terms of their successors shall then begin.

Section 2 The Congress shall assemble at least once in every year, and such meeting shall begin at noon on the 3d day of January, unless they shall by law appoint a different day.

Section 3 If, at the time fixed for the beginning of the term of the President, the President-elect shall have died, the Vice-President-elect shall become President. If a President shall not have been chosen before the time fixed for the beginning of his term, or if the President-elect shall have failed to qualify, then the Vice-President-elect shall act as President until a President shall have qualified; and the Congress may by law provide for the case wherein neither a President-elect nor a Vice-President-elect shall have qualified, declaring who shall then act as President, or the manner in which one who is to act shall be selected, and such persons shall act accordingly until a President or Vice-President shall have qualified.

Section 4 The Congress may by law provide for the case of the death of any of the persons from whom the House of Representatives may choose a President whenever the right of choice shall have devolved upon them, and for the case of the death of any of the persons from whom the Senate may choose a Vice-President whenever the right of choice shall have devolved upon them.

Section 5 Sections 1 and 2 shall take effect on the 15th day of October following the ratification of this article.

Section 6 This article shall be inoperative unless it shall have been ratified as an amendment to the Constitution by the Legislatures of three-fourths of the several States within seven years from the date of its submission.

Amendment XXI
[Adopted 1933]

Section 1 The eighteenth article of amendment to the Constitution of the United States is hereby repealed.

Section 2 The transportation or importation into any State, Territory, or Possession of the United States for delivery or use therein of intoxicating liquors, in violation of the laws thereof, is hereby prohibited.

Section 3 This article shall be inoperative unless it shall have been ratified as an amendment to the Constitution by conventions in the several States, as provided in the Constitution, within seven years from the date of submission thereof to the States by the Congress.

Amendment XXII
[Adopted 1951]

Section 1 No person shall be elected to the office of President more than twice, and no person who has held the office of President, or acted as President, for more than two years of a term to which some other person was elected President shall be elected to the office of President more than once. But this article shall not apply to any person holding the office of President when this article was proposed by the Congress, and shall not prevent any person who may be holding the office of President, or acting as President, during the term within which this article becomes operative from holding the office of President or acting as President during the remainder of such term.

Section 2 This article shall be inoperative unless it shall have been ratified as an amendment to the Constitution by the legislatures of three-fourths of the several States within seven years from the date of its submission to the States by the Congress.

Amendment XXIII
[Adopted 1961]

Section 1 The District constituting the seat of Government of the United States shall appoint in such manner as the Congress may direct:

A number of electors of President and Vice-President equal to the whole number of Senators and Representatives in Congress to which the District would be entitled if it were a State, but in no event more than the least populous State; they shall be in addition to those appointed by the States, but they shall be considered for the purposes of the election of President and Vice-President, to be electors appointed by a State; and they shall meet in the District and perform such duties as provided by the twelfth article of amendment.

Section 2 The Congress shall have the power to enforce this article by appropriate legislation.

Amendment XXIV
[Adopted 1964]

Section 1 The right of citizens of the United States to vote in any primary or other election for President or Vice-President, for electors for President or Vice-President, or for Senator or Representative in Congress, shall not be denied or abridged by the United States or any State by reason of failure to pay any poll tax or other tax.

Section 2   The Congress shall have the power to enforce this article by appropriate legislation.

Amendment XXV

[Adopted 1967]

Section 1   In case of the removal of the President from office or of his death or resignation, the Vice-President shall become President.

Section 2   Whenever there is a vacancy in the office of the Vice-President, the President shall nominate a Vice-President who shall take office upon confirmation by a majority vote of both Houses of Congress.

Section 3   Whenever the President transmits to the President pro tempore of the Senate and the Speaker of the House of Representatives his written declaration that he is unable to discharge the powers and duties of his office, and until he transmits to them a written declaration to the contrary, such powers and duties shall be discharged by the Vice-President as Acting President.

Section 4   Whenever the Vice-President and a majority of either the principal officers of the executive departments or of such other body as Congress may by law provide, transmit to the President pro tempore of the Senate and the Speaker of the House of Representatives their written declaration that the President is unable to discharge the powers and duties of his office, the Vice-President shall immediately assume the powers and duties of the office as Acting President.

Thereafter, when the President transmits to the President pro tempore of the Senate and the Speaker of the House of Representatives his written declaration that no inability exists, he shall resume the powers and duties of his office unless the Vice-President and a majority of either the principal officers of the executive department[s] or of such other body as Congress may by law provide, transmit within four days to the President pro tempore of the Senate and the Speaker of the House of Representatives their written declaration that the President is unable to discharge the powers and duties of his office. Thereupon Congress shall decide the issue, assembling within forty-eight hours for that purpose if not in session. If the Congress, within twenty-one days after receipt of the latter written declaration, or, if Congress is not in session, within twenty-one days after Congress is required to assemble, determines by two-thirds vote of both Houses that the President is unable to discharge the powers and duties of his office, the Vice-President shall continue to discharge the same as Acting President; otherwise, the President shall resume the powers and duties of his office.

Amendment XXVI

[Adopted 1971]

Section 1   The right of citizens of the United States, who are eighteen years of age or older, to vote shall not be denied or abridged by the United States or by any State on account of age.

Section 2   The Congress shall have power to enforce this article by appropriate legislation.

Amendment XXVII

[Adopted 1992]

No law, varying the compensation for the services of the Senators and Representatives, shall take effect, until an election of Representatives shall have intervened.

Tables

Territorial Expansion of the United States

Territory	Date Acquired	Square Miles	How Acquired
Original states and territories	1783	888,685	Treaty with Great Britain
Louisiana Purchase	1803	827,192	Purchase from France
Florida	1819	72,003	Treaty with Spain
Texas	1845	390,143	Annexation of independent nation
Oregon	1846	285,580	Treaty with Great Britain
Mexican Cession	1848	529,017	Conquest from Mexico
Gadsden Purchase	1853	29,640	Purchase from Mexico
Alaska	1867	589,757	Purchase from Russia
Hawaii	1898	6,450	Annexation of independent nation
The Philippines	1899	115,600	Conquest from Spain (granted independence in 1946)
Puerto Rico	1899	3,435	Conquest from Spain
Guam	1899	212	Conquest from Spain
American Samoa	1900	76	Treaty with Germany and Great Britain
Panama Canal Zone	1904	553	Treaty with Panama (returned to Panama by treaty in 1978)
Corn Islands	1914	4	Treaty with Nicaragua (returned to Nicaragua by treaty in 1971)
Virgin Islands	1917	133	Purchase from Denmark
Pacific Islands Trust (Micronesia)	1947	8,489	Trusteeship under United Nations (some granted independence)
All others (Midway, Wake, and other islands)		42	

Admission of States into the Union

	State	Date of Admission		State	Date of Admission
1.	Delaware	December 7, 1787	26.	Michigan	January 26, 1837
2.	Pennsylvania	December 12, 1787	27.	Florida	March 3, 1845
3.	New Jersey	December 18, 1787	28.	Texas	December 29, 1845
4.	Georgia	January 2, 1788	29.	Iowa	December 28, 1846
5.	Connecticut	January 9, 1788	30.	Wisconsin	May 29, 1848
6.	Massachusetts	February 6, 1788	31.	California	September 9, 1850
7.	Maryland	April 28, 1788	32.	Minnesota	May 11, 1858
8.	South Carolina	May 23, 1788	33.	Oregon	February 14, 1859
9.	New Hampshire	June 21, 1788	34.	Kansas	January 29, 1861
10.	Virginia	June 25, 1788	35.	West Virginia	June 20, 1863
11.	New York	July 26, 1788	36.	Nevada	October 31, 1864
12.	North Carolina	November 21, 1789	37.	Nebraska	March 1, 1867
13.	Rhode Island	May 29, 1790	38.	Colorado	August 1, 1876
14.	Vermont	March 4, 1791	39.	North Dakota	November 2, 1889
15.	Kentucky	June 1, 1792	40.	South Dakota	November 2, 1889
16.	Tennessee	June 1, 1796	41.	Montana	November 8, 1889
17.	Ohio	March 1, 1803	42.	Washington	November 11, 1889
18.	Louisiana	April 30, 1812	43.	Idaho	July 3, 1890
19.	Indiana	December 11, 1816	44.	Wyoming	July 10, 1890
20.	Mississippi	December 10, 1817	45.	Utah	January 4, 1896
21.	Illinois	December 3, 1818	46.	Oklahoma	November 16, 1907
22.	Alabama	December 14, 1819	47.	New Mexico	January 6, 1912
23.	Maine	March 15, 1820	48.	Arizona	February 14, 1912
24.	Missouri	August 10, 1821	49.	Alaska	January 3, 1959
25.	Arkansas	June 15, 1836	50.	Hawaii	August 21, 1959

Presidential Elections

Year	Number of States	Candidates	Parties	Popular Vote	% of Popular Vote	Electoral Vote	% Voter Participation[b]
1789	11	**George Washington**	No party			69	
		John Adams	designations			34	
		Other candidates				35	
1792	15	**George Washington**	No party			132	
		John Adams	designations			77	
		George Clinton				50	
		Other candidates				5	
1796	16	**John Adams**	Federalist			71	
		Thomas Jefferson	Democratic-Republican			68	
		Thomas Pinckney	Federalist			59	
		Aaron Burr	Democratic-Republican			30	
		Other candidates				48	
1800	16	**Thomas Jefferson**	Democratic-Republican			73	
		Aaron Burr	Democratic-Republican			73	
		John Adams	Federalist			65	
		Charles C. Pinckney	Federalist			64	
		John Jay	Federalist			1	
1804	17	**Thomas Jefferson**	Democratic-Republican			162	
		Charles C. Pinckney	Federalist			14	
1808	17	**James Madison**	Democratic-Republican			122	
		Charles C. Pinckney	Federalist			47	
		George Clinton	Democratic-Republican			6	
1812	18	**James Madison**	Democratic-Republican			128	
		DeWitt Clinton	Federalist			89	
1816	19	**James Monroe**	Democratic-Republican			183	
		Rufus King	Federalist			34	
1820	24	**James Monroe**	Democratic-Republican			231	
		John Quincy Adams	Independent-Republican			1	
1824	24	**John Quincy Adams**	Democratic-Republican	108,740	30.5	84	26.9
		Andrew Jackson	Democratic-Republican	153,544	43.1	99	

Presidential Elections, *Continued*

Year	Number of States	Candidates	Parties	Popular Vote	% of Popular Vote	Electoral Vote	% Voter Participation[b]
		Henry Clay	Democratic-Republican	47,136	13.2	37	
		William H. Crawford	Democratic-Republican	46,618	13.1	41	
1828	24	**Andrew Jackson**	Democratic	647,286	56.0	178	57.6
		John Quincy Adams	National Republican	508,064	44.0	83	
1832	24	**Andrew Jackson**	Democratic	688,242	54.5	219	55.4
		Henry Clay	National Republican	473,462	37.5	49	
		William Wirt	Anti-Masonic	101,051	8.0	7	
		John Floyd	Democratic			11	
1836	26	**Martin Van Buren**	Democratic	765,483	50.9	170	57.8
		William H. Harrison	Whig			73	
		Hugh L. White	Whig			26	
		Daniel Webster	Whig	739,795	49.1	14	
		W. P. Mangum	Whig			11	
1840	26	**William H. Harrison**	Whig	1,274,624	53.1	234	80.2
		Martin Van Buren	Democratic	1,127,781	46.9	60	
1844	26	**James K. Polk**	Democratic	1,338,464	49.6	170	78.9
		Henry Clay	Whig	1,300,097	48.1	105	
		James G. Birney	Liberty	62,300	2.3		
1848	30	**Zachary Taylor**	Whig	1,360,967	47.4	163	72.7
		Lewis Cass	Democratic	1,222,342	42.5	127	
		Martin Van Buren	Free Soil	291,263	10.1		
1852	31	**Franklin Pierce**	Democratic	1,601,117	50.9	254	69.6
		Winfield Scott	Whig	1,385,453	44.1	42	
		John P. Hale	Free Soil	155,825	5.0		
1856	31	**James Buchanan**	Democratic	1,832,955	45.3	174	78.9
		John C. Frémont	Republican	1,339,932	33.1	114	
		Millard Fillmore	American	871,731	21.6	8	
1860	33	**Abraham Lincoln**	Republican	1,865,593	39.8	180	81.2
		Stephen A. Douglas	Democratic	1,382,713	29.5	12	
		John C. Breckinridge	Democratic	848,356	18.1	72	
		John Bell	Constitutional Union	592,906	12.6	39	
1864	36	**Abraham Lincoln**	Republican	2,206,938	55.0	212	73.8
		George B. McClellan	Democratic	1,803,787	45.0	21	
1868	37	**Ulysses S. Grant**	Republican	3,013,421	52.7	214	78.1
		Horatio Seymour	Democratic	2,706,829	47.3	80	
1872	37	**Ulysses S. Grant**	Republican	3,596,745	55.6	286	71.3
		Horace Greeley	Democratic	2,843,446	43.9	a	
1876	38	**Rutherford B. Hayes**	Republican	4,036,572	48.0	185	81.8

Presidential Elections, *Continued*

Year	Number of States	Candidates	Parties	Popular Vote	% of Popular Vote	Electoral Vote	% Voter Participation[b]
		Samuel J. Tilden	Democratic	4,284,020	51.0	184	
1880	38	**James A. Garfield**	Republican	4,453,295	48.5	214	79.4
		Winfield S. Hancock	Democratic	4,414,082	48.1	155	
		James B. Weaver	Greenback-Labor	308,578	3.4		
1884	38	**Grover Cleveland**	Democratic	4,879,507	48.5	219	77.5
		James G. Blaine	Republican	4,850,293	48.2	182	
		Benjamin F. Butler	Greenback-Labor	175,370	1.8		
		John P. St. John	Prohibition	150,369	1.5		
1888	38	**Benjamin Harrison**	Republican	5,477,129	47.9	233	79.3
		Grover Cleveland	Democratic	5,537,857	48.6	168	
		Clinton B. Fisk	Prohibition	249,506	2.2		
		Anson J. Streeter	Union Labor	146,935	1.3		
1892	44	**Grover Cleveland**	Democratic	5,555,426	46.1	277	74.7
		Benjamin Harrison	Republican	5,182,690	43.0	145	
		James B. Weaver	People's	1,029,846	8.5	22	
		John Bidwell	Prohibition	264,133	2.2		
1896	45	**William McKinley**	Republican	7,102,246	51.1	271	79.3
		William J. Bryan	Democratic	6,492,559	47.7	176	
1900	45	**William McKinley**	Republican	7,218,491	51.7	292	73.2
		William J. Bryan	Democratic; Populist	6,356,734	45.5	155	
		John C. Wooley	Prohibition	208,914	1.5		
1904	45	**Theodore Roosevelt**	Republican	7,628,461	57.4	336	65.2
		Alton B. Parker	Democratic	5,084,223	37.6	140	
		Eugene V. Debs	Socialist	402,283	3.0		
		Silas C. Swallow	Prohibition	258,536	1.9		
1908	46	**William H. Taft**	Republican	7,675,320	51.6	321	65.4
		William J. Bryan	Democratic	6,412,294	43.1	162	
		Eugene V. Debs	Socialist	420,793	2.8		
		Eugene W. Chafin	Prohibition	253,840	1.7		
1912	48	**Woodrow Wilson**	Democratic	6,296,547	41.9	435	58.8
		Theodore Roosevelt	Progressive	4,118,571	27.4	88	
		William H. Taft	Republican	3,486,720	23.2	8	
		Eugene V. Debs	Socialist	900,672	6.0		
		Eugene W. Chafin	Prohibition	206,275	1.4		
1916	48	**Woodrow Wilson**	Democratic	9,127,695	49.4	277	61.6
		Charles E. Hughes	Republican	8,533,507	46.2	254	
		A. L. Benson	Socialist	585,113	3.2		
		J. Frank Hanly	Prohibition	220,506	1.2		
1920	48	**Warren G. Harding**	Republican	16,143,407	60.4	404	49.2
		James M. Cox	Democratic	9,130,328	34.2	127	

Presidential Elections, *Continued*

Year	Number of States	Candidates	Parties	Popular Vote	% of Popular Vote	Electoral Vote	% Voter Participation[b]
		Eugene V. Debs	Socialist	919,799	3.4		
		P. P. Christensen	Farmer-Labor	265,411	1.0		
1924	48	**Calvin Coolidge**	Republican	15,718,211	54.0	382	48.9
		John W. Davis	Democratic	8,385,283	28.8	136	
		Robert M. La Follette	Progressive	4,831,289	16.6	13	
1928	48	**Herbert C. Hoover**	Republican	21,391,993	58.2	444	56.9
		Alfred E. Smith	Democratic	15,016,169	40.9	87	
1932	48	**Franklin D. Roosevelt**	Democratic	22,809,638	57.4	472	56.9
		Herbert C. Hoover	Republican	15,758,901	39.7	59	
		Norman Thomas	Socialist	881,951	2.2		
1936	48	**Franklin D. Roosevelt**	Democratic	27,752,869	60.8	523	61.0
		Alfred M. Landon	Republican	16,674,665	36.5	8	
		William Lemke	Union	882,479	1.9		
1940	48	**Franklin D. Roosevelt**	Democratic	27,307,819	54.8	449	62.5
		Wendell L. Wilkie	Republican	22,321,018	44.8	82	
1944	48	**Franklin D. Roosevelt**	Democratic	25,606,585	53.5	432	55.9
		Thomas E. Dewey	Republican	22,014,745	46.0	99	
1948	48	**Harry S Truman**	Democratic	24,179,345	49.6	303	53.0
		Thomas E. Dewey	Republican	21,991,291	45.1	189	
		J. Strom Thurmond	States' Rights	1,176,125	2.4	39	
		Henry A. Wallace	Progressive	1,157,326	2.4		
1952	48	**Dwight D. Eisenhower**	Republican	33,936,234	55.1	442	63.3
		Adlai E. Stevenson	Democratic	27,314,992	44.4	89	
1956	48	**Dwight D. Eisenhower**	Republican	35,590,472	57.6	457	60.6
		Adlai E. Stevenson	Democratic	26,022,752	42.1	73	
1960	50	**John F. Kennedy**	Democratic	34,226,731	49.7	303	62.8
		Richard M. Nixon	Republican	34,108,157	49.5	219	
1964	50	**Lyndon B. Johnson**	Democratic	43,129,566	61.1	486	61.7
		Barry M. Goldwater	Republican	27,178,188	38.5	52	
1968	50	**Richard M. Nixon**	Republican	31,785,480	43.4	301	60.6
		Hubert H. Humphrey	Democratic	31,275,166	42.7	191	
		George C. Wallace	American Independent	9,906,473	13.5	46	
1972	50	**Richard M. Nixon**	Republican	47,169,911	60.7	520	55.2
		George S. McGovern	Democratic	29,170,383	37.5	17	
		John G. Schmitz	American	1,099,482	1.4		
1976	50	**Jimmy Carter**	Democratic	40,830,763	50.1	297	53.5
		Gerald R. Ford	Republican	39,147,793	48.0	240	
1980	50	**Ronald Reagan**	Republican	43,899,248	50.8	489	52.6
		Jimmy Carter	Democratic	35,481,432	41.0	49	
		John B. Anderson	Independent	5,719,437	6.6	0	
		Ed Clark	Libertarian	920,859	1.1	0	

Presidential Elections, *Continued*

Year	Number of States	Candidates	Parties	Popular Vote	% of Popular Vote	Electoral Vote	% Voter Participation[b]
1984	50	**Ronald Reagan**	Republican	54,455,075	58.8	525	53.1
		Walter Mondale	Democratic	37,577,185	40.6	13	
1988	50	**George Bush**	Republican	48,901,046	53.4	426	50.2
		Michael Dukakis	Democratic	41,809,030	45.6	111[c]	
1992	50	**Bill Clinton**	Democratic	44,908,233	43.0	370	55.0
		George Bush	Republican	39,102,282	37.4	168	
		Ross Perot	Independent	19,741,048	18.9	0	

Candidates receiving less than 1 percent of the popular vote have been omitted. Thus the percentage of popular vote given for any election year may not total 100 percent.

Before the passage of the Twelfth Amendment in 1804, the Electoral College voted for two presidential candidates; the runner-up became vice president.

Before 1824, most presidential electors were chosen by state legislatures, not by popular vote.

[a]Greeley died shortly after the election; the electors supporting him then divided their votes among minor candidates.

[b]Percent of voting-age population casting ballots.

[c]One elector from West Virginia cast her Electoral College presidential ballot for Lloyd Bentsen, the Democratic party's vice-presidential candidate.

Presidents, Vice Presidents, and Cabinet Members

The Washington Administration

President	George Washington	1789–1797
Vice President	John Adams	1789–1797
Secretary of State	Thomas Jefferson	1789–1793
	Edmund Randolph	1794–1795
	Timothy Pickering	1795–1797
Secretary of Treasury	Alexander Hamilton	1789–1795
	Oliver Wolcott	1795–1797
Secretary of War	Henry Knox	1789–1794
	Timothy Pickering	1795–1796
	James McHenry	1796–1797
Attorney General	Edmund Randolph	1789–1793
	William Bradford	1794–1795
	Charles Lee	1795–1797
Postmaster General	Samuel Osgood	1789–1791
	Timothy Pickering	1791–1794
	Joseph Habersham	1795–1797

The John Adams Administration

President	John Adams	1797–1801
Vice President	Thomas Jefferson	1797–1801
Secretary of State	Timothy Pickering	1797–1800
	John Marshall	1800–1801
Secretary of Treasury	Oliver Wolcott	1797–1800
	Samuel Dexter	1800–1801
Secretary of War	James McHenry	1797–1800
	Samuel Dexter	1800–1801
Attorney General	Charles Lee	1797–1801
Postmaster General	Joseph Habersham	1797–1801
Secretary of Navy	Benjamin Stoddert	1798–1801

The Jefferson Administration

President	Thomas Jefferson	1801–1809
Vice President	Aaron Burr	1801–1805
	George Clinton	1805–1809
Secretary of State	James Madison	1801–1809
Secretary of Treasury	Samuel Dexter	1801
	Albert Gallatin	1801–1809
Secretary of War	Henry Dearborn	1801–1809
Attorney General	Levi Lincoln	1801–1805
	Robert Smith	1805
	John Breckinridge	1805–1806
	Caesar Rodney	1807–1809
Postmaster General	Joseph Habersham	1801
	Gideon Granger	1801–1809
Secretary of Navy	Robert Smith	1801–1809

The Madison Administration

President	James Madison	1809–1817
Vice President	George Clinton	1809–1813
	Elbridge Gerry	1813–1817
Secretary of State	Robert Smith	1809–1811
	James Monroe	1811–1817
Secretary of Treasury	Albert Gallatin	1809–1813
	George Campbell	1814
	Alexander Dallas	1814–1816
	William Crawford	1816–1817
Secretary of War	William Eustis	1809–1812
	John Armstrong	1813–1814
	James Monroe	1814–1815
	William Crawford	1815–1817
Attorney General	Caesar Rodney	1809–1811
	William Pinkney	1811–1814
	Richard Rush	1814–1817
Postmaster General	Gideon Granger	1809–1814
	Return Meigs	1814–1817
Secretary of Navy	Paul Hamilton	1809–1813
	William Jones	1813–1814
	Benjamin Crowninshield	1814–1817

The Monroe Administration

President	James Monroe	1817–1825
Vice President	Daniel Tompkins	1817–1825
Secretary of State	John Quincy Adams	1817–1825
Secretary of Treasury	William Crawford	1817–1825
Secretary of War	George Graham	1817
	John C. Calhoun	1817–1825
Attorney General	Richard Rush	1817
	William Wirt	1817–1825
Postmaster General	Return Meigs	1817–1823
	John McLean	1823–1825
Secretary of Navy	Benjamin Crowninshield	1817–1818
	Smith Thompson	1818–1823
	Samuel Southard	1823–1825

Presidents, Vice Presidents, and Cabinet Members, *Continued*

The John Quincy Adams Administration

President	John Quincy Adams	1825–1829
Vice President	John C. Calhoun	1825–1829
Secretary of State	Henry Clay	1825–1829
Secretary of Treasury	Richard Rush	1825–1829
Secretary of War	James Barbour	1825–1828
	Peter Porter	1828–1829
Attorney General	William Wirt	1825–1829
Postmaster General	John McLean	1825–1829
Secretary of Navy	Samuel Southard	1825–1829

The Jackson Administration

President	Andrew Jackson	1829–1837
Vice President	John C. Calhoun	1829–1833
	Martin Van Buren	1833–1837
Secretary of State	Martin Van Buren	1829–1831
	Edward Livingston	1831–1833
	Louis McLane	1833–1834
	John Forsyth	1834–1837
Secretary of Treasury	Samuel Ingham	1829–1831
	Louis McLane	1831–1833
	William Duane	1833
	Roger B. Taney	1833–1834
	Levi Woodbury	1834–1837
Secretary of War	John H. Eaton	1829–1831
	Lewis Cass	1831–1837
	Benjamin Butler	1837
Attorney General	John M. Berrien	1829–1831
	Roger B. Taney	1831–1833
	Benjamin Butler	1833–1837
Postmaster General	William Barry	1829–1835
	Amos Kendall	1835–1837
Secretary of Navy	John Branch	1829–1831
	Levi Woodbury	1831–1834
	Mahlon Dickerson	1834–1837

The Van Buren Administration

President	Martin Van Buren	1837–1841
Vice President	Richard M. Johnson	1837–1841
Secretary of State	John Forsyth	1837–1841
Secretary of Treasury	Levi Woodbury	1837–1841
Secretary of War	Joel Poinsett	1837–1841
Attorney General	Benjamin Butler	1837–1838
	Felix Grundy	1838–1840
	Henry D. Gilpin	1840–1841
Postmaster General	Amos Kendall	1837–1840
	John M. Niles	1840–1841
Secretary of Navy	Mahlon Dickerson	1837–1838
	James Paulding	1838–1841

The William Harrison Administration

President	William H. Harrison	1841
Vice President	John Tyler	1841
Secretary of State	Daniel Webster	1841
Secretary of Treasury	Thomas Ewing	1841
Secretary of War	John Bell	1841
Attorney General	John J. Crittenden	1841
Postmaster General	Francis Granger	1841
Secretary of Navy	George Badger	1841

The Tyler Administration

President	John Tyler	1841–1845
Vice President	None	
Secretary of State	Daniel Webster	1841–1843
	Hugh S. Legaré	1843
	Abel P. Upshur	1843–1844
	John C. Calhoun	1844–1845
Secretary of Treasury	Thomas Ewing	1841
	Walter Forward	1841–1843
	John C. Spencer	1843–1844
	George Bibb	1844–1845
Secretary of Treasury	John Bell	1841
	John C. Spencer	1841–1843
	James M. Porter	1843–1844
	William Wilkins	1844–1845
Attorney General	John J. Crittenden	1841
	Hugh S. Legaré	1841–1843
	John Nelson	1343–1845
Postmaster General	Francis Granger	1841
	Charles Wickliffe	1841
Secretary of Navy	George Badger	1841
	Abel P. Upshur	1841
	David Henshaw	1843–1844
	Thomas Gilmer	1844
	John Y. Mason	1844–1845

Presidents, Vice Presidents, and Cabinet Members, *Continued*

The Polk Administration

President	James K. Polk	1845–1849
Vice President	George M. Dallas	1845–1849
Secretary of State	James Buchanan	1845–1849
Secretary of Treasury	Robert J. Walker	1845–1849
Secretary of War	William L. Marcy	1845–1849
Attorney General	John Y. Mason	1845–1846
	Nathan Clifford	1846–1848
	Isaac Toucey	1848–1849
Postmaster General	Cave Johnson	1845–1849
Secretary of Navy	George Bancroft	1845–1846
	John Y. Mason	1846–1849

The Taylor Administration

President	Zachary Taylor	1849–1850
Vice President	Millard Fillmore	1849–1850
Secretary of State	John M. Clayton	1849–1850
Secretary of Treasury	William Meredith	1849–1850
Secretary of War	George Crawford	1849–1850
Attorney General	Reverdy Johnson	1849–1850
Postmaster General	Jacob Collamer	1849–1850
Secretary of Navy	William Preston	1849–1850
Secretary of Interior	Thomas Ewing	1849–1850

The Fillmore Administration

President	Millard Fillmore	1850–1853
Vice President	None	
Secretary of State	Daniel Webster	1850–1852
	Edward Everett	1852–1853
Secretary of Treasury	Thomas Corwin	1850–1853
Secretary of War	Charles Conrad	1850–1853
Attorney General	John J. Crittenden	1850–1853
Postmaster General	Nathan Hall	1850–1852
	Sam D. Hubbard	1852–1853
Secretary of Navy	William A. Graham	1850–1852
	John P. Kennedy	1852–1853
Secretary of Interior	Thomas McKennan	1850
	Alexander Stuart	1850–1853

The Pierce Administration

President	Franklin Pierce	1853–1857
Vice President	William R. King	1853–1857
Secretary of State	William L. Marcy	1853–1857
Secretary of Treasury	James Guthrie	1853–1857
Secretary of War	Jefferson Davis	1853–1857
Attorney General	Caleb Cushing	1853–1857
Postmaster General	James Campbell	1853–1857
Secretary of Navy	James C. Dobbin	1853–1857
Secretary of Interior	Robert McClelland	1853–1857

The Buchanan Administration

President	James Buchanan	1857–1861
Vice President	John C. Breckinridge	1857–1861
Secretary of State	Lewis Cass	1857–1860
	Jeremiah S. Black	1860–1861
Secretary of Treasury	Howell Cobb	1857–1860
	Philip Thomas	1860–1861
	John A. Dix	1861
Secretary of War	John B. Floyd	1857–1861
	Joseph Holt	1861
Attorney General	Jeremiah S. Black	1857–1860
	Edwin M. Stanton	1860–1861
Postmaster General	Aaron V. Brown	1857–1859
	Joseph Holt	1859–1861
	Horatio King	1861
Secretary of Navy	Isaac Toucey	1857–1861
Secretary of Interior	Jacob Thompson	1857–1861

The Lincoln Administration

President	Abraham Lincoln	1861–1865
Vice President	Hannibal Hamlin	1861–1865
	Andrew Johnson	1865
Secretary of State	William H. Seward	1861–1865
Secretary of Treasury	Samuel P. Chase	1861–1864
	William P. Fessenden	1864–1865
	Hugh McCulloch	1865
Secretary of War	Simon Cameron	1861–1862
	Edwin M. Stanton	1862–1865
Attorney General	Edward Bates	1861–1864

Presidents, Vice Presidents, and Cabinet Members, *Continued*

	James Speed	1864–1865
Postmaster General	Horatio King	1861
	Montgomery Blair	1861–1864
	William Dennison	1864–1865
Secretary of Navy	Gideon Welles	1861–1865
Secretary of Interior	Caleb B. Smith	1861–1863
	John P. Usher	1863–1865

The Andrew Johnson Administration

President	Andrew Johnson	1865–1869
Vice President	None	
Secretary of State	William H. Seward	1865–1869
Secretary of Treasury	Hugh McCulloch	1865–1869
Secretary of War	Edwin M. Stanton	1865–1867
	Ulysses S. Grant	1867–1868
	Lorenzo Thomas	1868
	John M. Schofield	1868–1869
Attorney General	James Speed	1865–1866
	Henry Stanbery	1866–1868
	William M. Evarts	1868–1869
Postmaster General	William Dennison	1865–1866
	Alexander Randall	1866–1869
Secretary of Navy	Gideon Welles	1865–1869
Secretary of Interior	John P. Usher	1865
	James Harlan	1865–1866
	Orville H. Browning	1866–1869

The Grant Administration

President	Ulysses S. Grant	1869–1877
Vice President	Schuyler Colfax	1869–1873
	Henry Wilson	1873–1877
Secretary of State	Elihu B. Washburne	1869
	Hamilton Fish	1869–1877
Secretary of Treasury	George S. Boutwell	1869–1873
	William Richardson	1873–1874
	Benjamin Bristow	1874–1876
	Lot M. Morrill	1876–1877
Secretary of War	John A. Rawlins	1869
	William T. Sherman	1869
	William W. Belknap	1869–1876
	Alphonso Taft	1876
	James D. Cameron	1876–1877
Attorney General	Ebenezer Hoar	1869–1870

	Amos T. Ackerman	1870–1871
	G. H. Williams	1871–1875
	Edwards Pierrepont	1875–1876
	Alphonso Taft	1876–1877
Postmaster General	John A. J. Creswell	1869–1874
	James W. Marshall	1874
	Marshall Jewell	1874–1876
	James N. Tyner	1876–1877
Secretary of Navy	Adolph E. Borie	1869
	George M. Robeson	1869–1877
Secretary of Interior	Jacob D. Cox	1869–1870
	Columbus Delano	1870–1875
	Zachariah Chandler	1875–1877

The Hayes Administration

President	Rutherford B. Hayes	1877–1881
Vice President	William A. Wheeler	1877–1881
Secretary of State	William B. Evarts	1877–1881
Secretary of Treasury	John Sherman	1877–1881
Secretary of War	George W. McCrary	1877–1879
	Alex Ramsey	1879–1881
Attorney General	Charles Devens	1877–1881
Postmaster General	David M. Key	1877–1880
	Horace Maynard	1880–1881
Secretary of Navy	Richard W. Thompson	1877–1880
	Nathan Goff, Jr.	1881
Secretary of Interior	Carl Schurz	1877–1881

The Garfield Administration

President	James A. Garfield	1881
Vice President	Chester A. Arthur	1881
Secretary of State	James G. Blaine	1881
Secretary of Treasury	William Windom	1881
Secretary of War	Robert T. Lincoln	1881
Attorney General	Wayne MacVeagh	1881
Postmaster General	Thomas L. James	1881
Secretary of Navy	William H. Hunt	1881
Secretary of Interior	Samuel J. Kirkwood	1881

Presidents, Vice Presidents, and Cabinet Members, *Continued*

The Arthur Administration

President	Chester A. Arthur	1881–1885
Vice President	None	
Secretary of State	F. T. Frelinghuysen	1881–1885
Secretary of Treasury	Charles J. Folger	1881–1884
	Walter Q. Gresham	1884
	Hugh McCulloch	1884–1885
Secretary of War	Robert T. Lincoln	1881–1885
Attorney General	Benjamin H. Brewster	1881–1885
Postmaster General	Timothy O. Howe	1881–1883
	Walter Q. Gresham	1883–1884
	Frank Hatton	1884–1885
Secretary of Navy	William H. Hunt	1881–1882
	William E. Chandler	1882–1885
Secretary of Interior	Samuel J. Kirkwood	1881–1882
	Henry M. Teller	1882–1885

The Cleveland Administration

President	Grover Cleveland	1885–1889
Vice President	Thomas A. Hendricks	1885–1889
Secretary of State	Thomas F. Bayard	1885–1889
Secretary of Treasury	Daniel Manning	1885–1887
	Charles S. Fairchild	1887–1889
Secretary of War	William C. Endicott	1885–1889
Attorney General	Augustus H. Garland	1885–1889
Postmaster General	William F. Vilas	1885–1888
	Don M. Dickinson	1888–1889
Secretary of Navy	William C. Whitney	1885–1889
Secretary of Interior	Lucius G. C. Lamar	1885–1888
	William F. Vilas	1888–1889
Secretary of Agriculture	Norman J. Colman	1889

The Benjamin Harrison Administration

President	Benjamin Harrison	1889–1893
Vice President	Levi P. Morton	1889–1893
Secretary of State	James G. Blaine	1889–1892
	John W. Foster	1892–1893
Secretary of Treasury	William Windom	1889–1891
	Charles Foster	1891–1893

Secretary of War	Redfield Proctor	1889–1891
	Stephen B. Elkins	1891–1893
Attorney General	William H. H. Miller	1889–1891
Postmaster General	John Wanamaker	1889–1893
Secretary of Navy	Benjamin F. Tracy	1889–1893
Secretary of Interior	John W. Noble	1889–1893
Secretary of Agriculture	Jeremiah M. Rusk	1889–1893

The Cleveland Administration

President	Grover Cleveland	1893–1897
Vice President	Adlai E. Stevenson	1893–1897
Secretary of State	Walter Q. Gresham	1893–1895
	Richard Olney	1895–1897
Secretary of Treasury	John G. Carlisle	1893–1897
Secretary of War	Daniel S. Lamont	1893–1897
Attorney General	Richard Olney	1893–1895
	James Harmon	1895–1897
Postmaster General	Wilson S. Bissell	1893–1895
	William L. Wilson	1895–1897
Secretary of Navy	Hilary A. Herbert	1893–1897
Secretary of Interior	Hoke Smith	1893–1896
	David R. Francis	1896–1897
Secretary of Agriculture	Julius S. Morton	1893–1897

The McKinley Administration

President	William McKinley	1897–1901
Vice President	Garret A. Hobart	1897–1901
	Theodore Roosevelt	1901
Secretary of State	John Sherman	1897–1898
	William R. Day	1898
	John Hay	1898–1901
Secretary of Treasury	Lyman J. Gage	1897–1901
Secretary of War	Russell A. Alger	1897–1899
	Elihu Root	1899–1901
Attorney General	Joseph McKenna	1897–1898
	John W. Griggs	1898–1901
	Philander C. Knox	1901
Postmaster General	James A. Gary	1897–1898
	Charles E. Smith	1898–1901

Presidents, Vice Presidents, and Cabinet Members, *Continued*

Secretary of Navy	John D. Long	1897–1901
Secretary of Interior	Cornelius N. Bliss	1897–1899
	Ethan A. Hitchcock	1899–1901
Secretary of Agriculture	James Wilson	1897–1901

The Theodore Roosevelt Administration

President	Theodore Roosevelt	1901–1909
Vice President	Charles Fairbanks	1905–1909
Secretary of State	John Hay	1901–1905
	Elihu Root	1905–1909
	Robert Bacon	1909
Secretary of Treasury	Lyman J. Gage	1901–1902
	Leslie M. Shaw	1902–1907
	George B. Cortelyou	1907–1909
Secretary of War	Elihu Root	1901–1904
	William H. Taft	1904–1908
	Luke E. Wright	1908–1909
Attorney General	Philander C. Knox	1901–1904
	William H. Moody	1904–1906
	Charles J. Bonaparte	1906–1909
Postmaster General	Charles E. Smith	1901–1902
	Henry C. Payne	1902–1904
	Robert J. Wynne	1904–1905
	George B. Cortelyou	1905–1907
	George von L. Meyer	1907–1909
Secretary of Navy	John D. Long	1901–1902
	William H. Moody	1902–1904
	Paul Morton	1904–1905
	Charles J. Bonaparte	1905–1906
	Victor H. Metcalf	1906–1908
	Truman H. Newberry	1908–1909
Secretary of Interior	Ethan A. Hitchcock	1901–1907
	James R. Garfield	1907–1909
Secretary of Agriculture	James Wilson	1901–1909
Secretary of Labor and Commerce	George B. Cortelyou	1903–1904
	Victor H. Metcalf	1904–1906
	Oscar S. Straus	1906–1909
	Charles Nagel	1909

The Taft Administration

President	William H. Taft	1909–1913
Vice President	James S. Sherman	1909–1913
Secretary of State	Philander C. Knox	1909–1913
Secretary of Treasury	Franklin MacVeagh	1909–1913
Secretary of War	Jacob M. Dickinson	1909–1911
	Henry L. Stimson	1911–1913
Attorney General	George W. Wickersham	1909–1913
Postmaster General	Frank H. Hitchcock	1909–1913
Secretary of Navy	George von L. Meyer	1909–1913
Secretary of Interior	Richard A. Ballinger	1909–1911
	Walter L. Fisher	1911–1913
Secretary of Agriculture	James Wilson	1909–1913
Secretary of Labor and Commerce	Charles Nagel	1909–1913

The Wilson Administration

President	Woodrow Wilson	1913–1921
Vice President	Thomas R. Marshall	1913–1921
Secretary of State	William J. Bryan	1913–1915
	Robert Lansing	1915–1920
	Bainbridge Colby	1920–1921
Secretary of Treasury	William G. McAdoo	1913–1918
	Carter Glass	1918–1920
	David F. Houston	1920–1921
Secretary of War	Lindley M. Garrison	1913–1916
	Newton D. Baker	1916–1921
Attorney General	James C. McReynolds	1913–1914
	Thomas W. Gregory	1914–1919
	A. Mitchell Palmer	1919–1921
Postmaster General	Albert S. Burleson	1913–1921
Secretary of Navy	Josephus Daniels	1913–1921
Secretary of Interior	Franklin K. Lane	1913–1920
	John B. Payne	1920–1921
Secretary of Agriculture	David F. Houston	1913–1920
	Edwin T. Meredith	1920–1921
Secretary of Commerce	William C. Redfield	1913–1919
	Joshua W. Alexander	1919–1921
Secretary of Labor	William B. Wilson	1913–1921

The Harding Administration

President	Warren G. Harding	1921–1923

Presidents, Vice Presidents, and Cabinet Members, *Continued*

Vice President	Calvin Coolidge	1921–1923
Secretary of State	Charles E. Hughes	1921–1923
Secretary of Treasury	Andrew Mellon	1921–1923
Secretary of War	John W. Weeks	1921–1923
Attorney General	Harry M. Daugherty	1921–1923
Postmaster General	Will H. Hays	1921–1922
	Hubert Work	1922–1923
	Harry S. New	1923
Secretary of Navy	Edwin Denby	1921–1923
Secretary of Interior	Albert B. Fall	1921–1923
	Hubert Work	1923
Secretary of Agriculture	Henry C. Wallace	1921–1923
Secretary of Commerce	Herbert C. Hoover	1921–1923
Secretary of Labor	James J. Davis	1921–1923

The Coolidge Administration

President	Calvin Coolidge	1923–1929
Vice President	Charles G. Dawes	1925–1929
Secretary of State	Charles E. Hughes	1923–1925
	Frank B. Kellogg	1925–1929
Secretary of Treasury	Andrew Mellon	1923–1929
Secretary of War	John W. Weeks	1923–1925
	Dwight F. Davis	1925–1929
Attorney General	Henry M. Daugherty	1923–1924
	Harlan F. Stone	1924–1925
	John G. Sargent	1925–1929
Postmaster General	Harry S. New	1923–1929
Secretary of Navy	Edwin Derby	1923–1924
	Curtis D. Wilbur	1924–1929
Secretary of Interior	Hubert Work	1923–1928
	Roy O. West	1928–1929
Secretary of Agriculture	Henry C. Wallace	1923–1924
	Howard M. Gore	1924–1925
	William M. Jardine	1925–1929
Secretary of Commerce	Herbert C. Hoover	1923–1928
	William F. Whiting	1928–1929
Secretary of Labor	James J. Davis	1923–1929

The Hoover Administration

President	Herbert C. Hoover	1929–1933
Vice President	Charles Curtis	1929–1933
Secretary of State	Henry L. Stimson	1929–1933
Secretary of Treasury	Andrew Mellon	1929–1932
	Ogden L. Mills	1932–1933
Secretary of War	James W. Good	1929
	Patrick J. Hurley	1929–1933
Attorney General	William D. Mitchell	1929–1933
Postmaster General	Walter F. Brown	1929–1933
Secretary of Navy	Charles F. Adams	1929–1933
Secretary of Interior	Ray L. Wilbur	1929–1933
Secretary of Agriculture	Arthur M. Hyde	1929–1933
Secretary of Commerce	Robert P. Lamont	1929–1932
	Roy D. Chapin	1932–1933
Secretary of Labor	James J. Davis	1929–1930
	William N. Doak	1930–1933

The Franklin D. Roosevelt Administration

President	Franklin D. Roosevelt	1933–1945
Vice President	John Nance Garner	1933–1941
	Henry A. Wallace	1941–1945
	Harry S Truman	1945
Secretary of State	Cordell Hull	1933–1944
	Edward R. Stettinius, Jr.	1944–1945
Secretary of Treasury	William H. Woodin	1933–1934
	Henry Morgenthau, Jr.	1934–1945
Secretary of War	George H. Dern	1933–1936
	Henry A. Woodring	1936–1940
	Henry L. Stimson	1940–1945
Attorney General	Homer S. Cummings	1933–1939
	Frank Murphy	1939–1940
	Robert H. Jackson	1940–1941
	Francis Biddle	1941–1945
Postmaster General	James A. Farley	1933–1940
	Frank C. Walker	1940–1945
Secretary of Navy	Claude A. Swanson	1933–1940
	Charles Edison	1940
	Frank Knox	1940–1944
	James V. Forrestal	1944–1945
Secretary of Interior	Harold L. Ickes	1933–1945
Secretary of Agriculture	Henry A. Wallace	1933–1940
	Claude R. Wickard	1940–1945

Presidents, Vice Presidents, and Cabinet Members, *Continued*

Secretary of Commerce	Daniel C. Roper	1933–1939
	Harry L. Hopkins	1939–1940
	Jesse Jones	1940–1945
	Henry A. Wallace	1945
Secretary of Labor	Frances Perkins	1933–1945

The Truman Administration

President	Harry S Truman	1945–1953
Vice President	Alben W. Barkley	1949–1953
Secretary of State	Edward R. Stettinius, Jr.	1945
	James F. Byrnes	1945–1947
	George C. Marshall	1947–1949
	Dean G. Acheson	1949–1953
Secretary of Treasury	Fred M. Vinson	1945–1946
	John W. Snyder	1946–1953
Secretary of War	Robert P. Patterson	1945–1947
	Kenneth C. Royall	1947
Attorney General	Tom C. Clark	1945–1949
	J. Howard McGrath	1949–1952
	James P. McGranery	1952–1953
Postmaster General	Frank C. Walker	1945
	Robert E. Hannegan	1945–1947
	Jesse M. Donaldson	1947–1953
Secretary of Navy	James V. Forrestal	1945–1947
Secretary of Interior	Harold L. Ickes	1945–1946
	Julius A. Krug	1946–1949
	Oscar L. Chapman	1949–1953
Secretary of Agriculture	Clinton P. Anderson	1945–1948
	Charles F. Brannan	1948–1953
Secretary of Commerce	Henry A. Wallace	1945–1946
	W. Averell Harriman	1946–1948
	Charles W. Sawyer	1948–1953
Secretary of Labor	Lewis B. Schwellenbach	1945–1948
	Maurice J. Tobin	1948–1953
Secretary of Defense	James V. Forrestal	1947–1949
	Louis A. Johnson	1949–1950
	George C. Marshall	1950–1951
	Robert A. Lovett	1951–1953

The Eisenhower Administration

President	Dwight D. Eisenhower	1953–1961
Vice President	Richard M. Nixon	1953–1961
Secretary of State	John Foster Dulles	1953–1959
	Christian A. Herter	1959–1961
Secretary of Treasury	George M. Humphrey	1953–1957
	Robert B. Anderson	1957–1961
Attorney General	Herbert Brownell, Jr.	1953–1958
	William P. Rogers	1958–1961
Postmaster General	Arthur E. Summerfield	1953–1961
Secretary of Interior	Douglas McKay	1953–1956
	Fred A. Seaton	1956–1961
Secretary of Agriculture	Ezra T. Benson	1953–1961
Secretary of Commerce	Sinclair Weeks	1953–1958
	Lewis L. Strauss	1958–1959
	Frederick H. Mueller	1959–1961
Secretary of Labor	Martin P. Durkin	1953
	James P. Mitchell	1953–1961
Secretary of Defense	Charles E. Wilson	1953–1957
	Neil H. McElroy	1957–1959
	Thomas S. Gates, Jr.	1959–1961
Secretary of Health, Education, and Welfare	Oveta Culp Hobby	1953–1955
	Marion B. Folsom	1955–1958
	Arthur S. Flemming	1958–1961

The Kennedy Administration

President	John F. Kennedy	1961–1963
Vice President	Lyndon B. Johnson	1961–1963
Secretary of State	Dean Rusk	1961–1963
Secretary of Treasury	C. Douglas Dillon	1961–1963
Attorney General	Robert F. Kennedy	1961–1963
Postmaster General	J. Edward Day	1961–1963
	John A. Gronouski	1963
Secretary of Interior	Stewart L. Udall	1961–1963
Secretary of Agriculture	Orville L. Freeman	1961–1963
Secretary of Commerce	Luther H. Hodges	1961–1963
Secretary of Labor	Arthur J. Goldberg	1961–1962
	W. Willard Wirtz	1962–1963
Secretary of Defense	Robert S. McNamara	1961–1963
Secretary of Health, Education, and Welfare	Abraham A. Ribicoff	1961–1962
	Anthony J. Celebrezze	1962–1963

Presidents, Vice Presidents, and Cabinet Members, *Continued*

The Lyndon Johnson Administration

President	Lyndon B. Johnson	1963–1969
Vice President	Hubert H. Humphrey	1965–1969
Secretary of State	Dean Rusk	1963–1969
Secretary of Treasury	C. Douglas Dillon	1963–1965
	Henry H. Fowler	1965–1969
Attorney General	Robert F. Kennedy	1963–1964
	Nicholas Katzenbach	1965–1966
	Ramsey Clark	1967–1969
Postmaster General	John A. Gronouski	1963–1965
	Lawrence F. O'Brien	1965–1968
	Marvin Watson	1968–1969
Secretary of Interior	Stewart L. Udall	1963–1969
Secretary of Agriculture	Orville L. Freeman	1963–1969
Secretary of Commerce	Luther H. Hodges	1963–1964
	John T. Connor	1964–1967
	Alexander B. Trowbridge	1967–1968
	Cyrus R. Smith	1968–1969
Secretary of Labor	W. Willard Wirtz	1963–1969
Secretary of Defense	Robert F. McNamara	1963–1968
	Clark Clifford	1968–1969
Secretary of Health, Education, and Welfare	Anthony J. Celebrezze	1963–1965
	John W. Gardner	1965–1968
	Wilbur J. Cohen	1968–1969
Secretary of Housing and Urban Development	Robert C. Weaver	1966–1969
	Robert C. Wood	1969
Secretary of Transportation	Alan S. Boyd	1967–1969

The Nixon Administration

President	Richard M. Nixon	1969–1974
Vice President	Spiro T. Agnew	1969–1973
	Gerald R. Ford	1973–1974
Secretary of State	William P. Rogers	1969–1973
	Henry A. Kissinger	1973–1974
Secretary of Treasury	David M. Kennedy	1969–1970
	John B. Connally	1971–1972
	George P. Shultz	1972–1974
	William E. Simon	1974
Attorney General	John N. Mitchell	1969–1972
	Richard G. Kleindienst	1972–1973
	Elliot L. Richardson	1973
	William B. Saxbe	1973–1974
Postmaster General	Winton M. Blount	1969–1971
Secretary of Interior	Walter J. Hickel	1969–1970
	Rogers Morton	1971–1974
Secretary of Agriculture	Clifford M. Hardin	1969–1971
	Earl L. Butz	1971–1974
Secretary of Commerce	Maurice H. Stans	1969–1972
	Peter G. Peterson	1972–1973
	Frederick B. Dent	1973–1974
Secretary of Labor	George P. Shultz	1969–1970
	James D. Hodgson	1970–1973
	Peter J. Brennan	1973–1974
Secretary of Defense	Melvin R. Laird	1969–1973
	Elliot L. Richardson	1973
	James R. Schlesinger	1973–1974
Secretary of Health, Education, and Welfare	Robert H. Finch	1969–1970
	Elliot L. Richardson	1970–1973
	Casper W. Weinberger	1973–1974
Secretary of Housing and Urban Development	George Romney	1969–1973
	James T. Lynn	1973–1974
Secretary of Transportation	John A. Volpe	1969–1973
	Claude S. Brinegar	1973–1974

The Ford Administration

President	Gerald R. Ford	1974–1977
Vice President	Nelson A. Rockefeller	1974–1977
Secretary of State	Henry A. Kissinger	1974–1977
Secretary of Treasury	William E. Simon	1974–1977
Attorney General	William Saxbe	1974–1975
	Edward Levi	1975–1977
Secretary of Interior	Rogers Morton	1974–1975
	Stanley K. Hathaway	1975
	Thomas Kleppe	1975–1977
Secretary of Agriculture	Earl L. Butz	1974–1976
	John A. Knebel	1976–1977
Secretary of Commerce	Frederick B. Dent	1974–1975
	Rogers Morton	1975–1976
	Elliot L. Richardson	1976–1977
Secretary of Labor	Peter J. Brennan	1974–1975
	John T. Dunlop	1975–1976

Presidents, Vice Presidents, and Cabinet Members, *Continued*

	W. J. Usery	1976–1977
Secretary of Defense	James R. Schlesinger	1974–1975
	Donald Rumsfeld	1975–1977
Secretary of Health, Education, and Welfare	Casper Weinberger	1974–1975
	Forrest D. Mathews	1975–1977
Secretary of Housing and Urban Development	James T. Lynn	1974–1975
	Carla A. Hills	1975–1977
Secretary of Transportation	Claude Brinegar	1974–1975
	William T. Coleman	1975–1977

The Carter Administration

President	Jimmy Carter	1977–1981
Vice President	Walter F. Mondale	1977–1981
Secretary of State	Cyrus R. Vance	1977–1980
	Edmund Muskie	1980–1981
Secretary of Treasury	W. Michael Blumenthal	1977–1979
	G. William Miller	1979–1981
Attorney General	Griffin Bell	1977–1979
	Benjamin R. Civiletti	1979–1981
Secretary of Interior	Cecil D. Andrus	1977–1981
Secretary of Agriculture	Robert Bergland	1977–1981
Secretary of Commerce	Juanita M. Kreps	1977–1979
	Philip M. Klutznick	1979–1981
Secretary of Labor	F. Ray Marshall	1977–1981
Secretary of Defense	Harold Brown	1977–1981
Secretary of Health, Education, and Welfare	Joseph A. Califano	1977–1979
	Patricia R. Harris	1979
Secretary of Health and Human Services	Patricia R. Harris	1979–1981
Secretary of Education	Shirley M. Hufstedler	1979–1981
Secretary of Housing and Urban Development	Patricia R. Harris	1977–1979
	Moon Landrieu	1979–1981
Secretary of Transportation	Brock Adams	1977–1979
	Neil E. Goldschmidt	1979–1981
Secretary of Energy	James R. Schlesinger	1977–1979
	Charles W. Duncan	1979–1981

The Reagan Administration

President	Ronald Reagan	1981–1989
Vice President	George Bush	1981–1989
Secretary of State	Alexander M. Haig	1981–1982
	George P. Shultz	1982–1989
Secretary of Treasury	Donald Regan	1981–1985
	James A. Baker III	1985–1988
	Nicholas F. Brady	1988–1989
Attorney General	William F. Smith	1981–1985
	Edwin A. Meese III	1985–1988
	Richard L. Thornburgh	1988–1989
Secretary of Interior	James G. Watt	1981–1983
	William P. Clark, Jr.	1983–1985
	Donald P. Hodel	1985–1989
Secretary of Agriculture	John Block	1981–1986
	Richard E. Lyng	1986–1989
Secretary of Commerce	Malcolm Baldridge	1981–1987
	C. William Verity, Jr.	1987–1989
Secretary of Labor	Raymond J. Donovan	1981–1985
	William E. Brock	1985–1987
	Ann Dore McLaughlin	1987–1989
Secretary of Defense	Casper Weinberger	1981–1987
	Frank C. Carlucci	1987–1989
Secretary of Health and Human Services	Richard S. Schweiker	1981–1983
	Margaret Heckler	1983–1985
	Otis R. Bowen	1985–1989
Secretary of Education	Terrel H. Bell	1981–1984
	William J. Bennett	1985–1988
	Lauro F. Cavazos	1988–1989
Secretary of Housing and Urban Development	Samuel R. Pierce, Jr.	1981–1989
Secretary of Transportation	Drew Lewis	1981–1982
	Elizabeth Hanford Dole	1983–1987
	James H. Burnley IV	1987–1989
Secretary of Energy	James B. Edwards	1981–1982
	Donald P. Hodel	1982–1985
	John S. Herrington	1985–1989

The Bush Administration

President	George Bush	1989–1993
Vice President	Dan Quayle	1989–1993

Presidents, Vice Presidents, and Cabinet Members, *Continued*

Secretary of State	James A. Baker III	1989–1992
	Lawrence Eagleburger	1992–1993
Secretary of Treasury	Nicholas F. Brady	1989–1993
Attorney General	Richard L. Thornburgh	1989–1992
	William P. Barr	1992–1993
Secretary of Interior	Manuel Lujan, Jr.	1989–1993
Secretary of Agriculture	Clayton K. Yeutter	1989–1991
	Edward Madigan	1991–1993
Secretary of Commerce	Robert A. Mosbacher	1989–1992
	Barbara Hackman Franklin	1992–1993
Secretary of Labor	Elizabeth Hanford Dole	1989–1991
	Lynn Martin	1991–1993
Secretary of Defense	Richard B. Cheney	1989–1993
Secretary of Health and Human Services	Louis W. Sullivan	1989–1993
Secretary of Education	Lauro F. Cavazos	1989–1991
	Lamar Alexander	1991–1993
Secretary of Housing and Urban Development	Jack F. Kemp	1989–1993
Secretary of Transportation	Samuel K. Skinner	1989–1992
	Andrew H. Card	1992–1993
Secretary of Energy	James D. Watkins	1989–1993
Secretary of Veterans Affairs	Edward J. Derwinski	1989–1993

The Clinton Administration

President	Bill Clinton	1993–
Vice President	Albert Gore	1993–
Secretary of State	Warren M. Christopher	1993–
Secretary of Treasury	Lloyd Bentsen	1993–
Attorney General	Janet Reno	1993–
Secretary of Interior	Bruce Babbitt	1993–
Secretary of Agriculture	Mike Espy	1993–1994
Secretary of Commerce	Ronald H. Brown	1993–
Secretary of Labor	Robert B. Reich	1993–
Secretary of Defense	Les Aspin	1993–1994
	William J. Perry	1994–
Secretary of Health and Human Services	Donna E. Shalala	1993–
Secretary of Education	Richard W. Riley	1993–
Secretary of Housing and Urban Development	Henry G. Cisneros	1993–
Secretary of Transportation	Federico F. Peña	1993–
Secretary of Energy	Hazel O'Leary	1993–
Secretary of Veterans Affairs	Jesse Brown	1993–

Credits

Index

An Invitation to Respond

■ ■ ■ ■ ■ ■ ■

We would like to find out a little about your background and about your reactions to *Making America.* Your evaluation of the book will help us to meet the interests and needs of students in future editions. We invite you to share your reactions by completing the questionnaire below and returning it to *College Marketing, Houghton Mifflin Company, 222 Berkeley Street, Boston, MA 02116-3764.*

1. How do you rate this textbook in the following areas?

	Excellent	Good	Adequate	Poor
a. Understandable style of writing	❏	❏	❏	❏
b. Physical appearance/ readability	❏	❏	❏	❏
c. Fair coverage of topics	❏	❏	❏	❏
d. Comprehensiveness (covered major issues and time periods)	❏	❏	❏	❏
e. Individual Choices	❏	❏	❏	❏
f. Voices	❏	❏	❏	❏
g. Presentation of maps and artwork	❏	❏	❏	❏

2. Can you comment on or illustrate your above ratings?

_____

_____

3. What chapters or features did you particularly like?

_____

_____

_____

4. How effective did you find ECCO in helping you to understand each chapter?

_____

_____

_____

5. What chapters or features did you dislike or think should be changed?

_____

_____

_____

6. What material would you suggest adding or deleting?

_____

_____

_____

7. Are you a student at a community college or a four-year school?

_____

_____

8. Do you intend to major in history?   ❏ yes   ❏ no

9. Did you use the *Study Guide* that accompanies this textbook?   ❏ yes   ❏ no

10. We would appreciate any other comments or reactions you are willing to share.

_____

_____

_____

_____

_____